Reference mate
in the ...

A-Z LEEDS & BRADFORD

CONTENTS

Key to Map Pages	2-3	Index to Streets, Towns, Villages, Stations & selected Places of Interest	165-294
Large Scale Centres	4-7 & 164		
Map Pages	8-163	Index to Hospitals & Hospices	295-296

REFERENCE

Motorway	**M62**	Local Authority Boundary	— · — · —
Under Construction		Posttown Boundary	
Proposed		Postcode Boundary within Posttown	— — —
A Road	**A61**	Map Continuation 75 / Large Scale Centres 4	
Under Construction		Car Park (selected)	P
Proposed		Church or Chapel	†
B Road	**B6153**	Fire Station	■
Dual Carriageway		Hospital	**H**
One-way Street Traffic flow on A Roads is indicated by a heavy line on the driver's left.	→	House Numbers (A & B Roads only)	13
Large Scale Pages only	⇒	Information Centre	**i**
Restricted Access		National Grid Reference	⁴35
Pedestrianized Road		Park & Ride	King Lane P+
Leeds City Centre Loop Junctions are shown on Large Scale Pages only	①	Police Station	▲
Track / Footpath		Post Office	★
Residential Walkway		Toilet: without facilities for the Disabled with facilities for the Disabled for exclusive use by the Disabled	▽ ▽ ▽
Cycleway (selected)	•••	Viewpoint	※
Railway	Station / Level Crossing / Heritage Sta. / Tunnel	Educational Establishment	
		Hospital or Hospice	
Leeds Supertram Estimated Completion 2008	Stop	Industrial Building	
		Leisure or Recreational Facility	
Built-up Area	MANOR ST.	Place of Interest	
		Public Building	
		Shopping Centre or Market	
		Other Selected Buildings	

SCALE

Map Pages 8-163 1:18,103

0	¼	½ Mile
0	250 500	750 Metres

3½ inches (8.89 cm) to 1 mile   5.52 cm to 1 km

Map Pages 4-7 & 164 1:9,051

0	⅛	¼ Mile
0	100 200	300 Metres

7 inches (17.78 cm) to 1 mile   11.05 cm to 1 km

Copyright of Geographers' A-Z Map Company Ltd.

Head Office:
Fairfield Road, Borough Green, Sevenoaks, Kent, TN15 8PP
Telephone 01732 781000
www.a-zmaps.co.uk

Copyright © Geographers' A-Z Map Co. Ltd.   Edition 1 2004

Ordnance Survey® This product includes mapping data licensed from Ordnance Survey® with the permission of the Controller of Her Majesty's Stationery Office.

© Crown Copyright 2004. All rights reserved.
Licence number 100017302

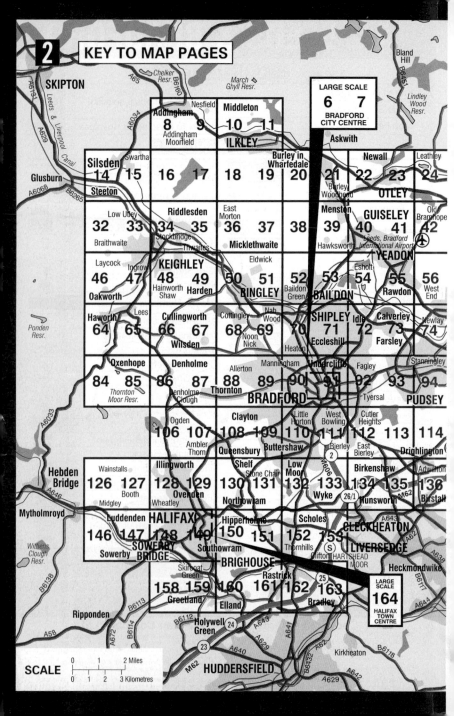

2 **KEY TO MAP PAGES**

SKIPTON

Chelker Resr.
March Ghyll Resr.

Bland Hill

Lindley Wood Resr.

LARGE SCALE
6 7
BRADFORD CITY CENTRE

Nesfield
Addingham
8   9
Addingham Moorfield

Middleton
10   11
ILKLEY

Askwith

Newall
Leathley

Glusburn

Silsden
Swartha
14   15
Steeton

16   17

18   19

Burley in Wharfedale
20   21
Burley Woodhead

22   23
Newall
24
UTLEY

Low Utley
32   33
Braithwaite

Riddlesden
34   35
Stockbridge
Thwaites

East Morton
36   37
Micklethwaite

38

Menston
39
Hawksworth

GUISELEY
40   41
Leeds, Bradford International Airport

Old Bramhope
42

Laycock
Ingrow
46   47
Oakworth

KEIGHLEY
48   49
Hainworth Shaw Harden

50   51
BINGLEY

Eldwick
52   53
Baildon Green

Esholt
54
BAILDON

55
Rawdon

YEADON

56
West End

Haworth
Lees
64   65

Cullingworth
66   67
Wilsden

Cottingley
68   69
Noon Nick

Nab Wood
70
Heaton

SHIPLEY
71
Eccleshill

Idle
72   73
Farsley

Calverley
Newlay
74

Ponden Resr.

Oxenhope
84   85
Thornton Moor Resr.

Denholme
86   87
Denholme Clough

Allerton
88   89
THORNTON

Manningham
90   91
BRADFORD

Undercliffe
Fagley
92   93
Tyersal

Stanningley
94
PUDSEY

Ogden
106 107
Ambler Thorn

Clayton
108 109
Queensbury Buttershaw

Little Horton
110 111
Bierley

West Bowling
East Bierley

Cutler Heights
112 113

114
Drighlington

Hebden Bridge

Wainstalls
126 127
Booth
Midgley

128 129
Ovenden
Wheatley

Illingworth

Shelf
130 131
Stone Chair
Northowram

Low Moor
132 133
Wyke

Birkenshaw
134 135
Hunsworth

136
Adwalton
Birstall

Mytholmroyd

Luddenden
146 147
Sowerby

HALIFAX
148 149
SOWERBY BRIDGE
Southowram

Hipperholme
150
151

Scholes
152
Thornhills
Clifton HARTSHEAD MOOR

CLECKHEATON

LIVERSEDGE
Heckmondwike

Withens Clough Resr.

BRIGHOUSE

Skircoat Green
158 159
Greetland

Rastrick
160 161
Elland

162 163
Bradley

LARGE SCALE
164
HALIFAX TOWN CENTRE

Ripponden

Holywell Green

Kirkheaton

SCALE
0   1   2 Miles
0 1 2   3 Kilometres

HUDDERSFIELD

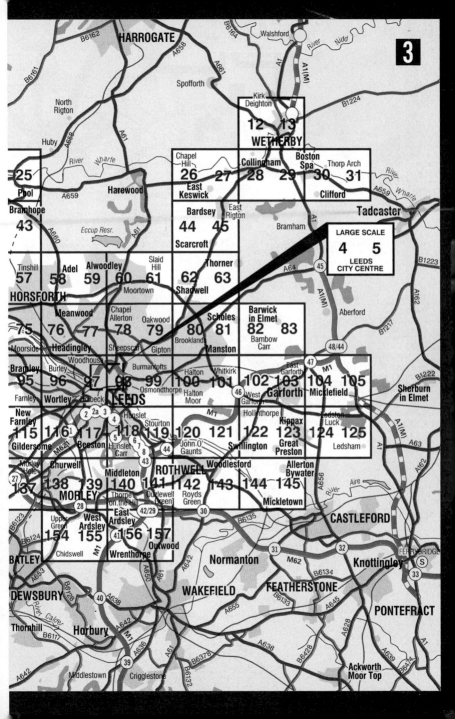

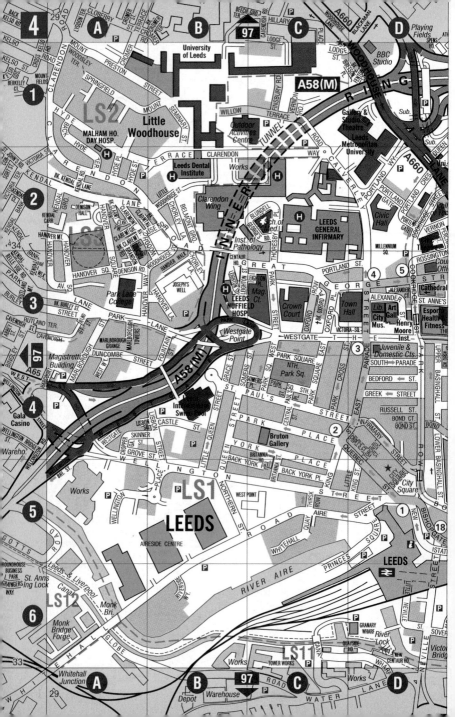

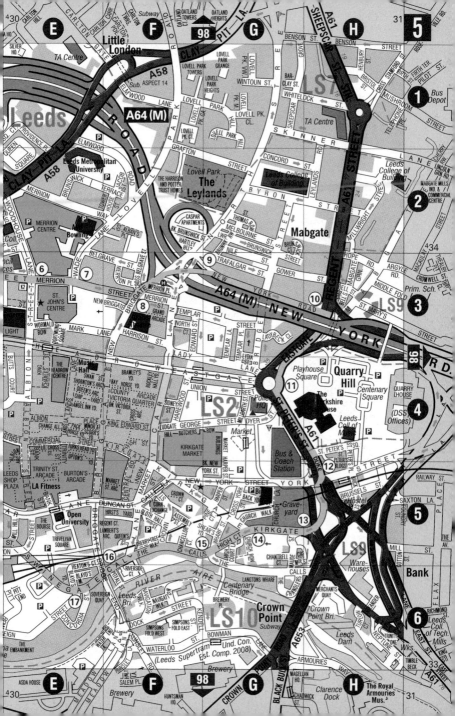

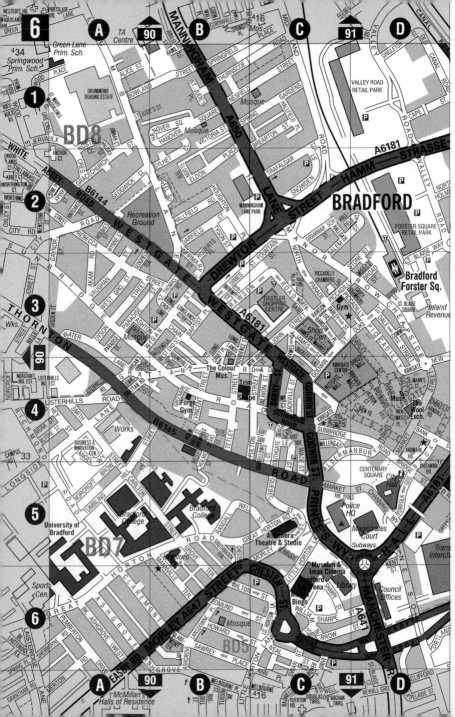

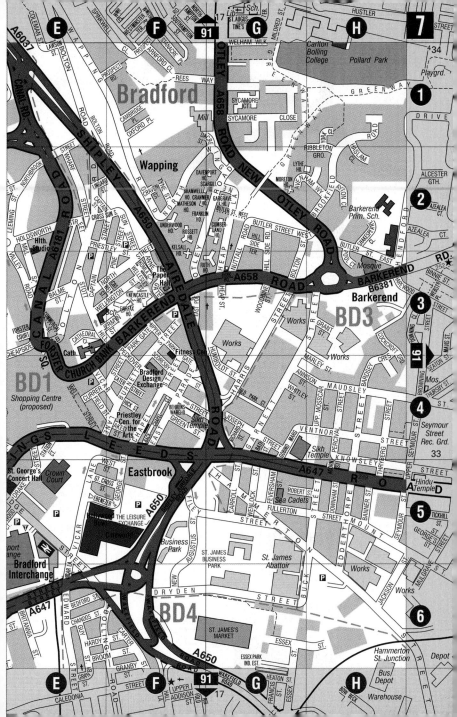

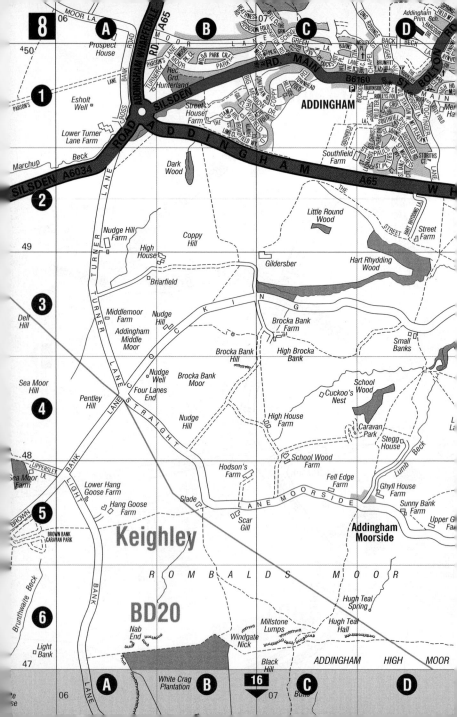

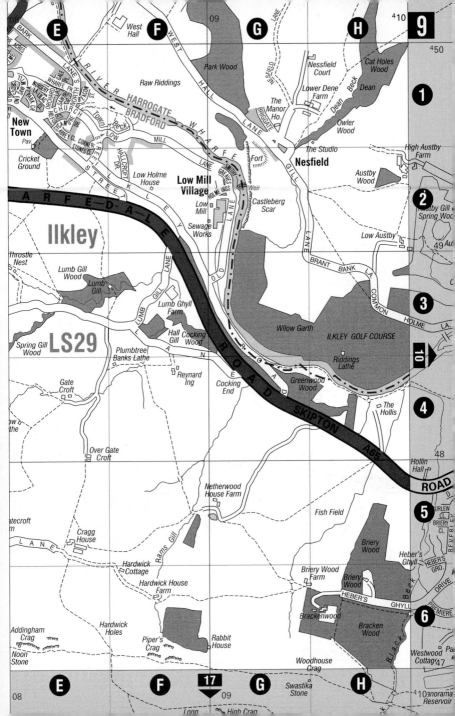

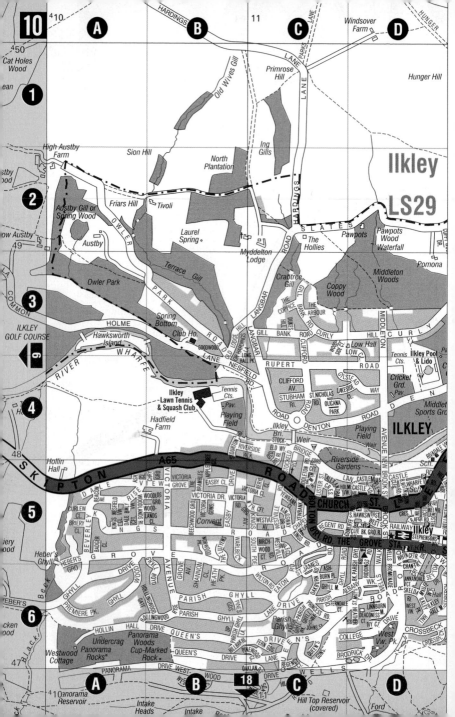

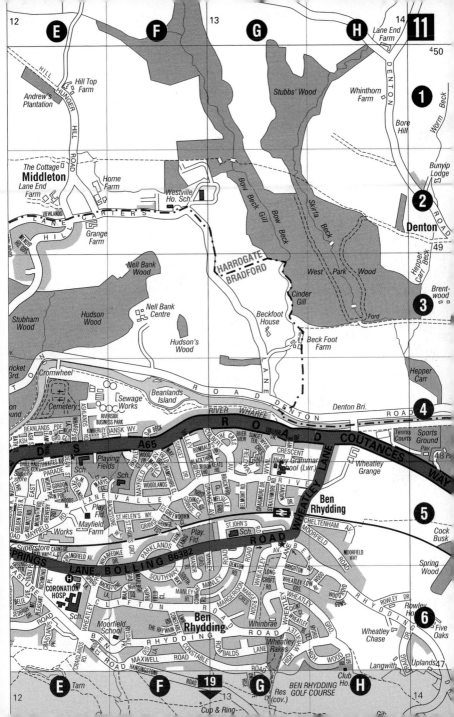

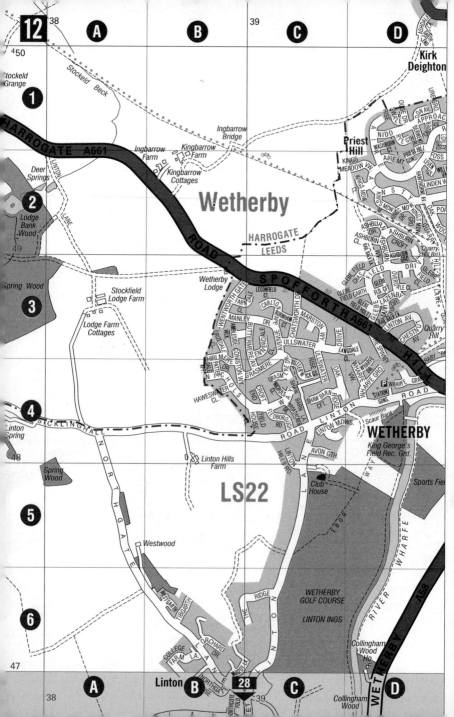

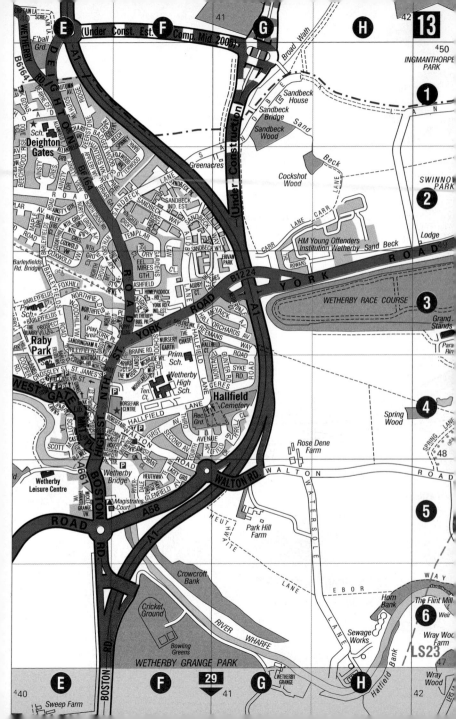

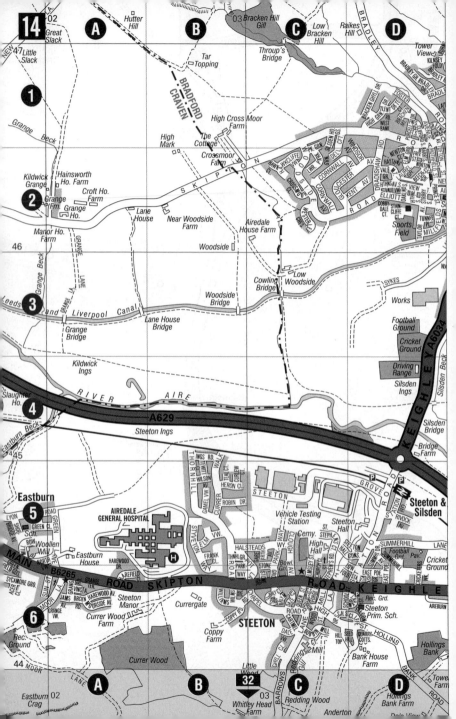

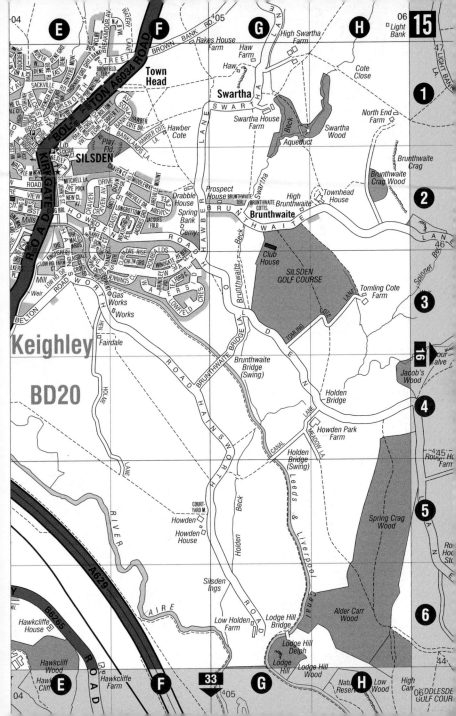

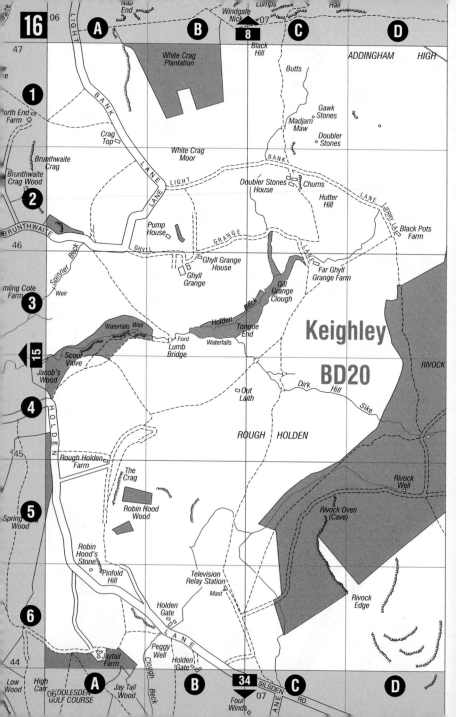

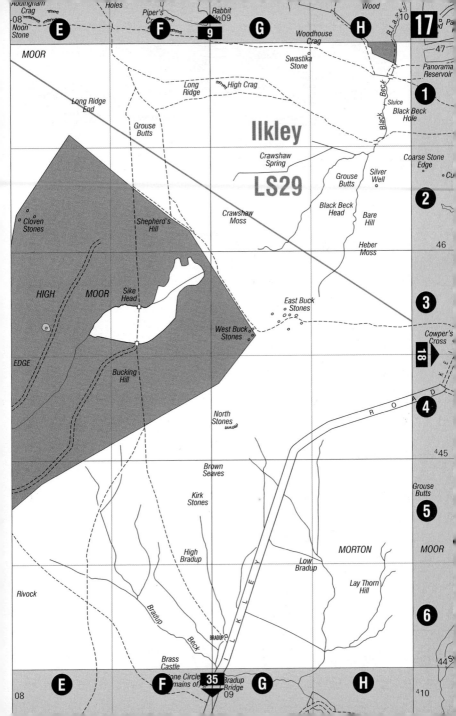

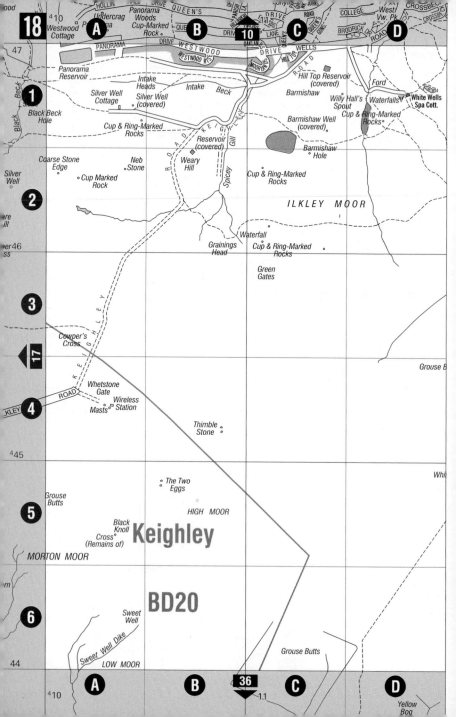

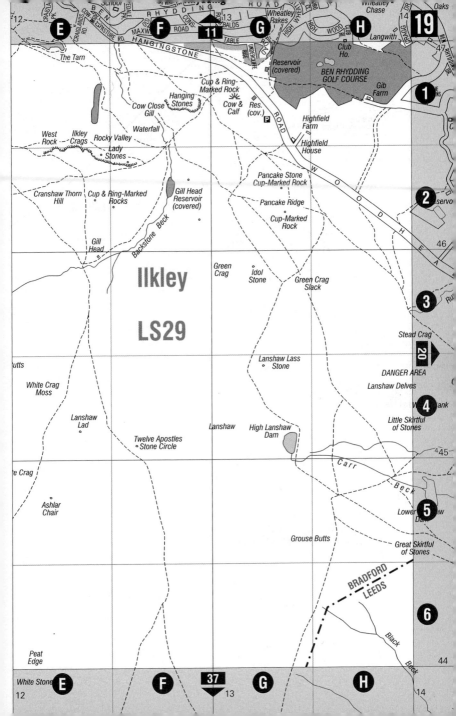

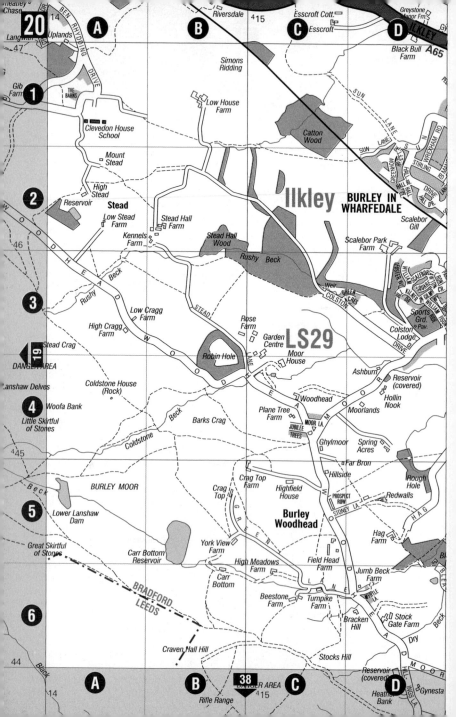

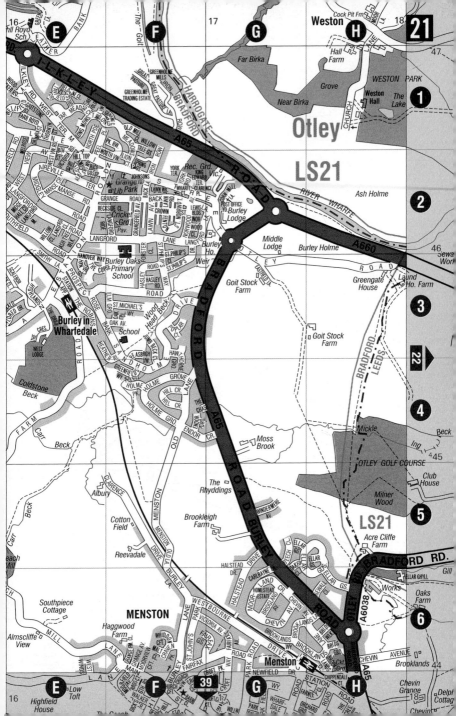

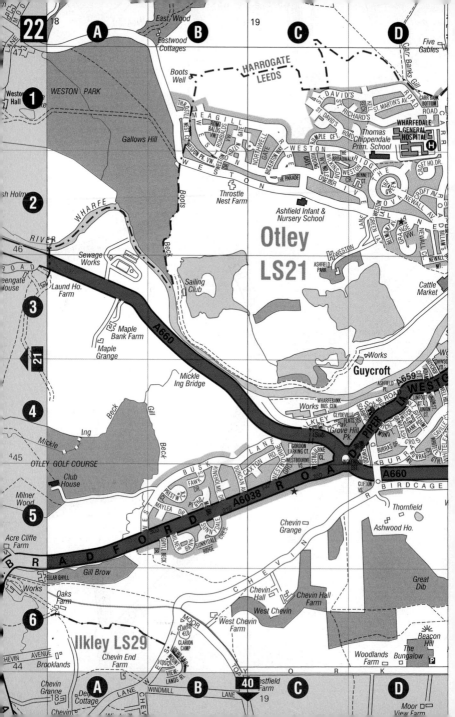

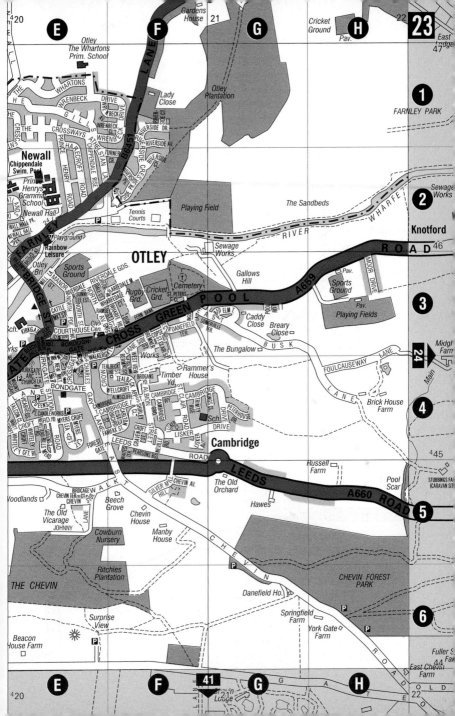

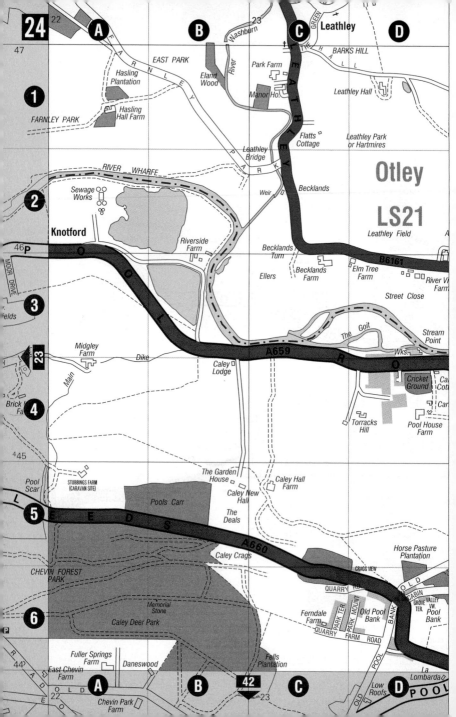

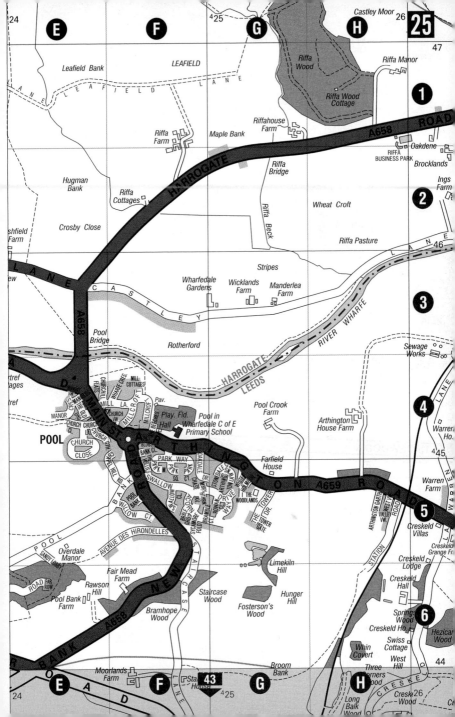

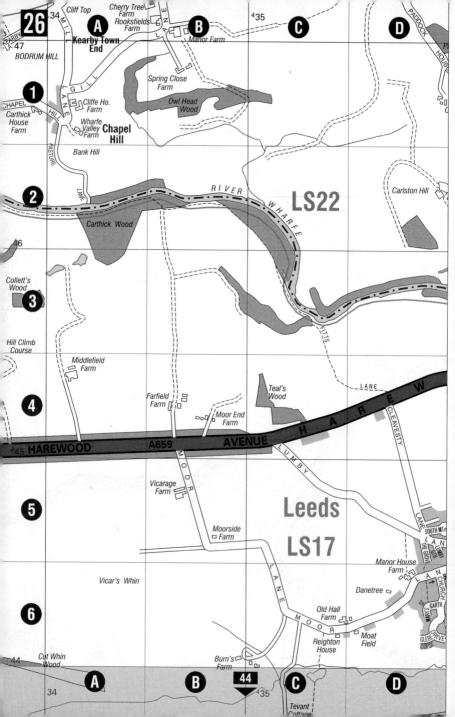

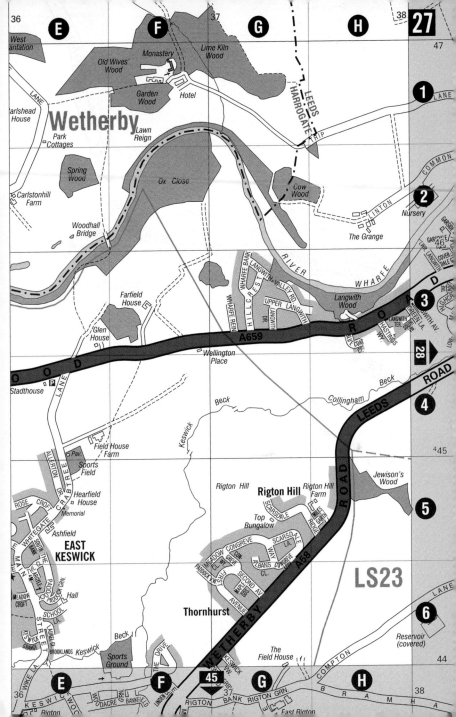

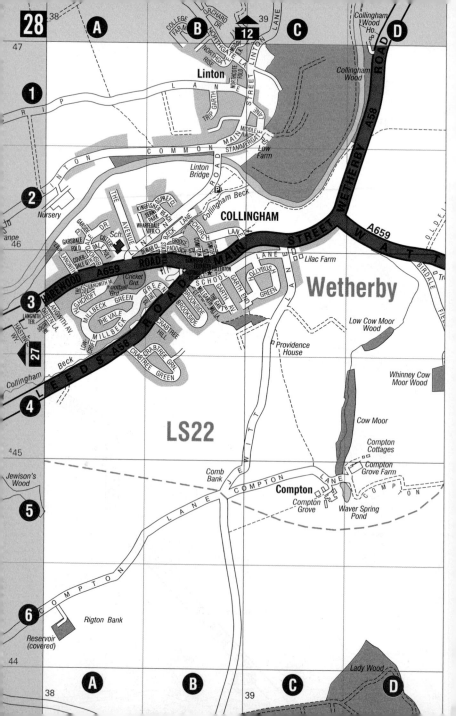

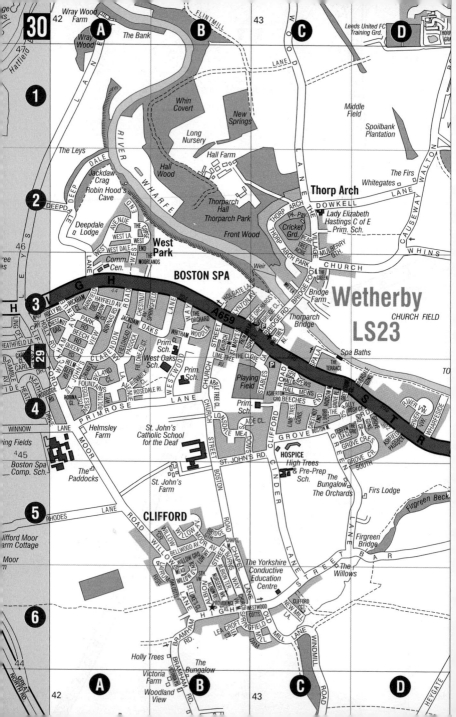

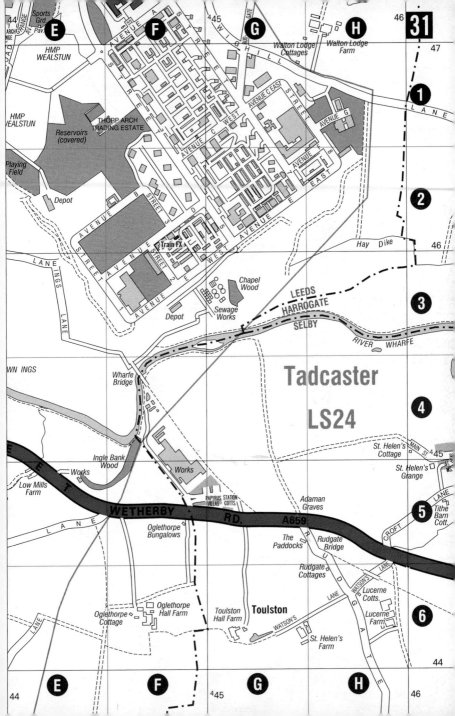

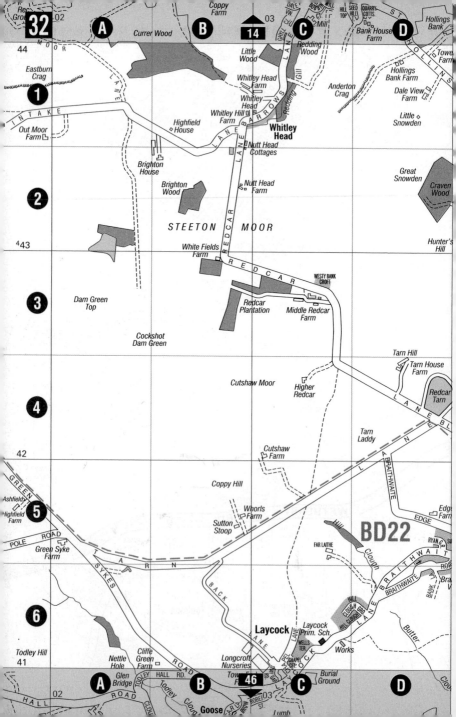

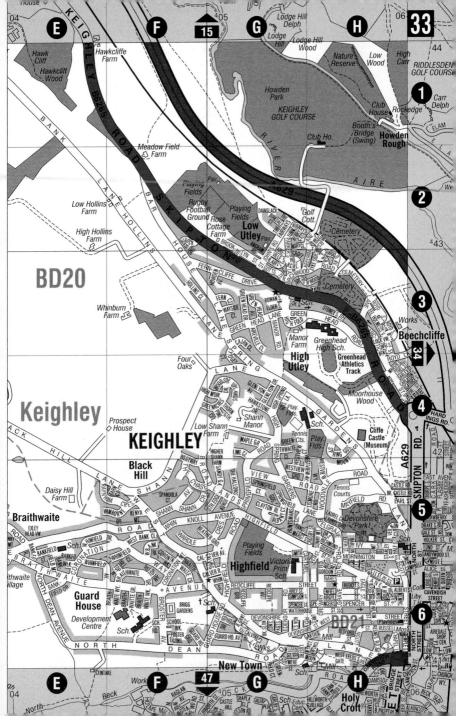

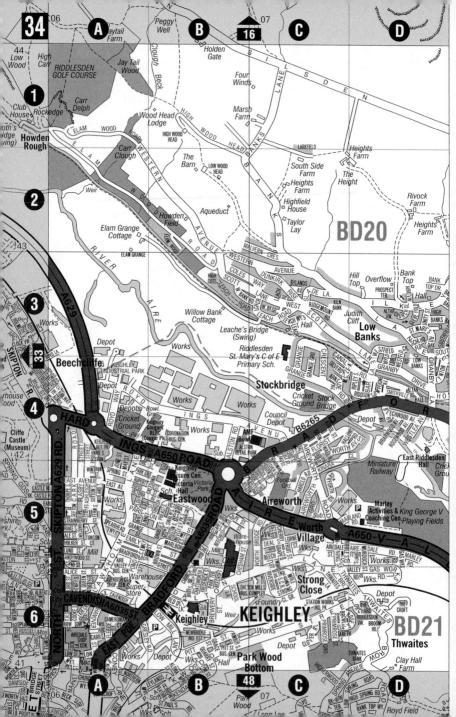

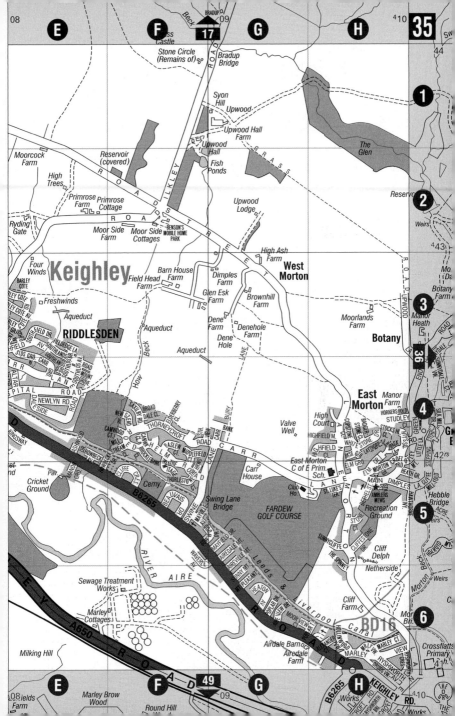

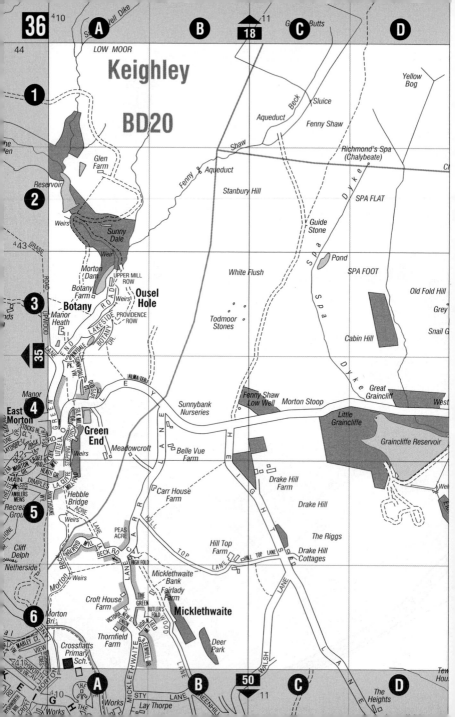

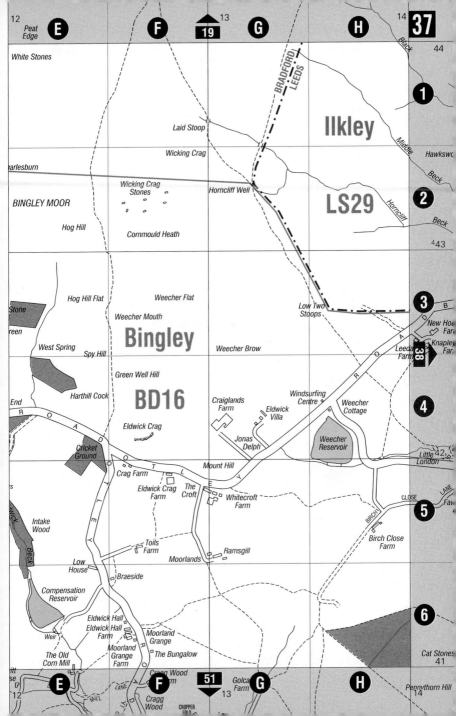

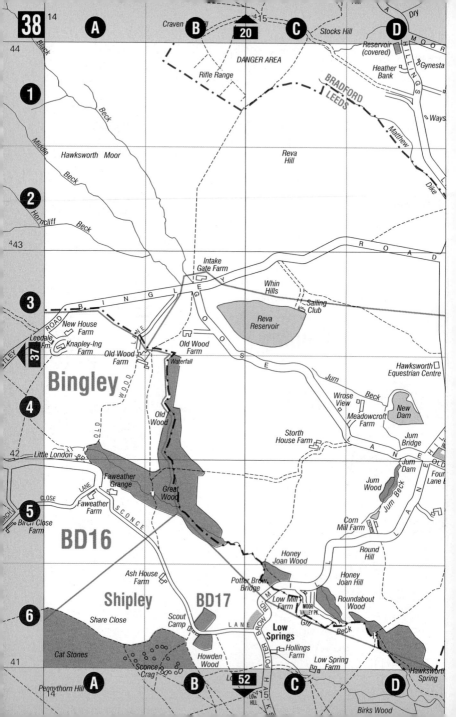

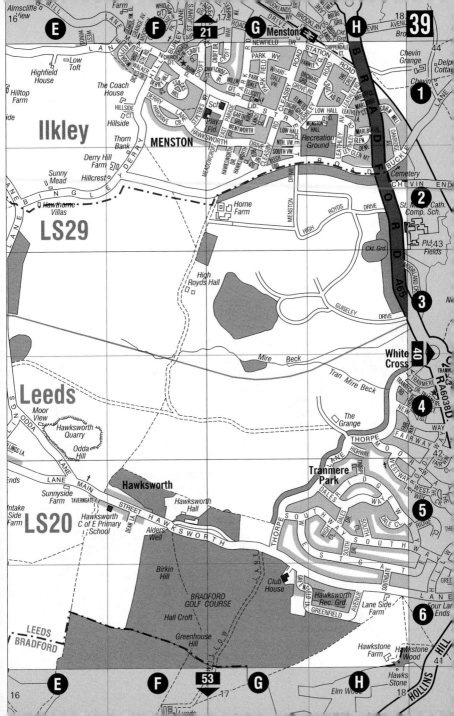

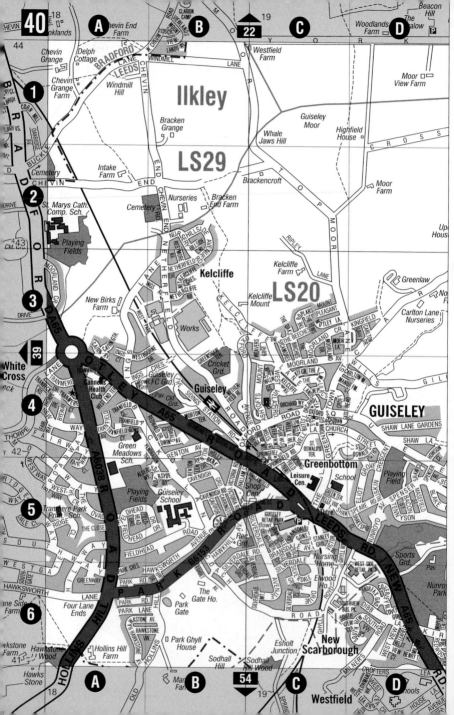

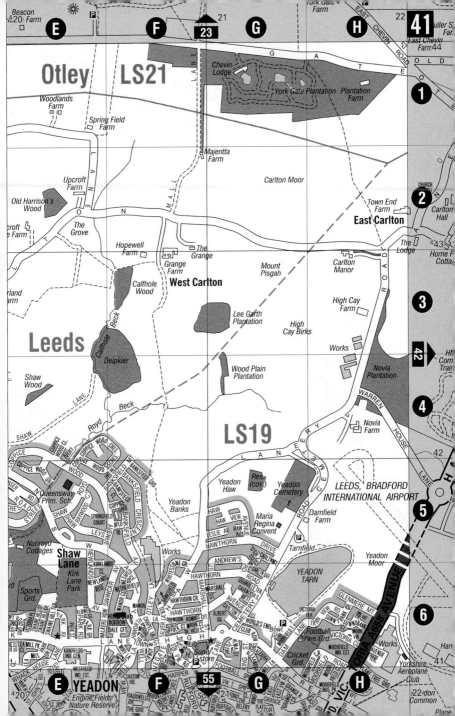

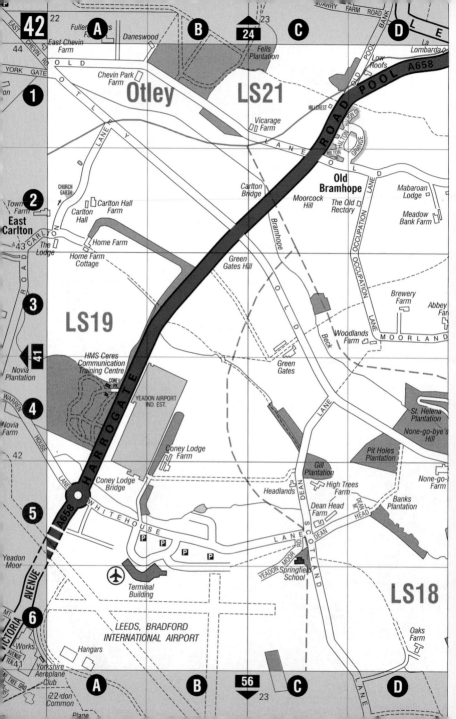

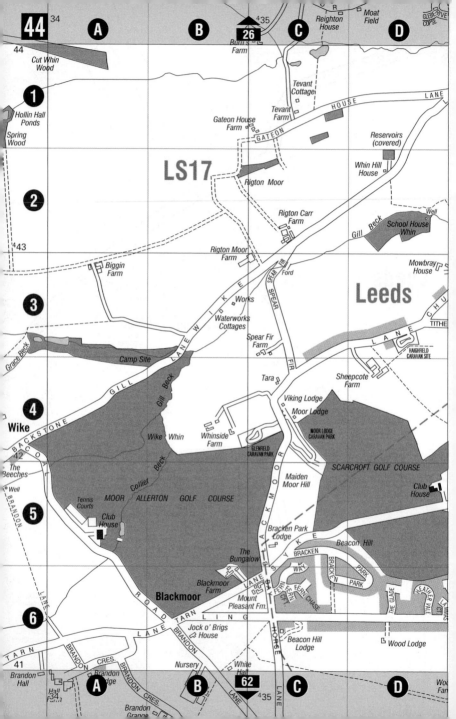

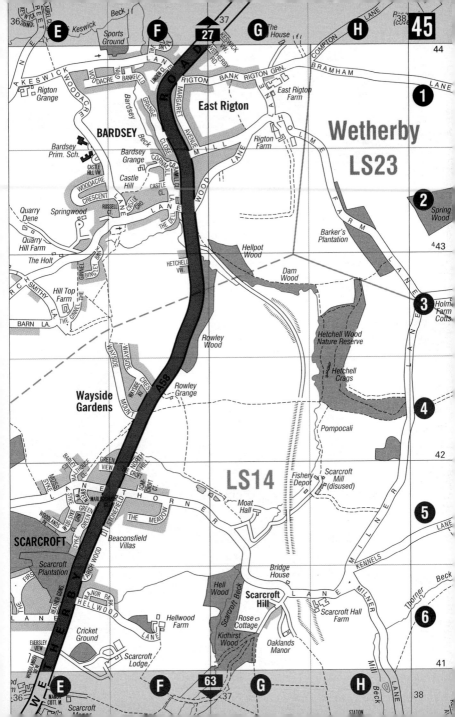

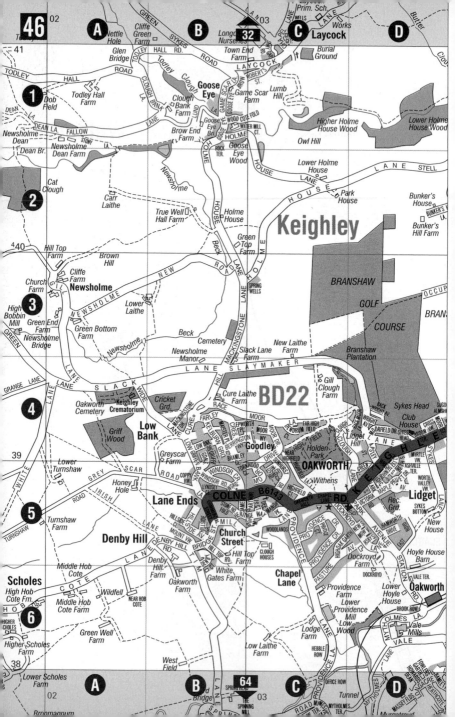

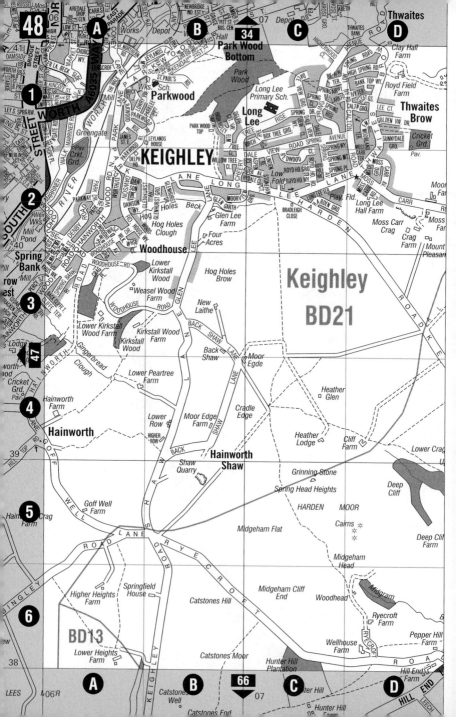

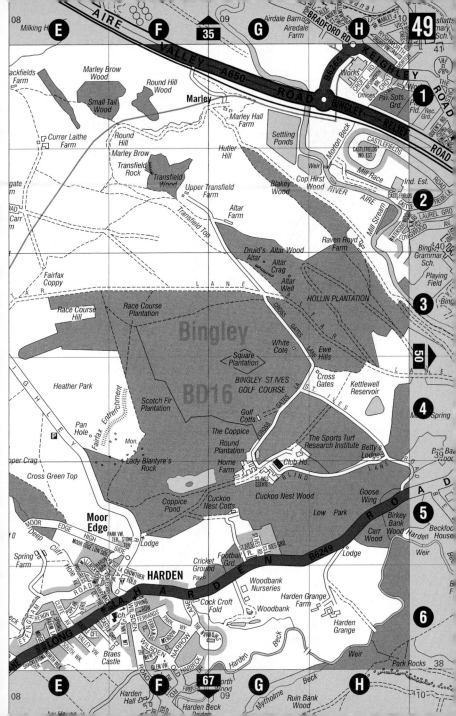

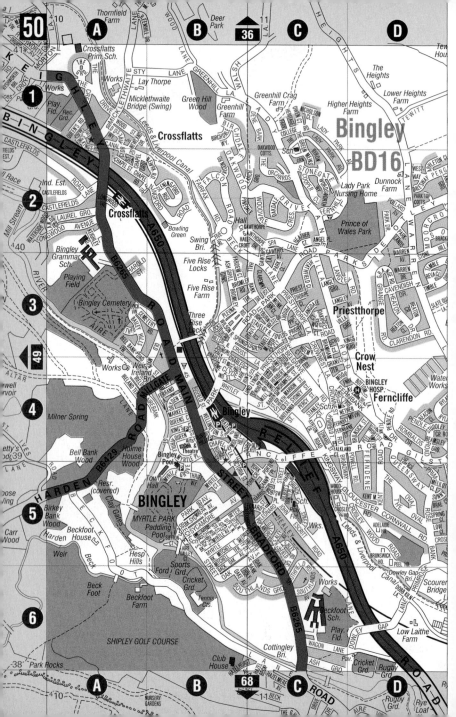

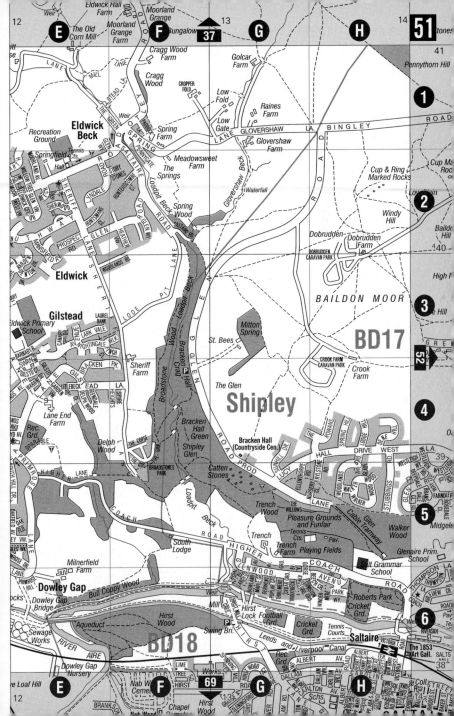

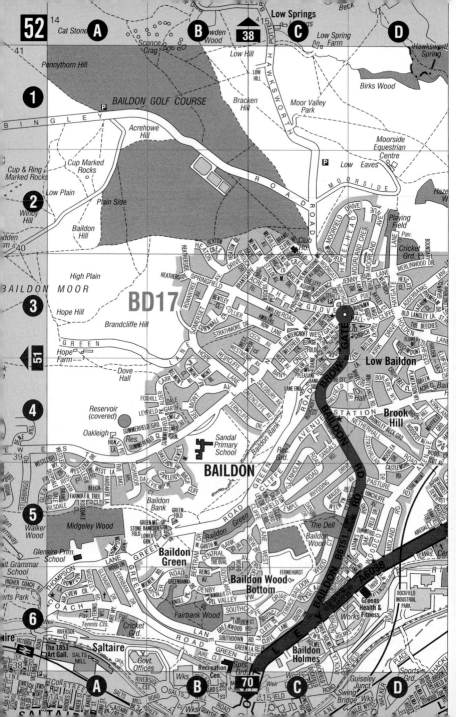

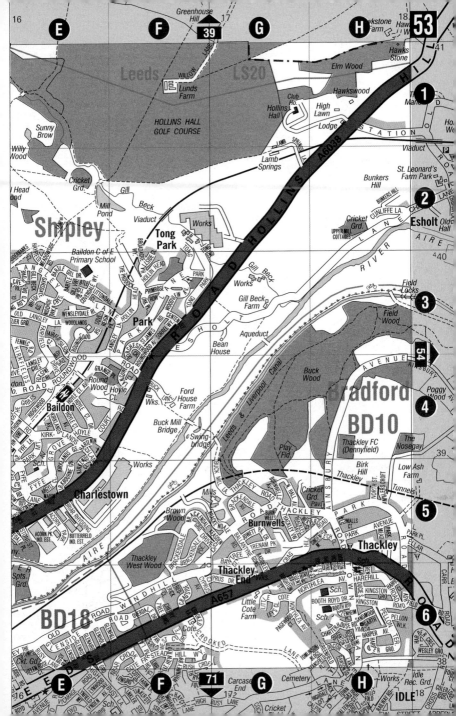

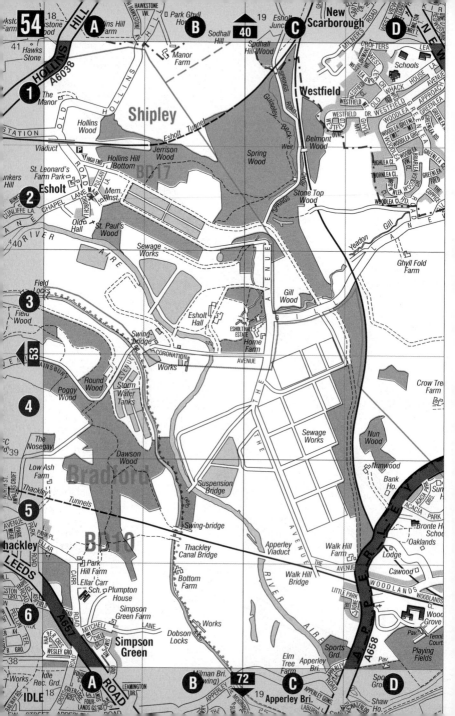

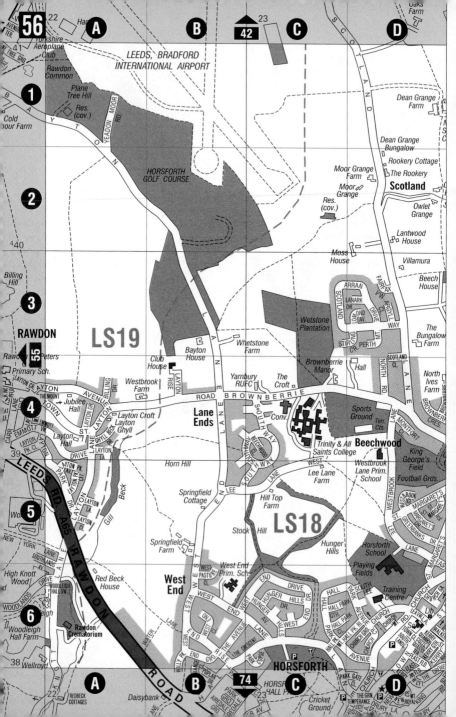

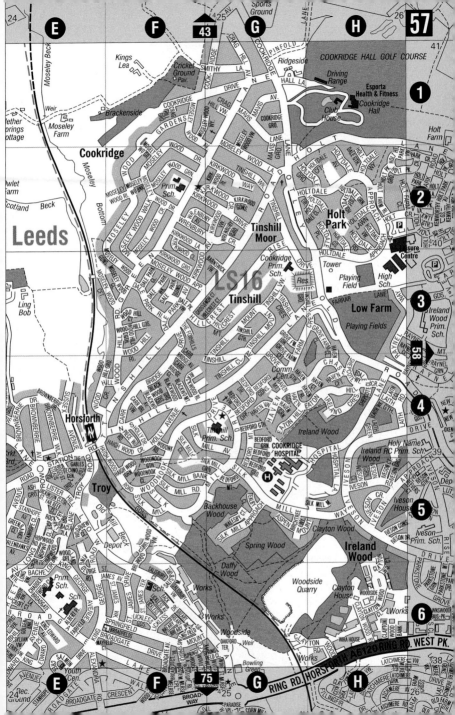

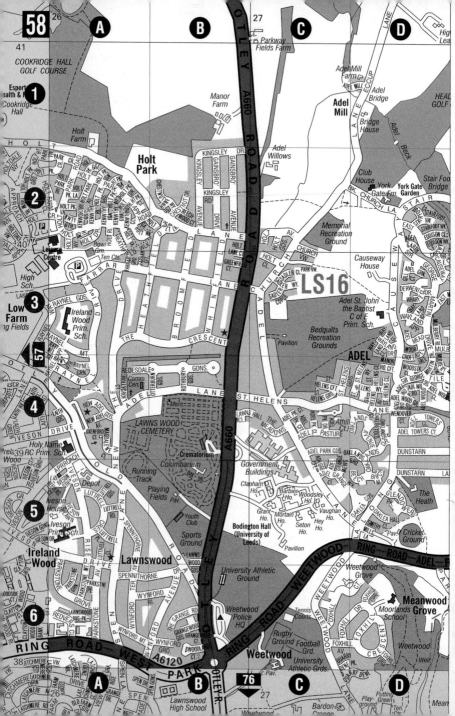

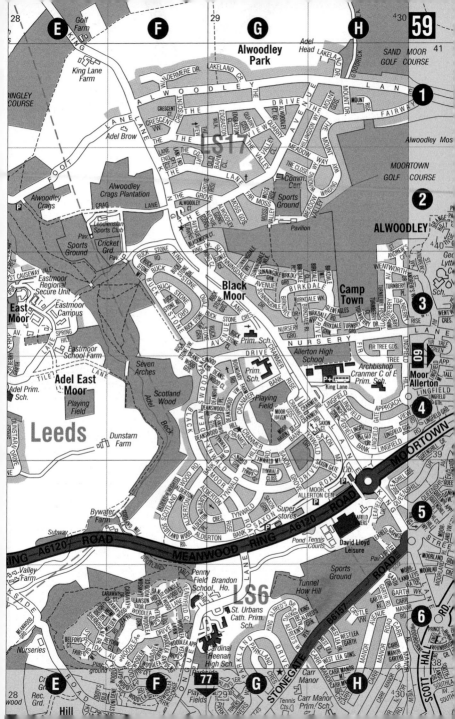

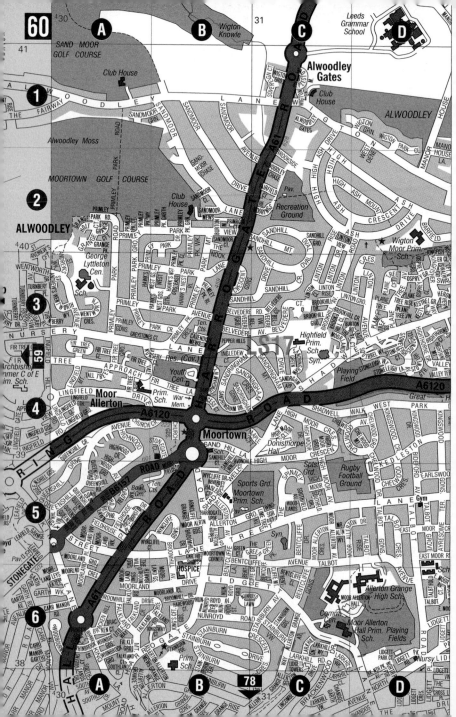

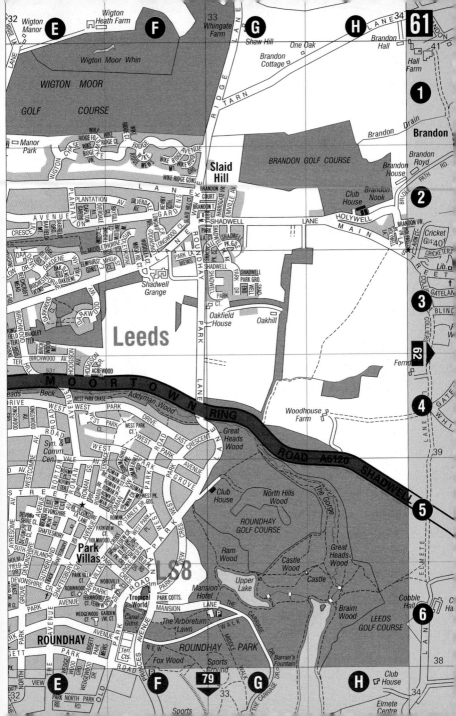

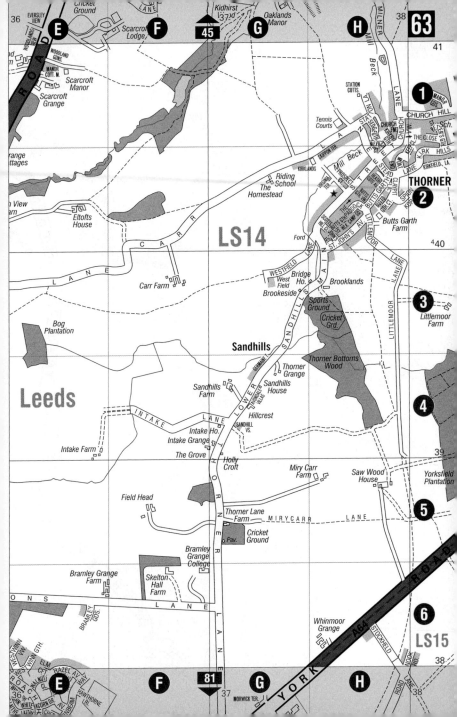

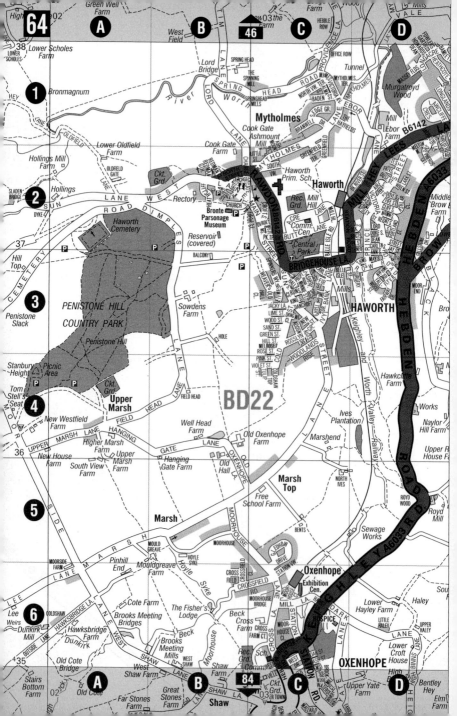

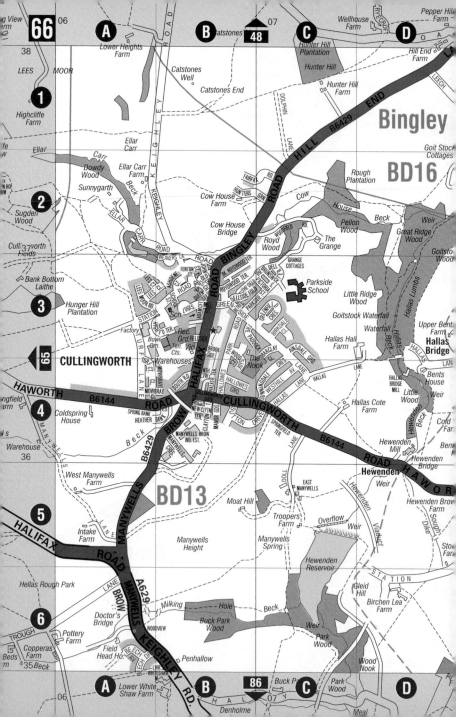

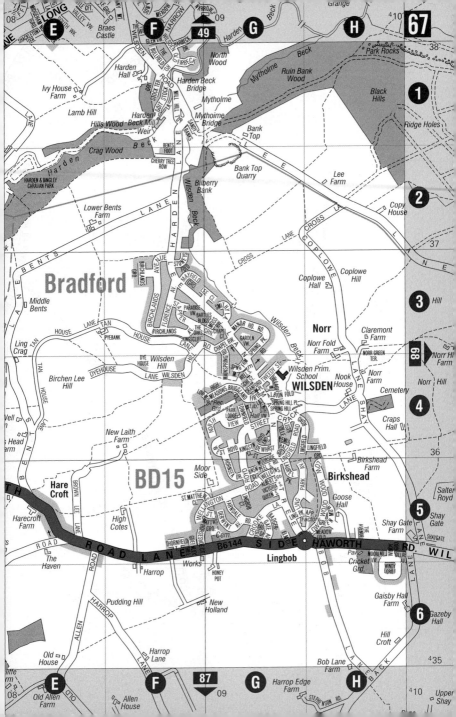

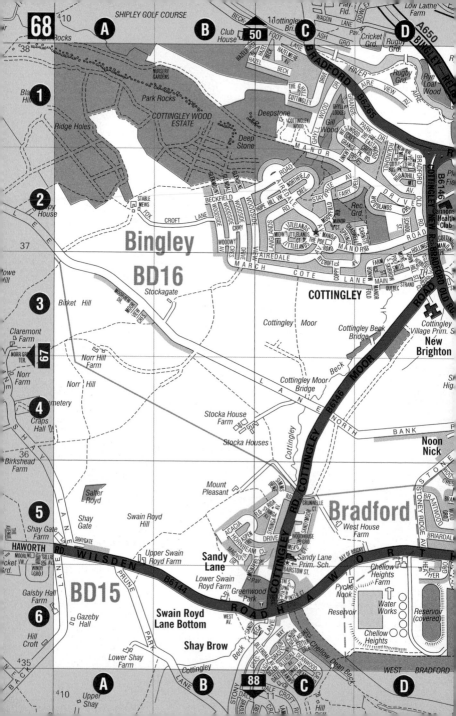

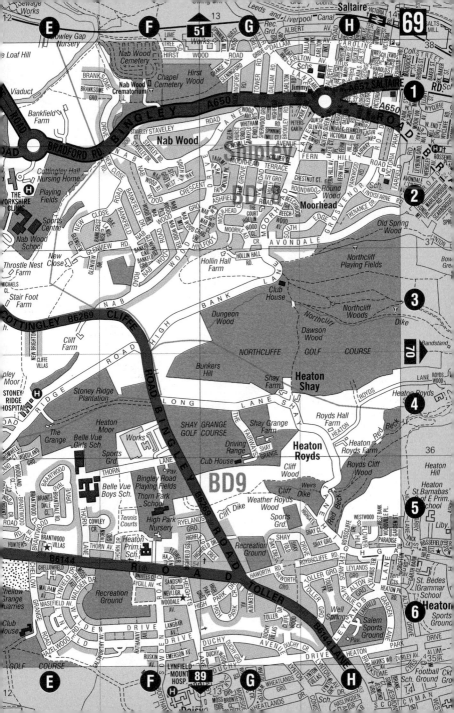

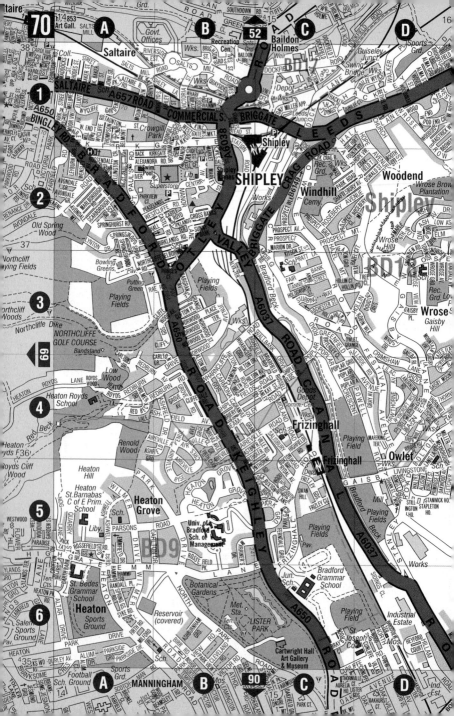

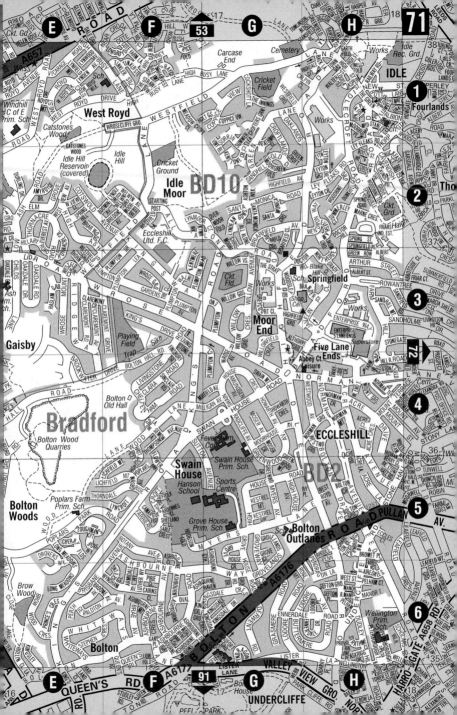

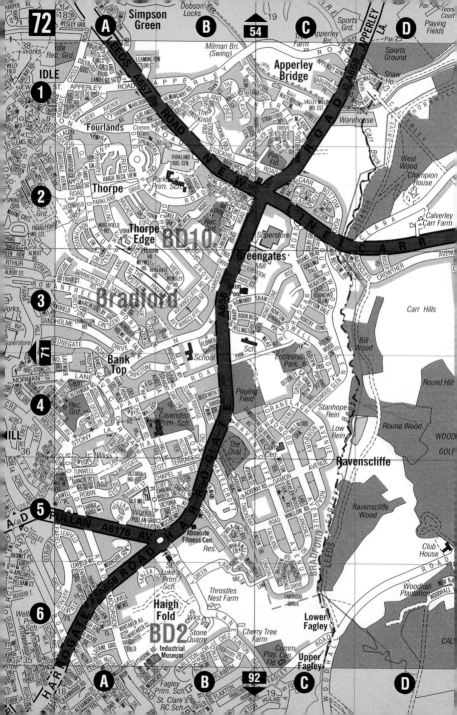

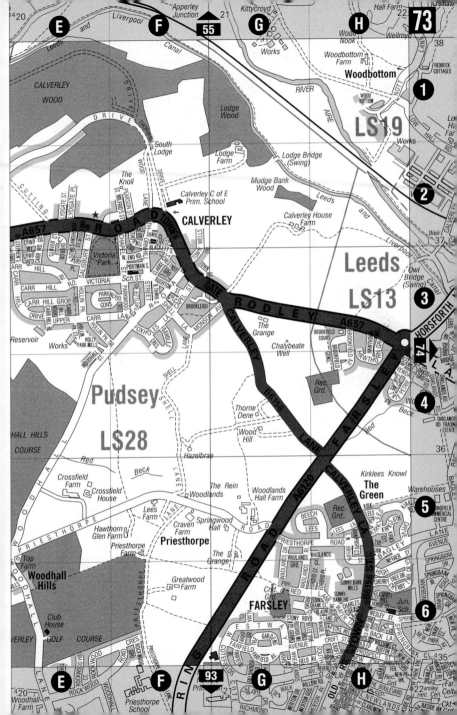

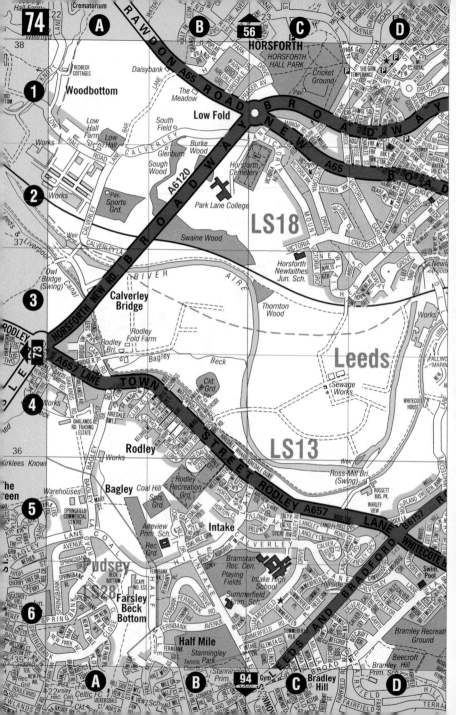

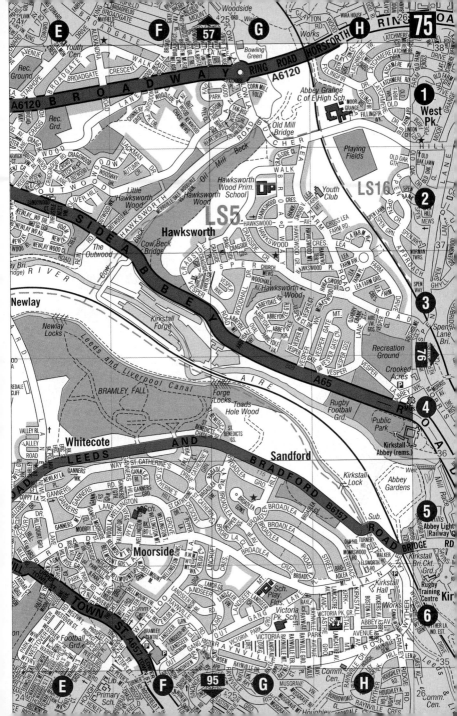

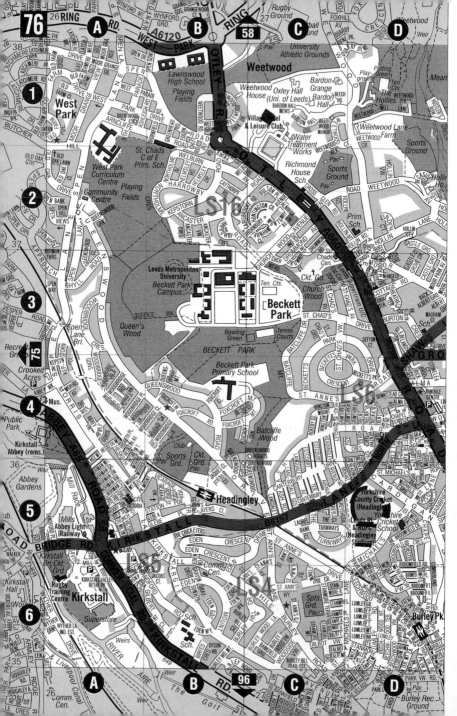

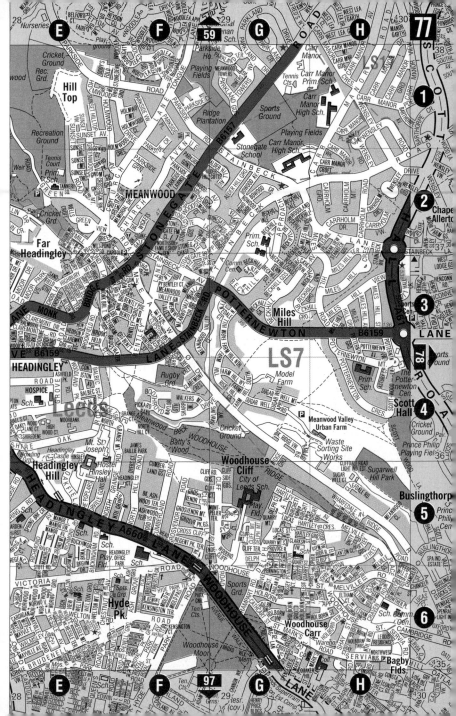

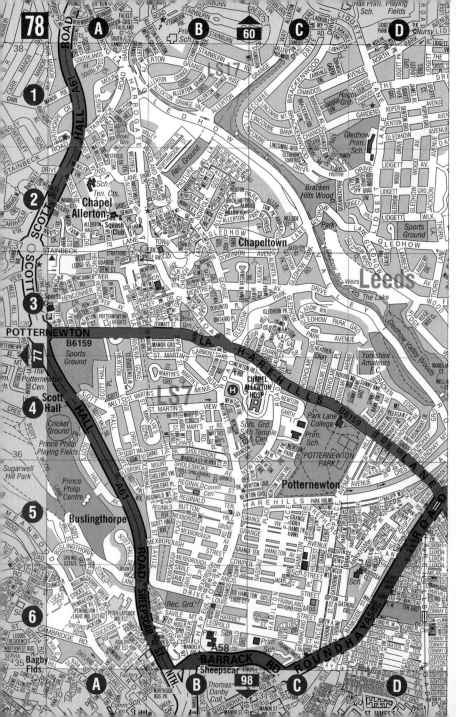

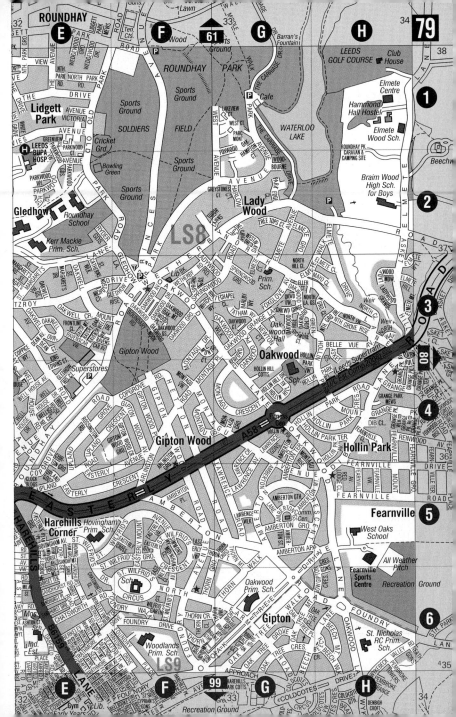

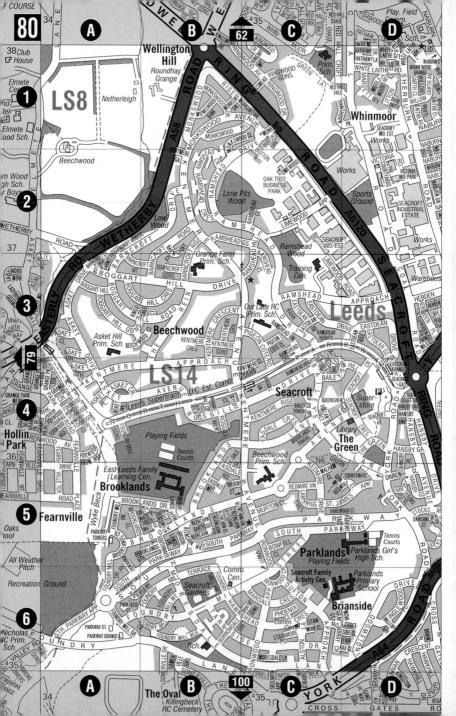

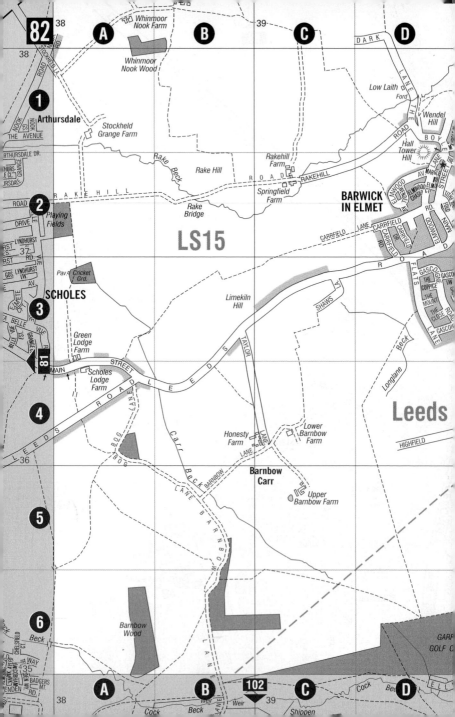

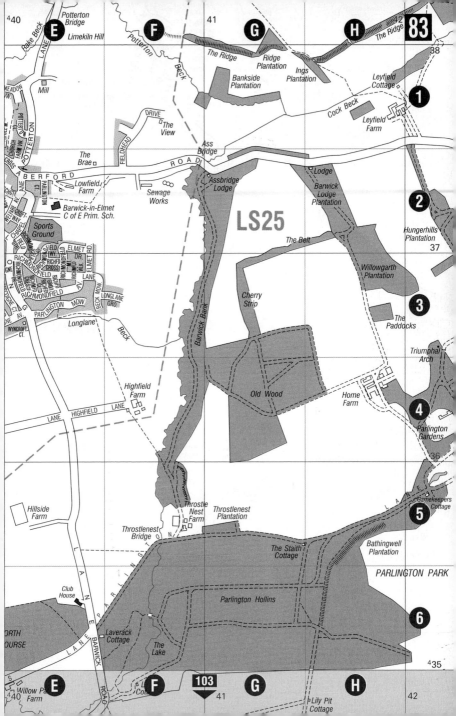

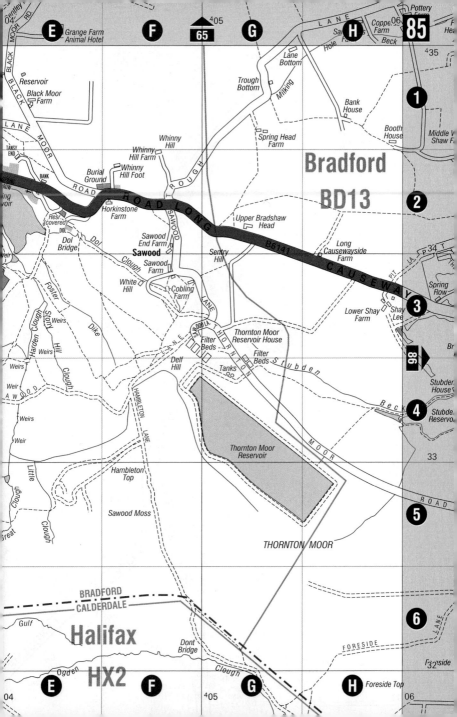

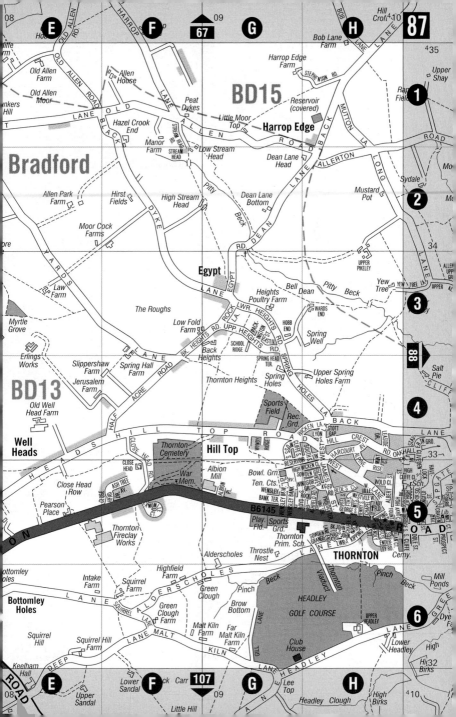

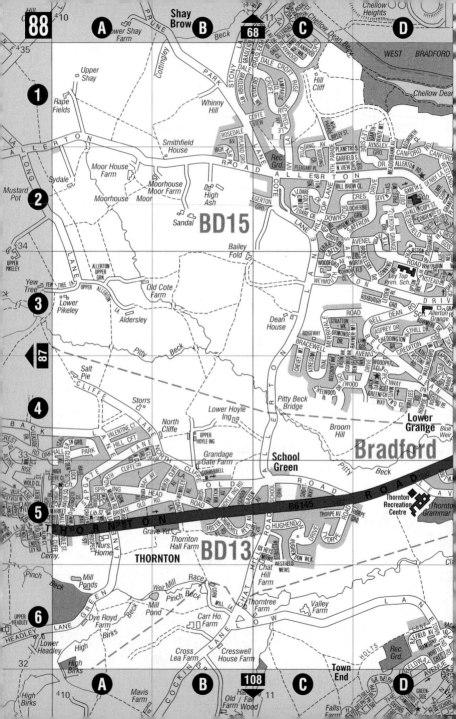

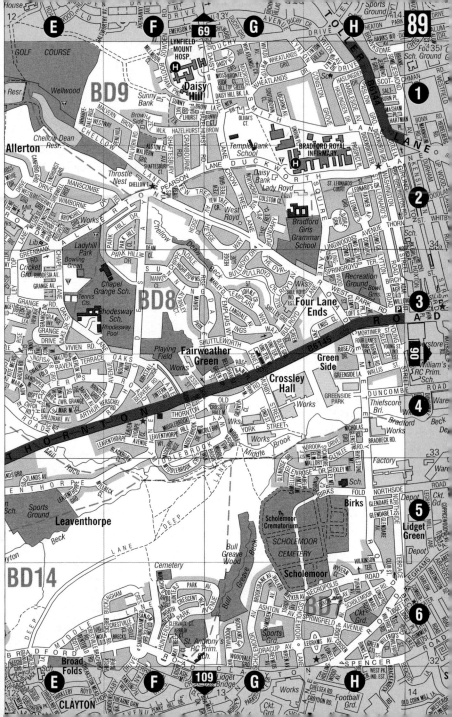

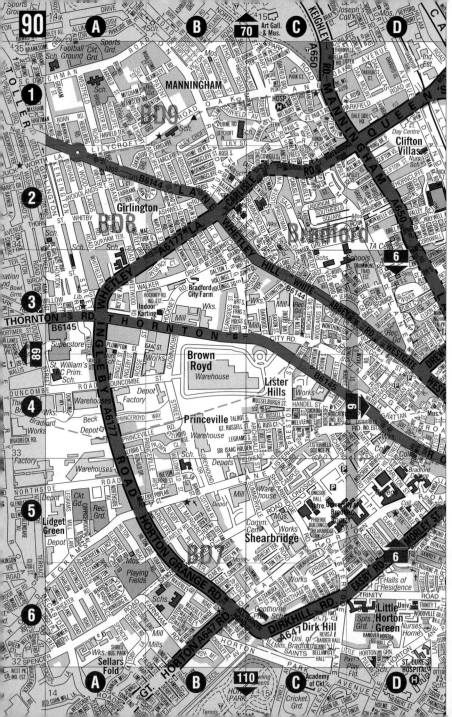

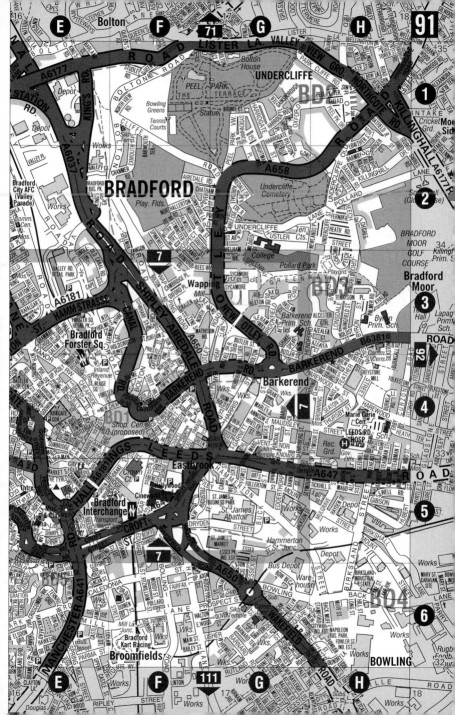

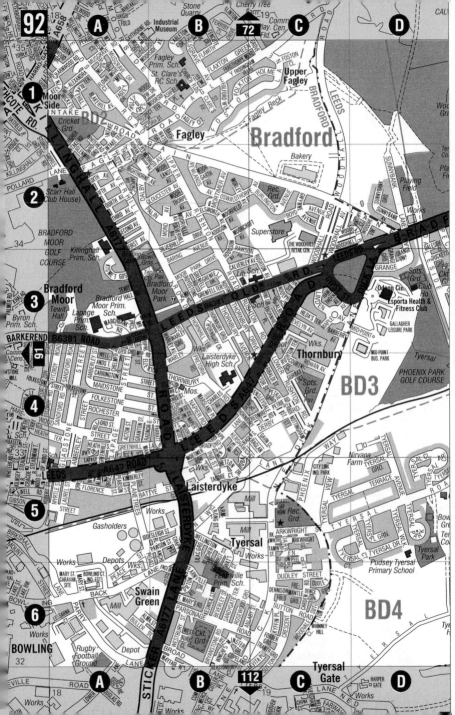

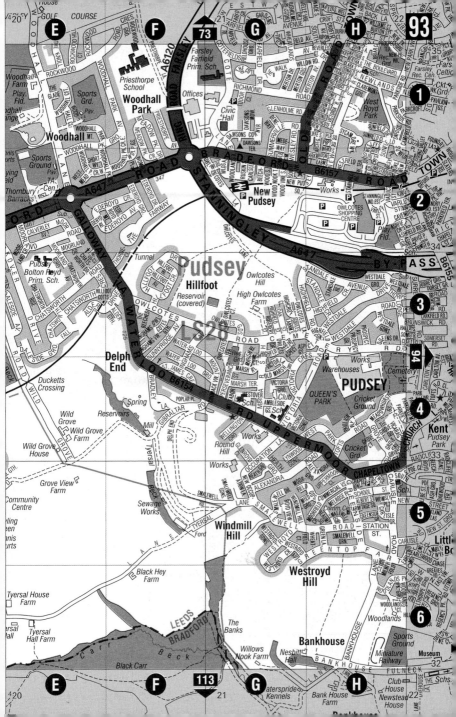

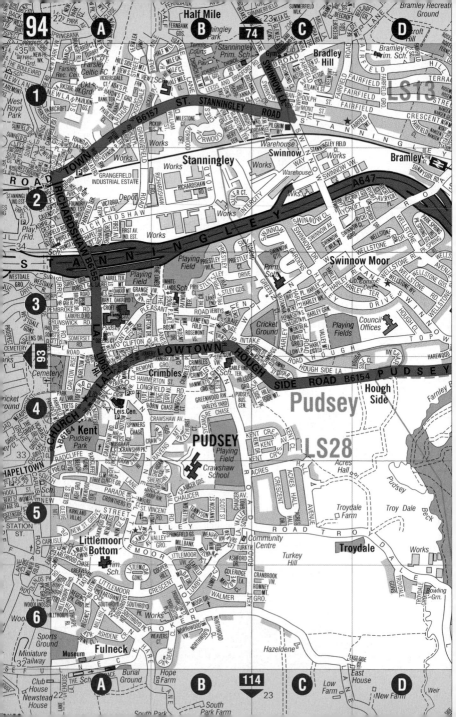

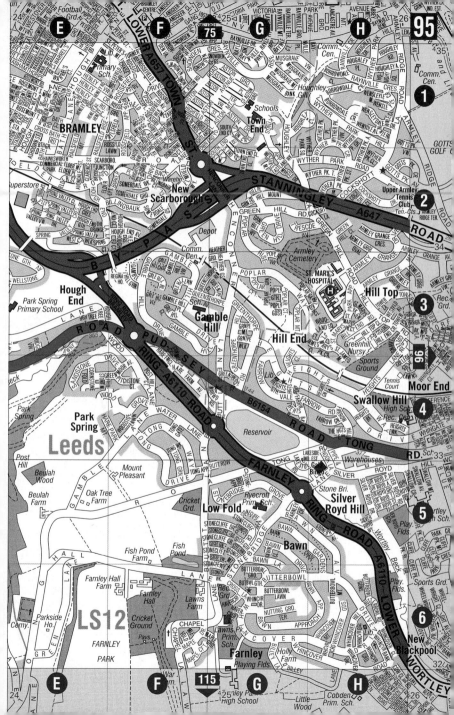

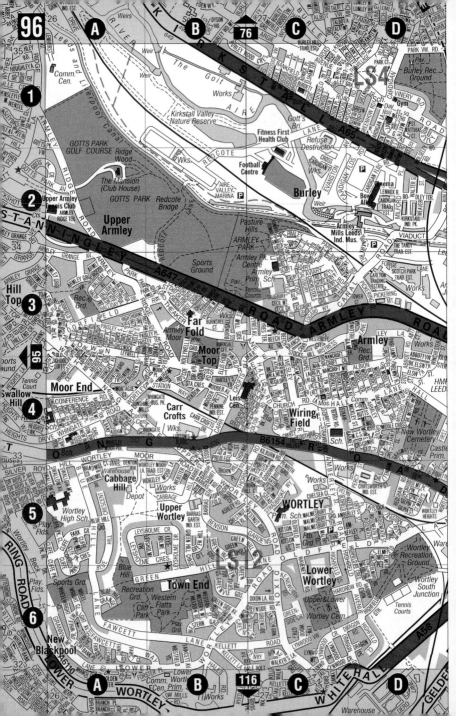

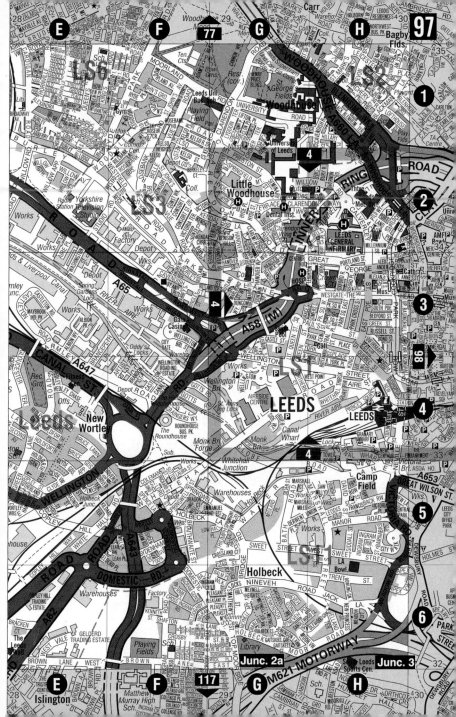

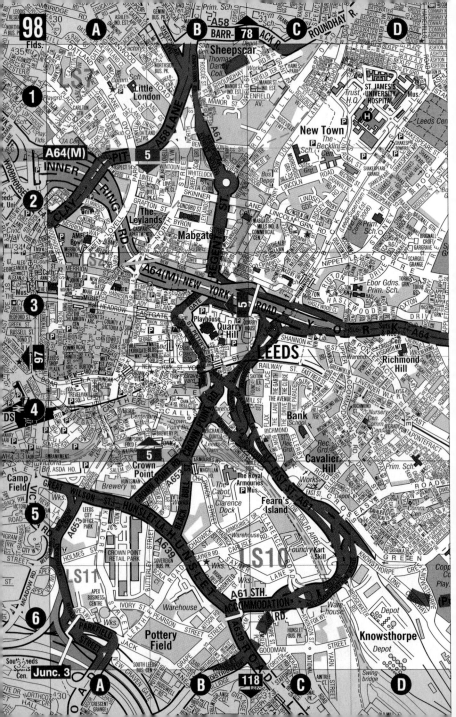

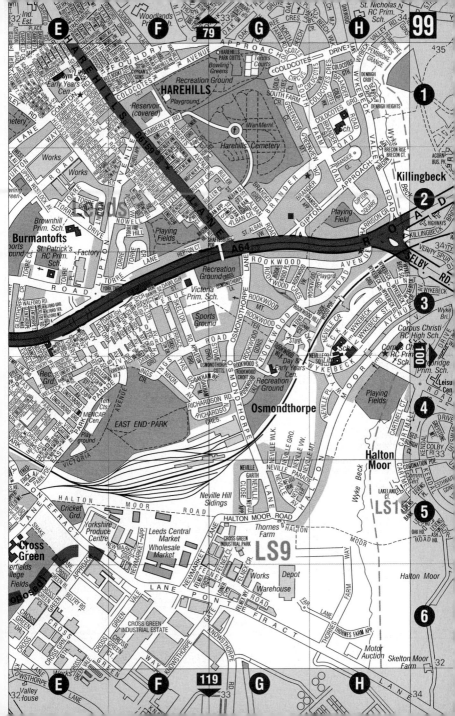

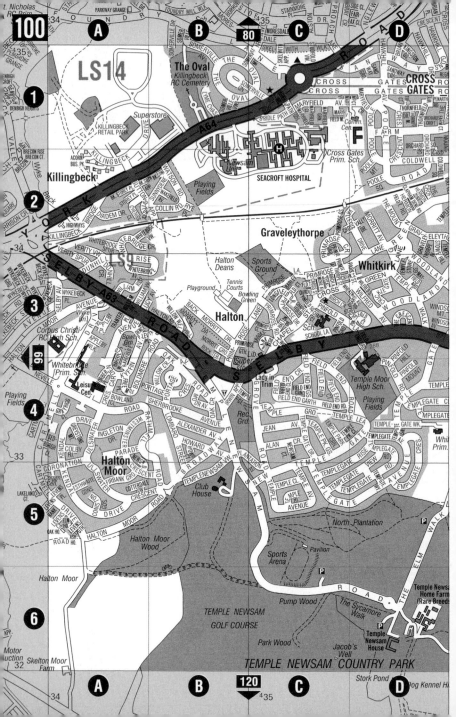

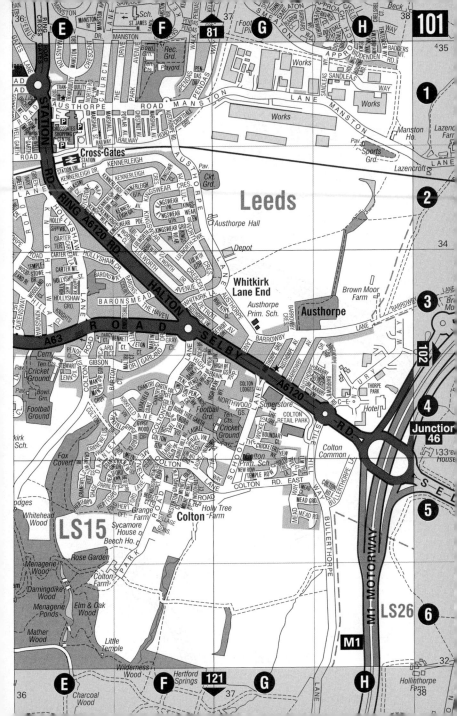

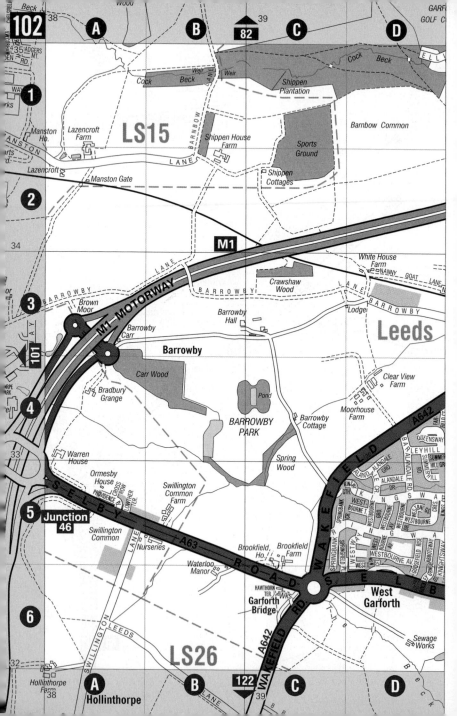

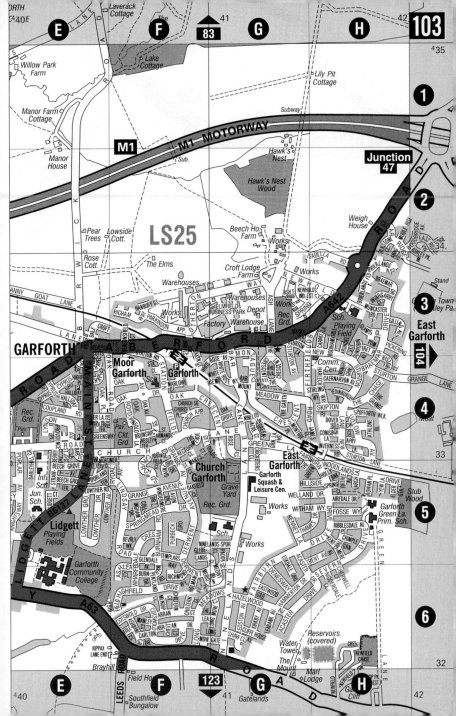

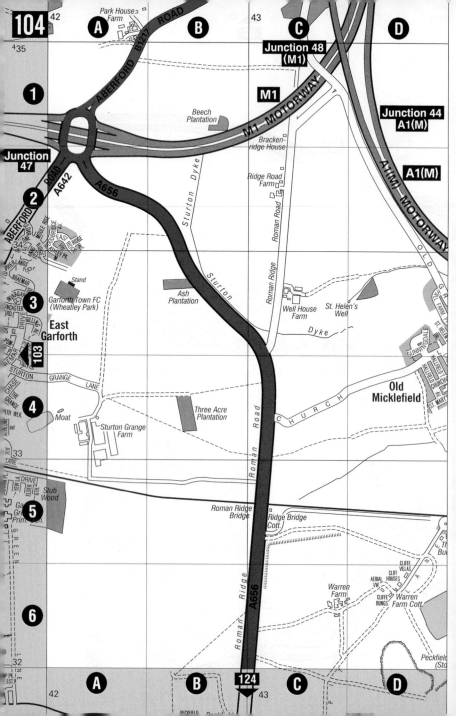

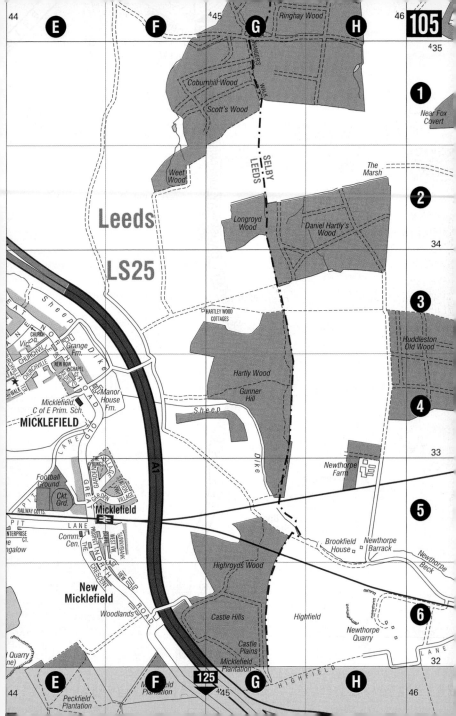

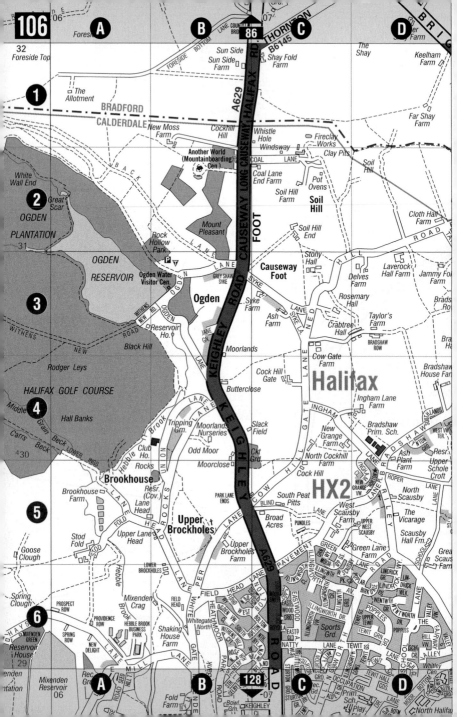

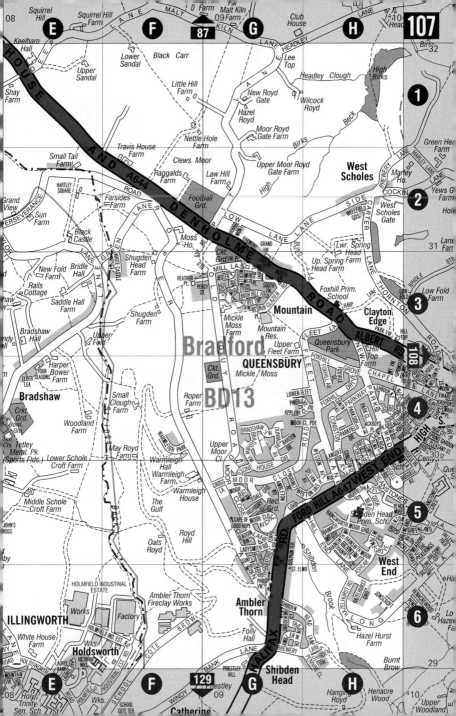

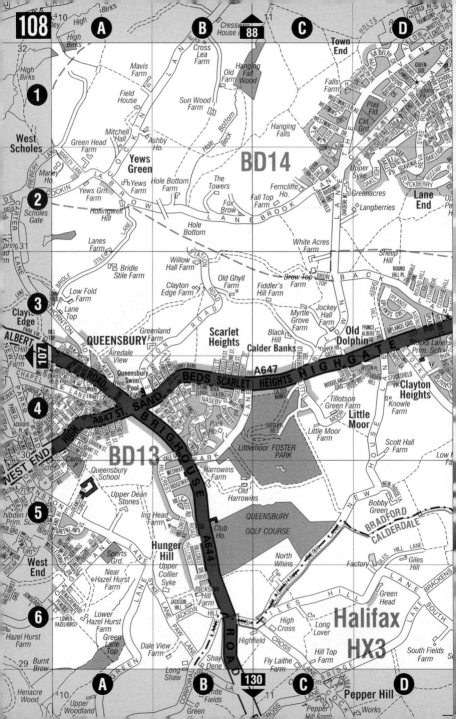

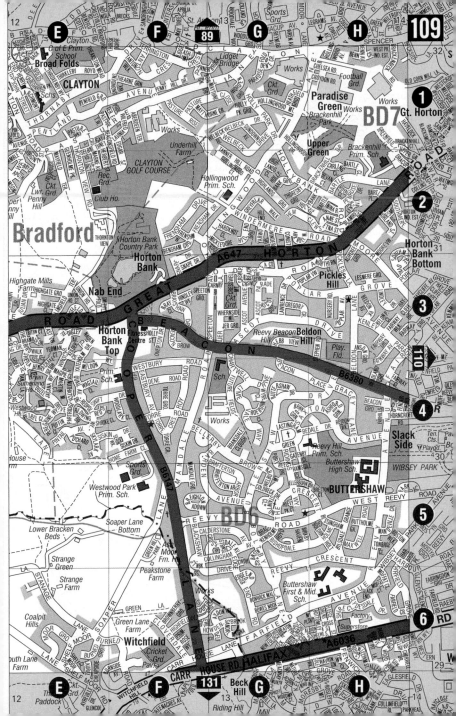

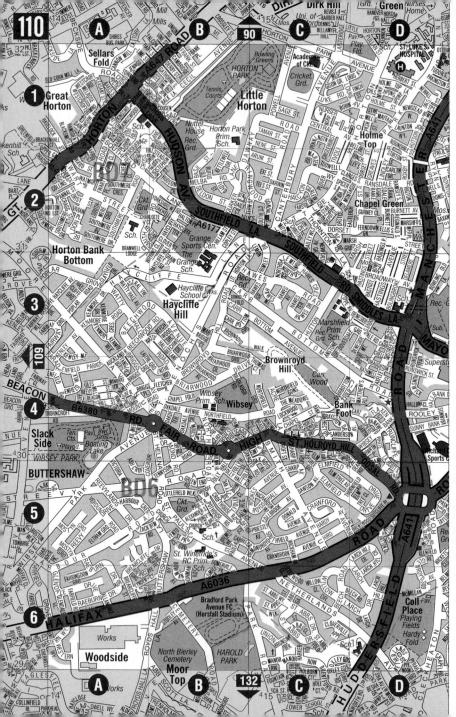

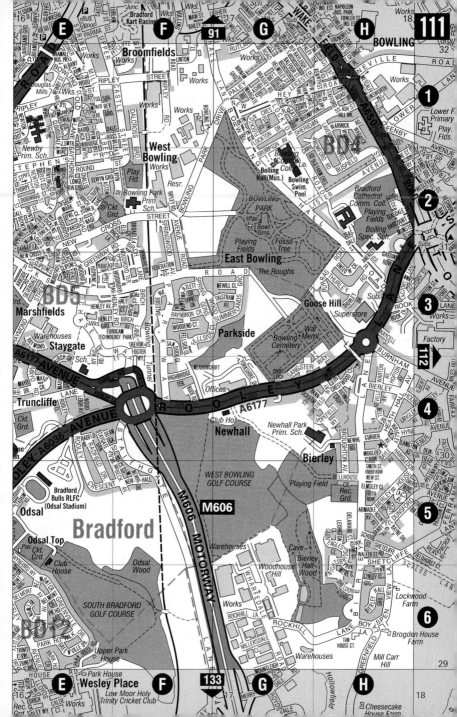

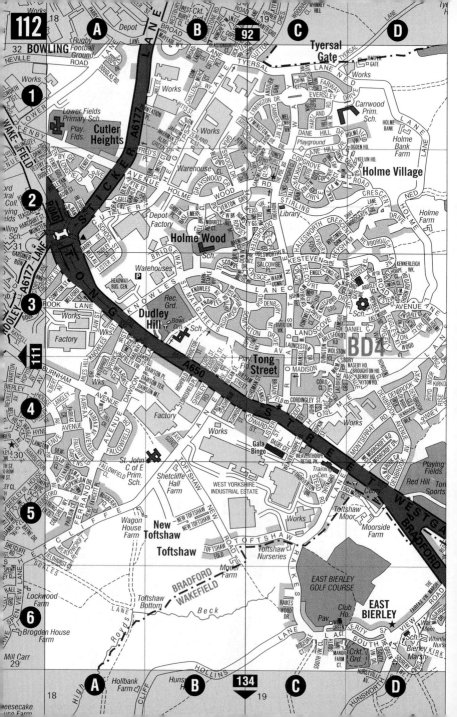

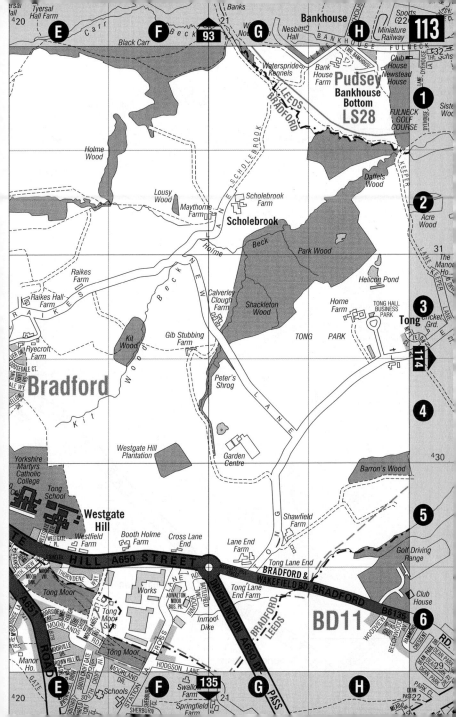

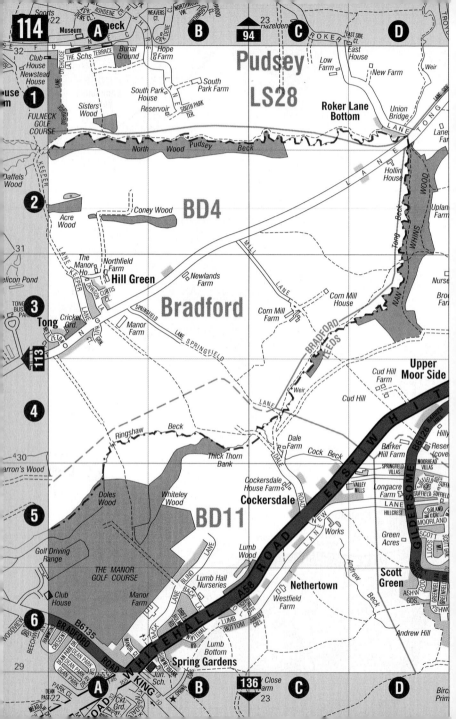

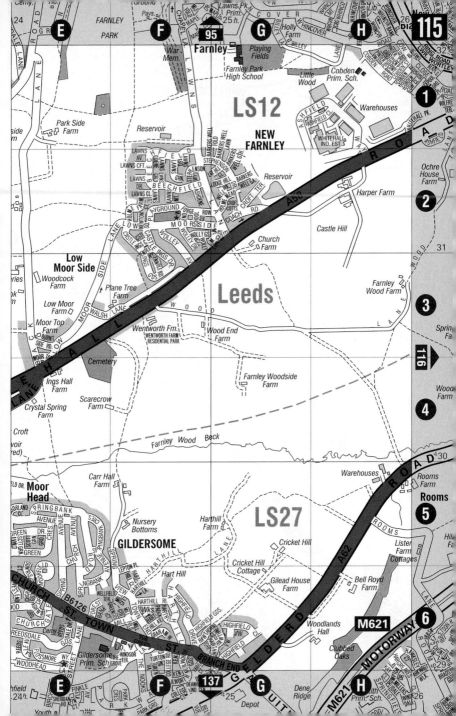

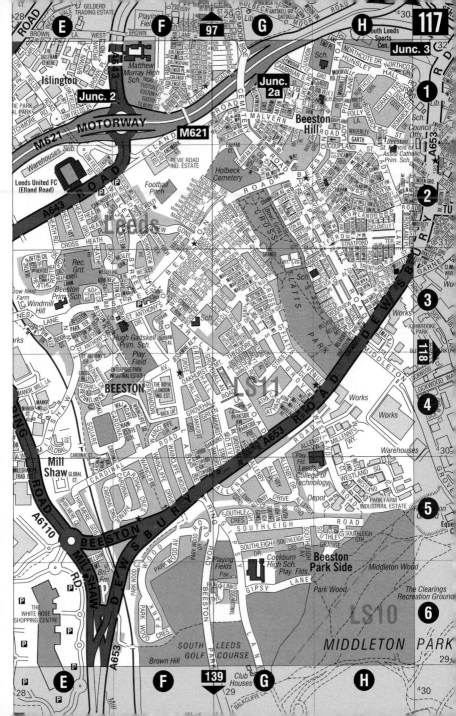

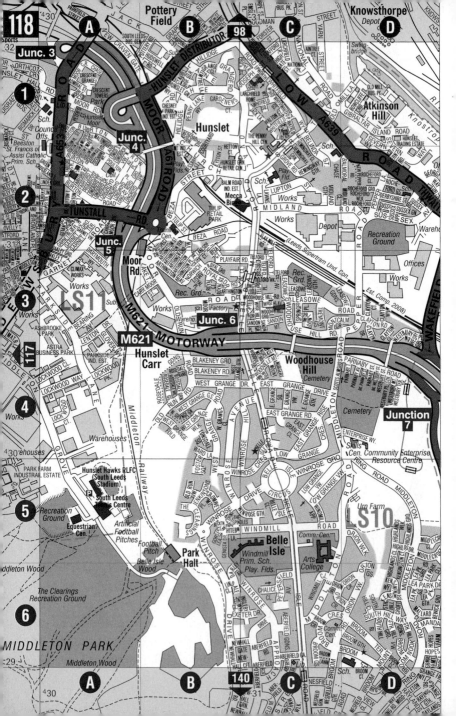

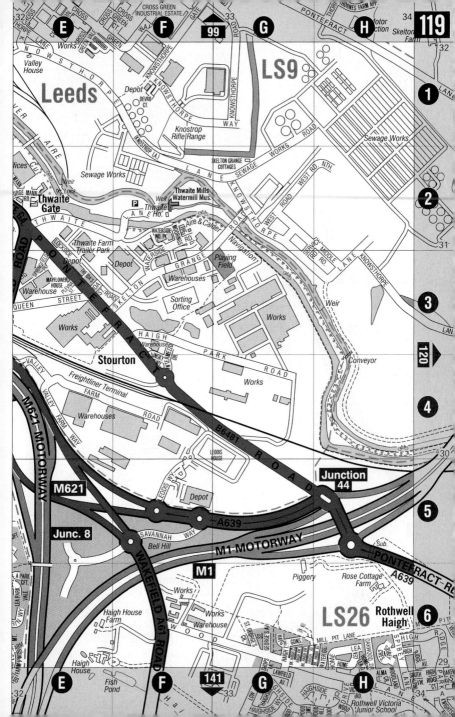

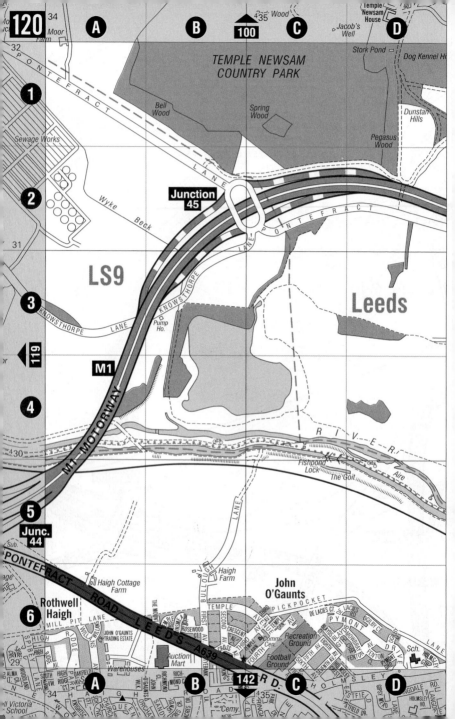

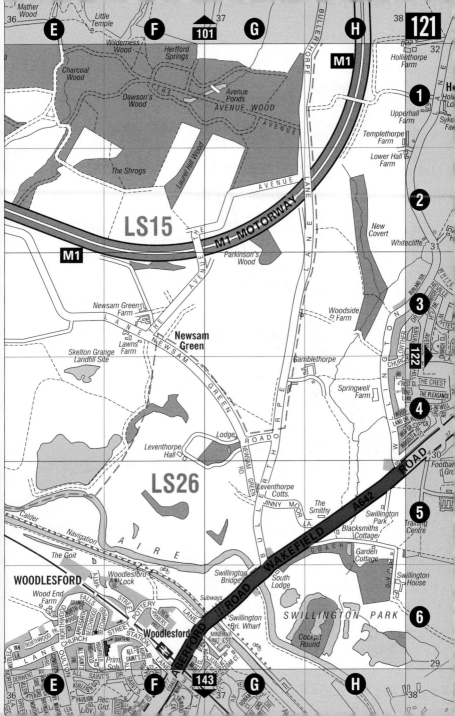

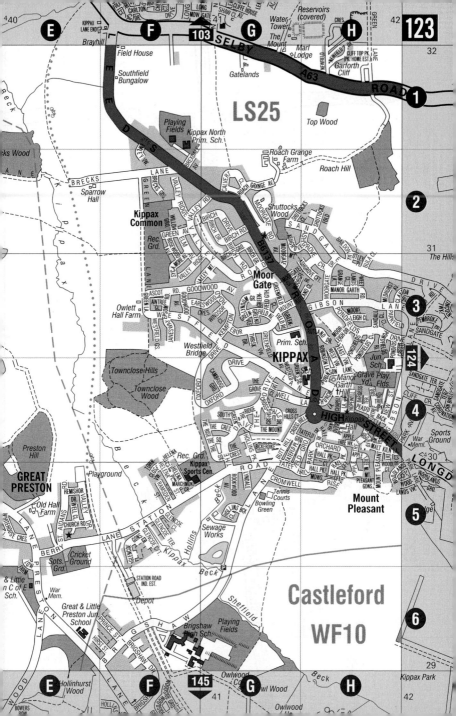

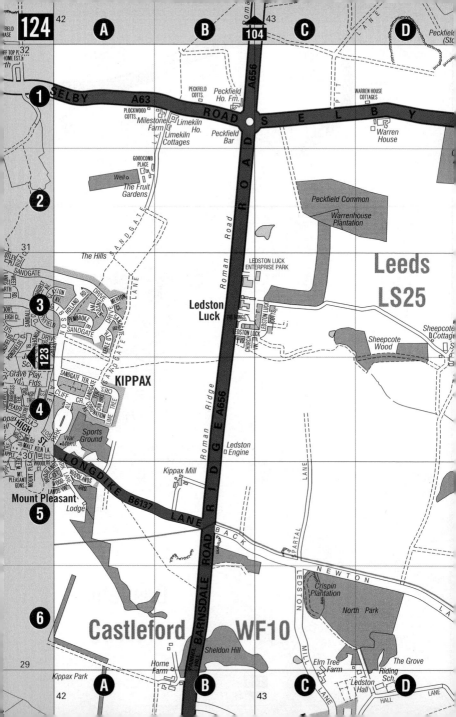

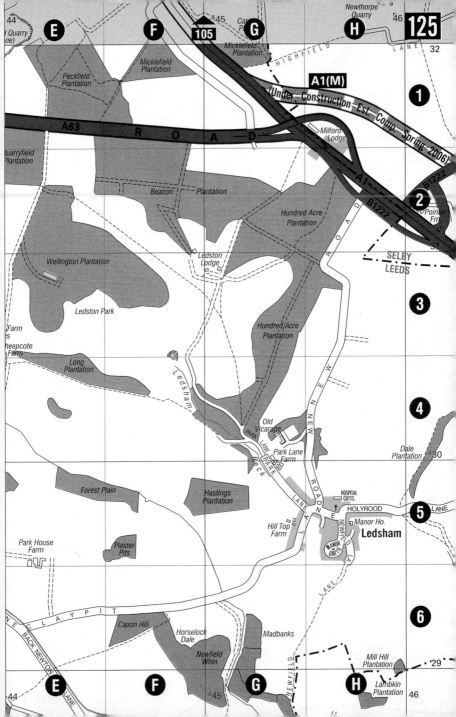

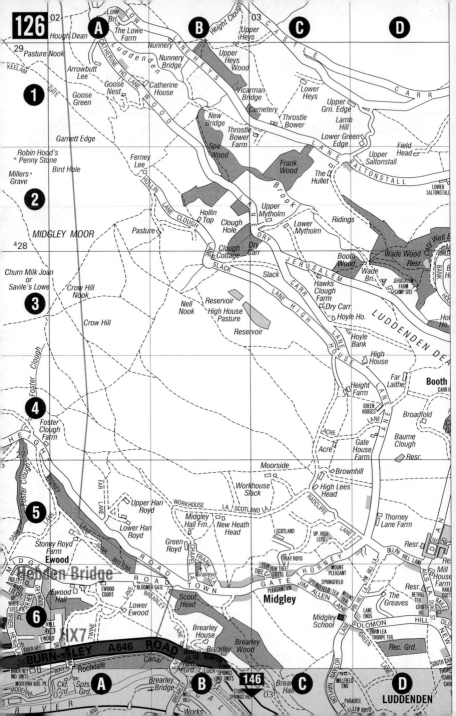

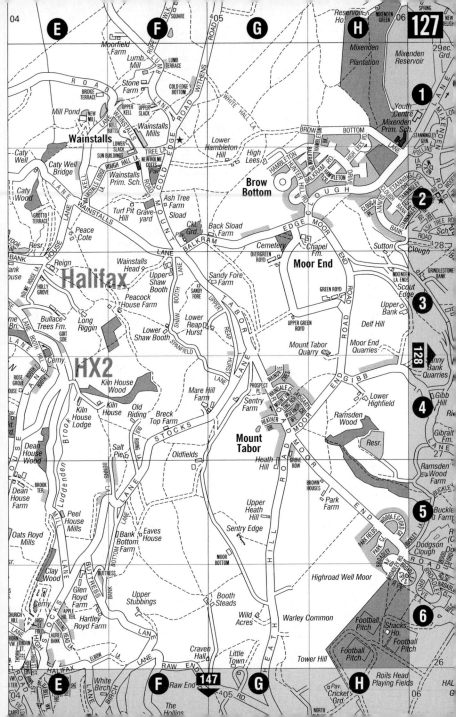

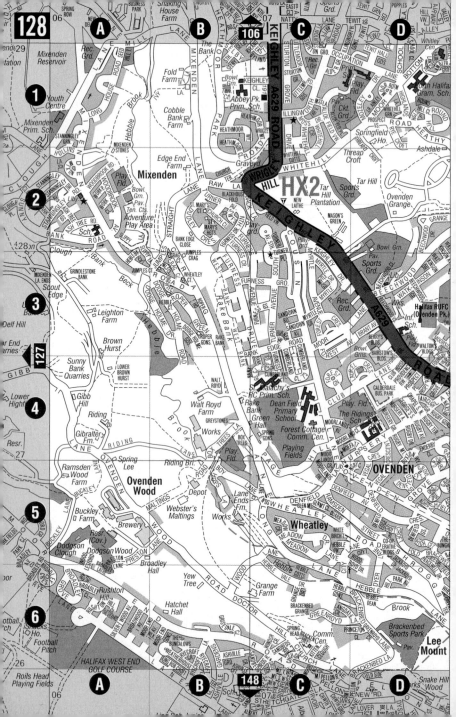

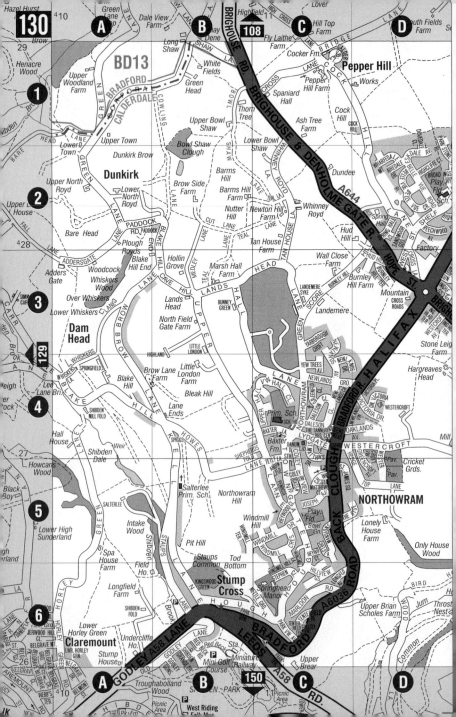

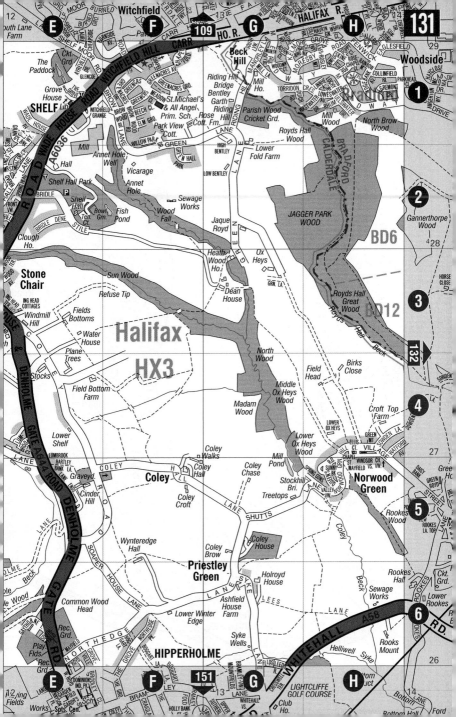

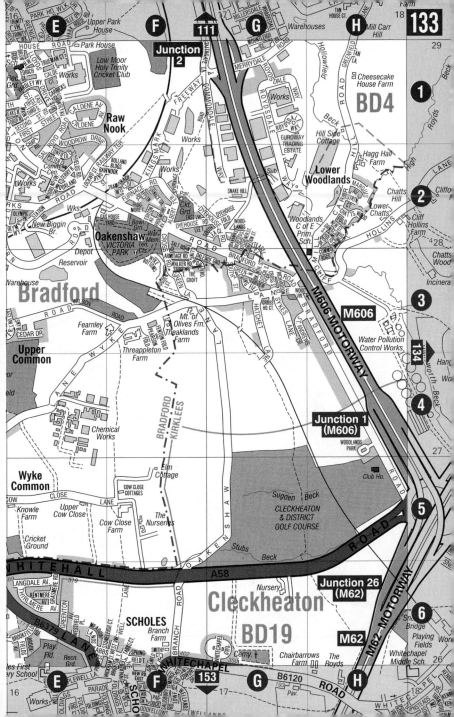

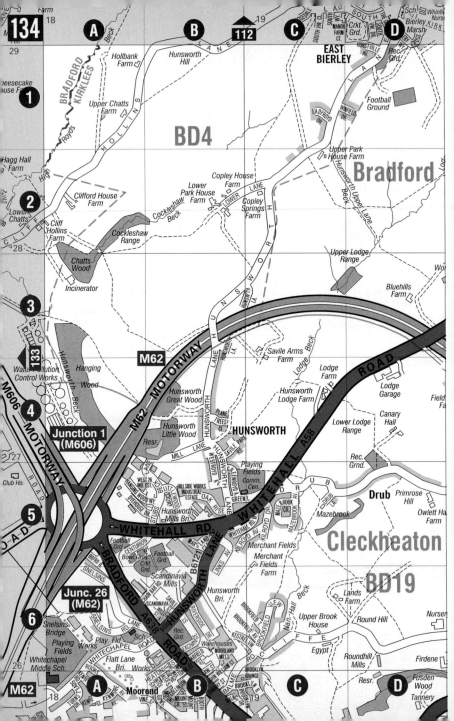

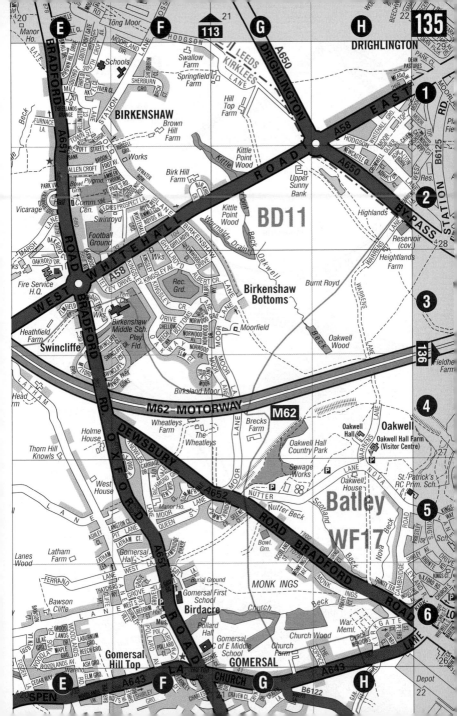

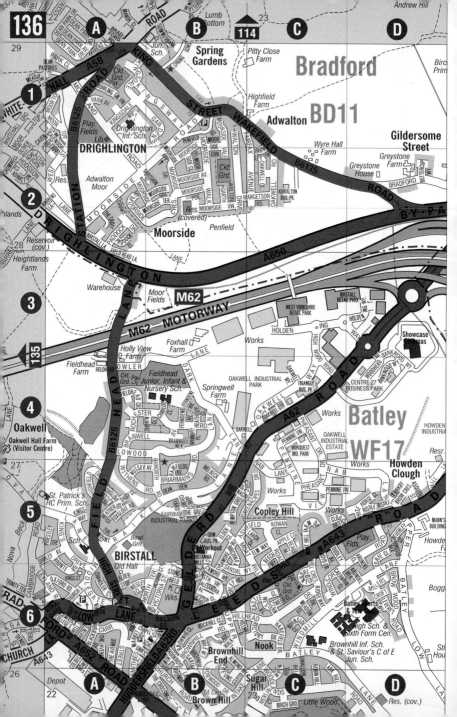

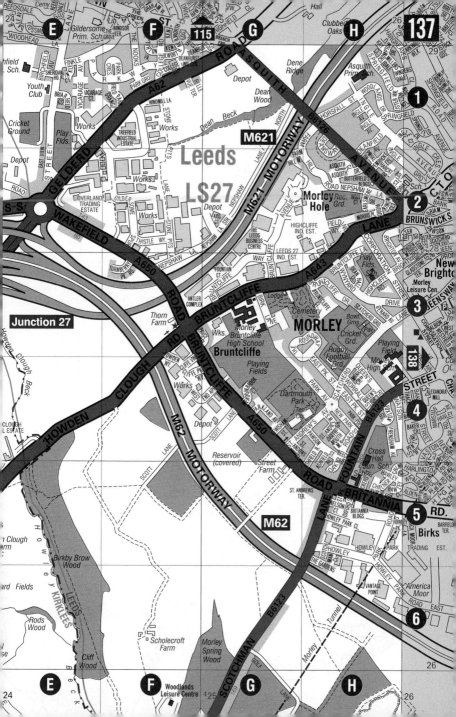

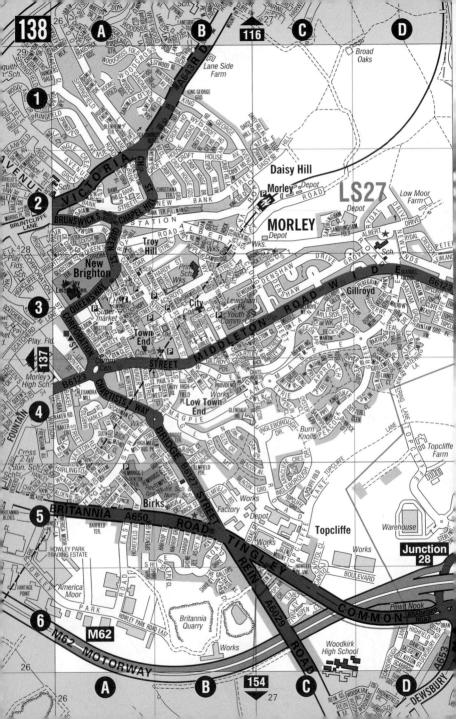

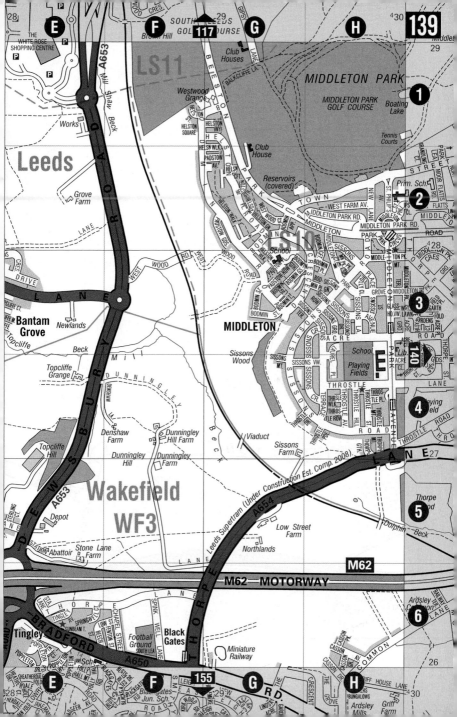

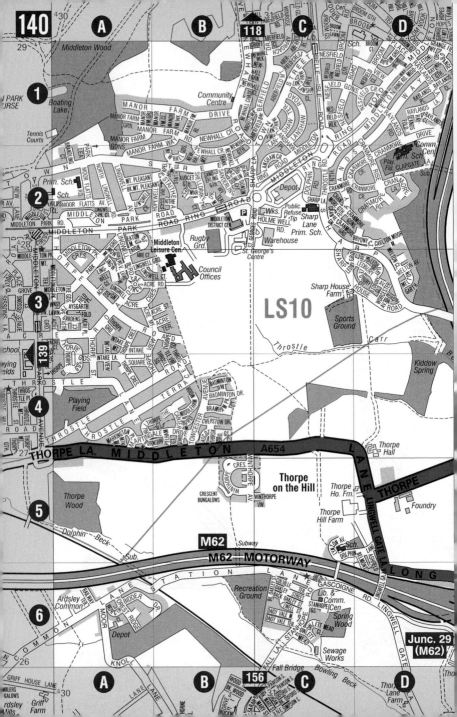

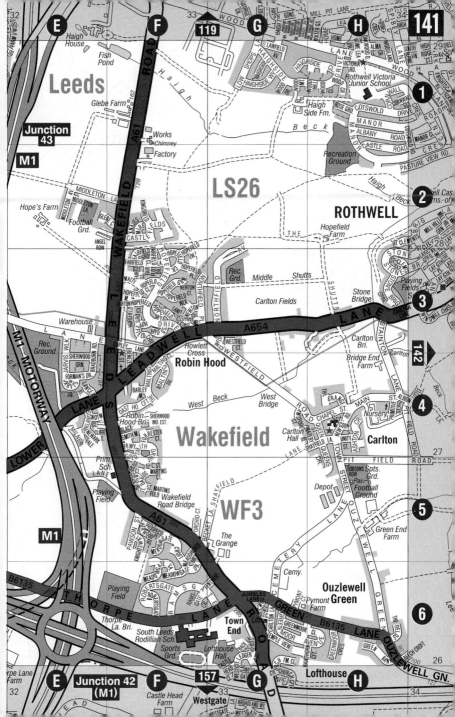

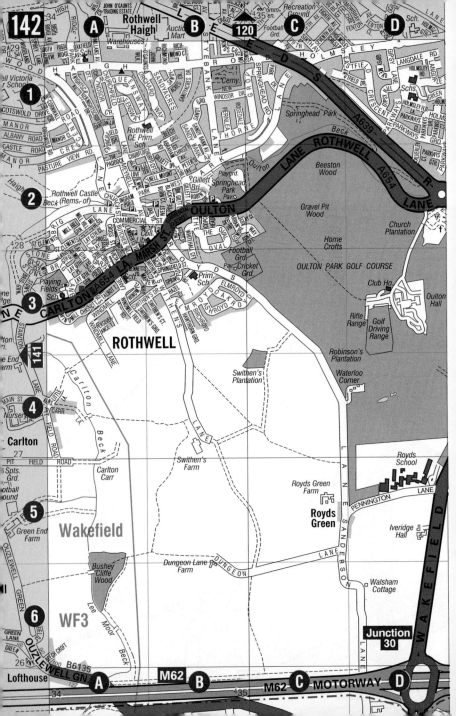

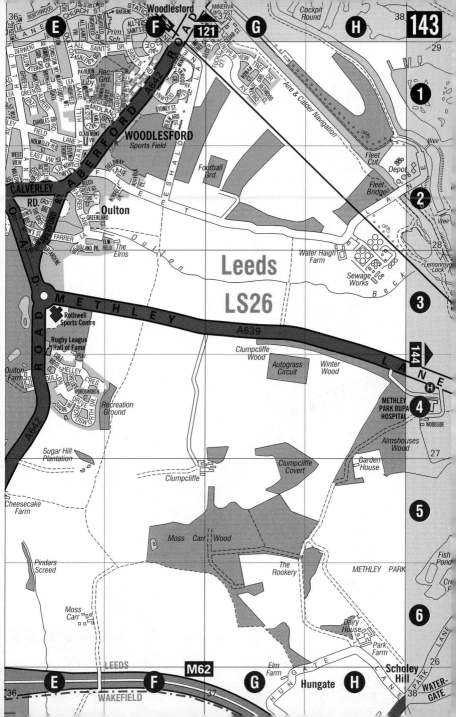

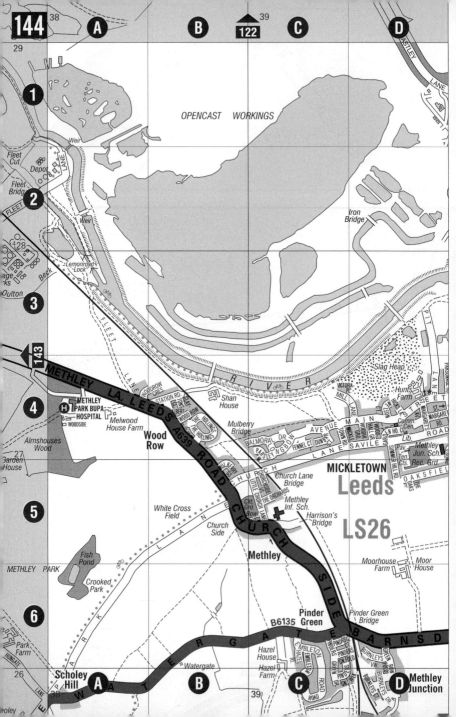

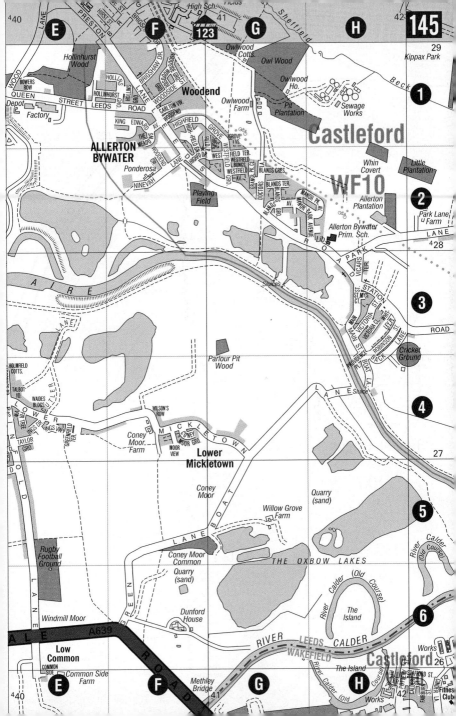

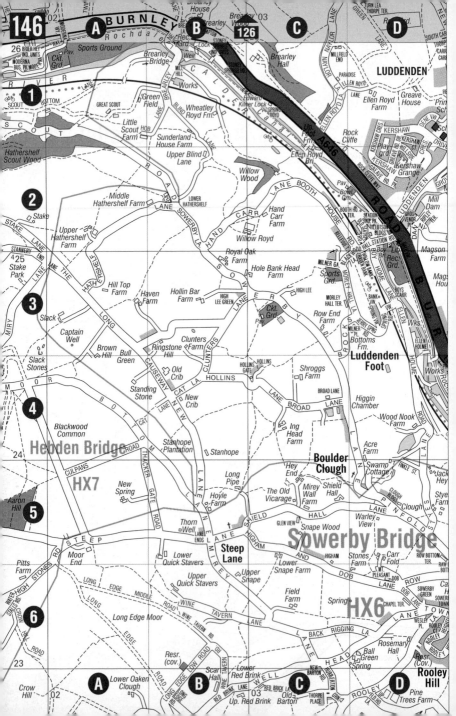

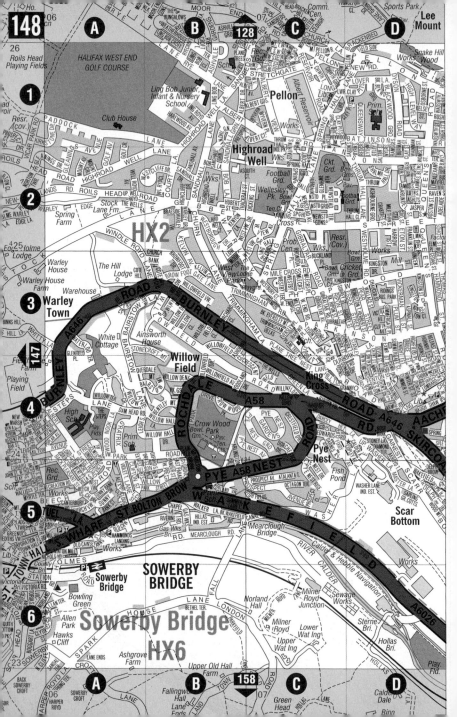

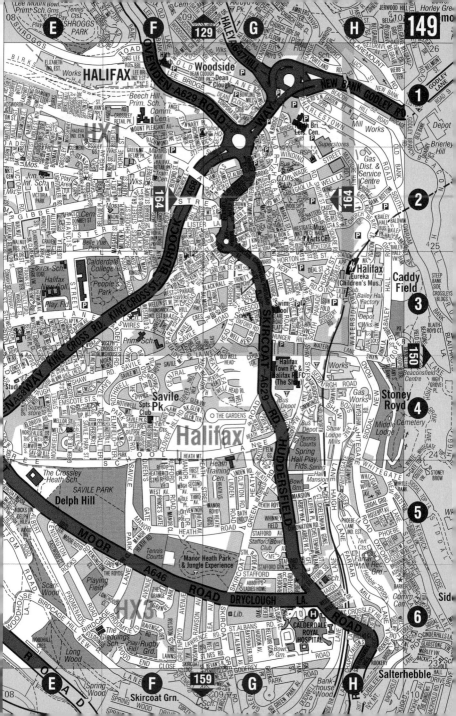

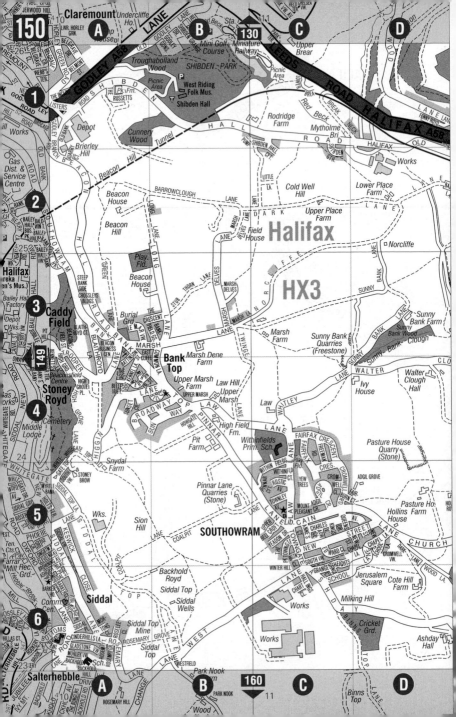

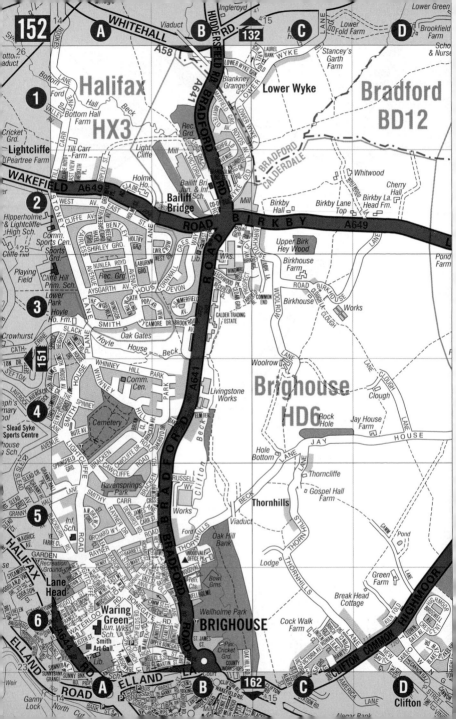

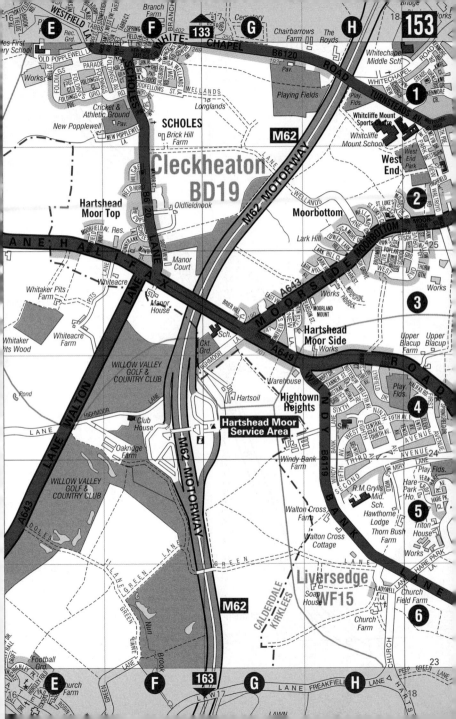

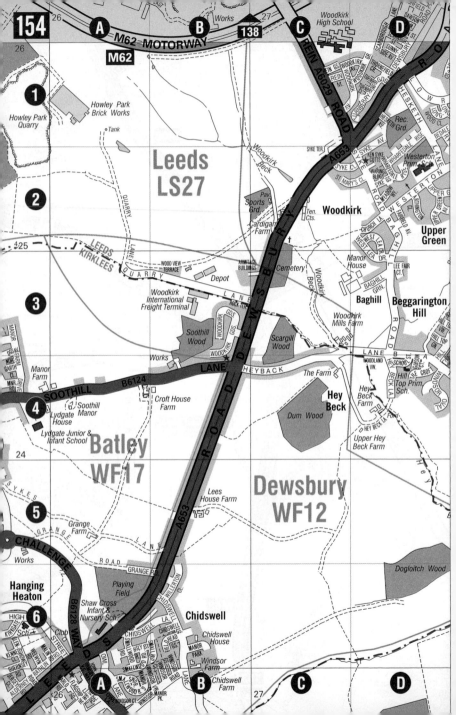

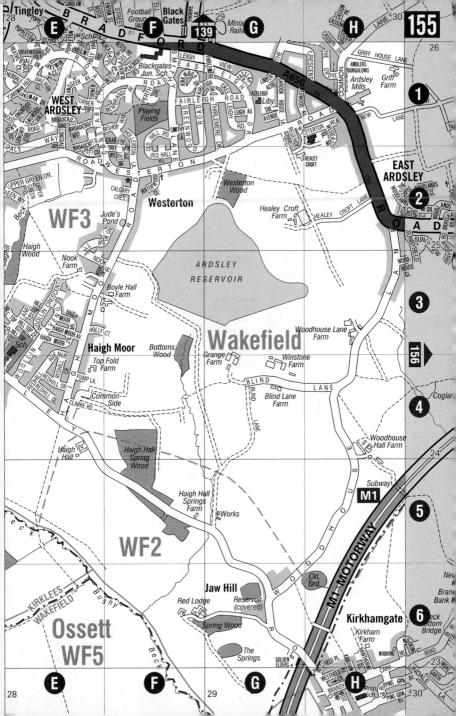

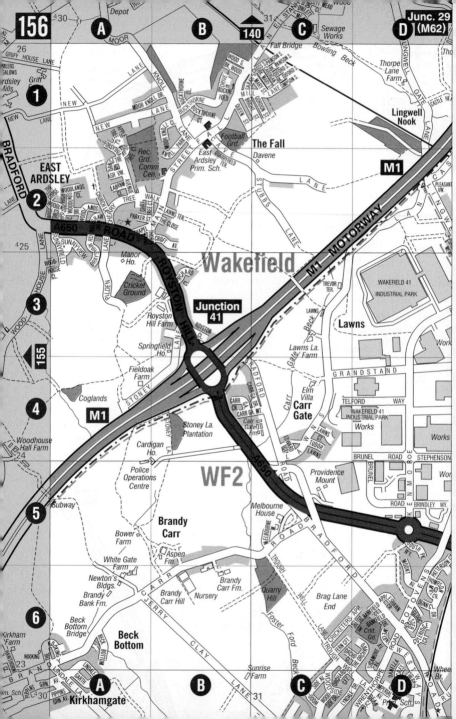

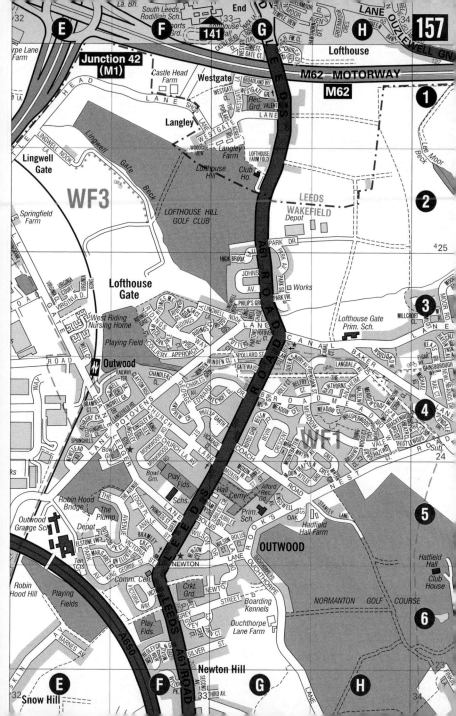

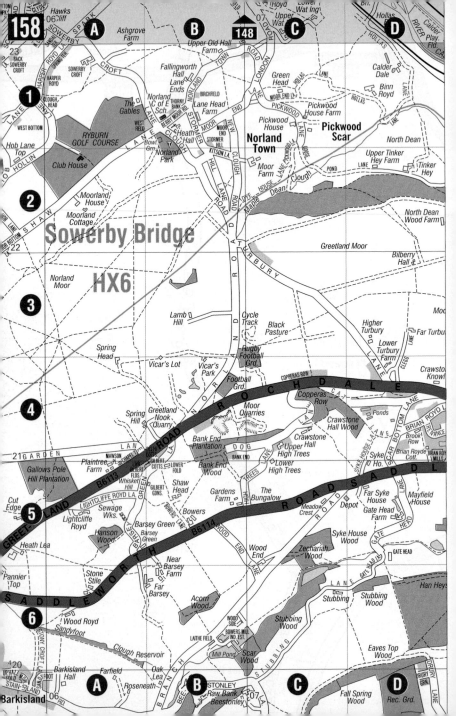

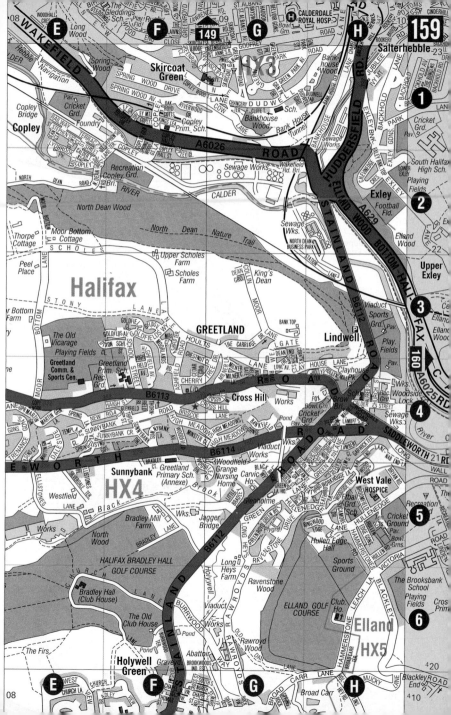

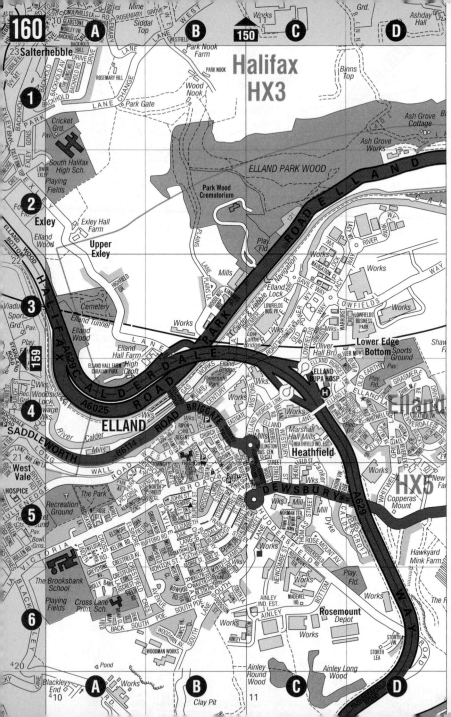

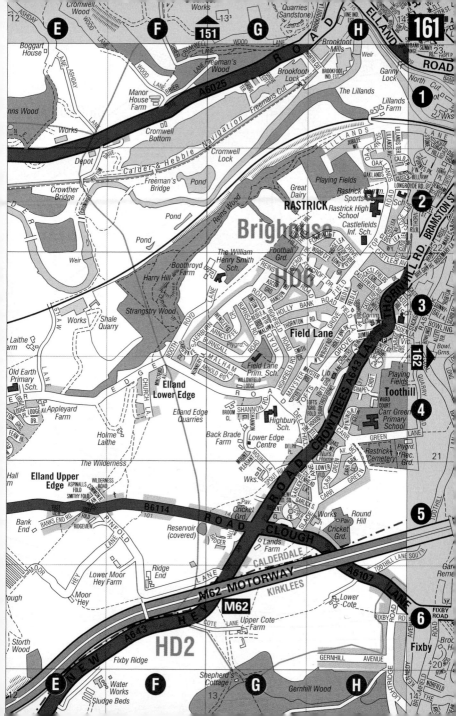

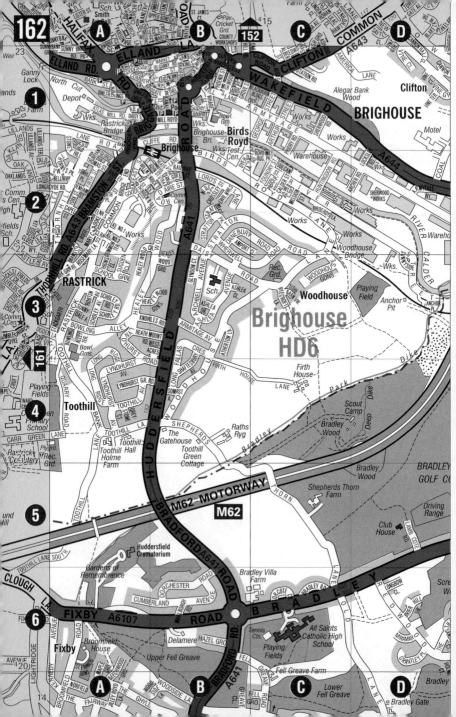

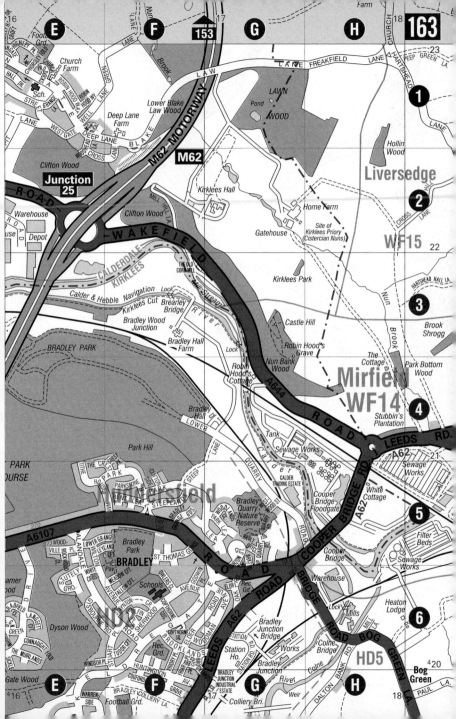

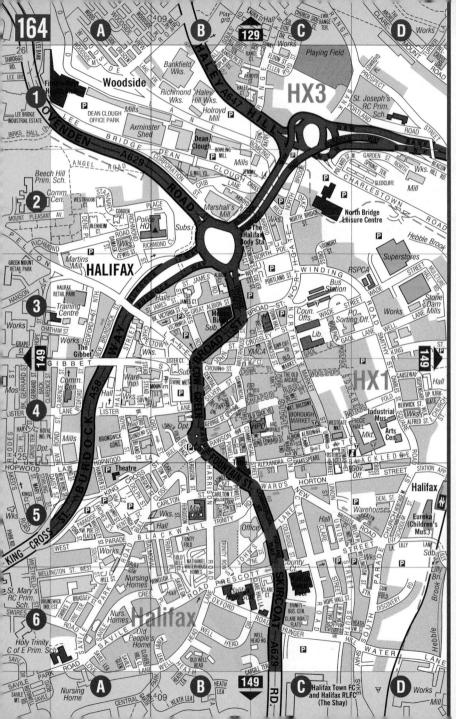

INDEX

Including Streets, Places & Areas, Industrial Estates, Selected Flats & Walkways, Stations and Selected Places of Interest.

HOW TO USE THIS INDEX

1. Each street name is followed by its Postcode District and then by its Locality abbreviation(s) and then by its map reference; e.g. **Abbey Av.** LS5: Leeds . . . 6H **75** is in the LS5 Postcode District and the Leeds Locality and is to be found in square 6H on page **75**. The page number is shown in bold type.

2. A strict alphabetical order is followed in which Av., Rd., St., etc. (though abbreviated) are read in full and as part of the street name; e.g. **Acrehowe Ri.** appears after **Acre Gro.** but before **Acre La.**

3. Streets and a selection of flats and walkways too small to be shown on the maps, appear in the index with the thoroughfare to which it is connected shown in brackets; e.g. **Abbey Gth.** LS19: Yead . . . . 1F **55** (off Well Hill)

4. Addresses that are in more than one part are referred to as not continuous.

5. Places and areas are shown in the index in **BLUE TYPE** and the map reference is to the actual map square in which the town centre or area is located and not to the place name shown on the map; e.g. **ADDINGHAM** **1D 8**

6. An example of a selected place of interest is **Abbey House Mus.** 4A **76**

7. An example of a station is **Baildon Station (Rail).** . . . .4E **53**.

8. Map references shown in brackets; e.g **Abbey St.** LS3: Leeds . . . 3F **97** (3A **4**) refer to entries that also appear on the large scale pages **4-7** & **164**.

GENERAL ABBREVIATIONS

All. : Alley	**Ent.** : Enterprise	**Nth.** : North
App. : Approach	**Est.** : Estate	**No.** : Number
Arc. : Arcade	**Fld.** : Field	**Pde.** : Parade
Av. : Avenue	**Flds.** : Fields	**Pk.** : Park
Bk. : Back	**Gdn.** : Garden	**Pas.** : Passage
Blvd. : Boulevard	**Gdns.** : Gardens	**Pl.** : Place
Bri. : Bridge	**Gth.** : Garth	**Prom.** : Promenade
B'way. : Broadway	**Ga.** : Gate	**Res.** : Residential
Bldgs. : Buildings	**Gt.** : Great	**Ri.** : Rise
Bungs. : Bungalows	**Grn.** : Green	**Rd.** : Road
Bus. : Business	**Gro.** : Grove	**Shop.** : Shopping
Cvn. : Caravan	**Hgts.** : Heights	**Sth.** : South
C'way. : Causeway	**Ho.** : House	**Sq.** : Square
Cen. : Centre	**Ho's.** : Houses	**Sta.** : Station
Chu. : Church	**Ind.** : Industrial	**St.** : Street
Circ. : Circle	**Info.** : Information	**Ter.** : Terrace
Cir. : Circus	**Junc.** : Junction	**Twr.** : Tower
Cl. : Close	**La.** : Lane	**Trad.** : Trading
Coll. : College	**Lit.** : Little	**Up.** : Upper
Comn. : Common	**Lwr.** : Lower	**Va.** : Vale
Cnr. : Corner	**Mnr.** : Manor	**Vw.** : View
Cott. : Cottage	**Mans.** : Mansions	**Vs.** : Villas
Cotts. : Cottages	**Mkt.** : Market	**Vis.** : Visitors
Ct. : Court	**Mdw.** : Meadow	**Wlk.** : Walk
Cres. : Crescent	**Mdws.** : Meadows	**W.** : West
Cft. : Croft	**M.** : Mews	**Yd.** : Yard
Dr. : Drive	**Mt.** : Mount	
E. : East	**Mus.** : Museum	

LOCALITY ABBREVIATIONS

Aber : **Aberford**	Dew : **Dewsbury**	Led : **Ledsham**
Add : **Addingham**	E Ard : **East Ardsley**	Leds : **Ledston**
Arth : **Arthington**	Ell : **Elland**	Leeds : **Leeds**
Bail : **Baildon**	F'ley : **Farnley**	Liv : **Liversedge**
Bard : **Bardsey**	Gar : **Garforth**	Men : **Menston**
Bar E : **Barwick in Elmet**	Guis : **Guiseley**	M'fld : **Micklefield**
Bat : **Batley**	Hal : **Halifax**	Mick : **Mickletown**
Bgly : **Bingley**	Hare : **Harewood**	Mir : **Mirfield**
B Spa : **Boston Spa**	Haw : **Haworth**	Morl : **Morley**
B'frd : **Bradford**	Heb B : **Hebden Bridge**	Otley : **Otley**
B'ham : **Bramham**	H'fth : **Horsforth**	Oxen : **Oxenhope**
B'hpe : **Bramhope**	Hud : **Huddersfield**	Pool : **Pool**
Brigh : **Brighouse**	I'ly : **Ilkley**	Pud : **Pudsey**
Burl W : **Burley in Wharfedale**	Keigh : **Keighley**	Rothw : **Rothwell**
C'frd : **Castleford**	Kild : **Kildwick**	S'cft : **Scarcroft**
Cleck : **Cleckheaton**	Kip : **Kippax**	Scho : **Scholes**
Coll : **Collingham**	Kirkby : **Kirkby Overblow**	Ship : **Shipley**
Den : **Denton**	Leat : **Leathley**	Sick : **Sicklinghall**

Locality Abbreviations

Sils : **Silsden**
Stee : **Steeton**
Swil : **Swillington**
Tad : **Tadcaster**

T'ner : **Thorner**
Wads : **Wadsworth**
Wake : **Wakefield**
W'ton : **Walton**

Weston : **Weston**
Weth : **Wetherby**
Yead : **Yeadon**

1853 Art Gallery, The 6A 52

A

Aachen Way HX1: Hal 4D 148
Abaseen Cl. BD3: B'frd 4H 91
Abbey Av. LS5: Leeds 6H 75
Abbey Cl. LS29: Add 1E 9
Abbey Ct. BD8: B'frd 2A 6
  LS18: H'fth 3D 74
Abbey Court Leisure 4H 71
Abbeydale Gdns. LS5: Leeds 3G 75
Abbeydale Gth. LS5: Leeds 3G 75
Abbeydale Gro. LS5: Leeds 3G 75
Abbeydale Mt. LS5: Leeds 3G 75
Abbeydale Oval LS5: Leeds 3G 75
Abbeydale Va. LS5: Leeds 3G 75
Abbeydale Way LS5: Leeds 3G 75
Abbey Gth. *LS19: Yead* *1F 55*
  (off Well Hill)
Abbey Gorse LS5: Leeds 4A 76
Abbey House Mus. 4A 76
Abbey La. HX2: Hal 2F 147
Abbey Lea BD15: B'frd 3E 89
Abbey Light Railway 5A 76
Abbey Mt. LS5: Leeds 6H 75
Abbey Rd. LS5: Leeds 3F 75
Abbey St. LS3: Leeds 3F 97 (3A 4)
Abbey Ter. LS5: Leeds 6H 75
Abbey Vw. LS5: Leeds 4A 76
Abbey Wlk. HX3: Hal 5G 149
  LS5: Leeds 4H 75
Abbey Wlk. Sth. HX3: Hal 5H 149
Abbotside Cl. BD10: B'frd 3A 72
Abbots Pl. HD2: Hud 6F 163
Abbotsway LS25: Gar 5D 102
Abbots Wood *BD9: B'frd* *6A 70*
  (off Heaton Rd.)
Abbott Ct. LS12: Leeds 3D 96
Abbott Rd. LS12: Leeds 4D 96
Abbott's Ladies Home HX3: Hal . . .6G 149
Abbott's Ter. *HX1: Hal* *2E 149*
  (off Leafland St.)
Abbott Vw. LS12: Leeds 3D 96
Abb Scott La. BD6: B'frd 1B 132
  BD12: B'frd 1B 132
Abelia Mt. BD7: B'frd 5G 89
Abel St. BD12: B'frd 3C 132
Aberdeen Dr. LS12: Leeds 4A 96
Aberdeen Gro. LS12: Leeds 4A 96
Aberdeen Pl. BD7: B'frd 6A 90
Aberdeen Rd. LS12: Leeds 4A 96
Aberdeen Ter. BD7: B'frd 5A 90
  BD14: B'frd 1F 109
Aberdeen Wlk. LS12: Leeds 4A 96
Aberfield Bank LS10: Leeds 1C 140
Aberfield Cl. LS10: Leeds 6C 118
Aberfield Crest LS10: Leeds 1C 140
Aberfield Dr. LS10: Leeds 1C 140
Aberfield Gdns. LS10: Leeds 6C 118
Aberfield Ga. LS10: Leeds 6C 118
Aberfield Mt. LS10: Leeds 1C 140
Aberfield Ri. LS10: Leeds 1C 140
Aberfield Rd. LS10: Leeds 6C 118
Aberfield Wlk. LS10: Leeds 1B 140
Aberford Rd. BD8: B'frd 2B 90
  LS15: Bar E 2E 83
  LS25: Aber, Gar 3F 103
  LS26: Rothw 2E 143
Abingdon St. BD8: B'frd 2B 90
Abraham Hill LS26: Rothw 2B 142
Abram St. BD5: B'frd 1E 111

Absolute Fitness Cen. 5B 72
Acacia Dr. BD15: B'frd 5B 68
  HX3: Hal 2A 152
Acacia Pk. Cres. BD10: Yead 5D 54
Acacia Pk. Dr. BD10: Yead 5D 54
Acacia Pk. Ter. BD10: Yead 5E 55
Acaster Dr. BD12: B'frd 1C 132
  LS25: Gar 5G 103
Accommodation Rd. LS9: Leeds . . .2C 98
Acer Cl. BD20: Stee 6A 14
Acer Way BD19: Cleck 1F 153
Ackroyd Ct. BD13: B'frd 5H 87
Ackroyd Pl. BD13: B'frd 4H 107
Ackroyd Sq. *BD13: B'frd* *4D 108*
  (off Highgate Rd.)
Ackroyd St. LS27: Morl 3B 138
Ackworth Av. LS19: Yead 1G 55
Ackworth Cres. LS19: Yead 1G 55
Ackworth Dr. LS19: Yead 1G 55
Ackworth Pl. LS19: Yead 1G 55
Ackworth St. BD5: B'frd 1E 111
Acomb Ter. BD12: B'frd 4C 132
Acorn Bus. Pk. LS14: Leeds 2A 100
Acorn Cl. BD6: B'frd 1G 131
Acorn Dr. LS14: Leeds 1E 81
Acorn Pk. BD17: Bail 5E 53
Acorn Pk. Ind. Est. BD17: Bail 5E 53
Acorn St. BD3: B'frd 5G 91 (5H 7)
  BD21: Keigh 2H 47
  HX1: Hal 2E 149
Acorn Way LS21: Pool 5F 25
Acre, The BD12: B'frd 2B 132
Acre Av. BD2: B'frd 4H 71
Acre Cl. LS10: Leeds 3A 140
  BD2: B'frd 4H 71
Acre Ct. LS10: Leeds 3H 139
Acre Cres. BD2: B'frd 4H 71
  LS10: Leeds 3A 140
Acre Fold LS29: Add 1C 8
Acre Gro. BD2: B'frd 4H 71
  LS10: Leeds 3A 140
Acrehowe Ri. BD17: Bail 3E 53
Acre La. BD2: B'frd 5H 71
  (not continuous)
  BD6: B'frd 4C 110
  BD16: Bgly 5A 36
  BD20: Keigh 5A 36
  BD22: Haw 2C 64
  HX2: Hal 4C 126
Acre Mt. LS10: Leeds 3A 140
Acre Pl. *BD6: B'frd* *4C 110*
  (off Acre La.)
  LS10: Leeds 3A 140
Acre Ri. BD17: Bail 3C 52
Acre Rd. LS10: Leeds 3H 139
Acres, The LS25: M'fld 1E 9
Acres Hall Av. LS28: Pud 5C 94
Acres Hall Cres. LS28: Pud 5C 94
Acres Hall Dr. LS28: Pud 5C 94
Acre Sq. LS10: Leeds 3A 140
Acres St. BD21: Keigh 1H 47
Acre St. LS10: Leeds 3B 140
Acre Ter. LS10: Leeds 3B 140
Acrewood Cl. LS17: Leeds 4E 61
Acton St. BD3: B'frd 4A 92
Adam Cft. BD13: B'frd 3B 66
Adams Cft. LS21: Otley 4D 22
Adams Gym 6F 77
Adam St. BD6: B'frd 4B 110
Adam's Wlk. LS6: Leeds 1F 97
Ada's Pl. LS28: Pud 1A 94
Ada St. BD13: B'frd 4H 107
  BD17: Bail 5E 53
  BD18: Ship 1H 69

Ada St. BD21: Keigh 6G 33
  HX3: Hal 6G 129
Addersgate La. HX3: Hal 3A 130
ADDINGHAM 1D 8
Addingham Gdns. LS12: Leeds 4A 96
ADDINGHAM MOORSIDE 5D 8
Addingham Wharfedale Rd.
  LS29: Add 1A 8
Addison Av. BD3: B'frd 2B 92
Addison Ct. LS15: Leeds 5F 101
Addison Dr. BD22: Haw 3C 64
Addi St. BD4: B'frd 2A 112
ADEL 4D 58
Adel Gth. LS16: Leeds 2D 58
Adel Grange Cl. LS16: Leeds 5C 58
Adel Grange Cft. LS16: Leeds 5C 58
Adel Grange M. LS16: Leeds 5C 58
  (not continuous)
Adel Grn. LS16: Leeds 3D 58
Adel La. LS16: Leeds 3C 58
Adel Mead LS16: Leeds 3D 58
ADEL MILL 1D 58
Adel Mill LS16: Leeds 1D 58
Adel Pk. Cl. LS16: Leeds 4C 58
Adel Pk. Ct. LS16: Leeds 4C 58
Adel Pk. Cft. LS16: Leeds 4C 58
Adel Pk. Dr. LS16: Leeds 4C 58
Adel Pk. Gdns. LS16: Leeds 4C 58
Adel Pasture LS16: Leeds 4C 58
Adel Towers Cl. LS16: Leeds 4D 58
Adel Towers Ct. LS16: Leeds 4D 58
Adel Va. LS16: Leeds 3D 58
Adel Wood Cl. LS16: Leeds 4D 58
Adel Wood Dr. LS16: Leeds 4D 58
Adel Wood Gdns. LS16: Leeds 4D 58
Adel Wood Gro. LS16: Leeds 4D 58
Adel Wood Pl. LS16: Leeds 4D 58
Adel Wood Rd. LS16: Leeds 4D 58
Adgil Cres. HX3: Hal 5C 150
Adgil Gro. HX3: Hal 5D 150
Admiral St. LS11: Leeds 1A 118
ADWALTON 1C 136
Adwalton Bus. Pk.
  BD11: B'frd 2C 136
Adwalton Cl. BD11: B'frd 2H 135
Adwalton Grn. BD11: B'frd 2H 135
Adwalton Gro. BD13: B'frd 4B 108
Adwalton Moor Bus. Pk.
  BD4: B'frd 6F 113
Adwick Pl. LS4: Leeds 1C 96
Aerial Vw. LS25: M'fld 6D 104
Agar St. BD8: B'frd 3H 89
  (not continuous)
Agar Ter. BD8: B'frd 3H 89
Agnes St. BD20: Keigh 4A 34
Ailsa Ho. *BD10: B'frd* *2A 72*
  (off Fairhaven Grn.)
Ails La. HX2: Hal 6D 126
Ainley Bottom HX5: Ell 6B 160
Ainley Ind. Est. HX5: Ell 6C 160
Ainley St. HX5: Ell 5B 160
Ainsbury Av. BD10: B'frd 5H 53
  (not continuous)
Ainsdale Gro. BD13: B'frd 3C 66
Ainsty Cres. LS22: Weth 2E 13
Ainsty Dr. LS22: Weth 2E 13
Ainsty Gth. LS22: Weth 2E 13
Ainsty Rd. LS22: Weth 2D 12
Ainsty Vw. LS22: Weth 2E 13
Aintree Cl. LS25: Kip 3F 123
Aintree Ct. LS10: Leeds 1C 118

Airdale Ter. LS13: Leeds 4B **74**
(off Airedale Cft.)
Airebank BD16: Bgly 4B **50**
Aireborough Leisure Cen. 5C **40**
Aireburn Av. BD20: Stee 6D **14**
Aire Cl. BD17: Bail 6B **52**
Aire Ct. BD20: Sils 3E **15**
(off Ings Way)
LS10: Leeds 3A **140**
Airedale Av. BD16: Bgly 2C **68**
Airedale Cliff LS13: Leeds 4E **75**
Airedale Coll. Mt. BD3: B'frd 2G **91**
(off Airedale College Rd.)
BD5: B'frd 2E **111**
(off Darnay La.)
Airedale Coll. Rd. BD3: B'frd 2G **91**
Airedale Coll. Ter. BD3: B'frd 2G **91**
Airedale Ct. LS14: Leeds 4B **80**
Airedale Cres. BD3: B'frd 2G **91**
Airedale Cft. LS13: Leeds 5B **74**
Airedale Dr. HX3: Hal 2D **130**
LS18: H'fth 1B **74**
LS25: Gar 5H **103**
Airedale Gdns. LS13: Leeds 5B **74**
Airedale Gro. LS18: H'fth 1B **74**
LS26: Rothw 1F **143**
Airedale M. BD20: Sils 2E **15**
Airedale Mt. BD20: Keigh 5G **35**
LS13: Pud 4A **74**
Airedale Pl. BD17: Bail 5E **53**
Airedale Quay LS13: Leeds 5C **74**
Airedale Rd. BD3: B'frd 2F **91**
BD21: Keigh 5D **34**
LS26: Rothw 1F **143**
Airedale Shop. Cen.
BD21: Keigh 6A **34**
Airedale St. BD2: B'frd 6H **71**
BD16: Bgly 4B **50**
BD21: Keigh 5C **34**
Airedale Ter. BD17: Bail 5D **52**
LS26: Rothw 1F **143**
LS27: Morl 3B **138**
(off South Pde.)
Airedale Vw. LS13: Leeds 4B **74**
(off Town St.)
LS19: Yead 4H **55**
LS26: Rothw 1F **143**
Airedale Wharf LS13: Leeds 4B **74**
Aire Gro. LS19: Yead 1G **55**
Aire Mt. LS22: Weth 2D **12**
Aire Pl. LS3: Leeds 2E **97**
Aire Rd. LS22: Weth 1D **12**
Aireside Cen. LS1: Leeds 4G **97** (5B **4**)
Aire St. BD10: B'frd 6G **53**
BD16: Bgly 1A **50**
BD21: Keigh 5B **34**
BD22: Haw 2D **64**
HD6: Brigh 2B **162**
LS1: Leeds 4H **97** (5C **4**)
Aire Valley Bus. Cen.
BD21: Keigh 6A **34**
Aire Valley Ct. BD16: Bgly 5B **50**
Aire Valley Marina LS4: Leeds 2B **96**
Aire Valley Rd. BD21: Keigh 5C **34**
Aire Vw. BD20: Keigh 3D **34**
BD20: Sils 2D **14**
LS19: Yead 1G **55**
Aire Vw. Av. BD16: Bgly 1D **68**
Aireview Cres. BD17: Bail 6A **52**
Aire Vw. Dr. BD20: Keigh 6G **35**
Aire Vw. Gdns. LS5: Leeds 3H **75**
Aire Vw. Nth. BD18: Ship 1A **70**
Aireview Ter. BD21: Keigh 1C **48**
LS13: Leeds 5C **74**
Aireville Av. BD9: B'frd 4B **70**
BD18: B'frd 4B **70**
Aireville Cl. BD18: B'frd 4B **70**
BD20: Keigh 3G **33**
Aireville Cres. BD9: B'frd 5B **70**
BD20: Sils 2F **15**
Aireville Dr. BD18: B'frd 4B **70**
BD20: Sils 2F **15**
Aireville Grange BD18: B'frd 4B **70**
Aireville Gro. BD18: B'frd 4B **70**

Aireville Mt. BD20: Keigh 5G **35**
BD20: Sils 2F **15**
Aireville Ri. BD9: B'frd 4B **70**
Aireville Rd. BD9: B'frd 4B **70**
Aireville St. BD20: Keigh 3G **33**
Aireville Ter. LS29: Burl W 2E **21**
Aire Way BD17: Bail 6A **52**
AIREWORTH 5C **34**
Aireworth Cl. BD21: Keigh 4C **34**
Aireworth Gro. BD21: Keigh 5C **34**
Aireworth Rd. BD21: Keigh 4C **34**
Airey St. BD21: Keigh 6G **33**
Airlie Av. LS8: Leeds 5D **78**
Airlie Pl. LS8: Leeds 5D **78**
AJ's Workhouse 1B **70**
(off Charles St.)
Akam Rd. BD1: B'frd 4D **90** (3A **6**)
Aked's Rd. HX1: Hal 3F **149** (5A **164**)
Akroyd Ct. HX3: Hal 1B **164**
AKROYDON 6G **129** (1B **164**)
Akroyd Pl. HX1: Hal 1G **149** (2B **164**)
Akroyd Ter. HX2: Hal 4D **148**
Alabama St. HX1: Hal 2D **148**
Alandale Cres. LS25: Gar 5D **102**
Alandale Dr. LS25: Gar 5D **102**
Alandale Gro. LS25: Gar 5D **102**
Alandale Rd. HD2: Hud 5E **163**
LS25: Gar 4D **102**
Alaska Pl. LS7: Leeds 3C **78**
Albans Cl. LS17: Bard 6G **27**
Albany Ct. BD20: Keigh 5G **33**
Albany Rd. LS26: Rothw 1H **141**
Albany St. BD5: B'frd 1E **111**
BD6: B'frd 4C **110**
HX3: Hal 4H **149**
LS12: Leeds 4A **96**
Albany Ter. HX3: Hal 4H **149**
LS12: Leeds 4A **96**
Albany Wlk. LS29: I'ly 6D **10**
Alberta Av. LS7: Leeds 3C **78**
Albert Av. BD10: B'frd 1A **72**
BD18: Ship 6G **51**
HX2: Hal 1C **148**
Albert Bldgs. BD10: B'frd 3H **71**
Albert Cres. BD11: B'frd 3F **135**
BD13: B'frd 4A **108**
Albert Dr. HX2: Hal 1B **148**
LS27: Morl 2D **138**
Albert Edward St. BD13: B'frd 4A **108**
Albert Gdns. HX2: Hal 1C **148**
Albert Gro. LS6: Leeds 3D **76**
Albert Pl. BD3: B'frd 3C **92**
LS18: H'fth 6E **57**
LS26: Mick 4B **144**
Albert Prom. HX3: Hal 5E **149**
Albert Rd. BD13: B'frd 3H **107**
BD18: Ship 1H **69**
HX2: Hal 1B **148**
HX6: Hal 4A **148**
LS26: Rothw 1E **143**
LS27: Morl 2B **138**
Albert Simmons Way
LS29: Burl W 2E **21**
Albert Sq. BD20: Sils 2E **15**
LS19: Yead 6G **41**
Albert St. BD6: B'frd 5B **110**
BD10: B'frd 3H **71**
BD12: B'frd 5C **132**
BD13: B'frd 4B **108**
(Brighouse Rd.)
BD13: B'frd 5H **87**
(Kipping La.)
BD15: B'frd 5G **67**
BD17: Bail 6C **52**
BD21: Keigh 6H **33**
BD22: Haw 1F **65**
(off Bingley Rd.)
HD6: Brigh 1C **162**

Albert St. HX1: Hal 2F **149**
HX5: Ell 5B **160**
LS28: Pud 5H **93**
Albert Ter. BD12: B'frd 5D **132**
(Craiglea Dr.)
BD12: B'frd 2F **133**
(Dyehouse Rd.)
BD18: Ship 6H **51**
LS19: Yead 6G **41**
(off Rockfield Ter.)
Albert Vw. HX2: Hal 1C **148**
Albert Wlk. BD18: Ship 1G **69**
Albert Way BD11: B'frd 3F **135**
Albion Arc. LS1: Leeds 4E **5**
Albion Av. LS12: Leeds 4D **96**
Albion Cl. LS23: B Spa 6B **30**
Albion Ct. BD1: B'frd 4E **91** (4D **6**)
HX1: Hal 3B **164**
Albion Fold BD15: B'frd 4G **67**
Albion Pk. LS12: Leeds 3E **97**
Albion Pl. BD13: B'frd 5G **87**
HD6: Brigh 6A **152**
(off Waterloo Rd.)
LS1: Leeds 3A **98** (4E **5**)
LS20: Guis 4C **40**
Albion Rd. BD10: B'frd 1H **71**
LS28: Pud 1A **94**
Albion St. BD1: B'frd 4E **91** (4C **6**)
BD6: B'frd 6G **109**
BD13: B'frd 4H **107**
(Alma St.)
BD13: B'frd 3B **86**
(Station Rd.)
BD22: Haw 1E **65**
HD6: Brigh 6A **152**
HX1: Hal 2G **149** (4C **164**)
(not continuous)
HX5: Ell 5C **160**
LS1: Leeds 3A **98** (4E **5**)
(not continuous)
LS2: Leeds 3A **98** (4E **5**)
LS21: Otley 4F **23**
LS23: B Spa 6B **30**
LS27: Morl 3A **138**
(not continuous)
WF3: Rothw 4H **141**
Albion Ter. LS23: B Spa 6B **30**
Albion Way LS12: Leeds 3E **97**
Albion Yd. BD1: B'frd 4E **91** (4D **6**)
Alcester Gth. BD3: B'frd 3H **91** (2H **7**)
Alcester Pl. LS8: Leeds 5D **78**
Alcester Rd. LS8: Leeds 5D **78**
Alcester Ter. LS8: Leeds 5D **78**
Alden Av. LS27: Morl 5A **138**
Alden Cl. LS27: Morl 5A **138**
Alden Ct. LS27: Morl 5A **138**
Alden Fold LS27: Morl 5A **138**
Alder Av. BD21: Keigh 2C **48**
Alder Carr BD17: Bail 4B **52**
Alder Dr. LS28: Pud 3E **93**
Alder Gth. LS28: Pud 3F **93**
Alder Gro. HX2: Hal 1C **128**
Alder Hill Av. LS6: Leeds 2G **77**
Alder Hill Cotts. LS6: Leeds 2F **77**
Alder Hill Gro. LS7: Leeds 2G **77**
Alderholt Dr. BD6: B'frd 1A **132**
Aldermanbury BD1: B'frd 4E **91** (5C **6**)
Alderney Rd. WF12: Dew 6A **154**
Alders, The LS7: Leeds 2B **78**
Alderscholes Cl. BD13: B'frd 5H **87**
(off Alderscholes La.)
Alderscholes La. BD13: B'frd 6F **87**
Aldersgate LS12: Leeds 4C **96**
(off Wesley Rd.)
Alderson St. BD6: B'frd 6G **109**
Aldersyde WF17: Bat 4A **136**
Aldersyde Rd. LS20: Guis 5B **40**
Aldersyde Way LS20: Guis 5B **40**
Alderton Bank LS17: Leeds 5F **59**
Alderton Cres. LS17: Leeds 5F **59**
Alderton Hgts. LS17: Leeds 5F **59**
Alderton Mt. LS17: Leeds 5F **59**
Alderton Pl. LS17: Leeds 5F **59**
Alderton Ri. LS17: Leeds 5G **59**

Alegar St. HD6: Brigh 1C 162
Alexander Av. LS15: Leeds 4B 100
Alexander Ct. BD20: Keigh 6H 35
  LS1: Leeds 3H 97 (3D 4)
Alexander Sq. BD14: B'frd 1D 108
Alexander St. BD6: B'frd 5B 110
  LS1: Leeds 3H 97 (3D 4)
Alexander Ter. HX1: Hal 2D 148
Alexandra Av. WF17: Bat 6B 136
Alexandra Cl. HX6: Ell 5A 148
Alexandra Cres. HX5: Ell 4D 160
  LS29: I'ly 5C 10
Alexandra Gro. LS6: Leeds 1E 97
  LS28: Pud 5H 93
Alexandra Mill LS27: Morl 4A 138
Alexandra Pl. LS29: I'ly 5C 10
  (off Alexandra Cres.)
Alexandra Rd. BD2: B'frd 4A 72
  BD18: Ship 2A 70
  LS6: Leeds 1E 97
  LS18: H'fth 6E 57
  LS28: Pud 5G 93
Alexandra Sq. BD18: Ship 1H 69
Alexandra St. BD7: B'frd 6C 90
  BD13: B'frd 4H 107
  HX1: Hal 2G 149 (5C 164)
Alexandra Ter. BD2: B'frd 1A 92
  LS19: Yead 6G 41
  (not continuous)
Alford Ter. BD7: B'frd 4A 90
Alfred St. HD6: Brigh 6B 152
  HX1: Hal 2D 148
  HX4: Hal 4H 159
  LS27: Morl 5C 116
Alfred St. E. HX1: Hal . . .2H 149 (4D 164)
Alhambra Theatre & Studio
  . . . . .5E 91 (5C 6)
Alice St. BD8: B'frd 3D 90 (1A 6)
  BD19: Cleck 6B 134
  BD21: Keigh 6A 34
  BD22: Haw 3C 64
Alkincote St. BD21: Keigh 1A 48
All Alone BD10: B'frd 2G 71
All Alone Rd. BD10: B'frd 2F 71
Allanbridge Cl. BD10: B'frd 2A 72
Allandale Av. BD6: B'frd 6A 110
Allandale Rd. BD6: B'frd 6A 110
Allanfield Gro. LS22: Weth 2E 13
Allanfield Ter. LS22: Weth 1E 13
Allan St. BD3: B'frd 5H 91
Allan Ter. HX6: Hal 6A 148
Allenby Cres. LS11: Leeds 5G 117
Allenby Dr. LS11: Leeds 5G 117
Allenby Gdns. LS11: Leeds 5G 117
Allenby Gro. LS11: Leeds 5G 117
Allenby Pl. LS11: Leeds 5G 117
Allenby Rd. LS11: Leeds 5G 117
Allenby Vw. LS11: Leeds 4H 117
Allen Cft. BD11: B'frd 2E 135
Allerby Grn. BD6: B'frd 6H 109
ALLERTON 2D 88
Allerton Av. LS17: Leeds 5B 60
ALLERTON BYWATER 1F 145
Allerton Cl. BD15: B'frd 2D 88
Allerton Ct. LS17: Leeds 5B 60
  (off Harrogate Rd.)
Allerton Cft. LS7: Leeds 4C 78
  (off Harehills La.)
Allerton Dr. LS17: Bard 4E 27
Allerton Grange Av. LS17: Leeds 6C 60
Allerton Grange Cl. LS17: Leeds 1A 78
Allerton Grange Cres.
  LS17: Leeds 1B 78
Allerton Grange Cft. LS8: Leeds 1C 78
Allerton Grange Dr. BD15: B'frd 2D 88
  LS17: Leeds 1B 78
Allerton Grange Gdns.
  LS17: Leeds 1B 78
Allerton Grange Ri. LS17: Leeds 1A 78
Allerton Grange Va. LS17: Leeds 1B 78
Allerton Grange Wlk. LS17: Leeds . . .1B 78
Allerton Grange Way LS17: Leeds . . .1B 78
Allerton Gro. LS17: Leeds 5B 60
Allerton Hall LS7: Leeds 2A 78

Allerton Hill LS7: Leeds 2A 78
Allerton La. BD13: B'frd 4C 88
  BD15: B'frd 4C 88
Allerton M. LS17: Leeds 6B 60
Allerton Pk. LS17: Leeds 2B 78
Allerton Pl. HX1: Hal 2E 149
  LS17: Leeds 5B 60
Allerton Rd. BD8: B'frd 2E 89
  BD15: B'frd 2H 87
  (Dean La.)
  BD15: B'frd 2H 87
  (Meadowbank Av.)
Allerton St. LS4: Leeds 1D 96
Allerton Ter. LS4: Leeds 1D 96
Allerton Up. Grn. BD15: B'frd 3A 88
Alliance St. LS12: Leeds 4A 96
Allinson St. LS12: Leeds 5E 97
Allison La. BD2: B'frd 5D 70
Alloe Fld. Pl. HX2: Hal 1C 128
Alloe Fld. Vw. HX2: Hal 1C 128
Allotments Rd. BD13: B'frd 2C 86
All Saints Circ. LS26: Rothw 1F 143
All Saints Dr. LS26: Rothw 1E 143
All Saints Rd. LS26: Rothw 6F 121
  BD7: B'frd 6B 90
  LS9: Leeds 3D 98
All Saints Ter. LS21: Keigh 6H 33
All Saint's Vw. LS26: Rothw 6E 121
All Souls' Rd. HX3: Hal . . .6G 129 (1B 164)
All Souls' St. HX3: Hal 6G 129
All Souls' Ter. HX3: Hal . . .6G 129 (1B 164)
Alma Cl. LS28: Pud 6G 73
Alma Cotts. BD13: B'frd 5G 107
  (off Moor Cl. La.)
  LS6: Leeds 4D 76
Alma Dr. BD18: Ship 1D 70
Alma Pl. BD3: B'frd 3B 92
  BD21: Keigh 2A 48
Alma Rd. LS6: Leeds 4D 76
Alma St. BD4: B'frd 6A 92
  (Buller St.)
  BD4: B'frd 1B 112
  (Inkerman St.)
  BD13: B'frd 4H 107
  BD18: Ship 1D 70
  BD21: Keigh 3A 48
  (not continuous)
  BD22: Haw 1C 64
  HX5: Ell 5C 160
  (off James St.)
  LS9: Leeds 2C 98
  LS19: Yead 6G 41
  LS26: Rothw 6E 121
Alma Ter. BD20: Keigh 4A 36
  BD21: Keigh 2A 48
  LS26: Rothw 1H 141
Alma Vs. LS26: Rothw 6F 121
Almond St. BD3: B'frd 5A 92
Almond Way WF17: Bat 6B 136
Almscliffe Pl. BD2: B'frd 5B 72
Almscliffe Ter. LS21: Otley 4F 23
Almsford BD13: B'frd 3B 86
Alnwick Vw. LS16: Leeds 2C 76
Alpha St. BD21: Keigh 6B 34
Alpine Ri. BD13: B'frd 4H 87
Alpine Ter. LS26: Rothw 1H 141
Alston Cl. BD9: B'frd 2F 89
Alston La. LS14: Leeds 6C 80
Alston Retail Pk. BD21: Keigh 4B 34
Alston Rd. BD21: Keigh 4B 34
Altar Dr. BD9: B'frd 6A 70
  BD20: Keigh 4E 35
Altar La. BD16: Bgly 3D 48
Altar Vw. BD16: Bgly 2A 50
  (off Sleningford Rd.)
  BD20: Keigh 3D 34
Altar Vs. BD20: Keigh 4D 34
Althorpe Gro. BD10: B'frd 3G 71
Alton Gro. BD9: B'frd 6H 69
  BD18: Ship 4B 70
Alum Cl. BD9: B'frd 6A 70
Alum Ct. BD9: B'frd 6A 70
Alvanley Ct. BD8: B'frd 3F 89

Alva Ter. BD18: Ship 3B 70
ALWOODLEY 3A 60
Alwoodley Chase LS17: Leeds 2C 60
Alwoodley Ct. LS17: Leeds 2F 59
Alwoodley Ct. Gdns. LS17: Leeds . . .1G 59
Alwoodley Gdns. LS17: Leeds 2G 59
ALWOODLEY GATES 1C 60
Alwoodley Gates LS17: Leeds 1C 60
Alwoodley La. LS17: Leeds 1F 59
ALWOODLEY PARK 1G 59
Amberley Ct. BD3: B'frd 5A 92
  (off Amberley St.)
Amberley Gdns. LS12: Leeds 5D 96
Amberley Rd. LS12: Leeds 5C 96
Amberley St. BD3: B'frd 4A 92
  (not continuous)
  LS12: Leeds 5C 96
Amberton App. LS8: Leeds 5G 79
Amberton Cl. LS8: Leeds 4G 79
Amberton Cres. LS8: Leeds 5G 79
Amberton Gdns. LS8: Leeds 5G 79
Amberton Gth. LS8: Leeds 5G 79
Amberton Gro. LS8: Leeds 5G 79
Amberton La. LS8: Leeds 5G 79
Amberton Mt. LS8: Leeds 5G 79
Amberton Pl. LS8: Leeds 5F 79
Amberton Rd. LS8: Leeds 5F 79
  LS9: Leeds 6G 79
Amberton St. LS8: Leeds 5G 79
Amberton Ter. LS8: Leeds 5G 79
Ambler Gro. HX2: Hal 1D 128
Amblers Bldgs. LS28: Pud 5A 94
  (off Amblers Ct.)
Amblers Bungs. WF3: E Ard 1H 155
Amblers Ct. LS28: Pud 5A 94
Amblers Cft. BD10: B'frd 5H 53
Amblers M. BD17: Bail 3C 52
  BD20: Keigh 5H 35
Amblers Row BD17: Bail 3C 52
Amblers Ter. HX3: Hal 6G 129
Ambler St. BD8: B'frd 2C 90
  BD21: Keigh 6B 34
AMBLER THORN 6G 107
Amblerthorne BD11: B'frd 2F 135
Ambler Way BD13: B'frd 6G 107
Ambleside Av. BD9: B'frd 1H 89
Ambleside Gdns. LS28: Pud 4G 93
Ambleside Gro. LS26: Rothw 1E 143
Ambleside Wlk. LS22: Weth 3B 12
Amble Tonia BD13: B'frd 2C 86
Ambleton Way BD13: B'frd 5G 107
Amelia St. BD18: Ship 6H 51
America La. HD6: Brigh 1C 162
America Moor La. LS27: Morl 5A 138
AMF Bowling
  Keighley 4B 34
  Leeds 2A 98 (2E 5)
Amisfield Rd. HX3: Hal 1F 151
Amos St. HX1: Hal 2D 148
Amport Cl. HD6: Brigh 2B 162
Amspool Ct. WF3: Rothw 4G 141
Amundsen Av. BD2: B'frd 4G 71
Amy Busfield Grn. LS29: Burl W 2E 21
Amyroyce Dr. BD18: Ship 2E 71
Amy St. BD16: Bgly 4C 50
  HX3: Hal 5E 129
Anaheim Dr. WF1: Wake 4H 157
Ancaster Cres. LS16: Leeds 2B 76
Ancaster Rd. LS16: Leeds 2B 76
Ancaster Vw. LS16: Leeds 2B 76
Anchorage, The BD16: Bgly 3B 50
Anchor Ct. BD8: B'frd 2A 6
Anchor Pl. HD6: Brigh 3D 162
Anderson Av. LS8: Leeds 1C 98
Anderson Ho. BD17: Bail 6B 52
  (off Fairview Ct.)
Anderson Mt. LS8: Leeds 1C 98
Anderson St. BD8: B'frd 2C 90
Anderton Fold HX3: Hal 5C 130
Andover Grn. BD4: B'frd 1C 112
Andrew Cl. HX3: Hal 5C 150
Andrew Cres. WF1: Wake 4F 157
Andrew Ho. LS28: Pud 6H 73
  (off Water La.)

Andrews Mnr. LS19: Yead 6F 41
(off Manor Sq.)
Andrew Sq. LS28: Pud 6H 73
Andrew St. LS28: Pud 1H 93
Anerley St. BD4: B'frd 3H 111
Angel Ct. LS3: Leeds 2F 97
Angel Inn Yd. LS1: Leeds 4E 5
Angel Pl. BD16: Bgly 2C 50
Angel Rd. HX1: Hal 1F 149
(Crossley Retail Pk.)
HX1: Hal 1F 149 (2A 164)
(Stannary Pl.)
Angel Row LS26: Rothw 2E 141
. . . . .3D 52
Angel Way BD7: B'frd 4D 90 (4A 6)
Angerton Way BD6: B'frd 1A 132
Anglesea Pl. BD22: Haw 4C 64
Angram Rd. BD20: Keigh 2G 33
Angus Av. BD12: B'frd 6C 132
Anlaby St. BD4: B'frd 6B 92
Annandale Vw. BD13: B'frd 3D 108
Anne Ga. BD1: B'frd 4F 91 (3F 7)
Anne's Ct. HX3: Hal 5C 150
Anne St. BD7: B'frd 2H 109
Annie St. BD18: Ship 3C 70
BD21: Keigh 4A 34
BD22: Haw 1F 65
HX6: Hal 5H 147
LS27: Morl 3B 138
WF1: Wake 5F 157
Anning Fold LS25: Gar 3H 103
Annison St. BD3: B'frd 4G 91 (4G 7)
Ann Pl. BD5: B'frd 6E 91 (6C 6)
Ann St. BD21: Keigh 1H 47
BD22: Haw 2D 64
Another World (Mountainboarding Cen.)
. . . . .2B 106
Anson Gro. BD7: B'frd 3H 109
Anstone Dr. BD5: B'frd 3C 110
Anthony La. BD16: Bgly 5F 49
Antler Complex LS27: Morl 3F 137
Anvil Ct. BD8: B'frd 2B 90
(off Carlisle St.)
BD13: B'frd 4B 66
Anvil St. BD8: B'frd 2B 90
(not continuous)
HD6: Brigh 6A 152
Apex Bus. Cen. LS11: Leeds 6A 98
Apex Vw. LS11: Leeds 6H 97
Apex Way LS11: Leeds 6A 98
APPERLEY BRIDGE 1B 72
Apperley Gdns. BD10: B'frd 1C 72
Apperley La. BD10: B'frd, Yead 1C 72
LS19: Yead 6D 54
Apperley Rd. BD10: B'frd 1A 72
(not continuous)
Appleby Cl. BD13: B'frd 4G 107
Appleby La. LS25: Gar 4H 103
Appleby Pl. LS15: Leeds 3A 100
Appleby Wlk. LS15: Leeds 3A 100
Appleby Way LS22: Weth 2E 13
LS27: Morl 2B 138
Apple Cl. WF17: Bat 5C 136
Applegarth BD14: B'frd 2E 109
LS26: Rothw 6E 121
Applehaigh Cl. BD10: B'frd 2A 72
Apple Ho. Ter. HX2: Hal 6E 127
Appleshaw Cres. WF2: Wake 6D 156
Apple St. BD21: Keigh 4G 47
BD22: Oxen 1C 84
Appleton Cl. BD12: B'frd 2F 133
BD16: Bgly 2D 50
LS9: Leeds 3D 98
Appleton Ct. LS9: Leeds 3D 98
Appleton Gro. LS9: Leeds 3F 99
Appleton Sq. LS9: Leeds 3D 98
Appleton Way LS9: Leeds 3D 98
Apple Tree Cl. LS23: B Spa 4B 30
WF3: E Ard 2A 156
Apple Tree Ct. WF3: E Ard 2A 156
Apple Tree Gdns. LS29: I'ly 5B 10
Apple Tree La. LS25: Kip 5H 123
Apple Tree Wlk. LS25: Kip 4H 123
Approach, The LS15: Scho 2H 81

Aprilia Ct. BD14: B'frd 6F 89
Apsley Cres. BD8: B'frd 2C 90
Apsley St. BD21: Keigh 2H 47
BD22: Haw 2D 64
BD22: Keigh 4D 46
Apsley Ter. BD22: Keigh 4D 46
(off Green La.)
Apsley Vs. BD8: B'frd 2D 90
Arbour, The LS29: I'ly 3C 10
Arcade, The LS29: I'ly 5D 10
(off Church St.)
Arc. Royale HX1: Hal 4C 164
(off Commercial St.)
Arcadia St. BD21: Keigh 2H 47
Archbell Av. HD6: Brigh 3B 162
Archer Rd. HD6: Brigh 2D 162
Archery Pl. LS2: Leeds 1H 97
Archery Rd. LS2: Leeds 1H 97
Archery St. LS2: Leeds 1H 97
Archery Ter. LS2: Leeds 1H 97
Arches, The HX3: Hal 6G 129 (1D 164)
Arches St. HX1: Hal 3F 149 (5A 164)
Archibald St. BD7: B'frd 4C 90
Arctic Pde. BD7: B'frd 1A 110
Arctic St. BD20: Keigh 3H 33
BD22: Haw 1E 65
Arden Ho. HX1: Hal 4F 149
(off Arden Rd.)
Ardennes Cl. BD2: B'frd 5F 71
Arden Rd. BD8: B'frd 4E 89
HX1: Hal 3F 149
Ardsley Cl. BD4: B'frd 3D 112
(not continuous)
Argent Way BD4: B'frd 3D 112
Argie Av. LS4: Leeds 6B 76
Argie Gdns. LS4: Leeds 1C 96
Argie Rd. LS4: Leeds 1C 96
Argie Ter. LS4: Leeds 1C 96
Argyle M. LS17: Bard 6E 27
Argyle Rd. LS9: Leeds 3B 98 (3H 5)
Argyle St. BD4: B'frd 2H 111
BD21: Keigh 6H 33
Argyll Cl. BD17: Bail 5E 53
LS18: H'fth 3D 56
Arkendale M. BD7: B'frd 2G 109
Arksey Pl. LS12: Leeds 3C 96
Arksey Ter. LS12: Leeds 3C 96
Arkwright St. BD4: B'frd 5C 92
BD14: B'frd 1D 108
Arkwright Wlk. LS27: Morl 1A 138
Arlesford Rd. BD4: B'frd 3C 112
Arley Gro. LS12: Leeds 3C 96
Arley Pl. LS12: Leeds 3C 96
Arley St. LS12: Leeds 3C 96
Arley Ter. LS12: Leeds 3C 96
Arlington Bus. Cen. LS11: Leeds 5D 116
Arlington Cres. HX2: Hal 4B 148
Arlington Gro. LS8: Leeds 4F 79
Arlington Rd. LS8: Leeds 5F 79
Arlington St. BD3: B'frd 5H 91
Armadale Av. BD4: B'frd 5H 111
Armgill La. BD2: B'frd 5D 70
Armidale Way BD2: B'frd 6F 71
Armitage, The BD20: Keigh 5F 35
Armitage Av. HD6: Brigh 3B 162
Armitage Bldgs. WF12: Dew 3B 154
Armitage Rd. BD12: B'frd 3F 133
HX1: Hal 4D 148
Armitage Sq. LS28: Pud 5H 93
Armitage St. LS26: Rothw 3A 142
ARMLEY 3D 96
Armley Grange Av. LS12: Leeds 2H 95
Armley Grange Cres. LS12: Leeds . . .2H 95
Armley Grange Dr. LS12: Leeds 3H 95
Armley Grange Mt. LS12: Leeds 3H 95
Armley Grange Oval LS12: Leeds 2H 95
Armley Grange Ri. LS12: Leeds 3H 95
Armley Grange Vw. LS12: Leeds 3A 96
Armley Grange Wlk.
LS12: Leeds 3A 96
Armley Gro. Pl. LS12: Leeds 4D 96
Armley Leisure Cen. 4B 96
Armley Lodge Rd. LS12: Leeds 2C 96

Armley Mills Leeds Industrial Mus.
. . . . .2D 96
Armley Pk. Ct. LS12: Leeds 3C 96
(off Stanningley Rd.)
Armley Pk. Rd. LS12: Leeds 2C 96
Armley Ridge Cl. LS12: Leeds 3A 96
Armley Ridge Rd. LS12: Leeds 6H 75
(not continuous)
Armley Ridge Ter. LS12: Leeds 2A 96
Armley Rd. LS12: Leeds 3C 96
(not continuous)
Armouries Dr. LS10: Leeds 5B 98
Armouries Way
LS10: Leeds 4B 98 (6G 5)
Armstrong St. BD4: B'frd 5B 92
LS28: Pud 1H 93
Armytage Rd. HD6: Brigh 1C 162
Armytage Way HD6: Brigh 2D 162
Arncliffe Av. BD22: Keigh 1G 47
Arncliffe Cres. HD6: Brigh 3G 161
LS27: Morl 5C 138
Arncliffe Gth. LS28: Pud 1H 93
Arncliffe Grange LS17: Leeds 5B 60
Arncliffe Gro. BD22: Keigh 2G 47
Arncliffe Path BD22: Keigh 1G 47
(off Arncliffe Av.)
Arncliffe Pl. BD22: Keigh 1G 47
(off Arncliffe Av.)
Arncliffe Rd. BD22: Keigh 2G 47
LS16: Leeds 1A 76
Arncliffe St. LS28: Pud 1H 93
Arncliffe Ter. BD7: B'frd 5B 90
Arndale Cen. LS6: Leeds 4D 76
Arndale Ho. BD1: B'frd 4D 6
Arndale Shop. Cen. BD18: Ship 2B 70
(off Market St.)
Anford Cl. BD3: B'frd 3F 91 (1F 7)
Arnold Pl. BD8: B'frd 3C 90
Arnold Royd HD6: Brigh 4G 161
Arnold St. BD8: B'frd 2C 90
HX1: Hal 2E 149
HX6: Hal 5H 147
Arnside Av. BD20: Keigh 4C 34
Arnside Rd. BD5: B'frd 3E 111
Arran Ct. LS25: Gar 6F 103
Arran Dr. LS18: H'fth 3D 56
LS25: Gar 6F 103
Arran Way LS26: Rothw 2B 142
Arthington Av. LS10: Leeds 3B 118
Arthington Cl. WF3: E Ard 2D 154
Arthington Ct. LS10: Leeds 3B 118
Arthington Gth. LS21: Arth 5H 25
Arthington Gro. LS10: Leeds 3B 118
Arthington La. LS21: Arth, Pool 4F 25
Arthington Lawns LS21: Pool 5G 25
Arthington Pl. LS10: Leeds 3B 118
Arthington St. BD8: B'frd 3C 90
LS10: Leeds 3B 118
Arthington Ter. LS10: Leeds 3B 118
Arthington Vw. LS10: Leeds 3B 118
Arthur Av. BD8: B'frd 4E 89
ARTHURSDALE 1H 81
Arthursdale Cl. LS15: Scho 2H 81
Arthursdale Dr. LS15: Scho 2H 81
Arthursdale Grange LS15: Scho 2H 81
Arthur St. BD10: B'frd 3H 71
BD16: Bgly 3B 50
BD22: Keigh 5C 46
HD6: Brigh 1C 162
LS28: Pud 1H 93
(New St.)
LS28: Pud 1A 94
(Town St.)
Arthur Ter. LS28: Pud 1H 93
(off Arthur St.)
Artist St. LS12: Leeds 4F 97
Arum St. BD5: B'frd 2C 110
Arundel Cl. WF17: Bat 5D 136
Arundel St. HX1: Hal 2D 148
LS25: Gar 3H 103
LS28: Pud 4A 94
Arundel Ter. LS15: Leeds 1E 101
(off Tranquility Av.)
Arundel Wlk. WF17: Bat 6D 136

Ascot Av. BD7: B'frd 3G 109
Ascot Dr. BD7: B'frd 3G 109
Ascot Gdns. BD7: B'frd 3G 109
  LS10: Leeds 4B 140
Ascot Gro. HD6: Brigh 3G 161
Ascot Pde. BD7: B'frd 3G 109
Ascot Rd. LS25: Kip 3F 123
Ascot Ter. LS9: Leeds 4D 98
Asda Ho. LS11: Leeds 5A 98 (6E 5)
Ash Av. LS6: Leeds 4D 76
Ashbourne Av. BD2: B'frd 6F 71
Ashbourne Bank BD2: B'frd 6F 71
Ashbourne Cl. BD2: B'frd 5F 71
Ashbourne Cres. BD2: B'frd 6F 71
  BD13: B'frd 4H 107
  LS25: Gar 6F 103
Ashbourne Dr. BD2: B'frd 6F 71
Ashbourne Gdns. BD2: B'frd 6F 71
Ashbourne Gth. BD2: B'frd 5G 71
Ashbourne Gro. BD2: B'frd 6F 71
  HX1: Hal 2D 148
Ashbourne Haven BD2: B'frd 6F 71
Ashbourne Mt. BD2: B'frd 6F 71
Ashbourne Oval BD2: B'frd 6F 71
Ashbourne Ri. BD2: B'frd 6F 71
Ashbourne Rd. BD2: B'frd 6F 71
  BD21: Keigh 3G 47
Ashbourne Way BD2: B'frd 5F 71
Ashbrooke Pk. LS11: Leeds 3A 118
Ashburn Cl. LS22: Weth 2D 12
Ashburn Cft. LS22: Weth 2D 12
Ashburn Dr. LS22: Weth 2D 12
Ashburn Gro. BD17: Bail 3C 52
  LS22: Weth 2D 12
Ashburnham Gro. BD9: B'frd 6B 70
Ashburn Pl. LS29: I'ly 6C 10
Ashburn Way LS22: Weth 2D 12
Ashbury Chase WF1: Wake 4E 157
Ashby Av. LS13: Leeds 1F 95
Ashby Cres. LS13: Leeds 2F 95
Ashby Mt. LS13: Leeds 1F 95
Ashby Sq. LS13: Leeds 1F 95
Ashby St. BD4: B'frd 1G 111
Ashby Ter. LS13: Leeds 1F 95
Ashby Vw. LS13: Leeds 1F 95
Ash Cl. HX3: Hal 1F 151
  LS29: I'ly 5A 10
Ash Ct. BD19: Cleck 1F 153
Ash Cres. LS6: Leeds 4D 76
Ash Cft. BD6: B'frd 5A 110
Ashdale La. LS22: Weth 1D 12
Ashday La. HX3: Hal 6C 150
Ashdene LS12: Leeds 2F 115
Ashdene Cl. LS28: Pud 6A 94
Ashdene Ct. BD13: B'frd 3B 66
Ashdene Cres. LS28: Pud 6A 94
Ashdown Cl. BD6: B'frd 4B 110
  HX2: Hal 3B 148
Ashdown Ct. BD18: Ship 2A 70
Ashdowne Pl. BD8: B'frd 2C 90
  (off E. Squire La.)
Ashdown St. LS13: Leeds 2E 95
Asherton Gro. LS23: B Spa 4C 30
Ashfield BD4: B'frd 4B 112
  LS12: Leeds 1A 116
  LS22: Weth 3F 13
Ashfield Av. BD9: Ship 4B 70
  LS27: Morl 5H 137
Ashfield Cl. HX3: Hal 5D 128
  LS12: Leeds 1H 115
  LS15: Leeds 5F 81
  WF17: Bat 6C 136
Ashfield Cl. BD16: Bgly 5C 50
Ashfield Cres. BD16: Bgly 5C 50
  LS28: Pud 2H 93
Ashfield Dr. BD9: Ship 4B 70
  BD17: Bail 3D 52
  HX3: Hal 5D 128
Ashfield Gro. BD9: B'frd 4A 70
  LS28: Pud 2H 93
Ashfield Paddock
  LS23: B Spa 4D 30
Ashfield Pk. LS6: Leeds 4E 77
  LS21: Otley 3C 22

Ashfield Pl. BD2: B'frd 1B 92
  LS21: Otley 4D 22
Ashfield Rd. BD10: B'frd 6H 53
  BD13: B'frd 5H 87
  BD18: Ship 2G 69
  HX4: Hal 4F 159
  LS27: Morl 4H 137
  LS28: Pud 2H 93
  WF17: Bat 5B 136
Ashfield St. BD21: Keigh 1H 47
  (off Minnie St.)
Ashfield Ter. BD12: B'frd 3D 132
  BD16: Bgly 5C 50
  BD22: Haw 3C 64
  HX4: Hal 3F 159
  LS15: Leeds 5F 81
  WF3: Leeds 5D 140
Ashfield Way LS12: Leeds 1G 115
Ashford Dr. LS28: Pud 5B 94
Ashford Grn. BD6: B'frd 4H 109
Ash Gdns. LS6: Leeds 4D 76
Ash Ghyll Gdns. BD16: Bgly 3B 50
Ash Gro. BD2: B'frd 6A 72
  BD11: B'frd 1E 135
  BD16: Bgly 6C 50
  BD19: Cleck 3H 153
  (W. End Rd.)
  BD19: Cleck 6E 135
  (Woodlands Rd.)
  BD20: Stee 6D 14
  BD21: Keigh 3G 47
  HD6: Brigh 6C 152
  LS6: Leeds 6F 77
  LS18: H'fth 5E 57
  LS21: Otley 4D 22
  LS28: Pud 5A 94
  LS29: I'ly 4E 11
Ashgrove BD7: B'frd 5D 90 (6A 6)
  BD10: B'frd 2C 72
Ashgrove Av. HX3: Hal 6H 149
Ashgrove Cres. LS25: Kip 2H 123
Ashgrove Cft. LS25: Kip 3H 123
Ashgrove M. LS13: Leeds 5B 74
Ashgrove Mt. LS25: Kip 2G 123
Ashgrove Pl. HX3: Hal 6A 150
Ash Gro. Ter. HD6: Brigh 2A 162
  (off Thomas St.)
Ash Hill Dr. LS17: Leeds 3B 62
Ash Hill Gdns. LS17: Leeds 3B 62
Ash Hill Gth. LS17: Leeds 3B 62
Ash Hill La. LS17: Leeds 3B 62
Ash Hill Wlk. BD4: B'frd 1H 111
Ash Ho. LS15: Leeds 5A 100
Ashington Cl. BD2: B'frd 6B 72
Ashlands Rd. LS29: I'ly 4E 11
Ashlar Cl. BD22: Haw 2D 64
Ashlar Gro. BD13: B'frd 6H 107
Ashlea Av. HD6: Brigh 3B 162
Ashlea Cl. HD6: Brigh 3B 162
  LS25: Gar 6F 103
Ashlea Ct. LS13: Leeds 6E 75
  (off Ashlea Ga.)
Ashlea Dr. HD6: Brigh 3B 162
Ashlea Ga. LS13: Leeds 6E 75
Ashlea Grn. LS13: Leeds 6E 75
Ashleigh Gdns. LS26: Rothw 1E 143
Ashleigh Rd. LS16: Leeds 1A 76
Ashleigh St. BD21: Keigh 5A 34
  HX3: Hal 4E 129
Ashley Cl. LS9: Leeds 1E 99
Ashley Cl. BD19: Cleck 5E 135
Ashley Ind. Est. LS7: Leeds 6A 78
Ashley La. BD17: Ship 1B 70
Ashley Pk. M. LS25: Gar 2A 104
Ashley Rd. BD12: B'frd 5C 132
  BD16: Bgly 5C 50
  LS9: Leeds 1D 98
  LS12: Leeds 5B 96
Ashley St. BD18: Ship 1B 70
  HX1: Hal 2D 148
Ashley Ter. LS9: Leeds 1E 99
Ashmead LS23: B Spa 6B 30

Ash M. BD10: B'frd 2C 72
Ashmore Gdns. BD4: B'frd 5H 111
Ash Mt. BD7: B'frd 6B 90
  BD21: Keigh 2G 47
Ashmount BD7: B'frd 1F 109
Ashmount Pl. BD22: Haw 2C 64
Ash Rd. LS6: Leeds 5C 76
Ashroyd LS26: Rothw 3B 142
Ash St. BD22: Oxen 6C 64
  LS29: I'ly 4E 11
Ash Ter. BD16: Bgly 5B 50
  LS6: Leeds 4D 76
  LS25: Gar 3G 103
Ashtofts Mt. LS20: Guis 4C 40
Ashton Av. BD7: B'frd 6G 89
  LS8: Leeds 6D 78
Ashton Ct. LS8: Leeds 5D 78
  (off Karnac Rd.)
  LS8: Leeds 6E 79
  (Ashton Rd.)
Ashton Cres. WF3: Rothw 4H 141
Ashton Gro. LS8: Leeds 1D 98
Ashton Ho. BD5: B'frd 6E 91
  (off Crosscombe Wlk.)
Ashton Mt. LS8: Leeds 1D 98
Ashton Pl. LS8: Leeds 1D 98
Ashton Rd. LS8: Leeds 6E 79
Ashton Rd. Ind. Est. LS8: Leeds 6E 79
Ashton St. BD1: B'frd 4D 90 (3A 6)
  LS8: Leeds 6D 78
Ashton Ter. LS8: Leeds 1D 98
  LS26: Rothw 3F 141
Ashton Vw. LS8: Leeds 1D 98
Ash Tree App. LS14: Leeds 5F 81
Ash Tree Av. BD13: B'frd 5F 87
Ash Tree Bank LS14: Leeds 4F 81
Ash Tree Cl. LS14: Leeds 4F 81
Ash Tree Gdns. HX2: Hal 2A 128
  LS14: Leeds 4F 81
Ash Tree Grange LS14: Leeds 4F 81
  (off Ash Tree Bank)
Ash Tree Gro. LS14: Leeds 4F 81
  LS25: Kip 4H 123
Ashtree Gro. BD7: B'frd 3H 109
Ash Tree Pk. LS25: Kip 4H 123
Ash Tree Rd. HX2: Hal 2A 128
Ash Tree Vw. LS14: Leeds 4F 81
  (off Ash Tree Gdns.)
Ash Tree Wlk. LS14: Leeds 4F 81
  (off Ash Tree Cl.)
  LS29: Burl W 2E 21
Ash Vw. LS6: Leeds 4D 76
  WF3: E Ard 2A 156
Ash Vs. LS15: Leeds 5F 81
Ashville Av. LS6: Leeds 6D 76
Ashville Cft. HX2: Hal 1B 148
Ashville Gdns. HX2: Hal 1B 148
Ashville Gro. HX2: Hal 6B 128
  LS6: Leeds 6D 76
Ashville Rd. LS4: Leeds 6D 76
Ashville St. HX3: Hal 6E 129
Ashville Ter. BD22: Keigh 5D 46
  LS6: Leeds 6D 76
  LS28: Pud 1H 93
  (off New St.)
Ashville Vw. LS6: Leeds 1E 97
Ashwell La. BD9: B'frd 5A 70
Ashwell Rd. BD8: B'frd 2B 90
  BD9: B'frd 5A 70
Ashwood LS14: Leeds 6D 62
Ashwood Dr. BD20: Keigh 4E 35
  LS27: Morl 6D 114
Ashwood Gdns. LS27: Morl 6D 114
Ashwood Gro. LS27: Morl 6E 115
Ashwood Pde. LS27: Morl 6D 114
  (off Ashwood Gdns.)
Ashwood St. BD4: B'frd 4B 112
Ashwood Ter. LS6: Leeds 5F 77
Ashwood Vs. LS6: Leeds 5F 77
Ashworth Pl. BD6: B'frd 4D 110
Asket Av. LS14: Leeds 4A 80
Asket Cl. LS14: Leeds 3A 80

Asket Cres. LS14: Leeds 4A 80
Asket Dr. LS14: Leeds 3A 80
Asket Gdns. LS8: Leeds 3H 79
Asket Gth. LS14: Leeds 4A 80
Asket Grn. LS14: Leeds 3A 80
Asket Hill LS8: Leeds 2H 79
Asket Pl. LS14: Leeds 4A 80
Asket Wlk. LS14: Leeds 4A 80
Askey Av. LS27: Morl 5B 138
Askey Cres. LS27: Morl 5B 138
Askrigg Dr. BD2: B'frd 6H 71
Aspect 14 LS7: Leeds 2A 98 (1F 5)
Aspect Gdns. LS28: Pud 3G 93
Aspect Ter. LS28: Pud 3G 93
Aspen Cl. BD21: Keigh 2C 48
Aspen Ct. WF3: Morl 6C 138
Aspen Mt. LS16: Leeds 5G 57
Aspen Ri. BD15: B'frd 5B 68
Aspinalls Fold HX5: Ell 5E 161
Aspinall St. HX1: Hal 3D 148
Asprey Dr. BD15: B'frd 3D 88
Asquith Av. LS27: Morl 1G 137
Asquith Bottom HX6: Hal 6H 147
Asquith Bldgs. BD12: B'frd 2F 133
(off Cleckheaton Rd.)
Asquith Cl. LS27: Morl 2H 137
Asquith Ct. HX2: Hal 2B 148
Asquith Dr. LS27: Morl 2H 137
Asquith St. WF17: Bat 5D 136
Asquith Ter. HX6: Hal 6H 147
Assembly St. LS2: Leeds 4A 98 (5F 5)
Astley Av. LS26: Swil 4A 122
Astley La. LS26: Swil 4B 122
Astley La. Ind. Est. LS26: Swil 5B 122
Astley Way LS26: Swil 5B 122
Aston Av. LS13: Leeds 1F 95
Aston Cres. LS13: Leeds 1G 95
Aston Dr. LS13: Leeds 1G 95
Aston Gro. LS13: Leeds 1G 95
Aston Mt. LS13: Leeds 1G 95
Aston Pl. LS13: Leeds 1G 95
Aston Rd. BD5: B'frd 2E 111
LS13: Leeds 1F 95
Aston St. LS13: Leeds 1F 95
Aston Ter. LS13: Leeds 1G 95
Aston Vw. LS13: Leeds 1F 95
Astor Gro. LS13: Leeds 1C 94
Astor St. LS13: Leeds 1C 94
Astra Bus. Pk. LS11: Leeds 3A 118
Astral Av. HX3: Hal 1F 151
Astral Cl. HX3: Hal 1F 151
Astral Vw. BD6: B'frd 3A 110
Astura Ct. LS7: Leeds 4H 77
Atalanta Ter. HX2: Hal 5C 148
Atha Cl. LS11: Leeds 4G 117
Atha Cres. LS11: Leeds 4G 117
Atha Ho. LS2: Leeds 1E 5
Atha St. LS11: Leeds 4G 117
Athelstan La. LS21: Otley 1E 23
Atherstone Rd. BD15: B'frd 4D 88
Atherton La. HD6: Brigh 3B 162
Athlone Gro. LS12: Leeds 4C 96
Athlone Ri. LS25: Gar 4H 103
Athlone St. LS12: Leeds 4C 96
Athlone Ter. LS12: Leeds 4C 96
Athol Cl. HX3: Hal 4E 129
Athol Cres. HX3: Hal 4E 129
Athol Gdns. HX3: Hal 4E 129
Athol Grn. HX3: Hal 4E 129
Athol Mt. HX3: Hal 4E 129
Athol Rd. BD9: B'frd 1B 90
HX3: Hal 4E 129
Athol St. BD21: Keigh 4C 34
HX3: Hal 4E 129
ATKINSON HILL 1D 118
Atkinson's Ct. HX1: Hal . . .1G 149 (3B 164)
Atkinson St. BD18: Ship 1B 70
LS10: Leeds 6C 98
Atlanta St. LS13: Leeds 1C 94
Atlas Mill Rd. HD6: Brigh 1A 162
Atlas St. BD8: B'frd 2B 90
Attlee Gro. WF1: Wake 5G 157
Auckland Rd. BD6: B'frd 4A 110
Audby Ct. LS22: Weth 3F 13

Audby La. LS22: Weth 2F 13
Aurelia Ho. BD8: B'frd 1C 90
Austell Ho. BD5: B'frd 1D 110
(off Park La.)
AUSTHORPE 3G 101
Austhorpe Av. LS15: Leeds 4G 101
Austhorpe Ct. LS15: Leeds 4G 101
(off Austhorpe Dr.)
Austhorpe Dr. LS15: Leeds 4G 101
Austhorpe Gdns. LS15: Leeds 3H 101
Austhorpe Gro. LS15: Leeds 4G 101
Austhorpe La. LS15: Leeds 2F 101
Austhorpe Rd. LS15: Leeds 1E 101
Austhorpe Vw. LS15: Leeds 3F 101
Austin Av. HD6: Brigh 5H 151
Austin St. BD21: Keigh 5B 34
Authorpe Rd. LS6: Leeds 3F 77
Autumn Av. LS6: Leeds 1E 97
LS22: Weth 1E 13
Autumn Cres. LS18: H'fth 2F 75
Autumn Gro. LS6: Leeds 1E 97
Autumn Pl. LS6: Leeds 1E 97
Autumn St. HX1: Hal 4D 148
LS6: Leeds 1E 97
Autumn Ter. LS6: Leeds 1E 97
Auty Sq. LS27: Morl 4B 138
Avenel Rd. BD15: B'frd 2D 88
Avenel Ter. BD15: B'frd 3D 88
Avenham Way BD3: B'frd . . .3G 91 (2G 7)
Avenue, The BD10: B'frd 4C 54
(not continuous)
BD14: B'frd 1C 108
BD15: B'frd 5H 67
BD16: Bgly 1D 68
BD17: B'frd 4C 54
HX3: Hal 1F 151
LS8: Leeds 1E 79
LS9: Leeds 4C 98 (5H 5)
LS15: Leeds, Swil 3F 121
(Newsam Grn. Rd.)
LS15: Leeds 6F 81
(Sandbed La.)
LS15: Scho 1H 81
LS17: Leeds 2F 59
LS18: H'fth 6B 56
LS22: Coll 2A 28
WF1: Wake 5E 157
WF3: E Ard 1G 155
WF17: Bat 6A 136
(not continuous)
Avenue A LS23: W'ton 1F 31
Avenue B LS23: W'ton 2E 31
Avenue C East LS23: W'ton 1G 31
Avenue Cres. LS8: Leeds 5D 78
Avenue C West LS23: W'ton 2F 31
Avenue D LS23: W'ton 3F 31
Avenue Des Hirondelles
LS21: Pool 5E 25
Avenue E East LS23: W'ton 2G 31
Avenue E West LS23: W'ton 3F 31
Avenue F LS23: W'ton 2G 31
Avenue G LS23: W'ton 1H 31
Avenue Gdns. LS17: Leeds 2G 59
Avenue Hill LS8: Leeds 5C 78
Avenue Lawns LS17: Leeds 2F 59
Avenue No. 1 HD6: Brigh 2A 162
Avenue No. 2 HD6: Brigh 2A 162
Avenue Rd. BD5: B'frd 2F 111
Avenue St. BD4: B'frd 4B 112
Avenue Ter. LS19: Yead 6H 41
Avenue Victoria LS8: Leeds 1E 79
Avenue Wlk. LS2: Leeds 6G 77
LS6: Leeds 6G 77
Averingcliffe Rd. BD10: B'frd 3B 72
Aviary Gro. LS12: Leeds 3C 96
Aviary Mt. LS12: Leeds 3C 96
Aviary Pl. LS12: Leeds 3C 96
Aviary Rd. LS12: Leeds 3C 96
Aviary Row LS12: Leeds 3C 96
Aviary St. LS12: Leeds 3C 96
Aviary Ter. LS12: Leeds 3C 96
Aviary Vw. LS12: Leeds 3C 96
Avocet Cl. BD8: B'frd 4E 89
Avocet Gth. LS10: Leeds 2B 140

Avon Cl. LS17: Leeds 3B 62
Avon Ct. LS17: Leeds 2A 62
Avondale BD20: Keigh 5G 33
Avondale Ct. LS17: Leeds 4B 60
Avondale Cres. BD18: Ship 2A 70
Avondale Dr. WF3: Wake 4H 157
Avondale Gro. BD18: Ship 2A 70
Avondale Mt. BD18: Ship 2A 70
Avondale Pl. HX3: Hal 5F 149
Avondale Rd. BD18: Ship 2G 69
Avondale St. LS13: Leeds 2E 95
Avondale Vs. LS14: T'ner 4G 63
Avon Dr. LS25: Gar 5F 103
Avon Gth. LS22: Weth 4C 12
Axis Ct. LS27: Morl 2G 137
Aydon Way HX3: B'frd 6G 109
Aygill Av. BD9: B'frd 6F 69
Aylesbury St. BD21: Keigh 3G 47
Aylesford Mt. LS15: Leeds 6H 81
Aylesham Ind. Est. BD12: B'frd 1D 132
Aynholme Cl. LS29: Add 1D 8
Aynholme Dr. LS29: Add 1D 8
Aynsley Gro. BD15: B'frd 1D 88
Ayresome Av. LS8: Leeds 5E 61
Ayresome Oval BD15: B'frd 4C 88
Ayresome Ter. LS8: Leeds 5D 60
Ayreville Dr. HX3: Hal 1E 131
Ayrton Cres. BD16: Bgly 4C 50
Aysgarth Av. HX3: Hal 3A 152
Aysgarth Cl. BD12: B'frd 5C 132
LS9: Leeds 4D 98
Aysgarth Cres. HX2: Hal 4G 127
Aysgarth Dr. LS9: Leeds 4D 98
Aysgarth Fold LS10: Leeds 3A 140
Aysgarth Pl. LS9: Leeds 4D 98
Aysgarth Wlk. LS9: Leeds 4D 98
Ayton Cl. BD3: B'frd 3G 91 (2H 7)
Ayton Ho. BD4: B'frd 4D 112
Azalea Ct. BD3: B'frd 3H 91 (2H 7)
(not continuous)

B

Bachelor La. LS18: H'fth 6E 57
Bk. Ada St. BD21: Keigh 6G 33
(off Devonshire St.)
Bk. Aireview Ter. BD21: Keigh 1C 48
Bk. Aireville St. BD20: Keigh 3G 33
Bk. Airlie Av. LS8: Leeds 5D 78
(off Airlie Av.)
Bk. Airlie Pl. LS8: Leeds 5D 78
(off Airlie Pl.)
Bk. Albert Gro. LS6: Leeds 3D 76
Bk. Albert Ter. LS6: Leeds 1E 97
(off Burley Lodge Rd.)
Bk. Alcester Pl. LS8: Leeds 5D 78
(off Alcester Pl.)
Bk. Alcester Rd. LS8: Leeds 5D 78
(off Alcester Rd.)
Bk. Alcester Ter. LS8: Leeds 5D 78
(off Alcester Ter.)
Bk. Allerton St. LS7: Leeds 2B 78
Bk. Alma St. LS19: Yead 6G 41
(off Alma St.)
Bk. Ann St. BD13: B'frd 2B 86
Bk. Archery Pl. LS2: Leeds 1H 97
(off Archery Pl.)
Bk. Archery Rd. LS2: Leeds 1H 97
(off Archery Rd.)
Bk. Archery St. LS2: Leeds 1H 97
(off Archery St.)
Bk. Archery Ter. LS2: Leeds 1H 97
(off Archery Ter.)
Bk. Ash Gro. LS6: Leeds 6F 77
(not continuous)
Bk. Ashgrove W.
BD7: B'frd 5D 90 (6A 6)
Bk. Ashley Av. LS9: Leeds 1E 99
(off Ashley Av.)
Bk. Ashley St. LS9: Leeds 1E 99
(off Ashley Rd.)
Bk. Ashville Av. LS6: Leeds 6E 77
(off Ashville Av.)

Bk. Ashville Gro. LS6: Leeds 6D 76
(off Ashville Gro.)
Bk. Ashville Rd. LS6: Leeds 6D 76
(off Ashville Rd.)
Bk. Ashville Ter. LS6: Leeds 6D 76
(off Ashville Ter.)
Bk. Ashwood Ter. LS6: Leeds 5F 77
Bk. Aston Pl. LS13: Leeds 1G 95
(off Aston Rd.)
Bk. Aston Rd. LS13: Leeds 1F 95
Bk. Aston St. LS13: Leeds 1F 95
Bk. Aston Ter. LS13: Leeds 1G 95
(off Aston Rd.)
Bk. Aston Vw. LS13: Leeds 1F 95
Bk. Athlone Av. LS12: Leeds 4C 96
Bk. Athlone Gro. LS12: Leeds 4C 96
(off Athlone St.)
Bk. Athlone Ter. LS12: Leeds 4C 96
(off Athlone St.)
Bk. Atlanta St. LS13: Leeds 1C 94
Bk. Austhorpe Rd. LS15: Leeds 1E 101
(off Austhorpe Rd.)
Bk. Autumn Rd. LS6: Leeds 1E 97
(off Autumn Ter.)
Bk. Autumn Ter. LS6: Leeds 1E 97
(off Autumn Ter.)
Bk. Aviary Rd. LS12: Leeds 3C 96
(off Aviary Gro.)
Bk. Aylesbury St. BD21: Keigh 3G 47
(off Queen's Rd.)
Bk. Bailey's Pl. LS16: Leeds 3D 76
Bk. Baker St. BD18: Ship 1A 70
Bk. Baldovan Ter. LS8: Leeds 5D 78
(off Baldovan Ter.)
Bk. Balfour St. BD16: Bgly 5B 50
BD21: Keigh 1H 47
Bk. Bank Ter. LS28: Pud 1A 94
Bk. Banstead St. LS8: Leeds 6D 78
(off Banstead Ter. E.)
Bk. Barden Pl. LS12: Leeds 4A 96
(off Whingate Rd.)
Bk. Barkly Gro. LS11: Leeds 3G 117
(off Barkly Gro.)
Bk. Barkly Pde. LS11: Leeds 4G 117
(off Barkly Pde.)
Bk. Barkly Ter. LS11: Leeds 3G 117
(off Barkly Ter.)
Bk. Barrowby Vw. LS15: Leeds 4G 101
Bk. Bath Rd. LS13: Leeds 1E 95
(off Cross Bath Rd.)
Bk. Beamsley Gro. LS6: Leeds 1E 97
(off Beamsley Gro.)
Bk. Beamsley Mt. LS6: Leeds 1E 97
(off Beamsley Mt.)
Bk. Beamsley Ter. LS6: Leeds 1E 97
(off Beamsley Ter.)
Bk. Beck La. LS29: Add 1D 8
Bk. Beech St. BD16: Bgly 5B 50
Bk. Beechwood Gro. LS4: Leeds 6D 76
Bk. Beechwood Rd. LS4: Leeds 6D 76
(off Beechwood Pl.)
Bk. Bellbrooke Gro. LS9: Leeds 1F 99
(off Bellbrooke Gro.)
Bk. Bellbrooke Pl. LS9: Leeds 1F 99
(off Bellbrooke Pl.)
Bk. Bellbrooke Ter. LS9: Leeds 1F 99
(off Bellbrooke St.)
Bk. Belvedere Av. LS11: Leeds 3H 117
(off Belvedere Av.)
Bk. Bentley Av. LS6: Leeds 3F 77
(off Bentley Gro.)
Bk. Bentley Gro. LS6: Leeds 3F 77
(off Bentley Gro.)
Bk. Berkeley Av. LS8: Leeds 6E 79
(off Berkeley Av.)
Bk. Berkeley Ter. LS8: Leeds 6E 79
(off Berkeley Ter.)
Bk. Beverley Ter. LS11: Leeds 2H 117
Bk. Blackwood Gro. HX1: Hal 1D 148
Bk. Blenheim Av. LS2: Leeds 1H 97
Bk. Blenheim Mt. BD8: B'frd 1C 90
Bk. Blenheim Ter. LS2: Leeds 1H 97
Bk. Boundary Ter. LS3: Leeds 2E 97
(off Burley Rd.)

Bk. Bower Rd. HX5: Ell 4C 160
Bk. Branch Pl. LS12: Leeds 1A 116
(off Branch Pl.)
Bk. Breary Av. LS18: H'fth 6F 57
Bk. Breary Ter. LS18: H'fth 6F 57
(off Breary Av.)
Bk. Briggate BD20: Sils 1E 15
Bk. Broad La. LS13: Leeds 5F 75
Bk. Broomfield Cres. LS6: Leeds ...5D 76
Bk. Broomfield Pl. LS6: Leeds 6D 76
(off Broomfield Pl.)
Bk. Broomfield Rd. BD21: Keigh ...6H 33
LS6: Leeds 6D 76
(off Newport Rd.)
Bk. Broomfield St. BD21: Keigh ...6H 33
Bk. Broughton Av. LS9: Leeds 1E 99
(off Broughton Av.)
Bk. Broughton Ter. LS9: Leeds 1E 99
(off Broughton Ter.)
Bk. Brudenell Gro. LS6: Leeds 6F 77
(off Brudenell Gro.)
Bk. Brudenell Mt. LS6: Leeds 6E 77
(off Brudenell Mt.)
Bk. Brudenell Rd. LS6: Leeds 6E 77
(off Brudenell Rd.)
Bk. Brunswick St.
LS2: Leeds 2A 98 (2F 5)
Bk. Burchett Gro. LS6: Leeds 5G 77
(off Burchett Gro.)
Bk. Burchett Pl. LS6: Leeds 5G 77
(off Burchett Pl.)
Bk. Burley Hill LS4: Leeds 1C 96
Bk. Burley Lodge Rd. LS6: Leeds ...1E 97
(off Burley Lodge Rd.)
Bk. Burley Lodge Ter. LS4: Leeds ...2E 97
(off Burley Lodge Ter.)
Bk. Burley St. LS3: Leeds 3A 4
Bk. Burlington Pl. LS11: Leeds 3H 117
(off Burlington Pl.)
Bk. Burlington Rd. LS11: Leeds 3H 117
(off Burlington Rd.)
Bk. Burton Cres. LS6: Leeds 3D 76
Bk. Burton Ter. LS11: Leeds 2A 118
Bk. Buxton St. BD21: Keigh 6B 34
(off Buxton St.)
Bk. Byrl St. BD21: Keigh 4A 34
(off Byrl St.)
Bk. Caister St. BD21: Keigh 3H 47
(off Oakfield Rd.)
Bk. Caledonia Rd. BD21: Keigh ...5B 34
(off Caledonia Rd.)
Bk. Camberley St. LS11: Leeds 2H 117
(off Camberley St.)
Bk. Carberry Pl. LS6: Leeds 1E 97
(off Carberry Pl.)
Bk. Carberry Rd. LS6: Leeds 1E 97
(off Carberry Rd.)
Bk. Carberry Ter. LS6: Leeds 1E 97
(off Carberry Ter.)
Bk. Carter Mt. LS15: Leeds 3E 101
(off Carter Mt.)
Bk. Cartmel Rd. BD21: Keigh ...6G 33
(off Devonshire St.)
Bk. Castle Rd. BD21: Keigh 5H 33
Bk. Cavendish Rd. BD10: B'frd ...2H 71
Bk. Cavendish St. BD21: Keigh ...6A 34
Bk. Cavendish Ter. HX1: Hal 2E 149
Bk. Chapel La. LS6: Leeds 5D 76
(off Broomfield Rd.)
Bk. Chapel St. BD1: B'frd 4F 91 (4F 7)
Bk. Charles St. HD6: Brigh 6A 152
(off Charles St.)
Bk. Charlton Rd. LS9: Leeds 4E 99
Bk. Chatsworth Rd. LS8: Leeds ...6E 79
(off Chatsworth Rd.)
Bk. Chestnut Av. LS15: Leeds 1F 101
(off Chestnut Av.)
Bk. Chiswick Ter. LS6: Leeds 1E 97
(off Burley Lodge Rd.)
Bk. Christ Chu. Vw. LS12: Leeds ...3B 96
(off Stanningley Rd.)
Bk. Church La. LS5: Leeds 5A 76
(off Hesketh Rd.)
LS16: Leeds 2D 58

Bk. Claremont Av. LS3: Leeds 2A 4
Bk. Claremont Gro. LS3: Leeds 2A 4
Bk. Claremont St. LS26: Rothw ...1E 143
Bk. Claremont Ter. LS3: Leeds 2A 4
Bk. Claremount Ter. HX3: Hal ...5G 129
Bk. Clarence Rd. LS18: H'fth 2D 74
Bk. Clarence St.
HX1: Hal 2F 149 (4A 164)
LS13: Leeds 2E 95
Bk. Clarendon Pl. HX1: Hal 2E 149
Bk. Clarkson Vw. LS6: Leeds 5G 77
(off Clarkson Vw.)
Bk. Cliffe Ter. BD21: Keigh 3A 48
Bk. Cliff Mt. LS6: Leeds 5G 77
(off Cliff Mt.)
Bk. Clifton Ter. LS9: Leeds 1F 99
(off Clifton Ter.)
Bk. Clipston Av. LS6: Leeds 3F 77
(off Clipston Av.)
Bk. Clock Vw. St. BD20: Keigh ...3H 33
(off Eel Holme Vw. St.)
Bk. Clough HX3: Hal 5C 130
Bk. Clovelly Pl. LS11: Leeds 2H 117
(off Clovelly Pl.)
Bk. Colenso Mt. LS11: Leeds 1F 117
(off Colenso Mt.)
Bk. Colenso Rd. BD21: Keigh 4C 34
(off Aireworth Rd.)
LS11: Leeds 1F 117
(off Colenso Rd.)
Bk. Colton Rd. LS12: Leeds 4C 96
Bk. Colwyn Vw. LS11: Leeds 3H 117
(off Colwyn Vw.)
Bk. Commercial St. HX1: Hal 4B 164
Bk. Compton St. BD21: Keigh 5B 34
(off Compton St.)
Bk. Conway St. LS8: Leeds 6D 78
(off Conway St.)
Bk. Cowper Gro. LS8: Leeds 6E 79
(off Cowper Gro.)
Bk. Cowper St. LS7: Leeds 6C 78
(off Cross Cowper St.)
Bk. Craggwood Rd. LS18: H'fth ...2E 75
Bk. Crag Rd. BD18: Ship 2C 70
Bk. Cranbrook Av. LS11: Leeds ...2G 117
(off Cranbrook Av.)
Bk. Cranbrook Ter. LS11: Leeds ...2G 117
(off Cranbrook Av.)
Bk. Crescent, The LS6: Leeds 6G 77
(off Woodhouse La.)
Bk. Croft Ho. La. BD20: Keigh ...3G 33
Bk. Cromer Av. BD21: Keigh 2H 47
(off Cromer Rd.)
Bk. Cromer Gro. BD21: Keigh 3H 47
(off Cromer Rd.)
Bk. Cromer Ter.
LS2: Leeds 1G 97 (1B 4)
Bk. Cromwell Ter. HX1: Hal 2F 149
Bk. Cross Flatts Av. LS11: Leeds ...3G 117
(off Cross Flatts Av.)
Bk. Cross Flatts Cres.
LS11: Leeds 3F 117
(off Cross Flatts Cres.)
Bk. Cross Flatts Gro.
LS11: Leeds 3G 117
(off Cross Flatts Gro.)
Bk. Cross Flatts Mt. LS11: Leeds ...3G 117
(off Cross Flatts Mt.)
Bk. Cross Flatts Pl. LS11: Leeds ...3F 117
(off Cross Flatts Pl.)
Bk. Cross Flatts Row
LS11: Leeds 3F 117
(off Cross Flatts Row)
Bk. Cross Grn. Cres. LS9: Leeds ...5D 98
(off Cross Grn. Cres.)
Bk. Cross Grn. La. LS9: Leeds ...5D 98
(off Cross Grn. La.)
Bk. Cross La. HX5: Ell 5A 160
(off Linden Rd.)
Bk. Cunliffe Rd. LS29: I'ly 5D 10
Bk. Dalton Gro. LS11: Leeds 3G 117
(off Dalton Gro.)
Bk. Dalton Rd. LS11: Leeds 3G 117
Bk. Dargai St. LS7: Leeds 6A 78

Bk. Dawlish Av. LS9: Leeds 3F **99**
    (off Dawlish Av.)
Bk. Dawlish Mt. LS9: Leeds 3F **99**
    (off Dawlish Mt.)
Bk. Dawlish Rd. LS9: Leeds 3F **99**
    (off Dawlish Rd.)
Bk. De Lacy Mt. LS5: Leeds 4A **76**
    (off Abbey Rd.)
Bk. Delph Mt. LS6: Leeds 5G **77**
    (off Delph Mt.)
Bk. Dent St. LS9: Leeds 4D **98**
    (off Dent St.)
Bk. Devonshire La. LS8: Leeds 5E **61**
Bk. Dorset Mt. LS8: Leeds 5E **79**
    (off Dorset Mt.)
Bk. Dorset Rd. LS8: Leeds 5E **79**
    (off Dorset Rd.)
Bk. Dorset Ter. LS8: Leeds 6E **79**
    (off Dorset Ter.)
Bk. Dudley Hill Rd. BD2: B'frd 1H **91**
Bk. East Pk. Rd. LS9: Leeds 4E **99**
    (off E. Park Rd.)
Bk. Eaton St. BD21: Keigh 3G **47**
    (off Queen's Rd.)
Bk. Ecclesburn Gro. LS9: Leeds 4F **99**
    (off Ecclesburn Gro.)
Bk. Ecclesburn St. LS9: Leeds 4E **99**
    (off Ecclesburn St.)
Bk. Edensor Rd. BD21: Keigh 6G **33**
    (off Devonshire Rd.)
Bk. Edinburgh Rd. LS12: Leeds 3A **96**
    (off Town St.)
Bk. Elford Pl. LS8: Leeds 6D **78**
    (off Elford Gro., not continuous)
Bk. Elizabeth St. BD5: B'frd 6E **91**
Bk. Ellers Gro. LS8: Leeds 5D **78**
    (off Ellers Gro.)
Bk. Ellers Rd. LS8: Leeds 5D **78**
    (off Ellers Rd.)
Bk. Elmfield Ter. HX1: Hal 4F **149**
Bk. Elsworth St. LS12: Leeds 4D **96**
Bk. Emily St. BD21: Keigh 5A **34**
    (off Cross Emily St.)
Bk. Eric St. BD21: Keigh 5A **34**
    (off Eric St.)
    LS13: Leeds 4E **75**
Bk. Eshald Pl. LS26: Rothw 1F **143**
Bk. Esmond Ter. LS12: Leeds 4C **96**
Bk. Estcourt Av. LS6: Leeds 4C **76**
    (off Ash Rd.)
Bk. Eversley Mt. HX2: Hal 3C **148**
Bk. Fairford Pl. LS11: Leeds 2A **118**
Bk. Ferguson St.
    HX1: Hal 3G **149** (4B **164**)
Back Fld. BD13: B'frd 5A **88**
    (off Havelock Sq.)
Bk. Field Ct. BD13: B'frd 5H **87**
    (off Bk. High St.)
Bk. Florist St. BD21: Keigh 4C **34**
    (off Florist St.)
Back Fold BD14: B'frd 6D **88**
    (off Oakfield Rd.)
Bk. Foster Rd. BD21: Keigh 3H **47**
    (off Oakfield Rd.)
Bk. Garton Rd. LS9: Leeds 4E **99**
    (off Garton Rd.)
Bk. Garton Ter. LS9: Leeds 4E **99**
    (off Garton Ter.)
Bk. Gathorne St. LS7: Leeds 6C **78**
    (off Gathorne St.)
Bk. Gerard St. HX1: Hal . . .2F **149** (4A **164**)
Bk. Giles St. Nth. BD5: B'frd 6D **90**
Bk. Giles St. Sth. BD5: B'frd 6D **90**
Bk. Gillett La. LS26: Rothw 2B **142**
Bk. Girlington Rd. BD8: B'frd 2H **89**
Bk. Gladstone Rd. HX1: Hal 2F **149**
Bk. Gladstone St. BD16: Bgly 5B **50**
Bk. Glebe Ter. LS16: Leeds 3D **76**
    (off Glebe Ter.)
Bk. Glen Ter. HX1: Hal 4F **149**
Bk. Glenthorpe Ter. LS9: Leeds 3E **99**
    (off Glenthorpe Ter.)
Bk. Glossop St. LS6: Leeds 5H **77**
    (off Glossop St.)
Bk. Gooder La. HD6: Brigh 2B **162**

Bk. Gordon Ter. LS6: Leeds 3F **77**
    (off Gordon Ter.)
Bk. Graham Gro. LS4: Leeds 6D **76**
Bk. Granby Gro. LS6: Leeds 5D **76**
    (off Granby Rd.)
Bk. Grange Av. LS7: Leeds 5B **78**
    (off Grange Av.)
Bk. Grange Cres. LS7: Leeds 5C **78**
    (off Grange Cres.)
Bk. Grange Ter. LS7: Leeds 5B **78**
    (off Grange Ter.)
Bk. Grange Vw. LS7: Leeds 5C **78**
    (off Grange Vw.)
Bk. Grant St. BD21: Keigh 6G **33**
Bk. Grassington Ter. BD21: Keigh . . .5A **34**
    (off Lawkholme La.)
Bk. Gt. Russell St. BD7: B'frd 4C **90**
Bk. Greaves St. BD5: B'frd 2D **110**
    (off Greaves St.)
Back Grn. LS27: Morl 6C **116**
Bk. Greenhow Wlk. LS4: Leeds 1D **96**
    (off Greenhow Rd.)
Bk. Greenmount Ter.
    LS11: Leeds 2H **117**
    (off Greenmount Ter.)
Bk. Grosvenor Ter. HX1: Hal 2E **149**
    LS6: Leeds 5F **77**
    (off Grosvenor Ter.)
Bk. Grouse St. BD21: Keigh 5B **34**
    (off Parson St.)
Bk. Grove Gdns. LS6: Leeds 3E **77**
    (off Grove Gdns.)
Bk. Grovehall Av. LS11: Leeds 4G **117**
Bk. Grovehall Dr. LS11: Leeds 4G **117**
Bk. Grove Rd. LS29: I'ly 5D **10**
Bk. Haigh Av. LS26: Rothw 6H **119**
Bk. Haigh St. LS26: Rothw 6G **119**
Bk. Haigh Vw. LS26: Rothw 6G **119**
Bk. Halliday Gro. LS12: Leeds 3A **96**
Bk. Halliday Pl. LS12: Leeds 3A **96**
Bk. Hamilton Av. LS7: Leeds 5C **78**
    (off Hamilton Av.)
Bk. Hamilton Vw. LS7: Leeds 5C **78**
    (off Hamilton Vw.)
Bk. Hanson La. HX1: Hal 1C **148**
    (off Hanson La., not continuous)
Bk. Harehills Av. LS7: Leeds 5C **78**
    (off Harehills Av.)
Bk. Harehills Pk. Vw. LS9: Leeds 1F **99**
    (off Harehills Pk. Vw.)
Bk. Harehills Pl. LS8: Leeds 6D **78**
    (off Harehills Pl.)
Bk. Hares Av. LS8: Leeds 5D **78**
    (off Hares Av.)
Bk. Hares Mt. LS8: Leeds 5C **78**
    (off Hares Mt.)
Bk. Hares Ter. LS8: Leeds 5D **78**
    (off Hares Ter.)
Bk. Hares Vw. LS8: Leeds 5C **78**
    (off Hares Vw.)
Bk. Harold Gro. LS6: Leeds 1E **97**
    (off Harold Gro.)
Bk. Hartley Av. LS6: Leeds 5H **77**
    (off Hartley Av.)
Bk. Hartley Gro. LS6: Leeds 5G **77**
    (off Hartley Gro.)
Bk. Hartley St. LS27: Morl 4C **138**
Bk. Hawksworth Gro.
    LS5: Leeds 3F **75**
Bk. Headingley Av. LS6: Leeds 4C **76**
    (off Ash Rd.)
Bk. Headingley Mt. LS6: Leeds 4C **76**
    (off Ash Rd.)
Bk. Heathfield Ter. LS6: Leeds 3D **76**
    (off Heathfield Ter.)
Bk. Heddon St. LS6: Leeds 3E **77**
    (off Heddon St.)
Bk. Heights Rd. BD13: B'frd 4F **87**
Bk. Hessle Av. LS6: Leeds 6E **77**
    (off Hessle Av.)
Bk. Hessle Mt. LS6: Leeds 6E **77**
    (off Hessle Mt.)
Bk. Hessle Ter. LS6: Leeds 6E **77**
    (off Hessle Ter.)

Bk. Hessle Vw. LS6: Leeds 6E **77**
    (off Hessle Vw.)
Bk. Highbury Ter. LS6: Leeds 3E **77**
    (off Highbury Ter.)
Bk. Highfield Rd. LS13: Leeds 1F **95**
Bk. High St. BD13: B'frd 5A **88**
    LS19: Yead 6F **41**
Bk. Highthorne Gro. LS12: Leeds 3A **96**
Bk. Hillcrest Av. LS7: Leeds 5C **78**
    (off Hillcrest Av.)
Bk. Hillcrest Vw. LS7: Leeds 5C **78**
    (off Hillcrest Vw.)
Bk. Hilltop Av. LS8: Leeds 5D **78**
    (off Hilltop Av.)
Bk. Hill Top Mt. LS8: Leeds 5D **78**
    (off Hill Top Mt.)
Bk. Hilton Pl. LS8: Leeds 5D **78**
    (off Hilton Pl.)
Bk. Hilton Rd. LS8: Leeds 5D **78**
    (off Hilton Rd.)
Backhold HX3: Hal 6A **150**
Backhold Dr. HX3: Hal 1A **160**
Backhold Dr. HX3: Hal 1H **159**
Backhold Hall HX3: Hal 6A **150**
Backhold La. HX3: Hal 1H **159**
Backhold Rd. HX3: Hal 1A **160**
Bk. Hollyshaw Ter. LS15: Leeds 3E **101**
Bk. Holywell La. LS17: Leeds 2H **61**
Bk. Hope Hall Ter.
    HX1: Hal 3G **149** (6C **164**)
Bk. Hovingham Gro. LS8: Leeds 5E **79**
    (off Hovingham Gro.)
Bk. Hovingham Mt. LS8: Leeds 5E **79**
    (off Hovingham Mt.)
Bk. Hovingham Ter. LS8: Leeds 5E **79**
    (off Hovingham Ter.)
Bk. Hyde Gro. BD21: Keigh 5B **34**
    (off Kirby St.)
Bk. Hyde Ter. LS2: Leeds 2G **97** (1A **4**)
Bk. Ibbetson Pl. LS1: Leeds 1C **4**
Bk. Ingledew Cres. LS8: Leeds 5F **61**
Bk. Irwell St. BD4: B'frd 6G **91**
Bk. Ivy Av. LS9: Leeds 3E **99**
    (off Ivy Av.)
Bk. Ivy Gro. LS9: Leeds 4F **99**
    (off Ivy Gro.)
Bk. Ivy Mt. LS9: Leeds 3E **99**
    (off Ivy Mt.)
Bk. Ivy St. LS9: Leeds 3E **99**
    (off Ivy St.)
Bk. John St. BD13: B'frd 5H **87**
Bk. Karnac Rd. LS8: Leeds 5D **78**
    (off Karnac Rd.)
Bk. Kelso Rd. LS2: Leeds 1F **97** (1A **4**)
Bk. Kendal La. LS3: Leeds 2A **4**
Bk. Kennerleigh Wlk.
    LS15: Leeds 2E **101**
    (off Kennerleigh Wlk.)
Bk. Kensington St. BD8: B'frd 2A **90**
    (off Kensington St.)
Bk. Kensington Ter. LS6: Leeds 6F **77**
Bk. Kings Av. LS6: Leeds 1E **97**
    (off Kings Av.)
Bk. Kirby St. BD21: Keigh 5B **34**
    (off Kirby St.)
Bk. Kirkgate BD18: Ship 2A **70**
Bk. Kitson St. LS9: Leeds 4D **98**
    (off Kitson St.)
Bk. Knowle Mt. LS4: Leeds 6D **76**
    (off Stanmore Hill)
Bk. Laisteridge La.
    BD7: B'frd 5C **90** (6A **6**)
Bk. Lake St. LS10: Leeds 3B **118**
Bk. Lambton Gro. LS8: Leeds 5D **78**
    (off Lambton Gro.)
Bk. Landseer Av. LS13: Leeds 6G **75**
    (off Raynville Rd.)
Bk. Landseer Gro. LS13: Leeds 6G **75**
    (off Raynville Rd.)
Bk. Landseer Ter. LS13: Leeds 6G **75**
    (off Raynville Rd.)
Back La. BD9: B'frd 5A **70**
    BD10: B'frd 1H **71**

Back La. BD11: B'frd 6B **114**
  BD13: B'frd 3D **108**
  (Sheep Hill La.)
  BD13: B'frd 4H **87**
  (West La.)
  BD14: B'frd 1E **109**
  BD15: B'frd 1H **87**
  BD20: Keigh 4H **35**
  BD20: Sils 1E **15**
  BD22: Keigh 6B **32**
  HX2: Hal 2A **106**
  (Causeway Foot)
  HX2: Hal 2B **128**
  (Keighley Rd.)
  LS11: Leeds 4F **117**
  LS12: Leeds 3E **115**
  LS13: Leeds 2F **95**
  LS18: H'fth 1D **74**
  LS19: Yead 1E **55**
  LS20: Guis 4A **40**
  LS25: Kip 4H **123**
  LS28: Pud 6H **73**
  LS29: Burl W 2F **21**
  WF3: Rothw 6G **141**
  WF10: Kip 4H **145**
Bk. Langdale Gdns. LS6: Leeds 5C **76**
  (off Kirkstall La.)
Bk. Langdale Ter. LS6: Leeds 5C **76**
  (off Kirkstall La.)
Bk. Laurel Mt. LS7: Leeds 4B **78**
Bk. Lime St. BD21: Keigh 4H **47**
  (off Ivy St. Sth.)
Bk. Linden Gro. LS11: Leeds 2A **118**
  (off Linden Gro.)
Bk. Lindum Ter. BD8: B'frd 1C **90**
  (off Oak La.)
Bk. Lodge La. LS11: Leeds 3H **117**
  (off Lodge La.)
Bk. Lombard St. LS19: Yead 3E **55**
Bk. Longroyd Ter. LS11: Leeds 2A **118**
  (off Longroyd Ter.)
Bk. Lord St. HX1: Hal 2F **149** (4A **164**)
Bk. Low La. LS18: H'fth 6F **57**
  (off Springfield Mt.)
Bk. Lucas St. LS6: Leeds 5G **77**
  (off Lucas St.)
Bk. Lunan Pl. LS8: Leeds 5D **78**
  (off Lunan Pl.)
Bk. Lunan Ter. LS8: Leeds 5D **78**
  (off Lunan Ter.)
Bk. Lyons St. BD13: B'frd 4B **108**
Bk. Lytton St. HX3: Hal 6G **129**
Bk. Mafeking Av. LS11: Leeds 4G **117**
  (off Mafeking Av.)
Bk. Mafeking Mt. LS11: Leeds 4G **117**
Bk. Malt St. BD22: Keigh 3G **47**
  (off Bracken Rd.)
Bk. Mannville Rd. BD21: Keigh 1G **47**
  (off Malsis Rd.)
Bk. Manor Dr. LS6: Leeds 5E **77**
  (off Manor Av.)
Bk. Manor Gro. LS7: Leeds 3B **78**
  (off Manor Gro.)
Bk. Manor St. BD2: B'frd 6H **71**
Bk. Market St. BD6: B'frd 4C **110**
Bk. Markham Av. LS8: Leeds 5D **78**
  (off Markham Av.)
Bk. Marshall Av. LS15: Leeds 1F **101**
  (off Marshall Av.)
Bk. Marshall St. LS15: Leeds 1E **101**
  (off Marshall St.)
Bk. Marshall Ter. LS15: Leeds 1E **101**
  (off Marshall Ter.)
Bk. Mary St. WF3: E Ard 1C **156**
Bk. Masham St. LS12: Leeds 4D **96**
  (off Bk. Middle Cross St.)
Bk. Mayville Av. LS6: Leeds 6E **77**
  (off Mayville Av.)
Bk. Mayville Pl. LS6: Leeds 6E **77**
  (off Mayville Pl.)
Bk. Mayville St. LS6: Leeds 6E **77**
  (off Mayville St.)
Bk. Mayville Ter. LS6: Leeds 6E **77**
  (off Mayville Ter.)

Bk. Meadow Vw. LS6: Leeds 6E **77**
  (off Meadow Vw.)
Bk. Methley Dr. LS7: Leeds 3B **78**
Bk. Mexborough Av. LS7: Leeds 5B **78**
  (off Mexborough Av.)
Bk. Mexborough Dr. LS7: Leeds 6B **78**
  (off Mexborough Dr.)
Bk. Mexborough Gro. LS7: Leeds 5B **78**
  (off Mexborough Gro.)
Bk. Mexborough St. LS7: Leeds 5B **78**
  (off Mexborough St.)
Bk. Meynell Av. LS26: Rothw 2A **142**
Bk. Middle Cross St. LS12: Leeds . . .4D **96**
Bk. Middleton Rd. LS29: I'ly 5C **10**
Bk. Middleton Vw. LS11: Leeds 2G **117**
Bk. Midland Rd. LS6: Leeds 6F **77**
  (off Midland Rd.)
Bk. Milan Av. LS8: Leeds 6D **78**
  (off Karnac Rd.)
Bk. Milan Rd. LS8: Leeds 6D **78**
  (off Milan Rd.)
Bk. Milan St. LS8: Leeds 6D **78**
  (off Milan St.)
Bk. Mill Hey BD22: Haw 2D **64**
  (off Mill Hey)
Bk. Milton Ter. HX1: Hal 2F **149**
Bk. Mitchell Ter. BD16: Bgly 5B **50**
Bk. Mitford Rd. LS12: Leeds 4D **96**
Bk. Model Rd. LS12: Leeds 4D **96**
Bk. Model Ter. LS12: Leeds 4D **96**
Bk. Model Vw. LS12: Leeds 4D **96**
Bk. Monk Bri. Dr. LS6: Leeds 3F **77**
  (off Monk Bri. Dr.)
Bk. Monk Bri. St. LS6: Leeds 3F **77**
  (off Monk Bri. St.)
Bk. Montpelier Ter. LS6: Leeds 5G **77**
  (off Montpelier Ter.)
Bk. Moorfield St. HX1: Hal 4E **149**
Bk. Moorfield Ter. LS12: Leeds 3A **96**
Bk. Morning St. BD21: Keigh 3H **47**
  (off Morning St.)
Bk. Morritt Dr. LS15: Leeds 3B **100**
Bk. Mt. Pleasant LS10: Leeds 2A **140**
Bk. Mount Royd BD8: B'frd 1C **90**
Bk. Mount Vw. LS6: Leeds 5F **77**
  (off Grosvenor Rd.)
Bk. Muff St. BD4: B'frd 6H **91**
Bk. Myrtle Av. BD16: Bgly 5B **50**
Bk. Myrtle Ter. BD22: Haw 6F **47**
Bk. Nansen St. LS13: Leeds 1C **94**
Bk. Nelson Rd. LS29: I'ly 5D **10**
Bk. Newport Gdns. LS6: Leeds 6D **76**
  (off Newport Rd.)
Bk. Newport Mt. LS6: Leeds 6D **76**
  (off Newport Rd.)
Bk. Newport Pl. LS6: Leeds 6D **76**
  (off Newport Rd.)
Bk. New St. BD12: B'frd 2H **133**
  (off Mill Carr Hill St.)
Bk. Newton Gro. LS7: Leeds 5C **78**
Bk. Newton La. WF10: Led, Leds . . .5B **124**
Bk. New York St.
  LS2: Leeds 4B **98** (5G **5**)
Bk. Nice Vw. LS8: Leeds 6D **78**
  (off Nice Vw.)
Bk. Norman Pl. LS8: Leeds 5E **61**
  (off Norman Pl.)
Bk. Norman Ter. LS8: Leeds 5E **61**
  (off Norman Ter.)
Bk. Northbrook St. LS7: Leeds 2B **78**
  (off Northbrook St.)
Bk. Northfield Pl. BD8: B'frd 2C **90**
  (off Carlisle Rd.)
Bk. North Pk. Av. LS8: Leeds 1D **78**
Bk. North St. BD12: B'frd 3G **133**
Bk. Norwood Gro. LS6: Leeds 6E **77**
  (off Norwood Gro.)
Bk. Norwood Pl. LS6: Leeds 6E **77**
  (off Norwood Pl.)
Bk. Norwood Rd. LS6: Leeds 6E **77**
  (off Norwood Rd.)
Bk. Norwood Ter. LS6: Leeds 6E **77**
Bk. Nowell Cres. LS9: Leeds 2F **99**
  (off Nowell Cres.)

Bk. Nowell Mt. LS9: Leeds 2F **99**
  (off Nowell Mt.)
Bk. Nowell Pl. LS9: Leeds 2F **99**
  (off Nowell Pl.)
Bk. Nowell Ter. LS9: Leeds 2F **99**
  (off Nowell Ter.)
Bk. Nunington St. LS12: Leeds 3D **96**
  (off Armley Pk. Rd.)
Bk. Nunington Vw. LS12: Leeds 2C **96**
  (off Armley Pk. Rd.)
Bk. Nunroyd Rd. LS17: Leeds 6B **60**
  (off Nunroyd Rd.)
Bk. Oakfield Ter. LS6: Leeds 3E **77**
  (off Brookfield Rd.)
Bk. Oakley St. WF3: E Ard 6C **140**
Bk. Oakley Ter. LS11: Leeds 3A **118**
  (off Oakley Ter.)
Bk. Oak Rd. LS7: Leeds 4B **78**
  (off Chapel Rd.)
Bk. Oakwood Av. LS8: Leeds 3F **79**
  (off Oakwood Dr.)
Bk. Oakwood Dr. LS8: Leeds 3F **79**
  (off Oakwood Dr.)
Bk. of the Mill BD16: Bgly 6E **49**
Bk. Osmondthorpe La.
  LS9: Leeds 3G **99**
  (off Osmondthorpe La.)
Bk. Otterburn St. BD21: Keigh 5A **34**
  (off Ashleigh St.)
Bk. Outwood La. LS18: H'fth 2E **75**
Bk. Overdale Ter. LS15: Leeds 3C **100**
  (off Overdale Ter.)
Bk. Oxford Pl. LS1: Leeds 3C **4**
Bk. Oxford St. WF3: E Ard 1C **156**
Bk. Paget St. BD21: Keigh 6G **33**
  (off Devonshire St.)
Bk. Parish Ghyll Rd. LS29: I'ly 6D **10**
Bk. Park Cres. LS8: Leeds 5F **61**
Bk. Parkfield Pl. LS11: Leeds 2G **117**
  (off Parkfield Pl.)
Bk. Parkfield Rd. LS11: Leeds 2G **117**
  (off Parkfield Rd.)
Bk. Park Ter. HX1: Hal 3E **149**
Bk. Park Vw. LS11: Leeds 2G **117**
  (off Park Vw.)
Bk. Park Vw. Av. LS4: Leeds 6D **76**
Bk. Parkville Rd. LS13: Leeds 6E **75**
Bk. Parnaby Av. LS10: Leeds 4D **118**
  (off Parnaby Av.)
Bk. Parnaby St. LS10: Leeds 4D **118**
Bk. Parnaby Ter. LS10: Leeds 4D **118**
  (off Parnaby Ter.)
Bk. Pasture Gro. LS7: Leeds 2B **78**
  (off Pasture Gro.)
Bk. Pasture Rd. LS8: Leeds 5D **78**
  (off Pasture Rd.)
Bk. Pawson St. WF3: E Ard 1C **156**
Bk. Pelham Rd. BD2: B'frd 6H **71**
Bk. Pleasant St. HX6: Hal 5A **148**
Bk. Pollard La. LS13: Leeds 4E **75**
Bk. Poplar Av. LS15: Leeds 1F **101**
  (off Poplar Av.)
Bk. Potternewton La. LS7: Leeds 3A **78**
Bk. Potters St. LS7: Leeds 3B **78**
  (off Potternewton La.)
Bk. Prospect Pl. BD21: Keigh 1H **47**
Bk. Prospect Ter. LS9: Leeds 4D **98**
Bk. Providence Av. LS6: Leeds 5G **77**
  (off Delph La.)
Bk. Quarry Mt. Ter.
  LS6: Leeds 5G **77**
  (off Quarry Mt. Ter.)
Bk. Queen St. HX4: Hal 5G **159**
Bk. Raglan Rd. LS2: Leeds 6G **77**
  (off Raglan Rd.)
Bk. Ravenscar Av. LS8: Leeds 3E **79**
  (off Ravenscar Av.)
Bk. Raynville Mt. LS13: Leeds 6G **75**
  (off Raynville Rd.)
Bk. Regent Pk. Ter. LS6: Leeds 5F **77**
  (off Regent Pk. Ter.)
Bk. Regent Ter. LS6: Leeds 1F **97**
Bk. Reginald Mt. LS7: Leeds 5B **78**
  (off Reginald Mt.)

Bk. Reginald Pl. *LS7: Leeds* 5B **78**
   (off Reginald Pl.)
Bk. Reginald Ter. *LS7: Leeds* 5B **78**
   (off Reginald St.)
Bk. Rhodes St. HX1: Hal 2F **149**
Bk. Ribble St. *BD21: Keigh* 5D **34**
   (off Ribble St.)
Bk. Richardson St. *BD12: B'frd* 3G **133**
   (off Richardson St.)
Bk. Richmond Mt. *LS6: Leeds* 5E **77**
   (off Manor Av.)
Bk. Ridge Mt. Ter. *LS6: Leeds* 5G **77**
   (off Cliff Rd.)
Bk. Ridge Vw. LS7: Leeds 4G **77**
Bk. Rigging La. HX6: Hal 6C **146**
Bk. Ripley St. *BD20: Keigh* 4D **34**
   (off Ripley St.)
Bk. Ripon St. HX1: Hal 3C **148**
Bk. Ripon Ter. HX3: Hal 6F **129**
Bk. River St. BD22: Haw 2D **64**
Back Rd. BD3: B'frd 2G **91**
   BD12: B'frd 3C **132**
Bk. Roberts St. LS26: Rothw 1E **143**
Bk. Rochester Ter. *LS6: Leeds* 5D **76**
   (off Broomfield Rd.)
Bk. Rokeby Gdns. *LS6: Leeds* 4C **76**
   (off Ash Rd.)
Bk. Roman Gro. LS8: Leeds 5E **61**
Bk. Roman Pl. LS8: Leeds 5F **61**
Bk. Roman St. LS8: Leeds 5F **61**
Bk. Rose Av. *LS18: H'fth* 2D **74**
   (off Rose St.)
Bk. Rosebank Cres. LS3: Leeds 1F **97**
Bk. Rosemont Wlk. LS13: Leeds 1E **95**
Bk. Rossall Rd. *LS8: Leeds* 5E **79**
   (off Rossall Rd.)
Bk. Rossington Rd. *LS8: Leeds* 5C **78**
   (off Spencer Pl.)
Bk. Roundhay Cres. *LS8: Leeds* 4D **78**
   (off Roundhay Cres.)
Bk. Roundhay Gro. *LS8: Leeds* 4D **78**
   (off Roundhay Gro., not continuous)
Bk. Roundhay Pl. *LS8: Leeds* 4D **78**
   (off Roundhay Pl.)
Bk. Roundhay Vw. *LS8: Leeds* 4D **78**
   (off Roundhay Vw.)
Back Row LS11: Leeds 5H **97**
Bk. Rowland Ter. *LS11: Leeds* 2A **118**
   (off Rowland Ter.)
Bk. Rowsley St. *BD21: Keigh* 6B **34**
   (off Rowsley St.)
Bk. Roydwood Ter. BD13: B'frd 3B **66**
Bk. Rupert St. *BD21: Keigh* 5A **34**
   (off Rupert St.)
Bk. Russell St. BD5: B'frd 6D **90** (6B **6**)
Bk. Ruthven Vw. *LS8: Leeds* 6E **79**
   (off Ruthven Vw.)
Bk. Rydal St. BD22: Keigh 1G **47**
Bk. Rylstone St. BD21: Keigh 5C **34**
Bk. St Alban Cres. *LS9: Leeds* 2G **99**
   (off St Alban Cres.)
Bk. St Elmo Gro. *LS9: Leeds* 3E **99**
   (off St Elmo Gro.)
Bk. St Ives Mt. LS12: Leeds 3A **96**
Bk. St Mary's Rd. LS7: Leeds 4B **78**
Bk. St Paul's Rd. BD18: Ship 2A **70**
Bk. Salisbury Gro. LS12: Leeds 3C **96**
Bk. Salisbury Ter. HX3: Hal 6F **129**
   LS12: Leeds 3C **96**
   (off Armley Lodge Rd.)
Bk. Saltaire Rd. BD18: Ship 1A **70**
Bk. Saltaire Rd. Nth.
   BD18: Ship 1A **70**
Bk. Sandhurst Gro. *LS8: Leeds* 6E **79**
   (off Sandhurst Gro.)
Bk. Sandhurst Pl. *LS8: Leeds* 6E **79**
   (off Sandhurst Pl.)
Bk. Sandhurst Rd. *LS8: Leeds* 6E **79**
   (off Sandhurst Rd.)
Bk. Savile Pde. HX1: Hal 4F **149**
Bk. Savile Pl. *LS7: Leeds* 6B **78**
   (off Savile Pl.)
Bk. Savile Rd. *LS7: Leeds* 6B **78**
   (off Savile Rd.)

Bk. School St. *LS27: Morl* 3B **138**
   (off School St.)
Bk. School Vw. *LS6: Leeds* 6E **77**
   (off School Vw.)
Bk. Seaforth Av. *LS9: Leeds* 1F **99**
   (off Seaforth Av.)
Bk. Seaforth Pl. *LS9: Leeds* 6E **79**
   (off Seaforth Pl.)
Bk. Seaforth Ter. *LS9: Leeds* 6E **79**
   (off Seaforth Ter.)
Bk. Sefton Av. *LS11: Leeds* 2G **117**
   (off Sefton Av.)
Bk. Sefton Ter. *LS11: Leeds* 2G **117**
   (off Sefton Ter.)
Bk. Shaftesbury Av. LS8: Leeds 6E **61**
Bk. Shaw La. BD21: Keigh 3B **48**
Bk. Shepherds *LS7: Leeds* 5C **78**
   (off Shepherd's La.)
Bk. Shepherd's Pl. *LS8: Leeds* 5D **78**
   (off Shepherd's Pl.)
Bk. Sholebroke Av. LS7: Leeds 4B **78**
Bk. Sholebroke Pl. *LS7: Leeds* 5B **78**
   (off Sholebroke Pl.)
Bk. Sholebroke Vw. *LS7: Leeds* 5B **78**
   (off Sholebroke Vw.)
Bk. Sidlaw Ter. *LS8: Leeds* 5D **78**
   (off Markham Av.)
Bk. Simpson St. BD21: Keigh 6G **33**
Bk. Sladen St. BD21: Keigh 6G **33**
Bk. Smith Row BD5: B'frd 2C **110**
Bk. South End Gro. LS13: Leeds 1G **95**
Bk. Southfield Sq. *BD8: B'frd* 2C **90**
   (off Southfield Sq.)
Bk. South Pde. HX5: Ell 6A **160**
   (not continuous)
Bk. Sowerby Cft. HX6: Hal 6H **147**
Bk. Spencer Mt. *LS7: Leeds* 5C **78**
   (off Spencer Mt.)
Bk. Springfield Mt. LS12: Leeds 3A **96**
Bk. Springfield Pl. BD1: B'frd 1B **6**
Bk. Springfield Rd. HX5: Ell 4C **160**
Bk. Spring Gro. Wlk.
   LS6: Leeds 1E **97**
   (off Spring Gro. Wlk.)
Bk. Stanley St. *LS9: Leeds* 1D **98**
   (off Stanley Av.)
Bk. Stanmore Pl. *LS4: Leeds* 6C **76**
   (off St Michaels La.)
Bk. Stanmore St. *LS4: Leeds* 6C **76**
   (off St Michaels La.)
Bk. Stonegate Rd. LS6: Leeds 2F **77**
Backstone Gill La. LS17: Leeds 4A **44**
Bk. Stone Hall Rd. BD2: B'frd 5H **71**
Backstone La. LS29: I'ly 6E **11**
Backstone Way LS29: I'ly 5F **11**
Bk. Storey Pl. LS14: Leeds 2A **100**
Bk. Stratford Av. *LS11: Leeds* 2G **117**
   (off Stratford Av.)
Bk. Stratford St. *LS11: Leeds* 2H **117**
   (off Stratford St.)
Bk. Stratford Ter. *LS11: Leeds* 2H **117**
   (off Stratford Ter.)
Bk. Strathmore Dr. *LS9: Leeds* 6E **79**
   (off Strathmore Dr.)
Bk. Sunnydene LS14: Leeds 2B **100**
Bk. Sutton App. LS14: Leeds 2A **100**
Bk. Sycamore Av. BD16: Bgly 5B **50**
Bk. Tamworth St. BD4: B'frd 5C **92**
Bk. Tempest Rd. *LS11: Leeds* 2G **117**
   (off Tempest Rd.)
Bk. Temple Vw. LS11: Leeds 2G **117**
Bk. Thornhill St. LS28: Pud 3F **73**
Bk. Thornville Row *LS6: Leeds* 6E **77**
   (off Thornville Row)
Bk. Tower Gro. LS12: Leeds 3A **96**
Bk. Trafford Av. *LS9: Leeds* 1F **99**
   (off Trafford Av.)
Bk. Trentham Pl. *LS11: Leeds* 3H **117**
   (off Trentham Pl.)
Bk. Trinity Ter. BD5: B'frd 6D **90**
Bk. Unity St. Nth. BD16: Bgly 5B **50**
Bk. Unity St. Sth. BD16: Bgly 5B **50**
Bk. Vicars Rd. *LS8: Leeds* 5D **78**
   (off Vicars Rd.)

Bk. Victoria Av. *LS9: Leeds* 3E **99**
   (off Victoria Av.)
Bk. Victoria Gro. *LS9: Leeds* 3F **99**
   (off Victoria Gro.)
Bk. Victoria St.
   HX1: Hal 2G **149** (3B **164**)
Bk. Victor Ter. HX1: Hal 1D **148**
Bk. Violet Ter. *HX6: Hal* 5A **148**
   (off Violet Ter.)
Bk. Wakefield Rd. HX6: Hal 5B **148**
Bk. Walmsley Rd. *LS6: Leeds* 6E **77**
   (off Walmsley Rd.)
Bk. Walnut St. *BD21: Keigh* 3H **47**
   (off Walnut St.)
Bk. Waverley Rd. HX5: Ell 6B **160**
Bk. Welburn Av. LS16: Leeds 2B **76**
Bk. Welton Av. *LS6: Leeds* 6E **77**
   (off Welton Rd.)
Bk. Welton Gro. *LS6: Leeds* 6E **77**
   (off Welton Gro.)
Bk. Welton Mt. *LS6: Leeds* 6E **77**
   (off Welton Mt.)
Bk. Welton Pl. *LS6: Leeds* 6E **77**
   (off Welton Pl.)
Bk. Wesley Rd. LS12: Leeds 4C **96**
Bk. Westbury St. LS10: Leeds 4D **118**
Bk. Westfield Rd. *LS3: Leeds* 2F **97**
   (off Westfield Rd.)
Bk. Westlock Av. *LS9: Leeds* 2E **99**
   (off Westlock Av.)
Bk. Westmorland Mt. LS13: Leeds ...5F **75**
Bk. Weston Rd. LS29: I'ly 5D **10**
Bk. Westover Rd. LS13: Leeds 6E **75**
Bk. West St. HX6: Hal 6H **147**
Bk. Wetherby Gro. *LS4: Leeds* 1C **96**
   (off Argie Av.)
Bk. Wetherby Rd. *LS8: Leeds* 3F **79**
   (off Wetherby Rd.)
Bk. Wheat St. *BD22: Keigh* 3G **47**
   (off Bracken Rd.)
Bk. Wickham St. *LS11: Leeds* 2G **117**
   (off Wickham St.)
Bk. William Av. *LS15: Leeds* 3A **100**
   (off William Av.)
Bk. William St. *HD6: Brigh* 2A **162**
   (off William St.)
Bk. Wilton Gro. *LS6: Leeds* 3E **77**
   (off Wilton Gro.)
Bk. Winfield Gro. *LS2: Leeds* 1H **97**
   (off Winfield Pl.)
Bk. Winston Gdns. *LS6: Leeds* 4C **76**
   (off Ash Rd.)
Bk. Winterburn St. *BD21: Keigh* 5A **34**
   (off Ashleigh St.)
Bk. Wolseley Ter. HX1: Hal 2D **148**
Bk. Woodbine Ter. LS6: Leeds 3E **77**
Bk. Woodland Pk. Rd. *LS6: Leeds* ...4E **77**
   (off Woodland Pk. Rd.)
Bk. Woodstock St. *LS2: Leeds* 1H **97**
   (off Bk. Blenheim Ter.)
Bk. Wood St. WF3: E Ard 1B **156**
Bk. Wright Av. BD22: Keigh 4D **46**
Bk. York Cres. *HX2: Hal* 4D **148**
   (off Up. Washer La.)
Bk. York Pl. LS1: Leeds 4G **97** (5B **4**)
   (not continuous)
Bk. York St. LS2: Leeds 4B **98** (5G **5**)
Bacon St. LS20: Guis 5D **40**
Baddeley Gdns. BD10: B'frd 6G **53**
Baden St. BD22: Haw 1C **64**
Baden Ter. *LS13: Leeds* 3E **95**
   (off Pudsey Rd.)
Badger Cl. LS29: I'ly 5A **10**
Badger Ga. BD15: B'frd 5G **67**
Badgergate Av. BD15: B'frd 5G **67**
Badger Hill HD6: Brigh 5G **161**
Badger La. HX3: Hal 2D **150**
Badgers Mt. LS15: Leeds 1H **101**
Badgerstone Cl. BD20: Keigh 4H **35**
Badgers Way BD2: B'frd 5E **71**
Badger Wood Glade LS22: Weth ...1E **13**
Badminton Dr. LS10: Leeds 4B **140**
Badminton Vw. LS10: Leeds 4B **140**
Badsworth Ct. BD14: B'frd 6F **89**

BAGBY FIELDS 6H 77
BAGHILL 3D 154
Baghill Grn. WF3: E Ard 3D 154
Baghill Rd. WF3: E Ard 3D 154
BAGLEY 5A 74
Bagley La. LS13: Pud 5A 74
 LS28: Pud 5H 73
Bagnall Ter. BD6: B'frd 4B 110
BAILDON 4C 52
Baildon Av. LS25: Kip 2H 123
Baildon Bri. BD17: Ship 1B 70
Baildon Chase LS14: Leeds 2E 81
Baildon Cl. LS14: Leeds 3E 81
Baildon Dr. LS14: Leeds 3E 81
BAILDON GREEN 5B 52
Baildon Grn. LS14: Leeds 3E 81
BAILDON HOLMES 6C 52
Baildon Holmes BD17: Bail 6C 52
Baildon Mills BD17: Bail 3C 52
 (off Straits)
Baildon Path LS14: Leeds 3E 81
Baildon Pl. LS14: Leeds 3E 81
Baildon Recreation Cen. 6B 52
Baildon Rd. BD17: Bail 4C 52
 LS14: Leeds 2E 81
Baildon Station (Rail) 4E 53
Baildon Wlk. LS14: Leeds 2E 81
BAILDON WOOD BOTTOM 6C 52
Baildon Wood Ct. BD17: Bail 6C 52
Bailes Rd. LS7: Leeds 4G 77
Bailey Hall Bank HX3: Hal 2H 149
Bailey Hall Bus. Pk. HX3: Hal 2H 149
Bailey Hall Rd. HX3: Hal 3H 149
Bailey Hall Vw. HX3: Hal 2H 149
Bailey Hills Rd. BD16: Bgly 3A 50
Bailey's Cl. LS14: Leeds 3C 80
Bailey's Hill LS14: Leeds 4C 80
Bailey's La. LS14: Leeds 4C 80
Bailey's Lawn LS14: Leeds 4C 80
Bailey St. BD4: B'frd 6F 91
Bailey Towers LS14: Leeds 4C 80
Bailey Wells Av. BD5: B'frd 2C 110
BAILIFF BRIDGE 2B 152
Bainbrigge Rd. LS6: Leeds 5D 76
Baines St. HX1: Hal 1E 149
 LS26: Rothw 3A 142
Baird St. BD5: B'frd 1E 111
Bairstow Ct. HX6: Hal 3A 148
Bairstow La. HX6: Hal 3A 148
Bairstow Mt. HX6: Hal 4B 148
Bairstow's Bldgs. HX2: Hal 4D 128
Bairstow St. BD15: B'frd 6C 68
Baker Cres. LS27: Morl 4A 138
Baker Fold HX1: Hal 2E 149
 (off Crossley Gdns.)
Baker La. WF3: Wake 3H 157
Baker Rd. LS27: Morl 4A 138
Baker St. BD2: B'frd 1H 91
 BD18: Ship 1A 70
 LS27: Morl 4A 138
Baker St. Nth. HX2: Hal 2E 129
Bakes St. BD7: B'frd 1A 110
Balbec Av. LS6: Leeds 4E 77
Balcony BD22: Haw 3B 64
Balcony Cotts. BD13: B'frd 5A 108
Balcony Ter. BD22: Haw 1F 65
 (off Halifax Rd.)
Baldovan Mt. LS8: Leeds 5D 78
Baldovan Pl. LS8: Leeds 5D 78
Baldovan Ter. LS8: Leeds 5D 78
Baldwin La. BD13: B'frd 3C 108
Baldwin Ter. HX3: Hal 2H 149
Bale Dr. BD10: B'frd 1F 71
Balfour St. BD4: B'frd 1G 111
 BD16: Bgly 5B 50
 BD21: Keigh 1H 47
Balkcliffe La. LS10: Leeds 1G 139
Balk La. BD7: B'frd 1B 110
Balkram Dr. HX2: Hal 2H 127
Balkram Edge HX2: Hal 2F 127
Balkram Rd. HX2: Hal 2H 127
Ballantyne Rd. BD10: B'frd 5G 53
Ball St. BD13: B'frd 5A 88

Balme La. BD12: B'frd 4D 132
Balme Rd. BD19: Cleck 6B 134
Balme St. BD1: B'frd 4F 91 (3E 7)
 BD12: B'frd 4C 132
Balmoral Chase LS10: Leeds 2D 118
Balmoral Dr. LS26: Mick 4C 144
Balmoral Pl. BD13: B'frd 6G 107
 HX1: Hal 3G 149 (5A 164)
Balmoral Ter. LS6: Leeds 3E 77
Balmoral Way LS19: Yead 1H 55
Balm Pl. LS11: Leeds 6G 97
Balm Rd. LS10: Leeds 3C 118
Balm Rd. Ind. Est. LS10: Leeds 2B 118
Balm Wlk. LS11: Leeds 6F 97
Bamburgh Cl. LS15: Leeds 6G 81
Bamburgh Rd. LS15: Leeds 6G 81
Bamford Ho. BD4: B'frd 4C 112
 (off Tong St.)
Bamlett Brow BD22: Haw 1D 64
Bancroft St. BD22: Haw 1F 65
 (off Halifax Rd.)
Bangor Gro. LS12: Leeds 1A 116
Bangor Pl. LS12: Leeds 1A 116
Bangor St. LS12: Leeds 1A 116
Bangor Ter. LS12: Leeds 1A 116
Bangor Vw. LS12: Leeds 1A 116
BANK 4C 98 (5H 5)
Bank BD10: B'frd 4A 72
 BD22: Oxen 2E 85
Bank Av. LS18: H'fth 1D 74
 LS27: Morl 2A 138
Bank Bottom HX3: Hal 2H 149
 HX7: Heb B 5A 126
Bank Bottom La. HX2: Hal 6F 127
Bank Cl. BD10: B'frd 4A 72
Bank Crest BD17: Bail 4C 52
Bank Dr. BD6: B'frd 4D 110
Bankcrest Ri. BD18: Ship 2E 69
Bank Edge Cl. HX2: Hal 2B 128
Bank Edge Gdns. HX2: Hal 4C 128
Bank Edge Rd. HX2: Hal 3C 128
Bank End HX4: Hal 4B 158
Banker St. LS4: Leeds 2D 96
Bankfield LS17: Bard 1F 45
Bankfield Av. BD18: Ship 2F 69
Bankfield Ct. WF2: Wake 6D 156
Bankfield Dr. BD18: Ship 2F 69
 BD22: Keigh 6E 33
 WF2: Wake 6D 156
Bankfield Gdns. HX3: Hal 3B 150
 LS4: Leeds 1C 96
Bankfield Grange HX4: Hal 4G 159
Bankfield Gro. BD18: Ship 2F 69
 LS4: Leeds 6C 76
Bankfield Mt. BD22: Keigh 5E 33
Bankfield Mus. & Gallery 6G 129
Bankfield Rd. BD18: Ship 2F 69
 BD22: Keigh 5E 33
 LS4: Leeds 1C 96
Bankfield St. BD22: Keigh 5E 33
Bankfield Ter. BD17: Bail 5D 52
 HX6: Hal 4G 147
 LS4: Leeds 1C 96
 LS28: Pud 4A 94
 (off Richardshaw Rd.)
Bankfield Wlk. BD22: Keigh 5E 33
Bankfield Yd. HX3: Hal 6F 129
 (off Boothtown Rd.)
BANK FOOT 4C 110
Bank Gdns. LS18: H'fth 1D 74
Bank Gdns. Cl. HX2: Leeds 4C 128
Bank Holme Ct. BD4: B'frd 3D 112
BANKHOUSE 6H 93
Bank Ho. BD3: B'frd 2G 7
Bankhouse LS28: Pud 6H 93
BANKHOUSE BOTTOM 1H 113
Bank Ho. Cl. LS27: Morl 2A 138
Bankhouse Ct. LS28: Pud 6H 93
Bank Ho. La. HX2: Hal 3D 126
Bankhouse La. HX3: Hal 1H 159
 LS28: Pud 6H 93
Bank Ho. Ter. HX3: Hal 1H 159
Banklands BD20: Sils 1E 15

Banklands Av. BD20: Sils 1F 15
Banklands La. BD20: Sils 1F 15
Bank La. BD22: Keigh 6D 32
 (Braithwaite Rd.)
 BD22: Keigh 5B 46
 (Windsor Rd.)
Bank Pde. LS21: Otley 4D 22
Bank Rd. HX6: Hal 6H 147
 (not continuous)
Banks, The HX6: Hal 4G 147
Banks End Rd. HX5: Ell 5E 161
Banksfield Av. LS19: Yead 5F 41
Banksfield Cl. LS19: Yead 5F 41
Banksfield Cres. LS19: Yead 5F 41
Banksfield Gro. LS19: Yead 5F 41
Banksfield Mt. LS19: Yead 5F 41
Banksfield Ri. LS19: Yead 5F 41
Banksfield Ter. LS19: Yead 6F 41
Bank Side BD17: Bail 4C 52
Bank Side St. LS8: Leeds 6D 78
 (not continuous)
Bankside Ter. BD17: Bail 5B 52
Banks La. BD20: Keigh 1C 34
Bank Sq. LS27: Morl 2A 138
Bank St. BD1: B'frd 4E 91 (4D 6)
 (not continuous)
 BD6: B'frd 4C 110
 BD18: Ship 2B 70
 BD19: Cleck 2H 153
 BD21: Keigh 6A 34
 (off Airedale Shop. Cen.)
 BD22: Haw 2C 64
 (off Main St.)
 HD6: Brigh 1A 162
 LS1: Leeds 4A 98 (4D 5)
 (Boar La.)
 LS1: Leeds 4E 5
 (Commercial St.)
 LS22: Weth 4E 13
 LS27: Morl 2A 138
Banks Vw. BD22: Keigh 5B 46
 (off Low Banks La.)
Bank Ter. HX2: Hal 1E 147
 (off High St.)
 LS27: Morl 2B 138
 LS28: Pud 1A 94
BANK TOP
 Bradford 4A 72
 Halifax 4B 150
Bank Top HX3: Hal 3A 150
 HX4: Hal 3G 159
Bank Top Dr. BD20: Keigh 3D 34
Bank Top Way BD21: Keigh 1D 48
Bank Vw. BD17: Bail 5B 52
 HX2: Hal 3D 146
Bank Vw. Ho. BD17: Bail 5C 52
 (off Bank Vw.)
Bank Vw. Ter. LS7: Leeds 3H 77
Bank Wlk. BD17: Bail 4C 52
Bankwell Fold BD6: B'frd 4D 110
Bankwood Way WF17: Bat 3D 136
Bannerman St. BD12: B'frd 2G 133
Banner St. BD3: B'frd 5G 91 (5H 7)
Bannockburn Ct. BD5: B'frd 4H 111
Banstead St. E. LS8: Leeds 6D 78
Banstead St. W. LS8: Leeds 6D 78
Banstead Ter. E. LS8: Leeds 6D 78
Banstead Ter. W. LS8: Leeds 6D 78
Bantam Cl. LS27: Morl 3D 138
BANTAM GROVE 3D 138
Bantam Gro. La. LS27: Morl 3D 138
Bantam Gro. Vw. LS27: Morl 3D 138
Bantree Ct. BD10: B'frd 5G 53
Baptist Fold BD13: B'frd 4A 108
Baptist Pl. BD1: B'frd 4D 90 (3B 6)
Baptist Way LS28: Pud 1C 94
Barberry Av. BD3: B'frd 3C 92
Barber St. HD6: Brigh 6B 152
Barclay Cl. BD13: B'frd 3C 66
Barclay St. LS7: Leeds 1G 5
BARCROFT 1F 65
Barcroft BD22: Haw 1F 65
Barcroft Gro. LS19: Yead 1E 55
Barden Av. BD6: B'frd 4F 109

Barden Cl. LS12: Leeds 4A 96
Barden Dr. BD16: Bgly 3E 51
Barden Grn. LS12: Leeds 4A 96
Barden Mt. LS12: Leeds 4A 96
Barden Pl. LS12: Leeds 4A 96
Barden St. BD8: B'frd 2B 90
Barden Ter. LS12: Leeds 4A 96
Bardon Hall Gdns. LS16: Leeds 1C 76
Bardon Hall M. LS16: Leeds 1C 76
BARDSEY .2F 45
Bardsey Cres. BD3: B'frd 4G 91 (4H 7)
Bardsey Ho. BD4: B'frd 6B 92
(off Parsonage Rd.)
Bare Head La. HX3: Hal 2H 129
Barfield Av. LS19: Yead 1E 55
Barfield Cres. LS17: Leeds 2D 60
Barfield Dr. LS19: Yead 1E 55
Barfield Gro. LS17: Leeds 2E 61
Barfield Mt. LS17: Leeds 2E 61
Barfield Rd. HX3: Hal 2E 151
Barfield Ter. LS27: Morl 5A 138
Bargess Ter. LS25: Kip 4H 123
Bargrange Av. BD18: Ship 3B 70
Barham Ter. BD10: B'frd 5B 72
Bar Ho. La. BD20: Keigh 2F 33
Bar Ho. Row LS21: Pool 6D 24
Baring Av. BD3: B'frd 3B 92
Barker Cl. HX3: Hal 6A 150
BARKEREND 4H 91
Barkerend Rd. BD1: B'frd 4F 91 (3F 7)
BD3: B'frd 4F 91 (3F 7)
Barker Hill LS12: Morl 4D 114
Barker Ho. HX3: Hal 6A 150
Barker Pl. LS13: Leeds 2F 95
Barkers Well Fold LS12: Leeds 2F 115
Barkers Well Gth. LS12: Leeds 2G 115
Barkers Well Ga. LS12: Leeds 2G 115
Barkers Well Lawn LS12: Leeds 2G 115
BARKISLAND 6A 158
Bark La. LS29: Add 1E 9
Barkly Av. LS11: Leeds 4G 117
Barkly Dr. LS11: Leeds 4G 117
Barkly Gro. LS11: Leeds 3G 117
Barkly Pde. LS11: Leeds 4G 117
Barkly Pl. LS11: Leeds 4G 117
Barkly Rd. LS11: Leeds 3F 117
Barkly St. LS11: Leeds 4G 117
Barkly Ter. LS11: Leeds 4G 117
Barkston Wlk. BD15: B'frd 4C 88
Bar La. BD20: Keigh 4D 34
LS18: H'fth 1A 74
LS23: B Spa 5D 30
LS25: Gar 4G 103
Barlby Way LS8: Leeds 3G 79
Barleycorn Yd. LS12: Leeds 4B 96
Barley Cote BD20: Keigh 3E 35
Barley Cote Av. BD20: Keigh 3D 34
Barley Cote Gro. BD20: Keigh 3E 35
Barley Cote Rd. BD20: Keigh 3E 35
Barley Ct. LS14: S'cft 5E 45
Barley Fld. Ct. LS15: Leeds 3C 100
Barleyfields Cl. LS22: Weth 2E 13
Barleyfields Ct. LS22: Weth 3E 13
Barleyfields La. LS22: Weth 3E 13
Barleyfields M. LS22: Weth 3E 13
Barleyfields Rd. LS22: Weth 3E 13
(not continuous)
Barleyfields Ter. LS22: Weth 3E 13
Barleyfields Wlk. LS22: Weth 4E 13
Barleyhill Cres. LS25: Gar 5E 103
Barleyhill La. LS25: Gar 4E 103
Barleyhill Rd. LS25: Gar 4D 102
Barley M. WF3: Rothw 4F 141
Barlow Rd. BD21: Keigh 3G 47
Barlow St. BD3: B'frd 4H 91
Barmby Pl. BD2: B'frd 2H 91
Barmby Rd. BD2: B'frd 2H 91
Barmby St. BD12: B'frd 3D 132
Bar Mt. LS25: Gar 4G 103
Barmouth Ter. BD3: B'frd 2F 91
Barnaby Rd. BD16: Bgly 3E 51
Barnard Cl. LS15: Leeds 6G 81

Barnard Rd. BD4: B'frd 6G 91
Barnard Ter. BD4: B'frd 6G 91
Barnard Way LS15: Leeds 6G 81
BARNBOW CARR 4C 82
Barnbow La. LS15: Scho 5B 82
Barnbrough St. LS4: Leeds 1C 96
Barnby Av. BD8: B'frd 4E 89
Barn Cl. LS29: Men 1F 39
Barncroft Cl. LS14: Leeds 2B 80
Barncroft Ct. LS14: Leeds 3A 80
Barncroft Dr. LS14: Leeds 3A 80
Barncroft Gdns. LS14: Leeds 3B 80
Barncroft Grange LS14: Leeds 3A 80
Barncroft Hgts. LS14: Leeds 2A 80
Barncroft Mt. LS14: Leeds 3A 80
Barncroft Ri. LS14: Leeds 3B 80
Barncroft Rd. LS14: Leeds 3B 80
Barncroft Towers LS14: Leeds 3A 80
Barnes Av. WF1: Wake 6E 157
Barnes Rd. BD8: B'frd 3H 89
Barnet Gro. LS27: Morl 5A 138
Barnet Rd. LS12: Leeds 4D 96
Barns, The LS29: I'ly 1A 20
Barnsdale Rd. LS26: Mick 6D 144
WF10: Kip, Leeds 6B 124
Barnsley Beck Gro. BD17: Bail 4D 52
Barnstaple Way BD4: B'frd 3B 112
Barn St. BD22: Oxen 1C 84
Barnswick Vw. LS16: Leeds 3G 57
Baron Cl. LS11: Leeds 1G 117
Baronscourt LS15: Leeds 3F 101
Baronsmead LS15: Leeds 3E 101
Baronsway LS15: Leeds 3E 101
Barrack Rd. LS7: Leeds 6B 78
Barrack St. LS7: Leeds 1B 98
Barraclough Bldgs. BD10: B'frd 2C 72
Barraclough Sq. BD12: B'frd 3C 132
Barraclough St. BD12: B'frd 1B 132
Barraclough Yd. LS26: Rothw 2A 142
(off Cross St.)
Barran Ct. LS8: Leeds 6D 78
Barran St. BD16: Bgly 4C 50
Barras Gth. Ind. Est. LS12: Leeds . . .5B 96
Barras Gth. Pl. LS12: Leeds 5B 96
Barras Gth. Rd. LS12: Leeds 5B 96
Barras Pl. LS12: Leeds 5B 96
Barras St. LS12: Leeds 5B 96
Barras Ter. LS12: Leeds 5B 96
Barrett St. BD20: Sils 2D 14
Barrington Cl. HX3: Hal 5C 150
Barrington Pde. BD19: Cleck 6E 135
BARROWBY 3B 102
Barrowby Av. LS15: Leeds 4G 101
Barrowby Cl. LS29: Men 1H 39
Barrowby Cres. LS15: Leeds 3G 101
Barrowby Dr. LS15: Leeds 4H 101
Barrowby La. LS15: Leeds 3G 101
LS25: Gar 3D 102
LS25: Leeds 3H 101
Barrowby Rd. LS15: Leeds 4H 101
Barrowclough La. HX3: Hal 2B 150
Barrows La. BD20: Stee 1B 32
Barr Ter. BD8: B'frd 3H 89
(off Washington St.)
Barry St. BD1: B'frd 4E 91 (4C 6)
Barsey Grn. La. HX4: Hal 5A 158
Barthorpe Av. LS17: Leeds 1H 77
Barthorpe Cl. BD4: B'frd 3D 112
Barthorpe Cres. LS17: Leeds 1A 78
Bartle Cl. BD7: B'frd 2H 109
Bartle Fold BD7: B'frd 1A 110
Bartle Gill Dr. BD17: Bail 3E 53
Bartle Gill Ri. BD17: Bail 3E 53
Bartle Gill Vw. BD17: Bail 3E 53
Bartle Gro. BD7: B'frd 2H 109
Bartle La. BD7: B'frd 2H 109
Bartle Pl. BD7: B'frd 2H 109
Bartles Bldgs. BD15: B'frd 3G 67
Bartle Sq. BD7: B'frd 1A 110
Barton Ct. LS15: Leeds 4E 101
Barton Gro. LS11: Leeds 1G 117
Barton Hill LS11: Leeds 1G 117
Barton Mt. LS11: Leeds 1G 117
Barton Pl. LS11: Leeds 1G 117

Barton Rd. LS11: Leeds 1G 117
Barton St. BD5: B'frd 2B 110
HD6: Brigh 6A 152
(off Manley St.)
Barton Ter. LS11: Leeds 1G 117
Barton Vw. LS11: Leeds 1G 117
Barum Top HX1: Hal 2G 149 (4B 164)
Barwick Grn. BD6: B'frd 4G 109
BARWICK IN ELMET 2D 82
Barwick Rd. LS15: Leeds 6D 80
LS25: Gar 3E 103
Barwick Sq. BD22: Haw 1F 65
Basil St. BD5: B'frd 2B 110
Baslow Gro. BD9: B'frd 1H 89
Batcliffe Dr. LS6: Leeds 3C 76
Batcliffe Mt. LS6: Leeds 4C 76
Bateman Fold BD12: B'frd 2H 133
(off Mill Carr Hill St.)
Bateman St. BD8: B'frd 2D 90
Bates Av. HX6: Hal 6F 147
Bateson St. BD10: B'frd 2C 72
Bath Cl. LS13: Leeds 1E 95
Bath Gro. LS13: Leeds 1E 95
Bath La. LS13: Leeds 2E 95
Bath Pl. HD6: Brigh 2A 152
HX3: Hal 6F 129 (1B 164)
Bath Rd. HX3: Hal 5G 149
LS11: Leeds 5G 97
LS13: Leeds 2E 95
Bath St. BD3: B'frd 4G 91 (4G 7)
BD21: Keigh 6H 33
HX1: Hal 3H 149 (5D 164)
HX5: Ell 5B 160
LS29: I'ly 4E 11
Batley Cl. BD17: Bail 3D 52
Batley Rd. WF2: E Ard 4D 154
WF3: E Ard 4D 154
Batley Sports & Tennis Cen. 6D 136
Batley St. HX3: Hal 6E 129
Batter La. LS19: Yead 3G 55
Battinson Rd. HX1: Hal 1D 148
Battinson's St. HX3: Hal 4A 150
Battlefield BD4: B'frd 6F 113
Battye St. BD4: B'frd 5A 92
Bavaria Pl. BD8: B'frd 2B 90
BAWN 6H 95
Bawn App. LS12: Leeds 6G 95
Bawn Av. LS12: Leeds 5G 95
Bawn Chase LS12: Leeds 5G 95
Bawn Dr. LS12: Leeds 5G 95
Bawn Gdns. LS12: Leeds 5G 95
Bawn La. LS12: Leeds 5G 95
Bawn Path LS12: Leeds 5H 95
(off Bawn Gdns.)
Bawn Va. LS12: Leeds 5G 95
(off Bawn Gdns.)
Bawn Wlk. LS12: Leeds 5H 95
(off Bawn Av.)
Bawson Ct. BD19: Cleck 6E 135
Baxandall St. BD5: B'frd 2D 110
Baxter La. HX3: Hal 4C 130
Bay Horse Ct. LS21: Otley 3E 23
(off Clapgate)
LS21: Otley 3E 23
(off Courthouse St.)
Bay Horse La. LS17: Leeds, S'cft . . .6C 44
Bay Horse Yd. LS1: Leeds 4F 5
LS28: Pud 6H 73
Bayne Dr. BD4: B'frd 5H 111
Bay of Biscay BD15: B'frd 5C 68
Bayswater Cres. LS8: Leeds 6D 78
Bayswater Gro. BD2: B'frd 1B 92
LS8: Leeds 6D 78
Bayswater Mt. LS8: Leeds 6D 78
Bayswater Pl. LS8: Leeds 6D 78
Bayswater Rd. LS8: Leeds 6C 78
Bayswater Row LS8: Leeds 6D 78
Bayswater Ter. HX3: Hal 6G 149
LS8: Leeds 6D 78
Bayswater Vw. LS8: Leeds 6D 78
Bayton La. LS18: H'fth 1A 56
LS19: H'fth, Yead 1H 55
Beacon Av. LS27: Morl 5B 138
Beacon Brow BD6: B'frd 3F 109

Beacon Bus. Cen. HX3: Hal 3A **150**
Beacon Cl. BD16: Bgly 4D **50**
Beacon Gro. BD6: B'frd 4H **109**
  LS27: Morl 5B **138**
Beacon Hill Rd.
  HX3: Hal 1H **149** (2D **164**)
    (not continuous)
Beacon Pl. BD6: B'frd 4G **109**
Beacon Ri. LS29: I'ly 5A **10**
Beacon Rd. BD6: B'frd 3F **109**
Beaconsfield Ct. LS25: Gar 3F **103**
Beaconsfield Rd. BD14: B'frd 1E **109**
Beaconsfield St. HX3: Hal 3A **150**
Beacon St. BD6: B'frd 4A **110**
  BD7: B'frd 3G **109**
  LS29: Add 1E **9**
Beacon Vw. LS27: Morl 5B **138**
    (off Tingley Comn.)
Beamsley Gro. BD16: Bgly 4D **50**
  LS6: Leeds 1E **97**
Beamsley Ho. BD18: Ship 4B **70**
    (off Bradford Rd.)
Beamsley Mt. LS6: Leeds 1E **97**
Beamsley Pl. LS6: Leeds 1E **97**
Beamsley Rd. BD9: B'frd 1B **90**
  BD18: Ship 4B **70**
Beamsley Ter. LS6: Leeds 1E **97**
Beamsley Vw. LS29: I'ly 5A **10**
Beamsley Wlk. BD9: B'frd 1A **90**
Beanland Ct. BD18: B'frd 4B **70**
    (off Aireville Av.)
Beanlands Pde. LS29: I'ly 4E **11**
Bean St. HX5: Ell 5E **161**
Bearing Av. LS11: Leeds 3A **118**
Bear Pit Gdns. LS6: Leeds 6D **76**
    (off Chapel La.)
Beatrice St. BD19: Cleck 6B **134**
  BD20: Keigh 4H **33**
  BD22: Oxen 1C **84**
Beaufort Gro. BD2: B'frd 6G **71**
Beaumont Av. LS8: Leeds 5E **61**
Beaumont Rd. BD8: B'frd 2B **90**
Beaumont Sq. LS28: Pud 5H **93**
Beauvais Dr. BD20: Keigh 5F **35**
Beaver Cl. BD22: Haw 1E **65**
BECK BOTTOM 6A **156**
Beck Bottom LS28: Pud 3C **72**
    (Carr Rd.)
  LS28: Pud 6A **74**
    (Coal Hill La.)
  WF2: Wake 6A **156**
Beckbury Cl. LS28: Pud 1H **93**
Beckbury St. LS28: Pud 1H **93**
Beckenham Pl. HX1: Hal 1C **148**
Becket La. WF3: Rothw 5G **141**
Beckett Ct. LS15: Leeds 5F **101**
BECKETT PARK 3D **76**
Beckett's Pk. Cres. LS6: Leeds ...4C **76**
Beckett's Pk. Dr. LS6: Leeds 4C **76**
Beckett's Pk. Rd. LS6: Leeds 4D **76**
Beckett St. LS9: Leeds 2C **98**
Beckfield Cl. HD6: Brigh 3B **152**
Beckfield Rd. BD16: Bgly 2B **68**
Beckfoot La. BD16: Bgly 5A **50**
BECK HILL 6H **109**
Beck Hill BD6: B'frd 6G **109**
Beckhill App. LS7: Leeds 3G **77**
Beckhill Av. LS7: Leeds 3G **77**
Beckhill Chase LS7: Leeds 3G **77**
Beckhill Cl. LS7: Leeds 3G **77**
Beckhill Dr. LS7: Leeds 2G **77**
Beckhill Fold LS7: Leeds 3G **77**
Beckhill Gdns. LS7: Leeds 3G **77**
Beckhill Gth. LS7: Leeds 3G **77**
Beckhill Ga. LS7: Leeds 3G **77**
Beckhill Grn. LS7: Leeds 3G **77**
Beckhill Gro. LS7: Leeds 3G **77**
Beckhill Lawn LS7: Leeds 3G **77**
Beckhill Pl. LS7: Leeds 2G **77**
Beckhill Row LS7: Leeds 2G **77**
Beckhill Va. LS7: Leeds 2G **77**
    (not continuous)
Beckhill Vw. LS7: Leeds 3G **77**
Beckhill Wlk. LS7: Leeds 2G **77**

Beck Ho's. BD16: Bgly 3C **50**
    (off Gawthorpe La.)
Beck La. BD16: Bgly 2B **50**
  LS22: Coll 2B **28**
Beck Mdw. LS15: Bar E 3E **83**
Beck Rd. BD16: Bgly 5A **36**
  LS8: Leeds 5D **78**
Beck Side BD21: Keigh 1A **48**
Beckside Cl. LS29: Add 1D **8**
  LS29: Burl W 2E **21**
Beckside Ct. BD20: Sils 2E **15**
Beckside Gdns.
  LS16: Leeds 2D **76**
Beckside La. BD7: B'frd 1A **110**
Beckside Rd. BD7: B'frd 6A **90**
Beckside Vw. LS27: Morl 3C **138**
Becks Rd. BD21: Keigh 1G **47**
Beck St. BD21: Keigh 1H **47**
Beckwith Dr. BD10: B'frd 4B **72**
Bedale HD6: Brigh 1D **154**
Bedale Av. HD6: Brigh 3G **161**
Bedale Dr. BD6: B'frd 4G **109**
Bede's Cl. BD13: B'frd 5H **87**
Bedford Cl. LS16: Leeds 4G **57**
Bedford Ct. LS8: Leeds 3G **79**
Bedford Dr. LS16: Leeds 4G **57**
Bedford Gdns. LS16: Leeds 4G **57**
Bedford Grn. LS16: Leeds 4G **57**
Bedford Gro. LS16: Leeds 5G **57**
Bedford Mt. LS16: Leeds 5G **57**
    (not continuous)
Bedford Pl. LS20: Guis 5C **40**
  LS21: Otley 3G **23**
Bedford Row LS10: Leeds 1B **118**
Bedford St. BD4: B'frd 5F **91** (6E **7**)
  BD21: Keigh 6H **33**
  HX1: Hal 2F **149** (4A **164**)
  HX5: Ell 5B **160**
  LS1: Leeds 3H **97** (4D **4**)
Bedford St. Nth.
  HX1: Hal 2F **149** (3A **164**)
Bedford Vw. LS16: Leeds 4G **57**
Bedivere Rd. BD8: B'frd 4F **89**
Beech Av. BD13: B'frd 6A **66**
  HX6: Hal 4H **147**
  LS12: Leeds 3C **96**
  LS18: H'fth 2E **75**
BEECHCLIFFE 4H **33**
Beech Cl. BD10: B'frd 5H **53**
  HX3: Hal 1F **131**
  LS9: Leeds 6H **79**
  LS29: Men 5G **21**
Beech Cres. BD3: B'frd 2H **91**
  BD17: Bail 6H **51**
  LS9: Leeds 6H **79**
Beech Cft. BD17: Bail 6B **52**
    (off Valley Vw.)
  WF3: Rothw 6H **141**
Beechcroft Cl. LS11: Leeds 4D **116**
Beechcroft Mead
  LS17: Leeds 3E **61**
Beechcroft Vw. LS11: Leeds 4D **116**
Beech Dr. BD13: B'frd 6A **66**
  LS12: Leeds 3C **96**
  LS18: H'fth 2D **74**
Beecher St. BD21: Keigh 5C **34**
  HX3: Hal 5F **129**
Beeches, The BD11: B'frd 2E **135**
  BD17: Bail 3D **52**
  BD19: Cleck 1F **153**
    (off Field Hurst)
  BD19: Cleck 2F **153**
    (off Scholes La.)
  LS20: Guis 3C **40**
  LS21: Pool 4F **25**
  LS22: Weth 3E **13**
    (off Barleyfields M.)
  LS22: Weth 3F **13**
    (York Rd.)
  LS28: Pud 3F **93**
Beeches End LS23: B Spa 4C **30**
Beeches Rd. BD21: Keigh 5C **34**
Beechfield LS12: Leeds 2F **115**

Beech Gro. BD3: B'frd 2H **91**
  BD14: B'frd 6E **89**
  BD16: Bgly 2E **51**
  BD19: Cleck 6E **135**
  BD20: Sils 2D **14**
  HX3: Hal 2A **152**
  LS6: Leeds 3D **76**
  LS26: Rothw 1B **142**
  LS27: Morl 4H **137**
  LS29: Men 2G **39**
Beech Gro. Av. LS25: Gar 5E **103**
Beech Gro. Gdns. LS26: Rothw ...2E **143**
Beech Gro. Ter. LS2: Leeds ..1H **97** (1B **4**)
  LS25: Gar 5E **103**
Beech Hill LS21: Otley 3E **23**
Beech Ho. LS16: Leeds 1C **76**
Beech La. LS9: Leeds 6G **79**
Beech Lees LS28: Pud 5G **73**
Beech Mt. LS9: Leeds 6H **79**
Beechmount Cl. BD17: Bail 3D **52**
Beech Rd. BD6: B'frd 6C **110**
  HX6: Hal 5A **148**
  LS23: B Spa 3A **30**
Beechroyd LS28: Pud 5A **94**
Beechroyd Ter. BD16: Bgly 5B **50**
Beech Spinney LS22: Weth 1F **13**
Beech Sq. BD14: B'frd 1E **109**
Beech St. BD16: Bgly 5B **50**
  BD20: Stee 6C **14**
  BD21: Keigh 5C **34**
  HX1: Hal 1F **149**
  HX5: Ell 5B **160**
  WF3: E Ard 6E **139**
Beech Ter. BD3: B'frd 3H **91**
Beechtree Ct. BD17: Bail 5A **52**
Beech Vw. HX6: Hal 4H **147**
Beech Vs. HX6: Hal 5A **148**
Beech Wlk. BD11: B'frd 3F **135**
  LS9: Leeds 6H **79**
  LS16: Leeds 5D **58**
Beech Way WF17: Bat 5C **136**
BEECHWOOD
  HX6 ....6F **147**
  LS14 ....3B **80**
  LS18 ....4D **56**
Beechwood LS26: Rothw 6E **121**
Beechwood Av. BD6: B'frd 3A **110**
  BD11: B'frd 6H **113**
  BD18: Ship 2G **69**
  BD20: Keigh 4D **34**
  HX2: Hal 2E **129**
  HX3: Hal 2D **130**
  HX6: Hal 6F **147**
  LS4: Leeds 6D **76**
Beechwood Cen. LS26: Rothw ...6E **121**
    (off Church St.)
Beechwood Cl. HX2: Hal 3D **128**
  LS18: H'fth 4C **56**
Beechwood Ct. LS4: Leeds 6D **76**
    (off Bk. Beechwood Gro.)
  LS14: Leeds 3A **80**
  LS16: Leeds 2B **58**
Beechwood Cres. HX6: Hal 6F **147**
  LS4: Leeds 6D **76**
Beechwood Dr. BD6: B'frd 3B **110**
  HX2: Hal 2D **128**
  HX6: Hal 6F **147**
Beechwood Gro. BD6: B'frd 3B **110**
  BD11: B'frd 6H **113**
  BD18: Ship 2G **69**
  HD2: Hud 6A **162**
  HX2: Hal 3D **128**
  LS4: Leeds 6D **76**
  LS29: I'ly 5B **10**
Beechwood Mt. LS4: Leeds 6D **76**
Beechwood Pk. HD6: Brigh 3B **152**
Beechwood Pl. LS4: Leeds 6D **76**
Beechwood Ri. LS22: Weth 2E **13**
Beechwood Rd. BD6: B'frd 3A **110**
  HX2: Hal 3D **128**
  LS4: Leeds 6D **76**
Beechwood Row LS4: Leeds 6D **76**
Beechwood St. LS4: Leeds 6D **76**
  LS28: Pud 2G **93**

Beechwood Ter. LS4: Leeds 6D 76
Beechwood Vw. LS4: Leeds 6D 76
Beechwood Vs. HX2: Hal 3D 128
Beechwood Wlk. LS4: Leeds 6D 76
Beecroft Cl. LS13: Leeds 6C 74
Beecroft Cres. LS13: Leeds 6D 74
Beecroft Gdns. LS13: Leeds 6C 74
Beecroft Mt. LS13: Leeds 6C 74
Beecroft St. BD21: Keigh 6B 34
   LS5: Leeds 6A 76
Beecroft Wlk. BD15: B'frd 4C 88
Beehive St. BD6: B'frd 6H 109
Beehive Yd. BD6: B'frd 6H 109
BEESTON 4F 117
Beeston LS11: Leeds 5E 117
BEESTON HILL 1G 117
Beestonley La. HX4: Hal 6B 158
Beeston Pk. Cft. LS11: Leeds 3E 117
Beeston Pk. Gth. LS11: Leeds 3E 117
Beeston Pk. Gro. LS11: Leeds 3E 117
Beeston Pk. Pl. LS11: Leeds 3E 117
BEESTON PARK SIDE 5G 117
Beeston Pk. Ter. LS11: Leeds 3E 117
Beeston Rd. LS11: Leeds 3F 117
Beeston Royd Ind. Est.
   LS12: Leeds 2C 116
BEESTON ROYDS 3B 116
Beevers Cotts. LS25: Gar 3E 103
Beevers Ct. LS16: Leeds 5A 58
BEGGARINGTON HILL 3D 154
Behrens Warehouse
   BD1: B'frd 4F 7
Bela Av. BD4: B'frd 3A 112
Belcross Dr. HX3: Hal 6H 129 (1D 164)
BELDON HILL 3G 109
Beldon La. BD7: B'frd 4H 109
Beldon Pk. Av. BD7: B'frd 3H 109
Beldon Pk. Cl. BD7: B'frd 3H 109
Beldon Pl. BD2: B'frd 1H 91
Beldon Rd. BD7: B'frd 2A 110
Belfast St. HX1: Hal 3D 148
Belford Cl. BD4: B'frd 2B 112
Belford Ct. LS6: Leeds 6E 59
Belfry, The LS19: Yead 1G 55
Belfry Ct. WF1: Wake 4G 157
Belfry Rd. LS9: Leeds 6E 99
Belgrave Av. HX3: Hal 1H 149
Belgrave Cl. HX3: Hal 1H 149
Belgrave Cres. HX3: Hal 1H 149
Belgrave Dr. HX3: Hal 6A 130
Belgrave Gdns. HX3: Hal 6H 129
Belgrave M. LS19: Yead 3E 55
Belgrave Mt. HX3: Hal 6H 129
Belgrave Pk. HX3: Hal 6H 129
Belgrave Rd. BD16: Bgly 3C 50
   BD21: Keigh 5H 33
Belgrave St. HX6: Hal 5H 147
   LS2: Leeds 3A 98 (3E 5)
Belgravia Gdns. LS8: Leeds 2G 79
Belinda St. LS10: Leeds 1C 118
Bell Bank Vw. BD16: Bgly 3A 50
Bellbrooke Av. LS9: Leeds 1F 99
Bellbrooke Gro. LS9: Leeds 1F 99
Bellbrooke Pl. LS9: Leeds 1F 99
Bellbrooke St. LS9: Leeds 1E 99
Bell Dean Rd. BD8: B'frd 3D 88
   BD15: B'frd 3D 88
BELLE ISLE 5C 118
Belle Isle BD22: Haw 3C 64
Belle Isle Cir. LS10: Leeds 5C 118
Belle Isle Cl. LS10: Leeds 5C 118
Belle Isle Pde. LS10: Leeds 4C 118
Belle Isle Rd. BD22: Haw 2C 64
   LS10: Leeds 3C 118
Bellerby Brow BD6: B'frd 4F 109
Belle Vw. BD13: B'frd 6A 108
Belle Vw. Ter. LS23: B Spa 6B 30
                  (off Albion St.)
Belle Vue BD2: B'frd 4A 72
   BD8: B'frd 2D 90
   LS29: I'ly 6E 11
Belle Vue Av. LS8: Leeds 3H 79
   LS15: Scho 2H 81

Belle Vue Ct. LS3: Leeds 2F 97
                (off Consort Ter.)
Belle Vue Cres. HX3: Hal 2D 130
Belle Vue Dr. LS28: Pud 6G 73
Belle Vue Est. LS15: Scho 3H 81
Bellevue Pl. HX1: Hal 2E 149
Belle Vue Ri. HX3: Hal 2D 130
Belle Vue Rd. HX3: Hal 2D 130
   LS3: Leeds 2F 97 (3A 4)
   LS15: Scho 3H 81
Belle Vue Ter. BD21: Keigh 1B 48
                (off Feather St.)
   LS20: Guis 5C 40
   LS27: Morl 1F 137
Bellevue Ter. HX2: Hal 2C 146
   LS27: Morl 4A 150
Bell Gro. LS13: Leeds 6E 75
Bell Hall Mt. HX1: Hal 4E 149
Bell Hall Ter. HX1: Hal 4E 149
Bell Ho. Av. BD4: B'frd 4H 111
Bellhouse Cres. BD4: B'frd 5H 111
Bell La. LS13: Leeds 6E 75
Bellmount Cl. LS13: Leeds 6F 75
Bellmount Gdns. LS13: Leeds 5E 75
Bellmount Grn. LS13: Leeds 6F 75
Bellmount Pl. LS13: Leeds 5E 75
Bellmount Vw. LS13: Leeds 6F 75
Bell Rd. LS13: Leeds 6E 75
Bell Row HD6: Brigh 2A 162
Bellshaw St. BD8: B'frd 4G 89
Bell St. BD12: B'frd 3C 132
   HX3: Hal 6H 129
   LS2: Leeds 3B 98 (3H 5)
Bellwood Av. LS23: B Spa 5B 30
Belmont Av. BD12: B'frd 6E 111
   BD17: Bail 4B 52
   LS21: Otley 2D 22
Belmont Cl. BD17: Bail 4B 52
Belmont Cres. BD12: B'frd 6E 111
   BD18: Ship 1A 70
Belmont Gdns. BD12: B'frd 6E 111
Belmont Gro. BD6: B'frd 6D 110
   LS2: Leeds 2G 97 (2B 4)
   LS19: Yead 2G 55
Belmont Pl. HX1: Hal 3E 149
Belmont Ri. BD12: B'frd 6E 111
   BD17: Bail 4B 52
Belmont Rd. LS29: I'ly 5G 11
Belmont St. BD2: B'frd 4A 72
   HX3: Hal 1A 150
   HX6: Hal 5A 148
Belmont Ter. BD18: Ship 1A 70
   HX2: Hal 4E 147
   WF3: Leeds 5D 140
Belton Cl. BD7: B'frd 2A 110
Belton Rd. BD20: Sils 3E 15
Belvedere Av. LS11: Leeds 3H 117
   LS17: Leeds 3B 60
Belvedere Ct. LS7: Leeds 4C 78
             (off Harehills La.)
   LS17: Leeds 3C 60
Belvedere Gdns. LS17: Leeds 3C 60
Belvedere Gro. LS17: Leeds 3B 60
Belvedere Mt. LS11: Leeds 3H 117
Belvedere Rd. LS17: Leeds 3B 60
Belvedere St. BD8: B'frd 3B 90
Belvedere Ter. BD8: B'frd 3B 90
   LS11: Leeds 3H 117
Belvedere Vw. LS17: Leeds 3C 60
Belvoir Gdns. HX3: Hal 6G 149
Bempton Ct. BD7: B'frd 1B 110
Bempton Gro. WF17: Bat 5B 136
Bempton Ho. BD10: B'frd 3A 72
               (off Savile Av.)
Bempton Pl. BD7: B'frd 1B 110
Benbow Av. BD10: B'frd 4C 72
Benn Av. BD7: B'frd 1H 109
Benn Cres. BD7: B'frd 1H 109
Bennett Ct. LS15: Leeds 3F 101
   LS21: Otley 2D 22
Bennett Rd. LS6: Leeds 4D 76
Bennett St. HX3: Hal 3A 150

Bennetts Yd. LS26: Rothw 3A 142
Benns La. HX2: Hal 5E 127
BEN RHYDDING 5F 11
Ben Rhydding Dr. LS29: I'ly 5G 11
Ben Rhydding Rd. LS29: I'ly 6E 11
Ben Rhydding Station (Rail) 5G 11
Benson Gdns. LS12: Leeds 5B 96
Benson's Mobile Home Pk.
   BD20: Keigh 2F 35
Benson St. LS7: Leeds 1B 98 (1G 5)
Bentcliffe Av. LS17: Leeds 5B 60
Bentcliffe Cl. LS17: Leeds 6C 60
Bentcliffe Ct. LS17: Leeds 6C 60
Bentcliffe Dr. LS17: Leeds 5C 60
Bentcliffe Gdns. LS17: Leeds 6C 60
Bentcliffe Gro. LS17: Leeds 6C 60
Bentcliffe La. LS17: Leeds 6B 60
Bentcliffe Mt. LS17: Leeds 6C 60
Bentcliff Wlk. BD15: B'frd 4D 88
Bentfield Cotts. BD14: B'frd 6E 89
Bent Lea HD2: Hud 5F 163
Bentley Av. HX3: Hal 2A 152
Bentley Cl. BD17: Bail 3B 52
Bentley Ct. LS7: Leeds 3F 77
Bentley Gdns. LS7: Leeds 3F 77
Bentley Gro. LS6: Leeds 3F 77
Bentley La. LS6: Leeds 3F 77
Bentley Mt. HX6: Hal 4B 148
   LS6: Leeds 3F 77
Bentley Pde. LS6: Leeds 3F 77
Bentley Royd Cl. HX6: Hal 6G 147
Bentley Sq. LS26: Rothw 2E 143
Bentley St. BD12: B'frd 4D 132
Benton Pk. Av. LS19: Yead 2G 55
Benton Pk. Cres. LS19: Yead 2G 55
Benton Pk. Dr. LS19: Yead 2G 55
Benton Pk. Rd. LS19: Yead 2G 55
Bents BD22: Oxen 5C 64
Bents Foot BD16: B'frd 2F 67
Bents La. BD15: B'frd 5E 67
Benyon Pk. Way LS12: Leeds 1D 116
Beresford Rd. BD6: B'frd 6B 110
Beresford St. BD12: B'frd 2G 133
Berkeley Av. LS8: Leeds 6E 79
Berkeley Ct. LS2: Leeds 2F 97 (1A 4)
Berkeley Cres. LS8: Leeds 6E 79
Berkeley Gro. LS8: Leeds 6E 79
Berkeley Ho. BD4: B'frd 2C 112
             (off Stirling Cres.)
Berkeley Mt. LS8: Leeds 6E 79
Berkeley Rd. LS8: Leeds 6E 79
Berkeley St. LS8: Leeds 6E 79
Berkeley Ter. LS8: Leeds 6E 79
Berkeley Vw. LS8: Leeds 6E 79
Berking Av. LS9: Leeds 3D 98
Berking Row LS9: Leeds 3D 98
Bermondsey M. LS21: Otley 4F 23
Bermondsey St. LS21: Otley 4F 23
Bernard St. LS26: Rothw 1F 143
Berrington Way BD22: Keigh 4B 46
Berry La. BD21: Keigh 2H 47
   HX1: Hal 2H 149
   LS26: Kip 5E 123
Berry Moor Rd. HX6: Hal 1B 158
Berry's Bldgs. HX2: Hal 3D 128
Berry St. BD21: Keigh 6B 34
Bertha St. LS28: Pud 1H 93
Bertie St. BD4: B'frd 2A 112
Bertram Dr. BD17: Bail 6B 52
Bertram St. BD8: B'frd 1C 90
Bertrand St. LS11: Leeds 6G 97
Berwick St. HX1: Hal 2H 149 (4D 164)
Bescaby Gro. BD17: Bail 4E 53
Besha Av. BD12: B'frd 1D 132
Besha Gro. BD12: B'frd 1D 132
Bessbrook St. LS10: Leeds 2B 118
Bessingham Gdns.
   BD6: B'frd 5H 109
Best La. BD22: Oxen 1C 84
Beswick Cl. BD3: B'frd 4B 92
Bethel Rd. BD18: Ship 1D 70
Bethel St. BD20: Keigh 5H 35
   HD6: Brigh 1B 162
   HX3: Hal 5E 129

Bethel Ter.—Blackhouse Fold

Bethel Ter. HX2: Hal 6D **126**
HX6: Hal 6B **148**
Beulah Gro. LS6: Leeds 6H **77**
Beulah Mt. LS6: Leeds 6H **77**
Beulah Pl. HX2: Hal 4E **147**
Beulah St. LS6: Leeds 6H **77**
Beulah Ter. *LS6: Leeds 6H 77*
(off Beulah St.)
LS15: Leeds 1E 101
(off Austhorpe Rd.)
Beulah Vw. LS6: Leeds 6H **77**
Bevan Ct. BD7: B'frd 2H **109**
Beverley Av. BD12: B'frd 5D **132**
LS11: Leeds 2H **117**
Beverley Cl. HX5: Ell 4D **160**
Beverley Ct. LS17: Leeds 5B **60**
LS28: Pud 1H **93**
Beverley Dr. BD12: B'frd 5D **132**
Beverley Gdns. WF17: Bat 5D **136**
Beverley Mt. LS11: Leeds 2H **117**
Beverley Pl. HX3: Hal 6F **129**
Beverley Ri. LS29: I'ly 5A **10**
Beverley St. BD4: B'frd 6B **92**
Beverley Ter. HX3: Hal 6F **129**
(not continuous)
LS11: Leeds 2H **117**
Beverley Vw. LS11: Leeds 2H **117**
Beverley Wlk. LS25: Gar 5F **103**
Bevin Cl. WF1: Wake 4G **157**
Bevin Cres. WF1: Wake 4G **157**
Bewerley Cres. BD6: B'frd 1A **132**
Bewick Ct. BD13: B'frd 3D **108**
Bewick Gro. LS10: Leeds 6D **118**
Bexley Av. LS8: Leeds 1D **98**
Bexley Gro. LS8: Leeds 1D **98**
Bexley Mt. LS8: Leeds 1D **98**
Bexley Pl. LS9: Leeds 1D **98**
Bexley Rd. LS8: Leeds 1D **98**
Bexley Ter. LS8: Leeds 1D **98**
Bexley Vw. LS8: Leeds 1D **98**
Beza Ct. LS10: Leeds 3B **118**
Beza Rd. LS10: Leeds 2B **118**
Beza St. LS10: Leeds 2B **118**
Bickerdike Pl. *WF10: Kip 3H 145*
(off St Mary's Ct.)
Bickerdike Ter. LS25: Kip 4G **123**
Bickerdyke Bldgs. *LS26: Mick 4D 144*
(off Main Street)
Bickerton Way LS21: Otley 2C **22**
Biddenden Rd. LS15: Leeds 1H **101**
Bidder Dr. WF3: E Ard 6A **140**
Bideford Av. LS8: Leeds 4D **60**
Bideford Mt. BD4: B'frd 2C **112**
BIERLEY **4H 111**
Bierley Hall Gro. BD4: B'frd 6H **111**
Bierley Ho. Av. BD4: B'frd 4H **111**
Bierley La. BD4: B'frd 6H **111**
Bierley Vw. BD4: B'frd 4A **112**
Big Mdw. Dr. LS29: Add 1B **8**
Bilberry Cl. BD14: B'frd 2E **109**
Bilberry Ri. BD22: Haw 3D **64**
Billam's Hill LS21: Otley 2D **22**
Billey La. LS12: Leeds 6G **95**
(not continuous)
Billingbauk Ct. LS13: Leeds 2F **95**
Billingbauk Dr. LS13: Leeds 2F **95**
Billing Ct. LS19: Yead 4H **55**
Billing Dr. LS19: Yead 4A **56**
Billingsley Ter. BD4: B'frd 1H **111**
Billing Vw. BD10: B'frd 2A **72**
LS19: Yead 4H **55**
Billingwood Dr. LS19: Yead 4H **55**
Bilsdale Grange BD6: B'frd 5H **109**
Bilsdale Way BD17: Bail 5A **52**
Bilton Pl. BD8: B'frd 3C **90**
BINGLEY **4B 50**
Bingley Arts Cen. & Little Theatre **4B 50**
Bingley Bank LS17: Bard 3E **45**
Bingley Pool **5B 50**
Bingley Relief Rd. BD16: Bgly 1H **49**
Bingley Rd. BD9: B'frd 4F **69**
BD13: B'frd 3B **66**
BD17: Bail 1H **51**
Bingley Rd. BD18: Ship 1F **69**
BD21: Haw 1F **65**
BD22: Haw 1F **65**
LS20: Guis 3A **38**
LS29: Bgly, Guis 3A **38**
LS29: Men 2E **39**
Bingley Station (Rail) **4B 50**
Bingley St. BD8: B'frd 4A **90**
LS3: Leeds 3F **97** (4A **4**)
Binks Fold BD12: B'frd 5D **132**
Binks St. WF1: Wake 5G **157**
Binnie St. BD3: B'frd 4H **91** (3H **7**)
Binns Fold *BD15: B'frd 4G 67*
(off Main Rd.)
Binns Hill HX2: Hal 3H **147**
Binns Hill La. HX6: Hal 3H **147**
Binns La. BD7: B'frd 6H **89**
Binns St. BD16: Bgly 3C **50**
Binns Top La. HX3: Hal 6C **150**
HX5: Hal 1D **160**
Binswell Fold BD17: Bail 3C **52**
Bircham Cl. BD16: Bgly 2E **51**
Birch Av. BD5: B'frd 3F **111**
LS15: Leeds 3C **100**
Birch Cliff BD17: Bail 5B **52**
Birch Cl. BD5: B'frd 3F **111**
HD6: Brigh 6C **152**
Birch Cl. La. BD16: Bgly 5H **37**
Birch Ct. BD11: B'frd 1F **135**
LS27: Morl 5B **138**
Birch Cres. LS15: Leeds 3C **100**
Birchdale BD16: Bgly 1B **50**
Birch Dr. LS25: Kip 2G **123**
Birches, The LS16: B'hpe 3H **43**
LS20: Guis 3C **40**
Birchfield HX6: Hal 1B **158**
Birchfield Av. LS27: Morl 1E **137**
Birchfields Av. LS14: Leeds 1E **81**
Birchfields Cl. LS14: Leeds 2E **81**
Birchfields Ct. LS14: Leeds 1E **81**
Birchfields Cres. LS14: Leeds 1E **81**
Birchfields Gth. LS14: Leeds 1E **81**
Birchfields Ri. LS14: Leeds 2E **81**
Birch Gro. BD5: B'frd 4E **111**
BD21: Keigh 3H **47**
LS25: Kip 3G **123**
WF17: Bat 6C **136**
Birch Hill Ri. LS18: H'fth 1G **75**
Birch Ho. LS7: Leeds 2B **78**
Birchlands Av. BD15: B'frd 3F **67**
Birchlands Gro. BD15: B'frd 3F **67**
Birch La. BD5: B'frd 2E **111**
(not continuous)
HX2: Hal 1E **147**
Birch M. LS16: Leeds 5D **58**
Birch Rd. LS25: Kip 2G **123**
Birchroyd LS26: Rothw 3B **142**
Birch St. BD8: B'frd 3H **89**
(not continuous)
LS27: Morl 5B **138**
Birch Tree Gdns. BD21: Keigh 1C **48**
Birchtree Way LS16: Leeds 5G **57**
Birch Way BD5: B'frd 3F **111**
Birchwood Av. BD20: Keigh 3H **33**
LS17: Leeds 4E **61**
WF17: Bat 5B **136**
Birchwood Ct. LS29: I'ly 5C **10**
Birchwood Dr. BD20: Keigh 3G **33**
Birchwood Hill LS17: Leeds 3E **61**
Birchwood Mt. LS17: Leeds 3E **61**
Birchwood Rd. BD20: Keigh 3G **33**
BIRDACRE **6F 135**
Birdale Fld. La. LS22: Coll 3D **28**
Birdcage HX3: Hal 1H **149**
Birdcage Ct. LS21: Otley 5E **23**
Birdcage Hill HX3: Hal 6E **149**
Birdcage La. HX3: Hal 6E **149**
Birdcage Wlk. LS21: Otley 5D **22**
Bird Holme La. HX3: Hal 6D **130**
BIRDS ROYD **2B 162**
Birds Royd La. HD6: Brigh 2B **162**
Birdswell Av. HD6: Brigh 6D **152**
Birdwalk, The BD13: B'frd 3E **109**
Birfed Cres. LS4: Leeds 6B **76**
Birkby Brow Cres. WF17: Bat 5D **136**
Birkby Haven BD6: B'frd 5G **109**
Birkby La. BD19: Brigh 2B **152**
HD6: Brigh 2B **152**
Birkby St. BD12: B'frd 3D **132**
Birkdale Cl. BD13: B'frd 3C **66**
LS17: Leeds 3H **59**
Birkdale Ct. BD20: Keigh 2G **33**
Birkdale Dr. LS17: Leeds 3G **59**
Birkdale Grn. LS17: Leeds 3H **59**
Birkdale Gro. HX2: Hal 6D **106**
LS17: Leeds 3G **59**
Birkdale Mt. LS17: Leeds 3H **59**
Birkdale Pl. LS17: Leeds 3G **59**
Birkdale Ri. LS17: Leeds 3G **59**
Birkdale Wlk. LS17: Leeds 3G **59**
Birkdale Way LS17: Leeds 3H **59**
BIRKENSHAW **1E 135**
BIRKENSHAW BOTTOMS **3G 135**
Birkenshaw La. BD11: B'frd 2F **135**
Birkhey Cl. HD6: Brigh 3C **152**
Birkhill Cres. BD11: B'frd 2F **135**
Birkhouse La. HD6: Brigh 3C **152**
Birkhouse Rd. HD6: Brigh 2C **152**
Birklands Rd. BD18: Ship 2B **70**
Birklands Ter. BD18: Ship 2B **70**
Birk La. LS27: Morl 3G **137**
Birk Lea St. BD5: B'frd 1F **111**
BIRKS
Bradford **5H 89**
Leeds **5B 138**
Birks Av. BD7: B'frd 6H **89**
Birks Fold BD7: B'frd 5H **89**
Birks Hall La. HX1: Hal 1E **149**
Birkshall La. BD4: B'frd 5H **91**
Birks Hall St. HX1: Hal 1E **149**
Birks Hall Ter. HX1: Hal 1E **149**
BIRKSHEAD **5H 67**
Birksland Ind. Est. BD4: B'frd 6H **91**
Birksland Moor BD11: B'frd 4F **135**
Birksland St. BD3: B'frd 6H **91**
Birkwith Cl. LS14: Leeds 1D **80**
Birnam Gro. BD4: B'frd 1G **111**
Birr Rd. BD9: B'frd 6B **70**
BIRSTALL **5A 136**
Birstall La. BD11: B'frd 2A **136**
Birstall Retail Pk. WF17: Bat 3C **136**
BIRSTALL SMITHIES **6A 136**
Bishopdale Dr. LS22: Coll 3A **28**
Bishopdale Holme BD6: B'frd 5G **109**
Bishopgate St. LS1: Leeds 4H **97** (5D **4**)
Bishop St. BD9: B'frd 6B **70**
Bishop Way WF3: E Ard 1F **155**
Bismarck Ct. LS11: Leeds 1H **117**
Bismarck Dr. LS11: Leeds 1H **117**
Bismarck St. LS11: Leeds 1H **117**
Bittern Ct. BD13: B'frd 3E **109**
Bittern Ri. LS27: Morl 4C **138**
Blackberry Way BD14: B'frd 2D **108**
Blackbird Gdns. BD8: B'frd 4D **88**
Black Brook Way HX4: Hal 5G **159**
Black Bull St. LS10: Leeds 5B **98**
Black Bull Yd. *LS26: Rothw 2B 142*
(off Commercial St.)
Blackburn Bldgs. HD6: Brigh 1C **162**
Blackburn Cl. BD8: B'frd 4F **89**
HX3: Hal 4D **128**
Blackburn Ct. LS26: Rothw 2B **142**
Blackburn Ho. HX3: Hal 4E **129**
Blackburn Rd. HD6: Brigh 5H **151**
WF17: Bat 6A **136**
Black Dyke La. BD13: B'frd 1F **87**
Black Edge La. BD13: B'frd 5B **86**
Blackett St. LS28: Pud 2F **73**
BLACK GATES **6F 139**
Blackgates Ct. WF3: E Ard 1F **155**
Blackgates Cres. WF3: E Ard 1F **155**
Blackgates Dr. WF3: E Ard 1F **155**
Blackgates Fold WF3: E Ard 1F **155**
Blackgates Ri. WF3: E Ard 1F **155**
Blackgates Rd. WF3: E Ard 1F **155**
BLACK HILL **5F 33**
Black Hill La. BD20: Keigh 4D **32**
Blackhouse Fold HX2: Hal 2B **128**

180 A-Z Leeds & Bradford

Blackledge HX1: Hal 2H **149** (4D **164**)
Blackley Rd. HX5: Ell 6H **159**
Blackman La. LS2: Leeds 1H **97** (1D **4**)
Blackmires BD13: B'frd 5H **107**
   HX2: Hal 2E **129**
BLACK MOOR 3G **59**
BLACKMOOR 6B **44**
Blackmoor Ct. LS17: Leeds 2F **59**
Blackmoor La. LS17: Bard, S'cft ...5C **44**
Black Moor Rd. BD22: Oxen 1E **85**
   LS17: Leeds 4F **59**
Black Moor Top BD22: Haw 3D **64**
Blackpool Ct. LS12: Leeds 1A **116**
Blackpool Pl. LS12: Leeds 1A **116**
Blackpool St. LS12: Leeds 1A **116**
Blackpool Ter. LS12: Leeds 1A **116**
Blackpool Vw. LS12: Leeds 1A **116**
Blackshaw Beck La. BD13: B'frd 6C **108**
Blackshaw Dr. BD6: B'frd 5F **109**
Blacksmith Fold BD7: B'frd 1A **110**
Blacksmith M. WF3: Rothw 4F **141**
Blackstone Av. BD12: B'frd 5C **132**
Black Swan Ginnell HX1: Hal 4B **164**
Black Swan Pas.
   HX1: Hal 2G **149** (4B **164**)
Blackthorn Ct. LS10: Leeds 5B **118**
Blackthorn Rd. LS29: I'ly 4F **11**
Blackwall HX1: Hal 3G **149** (5B **164**)
Blackwall La. HX6: Hal 4G **147**
Blackwall Ri. HX6: Hal 4G **147**
Blackwood Av. LS16: Leeds 4F **57**
Blackwood Gdns. LS16: Leeds 4F **57**
Blackwood Gro. HX1: Hal 1D **148**
   LS16: Leeds 4F **57**
Blackwood Hall La. HX2: Hal 3C **146**
Blackwood Mt. LS16: Leeds 4F **57**
Blackwood Ri. LS16: Leeds 4F **57**
Blairsville Gdns. LS13: Leeds 5D **74**
Blairsville Gro. LS13: Leeds 5E **75**
Blaithroyd Ct. HX3: Hal 3A **150**
Blaithroyd La. HX3: Hal 3A **150**
Blake Cres. LS20: Guis 5D **40**
Blake Gro. LS7: Leeds 3B **78**
Blake Hill HX3: Hal 4A **130**
Blakehill Av. BD2: B'frd 1A **92**
Blake Hill End HX3: Hal 2B **130**
Blakehill Ter. BD2: B'frd 1A **92**
Blakelaw Dr. HD6: Brigh 6D **152**
Blake Law La. HD6: Brigh 1F **163**
Blakeney Gro. LS10: Leeds 4B **118**
Blakeney Rd. LS10: Leeds 4B **118**
Blamires Pl. BD7: B'frd 2H **109**
Blamires St. BD7: B'frd 2H **109**
Blanche St. BD4: B'frd 5B **92**
Blandford Gdns. LS2: Leeds 1H **97**
Blandford Gro. LS2: Leeds 1H **97**
   (off Bk. Blenheim Ter.)
Blands Av. WF10: Kip 2G **145**
Blands Cres. WF10: Kip 2G **145**
Blands Gro. WF10: Kip 2G **145**
Blands Ter. WF10: Kip 2G **145**
Bland St. HX1: Hal 2F **149** (4A **164**)
Blantyre Ct. BD13: B'frd 3B **66**
Blayds Gth. LS26: Rothw 6C **120**
Blayd's M. LS1: Leeds 4A **98** (6E **5**)
Blayds St. LS9: Leeds 4D **98**
Blayd's Yd. LS1: Leeds 4A **98** (6E **5**)
Bleach Mill La. LS29: Men 6D **20**
Blencarn Cl. LS14: Leeds 5B **80**
Blencarn Gth. LS14: Leeds 5B **80**
Blencarn Lawn LS14: Leeds 5B **80**
Blencarn Path LS14: Leeds 5B **80**
Blencarn Rd. LS14: Leeds 5B **80**
Blencarn Vw. LS14: Leeds 5B **80**
Blencarn Wlk. LS14: Leeds 5B **80**
Blenheim Av. LS2: Leeds 1H **97**
Blenheim Ct. HX1: Hal 2A **164**
   LS2: Leeds 1H **97**
   (off Blenheim Wlk.)
Blenheim Cres. LS2: Leeds 1H **97**
   (off Blenheim Av.)
Blenheim Gro. LS2: Leeds 1H **97**
Blenheim Mt. BD8: B'frd 1C **90**
Blenheim Pl. BD10: B'frd 6H **53**

Blenheim Rd. BD8: B'frd 2C **90**
Blenheim Sq. LS2: Leeds 1H **97**
Blenheim St. *BD20: Stee* 6C **14**
   (off Barrows La.)
   BD21: Keigh 2H **47**
   (off Victoria Rd.)
Blenheim Ter. LS2: Leeds 1H **97**
   (off Bk. Blenheim Ter.)
   LS27: Morl 1A **138**
Blenheim Vw. LS2: Leeds 1H **97**
Blenheim Wlk. LS2: Leeds 1H **97**
Blenkinsop Ct. *LS27: Morl* 5B **138**
   (off Britannia Rd.)
Blind La. BD11: B'frd 6B **114**
   BD13: B'frd 2G **107**
   BD16: Bgly 5G **49**
   HX2: Hal 1B **146**
   (Brearley La.)
   HX2: Hal 5C **106**
   (Cow Hill Ga. La.)
   LS17: Leeds 3A **62**
Bloomer Ga. HX7: Heb B 6A **126**
Bloomfield Sq. *LS21: Otley* 4E **23**
   (off Gay La.)
Blucher St. BD4: B'frd 5B **92**
Bluebell Cl. BD15: B'frd 3D **88**
   BD18: Ship 4D **70**
Bluebell Ct. WF17: Bat 5A **136**
Bluebell Wlk. HX2: Hal 1E **147**
Bluebird Wlk. BD16: Bgly 3E **51**
Bluecoat Ct. LS22: Coll 3H **27**
Blue Hill BD13: B'frd 1B **86**
Blue Hill Cres. LS12: Leeds 5A **96**
Blue Hill Grange LS12: Leeds 6A **96**
Blue Hill Gro. LS12: Leeds 5A **96**
Blue Hill La. LS12: Leeds 5A **96**
Blundell St. LS1: Leeds 2H **97** (2C **4**)
Blythe Av. BD8: B'frd 1D **90**
Blythe St. BD7: B'frd 4C **90** (4A **6**)
Boar La. LS1: Leeds 4H **97** (5D **4**)
Boat La. LS26: Mick 5G **145**
   WF10: Kip 4H **145**
Bobbin Mill Cl. *BD20: Stee* 6C **14**
   (off Bobbin Mill Ct.)
Bobbin Mill Ct. BD20: Stee 6C **14**
Bob La. BD15: B'frd 6H **67**
   HX2: Hal 2B **148**
BOCKING 1F **65**
Bodiham Hill LS25: Gar 3H **103**
Bodington Hall (University of Leeds)
   ....5C **58**
Bodley Ter. LS4: Leeds 2D **96**
Bodmin App. LS10: Leeds 2G **139**
Bodmin Av. BD18: Ship 2F **71**
Bodmin Cres. LS10: Leeds 2G **139**
Bodmin Cft. LS10: Leeds 2H **139**
Bodmin Gdns. LS10: Leeds 3G **139**
Bodmin Gth. LS10: Leeds 3G **139**
Bodmin Pl. LS10: Leeds 3H **139**
   (not continuous)
Bodmin Rd. LS10: Leeds 1F **139**
Bodmin Sq. LS10: Leeds 3G **139**
Bodmin St. LS10: Leeds 3G **139**
Bodmin Ter. LS10: Leeds 3G **139**
Body Balance 1C **94**
Bodylines Gym 2C **98**
   (in Mabgate Mills Industrial &
   Commercial Cen.)
Body Mania Fitness 2B **142**
   (off Marsh St.)
Bodytech 2B **142**
   (in Middleton District Cen.)
Bogart La. HX3: Hal 6F **131**
   (not continuous)
Boggart Hill LS14: Leeds 3A **80**
Boggart Hill Cres. LS14: Leeds ...3A **80**
Boggart Hill Dr. LS14: Leeds 3A **80**
Boggart Hill Gdns. LS14: Leeds ...3A **80**
Boggart Hill Rd. LS14: Leeds 3A **80**
Boggart Wood Vw. BD8: B'frd 4D **88**
BOG GREEN 6H **163**
Bog Grn. La. HD5: Hud 6H **163**
Bog La. LS15: Scho 4A **82**

BOGTHORN 3F **47**
Boland Ct. BD22: Keigh 4E **47**
Boldmere Rd. LS15: Leeds 4A **100**
Boldron Holt BD6: B'frd 5H **109**
Boldshay St. BD3: B'frd 3H **91**
Bold St. BD8: B'frd 2C **90**
Bolehill Pk. HD6: Brigh 3G **151**
Bolingbroke Ct. *BD5: B'frd* 6E **91**
   (off Elsdon Gro.)
Bolingbroke St. BD5: B'frd 3D **110**
Bolland Bldgs. BD12: B'frd 2F **133**
Bolland St. BD12: B'frd 2E **133**
Bolling Hall (Mus.) 2G **111**
Bolling Rd. BD4: B'frd 5F **91** (6E **7**)
   LS29: I'ly 6F **11**
Bolsover Cl. LS25: Gar 4H **103**
Boltby La. BD6: B'frd 5G **109**
BOLTON 6F **71**
Bolton Bri. Ct. *LS29: I'ly* 5C **10**
   (off Bolton Bri. Rd.)
Bolton Bri. Rd. LS29: I'ly 5C **10**
Bolton Brow HX6: Hal 5A **148**
Bolton Ct. BD3: B'frd 1G **91**
Bolton Cres. BD2: B'frd 5H **71**
Bolton Dr. BD2: B'frd 4H **71**
Bolton Grange LS19: Yead 1G **55**
Bolton Gro. BD2: B'frd 5H **71**
Bolton Hall Rd. BD2: B'frd 4D **70**
   (not continuous)
Bolton La. BD3: B'frd 4G **91** (3G **7**)
   BD12: B'frd 1C **132**
   (not continuous)
   BD2: B'frd 1F **91**
   BD3: B'frd 1F **91** (1E **7**)
   BD20: Sils 1E **15**
   LS19: Yead 1G **55**
   LS29: Add 1D **8**
Bolton Outlanes 5G **71**
BOLTON OUTLANES 5G **71**
Bolton Rd. BD1: B'frd 4F **91** (3E **7**)
Bolton Ter. BD20: Sils 1E **15**
Bolton Way LS23: B Spa 4A **30**
BOLTON WOODS 5E **71**
Bolus Cl. WF1: Wake 5G **157**
Bolus La. WF1: Wake 5F **157**
Bond Ct. LS1: Leeds 4D **4**
   LS6: Leeds 4D **4**
   (off Alexandra Rd.)
Bondgate LS21: Otley 4E **23**
Bond St. HD6: Brigh 6A **152**
   HX1: Hal 6A **164**
   LS1: Leeds 3H **97** (4D **4**)
   WF17: Bat 6A **136**
Bonegate Av. HD6: Brigh 6B **152**
Bonegate Rd. HD6: Brigh 6A **152**
Bonn Rd. BD9: B'frd 1A **90**
Bonwick Mall BD6: B'frd 6G **109**
BOOTH 4E **127**
Bootham Pk. BD9: B'frd 1F **89**
Booth Hill HX2: Hal 3E **127**
Booth Ho. Rd. HX2: Hal 2C **146**
Booth Ho. Ter. HX2: Hal 2C **146**
Boothman Wlk. BD21: Keigh 2G **47**
Booth Royd BD10: B'frd 6H **53**
Booth Royd Dr. BD10: B'frd 6H **53**
Boothroyd Dr. LS6: Leeds 4F **77**
Booth Royd La. HD6: Brigh 3F **161**
Booth's Bldgs. *HD6: Brigh* 2B **152**
   (off Wyke Old La.)
Booth St. BD10: B'frd 2H **71**
   BD13: B'frd 4H **107**
   BD18: Ship 2D **70**
   BD19: Cleck 6B **134**
   LS29: Burl W 2E **21**
Booth's Yd. LS28: Pud 4A **94**
Booth Ter. HX2: Hal 4E **127**
BOOTHTOWN 6E **129**
Boothtown Rd. HX3: Hal 4F **129**
Boroughgate LS21: Otley 3E **23**
Borough Mkt. HX1: Hal 4C **164**
Borrin's Way BD17: Bail 4D **52**
Borrough Av. LS8: Leeds 1C **78**
Borrough Vw. LS8: Leeds 1C **78**

Borrowdale Cl. LS12: Leeds 1H 95
Borrowdale Cres. LS12: Leeds 1H 95
Borrowdale Cft. LS19: Yead 6F 41
Borrowdale Ter. LS14: Leeds 6B 80
Boston Av. LS5: Leeds 6H 75
Boston M. LS23: B Spa 4C 30
Boston Rd. LS22: Weth 5E 13
   LS23: B Spa 5B 30
BOSTON SPA 3C 30
Boston St. HX1: Hal 2D 148
   HX6: Hal 6G 147
Boston Towers LS9: Leeds 2C 98
   (off Lindsey Gdns.)
Boston Wlk. BD6: B'frd 5H 109
Bosworth Cl. BD15: B'frd 1D 88
BOTANY 4A 36
Botany Av. BD2: B'frd 5F 71
Botany Dr. BD20: Keigh 3A 36
BOTTOMLEY HOLES 6E 87
Bottomley St. BD5: B'frd 1D 110
   BD6: B'frd 6H 109
   HD6: Brigh 5B 152
Bottoms HX3: Hal 6H 149
Bottoms La. BD11: B'frd 3F 135
BOULDER CLOUGH 5D 146
Boulevard, The HX1: Hal 6A 164
   (off Park Rd.)
   LS12: Leeds 2D 116
   LS28: Pud 1H 93
Boundary, The BD8: B'frd 2G 89
Boundary Cl. BD17: Bail 2D 52
   LS15: Leeds 4G 101
Boundary Farm Rd. LS17: Leeds ...4G 59
Boundary Pl. BD2: B'frd 1H 91
   (off Baker St.)
   LS7: Leeds 1C 98
Boundary St. LS7: Leeds 1C 98
Bourbon Cl. BD6: B'frd 5B 110
Bourne St. BD10: B'frd 6H 53
Bourse, The LS1: Leeds 5E 5
Bowater Ct. BD4: B'frd 3D 112
Bow Beck BD4: B'frd 6G 91 (6H 7)
Bowbridge Rd. BD5: B'frd 1E 111
Bowcliffe Rd. LS10: Leeds 1D 118
Bower Grn. BD3: B'frd 4A 92
Bower Rd. LS15: Leeds 6G 81
Bowers La. HX4: Hal 5B 158
Bowers Mill Ind. Est. HX4: Hal 6B 158
Bowers Row LS26: Kip 1E 145
Bower St. BD5: B'frd 6C 6
Bowes Nook BD6: B'frd 6G 109
Bowfell Cl. LS14: Leeds 5C 80
Bow Grn. BD14: B'frd 1F 109
Bowland Av. BD17: Bail 6G 51
   (not continuous)
Bowland Cl. LS15: Leeds 4A 100
Bowland St. BD1: B'frd 3D 90 (1A 6)
Bowler Cl. BD12: B'frd 1C 132
BOWLING 1H 111
Bowling All. HD6: Brigh 3A 162
Bowling All. Ter. HD6: Brigh 3A 162
Bowling Bk. La. BD4: B'frd 6G 91
Bowling Ct. HD6: Brigh 6H 151
Bowling Ct. Ind. Est. BD4: B'frd ...6A 92
Bowling Dyke HX3: Hal ...1G 149 (1C 164)
Bowling Grn. Fold BD12: B'frd 4C 132
Bowling Grn. Ter. LS11: Leeds 6H 97
Bowling Grn. Vw. BD11: B'frd 1A 136
Bowling Hall Rd. BD4: B'frd 1G 111
Bowling Mill HX3: Hal ...1G 149 (2B 164)
Bowling Old La. BD5: B'frd 3D 110
   (not continuous)
Bowling Pk. Cl. BD4: B'frd 1F 111
Bowling Pk. Dr. BD4: B'frd 2F 111
Bowling Swimming Pool 2G 111
Bowl Shaw La. HX3: Hal 1B 130
Bowman Av. BD6: B'frd 6B 110
Bowman Gro. HX1: Hal 2E 149
Bowman La. LS10: Leeds 4B 98 (6G 5)
Bowman Pl. HX1: Hal 2E 149
Bowman Rd. BD6: B'frd 6B 110
Bowman St. HX1: Hal 2E 149
Bowman Ter. HX1: Hal 2E 149
Bowmere Dr. BD15: B'frd 3D 88

Bownas Rd. LS23: B Spa 3A 30
Bowness Av. BD10: B'frd 5B 72
Bowood Av. LS7: Leeds 2G 77
Bowood Cres. LS7: Leeds 2G 77
Bowood Gro. LS7: Leeds 2G 77
Bow St. BD21: Keigh 6A 34
   LS9: Leeds 4C 98
Bowwood Dr. BD20: Keigh 5F 35
Boxhall Rd. HX5: Ell 4B 160
Box Tree Cl. BD8: B'frd 2G 89
Box Tree Gro. BD21: Keigh 1C 48
Box Trees HX2: Hal 4B 128
Box Trees La. HX2: Hal 4B 128
Boxwood Rd. HX5: Ell 6B 160
Boyd Av. BD3: B'frd 2C 92
Boy Home La. HX2: Hal 3D 146
Boy La. BD4: B'frd 6H 111
   HX3: Hal 5B 128
Boyle, The LS15: Bar E 1D 82
Boyne St. HX1: Hal ...2F 149 (4A 164)
Boynton St. BD5: B'frd 2D 110
   (not continuous)
Boynton Ter. BD5: B'frd 2E 111
Boys La. HX3: Hal 4H 149
Boys Scarr HX2: Hal 3D 146
Bracewell Av. BD15: B'frd 3C 88
Bracewell Bank HX3: Hal 5D 128
Bracewell Dr. HX3: Hal 5D 128
Bracewell Gro. HX3: Hal 6E 129
Bracewell Mt. HX3: Hal 5D 128
   (off Bracewell Hill)
Bracewell St. BD21: Keigh 6C 34
Bracken Av. HD6: Brigh 4A 152
BRACKEN BANK 4F 47
Bracken Bank Av. BD22: Keigh 5F 47
Bracken Bank Cres. BD22: Keigh ..4F 47
Bracken Bank Gro. BD22: Keigh ...4F 47
Bracken Bank Wlk. BD22: Keigh ...5F 47
Bracken Bank Way BD22: Keigh ...4F 47
Brackenbeck Rd. BD7: B'frd 1H 109
Brackenbed Grange HX2: Hal 6C 128
Brackenbed La. HX2: Hal 6D 128
Brackenbed Ter. HX2: Hal 6D 128
   (off Brackenbed La.)
Bracken Cl. HD6: Brigh 4A 152
Bracken Ct. LS12: Leeds 6E 97
   LS17: Leeds 6A 60
Brackendale BD10: B'frd 5F 53
Brackendale Av. BD10: B'frd 5G 53
Brackendale Dr. BD10: B'frd 5F 53
Brackendale Gro. BD10: B'frd 5F 53
Brackendale Pde. BD10: B'frd 5F 53
Bracken Edge BD10: B'frd 2A 72
   LS8: Leeds 4D 78
Bracken Ghyll Dr. BD20: Sils 1D 14
Bracken Hall (Countryside Cen.) ...4G 51
Brackenhall Ct. BD7: B'frd 1H 109
Bracken Hill HX2: Hal 6C 128
   LS15: Leeds 6A 60
Brackenhill Dr. BD7: B'frd 2H 109
Brackenholme Royd BD6: B'frd 5G 109
Brackenhurst Dr. LS17: Leeds 5A 60
Brackenhurst Pl. LS17: Leeds 5A 60
Bracken Mt. BD20: Sils 1D 14
Bracken Pk. BD16: Bgly 4E 51
   (Gilstead La.)
   BD16: Bgly 2D 50
   (Southway)
   LS14: S'cft 5C 44
   BD20: Stee 6A 14
   BD22: Keigh 3G 47
   HD6: Brigh 4A 152
Brackens La. HX3: Hal 6D 108
Brackens St. BD21: Keigh 3H 47
Bracken Way HX5: Ell 4D 160
Brackenwood Cl. LS8: Leeds 2C 78
   LS29: I'ly 5G 11
Brackenwood Ct. WF1: Wake 4H 157
Brackenwood Dr. LS8: Leeds 1C 78
Brackenwood Grn. LS8: Leeds 1C 78
Brackenwood Rd. WF1: Wake 4H 157
Bradbeck Rd. BD7: B'frd 4H 89
Bradburn Rd. WF3: Rothw 4E 141
Bradfield Cl. HD2: Hud 6E 163

BRADFORD 4E 91 (3C 6)
Bradford & Wakefield Rd.
   BD4: B'frd 6G 113
Bradford Bulls RLFC (Odsal Stadium)
   ....5E 111
Bradford Bus. Pk. BD1: B'frd 2E 91
Bradford Cathedral Church of St Peter
   ....4F 91 (3E 7)
Bradford City AFC (Valley Parade)
   ....2D 90
Bradford City Farm 3B 90
Bradford College
   McMillan Building 6D 90
   McMillan Halls of Residence
   ....6D 90 (6A 6)
Bradford Design Exchange 4F 7
Bradford Forster Square Station (Rail)
   ....4E 91 (3D 6)
Bradford Ice Arena 5E 91 (6C 6)
Bradford Industrial & Horses at Work Mus.
   ....6B 72
Bradford Interchange Station (Rail)
   ....5F 91 (5E 7)
Bradford Kart Racing 6F 91
Bradford La. BD3: B'frd 4B 92
BRADFORD MOOR 3A 92
Bradford Old Rd. BD16: Bgly 2D 68
   (not continuous)
   HX3: Hal 4G 129
Bradford Pk. Avenue FC (Horsfall Stadium)
   ....6B 110
Bradford Rd. BD3: Pud 2D 92
   BD4: B'frd 5D 112
   BD10: B'frd 4G 71
   BD11: B'frd 2D 136
    (Buttercup Way)
   BD11: B'frd 3E 135
    (Whitehall Rd. E.)
   BD11: B'frd 6H 113
    (Woodview)
   BD12: B'frd 3G 133
   BD14: B'frd 6E 89
   BD16: Bgly 5C 50
   BD18: Ship 2A 70
   BD19: B'frd, Cleck 3E 135
   BD19: Cleck 5A 134
   BD20: Keigh 4C 34
   BD21: Keigh 6B 34
   HD2: Hud 5B 162
   HD6: Brigh 1B 162
    (King St.)
   HD6: Brigh 1B 152
    (Mayfield Gro.)
   HX3: Hal 4C 130
    (Oaklands Av.)
   HX3: Hal 6C 130
    (Pk. View Av.)
   LS20: Guis, Men 1H 39
   LS21: Otley 5H 21
   LS28: Pud 2D 92
   LS29: Burl W 3G 21
   LS29: Men 1H 39
   WF1: Wake 5C 156
   WF2: Wake 4C 156
    (not continuous)
   WF3: E Ard 6D 138
   WF17: Bat 5G 155
Bradford St. BD21: Keigh 5A 34
Bradlaugh Rd. BD6: B'frd 4B 110
Bradlaugh Ter. BD6: B'frd 4C 110
Bradleigh Cl. BD21: Keigh 2C 48
BRADLEY 6F 163
Bradley Av. BD20: Sils 1D 14
Bradley Colliery La. HD2: Hud 6F 163
Bradley Ct. HX4: Hal 5F 159
Bradley Dr. BD20: Sils 1D 14
Bradley Grange Gdns.
   HD2: Hud 5F 163
Bradley Gro. BD20: Sils 1D 14
BRADLEY HILL 1C 94
Bradley Hill Vw. LS28: Leeds 1C 94
   (off Swinnow La.)
Bradley Junc. Ind. Est.
   HD2: Hud 6G 163

Bradley La. HX4: Hal 5F **159**
  LS28: Pud 4F **93**
Bradley Quarry Cl. HD2: Hud 5G **163**
Bradley Quarry Nature Reserve
  . . . . .5G **163**
Bradley Ri. BD20: Sils 1D **14**
Bradley Rd. BD20: Sils 1D **14**
  HD2: Hud 6C **162**
Bradley St. BD9: B'frd 5C **70**
  BD16: Bgly 4B **50**
Bradley Ter. LS17: Leeds 3E **61**
Bradley Vw. HX4: Hal 6E **159**
BRADSHAW 4D **106**
Bradshaw La. HX2: Hal 5D **106**
Bradshaw Row HX2: Hal 3D **106**
Bradshaw Vw. BD13: B'frd 4G **107**
  HX2: Hal 6C **106**
          (off Moor Top Gdns.)
Bradstock Gdns. LS27: Morl 1A **138**
Bradup BD20: Keigh 6G **17**
Brae Av. BD2: B'frd 6F **71**
Braemar Dr. LS25: Gar 3H **103**
Braeside HX2: Hal 2B **148**
Brafferton Arbor BD6: B'frd 5G **109**
Braine Rd. LS22: Weth 3F **13**
BRAITHWAITE 5E **33**
Braithwaite Av. BD22: Keigh 6E **33**
Braithwaite Cres. BD22: Keigh . . .6F **33**
Braithwaite Dr. BD22: Keigh 6F **33**
Braithwaite Edge Rd.
  BD22: Keigh 5D **32**
Braithwaite Gro. BD22: Keigh 6F **33**
Braithwaite Rd. BD22: Keigh 6D **32**
Braithwaite Row LS10: Leeds 3C **118**
Braithwaite St. LS11: Leeds 5F **97**
Braithwaite Wlk. BD22: Keigh 6F **33**
Braithwaite Way BD22: Keigh 6F **33**
Bramall Bus. Pk. BD5: B'frd 1E **111**
Bramble Av. LS23: B Spa 4H **29**
Bramble Cl. BD14: Clay 2E **109**
  BD22: Haw 3D **64**
Bramble Ct. LS21: Pool 5F **25**
  WF1: Wake 4E **157**
Bramble Gro. HX5: Ell 4D **160**
  LS21: Pool 5F **25**
Bramble M. LS17: Leeds 2G **61**
Brambles, The LS29: I'ly 5B **10**
Bramble Wlk. WF17: Bat 6B **136**
Brambling Dr. BD13: B'frd 3E **109**
Brambling M. LS27: Morl 3C **138**
Bramham Dr. BD17: Bail 3D **52**
Bramham La. LS23: Bard 1H **45**
Bramham Pk. Ct. LS10: Leeds 4B **140**
Bramham Rd. BD16: Bgly 3C **50**
  LS23: B Spa, B'ham 6B **30**
Bramham's Yd. LS25: Kip 4H **123**
BRAMHOPE 2G **43**
Bramleigh Dr. LS27: Morl 1A **138**
Bramleigh Gro. LS27: Morl 1A **138**
BRAMLEY 6F **75**
Bramley Baths (Swimming Pool) . .6D **74**
Bramley Cen. LS13: Leeds 6F **75**
Bramley Cl. BD22: Keigh 4B **46**
Bramley Cres. WF1: Wake 5F **157**
Bramley Gdns. LS14: Leeds 6E **63**
Bramley La. HX3: Hal 1E **151**
Bramley Station (Rail) 2D **94**
Bramley St. BD5: B'frd 6E **91**
           (not continuous)
Bramley's Yd. LS1: Leeds 4F **5**
Bramley Vw. HX3: Hal 1G **151**
Brampton HX2: Hal 6B **126**
Bramstan Av. LS13: Leeds 6C **74**
Bramstan Cl. LS13: Leeds 6C **74**
Bramstan Gdns.
  LS13: Leeds 6C **74**
Bramston Gdns. HD6: Brigh 3A **162**
Bramston St. HD6: Brigh 2A **162**
Bramwell Ho. BD3: B'frd 2F **7**
Brancepeth Pl. LS12: Leeds 4E **97**
Branch Cl. LS12: Leeds 1A **116**
Branch End LS27: Morl 6F **115**
Branch Pl. LS12: Leeds 1A **116**

Branch Rd. BD19: Cleck 6F **133**
  HX4: Hal 6B **158**
  LS12: Leeds 1A **116**
            (Branch Pl.)
  LS12: Leeds 3C **96**
           (Stocks Hill)
Branch St. LS12: Leeds 1A **116**
Brander App. LS9: Leeds 2H **99**
Brander Cl. BD10: B'frd 3H **71**
  LS9: Leeds 2H **99**
Brander Dr. LS9: Leeds 2G **99**
Brander Gro. LS9: Leeds 2G **99**
Brander Rd. LS9: Leeds 1H **99**
Brander St. LS9: Leeds 1H **99**
Brandfort St. BD7: B'frd 6A **90**
Brandling Ct. LS10: Leeds 2A **140**
BRANDON 2A **62**
Brandon Ct. LS17: Leeds 2G **61**
Brandon Cres. LS17: S'cft 6A **44**
Brandon La. LS17: Leeds 5A **44**
  LS17: S'cft 6B **44**
Brandon Rd. LS3: Leeds 3G **97** (3A **4**)
Brandon St. LS12: Leeds 4F **97**
Brandon Ter. LS17: Leeds 2F **61**
Brandon Vw. LS17: Leeds 2H **61**
Brandon Way LS7: Leeds 4B **78**
BRANDY CARR 5B **156**
Brandy Carr Rd. WF2: Wake 6H **155**
Branksome Cl. BD9: B'frd 1H **89**
Branksome Cres. BD9: B'frd 1H **89**
Branksome Dr. BD18: Ship 1E **69**
Branksome Gro. BD18: Ship 1E **69**
Branksome Pl. LS3: Leeds 3A **4**
  LS6: Leeds 1E **97**
Bransby Cl. LS28: Pud 1A **94**
Bransby Ct. LS28: Pud 1A **94**
Bransby Ri. LS28: Pud 6A **74**
Bransdale Av. LS20: Guis 5C **40**
Bransdale Cl. BD17: Bail 5A **52**
  LS20: Guis 5C **40**
Bransdale Clough BD6: B'frd 4G **109**
Bransdale Gdns. LS20: Guis 5C **40**
Bransdale Gth. LS20: Guis 5C **40**
Branshaw Dr. BD22: Keigh 2E **47**
Branshaw Gro. BD22: Keigh 2E **47**
Branshaw Mt. BD22: Keigh 2E **47**
Bran St. BD21: Keigh 3H **47**
Brant Av. HX2: Hal 3D **128**
Brant Bank La. LS29: I'ly 3H **9**
Brantcliffe Dr. BD17: Bail 3B **52**
Brantcliffe Way BD17: Bail 2C **52**
Brantdale Cl. BD9: B'frd 5E **69**
Brantdale Rd. BD9: B'frd 5E **69**
Brantford St. LS7: Leeds 3B **78**
Brantwood Av. BD9: B'frd 5E **69**
Brantwood Cl. BD9: B'frd 5E **69**
Brantwood Cres. BD9: B'frd 5D **68**
Brantwood Dr. BD9: B'frd 5E **69**
Brantwood Gro. BD9: B'frd 5D **68**
Brantwood Oval BD9: B'frd 5E **69**
Brantwood Rd. BD9: B'frd 5D **68**
Brantwood Vs. BD9: B'frd 5E **69**
Branwell Av. WF17: Bat 4A **136**
Branwell Ct. BD9: B'frd 1G **89**
Branwell Dr. BD22: Haw 1C **64**
Branwell Lodge BD7: B'frd 2A **110**
Branwell Wlk. WF17: Bat 4B **136**
Branxholme Ind. Est. HD6: Brigh . .3G **152**
Brassey Rd. BD4: B'frd 1G **111**
Brassey St. HX1: Hal 3F **149** (6A **164**)
Brassey Ter. BD4: B'frd 1G **111**
Brathay Gdns. LS14: Leeds 6C **80**
Braybrook Ct. BD8: B'frd 6C **70**
Bray Cl. BD7: B'frd 3F **109**
Braybrook Dr. BD7: B'frd 3F **109**
Brayshaw Fold BD12: B'frd 1E **133**
Brayshaw Rd. WF3: E Ard 3A **156**
Brayton App. LS14: Leeds 4E **81**
Brayton Cl. LS14: Leeds 4E **81**
Brayton Gth. LS14: Leeds 4E **81**
Brayton Grange LS14: Leeds 4F **81**
Brayton Grn. LS14: Leeds 4E **81**
           (not continuous)
Brayton Gro. LS14: Leeds 4E **81**

Brayton Pl. LS14: Leeds 4F **81**
Brayton Sq. LS14: Leeds 4F **81**
Brayton Ter. LS14: Leeds 4E **81**
Brayton Wlk. LS14: Leeds 4E **81**
Breakmoor Av. BD20: Sils 1E **15**
Break Neck HX3: Hal 1C **150**
Breaks Fold BD12: B'frd 5D **132**
Breaks Rd. BD12: B'frd 1E **133**
Brearcliffe Cl. BD6: B'frd 5B **110**
Brearcliffe Dr. BD6: B'frd 6A **110**
Brearcliffe Gro. BD6: B'frd 6A **110**
Brearcliffe Rd. BD6: B'frd 6B **110**
Brearcliffe St. BD6: B'frd 6A **110**
Brearley La. HX2: Hal 1B **146**
  HX7: Heb B 6A **126**
Brearley La. Top HX2: Hal 6B **126**
Brearton St. BD1: B'frd 3E **91** (1C **6**)
Breary Av. LS18: H'fth 6F **57**
           (not continuous)
Breary Ct. LS16: B'hpe 2G **43**
Breary La. LS16: B'hpe 2G **43**
Breary La. E. LS16: B'hpe 2H **43**
Breary Ri. LS16: B'hpe 2G **43**
Breary Ter. LS18: H'fth 6F **57**
Breary Wlk. LS18: H'fth 6F **57**
Breck Lea HX6: Hal 6G **147**
Brecks BD14: B'frd 6F **89**
Brecks Gdns. LS25: Kip 2F **123**
Brecks La. LS26: Kip 1C **122**
Brecks Rd. BD14: B'frd 6F **89**
Breck Willows HX6: Hal 6F **147**
Brecon App. LS9: Leeds 2H **99**
Brecon Cl. BD10: B'frd 2H **71**
Brecon Ct. LS9: Leeds 2H **99**
Brecon Ri. LS9: Leeds 2H **99**
Bredon Av. BD18: Ship 2F **71**
Breighton Adown BD6: B'frd 5F **109**
Bremit Wlk. BD6: B'frd 5B **110**
Bremner St. LS21: Otley 3F **23**
Brendon Ct. BD4: B'frd 2B **112**
Brendon Ho. BD4: B'frd 3C **112**
          (off Landscove Av.)
Brendon Wlk. BD4: B'frd 3B **112**
           (not continuous)
Brentford Rd. BD12: B'frd 6C **110**
Brentwood Ct. LS16: Leeds 1A **76**
Brentwood Gdns. BD6: B'frd 5D **110**
Brentwood Gro. LS12: Leeds 4C **96**
Brentwood St. LS12: Leeds 4C **96**
Brentwood Ter. LS12: Leeds 4C **96**
Brett Gdns. LS11: Leeds 1H **117**
Bretton Ct. BD6: B'frd 5H **109**
Brewery La. BD13: B'frd 6G **107**
           (Ambler Way)
  BD13: B'frd 2H **107**
           (Carter La.)
Brewery Pl. LS10: Leeds 4B **98** (6G **5**)
Brewery Rd. BD21: Keigh 4G **47**
  LS29: I'ly 5E **11**
Brewery St. BD21: Keigh 6B **34**
  HX3: Hal 5G **129**
Brexdale Av. LS25: Kip 2F **123**
Brian Cres. LS15: Leeds 6D **80**
Brian Pl. LS15: Leeds 6D **80**
Brian Royd La. HX4: Hal 4D **158**
Brian Royd Mills HX4: Hal 4D **158**
BRIANSIDE 6C **80**
Brian Vw. LS15: Leeds 6E **81**
Briar Cl. HX5: Ell 6A **160**
  LS28: Pud 1H **93**
Briardale Rd. BD9: B'frd 5D **68**
Briardene LS26: Rothw 3E **143**
Briarfield Av. BD10: B'frd 2G **71**
Briarfield Cl. BD10: B'frd 2G **71**
  LS29: I'ly 6F **11**
Briarfield Gdns. BD18: Ship 3B **70**
  LS27: Morl 1E **137**
Briarfield Gro. BD10: B'frd 2G **71**
Briarfield Rd. BD18: Ship 4C **70**
Briar Ga. LS22: Weth 2E **13**
Briarlea Cl. LS19: Yead 2D **54**
Briarmains Rd. WF17: Bat 5B **136**
Briar Rhydding BD17: Bail 5E **53**
Briarsdale Ct. LS8: Leeds 6G **79**

Briarsdale Cft. LS8: Leeds 6G 79
Briarsdale Gth. LS8: Leeds 6G 79
Briarsdale Hgts. LS9: Leeds 6G 79
Briar Wood BD18: Ship 2E 71
Briarwood Av. BD6: B'frd 4B 110
  BD20: Keigh 4D 34
Briarwood Cl. WF1: Wake 4H 157
Briarwood Cres. BD6: B'frd 4B 110
Briarwood Dr. BD6: B'frd 4B 110
Briarwood Gro. BD6: B'frd 3B 110
Brick & Tile Ter. HD6: Brigh 2A 162
Brickfield Gro. HX2: Hal 2E 129
Brickfield La. HX2: Hal 2E 129
Brickfield Ter. HX2: Hal 2E 129
Brick Mill Rd. LS28: Pud 5B 94
Brick Row BD12: B'frd 4C 132
Brick St. BD19: Cleck 2H 153
  BD21: Keigh 1A 48
  LS9: Leeds 4B 98 (5H 5)
Brick Ter. HD6: Brigh 2B 162
Bridge Av. LS21: Otley 3E 23
Bridge Cl. LS23: B Spa 3C 30
Bridge Ct. LS11: Leeds 6G 97
  LS27: Morl 4B 138
Bridge End HD6: Brigh 2A 162
  LS1: Leeds 4A 98 (5E 5)
  (not continuous)
Bridge Fold LS5: Leeds 5H 75
Bridge Foot LS23: B Spa 3C 30
Bridge Gth. LS23: B Spa 5B 30
Bridgegate Way BD10: B'frd 4B 72
Bridgehouse La. BD22: Haw 3C 64
Bridge La. HX3: Hal 1C 130
  LS29: I'ly 4C 10
Bridge Paddock LS22: Coll 2B 28
  HD5: Hud 6G 163
  HD6: Brigh 1A 162
  LS5: Leeds 5H 75
  LS11: Leeds 6G 97
  LS13: Leeds 4A 74
  LS23: B Spa 3C 30
Bridge St. BD1: B'frd 5E 91 (5D 6)
  BD13: B'frd 5A 88
  BD20: Sils 1E 15
  BD21: Keigh 1H 47
  BD22: Keigh 5B 46
  HX6: Hal 6H 147
  LS2: Leeds 3B 98 (4G 5)
  LS21: Otley 3E 23
  LS27: Morl 4B 138
Bridge Ter. HX2: Hal 1E 127
  LS17: Leeds 3C 62
  LS27: Morl 4B 138
Bridge Vw. LS13: Leeds 4A 74
Bridgewater Apartments
  BD5: B'frd 6E 91
  (off Park Rd.)
Bridgewater Ct. LS6: Leeds 3F 77
Bridgewater Rd. LS9: Leeds 6D 98
Bridgway BD4: B'frd 3B 112
Bri. Wood Cl. LS18: H'fth 6F 57
Bri. Wood Vw. LS18: H'fth 5F 57
Bridgland Av. LS29: Men 6G 21
Bridgwater Rd. BD9: B'frd 1A 90
Bridle Dene HX3: Hal 2E 131
Bridle Path Rd. LS15: Leeds 1C 100
  LS17: Leeds 2H 61
Bridle Path Wlk. LS15: Leeds 1C 100
Bridle Stile HX3: Hal 2E 131
Bridle Stile La. BD13: B'frd 3A 108
Brierdene BD20: Sils 1E 15
Brier Hey HX7: Heb B 6A 126
Brier Hey Cl. HX7: Heb B 6A 126
Brier Hey Ind. Units
  HX7: Heb B 1A 146
Brier Hey La. HX7: Heb B 6A 126
Brier Hill Cl. BD19: Cleck 3G 153
Brier Hill Vw. HD2: Hud 6D 162
Brierlands CI. LS25: Gar 3H 103
Brierlands Fold LS25: Gar 3H 103
Brier La. HD6: Brigh 1F 161
Brierley Cl. BD18: Ship 3C 70

Brier St. BD21: Keigh 3H 47
  HX3: Hal 5G 129
Briery Cl. LS29: I'ly 5A 10
Briery Fld. BD18: Ship 4B 70
Briggate BD17: Ship 1B 70
  BD18: Ship 2B 70
  BD20: Sils 1E 15
  HD6: Brigh 1A 162
  (not continuous)
  HX5: Ell 4B 160
  LS1: Leeds 4A 98 (5E 5)
  LS29: I'ly 1G 9
Brigg Gdns. BD22: Keigh 6F 33
Briggland Ct. BD15: B'frd 4G 67
Briggs Av. BD6: B'frd 4A 110
Briggs Bldgs. LS27: Morl 3B 138
  (off Melbourne St.)
Briggs Gro. BD6: B'frd 4A 110
Briggs Pl. BD6: B'frd 4A 110
Briggs St. BD13: B'frd 4H 107
Briggs Vs. BD13: B'frd 4A 108
  (off Briggs St.)
BRIGHOUSE 6A 152
Brighouse & Denholme Ga. Rd.
  HX3: Hal 1C 130
  (Pepper Hill)
  HX3: Hal 3D 130
  (Stone Chair)
Brighouse & Denholme Rd.
  BD13: B'frd 5C 86
Brighouse Pool 1B 162
Brighouse Rd. BD12: B'frd 2D 132
  BD13: B'frd 4B 108
  HX3: Hal 2E 151
  (Barfield Rd.)
  HX3: Hal 4B 108
  (Brighouse & Denholme Ga. Rd.)
Brighouse Station (Rail) 2B 162
Brighouse Wood La. HD6: Brigh . . .6H 151
Brighouse Wood Row
  HD6: Brigh 6H 151
  (off Brighouse Wood La.)
Brighton Av. LS27: Morl 2H 137
Brighton Cliff LS13: Leeds 1E 95
Brighton Gro. HX1: Hal 1E 149
  (off Pellon La.)
  LS13: Leeds 2F 95
Brighton Rd. LS29: I'ly 6G 11
Brighton St. BD10: B'frd 6G 53
  BD17: Ship 1B 70
  HX3: Hal 6E 129
Brighton Ter. BD19: Cleck 1F 153
Bright St. BD4: B'frd 3A 112
  BD13: B'frd 4B 108
  BD14: B'frd 1D 108
  BD15: B'frd 2D 88
  BD22: Haw 2D 64
  HX6: Hal 4H 147
  LS27: Morl 3H 137
  LS28: Pud 1B 94
  WF3: E Ard 1B 156
Brignall Cft. LS9: Leeds 2D 98
Brignall Gth. LS9: Leeds 2D 98
Brignall Way LS9: Leeds 2D 98
Brigshaw Dr. WF10: Kip 6F 123
Brigshaw La. WF10: Kip 6F 123
Brindley Gro. BD8: B'frd 4E 89
Brindley Rd. BD20: Sils 3F 15
Brindley Way WF2: Wake 5D 156
Brinsmead Ct. LS26: Rothw 6B 120
Brisbane Av. BD2: B'frd 6E 71
Briscoe La. HX4: Hal 4F 159
Bristol Av. BD20: Keigh 5F 35
  (off Ford Rd.)
Bristol St. HX3: Hal 6H 149
  LS7: Leeds 2B 98 (1H 5)
Britannia Bldgs. LS27: Morl 5H 137
Britannia CI. LS28: Pud 1B 94
Britannia Ct. LS13: Leeds 3C 94
Britannia Ho. BD1: B'frd 5D 6
  (off Bridge St.)
  LS1: Leeds 4C 4
Britannia M. LS28: Pud 3C 94
Britannia Mills WF17: Bat 5B 136

Britannia Rd. LS27: Morl 5H 137
Britannia Sq. LS27: Morl 5H 137
Britannia St. BD5: B'frd 5F 91 (6E 7)
  BD16: Bgly 4C 50
  LS1: Leeds 4H 97 (5C 4)
  LS28: Pud 1B 94
Broadacres Cl. LS22: Weth 4C 12
Broadacre Way BD17: Bail 3F 53
Broad Carr La. HX4: Hal 6G 159
Broad Carr Ter. HX4: Ell 6H 159
Broadcroft Chase WF3: E Ard 2E 155
Broadcroft Dr. WF3: E Ard 2E 155
Broadcroft Gro. WF3: E Ard 1E 155
Broadcroft Way WF3: E Ard 1E 155
Broad Dale Cl. BD20: Keigh 4F 35
Broadfield Cl. BD4: B'frd 4C 112
Broadfields LS18: H'fth 6F 57
Broadfield Way LS29: Add 1B 8
BROAD FOLDS 6E 89
Broadfolds BD14: B'frd 1E 109
Broadgate Av. LS18: H'fth 1F 75
Broadgate Ct. LS18: H'fth 1F 75
Broadgate Cres. LS18: H'fth 1E 75
Broadgate Dr. LS18: H'fth 6F 57
Broadgate La. LS18: H'fth 6E 57
Broadgate M. LS18: H'fth 1F 75
Broadgate Ri. LS18: H'fth 1F 75
Broadgate Wlk. LS18: H'fth 1E 75
Broad Ings Way HX3: Hal 2E 131
Broadlands BD20: Keigh 5F 33
Broadlands St. BD4: B'frd 1B 112
Broadland Way WF3: Wake 1G 157
Broad La. BD4: B'frd 6B 92
  HX2: Hal 4C 146
  (not continuous)
  LS5: Leeds 5E 75
  LS13: Leeds 1C 94
Broad La. Cl. LS13: Leeds 5G 75
Broadlea Av. LS13: Leeds 5G 75
Broadlea Cl. LS13: Leeds 5G 75
Broadlea Cres. BD5: B'frd 2F 111
  LS13: Leeds 5G 75
Broadlea Gdns. LS13: Leeds 5G 75
Broadlea Gro. LS13: Leeds 5G 75
Broadlea Hill LS13: Leeds 5G 75
Broadlea Mt. LS13: Leeds 6H 75
Broadlea Oval LS13: Leeds 6G 75
Broadlea Pl. LS13: Leeds 6G 75
Broadlea Rd. LS13: Leeds 5G 75
Broadlea St. LS13: Leeds 5G 75
Broadlea Ter. LS13: Leeds 5G 75
Broadlea Vw. LS13: Leeds 5F 75
Broadley Av. HX2: Hal 6H 127
Broadley Cl. HX2: Hal 6A 128
Broadley Cres. HX2: Hal 6H 127
Broadley Gro. HX2: Hal 6A 128
Broadley Laithe HX2: Hal 6A 128
Broadley Rd. HX2: Hal 6H 127
Broadmeadows WF1: Wake 4G 157
Broad Oak HX3: Hal 3F 151
Broad Oak La. HX3: Hal 3F 151
Broad Oak Pl. HX3: Hal 3F 151
Broad Oak St. HX3: Hal 3F 151
Broad Oak Ter. HX3: Hal 3F 151
Broadstones Pk. BD16: Bgly 5F 51
Broadstone Way BD4: B'frd 4C 112
Broad St. BD1: B'frd 4E 91 (3D 6)
  HX1: Hal 2G 149 (4B 164)
  LS28: Pud 6G 73
Broad Tree Rd. HX3: Hal 5E 129
Broad Wlk. LS2: Leeds 6G 77
Broadwalk, The LS21: Otley 2C 22
Broadwater Dr. BD2: B'frd 4E 71
  BD18: Ship 4E 71
Broadway BD1: B'frd 5E 91 (5D 6)
  BD16: Bgly 4C 50
  HX3: Hal 4A 150
  HX6: Hal 6E 147
  LS5: Leeds 2G 75
  LS15: Leeds 5B 100
  LS18: H'fth 3A 74
  LS20: Guis 5A 40
Broadway Av. BD5: B'frd 3D 110
  LS4: Leeds 1E 97

Broadway Cl. BD5: B'frd 3D **110**
Broadway Ct. HX6: Hal 6E **147**
Broadway Dr. LS18: H'fth 1D **74**
Broadwood Av. HX2: Hal 6A **128**
Brocklesby Dr. BD15: B'frd 3D **88**
Brocklyn Yd. HX1: Hal 5D **164**
Brocks HX2: Hal 4C **146**
Brockwell Gdns. HX6: Hal 6G **147**
Brockwell Ga. HX6: Hal 6G **147**
Brockwell La. HX6: Hal 6F **147**
   (not continuous)
Brodley Cl. HX3: Hal 1E **151**
Brodrick Ct. LS6: Leeds 4D **76**
Brodrick Dr. LS29: I'ly 6D **10**
Brodwell Grange LS18: H'fth 1G **75**
Brogans Yd. LS21: Otley 4F **23**
Broken Way BD5: B'frd 3D **110**
   (off Manchester Rd.)
Bromet Pl. BD2: B'frd 5H **71**
Bromford Rd. BD4: B'frd 1H **111**
Bromley Gro. BD22: Keigh 2E **47**
Bromley Rd. BD16: Bgly 3B **50**
   BD18: Ship 1G **69**
Brompton Av. BD4: B'frd 2G **111**
Brompton Gro. LS11: Leeds 3H **117**
Brompton Mt. LS11: Leeds 3H **117**
Brompton Rd. BD4: B'frd 1G **111**
Brompton Row LS11: Leeds 3H **117**
Brompton Ter. BD4: B'frd 1G **111**
   LS11: Leeds 3H **117**
Brompton Vw. LS11: Leeds 3H **117**
Bronshill Gro. BD15: B'frd 2E **89**
Bronte Cl. BD9: B'frd 1G **89**
   BD19: Cleck 6F **135**
Bronte Dr. BD22: Keigh 4E **47**
Bronte Ho. BD4: B'frd 1C **112**
   (off Eversley Dr.)
   LS7: Leeds 6A **78**
Bronte Old Rd. BD13: B'frd 5A **88**
Bronte Parsonage Mus. **2B 64**
Bronte Pl. BD13: B'frd 5A **88**
Bronte Rd. WF17: Bat 6A **136**
Bronte St. BD21: Keigh 5B **34**
   BD22: Haw 2B **64**
Bronte Vs. BD22: Haw 1F **65**
Brooke Grn. HX3: Hal 1E **151**
Brooke St. HD6: Brigh 2A **162**
Brookeville HX3: Hal 2F **151**
   (off Brighouse Rd.)
Brookeville Av. HX3: Hal 2E **151**
Brookfield Av. BD18: Ship 1D **70**
   BD19: Cleck 6B **134**
   LS8: Leeds 5D **78**
   LS13: Leeds 3H **73**
Brookfield Ct. LS13: Leeds 3H **73**
Brookfield Gdns. LS13: Leeds 4H **73**
Brookfield Pl. LS6: Leeds 3E **77**
Brookfield Rd. BD3: B'frd 3G **91** (2H **7**)
   BD18: Ship 1D **70**
   LS6: Leeds 3E **77**
Brookfields Av. BD12: Cleck 6E **133**
Brookfields Rd. BD12: Cleck 6E **133**
Brookfield St. LS10: Leeds 6B **98**
Brookfield Ter. BD19: Cleck 6C **134**
   LS6: Leeds 3E **77**
   (off Brookfield Rd.)
   LS10: Leeds 6B **98**
Brookfield Vw. BD19: Cleck 6C **134**
BROOKFOOT **6H 151**
Brookfoot Av. BD11: B'frd 2E **135**
Brookfoot Bus. Pk. HD6: Brigh 6H **151**
Brookfoot Ind. Est. HD6: Brigh 1H **161**
Brookfoot La. HD6: Brigh 6H **151**
   HX3: Brigh 6F **151**
Brookfoot Old La. HD6: Brigh 6H **151**
Brook Grain Hill HD6: Brigh 3A **162**
BROOK HILL **4D 52**
Brook Hill BD17: Bail 4D **52**
Brookhill Av. LS17: Leeds 3C **60**
Brookhill Cl. LS17: Leeds 3C **60**
Brookhill Cres. LS17: Leeds 3C **60**
Brookhill Dr. LS17: Leeds 3C **60**
Brookhill Gro. LS17: Leeds 3C **60**
BROOKHOUSE **5A 106**

Brookhouse Gdns. BD10: B'frd 1D **72**
BROOKLANDS **5B 80**
BROOKLANDS HD2: Hud 6F **163**
   HX3: Hal 2F **151**
   LS17: Bard 6E **27**
Brooklands Av. BD13: B'frd 5B **88**
   LS14: Leeds 5B **80**
   LS29: Men 6H **21**
Brooklands Cl. LS14: Leeds 5A **80**
Brooklands Ct. LS14: Leeds 5B **80**
Brooklands Cres. LS14: Leeds 5A **80**
   LS19: Yead 1F **55**
Brooklands Dr. LS14: Leeds 5A **80**
   LS19: Yead 1F **55**
Brooklands Gth. LS14: Leeds 5B **80**
Brooklands Gro. LS29: Men 6H **21**
Brooklands La. LS14: Leeds 5A **80**
   LS29: Men 6G **21**
Brooklands Towers LS14: Leeds 4C **80**
Brooklands Vw. LS14: Leeds 5B **80**
   (not continuous)
Brooklands Wlk. LS29: Men 6H **21**
Brooklands Way LS29: Men 6G **21**
Brook La. BD4: B'frd 2C **108**
Brooklea HX3: Hal 2G **151**
Brookleigh LS28: Pud 3F **73**
Brooklyn Av. LS12: Leeds 4C **96**
Brooklyn Ct. BD19: Cleck 6B **134**
Brooklyn Dr. BD19: Cleck 6B **134**
Brooklyn Grange BD19: Cleck 6C **134**
Brooklyn Pl. LS12: Leeds 4C **96**
Brooklyn Rd. BD19: Cleck 6B **134**
Brooklyn St. BD20: Keigh 2G **33**
   LS12: Leeds 4C **96**
Brooklyn Ter. HD6: Brigh 4G **151**
   LS12: Leeds 4C **96**
Brook Row BD22: Keigh 6D **46**
Brookroyd Av. HD6: Brigh 3B **152**
Brookroyd La. WF17: Bat 6B **136**
Brooksbank Av. BD7: B'frd 6G **89**
Brooksbank Dr. LS15: Leeds 3C **100**
Brooksbank Gdns. HX5: Ell 5B **160**
Brookside BD13: B'frd 3B **66**
   LS17: Leeds 2C **60**
   LS22: Coll 3B **28**
Brookside Fold BD22: Oxen 1C **84**
Brooks Ter. BD13: B'frd 3D **108**
Brook St. BD12: B'frd 2H **133**
   BD21: Keigh 2H **47**
   HX2: Hal 6E **127**
   (off High St.)
   HX5: Ell 5C **160**
   LS29: I'ly 5D **10**
Brooks Yd. HD2: Hud 5G **163**
Brook Ter. HX2: Hal 5E **127**
Brookwater Cl. HX3: Hal 6H **149**
Brookwoods Ind. Est. HX4: Hal 6G **159**
Broom Cl. HD6: Brigh 4G **161**
   LS10: Leeds 6D **118**
Broom Ct. LS10: Leeds 1D **140**
Broom Cres. LS10: Leeds 6C **118**
Broom Cft. BD14: B'frd 1D **108**
Broom Cross LS10: Leeds 6C **118**
Broome Av. BD2: B'frd 6E **71**
Broomfield BD14: B'frd 2C **108**
   BD19: Cleck 3H **153**
   (off W. End Dr.)
   HX5: Ell 5H **159**
   LS16: Leeds 3B **58**
Broomfield Cres. LS6: Leeds 5D **76**
Broomfield Pl. BD14: B'frd 2C **108**
   BD21: Keigh 6H **33**
   LS6: Leeds 6D **76**
Broomfield St. BD13: B'frd 4A **108**
   BD21: Keigh 6H **33**
   LS6: Leeds 6D **76**
Broomfield Ter. BD19: Cleck 3H **153**
   LS6: Leeds 6D **76**
Broomfield Vw. LS6: Leeds 6D **76**

Broom Gdns. LS10: Leeds 6C **118**
Broom Gth. LS10: Leeds 6D **118**
Broom Gro. LS10: Leeds 1D **140**
Broomhill BD21: Keigh 6D **34**
Broomhill Av. BD21: Keigh 2G **47**
   LS17: Leeds 5B **60**
Broomhill Cres. LS17: Leeds 5B **60**
Broomhill Dr. BD21: Keigh 2G **47**
   LS17: Leeds 6A **60**
Broomhill Gro. BD21: Keigh 2G **47**
Broomhill Mt. BD21: Keigh 2G **47**
Broom Hill Rd. LS9: Leeds 2F **99**
Broomhill St. BD21: Keigh 3G **47**
Broomhill Wlk. BD21: Keigh 2G **47**
Broomhill Way BD21: Keigh 2G **47**
Broom Lawn LS10: Leeds 6C **118**
Broom Mt. LS10: Leeds 1D **140**
Broom Nook LS10: Leeds 6D **118**
Broom Pl. LS10: Leeds 6D **118**
Broom St. BD4: B'frd 5F **91** (6E **7**)
   BD19: Cleck 3H **153**
Broom Ter. BD22: Keigh 4D **46**
   LS10: Leeds 6D **118**
Broom Vw. LS10: Leeds 6D **118**
Broom Wlk. LS10: Leeds 1D **140**
Broster Av. BD22: Keigh 6F **33**
Brougham Rd. HX3: Hal 6G **129**
Brougham St. HX3: Hal 6G **129**
Brougham Ter. HX3: Hal 5G **129**
Broughton Av. BD4: B'frd 4H **111**
   LS9: Leeds 1E **99**
Broughton Ho. BD4: B'frd 4D **112**
Broughton Ter. LS9: Leeds 1E **99**
   LS28: Pud 3A **94**
Brow, The BD17: Bail 4C **52**
   (off Bank Wlk.)
BROW BOTTOM **2G 127**
Brow Bottom La. HX2: Hal 1G **127**
Browcliff BD20: Sils 1E **15**
Brow Cotts. HD6: Hal 4F **151**
Browfield Ter. BD20: Sils 1E **15**
Browfield Vw. BD22: Keigh 2E **47**
Browfoot Dr. HX2: Hal 3B **148**
Brow Foot Ga. HX2: Hal 3B **148**
   (off Brow Foot Ga. La.)
Brow Foot Ga. La. HX2: Hal 3B **148**
Browgate BD17: Bail 4C **52**
Brow La. BD14: B'frd 2A **108**
   HX3: Hal 1E **129**
   (Holmfield Ind. Est. Rd.)
   HX3: Hal 3A **130**
   (Whiskers La.)
   HX3: Hal 1F **131**
   (Witchfield Hill)
Brow Mills Ind. Est. HX3: Hal 3F **151**
Brown Av. LS11: Leeds 1E **117**
Brown Bank Cvn. Pk. BD20: Sils 5A **8**
Brown Bank La. BD20: Sils 1F **15**
Brownberrie Av. LS18: H'fth 4E **57**
Brownberrie Cres. LS18: H'fth 4D **56**
Brownberrie Dr. LS18: H'fth 4E **57**
   (not continuous)
Brownberrie Gdns. LS18: H'fth 4D **56**
Brownberrie La. LS18: H'fth 4B **56**
Brownberrie Wlk. LS18: H'fth 4E **57**
Brownberry Gro. HX3: Hal 6F **109**
BROWN HILL **6B 136**
Brown Hill Av. LS9: Leeds 1E **99**
Brown Hill Cl. BD11: B'frd 6E **113**
Brownhill Cl. WF17: Bat 6B **136**
Brown Hill Cres. LS9: Leeds 1E **99**
Brown Hill Dr. BD11: B'frd 1E **135**
BROWNHILL END **6B 136**
Brownhill Gth. WF17: Bat 6B **136**
Brownhill Rd. WF17: Bat 6B **136**
Brown Hill Ter. LS9: Leeds 1E **99**
Brown Ho's. HX2: Hal 5H **127**
Browning Av. HX3: Hal 6H **149**
Browning St. BD3: B'frd 4H **91** (4H **7**)
Brown La. E. LS11: Leeds 6E **97**
Brown La. W. LS12: Leeds 6E **97**
Brownlea Cl. LS19: Yead 2D **54**

Brown Lee La.—Burns Hill

Brown Lee La. BD15: B'frd 5E **67**
Brown Pl. LS11: Leeds 1E **117**
Brown Rd. LS11: Leeds 1E **117**
BROWN ROYD 4B **90**
Brownroyd Fold BD5: B'frd 3B **110**
BROWNROYD HILL 3C **110**
Brownroyd Hill Rd. BD6: B'frd 4B **110**
Brownroyd St. BD7: B'frd 5B **90**
BD8: B'frd 3B **90**
Brownroyd Wlk. BD6: B'frd 3B **110**
Brown Springs BD22: Keigh 3E **47**
Brown St. BD21: Keigh 5B **34**
Brow Rd. BD22: Haw 3D **64**
Browsfield Rd. LS29: Add 1B **8**
Browsholme St. BD21: Keigh 1A **48**
Brow St. BD21: Keigh 1B **48**
Brow Top BD14: B'frd 3C **108**
Brow Top Rd. BD22: Haw 3D **64**
Brow Wood Cres. BD2: B'frd 6E **71**
Brow Wood Ri. HX3: Hal 1F **131**
Brow Wood Rd. HX3: Hal 1F **131**
WF17: Bat 6D **136**
Brow Wood Ter. BD6: B'frd 6H **109**
Bruce Gdns. LS12: Leeds 4E **97**
Bruce Lawn LS12: Leeds 4E **97**
Bruce St. HX1: Hal 3D **148**
Brudenell Av. LS6: Leeds 6F **77**
Brudenell Gro. LS6: Leeds 6F **77**
Brudenell Mt. LS6: Leeds 6E **77**
Brudenell Rd. LS6: Leeds 6E **77**
Brudenell St. LS6: Leeds 6F **77**
Brudenell Vw. LS6: Leeds 6F **77**
Brumfitt Hill LS29: Add 1D **8**
Brunel Cl. BD9: B'frd 1A **90**
Brunel Ct. BD3: B'frd 1G **91**
*HX3: Hal 5F **129***
(off See Mill La.)
Brunel Gdns. *BD5: B'frd 2C **110***
(off Ida St.)
Brunel Rd. WF2: Wake 4D **156**
Brunswick Arc. *BD21: Keigh 6A **34***
(off Airedale Shop. Cen.)
Brunswick Ct. LS2: Leeds 2B **98** (2G **5**)
Brunswick Gdns.
HX1: Hal 2F **149** (4A **164**)
LS25: Gar 4F **103**
Brunswick Ho. BD16: Bgly 5D **50**
Brunswick Ind. Est.
HX1: Hal 3F **149** (6A **164**)
Brunswick Pl. BD10: B'frd 2B **72**
LS27: Morl 3B **138**
Brunswick Rd. BD10: B'frd 2B **72**
LS28: Pud 3A **94**
Brunswick Row LS2: Leeds 2B **98** (2G **5**)
Brunswick St. BD13: B'frd 4B **108**
(Sand Beds)
BD13: B'frd 3C **66**
(Victoria St.)
BD16: Bgly 4D **50**
LS27: Morl 2A **138**
Brunswick Ter. BD12: B'frd 6C **110**
LS2: Leeds 2A **98** (2E **5**)
(not continuous)
LS27: Morl 3C **138**
BRUNTCLIFFE 3F **137**
Bruntcliffe Av. LS27: Morl 3G **137**
Bruntcliffe Cl. LS27: Morl 3H **137**
Bruntcliffe Dr. LS27: Morl 3H **137**
Bruntcliffe La. LS27: Morl 3G **137**
Bruntcliffe Rd. LS27: Morl 3F **137**
Bruntcliffe Way LS27: Morl 3G **137**
BRUNTHWAITE 2G **15**
Brunthwaite Bri. La. BD20: Sils 4F **15**
Brunthwaite Cotts. BD20: Sils 2G **15**
Brunthwaite La. BD20: Sils 2G **15**
Brunthwaite Ter. BD20: Sils 2G **15**
Brussels Ct. HX1: Hal 5C **164**
Brussels St. LS9: Leeds 4B **98** (5H **5**)
Bruton Gallery 3H **97** (4C **4**)
Bryan Rd. HX5: Ell 5H **159**
Bryanstone Rd. BD4: B'frd 6B **92**
Bryan St. LS28: Pud 5H **73**
Bryan St. Nth. LS28: Pud 5H **73**
Bryant St. HD6: Brigh 2A **162**
Bryngate LS26: Rothw 1E **143**
Bryony Ct. LS10: Leeds 2D **140**
Bubwith Gro. *HX2: Hal 3C **148***
(off Trimmingham Rd.)
Buchan Towers BD5: B'frd 6C **6**
Buckden Ct. BD20: Sils 1E **15**
Buckfast Ct. BD10: B'frd 2H **71**
Buckingham Av. LS6: Leeds 5E **77**
Buckingham Cres. BD14: B'frd 6F **89**
Buckingham Dr. LS6: Leeds 5E **77**
Buckingham Gro. LS6: Leeds 5E **77**
Buckingham Ho. *LS6: Leeds 5E **77***
(off Headingley La.)
Buckingham Mt. LS6: Leeds 6E **77**
Buckingham Rd. LS6: Leeds 6E **77**
Buckland Pl. HX1: Hal 3C **148**
Buckland Rd. BD8: B'frd 3H **89**
Buck La. BD17: Bail 4F **53**
Buckle La. LS29: Men 2H **39**
Buckley Av. LS11: Leeds 2H **117**
Buckley La. HX2: Hal 5A **128**
(not continuous)
Buck Mill La. BD10: B'frd 5G **53**
Buck Stone Av. LS17: Leeds 3F **59**
Buck Stone Cl. LS17: Leeds 3G **59**
Buck Stone Cres. LS17: Leeds 3G **59**
Buck Stone Dr. LS17: Leeds 3F **59**
Buckstone Dr. LS19: Yead 4E **55**
(not continuous)
Buck Stone Gdns. LS17: Leeds 3G **59**
Buckstone Gth. BD20: Keigh 4H **35**
Buck Stone Grn. LS17: Leeds 3F **59**
Buck Stone Gro. LS17: Leeds 3F **59**
Buck Stone Mt. LS17: Leeds 3F **59**
Buck Stone Oval LS17: Leeds 3F **59**
Buck Stone Ri. LS17: Leeds 3F **59**
Buck Stone Rd. LS17: Leeds 3F **59**
Buck Stone Vw. LS17: Leeds 3F **59**
Buck Stone Way LS17: Leeds 3F **59**
Buck St. BD3: B'frd 5G **91** (6G **7**)
BD13: B'frd 3C **86**
Buckthorne Cl. WF3: E Ard 1B **156**
Buckthorne Ct. WF3: E Ard 1B **156**
Buckthorne Dr. WF3: E Ard 1B **156**
Buckthorne Fold WF3: E Ard 1B **156**
Buckton Cl. LS11: Leeds 1G **117**
Buckton Mt. LS11: Leeds 1G **117**
Buckton Vw. LS11: Leeds 1G **117**
Bude Rd. BD5: B'frd 4F **111**
LS11: Leeds 2H **117**
Bula Cl. LS25: Kip 3H **123**
Bull Cl. La. HX1: Hal 3F **149** (5A **164**)
Buller Cl. LS9: Leeds 2G **99**
Buller Ct. LS9: Leeds 2G **99**
Buller Gro. LS9: Leeds 2F **99**
Buller St. BD4: B'frd 6A **92**
LS26: Rothw 1E **143**
Bullerthorpe La. LS15: Leeds 5H **101**
LS26: Swil 5G **121**
Bullfield, The BD16: Bgly 1F **67**
Bull Grn. HX1: Hal 2G **149** (4B **164**)
Bull Hill BD22: Oxen 2C **84**
Bullough La. LS26: Rothw 6B **120**
Bullroyd Av. BD8: B'frd 3G **89**
Bullroyd Cres. BD8: B'frd 3G **89**
Bullroyd Dr. BD8: B'frd 3G **89**
Bull Royd Ind. Est. BD8: B'frd 3G **89**
Bullroyd La. BD8: B'frd 3G **89**
Bundria Ct. BD8: B'frd 1C **90**
Bungalow, The BD5: B'frd 1E **111**
Bungalows, The HX2: Hal 6B **128**
HX3: Hal 1A **160**
(Backhold Av.)
HX3: Hal 5D **128**
(Ovenden Grn.)
HX6: Hal 5G **147**
*LS15: Leeds 6F **81***
(off Church La.)
LS25: Leds 3B **124**
LS25: M'fld 5E **105**
Bunkers Hill BD17: B'frd 2H **53**
Bunker's Hill La. BD22: Keigh 2D **46**
Bunney Grn. HX3: Hal 3B **130**
Bunting Dr. BD13: B'frd 3D **108**
Burberry Cl. BD4: B'frd 5A **112**
Burchett Gro. LS6: Leeds 5G **77**
Burchett Pl. LS6: Leeds 5G **77**
Burchett Ter. LS6: Leeds 5H **77**
Burdale Pl. BD7: B'frd 5B **90**
Burdett Ter. LS4: Leeds 1C **96**
Burdock Way HX1: Hal 3F **149** (5A **164**)
Burghley M. LS10: Leeds 4B **140**
Burland Ter. LS26: Swil 3A **122**
Burleigh St. HX1: Hal 4D **148**
BURLEY 1D **96**
Burley Ct. BD20: Stee 6C **14**
Burley Grange Rd. LS4: Leeds 1C **96**
Burley Hill Cres. LS4: Leeds 6B **76**
Burley Hill Dr. LS4: Leeds 6B **76**
Burley Hill Trad. Est. LS4: Leeds 6C **76**
BURLEY IN WHARFEDALE 2F **21**
Burley in Wharfedale Station (Rail)
3E **21**
Burley La. LS18: H'fth 1D **74**
LS29: Men 1F **39**
Burley Lodge Pl. *LS6: Leeds 2E **97***
(off Burley Lodge Rd.)
Burley Lodge Rd. LS6: Leeds 1E **97**
Burley Lodge St. LS6: Leeds 2E **97**
Burley Lodge Ter. LS6: Leeds 1E **97**
Burley M. BD20: Stee 6C **14**
Burley Park Station (Rail) 6D **76**
Burley Pl. LS4: Leeds 2D **96**
Burley Rd. LS3: Leeds 1E **97**
LS4: Leeds 6C **76**
LS29: Men 5G **21**
Burley St. BD2: B'frd 5D **70**
HX5: Ell 5B **160**
LS3: Leeds 3F **97** (3A **4**)
Burley Wood Cres. LS4: Leeds 6B **76**
BURLEY WOODHEAD 5C **20**
Burley Wood La. LS4: Leeds 6C **76**
Burley Wood Mt. LS4: Leeds 6B **76**
Burley Wood Vw. LS4: Leeds 6C **76**
Burlington Av. BD3: B'frd 2C **92**
Burlington Pl. LS11: Leeds 3H **117**
Burlington Rd. LS11: Leeds 3H **117**
Burlington St. BD8: B'frd 2D **90**
HX1: Hal 2D **148**
Burmah St. HX1: Hal 2D **148**
BURMANTOFTS 2D **98**
Burmantofts St. LS9: Leeds 3C **98**
Burned Gro. HX3: Hal 6E **109**
Burned Rd. HX3: Hal 6E **109**
Burneston Gdns. BD6: B'frd 5G **109**
Burnett Av. BD5: B'frd 2D **110**
Burnett Pl. BD5: B'frd 2D **110**
Burnett Ri. BD13: B'frd 5G **107**
Burnett St. BD1: B'frd 4F **91** (4F **7**)
Burnham Av. BD4: B'frd 3H **111**
Burnham Ct. LS22: Weth 3C **12**
Burnham Rd. LS25: Gar 6F **103**
Burnholme BD13: B'frd 3B **86**
Burniston Cl. BD15: B'frd 5G **67**
Burnley Hill HX3: Hal 3C **130**
Burnley Hill Ter. HX3: Hal 3D **130**
Burnley Rd. HX2: Hal 3D **146**
HX6: Hal 4E **147**
HX7: Heb B 6A **126**
Burnleys Ct. LS26: Mick 6D **144**
Burnleys Dr. LS26: Mick 6D **144**
Burnleys Vw. LS26: Mick 6D **144**
Burnleyville BD19: Cleck 6F **135**
Burnsall Ct. LS12: Leeds 3B **96**
Burnsall Cft. LS12: Leeds 3B **96**
Burnsall Gdns. LS12: Leeds 3B **96**
Burnsall Grange *LS12: Leeds 4B **96***
(off Gelder Rd.)
Burnsall Ho. *BD10: B'frd 3A **72***
(off Rowantree Dr.)
Burnsall M. BD20: Sils 1D **14**
Burnsall Rd. BD3: B'frd 4H **91**
(not continuous)
HD6: Brigh 3G **161**
Burns Ct. WF17: Bat 5H **135**
Burnsdale BD15: B'frd 6C **68**
Burnshaw M. LS10: Leeds 4A **140**
Burns Hill LS29: Add 1C **8**

Burnside LS29: Add ...1D 8
Burnside Av. HX3: Hal ...6F 109
Burnside Cl. WF17: Bat ...6C 136
Burns HX3: Hal ...3D 128
Burns Way LS23: B Spa ...5B 30
BURNWELLS ...5G 53
Burnwells BD10: B'frd ...5G 53
Burnwells Av. BD10: B'frd ...5G 53
Burrage St. BD16: Bgly ...4B 50
Burras Av. LS21: Otley ...4D 22
Burras Dr. LS21: Otley ...4D 22
Burras La. LS21: Otley ...4D 22
Burras Rd. BD4: B'frd ...3H 111
Burrell Cl. LS27: Weth ...4G 13
Burrow St. BD5: B'frd ...5E 91 (6C 6)
Burr Tree Dr. LS15: Leeds ...4F 101
Burr Tree Gth. LS15: Leeds ...4F 101
Burr Tree Va. LS15: Leeds ...4F 101
Burrwood Ter. HX4: Hal ...6F 159
Burrwood Way HX4: Hal ...6F 159
Burton Av. LS11: Leeds ...2A 118
Burton Cres. LS6: Leeds ...3D 76
Burton Ho. LS17: Leeds ...3D 60
Burton M. LS17: Leeds ...2B 60
Burton Rd. LS11: Leeds ...2A 118
Burton Row LS11: Leeds ...1A 118
Burton's Arc. LS1: Leeds ...4A 98 (5E 5)
Burton St. BD4: B'frd ...1G 111
  BD20: Keigh ...3H 33
  HX2: Hal ...2E 129
  LS11: Leeds ...1A 118
  LS28: Pud ...6H 73
Burton Ter. LS11: Leeds ...2A 118
Burton Way LS9: Leeds ...2E 99
Bury La. BD20: Keigh ...4G 35
Busely Ct. LS27: Morl ...2H 137
Busfield St. BD4: B'frd ...2H 111
  BD16: Bgly ...4B 50
Bush Hill Fold BD13: B'frd ...3G 107
Business & Innovation Cen.
  BD7: B'frd ...4A 6
BUSLINGTHORPE ...5A 78
Buslingthorpe Grn. LS7: Leeds ...6A 78
Buslingthorpe La. LS7: Leeds ...5A 78
Buslingthorpe Va. LS7: Leeds ...5A 78
Bussey Ct. LS6: Leeds ...6G 77
Busy La. BD18: Ship ...6E 53
Butcher Hill LS5: Leeds ...1G 75
  LS16: Leeds ...1G 75
Butcher La. LS26: Rothw ...2A 142
Butchers Row LS2: Leeds ...4F 5
Butcher St. BD7: B'frd ...5D 90 (4A 6)
Bute Av. HD6: Brigh ...4A 152
Bute St. BD2: B'frd ...5D 70
Butler La. BD17: Bail ...4D 52
  (not continuous)
Butler's Fold BD16: Bgly ...6B 36
Butler St. E. BD3: B'frd ...3G 91 (2H 7)
Butler St. W. BD3: B'frd ...3G 91 (2G 7)
  (not continuous)
Butterbowl Dr. LS12: Leeds ...6G 95
Butterbowl Gdns. LS12: Leeds ...6H 95
Butterbowl Gth. LS12: Leeds ...6G 95
Butterbowl Gro. LS12: Leeds ...6G 95
Butterbowl Lawn LS12: Leeds ...6G 95
Butterbowl Mt. LS12: Leeds ...6H 95
Butterbowl Rd. LS12: Leeds ...6H 95
Buttercup Way BD11: B'frd ...2D 136
Butterfield Homes BD16: Bgly ...3D 68
  (off Cottingley Moor Rd.)
Butterfield Ind. Est. BD17: Bail ...5E 53
Butterfield's Bldgs. LS27: Morl ...2H 137
Butterfield St. LS9: Leeds ...4D 98
Butterley St. LS10: Leeds ...6A 98
Buttermead Cl. BD6: B'frd ...6A 110
Buttermere Av. LS22: Weth ...3C 12
Buttermere Rd. BD2: B'frd ...6G 71
BUTTERSHAW ...5G 109
Buttershaw Dr. BD6: B'frd ...5G 109
Buttershaw La. BD6: B'frd ...6B 110
  WF15: Liv ...4H 153
Butterwick Gdns. LS22: Weth ...4C 12
Butt Hill LS25: Kip ...4G 123

Buttholme Ga. BD6: B'frd ...5H 109
Butt La. BD10: B'frd ...1H 71
  BD22: Haw ...2C 64
  LS12: Leeds ...5F 95
  LS13: Leeds ...4G 95
Button Hill LS7: Leeds ...5B 78
Buttress HX2: Hal ...6E 127
Buttress La. HX2: Hal ...6E 127
Butt Row LS12: Leeds ...5G 95
Butts, The BD20: Keigh ...5H 35
  (off Morton La.)
Butts Ct. LS1: Leeds ...3A 98 (4E 5)
Butts Gth. LS14: T'ner ...2H 63
Butts Gth. Ct. LS14: T'ner ...2H 63
Butts Gth. Vw. LS14: T'ner ...2H 63
Butts Gth. Wlk. LS14: T'ner ...2H 63
Butts Grn. La. HX2: Hal ...2F 147
Butts Grn. Rd. HX2: Hal ...2E 147
Butts Hill BD19: Cleck ...6F 135
Butts La. LS20: Guis ...4C 40
Butts Mt. LS12: Leeds ...4D 96
Butts Ter. LS20: Guis ...4C 40
Buxton Av. BD9: B'frd ...5C 70
Buxton La. BD9: B'frd ...5C 70
Buxton St. BD9: B'frd ...1B 90
  BD21: Keigh ...6B 34
  HX3: Hal ...6E 129
Byeway LS20: Guis ...4A 40
Byland HX2: Hal ...6C 106
Byland Cl. LS23: B Spa ...4A 30
Byland Gro. BD15: B'frd ...1B 88
Bylands Av. BD20: Keigh ...3C 34
Byrl St. BD21: Keigh ...5B 34
Byron Av. HX6: Hal ...4H 147
Byron Ho. LS29: I'ly ...5F 11
Byron M. BD16: Bgly ...2C 50
Byron St. BD3: B'frd ...3H 91
  HX1: Hal ...2D 148
  HX6: Hal ...4H 147
  LS2: Leeds ...2B 98 (2G 5)
Byron Ter. HX6: Hal ...4H 147
  (off Byron St.)
Bywater Row BD11: B'frd ...2F 135

C

CABBAGE HILL ...5A 96
Cabbage Hill LS12: Leeds ...5B 96
Cabin Rd. LS21: Pool ...6D 24
CACKLESHAW ...5E 47
Cad Beeston LS11: Leeds ...2G 117
Cad Beeston M. LS11: Leeds ...2G 117
CADDY FIELD ...3H 149
Cadman Cl. LS27: Morl ...4A 138
Cadney Cft. HX1: Hal ...5B 164
Caernarvon Av. LS26: Gar ...4H 103
Caernarvon Cl. WF17: Bat ...6C 136
Cain Cl. LS9: Leeds ...4D 98
  (not continuous)
Cain La. HX3: Hal ...5C 150
Cairn Av. LS20: Guis ...3A 40
Cairn Cl. BD20: Keigh ...3G 33
Cairn Gth. LS20: Guis ...3A 40
Cairns Cl. BD2: B'frd ...6F 71
Cairn Vw. LS29: I'ly ...4F 11
  (off Hauxley Ct.)
Caister Cl. WF17: Bat ...5C 136
Caister Gro. BD21: Keigh ...3H 47
  (off Caister Way)
Caister St. BD21: Keigh ...3H 47
Caister Way BD21: Keigh ...3H 47
Caistor Gth. BD10: B'frd ...3A 72
  (off Rowantree Dr.)
Calde Ct. BD12: B'frd ...1E 133
Caldene Av. BD12: B'frd ...1E 133
Calder Av. HX2: Hal ...4D 148
CALDER BANKS ...4C 108
Calder Banks BD13: B'frd ...4C 108
Calder Cl. HX4: Hal ...4H 159
  (off Calder St.)
  LS22: Weth ...1D 12

Caldercroft HX5: Ell ...5C 160
Calderdale Bus. Pk. HX2: Hal ...4D 128
Calderdale Rd. HX5: Ell ...4A 160
Calderdale Way HX4: Ell ...4A 160
Calder Ho. HX5: Ell ...4B 160
  (off Southgate)
Calderstone Av. BD6: B'frd ...5F 109
Calder St. HD6: Brigh ...2C 162
  HX4: Hal ...4H 159
  WF10: C'frd ...6H 145
Calder Ter. HX3: Hal ...2E 159
Calder Trad. Est. HD6: Brigh ...3B 152
  WF14: Hud ...5G 163
Calder Vw. HD6: Brigh ...2H 161
Calder Vw. Ct. HX3: Hal ...1C 130
Calder Way BD20: Sils ...3E 15
Caledonia Rd. BD21: Keigh ...5B 34
Caledonia St. BD5: B'frd ...6E 91
Calgary Cres. WF3: E Ard ...2F 155
Calgary Pl. LS7: Leeds ...3B 78
California M. LS27: Morl ...1B 138
California St. LS27: Morl ...3B 138
Call La. LS1: Leeds ...4A 98 (6F 5)
Calls, The LS1: Leeds ...4A 98 (5F 5)
Calpin Cl. BD10: B'frd ...1H 71
Calton Gro. BD21: Keigh ...1D 48
Calton Rd. BD21: Keigh ...1D 48
Calton St. BD21: Keigh ...2H 47
  (not continuous)
Calver Av. BD21: Keigh ...5F 33
Calver Gro. BD21: Keigh ...6G 33
CALVERLEY ...2E 73
Calverley Av. BD3: B'frd ...3B 92
  LS13: Leeds ...6D 74
CALVERLEY BRIDGE ...3A 74
Calverley Ct. LS13: Leeds ...6D 74
  LS26: Rothw ...2D 142
Calverley Cutting LS28: Pud ...1D 72
Calverley Dr. LS13: Leeds ...6D 74
Calverley Gdns. LS13: Leeds ...5C 74
Calverley Gth. LS13: Leeds ...6D 74
Calverley Gro. LS13: Leeds ...6D 74
Calverley La. LS13: Leeds ...5B 74
  LS18: H'fth ...2A 74
  LS28: Pud ...3G 73
  (not continuous)
Calverley Moor Av. LS28: Pud ...2E 93
Calverley Rd. LS26: Rothw ...2E 143
Calverley St. LS1: Leeds ...2H 97 (2C 4)
Calverley Ter. LS13: Leeds ...6D 74
Calver Rd. BD21: Keigh ...6G 33
Calversyke St. BD21: Keigh ...6G 33
Calvert Cl. LS25: Kip ...2G 123
Camargue Fold BD2: B'frd ...5F 71
Camberley Cl. LS28: Pud ...5A 94
Camberley Mt. BD4: B'frd ...1C 112
Camberley St. LS11: Leeds ...2A 118
Camberley Way LS28: Pud ...5A 94
Camborne Way BD22: Keigh ...2E 47
Cambrian Bar BD12: B'frd ...1B 132
Cambrian St. LS11: Leeds ...1G 117
Cambrian Ter. LS11: Leeds ...1G 117
CAMBRIDGE ...4F 23
Cambridge Chase BD19: Cleck ...5F 135
Cambridge Cl. LS27: Morl ...2B 138
Cambridge Ct. LS27: Morl ...3B 138
Cambridge Dr. LS13: Leeds ...6D 74
  LS21: Otley ...4F 23
Cambridge Gdns. LS13: Leeds ...6D 74
Cambridge Gro. LS21: Otley ...4F 23
  LS25: Kip ...4G 123
Cambridge Pl. BD3: B'frd ...3F 91 (1F 7)
  BD13: B'frd ...4A 108
  HX3: Hal ...6A 150
Cambridge Rd. LS7: Leeds ...6H 77
  WF17: Bat ...6H 135
Cambridge St. BD7: B'frd ...1B 110
  BD13: B'frd ...4B 108
  BD14: B'frd ...1D 108
  LS20: Guis ...4C 40
  LS21: Otley ...4E 23
Cambridge Ter. HX3: Hal ...6A 150
  (off Cambridge Pl.)
  LS21: Otley ...4E 23

Cambridge Way LS21: Otley 4F 23
Camden St. HX6: Hal 6H 147
Camden Ter. BD8: B'frd 2D 90
Camellia Ct. BD18: Ship 4D 70
Camellia Mt. BD7: B'frd 5G 89
Cameron Av. BD12: B'frd 6B 132
Cameronian Ct. BD21: Keigh 6A 34
Camerton Grn. BD5: B'frd 3F 111
Camm La. HD6: Brigh 5D 152
Camm St. HD6: Brigh 6B 152
Camomile St. BD13: B'frd 5F 87
Campbell St. BD13: B'frd 4B 108
   BD21: Keigh 6A 34
   LS28: Pud 1H 93
CAMP FIELD 5H 97
Camp Rd. LS16: B'hpe 4F 43
Camp Sq. LS14: T'ner 2H 63
CAMP TOWN 3H 59
Campus Rd. BD7: B'frd 5C 90 (4A 6)
Camwood Ct. BD20: Keigh 4F 35
Canada Cres. LS19: Yead 3G 55
Canada Dr. LS19: Yead 2G 55
Canada Rd. LS19: Yead 2G 55
Canada Ter. LS19: Yead 3G 55
Canalbank Vw. LS13: Leeds 4B 74
Canal Ct. WF3: Wake 3H 157
Canal La. BD20: Sils 4G 15
   WF3: Wake 3G 157
Canal Pl. LS12: Leeds 4F 97
Canal Rd. BD2: B'frd 4C 70 (1D 6)
   BD16: Bgly 1A 50
   BD20: Keigh 4C 34
   HX6: Hal 5C 148
   LS12: Leeds 3C 96
   LS13: Leeds 4A 74
Canal St. HD6: Brigh 1B 162
   HX3: Hal 3H 149
   LS12: Leeds 4E 97
Canal Vw. HX6: Hal 5G 147
Canal Wharf LS5: Leeds 6H 75
   LS11: Leeds 4H 97 (6C 4)
Canary Dr. BD16: Bgly 3E 51
Canary St. BD19: Cleck 6B 134
Canberra Ct. BD22: Haw 1F 65
Canberra Dr. BD22: Haw 1F 65
Candleworks Yd.
   LS21: Otley 4E 23
Canford Dr. BD15: B'frd 2D 88
Canford Gro. BD15: B'frd 2E 89
Canford Rd. BD15: B'frd 2D 88
Canker La. HX3: Hal 4E 129
Canning St. BD4: B'frd 6G 91
Cannon Hall Cl. HD6: Brigh 6D 152
Cannon Hall Dr. HD6: Brigh 1D 162
Cannon Mill La. BD7: B'frd 1A 110
Cannons Health Club
   Cottingley New Rd. 2D 68
   Otley Rd. 4A 40
Cannon St. BD16: Bgly 5C 50
Cannon Wlk. LS2: Leeds 1G 97
Canonbury Ter. LS11: Leeds 2E 117
Canon St. HX1: Hal 4D 148
Canter, The LS10: Leeds 4B 140
Canterbury Av. BD5: B'frd 2C 110
Canterbury Cres. HX3: Hal 6F 129
Canterbury Dr. LS6: Leeds 5C 76
Canterbury Ho. HX6: Hal 5A 148
Canterbury Rd. LS6: Leeds 5C 76
Canwick Cl. BD20: Keigh 4F 35
Cape Ind. Est. LS28: Pud 6A 74
Capel Ct. LS28: Pud 3F 73
Capel St. HD6: Brigh 2A 162
   LS28: Pud 3F 73
Cape of Good Hope BD13: B'frd . . .5G 107
Cape St. BD1: B'frd 3E 91 (1D 6)
Capitol Blvd. LS27: Morl 6C 138
Capitol Cl. LS27: Morl 5C 138
Capitol Pde. LS6: Leeds 2F 77
Captain St. BD1: B'frd 4F 91 (2E 7)
Caraway Ct. LS6: Leeds 6F 59
Caraway Dr. LS6: Leeds 6F 59
Caraway M. LS6: Leeds 6F 59
Carberry Pl. LS6: Leeds 1E 97
Carberry Rd. LS6: Leeds 1E 97

Carberry Ter. LS6: Leeds 1E 97
   (off Carberry Pl.)
Cardan Dr. LS29: I'ly 5G 11
Carden Av. LS15: Leeds 4A 100
Carden Rd. BD4: B'frd 6C 92
Cardigan Av. LS27: Morl 5A 138
Cardigan Ct. LS6: Leeds 5E 77
Cardigan Flds. Rd. LS4: Leeds 2C 96
Cardigan La. LS4: Leeds 1D 96
   (not continuous)
   LS6: Leeds 6E 77
Cardigan Rd. LS6: Leeds 5D 76
Cardigan St. BD3: B'frd 4B 108
Cardigan Ter. WF3: E Ard 1C 156
Cardigan Trad. Est. LS4: Leeds 2D 96
Cardinal Av. LS11: Leeds 5F 117
Cardinal Ct. LS11: Leeds 4E 117
Cardinal Cres. LS11: Leeds 5F 117
Cardinal Gdns. LS11: Leeds 5E 117
Cardinal Gro. LS11: Leeds 5E 117
Cardinal Rd. LS11: Leeds 5E 117
Cardinal Sq. LS11: Leeds 4F 117
Cardinal Wlk. LS11: Leeds 4E 117
Carisbrooke Cres. BD6: B'frd 5B 110
Carisbrooke La. LS25: Gar 3H 103
Carisbrooke Rd. LS16: Leeds 2B 76
Cark Rd. BD21: Keigh 5A 34
Carlby Gro. BD21: Keigh 1G 47
   (off Carlby St.)
Carlby St. BD22: Keigh 1G 47
Carlecotes Ho. BD4: B'frd 1C 112
   (off Ned La.)
Carleton Cl. LS23: B Spa 3H 29
Carleton Dr. LS23: B Spa 4H 29
Carleton St. BD20: Keigh 4H 33
Carling Cl. BD7: B'frd 2H 109
Carlisle Av. LS19: Yead 1G 55
Carlisle Dr. LS28: Pud 5H 93
Carlisle Gro. LS28: Pud 5H 93
Carlisle Pl. BD8: B'frd 2C 90
Carlisle Rd. BD8: B'frd 2B 90
   LS10: Leeds 5B 98
   LS28: Pud 5H 93
Carlisle St. BD8: B'frd 2C 90
   BD21: Keigh 6B 34
   HX2: Hal 1C 148
   LS28: Pud 2G 93
Carlisle Ter. BD8: B'frd 2C 90
Carlrayne La. LS29: Men 6G 21
CARLTON 4H 141
Carlton App. LS22: Weth 3C 12
Carlton Av. BD18: Ship 1G 69
   LS28: Pud 4A 94
Carlton Carr LS7: Leeds 1A 98 (1E 5)
Carlton Cl. LS7: Leeds 1A 98
   (off Carlton Hill)
Carlton Ct. LS12: Leeds 1E 117
Carlton Cft. LS7: Leeds 1A 98
   (off Carlton Hill)
Carlton Dr. BD9: B'frd 5B 70
   BD17: Bail 3C 52
   BD18: Ship 4A 70
   LS20: Guis 3D 40
   LS25: Gar 6F 103
Carlton Gdns. LS7: Leeds 1A 98
Carlton Gth. LS7: Leeds 1A 98
   LS17: Leeds 2E 61
Carlton Ga. LS7: Leeds 1A 98 (1E 5)
Carlton Grange LS19: Yead 6G 41
Carlton Gro. BD5: B'frd 2D 110
   BD18: Ship 4B 70
   HX5: Ell 4D 160
   LS7: Leeds 1A 98
Carlton Hill LS7: Leeds 1A 98 (1E 5)
Carlton Ho. LS20: Guis 3D 40
Carlton La. LS20: Guis 3D 40
   LS26: Rothw 3H 141
   WF3: Rothw 6G 141
Carlton M. LS20: Guis 4D 40
Carlton Mill HX6: Hal 5A 148
   (off Old Cawsey)
Carlton Moor M. LS10: Leeds 2D 140
Carlton Mt. LS19: Yead 5G 41
Carlton Pde. LS7: Leeds 1A 98 (1F 5)

Carlton Pl. HX1: Hal 3G 149 (5B 164)
   LS7: Leeds 1A 98
Carlton Ri. LS7: Leeds 1A 98
   LS28: Pud 4A 94
Carlton Rd. BD18: Ship 1G 69
Carlton Row LS12: Leeds 4A 96
Carlton St. BD7: B'frd 5D 90 (5A 6)
   BD22: Haw 2D 64
   HX1: Hal 3G 149 (5B 164)
   LS21: Otley 4F 23
Carlton Ter. HX1: Hal 3G 149 (5B 164)
   LS19: Yead 6G 41
   LS28: Pud 3A 94
Carlton Towers
   LS7: Leeds 1A 98 (1F 5)
Carlton Trad. Est.
   LS12: Leeds 3D 96
Carlton Vw. LS7: Leeds 1A 98
   WF10: Kip 1F 145
Carlton Wlk. BD18: Ship 1H 69
   LS7: Leeds 1A 98
Carmel Rd. HX3: Hal 5G 129
Carmona Av. BD18: Ship 4B 70
Carmona Gdns. BD18: Ship 4B 70
Carnaby Rd. BD7: B'frd 3G 109
Carnation St. BD3: B'frd 5A 92
Carnegie Ct. LS29: I'ly 5E 11
Carnegie Dr. BD18: Ship 2C 70
Carnoustie Gro. BD16: Bgly 2D 68
Caroline St. BD18: Ship 1H 69
Carperley Cres. BD13: B'frd 3C 86
Carr Bank BD20: Keigh 4G 35
Carr Bank Bottom LS21: Otley 1D 22
Carr Bottom Av. BD5: B'frd 3B 110
Carrbottom Fold BD5: B'frd 4C 110
Carr Bottom Gro. BD5: B'frd 3B 110
   BD10: B'frd 2C 72
Carr Bottom Rd. BD5: B'frd 3B 110
   BD10: B'frd 2C 72
Carr Bri. Av. LS16: Leeds 4F 57
Carr Bri. Cl. LS16: Leeds 4F 57
Carr Bri. Dr. LS16: Leeds 4F 57
Carr Bri. Vw. LS16: Leeds 4F 57
Carr Cl. LS19: Yead 4H 55
CARR CROFTS 4B 96
Carr Crofts LS12: Leeds 4B 96
Carr Crofts Dr. LS12: Leeds 4B 96
Carr Croft's Ter. LS12: Leeds 4B 96
Carr Fld. Dr. HX2: Hal 1E 147
Carr Hall Rd. BD12: B'frd 4C 132
Carrfield Dr. LS15: Bar E 2D 82
Carrfield La. LS15: Bar E 2C 82
Carrfield Rd. LS15: Bar E 2D 82
CARR GATE 4C 156
Carr Ga. Cres. WF2: Wake 4B 156
Carr Ga. Dr. WF2: Wake 4B 156
Carr Ga. Mt. WF2: Wake 4B 156
Carr Grn. Av. HD6: Brigh 5H 161
Carr Grn. Cl. HD6: Brigh 5H 161
Carr Grn. Dr. HD6: Brigh 5H 161
Carr Grn. La. HD6: Brigh 4H 161
Carr Gro. BD20: Keigh 4E 35
Carr Hall Rd. BD12: B'frd 4C 132
Carr Hill Av. LS28: Pud 3E 73
Carr Hill Dr. LS28: Pud 3E 73
Carr Hill Gro. LS28: Pud 3E 73
Carr Hill Nook LS28: Pud 3E 73
Carr Hill Ri. LS28: Pud 3E 73
Carr Hill Rd. LS28: Pud 3E 73
Carrholm Cres. LS7: Leeds 2H 77
Carrholm Dr. LS7: Leeds 2H 77
Carrholm Grn. BD6: B'frd 1B 132
Carrholm Gro. LS7: Leeds 2H 77
Carrholm Mt. LS7: Leeds 2H 77
Carrholm Rd. LS7: Leeds 2H 77
Carrholm Vw. LS7: Leeds 2H 77
Carr Ho. HX2: Hal 4E 127
CARR HOUSE GATE 3C 132
Carr Ho. Ga. BD12: B'frd 3C 132
Carr Ho. Gro. BD12: B'frd 3C 132
Carr Ho. La. BD12: B'frd 2B 132
   (not continuous)
   HX3: Hal 6F 109
Carr Ho. Mt. BD12: B'frd 3C 132
Carr Ho. Rd. HX3: Hal 1F 131
Carriage Dr. BD19: Cleck 5F 135

Carriage Dr., The HX4: Hal 3G 159
  LS8: Leeds 6G 61
       (not continuous)
Carricks Cl. BD12: B'frd 1E 133
Carrier St. HX1: Hal 2G 149 (4C 164)
Carrington St. BD3: B'frd 4A 92
       (not continuous)
Carrington Ter. LS20: Guis 5B 40
Carr La. BD12: B'frd 3D 132
  BD13: B'frd 1C 86
  BD16: Bgly 5A 36
  BD18: Ship 1C 70
  BD20: Keigh 4G 35
       (Carr Bank)
  BD20: Keigh 4E 35
       (Carr Gro.)
  LS14: Leeds 3C 62
  LS19: Yead 4H 55
  LS22: Weth 2G 13
  WF3: Rothw 4A 142
Carr Mnr. Av. LS17: Leeds 1H 77
Carr Mnr. Cres. LS17: Leeds 6H 59
Carr Mnr. Cft. LS17: Leeds 2H 77
Carr Mnr. Dr. LS17: Leeds 1H 77
Carr Mnr. Gdns. LS17: Leeds 1H 77
Carr Mnr. Gth. LS17: Leeds 6H 59
Carr Mnr. Gro. LS17: Leeds 1H 77
Carr Mnr. Mt. LS17: Leeds 1H 77
Carr Mnr. Pde. LS17: Leeds 1H 77
Carr Mnr. Pl. LS17: Leeds 1H 77
Carr Mnr. Rd. LS17: Leeds 2H 77
Carr Mnr. Vw. LS17: Leeds 6H 59
Carr Mnr. Wlk. LS17: Leeds 2H 77
Carr Moor Side LS11: Leeds 2A 118
Carr Moor St. LS10: Leeds 3B 118
Carroll St. BD3: B'frd 5G 91 (5G 7)
Carr Rd. BD12: B'frd 4C 132
  LS28: Pud 2D 72
Carr Row BD12: B'frd 4C 132
Carr St. BD5: B'frd 3D 110
  BD21: Keigh 6A 34
  HD6: Brigh 5A 152
  WF17: Bat 6A 136
Carr Ter. HX2: Hal 1D 146
Carr Vw. HX2: Hal 1D 146
Carr Wood Cl. LS28: Pud 3E 73
Carr Wood Gdns. LS28: Pud 3E 73
Carr Wood Way LS28: Pud 2E 73
Carter Av. LS15: Leeds 3E 101
Carter La. BD13: B'frd 2H 107
  LS15: Leeds 2E 101
Carter Mt. LS15: Leeds 3E 101
Carter's La. LS29: I'ly 2E 11
Carter St. BD4: B'frd 5F 91 (6F 7)
Carter Ter. LS15: Leeds 2E 101
Cart Ga. BD6: B'frd 4D 110
Cartmell Ct. LS15: Leeds 4H 99
Cartmell Dr. LS15: Leeds 4H 99
Cartmel Rd. BD21: Keigh 5G 33
Carton Cft. BD5: B'frd 2E 111
       (off New Cross St.)
Cartwright Hall Art Gallery & Mus.
   . . . . .6C 70
Caryl Rd. BD4: B'frd 2G 111
Cashmere St. BD21: Keigh 6G 33
Caspar Apartments
  LS2: Leeds 2A 98 (2F 5)
Casson Av. WF3: E Ard 6H 139
Casson Dr. WF3: E Ard 6H 139
Casson Fold HX3: Hal 5C 130
Casson Gro. WF3: E Ard 6H 139
Castle Av. HD6: Brigh 3H 161
Castle Carr Rd. HX2: Wads, Hal . . .1C 126
Castle Cl. LS17: Bard 2F 45
  WF17: Bat 6C 136
Castle Cft. BD16: Bgly 6E 49
CASTLEFIELDS 2H 49
Castlefields LS26: Rothw 2F 141
Castlefields Cres. HD6: Brigh 3H 161
Castlefields Dr. HD6: Brigh 3H 161
Castlefields Ind. Est.
  BD16: Bgly 2H 49
Castlefields La. BD16: Bgly 2H 49
  HD6: Brigh 3H 161

Castlefields Rd. BD16: Bgly 1H 49
  HD6: Brigh 3H 161
Castle Ga. LS22: Weth 4E 13
  LS29: I'ly 5D 10
Castlegate Dr. BD10: B'frd 3A 72
Castlegate Ho. HX5: Ell 4B 160
       (off Crown St.)
Castle Grange LS19: Yead 1H 55
Castle Gro. BD16: Bgly 6E 49
Castle Gro. Av. LS6: Leeds 2D 76
Castle Gro. Dr. LS6: Leeds 3D 76
Castle Head Cl. WF3: Rothw 1G 157
Castle Head La. WF3: E Ard 1D 156
  WF3: Wake 2D 156
Castle Hill BD22: Keigh 1G 47
  HD6: Brigh 3H 161
  LS29: I'ly 5D 10
Castle Hill Vw. LS17: Bard 2E 45
Castle Ings Cl. LS12: Leeds 2F 115
Castle Ings Dr. LS12: Leeds 2F 115
Castle Ings Gdns.
  LS12: Leeds 2F 115
Castle M. BD18: Ship 2B 70
Castlemore Rd. BD17: Bail 5D 52
Castle Pl. HD6: Brigh 3A 162
Castlerigg Grn. BD6: B'frd 1H 131
Castle Rd. BD18: Ship 2B 70
  BD21: Keigh 5H 33
  LS26: Rothw 2H 141
  LS29: I'ly 5D 10
       (not continuous)
Castle St. BD5: B'frd 6G 91
  LS1: Leeds 3G 97 (4B 4)
Castle Ter. HD6: Brigh 3H 161
       (off Castle Av.)
Castleton Cl. LS12: Leeds 4F 97
Castleton Rd. LS12: Leeds 3E 97
Castle Vw. LS17: Leeds 6H 59
Castle Wood Cl. LS18: H'fth 1F 75
Castle Yd. LS29: I'ly 5D 10
Castley La. LS21: Leat 2B 38
Cater St. BD1: B'frd 4F 91 (4F 7)
Cathcart St. HX3: Hal 6F 129
Cathedral Cl. BD1: B'frd 4F 91 (3E 7)
Catherine Cres. HX5: Ell 5B 160
Catherine Gro. LS11: Leeds 2H 117
Catherine Ho. La. HX2: Hal 1A 126
CATHERINE SLACK 1F 129
Catherine Slack HD6: Brigh 3H 151
Catherine St. BD21: Keigh 2H 47
       (not continuous)
  HD6: Brigh 5A 152
  HX5: Ell 5B 160
Cat La. HX2: Hal 8A 146
  HX4: Hal 4C 158
  HX7: Hal 4A 146
       (not continuous)
Catstones Wood BD18: Ship 2E 71
Cattle Mkt. St. LS21: Otley 3E 23
Cauldwell Gdns. BD5: B'frd 1E 111
Causeway HX1: Hal 2H 149 (4D 164)
CAUSEWAY FOOT 3C 106
Causeway Foot HX2: Hal 2B 106
Cautley Rd. LS9: Leeds 5D 98
Cavalier App. LS9: Leeds 5D 98
Cavalier Cl. LS9: Leeds 5D 98
Cavalier Ct. LS9: Leeds 5D 98
Cavalier Dr. BD10: B'frd 1C 72
Cavalier Gdns. LS9: Leeds 5D 98
Cavalier Ga. LS9: Leeds 5D 98
Cavalier Grn. LS9: Leeds 5D 98
CAVALIER HILL 4C 98
Cavalier M. LS9: Leeds 5D 98
Cavalier Vw. LS9: Leeds 5D 98
Cave Hill HX3: Hal 3B 130
Cave La. WF3: E Ard 1A 156
Cavendish App. BD11: B'frd 1A 136
Cavendish Ct. BD10: B'frd 4A 72
       (off Cavendish Rd.)
  BD11: B'frd 1A 136
       (off Cavendish App.)

Cavendish Ct. Shop. Cen.
  BD21: Keigh 6A 34
Cavendish Dr. BD16: Bgly 3D 50
  LS20: Guis 5B 40
Cavendish Gro. LS20: Guis 5B 40
Cavendish M. BD11: B'frd 1A 136
  LS17: Leeds 3B 60
Cavendish Pl. LS28: Pud 2H 93
Cavendish Ri. LS28: Pud 4C 94
Cavendish Rd. BD2: B'frd 4A 72
  BD10: B'frd 4A 72
       (Park Rd.)
  BD10: B'frd 2H 71
       (Thorp Gth.)
  LS2: Leeds 1H 97 (1C 4)
  LS20: Guis 5B 40
Cavendish Sq. LS28: Pud 2A 94
Cavendish St. BD21: Keigh 6A 34
  HX1: Hal 2E 149
  LS3: Leeds 3F 97 (3A 4)
  LS19: Yead 6G 41
  LS28: Pud 4C 94
Cavendish Ter. HX1: Hal 2E 149
       (not continuous)
Cawcliffe Dr. HD6: Brigh 4A 152
Cawcliffe Rd. HD6: Brigh 5A 152
Cawood Haven BD6: B'frd 5G 109
Caxton Rd. LS21: Otley 5C 22
Caxton St. LS22: Weth 4E 13
Caygill Ter. HX1: Hal 4G 149 (6C 164)
Caythorpe Rd. LS16: Leeds 2B 76
Caythorpe Wlk. BD10: B'frd 4A 72
Cecil Av. BD7: B'frd 1B 110
  BD17: Bail 3C 52
  HX3: Hal 1G 151
Cecil Gro. LS12: Leeds 3C 96
Cecil Mt. LS12: Leeds 3C 96
Cecil Rd. LS12: Leeds 3C 96
Cecil St. BD22: Haw 1F 65
  LS12: Leeds 3C 96
Cedar Av. LS12: Leeds 4B 96
Cedar Cl. LS17: Leeds 5B 60
       (off Harrogate Rd.)
  LS26: Rothw 6G 121
Cedar Covert LS22: Weth 1E 13
Cedar Dr. BD12: B'frd 3E 133
  HD6: Brigh 3B 152
  HX4: Hal 4F 159
Cedar Mt. LS12: Leeds 4B 96
Cedar Pl. LS12: Leeds 4B 96
Cedar Ridge LS25: Gar 2H 103
Cedar Rd. LS12: Leeds 4B 96
Cedars, The LS16: B'hpe 3H 43
Cedar St. BD16: Bgly 2A 50
  BD21: Keigh 3H 47
  HX1: Hal 3D 148
  LS12: Leeds 4B 96
Cedar Ter. LS12: Leeds 4B 96
Cedar Way BD19: Cleck 6E 135
Cemetery La. BD20: Keigh 3H 33
  HX6: Hal 5G 147
  WF3: Rothw 6G 141
Cemetery Rd. BD6: B'frd 6B 110
  BD7: B'frd 3H 89
  BD8: B'frd 3H 89
  BD12: B'frd 6B 110
  BD16: Bgly 3A 50
  BD22: Haw 3A 64
  LS11: Leeds 1G 117
  LS19: Yead 6G 41
  LS28: Pud 5C 94
Centaur Ho. LS1: Leeds 3G 97 (3B 4)
Centenary Rd. BD17: Bail 3F 53
Centenary Sq. BD1: B'frd 5E 91 (5D 6)
  LS2: Leeds 3B 98 (4H 5)
Central Av. BD5: B'frd 1C 110
  BD17: Bail 5B 52
  BD18: Ship 2B 70
  BD22: Keigh 4F 47
  WF15: Liv 4H 153
Central Bldgs. HX6: Hal 5H 147
       (off Town Hall St.)

Central Dr. BD22: Keigh 4F 47
Central Pk. HX1: Hal 4F 149 (6A 164)
  LS11: Leeds 5H 97
Central Pl. BD14: B'frd 1D 108
  (off Clayton La.)
Central Rd. LS1: Leeds 4A 98 (5F 5)
Central St. HX1: Hal 2G 149 (4B 164)
  LS1: Leeds 3H 97 (4C 4)
Centre 27 Bus. Pk. WF17: Bat 4D 136
Centre St. BD5: B'frd 2C 110
Centurion Way BD19: Cleck 5A 134
Century Pl. BD8: B'frd 2C 90
Century Rd. HX5: Ell 4B 160
Century St. BD21: Keigh 3A 48
  (off Percy St.)
Century Way LS15: Leeds 4H 101
Ceres Rd. LS22: Weth 4G 13
Chaddle Wood Cl. LS18: H'fth 6E 57
Chadwell Spring BD16: Bgly 2C 68
Chadwick St. LS10: Leeds ...5B 98 (6G 5)
  (not continuous)
Chadwick St. Sth. LS10: Leeds 5B 98
Chaffinch Rd. BD8: B'frd 4E 89
Chain Bar Rd. BD19: Cleck 6A 134
Chain St. BD1: B'frd 4D 90 (3B 6)
Chalfont Rd. LS16: Leeds 1B 76
Chalice Cl. LS10: Leeds 6C 118
Challenge Way BD4: B'frd 1B 112
  WF17: Dew 5A 154
Challis Gro. BD5: B'frd 2E 111
Chalner Av. LS27: Morl 5H 137
Chalner Cl. LS27: Morl 5H 137
Chancellor Ct. LS2: Leeds ...4A 98 (5F 5)
Chancellor St. LS6: Leeds 6H 77
Chancery Ter. HX3: Hal 1G 159
Chandler Cl. WF17: Bat 6A 136
Chandlers, The LS2: Leeds 6G 5
Chandlers Cl. WF1: Wake 4F 157
Chandlers Wharf LS13: Leeds 3A 74
Chandos Av. LS8: Leeds 1C 78
Chandos Fold LS8: Leeds 2C 78
Chandos Gdns. LS8: Leeds 1C 78
Chandos Gth. LS8: Leeds 1C 78
Chandos Grn. LS8: Leeds 1C 78
Chandos Pl. LS8: Leeds 1D 78
Chandos Ri. BD4: B'frd 5F 91 (6E 7)
  BD21: Keigh 2H 47
  (not continuous)
Chandos Ter. LS8: Leeds 1D 78
Chandos Wlk. LS8: Leeds 1C 78
Change All. LS1: Leeds 4E 5
Changegate BD22: Haw 2B 64
Changegate BD22: Haw 2B 64
Change La. HX3: Hal 1A 160
Channing Way BD1: B'frd ...5E 91 (5D 6)
  (not continuous)
Chantrell Ct. LS2: Leeds 4B 98 (5G 5)
Chantry Cl. LS29: I'ly 6D 10
Chantry Cl. LS27: Morl 2B 138
Chantry Cft. LS15: Leeds 4F 101
Chantry Dr. LS29: I'ly 5D 10
Chantry Gth. LS15: Leeds 4F 101
CHAPEL ALLERTON 3H 77
Chapel Allerton Lawn Tennis &
  Squash Club 2A 78
Chapel Cl. HX3: Hal 1F 131
  HX4: Hal 6F 159
  LS25: Gar 4E 103
Chapel Ct. BD13: B'frd 3D 108
  (off Chapel La.)
  BD15: B'frd 3G 67
  HD6: Brigh 1B 162
  (off Park St.)
  LS15: Leeds 3C 100
  LS25: M'fld 4E 105
Chapel Cft. BD22: Keigh 6C 32
  HD6: Brigh 4H 161
Chapel Fold BD6: B'frd 4B 110
  BD12: Brigh 1C 152
  HX3: Hal 1F 131
  LS6: Leeds 6D 76
  LS11: Leeds 3E 117
  LS12: Leeds 4C 96
  (off Wesley Rd.)

Chapel Fold LS15: Leeds 3C 100
  LS28: Pud 5A 94
  (off Littlemoor Rd.)
CHAPEL GREEN 2D 110
Chapel Grn. LS28: Pud 5H 93
Chapel Gro. BD16: Bgly 2A 50
CHAPEL HILL 1A 26
Chapel Hill LS10: Leeds 2B 140
  LS19: Yead 6F 41
  LS22: Kirkby 1A 26
  LS27: Morl 2A 138
Chapel Hill Rd. LS21: Pool 5F 25
  (off Burnside)
Chapel La. BD13: B'frd 4H 107
  (Foxhill Grn.)
  BD13: B'frd 3D 108
  (Stocks La.)
  BD15: B'frd 3E 89
  BD16: Bgly 4B 50
  BD17: B'frd 2A 54
  BD21: Keigh 6H 33
  BD22: Keigh 6C 32
  (Chapel Cft.)
  BD22: Keigh 6C 46
  (Dockroyd La.)
  HX2: Hal 5B 126
  HX3: Hal 5C 150
  (Edward Cl., not continuous)
  HX3: Hal 6H 149
  (Falcon St.)
  HX6: Hal 5B 148
  LS6: Leeds 5D 76
  (not continuous)
  LS12: Leeds 6F 95
  (Maple Dr.)
  LS12: Leeds 4C 96
  (Stocks Hill)
  LS15: Bar E 2E 83
  LS19: Yead 6F 41
  LS23: B Spa 5B 30
  LS25: Gar 4E 103
  LS25: Kip 4H 123
  LS29: I'ly 5C 10
  WF17: Bat 6A 136
Chapel M. LS23: B Spa 5B 30
Chapel Pl. LS6: Leeds 4D 76
Chapel Rd. BD12: B'frd 1D 132
  (not continuous)
  BD16: Bgly 2A 50
  BD20: Stee 6C 14
  LS7: Leeds 4B 78
Chapel Row BD15: B'frd 3G 67
  LS21: Pool 4E 25
  (off Main St.)
Chapel Sq. LS6: Leeds 4D 76
  (off Chapel St.)
Chapel St. BD1: B'frd 4F 91 (4F 7)
  BD2: B'frd 5B 72
  BD5: B'frd 1D 110
  BD6: B'frd 4C 110
  BD13: B'frd 4A 108
  (Albert Edward St.)
  BD13: B'frd 5H 87
  (Bk. John St.)
  BD13: B'frd 3B 86
  (Main Rd.)
  BD16: Bgly 2A 50
  BD20: Sils 1E 15
  HD6: Brigh 4G 151
  HX2: Hal 1C 148
  HX3: Hal 4H 131
  HX4: Hal 6F 159
  LS6: Leeds 4D 76
  LS13: Leeds 4A 74
  LS15: Leeds 3C 100
  LS19: Yead 3F 41
  LS28: Pud 2A 94
  (Richardshaw La.)
  LS28: Pud 2F 73
  (Thornhill La.)
  LS29: Add 1D 8

Chapel St. WF3: E Ard 6F 139
  (Fenton St.)
  WF3: E Ard 2A 156
  (Thorpe Rd.)
  WF3: Rothw 4H 141
Chapel St. Nth. HX3: Hal 4D 128
Chapel Ter. BD13: B'frd 5H 87
  BD15: B'frd 2D 88
  HX4: Hal 4A 158
  HX6: Hal 6D 146
  LS6: Leeds 4D 76
  (off Chapel St.)
CHAPELTOWN 2B 78
Chapeltown HX1: Hal 2G 149 (3A 164)
  LS28: Pud 5H 93
Chapeltown Bus. Cen. LS7: Leeds ..5B 78
  (off Chapeltown Rd.)
Chapeltown Rd. LS7: Leeds 6B 78
Chapel Wlk. BD2: B'frd 5B 72
Chapel Yd. LS15: Leeds 5F 101
  (off Meynell Rd.)
  LS26: Rothw 2E 143
Chapman St. BD4: B'frd 5B 92
Charles Av. BD3: B'frd 4B 92
  HX3: Hal 5C 150
  LS9: Leeds 5D 98
  WF1: Wake 4F 157
Charles Ct. BD22: Oxen 1C 84
  (off Station Rd.)
Charles Gdns. LS11: Leeds 6G 97
Charles Gro. LS26: Rothw 1E 143
Charles St. BD1: B'frd 4E 91 (4D 6)
  (not continuous)
  BD13: B'frd 4H 107
  BD16: Bgly 4B 50
  BD17: Ship 1B 70
  BD19: Cleck 6F 135
  HD6: Brigh 6A 152
  HX1: Hal 2H 149 (4D 164)
  HX5: Ell 5B 160
  HX6: Hal 5H 147
  LS18: H'fth 1D 74
  LS21: Otley 4E 23
  LS27: Morl 3B 138
  LS28: Pud 6H 73
CHARLESTOWN 5E 53
Charlestown Rd.
  HX3: Hal 1H 149 (2D 164)
Charlesworth Gro. HX2: Hal 1C 148
Charlesworth Ter. HX2: Hal 1C 148
Charlotte Cl. WF17: Bat 4B 136
  BD22: Haw 1D 64
Charlotte Gro. LS15: Leeds 3D 100
Charlton Cl. BD2: B'frd 5H 71
Charlton Ct. HX2: Hal 1C 148
  (off Reservoir Rd.)
Charlton Gro. BD20: Sils 3F 15
  LS9: Leeds 4E 99
Charlton Pl. LS9: Leeds 4E 99
Charlton Rd. LS9: Leeds 4E 99
Charlton St. LS9: Leeds 4E 99
Charnley Dr. LS7: Leeds 3C 78
Charnwood Cl. BD2: B'frd 1A 92
Charnwood Gro. BD2: B'frd 1A 92
Charnwood Rd. BD2: B'frd 1A 92
Chart Cl. LS25: Gar 4E 103
Charterhouse Rd. BD10: B'frd 6H 53
Charteris Rd. BD8: B'frd 4E 89
Chartist's Ct. LS27: Morl 4A 138
  (off Gt. Northern St.)
Chartists Way LS27: Morl 4A 138
Chartwell Ct. LS17: Leeds 2F 61
Chartwell Dr. BD6: B'frd 4G 109
Charville Gdns. LS17: Leeds 4B 62
Chase, The BD20: Keigh 5F 33
  LS19: Yead 3E 55
  LS22: Weth 3F 13
  LS25: Gar 4H 103
  LS29: Burl W 4F 21
Chase Av. LS27: Morl 6B 138
Chase Cl. LS27: Morl 6B 138
Chase Way BD5: B'frd 3E 111
Chassum Gro. BD9: B'frd 1A 90

Chatham St.—Church Hill Mt.

Chatham St. BD3: B'frd . . . 2F 91
HX1: Hal . . . 2F 149 (3A 164)
HX6: Hal . . . 4H 147
Chat Hill Rd. BD13: B'frd . . . 6B 88
Chatswood Av. LS11: Leeds . . . 5F 117
Chatswood Cres. LS11: Leeds . . . 5F 117
Chatswood Dr. LS11: Leeds . . . 4F 117
Chatsworth Av. LS28: Pud . . . 3E 93
Chatsworth Cl. LS8: Leeds . . . 6E 79
Chatsworth Ct. *BD8: B'frd . . . 3A 90*
(off Girlington Rd.)
Chatsworth Cres. LS28: Pud . . . 3E 93
Chatsworth Dr. LS22: Weth . . . 3C 12
LS28: Pud . . . 3E 93
Chatsworth Fall LS28: Pud . . . 3E 93
Chatsworth M. LS27: Morl . . . 4C 138
Chatsworth Pl. BD8: B'frd . . . 1B 90
Chatsworth Ri. LS28: Pud . . . 3E 93
Chatsworth Rd. LS8: Leeds . . . 6E 79
LS28: Pud . . . 3E 93
Chatsworth St. BD21: Keigh . . . 6B 34
Chatts Wood Fold BD12: B'frd . . . 2H 133
Chaucer Av. LS28: Pud . . . 5B 94
Chaucer Gdns. LS28: Pud . . . 5B 94
Chaucer Gro. LS28: Pud . . . 5B 94
Chaucer St. HX1: Hal . . . 3D 148
Cheapside BD1: B'frd . . . 4E 91 (3D 6)
HX1: Hal . . . 2G 149 (4C 164)
HX3: Hal . . . 1E 131
LS27: Morl . . . 2A 138
(off Chapel Hill)
Cheddington Gro. BD15: B'frd . . . 3D 88
Chellowfield Ct. BD9: B'frd . . . 6E 69
Chellow Gdns. *BD15: B'frd . . . 1C 88*
(off Deanwood Cres.)
Chellow Grange Rd. BD9: B'frd . . . 6E 69
Chellow La. BD9: B'frd . . . 1E 89
Chellow St. BD5: B'frd . . . 3D 110
Chellow Ter. BD9: B'frd . . . 2F 89
BD11: B'frd . . . 3F 135
Chelmsford Rd. BD3: B'frd . . . 3A 92
(not continuous)
Chelmsford Ter. BD3: B'frd . . . 4A 92
Chelsea Cl. LS12: Leeds . . . 5C 96
Chelsea Mans. HX3: Hal . . . 5C 130
Chelsea Rd. BD7: B'frd . . . 1H 109
Chelsea St. BD21: Keigh . . . 1H 47
Chelsea Vw. *HX3: Hal . . . 6C 130*
(off Bradford Rd.)
Chelsfield Ct. LS15: Leeds . . . 6H 81
Chelsfield Way LS15: Leeds . . . 6H 81
Cheltenham Av. LS29: I'ly . . . 5H 11
Cheltenham Ct. HX3: Hal . . . 5H 149
Cheltenham Gdns. HX3: Hal . . . 5H 149
Cheltenham Pl. HX3: Hal . . . 5H 149
Cheltenham Rd. BD2: B'frd . . . 4F 71
Cheltenham St. LS12: Leeds . . . 5D 96
Chelwood Av. LS8: Leeds . . . 4D 60
Chelwood Cres. LS8: Leeds . . . 5D 60
Chelwood Dr. BD15: B'frd . . . 4C 88
LS8: Leeds . . . 4D 60
Chelwood Gro. LS8: Leeds . . . 4D 60
Chelwood Mt. LS8: Leeds . . . 4D 60
Chelwood Pl. LS8: Leeds . . . 4C 60
Chenies Cl. LS14: Leeds . . . 2A 100
Chepstow Cl. LS25: Gar . . . 4H 103
Chepstow Dr. LS10: Leeds . . . 4B 140
Cheriton Dr. BD13: B'frd . . . 4B 108
Cherry Ct. *HX1: Hal . . . 1E 149*
(off Crossley Gdns.)
LS6: Leeds . . . 3F 77
LS9: Leeds . . . 2C 98
(off Cherry Pl.)
Cherry Flds. BD2: B'frd . . . 5E 71
Cherry Gro. LS6: Leeds . . . 4F 77
LS29: I'ly . . . 5B 10
Cherry Lea Ct. LS19: Yead . . . 2F 55
Cherry Pl. LS9: Leeds . . . 2C 98
Cherry Ri. LS14: Leeds . . . 1E 81
Cherry Row LS9: Leeds . . . 2C 98 (2H 5)
Cherry St. BD21: Keigh . . . 5C 34
BD22: Haw . . . 1E 65
Cherry Tree Av. BD10: B'frd . . . 2B 72
Cherry Tree Ct. WF3: E Ard . . . 2A 156
Cherry Tree Cres. LS28: Pud . . . 6H 73
Cherry Tree Dr. HX4: Hal . . . 4F 159
LS28: Pud . . . 6H 73
Cherry Tree Gdns. BD10: B'frd . . . 6F 53
Cherry Tree Ri. BD21: Keigh . . . 2B 48
Cherry Tree Row BD16: B'frd . . . 2F 67
Cherry Tree Wlk. LS2: Leeds . . . 5F 5
WF3: E Ard . . . 2A 156
Cherrywood Cl. LS14: Leeds . . . 6D 62
Cherrywood Gdns. LS14: Leeds . . . 6D 62
Chervana Ct. BD4: B'frd . . . 1C 112
Cherwell Cft. LS25: Gar . . . 6H 103
Cherwell Dr. BD6: B'frd . . . 6H 109
Chesham St. BD21: Keigh . . . 6B 34
Chesney Av. LS10: Leeds . . . 1B 118
Chesney Pk. Ind. Est.
LS10: Leeds . . . 1B 118
Chester Cl. HX3: Hal . . . 6F 129
Chester Ct. HX3: Hal . . . 6F 129
Chester Gro. HX3: Hal . . . 6F 129
Chester Pl. HX3: Hal . . . 6F 129
Chester Rd. HX3: Hal . . . 6F 129
Chester St. BD5: B'frd . . . 5E 91 (5B 6)
BD7: B'frd . . . 5D 90 (6C 6)
HX3: Hal . . . 6F 129
HX6: Hal . . . 5H 147
LS12: Leeds . . . 3C 96
Chester Ter. HX3: Hal . . . 6F 129
Chesterton Ct. LS15: Leeds . . . 5F 101
Chestnut Av. LS6: Leeds . . . 6E 77
LS15: Leeds . . . 1F 101
LS22: Weth . . . 3D 12
LS23: B Spa . . . 3A 30
Chestnut Cl. BD22: Keigh . . . 1F 47
HX4: Hal . . . 4F 159
LS7: Leeds . . . 4C 78
(off Harehills La.)
LS29: I'ly . . . 6G 11
Chestnut Ct. BD18: Ship . . . 2H 69
Chestnut Dr. LS16: Leeds . . . 2B 58
Chestnut End LS23: B Spa . . . 4C 30
Chestnut Gdns. LS12: Leeds . . . 5C 96
LS27: Morl . . . 6A 116
Chestnut Gro. BD2: B'frd . . . 5E 71
LS6: Leeds . . . 6E 77
LS23: B Spa . . . 3A 30
LS26: Rothw . . . 1G 143
LS28: Pud . . . 3F 73
Chestnut Pl. LS6: Leeds . . . 6E 77
Chestnut Ri. LS12: Leeds . . . 5B 96
Chestnut St. HX1: Hal . . . 3D 148
LS6: Leeds . . . 6E 77
Chestnut Vw. LS27: Morl . . . 6A 116
Chestnut Way LS16: Leeds . . . 2B 58
Chevet Mt. BD15: B'frd . . . 4C 88
Chevin Av. LS21: Otley . . . 5F 23
LS29: Men . . . 6H 21
(Bradford Rd.)
LS29: Men . . . 6G 21
(Bridgland Av.)
Chevin Ct. *LS21: Otley . . . 3E 23*
(off Courthouse St.)
Chevinedge Cres. HX3: Hal . . . 2H 159
Chevin End LS29: Guis, Men . . . 2H 39
Chevin End Rd. LS29: Guis . . . 2B 40
Chevington Ct. LS19: Yead . . . 4E 55
Chevins Cl. WF17: Bat . . . 6B 136
Chevin Side LS21: Otley . . . 5E 23
Chevin Ter. LS21: Otley . . . 5E 23
Chevin Vw. *LS21: Pool . . . 4E 25*
(off Main St.)
Cheviot Ct. LS25: Gar . . . 6F 103
Cheviot Ga. BD12: B'frd . . . 1B 132
Cheyne Wlk. BD22: Keigh . . . 1G 47
Chichester St. LS12: Leeds . . . 3C 96
CHIDSWELL . . . 6A 154
Chidswell Gdns. WF12: Dew . . . 6B 154
Chidswell La. WF12: Dew . . . 6B 154
Childs La. BD18: Ship . . . 3E 71
Chiltern Cl. LS25: Gar . . . 6F 103
Chiltern Ct. LS13: Leeds . . . 4A 74
LS25: Gar . . . 6F 103
Chilver Dr. BD4: B'frd . . . 3E 113
Chippendale Ct. LS29: Men . . . 1H 39
Chippendale Ri. BD8: B'frd . . . 3F 89
LS21: Otley . . . 2E 23
Chippendale Swimming Pool . . . 2E 23
Chirton Gro. LS8: Leeds . . . 4E 79
Chislehurst Pl. BD5: B'frd . . . 2C 110
Chiswick St. LS6: Leeds . . . 1E 97
Chiswick Ter. *LS6: Leeds . . . 1E 97*
(off Chiswick Vw.)
Chorley La. LS2: Leeds . . . 2G 97 (2B 4)
LS3: Leeds . . . 3G 97 (3B 4)
Chrisharben Pk. BD14: B'frd . . . 1E 109
Chrismoor BD10: B'frd . . . 2G 71
Christ Chu. Av. LS12: Leeds . . . 3B 96
Christ Chu. Mt. LS12: Leeds . . . 3B 96
Christ Chu. Pde. LS12: Leeds . . . 3B 96
Christ Chu. Pl. LS12: Leeds . . . 3B 96
Christ Chu. Rd. LS12: Leeds . . . 3B 96
Christ Chu. Ter. LS12: Leeds . . . 3B 96
Christ Chu. Vw. LS12: Leeds . . . 3B 96
Christiana Ter. LS27: Morl . . . 2B 138
Christopher Cl. BD20: Sils . . . 2E 15
Christopher Rd. LS6: Leeds . . . 6H 77
Christopher St. BD5: B'frd . . . 2C 110
Christopher Ter. BD5: B'frd . . . 2C 110
Church App. LS25: Gar . . . 4F 103
Church Av. LS6: Leeds . . . 2F 77
LS18: H'fth . . . 6D 56
LS26: Swil . . . 3A 122
LS27: Morl . . . 5E 115
Church Bank BD1: B'frd . . . 4F 91 (4E 7)
HX2: Hal . . . 3B 148
HX6: Hal . . . 5A 148
Church C'way. LS23: B Spa . . . 3C 30
Church Cl. BD20: Stee . . . 6C 14
BD22: Keigh . . . 5B 46
(off Commercial St.)
HX2: Hal . . . 2B 128
HX6: Hal . . . 6E 147
LS14: Leeds . . . 5D 80
(not continuous)
LS21: Pool . . . 4E 25
LS25: M'fld . . . 3E 105
LS26: Swil . . . 3A 122
Church Ct. BD7: B'frd . . . 6H 89
BD20: Keigh . . . 3D 34
LS19: Yead . . . 1F 55
Church Cres. LS17: Leeds . . . 4A 60
LS18: H'fth . . . 6D 56
LS19: Yead . . . 1E 55
LS26: Swil . . . 4B 122
Church Cft. LS29: Men . . . 1F 39
Church Dr. LS17: Bard . . . 6D 26
Church Farm LS14: T'ner . . . 1H 63
Church Farm Cl. WF3: Rothw . . . 1G 157
Church Farm Gth.
LS17: Leeds . . . 3B 62
Church Farm Vw. LS15: Bar E . . . 2E 83
Churchfield Cft. LS26: Rothw . . . 2B 142
Churchfield Gro. LS26: Rothw . . . 1A 142
Churchfield La. LS26: Rothw . . . 1A 142
Churchfield Rd. LS26: Rothw . . . 2A 142
Church Flds. BD2: B'frd . . . 1B 92
Churchfields Rd. HD6: Brigh . . . 6A 152
Church Gdns. LS17: Leeds . . . 4B 60
LS25: Gar . . . 4F 103
LS27: Morl . . . 6E 115
CHURCH GARFORTH . . . 5F 103
Church Gth. LS19: Yead . . . 2A 42
LS21: Pool . . . 4E 25
Church Ga. LS18: H'fth . . . 6D 56
Churchgate LS16: B'hpe . . . 2F 43
LS27: Morl . . . 6E 115
Church Grn. *BD8: B'frd . . . 2C 90*
(off Conduit St.)
HX2: Hal . . . 6C 128
Church Gro. LS6: Leeds . . . 2E 77
LS18: H'fth . . . 6D 56
Church Hill BD17: Bail . . . 3D 52
HX2: Hal . . . 6E 127
LS14: T'ner . . . 1H 63
LS16: B'hpe . . . 2F 43
Church Hill Gdns. LS28: Pud . . . 1B 94
Church Hill Grn. LS28: Pud . . . 1B 94
Church Hill Mt. LS28: Pud . . . 1B 94

A-Z Leeds & Bradford 191

Church Ho. *HX5: Ell* *4B 160*
(off Church St.)
HX5: Ell *4B 160*
(off Southgate)
Churchill Flats LS21: Pool 4E 25
Churchill Gdns. *LS2: Leeds* 1H 97
(off Bk. Blenheim Ter.)
Churchill Rd. BD13: B'frd 5B 88
Church La. BD6: B'frd 5B 110
BD17: B'frd 2A 54
BD19: Cleck 6G 135
HD6: Brigh 1A 162
(Churchfields Rd.)
HD6: Brigh 1A 162
(Gooder St.)
HX2: Hal 6C 128
HX3: Hal 5D 150
HX4: Hal 6E 159
(not continuous)
HX5: Brigh 4F 161
LS2: Leeds 4B 98 (5G 5)
LS6: Leeds 2F 77
LS7: Leeds 3B 78
LS15: Leeds 1E 101
LS16: Leeds 3C 58
LS17: Bard 3D 44
LS18: H'fth 6D 56
LS21: Otley 4E 23
LS21: Pool 4E 25
LS21: Weston 1H 21
LS22: Coll 2B 28
LS25: Gar 4F 103
LS25: Kip 4H 123
LS25: M'fld 4C 104
LS26: Mick 5C 144
LS26: Swil 4H 121
LS28: Pud 4A 94
WF1: Wake 4F 157
WF3: E Ard 2A 156
(Cherry Tree Wlk.)
WF3: E Ard 2D 154
(W. Lea Dr.)
WF15: Liv 6H 153
WF17: Bat 6G 135
Church La. Av. WF1: Wake 4F 157
Church Mdws. WF17: Bat 6H 135
Church M. *BD6: B'frd* 6G 109
(off Church St.)
LS5: Leeds 3G 75
LS23: B Spa 3B 30
Church Mt. LS18: H'fth 6D 56
Church Paddocks HD6: Brigh 1E 163
Church Pl. HX1: Hal 2F 149 (4A 164)
LS25: Gar 4F 103
Church Rd. BD6: B'frd 5B 110
LS12: Leeds 4C 96
LS18: H'fth 1D 74
LS26: Kip 5E 123
WF17: Bat 6B 136
Church Row LS2: Leeds 4B 98 (5G 5)
Church Side LS26: Mick 5C 144
Church Side Cl.
HX3: Hal 6G 129 (1C 164)
Church Side Dr.
HX3: Hal 6G 129 (1C 164)
Churchside Vs. LS26: Mick 5C 144
Church Sq. LS25: Gar 4F 103
CHURCH STREET 5C 46
Church St. BD6: B'frd 6G 109
BD8: B'frd 2B 90
BD13: B'frd 3B 66
BD16: Bgly 5C 50
BD18: Ship 1D 70
BD21: Keigh 6B 34
(Bradford Rd.)
BD21: Keigh 1H 47
(Water La.)
BD22: Haw 2B 64
HD6: Brigh 3H 161
(Berry La.)
HX1: Hal 2H 149 (4D 164)
(Lily La.)
HX1: Hal 3H 149 (5D 164)
HX4: Hal 4H 159

Church St. HX5: Ell 4B 160
LS5: Leeds 5A 76
LS10: Leeds 2B 118
LS19: Yead 1E 55
LS20: Guis 4C 40
LS22: Weth 4E 13
LS23: B Spa 4B 30
LS26: Rothw 2A 142
(Ingram Pde.)
LS26: Rothw 6E 121
(Northwood Falls)
LS27: Morl 2A 138
(Bank Sq.)
LS27: Morl 2A 138
(West End)
LS29: Add 1E 9
LS29: I'ly 5C 10
WF17: Bat 6A 136
Church Ter. HX2: Hal 2B 128
HX6: Hal 6E 147
Church Vw. BD19: Cleck 1H 153
HX3: Hal 5H 131
HX6: Hal 5A 148
LS14: T'ner 1H 63
LS16: Leeds 2C 58
LS21: Pool 4F 25
LS25: Leds 3B 124
LS29: Men 1F 39
Church Vw. M. LS23: B Spa 6B 30
Churchville LS25: M'fld 4E 105
Churchville La. LS25: M'fld 4D 104
Churchville Dr. LS25: M'fld 4E 105
Churchville Ter. LS25: M'fld 4E 105
Church Wlk. HX3: Hal 5C 130
LS2: Leeds 4B 98 (5G 5)
LS27: Morl 2A 138
Church Way BD21: Keigh 1A 48
Church Wood Av. LS16: Leeds 3C 76
Church Wood Mt. LS16: Leeds 2C 76
Church Wood Rd. LS16: Leeds 3C 76
Churn La. HX2: Hal 2B 148
Churn Milk La. HX3: Hal 3E 129
CHURWELL 5C 116
Cinderhills La. HX3: Hal 6A 150
Cinder La. LS23: B Spa 5C 30
WF10: C'frd 6H 145
Cineworld 5F 91 (5F 7)
CITY 3B 138
City Ga. LS3: Leeds 3F 97
City La. HX3: Hal 6C 128
City Link Ind. Pk. BD4: Pud 5C 92
City Mills *LS27: Morl* 3B 138
(off Peel St.)
City Mus. 3H 97 (3D 4)
City Pk. Ind. Est. LS12: Leeds 2C 116
City Rd. BD1: B'frd 3C 90
BD8: B'frd 3C 90 (2A 6)
City Sports 4H 91
(in Greystone Mill)
City Sq. LS1: Leeds 4H 97 (5D 4)
City Ter. HX3: Hal 5D 128
City Varieties Music Hall 3A 98 (4E 5)
City Wlk. LS11: Leeds 5H 97
Cityway Ind. Est. BD4: B'frd 6H 91
City West One Office Pk.
LS12: Leeds 2D 116
Claggate LS21: Otley 3E 23
Claggate La. LS10: Leeds 2D 140
Clapham Dene Rd. LS15: Leeds 2D 100
Clapham St. BD13: B'frd 3C 86
Clapton Av. HX1: Hal 3E 149
Clapton Gro. HX1: Hal 3E 149
Clapton Mt. *HX1: Hal* 3E 149
(off King Cross St.)
Clara Dr. LS28: Pud 2D 72
Clara Rd. BD2: B'frd 4F 71
Clara St. HD6: Brigh 2A 162
LS28: Pud 1H 93
Clare Ct. HX1: Hal 6C 164
Clare Cres. BD12: B'frd 5C 132
Clare Hall La. HX1: Hal . . .3G 149 (6C 164)
Claremont BD7: B'frd 5D 90 (6A 6)
BD12: B'frd 5C 132
LS28: Pud 4B 94

Claremont Av. BD18: Ship 3E 71
LS3: Leeds 2G 97 (2A 4)
Claremont Ct. LS6: Leeds 3E 77
Claremont Cres. BD18: Ship 3E 71
LS6: Leeds 4F 77
Claremont Dr. LS6: Leeds 3E 77
Claremont Gdns. BD16: Bgly 3C 50
LS28: Pud 1H 93
Claremont Gro. BD18: Ship 3F 71
LS3: Leeds 2G 97 (2A 4)
LS28: Pud 4A 94
Claremont Pl. LS12: Leeds 4A 96
Claremont Rd. BD18: Ship 3E 71
LS6: Leeds 4F 77
Claremont St. HX5: Ell 5C 160
HX6: Hal 4A 148
LS12: Leeds 4A 96
LS26: Rothw 1E 143
Claremont Ter. BD7: B'frd . . .5D 90 (6B 6)
LS12: Leeds 4A 96
Claremont Vw. LS3: Leeds . . .2G 97 (2A 4)
LS26: Rothw 1E 143
Claremont Vs. *HX6: Hal* 5A 148
(off Victoria Av.)
CLAREMOUNT 1H 149
Claremount LS6: Leeds 3E 77
Claremount Ho. *HX3: Hal* 1H 149
(off Claremount Rd.)
Claremount Rd.
HX3: Hal 5F 129 (1D 164)
Claremount Ter. HX3: Hal 5G 129
LS29: Burl W 5F 21
Clarence Dr. LS18: H'fth 2D 74
Clarence Gdns. LS18: H'fth 2D 74
Clarence Gro. LS18: H'fth 2D 74
Clarence M. LS18: H'fth 2D 74
Clarence Pl. LS29: Burl W 2F 21
Clarence Rd. BD18: Ship 1H 69
LS10: Leeds 5C 98
LS18: H'fth 2D 74
Clarence St. HX1: Hal 2F 149 (4A 164)
LS13: Leeds 2E 95
Clarence Ter. LS28: Pud 3A 94
Clarendon Pl. BD13: B'frd 5G 107
HX1: Hal 2E 149
LS2: Leeds 1G 97 (1A 4)
Clarendon Rd. BD16: Bgly 3D 50
LS2: Leeds 1G 97 (1A 4)
LS23: B Spa 4A 30
Clarendon St. BD21: Keigh 2H 47
BD22: Haw 3C 64
Clarendon Ter. LS28: Pud 5A 94
Clarendon Way LS2: Leeds . . .2G 97 (2A 4)
Clare Rd. BD12: B'frd 5C 132
HX1: Hal 3G 149 (5C 164)
Clare Rd. Flats
HX1: Hal 3G 149 (6C 164)
Clare Royd HX3: Hal 2A 152
Clare St. HX1: Hal 3G 149 (5C 164)
Clarges St. BD5: B'frd 2C 110
Clarion Camp LS29: Men 6B 22
Clarion Fld. LS29: Men 6B 22
Clark Av. LS9: Leeds 4D 98
Clark Cres. LS9: Leeds 4D 98
Clarke Rd. WF3: E Ard 4E 155
Clarke St. LS28: Pud 3F 73
Clark Gro. LS9: Leeds 5D 98
Clark La. LS9: Leeds 4D 98
(not continuous)
Clark Mt. LS9: Leeds 4D 98
Clark Rd. LS9: Leeds 5D 98
Clark Row LS9: Leeds 5D 98
Clarkson Ter. LS27: Morl 5C 116
Clarkson Vw. LS6: Leeds 5G 77
Clark Spring Cl. LS27: Morl 6A 116
Clark Spring Ri. LS27: Morl 6B 116
Clark Ter. LS9: Leeds 4D 98
Clark Vw. LS9: Leeds 5D 98
Classic Gym, The 3C 6
Clay Brow *BD22: Haw* 1C 64
(off Nth. View Ter.)
Clayfield Dr. BD7: B'frd 3A 110
Clay Hill Dr. BD12: B'frd 4D 132
(not continuous)

Clay Ho. La. HX4: Hal 4G 159
Claymore Ri. BD20: Sils 3F 15
Clay Pit La. LS2: Leeds 2A 98 (2E 5)
   LS7: Leeds 2A 98 (1F 5)
Claypit La. LS14: T'ner 2H 63
   LS25: Leds 6E 125
Clay Pits La. HX1: Hal 1C 148
Clay Royd La. HX3: Hal 4E 151
Clay St. HX1: Hal 2D 148
   HX6: Hal 5A 148
           (Bk. Pleasant St.)
   HX6: Hal 5H 147
            (John St. W.)
CLAYTON 1D 108
Clayton Av. LS25: Kip 3H 123
Clayton Cl. LS10: Leeds 3D 118
Clayton Ct. LS10: Leeds 3D 118
   LS16: Leeds 1H 75
Clayton Dr. LS10: Leeds 3D 118
CLAYTON EDGE 3H 107
Clayton Grange LS16: Leeds 1H 75
Clayton Gro. LS19: Yead 6F 41
CLAYTON HEIGHTS 4D 108
Clayton La. BD5: B'frd 1E 111
   BD14: B'frd 2D 108
Clayton Ri. BD20: Keigh 5G 33
   WF1: Wake 4F 157
Clayton Rd. BD7: B'frd 1G 109
   LS10: Leeds 3D 118
Claytons Cl. LS26: Mick 4B 144
Clayton St. LS26: Rothw 2B 142
Clayton Ter. BD13: B'frd 4B 66
Clayton Way LS10: Leeds 3D 118
Clayton Wood Bank LS16: Leeds . . .6H 57
Clayton Wood Cl. LS16: Leeds 6H 57
Clayton Wood Ct. LS16: Leeds 6H 57
Clayton Wood Ri. LS16: Leeds 6H 57
Clayton Wood Rd. LS16: Leeds 6G 57
Clearings, The LS10: Leeds 5B 118
Cleasby Rd. LS29: Men 2G 39
Cleavesty La. LS17: Bard 4D 26
Cleckheaton Rd. BD6: B'frd 1D 132
   BD12: B'frd 1D 132
Cleeve Hill LS19: Yead 3F 55
Clegg La. HX4: Hal 4D 158
Clegg St. BD12: B'frd 5C 132
Clement Ct. HX1: Hal 2E 149
Clement St. BD8: B'frd 3H 89
   HX6: Hal 5H 147
Clement Ter. LS26: Rothw 3A 142
   LS27: Morl 3B 138
           (off Ackroyd St.)
Clervaux Ct. BD14: B'frd 6F 89
Cleveden Pl. HX3: Hal 5E 129
Clevedon Ho. BD8: B'frd 2C 90
           (off Trenton Dr.)
Cleveland Av. HX3: Hal 5H 149
Cleveland Rd. BD9: B'frd 6B 70
Cleveland Ter. BD16: Bgly 3F 49
         (off Elizabeth St.)
Cleveleys Av. HX6: Hal 4H 147
          (off Edward St.)
   LS11: Leeds 1F 117
Cleveleys Ct. LS11: Leeds 1F 117
          (off Cleveleys Av.)
Cleveleys Gdns. HX6: Hal 4H 147
Cleveleys Mt. LS11: Leeds 1F 117
Cleveleys Rd. LS11: Leeds 1F 117
Cleveleys St. LS11: Leeds 1F 117
          (off Cleveleys Rd.)
Cleveleys Ter. LS11: Leeds 1F 117
Clifby HX2: Hal 1B 148
Cliff Ct. LS6: Leeds 5G 77
   LS25: Kip 4A 124
Cliffdale Rd. LS7: Leeds 5H 77
Cliffdale Rd. Light Ind. Est.
   LS7: Leeds 5H 77
Cliffe HX2: Hal 3H 147
Cliffe Av. BD16: Bgly 6E 49
   BD17: Bail 5C 52
   HX3: Hal 2A 152
Cliffe Bungs. LS25: M'fld 6D 104
Cliffe Castle (Mus.) 4H 33

Cliffe Ct. LS19: Yead 6G 41
          (off Harper La.)
Cliffe Cres. BD20: Keigh 5F 35
Cliffe Dr. LS19: Yead 4E 55
         (not continuous)
Cliffe Gdns. BD18: Ship 3B 70
Cliffe Ho. Av. LS25: Gar 6G 103
Cliffe La. BD13: B'frd 4A 88
   BD17: Bail 6C 52
   BD19: Cleck 6C 134
   LS19: Yead 5G 55
         (not continuous)
Cliffe La. Sth. BD17: Bail 6C 52
Cliffe La. W. BD17: Bail 5C 52
Cliffe Mill Fold BD20: Keigh 5A 36
Cliffe Mt. BD20: Cleck 6E 135
Cliffe Pk. Chase LS12: Leeds 5A 96
Cliffe Pk. Cl. LS12: Leeds 5A 96
Cliffe Pk. Cres. LS12: Leeds 5A 96
Cliffe Pk. Dr. LS12: Leeds 5A 96
Cliffe Pk. Mt. LS12: Leeds 5A 96
Cliffe Pk. Ri. LS12: Leeds 5A 96
Cliffe Pk. Way LS27: Morl 4F 137
Cliffe Rd. BD3: B'frd 1F 91
   BD21: Keigh 3H 47
   HD6: Brigh 1A 162
Cliffestone Dr. BD20: Keigh 5H 35
Cliffe St. BD13: B'frd 4G 87
   BD21: Keigh 5H 33
Cliffe Ter. BD8: B'frd 2D 90
   BD13: B'frd 3C 86
          (off Station Rd.)
   BD17: Bail 6C 52
   BD21: Keigh 3A 48
   HX3: Hal 1G 159
   HX6: Hal 4G 147
   LS22: Weth 4E 13
        (off Highcliffe Ct.)
   LS25: M'fld 5F 105
   WF3: Rothw 4E 141
Cliffe Vw. BD15: B'frd 1C 88
   BD21: Keigh 4F 137
Cliffe Vs. BD16: Bgly 4E 69
   LS25: M'fld 6D 104
Cliffe Wood Av. BD18: Ship 3B 70
Cliffe Wood Cl. BD9: B'frd 6G 69
Cliff Gdns. HX2: Hal 4C 148
Cliff Hill La. HX2: Hal 3H 147
Cliff Hollins La. BD4: B'frd 3H 133
   BD12: B'frd 3H 133
Cliff Ho's. LS25: M'fld 6D 104
Cliff La. LS6: Leeds 5F 77
         (not continuous)
Cliff Mt. LS6: Leeds 5G 77
Cliff Mt. Ter. LS6: Leeds 5G 77
CLIFFORD 6B 30
Clifford Av. LS29: I'ly 4C 10
Clifford Cl. BD2: B'frd 4D 70
Clifford Ct. LS23: B Spa 6C 30
Clifford Moor Rd. LS23: B Spa 3H 29
Clifford Pl. LS27: Morl 6B 116
Clifford Rd. BD17: Bail 5C 52
   LS23: B Spa 4C 30
   LS29: I'ly 3C 10
Clifford St. BD5: B'frd 6E 91 (6D 6)
   BD20: Sils 1D 14
Cliff Rd. LS6: Leeds 5G 77
Cliff Rd. Gdns. LS6: Leeds 5G 77
Cliff Side Gdns. LS6: Leeds 5G 77
Cliff St. BD22: Haw 2D 64
Cliff Ter. LS6: Leeds 5G 77
Cliff Top Pk. (Pk. Home Est.)
   LS25: Gar 1H 123
Cliff Va. Rd. BD18: Ship 4B 70
CLIFTON 1D 162
Clifton Av. HX1: Hal 3D 148
   LS9: Leeds 2E 99
Clifton Comn. HD6: Brigh 1C 162
Clifton Ct. LS28: Pud 3A 94
          (off Clifton Rd.)
Clifton Dr. LS28: Pud 3A 94
Clifton Gro. LS9: Leeds 2E 99
Clifton Hill LS28: Pud 3A 94
Clifton M. LS28: Pud 3A 94

Clifton Mt. LS9: Leeds 1E 99
Clifton Pl. BD18: Ship 3B 70
   LS28: Pud 3A 94
Clifton Rd. HD6: Brigh 1B 162
         (not continuous)
   HX3: Hal 5G 149
   LS28: Pud 3A 94
   LS29: I'ly 6E 11
Clifton Side HD2: Hud 5F 163
Clifton St. BD8: B'frd 2D 90
   BD13: B'frd 4A 108
   BD22: Keigh 1G 47
   HX3: Hal 6E 129
   HX6: Hal 5A 148
Clifton Ter. LS9: Leeds 2E 99
   LS29: I'ly 5D 10
         (off Leeds Rd.)
CLIFTON VILLAS 2C 90
Clifton Vs. BD8: B'frd 2D 90
   LS21: Otley 5D 22
Climax Works LS11: Leeds 3A 118
Clipston Av. LS6: Leeds 3F 77
Clipstone Mt. LS6: Leeds 3F 77
Clipstone St. BD5: B'frd 3E 111
Clipstone Ter. LS6: Leeds 3F 77
Clipston St. LS6: Leeds 3F 77
Cliveden Av. BD13: B'frd 4A 88
Clive Mt. Ho. LS5: Leeds 6H 75
          (off Broad La.)
Clive Pl. BD7: B'frd 6B 90
Clive Ter. BD7: B'frd 6B 90
Cloberry St. LS2: Leeds 1G 97 (1A 4)
Clock Bldgs. LS8: Leeds 5E 79
Clock La. BD13: B'frd 2B 86
Clock Vw. St. BD20: Keigh 3H 33
Clog Bri. BD20: Sils 2E 15
Clog Sole Rd. HD6: Brigh 5H 151
Cloisters, The HX1: Hal 4E 149
        (off Constitutional St.)
Close, The BD2: B'frd 3F 71
   LS9: Leeds 4C 98
   LS14: T'ner 1H 63
   LS15: Bar E 3D 82
   LS17: Bard 6E 27
   LS17: Leeds 2G 59
   LS20: Guis 5A 40
   LS22: Coll 3B 28
   LS23: B Spa 3B 30
   LS25: Kip 4G 123
   WF3: E Ard 2B 156
Close Head BD13: B'frd 5F 87
Close Head Dr. BD13: B'frd 5F 87
Close Head La. BD13: B'frd 4F 87
Close Lea HD6: Brigh 2H 161
Close Lea Av. HD6: Brigh 2H 161
Close Lea Dr. HD6: Brigh 2H 161
Close Lea Way HD6: Brigh 2H 161
Closes Pl. HD6: Brigh 2A 162
          (off Closes Rd.)
Closes Rd. HD6: Brigh 2H 161
Cloth Hall St. LS2: Leeds 4A 98 (5F 5)
Cloudsdale Av. BD5: B'frd 1E 111
Clough Av. BD20: Stee 5C 14
Clough Bank HX2: Hal 2H 127
Clough Bank La. BD22: Keigh 1A 46
Clough Bldgs. HX6: Hal 5D 146
Clough Ct. BD13: B'frd 5C 86
Clough Dr. WF17: Bat 5C 136
Clough Ga. BD22: Keigh 5D 46
          (off Clough La.)
Clough Head HX6: Hal 1A 158
Clough Ho's. BD22: Keigh 5C 46
Clough La. BD22: Keigh 4C 46
   HD2: Hud 5G 161
   HD6: Brigh 3C 152
          (Birkhouse La.)
   HD6: Brigh 5G 161
          (Slade La.)
   HX2: Hal 2B 126
          (Hollin La.)
   HX2: Hal 2H 127
          (Moor End Rd.)
Clough Pl. HX2: Hal 2H 127
Clough Rd. HX6: Hal 1B 158

Clough St. BD5: B'frd 2E **111**
  LS27: Morl 3B **138**
Clough Ter. HX6: Hal 5A **148**
Clovelly Av. LS11: Leeds 2H **117**
Clovelly Gro. LS11: Leeds 2H **117**
Clovelly Pl. LS11: Leeds 2H **117**
Clovelly Row LS11: Leeds 2H **117**
Clovelly Ter. LS11: Leeds 2H **117**
Clover Ct. LS28: Pud 3E **73**
Clover Cres. LS28: Pud 2E **73**
Cloverdale HX3: Hal 6F **109**
  HX1: Hal 3F **149** (6A **164**)
Clover Hill Cl.
Clover Hill Rd. HX1: Hal 4F **149**
Clover Hill Ter. HX1: Hal 4F **149**
Clover Hill Vw. HX1: Hal 4F **149**
Clover Hill Wlk. HX1: Hal 4F **149**
Clover Ri. BD21: Keigh 6C **34**
Clover St. BD5: B'frd 2B **110**
Cloverville App.
  BD6: B'frd 6C **110**
Club Ho's. HX2: Hal 4D **128**
Club La. HX2: Hal 4C **128**
  LS13: Leeds 4A **74**
Club Row BD15: B'frd 4G **67**
               (off Main St.)
  LS7: Leeds 2A **78**
  LS19: Yead 6G **41**
Club St. BD7: B'frd 6H **89**
Clunters La. HX2: Hal 4B **146**
Clyde App. LS12: Leeds 5E **97**
Clyde Chase LS12: Leeds 5E **97**
              (off Clyde Vw.)
Clyde Ct. LS12: Leeds 5E **97**
Clyde Gdns. LS12: Leeds 5E **97**
Clyde Grange LS12: Leeds 5E **97**
Clydesdale Dr. BD6: B'frd 6H **109**
Clyde St. BD16: Bgly 4B **50**
  HX6: Hal 6H **147**
Clyde Vw. LS12: Leeds 5E **97**
Clydeville Flats
  LS21: Otley 4C **22**
Clyde Wlk. LS12: Leeds 5E **97**
Coach La. BD13: B'frd 5B **88**
Coach Rd. BD17: Bail 6A **52**
  HD6: Brigh 4H **151**
  HD6: Hal 2G **151**
  HX3: Hal 2G **151**
  LS12: Leeds 2G **115**
  LS20: Guis 6B **40**
  LS26: Swil 5H **121**
  WF1: Wake 4G **157**
Coach Row BD3: B'frd 3A **92**
Coal Hill Dr. LS13: Leeds 5B **74**
Coal Hill Fold LS13: Leeds 5B **74**
Coal Hill Gdns. LS13: Leeds 5B **74**
Coal Hill Ga. LS13: Leeds 5B **74**
           (off Coal Hill Dr.)
Coal Hill Grn. LS13: Leeds 5B **74**
Coal Hill La. LS13: Leeds 6B **74**
  LS28: Pud 5A **74**
Coal La. HX2: Hal 2C **106**
Coal Pit La. HD6: Brigh 2D **162**
Coalpit La. HX3: Hal 5A **150**
Coal Rd. LS14: Leeds 4C **62**
  LS17: Leeds 3C **62**
  LS17: Leeds, S'cft 4A **44**
Coates St. BD5: B'frd 2D **110**
Coates Ter. BD5: B'frd 1D **110**
Cobbydale Cl. BD20: Sils 2D **14**
Cobden Av. LS12: Leeds 1H **115**
Cobden Ct. HX1: Hal 2A **164**
Cobden Gro. LS12: Leeds 1H **115**
Cobden Pl. LS12: Leeds 1H **115**
Cobden Rd. LS12: Leeds 1H **115**
Cobden St. BD6: B'frd 2H **71**
  BD13: B'frd 8B **108**
  BD14: B'frd 1D **108**
  BD15: B'frd 2D **88**
  HX6: Hal 4G **147**
         (off Sowerby New Rd.)
  LS12: Leeds 1H **115**
  LS27: Morl 2A **138**

Cobden Ter. HX3: Hal 1E **151**
  HX5: Ell 6B **160**
            (off Savile Rd.)
  LS12: Leeds 1H **115**
Cobham Pde. WF1: Wake 5F **157**
Cobham Wlk. LS15: Leeds 1H **101**
Cockburn Cl. LS11: Leeds 2A **118**
Cockburn Way LS11: Leeds 2A **118**
Cockcroft Gro. BD3: B'frd ...4G **91** (3H 7)
Cockcroft Ho. LS6: Leeds 6D **76**
           (off Chapel La.)
COCKERSDALE 5C **114**
Cock Hill HX3: Hal 1D **130**
Cock Hill La. HX3: Hal 1C **130**
Cocking La. LS29: Add 4A **8**
Cockin La. BD14: B'frd 2H **107**
Cockshott Cl. LS12: Leeds 2H **95**
Cockshott Dr. LS12: Leeds 2H **95**
Cockshott Hill LS28: Pud 6H **73**
Cockshott La. BD10: B'frd 1G **71**
  LS12: Leeds 2H **95**
          (not continuous)
Cockshott Pl. LS12: Leeds 2H **95**
Colbeck Row WF17: Bat 6A **136**
Colbert Av. LS29: I'ly 4F **11**
Colby Ri. LS15: Leeds 4A **100**
Coldbeck Dr. BD6: B'frd 5G **109**
Coldcotes Av. LS9: Leeds 1F **99**
Coldcotes Cir. LS9: Leeds 1G **99**
Coldcotes Cl. LS9: Leeds 1G **99**
Coldcotes Cres. LS9: Leeds 1H **99**
Coldcotes Dr. LS9: Leeds 1G **99**
Coldcotes Gth. LS9: Leeds 1H **99**
Coldcotes Gro. LS9: Leeds 1H **99**
Coldcotes Vw. LS9: Leeds 1H **99**
Coldcotes Wlk. LS9: Leeds 1H **99**
Cold Edge Bottom HX2: Hal 1F **127**
Cold Edge Rd. HX2: Hal 2F **127**
          (Mt. Tabor Rd.)
  HX2: Hal 6C **84**
           (Nab Water La.)
Coldshaw BD22: Oxen 6A **64**
Coldshaw Top BD22: Haw 4C **64**
Cold St. BD22: Haw 4C **64**
Coldwell Rd. LS15: Leeds 2D **100**
Coldwell Sq. LS15: Leeds 2D **100**
Coleman St. BD3: B'frd 2F **91** (1E 7)
  LS12: Leeds 5F **97**
Colenso Gdns. LS11: Leeds 6F **97**
Colenso Gro. BD21: Keigh 4C **34**
          (off Aireworth Cl.)
  LS11: Leeds 1F **117**
Colenso Mt. LS11: Leeds 1F **117**
Colenso Pl. LS11: Leeds 1F **117**
Colenso Rd. LS11: Leeds 1F **117**
Colenso Ter. LS11: Leeds 1F **117**
Colenso Wlk. BD21: Keigh 4C **34**
           (off Florist St.)
Colenso Way BD21: Keigh 4C **34**
          (off Cornwall Rd.)
Coleridge Cl. LS26: Rothw 4E **143**
Coleridge Cres. WF2: Wake 6D **156**
Coleridge Gdns. BD10: B'frd 1A **72**
Coleridge La. LS28: Pud 6B **94**
Coleridge St.
  HX1: Hal 3G **149** (5C **164**)
Coleshill Way BD4: B'frd 5A **112**
Coles Way BD20: Keigh 3B **34**
COLEY 5F **131**
Coley Hall La. HX3: Hal 5F **131**
Coley Rd. HX3: Hal 3E **131**
Coley Vw. HX3: Hal 1F **151**
           (Drive, The)
  HX3: Hal 4C **130**
         (St Matthew's La.)
Colindale Cl. BD10: B'frd 3C **72**
Collbrook Av. BD6: B'frd 5C **110**
College Cl. LS27: Morl 1F **137**
College Dr. LS29: I'ly 6D **10**
College Farm La. LS22: Coll 6B **12**
College Lawns LS11: Leeds 3H **95**
College Rd. BD16: Bgly 1C **50**
  LS27: Morl 1F **137**
College St. WF17: Bat 6A **136**

College Ter. HX1: Hal 4D **148**
           (off Saville Pk.)
College Vw. LS12: Leeds 4H **95**
College Wlk. BD21: Keigh 6A **34**
       (off Airedale Shop. Cen.)
Collier Cl. BD18: Ship 2G **69**
Colliers La. BD17: Bail 3B **52**
Colliers La. LS17: Leeds 3A **62**
Colliery App. WF3: Wake 3F **157**
Collinfield Ri. BD6: B'frd 1H **131**
COLLINGHAM 3B **28**
Collingham Av. BD6: B'frd 5G **109**
Collingham Dr. LS25: Gar 5F **103**
COLLINGHAM FIELDS 3D **28**
Collingwood Ct. BD5: B'frd 2E **111**
           (off Ladywell Cl.)
Collin Moor La. HX4: Hal 3G **159**
Collin Rd. LS14: Leeds 2B **100**
Collins Cl. BD22: Haw 1E **65**
Collins St. BD4: B'frd 1H **111**
  BD7: B'frd 2A **110**
COLL PLACE 6D **110**
Coll Pl. BD6: B'frd 5D **110**
Colmore Gro. LS12: Leeds 6D **96**
Colmore Rd. LS12: Leeds 6D **96**
Colmore St. LS12: Leeds 5D **96**
Colne Rd. BD22: Keigh 5B **46**
Colour Mus., The 4D **90** (4B **6**)
Colston Cl. BD8: B'frd 2G **89**
Colston Dr. LS29: Burl W 3C **20**
COLTON 5F **101**
Colton Ct. LS15: Leeds 4F **101**
Colton Cft. LS15: Leeds 4F **101**
Colton Gth. LS15: Leeds 4F **101**
Colton La. LS15: Leeds 4F **101**
Colton Lodges LS15: Leeds 4G **101**
Colton Retail Pk. LS15: Leeds 4G **101**
Colton Rd. LS12: Leeds 4C **96**
  LS15: Leeds 4E **101**
Colton Rd. E. LS15: Leeds 5G **101**
          (not continuous)
Colton St. LS12: Leeds 4C **96**
Columbus St. HX3: Hal 6E **129**
Colville Ter. LS11: Leeds 1H **117**
  WF3: E Ard 6C **140**
Colwyn Av. LS11: Leeds 3H **117**
Colwyn Mt. LS11: Leeds 3H **117**
Colwyn Pl. LS11: Leeds 3H **117**
Colwyn Rd. LS11: Leeds 3H **117**
Colwyn Ter. LS11: Leeds 3H **117**
Colwyn Vw. LS11: Leeds 3H **117**
Colyton Mt. BD15: B'frd 2C **88**
Commerce Ct. BD4: B'frd 1G **111**
Commerce St. BD1: B'frd 4E **91** (3D **6**)
Commercial Bldgs. BD12: B'frd ...3H **133**
Commercial Rd. LS5: Leeds 5A **76**
Commercial St. BD1: B'frd 3E **7**
  BD13: B'frd 4H **107**
             (Alma St.)
  BD13: B'frd 3B **86**
             (Main Rd.)
  BD13: B'frd 5A **88**
           (Market St.)
  BD18: Ship 1B **70**
  BD22: Keigh 5B **46**
  HD6: Brigh 1A **162**
  HX1: Hal 2G **149** (4B **164**)
          (not continuous)
  LS1: Leeds 3A **98** (4E **5**)
  LS26: Rothw 2A **142**
  LS27: Morl 3A **138**
Commercial Vs. LS28: Pud 5H **93**
Commercial Way LS28: Pud 3B **94**
Commondale Way BD4: B'frd 1G **133**
Common End HD6: Brigh 3C **152**
Common Holme La. LS29: I'ly 3H **9**
Common La. HX3: Hal 4H **155**
  WF3: E Ard 1H **155**
Common Rd. BD12: B'frd 1B **132**
  HX5: Ell 5E **161**
Common Rd. Ind. Est.
  BD12: B'frd 1D **132**

Common Side. LS26: Mick 6E **145**
Common Ter. HD6: Brigh 2A **162**
Community Sports Cen. 2A **152**
Como Av. BD8: B'frd 2H **89**
Como Dr. BD8: B'frd 3H **89**
Como Gdns. BD8: B'frd 2H **89**
Como Gro. BD8: B'frd 2H **89**
Compeigne Av. BD20: Keigh 4D **34**
COMPTON 5C **28**
Compton Av. LS9: Leeds 1E **99**
Compton Ct. LS22: Coll 2B **28**
Compton Cres. LS9: Leeds 1E **99**
Compton Gro. LS9: Leeds 1E **99**
Compton La. LS22: Coll 5C **28**
      (not continuous)
  LS23: Bard, Coll 6H **27**
  LS23: Coll 5D **28**
Compton Mt. LS9: Leeds 1E **99**
Compton Pl. LS9: Leeds 1E **99**
Compton Rd. LS9: Leeds 1E **99**
Compton Row LS9: Leeds 1E **99**
Compton St. BD4: B'frd 3A **112**
  BD21: Keigh 5B **34**
  LS9: Leeds 1E **99**
Compton Ter. LS9: Leeds 1E **99**
Compton Vw. LS9: Leeds 1E **99**
Concordia St. LS1: Leeds 4A **98** (6E **5**)
Concord St. LS2: Leeds 2B **98** (2G **5**)
Concrete St. HX3: Hal 6E **129**
Condor Cl. BD13: B'frd 3E **109**
Conduit Pl. BD8: B'frd 2C **90**
Conduit St. BD8: B'frd 2C **90**
Coney La. BD21: Keigh 6A **34**
  HX2: Hal 1E **129**
Coney Moor Gro. LS26: Mick 4F **145**
Coney Pk. LS19: Yead 4A **42**
Conference Pl. LS12: Leeds 4A **96**
Conference Rd. LS12: Leeds 4A **96**
Conference Ter. LS12: Leeds 4A **96**
Congress Mt. LS12: Leeds 4A **96**
Congress St. LS12: Leeds 4A **96**
Congreve App. LS17: Bard 6G **27**
Congreve Way LS17: Bard 5G **27**
Conisborough La. LS25: Gar 4H **103**
Coniston Av. BD13: B'frd 4H **107**
  LS6: Leeds 4E **77**
Coniston Cl. BD13: B'frd 4H **107**
  HX5: Ell 4D **160**
Coniston Ct. WF3: Wake 3F **157**
Coniston Gdns. LS15: Leeds 5A **100**
Coniston Gro. BD9: B'frd 1H **89**
  BD17: Bail 6G **51**
Coniston Ho. HX5: Ell 4B **160**
      (off Crown St.)
Coniston Rd. BD7: B'frd 2G **109**
  LS26: Rothw 6E **121**
Coniston Way LS22: Weth 3B **12**
  LS26: Rothw 1E **143**
Connaught Fold HD2: Hud 6E **163**
Connaught Rd. LS29: I'ly 6F **11**
Consort St. LS3: Leeds 2F **97** (2A **4**)
Consort Ter. LS3: Leeds 2F **97**
Consort Vw. LS3: Leeds 2F **97**
Consort Wlk. LS3: Leeds 2F **97**
      (not continuous)
Constable Gro. WF3: Wake 3H **157**
Constable Rd. LS29: I'ly 6F **11**
  WF3: E Ard 1E **155**
Constance Gdns. LS7: Leeds 1H **97**
Constance St. BD18: Ship 1H **69**
Constance Way LS7: Leeds 1H **97**
Constitutional St. HX1: Hal 4E **149**
Conway Av. LS8: Leeds 6D **78**
Conway Dr. LS8: Leeds 6D **78**
Conway Gro. LS8: Leeds 6D **78**
Conway Mt. LS8: Leeds 6D **78**
Conway Pl. LS8: Leeds 6D **78**
Conway Rd. LS8: Leeds 6D **78**
Conway St. BD4: B'frd 3E **149**
  HX1: Hal 3E **149**
  LS8: Leeds 6D **78**
  LS28: Pud 2H **93**
Conway Ter. LS8: Leeds 6D **78**
Conway Vw. LS8: Leeds 6D **78**

Cooke St. BD21: Keigh 6A **34**
Cook La. BD21: Keigh 6A **34**
COOKRIDGE 2F **57**
Cookridge Av. LS16: Leeds 1G **57**
Cookridge Dr. LS16: Leeds 1F **57**
Cookridge Gro. LS16: Leeds 1G **57**
Cookridge La. LS16: Leeds 5F **43**
Cookridge St. LS1: Leeds 3H **97** (3D **4**)
  LS2: Leeds 3H **97** (2D **4**)
Cookson St. HD6: Brigh 6H **151**
Coombe Hill BD13: B'frd 3D **108**
Co-op Bldgs. HD6: Brigh 2B **152**
Co-operation St. LS12: Leeds 1A **116**
Co-operative Bldgs. HX3: Hal 5D **128**
Co-operative St. BD21: Keigh 4G **47**
  LS27: Morl 5C **116**
      (Fountain St.)
  LS27: Morl 2A **138**
      (Queen's Prom.)
  WF3: Rothw 6G **141**
Co-operative Yd. BD19: Cleck 6B **134**
      (off Heaton St.)
Cooper Bri. Rd. WF14: Hud 5H **163**
Cooper Cl. BD16: Bgly 2C **50**
Cooper Flds. HX2: Hal 3E **147**
Cooper Gro. HX3: B'frd 6F **109**
Cooper Hill LS28: Pud 6B **94**
Cooper La. BD6: B'frd 3F **109**
Cooper Rd. LS22: Weth 4E **13**
Copeland St. BD4: B'frd 6B **92**
Copgrove Cl. BD4: B'frd 2C **112**
Copgrove Ct. BD4: B'frd 2C **112**
Copgrove Rd. BD4: B'frd 2C **112**
  LS8: Leeds 5E **79**
COPLEY 1E **159**
Copley Av. HX2: Hal 4D **148**
Copley Circ. HX3: Hal 2E **159**
Copley Cl. HX3: Hal 2F **159**
Copley Glen HX3: Hal 1F **159**
Copley Hall St. HX3: Hal 2F **159**
Copley Hall Ter. HX3: Hal 1F **159**
COPLEY HILL 5C **136**
Copley Hill LS12: Leeds 5E **97**
  WF17: Bat 6B **136**
Copley Hill Trad. Est. LS12: Leeds . .6E **97**
Copley Hill Way LS12: Leeds 6E **97**
Copley La. HX3: Hal 2E **159**
  WF3: Rothw 3F **141**
Copley Mill Ho. HX3: Hal 1E **159**
      (off St Stephen's St.)
Copley Mt. HX3: Hal 1F **159**
Copley St. BD5: B'frd 2B **110**
  LS12: Leeds 5E **97**
Copley Ter. HX3: Hal 1F **159**
Copley Vw. HX3: Hal 1F **159**
Copley Wood Ter. HX3: Hal 1F **159**
Copley Yd. LS12: Leeds 5E **97**
Coplow La. BD15: B'frd 2H **67**
Copperas Row HX4: Hal 4C **158**
Copperfield Av. LS9: Leeds 5D **98**
Copperfield Cres. LS9: Leeds 5D **98**
Copperfield Dr. LS9: Leeds 5D **98**
Copperfield Gro. LS9: Leeds 5D **98**
Copperfield Mt. LS9: Leeds 5E **99**
Copperfield Pl. LS9: Leeds 5D **98**
Copperfield Row LS9: Leeds 5D **98**
Copperfield Ter. LS9: Leeds 5D **98**
Copperfield Vw. LS9: Leeds 5D **98**
Copperfield Wlk. LS9: Leeds 5D **98**
Coppice, The BD19: Bat 6H **135**
  HX1: Hal 4F **149**
  LS15: Bar E 3D **82**
  LS19: Yead 2D **54**
  LS29: I'ly 3C **10**
Coppice Grange LS19: Yead 5F **41**
Coppice Head LS26: Rothw 2B **142**
Coppice Vw. BD10: B'frd 1G **71**
Coppice Way LS8: Leeds 3E **79**
Coppice Wood Av. LS19: Yead 5E **41**
  LS20: Guis, Yead 5E **41**
Coppicewood Av. BD7: B'frd 5A **90**
Coppice Wood Cl. LS20: Guis 4E **41**
Coppice Wood Cres. LS19: Yead . . .5E **41**

Coppice Wood Gro. LS20: Guis 5E **41**
Coppicewood Gro. BD7: B'frd 5A **90**
Coppice Wood Ri. LS19: Yead 5F **41**
Coppies, The BD12: B'frd 3B **132**
Copplestone Wlk. BD4: B'frd 3C **112**
Coppy Cl. BD16: Bgly 3C **68**
Coppy La. LS13: Leeds 5E **75**
Coppy Rd. BD20: Stee 6B **14**
  LS29: Add 1C **8**
Coppy Row BD22: Keigh 5B **46**
Coppy Wood Dr. LS29: I'ly 2D **10**
Copse, The BD16: Bgly 4F **51**
  BD19: Cleck 2F **153**
  LS23: B Spa 2A **30**
  LS29: Burl W 3E **21**
  WF3: E Ard 2H **155**
Copthorne Gdns. HD2: Hud 6F **163**
Copthorne Sq. HD2: Hud 6F **163**
Copt Royd Gro. LS19: Yead 6E **41**
Copy Nook HX4: Hal 4E **159**
Copy St. BD15: B'frd 2D **88**
Corban St. BD4: B'frd 2A **112**
Cordingley Cl. BD4: B'frd 4C **112**
Cordingley St. BD4: B'frd 4C **112**
Corfe Cl. WF17: Bat 5D **136**
Coriander Cl. BD15: B'frd 3C **88**
Corner Ho. Shops
  LS17: Leeds 5B **60**
Cornerstones Cl. LS29: Add 1E **9**
Corn Exchange LS2: Leeds 5F **5**
Corn Mkt. HX1: Hal 2G **149** (4C **164**)
Corn Mill LS29: Men 1H **39**
Cornmill Cl. LS17: Bard 2F **45**
Corn Mill Ct. LS13: Leeds 3F **95**
Corn Mill Fold LS18: H'fth 1G **75**
Corn Mill La. BD14: B'frd 6B **88**
  LS29: Burl W 2G **21**
Cornmill La. LS17: Bard 2F **45**
Cornstone Fold LS12: Leeds 4E **95**
Corn St. BD21: Keigh 3G **47**
Cornus Gdns. LS10: Leeds 5B **118**
Cornwall Av. BD20: Sils 2C **14**
Cornwall Cl. LS26: Rothw 1H **141**
Cornwall Cres. BD17: Bail 3B **52**
  HD6: Hal 3B **152**
  LS26: Rothw 1H **141**
Cornwall Ho. HX5: Ell 5B **160**
      (off Crown St.)
Cornwall Pl. BD8: B'frd 2D **90** (1B **6**)
Cornwall Rd. BD8: B'frd 2D **90** (1B **6**)
  BD16: Bgly 5D **50**
  BD21: Keigh 4C **34**
Cornwall Ter. BD8: B'frd 2D **90** (1B **6**)
Coronation Av. BD17: B'frd 3B **54**
  LS25: Kip 4A **124**
Coronation Bungs. LS25: Kip 4A **124**
Coronation Bus. Cen.
  BD21: Keigh 4B **34**
Coronation Mt. BD22: Keigh 6F **33**
Coronation Pde. LS15: Leeds 5A **100**
Coronation Rd. HX3: Hal 5G **149**
Coronation St. BD12: B'frd 3G **133**
  HX4: Hal 4G **159**
  HX5: Ell 3B **160**
  WF3: Rothw 4H **141**
Coronation Ter. WF17: Bat 6B **136**
Coronation Wlk.
  BD22: Keigh 5F **33**
Coronation Way BD22: Keigh 6E **33**
Corporal La. BD13: B'frd 1A **130**
  HX3: Hal 1A **130**
Corporation St. BD2: B'frd 6A **72**
  HX1: Hal 1G **149** (2B **164**)
  HX6: Hal 5H **147**
  LS27: Morl 2H **137**
Corrance Rd. BD12: B'frd 6D **132**
Corrie Fold BD13: B'frd 5A **88**
      (off Corrie St.)
Corrie St. BD13: B'frd 5A **88**
Cote, The LS28: Pud 1G **93**
Cote Farm La. BD10: B'frd 6F **53**
Cotefields Av. LS28: Pud 6G **73**
Cote Hill HX2: Hal 3A **148**
Cote Hill Fold HX2: Hal 3B **148**

Cote La. BD15: B'frd 2C **88**
  HD6: Hud 6G **161**
  LS28: Pud 1G **93**
Coteroyd Av. LS27: Morl 5C **116**
Coteroyd Dr. LS27: Morl 6C **116**
Cotewall Rd. BD5: B'frd 2D **110**
Cotswold Av. BD18: Ship 2E **71**
Cotswold Dr. LS25: Gar 6F **103**
  LS26: Rothw 1H **141**
Cotswold Rd. LS26: Rothw 1A **142**
Cottage Grn. BD8: B'frd 3H **89**
           (off Lane Ends Cl.)
Cottage Rd. BD10: B'frd 2B **72**
  LS6: Leeds 3D **76**
Cottage Road Cinema 3D **76**
Cottam Av. BD7: B'frd 5B **90**
Cottam Ter. BD7: B'frd 5B **90**
Cotterdale BD15: B'frd 6C **68**
Cotterdale Holt LS22: Coll 2A **28**
Cotterdale Vw. LS15: Leeds 5A **100**
COTTINGLEY
  Bingley 2C **68**
  Leeds 4D **116**
Cottingley App. LS11: Leeds 4D **116**
Cottingley Bus. Pk. BD16: Bgly 2D **68**
Cottingley Chase LS11: Leeds 4C **116**
Cottingley Cliffe Rd. BD16: Bgly . . .3E **69**
Cottingley Ct. LS11: Leeds 4D **116**
Cottingley Cres. LS11: Leeds 4D **116**
Cottingley Dr. BD16: Bgly 1C **68**
  LS11: Leeds 3C **116**
Cottingley Fold LS11: Leeds 3C **116**
Cottingley Gdns. LS11: Leeds 4D **116**
Cottingley Grn. LS11: Leeds 4D **116**
Cottingley Gro. LS11: Leeds 4D **116**
Cottingley Hall Crematorium
  LS11: Leeds 3D **116**
Cottingley Hgts. LS11: Leeds 4D **116**
Cottingley Mnr. Pk. BD16: Bgly 2D **68**
Cottingley Moor Rd. BD16: Bgly 5C **68**
Cottingley New Rd. BD16: Bgly 2D **68**
Cottingley Rd. BD15: B'frd 6C **68**
  LS11: Leeds 3C **116**
Cottingley Springs Cvn. Pk.
  LS27: Morl 4A **116**
Cottingley Station (Rail) 4C **116**
Cottingley Ter. BD8: B'frd 2D **90**
Cottingley Towers LS11: Leeds . . .4D **116**
Cottingley Va. LS11: Leeds 4D **116**
Cottingley Wood BD16: Bgly 1C **68**
Cotton St. LS9: Leeds 4C **98** (5H **5**)
Couford Gro. HD2: Hud 6F **163**
Cougar Pk. 4B **34**
Coulsdon Ho. BD8: B'frd 2C **90**
           (off Trenton Dr.)
Coultas Cl. LS29: Men 1H **39**
County Arc. LS1: Leeds 3A **98** (4F **5**)
County Bri. BD13: B'frd 6B **86**
County Workshops HD6: Brigh 6B **152**
Coupland Pl. LS11: Leeds 1H **117**
Coupland Rd. LS11: Leeds 1H **117**
  LS25: Gar 4E **103**
Coupland St. LS11: Leeds 2H **117**
Court, The BD18: Ship 2G **69**
  LS17: Leeds 2F **59**
Courtenay Cl. BD3: B'frd 4C **92**
Courtenays LS14: Leeds 5D **80**
Courthouse St. LS21: Otley 3E **23**
Court La. HX2: Hal 2B **148**
Courtney Ho. BD8: B'frd 2D **90**
           (off Trenton Dr.)
Courts Leet BD12: B'frd 3C **132**
Court Yard, The BD17: Bail 3D **52**
           (off East Pde.)
Courtyard, The BD7: B'frd 3G **109**
  LS10: Leeds 1B **118**
  WF3: Bat 5B **136**
Courtyard M. BD20: Sils 5F **15**
Courtyards, The LS14: Leeds 2D **80**
Cousen Av. BD7: B'frd 6H **89**
Cousen Pl. BD7: B'frd 1B **110**
Cousen Rd. BD7: B'frd 1B **110**
Cousin La. HX2: Hal 2C **128**
Coutances Way LS29: I'ly 4H **11**

Coventry St. BD4: B'frd 1H **111**
  HX2: Hal 2C **148**
Coverdale Gth. LS22: Coll 3A **28**
Coverdale Way BD17: Bail 3E **53**
Cover Dr. BD6: B'frd 5A **110**
Coverley Gth. LS19: Yead 6D **40**
Coverley Ri. LS19: Yead 6D **40**
Covet, The BD10: B'frd 1B **72**
Cow Cl. Cotts. BD12: B'frd 5F **133**
Cow Cl. Gro. LS12: Leeds 1A **116**
Cow Cl. La. BD12: B'frd 5E **133**
Cow Cl. Rd. LS12: Leeds 1H **115**
Cowdray Dr. BD19: Cleck 1F **153**
Cowgill St. BD8: B'frd 2C **90**
Cow Grn. HX1: Hal 2G **149** (4B **164**)
Cow Hill Ga. La. HX2: Hal 5C **106**
Cow La. HX3: Brigh 5F **151**
  HX3: Hal 1G **159**
Cowley Cres. BD9: B'frd 5E **69**
Cowley Rd. LS13: Leeds 4B **74**
Cowling La. HX3: Hal 1B **130**
Cowpasture Rd. LS29: I'ly 5D **10**
Cowper Av. LS9: Leeds 1E **99**
Cowper Cres. LS9: Leeds 1E **99**
Cowper Gro. LS8: Leeds 6E **79**
Cowper Mt. LS9: Leeds 1E **99**
Cowper Rd. LS9: Leeds 1E **99**
Cowper St. LS7: Leeds 5B **78**
Cowper Ter. LS9: Leeds 1E **99**
Cowroyd Pl. HX3: Hal 6H **129** (1D **164**)
Coxwold Hill LS22: Weth 2E **13**
Coxwold Vw. LS22: Weth 2E **13**
Coxwold Wlk. BD15: B'frd 6G **67**
Crab La. LS12: Leeds 3C **96**
Crabtree Gdns. LS22: Coll 3A **28**
Crabtree Hill LS22: Coll 3B **28**
Crabtree La. LS17: Bard 5E **27**
Crabtree Pl. BD7: B'frd 1B **110**
Crabtree St. BD7: B'frd 1A **110**
  HX1: Hal 2D **148**
Crabtree Way WF3: E Ard 2F **155**
Crack La. BD15: B'frd 4G **67**
Cracoe Rd. BD3: B'frd 5H **91**
Crag Av. HX2: Hal 3B **128**
Crag Ct. HX2: Hal 3B **128**
Cragg Av. LS18: H'fth 1D **74**
Cragg Dr. LS29: I'ly 6H **11**
Cragg La. BD7: B'frd 2A **110**
  BD13: B'frd 6C **86**
           (Cragg Top)
  BD13: B'frd 6D **86**
           (New Cl.)
Cragg Rd. LS18: H'fth 1E **75**
Cragg St. BD7: B'frd 2A **110**
Cragg Ter. BD7: B'frd 2A **110**
  LS18: H'fth 1D **74**
        (not continuous)
  LS19: Yead 5F **55**
Cragg Top BD13: B'frd 6C **86**
Cragg Vw. BD20: Sils 1E **15**
  LS21: Pool 6D **24**
  LS28: Add 1D **8**
         (off Bolton Rd.)
Craggwell Ter. LS18: H'fth 2E **75**
         (off Wood La.)
Craggwood Cl. LS18: H'fth 2E **75**
Craggwood Rd. LS18: H'fth 2E **75**
Craggwood Ter. LS18: H'fth 2E **75**
        (off Craggwood Rd.)
Crag Hill Av. LS16: Leeds 6G **43**
Crag Hill Rd. BD10: B'frd 5G **53**
Crag Hill Vw. LS16: Leeds 1G **57**
Crag La. HX2: Hal 3B **128**
  LS17: Leeds 2E **59**
Crag Pl. BD21: Keigh 3A **48**
Crag Rd. BD18: Ship 2C **70**
Cragside BD10: B'frd 6F **53**
Cragside Cl. LS5: Leeds 2G **75**
Cragside Cres. LS5: Leeds 2G **75**
Cragside Gdns. LS5: Leeds 3G **75**
Cragside Gro. LS5: Leeds 3F **75**
Cragside Mt. LS5: Leeds 2G **75**
Cragside Pl. LS5: Leeds 2G **75**

Cragside Wlk. LS5: Leeds 3F **75**
Crag Vw. BD10: B'frd 3A **72**
Craiglands HX3: Hal 1F **151**
Craiglands Pk. LS29: I'ly 6E **11**
Craiglands Rd. LS29: I'ly 6E **11**
Craiglea Dr. BD12: B'frd 5D **132**
Craigmore Ct. BD4: B'frd 3D **112**
Craigmore Dr. LS29: I'ly 5G **11**
Craig Vw. BD18: Ship 2F **69**
Crake Dr. BD6: B'frd 4E **109**
Cranbourne Rd. BD9: B'frd 1F **89**
Cranbrook Av. BD6: B'frd 5C **110**
  LS11: Leeds 2G **117**
Cranbrook Pl. BD5: B'frd 2E **111**
Cranbrook St. BD5: B'frd 2E **111**
  BD14: B'frd 1D **108**
Cranbrook Vw. LS28: Pud 6C **94**
Cranewells Dr. LS15: Leeds 5F **101**
Cranewells Grn. LS15: Leeds 5E **101**
Cranewells Ri. LS15: Leeds 5E **101**
Cranewells Va. LS15: Leeds 5E **101**
Cranewells Vw. LS15: Leeds 4E **101**
Cranford Pl. BD15: B'frd 4G **67**
Cranleigh Mt. BD21: Keigh 2G **47**
Cranmer Bank LS17: Leeds 4G **59**
Cranmer Cl. LS17: Leeds 4G **59**
Cranmer Gdns. LS17: Leeds 4G **59**
Cranmer Ho. BD3: B'frd 2F **7**
Cranmer Ri. LS17: Leeds 3G **59**
Cranmer Rd. BD3: B'frd 2F **91**
  LS17: Leeds 4G **59**
        (not continuous)
Cranmore Cres. LS10: Leeds 2D **140**
Cranmore Dr. LS10: Leeds 2D **140**
Cranmore Gdns. LS10: Leeds 2C **140**
Cranmore Grn. LS10: Leeds 2C **140**
Cranmore Gro. LS10: Leeds 2C **140**
Cranmore La. LS10: Leeds 2D **140**
Cranmore Ri. LS10: Leeds 2D **140**
Cranmore Rd. LS10: Leeds 2C **140**
Cranswick Ho. BD10: B'frd 3A **72**
        (off Summerfield Rd.)
Craven Av. BD13: B'frd 5A **88**
  BD20: Sils 2E **15**
Craven Cl. BD19: Cleck 6G **135**
Craven Ct. BD8: B'frd 3H **89**
         (off Lane Ends Cl.)
  BD20: Sils 2F **15**
  HX1: Hal 2E **149**
Craven Cres. LS29: Add 1C **8**
Craven Dr. BD19: Cleck 6G **135**
  BD20: Sils 2E **15**
Craven Edge HX1: Hal 3E **149**
Craven Gro. BD20: Sils 2F **15**
Craven La. BD19: Cleck 6G **135**
Craven Mt. HX1: Hal 3E **149**
         (off Lister La.)
Craven Pk. LS29: Men 6F **21**
Craven Pl. HX1: Hal 3E **149**
        (off Hopwood La.)
Craven Rd. BD21: Keigh 5C **34**
  LS6: Leeds 6H **77**
Craven St. BD3: B'frd 3F **91** (2F **7**)
  LS21: Otley 4F **23**
Craven Ter. BD2: B'frd 6A **72**
  HX1: Hal 3E **149**
  LS21: Otley 4F **23**
        (off Craven St.)
Crawford Av. BD6: B'frd 5C **110**
Crawford St. BD4: B'frd 1G **111**
Crawshaw Av. LS28: Pud 4B **94**
Crawshaw Cl. LS28: Pud 4A **94**
Crawshaw Gdns. LS28: Pud 4B **94**
Crawshaw Hill LS28: Pud 4A **94**
Crawshaw Pk. LS28: Pud 4A **94**
Crawshaw Ri. LS28: Pud 5A **94**
Crawshaw Rd. LS28: Pud 4A **94**
Crediton Av. BD15: B'frd 3D **88**
Crediton Ct. BD15: B'frd 3D **88**
Crescent, The BD6: B'frd 5G **109**
  BD11: B'frd 6E **113**
  BD16: Bgly 1A **50**
  BD17: Bail 5C **52**

Crescent, The HD6: Brigh 6B **152**
(off Bonegate Rd.)
HX3: Hal 1F **151**
(Leeds Rd.)
HX3: Hal 3B **150**
(Stub Thorn La.)
LS6: Leeds 6G **77**
(off Woodhouse La.)
LS13: Leeds 6E **75**
LS15: Leeds 3D **100**
LS16: Leeds 3A **58**
LS17: Leeds 1F **59**
LS18: H'fth 6B **56**
LS20: Guis 5A **40**
LS21: Otley 1E **23**
LS25: Gar 3G **103**
LS25: Kip 4G **123**
LS25: M'fld 5E **105**
LS28: Pud 3B **94**
LS29: Burl W 3E **21**
LS29: I'ly 4G **11**
LS29: Men 1H **39**
WF3: E Ard 1G **155**
Crescent Av. LS26: Rothw 6B **120**
Crescent Bungs. WF3: Leeds 5B **140**
Crescent Ct. LS17: Leeds 1F **59**
Crescent Gdns. LS17: Leeds 3B **60**
Crescent Grange LS11: Leeds 1A **118**
Crescent Ter. LS29: I'ly 5D **10**
Crescent Towers LS11: Leeds 1A **118**
Crescent Vw. BD22: Keigh 4G **47**
LS17: Leeds 1F **59**
Crescent Wlk. BD14: B'frd 6F **89**
Creskeld Cres. LS16: B'hpe 2H **43**
Creskeld Dr. LS16: B'hpe 1G **43**
Creskeld Gdns. LS16: B'hpe 2G **43**
Creskeld Gth. LS16: B'hpe 2H **43**
Creskeld La. LS16: Arth, B'hpe 1H **43**
(not continuous)
LS21: Arth 1H **43**
Creskeld Pk. LS16: B'hpe 2H **43**
Creskeld Vw. LS16: B'hpe 2G **43**
Creskeld Way BD15: B'frd 1C **88**
Cressingham Vs. BD13: B'frd 4B **66**
(off Cullingworth Ga.)
Cresswell Mt. BD7: B'frd 3G **109**
Cresswell Pl. BD7: B'frd 3G **109**
Cresswell Ter. BD7: B'frd 3G **109**
HX3: Hal 1G **151**
Crest, The BD7: Hud 5E **163**
LS25: Kip 4G **123**
LS26: Swil 4A **122**
Crest Av. BD12: B'frd 6C **132**
Crestfield Av. HX5: Ell 5A **160**
Crestfield Cres. HX5: Ell 6A **160**
Crestfield Dr. HX2: Hal 4C **148**
HX5: Ell 6A **160**
Crestfield Rd. HX5: Ell 6A **160**
Crest Pl. HD6: Brigh 3A **151**
(off Halifax Rd.)
Crest Vw. HD6: Brigh 4G **151**
Crestville Cl. BD14: B'frd 6F **89**
Crestville Rd. BD14: B'frd 6E **89**
Crestville Ter. BD14: B'frd 6F **89**
Crestwood Cl. BD5: B'frd 4H **111**
Crib La. HX1: Hal 1G **149** (2B **164**)
Cricketers, The LS5: Leeds 5B **76**
Cricketers App. WF2: Wake 6C **156**
Cricketers Cl. LS25: Gar 4G **103**
Cricketers Fold LS17: Leeds 3A **62**
Cricketers Grn. LS19: Yead 1G **55**
Cricketers Ter. LS12: Leeds 4C **96**
Cricketers Vw. LS17: Leeds 3A **62**
Cricketers Wlk. BD20: Stee 6D **14**
LS15: Leeds 4G **101**
Cricklegate LS15: Leeds 3D **100**
Crimble Cl. HX3: Hal 2G **151**
CRIMBLES 4B **94**
Crimbles Ct. LS28: Pud 4B **94**
Crimbles Pl. LS28: Pud 4B **94**
Crimbles Rd. LS28: Pud 4B **94**
Crimbles Ter. LS28: Pud 4B **94**
Crimple Grn. LS25: Gar 5H **103**
Crimshaw La. BD18: Ship 4D **70**

Cripplegate HX1: Hal 2H **149**
Critchell Ho. BD5: B'frd 6E **91**
(off Swan La.)
Croft, The BD11: B'frd 2A **136**
BD12: B'frd 3F **133**
BD17: Bail 4C **52**
BD21: Keigh 6D **34**
LS14: S'cft 5F **45**
LS15: Leeds 2D **100**
LS22: Coll 3A **28**
LS26: Rothw 2E **143**
WF3: E Ard 4D **154**
Croft Av. BD16: Bgly 1H **49**
LS28: Pud 6H **73**
WF3: E Ard 2B **156**
Croft Bank BD11: B'frd 2E **135**
Croft Bri. LS26: Rothw 2E **143**
Croft Cl. LS29: Men 1F **39**
Croft Cotts. LS12: Leeds 2G **115**
Croft Ct. LS18: H'fth 6E **57**
LS29: Men 1G **39**
Croftdale Gro. LS15: Leeds 1F **101**
Croft Dr. LS29: Men 1G **39**
Croft End LS22: Weth 4C **12**
Crofters Grn. BD10: B'frd 1G **71**
Crofters Lea LS19: Yead 1D **54**
Croft Fld. BD20: Sils 3E **15**
Croft Foulds Ct. LS25: Gar 4F **103**
Croft Head BD20: Guis 4C **40**
Croft Ho. HX2: Hal 6D **126**
HX5: Ell 4B **160**
(off Southgate)
Croft Ho. Av. LS27: Morl 2B **138**
Croft Ho. Cl. LS27: Morl 1B **138**
Crofthouse Cl. BD6: B'frd 5B **110**
Croft Ho. Ct. LS28: Pud 3A **94**
Croft Ho. Dr. LS21: Otley 2D **22**
LS27: Morl 2B **138**
Croft Ho. Fold LS29: Add 1E **9**
Croft Ho. Gdns. LS27: Morl 2B **138**
Croft Ho. Gro. LS27: Morl 2B **138**
Croft Ho. La. BD20: Keigh 3G **33**
LS27: Morl 2B **138**
Croft Ho. M. LS27: Morl 2B **138**
Croft Ho. Mt. LS27: Morl 1B **138**
Croft Ho. Ri. LS27: Morl 1B **138**
Croft Ho. Rd. LS27: Morl 2B **138**
Crofthouse Rd. BD6: B'frd 5B **110**
Croft Ho. Vw. LS27: Morl 2B **138**
Croft Ho. Wlk. LS27: Morl 1B **138**
Croft Ho. Way LS27: Morl 1B **138**
Croftlands BD10: B'frd 1G **71**
Croft La. LS24: Tad 5H **31**
Cft. Leigh Ct. BD5: B'frd 4G **111**
Crofton Ct. BD9: B'frd 5H **69**
(off Crofton Rd.)
Crofton Ri. LS17: Leeds 3C **62**
Crofton Rd. BD9: B'frd 6A **70**
LS17: Leeds 3C **62**
Croft Pl. BD6: B'frd 4H **109**
BD22: Haw 1F **65**
HD6: Brigh 5B **152**
Croft Ri. HX3: Hal 5D **128**
LS29: Men 1G **39**
Croft Rd. BD16: Bgly 1H **49**
BD20: Keigh 5H **35**
Croft Row BD13: B'frd 1A **86**
Croft's Ct. LS1: Leeds 3H **97** (4D **4**)
Croftside Cl. LS14: Leeds 6D **80**
Croft St. BD5: B'frd 5E **91** (6D **6**)
(not continuous)
BD6: B'frd 4C **110**
BD10: B'frd 1A **72**
BD11: B'frd 2E **135**
(not continuous)
BD18: Ship 2B **70**
BD20: Stee 6C **14**
BD21: Keigh 1H **47**
BD22: Haw 2C **64**
HD6: Brigh 1A **162**
HX6: Hal 5A **148**
LS21: Otley 4F **23**
LS28: Pud 6H **73**

Croft Ter. BD22: Keigh 5D **46**
(off Dockroyd La.)
LS12: Leeds 2G **115**
Croft Way LS29: Men 1G **39**
Croftway LS15: Bar E 2E **83**
Cromack Vw. LS28: Pud 4G **93**
Cromer Av. BD21: Keigh 2H **47**
(off Cromer Rd.)
Cromer Gro. BD21: Keigh 2H **47**
Cromer Pl. LS2: Leeds 1G **97** (1A **4**)
(not continuous)
Cromer Rd. BD21: Keigh 2H **47**
LS2: Leeds 1G **97** (1A **4**)
Cromer St. BD21: Keigh 2H **47**
HX1: Hal 4D **148**
LS2: Leeds 1G **97** (1A **4**)
Cromer Ter. LS2: Leeds 2G **97** (1A **4**)
Crompton Dr. LS27: Morl 1H **137**
Cromwell Bottom Dr. HD6: Ell 2E **161**
Cromwell Cl. HX3: Hal 5C **150**
Cromwell Ct. BD9: B'frd 4E **69**
BD11: B'frd 2H **135**
Cromwell Hgts. LS9: Leeds 3C **98**
(off Cromwell St.)
Cromwell M. LS9: Leeds 2C **98**
Cromwell Mt. LS9: Leeds 2C **98**
LS10: Leeds 5B **118**
Cromwell Ri. LS25: Kip 5G **123**
Cromwell Rd. HX3: Hal 5C **150**
Cromwells Mt. HX2: Hal 2H **147**
Cromwell St. LS9: Leeds 3C **98** (3H **5**)
Cromwell Ter. HX1: Hal 2F **149**
(not continuous)
Cromwell Vw. HX3: Hal 5D **150**
Cromwell Wood La. HD6: Brigh 1F **161**
Crooked La. BD10: B'frd 6F **53**
(not continuous)
HX3: Hal 1F **129**
Crooke La. BD15: B'frd 5G **67**
Crook Farm Cvn. Pk. BD17: Bail 4H **51**
Cropper Fold BD16: Bgly 1F **51**
Cropper Ga. LS1: Leeds 3G **97** (4A **4**)
Cropredy Cl. BD13: B'frd 4B **108**
Crosby Av. LS11: Leeds 1F **117**
Crosby Pl. LS11: Leeds 6G **97**
Crosby Rd. LS11: Leeds 1F **117**
Crosby St. BD21: Keigh 5H **33**
LS11: Leeds 6F **97**
Crosby Ter. LS11: Leeds 6G **97**
Crosby Vw. LS11: Leeds 6G **97**
Croscombe Wlk. BD5: B'frd 6E **91**
Crosley Ho. BD16: Bgly 5C **50**
Crosley Vw. BD16: Bgly 5D **50**
Crosley Wood Rd. BD16: Bgly 5D **50**
Cross, The LS15: Bar E 2D **82**
LS16: B'hpe 2F **43**
Cross Albert Pl. LS12: Leeds 5D **96**
Cross Arc. LS1: Leeds 4F **5**
Cross Aston Gro. LS13: Leeds 1G **95**
Cross Av. LS26: Rothw 6B **120**
Cross Aysgarth Mt. LS9: Leeds 3D **98**
Cross Bank Rd. LS29: Add 1A **8**
Cross Banks BD18: Ship 2B **70**
Cross Banstead St. LS8: Leeds 6D **78**
Cross Bath Rd. LS13: Leeds 1E **95**
Crossbeck Cl. LS29: I'ly 6D **10**
Crossbeck Rd. LS29: I'ly 6D **10**
Cross Belgrave St.
LS2: Leeds 3A **98** (3F **5**)
Cross Bellbrooke Av. LS9: Leeds 1F **99**
(off Bellbrooke Av.)
Cross Bell St. LS9: Leeds 3H **5**
Cross Bentley La. LS6: Leeds 3F **77**
Cross Burley Lodge Rd.
LS6: Leeds 1E **97**
(off Burley Rd.)
Cross Cardigan Ter. LS4: Leeds 2C **96**
Cross Catherine St. LS9: Leeds 4C **98**
Cross Chancellor St. LS6: Leeds 6H **77**
Cross Chapel St. LS6: Leeds 4D **76**
Cross Chestnut Gro. LS6: Leeds 6E **77**
(off Chestnut Av.)
Cross Cliff Rd. LS6: Leeds 5F **77**
Cross Conway Mt. LS8: Leeds 6D **78**

Cross Cowper St. LS7: Leeds 6B 78
Crossdale Av. BD6: B'frd 5G 109
Cross Dawlish Gro. LS9: Leeds 3F 99
Cross Easy Rd. LS9: Leeds 5D 98
Cross Elford St. LS8: Leeds 6D 78
Cross Emily St. BD21: Keigh 5A 34
Cross End Fold LS29: Add 1E 9
Cross Farm Ct. BD22: Oxen 6C 64
Crossfield Cl. BD22: Oxen 6B 64
Crossfield Rd. BD22: Oxen 6B 64
Crossfield St. LS2: Leeds 6G 77
CROSSFLATTS 1A 50
Cross Flatts Av. LS11: Leeds 3G 117
Cross Flatts Cres. LS11: Leeds 3F 117
Cross Flatts Dr. LS11: Leeds 2F 117
Cross Flatts Gro. LS11: Leeds 3F 117
Cross Flatts Mt. LS11: Leeds 3G 117
Cross Flatts Pde. LS11: Leeds 3F 117
Cross Flatts Pl. LS11: Leeds 3F 117
Cross Flatts Rd. LS11: Leeds 3F 117
Cross Flatts Row LS11: Leeds 3F 117
Crossflatts Station (Rail) 2A 50
Cross Flatts St. LS11: Leeds 3F 117
Cross Flatts Ter. LS11: Leeds 3F 117
Cross Francis St. LS7: Leeds 6B 78
Crossgate LS21: Otley 4E 23
CROSS GATES 1E 101
Cross Gates Av. LS15: Leeds 6E 81
Cross Gates La. BD16: Bgly 3G 49
LS15: Leeds 6D 80
Cross Gates Rd. LS15: Leeds 1C 100
(not continuous)
Crossgates Shop. Cen.
LS15: Leeds 1E 101
Cross Gates Station (Rail) 2E 101
Cross Glen Rd. LS16: Leeds 2C 76
Cross Granby Ter. LS6: Leeds 4D 76
Cross Grange Av. LS15: Leeds 6C 78
Cross Grasmere St. LS12: Leeds . . .4D 96
CROSS GREEN 6E 99
Cross Grn. BD4: B'frd 1C 112
LS21: Otley 3F 23
Cross Grn. App. LS9: Leeds 6E 99
Cross Grn. Av. LS9: Leeds 5D 98
Cross Grn. Cl. LS9: Leeds 6E 99
Cross Grn. Ct. LS9: Leeds 6F 99
Cross Grn. Cres. LS9: Leeds 5D 98
Cross Grn. Dr. LS9: Leeds 6E 99
Cross Grn. Gth. LS9: Leeds 6E 99
Cross Grn. Gro. LS9: Leeds 5D 98
Cross Grn. Ind. Est. LS9: Leeds . . .6F 99
Cross Green Ind. Pk. LS9: Leeds . . .5G 99
Cross Grn. La. LS9: Leeds 5C 98
LS15: Leeds 3C 100
Cross Grn. Ri. LS9: Leeds 6E 99
Cross Grn. Rd. LS9: Leeds 5D 98
Cross Grn. Row LS9: Leeds 2E 77
Cross Grn. Va. LS9: Leeds 1E 119
Cross Grn. Way LS9: Leeds 6E 99
Cross Greenwood Mt. LS6: Leeds . . .2E 77
Cross Hartley Av. LS6: Leeds 5G 77
(off Delph La.)
Cross Heath Gro. LS11: Leeds 2E 117
Cross Henley Rd. LS13: Leeds 1E 95
CROSS HILL 4G 159
Cross Hill HX4: Hal 4G 159
LS11: Leeds 4E 117
Cross Hill La. WF15: Liv 2H 163
Cross Hills HX1: Hal 1G 149 (2C 164)
LS25: Kip 4G 123
Cross Hills Cl. LS25: Kip 4G 123
Cross Hills Dr. LS25: Kip 4G 123
Cross Hills Gdns. LS25: Kip 4G 123
Crosshills Mt. HX4: Hal 4G 159
Cross Hilton Gro. LS8: Leeds 5D 78
Cross Ho. Ct. BD12: B'frd 3G 133
Cross Ingledew Cres. LS8: Leeds . . .5F 61
Cross Ingram Rd. LS11: Leeds 6F 97
Crossings, The WF17: Bat 6B 136
Cross Kelso Rd. LS2: Leeds . . .2F 97 (1A 4)
Crossland Ct. BD12: B'frd 3C 132
(off Carr Ho. La.)
LS11: Leeds 5G 97
Crossland Rd. LS27: Morl 6B 116

Crossland Ter. LS11: Leeds 2A 118
Cross La. BD7: B'frd 1B 110
(Balk La.)
BD7: B'frd 2A 110
(Low Grn.)
BD11: B'frd 6F 113
BD13: B'frd 5G 107
BD15: B'frd 3G 67
BD16: Bgly 3B 50
BD22: Oxen 6C 64
HD6: Brigh 2E 163
HX3: Hal 1C 130
(Brighouse & Denholme Ga. Rd.)
HX3: Hal 3D 130
(West St.)
HX5: Ell 5A 160
LS12: Leeds 6G 95
(Stonebridge La.)
LS12: Leeds 4B 96
(Up. Wortley Rd.)
LS20: Guis 1D 40
Cross Lea Farm Rd. LS5: Leeds 2H 75
Cross Leeds St. BD21: Keigh 6A 34
(off North St.)
BD21: Keigh 6H 33
(Leeds St.)
Crossley Bri. BD22: Oxen 2D 84
Crossley Cl. HX1: Hal 2E 149
(off Crossley Gdns.)
Crossley Gdns. HX1: Hal 2E 149
(Bowman Ter.)
HX1: Hal 1E 149
(Halifax Ind. Cen.)
CROSSLEY HALL 4G 89
Crossley Hall M. BD8: B'frd 4G 89
Crossley Hall St. BD8: B'frd 4F 89
Crossley Hill HX3: Hal 6H 149
Crossley Hill La. HX3: Hal 6H 149
(off Crossley Hill)
Crossley Retail Pk. HX1: Hal 1F 149
Crossleys Bldgs. HX3: Hal 3A 150
Crossley St. BD7: B'frd 6B 90
BD13: B'frd 4B 108
HD6: Brigh 2B 162
HX1: Hal 2G 149 (3B 164)
LS22: Weth 4E 13
Crossley Ter. Nth. HX3: Hal 3E 129
Crossley Ter. Sth. HX3: Hal 3E 129
Cross Lidgett Pl. LS8: Leeds 1D 78
Cross Lister St. BD21: Keigh 1G 47
(off Lister St.)
Cross Louis St. LS7: Leeds 6B 78
Cross Maude St. LS2: Leeds 5G 5
Cross Mitford Rd. LS12: Leeds 4D 96
Crossmoor Cl. BD20: Sils 2C 14
Cross Osmondthorpe La.
LS9: Leeds 3G 99
Cross Pk. St. LS15: Leeds 3C 100
Cross Peel St. LS27: Morl 3B 138
Cross Pl. HD6: Brigh 5B 152
(off Cross St.)
Cross Platts HX3: Hal 5E 151
Cross Quarry St. LS6: Leeds 5G 77
Cross Roundhay Av. LS8: Leeds . . .4D 78
Cross River St. BD21: Keigh 4C 34
(off Dale St.)
Cross Rd. BD8: B'frd 2B 90
BD10: B'frd 1A 72
BD12: B'frd 2F 133
LS18: H'fth 1C 74
CROSS ROADS 1E 65
Cross Roads BD22: Haw 1F 65
HX3: Hal 3D 130
Cross Roseville Rd. LS8: Leeds 6C 78
(off Bayswater Pl.)
Cross Rosse St. BD18: Ship 1B 70
Cross Row LS15: Swil 5A 102
Cross Rydal St. BD21: Keigh 1G 47
Cross St Michaels La.
LS6: Leeds 5D 76
Cross Speedwell St. LS6: Leeds . . .6H 77
Cross Stamford St.
LS7: Leeds 2B 98 (1H 5)

Cross St. BD6: B'frd 6H 109
BD12: B'frd 3G 133
BD14: B'frd 1E 109
HD6: Brigh 5A 152
HX1: Hal 3H 149 (5D 164)
(Horton St.)
HX1: Hal 2G 149 (3C 164)
(Winding Rd.)
HX4: Hal 4H 159
LS15: Leeds 3C 100
LS22: Weth 4E 13
LS26: Rothw 2A 142
WF3: E Ard 1C 156
Cross St. W. HX2: Hal 1C 148
Cross Sun St. BD1: B'frd 3F 91 (2E 7)
Cross Ter. LS26: Rothw 2A 142
Cross Valley Dr. LS15: Leeds 2D 100
Cross Vw. BD22: Keigh 4D 46
Crossway BD16: Bgly 2B 68
Crossways, The LS21: Otley 1E 23
Cross Wellington St. BD1: B'frd 3F 7
Cross Westfield Rd. LS3: Leeds 2F 97
(off Westfield Rd.)
Cross Wingham St. LS7: Leeds 1B 98
Cross Woodstock St. LS2: Leeds . . .1H 97
(off Blenheim Wlk.)
Cross Woodview St.
LS11: Leeds 3H 117
(off Woodview St.)
Cross York St. LS2: Leeds 4B 98 (5G 5)
Crowgill Rd. BD18: Ship 1B 70
Crow Hill Rd. HX7: Hal 6A 146
Crow La. LS21: Otley 4E 23
Crown Ct. LS2: Leeds 4A 98 (5F 5)
Crown Dr. BD12: B'frd 3C 132
CROW NEST 4C 50
Crow Nest Cotts. HX3: Hal 2G 151
Crow Nest Dr. LS11: Leeds 3E 117
Crow Nest La. LS11: Leeds 3D 116
Crownest La. BD16: Bgly 3C 50
Crow Nest M. LS11: Leeds 3E 117
Crownest Rd. BD16: Bgly 4C 50
CROWN POINT 4B 98 (6G 5)
Crown Point Retail Pk.
LS10: Leeds 5A 98
Crown Point Rd.
LS2: Leeds 4B 98 (6G 5)
LS9: Leeds 4B 98 (6G 5)
LS10: Leeds 5A 98
Crown Rd. HX3: Hal 5F 129
Crown St. BD1: B'frd 4C 90
BD12: B'frd 3C 132
HD6: Brigh 6A 152
HX1: Hal 2G 149 (4B 164)
HX5: Ell 5A 160
LS2: Leeds 4A 98 (5F 5)
LS29: Burl W 2F 21
Crown Ter. HX1: Hal 3D 148
(off Queen's Rd.)
Crowther Av. LS28: Pud 3D 72
Crowther Fold BD16: Bgly 6F 49
Crowther Pl. LS6: Leeds 6H 77
Crowthers St. BD12: B'frd 3C 132
Crowther St. BD10: B'frd 2B 72
Crowthers Yd. LS28: Pud 5A 94
Crow Tree Cl. BD17: Bail 4D 52
Crow Tree La. BD8: B'frd 2G 89
Crowtrees Cl. LS19: Yead 3G 55
Crowtrees Cres. HD6: Brigh 3H 161
Crowtrees La. HD6: Brigh 4H 161
Crowtrees Pde. HD6: Brigh 4H 161
(off Crowtrees La.)
Crowtrees Pk. LS19: Yead 3F 55
Crow Trees Pk. HD6: Brigh 3H 161
Crow Wood Pk. HX2: Hal 4B 148
Croydon Rd. BD7: B'frd 1H 109
Croydon St. BD13: B'frd 4A 108
LS11: Leeds 5F 97
Crumack La. BD22: Oxen 6E 65
Crunwelle St. BD15: B'frd 5C 68
Crystal Ct. HX1: Hal 2E 149
(off Hanson La.)
Crystal Ter. BD4: B'frd 2A 112
Cuckoo Nest BD7: B'frd 4C 90

Cuckoo Nest Ind. Est. BD7: B'frd 4C **90**
Cuckoo Pk. La. BD22: Oxen 5E **65**
Cudbear St. LS10: Leeds 5B **98**
CULLINGWORTH 4B **66**
Cullingworth Ga. BD13: B'frd 4B **66**
Cullingworth Rd. BD13: B'frd 4B **66**
Culpans Rd. HX7: Hal 5A **146**
Culver St. HX1: Hal 2G **149** (3C **164**)
Cumberland Av. HD2: Hud 6A **162**
Cumberland Cl. HX2: Hal 3C **128**
Cumberland Ct. HX2: Hal 4C **128**
  LS6: Leeds 6D **76**
Cumberland Ho. BD3: B'frd 2G **7**
Cumberland Rd. BD7: B'frd 6A **90**
  LS6: Leeds 5F **77**
Cunliffe La. BD17: B'frd 2H **53**
Cunliffe Rd. BD8: B'frd 1C **90**
  LS29: I'ly 5D **10**
Cunliffe Ter. BD8: B'frd 1D **90**
Cunliffe Vs. BD8: B'frd 6D **70**
Cupstone Cl. BD20: Keigh 4H **35**
Cure Hill BD22: Keigh 4B **46**
Curlew Cl. LS29: I'ly 5A **10**
Curlew Dr. BD20: Stee 5B **14**
Curlew Ri. LS27: Morl 4D **138**
Curlew St. BD5: B'frd 2C **110**
Curly Hill LS29: I'ly 3C **10**
Currer Av. BD4: B'frd 4H **111**
Currerbell M. BD13: B'frd 5B **88**
Currer St. BD1: B'frd 4F **91** (4E **7**)
  BD12: B'frd 3G **133**
Currer Wlk. BD20: Stee 5B **14**
Curtis Ct. BD13: B'frd 3B **66**
                           (off Halifax Rd.)
Curzon Rd. BD3: B'frd 4H **91**
                           (not continuous)
Curzon St. HD2: Hud 5G **163**
Cuthberts Cl. BD13: B'frd 5H **107**
Cut La. HX3: Hal 2B **130**
CUTLER HEIGHTS 1A **112**
Cutler Hgts. La. BD4: B'frd 2A **112**
Cutler La. LS26: Mick 4E **145**
Cutler Pl. BD4: B'frd 1B **112**
Cyprus Av. BD10: B'frd 6F **53**
Cyprus Dr. BD10: B'frd 6G **53**
Cyprus Gro. LS25: Gar 4E **103**
Cyprus Rd. LS25: Gar 4E **103**
Cyprus Ter. LS25: Gar 4E **103**
Czar St. LS11: Leeds 6G **97**

D

Dacre St. BD3: B'frd 3F **91** (1G **7**)
Daffels Wood Cl. BD4: B'frd 5H **111**
Daffil Av. LS27: Morl 6B **116**
Daffil Grange M. LS27: Morl 6B **116**
Daffil Grange Way LS27: Morl 6B **116**
Daffil Gro. LS27: Morl 6B **116**
Daffil Rd. LS27: Morl 6B **116**
Daffodil Ct. BD15: B'frd 3D **88**
Daily Ct. BD5: B'frd 2B **110**
Daisy Bank HX1: Hal 4F **149**
  HX3: Hal 5A **132**
Daisy Cl. WF17: Bat 5A **136**
Daisy Cft. BD20: Sils 2F **15**
Daisyfield Grange LS13: Leeds 2F **95**
                           (off Rossefield App.)
Daisyfield Rd. LS13: Leeds 1F **95**
DAISY HILL
  Bradford 1G **89**
  Leeds 2C **138**
Daisy Hill BD12: B'frd 4C **132**
  BD20: Sils 2F **15**
  LS27: Morl 2C **138**
Daisy Hill Av. LS27: Morl 1C **138**
Daisy Hill Bk. La. BD9: B'frd 1G **89**
Daisy Hill Cl. LS27: Morl 1B **138**
Daisy Hill Gro. BD9: B'frd 1G **89**
Daisy Hill La. BD9: B'frd 1G **89**
Daisy Lea HX6: Hal 5F **147**
Daisy Mt. HX6: Hal 4G **147**
Daisy Pl. BD18: Ship 1H **69**
                           (off Saltaire Rd.)

Daisy Rd. HD6: Brigh 2B **162**
Daisy Row LS13: Leeds 2F **95**
Daisy St. BD7: B'frd 2A **110**
  BD22: Haw 1E **65**
  HD6: Brigh 1A **162**
  HX1: Hal 3F **149** (5A **164**)
Daisy Va. M. WF3: E Ard 6C **140**
Daisy Va. Ter. WF3: E Ard 6C **140**
Dalby Av. BD3: B'frd 2A **92**
Dalby St. BD3: B'frd 3A **92**
Dalcross Gro. BD5: B'frd 1F **111**
Dalcross St. BD5: B'frd 1E **111**
Dale Cl. LS20: Guis 5H **39**
Dale Ct. LS29: I'ly 4G **11**
Dale Cres. BD20: Stee 6C **14**
Dale Cft. LS25: Gar 3E **103**
  LS29: I'ly 5A **10**
Dale Cft. Ri. BD15: B'frd 1B **88**
Dale Gth. BD17: Bail 4B **52**
Dale Gro. BD10: B'frd 6E **53**
Dale Pk. Av. LS16: Leeds 3F **57**
Dale Pk. Cl. LS16: Leeds 3F **57**
Dale Pk. Gdns. LS16: Leeds 3F **57**
Dale Pk. Ri. LS16: Leeds 3F **57**
Dale Pk. Vw. LS16: Leeds 3F **57**
Dale Pk. Wlk. LS16: Leeds 3F **57**
Dales Dr. LS20: Guis 5H **39**
Daleside Av. LS28: Pud 3E **93**
Daleside Cl. LS28: Pud 2D **92**
Daleside Gro. BD12: B'frd 3F **133**
  LS28: Pud 3E **93**
Dale Side Ho. BD8: B'frd 1D **90**
Daleside Rd. BD18: Ship 6D **52**
  BD20: Keigh 4E **35**
  LS28: Pud 2D **92**
Daleside Wlk. BD5: B'frd 3F **111**
Daleson Cl. HX3: Hal 4C **130**
Dale St. BD1: B'frd 4E **91** (3D **6**)
  BD18: Ship 2B **70**
  BD21: Keigh 4C **34**
  HX6: Hal 5H **147**
Dales Way LS20: Guis 5H **39**
Dalesway BD16: Bgly 2D **50**
Dale Ter. HX6: Hal 5H **147**
                           (off Greenups Ter.)
Dale Vw. BD20: Sils 1E **15**
  BD20: Stee 6C **14**
  HX2: Hal 2D **146**
  LS29: I'ly 5A **10**
Dale Vw. Cl. BD21: Keigh 1C **48**
Daleview Ct. BD17: Bail 5A **52**
Dale Vw. Gro. BD21: Keigh 1C **48**
Dale Vw. Rd. BD21: Keigh 2C **48**
Dale Vw. Way BD21: Keigh 1C **48**
Dale Vs. LS18: H'fth 2C **75**
Dallam Av. BD18: Ship 1G **69**
Dallam Gro. BD18: Ship 6G **51**
Dallam Rd. BD18: Ship 1G **69**
Dallam Wlk. BD18: Ship 1H **69**
Dalton Av. LS11: Leeds 3G **117**
Dalton Bank Rd. HD5: Hud 6H **163**
Dalton Gro. LS11: Leeds 3G **117**
Dalton La. BD21: Keigh 6B **34**
Dalton Mills Bus. Complex
  BD21: Keigh 6C **34**
Dalton Rd. BD21: Keigh 6C **34**
  LS11: Leeds 3G **117**
Dalton St. HX6: Hal 4H **147**
Dalton Ter. BD8: B'frd 3B **90**
  BD21: Keigh 5C **34**
                           (off Surrey St.)
Damask St. HX1: Hal 1F **149** (2A **164**)
Demems BD22: Keigh 5F **47**
Demems La. BD22: Keigh 5F **47**
Demems Rd. BD21: Keigh 5G **47**
Demems Station
  Vintage Carriages Trust Mus. of
  Rail Travel 5G **47**
DAM HEAD 4A **130**
Dam Head Rd. HX6: Hal 4A **148**
Dam La. LS19: Yead 6G **41**
Damon Av. BD10: B'frd 5C **72**

Damside BD21: Keigh 1H **47**
Damson Ct. BD14: B'frd 2E **109**
Danby Av. BD4: B'frd 5H **111**
Danby Wlk. LS9: Leeds 4D **98**
Dancroft BD22: Haw 3C **64**
Danebury Rd. HD6: Brigh 2B **162**
Dane Ct. BD4: B'frd 2C **112**
Danefield Ter. LS21: Otley 3F **23**
Dane Hill Dr. BD4: B'frd 1C **112**
Danella Cres. WF2: Wake 6D **156**
Daniel Cl. BD21: Keigh 4G **47**
Daniel Ct. BD4: B'frd 3D **112**
Daniel St. BD3: B'frd 4B **92**
Dan La. BD13: B'frd 4E **109**
Dansk Way LS29: I'ly 4F **11**
Danum Dr. BD17: Bail 5C **52**
Danum Ter. HX3: Hal 4C **130**
Darcey Hey La. HX2: Hal 4C **148**
Darcy Ct. LS15: Leeds 3E **101**
Darfield Av. LS8: Leeds 6E **79**
Darfield Cres. LS8: Leeds 6E **79**
Darfield Gro. LS8: Leeds 6D **78**
Darfield Ho. BD10: B'frd 3A **72**
                           (off Summerfield Rd.)
Darfield Pl. LS8: Leeds 6E **79**
Darfield Rd. LS8: Leeds 6E **79**
Darfield St. BD1: B'frd 3D **90** (2B **6**)
  LS8: Leeds 6E **79**
Dark La. BD22: Oxen 6C **64**
  HX2: Hal 3H **147**
  HX3: Hal 2C **150**
                           (Barrowclough La.)
  HX3: Hal 5D **150**
                           (Church La.)
  HX7: Heb B 5A **126**
  LS15: Bar E 1D **82**
  WF17: Bat 4B **136**
Darkwood Cl. LS17: Leeds 3E **61**
Darkwood Way LS17: Leeds 3E **61**
Darley Av. LS10: Leeds 6B **118**
Darley Mall BD1: B'frd 4D **6**
Darley St. BD1: B'frd 4E **91** (3C **6**)
                           (not continuous)
  BD20: Keigh 4H **33**
Darnay La. BD5: B'frd 2E **111**
Darnes Av. HX2: Hal 4C **148**
Darnley La. LS15: Leeds 5E **101**
Darnley Rd. LS16: Leeds 2B **76**
Darren St. BD4: B'frd 5C **92**
Dartmouth M. LS27: Morl 4H **137**
Dartmouth Av. LS27: Morl 5A **138**
Dartmouth Ter. BD8: B'frd 1C **90**
Dartmouth Way LS11: Leeds 3A **118**
Darwin St. BD5: B'frd 2C **110**
Davenport Ho. BD3: B'frd 2G **7**
David Lloyd Leisure 5H **59**
David St. LS11: Leeds 5H **97**
Davies Av. LS8: Leeds 1D **78**
Dawlish Av. LS9: Leeds 3F **99**
Dawlish Cres. LS9: Leeds 3F **99**
Dawlish Gro. LS9: Leeds 4F **99**
Dawlish Mt. LS9: Leeds 3F **99**
Dawlish Pl. LS9: Leeds 3F **99**
Dawlish Rd. LS9: Leeds 3F **99**
Dawlish Row LS9: Leeds 3F **99**
Dawlish St. LS9: Leeds 3F **99**
Dawlish Ter. LS9: Leeds 3F **99**
Dawlish Wlk. LS9: Leeds 4F **99**
Dawnay Rd. BD5: B'frd 2B **110**
Dawrah Rd. BD20: Keigh 2G **33**
Dawson Av. BD6: B'frd 5C **110**
Dawson Hill LS27: Morl 2A **138**
Dawson La. BD4: B'frd 4A **112**
                           (Dawson Mt.)
  BD4: B'frd 3A **114**
                           (Keeper La.)
  LS26: Rothw 1A **142**
Dawson Mt. BD4: B'frd 4A **112**
Dawson Pl. BD4: B'frd 4B **112**
  BD21: Keigh 2A **48**
Dawson Rd. BD21: Keigh 2A **48**
  LS11: Leeds 2G **117**
Dawsons Cnr. LS28: Pud 1G **93**

Dawsons Ct. LS14: Leeds 5D **80**
Dawsons Mdw. LS28: Pud 1G **93**
Dawsons Ter. LS28: Pud 1G **93**
Dawson St. BD4: B'frd 3A **112**
  BD10: B'frd 6H **53**
  LS28: Pud 2H **93**
  WF3: E Ard 6D **138**
Dawsons Yd. LS21: Otley 4D **22**
Dawson Ter. BD4: B'frd 4A **112**
Dawson Way BD21: Keigh 2A **48**
Deaconess Cl. LS29: I'ly 6D **10**
Dealburn Rd. BD12: B'frd 2D **132**
Deal St. BD21: Keigh 5C **46**
  HX1: Hal 3H **149** (5D **164**)
Dean Av. LS8: Leeds 3E **79**
Dean Beck Av. BD6: B'frd 4E **111**
Dean Beck Ct. BD6: B'frd 5F **111**
Dean Cl. BD8: B'frd 3F **89**
  WF2: Wake 6D **156**
Dean Clough 1G **149** (1B **164**)
Dean Clough HX3: Hal . . .1G **149** (2B **164**)
Dean Clough Galleries *1B 164*
  (in Dean Clough)
Dean Clough Office Pk.
  HX3: Hal 1G **149** (1A **164**)
Dean Ct. HX3: Hal 1E **159**
  LS8: Leeds 3E **79**
Dean End HX4: Hal 3G **159**
Deanery Bldg. BD10: B'frd 4A **72**
Deanfield Av. LS27: Morl 1H **137**
Dean Hall Cl. LS27: Morl 3H **137**
Dean Head LS18: H'fth 5C **42**
Dean Ho. HX2: Hal 5D **126**
Deanhurst Gdns. LS27: Morl 1F **137**
Deanhurst Ind. Cen. LS27: Morl 1F **137**
Dean La. BD13: B'frd 2G **87**
  BD22: Keigh 1A **46**
  (not continuous)
  HX6: Hal 6E **147**
  LS18: H'fth, Yead 5C **42**
  LS20: Guis 5F **39**
Dean M. LS18: H'fth 5D **42**
Dean Pk. Av. BD11: B'frd 6A **114**
Dean Pk. Dr. BD11: B'frd 6A **114**
Dean Pastures BD11: B'frd 1A **136**
Dean Rd. BD6: B'frd 5D **110**
Dean's Ter. HX3: Hal 4F **129**
Deanstones Cres. BD13: B'frd 5A **108**
Deanstones La. BD13: B'frd 5H **107**
Dean St. BD22: Haw 2D **64**
  HX4: Hal 5G **159**
  HX5: Ell 5B **160**
  LS29: I'ly 4E **11**
Deansway LS27: Morl 1H **137**
Deanswood Cl. LS17: Leeds 4G **59**
Deanswood Dr. LS17: Leeds 4F **59**
Deanswood Gdns. LS17: Leeds 4F **59**
Deanswood Gth. LS17: Leeds 4G **59**
Deanswood Grn. LS17: Leeds 4F **59**
Deanswood Hill LS17: Leeds 4F **59**
Deanswood Pl. LS17: Leeds 4G **59**
Deanswood Ri. LS17: Leeds 4G **59**
Deanswood Vw. LS17: Leeds 4G **59**
Dean Vw. WF17: Bat 5B **136**
Deanwood Av. BD15: B'frd 1C **88**
Deanwood Cres. BD15: B'frd 6C **68**
Deanwood Wlk. BD15: B'frd 1C **88**
Dearden St. HX6: Hal 4H **147**
Dearne Cft. LS22: Weth 1E **13**
Dee Ct. BD22: Keigh 5C **46**
Deep Dale LS23: B Spa 2A **30**
Deepdale Cl. BD17: Bail 5A **52**
Deepdale La. LS23: B Spa 2H **29**
Deep La. BD13: B'frd 1E **107**
  BD14: B'frd 6E **89**
  HD6: Brigh 1E **163**
  HX2: Hal 2F **147**
Deerstone Ridge LS22: Weth 1E **13**
Defarge Ct. *BD5: B'frd* *6C 52*
  (off Newton St.)
Deighton Cl. LS22: Weth 3F **13**
DEIGHTON GATES **1E 13**
Deighton Rd. LS22: Weth 1E **13**
Deighton Vw. LS6: Leeds 6E **59**

De Lacies Ct. LS26: Rothw 6C **120**
De Lacies Rd. LS26: Rothw 6C **120**
De Lacy Av. BD4: B'frd 5H **111**
De Lacy Mt. LS5: Leeds 5A **76**
Delamere St. BD5: B'frd 3D **110**
Delaware Ct. BD4: B'frd 5H **111**
Delf Cl. HX3: B'frd 6G **109**
Delf Hill HD6: Brigh 4G **161**
Delius Av. BD10: B'frd 4C **72**
Dell, The BD13: B'frd 3B **66**
Dell Ct. Bard 2F **45**
Dell Cft. BD20: Sils 2C **14**
Dellside Fold BD13: B'frd 3B **66**
Delph Cotts. HX4: Hal 4B **158**
Delph Ct. LS6: Leeds 5G **77**
Delph Cres. BD14: B'frd 1D **108**
Delph Cft. Vw. BD21: Keigh 1B **48**
Delph Dr. BD14: B'frd 1D **108**
Delph End LS28: Pud 4F **93**
Delph Gro. BD14: B'frd 1D **108**
DELPH HILL
  Bradford 2C **132**
  Halifax 5E **149**
Delph Hill BD17: Bail 3C **52**
  HX2: Hal 5E **149**
Delph Hill Fold HX2: Hal 5D **148**
Delph Hill La. HX2: Hal 5D **126**
Delph Hill Rd. HX2: Hal 5D **148**
Delph Hill Ter. *HX2: Hal* 5D **148**
  (off Delph Hill Rd.)
Delph Ho. BD21: Keigh 2A **48**
Delph La. LS6: Leeds 5G **77**
Delph Mt. LS6: Leeds 5G **77**
Delph Pl. HD6: Brigh 4G **161**
Delph St. HX1: Hal 3F **149** (5A **164**)
Delph Ter. BD4: B'frd 1D **108**
  HX4: Hal 4B *158*
  (off Barsey Grn. La.)
Delph Vw. LS6: Leeds 5G **77**
Delphwood Cl. BD16: Bgly 4E **51**
Delverne Gro. BD2: B'frd 6A **72**
Demontfort Ho. *BD4: B'frd* *1C 112*
  (off Ned La.)
Denbigh App. LS9: Leeds 1H **99**
Denbigh Cl. LS9: Leeds 1H **99**
Denbigh Hgts. LS9: Leeds 1H **99**
Denbrook Av. BD4: B'frd 4D **112**
Denbrook Cl. BD4: B'frd 4D **112**
Denbrook Cres. BD4: B'frd 5D **112**
Denbrook Wlk. BD4: B'frd 4D **112**
Denbrook Way BD4: B'frd 4D **112**
Denbury Mt. BD4: B'frd 3C **112**
Denby Cl. WF17: Bat 6H **135**
Denby Ct. BD22: Keigh 5B **46**
Denby Dr. BD17: Bail 6B **52**
DENBY HILL **5A 46**
Denby Hill Rd. BD22: Keigh 5B **46**
Denby Ho. *BD4: B'frd* 4D **112**
  BD17: Bail *6C 52*
  (off Denby Dr.)
Denby La. BD15: B'frd 2D **88**
Denby Mt. BD22: Oxen 1C **84**
Denby Pl. HX6: Hal 4H **147**
Denby Rd. BD21: Keigh 2A **48**
Denby St. BD8: B'frd 3C **90**
Dence Grn. BD4: B'frd 6C **92**
Dence Pl. LS15: Leeds 3A **100**
Dendrum Cl. BD22: Keigh 4C **46**
Dene Bank BD16: Bgly 1C **50**
Dene Cl. HX5: Ell 6A **160**
Dene Cres. BD7: B'frd 1G **109**
Dene Gro. BD20: Sils 1E **15**
Dene Hill BD17: Bail 4H **51**
Denehill BD9: B'frd 1F **89**
Dene Ho. Ct. LS2: Leeds 1H **97**
Dene Mt. BD15: B'frd 2E **89**
Dene Pl. HX1: Hal 1F **149** (2A **164**)
Dene Rd. BD6: B'frd 4F **109**
Deneside Mt. BD5: B'frd 3D **110**
Deneside Ter. BD5: B'frd 3D **110**
Denesway LS25: Gar 6G **103**
Dene Vw. HX2: Hal 1D **146**
Deneway LS28: Pud 1G **93**
Denfield Av. HX3: Hal 5C **128**

Denfield Cres. HX3: Hal 5D **128**
Denfield Edge HX3: Hal 5D **128**
Denfield Gdns. HX3: Hal 5D **128**
Denfield La. HX3: Hal 5C **128**
Denfield Sq. HX3: Hal 5D **128**
Denham Av. LS27: Morl 5A **138**
Denham St. HD6: Brigh 2A **162**
DENHOLME **2C 86**
DENHOLME CLOUGH **5C 86**
DENHOLME GATE **6B 86**
Denholme Ga. BD13: B'frd 4C **86**
Denholme Ga. Rd. HX3: Hal 5E **131**
Denholme House **4C 86**
Denholme Rd. BD22: Oxen 1D **84**
Denison Hall LS3: Leeds 2G **97** (2A **4**)
Denison Rd. LS3: Leeds 3G **97** (3A **4**)
Denison St. LS19: Yead 6F **41**
Dennil Cres. LS15: Leeds 5F **81**
Dennil Rd. LS15: Leeds 6F **81**
Dennison Fold BD4: B'frd 6C **92**
Dennison Hill LS21: Otley 3F **23**
Dennistead Cres. LS6: Leeds 4D **76**
Denshaw Dr. LS27: Morl 3C **138**
Denshaw Gro. LS27: Morl 3C **138**
Denshaw La. WF3: Leeds 4F **139**
DENTON **2H 11**
Denton Av. LS8: Leeds 1D **78**
Denton Dr. BD16: Bgly 3E **51**
Denton Gro. LS8: Leeds 1D **78**
Denton Rd. LS29: Den 1H **11**
  LS29: I'ly 4C **10**
  (Clifford Rd.)
  LS29: I'ly 5G **11**
  (Manley Rd.)
Denton Row BD13: B'frd 3B **86**
  LS12: Leeds 5A **96**
Denton Ter. LS27: Morl 5A **138**
Dent St. LS9: Leeds 4D **98**
Derby Pl. BD3: B'frd 4B **92**
  LS19: Yead 3F *55*
  (off North St.)
Derby Rd. BD3: B'frd 4C **92**
  LS19: Yead 3F **55**
Derbyshire St. LS10: Leeds 2D **118**
Derby St. BD7: B'frd 1B **110**
  BD13: B'frd 4H **107**
  BD14: B'frd 1D **108**
  HX6: Hal 5B **148**
Derby Ter. BD10: B'frd 1C **72**
Derry Hill LS29: Men 2F **39**
Derry Hill Gdns. LS29: Men 1F **39**
Derry La. LS29: Men 1F **39**
Derwent Av. BD15: B'frd 5G **67**
  BD17: Bail 6G **51**
  (not continuous)
  LS25: Gar 5F **103**
  LS26: Rothw 1E **143**
Derwent Dr. BD20: Sils 3E **15**
Derwent Dr. LS16: Leeds 3D **58**
Derwent Ho. HX3: Hal 6E **129**
Derwent Pl. BD13: B'frd 3G **107**
  LS11: Leeds 5G **97**
Derwent Ri. LS22: Weth 1D **12**
Derwent Rd. BD2: B'frd 6G **71**
  BD21: Keigh 5D **34**
Derwentwater Gro. LS6: Leeds 4D **76**
Derwentwater Ter. LS6: Leeds 4D **76**
Derwent Way LS15: Leeds 3F **101**
Devon Cl. LS2: Leeds 1H **97**
Devon Rd. LS2: Leeds 1H **97**
Devonshire Av. LS8: Leeds 6E **61**
Devonshire Cl. LS8: Leeds 5E **61**
  (not continuous)
Devonshire Cres. LS8: Leeds 6E **61**
Devonshire Gdns. LS2: Leeds 6H **77**
Devonshire La. LS8: Leeds 5E **61**
Devonshire Pl. LS19: Yead 6F **41**
Devonshire St. BD21: Keigh 6G **33**
Devonshire St. W. BD21: Keigh 6G **33**
Devonshire Ter. BD9: B'frd 1C **90**
Devon St. HX1: Hal 3D **148**
Devon Way HD6: Brigh 3B **152**
Devro Ct. LS9: Leeds 1F **119**

Dewar Cl. LS22: Coll 2B 28
Dewfield Cl. BD4: B'frd 4A 112
Dewhirst Cl. BD17: Bail 5D 52
Dewhirst Pl. BD4: B'frd 6B 92
Dewhirst Rd. BD17: Bail 5D 52
   HD6: Brigh 5A 152
Dewhirst St. BD15: B'frd 4G 67
Dewsbury Rd. BD19: Cleck 4F 135
   HD6: Brigh 5C 160
   HX5: Ell 5C 160
   LS11: Leeds 5A 98
             (Meadow La.)
   LS11: Leeds 6F 117
            (Pk. Wood Cl.)
   WF3: Dew, E Ard, Leeds, Morl
   . . . . .5E 139
   WF12: Dew, E Ard 3B 154
   WF17: Bat 4F 135
Diadem Dr. LS14: Leeds 2A 100
Dial St. LS9: Leeds 5D 98
Diamond St. BD22: Keigh 3G 47
   HX1: Hal 1E 149
Diamond Ter. HX1: Hal 1E 149
   HX2: Hal 4D 148
Dibb La. LS19: Yead 6D 40
Dib Cl. LS8: Leeds 4H 79
Dib La. LS8: Leeds 4H 79
Dickens St. BD5: B'frd 2E 111
   HX2: Hal 2C 148
Dickinson St. LS18: H'fth 5E 57
Dick La. BD3: B'frd 4C 92
   BD4: B'frd 1B 112
Dick's Gth. Rd. LS29: Men 1F 39
Digby Rd. LS29: Men 1G 39
Digley Av. BD6: B'frd 3E 109
Digpal Rd. LS27: Leeds 4C 116
Dimples La. BD20: Keigh 5H 35
   BD22: Haw 2B 64
Dinsdale Bldgs. *LS19: Yead* 1E 55
             (off Back La.)
DIRK HILL 6C 90
Dirkhill Rd. BD7: B'frd 6C 90
Dirkhill St. BD7: B'frd 6B 90
Discovery Rd. HX1: Hal . . .3H 149 (6D 164)
Dispensary Wlk.
   HX1: Hal 2H 149 (4D 164)
Disraeli Gdns. LS11: Leeds 1H 117
Disraeli Ter. LS11: Leeds 1H 117
Dixon Av. BD7: B'frd 6H 89
Dixon Cl. BD20: Stee 6C 14
   HX4: Hal 3E 159
Dixon La. LS12: Leeds 6C 96
Dixon La. Rd. LS12: Leeds 6C 96
Dob HX6: Hal 6D 146
Dobb Kiln La. BD16: Bgly 6D 50
Dob La. HX6: Hal 6D 146
Dobrudden Cvn. Pk. BD17: Bail . . .2H 51
Dobson Av. LS11: Leeds 2A 118
Dobson Gro. LS11: Leeds 2A 118
Dobson Pl. LS11: Leeds 2A 118
Dobsons Row WF3: Rothw 5H 141
Dobsons Wharf BD20: Sils 3E 15
Dobson Ter. LS11: Leeds 2A 118
Dobson Vw. LS11: Leeds 2A 118
Dockfield Ind. Pk. BD17: Ship 6D 52
Dockfield Pl. BD17: Ship 1C 70
Dockfield Rd. BD17: Ship 1C 70
Dockfield Ter. BD17: Ship 1C 70
Dock La. BD17: Ship 6C 52
   BD18: Ship 1C 70
Dockroyd BD22: Keigh 6D 46
Dockroyd La. BD22: Keigh 5C 46
Dock St. LS10: Leeds 4A 98 (6F 5)
Doctor Hill BD10: B'frd 2H 71
            (Evesham Gro.)
   BD10: B'frd 3G 71
            (Highfield Rd.)
   HX2: Hal 6B 128
Doctor La. BD10: B'frd 6H 53
Doctors La. WF10: Kip 2G 145
Dodge Holme Cl. HX2: Hal 3B 128
Dodge Holme Ct. *HX2: Hal* 3B 128
       (off Dodge Holme Rd.)
Dodge Holme Dr. HX2: Hal 3A 128

Dodge Holme Gdns. HX2: Hal 3B 128
Dodge Holme Rd. HX2: Hal 3B 128
Dodgson Av. LS7: Leeds 6C 78
Dodgson St. HX5: Ell 6B 160
Doe Pk. BD13: B'frd 2D 86
Dog Kennel La. HX3: Hal 4A 150
Dog La. HX4: Hal 4B 158
Dol BD22: Oxen 2E 85
Doles La. HD6: Brigh 5E 153
Dole St. BD13: B'frd 5A 88
Dolfin Pl. HD2: Hud 6F 163
Doll La. BD13: B'frd 5C 66
Dolly La. LS9: Leeds 1C 98
Dolphin Ct. LS9: Leeds 4C 98
   LS13: Leeds 2D 94
Dolphin La. BD16: B'frd 1C 66
   WF3: E Ard, Leeds 5C 140
          (not continuous)
Dolphin Rd. LS10: Leeds 2C 140
Dolphin St. LS9: Leeds 4C 98
Dolphin Ter. BD13: B'frd 5G 107
Dombey St. HX1: Hal 2E 149
Domestic La. LS12: Leeds 6F 97
Domestic St. LS11: Leeds 5F 97
Dominion Av. LS7: Leeds 3B 78
Dominion Cl. LS7: Leeds 3B 78
Dominion Ind. Pk. HX3: Hal 1E 151
Donald Aldred Dr. LS29: Burl W . . .3E 21
Donald Av. BD6: B'frd 5C 110
Donald St. LS28: Pud 1H 93
Don Av. LS22: Weth 1D 12
Doncaster St. HX3: Hal 6H 149
Don Ct. BD20: Sils 2E 15
Donisthorpe St. BD5: B'frd 2D 110
   LS10: Leeds 6C 98
Don St. BD21: Keigh 5H 33
Dorchester Ct. BD4: B'frd 2C 112
Dorchester Cres. BD4: B'frd 2C 112
   BD17: Bail 3F 53
Dorchester Dr. HX2: Hal 4C 148
   LS19: Yead 1H 55
Dorchester Rd. HD2: Hud 6B 162
Dorian Cl. BD10: B'frd 3B 72
Dorothy St. BD21: Keigh 4G 47
Dorset Av. LS8: Leeds 5E 79
Dorset Cl. BD5: B'frd 2C 110
Dorset Gro. LS28: Pud 3A 94
Dorset Mt. LS8: Leeds 6E 79
Dorset Rd. LS8: Leeds 5E 79
Dorset St. BD5: B'frd 2C 110
   LS8: Leeds 5E 79
Dorset Ter. LS8: Leeds 6E 79
Dortmund Sq. LS2: Leeds 3E 5
Dotterel Glen LS27: Morl 4D 138
Douglas Av. WF17: Bat 3A 154
Douglas Cres. BD18: Ship 3D 70
Douglas Dr. BD4: B'frd 1A 112
Douglas Rd. BD4: B'frd 1A 112
Douglas St. BD22: Haw 1E 65
   HX3: Hal 5F 129
Douglas Towers BD5: B'frd 6C 6
Dove Cl. LS22: Weth 1E 13
Dovedale Cl. HX3: Hal 1D 130
Dovedale Gdns. LS15: Leeds 1H 101
Dovedale Gth. LS15: Leeds 6H 81
Dover St. BD3: B'frd 2F 91
   LS25: Gar 4H 103
Dovesdale Gro. BD5: B'frd 3C 110
Dovesdale Rd. BD5: B'frd 3D 110
Dove St. BD18: Ship 1H 69
   BD22: Haw 2D 64
Dowkell La. LS23: B Spa 2C 30
Dowker St. HX1: Hal 4D 148
DOWLEY GAP 5E 51
Dowley Gap La. BD16: Bgly 6D 50
Downham St. BD3: B'frd 5G 91 (5H 7)
Downing Cl. BD3: B'frd 4H 91 (3H 7)
Downside Cres. BD15: B'frd 2C 88
Dracup Av. BD7: B'frd 6G 89
Dracup Rd. BD7: B'frd 2H 109
Dradishaw Rd. BD20: Sils 2D 14
Dragon Cl. LS12: Leeds 5F 97
Dragon Cres. LS12: Leeds 6D 96
Dragon Dr. LS12: Leeds 6C 96

Dragon Rd. LS12: Leeds 6D 96
Dragons Health Club 6F 41
Drake Fold BD12: B'frd 4C 132
Drake La. BD11: B'frd 2A 136
Drakes Ind. Est. HX3: Hal 3E 129
Drake St. BD1: B'frd 5F 91 (5E 7)
   BD21: Keigh 5A 34
Draughton Gro. BD5: B'frd 4D 110
Draughton St. BD5: B'frd 4D 110
Draycott Wlk. BD4: B'frd 3C 112
Drayton Mnr. Yd. *LS11: Leeds* 1A 118
           (off Moor Cres.)
Drewry Rd. BD21: Keigh 6H 33
Drewton St. BD1: B'frd 4D 90 (3B 6)
Driftholme Rd. BD11: B'frd 6B 114
DRIGHLINGTON 1A 136
Drighlington By-Pass BD4: B'frd . . .6G 113
   BD11: B'frd 1G 135
   WF17: B'frd 1G 135
Drill Hall Bus. Cen. LS29: I'ly 5E 11
Drill Pde. BD8: B'frd 2D 90
Drill St. BD21: Keigh 6A 34
   BD22: Haw 3C 64
Drive, The BD10: B'frd 3B 72
   BD13: B'frd 3A 86
   BD16: Bgly 1A 50
   HX3: Hal 1F 151
   LS8: Leeds 1D 78
   LS9: Leeds 4C 98
   LS15: Leeds 1F 101
   LS16: Leeds 4A 58
   LS17: Bard 1F 45
   LS17: Leeds 1F 59
   LS25: Kip 5G 123
   LS26: Swil 4A 122
   LS29: Burl W 3E 21
Driver Pl. LS12: Leeds 5E 97
Driver St. LS12: Leeds 5F 97
Driver Ter. BD20: Sils 1E 15
   LS12: Leeds 5E 97
Drove Rd. Ho. *BD5: B'frd* 2E 111
       (off Bowling Old La.)
Drovers Way BD2: B'frd 5E 71
DRUB 5C 134
Drub La. BD19: Cleck 5C 134
Druggist La. LS29: Add 1D 8
Druids St. BD14: B'frd 1D 108
Druids Vw. Av. BD16: Bgly 6H 35
Drummond Av. LS16: Leeds 3C 76
Drummond Ct. LS16: Leeds 3C 76
Drummond Rd. BD8: B'frd 2C 90
   LS16: Leeds 2C 76
Drummond Trad. Est.
   BD8: B'frd 3D 90 (1A 6)
Drury Av. LS18: H'fth 1D 74
Drury Cl. LS18: H'fth 1D 74
Drury La. HX4: Hal 6D 158
   LS18: H'fth 1D 74
           (not continuous)
Dry Carr La. HX2: Hal 2C 126
Dryclough Cl. HX3: Hal 6G 149
Dryclough La. HX3: Hal 6G 149
Dryden St. BD1: B'frd 5F 91 (6F 7)
   BD16: Bgly 4B 50
Dubb La. BD16: Bgly 4B 50
Duchy Av. BD9: B'frd 6G 69
Duchy Cres. BD9: B'frd 6G 69
Duchy Dr. BD9: B'frd 1G 89
           (not continuous)
Duchy Gro. BD9: B'frd 6G 69
Duchy Vs. BD9: B'frd 6G 69
Duchywood BD9: B'frd 6G 69
Ducie St. BD10: B'frd 6H 53
Duckett Gro. LS28: Pud 3D 92
Duckett La. BD1: B'frd 4E 91 (3C 6)
Ducking Well Cl. BD22: Haw 3C 64
Duckworth Gro. BD9: B'frd 1H 89
Duckworth La. BD9: B'frd 2G 89
Duckworth Ter. BD9: B'frd 1H 89
Dudley Av. WF17: Bat 5C 136
Dudley Cres. HX2: Hal 2B 128
Dudley Gro. BD4: B'frd 6C 92
DUDLEY HILL 3A 112
Dudley Hill Rd. BD2: B'frd 6H 71

Dudley St. BD4: B'frd 6C **92**
(Dennison Fold)
BD4: B'frd 2A **112**
(School St.)
BD4: B'frd 2A **112**
(Wakefield Rd.)
Dudwell Av. HX3: Hal 1H **159**
Dudwell Gro. HX3: Hal 1G **159**
Dudwell La. HX3: Hal 1G **159**
Dufton App. LS14: Leeds 6C **80**
Duich Rd. BD6: B'frd 1G **131**
Duinen St. BD5: B'frd 6F **91**
Dukes Hill LS29: I'ly 3C **10**
Duke St. BD1: B'frd 4E **91** (3D 6)
BD20: Keigh 4H **33**
BD22: Haw 2D **64**
HX2: Hal 6D **126**
HX5: Ell 5B **160**
LS9: Leeds 4B **98** (5H 5)
Dulverton Cl. LS11: Leeds 4D **116**
Dulverton Ct. LS11: Leeds 4D **116**
Dulverton Gdns. LS11: Leeds 3C **116**
Dulverton Gth. LS11: Leeds 4C **116**
Dulverton Grn. LS11: Leeds 4D **116**
(Dulverton Cl.)
LS11: Leeds 4C **116**
(Dulverton Gro.)
Dulverton Gro. BD4: B'frd 2B **112**
LS11: Leeds 4C **116**
Dulverton Pl. LS11: Leeds 4C **116**
Dulverton Sq. LS11: Leeds 4D **116**
Dunbar Ct. LS26: Mick 4C **144**
Dunbar Cft. BD13: B'frd 4B **108**
Duncan Av. LS21: Otley 5B **22**
Duncan St. BD5: B'frd 6E **91**
LS1: Leeds 4A **98** (5F 5)
Dunce Pk. Cl. HX5: Ell 6B **160**
Duncombe Rd. BD8: B'frd 4H **89**
Duncombe St. BD8: B'frd 4A **90**
LS1: Leeds 3G **97** (4A 4)
Duncombe Way BD8: B'frd 4A **90**
Dundas St. BD21: Keigh 1B **48**
HX1: Hal 4D **148**
Dungeon La. LS26: Rothw 6B **142**
Dunhill Cres. LS9: Leeds 3A **100**
Dunhill Ri. LS9: Leeds 3A **100**
Dunkhill Cft. BD10: B'frd 2H **71**
DUNKIRK 2A **130**
Dunkirk Cres. HX1: Hal 3C **148**
Dunkirk Gdns. HX1: Hal 4C **148**
Dunkirk Hill LS12: Leeds 2D **96**
Dunkirk La. HX1: Hal 4C **148**
Dunkirk Ri. BD20: Keigh 3C **34**
Dunkirk St. HX1: Hal 3C **148**
Dunkirk Ter. HX1: Hal 3D **148**
Dunlin Cl. LS27: Morl 4D **138**
Dunlin Ct. LS10: Leeds 2B **140**
Dunlin Cft. LS10: Leeds 2B **140**
Dunlin Dr. LS10: Leeds 2B **140**
Dunlin Fold LS10: Leeds 2B **140**
Dunlin Way BD8: B'frd 4E **89**
Dunmore Av. BD13: B'frd 4G **107**
Dunn Cl. WF2: Wake 6D **156**
Dunningley La. WF3: Leeds 4F **139**
Dunnington Wlk. BD6: B'frd 1A **132**
Dunnock Av. BD13: B'frd 4D **108**
Dunnock Cft. LS27: Morl 4C **138**
Dunrobin Av. LS25: Gar 4H **103**
Dunsford Av. BD4: B'frd 5H **111**
Dunstarn Dr. LS16: Leeds 4D **58**
Dunstarn Gdns. LS16: Leeds 4E **59**
Dunstarn La. LS16: Leeds 5D **58**
Durban Av. LS11: Leeds 3F **117**
Durban Cres. LS11: Leeds 3F **117**
Durham Cft. LS28: Pud 6H **73**
Durham Rd. BD8: B'frd 2A **90**
Durham St. HX2: Hal 1C **148**
Durham Ter. BD8: B'frd 2A **90**
Durkheim Ct. BD3: B'frd 4A **92**
(off Amberley St.)
Durley Av. BD9: B'frd 6A **70**
Durling Dr. BD18: Ship 2E **71**
Durlston Gro. BD12: B'frd 3D **132**
Durlston Ter. BD12: B'frd 3D **132**

Durrance St. BD22: Keigh 1F **47**
Durrant Cl. LS22: Weth 4F **13**
Dutton Grn. LS14: Leeds 1C **80**
Dutton Way LS14: Leeds 2C **80**
Duxbury Ri. LS7: Leeds 1H **97**
Dye Ho. BD15: B'frd 4F **67**
Dyehouse Dr. BD19: Cleck 5A **134**
Dyehouse Fold BD12: B'frd 2G **133**
Dye Ho. La. HX6: Hal 2C **158**
Dyehouse La. BD15: B'frd 4E **67**
HD6: Brigh 2B **162**
LS28: Pud 1A **114**
(not continuous)
Dyehouse Rd. BD12: B'frd 2F **133**
Dyer La. HX3: Hal 6D **128**
Dyers Ct. LS6: Leeds 5F **77**
Dyer St. LS2: Leeds 3B **98** (4G 5)
Dyke BD22: Haw 2A **64**
Dyke Nook BD22: Oxen 3A **84**
Dyson Ho. LS4: Leeds 6B **76**
Dyson Pl. HX3: Hal 6A **150**
(off Ashgrove Av.)
Dyson Rd. HX1: Hal 1D **148**
Dyson St. BD1: B'frd 4D **90** (3A 6)
BD9: B'frd 5A **70**
HD6: Brigh 6A **152**

E

Eaglesfield Dr. BD6: B'frd 1H **131**
Eagle St. BD21: Keigh 6H **33**
BD22: Haw 2D **64**
Earlsmere Dr. LS27: Morl 2H **137**
Earl St. BD21: Keigh 5H **33**
BD22: Haw 3C **64**
Earlswood BD12: B'frd 4D **132**
Earlswood Av. LS8: Leeds 5D **60**
Earlswood Chase LS28: Pud 5A **94**
Earlswood Cres. LS25: Kip 3F **123**
Earlswood Mead LS28: Pud 5H **93**
Earl Ter. HX3: Hal 5E **129**
Easby Cl. LS29: I'ly 5B **10**
Easby Dr. LS29: I'ly 5B **10**
Easby Rd. BD7: B'frd 6D **90** (6A 6)
Easdale Cl. LS14: Leeds 4B **80**
Easdale Cres. LS14: Leeds 4C **80**
Easdale Mt. LS14: Leeds 5B **80**
Easdale Rd. LS14: Leeds 5B **80**
EAST ARDSLEY 2A **156**
East Av. BD21: Keigh 5A **34**
(not continuous)
EAST BIERLEY 6D **112**
East Bolton HX2: Hal 6C **106**
Eastbourne Rd. BD9: B'frd 4B **70**
EAST BOWLING 3G **111**
EASTBROOK 5F **91** (5F 7)
EASTBURN 6A **14**
Eastbury Av. BD6: B'frd 4F **109**
E. Busk La. LS21: Otley 3G **23**
East Byland HX2: Hal 1C **128**
EAST CARLTON 2H **41**
East C'way. LS16: Leeds 2D **58**
E. Causeway Cl. LS16: Leeds 2D **58**
E. Causeway Cres. LS16: Leeds 3D **58**
E. Causeway Va. LS16: Leeds 3E **59**
E. Chevin Rd. LS21: Otley 5F **23**
East Ct. LS28: Pud 6H **73**
(off Ebenezer St.)
East Cft. BD12: B'frd 5D **132**
East Croft M. BD12: B'frd 5D **132**
(off Garden Fld.)
Eastdean Bank LS14: Leeds 3C **80**
Eastdean Dr. LS14: Leeds 3C **80**
Eastdean Gdns. LS14: Leeds 3D **80**
Eastdean Ga. LS14: Leeds 4D **80**
Eastdean Grange LS14: Leeds 4D **80**
Eastdean Gro. LS14: Leeds 3D **80**
Eastdean Ri. LS14: Leeds 3D **80**
Eastdean Rd. LS14: Leeds 3C **80**
East Dene BD20: Sils 1E **15**
Easterly Av. LS8: Leeds 5E **79**
Easterly Cl. LS8: Leeds 6F **79**
Easterly Cres. LS8: Leeds 5E **79**

Easterly Cross LS8: Leeds 5F **79**
Easterly Gth. LS8: Leeds 5F **79**
Easterly Gro. LS8: Leeds 5E **79**
Easterly Mt. LS8: Leeds 5F **79**
Easterly Rd. LS8: Leeds 5E **79**
Easterly Sq. LS8: Leeds 5F **79**
Easterly Vw. LS8: Leeds 5E **79**
Eastfield BD13: B'frd 3B **86**
Eastfield Cres.
LS26: Rothw 1D **142**
Eastfield Dr. LS26: Rothw 1D **142**
Eastfield Gdns. BD4: B'frd 2C **112**
Eastfield La.
LS29: Burl W 3G **21**
E. Field St. LS9: Leeds 4C **98**
E. Fountains HX2: Hal 6B **106**
(off Field Head La.)
EAST GARFORTH 3H **103**
East Garforth Station (Rail) 4G **103**
Eastgate HX5: Ell 4B **160**
LS2: Leeds 3A **98** (4F 5)
LS16: B'hpe 2F **43**
Eastgate Cl. LS16: B'hpe 2F **43**
E. Grange Cl. LS10: Leeds 4C **118**
E. Grange Dr. LS10: Leeds 4C **118**
E. Grange Gth. LS10: Leeds 4C **118**
E. Grange Ri. LS10: Leeds 4C **118**
E. Grange Rd. LS10: Leeds 4C **118**
E. Grange Sq. LS10: Leeds 4C **118**
E. Grange Vw. LS10: Leeds 4C **118**
Easthorpe Ct. BD2: B'frd 5B **72**
EAST KESWICK 6E **27**
E. King St. LS9: Leeds 4C **98** (6H 5)
Eastland Wlk. LS13: Leeds 2G **95**
East Leeds Leisure Cen. 4A **100**
Eastleigh WF3: E Ard 1G **155**
Eastleigh Ct. WF3: E Ard 1G **155**
Eastleigh Dr. WF3: E Ard 1F **155**
Eastleigh Gro. BD5: B'frd 2C **110**
E. Manywells BD13: B'frd 5C **66**
EAST MOOR 3D **58**
E. Moor Av. LS8: Leeds 6D **60**
E. Moor Cl. LS8: Leeds 6D **60**
E. Moor Cres. LS8: Leeds 5D **60**
E. Moor Dr. LS8: Leeds 6E **61**
Eastmoor Ho. BD4: B'frd 3D **112**
E. Moor La. LS16: Leeds 3D **58**
E. Moor Rd. LS8: Leeds 5D **60**
EAST MORTON 5H **35**
East Mt. HD6: Brigh 6A **152**
E. Mount Pl. HD6: Brigh 6A **152**
East Pde. BD1: B'frd 4F **91** (4F 7)
(not continuous)
BD17: Bail 3D **52**
BD20: Stee 6D **14**
BD21: Keigh 6A **34**
HX6: Hal 5B **148**
LS1: Leeds 3H **97** (4D 4)
LS29: I'ly 5E **11**
LS29: Men 1G **39**
East Pk. Dr. LS9: Leeds 4D **98**
East Pk. Gro. LS9: Leeds 4E **99**
East Pk. Mt. LS9: Leeds 4E **99**
East Pk. Pde. LS9: Leeds 4E **99**
East Pk. Pl. LS9: Leeds 4E **99**
East Pk. Rd. HX3: Hal 6E **129**
LS9: Leeds 4D **98**
East Pk. St. LS9: Leeds 4E **99**
LS27: Morl 4H **137**
East Pk. Ter. LS9: Leeds 4E **99**
East Pk. Vw. LS9: Leeds 4E **99**
East Riddlesden Hall 4D **34**
E. Ridge Vw. LS25: Gar 2A **104**
EAST RIGTON 1F **45**
East Rd. BD12: B'frd 1E **133**
East Royd BD22: Keigh 5D **46**
HX3: Hal 6E **131**
(off Groveville)
E. Side Ct. LS28: Pud 6D **94**
E. Squire La. BD8: B'frd 2C **90**
East St. HD6: Brigh 2A **162**
HX3: Hal 2A **152**
LS9: Leeds 4B **98** (6H 5)
East Ter. BD22: Haw 1E **65**

East Vw. BD12: B'frd 2F **133**
BD13: B'frd 3E **109**
(Lingfield Ter.)
BD13: B'frd 3G **87**
(Up. Heights Rd.)
BD19: Cleck 3G **153**
BD20: Sils 2E **15**
HX3: Hal 2A **152**
HX5: Ell 5E **161**
HX6: Hal 4A **148**
LS15: Leeds 1E **101**
LS19: Yead 1G **55**
LS25: Kip 3H **123**
LS25: M'fld 6F **105**
LS26: Rothw 2E **143**
LS27: Morl 2E **137**
LS28: Pud 6A **94**
East Vw. Cotts. *LS28: Pud* *3B* **94**
(off Lane End)
East Vw. Rd. LS19: Yead 1G **55**
East Vw. Ter. BD12: B'frd 3E **133**
LS21: Otley *4F* **23**
(off Carlton St.)
Eastwood Av. HX2: Hal 6C **106**
HX6: Hal 6F **147**
Eastwood Cl. HX2: Hal 6C **106**
Eastwood Ct. HX3: Hal 5E **149**
Eastwood Cres. BD16: Bgly 1D **68**
LS14: Leeds 5F **81**
Eastwood Dr. LS14: Leeds 4F **81**
Eastwood Gdns. LS14: Leeds . . .5E **81**
Eastwood Gth. LS14: Leeds 5F **81**
Eastwood Gro. HX2: Hal 6C **106**
LS25: Gar 6G **103**
Eastwood La. LS14: Leeds 5F **81**
Eastwood Nook LS14: Leeds 5F **81**
Eastwood's Farm *HX2: Hal* *6C* **106**
(off Causeway Foot)
Eastwood St. BD4: B'frd 6F **91**
HD6: Brigh 6B **152**
HX3: Hal 5E **129**
Easy Rd. LS9: Leeds 5D **98**
Eaton Hill LS16: Leeds 4G **57**
Eaton M. LS10: Leeds 2A **140**
Eaton Rd. LS29: I'ly 6C **10**
Eaton Sq. LS10: Leeds 3A **140**
Eaton St. BD21: Keigh 3G **47**
Ebberston Gro. LS6: Leeds 6F **77**
Ebberston Pl. LS6: Leeds 6F **77**
Ebberston Ter. LS6: Leeds 6F **77**
Ebenezer Pl. BD7: B'frd 1A **110**
Ebenezer St. BD1: B'frd 5F **91** (5E **7**)
LS28: Pud 6H **73**
WF3: Rothw 4F **141**
Ebor Ct. *BD21: Keigh* *1H* **47**
(off Aireworth St.)
Ebor La. BD22: Haw 1C **64**
Ebor Mt. LS6: Leeds 1F **97**
LS25: Kip 3G **123**
Ebor Pl. LS6: Leeds 1F **97**
Ebor St. LS6: Leeds 1F **97**
Ebor Ter. *LS10: Leeds* *3C* **118**
(off Woodhouse Hill Rd.)
Ebor Way LS22: Weth 5C **12**
(Linton La.)
LS22: Weth 6H **13**
(Watersole La.)
Ebridge Ct. *BD16: Bgly* *4C* **50**
(off Edward St.)
Ecclesburn Av. LS9: Leeds 4E **99**
Ecclesburn Rd. LS9: Leeds 4E **99**
Ecclesburn St. LS9: Leeds 4E **99**
Ecclesburn Ter. LS9: Leeds 4E **99**
Eccles Ct. BD2: B'frd 5H **71**
ECCLESHILL 4H **71**
Eccleshill Swimming Pool 3B **72**
Eccup La. LS16: Leeds 1D **58**
Edale Gro. BD13: B'frd 5G **107**
Edale Way LS16: Leeds 4H **57**
Edderthorpe St. BD3: B'frd . .5G **91** (5H **7**)
Eddison Cl. LS16: Leeds 2D **58**
Eddison St. LS28: Pud 1H **93**
Eddison Wlk. LS16: Leeds 2D **58**
Eden Cl. BD12: B'frd 4D **132**

Eden Cres. LS4: Leeds 5B **76**
Eden Dr. LS4: Leeds 6B **76**
Eden Gdns. LS4: Leeds 6B **76**
Eden Gro. LS4: Leeds 6B **76**
Eden Mt. LS4: Leeds 5B **76**
Eden Rd. LS4: Leeds 5B **76**
Edensor Rd. BD21: Keigh 6G **33**
Eden Wlk. LS4: Leeds 6B **76**
Eden Way LS4: Leeds 6B **76**
Ederoyd Av. LS28: Pud 2F **93**
Ederoyd Cres. LS28: Pud 2E **93**
Ederoyd Dr. LS28: Pud 2F **93**
Ederoyd Gro. LS28: Pud 2F **93**
Ederoyd Mt. LS28: Pud 2F **93**
Ederoyd Ri. LS28: Pud 2E **93**
Edgar St. BD14: B'frd 1F **109**
Edgbaston Cl. LS17: Leeds 1G **59**
Edgbaston Wlk. LS17: Leeds 1G **59**
Edgebank Av. BD6: B'frd 1H **131**
Edge Bottom BD13: B'frd 2B **86**
Edge End BD13: B'frd 2C **86**
Edge End Gdns. BD6: B'frd 6G **109**
Edge End Rd. BD6: B'frd 5G **109**
Edgehill Cl. BD13: B'frd 4B **108**
Edgeholme La. HX2: Hal 2H **147**
Edgemoor Cl. BD4: B'frd 5C **112**
HX3: Hal 5F **149**
Edge Nook *BD6: B'frd* *4A* **110**
(off Windmill Hill)
Edgerton Rd. LS16: Leeds 1B **76**
Edgware Av. LS8: Leeds 1D **98**
Edgware Gro. LS8: Leeds 1D **98**
Edgware Mt. LS8: Leeds 1D **98**
Edgware Pl. LS8: Leeds 1D **98**
Edgware Row LS8: Leeds 1D **98**
Edgware St. LS8: Leeds 1D **98**
Edgware Ter. LS8: Leeds 1D **98**
Edgware Vw. LS8: Leeds 1D **98**
Edinburgh Av. LS12: Leeds 3A **96**
Edinburgh Gro. LS12: Leeds 3A **96**
Edinburgh Pl. LS12: Leeds 3A **96**
LS25: Gar 4H **103**
Edinburgh Rd. LS12: Leeds 3A **96**
Edinburgh Ter. LS12: Leeds 3A **96**
Ediths Vw. HX6: Hal 5H **147**
Edlington Cl. BD4: B'frd 2C **112**
Edmonton Pl. LS7: Leeds 3B **78**
Edmund St. BD5: B'frd 5D **90** (6B **6**)
Edrich Cl. BD12: B'frd 1E **133**
Edroyd Pl. LS28: Pud 6H **73**
Edroyd St. LS28: Pud 6H **73**
Education Rd. LS7: Leeds 6A **78**
Edward Cl. HX3: Hal 5C **150**
Edward Ct. WF2: Wake 4C **156**
Edward Dr. WF1: Wake 4F **157**
Edwards Rd. HX2: Hal 4C **148**
Edward St. BD4: B'frd 5F **91** (6E **7**)
(Bedford St.)
BD4: B'frd 4C **112**
(Lister St.)
BD16: Bgly 4C **50**
BD18: Ship 6H **51**
HD6: Brigh 1C **162**
(Albert St.)
HD6: Brigh 6A **152**
(Lightcliffe Rd.)
HX6: Hal 5H **147**
LS2: Leeds 3A **98** (3F **5**)
Edward Turner Cl. BD12: B'frd . . .1C **132**
Edwin Av. LS20: Guis 4B **40**
Edwin Rd. LS6: Leeds 1E **97**
Eel Holme Vw. St. BD20: Keigh . .3H **33**
Eel Mires Gth. LS22: Weth 3F **13**
Effingham Rd. BD16: Bgly 6E **49**
Egerton Gro. BD15: B'frd 2C **88**
Egerton St. HX6: Hal 5H **147**
Egerton Ter. *LS19: Yead* *4H* **55**
(off Town St.)
Eggleston Dr. BD4: B'frd 3D **112**
Egglestone Sq. LS23: B Spa 4A **30**
Eggleston St. LS13: Leeds 4B **74**
Egham Grn. BD10: B'frd 2H **71**
(off Ley Fleaks Rd.)
Egremont Cres. BD6: B'frd 1H **131**

Egremont St. HX6: Hal 6G **147**
Egremont Ter. *HX6: Hal* *6G* **147**
(off Egremont St.)
EGYPT 3G **87**
Egypt Rd. BD13: B'frd 3G **87**
Eider Cl. BD13: B'frd 4E **109**
Eighth Av. LS12: Leeds 5D **96**
LS26: Rothw 6C **120**
WF15: Liv 4H **153**
Eightlands Av. LS13: Leeds 1F **95**
Eightlands La. LS13: Leeds 1F **95**
Ekota Pl. LS8: Leeds 5D **78**
Elam Grange BD20: Keigh 2A **34**
Elam Wood BD20: Keigh 2B **34**
Elam Wood Rd. BD20: Keigh 1A **34**
Eland Ho. *HX5: Ell* *4B* **160**
(off Southgate)
Elbow La. BD2: B'frd 1H **91**
HX2: Hal 6E **127**
Elder Bank *BD13: B'frd* *3B* **66**
(off Keighley Rd.)
Elderberry Cl. BD20: Keigh 4F **35**
Elder Cl. WF17: Bat 5B **136**
Elder Cft. LS13: Leeds 2E **95**
Elder Gth. LS25: Gar 5H **103**
Elder La. HD2: Hud 6G **163**
Elder Lea HX3: Hal 4E **107**
Elder Mt. LS13: Leeds 2E **95**
Elder Pl. LS13: Leeds 2E **95**
Elder Ri. LS26: Rothw 1G **143**
Elder Rd. HD2: Hud 6F **163**
LS13: Leeds 2E **95**
Elder St. BD10: B'frd 2C **72**
BD20: Keigh 3G **33**
LS13: Leeds 2E **95**
Elderwood Gdns. BD10: B'frd 4C **72**
Eldon Pl. LS20: Guis 4C **40**
Eldon Pl. BD1: B'frd 3D **90** (2B **6**)
BD4: B'frd 1B **112**
Eldon St. HX3: Hal 6G **129** (1C **164**)
Eldon Ter. BD1: B'frd 3D **90** (2B **6**)
LS2: Leeds 1H **97**
Eldroth Mt. HX1: Hal 4E **149**
Eldroth Rd. HX1: Hal 4E **149**
ELDWICK 3D **50**
ELDWICK BECK 2E **51**
Eldwick Cft. BD16: Bgly 2E **51**
Eleanor Dr. LS28: Pud 2D **72**
Eleanor St. HD6: Brigh 2A **162**
Eleventh Av. WF15: Liv 4H **153**
Elford Gro. LS8: Leeds 6D **78**
Elford Pl. E. LS8: Leeds 6D **78**
Elford Pl. W. LS8: Leeds 6D **78**
Elford Rd. LS8: Leeds 6D **78**
Elgar Wlk. WF3: Wake 4H **157**
Elia St. BD21: Keigh 5B **34**
Eliot Gro. LS20: Guis 5D **40**
Eli St. BD5: B'frd 2F **111**
Elizabethan Manor House Art Gallery &
Mus. 5D **10**
Elizabeth Av. BD12: B'frd 3D **132**
Elizabeth Cl. BD12: B'frd 3D **132**
Elizabeth Ct. LS22: Coll 3B **28**
Elizabeth Cres. BD12: B'frd 3D **132**
Elizabeth Dr. BD12: B'frd 3D **132**
Elizabeth Gro. LS27: Morl 2C **138**
Elizabeth Ho. *HX2: Hal* *4C* **128**
(off Furness Pl.)
Elizabeth Ind. Est.
HX3: Hal 1E **149**
Elizabeth Pl. LS14: Leeds 4C **80**
Elizabeth St. BD5: B'frd 6E **91**
BD12: B'frd 3D **132**
BD16: Bgly 4C **50**
BD21: Keigh 6C **34**
BD22: Keigh 5D **46**
HX4: Hal 4H **159**
HX5: Ell 5B **160**
LS6: Leeds 6E **77**
ELLAND 5B **160**
Elland Baths 5B **160**
Elland Bri. HX5: Ell 4B **160**
Elland Fitness Cen. *5B* **160**
(off Southgate)

Elland Hall Farm Cvn. Pk.
HX4: Ell 4A 160
Elland La. HD6: Brigh 1A 162
HX5: Ell 4C 160
(not continuous)
ELLAND LOWER EDGE 4F 161
Elland Riorges Link HX5: Ell 4C 160
Elland Road 2E 117
Elland Rd. HD6: Brigh 6H 151
HX5: Ell 4C 160
(Elland Riorges Link)
HX5: Ell 2C 160
(Park Rd.)
LS11: Leeds 3D 116
(Crow Nest La.)
LS11: Leeds 6B 116
(Millshaw Pk. Way)
LS11: Leeds 1F 117
(Tilbury Rd.)
LS27: Morl 6B 116
Elland Rd. Ind. Pk. LS11: Leeds . .2D 116
Elland Ter. LS11: Leeds 6H 97
ELLAND UPPER EDGE 5E 161
Elland Way LS11: Leeds 3D 116
Elland Wood Bottom HX3: Hal 2H 159
HX4: Hal 2H 159
Ellar Carr Rd. BD10: B'frd 5A 54
BD13: B'frd 2A 66
Ellar Gdns. LS29: Men 5G 21
Ellar Ghyll LS21: Otley 6A 22
Ella St. BD21: Keigh 5B 34
Ellen Holme HX2: Hal 3D 146
Ellen Holme Rd. HX2: Hal 3D 146
Ellen Royd La. HX2: Hal 1C 146
Ellen Royd St. HX3: Hal . . .1G 149 (1C 164)
Ellen St. BD16: Bgly 4C 50
Ellenthorpe Rd. BD17: Bail 5G 51
Ellerburn Dr. BD6: B'frd 5G 109
Ellerby La. LS9: Leeds 5C 98
Ellerby Rd. LS9: Leeds 4C 98
Eller Ct. LS8: Leeds 3G 79
Ellercroft Av. BD7: B'frd 5A 90
Ellercroft Rd. BD7: B'frd 5A 90
Ellercroft Ter. BD7: B'frd 5A 90
Ellers Gro. LS8: Leeds 5D 78
Ellers Rd. LS8: Leeds 5D 78
Ellerton St. BD3: B'frd 4A 92
Ellicott Ct. LS29: Men 1G 39
Ellinthorpe St. BD4: B'frd 6H 91
Elliot Ct. BD13: B'frd 4H 107
Elliott St. BD18: Ship 1A 70
BD20: Sils 2D 14
Ellis Ct. HX3: Hal 4H 131
Ellis Fold LS12: Leeds 4B 96
Ellis La. LS25: Bar E 1D 102
Ellison Fold BD17: Bail 3C 52
Ellison St. HX3: Hal 6E 129
Ellis St. BD5: B'frd 2D 110
Ellis Ter. LS16: Leeds 3D 76
(off Glebe Ter.)
Ellistones Gdns. HX4: Hal 4E 159
Ellistones La. HX4: Hal 5E 159
Ellistones Pl. HX4: Hal 5E 159
Ellton Gro. BD6: B'frd 4A 110
Ellwood Cl. LS7: Leeds 2F 77
Elm Av. HX6: Hal 4H 147
LS25: Kip 2F 123
Elm Ct. BD11: B'frd 3F 135
BD15: B'frd 5G 67
Elm Cres. BD20: Keigh 5H 35
Elm Cft. LS14: Leeds 1E 81
Elmet Dr. LS15: Bar E 2E 83
Elmete Av. LS8: Leeds 2G 79
LS15: Scho 3H 81
Elmete Cl. LS8: Leeds 3H 79
Elmete Ct. LS8: Leeds 3G 79
Elmete Cft. LS15: Scho 3H 81
Elmete Dr. LS8: Leeds 2H 79
Elmete Grange LS29: Men 1G 39
Elmete Gro. LS8: Leeds 2G 79
Elmete Hill LS8: Leeds 3H 79
Elmete La. LS8: Leeds 2H 79
LS17: Leeds 6A 62
Elmete Mt. LS8: Leeds 3H 79

Elmete Wlk. LS8: Leeds 3G 79
Elmete Way LS8: Leeds 3H 79
Elmet Rd. LS15: Bar E 3E 83
Elmet Towers LS14: Leeds 5E 81
Elmfield BD17: Bail 3D 52
LS26: Rothw 2F 143
Elmfield Bus. Pk. LS25: Gar 3G 103
Elmfield Ct. BD11: B'frd 3E 135
LS27: Morl 4B 138
Elmfield Dr. BD6: B'frd 5C 110
Elmfield Gro. LS12: Leeds 5D 96
Elmfield Pde. LS27: Morl 5B 138
Elmfield Pl. LS12: Leeds 5D 96
Elmfield Rd. LS12: Leeds 5D 96
LS27: Morl 5B 138
Elmfield Ter. HX1: Hal 4F 149
Elmfield Way LS13: Leeds 2F 95
Elm Gdns. HX3: Hal 4G 149
Elm Gro. BD18: Ship 2E 71
BD19: Cleck 6E 135
BD20: Keigh 5H 35
BD20: Sils 2D 14
BD21: Keigh 3G 47
HX3: Hal 1F 131
LS29: Burl W 3F 21
Elm Ho. LS7: Leeds 2C 78
(off Allerton Pk.)
LS15: Leeds 5A 100
Elmhurst Cl. LS17: Leeds 3E 61
Elmhurst Gdns. LS17: Leeds 3E 61
Elm Pl. HX1: Hal 2D 148
HX6: Hal 4H 147
Elm Rd. BD18: Ship 2D 70
Elmroyd LS26: Rothw 3B 142
Elms, The LS7: Leeds 3B 78
LS20: Guis 4C 40
Elmsley St. BD20: Stee 6C 14
Elm St. BD22: Oxen 6C 64
LS6: Leeds 5H 77
Elm Ter. HD6: Brigh 4B 152
LS21: Otley 3G 23
Elmton Cl. LS10: Leeds 6B 118
Elm Tree Av. BD6: B'frd 5C 110
Elm Tree Cl. BD6: B'frd 5D 110
BD21: Keigh 1B 48
LS15: Leeds 5G 101
LS28: Pud 5A 94
Elm Tree Gdns. BD6: B'frd 4C 110
Elmtree La. LS10: Leeds 1B 118
Elm Vw. BD20: Stee 5B 14
HX3: Hal 5G 149
(off Skircoat Grn. Rd.)
Elm Wlk., The LS15: Leeds 6D 100
Elmwood Av. LS15: Bar E 2D 82
Elmwood Chase LS15: Bar E 2D 82
Elmwood Ct. LS15: Bar E 2D 82
Elmwood Dr. BD22: Keigh 3F 47
HD6: Brigh 4A 152
Elmwood La. LS7: Leeds . . .2A 98 (1F 5)
LS15: Bar E 2D 82
Elmwood Pl. BD2: B'frd 2A 92
(off Fagley Rd.)
Elmwood Rd. BD22: Keigh 4F 47
LS2: Leeds 2A 98 (1E 5)
Elm Wood St. HD6: Brigh 5B 152
Elmwood St. HX1: Hal 4E 149
Elmwood Ter. BD22: Keigh 4F 47
LS22: Coll 3B 28
Elsdon Gro. BD5: B'frd 6E 91
Elsham Ter. LS4: Leeds 1C 96
Elsie St. BD20: Keigh 3H 33
BD22: Haw 1F 65
Elsinore Av. HX5: Ell 5A 160
Elsinore Ct. HX5: Ell 5A 160
Elston Dr. BD20: Keigh 5F 35
(off Ford Rd.)
Elstone Vw. WF1: Wake 6E 157
Elsworth Av. BD3: B'frd 2B 92
Elsworth Ho. LS5: Leeds 6H 75
Elsworth St. BD4: B'frd 6G 91
LS12: Leeds 4D 96
Eltham Av. LS6: Leeds 6H 77
Eltham Cl. LS6: Leeds 6H 77

Eltham Ct. LS6: Leeds 6H 77
Eltham Dr. LS6: Leeds 6H 77
Eltham Gdns. LS6: Leeds 6H 77
Eltham Gro. BD6: B'frd 5A 110
Eltham Ri. LS6: Leeds 6H 77
Elvaston Rd. LS27: Morl 4A 138
Elvey Cl. BD2: B'frd 5B 72
Elwell Cl. HX3: B'frd 6F 109
Elwell St. WF3: E Ard 6C 140
Elwyn Gro. BD5: B'frd 2E 111
Elwyn Rd. BD5: B'frd 2F 111
Ely St. HX4: Hal 5H 159
LS12: Leeds 3C 96
Embankment, The
LS1: Leeds 4A 98 (6E 5)
Emblem Ct. BD13: B'frd 5H 107
Embleton Rd. LS26: Mick 6C 144
Emerald St. BD22: Keigh 3G 47
Emerson Av. BD9: B'frd 6F 69
Emily Ct. BD7: B'frd 2B 110
(off Oakwell Cl.)
Emily Hall Gdns. BD15: B'frd 4G 67
Emily St. BD21: Keigh 5A 34
BD22: Haw 2D 64
(off Victoria Rd.)
Emley Vw. LS25: Kip 2F 123
Emmanuel Trad. Est. LS12: Leeds . .5G 97
Emmeline Cl. BD10: B'frd 1H 71
Emmet Cl. BD11: B'frd 2F 135
Emmfield Dr. BD9: B'frd 5A 70
Emm La. BD9: B'frd 6A 70
Emmott Dr. LS19: Yead 4H 55
Emmott Farm Fold BD22: Haw 3C 64
Emmott Vw. LS19: Yead 4H 55
Empire Bus. Cen. HX2: Hal 3E 129
Empsall Row HD6: Brigh 6B 152
(off Camm St.)
Emscote Av. HX1: Hal 4E 149
Emscote Gdns. HX1: Hal 4E 149
Emscote Gro. HX1: Hal 4E 149
Emscote Pl. HX1: Hal 4E 149
Emscote St. Sth. HX1: Hal 4E 149
Emsley Cl. BD4: B'frd 5H 111
Emsley Pl. LS10: Leeds 6C 98
Emsley's Vis. Cen. 2E 55
Emville Av. LS17: Leeds 2G 61
Endecliffe M. LS6: Leeds 5G 77
Enderby Cl. HX3: Hal 4D 128
Enderley Rd. BD13: B'frd 5H 87
Endor Cres. LS29: Burl W 4F 21
Endor Gro. LS29: Burl W 4F 21
Endsleigh Pl. BD14: B'frd 1D 108
Enfield LS19: Yead 1F 55
Enfield Av. LS7: Leeds 1C 98
Enfield Dr. BD6: B'frd 4A 110
Enfield Pde. BD6: B'frd 4A 110
Enfield Rd. BD17: Bail 5C 52
Enfield St. BD21: Keigh 6H 33
LS7: Leeds 1B 98
Enfield Ter. LS7: Leeds 1C 98
Enfield Wlk. BD6: B'frd 4A 110
Engine Fields Nature Reserve 1E 55
Englefield Cl. BD4: B'frd 3C 112
Englefield Cres. BD4: B'frd 3C 112
Ennerdale Cl. LS22: Weth 3C 12
Ennerdale Dr. BD2: B'frd 6H 71
HX5: Ell 4D 160
Ennerdale Rd. BD2: B'frd 6G 71
LS12: Leeds 3F 115
Ennerdale Way LS12: Leeds 2F 115
Enterprise 5 La. Ends BD10: B'frd . .3H 71
Enterprise Ct. BD4: B'frd 4A 112
LS25: M'fld 5E 105
Enterprise Pk. Ind. Est.
LS11: Leeds 4F 117
Enterprise Way BD10: B'frd 3H 71
LS10: Leeds 4D 118
Envoy St. LS11: Leeds 1A 118
Epsom Rd. LS25: Kip 3F 123
Epworth Pl. BD22: Keigh 4B 46
LS10: Leeds 1C 118
Equity Chambers BD1: B'frd 3D 6
Eric St. BD21: Keigh 5A 34
LS13: Leeds 4E 75

Erivan Pk. LS22: Weth 3G 13
Escroft Cl. BD12: B'frd 6D 132
Eshald La. LS26: Rothw 2F 143
Eshald Mans. LS26: Rothw 1F 143
Eshald Pl. BD7: B'frd 1F 143
ESHOLT 2A 54
Esholt Av. LS20: Guis 6B 40
Esholt Hall Est. BD17: B'frd 3C 54
Esholt La. BD17: Bail, B'frd 3F 53
Eshton Av. BD12: B'frd 2F 133
Eskdale Av. HX3: Hal 2D 130
Eskdale Cl. LS20: Guis 5C 40
Eskdale Cft. LS20: Guis 5C 40
Eskdale Gro. LS25: Gar 5G 103
Eskdale Ho. HX6: Hal 6H 147
(off Quarry Hill)
Eskdale Ri. BD15: B'frd 3D 88
Esk Gdns. LS22: Weth 1E 13
Eskine Pde. BD6: B'frd 1H 131
Esmond St. BD7: B'frd 2H 109
LS12: Leeds 4C 96
Esmond Ter. LS12: Leeds 4C 96
Esporta Health & Fitness Club
Bradford 3D 92
Cookridge 1H 57
Leeds 3D 4
Essex Pk. Ind. Est.
BD4: B'frd 5G 91 (6G 7)
Essex St. BD4: B'frd 5G 91 (6G 7)
HX1: Hal 3D 148
Estcourt Av. LS6: Leeds 4C 76
Estcourt Gro. BD7: B'frd 6A 90
Estcourt Rd. BD7: B'frd 6A 90
Estcourt Ter. LS6: Leeds 4C 76
Esthwaite Gdns. LS15: Leeds 5A 100
Ethel St. BD20: Keigh 4H 33
Etna St. BD7: B'frd 2H 109
Eton St. HX1: Hal 2D 148
Eureka Children's Mus.
. . . . .3H 149 (5D 164)
Eurocam Technology Pk.
BD5: B'frd 3E 111
Euroway Trad. Est. BD4: B'frd 1G 133
Euston Gro. LS11: Leeds 1F 117
Euston Mt. LS11: Leeds 1F 117
Euston Ter. LS11: Leeds 1F 117
Evanston Av. LS4: Leeds 2C 96
Evelyn Av. BD3: B'frd 3C 92
Evelyn Pl. LS12: Leeds 5C 96
Evelyn Ter. BD13: B'frd 3G 107
Evens Ter. BD5: B'frd 3E 111
Everest Av. BD18: Ship 2E 71
Evergreen Wlk. BD16: Bgly 2A 50
(off Canal Rd.)
Everleigh St. LS9: Leeds 3E 99
Eversley Dr. BD4: B'frd 1C 112
Eversley Mt. HX2: Hal 3C 148
(off Bk. Eversley Mt.)
Eversley Pl. HX2: Hal 3C 148
Eversley Vw. LS14: S'cft 6E 45
Evesham Gro. BD10: B'frd 2H 71
Ewart Pl. BD7: B'frd 2A 110
Ewart St. BD7: B'frd 2A 110
BD13: B'frd 4A 108
EWOOD 6A 126
Ewood Cl. HX7: Heb B 6A 126
Ewood Dr. HX7: Heb B 6A 126
Ewood Hall Av. HX7: Heb B 6A 126
Exchange St. BD19: Cleck 6B 134
HX4: Hal 5H 159
Exe St. BD5: B'frd 2C 110
Exeter St. LS10: Leeds 6B 118
Exeter St. HX3: Hal 6H 149
HX6: Hal 5A 148
Exhibition Rd. BD18: Ship 1H 69
EXLEY 2H 159
Exley Av. BD21: Keigh 3G 47
Exley Bank HX3: Hal 1H 159
Exley Bank Top HX3: Hal 2H 159
Exley Cres. BD21: Keigh 2G 47
(not continuous)
Exley Dr. BD21: Keigh 2G 47

Exley Gdns. HX3: Hal 2H 159
Exley Gro. BD21: Keigh 2G 47
EXLEY HEAD 2F 47
Exley Head Vw. BD22: Keigh 5E 33
Exley La. HX3: Hal 2H 159
HX5: Hal 2A 160
Exley Mt. BD7: B'frd 5H 89
BD21: Keigh 2G 47
Exley Rd. BD21: Keigh 2G 47
Exley St. BD22: Keigh 1G 47
Exley Way BD21: Keigh 3G 47
(not continuous)
Exmoor St. HX1: Hal 3D 148
Exmouth Pl. BD3: B'frd 2F 91
Eyres Av. LS12: Leeds 3C 96
Eyres Gro. LS12: Leeds 3C 96
(off Eyres Ter.)
Eyres Mill Side LS12: Leeds 3B 96
Eyres St. LS12: Leeds 3C 96
(off Eyres Ter.)
Eyres Ter. LS12: Leeds 3C 96
Eyrie App. LS27: Morl 4C 138

F

Factory La. BD4: B'frd 3H 111
Factory St. BD4: B'frd 3A 112
FAGLEY 1A 92
Fagley Cres. BD2: B'frd 1A 92
Fagley Cft. BD2: B'frd 1B 92
Fagley Dr. BD2: B'frd 1A 92
Fagley La. BD2: B'frd 5B 72
Fagley Pl. BD2: B'frd 2A 92
Fagley Rd. BD2: B'frd 2A 92
Fagley Ter. BD2: B'frd 2A 92
Fair Bank BD18: Ship 3C 70
Fairbank Rd. BD18: Ship 3C 70
(off Fair Bank)
Fairbank Rd. BD8: B'frd 2A 90
Fairbank Ter. BD8: B'frd 2A 90
Fairburn Ct. HX3: Hal 5C 150
Fairburn Dr. LS25: Gar 4G 103
Fairburn Gdns. BD2: B'frd 5A 72
Fairburn Ho. LS18: H'fth 2D 74
(off Regent Cres.)
Fairburn St. WF10: C'frd 6H 145
Fairclough Gro. HX3: Hal 4D 128
Fairfax Av. BD4: B'frd 4A 112
BD11: B'frd 1C 136
LS29: Men 6G 21
Fairfax Cl. LS14: Leeds 6D 80
Fairfax Ct. LS11: Leeds 2G 117
Fairfax Cres. BD4: B'frd 4A 112
HX3: Hal 4C 150
Fairfax Flats LS21: Otley 4F 23
(off Fairfax St.)
Fairfax Gdns. LS29: Men 6F 21
Fairfax Gro. LS19: Yead 6D 40
Fairfax Ho. BD1: B'frd 3F 7
Fairfax Rd. BD13: B'frd 2B 66
BD16: Bgly 2B 50
LS11: Leeds 2G 117
LS29: Men 6F 21
Fairfax St. BD4: B'frd 6F 91
BD20: Sils 2D 14
BD22: Haw 2D 64
LS21: Otley 4F 23
Fairfax Vw. BD4: B'frd 6D 112
LS18: H'fth 3D 56
Fairfield BD13: B'frd 3B 86
LS18: H'fth 6E 57
LS25: Gar 4D 102
Fairfield Av. LS13: Leeds 1C 94
LS28: Pud 3A 94
WF3: E Ard 2D 154
Fairfield Cl. LS13: Leeds 1D 94
LS26: Rothw 3F 141
Fairfield Ct. BD17: Bail 3E 53
LS17: Leeds 2C 60
Fairfield Cres. LS13: Leeds 1C 94
Fairfield Dr. BD17: Bail 3E 53
LS26: Rothw 3F 141
Fairfield Gdns. LS26: Rothw 3F 141

Fairfield Gro. LS13: Leeds 1D 94
LS26: Rothw 3F 141
Fairfield Hill LS13: Leeds 1D 94
Fairfield La. LS26: Rothw 3F 141
Fairfield Mt. LS13: Leeds 1D 94
Fairfield Ri. HD6: Brigh 3B 152
Fairfield Rd. BD8: B'frd 2B 90
BD12: B'frd 4D 132
LS13: Leeds 1C 94
Fairfield Sq. LS13: Leeds 1D 94
Fairfield St. BD4: B'frd 4B 112
LS13: Leeds 1C 94
Fairfield Ter. LS13: Leeds 1D 94
Fairford Av. LS11: Leeds 2A 118
Fairford Ct. BD2: B'frd 6H 71
Fairford Mt. LS6: Leeds 6E 59
Fairford Ter. LS11: Leeds 2A 118
Fairhaven Grn. BD10: B'frd 2A 72
Fair Isle Ct. BD21: Keigh 6A 34
(off Alice St.)
Fairlands Cl. HX2: Hal 1D 128
Fairleigh Cres. WF3: E Ard 1F 155
Fairleigh Rd. WF3: E Ard 1F 155
Fairless Av. HX3: Hal 2A 152
Fairmount BD9: B'frd 1C 90
Fairmount Pk. BD18: Ship 2G 69
(not continuous)
Fairmount Ter. BD21: Keigh 1D 48
Fair Rd. BD6: B'frd 4B 110
Fair Vw. LS11: Leeds 4D 116
Fairview BD12: B'frd 3G 133
Fairview Ct. BD17: Bail 6B 52
Fairview Ter. HX3: Hal 6E 129
Fairway BD7: B'frd 4H 109
BD10: Yead 6E 55
BD18: Ship 2H 69
LS20: Guis 4H 39
Fairway, The HD2: Hud 6A 162
HX2: Hal 6D 106
LS17: Leeds 1H 59
LS28: Pud 2F 93
Fairway Av. BD7: B'frd 4H 109
Fairway Cl. BD7: B'frd 4H 109
LS20: Guis 5A 40
Fairway Cres. BD22: Haw 3D 64
Fairway Dr. BD7: B'frd 3H 109
Fairway Gro. BD7: B'frd 3H 109
Fairway Ind. Pk. WF17: Bat 5B 136
Fairways, The BD9: B'frd 4G 69
BD20: Keigh 2G 33
Fairway Wlk. BD7: B'frd 3H 109
FAIRWEATHER GREEN 4F 89
Fairweather M. BD8: B'frd 4G 89
Fairwood Gro. BD10: B'frd 6C 72
Fairy Dell BD16: Bgly 2C 68
Falcon Cliffe BD20: Stee 6D 14
Falcon Cl. LS21: Otley 4E 23
Falcon M. BD8: B'frd 3E 89
LS27: Morl 4C 138
Falcon Rd. BD16: Bgly 2B 50
Falcon St. BD7: B'frd 6B 90
HX3: Hal 6H 149
Falkland Ct. BD16: Bgly 4C 50
LS17: Leeds 6A 60
Falkland Cres. LS17: Leeds 6A 60
Falkland Gdns. LS17: Leeds 6B 60
Falkland Gro. LS17: Leeds 6A 60
Falkland Mt. LS17: Leeds 6A 60
Falkland Ri. LS17: Leeds 6A 60
Falkland Rd. BD10: B'frd 5C 72
LS17: Leeds 6A 60
FALL, THE .1B 156
Fall Brow Cl. BD14: B'frd 2C 108
Fall La. HX3: Hal 2H 129
HX6: Hal 6B 148
WF3: E Ard 1B 156
Fallow Cft. HD2: Hud 6F 163
Fallowfield Cl. BD4: B'frd 5A 112
Fallowfield Dr. BD4: B'frd 4A 112
Fallowfield Gdns. BD4: B'frd 4A 112
Fallow La. BD22: Keigh 1A 46
Fall St. LS13: Leeds 4F 75
Fallswood Gro. LS13: Leeds 5F 75
Fallwood Marina LS13: Leeds 4D 74

Fallwood St. BD22: Haw 3D 64
Falmers Cotts. LS6: Leeds 5F 77
(off Cliff La.)
Falmouth Av. BD3: B'frd 2F 91
Falsgrave Av. BD2: B'frd 1B 92
Faltis Sq. BD10: B'frd 3A 72
Fanny St. BD18: Ship 6H 51
BD21: Keigh 1H 47
Farcliffe Pl. BD8: B'frd 2B 90
Farcliffe Rd. BD8: B'frd 2B 90
Farcliffe Ter. BD8: B'frd 2B 90
Far Cft. Ter. LS12: Leeds 5D 96
Far Crook BD10: B'frd 6F 53
Fardene St. BD20: Sils 1D 14
Fardew Ct. BD16: Bgly 3B 50
Farfield Av. BD6: B'frd 6G 109
LS28: Pud 6G 73
Farfield Cres. BD6: B'frd 6H 109
Farfield Dr. LS28: Pud 1G 93
Farfield Gro. BD6: B'frd 6H 109
LS28: Pud 6G 73
Farfield Ri. LS28: Pud 6G 73
Farfield Rd. BD6: B'frd 6A 110
BD17: Bail 5D 52
BD18: Ship 2H 69
Farfield St. BD9: B'frd 1A 90
BD19: Cleck 6B 134
Farfield Ter. BD9: B'frd 1A 90
FAR FOLD 3B 96
FAR HEADINGLEY 3F 77
Far High Fld. BD22: Keigh 4C 46
Farhills BD6: B'frd 4H 109
Far Laithe BD22: Keigh 5C 32
Far La. HX2: Heb B 5A 126
LS9: Leeds 6H 99
Farlea Dr. BD2: B'frd 6A 72
Farleton Dr. BD2: B'frd 6B 72
Farley Cres. BD22: Keigh 4B 46
Far Low Bank BD22: Keigh 4B 46
(off Kelburn Gro.)
Farm Ct. LS15: Leeds 1D 100
Far Mead Cft. LS29: Burl W 1E 21
Farm Hill Ct. BD10: B'frd 4H 71
Farm Hill Cres. LS7: Leeds 4G 77
Farm Hill M. LS27: Morl 2G 137
Farm Hill Nth. LS7: Leeds 3G 77
Farm Hill Ri. LS7: Leeds 4G 77
Farm Hill Rd. BD10: B'frd 3H 71
LS27: Morl 1H 137
Farm Hill Sth. LS7: Leeds 4G 77
Farm Hill Way LS7: Leeds 4G 77
Farm Mt. LS15: Leeds 1E 101
Far Moss LS17: Leeds 2G 59
Farm Rd. LS15: Leeds 1D 100
Farmstead Rd. BD10: B'frd 3A 72
Farndale App. LS14: Leeds 4E 81
Farndale Cl. LS14: Leeds 4E 81
LS22: Weth 3B 12
Farndale Ct. LS14: Leeds 4E 81
LS25: Gar 6F 103
Farndale Gdns. LS14: Leeds 3E 81
Farndale Gth. LS14: Leeds 3E 81
Farndale Pl. LS14: Leeds 3E 81
Farndale Rd. BD15: B'frd 5G 67
BD17: Bail 5A 52
Farndale Sq. LS14: Leeds 4E 81
Farndale Ter. LS14: Leeds 4E 81
Farndale Vw. LS14: Leeds 3E 81
(off Farndale Gdns.)
Farnham Cl. BD17: Bail 3D 52
LS14: Leeds 6D 62
LS16: Leeds 2C 76
Farnham Cft. LS14: Leeds 6D 62
Farnham Rd. BD7: B'frd 6B 90
FARNLEY .6G 95
Farnley Cl. LS29: Men 1H 39
Farnley Cres. LS12: Leeds 5G 95
Farnley La. LS21: Otley 2E 23
Farnley Pk. LS21: F'ley 1A 24
Farnley Rd. LS29: Men 1G 39
Farnley Vw. BD11: B'frd 2C 136
Far Peat La. BD22: Oxen 4B 84
Farrar Bldgs. BD12: B'frd 4C 132
(off Brick Row)

Farrar Ct. LS13: Leeds 6E 75
Farrar Cft. LS16: Leeds 3A 58
Farrar Gro. LS16: Leeds 3A 58
Farrar La. LS16: Leeds 3H 57
(not continuous)
Farrar Mill La. HX3: Hal 5H 149
Farra St. BD22: Oxen 1C 84
Far Reef Cl. LS18: H'fth 5E 57
Farrer La. LS26: Rothw 2E 143
Farriers Ct. BD11: B'frd 1A 136
LS22: Weth 4F 13
Farriers Cft. BD2: B'frd 5F 71
Farrier Way WF3: Rothw 4F 141
Farringdon Cl. BD4: B'frd 1B 112
Farringdon Dr. BD4: B'frd 2C 112
Farringdon Gro. BD6: B'frd 6A 110
Farringdon Sq. BD4: B'frd 1C 112
Far Row LS21: Pool 6E 25
Farrow Bank LS12: Leeds 4G 95
Farrow Grn. LS12: Leeds 4H 95
Farrow Hill LS12: Leeds 4H 95
Farrow Rd. LS12: Leeds 4G 95
Farrow Va. LS12: Leeds 4G 95
Far Royd HX3: Hal 3E 129
FAR ROYDS 1C 116
Farr Royd LS29: Burl W 1E 21
Farside Grn. BD5: B'frd 2C 110
FARSLEY .6H 73
FARSLEY BECK BOTTOM 6A 74
Fartown LS28: Pud 5H 93
Fartown Cl. LS28: Pud 6A 94
Far Vw. HX2: Hal 1C 128
Farway BD4: B'frd 1C 112
Far Well LS19: Yead 4H 55
Far Well Fold LS19: Yead 4H 55
Far Well Rd. LS19: Yead 4H 55
Fascination Pl. BD13: B'frd 3G 107
(off Mill La.)
Faulkland Ho. BD8: B'frd 1A 6
Fawcett Av. LS12: Leeds 6B 96
Fawcett Bank LS12: Leeds 6A 96
Fawcett Cl. LS12: Leeds 6A 96
Fawcett Dr. LS12: Leeds 6A 96
Fawcett Gdns. LS12: Leeds 6A 96
Fawcett La. LS12: Leeds 6A 96
Fawcett Pl. BD4: B'frd 5A 112
LS12: Leeds 6A 96
Fawcett Rd. LS12: Leeds 6A 96
Fawcett Va. LS12: Leeds 6A 96
Fawcett Vw. LS12: Leeds 6A 96
(off Fawcett Dr.)
Fawcett Way LS12: Leeds 6A 96
Fawkes Dr. LS21: Otley 5B 22
Faxfleet St. BD5: B'frd 4D 110
Faye Gdns. BD4: B'frd 4B 112
Fearnley Cl. LS12: Leeds 4D 96
Fearnley Cft. BD19: Cleck 6F 135
Fearnley Pl. LS12: Leeds 4D 96
Fearnsides St. BD8: B'frd 3B 90
Fearnsides Ter. BD8: B'frd 3B 90
FEARN'S ISLAND 5C 98
FEARNVILLE 5H 79
Fearnville Av. LS8: Leeds 5H 79
Fearnville Cl. LS8: Leeds 4H 79
Fearnville Dr. BD4: B'frd 6B 92
LS8: Leeds 5H 79
Fearnville Gro. LS8: Leeds 4H 79
Fearnville Mt. LS8: Leeds 4H 79
Fearnville Pl. LS8: Leeds 4A 80
Fearnville Rd. LS8: Leeds 4H 79
Fearnville Sports Cen. 5H 79
Fearnville Ter. LS8: Leeds 4A 80
Fearnville Vw. LS8: Leeds 5H 79
Feast Fld. LS18: H'fth 6D 56
Featherbank Av. LS18: H'fth 2D 74
Featherbank Ct. LS18: H'fth 2D 74
(off Featherbank Av.)
Featherbank Gro. LS18: H'fth 1D 74
Featherbank La. LS18: H'fth 1D 74
Featherbank Mt. LS18: H'fth 1D 74
Featherbank Ter. LS18: H'fth 2D 74
Featherbank Wlk. LS18: H'fth 2D 74
Featherbed Cl. HX4: Hal 5H 159

Featherbed La. HX4: Hal 5H 159
Feather Rd. BD3: B'frd 4H 91
Feather St. BD21: Keigh 1B 48
Federation St. BD5: B'frd 3F 111
Felbrigg Av. BD22: Keigh 1F 47
Felcourt Dr. BD4: B'frd 3C 112
Felcourt Fold BD4: B'frd 3C 112
Fell Cres. BD22: Keigh 1F 47
Fell Greave Rd. HD2: Hud 6B 162
Fell Gro. BD22: Keigh 1F 47
HD2: Hud 6C 162
Fell La. BD22: Keigh 2E 47
Fellside Cl. BD5: B'frd 3F 111
Fellwood Av. BD22: Haw 1E 65
Fellwood Cl. BD22: Haw 1E 65
Felnex Cl. LS9: Leeds 6G 99
Felnex Cres. LS9: Leeds 6G 99
Felnex Rd. LS9: Leeds 6F 99
Felnex Sq. LS9: Leeds 6F 99
Felnex Way LS9: Leeds 6G 99
Fenby Av. BD4: B'frd 1H 111
(not continuous)
Fenby Cl. BD4: B'frd 2A 112
(not continuous)
Fenby Gdns. BD4: B'frd 2A 112
Fenby Gro. BD4: B'frd 2A 112
Fencote Cres. BD2: B'frd 6B 72
Fencote Ho. BD10: B'frd 3A 72
(off Rowantree Dr.)
Fender Rd. BD6: B'frd 4H 109
Fenned Rd. BD17: Bail 3E 53
Fennel Ct. LS26: Mick 4C 144
Fenny Royd HX3: Hal 1D 150
Fenton Av. LS26: Rothw 6D 120
Fenton Cl. LS26: Rothw 6D 120
Fenton Fold BD12: B'frd 3F 133
Fenton Rd. HX1: Hal 4D 148
Fentonsgate WF3: Rothw 6G 141
Fenton St. LS1: Leeds 2H 97 (1D 4)
LS29: Burl W 2F 21
WF3: E Ard 6F 139
Fenwick Dr. BD6: B'frd 6H 109
Fenwick Ho. BD5: B'frd 4F 111
(off Parkway)
Ferguson St. HX1: Hal . . .3G 149 (5B 164)
Fern Bank HX6: Hal 6H 147
LS21: Otley 3F 23
Fernbank Av. BD16: Bgly 4D 50
BD22: Keigh 3F 47
LS13: Pud 6B 74
Fernbank Cl. LS13: Leeds 6B 74
Fernbank Dr. BD16: Bgly 4C 50
BD17: Bail 6A 52
LS13: Leeds 6B 74
Fernbank Gdns. LS13: Pud 6B 74
Fernbank Pl. LS13: Leeds 6B 74
Fernbank Rd. BD3: B'frd 2H 91
LS13: Leeds 6B 74
Fernbank St. BD16: Bgly 4C 50
Fern Bank Ter. LS19: Yead 6E 41
(off Park Av.)
Fernbank Ter. BD16: Bgly 4C 50
Fernbank Wlk. LS13: Leeds 6B 74
Fern Chase LS14: S'cft 6C 44
FERNCLIFFE 4D 50
Ferncliffe Ct. BD18: Ship 1H 69
Ferncliffe Dr. BD17: Bail 4B 52
BD20: Keigh 3F 33
Ferncliffe Rd. BD16: Bgly 4B 50
BD18: Ship 1H 69
LS13: Leeds 1E 95
Ferncliffe Ter. LS13: Leeds 1D 94
Fern Ct. BD20: Keigh 3G 33
Fern Cft. LS14: S'cft 6C 44
WF2: Wake 6C 156
WF15: Liv 5H 153
Ferndale BD14: B'frd 2C 108
Ferndale Av. BD14: B'frd 2C 108
Ferndale Ct. LS29: I'ly 6C 10
Ferndale Gro. BD9: B'frd 5C 70
Ferndene BD16: Bgly 4D 50
Ferndene Av. WF17: Bat 4B 136
Ferndene Wlk. WF17: Bat 4B 136

Ferndown Grn. BD5: B'frd 2D **110**
Fernfield Ter. HX3: Hal 5G **129**
Fern Gdns. LS29: I'ly 6C **10**
Fernhill BD16: Bgly 2C **50**
Fern Hill Av. BD18: Ship 2H **69**
Fern Hill Gro. BD18: Ship 2H **69**
Fern Hill Mt. BD18: Ship 2H **69**
Fern Hill Rd. BD18: Ship 2H **69**
Ferniehurst BD17: Bail 6C **52**
Fern Lea BD13: B'frd 4B **108**
                                     (off Scarlet Hgts.)
Fernlea LS26: Rothw 1B **142**
Fern Lea St. HX6: Hal 4H **147**
Fern Lea Vw. LS28: Pud 1A **94**
Fernley Gdns. BD12: B'frd 3C **132**
Fern Pl. BD18: Ship 1H **69**
                                      (off George St.)
Fern Ri. HX5: Ell 4D **160**
Fern St. BD4: B'frd 2B **112**
  BD21: Keigh 5A **34**
  HX3: Hal 5F **129**
Fern Ter. BD8: B'frd 1C **90**
  BD20: Keigh 4D **34**
                                       (off Carr La.)
  LS28: Pud 1A **94**
Fern Way LS14: S'cft 6C **44**
Fernwood LS8: Leeds 6E **61**
Fernwood Ct. LS8: Leeds 6E **61**
Ferrand Av. BD14: B'frd 5A **112**
  BD19: Cleck 6E **135**
Ferrand Rd. BD18: Ship 1H **69**
Ferrands Cl. BD16: Bgly 6F **49**
Ferrands Pk. Way BD16: Bgly 6F **49**
Ferriby Cl. BD2: B'frd 6B **72**
Ferriby Towers LS9: Leeds 2C **98**
                                    (off Granville Rd.)
Festival Av. BD18: Ship 4D **70**
Feversham St. BD3: B'frd . . .5G **91** (5G **7**)
Fewston Av. LS9: Leeds 5D **98**
Fewston Ct. LS9: Leeds 5D **98**
Fidler Cl. LS25: Gar 4E **103**
Fidler La. LS25: Gar 4E **103**
Field Cl. HX3: Hal 6D **128**
Field Ct. BD13: B'frd 5A **88**
Fieldedge La. BD20: Keigh 3E **35**
Field End LS15: Leeds 4C **100**
Fld. End Cl. LS15: Leeds 4C **100**
Fld. End Cres. LS15: Leeds 4C **100**
Fld. End Gdns. LS15: Leeds 4C **100**
Fld. End Gth. LS15: Leeds 4C **100**
Fld. End Gro. LS15: Leeds 3D **100**
Fld. End Mt. LS15: Leeds 4C **100**
Fld. End Rd. LS15: Leeds 4C **100**
Fieldfare Dr. BD13: B'frd 4D **108**
Fieldfares, The BD20: Sils 2E **15**
                                    (off Mallards, The)
Fieldgate Rd. BD10: B'frd 2B **72**
Field Head BD22: Oxen 4B **64**
  HX2: Hal 6B **106**
Fieldhead WF17: Bat 4A **136**
Fieldhead Bus. Cen. BD7: B'frd 4C **90**
                                   (off Gt. Russell Ct.)
Fieldhead Ct. LS23: B Spa 4A **30**
Fieldhead Cres. WF17: Bat 4A **136**
Fieldhead Dr. LS15: Bar E 2F **83**
  LS20: Guis 5A **40**
Fieldhead Gdns. WF12: Dew 6B **154**
Fieldhead Gro. LS20: Guis 5A **40**
Fld. Head La. BD11: B'frd 3A **136**
  BD22: Oxen 4A **64**
  HX2: Hal 6B **106**
  WF17: Bat, B'frd 5A **136**
Fieldhead Paddock LS23: B Spa . . .3A **30**
Fieldhead Rd. LS20: Guis 5A **40**
Fieldhead St. BD7: B'frd 5C **90**
Fld. Head Way HX2: Hal 6B **106**
Field Ho. Cl. LS22: Weth 4C **12**
Fieldhouse Cl. LS17: Leeds 5A **60**
Field Ho. Cotts. HX1: Hal 4E **149**
                                   (off Carlton Ho. Ter.)
Fieldhouse Ct. BD14: B'frd 2E **109**

Fieldhouse Dr. LS17: Leeds 5A **60**
Fieldhouse Gro. LS28: Pud 1G **93**
Fieldhouse Lawn
  LS17: Leeds 5A **60**
Fieldhouse St. BD3: B'frd 4B **92**
Fieldhouse Wlk. LS17: Leeds 5A **60**
                                       (not continuous)
Field Hurst BD19: Cleck 2F **153**
Fieldhurst BD4: B'frd 5A **112**
Fielding Ga. LS12: Leeds 3D **96**
Fielding Ga. M. LS12: Leeds 3D **96**
Fielding Way LS27: Morl 2H **137**
FIELD LANE 3G **161**
Fld. Pk. Grange LS27: Morl 1F **137**
Field La. HD6: Brigh 3H **161**
Fields, The WF3: Rothw 6H **141**
Field Side HX1: Hal 1D **148**
Fieldside BD13: B'frd 3B **66**
Fields Rd. BD12: B'frd 2E **133**
Field St. BD1: B'frd 4F **91** (4E **7**)
Field Ter. LS15: Leeds 3C **100**
                                         (Cross St.)
  LS15: Leeds 2D **100**
                                       (Hermon Rd.)
Field Top HD6: Brigh 2B **152**
Fld. Top Rd. HD6: Brigh 3H **161**
Field Vw. HX2: Hal 2C **128**
  HX3: Hal 5D **128**
Fieldway BD14: B'frd 6D **88**
  LS29: I'ly 4G **11**
Fieldway Av. LS13: Leeds 5C **74**
Fieldway Chase LS26: Rothw 2F **143**
Fieldway Cl. LS13: Leeds 5C **74**
Fieldway Ri. LS13: Leeds 5C **74**
Fife St. BD22: Haw 2D **64**
Fifth Av. BD3: B'frd 2A **92**
  LS26: Rothw 6C **120**
Fifth Av. E. WF15: Liv 4H **153**
Fifth Av. W. WF15: Liv 5H **153**
Fifth St. BD12: B'frd 1D **132**
Filey St. BD1: B'frd 5F **91** (5F **7**)
Fillingfir Dr. LS16: Leeds 1H **75**
Fillingfir Rd. LS16: Leeds 1H **75**
Fillingfir Wlk. LS16: Leeds 1H **75**
Finch Cl. BD16: Bgly 3E **51**
Finchley St. BD5: B'frd 2D **110**
Finchley Way LS27: Morl 4A **138**
Finch St. BD5: B'frd 1D **110**
Findon Ter. BD10: B'frd 5C **72**
Fink Hill LS18: H'fth 1C **74**
Finkil St. HD6: Brigh 4G **151**
Finkin La. WF3: Wake 6H **157**
Finkle Cl. LS27: Morl 1E **137**
Finkle La. LS27: Morl 1E **137**
Finkle St. HX6: Hal 5D **146**
Finsbury Dr. BD2: B'frd 4F **71**
Finsbury Rd. LS1: Leeds 2H **97** (1C **4**)
Firbank Grn. BD2: B'frd 6B **72**
Firbank Gro. LS15: Leeds 5A **100**
Firbeck BD16: Bgly 1F **67**
Firethorn Cl. BD8: B'frd 3A **90**
First Av. BD3: B'frd 2A **92**
  BD21: Keigh 1H **47**
  HX3: Hal 5F **149**
  LS12: Leeds 4D **96**
  LS17: Bard 6G **27**
  LS19: Yead 2G **55**
  LS22: Weth 4F **13**
  LS26: Rothw 6B **120**
  LS28: Pud 2A **94**
  WF15: Liv 4H **153**
First Av. Ind. Est. LS28: Pud 2A **94**
Fir St. BD21: Keigh 3H **47**
  BD22: Haw 3C **64**
First St. BD12: B'frd 1E **133**
Firth Av. HD6: Brigh 6A **152**
  LS11: Leeds 3G **117**
Firth Carr BD18: B'frd 4B **70**
Firthfields LS25: Gar 4G **103**
Firth Gro. LS11: Leeds 3G **117**
Firth Ho. La. HD6: Brigh 4B **162**
Firth La. BD15: B'frd 4G **67**
Firth Mt. LS11: Leeds 3G **117**

Firth Rd. BD9: B'frd 6A **70**
  LS11: Leeds 3G **117**
Firths Ter. HX3: Hal 5D **128**
                                     (off Ramsden St.)
Firth St. BD13: B'frd 5H **87**
  HD6: Brigh 2A **162**
  LS7: Leeds 2B **98** (1H **5**)
Firth Ter. LS9: Leeds 2C **98** (1H **5**)
  LS11: Leeds 3G **117**
Fir Tree App. LS17: Leeds 3H **59**
Firtree Av. LS25: Gar 5H **103**
Fir Tree Cl. LS17: Leeds 3A **60**
Fir Tree Gdns. BD10: B'frd 3B **72**
  LS17: Leeds 3H **59**
Fir Tree Grn. LS17: Leeds 3A **60**
Fir Tree Gro. LS17: Leeds 4A **60**
Fir Tree La. LS17: Leeds 4B **60**
Fir Tree Ri. LS17: Leeds 4A **60**
Fir Tree Va. LS17: Leeds 4A **60**
Fir Tree Vw. LS26: Mick 4E **145**
Fish St. LS1: Leeds 3A **98** (4F **5**)
Fitness Fast 5B **160**
                                      (off Burley St.)
Fitness Finesse Health & Exercise Cen.
  . . . . .3F **109**
Fitness First Health Club
  Halifax 1F **149** (1A **164**)
  Leeds .2C **96**
Fitness Studio, The 1B **162**
                                       (off Park Row)
Fitts La. LS17: Bard 3C **26**
Fitzgerald St. BD5: B'frd 6D **90**
Fitzroy Dr. LS8: Leeds 3E **79**
Fitzroy Rd. BD3: B'frd 4H **91**
                                       (not continuous)
Fitzwilliam St. BD4: B'frd 6F **91**
FIVE LANE ENDS 3H **71**
Five Oaks BD17: Bail 5A **52**
Five Ri. BD16: Bgly 2B **50**
FIXBY 6A **162**
Fixby Av. HX2: Hal 4C **148**
Fixby Fold HX5: Ell 5E **161**
Fixby Rd. HD2: Hud 6H **161**
Flagship Sq. WF12: Dew 6A **154**
FLAPPIT SPRINGS 3G **65**
Flasby Av. BD20: Keigh 5F **35**
                                       (off Ford Rd.)
Flasby St. BD21: Keigh 5A **34**
Flat Nook BD16: Bgly 4D **50**
Flats, The LS19: Yead 1G **55**
Flats La. LS15: Bar E 3D **82**
Flawith Dr. BD2: B'frd 1B **92**
Flaxen Cl. BD6: B'frd 4D **110**
Flaxman Rd. BD2: B'frd 5A **72**
Flax Mill Rd. LS10: Leeds 2C **118**
Flax Pl. LS9: Leeds 4C **98** (6H **5**)
Flaxton Cl. LS11: Leeds 2H **117**
Flaxton Gdns. LS11: Leeds 2H **117**
Flaxton Grn. BD2: B'frd 1B **92**
Flaxton Pl. BD7: B'frd 5B **90**
Flaxton St. LS11: Leeds 2H **117**
Flaxton Vw. LS11: Leeds 2H **117**
Fledborough Rd. LS22: Weth 4C **12**
Fleece St. BD6: B'frd 6H **109**
  BD21: Keigh 6A **34**
Fleet La. BD13: B'frd 3H **107**
  LS26: Mick 3A **144**
  LS26: Rothw 2F **143**
                                       (not continuous)
Fletcher Av. BD20: Sils 1E **15**
Fletcher Cres. HD6: Brigh 5G **161**
Fletcher La. BD2: B'frd 5D **70**
Fletcher Rd. BD6: B'frd 4B **110**
Fletton Ter. BD2: B'frd 1H **91**
Flexbury Av. LS27: Morl 4A **138**
Flintmill La. LS23: B Spa 1B **30**
Flinton Gro. BD2: B'frd 6B **72**
Flockton Av. BD4: B'frd 1G **111**
Flockton Cl. BD4: B'frd 1G **111**
Flockton Cres. BD4: B'frd 1G **111**
Flockton Dr. BD4: B'frd 1G **111**
Flockton Gro. BD4: B'frd 1G **111**
Flockton Rd. BD4: B'frd 1G **111**

Flockton Ter. BD4: B'frd 1G 111
Floral Av. LS7: Leeds 3A 78
Florence Av. BD15: B'frd 3F 67
   LS9: Leeds 1E 99
Florence Gro. LS9: Leeds 1E 99
Florence Mt. LS9: Leeds 1E 99
Florence Pl. LS9: Leeds 1E 99
Florence St. BD3: B'frd 5A 92
   HX1: Hal 2E 149
   LS9: Leeds 1E 99
Florence Ter. LS27: Morl 4B 138
   (off South Pde.)
Florida Rd. BD15: B'frd 5C 68
Florist St. BD21: Keigh 4C 34
Flossmore Way LS27: Morl 6E 115
Flower Acre HX5: Ell 5B 160
Flower Bank BD2: B'frd 5F 71
   HX6: Hal 6F 147
Flower Cl. LS19: Yead 6E 41
Flower Ct. BD2: B'frd 1A 92
   LS18: H'fth 1D 74
Flower Cft. BD21: Keigh 2F 47
Flowerfields HX3: Hal 6G 131
Flower Gth. BD10: B'frd 3B 72
   LS18: H'fth 2D 74
   (off Regent Rd.)
Flower Haven BD9: B'frd 5F 69
Flower Hill BD9: B'frd 5H 69
Flower Mt. BD17: Bail 3D 52
   LS19: Yead 6G 41
   (off Alexandra Ter.)
Flowerpot La. BD13: B'frd 5G 107
Floyd St. BD5: B'frd 2B 110
Fold, The BD22: Haw 2B 64
   LS15: Leeds 5G 81
Foldings Av. BD19: Cleck 1F 153
Foldings Cl. BD19: Cleck 1E 153
Foldings Ct. BD19: Cleck 1E 153
Foldings Gro. BD19: Cleck 1E 153
Foldings Pde. BD19: Cleck 1E 153
Foldings Rd. BD19: Cleck 1E 153
Folkestone St. BD3: B'frd 4H 91
   (not continuous)
Folkton Holme BD3: B'frd 1B 92
Folly Hall Av. BD6: B'frd 5B 110
Folly Hall Cl. BD6: B'frd 5B 110
Folly Hall Gdns., The BD6: B'frd .5B 110
Folly Hall Mt. WF3: E Ard 1E 155
Folly Hall Rd. BD6: B'frd 5B 110
   WF3: E Ard 1E 155
Folly Hall Wlk. BD6: B'frd 5B 110
Folly La. LS11: Leeds 1H 117
Folly Vw. Rd. BD22: Haw 3D 64
Fontmell Cl. BD4: B'frd 3C 112
Football LS19: Yead 6G 41
Football Centre 2C 96
Forber Gro. BD4: B'frd 6C 92
Forber Pl. LS15: Leeds 4A 100
Forbes Ho. *BD4: B'frd* 2C 112
   (off Stirling Cres.)
Ford BD13: B'frd 5G 107
Ford Hill BD13: B'frd 5G 107
Ford St. BD21: Keigh 4C 34
Fore La. HX6: Hal 6G 147
Fore La. Av. HX6: Hal 6F 147
Foreside Bottom La.
   BD13: B'frd 1B 106
Foreside La. BD13: B'frd 6H 85
Forest Av. HX2: Hal 3C 128
Forest Bank LS27: Morl 6E 115
Forest Cres. HX2: Hal 3C 128
Forester Ct. *BD13: B'frd* 3B 86
   (off Main Rd.)
Forester Sq. BD13: B'frd 3B 86
Forest Ga. LS21: Otley 4E 23
Forest Grn. HX2: Hal 4C 128
Forest Gro. HX2: Hal 4D 128
Forest Ridge WF3: E Ard 6A 140
Forge Gym 4B 6
Forge La. LS12: Leeds 3D 96
Forge Row LS12: Leeds 2F 115
Forge Vw. BD20: Stee 6C 14
Forman's Dr. WF3: Rothw 4E 141
Forrester Ct. WF3: Rothw 4F 141

Forrest Ter. *LS21: Otley* 4D 22
   (off Piper La.)
Forrest Vs. *LS21: Otley* 4D 22
   (off Piper La.)
Forster Cl. LS29: Burl W 2F 21
Forster Ct. BD1: B'frd 4E 91 (3E 7)
Forster Pl. LS12: Leeds 1A 116
Forster Sq. BD1: B'frd 4F 91 (4E 7)
Forster Sq. Retail Pk.
   BD1: B'frd 3E 91 (2D 6)
Forster St. LS10: Leeds 6C 98
Forsythia Av. WF3: E Ard 1A 156
Forth Ct. LS11: Leeds 5G 97
Foss Av. LS22: Weth 2D 12
Fosse Way LS25: Gar 5H 103
Foster Av. BD13: B'frd 5B 88
   BD20: Sils 1D 14
Foster Cl. LS27: Morl 2A 138
Foster Cres. LS27: Morl 2A 138
Foster Gdns. BD22: Keigh 6F 33
Foster Pk. BD13: B'frd 2C 86
Foster Pk. Gro. BD13: B'frd 2C 86
Foster Pk. Rd. BD13: B'frd 2C 86
Foster Pk. Vw. BD13: B'frd 2C 86
   (not continuous)
Foster Rd. BD21: Keigh 3H 47
Foster's Ct. HX1: Hal 4C 164
Foster Sq. BD13: B'frd 3B 86
   LS10: Leeds 5B 118
Foster St. BD13: B'frd 4A 108
   LS27: Morl 2A 138
Foster Ter. LS13: Leeds 6F 75
Foston Cl. BD2: B'frd 1C 92
Foston La. BD2: B'frd 1B 92
Foulcauseway La. LS21: Otley ...4H 23
Foulds Ter. BD16: Bgly 3C 50
Foundry App. LS9: Leeds 1F 99
Foundry Av. LS9: Leeds 6F 79
Foundry Dr. LS9: Leeds 6F 79
Foundry Hill BD16: Bgly 4B 50
Foundry Ind. Est. LS28: Pud 2A 94
Foundry La. BD4: B'frd 6H 91
   LS9: Leeds 6H 79
   LS14: Leeds 6A 80
   LS28: Pud 1A 94
Foundry Mill Cres. LS14: Leeds ..6B 80
Foundry Mill Dr. LS14: Leeds 6A 80
   (not continuous)
Foundry Mill Gdns. LS14: Leeds ..4A 80
Foundry Mill Mt. LS14: Leeds 6B 80
Foundry Mill St. LS14: Leeds 6B 80
Foundry Mill Ter. LS14: Leeds ...6B 80
Foundry Mill Vw. LS14: Leeds ...6B 80
Foundry Mill Wlk. LS14: Leeds ..6B 80
Foundry Pl. LS9: Leeds 6F 79
Foundry Rd. LS28: Pud 2A 94
Foundry St. HD6: Brigh 2C 162
   HX1: Hal 1G 149 (2C 164)
   HX6: Hal 6H 147
   LS9: Leeds 4C 98 (5H 5)
   LS11: Leeds 5H 97
Foundry St. Nth. HX3: Hal 4D 128
Foundry Wlk. LS8: Leeds 6E 79
Fountain Ct. LS27: Morl 3G 137
Fountains Av. LS23: B Spa 4A 30
Fountain St. BD1: B'frd 4E 91 (3C 6)
   BD12: B'frd 1C 132
   BD13: B'frd 5H 87
   (Kipping La.)
   BD13: B'frd 4A 108
   (Union St.)
   HX1: Hal 2G 149 (5B 164)
   LS1: Leeds 3G 97 (4B 4)
   LS27: Morl 5H 137
   (Britannia Rd.)
   LS27: Morl 5C 116
   (William St.)
Fountain Ter. BD12: B'frd 4D 132
Fountain Way BD18: Ship 2C 70
FOURLANDS 1A 72
Fourlands Ct. BD10: B'frd 1A 72
Fourlands Cres. BD10: B'frd 1A 72
Fourlands Dr. BD10: B'frd 1A 72
Fourlands Gdns. BD10: B'frd 1A 72

Fourlands Gro. BD10: B'frd 1A 72
Fourlands Rd. BD10: B'frd 1A 72
FOUR LANE ENDS 3H 89
Four Lanes Bus. Pk. BD8: B'frd ..3H 89
Four Seasons HX2: Hal 4E 107
Fourteenth Av. LS12: Leeds 5D 96
Fourth Av. BD3: B'frd 2A 92
   BD21: Keigh 1G 47
   LS22: Weth 4F 13
   LS26: Rothw 6C 120
   WF15: Liv 4H 153
Fourth St. BD12: B'frd 1E 133
Fowlers Gth. BD22: Haw 1D 64
Fowler's Pl. LS28: Pud 1A 94
Fowler St. BD4: B'frd 6H 91
Fowler St. Ind. Est. BD4: B'frd ..6H 91
Fox Ct. HX4: Hal 4H 159
Fox Cft. Cl. BD13: B'frd 6G 107
Foxcroft Cl. LS6: Leeds 4B 76
Foxcroft Dr. HD6: Brigh 3H 161
Foxcroft Grn. LS6: Leeds 4B 76
Fox Croft La. BD16: Bgly 2A 68
Foxcroft Mt. LS6: Leeds 4B 76
Foxcroft Rd. LS6: Leeds 4B 76
Foxcroft Wlk. LS6: Leeds 4B 76
Foxcroft Way LS6: Leeds 4B 76
Foxglove Av. LS8: Leeds 5G 79
Foxglove Rd. WF17: Bat 5A 136
Foxhill BD17: Bail 4B 52
   LS22: Weth 3E 13
Foxhill Av. BD13: B'frd 4H 107
   LS16: Leeds 6C 58
Foxhill Cl. BD13: B'frd 4H 107
Foxhill Ct. LS16: Leeds 6C 58
Foxhill Cres. LS16: Leeds 6D 58
Foxhill Dr. BD13: B'frd 4H 107
   LS16: Leeds 6C 58
Foxhill Grn. LS16: Leeds 6D 58
Foxhill Gro. BD13: B'frd 4H 107
   LS16: Leeds 6D 58
Foxhills, The LS16: Leeds 3F 57
Foxholes Cres. LS28: Pud 3F 73
Foxholes La. LS28: Pud 3F 73
Foxstone Ri. BD17: Bail 4E 53
Fox St. BD16: Bgly 4B 50
   BD19: Cleck 2H 153
Foxton Gdns. LS27: Morl 4H 137
Fox Way LS10: Leeds 6C 98
Foxwood LS8: Leeds 1G 79
Foxwood Av. LS8: Leeds 4A 80
Foxwood Cl. LS8: Leeds 4A 80
Foxwood Farm Way LS8: Leeds ..4A 80
Foxwood Gro. LS8: Leeds 4A 80
Foxwood Ho. *BD4: B'frd* 6B 92
   (off Westbury St.)
Foxwood Ri. LS8: Leeds 4A 80
Foxwood Wlk. LS8: Leeds 4A 80
   LS22: Weth 2F 13
Fraisthorpe Mead BD2: B'frd 1B 92
Frances St. BD21: Keigh 5G 33
   HD6: Brigh 6A 152
   HX5: Ell 5B 160
   LS28: Pud 1H 93
Francis Cl. BD12: B'frd 5C 132
   HX1: Hal 2E 149
Francis Ct. *LS7: Leeds* 6B 78
   (off Francis St.)
Francis Gro. LS11: Leeds 2H 117
Francis Ho. *BD2: B'frd* 1H 91
   (off Hatfield Rd.)
Francis Sq. *BD13: B'frd* 3B 66
   (off Station Rd.)
Francis St. BD4: B'frd 6G 91 (6G 7)
   HX1: Hal 2E 149
   LS7: Leeds 6B 78
Frankland Gro. LS7: Leeds 6C 78
Frankland Pl. LS7: Leeds 6C 78
   (not continuous)
Frank La. HX2: Hal 5B 126
Franklin Ho. BD3: B'frd 2F 7
Franklin St. HX1: Hal 2D 148
Frank Parkinson Ct.
   LS20: Guis 4C 40
   (off Kelcliffe Av.)

Frank Parkinson Homes
LS20: Guis 4C **40**
(off Oxford St.)
Frank Pl. BD7: B'frd 1B 110
Frank St. BD7: B'frd 1B 110
HX1: Hal · 3E **149**
Fraser Av. LS18: H'fth 1B 74
Fraser Rd. LS28: Pud 3D 72
Fraser St. BD8: B'frd 3C 90
LS9: Leeds 2D 98
Freakfield La. HD6: Liv 1H **163**
Fred Atkinson Way BD17: Bail 6D 52
Frederick Av. LS9: Leeds 5E 99
Frederick Cl. BD10: B'frd 6F 53
Frederick St. BD21: Keigh 6B 34
LS28: Pud 6G 73
Fred's Pl. BD4: B'frd 2A 112
Fred St. BD21: Keigh 1H 47
Freeman Rd. HX3: Hal 4C 150
Freemans Way LS22: Weth 3F 13
Freemantle Pl. LS15: Leeds 4A 100
Freemont St. LS13: Leeds 1C 94
Free School La. HX1: Hal 4E 149
Freestone M. LS12: Leeds 4E 95
Fremantle Gro. BD4: B'frd 6C 92
Frensham Av. LS27: Morl 4H 137
Frensham Dr. BD7: B'frd 2F 109
Frensham Gro. BD7: B'frd 2F 109
Frensham Way BD7: B'frd 2F 109
Freshfield Gdns. BD15: B'frd 2D 88
Friar Cl. BD10: B'frd 3A 72
Friar Pl. HD2: Hud 6F 163
Friars Ind. Est. BD10: B'frd 2H 71
Friary Ct. WF17: Bat 6H 135
FRIENDLY 4H 147
Friendly Av. HX6: Hal 4G 147
Friendly Fold HX3: Hal 5E 129
Friendly Fold Ho. *HX3: Hal* 5E **129**
(off Lentilfield St.)
Friendly Fold Rd. HX3: Hal 5E 129
Friendly St. BD13: B'frd 5H 87
HX3: Hal 5E 129
Frimley Dr. BD5: B'frd 3C 110
Frith Row BD4: B'frd 5H 111
Frith St. BD22: Haw 1E 65
FRIZINGHALL 4C 70
Frizinghall Rd. BD9: B'frd 6C 70
Frizinghall Station (Rail) 5C 70
Frizley Gdns. BD9: B'frd 5C 70
Frodingham Vs. BD2: B'frd 1B 92
Frogmore Av. BD12: B'frd 2F 133
Frogmore Ter. BD12: B'frd 2F 133
Frontline Cl. LS8: Leeds 3E 79
Front Row LS11: Leeds 5H 97
(not continuous)
Front St. LS11: Leeds 5H 97
Front Vw. HX3: Hal 2E 131
Fruit St. BD21: Keigh 5C 34
Fuchsia Cft. LS26: Rothw 1G 143
Fulford Wlk. BD2: B'frd 1B 92
Fulham Pl. LS11: Leeds 2H 117
Fulham Sq. *LS11: Leeds* 2H **117**
(off Fulham St.)
Fulham St. LS11: Leeds 2H 117
Fullerton St. BD3: B'frd 5G **91** (5G **7**)
Fullerton Ter. LS22: Coll 3B 28
Fulmar Ct. LS10: Leeds 2B 140
Fulmar M. BD8: B'frd 4E 89
FULNECK 6A 94
Fulneck LS28: Pud 1H 113
Fulneck Cl. LS11: Leeds 6G 117
Fulneck Moravian Settlement &
Moravian Mus. 6A 94
Fulton Pl. LS16: Leeds 2C 76
Fulton St. BD1: B'frd 4D **90** (4C **6**)
Furnace Gro. BD12: B'frd 2F 133
Furnace Inn St. BD4: B'frd 6B 92
Furnace Rd. BD12: B'frd 2F 133
(not continuous)
Furness Av. HX2: Hal 2B 128
Furness Cres. HX2: Hal 2B 128
Furness Dr. HX2: Hal 2B 128
Furness Gdns. HX2: Hal 3C 128

Furness Gro. HX2: Hal 3B 128
Furness Pl. HX2: Hal 4C 128
Fusden La. BD19: Cleck 6E 135
Future Bodies Gym & Fitness Cen.
. . . . .3B **138**
(in Peel Mills Business Cen.)
Future Flds. BD6: B'frd 4G 109
Futures Way BD4: B'frd 6F 91
Fyfe Cres. BD17: Bail 5D 52
Fyfe Gro. BD17: Bail 5E 53
Fyfe La. BD17: Bail 5E 53

G

Gable End Ter. LS28: Pud 4B 94
Gables, The *BD17: Bail* 5E **53**
(off Dewhirst Rd.)
BD17: Bail 4E 53
(Kirklands Rd.)
BD21: Keigh 6G **33**
(off W. Leeds St.)
LS18: H'fth 5E 57
Gainest HX2: Hal 4D 148
Gainford Dr. LS25: Gar 5F 103
Gain La. BD3: B'frd 2B 92
Gainsborough Cl. BD3: B'frd 1G 91
Gainsborough Pl. *LS12: Leeds* 2G **115**
(off Well Holme Mead)
Gainsborough Way WF3: Wake 4H 157
Gainsbro' Av. LS16: Leeds 2B 58
Gainsbro' Dr. LS16: Leeds 2B 58
GAISBY 4D 70
Gaisby La. BD2: Ship 5C 70
Gaisby Mt. BD18: Ship 4D 70
Gaisby Pl. BD18: Ship 3D 70
Gaisby Ri. BD18: Ship 3D 70
Gaitskell Ct. LS11: Leeds 6G 97
Gaitskell Grange LS11: Leeds 6G 97
Gaitskell Wlk. LS11: Leeds 6G 97
Gala Bingo
Silver Royd Hill 5H 95
Tong Street 4C 112
Gala Casino 3F **97** (4A **4**)
Galefield Grn. BD6: B'frd 1H 131
Gale St. BD21: Keigh 5A 34
BD22: Haw 1F 65
Gallagher Leisure Pk. BD3: Pud 3D 92
Gallery & Studio Theatre 2H **97** (1D **4**)
Gallops, The LS27: Morl 6B 138
Galloway Ct. LS28: Pud 3E 93
Galloway La. LS28: Pud 2E 93
Galloway Rd. BD10: B'frd 2B 72
Galsworthy Av. BD9: B'frd 6E 69
GAMBLE HILL 3F 95
Gamble Hill LS13: Leeds 3F 95
Gamble Hill Chase LS13: Leeds 3F 95
Gamble Hill Cl. LS13: Leeds 3F 95
Gamble Hill Cft. *LS13: Leeds* 3F **95**
(off Gamble Hill Vw.)
Gamble Hill Cross *LS13: Leeds* 3F **95**
(off Gamble Hill Lawn)
Gamble Hill Dr. LS13: Leeds 3F 95
Gamble Hill Fold *LS13: Leeds* 3F **95**
(off Gamble Hill Dr.)
Gamble Hill Grange
LS13: Leeds 3F **95**
(off Gamble Hill Lawn)
Gamble Hill Grn. LS13: Leeds 3F 95
Gamble Hill Lawn LS13: Leeds 3F 95
Gamble Hill Path *LS13: Leeds* 3F **95**
(off Gamble Hill Grn.)
Gamble Hill Pl. LS13: Leeds 3F 95
Gamble Hill Ri. LS13: Leeds 3F 95
Gamble Hill Va. LS13: Leeds 3F 95
Gamble Hill Vw. LS13: Leeds 3F 95
Gamble Hill Wlk. *LS13: Leeds* 3F **95**
(off Gamble Hill Ri.)
Gamble La. LS12: Leeds 5E 95
Gambles Hill LS28: Pud 6H 73
Gamel Vw. BD20: Stee 5B 14
Game Scar La. BD22: Keigh 1B 46
Gang, The *LS12: Leeds* 4C **96**
(off Town St.)

Gangster's Gym & Smokey's Place
. . . . .1D 96
Ganners Cl. LS13: Leeds 5E 75
Ganners Gth. LS13: Leeds 5F 75
Ganners Grn. LS13: Leeds 5E 75
Ganners Gro. LS13: Leeds 5F 75
Ganners Hill LS13: Leeds 5F 75
Ganners La. LS13: Leeds 5E 75
Ganners Mt. LS13: Leeds 5E 75
Ganners Ri. LS13: Leeds 5E 75
Ganners Rd. LS13: Leeds 5E 75
Ganners Wlk. LS13: Leeds 5E 75
Ganners Way LS13: Leeds 5E 75
Gannerthorpe Cl. BD12: B'frd 4C 132
Ganny Rd. HD6: Brigh 1B 162
Ganton Cl. LS6: Leeds 5H 77
Gant Pl. BD2: B'frd 6F 71
Gaol La. HX1: Hal 2G **149** (3C **164**)
(not continuous)
Garden Cl. BD12: B'frd 3C 132
Gardeners Ct. LS10: B'frd 1B 118
Gardener's Sq. HX3: Hal 1E 151
Garden Fld. BD12: B'frd 4C 132
Garden Fold HX3: Hal 1E 151
Garden Ho. Cl. LS26: Mick 4D 144
Garden Ho. La. WF3: E Ard 1G 155
Gardenhurst LS6: Leeds 5E 77
Garden La. BD9: B'frd 6H 69
HX4: Hal 4A 158
Garden Rd. HD6: Brigh 5H 151
Gardens, The BD16: Bgly 4F 51
HX1: Hal 4G 149
LS10: Leeds 3A 140
LS27: Morl 5H 137
LS28: Pud 6G 73
Garden St. BD9: B'frd 5H 69
BD22: Haw 1F 65
Garden St. Nth.
HX3: Hal 1H **149** (2D **164**)
Garden Ter. BD9: B'frd 6A 70
Garden Vw. BD15: B'frd 3G 67
BD16: Bgly 4E 51
Garden Vw. Ct. LS8: Leeds 6F 61
Garden Village LS25: M'fld 5E 105
Gardiner Row BD4: B'frd 3H 111
Gare Forth Av. BD20: Stee 5C 14
Garfield Av. BD8: B'frd 1B 90
Garfield Ho. *BD5: B'frd* 1D **110**
(off Hutson St.)
Garfield Pl. *BD15: B'frd* 2C **88**
(off North Vw.)
Garfield St. BD15: B'frd 2C 88
HX3: Hal 6E 129
Garfit Hill BD19: Bat 6H 135
GARFORTH 4E 103
GARFORTH BRIDGE 6C 102
Garforth Rd. BD21: Keigh 5C 34
Garforth Squash & Leisure Cen. . . .5G 103
Garforth Station (Rail) 4F 103
Garforth St. BD15: B'frd 2D 88
Gargrave App. LS9: Leeds 3D 98
Gargrave Ct. LS9: Leeds 2D 98
Gargrave Ho. BD3: B'frd 2G 7
Gargrave Pl. LS9: Leeds 2D 98
Garibaldi St. BD3: B'frd 4G 92
(not continuous)
Garland Dr. LS15: Leeds 4F 101
Garlick St. HD6: Brigh 5G 161
Garmont M. LS7: Leeds 3B 78
Garmont Rd. LS7: Leeds 3B 78
Garnet Av. LS11: Leeds 2A 118
Garnet Cres. LS11: Leeds 2A 118
Garnet Gro. LS11: Leeds 2A 118
Garnet Pde. LS11: Leeds 2A 118
Garnet Pl. LS11: Leeds 2A 118
Garnet Rd. LS11: Leeds 3A 118
Garnet Ter. LS11: Leeds 2A 118
Garnett St. BD3: B'frd 4G **93** (4G **7**)
LS21: Otley 3E 23
Garnett St. LS11: Leeds 2A 118
Garrowby Ho. *BD10: B'frd* 1H **71**
(off Thorp Gth.)
Garsdale Av. BD10: B'frd 2A 72

Garsdale Cres. BD17: Bail 3E 53
Garsdale Fold LS22: Coll 2A 28
Garth, The LS9: Leeds 4C 98
  LS22: Coll 3B 28
  LS25: Gar 4G 103
Garth Av. LS17: Leeds 6H 59
  LS22: Coll 3B 28
Gth. Barn Cl. BD9: B'frd 6A 70
Garth Dr. LS17: Leeds 6H 59
Garth End LS22: Coll 3B 28
  LS22: Weth 1D 12
Garth Fold BD10: B'frd 1H 71
Garth Gro. LS29: Men 1G 39
Garthland Way BD4: B'frd 2A 112
Garth Rd. LS17: Leeds 6H 59
Garth St. BD21: Keigh 6H 33
Garthwaite Mt. BD15: B'frd 1D 88
Garth Wlk. LS17: Leeds 6H 59
Garton Av. LS9: Leeds 4E 99
Garton Dr. BD10: B'frd 4B 72
Garton Gro. LS9: Leeds 4E 99
Garton Rd. LS9: Leeds 4E 99
Garton Ter. LS9: Leeds 4E 99
Garton Vw. LS9: Leeds 4E 99
Garvey Vw. BD5: B'frd 1E 111
Garwick Ter. HX4: Hal 4H 159
Gascoigne Av. LS15: Bar E 3D 82
Gascoigne Ct. LS15: Bar E 3E 83
Gascoigne Rd. LS15: Bar E 3D 82
  WF3: E Ard 6C 140
Gascoigne Vw. LS15: Bar E 3D 82
Gashouse La. LS22: Weth 4F 13
Gas Ho. Yd. BD12: B'frd 2E 133
Gas Works La. HX5: Ell 4B 160
Gas Works Rd. BD21: Keigh 5D 34
  (not continuous)
  HX6: Hal 5B 148
Gas Works Yd. LS26: Rothw 2B 142
  (off Commercial St.)
Gatefield Mt. BD6: B'frd 1A 132
Gate Head HX4: Hal 5D 158
Ga. Head La. HX4: Hal 6D 158
Gate Ho. Ct. LS26: Rothw 6G 121
Gateland Dr. LS17: Leeds 3A 62
Gateland La. LS17: Leeds 4A 62
Gatenby Cl. BD6: B'frd 4G 109
Gateon Ho. La. LS17: Bard 1C 44
Gateway BD16: Bgly 6E 49
Gate Way Dr. LS19: Yead 6E 41
Gateways WF1: Wake 4G 157
Gateways, The BD12: B'frd 2C 132
Gathorne Cl. LS8: Leeds 6C 78
Gathorne St. BD7: B'frd 1B 110
  HD6: Brigh 6B 152
  LS8: Leeds 6C 78
  (not continuous)
Gathorne Ter. LS8: Leeds 6C 78
Gaukroger La. HX1: Hal 4H 149
Gavin Cl. BD3: B'frd 4C 92
Gawcliffe Rd. BD18: Ship 3C 70
Gawthorpe BD16: Bgly 2B 50
Gawthorpe Av. BD16: Bgly 2C 50
Gawthorpe Dr. BD16: Bgly 2C 50
Gawthorpe La. BD16: Bgly 3C 50
Gay La. LS21: Otley 4E 23
Gayle Cl. BD12: B'frd 5C 132
Gaynor St. BD1: B'frd 4D 90 (2A 6)
Gaythorne Rd. BD2: B'frd 6A 72
  BD5: B'frd 2E 111
Gaythorne Ter. BD14: B'frd 1E 109
  HX3: Hal 6E 131
Geelong Cl. BD2: B'frd 6F 71
Gelderd Bus. Pk. LS12: Leeds 1D 116
Gelderd Cl. LS12: Leeds 1D 116
Gelderd La. LS12: Leeds 1D 116
Gelderd Pl. LS12: Leeds 6E 97
Gelderd Rd. LS12: Leeds 2D 116
  LS12: Morl 5H 115
  LS27: Leeds, Morl 2E 137
  WF17: Bat 6B 136
Gelderd Trad. Est. LS12: Leeds 6E 97
Gelder Pl. LS12: Leeds 4B 96
Gemini Bus. Pk. LS7: Leeds 6B 78
Genista Dr. LS10: Leeds 5B 118

George Mann Rd. LS10: Leeds 2E 119
George Mann Way LS10: Leeds 2D 118
George Sq. HX1: Hal 2G 149 (4B 164)
George's Sq. BD13: B'frd 3B 66
  BD21: Keigh 1H 47
George's St. HX3: Hal 4D 128
George St. BD1: B'frd 5F 91 (5F 7)
  BD13: B'frd 2C 86
    (Foster Pk.)
  BD13: B'frd 5H 87
    (James St.)
  BD17: Bail 6C 52
  BD18: Ship 4B 70
  HD6: Brigh 1C 162
    (Armytage Rd.)
  HD6: Brigh 2A 162
    (Bryant St.)
  HX1: Hal 2G 149 (4B 164)
  HX3: Hal 2F 151
  HX4: Hal 4H 159
  HX5: Ell 5B 160
  HX6: Hal 6H 147
  LS2: Leeds 3A 98 (4F 5)
  LS19: Yead 3F 55
  LS29: Add 1D 8
  WF1: Wake 4F 157
Geraldton Av. BD2: B'frd 6E 71
Gerard Av. LS27: Morl 3H 137
Gerard Ho. BD10: B'frd 2A 72
    (off Fairhaven Grn.)
Gerard St. HX1: Hal 2F 149 (4A 164)
Germaine Ter. LS14: T'ner 4G 63
Gernhill Av. HD2: Hud 6H 161
Ghyll, The BD16: Bgly 1C 68
  HD2: Hud 6A 162
Ghyllbank BD20: Sils 1E 15
Ghyll Beck Dr. LS19: Yead 4A 56
  LS21: Otley 5B 22
Ghyll Cl. BD20: Stee 6C 14
Ghyll Dr. BD22: Haw 3C 64
Ghyll Grange La. BD20: Sils 2A 16
Ghyll Lodge BD16: Bgly 1C 68
Ghyll M. LS29: I'ly 6C 10
Ghyll Mt. LS19: Yead 1D 54
Ghyll Rd. LS6: Leeds 3A 76
Ghyll Royd LS20: Guis 5C 40
  (not continuous)
  LS29: I'ly 5B 10
Ghyllroyd LS19: Yead 2E 55
Ghyllroyd Av. BD11: B'frd 2F 135
Ghyllroyd Dr. BD11: B'frd 2F 135
Ghyll Wood LS29: I'ly 6A 10
Ghyll Wood Dr. BD16: Bgly 1C 68
Gibbet, The 3A 164
Gibbet St. HX1: Hal 2E 149
  HX2: Hal 2B 148
Gibb La. HX2: Hal 4H 127
Gibraltar HX1: Hal 3C 148
Gibraltar Av. HX1: Hal 3C 148
Gibraltar Island Rd. LS10: Leeds 1D 118
Gibraltar Rd. HX1: Hal 2C 148
  LS28: Pud 4F 93
Gibson Ct. WF3: E Ard 4D 154
Gibson Dr. LS15: Leeds 4E 101
Gibson La. LS25: Kip 3H 123
Gibson St. BD3: B'frd 5H 91
Gilbert Chase LS5: Leeds 6A 76
Gilbert Cl. LS5: Leeds 6B 76
Gilbert Cotts. HX4: Hal 5B 158
Gilbert Gdns. HX4: Hal 5B 158
Gilbert Mt. LS5: Leeds 6B 76
Gilbert St. LS28: Pud 1H 93
GILDERSOME 6E 115
Gildersome La. LS12: Morl 5D 114
  LS27: Morl 5D 114
Gildersome Spur LS27: Morl 2F 137
GILDERSOME STREET 2D 136
Giles Hill La. HX3: Hal 6C 108
  (not continuous)
Giles St. BD5: B'frd 6D 90
Giles' Wlk. BD16: Bgly 5E 51
Gill Bank Rd. LS29: I'ly 3C 10
Gill Beck Cl. BD17: Bail 3E 53

Gill Cl. LS29: Add 1B 8
Gillett Dr. LS26: Rothw 2B 142
Gillett La. LS26: Rothw 2B 142
Gilling Av. LS25: Gar 3H 103
Gillingham Grn. BD4: B'frd 2C 112
Gill La. BD13: B'frd 6G 87
  BD22: Keigh 3A 46
  LS19: Yead 3C 54
  LS22: Kirkby 1A 26
  LS29: I'ly 2G 9
Gillrene Av. BD15: B'frd 5H 67
Gillroyd Mt. LS27: Morl 3C 138
Gillroyd Pde. LS27: Morl 4B 138
Gillroyd Pl. LS27: Morl 4B 138
Gillroyd Ri. BD7: B'frd 4B 90
Gillroyd Ter. LS27: Morl 3C 138
Gills, The LS21: Otley 1E 23
  LS27: Morl 3C 138
Gill's Ct. HX1: Hal 2G 149 (4C 164)
Gillstone Dr. BD22: Haw 2D 64
Gilmour St. HX3: Hal 6E 129
Gilpin Pl. LS12: Leeds 5D 96
Gilpin St. BD3: B'frd 3H 91
  LS12: Leeds 5D 96
Gilpin Ter. LS12: Leeds 5D 96
Gilpin Vw. LS12: Leeds 5D 96
GILROYD 3C 138
GILSTEAD 3E 51
Gilstead Ct. BD16: Bgly 4E 51
Gilstead Dr. BD16: Bgly 4E 51
Gilstead La. BD16: Bgly 4D 50
Gilstead Way LS29: I'ly 4C 10
Gilynda Cl. BD8: B'frd 4G 89
Ginnel, The LS17: Bard 3E 45
  (not continuous)
  LS22: Weth 4E 13
Gipsy Hill LS26: Rothw 1D 142
Gipsy La. LS11: Leeds 5G 117
  LS26: Rothw 1D 142
Gipsy Mead LS26: Rothw 1D 142
Gipsy St. BD3: B'frd 3C 92
GIPTON 6F 79
Gipton App. LS9: Leeds 2G 99
Gipton Av. LS7: Leeds 6C 78
Gipton Ga. E. LS9: Leeds 6G 79
Gipton Ga. W. LS9: Leeds 6F 79
Gipton Sq. LS9: Leeds 2H 99
Gipton St. LS8: Leeds 6C 78
GIPTON WOOD 4F 79
Gipton Wood Av. LS8: Leeds 4F 79
Gipton Wood Cres. LS8: Leeds 4F 79
Gipton Wood Gro. LS8: Leeds 4F 79
Gipton Wood Pl. LS8: Leeds 4F 79
Gipton Wood Rd. LS8: Leeds 4F 79
GIRLINGTON 2A 90
Girlington Rd. BD8: B'frd 2H 89
Gisbourne Rd. HD2: Hud 6E 163
Gisburn St. BD21: Keigh 5H 33
Glade, The BD17: Bail 5H 51
  LS14: S'cft 6D 44
  LS28: Pud 1E 93
Gladstone Ct. LS28: Pud 1B 94
  (off Gladstone Ter.)
Gladstone Cres. LS19: Yead 2F 55
Gladstone Pl. BD13: B'frd 3B 86
  BD22: Keigh 5D 46
  (off Keighley Rd.)
Gladstone Rd. HX1: Hal 2E 149
  LS19: Yead 3F 55
Gladstone Sq. LS27: Morl 3B 138
  (off Middleton Rd.)
Gladstone St. BD3: B'frd 5A 92
  BD13: B'frd 4B 108
  BD15: B'frd 2D 88
  BD16: Bgly 5B 50
  BD21: Keigh 1H 47
  LS28: Pud 6H 73
Gladstone Ter. LS27: Morl 3A 138
  LS28: Pud 1B 94
Gladstone Vw. HX3: Hal 6A 150
Gladstone Vs. LS17: Leeds 4A 62
Glaisdale Cl. BD20: Sils 3E 15
Glaisdale Ct. BD15: B'frd 6C 68
Glaisdale Gro. HX3: Hal 2F 151

Glamis Cl. LS25: Gar 3H **103**
Glanville Ter. LS26: Rothw 2A **142**
Glasshouse St. LS10: Leeds 6B **98**
Glasshouse Vw.
   LS10: Leeds 3H **139**
Glastonbury Ct. BD4: B'frd 6B **92**
Glazier Rd. BD13: B'frd 3G **107**
Gleanings Av. HX2: Hal 2A **148**
Gleanings Dr. HX2: Hal 2H **147**
Glebe Av. LS5: Leeds 5B **76**
Glebe Ct. LS26: Rothw 2F **141**
Glebe Fld. Chase LS22: Weth 3D **12**
Glebe Fld. Cl. LS22: Weth 3D **12**
Glebe Fld. Cft. LS22: Weth 3D **12**
Glebe Fld. Dr. LS22: Weth 3D **12**
Glebe Fld. Gth. LS22: Weth 3D **12**
Glebe Fld. Holt LS22: Weth 3D **12**
Glebe Fold BD20: Keigh 3D **34**
Glebe Gdns. HX1: Hal 4E **149**
Glebelands Cl. LS25: Gar 5F **103**
Glebelands Dr. LS6: Leeds 3D **76**
Glebe Mt. LS28: Pud 5A **94**
Glebe Pl. LS5: Leeds 5B **76**
Glebe St. LS28: Pud 5A **94**
Glebe Ter. LS16: Leeds 2D **76**
Gledcliffe HX3: Hal 2D **164**
Gledhill Rd. BD3: B'frd 5H **91**
Gledhills Yd. HX1: Hal 4D **148**
         (off King Cross Rd.)
GLEDHOW 2D **78**
Gledhow Av. LS8: Leeds 1D **78**
Gledhow Ct. LS7: Leeds 2C **78**
Gledhow Dr. BD22: Oxen 5C **64**
Gledhow Grange Vw. LS8: Leeds . .2D **78**
Gledhow Grange Wlk. LS8: Leeds . .2D **78**
Gledhow La. LS7: Leeds 2B **78**
   LS8: Leeds 2C **78**
Gledhow La. End LS7: Leeds 2B **78**
Gledhow Mt. LS8: Leeds 1C **78**
Gledhow Pk. Av. LS7: Leeds 3C **78**
Gledhow Pk. Cres. LS7: Leeds 3C **78**
Gledhow Pk. Dr. LS7: Leeds 3B **78**
Gledhow Pk. Gro. LS7: Leeds 3C **78**
Gledhow Pk. Rd. LS7: Leeds 3C **78**
Gledhow Pk. Vw. LS7: Leeds 3C **78**
Gledhow Pl. LS8: Leeds 1C **98**
Gledhow Ri. LS8: Leeds 3F **79**
Gledhow Rd. LS8: Leeds 1C **98**
Gledhow Ter. LS8: Leeds 1C **98**
Gledhow Towers LS8: Leeds 2C **78**
Gledhow Valley Rd. LS7: Leeds . . .1B **78**
   LS8: Leeds 1B **78**
Gledhow Wood Av. LS8: Leeds 2D **78**
Gledhow Wood Cl. LS8: Leeds 2D **78**
Gledhow Wood Ct. LS8: Leeds 4E **79**
Gledhow Wood Gro. LS8: Leeds . . .2D **78**
Gledhow Wood Rd. LS8: Leeds 3D **78**
Glenaire BD18: Ship 6E **53**
Glenaire Dr. BD17: Bail 6A **52**
Glenbrook Dr. BD7: B'frd 4G **89**
Glencoe HX3: Hal 1E **131**
Glencoe Cl. LS25: Kip 5F **123**
Glencoe Cft. LS25: Kip 5F **123**
Glencoe Gdns. LS25: Kip 5F **123**
Glencoe Ter. LS25: Kip 5F **123**
Glencoe Vw. LS9: Leeds 5D **98**
Glendale BD16: Bgly 2B **68**
            (Beckfield Rd.)
   BD16: Bgly 4E **51**
            (Gilstead La.)
Glendale Av. LS25: Gar 5F **103**
Glendale Cl. BD6: B'frd 6A **110**
Glendale Dr. BD6: B'frd 6A **110**
Glendale Ho. LS27: Morl 4B **138**
Glendale Studio 4E **149**
Glendare Av. BD7: B'frd 5H **89**
Glendare Rd. BD7: B'frd 5H **89**
Glendare Ter. BD7: B'frd 5H **89**
Glen Dene LS29: Men 1H **39**
Glendene BD16: Bgly 2B **68**
Glendower Pk. LS16: Leeds 5D **58**
Glen Eagles Cl. BD4: B'frd 5H **111**
Gleneagles Rd. LS17: Leeds 3H **59**

Glenfield BD18: Ship 6E **53**
   HX4: Hal 4F **159**
Glenfield Av. BD6: B'frd 5D **110**
   LS22: Weth 5F **13**
Glenfield Cvn. Pk. LS17: Bard 4C **44**
Glenfield Mt. BD6: B'frd 5D **110**
Glenfield Pl. HX6: Hal 3A **148**
Glen Gth. BD21: Keigh 2B **48**
Glen Gro. LS27: Morl 4B **138**
Glenholm BD18: Ship 6E **53**
Glenholme Heath HX1: Hal 2C **148**
Glenholme Pk. BD14: B'frd 2E **109**
Glenholme Rd. BD8: B'frd 2B **90**
   LS28: Pud 1G **93**
Glenholm Rd. BD17: Bail 5C **52**
Glenhurst BD4: B'frd 4B **112**
Glenhurst Av. BD21: Keigh 2A **48**
Glenhurst Dr. BD21: Keigh 2B **48**
Glenhurst Gro. BD21: Keigh 2B **48**
Glenhurst Rd. BD18: Ship 1G **69**
Glen Lea HX6: Hal 4H **147**
Glenlea Cl. LS28: Leeds 6C **74**
Glenlea Gdns. LS28: Leeds 6C **74**
Glen Lee La. BD21: Keigh 3B **48**
Glenlee Rd. BD7: B'frd 4H **89**
Glenlow Rd. WF12: Dew 6A **154**
Glenlyon Dr. BD20: Keigh 4G **33**
Glenlyon Rd. BD20: Keigh 4G **33**
Glenmere Mt. LS19: Yead 6H **41**
Glenmore Cl. BD2: B'frd 2A **92**
Glenmore Ct. LS16: B'hpe 2G **43**
Glen Mt. HX3: Hal 5C **128**
   LS27: Morl 4B **138**
   LS29: Men 2H **39**
Glenmount BD16: Bgly 2B **68**
Glen Mt. Cl. HX3: Hal 5C **128**
Glenmount Ter. LS27: Morl 5C **138**
Glen Ri. BD17: Bail 5H **51**
Glen Rd. BD16: Bgly 2E **51**
   BD17: Bail 3F **51**
   LS16: Leeds 2C **76**
   LS27: Morl 4C **138**
Glenrose Dr. BD7: B'frd 5G **89**
Glenroyd BD18: Ship 6E **53**
Glenroyd Av. BD6: B'frd 5D **110**
Glenroyd Cl. LS28: Pud 4G **93**
Glensdale Gro. LS9: Leeds 4D **98**
Glensdale Mt. LS9: Leeds 4D **98**
Glensdale Rd. LS9: Leeds 4D **98**
Glensdale St. LS9: Leeds 4D **98**
Glensdale Ter. LS9: Leeds 4D **98**
Glenside Av. BD18: Ship 6E **53**
Glenside Rd. BD18: Ship 6E **53**
Glenstone Gro. BD7: B'frd 4H **89**
Glen Ter. HX1: Hal 4F **149**
   HX3: Hal 2E **151**
         (off Waverley Cres.)
Glenthorpe Av. LS9: Leeds 3E **99**
Glenthorpe Cres. LS9: Leeds 3E **99**
Glenthorpe Ter. LS9: Leeds 3E **99**
Glenton Sq. BD9: B'frd 1B **90**
Glen Vw. BD16: Bgly 6F **49**
   HX1: Hal 4F **149**
   HX6: Hal 5C **146**
Glenview Av. BD9: B'frd 6G **69**
Glenview Cl. BD18: Ship 2E **69**
Glenview Dr. BD18: Ship 3E **69**
Glenview Gro. BD18: Ship 2F **69**
Glen Vw. Rd. BD16: Bgly 2E **51**
Glenview Rd. BD18: Ship 3E **69**
Glenview Ter. BD18: Ship 1H **69**
Glen Way BD16: Bgly 2F **51**
            (Glen Rd.)
   BD16: Bgly 1E **51**
         (Green, The)
Glenwood Av. BD17: Bail 6G **51**
Global Av. LS11: Leeds 4E **117**
Global Ct. LS11: Leeds 5E **117**
Globe Fold BD8: B'frd 3C **90**
Globe Rd. LS11: Leeds 4G **97** (6A **4**)
Glossop Gro. LS6: Leeds 5H **77**
        (off Glossop Vw.)
Glossop Mt. LS6: Leeds 5H **77**
Glossop St. LS6: Leeds 5H **77**

Glossop Vw. LS6: Leeds 5H **77**
Gloucester Av. BD3: B'frd 2B **92**
   BD20: Sils 2C **14**
Gloucester Ct. LS12: Leeds 4E **97**
   WF2: Wake 6D **156**
Gloucester Rd. BD16: Bgly 5D **50**
Gloucester Ter. LS12: Leeds 3E **97**
Glover Cl. BD5: B'frd 1E **111**
Glovershaw La. BD16: Bgly 1G **51**
Glover Way LS11: Leeds 3A **118**
Glydegate BD5: B'frd 5E **91** (5C **6**)
Glyndon Ct. HD6: Brigh 3B **162**
Glynn Ter. BD8: B'frd 3B **90**
G Mill Yd. HX1: Hal 2B **164**
        (off Corporation St.)
Gobind Marg BD3: B'frd 4G **91** (4G **7**)
Godfrey Rd. HX3: Hal 1G **159**
Godfrey St. BD8: B'frd 4F **89**
Godley Branch Rd. HX3: Hal 1A **150**
Godley Gdns. HX3: Hal 6B **130**
Godley La. HX3: Hal 1A **150**
Godley Rd. HX3: Hal 1H **149** (2D **164**)
Godwin Pl. HD2: Hud 6F **163**
Godwin St. BD1: B'frd 4E **91** (4C **6**)
Goff Well La. BD16: Keigh 4A **48**
   BD21: Keigh 4A **48**
Gog Hill HX5: Ell 4B **160**
Goit Side BD1: B'frd 4D **90** (4B **6**)
         (not continuous)
   HX2: Hal 3E **127**
Goit Stock La. BD16: Bgly 1F **67**
Goit Stock Ter. BD16: Bgly 1F **67**
Goldcrest Av. BD8: B'frd 4D **88**
Golden Bank LS18: H'fth 6E **57**
Golden Butts Rd. LS29: I'ly 5E **11**
Golden Elders WF2: E Ard 6G **155**
Golden Ter. LS12: Leeds 1A **116**
Golden Vw. Dr. BD21: Keigh 1D **48**
Goldfields Av. HX4: Hal 3F **159**
Goldfields Cl. HX4: Hal 3F **159**
Goldfields Vw. HX4: Hal 3F **159**
Goldfields Way HX4: Hal 3F **159**
Goldsmith Dr. WF3: Rothw 4F **141**
Golf Av. HX2: Hal 2A **148**
Golf Cres. HX2: Hal 2A **148**
Golf La. LS27: Morl 6G **137**
GOMERSAL 6F **135**
GOMERSAL HILL TOP 6F **135**
Gondal Ct. BD5: B'frd 2C **110**
Goodcomb Pl. LS25: Gar 2A **124**
Gooder La. HD6: Brigh 2A **162**
Gooder St. HD6: Brigh 1A **162**
GOODLEY 4C **46**
Goodman St. LS10: Leeds 6C **98**
Goodrick La. LS17: Leeds 1H **59**
Goodwin Ho. BD13: B'frd 4A **108**
         (off Minstrel Dr.)
Goodwin Rd. LS12: Leeds 5C **96**
Goodwood LS29: I'ly 3B **10**
Goodwood Av. LS25: Kip 3F **123**
GOODY CROSS 3C **122**
Goody Cross La. LS26: Swil 3B **122**
Goody Cross Va. LS26: Swil 3B **122**
Goose Cote La. BD22: Keigh 4E **47**
Goose Cote Way BD22: Keigh 4E **47**
Goosedale Ct. BD4: B'frd 4E **113**
GOOSE EYE 1B **46**
Goose Eye BD22: Keigh 1B **46**
Goose Eye Brow BD22: Keigh 1B **46**
Goosefield Ri. LS25: Gar 6D **102**
GOOSE HILL 3H **111**
Goose La. LS20: Guis 3B **38**
Goose Pond La. HX6: Hal 2C **158**
Gordon Dr. LS6: Leeds 3E **77**
Gordon Larking Ct. LS21: Otley 4C **22**
Gordon Pl. LS6: Leeds 3F **77**
Gordon St. BD5: B'frd 6F **91**
   BD14: B'frd 1D **108**
   BD21: Keigh 6H **33**
   BD22: Haw 1E **65**
   HX3: Hal 5F **129**
   HX5: Ell 5B **160**
   HX6: Hal 6G **147**
   LS29: I'ly 5E **11**

Gordon St. WF3: E Ard 1C **156**
Gordon Ter. BD10: B'frd 6H **53**
  LS6: Leeds 3F **77**
Gordon Vw. LS6: Leeds 3F **77**
Gorse Av. BD17: Bail 6G **51**
Gorse Lea LS10: Leeds 5B **118**
Gothic St. BD13: B'frd 4A **108**
Gotts Pk. Av. LS12: Leeds 2H **95**
Gotts Pk. Cres. LS12: Leeds 2H **95**
Gotts Pk. Vw. LS12: Leeds 1H **95**
Gotts Rd. LS12: Leeds 4F **97** (5A 4)
Gotts Ter. BD20: Keigh 3G **33**
Gott St. BD22: Haw 1F **65**
Goulbourne St. BD21: Keigh 1H **47**
Gower St. BD5: B'frd 1E **111**
  LS2: Leeds 3B **98** (3G 5)
Gracechurch St. BD8: B'frd . .3D **90** (2A 6)
Grace St. BD21: Keigh 6B **34**
  LS1: Leeds 3G **97** (4B 4)
Gracey La. BD6: B'frd 4H **109**
Grady Cl. BD10: B'frd 3H **71**
Grafton Cl. BD17: Bail 3D **52**
Grafton Pl. HX3: Hal 4E **129**
Grafton Rd. BD21: Keigh 2G **47**
Grafton St. BD5: B'frd 6E **91**
  BD21: Keigh 2H **47**
  LS7: Leeds 2A **98** (2F 5)
Grafton Vs. LS15: Leeds 5F **81**
Graham Av. LS4: Leeds 6D **76**
Graham Gro. LS4: Leeds 6D **76**
Graham Ho. LS5: Leeds 6H **75**
(off Broad La.)
Graham Mt. LS4: Leeds 6D **76**
Graham St. BD9: B'frd 1A **90**
  LS4: Leeds 6D **76**
Graham Ter. LS4: Leeds 6D **76**
Graham Vw. LS4: Leeds 6D **76**
Graham Wlk. LS27: Morl 6F **115**
Graingers Way LS12: Leeds . .4F **97** (6A 4)
Grain St. BD5: B'frd 3B **110**
Grammar School Pl. HD6: Brigh . .3H **161**
(off Church St.)
Grammar School St.
  BD1: B'frd 3E **91** (2C 6)
Granary Ct. BD2: B'frd 4A **72**
Granary Wharf LS1: Leeds . . .4H **97** (6D 4)
Granby Av. LS6: Leeds 5D **76**
Granby Cl. LS6: Leeds 5D **76**
(off St Michael's Rd.)
Granby Dr. BD20: Keigh 4D **34**
Granby Gro. LS6: Leeds 5D **76**
Granby La. BD20: Keigh 4D **34**
Granby Mt. LS6: Leeds 4D **76**
Granby Pl. LS6: Leeds 4D **76**
Granby Rd. LS6: Leeds 5D **76**
Granby St. BD4: B'frd 6F **91** (6E 7)
(not continuous)
  BD13: B'frd 4A **108**
  LS6: Leeds 4D **76**
Granby Ter. LS6: Leeds 4D **76**
Granby Vw. LS6: Leeds 4D **76**
Grandage Ter. BD8: B'frd 3B **90**
Grand Arc. LS1: Leeds 3F **5**
Grandsmere Pl. HX3: Hal 5F **149**
Grandstand Rd. WF2: Wake 4C **156**
  WF3: Wake 4C **156**
Grand Theatre & Opera House
. . . . .3A **98** (3F 5)
Grand Vw. BD13: B'frd 2G **107**
  HX3: Hal 6E **129**
(off Ovenden Av.)
  HX6: Hal 6H **147**
(off Clyde St.)
Grange, The HX3: Hal 6F **149**
  LS11: Leeds 3G **117**
  LS13: Leeds 2E **95**
  LS25: Gar 4H **103**
  WF3: Rothw 4H **141**
Grange Av. BD3: Pud 3D **92**
  BD4: B'frd 5E **113**
  BD15: B'frd 3E **89**
  BD18: Ship 1G **69**
  HX2: Hal 2D **128**
  LS7: Leeds 5C **78**

Grange Av. LS19: Yead 1G **55**
  LS23: W'ton 1E **31**
  LS25: Gar 4F **103**
  LS29: I'ly 5F **11**
  LS29: Men 6F **21**
Grange Bank HX3: Hal 1E **131**
Grange Bldgs. LS27: Morl 6C **138**
(off Hodgson St.)
Grange Cl. LS10: Leeds 1B **118**
  LS17: Bard 1F **45**
  LS18: H'fth 1B **74**
  LS29: I'ly 5F **11**
Grange Cotts. BD13: B'frd 3C **66**
Grange Ct. BD16: Bgly 2C **68**
  HX3: Hal 6C **150**
  LS6: Leeds 4F **77**
  LS15: Scho 3H **81**
  LS17: Leeds 2A **60**
  LS26: Rothw 6E **121**
Grange Cres. BD20: Keigh 4C **34**
  LS7: Leeds 5C **78**
  LS19: Yead 1G **55**
Grange Cft. LS17: Leeds 2A **60**
Grange Dr. BD15: B'frd 3E **89**
  LS18: H'fth 1B **74**
Grange Est. LS29: I'ly 5F **11**
Grange Farm Cl. LS29: Men 6F **21**
Grangefield Av. LS29: Burl W 2F **21**
Grangefield Ct. LS25: Gar 4F **103**
Grangefield Ind. Est. LS28: Pud 2A **94**
Grangefield Rd. LS28: Pud 1A **94**
(not continuous)
Grange Flds. Mt. LS10: Leeds 6D **118**
Grange Flds. Rd. LS10: Leeds 1D **140**
Grange Flds. Way LS10: Leeds 1D **140**
Grange Fold BD15: B'frd 3D **88**
Grange Gro. BD3: Pud 3D **92**
  BD20: Keigh 4C **34**
Grange Hgts. HX3: Hal 6C **150**
Grange Holt LS17: Leeds 2A **60**
Grange La. BD20: Kild 2A **14**
  BD22: Keigh 4A **46**
  HD6: Brigh 1E **163**
  LS25: Kip 3H **123**
Grange Mt. LS19: Yead 1G **55**
Grange Pk. BD17: Bail 4E **53**
  HX3: Hal 6F **149**
Grange Pk. Av. LS8: Leeds 4H **79**
Grange Pk. Cl. LS8: Leeds 4A **80**
  LS27: Morl 6B **116**
  WF10: Kip 2G **145**
Grange Pk. Ct. LS27: Morl 6B **116**
(off Grange Pk. Dr.)
Grange Pk. Cres. LS8: Leeds 4H **79**
Grange Pk. Dr. BD16: Bgly 1C **68**
  LS27: Morl 6B **116**
Grange Pk. Gro. LS8: Leeds 4H **79**
Grange Pk. M. LS8: Leeds 4H **79**
  LS27: Morl 6B **116**
Grange Pk. Pl. LS8: Leeds 4H **79**
Grange Pk. Ri. LS8: Leeds 4H **79**
Grange Pk. Rd. BD16: Bgly 1C **68**
  LS8: Leeds 4H **79**
Grange Pk. Ter. LS8: Leeds 4A **80**
Grange Pk. Wlk. LS8: Leeds 4H **79**
Grange Pk. Way LS27: Morl 6B **116**
Grange Rd. BD15: B'frd 3E **89**
  BD16: Bgly 3D **50**
  BD20: Keigh 4C **34**
  BD20: Stee 6A **14**
  LS10: Leeds 1B **118**
  LS19: Yead 1G **55**
  LS29: Burl W 2F **21**
  WF1: Dew 5A **154**
Grange Rd., The
  LS16: Leeds 6B **58**
Grange Sports Cen. 3B **110**
Grange St. BD21: Keigh 5A **34**
  HX3: Hal 6E **129**
  LS27: Morl 5C **116**
Grange Ter. BD15: B'frd 3E **89**
  BD18: Ship 3B **70**
  BD20: Stee 6A **14**
  LS7: Leeds 5B **78**

Grange Ter. LS19: Yead 1G **55**
(off Grange Rd.)
  LS27: Morl 6B **116**
  LS28: Pud 3A **94**
Grange Vw. BD3: Pud 3D **92**
  BD20: Stee 6A **14**
  LS7: Leeds 5C **78**
  LS15: Leeds 5F **101**
  LS21: Otley 2D **22**
  LS22: Weth 5E **13**
  LS28: Pud 3A **94**
Grange Vw. Gdns. LS17: Leeds 6B **62**
Grange Way BD15: B'frd 3E **89**
Grangewood Ct. LS16: Leeds 6B **58**
Grangewood Gdns. LS16: Leeds . . .6B **58**
Grange Yd. HX6: Hal 5A **148**
(off Wharf St.)
Granhamthorpe LS13: Leeds 1E **95**
Granny Av. LS27: Morl 5C **116**
Granny Hall La. HD6: Brigh 5H **151**
Granny Hall La. HD6: Brigh 5H **151**
Granny Hall Pk. HD6: Brigh 5H **151**
Granny Hill HX2: Hal 4C **148**
Granny La. LS12: Leeds 6A **96**
Granny Pl. LS27: Morl 5C **116**
Grant Av. LS7: Leeds 1C **98**
Grantham Pl. BD7: B'frd 6C **90**
  HX3: Hal 5F **129**
Grantham Rd. BD7: B'frd 6C **90** (6A 6)
  HX3: Hal 5F **129**
Grantham Ter. BD7: B'frd 6C **90**
Grantham Towers LS9: Leeds 2C **98**
(off Lindsey Gdns.)
Grantley Pl. HD2: Hud 6D **162**
Granton St. BD3: B'frd 4A **92**
Grant St. BD3: B'frd 4G **91** (3H 7)
  BD21: Keigh 6G **33**
  BD22: Oxen 1C **84**
Granville Ct. LS21: Otley 4D **22**
(off Granville Mt.)
Granville Mt. LS21: Otley 4D **22**
Granville Pl. BD15: B'frd 2D **88**
  LS21: Otley 4D **22**
Granville Rd. BD9: B'frd 4B **70**
  BD18: B'frd 4B **70**
  LS9: Leeds 2C **98**
Granville St. BD14: B'frd 6E **89**
  BD21: Keigh 6H **33**
(off Drewery Rd.)
  HX5: Ell 5B **160**
  LS28: Pud 3G **93**
(Cemetery Rd.)
  LS28: Pud 1B **94**
(Gladstone Ter.)
Granville Ter. BD16: Bgly 4C **50**
  BD18: Ship 4B **70**
  LS19: Yead 6G **41**
  LS20: Guis 3D **40**
  LS21: Otley 4D **22**
Grape St. BD15: B'frd 2E **89**
  BD21: Keigh 5C **34**
  HX1: Hal 2F **149** (3A 6)
  LS10: Leeds 6B **98**
Grasleigh Av. BD15: B'frd 1C **88**
Grasleigh Way BD15: B'frd 1B **88**
Grasmere Av. LS22: Weth 4C **12**
Grasmere Cl. LS12: Leeds 5D **96**
Grasmere Ct. LS12: Leeds 4D **96**
Grasmere Dr. HX5: Ell 4D **160**
  LS22: Weth 4C **12**
Grasmere Pl. HX3: Hal 3E **129**
Grasmere Rd. BD2: B'frd 6G **71**
  BD12: Cleck 6E **133**
  LS12: Leeds 5D **96**
Grass Rd. BD20: Keigh 2G **35**
Gratrix La. HX6: Hal 4A **148**
Grattan Rd. BD1: B'frd 4D **90** (4A 6)
GRAVELEYTHORPE 3C **100**
Graveleythorpe La. LS15: Leeds . . .2D **100**
Graveleythorpe Rd. LS15: Leeds . . .2D **100**
Gray Av. BD18: Ship 4D **70**
Gray Ct. LS15: Leeds 3F **101**

Grayrigg Cl. LS15: Leeds 4A 100
Grayshon Dr. BD6: B'frd 4C 110
Grayshon St. BD11: B'frd 2B 136
Grayson Crest LS4: Leeds 6B 76
Grayson Hgts. LS4: Leeds 6B 76
Grayswood Cres. BD4: B'frd 2B 112
Grayswood Dr. BD4: B'frd 1B 112
Gt. Albion St. HX1: Hal . . .2G 149 (3B 164)
Gt. Cross St. BD1: B'frd 5F 91 (5E 7)
Gt. Edge Rd. HX2: Hal 2F 147
Greater Elland Historical Society
. . . . .4B 160
(off Northgate)
Gt. George St. LS1: Leeds . . .3H 97 (3C 4)
LS2: Leeds 3H 97 (3D 4)
GREAT HORTON 1A 110
Gt. Horton Rd. BD7: B'frd 3F 109
Gt. Northern Rd. BD21: Keigh 1A 48
Gt. Northern St. LS27: Morl 4A 138
Great North Rd.
LS23: B Spa, Coll, Weth 2F 29
LS25: M'fld 2D 104
Gt. Pasture LS29: Burl W 1F 21
Gt. Pasture La. LS29: Burl W 1F 21
GREAT PRESTON 5E 123
Gt. Russell Ct. BD7: B'frd 4C 90
Gt. Russell St. BD7: B'frd 4B 90
Great Scout HX2: Hal 1A 146
Gt. Wilson St. LS11: Leeds 5H 97
Greave Cl. HD2: Hud 6B 162
Greave Ho. Dr. HX2: Hal 2D 146
Greave Ho. Flds. HX2: Hal 1E 147
Greave Ho. Pk. HX2: Hal 2D 146
Greaves St. BD5: B'frd 2D 110
Greaves Yd. LS28: Pud 6A 94
Grebe Cl. BD13: B'frd 4E 109
Greek St. LS1: Leeds . . .3H 97 (4D 4)
GREEN, THE
   Leeds 5C 80
   Pudsey 5H 73
Green, The BD4: B'frd 6D 112
   BD10: B'frd 1H 71
   BD16: Bgly 1C 50
      (College Rd.)
   BD16: Bgly 4F 51
      (Gardens, The)
   BD16: Bgly 1E 51
      (Stead La.)
   BD16: Bgly 6A 36
      (Victoria St.)
   HD2: Hud 6D 162
   LS14: Leeds 5C 80
      (not continuous)
   LS17: Leeds 5C 60
   LS18: H'fth 1D 74
   LS20: Guis 5C 40
   LS21: Leat 1C 24
   LS21: Otley 2D 22
   LS23: B Spa 3C 30
   LS25: Gar 5G 103
   LS25: Kip 4G 123
   LS27: Morl 6F 115
   LS28: Pud 5H 73
   LS29: Add 1C 8
   WF2: Wake 6D 156
   WF17: Bat 5B 136
Greenacre Av. BD12: B'frd 5D 132
Green Acre Cl. BD17: Bail 4D 52
Greenacre Cl. BD12: B'frd 5D 132
Greenacre Ct. LS25: Gar 4G 103
Greenacre Dr. BD12: B'frd 5D 132
Greenacre Pk. LS19: Yead 2F 55
Greenacre Pk. Av. LS19: Yead . .2F 55
Greenacre Pk. M. LS19: Yead 2G 55
Greenacre Pk. Ri. LS19: Yead . . .2F 55
Green Acres LS29: Burl W 3D 20
Greenacres HX3: Hal 1F 131
Greenacres Av. HX3: Hal 1F 131
Greenacres Dr. BD20: Keigh 4G 33
   HX3: Hal 1F 131
   WF17: Bat 5B 136
Greenacres Gro. HX3: Hal 1F 131
Greenacre Way BD12: B'frd 5D 132
Greenaire Pl. BD1: B'frd 4D 90 (4B 6)

Green Av. BD20: Sils 1D 14
   LS25: Kip 2F 123
Green Bank WF3: Rothw 6H 141
Greenbank BD17: Bail 6B 52
Greenbank Rd. BD15: B'frd 3E 89
Greenbanks Av. LS18: H'fth 5E 57
Greenbanks Cl. LS18: H'fth 5E 57
Greenbanks Dr. LS18: H'fth 5D 56
GREENBOTTOM 5C 40
Green Chase LS6: Leeds 2E 77
Greencliffe Av. BD17: Bail 4B 52
Green Cl. BD8: B'frd 3G 89
   BD20: Stee 5A 14
   LS6: Leeds 2F 77
Green Ct. BD7: B'frd 6H 89
   BD19: Cleck 1F 153
   LS15: Scho 2H 81
   LS17: Leeds 5B 60
Green Cres. LS6: Leeds 2E 77
Greencroft Av. HX3: Hal 4D 130
Greencroft Cl. BD10: B'frd 2G 71
Greendown Cl. LS29: I'ly 5F 11
Green Dragon Yd. LS1: Leeds 3D 4
GREEN END 4A 36
Green End BD14: B'frd 1D 108
   HD6: Brigh 2A 162
Grn. End Rd. BD6: B'frd 5B 110
   BD20: Keigh 4A 36
Greenfell Cl. BD22: Keigh 1F 47
Greenfield BD22: Haw 2C 64
Greenfield Av. BD18: Ship 3C 70
   HX3: Hal 2A 152
   LS20: Guis 6H 39
   LS25: Kip 3G 123
   LS27: Morl 6D 114
Greenfield Cl. HX3: Hal 4C 130
   LS25: Kip 3G 123
   LS29: Burl W 4F 21
Greenfield Ct. BD21: Keigh 6G 33
   LS16: Leeds 3B 58
Greenfield Cres. BD13: B'frd 3C 66
Greenfield Dr. BD19: Cleck 1F 153
   LS27: Morl 6D 114
Greenfield Gdns. BD20: Stee 5A 14
Greenfield Gth. LS25: Kip 3G 123
Greenfield La. BD4: B'frd 1H 133
   BD7: B'frd 1H 109
   BD10: B'frd 6H 53
   LS20: Guis 6G 39
   HX3: Hal 2A 152
Greenfield Pl. BD8: B'frd 2C 90
   HX3: Hal 2A 152
Greenfield Ri. LS25: Kip 3G 123
Greenfield Rd. LS9: Leeds 4C 98
Greenfields Way LS29: Burl W 4F 21
Greenfield Ter. BD22: Haw 2C 64
   LS26: Mick 4E 145
Greenfield Va. LS25: Kip 3G 123
Greenfield Vw. LS25: Kip 3G 123
Greenfinch Way BD15: B'frd 4D 88
Green Fold BD17: Bail 5B 52
Greenfold La. LS22: Weth 4F 13
Greengate BD20: Sils 1D 14
   LS26: Rothw 1E 143
Greengate Rd. BD21: Keigh 1A 48
GREENGATES 2C 72
Greengates Av. BD12: B'frd 6C 132
Green Hall Pk. HX3: Hal 2F 131
Greenhead Athletics Track 4H 33
Green Head Av. BD20: Keigh 3G 33
Green Head Dr. BD20: Keigh 3G 33
Green Head La. BD20: Keigh 3G 33
Greenhead La. HD6: Brigh 5G 161
Green Head Rd. BD20: Keigh 3G 33
Greenhead Rd. LS16: Leeds 1B 76
Green Hill HX2: Hal 3H 147
Grn. Hill Chase LS12: Leeds 5B 96
Grn. Hill Cl. LS12: Leeds 2H 95
Grn. Hill Cres. LS12: Leeds 5B 96
Grn. Hill Ct. LS12: Leeds 5B 96
Grn. Hill Dr. LS13: Leeds 2G 95
Greenhill Dr. BD16: Bgly 6A 36
Grn. Hill Gdns. LS12: Leeds 5B 96
Grn. Hill Holt LS12: Leeds 5B 96
Grn. Hill La. LS12: Leeds 6A 96

Greenhill La. BD3: B'frd 4A 92
   BD16: Bgly 1B 50
Grn. Hill Mt. LS13: Leeds 2G 95
Grn. Hill Pk. HX3: Hal 5F 109
Grn. Hill Pl. LS13: Leeds 2G 95
Grn. Hill Rd. LS13: Leeds 2G 95
Greenhills LS19: Yead 4G 55
Greenhill St. BD3: B'frd 4A 92
Grn. Hill Way LS13: Leeds 2G 95
Greenholme Cl. LS29: Burl W 1F 21
Greenholme Mills
   LS29: Burl W 1F 21
Greenholme Trad. Est.
   LS29: Burl W 1F 21
Green Ho's. HX2: Hal 4D 126
Greenhow Gdns. LS4: Leeds 1D 96
Greenhow Pk. LS29: Burl W 2D 20
Greenhow Rd. LS4: Leeds 1D 96
Greenhow Wlk. LS4: Leeds 1D 96
Greenland Av. BD13: B'frd 5A 108
Greenland Ct. LS26: Rothw 2E 143
Greenland Vs. BD13: B'frd 5A 108
Green La. BD2: B'frd 6B 72
   BD7: B'frd 6B 90
   BD8: B'frd 2C 90 (1A 6)
   BD10: B'frd 1A 72
      (Apperley Rd.)
   BD10: B'frd 2G 71
      (Sandhill Fold)
   BD12: B'frd 5B 132
      (Huddersfield Rd.)
   BD12: B'frd 3F 133
      (Walker Rd.)
   BD13: B'frd 5A 88
      (Bronte Old Rd.)
   BD13: B'frd 1A 130
      (Corporal La.)
   BD13: B'frd 3F 107
      (White Castle Ct.)
   BD17: Bail 6A 52
      (Green Rd., not continuous)
   BD17: Bail 3A 52
      (Somerset Av.)
   BD19: Cleck 5B 134
   BD20: Stee 5A 14
   BD22: Keigh 5D 46
      (Keighley Rd.)
   BD22: Keigh 3A 46
      (Whitehill Rd.)
   BD22: Oxen 3D 84
   HD6: Brigh 4G 151
   HD6: Brigh, Liv 6F 153
   HX2: Hal 5C 106
      (Pavement La.)
   HX2: Hal 4C 148
      (Ryburn Vw.)
   HX2: Hal 6D 126
      (Solomon Hill)
   HX3: Hal 3A 150
      (Bank Top)
   HX3: Hal 2A 130
      (Paddock La.)
   HX3: Hal 6F 109
      (Soaper La.)
   HX3: Hal 1F 131
      (Willow Pk. Dr.)
   HX4: Hal 5G 159
   LS11: Leeds 4F 117
   LS12: Leeds 5E 97
      (Sutherland St.)
   LS12: Leeds 6E 95
      (Tong Rd.)
   LS14: Leeds 1C 80
   LS15: Leeds 2D 100
   LS16: Leeds 3F 57
   LS18: H'fth 2D 74
   LS19: Yead 2F 55
   LS21: Otley 2D 22
   LS22: Coll 3A 28
   LS23: B Spa 4C 30
   LS25: Gar 4G 103
      (Greenacre Ct.)

Green La. LS25: Gar 5H **103**
(Severn Dr.)
LS25: Kip 2F **123**
LS26: Mick 6F **145**
LS28: Pud 5H **93**
LS29: Add 1C **8**
LS29: Burl W 1E **21**
(Leather Bank)
LS29: Burl W 5B **20**
(Woodhead)
WF3: Rothw 6G **141**
Green La. Ho. HX4: Hal 5G **159**
Green La. Vs. LS25: Gar 4G **103**
Green Lea LS26: Rothw 1D **142**
Greenlea Av. LS19: Yead 1D **54**
Green Lea Cl. LS23: B Spa 4C **30**
Greenlea Cl. LS19: Yead 2D **54**
Greenlea Fold LS19: Yead 2D **54**
Greenlea Mt. LS19: Yead 1D **54**
Greenlea Rd. LS19: Yead 1D **54**
Greenley Hill BD15: B'frd 5F **67**
Green Mdw. BD15: B'frd 5H **67**
Greenmoor Av. LS12: Leeds 4F **95**
WF3: Rothw 6G **141**
Greenmoor Cl. WF3: Rothw 6G **141**
Greenmoor Cres. WF3: Rothw 6H **141**
Green Mt. BD4: B'frd 2B **112**
BD17: Bail 5A **52**
HX3: Hal 4H **131**
Greenmount Ct. *LS11: Leeds* 2H **117**
(off Fulham St.)
Greenmount La. LS11: Leeds 2H **117**
Greenmount Pl. LS11: Leeds 2H **117**
Green Mt. Retail Pk.
HX1: Hal 2F **149** (3A **164**)
Greenmount Rd. BD13: B'frd 5A **88**
Greenmount St. LS11: Leeds 2H **117**
Greenmount Ter. LS11: Leeds 2H **117**
Greenock Pl. LS12: Leeds 3A **96**
Greenock Rd. LS12: Leeds 3A **96**
Greenock St. LS12: Leeds 3A **96**
Greenock Ter. LS12: Leeds 3A **96**
Green Pk. LS17: Leeds 5C **60**
Green Pk. Av. HX3: Hal 1G **159**
Green Pk. Dr. HX3: Hal 1G **159**
Green Pk. Ga. HX3: Hal 1G **159**
Green Pk. Rd. HX3: Hal 1G **159**
Green Pk. St. HX3: Hal 6G **149**
Grn. Pasture Cl. LS9: Leeds 3G **99**
Green Pl. BD2: B'frd 1H **91**
Green Rd. BD17: Bail 5A **52**
LS6: Leeds 1E **77**
Green Row BD10: B'frd 3H **71**
LS6: Leeds 2E **77**
Green Row Fold LS26: Mick 6D **144**
Green Royd HX2: Hal 3H **127**
HX3: Hal 5A **132**
HX4: Hal 5G **159**
(not continuous)
Greenroyd Av. BD19: Cleck 5B **134**
HX3: Hal 6F **149**
Greenroyd Cl. HX3: Hal 1F **159**
Greenroyd Cres. HX2: Hal 6D **128**
Greenroyd La. HX2: Hal 6C **128**
Greenroyd Ter. HX3: Hal 1G **159**
Greenshank M. LS27: Morl 3D **138**
Greenshaw Ter. LS20: Guis 4B **40**
Greens Health & Fitness 6D **52**
GREEN SIDE 4H **89**
Greenside BD12: B'frd 3G **133**
BD14: B'frd 1D **108**
LS19: Yead 2E **55**
(off Warm La.)
LS28: Pud 5H **93**
Grn. Side Av. LS12: Leeds 6B **96**
Greenside Cl. LS12: Leeds 6C **96**
Greenside Ct. LS27: Morl 6F **115**
Greenside Dr. LS12: Leeds 6C **96**
Greenside Gro. LS28: Pud 5H **93**
Greenside La. BD8: B'frd 4H **89**
BD13: B'frd 3B **66**
Greenside Pk. BD8: B'frd 4H **89**
Greenside Rd. LS12: Leeds 6C **96**
Grn. Side Ter. LS12: Leeds 6B **96**

Greenside Wlk. LS12: Leeds 6B **96**
Green's Sq. HX2: Hal 1C **148**
Green's Ter. BD12: B'frd 3F **133**
Green St. BD1: B'frd 4F **91** (4F **7**)
BD12: B'frd 2H **133**
BD22: Haw 3C **64**
BD22: Oxen 1C **84**
Greensway LS25: Gar 4E **103**
Grn. Sykes Rd. BD22: Keigh 5A **32**
Green Ter. *BD2: B'frd* 1H **91**
(off Idle Rd.)
LS11: Leeds 2A **118**
LS20: Guis 5C **40**
Green Ter. Sq. HX1: Hal 4E **149**
Greenthorpe Ct. LS13: Leeds 4G **95**
Greenthorpe Hill LS13: Leeds 4G **95**
Greenthorpe Mt. LS13: Leeds 3G **95**
Greenthorpe Rd. LS13: Leeds 3G **95**
Greenthorpe St. LS13: Leeds 4G **95**
Greenthorpe Wlk. LS13: Leeds 3G **95**
Greenthwaite Cl. BD20: Keigh 4G **33**
Greenton Av. BD19: Cleck 6E **133**
Greenton Cres. BD13: B'frd 5H **107**
Green Top LS12: Leeds 6B **96**
Greentop LS28: Pud 5H **93**
Grn. Top Gdns. LS12: Leeds 6B **96**
Green Top St. BD8: B'frd 4G **89**
Greentrees BD6: B'frd 1B **132**
Greenups Mill *HX6: Hal* 5A **148**
(off Old Cawsey)
Greenups Ter. HX6: Hal 5H **147**
Green Vw. LS6: Leeds 2E **77**
LS14: S'cft 5E **45**
Greenview Cl. LS9: Leeds 1G **99**
Greenview Ct. LS8: Leeds 1E **79**
Greenview Mt. LS9: Leeds 1G **99**
Greenville Av. LS12: Leeds 6B **96**
Greenville Dr. BD12: B'frd 6E **111**
Greenville Gdns. LS12: Leeds 6B **96**
Green Way HX2: Hal 5C **106**
LS14: S'cft 5E **45**
Greenway BD3: B'frd 3G **91** (1G **7**)
LS15: Leeds 2E **101**
LS20: Guis 6A **40**
Greenway Cl. LS15: Leeds 2E **101**
Greenway Dr. BD15: B'frd 4D **88**
Greenway Rd. BD5: B'frd 3E **111**
Greenwell Row BD14: B'frd 1D **108**
Greenwood Av. BD2: B'frd 1E **77**
Greenwood Ct. BD1: B'frd 5E **91** (5E **7**)
LS6: Leeds 1E **77**
Greenwood Dr. BD2: B'frd 5G **71**
Greenwood Mt. BD2: B'frd 5G **71**
LS6: Leeds 2E **77**
Greenwood Pk. LS6: Leeds 2E **77**
Greenwood Rd. BD17: Bail 6B **52**
WF3: E Ard 1F **155**
Greenwood Row *LS27: Morl* 3B **138**
(off Commercial St.)
LS28: Pud 4B **94**
Greenwood's Ter. HX3: Hal 6D **128**
GREETLAND 4F **159**
Greetland Community & Sports Cen.
. . . . .4E **159**
Greetland Rd. HX4: Hal 5A **158**
Gregory Cl. BD14: B'frd 1E **109**
Gregory Cres. BD7: B'frd 3G **109**
Grenfell Dr. BD3: B'frd 3B **92**
Grenfell Rd. BD3: B'frd 3B **92**
Grenfell Ter. BD3: B'frd 3B **92**
Gresham Av. BD2: B'frd 5F **71**
Gresley Ho. *LS18: H'hth* 4E **57**
(off Sussex Av.)
Gresley Rd. BD21: Keigh 6A **34**
Grey Cl. WF1: Wake 6F **157**
Grey Ct. WF1: Wake 6F **157**
Greycourt Cl. BD10: B'frd 3G **71**
HX1: Hal 3E **149**
Greycourt Ho. *HX1: Hal* 3E **149**
(off King Cross Rd.)
Greyfriar Wlk. BD7: B'frd 2G **109**
Greyhound Dr. BD7: B'frd 5B **90**

Grey Scar Rd. BD22: Keigh 5A **46**
Grey Shaw Syke HX2: Hal 3B **106**
Greyshiels Av. LS6: Leeds 5C **76**
Greyshiels Cl. LS6: Leeds 5C **76**
Greystone Av. HX5: Ell 6A **160**
Greystone Cl. LS23: B Spa 4C **30**
LS29: Burl W 1E **21**
Greystone Ct. HD6: Brigh 4A **162**
Greystone Cres. BD10: B'frd 3A **72**
Greystone Mill BD3: B'frd 4H **91**
Greystone Mt. LS15: Leeds 4A **100**
Greystones HX2: Hal 4B **128**
Greystones Ct. LS8: Leeds 2G **79**
LS17: Leeds 3A **60**
Greystones Dr. BD22: Keigh 5F **47**
Greystones Mt. BD22: Keigh 5F **47**
Greystones Ri. BD22: Keigh 4F **47**
Greystones Rd. HX2: Hal 2E **147**
Grey St. WF1: Wake 6F **157**
Griffe Dr. BD12: B'frd 6C **132**
Griffe Gdns. BD22: Keigh 4B **46**
Griffe Head Cres. BD12: B'frd 5C **132**
Griffe Head Rd. BD12: B'frd 5C **132**
Griffe Rd. BD12: B'frd 5C **132**
Griffe Ter. BD12: B'frd 6C **132**
Griffe Vw. BD22: Keigh 4B **46**
Griff Ho. La. WF3: E Ard 1H **155**
Grimthorpe Av. LS6: Leeds 4C **76**
Grimthorpe Pl. LS6: Leeds 4D **76**
Grimthorpe St. LS6: Leeds 4C **76**
Grimthorpe Ter. LS6: Leeds 4D **76**
Grindlestone Bank HX2: Hal 3A **128**
Grisedale Cl. HX2: Hal 6B **128**
Gritstone Cl. LS29: Burl W 1E **21**
Grizedale Cl. LS22: Weth 3B **12**
Grosmont Pl. LS13: Leeds 6E **75**
Grosmont Rd. LS13: Leeds 1E **95**
Grosmont Ter. LS13: Leeds 6E **75**
Grosvenor Av. BD18: Ship 1H **69**
Grosvenor Ct. *LS16: Leeds* 3F **57**
(off Tinshill Rd.)
Grosvenor Hill LS7: Leeds 1A **98**
Grosvenor M. LS19: Yead 3E **55**
Grosvenor Mt. LS6: Leeds 5F **77**
Grosvenor Pk. LS7: Leeds 2A **78**
Grosvenor Pk. Gdns. LS6: Leeds . .5F **77**
Grosvenor Pl. HX2: Hal 2D **146**
Grosvenor Rd. BD8: B'frd 2D **90**
BD18: Ship 2H **69**
LS6: Leeds 5F **77**
Grosvenor St. BD8: B'frd 2D **90**
HX5: Ell 5B **160**
Grosvenor Ter. BD8: B'frd 2D **90**
HX1: Hal 2E **149**
(not continuous)
LS6: Leeds 5F **77**
LS21: Otley 3F **23**
LS22: Weth 3E **13**
Grotto Ter. HX2: Hal 2E **127**
Grouse Moor La. BD13: B'frd 3G **107**
Grouse St. BD21: Keigh 5B **34**
Grove, The BD10: B'frd 2B **72**
(New Line)
BD10: B'frd 2H **71**
(Woodbine Ter.)
BD13: B'frd 4H **107**
(off New Pk. Rd.)
BD16: Bgly 1A **50**
BD17: Bail 3C **52**
BD18: Ship 2G **69**
HX3: Hal 1F **151**
(Bramley La.)
HX3: Hal 1E **131**
(Wade Ho. Rd.)
LS17: Bard 5D **26**
LS17: Leeds 2F **59**
LS18: H'hth 1D **74**
LS19: Yead 1F **55**
LS23: B Spa 4D **30**
LS25: Kip 4G **123**
LS26: Swil 3B **122**
LS27: Morl 6F **115**
LS28: Pud 4H **93**
LS29: I'ly 5C **10**

Grove, The WF3: E Ard 1H **155**
Grove Av. BD18: Ship 4B **70**
  HX3: Hal 5D **128**
  LS6: Leeds 3E **77**
  LS28: Pud 4H **93**
  LS29: I'ly 6B **10**
Grove Cl. BD2: B'frd 5G **71**
  BD19: Cleck 6F **135**
Grove Cotts. HD6: Brigh 1G **161**
Grove Ct. HX3: Hal 4E **129**
  LS6: Leeds 3E **77**
  LS28: Pud 4H **93**
Grove Cres. HX2: Hal 2D **146**
  LS23: B Spa 4D **30**
Grove Cres. Sth.
  LS23: B Spa 4D **30**
Grove Cft. HX3: Hal 5D **128**
Grove Dr. HX3: Hal 5D **128**
Grove Edge HX3: Hal 5D **128**
Grove Farm Cl. LS16: Leeds 3H **57**
Grove Farm Cres. LS16: Leeds 4G **57**
Grove Farm Cft. LS16: Leeds 3G **57**
Grove Farm Dr. LS16: Leeds 3G **57**
Grove Gdns. HX3: Hal 5E **129**
  LS6: Leeds 3E **77**
  LS23: B Spa 4D **30**
Grovehall Av. LS11: Leeds 4F **117**
Grovehall Dr. LS11: Leeds 4F **117**
Grovehall Pde. LS11: Leeds 4F **117**
Grovehall Rd. LS11: Leeds 4F **117**
Grove Ho. LS7: Leeds 5C **78**
  (off Woodland Gro.)
Grove Ho. Cl. LS8: Leeds 3H **79**
  (off Nth. Grove Cl.)
Grove Ho. Cres. BD2: B'frd 5G **71**
Grove Ho. Dr. BD2: B'frd 5G **71**
Grove Ho. Rd. BD2: B'frd 5G **71**
Grovelands BD2: B'frd 5G **71**
Grove La. BD19: Cleck 6F **135**
  LS6: Leeds 3D **76**
Grove Mill Ct. LS21: Otley 4C **22**
Grove Mill La. HX3: Hal 5E **129**
Grove Pk. HX3: Hal 4E **129**
Grove Pl. LS23: B Spa 4D **30**
Grove Prom., The LS29: I'ly 5D **10**
  (off Bk. Grove Rd.)
Grove Ri. LS17: Leeds 2F **59**
Grove Rd. BD16: Bgly 5B **50**
  BD18: Ship 4B **70**
  LS6: Leeds 4E **77**
  LS10: Leeds 2C **118**
  LS15: Leeds 4C **100**
  LS18: H'fth 1D **74**
  LS23: B Spa 4C **30**
  LS28: Pud 4H **93**
  LS29: I'ly 5A **10**
  LS29: Men 1G **39**
Grove Row HX2: Hal 4G **127**
Grove Royd HX3: Hal 5E **129**
Grover Ter. LS21: Pool 6D **24**
Grove Sq. BD19: Cleck 6F **135**
  HX3: Hal 5D **128**
Grove St. HD6: Brigh 1B **162**
  HX2: Hal 4D **128**
  HX6: Hal 5B **148**
  LS1: Leeds 4B **4**
  LS28: Pud 1A **94**
Grove St. Sth. HX1: Hal 2D **148**
Grove Ter. BD7: B'frd 5D **90** (5B **6**)
  BD11: B'frd 3E **135**
  HD6: Brigh 1G **161**
  LS23: B Spa 4C **30**
  LS28: Pud 4H **93**
Grove Vs. WF10: Kip 1G **145**
Groveville HX3: Hal 6E **131**
Groveway BD2: B'frd 5G **71**
Grovewood LS6: Leeds 3D **76**
Grunberg Pl. LS6: Leeds 4D **76**
Grunberg St. LS6: Leeds 4D **76**
GUARD HOUSE 6E **33**
Guard Ho. Av. BD22: Keigh 6G **33**
Guard Ho. Dr. BD22: Keigh 6G **33**
Guard Ho. Gro. BD22: Keigh 6F **33**
Guard Ho. Rd. BD22: Keigh 6G **33**

Guardian Ct. LS29: I'ly 5D **10**
  (off Wells Prom.)
Guardian M. LS12: Leeds 6C **96**
  (off Lynwood Vw.)
Guernsey Rd. WF12: Dew 6A **154**
Guide Post Farm HX2: Hal 6C **106**
  (off Keighley Rd.)
Guild Way HX2: Hal 2H **147**
Guillemot App. LS27: Morl 4D **138**
GUISELEY 4C **40**
Guiseley Dr. LS29: Men 3H **39**
Guiseley Retail Pk. LS20: Guis 5C **40**
Guiseley Station (Rail) 4B **40**
Guiseley Theatre 5C **40**
Gunter Rd. LS22: Weth 4G **13**
Gurbax Ct. BD3: B'frd 4C **92**
Gurney Cl. BD5: B'frd 2D **110**
GUYCROFT 4D **22**
Guycroft LS21: Otley 4D **22**
Guy St. BD4: B'frd 5F **91** (6E **7**)
Gwynne Av. BD3: B'frd 2C **92**
Gym and Tonic 5D **60**
Gym Health & Fitness Club, The . . .1E **99**
Gypsy Wood Cl. LS15: Leeds 4F **101**
Gypsy Wood Crest LS15: Leeds 4F **101**

H

Hadassah St. HX3: Hal 5H **149**
Haddon Av. HX3: Hal 6G **149**
  LS4: Leeds 1C **96**
Haddon Pl. LS4: Leeds 1C **96**
Haddon Rd. LS4: Leeds 1D **96**
Hadleigh Ct. LS17: Leeds 5B **60**
Hag Farm Rd. LS29: Burl W 5D **20**
Hag La. HX3: Hal 4G **129**
Haigh Av. LS26: Rothw 6G **119**
Haigh Beck Vw. BD10: B'frd 2A **72**
Haigh Cnr. BD10: B'frd 2B **72**
Haighfield Cvn. Site LS17: Bard 3D **44**
HAIGH FOLD 5B **72**
Haigh Fold BD2: B'frd 6A **72**
Haigh Gdns. LS26: Rothw 6G **119**
Haigh Hall BD10: B'frd 2B **72**
Haigh Hall Rd. BD10: B'frd 2B **72**
Haigh La. HX3: Hal 5H **149**
HAIGH MOOR 3E **155**
Haigh Moor Av. WF3: E Ard 3E **155**
Haigh Moor Cres. WF3: E Ard 3E **155**
Haigh Moor Rd. WF3: E Ard 4E **155**
Haigh Moor Vw. WF3: E Ard 3E **155**
Haigh Pk. Rd. LS10: Leeds 3F **119**
Haigh Rd. LS26: Rothw 1A **142**
Haighside LS26: Rothw 1G **141**
Haighside Cl. LS26: Rothw 1G **141**
Haighside Dr. LS26: Rothw 1G **141**
Haighside Way LS26: Rothw 1G **141**
Haigh St. BD4: B'frd 2H **111**
  HD6: Brigh 6A **152**
  HX1: Hal 1D **148**
  HX4: Hal 4F **159**
Haigh Ter. LS26: Rothw 6G **119**
Haigh Vw. LS26: Rothw 6G **119**
Haigh Wood Cres. LS16: Leeds 4F **57**
Haigh Wood Grn. LS16: Leeds 5F **57**
Haigh Wood Rd. LS16: Leeds 4E **57**
Haincliffe Pl. BD21: Keigh 3H **47**
Haincliffe Rd. BD21: Keigh 3H **47**
Haines Pk. LS7: Leeds 1C **98**
Hainsworth Ct. LS28: Pud 6H **73**
  (off Ebenezer St.)
Hainsworth Moor Cres.
  BD13: B'frd 5H **107**
Hainsworth Moor Dr.
  BD13: B'frd 5H **107**
Hainsworth Moor Gth.
  BD13: B'frd 5H **107**
Hainsworth Moor Gro.
  BD13: B'frd 5H **107**
Hainsworth Moor Vw.
  BD13: B'frd 5H **107**
Hainsworth Rd. BD20: Sils 3E **15**
Hainsworth Sq. LS28: Pud 6H **73**

Hainsworth St. BD20: Sils 2E **15**
  (off Howden Rd.)
  LS12: Leeds 5E **97**
  LS26: Rothw 3A **142**
HAINWORTH 4H **47**
Hainworth Crag Rd. BD21: Keigh . . .5G **47**
Hainworth La. BD21: Keigh 4H **47**
Hainworth Rd. BD21: Keigh 4H **47**
HAINWORTH SHAW 4B **48**
Hainworth Wood Rd. BD21: Keigh . . .4H **47**
Hainworth Wood Rd. Nth.
  BD21: Keigh 2A **48**
Halcyon Hill LS7: Leeds 1A **78**
Halcyon Way BD5: B'frd 2C **110**
Hale Rd. LS12: Leeds 6B **96**
Halesworth Cres. BD4: B'frd 3C **112**
Haley Ct. HX3: Hal 1B **164**
Haley Hill HX3: Hal 6G **129** (1B **164**)
Haley's Yd. LS13: Leeds 6E **75**
Half Acre Rd. BD13: B'frd 4F **87**
Half Ho. La. HD6: Brigh 4F **151**
HALF MILE 6B **74**
Half Mile LS13: Pud 6B **74**
  LS28: Pud 1B **94**
Half Mile Cl. LS28: Pud 1B **94**
Half Mile Ct. LS28: Pud 1B **94**
Half Mile Gdns. LS13: Pud 1B **94**
Half Mile Grn. LS28: Pud 1B **94**
Half Mile La. LS13: Pud 6B **74**
  LS28: Pud 6B **74**
Half St. BD21: Keigh 5H **33**
HALIFAX 2G **149** (4C **164**)
Halifax Antiques Cen. 2D **148**
  (off Queen Rd.)
Halifax Body Station, The 2C **164**
Halifax Ind. Cen. HX1: Hal 1E **149**
Halifax La. HX2: Hal 1E **147**
Halifax Old Rd. HX3: Hal 1D **150**
Halifax Retail Pk.
  HX1: Hal 2F **149** (3A **164**)
Halifax Rd. BD6: B'frd 6G **109**
  BD13: B'frd 5H **65**
  (Haworth Rd.)
  BD13: B'frd 1B **106**
  (Long Causeway)
  BD13: B'frd 4B **86**
  (Old Rd.)
  BD13: B'frd 1G **129**
  (Queensbury Rd.)
  BD19: Cleck 2E **153**
  BD21: Haw 1F **65**
  BD21: Keigh 4H **47**
  BD22: B'frd, Haw 1F **65**
  BD22: Haw 6F **47**
  HD6: Brigh 3F **151**
  HX3: Hal 4D **130**
  (Bradford Rd.)
  HX3: Hal 1D **150**
  (Halifax Old Rd.)
  HX3: Hal 3F **151**
  (Westminster Rd.)
  HX4: Hal 3H **159**
  HX5: Ell 4A **160**
  WF15: Liv 2E **153**
Halifax RUFC (Ovenden Pk.) 3D **128**
Halifax Ski & Snowboarding Cen. 4G **129**
Halifax Station (Rail) 4H **149** (5D **164**)
Halifax Swimming Pool
   . . . . .3G **149** (6C **164**)
Halifax Town FC & Halifax RLFC
  (Shay, The) 4G **149** (6C **164**)
Hallamfield LS20: Guis 5C **40**
Hallam St. LS20: Guis 5B **40**
HALLAS BRIDGE 3D **66**
Hallas Bridge Mill
  BD13: B'frd 4D **66**
Hallas La. BD13: B'frd 4C **66**
  (not continuous)
Hall Av. BD2: B'frd 4B **72**
Hallbank Cl. BD5: B'frd 4D **110**
Hall Bank Dr. BD16: Bgly 3C **50**
Hallbank Dr. BD5: B'frd 4D **110**
Hallcliffe BD17: Bail 3D **52**

Hall Cl. HX3: Hal 4C 130
  LS16: B'hpe 1G 43
  LS23: B Spa 4C 30
  LS29: Burl W 2D 20
Hall Cl. LS7: Leeds 5B 78
Hall Cft. BD20: Sils 1E 15
Hallcroft BD16: Bgly 2B 50
Hallcroft Dr. LS29: Add 2F 9
Hall Dr. LS16: B'hpe 1F 43
  LS29: Burl W 2D 20
Hall Farm Pk. LS25: M'fld 3D 104
HALLFIELD 4F 13
Hallfield Av. LS25: M'fld 4D 104
Hallfield Ct. LS22: Weth 3F 13
Hallfield Cres. LS22: Weth 3F 13
Hallfield Dr. BD17: Bail 4C 52
Hallfield La. LS22: Weth 3F 13
Hallfield Pl. BD1: B'frd 3E 91 (1C 6)
Hallfield Rd. BD1: B'frd . . .3D 90 (2B 6)
Hallfield St. BD1: B'frd 3E 91 (2C 6)
Hallfield Ter. LS25: M'fld 4D 104
Hallgate BD1: B'frd 3E 91 (2C 6)
Hall Gro. LS6: Leeds 1F 97
Halliday Av. LS12: Leeds 3A 96
Halliday Ct. LS25: Gar 4E 103
Halliday Dr. LS12: Leeds 3A 96
Halliday Gro. LS12: Leeds 3A 96
Halliday Mt. LS12: Leeds 3A 96
Halliday Pl. LS12: Leeds 3A 96
Halliday Rd. LS12: Leeds 3A 96
  LS25: Gar 4E 103
Halliday St. LS28: Pud 3A 94
Hall Ings BD1: B'frd 5E 91 (5D 6)
  HX3: Hal 6C 150
Hall La. BD4: B'frd 6F 91 (6F 7)
  BD18: Ship 1C 70
    (not continuous)
  HX3: Hal 3B 130
  LS7: Leeds 4B 78
  LS12: Leeds 5E 95
    (Green La.)
  LS12: Leeds 4C 96
    (Strawberry Rd.)
  LS16: Leeds 1G 57
  LS18: H'fth 1B 74
  LS21: Leat 1C 24
  WF10: Leds 6D 124
Hall M. LS23: B Spa 4C 30
Hall Orchards Av. LS22: Weth 3F 13
Hallowes Gro. BD13: B'frd 4B 66
Hallowes Pk. Rd. BD13: B'frd 4B 66
Hallows, The BD20: Keigh 5G 33
Hallows Rd. BD21: Keigh 4C 34
Hall Pk. Av. LS18: H'fth 6C 56
Hall Pk. Cl. LS18: H'fth 6C 56
Hall Pk. Ct. LS25: Kip 4H 123
Hall Pk. Cft. LS25: Kip 5H 123
Hall Pk. Gth. LS18: H'fth 6C 56
Hall Pk. Mdws. LS25: Kip 5H 123
Hall Pk. Mt. LS18: H'fth 6C 56
Hall Pk. Orchard LS25: Kip 5H 123
Hall Pk. Ri. LS18: H'fth 6D 56
  LS25: Kip 4H 123
Hall Pl. LS9: Leeds 4D 98
Hall Ri. LS16: B'hpe 2G 43
  LS29: Burl W 2D 20
Hall Ri. Cl. LS16: B'hpe 2G 43
Hall Ri. Cft. LS16: B'hpe 2G 43
Hall Rd. BD2: B'frd 4A 72
  LS12: Leeds 4C 96
  LS26: Swil 4B 122
Hall Royd BD18: Ship 2A 70
Hallside Cl. BD17: Bail 3F 53
Hall Sq. LS28: Pud 2F 73
Hall Stone Ct. HX3: Hal 2E 131
Hall St. BD6: B'frd 4C 110
  BD22: Haw 3C 64
  BD22: Keigh *5D 46*
    (off Clough La.)
  HD6: Brigh 1B 162
  HX1: Hal 2F 149 (4A 164)
Hall St. Nth. HX3: Hal 5F 129
Hall Ter. BD2: B'frd 4A 72
  BD20: Keigh 4D 34

Hallwood Grn. BD10: B'frd 4C 72
Halstead Dr. LS29: Men 6G 21
Halstead Pl. BD7: B'frd 2B 110
Halsteads Way BD20: Stee 5B 14
HALTON 3B 100
Halton Dr. LS15: Leeds 3C 100
Halton Hill LS15: Leeds 3C 100
HALTON MOOR 4A 100
Halton Moor Av. LS9: Leeds 5H 99
Halton Moor Rd. LS9: Leeds 5E 99
    (not continuous)
  LS15: Leeds 5A 100
Hambledon Av. BD4: B'frd 4H 111
Hambleton Bank HX2: Hal 1H 127
Hambleton Cres. HX2: Hal 2H 127
Hambleton Dr. HX2: Hal 2G 127
Hambleton La. BD22: Oxen 4F 85
Hamilton Av. LS7: Leeds 5C 78
Hamilton Gdns. LS7: Leeds 6B 78
Hamilton Pl. LS7: Leeds 6C 78
Hamilton St. BD7: B'frd 3D 90 (1B 6)
Hamilton Ter. LS7: Leeds 6C 78
  LS21: Otley *3F 23*
    (off North Av.)
Hamilton Vw. LS7: Leeds 5C 78
Hammersmere Leach La.
  HX4: Ell 6H 159
  HX5: Ell 6H 159
Hammerstones Rd. HX5: Ell 5H 159
Hammerton Cl. HX5: Ell 4B 160
Hammerton Dr. LS25: Gar 6G 103
Hammerton Gro. LS28: Pud 4B 94
Hammerton St. BD3: B'frd . . .5G 91 (5G 7)
  LS28: Pud 4A 94
Hammond Cres. BD11: B'frd 6H 113
Hammond Pl. BD9: B'frd 6A 70
Hammonds Landing HX6: Hal 5A 148
Hammond Sq. BD9: B'frd 6A 70
Hammond St. HX1: Hal 3D 148
Hamm Strasse BD1: B'frd . . .3E 91 (2D 6)
Hampden Pl. BD5: B'frd 1D 110
  HX1: Hal 2F 149
Hampden St. BD5: B'frd 1D 110
Hampshire Cl. LS29: I'ly 5F 11
Hampton Ct. *LS29: I'ly* *5C 10*
    (off Grove Rd.)
Hampton Pl. BD10: B'frd 1H 71
  LS9: Leeds 4D 98
Hampton St. HX1: Hal 4D 148
  LS9: Leeds 4C 98
Hampton Ter. LS9: Leeds 4D 98
Hanworth Dr. BD22: Keigh 5D 46
Hanbury Gdns. LS25: Gar 3F 103
Hand Carr La. HX2: Hal 2B 146
Handel St. BD7: B'frd 4C 90
HANGING HEATON 6A 154
Hangingstone Rd. LS29: I'ly 6F 11
Hanging Wood Way BD19: Cleck . .5A 134
Hangram St. HD6: Brigh 1B 162
Hanley Rd. LS27: Morl 4A 138
Hannah Ct. BD12: B'frd 4C 132
Hanover Av. LS3: Leeds 3G 97 (2A 4)
Hanover Ct. LS27: Morl 2B 138
Hanover Gdns. BD5: B'frd 6D 90
  LS29: Burl W 3E 21
Hanover Ho. *HX2: Hal* *4C 148*
    LS19: Yead *5D 40*
    (off Harper La.)
Hanover La. LS3: Leeds 3G 97 (3A 4)
Hanover Mt. LS3: Leeds 2F 97 (3A 4)
Hanover Pl. LS25: Kip 4H 123
Hanover Sq. BD1: B'frd 3D 90 (1B 6)
  BD12: B'frd 4C 132
  LS3: Leeds 2G 97 (2A 4)
Hanover St. BD21: Keigh 6A 34
  HX1: Hal 3F 149 (5A 164)
  HX6: Hal 5B 148
Hanover Wlk. LS3: Leeds 3G 97 (3A 4)
Hanover Way LS3: Leeds 3G 97 (3A 4)
  LS29: Burl W 3E 21
Hansby Av. LS14: Leeds 4D 80

Hansby Bank LS14: Leeds 4D 80
Hansby Cl. LS14: Leeds 5D 80
Hansby Dr. LS14: Leeds 4D 80
Hansby Gdns. LS14: Leeds 5D 80
Hansby Ga. LS14: Leeds 4D 80
Hansby Grange LS14: Leeds 4D 80
Hansby Pl. LS14: Leeds 5D 80
Hanson Ct. BD12: B'frd 5C 132
Hanson Fold BD12: B'frd 4C 132
Hanson La. HX1: Hal 2C 148 (3A 164)
Hanson Mt. BD12: B'frd 5C 132
Hanson Pl. BD12: B'frd 4C 132
Hanson Rd. HD6: Brigh 3G 161
Hanson Sports Cen. 5G 71
Hanworth Rd. BD12: B'frd 1D 132
Hapsburg Ct. *BD5: B'frd* *6E 91*
    (off Elsdon Gro.)
Harbeck Dr. BD16: Bgly 6F 49
Harborough Grn.
  BD10: B'frd *1C 72*
    (off Leavens, The)
Harbour Cres. BD6: B'frd 5A 110
Harbour Pk. BD6: B'frd 5H 109
Harbour Rd. BD6: B'frd 5H 109
Harclo Rd. BD21: Keigh 5C 34
Harcourt Av. BD13: B'frd 4H 87
Harcourt Dr. LS27: Morl 2H 137
  LS29: Add 1D 8
Harcourt Pl. LS1: Leeds 3F 97 (4A 4)
Harcourt St. BD4: B'frd 2H 111
Hardaker La. BD17: Bail 5A 52
Hardaker St. BD8: B'frd 3D 90 (2A 6)
HARDEN 6F 49
Harden & Bingley Cvn. Pk.
  BD16: Bgly 2E 67
Harden Brow La. BD16: Bgly 6E 49
Harden Gro. BD10: B'frd 6C 72
  BD21: Keigh 2C 48
Harden La. BD15: B'frd 2F 67
  BD16: B'frd 2F 67
Harden Rd. BD16: Bgly 6F 49
  BD21: Keigh 2C 48
Hardgate La. BD21: Haw 3F 65
  BD22: Haw 2F 65
    (not continuous)
Hardhill Ho's. *BD16: Bgly* *6F 49*
    (off Wilsden Rd.)
Hardings La. LS29: I'ly 3B 10
Hard Ings Rd. BD21: Keigh 4A 34
Hardknot Cl. BD7: B'frd 2G 109
Hardnaze BD22: Oxen 2A 84
Hard Nese La. BD22: Oxen 2A 84
    (not continuous)
Hardrow Grn. LS12: Leeds 6D 96
Hardrow Gro. LS12: Leeds 6D 96
Hardrow Rd. LS12: Leeds 6C 96
Hardrow Ter. LS12: Leeds 6D 96
Hardwick Cft. LS7: Leeds 3B 78
Hardwick St. BD21: Keigh 1G 47
Hardy Av. BD6: B'frd 5C 110
  LS27: Morl 5C 116
Hardy Ct. LS27: Morl 3B 138
Hardy Gro. LS11: Leeds 2G 117
Hardy Pl. HD6: Brigh 4G 151
Hardy St. BD4: B'frd 5F 91 (6E 7)
  BD6: B'frd 4C 110
  HD6: Brigh 6B 152
  LS11: Leeds 2G 117
  LS27: Morl 3B 138
Hardy Ter. *BD6: B'frd* *4C 110*
    (off Hardy St.)
  LS11: Leeds 2H 117
Hardy Vw. LS11: Leeds 2G 117
HARE CROFT 5E 67
Harecroft Rd. LS21: Otley 2E 23
Hare Farm Av. LS12: Leeds 4F 95
Hare Farm Cl. LS12: Leeds 3F 95
Harefield Cl. BD20: Stee 6A 14
Harefield Dr. WF17: Bat 6C 136
Harefield E. LS15: Leeds 4A 100
Harefield W. LS15: Leeds 4A 100
Harehill Cl. BD10: B'frd 6H 53
Harehill Rd. BD10: B'frd 6H 53
HAREHILLS 1F 99

Harehills Av. LS7: Leeds 5C 78
  LS8: Leeds 5C 78
HAREHILLS CORNER 5D 78
Harehills La. LS7: Leeds 4C 78
  LS8: Leeds 4C 78
  LS9: Leeds 5E 79
Harehills Pk. Av. LS9: Leeds 1F 99
Harehills Pk. Cotts. LS9: Leeds 1G 99
Harehills Pk. Rd. LS9: Leeds 1F 99
Harehills Pk. Ter. LS9: Leeds 1F 99
Harehills Pk. Vw. LS9: Leeds 1F 99
Harehills Pl. LS8: Leeds 6D 78
Harehills Rd. LS8: Leeds 5D 78
Hare La. LS28: Pud 6A 94
Hare Pk. Av. WF15: Liv 5H 153
Hare Pk. Cl. WF15: Liv 5H 153
Hare Pk. La. WF15: Liv 6H 153
Hare Pk. Mt. LS12: Leeds 4E 95
Hares Av. LS8: Leeds 5D 78
Hares Mt. LS8: Leeds 5C 78
Hares Rd. LS8: Leeds 5C 78
Hares Ter. LS8: Leeds 5D 78
Hare St. HX1: Hal 2D 148
Hares Vw. LS8: Leeds 5D 78
Harewood Av. BD20: Stee 6A 14
  HX2: Hal 1B 148
  LS17: Bard, Hare 4A 26
Harewood Ct. LS14: Leeds 5C 80
  LS17: Leeds 6B 60
Harewood Cres. BD22: Keigh 4E 47
Harewood Dr. BD20: Stee 5A 14
Harewood Pl. HX2: Hal 3C 148
Harewood Ri. BD22: Keigh 4F 47
Harewood Rd. BD22: Keigh 5E 47
  LS17: Bard 4C 26
  LS22: Coll 4C 26
Harewood St. BD3: B'frd 4H 91 (3H 7)
    (not continuous)
  LS2: Leeds 3A 98 (4F 5)
Harewood Way LS13: Leeds 3D 94
Hargrave Cres. LS29: Men 1F 39
Hargreaves WF3: Wake 4H 157
Hargreaves Cl. LS27: Morl 6H 115
Hargreaves St. LS26: Rothw 2B 142
Harker Rd. BD12: B'frd 6C 110
Harker Ter. LS28: Pud 2H 93
Harland Cl. BD2: B'frd 1E 91
Harland Sq. LS2: Leeds 6G 77
    (off Moorfield St.)
Harlech Av. LS11: Leeds 3H 117
Harlech Cres. LS11: Leeds 3H 117
Harlech Mt. LS11: Leeds 3H 117
Harlech Pk. Ct. LS11: Leeds 3H 117
Harlech Rd. LS11: Leeds 3H 117
Harlech St. LS11: Leeds 3H 117
Harlech Ter. LS11: Leeds 3H 117
Harlech Way LS25: Gar 4H 103
Harley Av. LS13: Leeds 3C 94
Harley Ct. LS13: Leeds 3C 94
Harley Dr. LS13: Leeds 3C 94
Harley Gdns. LS13: Leeds 3C 94
Harley Grn. LS13: Leeds 3C 94
Harley Pl. HD6: Brigh 2A 162
    (off Harley St.)
Harley Ri. LS13: Leeds 3C 94
Harley Rd. LS13: Leeds 3C 94
Harley St. HD6: Brigh 2A 162
Harley Ter. LS13: Leeds 3C 94
Harley Vw. LS13: Leeds 3C 94
Harley Wlk. LS13: Leeds 3C 94
Harlington Ct. LS27: Morl 5A 138
Harlington Rd. LS27: Morl 5A 138
Harlow Ct. LS8: Leeds 2G 79
Harlow Rd. BD7: B'frd 6A 90
Harmon Cl. BD4: B'frd 5A 112
Harmony Pl. BD13: B'frd 2G 107
Harold Av. LS6: Leeds 1E 97
Harold Ct. BD12: B'frd 2C 132
Harold Gdns. LS27: Morl 3C 138
Harold Gro. LS6: Leeds 1E 97
Harold Mt. LS6: Leeds 1E 97
Harold Pl. BD18: Ship 1H 69
  LS6: Leeds 1E 97

Harold Rd. LS6: Leeds 1E 97
Harold Sq. LS6: Leeds 1E 97
Harold St. BD16: Bgly 3A 50
  LS6: Leeds 1E 97
Harold Ter. LS6: Leeds 1E 97
Harold Vw. LS6: Leeds 1E 97
Harold Wlk. LS6: Leeds 1E 97
Harper Av. BD10: B'frd 6H 53
Harper Cres. BD10: B'frd 6A 54
Harper Ga. BD4: B'frd 1D 112
Harper Gro. BD10: B'frd 6H 53
Harper La. LS19: Yead 1F 55
Harper Rock LS19: Yead 1F 55
    (off Harper La.)
Harper Royd HX6: Hal 1A 158
Harper Royd La. HX6: Hal 6H 147
Harper St. LS2: Leeds 4B 98 (5G 5)
Harper Ter. LS19: Yead 1F 55
    (off Harper La.)
Harp La. BD13: B'frd 3H 107
Harrier Cl. BD8: B'frd 4D 88
Harrier Way LS27: Morl 3D 138
Harriet St. BD8: B'frd 3B 90
  HD6: Brigh 5A 152
  LS7: Leeds 6B 78
Harris Ct. BD7: B'frd 2A 110
Harrison and Potter Trust Homes, The
  LS2: Leeds 2F 5
Harrison Cres. LS9: Leeds 2H 99
Harrison Potter Trust Almshouse
  LS2: Leeds 6G 77
    (off Raglan Rd.)
Harrison Rd. HX1: Hal 3G 149 (5B 164)
Harrison's Av. LS28: Pud 1B 94
Harrison St. BD16: Bgly 6C 50
  LS1: Leeds 3A 98 (3F 5)
Harris St. BD1: B'frd 4G 91 (4G 7)
  BD16: Bgly 5C 50
Harrogate Av. BD3: B'frd 1G 91
Harrogate Pde. LS17: Leeds 5B 60
Harrogate Pl. BD3: B'frd 1G 91
Harrogate Rd. BD2: B'frd 1H 91
  BD10: B'frd 5B 72
  LS7: Leeds 1A 78
  LS16: Yead 5A 42
  LS17: Leeds 1A 78
  LS19: B'hpe, Yead 5A 42
  LS19: Yead 3F 55
    (not continuous)
  LS21: Leat 2F 25
  LS22: Weth 1A 12
Harrogate St. BD3: B'frd 1G 91
Harrogate Ter. BD3: B'frd 1G 91
Harrogate Vw. LS17: Leeds 2G 61
Harrop Av. LS27: Morl 5B 138
HARROP EDGE 1H 87
Harrop Gro. LS27: Morl 5B 138
Harrop La. BD15: B'frd 6E 67
Harrop Ter. LS27: Morl 5B 138
Harrowby Cres. LS16: Leeds 2B 76
Harrowby Rd. LS16: Leeds 2B 76
Harrows, The BD20: Keigh 5F 35
Harrow St. HX1: Hal 2D 148
Harry La. BD14: B'frd 1C 108
  BD22: Oxen 6C 64
Harry St. BD4: B'frd 2A 112
Harthill LS27: Morl 6F 115
Harthill Av. LS27: Morl 6F 115
Harthill Cl. LS27: Morl 6F 115
Harthill La. LS27: Morl 6F 115
Harthill Paddock LS27: Morl 6F 115
Harthill Pde. LS27: Morl 6F 115
    (off Town St.)
Harthill Ri. LS27: Morl 6F 115
Hartington St. BD21: Keigh 5A 34
Hartington Ter. BD7: B'frd 6A 90
Hartland Rd. BD4: B'frd 1C 112
Hartley Av. LS6: Leeds 5G 77
Hartley Bank La. HX3: Hal 5E 131
Hartley Cres. LS6: Leeds 5G 77
Hartley Gdns. LS6: Leeds 5H 77
Hartley Gro. LS6: Leeds 5G 77
Hartley Hill LS2: Leeds 2A 98 (2F 5)
Hartley Pl. LS27: Morl 4B 138

Hartley's Bldgs. LS27: Morl 4B 138
Hartley Sq. BD13: B'frd 2E 107
Hartley's Sq. BD20: Keigh 4H 35
Hartley's St. BD4: B'frd 6G 91
  HX1: Hal 1E 149
  LS27: Morl 3B 138
    (California St.)
  LS27: Morl 6B 116
    (Grange Pk. Dr.)
Hartley's Yd. LS12: Leeds 4B 96
Hartley Wood Cotts. LS25: M'fld . . .3G 105
Hartlington Ct. BD17: Bail 4E 53
Hartman Pl. BD9: B'frd 1H 89
Hart Rhydding La. LS29: Add 2D 8
Hartshead Hall La. WF15: Liv 3H 163
Hartshead La. WF15: Liv 1H 163
HARTSHEAD MOOR SIDE 3G 153
HARTSHEAD MOOR TOP 3F 153
Hart St. BD7: B'frd 1A 110
Hartwell Rd. LS6: Leeds 1E 97
Harvest Ct. HX1: Hal 2F 149 (4A 164)
Harvest Cft. LS29: Burl W 2D 20
Harvest Mt. BD10: B'frd 1F 71
Harwill App. LS27: Morl 6C 116
Harwill Av. LS27: Morl 6C 116
Harwill Cft. LS27: Morl 6C 116
Harwill Gro. LS27: Morl 6C 116
Harwill Ri. LS27: Morl 6C 116
Harwill Rd. LS27: Morl 6C 116
Haselbury Apartments BD5: B'frd 6E 91
    (off Croscombe Wlk.)
Haslam Cl. BD3: B'frd 3G 91 (1H 7)
Haslam Gro. BD18: Ship 3E 71
Haslemere Cl. BD4: B'frd 2B 112
Haslewood Cl. LS9: Leeds 3C 98
Haslewood Ct. LS9: Leeds 3D 98
Haslewood Dene LS9: Leeds 3D 98
Haslewood Dr. LS9: Leeds 3C 98
Haslewood Gdns. LS9: Leeds 3D 98
Haslewood Grn. LS9: Leeds 3D 98
Haslewood M. LS9: Leeds 3D 98
Haslewood Pl. LS9: Leeds 3D 98
Haslewood Sq. LS9: Leeds 3D 98
Haslewood Vw. LS9: Leeds 3D 98
Hasley Rd. LS29: Burl W 3F 21
Haslingden Dr. BD9: B'frd 1H 89
Hastings Av. BD5: B'frd 3D 110
Hastings Ct. LS17: Leeds 3A 62
  LS22: Coll 3B 28
Hastings Pl. BD5: B'frd 2D 110
Hastings St. BD5: B'frd 3D 110
Hastings Ter. BD5: B'frd 3D 110
Hastings Way LS22: Coll 3H 27
Hatchet La. BD12: B'frd 3G 133
Hatfield Rd. BD2: B'frd 1H 91
Hathaway Av. BD9: B'frd 6F 69
Hathaway Dr. LS14: Leeds 6D 62
Hathaway La. LS14: Leeds 1D 80
Hathaway M. LS14: Leeds 6D 62
Hathaway Wlk. LS14: Leeds 1D 80
Hathershelf La. HX2: Hal 3A 146
Hatters Fold HX1: Hal 2H 149 (4D 164)
    (not continuous)
Hatton Cl. BD6: B'frd 5D 110
Haugh End La. HX6: Hal 6G 147
Haugh Shaw Cft. HX1: Hal 4E 149
Haugh Shaw Rd. HX1: Hal 4E 149
Haugh Shaw Rd. W. HX1: Hal 4D 148
Hauxley Ct. LS29: I'ly 5F 11
Hauxwell Dr. LS19: Yead 1F 55
Havelock Sq. BD13: B'frd 5A 88
Havelock St. BD7: B'frd 1A 110
  BD13: B'frd 5A 88
Haven, The BD10: B'frd 3A 72
  LS15: Leeds 3F 101
Haven Chase LS16: Leeds 4G 57
Haven Cl. LS16: Leeds 3H 57
Haven Ct. LS16: Leeds 4H 57
Haven Cft. LS16: Leeds 4H 57
Haven Gdns. LS16: Leeds 4G 57
Haven Gth. LS16: Leeds 4G 57
Haven Grn. LS16: Leeds 4G 57
Haven Mt. LS16: Leeds 4G 57
Haven Ri. LS16: Leeds 4G 57

Haven Vw.—Heather Ct.

Haven Vw. LS16: Leeds 4G 57
Havercroft LS12: Leeds 6G 95
Havercroft Gdns. LS12: Leeds 6G 95
Haw Av. LS19: Yead 5G 41
Hawber Cote Dr. BD20: Sils 1F 15
Hawber Cote La. BD20: Sils 1F 15
Hawber La. BD20: Sils 2F 15
Hawes Av. BD5: B'frd 3C 110
Hawes Cres. BD5: B'frd 3C 110
(not continuous)
Hawes Dr. BD5: B'frd 3C 110
Hawes Gro. BD5: B'frd 3C 110
Hawes Mt. BD5: B'frd 3C 110
Hawes Rd. BD5: B'frd 3B 110
Hawes Ter. BD5: B'frd 3C 110
Haweswater Cl. LS22: Weth 4B 12
Hawkcliffe Vw. BD20: Sils 2C 14
Hawke Way BD12: B'frd 1E 133
Hawkhill Av. LS15: Leeds 1D 100
LS20: Guis 5B 40
Hawkhill Dr. LS15: Leeds 6D 80
Hawkhill Gdns. LS15: Leeds 6D 80
Hawkhills LS7: Leeds 2C 78
Hawkhurst Rd. LS12: Leeds 5C 96
Hawkins Dr. LS7: Leeds 1A 98
Hawksbridge La. BD22: Oxen 6A 64
Hawkshead Cl. BD5: B'frd 6E 91
Hawkshead Cres. LS14: Leeds 6B 80
Hawkshead Dr. BD5: B'frd 6E 91
Hawkshead Wlk. BD5: B'frd 6E 91
Hawksley Ct. LS27: Morl 6H 115
Hawk's Nest Gdns. E.
LS17: Leeds 3B 60
Hawk's Nest Gdns. Sth.
LS17: Leeds 3B 60
Hawk's Nest Gdns. W.
LS17: Leeds 3B 60
Hawk's Nest Ri. LS17: Leeds 3B 60
Hawkstone Av. LS20: Guis 6A 40
Hawkstone Dr. BD20: Keigh 4G 33
Hawkstone Vw. LS20: Guis 6A 40
Hawk St. *BD21: Keigh 5B 34*
(off Pheasant St.)
Hawks Wood Av. BD9: B'frd 6H 69
Hawkswood Av. LS5: Leeds 2G 75
Hawkswood Cres. LS5: Leeds 2G 75
Hawkswood Gro. LS5: Leeds 2G 75
Hawkswood Mt. LS5: Leeds 2G 75
Hawkswood Pl. LS5: Leeds 3G 75
Hawkswood St. LS5: Leeds 3H 75
Hawkswood Ter. LS5: Leeds 3H 75
Hawkswood Vw. LS5: Leeds 2G 75
HAWKSWORTH
LS5 3G 75
LS20 5F 39
Hawksworth Av. LS20: Guis 6B 40
Hawksworth Cl. LS29: Men 2G 39
Hawksworth Commercial Pk.
LS13: Leeds 2E 95
Hawksworth Dr. LS20: Guis 6B 40
LS29: Men 1F 39
Hawksworth Gro. LS5: Leeds 3F 75
Hawksworth La. LS20: Guis 5F 39
Hawksworth Rd. BD17: Bail 1C 52
LS18: H'fth 2F 75
Hawksworth St. LS29: I'ly 5D 10
Haw La. LS19: Yead 6F 41
Hawley Cl. LS27: Morl 5H 137
Hawley Ter. BD10: B'frd 5C 72
Hawley Way LS27: Morl 5H 137
HAWORTH 2D 64
Haworth Ct. *LS19: Yead 6F 41*
(off Chapel La.)
Haworth Gro. BD9: B'frd 6G 69
Haworth La. LS19: Yead 6F 41
Haworth Rd. BD9: B'frd 6G 69
BD13: B'frd 3G 65
BD15: B'frd 6C 68
(Cottingley Rd.)
BD15: B'frd 5D 66
(Cullingworth Rd.)
BD15: B'frd 5H 67
(Lane Side)
BD21: B'frd 3F 65
Haworth Rd. BD22: Haw 1E 65
WF17: Bat 5B 136
Haworth Station
Vintage Carriages Trust Mus. of
Rail Travel 2C 64
Hawthorn Av. LS19: Yead 6F 41
LS21: Pool 5F 25
Hawthorn Cl. HD6: Brigh 6C 152
LS29: Add 1B 8
Hawthorn Cres. BD17: Bail 4D 52
LS7: Leeds 2B 78
LS19: Yead 6F 41
Hawthorn Cft. WF3: Rothw 6G 141
Hawthorn Dr. BD10: B'frd 2A 72
LS13: Leeds 3H 73
LS19: Yead 5G 41
Hawthorne Av. BD3: B'frd 3C 92
BD18: Ship 4D 70
LS22: Weth 2D 12
Hawthorne Cl. LS27: Morl 6F 115
WF2: Wake 6H 155
Hawthorne Dr. LS27: Morl 6G 115
Hawthorne Gdns. LS16: Leeds 2B 58
Hawthorne Gro. LS29: Burl W 3F 21
Hawthorne Mills *LS12: Leeds 1A 116*
(off Cow Cl. Gro.)
Hawthorne St. BD20: Sils 2D 14
Hawthorne Vw. LS27: Morl 6G 115
Hawthorne Way BD20: Keigh 5A 36
Hawthorn Gro. LS13: Leeds 4H 73
LS26: Rothw 3B 142
Hawthorn La. LS7: Leeds 2B 78
Hawthorn Mt. LS7: Leeds 2B 78
Hawthorn Pk. LS14: Leeds 1D 80
Hawthorn Ri. LS14: Leeds 1E 81
Hawthorn Rd. LS7: Leeds 2B 78
LS19: Yead 6F 41
Hawthorns, The WF1: Wake 4H 157
Hawthorn St. BD3: B'frd 3C 92
HX1: Hal 4E 149
HX3: Hal 1F 151
Hawthorn Ter. *HX1: Hal 4E 149*
(off Hawthorn St.)
LS25: Swil 6C 102
Hawthorn Va. LS7: Leeds 2B 78
Hawthorn Vw. BD17: Bail 4E 53
LS7: Leeds 2B 78
Haw Vw. LS19: Yead 5G 41
Haycliffe Av. BD7: B'frd 3A 110
Haycliffe Dr. BD7: B'frd 3H 109
Haycliffe Gro. BD7: B'frd 3A 110
HAYCLIFFE HILL 3B 110
Haycliffe Hill Rd. BD5: B'frd 3B 110
Haycliffe La. BD6: B'frd 3A 110
Haycliffe Rd. BD5: B'frd 2B 110
Haycliffe Ter. BD5: B'frd 2B 110
Hayclose Mead BD6: B'frd 1A 132
Hay Cft. BD10: B'frd 1F 71
Hayden St. BD3: B'frd 5H 91
Haydn Av. WF3: Wake 3H 157
Haydn Cl. LS27: Morl 3A 138
Haydn Ct. LS27: Morl 3A 138
Haydn Pl. BD13: B'frd 4A 108
Haydn's Ter. LS28: Pud 1A 94
Hayfield Av. LS23: B Spa 3A 30
Hayfield Cl. BD17: Bail 3E 53
Hayfields, The BD22: Haw 1C 64
Hayfields Cl. BD22: Keigh 2E 47
Hayfield Ter. LS12: Leeds 5C 96
Hayhills Rd. BD20: Sils 1E 15
Hayleigh Av. LS13: Leeds 6E 75
Hayleigh Mt. LS13: Leeds 6E 75
Hayleigh St. LS13: Leeds 6E 75
Hayleigh Ter. LS13: Leeds 1E 95
Haynes St. BD21: Keigh 1B 48
Hays La. HX2: Hal 6A 106
Haythorns Av. BD20: Sils 2D 14
Haythorns Mt. BD20: Sils 2D 14
Hayton Dr. LS22: Weth 5F 13
Haywain, The LS29: I'ly 6F 11
Hazebrouck Dr. BD17: Bail 3B 52
Hazel Av. LS14: Leeds 1E 81
Hazel Beck BD16: Bgly 1B 68
Hazel Cl. BD11: B'frd 1E 135
Hazel Ct. *HX2: Hal 4C 128*
(off Cumberland Cl.)
LS26: Rothw 3B 142
Hazel Cft. BD18: Ship 3C 70
Hazelcroft BD2: B'frd 5B 72
Hazel Dene *HX4: Hal 6F 159*
(off Cross St.)
Hazeldene BD13: B'frd 5H 107
Hazel Gro. HD2: Hud 6B 162
HX3: Hal 2A 152
Hazelheads BD17: Bail 3C 52
Hazelhurst Av. BD16: Bgly 1B 68
Hazelhurst Brow BD9: B'frd 1F 89
Hazelhurst Ct. BD3: B'frd 5A 92
LS28: Pud 4B 94
Hazelhurst Gro. BD13: B'frd 6H 107
Hazelhurst Rd. BD9: B'frd 1F 89
BD13: B'frd 6H 107
Hazelhurst Ter. BD9: B'frd 1F 89
Hazelmere Av. BD16: Bgly 1C 68
Hazel Mt. BD18: Ship 2C 70
Hazel Ri. LS26: Mick 6C 144
Hazel Wlk. BD9: B'frd 1F 89
Hazelwood Av. BD20: Keigh 4D 34
LS25: Gar 6G 103
Hazelwood Ct. HX1: Hal 4G 149
WF1: Wake 4H 157
Hazelwood Rd. BD9: B'frd 6E 69
WF1: Wake 4H 157
HEADINGLEY 4D 76
Headingley 5D 76
Headingley Av. LS6: Leeds 4C 76
Headingley Ct. LS6: Leeds 5F 77
Headingley Cres. LS6: Leeds 5D 76
HEADINGLEY HILL 5E 77
Headingley La. LS6: Leeds 5E 77
Headingley Mt. LS6: Leeds 4C 76
Headingley Office Pk. LS6: Leeds 5F 77
Headingley Ri. *LS6: Leeds 6F 77*
(off Welton Rd.)
Headingley Stadium 5D 76
Headingley Station (Rail) 5B 76
Headingley Ter. LS6: Leeds 5F 77
Headingley Vw. LS6: Leeds 5D 76
Headland Gro. BD6: B'frd 4H 109
Headley La. BD13: B'frd 1G 107
Headrow, The LS1: Leeds 3H 97 (3D 4)
Headrow Cen., The
LS1: Leeds 3A 98 (4E 5)
Headway Bus. Cen. BD4: B'frd 3A 112
Healey Av. BD16: Bgly 5C 50
Healey Cft. WF3: E Ard 2H 155
Healey Cft. La. WF3: E Ard 2H 155
Healey La. BD16: Bgly 5C 50
Healey Wood Bottom *HD6: Brigh 2B 162*
(off Gooder La.)
Healey Wood Cres. HD6: Brigh 3A 162
Healey Wood Gdns. HD6: Brigh 3A 162
Healey Wood Gro. HD6: Brigh 3B 162
Healey Wood Rd. HD6: Brigh 3A 162
Heap La. BD3: B'frd 4G 91 (3G 7)
Heap St. BD3: B'frd 4G 91 (3G 7)
HX3: Hal 5G 129
Heartbeat Fitness Cen. 4F 7
Heath Av. HX3: Hal 5F 149
Heathcliff BD22: Haw 2B 64
Heathcliffe Cl. WF17: Bat 4B 136
Heathcote Av. LS14: T'ner 2H 63
Heathcote Ri. BD22: Haw 1D 64
Heath Cres. HX1: Hal 4G 149
LS11: Leeds 2E 117
Heathcroft Bank LS11: Leeds 3E 117
Heathcroft Cres. LS11: Leeds 3E 117
Heathcroft Dr. LS11: Leeds 3E 117
Heathcroft Lawn LS11: Leeds 3E 117
Heathcroft Ri. LS11: Leeds 3E 117
Heathcroft Va. LS11: Leeds 3E 117
Heath Dr. LS23: B Spa 4H 29
Heatherbank Av. BD22: Keigh 3F 47
Heather Bank Cl. BD13: B'frd 4B 66
Heather Cl. WF1: Wake 4H 157
Heather Ct. BD16: Bgly 2C 50
LS29: I'ly 6D 10
WF1: Wake 4H 157

Heather Ct.—Herbert Pl.

Heather Ct. WF17: Bat 5A **136**
Heathercroft LS7: Leeds 3C **78**
Heatherdale Ct. WF3: E Ard 1E **155**
Heatherdale Dr. WF3: E Ard 1E **155**
Heatherdale Fold WF3: E Ard 1E **155**
Heatherdale Rd. WF3: E Ard 1D **154**
Heather Dr. HX2: Hal 4G **127**
Heather Gdns. LS13: Leeds 3G **95**
LS14: S'cft 6E **45**
Heather Gro. BD9: B'frd 6D **68**
BD21: Keigh 5F **33**
LS13: Leeds 2G **95**
Heatherlands Av. BD13: B'frd 1B **86**
Heather Pl. BD13: B'frd 3F **107**
Heather Ri. LS29: Burl W 3E **21**
Heather Rd. BD17: Bail 3D **52**
Heatherside BD17: Bail 3B **52**
Heatherstones HX3: Hal 5F **149**
Heather Va. LS14: S'cft 6D **44**
Heather Vw. BD16: Bgly 2F **51**
HX5: Ell 4D **160**
HEATHFIELD **4C 160**
Heathfield LS16: Leeds 3A **58**
Heathfield Av. HX5: Ell 4D **160**
Heathfield Cl. BD16: Bgly 3C **50**
WF3: E Ard 2F **155**
Heathfield Gro. BD7: B'frd 1G **109**
*HX3: Hal 5G **149***
(off Heath Rd.)
Heathfield Ind. Est. HX5: Ell 4C **160**
Heathfield La. LS23: B Spa 3H **29**
Heathfield Pl. HX3: Hal 5G **149**
Heathfield St. HX5: Ell 5C **160**
Heathfield Ter. HX3: Hal 5G **149**
LS6: Leeds 3D **76**
Heathfield Wlk. LS16: Leeds 2A **58**
Heath Gdns. HX3: Hal 5G **149**
Heath Gro. BD20: Keigh 5H **35**
LS11: Leeds 2E **117**
LS28: Pud 5G **93**
Heath Hall HX1: Hal 4G **149**
Heath Hall Av. BD4: B'frd 4H **111**
Heath Hill Rd. HX2: Hal 1G **147**
Heath La. HX3: Hal 5G **149**
Heath Lea HX1: Hal 4G **149** (6B **164**)
Heathmoor Cl. BD10: B'frd 1G **71**
HX2: Hal 1B **128**
Heathmoor Mt. HX2: Hal 1B **128**
Heathmoor Pk. Rd. HX2: Hal 6B **106**
Heathmoor Way HX2: Hal 1B **128**
Heath Mt. HX3: Hal 5F **149**
LS11: Leeds 2E **117**
Heath Mt. Rd. HD6: Brigh 3A **162**
Heathness Rd. LS29: Add 1B **8**
Heath Pk. LS29: I'ly 6B **10**
Heath Pk. Av. HX1: Hal 4G **149**
Heath Pl. LS11: Leeds 2E **117**
Heath Ri. LS11: Leeds 3E **117**
Heath Rd. BD3: B'frd 2H **91**
HX3: Hal 5G **149**
LS11: Leeds 2E **117**
Heath Royd HX3: Hal 5G **149**
Heath St. BD3: B'frd 4A **92**
BD16: Bgly 4C **50**
HX3: Hal 5F **149**
Heath Ter. BD3: B'frd 4H **91**
Heath Vw. HX1: Hal 6C **164**
Heath Vw. St. HX1: Hal 3H **149** (6C **164**)
(not continuous)
Heath Vs. HX3: Hal 5G **149**
Heathy Av. HX2: Hal 2E **129**
Heathy La. HX2: Hal 1D **128**
Heation Royds La. BD18: Ship 4H **69**
HEATON **6A 70**
Heaton Av. BD20: Keigh 6G **35**
LS12: Leeds 6C **96**
Heaton Cl. BD16: Bgly 3D **50**
BD17: Bail 2B **52**
Heaton Ct. *BD16: Bgly 5B **50***
(off Beechroyd Ter.)
Heaton Cres. BD16: Bgly 3D **50**
BD17: Bail 2B **52**
Heaton Dr. BD16: Bgly 3D **50**
BD17: Bail 2B **52**
HEATON GROVE **5B 70**
Heaton Gro. BD9: B'frd 5B **70**
BD18: Ship 2C **70**
Heaton Hill BD6: B'frd 6G **109**
Heaton Pk. Dr. BD9: B'frd 6H **69**
Heaton Pk. Rd. BD9: B'frd 6H **69**
Heaton Rd. BD9: B'frd 6A **70**
HEATON ROYDS **4H 69**
Heaton Royds La.
BD9: B'frd, Ship 4H **69**
Heaton's Ct. LS1: Leeds 4A **98** (6E **5**)
HEATON SHAY **4G 69**
Heaton St. BD4: B'frd 6G **91** (6G **7**)
BD19: Cleck 6B **134**
HD6: Brigh 1A **162**
Heatons Yd. HD6: Brigh 2B **162**
Hebble Brook Bus. Pk. HX2: Hal 6A **106**
Hebble Brook Cl. HX2: Hal 3A **128**
Hebble Cotts. HX3: Hal 6C **128**
Hebble Ct. HX2: Hal 3B **128**
Hebble Dean HX2: Hal 6D **128**
Hebble Gdns. HX2: Hal 6C **128**
Hebble La. HX3: Hal 6D **128**
Hebble Row *BD22: Haw 6C **46***
Hebble Va. Dr. HX2: Hal 5C **128**
Hebble Vw. HX3: Hal 5C **128**
Hebb Vw. BD6: B'frd 3G **109**
Hebden App. LS14: Leeds 3D **80**
Hebden Bridge Rd. BD22: Oxen 3A **84**
Hebden Chase LS14: Leeds 3D **80**
Hebden Cl. LS14: Leeds 3D **80**
Hebden Grn. LS14: Leeds 3D **80**
Hebden Path LS14: Leeds 3D **80**
Hebden Pl. LS14: Leeds 3D **80**
Hebden Rd. BD22: Haw 3D **64**
Hebden Wlk. LS14: Leeds 3D **80**
Heber Cl. BD20: Sils 3F **15**
Heber's Ghyll Dr. LS29: I'ly 6H **9**
Heber's Gro. LS29: I'ly 6A **10**
Heber St. BD21: Keigh 1H **47**
Hector Cl. BD6: B'frd 4C **110**
Heddon Cl. BD5: B'frd 6E **91**
Heddon Gro. BD5: B'frd 6E **91**
Heddon Pl. LS6: Leeds 3E **77**
Heddon St. LS6: Leeds 3E **77**
Heddon Wlk. *BD5: B'frd 6E **91***
(off Heddon Cl.)
Hedge Cl. BD8: B'frd 2F **89**
Hedge Nook BD12: B'frd 3C **132**
Hedge Side BD8: B'frd 3G **89**
Hedge Top La. HX3: Hal 4C **130**
Hedge Way BD8: B'frd 2G **89**
Hedley Chase LS12: Leeds 4E **97**
Hedley Cres. WF1: Wake 6F **157**
Hedley Gdns. LS12: Leeds 4E **97**
Hedley Grn. LS12: Leeds 4E **97**
Heidelberg Rd. BD9: B'frd 1A **90**
Height Grn. HX6: Hal 5H **147**
Height La. BD22: Oxen 1D **84**
Height Rd. HX7: Heb B, Wads 4A **126**
Heights Bank LS12: Leeds 4H **95**
Heights Cl. LS12: Leeds 4G **95**
Heights Ct. WF15: Liv 4H **153**
Heights Dr. LS12: Leeds 3G **95**
Heights E., The LS12: Leeds 4H **95**
Heights Gth. LS12: Leeds 4G **95**
Heights Grn. LS12: Leeds 4H **95**
Heights La. BD9: B'frd 6F **69**
BD16: Bgly 4B **36**
LS12: Leeds 4H **95**
Heights Pde. LS12: Leeds 4G **95**
Heights Wlk. LS12: Leeds 4H **95**
Heights Way LS12: Leeds 4G **95**
Heights W., The LS12: Leeds 4G **95**
Helena Ct. LS25: Kip 4F **123**
Helena Pl. LS25: Kip 5F **123**
Helena St. LS25: Kip 5F **123**
Helena Way BD4: B'frd 5A **112**
Helen Rose Ct. BD18: Ship 6E **53**
Helen St. BD18: Ship 1H **69**
Helen Ter. HD6: Brigh 6H **151**
Hellewell St. BD6: B'frd 6H **109**
Hellwood La. LS14: S'cft 6E **45**
Helmshore Dr. BD8: B'frd 3F **89**
Helmsley Ct. LS10: Leeds 3A **140**
Helmsley Dr. LS16: Leeds 2B **76**
Helmsley Rd. LS16: Leeds 2B **76**
LS23: B Spa 4A **30**
Helmsley St. BD4: B'frd 1G **111**
Helston Cft. LS10: Leeds 2G **139**
Helston Gth. LS10: Leeds 2G **139**
Helston Grn. LS10: Leeds 2G **139**
Helston Pl. LS10: Leeds 2G **139**
Helston Rd. LS10: Leeds 1G **139**
Helston Sq. LS10: Leeds 1F **139**
Helston St. LS10: Leeds 1F **139**
Helston Wlk. LS10: Leeds 2G **139**
(not continuous)
Helston Way LS10: Leeds 1G **139**
Hembrigg Gdns. LS27: Morl 5B **138**
Hembrigg Ter. LS27: Morl 5A **138**
Hemingway Cl. LS10: Leeds 1C **118**
Hemingway Gth. LS10: Leeds 2C **118**
Hemingway Grn. LS10: Leeds 2C **118**
Hemingway Rd. BD10: B'frd 1B **72**
Hemishor Dr. LS26: Kip 5E **123**
Hemsby Gro. *BD21: Keigh 3H **47***
(off Hemsby St.)
Hemsby St. BD21: Keigh 3H **47**
Henacrewood Ct. BD13: B'frd 6A **108**
Henage St. BD13: B'frd 4H **107**
Henbury St. LS7: Leeds 2B **98** (1H **5**)
Henconner Av. LS7: Leeds 3A **78**
Henconner Cres. LS7: Leeds 3A **78**
Henconner Dr. LS7: Leeds 3A **78**
Henconner Gdns. LS7: Leeds 3A **78**
Henconner Gth. LS7: Leeds 3A **78**
Henconner Gro. LS7: Leeds 3A **78**
Henconner La. LS7: Leeds 3A **78**
LS13: Leeds 2G **95**
Henconner Rd. LS7: Leeds 3A **78**
Henderson Pl. BD6: B'frd 4C **110**
Hendford Dr. BD3: B'frd 4G **91** (3H **7**)
Hen Holme La. BD20: Sils 3E **15**
Henley Av. BD5: B'frd 3E **111**
LS13: Leeds 1E **95**
LS19: Yead 4H **55**
Henley Cl. LS19: Yead 4H **55**
Henley Ct. BD5: B'frd 3F **111**
Henley Cres. LS13: Leeds 1E **95**
LS19: Yead 4H **55**
Henley Dr. LS19: Yead 4G **55**
Henley Gro. BD5: B'frd 3E **111**
LS13: Leeds 1E **95**
Henley Hill LS19: Yead 4G **55**
Henley Mt. LS19: Yead 4H **55**
Henley Pl. LS13: Leeds 1E **95**
Henley Rd. BD5: B'frd 3F **111**
LS13: Leeds 1E **95**
Henley St. LS13: Leeds 1E **95**
Henley Ter. LS13: Leeds 1E **95**
Henley Vw. LS13: Leeds 1E **95**
LS19: Yead 4G **55**
Henley Vs. *LS19: Yead 4G **55***
(off Well La.)
Henry Av. LS12: Leeds 6C **96**
Henry Moore Foundation Studio, The
1B 164
(in Dean Clough)
Henry Moore Institute **3D** 4
Henry Pl. LS27: Morl 3A **138**
Henry Price Bldgs. LS2: Leeds 1G **97**
Henry St. BD13: B'frd 5H **87**
BD14: B'frd 1E **109**
BD21: Keigh 6A **34**
HD6: Brigh 5A **152**
HX1: Hal 3F **149** (5A **164**)
Henry Ter. LS19: Yead 6D **40**
HENSHAW **1E 55**
Henshaw Av. LS19: Yead 1F **55**
Henshaw Cres. LS19: Yead 1F **55**
Henshaw La. LS19: Yead 2E **55**
Henshaw Oval LS19: Yead 1F **55**
Hepton Ct. LS9: Leeds 3F **99**
Hepworth Av. LS27: Morl 5B **116**
Hepworth Cres. LS27: Morl 5B **116**
Herbalist St. LS12: Leeds 5E **97**
Herbert Pl. BD3: B'frd 3C **92**

A-Z Leeds & Bradford 219

Herbert St. BD5: B'frd 1D **110**
  BD14: B'frd 2E **109**
  BD16: Bgly 4C **50**
                (Mornington Rd.)
  BD16: Bgly 3D **68**
                 (Town Hill St.)
  BD18: Ship 6H **51**
  HX1: Hal 3D **148**
Hereford St. LS12: Leeds 3C **96**
Hereford Way BD4: B'frd 1G **111**
Heritage M. HX1: Hal 5D **164**
Heritage Pk. BD16: Bgly 1C **50**
Heritage Way BD22: Keigh 5B **46**
HERMIT HOLE 5G **47**
Hermit St. BD22: Keigh 5G **47**
Hermon Av. HX1: Hal 3E **149**
Hermon Gro. HX1: Hal 3E **149**
Hermon Rd. LS15: Leeds 2D **100**
Hermon St. LS15: Leeds 2D **100**
Heron Cl. BD13: B'frd 3G **107**
  BD16: Bgly 6E **49**
  BD20: Stee 5B **14**
  LS17: Leeds 3D **60**
Heron Ct. LS27: Morl 3D **138**
Heron Gro. LS17: Leeds 3D **60**
Herries Ct. *LS29: Men* 1H **39**
              (off Leathley Rd.)
Herschel Rd. BD8: B'frd 4F **89**
Hertford Chase BD15: Leeds 5E **101**
Hertford Cl. LS15: Leeds 5F **101**
Hertford Cft. LS15: Leeds 5F **101**
Hertford Fold LS15: Leeds 5E **101**
Hertford Lawn LS15: Leeds 5E **101**
Heshbon St. BD4: B'frd 2A **112**
Hesketh Av. LS5: Leeds 4A **76**
  WF3: E Ard 1D **154**
Hesketh La. WF3: E Ard 1D **154**
Hesketh Mt. LS5: Leeds 4A **76**
Hesketh Pl. HX3: Hal 2A **152**
  LS5: Leeds 4A **76**
Hesketh Rd. LS5: Leeds 4A **76**
Hesketh Ter. LS5: Leeds 5A **76**
Hessle Av. LS6: Leeds 6E **77**
Hessle Mt. LS6: Leeds 6E **77**
Hessle Pl. LS6: Leeds 6E **77**
Hessle Rd. LS6: Leeds 6E **77**
Hessle St. LS6: Leeds 6E **77**
Hessle Ter. LS6: Leeds 6E **77**
Hessle Vw. LS6: Leeds 6E **77**
Hessle Wlk. LS6: Leeds 6E **77**
Hetchell Vw. LS17: Bard 3F **45**
Hetchell Wood Nature Reserve 3H **45**
Hetton Cl. LS10: Leeds 2B **118**
Hetton Dr. BD3: B'frd 5B **92**
Hetton Rd. LS8: Leeds 4F **79**
Heuthwaite Av. LS22: Weth 5F **13**
Heuthwaite La. LS22: Weth 5G **13**
Hew Clews BD7: B'frd 2G **109**
HEWENDEN 5D **66**
Hew Royd BD10: B'frd 1F **71**
Heyback La. WF3: E Ard 3D **154**
  WF12: E Ard 4C **154**
HEY BECK 4C **154**
Hey Beck La. WF3: E Ard 4D **154**
Heybeck Wlk. BD4: B'frd 3D **112**
Heydon Cl. LS6: Leeds 6F **59**
Heyford Ct. BD2: B'frd 6D **70**
Heygate Cl. BD17: Bail 3D **52**
Heygate La. BD17: Bail 3D **52**
  LS23: B'ham 6D **30**
Hey La. BD22: Keigh 1A **64**
Heys Av. BD13: B'frd 5B **88**
Heys Cres. BD13: B'frd 5C **88**
Heysham Dr. BD4: B'frd 2C **112**
Heys Ho. *HX2: Hal* 1C **148**
          (off Reservoir Rd.)
Heys La. HX2: Hal 1B **126**
Hey St. BD7: B'frd 4D **90** (4A **6**)
  HD6: Brigh 5B **152**
Heywood Cl. HX3: Hal 5C **130**
Heywood Ct. HX3: Hal 5C **130**
Heywood M. HX1: Hal 1C **148**
Hicks La. LS26: Mick 4D **144**
Hick St. BD1: B'frd 4F **91** (4F **7**)

Hi Energy Dance, Health & Fitness Cen.
  . . . . .6H **33**
          (off Devonshire St.)
Higgin La. HX3: Hal 4A **150**
Higham HX6: Hal 5C **146**
Higham and Dob La. HX6: Hal 5C **146**
Higham Way LS25: Gar 3F **103**
High Ash BD18: Ship 2E **71**
High Ash Av. LS17: Leeds 2C **60**
High Ash Cres. LS17: Leeds 2C **60**
High Ash Dr. LS17: Leeds 2C **60**
High Ash Mt. LS17: Leeds 2C **60**
High Ash Pk. BD15: B'frd 2B **88**
High Bank App. LS15: Leeds 4F **101**
High Bank Cl. LS15: Leeds 4F **101**
High Bank Gdns.
  LS15: Leeds 4G **101**
High Bank Ga. LS15: Leeds 4F **101**
High Bank La. BD18: Ship 3F **69**
High Banks Cl. BD20: Keigh 3D **34**
High Bank St. *LS28: Pud* 6H **73**
          (off Low Bank St.)
High Bank Vw. LS15: Leeds 4F **101**
High Bank Way LS15: Leeds 4F **101**
High Bentley HX3: Hal 1G **131**
High Binns La. BD22: Oxen 1D **84**
Highbridge Ter. BD5: B'frd 4F **111**
High Brook Fall WF3: Wake 3G **157**
Highbury Cl. BD13: B'frd 5G **107**
  LS6: Leeds 3E **77**
Highbury La. LS6: Leeds 3E **77**
Highbury Mt. LS6: Leeds 3E **77**
Highbury Pl. LS6: Leeds 3E **77**
  LS13: Leeds 3C **94**
Highbury Rd. LS6: Leeds 3E **77**
Highbury St. LS6: Leeds 3E **77**
Highbury Ter. LS6: Leeds 3E **77**
High Busy La. BD10: B'frd 1F **71**
  BD18: Ship 1E **71**
High Cliffe *LS4: Leeds* 6C **76**
          (off St Michael's La.)
High Cliffe Ct. BD13: B'frd 5A **88**
Highcliffe Ct. HX3: Hal 2D **130**
  LS22: Weth 4F **13**
Highcliffe Dr. HX2: Hal 2B **148**
Highcliffe Ind. Est. LS27: Morl 2H **137**
Highcliffe Rd. LS27: Morl 3H **137**
High Cliffe Ter. LS22: Weth 4E **13**
High Cl. LS19: Yead 4F **55**
  LS20: Guis 5H **39**
High Cote BD20: Keigh 3B **34**
High Ct. LS2: Leeds 4B **98** (5G **5**)
High Ct. La. LS2: Leeds 4B **98** (5G **5**)
High Cft. BD13: B'frd 4A **108**
  HX3: Hal 5D **128**
  LS29: Add 1D **8**
Highcroft Cl. LS22: Coll 3A **28**
Highcroft Cl. LS28: Pud 3G **93**
Highcroft Gdns. BD21: Keigh 1D **48**
High Cross La. BD13: Hal 6B **108**
  HX3: Hal 6B **108**
Highdale Cft. BD10: B'frd 1H **71**
High End BD17: B'frd 2A **54**
Higher Brockwell HX6: Hal 6F **147**
Higher Coach Rd. BD16: Bail, Bgly . . .5E **51**
  BD17: Bail 5G **51**
Higher Downs BD8: B'frd 3F **89**
Higher Grange Rd. LS28: Pud 3A **94**
Higher Intake Rd. BD2: B'frd 1A **92**
Higher Row BD21: Keigh 4B **48**
Higher Scholes BD22: Keigh 6A **46**
Higher School St. BD18: Ship 1H **69**
Higher Shann Farm
  BD20: Keigh 4G **33**
Higherwood Cl. BD21: Keigh 1C **48**
Highfell Ri. BD22: Keigh 2E **47**
High Fernley Cl. BD12: B'frd 3C **132**
High Fernley Rd. BD12: B'frd 4A **132**
         (not continuous)
HIGHFIELD 6G **33**
Highfield BD4: B'frd 4B **112**
  HX3: Hal 2D **130**

Highfield *LS23: B Spa* 3C **30**
          (off Bridge Rd.)
  WF3: E Ard 6D **138**
Highfield Av. BD10: B'frd 2G **71**
  HD6: Brigh 1B **152**
  HX3: Hal 6F **109**
  HX4: Hal 4F **159**
  LS12: Leeds 5C **96**
Highfield Cl. BD20: Keigh 4H **35**
  LS12: Leeds 6D **96**
  LS27: Morl 6G **115**
Highfield Ct. BD22: Keigh 5C **46**
  LS12: Leeds 6C **96**
         (off Highfield Av.)
Highfield Cres. BD9: B'frd 5F **69**
  BD17: Bail 3C **52**
  LS12: Leeds 5D **96**
  LS26: Rothw 6E **121**
  LS28: Pud 3H **93**
  WF10: Kip 2F **145**
         (off Highfield Dr.)
Highfield Dr. BD9: B'frd 5F **69**
  HX2: Hal 1E **147**
  LS19: Yead 4G **55**
  LS25: Gar 6F **103**
  LS27: Morl 6F **115**
  WF10: Kip 2F **145**
  WF17: Bat 5A **136**
Highfield Gdns. BD9: B'frd 6F **69**
  LS12: Leeds 5C **96**
  LS27: Morl 6F **115**
Highfield Gth. LS12: Leeds 6D **96**
Highfield Grn. LS28: Pud 3H **93**
  WF10: Kip 1F **145**
Highfield Gro. BD10: B'frd 3G **71**
  HX5: Hal 3A **160**
  WF10: Kip 1F **145**
High Fld. La. BD22: Keigh 4C **46**
Highfield La. BD20: Sils 1E **15**
  BD21: Keigh 5G **33**
  BD22: Keigh 5C **46**
  LS15: Bar E 4D **82**
  LS25: M'fld 1G **125**
  LS26: Rothw 6E **121**
Highfield M. BD17: Bail 3C **52**
  BD20: Keigh 4H **35**
  LS25: Gar 6F **103**
Highfield Mt. LS26: Rothw 1E **143**
Highfield Pl. *BD8: B'frd* 2C **90**
         (off Church St.)
  HX1: Hal 3D **148**
         (not continuous)
  LS25: Gar 4E **103**
  LS27: Morl 4B **138**
  WF10: Kip 1G **145**
Highfield Rd. BD2: B'frd 4G **71**
  BD9: B'frd 4C **70**
  BD10: B'frd 4G **71**
  BD19: Cleck 2H **153**
  BD21: Keigh 6G **33**
  HD6: Brigh 3G **161**
  HX2: Hal 1E **147**
  HX5: Ell 5B **160**
  LS13: Leeds 1F **95**
  LS28: Pud 3G **93**
High Flds. HX6: Hal 5C **148**
Highfield St. BD21: Keigh 6H **33**
  LS13: Leeds 1F **95**
  LS28: Pud 3G **93**
Highfield Ter. BD13: B'frd 3B **66**
          (Station Rd.)
  BD13: B'frd 5H **107**
          (West End)
  BD16: Bgly 4C **50**
  BD18: Ship 1G **69**
  HX1: Hal 3D **148**
         (off Highfield Pl.)
  LS19: Yead 4G **55**
  LS28: Pud 4G **93**
Highfield Vw. LS27: Morl 6G **115**
High Fold BD16: Bgly 5A **36**
  BD17: Bail 3C **52**
  BD20: Keigh 4H **35**
         (off Stocks Hill Cl.)

High Fold—Hillthorpe Ter.

High Fold BD22: Keigh 2F 47
Highfold LS19: Yead 2E 55
High Fold La. BD20: Keigh 3G 33
Highgate BD9: B'frd 5H 69
BD13: B'frd 5C 86
Highgate Cl. BD13: B'frd 3E 109
Highgate Gro. BD13: B'frd 3E 109
Highgate Rd. BD13: B'frd 4C 108
High Ga. St. LS10: Leeds 1C 118
High Grn. Dr. BD20: Sils 1D 14
High Gro. La. HX3: Hal 4A 150
High Grove Pl. HX3: Hal 4A 150
High Holly Gth. BD21: Keigh 1B 48
High Ho. Av. BD2: B'frd 5G 71
High Ho. La. HX2: Hal 3C 126
High Ho. M. LS29: Add 1D 8
High Ho. Rd. BD2: B'frd 5G 71
Highland HX3: Hal 3B 130
Highlands LS29: Burl W 3E 21
Highlands Cl. BD7: B'frd 2G 109
LS10: Leeds 5D 118
Highlands Dr. LS10: Leeds 5D 118
Highlands Gro. BD7: B'frd 2G 109
LS10: Leeds 5D 118
Highlands La. HX2: Hal 1D 128
Highlands Pk. HX2: Hal 1D 128
Highlands Wlk. LS10: Leeds 5D 118
Highland Ville HX3: Hal 1F 151
High La. HX2: Hal 1H 147
Highlea Cl. LS19: Yead 2D 54
High Lee HX2: Hal 3C 146
High Lee Grn. HX2: Hal 3B 146
High Lees Rd. HX2: Hal 2H 127
High Level Way HX1: Hal 1D 148
Highley Hall Cft. HD6: Brigh 6D 152
Highley Pk. HD6: Brigh 1E 163
High Mdw. BD20: Keigh 4G 33
High Mdws. BD15: B'frd 4G 67
HX4: Hal 4G 159
High Mill Bus. Pk. LS27: Morl 4A 138
High Moor Av. LS17: Leeds 5C 60
High Moor Cl. LS17: Leeds 4C 60
High Moor Ct. LS17: Leeds 5C 60
High Moor Cres. LS17: Leeds 4C 60
Highmoor Cres. HD6: Brigh 6D 152
High Moor Dr. LS17: Leeds 4C 60
High Moor Gro. LS17: Leeds 4C 60
Highmoor La. HD6: Brigh 6D 152
(not continuous)
Highmoor Wlk. BD17: Bail 5A 52
High Oak Gth. BD22: Keigh 5C 46
High Pk. Cres. BD9: B'frd 6G 69
High Pk. Dr. BD9: B'frd 6G 69
High Pk. Gro. BD9: B'frd 6G 69
High Pastures BD22: Keigh 2E 47
High Poplars BD2: B'frd 5F 71
High Ridge Av. LS26: Rothw 6H 119
High Ridge Ct. LS26: Rothw 1A 142
High Ridge Pk. LS26: Rothw 6H 119
High Ridge Way LS16: B'hpe 3H 43
HIGHROAD WELL 2B 148
Highroad Well HX2: Hal 2B 148
Highroad Well Ct. HX2: Hal 2B 148
Highroad Well La. HX2: Hal 2A 148
High Royd HX2: Hal 4F 147
High Royds Dr. LS29: Men 2H 39
High Spring Gdns. La.
BD20: Keigh 4G 33
High Spring Rd. BD21: Keigh 1D 48
High Stones Rd. HX7: Heb B 6A 146
High St. BD6: B'frd 4B 110
BD10: B'frd 1H 71
BD13: B'frd 4A 108
(Queensbury)
BD13: B'frd 5H 87
(Thornton)
BD20: Stee 6C 14
BD21: Keigh 6H 33
HD6: Brigh 6A 152
HX1: Hal 3F 149 (5A 164)
(not continuous)
HX2: Hal 6E 127
HX4: Hal 5H 159
LS19: Yead 6F 41
High St. LS22: Weth 5E 13
LS23: B Spa 3H 29
(Boston Spa)
LS23: B Spa 6B 30
(Clifford)
LS25: Kip 4H 123
LS27: Morl 5A 138
LS28: Pud 6H 73
WF12: Dew 6A 154
WF17: Bat 6A 136
WF17: Dew 6A 154
High St. Ct. HX2: Hal 6E 127
High St. Fold HX2: Hal 6E 127
High St. Pl. BD10: B'frd 1H 71
BD13: B'frd 4A 108
(off High St.)
High Sunderland La. HX3: Hal 6H 129
Highthorne Av. BD3: B'frd 2A 92
Highthorne Ct. LS17: Leeds 3D 60
Highthorne Dr. LS17: Leeds 3D 60
Highthorne Gro. LS12: Leeds 3A 96
LS17: Leeds 3E 61
Highthorne Mt. LS17: Leeds 3D 60
Highthorne St. LS12: Leeds 3A 96
Highthorne Vw. LS12: Leeds 3A 96
HIGHTOWN HEIGHTS 4H 153
High Trees La. HX4: Hal 5C 158
HIGH UTLEY 4G 33
Highway LS20: Guis 4H 39
Highways LS14: Leeds 2A 100
High Wheatley LS29: I'ly 6G 11
High Wicken Cl. BD13: B'frd 5H 87
High Wood LS29: I'ly 6H 11
Highwood Av. LS17: Leeds 4A 60
High Wood Ct. LS6: Leeds 4E 77
Highwood Cres. LS17: Leeds 4A 60
Highwood Gro. LS17: Leeds 5A 60
High Wood Head BD20: Keigh 1B 34
High Woodlands WF3: E Ard 2A 156
High Wood Rd. WF17: Bat 3C 136
Hilda St. BD9: B'frd 5A 70
Hillam Rd. BD2: B'frd 6D 70
Hillam St. BD5: B'frd 2B 110
Hillary Pl. LS2: Leeds 1H 97 (1C 4)
Hillary Rd. BD18: Ship 2E 71
Hillas Ct. HX3: Hal 6H 149
Hillas Ind. Est. HX6: Hal 5B 148
Hillbrook Ri. LS29: I'ly 6B 10
Hill Brow Cl. BD15: B'frd 2C 88
Hill Cl. BD17: Bail 5B 52
Hill Clough BD22: Keigh 6C 32
Hill Clough Gro.
BD22: Keigh 6C 32
Hillcote Dr. BD5: B'frd 1E 111
Hill Ct. Av. LS13: Leeds 5E 75
Hillcourt Cft. LS13: Leeds 5E 75
Hillcourt Dr. LS13: Leeds 5E 75
Hill Ct. Fold LS13: Leeds 5E 75
Hillcourt Gro. LS13: Leeds 5E 75
Hill Ct. Vw. LS13: Leeds 5D 74
Hill Cres. HX3: Hal 4B 150
LS19: Yead 2G 55
LS29: Burl W 4F 21
WF17: Bat 5C 136
Hill Crest *HX6: Hal 4H 147*
(off Dalton St.)
LS26: Swil 4A 122
Hillcrest LS16: B'hpe 1C 42
LS22: Coll 3G 27
LS27: Morl 5D 114
Hill Crest Av. BD13: B'frd 2C 86
HX6: Hal 4H 147
(off Dearden St.)
Hillcrest Av. BD13: B'frd 5B 108
BD20: Sils 1E 15
LS7: Leeds 6C 78
Hillcrest Cl. LS26: Swil 4H 121
Hill Crest Dr. BD13: B'frd 2B 86
Hillcrest Dr. BD13: B'frd 5B 108
Hill Crest Mt. BD13: B'frd 2B 86
Hillcrest Mt. BD19: Cleck 2F 153
LS16: Leeds 3G 57
Hillcrest Pl. LS7: Leeds 5C 78
Hillcrest Ri. LS16: Leeds 3F 57
Hill Crest Rd. BD13: B'frd 2B 86
(Hill Crest Mt.)
BD13: B'frd 4H 87
(West La.)
Hillcrest Rd. BD13: B'frd 5B 108
Hill Crest Vw. BD13: B'frd 2B 86
Hillcrest Vw. LS7: Leeds 5C 78
Hill Cft. BD13: B'frd 4A 88
HILL END 3G 95
Hill End BD7: B'frd 2G 109
Hill End Cl. HX3: Hal 5A 132
(Station Rd.)
HX3: Hal 2E 151
(Sutcliffe Wood La.)
LS12: Leeds 3H 95
Hill End Cres. LS12: Leeds 3H 95
Hill End Gro. BD7: B'frd 2G 109
Hill End La. BD13: B'frd 5H 107
BD16: Bgly, B'frd 1C 66
Hill End Rd. LS12: Leeds 3H 95
Hillesley Rd. WF12: Dew 6A 154
HILLFOOT 3F 93
Hillfoot BD18: Ship 2G 69
Hillfoot Av. LS28: Pud 3F 93
Hillfoot Cotts. LS28: Pud 3E 93
Hillfoot Cres. LS28: Pud 3F 93
Hillfoot Dr. LS28: Pud 3F 93
Hillfoot Ri. LS28: Pud 3F 93
HILL GREEN 3A 114
Hill Grn. Ct. BD4: B'frd 3A 114
Hillhead Dr. WF17: Bat 6B 136
Hill Ho. Edge La.
BD22: Oxen 2B 84
Hill Ho. La. BD22: Oxen 2C 84
Hillidge Rd. LS10: Leeds 1B 118
(not continuous)
Hillidge Sq. LS10: Leeds 1B 118
Hillingdon Way
LS17: Leeds 1G 59
Hillings La. LS20: Guis 4D 38
LS29: Men 1D 38
Hill Lands BD12: B'frd 2C 132
Hill Pk. Av. HX3: Hal 6D 128
Hill Ri. Av. LS13: Leeds 5E 75
Hill Ri. Gro. LS13: Leeds 5E 75
Hill Rd. HX3: Hal 2A 150
Hillside LS25: Gar 5G 103
Hillside Av.
BD22: Keigh 5B 46
HX2: Hal 2D 146
LS20: Guis 2B 40
Hillside Bldgs. *LS11: Leeds 2G 117*
(off Beeston Rd.)
Hillside Cl. LS29: Add 1C 8
Hillside Ct. LS7: Leeds 2C 78
LS29: Men 1F 39
Hillside Gro. BD22: Keigh 5B 46
LS28: Pud 4B 94
Hill Side Mt. LS28: Pud 1A 94
Hillside Mt. LS28: Pud 4C 94
Hillside Ri. LS20: Guis 2B 40
Hill Side Rd. BD3: B'frd 4G 91 (3G 7)
Hillside Rd. BD16: Bgly 3B 50
BD18: Ship 3C 70
LS7: Leeds 2B 78
Hill Side Ter. BD3: B'frd 4G 91 (2G 7)
Hillside Ter. BD17: Bail 4C 52
Hillside Vw. HX6: Hal 5G 147
LS28: Pud 4C 94
Hillside Works Ind. Est.
BD19: Cleck 5B 134
Hill St. BD4: B'frd 6H 91
BD6: B'frd 4A 110
BD22: Haw 3C 64
HX1: Hal 3F 149 (6A 164)
LS9: Leeds 2C 98
LS11: Leeds 2H 117
Hillthorpe LS28: Pud 6A 94
Hillthorpe Ct. LS10: Leeds 4A 140
Hillthorpe Ri. LS28: Pud 6A 94
Hillthorpe Rd. LS28: Pud 6A 94
Hillthorpe Sq. LS28: Pud 6A 94
Hillthorpe St. LS28: Pud 6A 94
Hillthorpe Ter. LS28: Pud 6A 94

HILL TOP
BD13 . . . . .4G 87
LS6 . . . . .1E 77
LS12 . . . . .3H 95
Hill Top BD13: B'frd 3H 107
BD16: Bgly 3E 69
BD20: Stee 6C 14
HX2: Hal 4C 148
HX6: Hal 4G 147
LS29: Burl W 2E 21
LS29: I'ly 1C 18
Hilltop Av. LS8: Leeds 5D 78
Hill Top Cl. LS14: Leeds 3H 95
WF3: E Ard 3E 155
Hill Top Cotts. BD9: B'frd 1G 89
Hill Top Ct. WF3: E Ard 3E 155
Hill Top Fold BD12: B'frd 1D 132
(off Low Moor St.)
Hill Top Gdns. WF3: E Ard 3E 155
Hill Top Grn. WF3: E Ard 3D 154
Hill Top Gro. BD15: B'frd 2C 88
WF3: E Ard 3E 155
Hill Top La. BD15: B'frd 2C 88
BD16: Bgly 5B 36
(not continuous)
WF3: E Ard 3D 154
Hill Top Mt. LS8: Leeds 5D 78
LS8: Leeds 5D 78
Hill Top Pl. LS6: Leeds 1F 97
LS8: Leeds 5D 78
Hill Top Rd. BD13: B'frd 4F 87
BD21: Keigh 6G 47
BD22: Keigh 5B 46
LS6: Leeds 1F 97
LS12: Leeds 3H 95
Hill Top St. LS6: Leeds 1F 97
Hill Top Vw. WF3: E Ard 3D 154
Hill Top Wlk. BD22: Keigh 6F 33
Hill Top Way BD22: Keigh 6F 33
Hill Vw. HX2: Hal 6D 106
Hill Vw. Av. LS7: Leeds 2B 78
Hillview Gdns. HX3: Hal 6C 130
Hill Vw. Mt. LS7: Leeds 2B 78
Hill Vw. Pl. LS7: Leeds 2B 78
Hill Vw. Ri. BD4: B'frd 1C 112
Hill Vw. Ter. LS7: Leeds 2B 78
Hillway LS20: Guis 6A 40
Hillworth Ho. BD21: Keigh 1H 47
(off Oakworth Rd.)
Hillworth Village BD21: Keigh 1H 47
Hilton Av. BD18: Ship 4B 70
Hilton Ct. LS16: B'hpe 1C 42
Hilton Cres. BD17: Bail 5C 52
Hilton Dr. BD18: Ship 4B 70
Hilton Grange LS16: B'hpe 1C 42
Hilton Gro. BD7: B'frd 5A 90
BD18: Ship 4B 70
LS8: Leeds 4D 78
Hilton M. LS16: B'hpe 2C 42
Hilton Pl. LS8: Leeds 5D 78
Hilton Rd. BD7: B'frd 5A 90
BD18: Ship 4B 70
LS8: Leeds 5D 78
Hilton St. LS8: Leeds 5D 78
Hilton Ter. LS8: Leeds 5D 78
Hinchcliffe St. BD3: B'frd 3H 91
Hinchliffe Av. BD17: Bail 5D 52
Hindle Pl. LS27: Morl 6B 116
Hindley Wlk. BD7: B'frd 3F 109
Hind St. BD8: B'frd 3C 90 (2A 6)
BD12: B'frd 5C 132
Hinsley Ct. LS6: Leeds 4E 77
Hions Cl. HD6: Brigh 3A 162
HIPPERHOLME 1F 151
Hipswell St. BD3: B'frd 3A 92
Hird Av. BD6: B'frd 5C 110
Hird Rd. BD12: B'frd 1D 132
Hird St. BD17: Ship 1B 70
BD21: Keigh 2G 47
(not continuous)
LS11: Leeds 2G 117
Hirst Fold BD12: B'frd 4C 132
(off Town Ga.)
Hirst La. BD18: Ship 6G 51
Hirst Lodge Ct. BD2: B'frd 4F 71

Hirst Mill Cres. BD18: Ship 6G 51
Hirst St. WF10: Kip 6E 123
Hirst's Yd. LS1: Leeds 5F 5
Hirst Wood Cres. BD18: Ship 1G 69
Hirst Wood Rd. BD18: Ship 1F 69
Hive BD22: Keigh 1G 47
HMP Leeds LS12: Leeds 4D 96
HMP Wealstun LS23: W'ton 1E 31
HM Young Offenders Institution Wetherby
LS22: Weth 2G 13
Hobb End BD13: B'frd 3G 87
Hobberley La. LS17: Leeds 3B 62
Hob Cote La. BD22: Keigh 6A 46
Hob La. HX2: Hal 1A 146
HX6: Hal 2A 158
Hobson Fold BD12: B'frd 5D 132
Hockney Rd. BD8: B'frd 3B 90
Hockney Rd. Ind. Est. BD8: B'frd 3B 90
Hodgson Av. BD3: B'frd 3B 92
LS17: Leeds 4E 61
Hodgson Cres. LS17: Leeds 4E 61
Hodgson Fold BD2: B'frd 5F 71
LS29: Add 1B 8
Hodgson La. BD11: B'frd 6F 113
(Cross La.)
BD11: B'frd 1H 135
(Whitehall Rd.)
Hodgson Pl. LS27: Morl 6B 116
Hodgson St. LS27: Morl 6C 138
Hodgson Yd. BD2: B'frd 4A 72
HOLBECK 6G 97
Holbeck La. LS11: Leeds 5F 97
Holbeck Moor Rd. LS11: Leeds 6G 97
Holbeck Towers LS11: Leeds 6G 97
Holborn App. LS6: Leeds 6G 77
Holborn Ct. BD12: B'frd 1C 132
LS6: Leeds 6H 77
Holborn Gdns. LS6: Leeds 6G 77
Holborn Grn. LS6: Leeds 6G 77
Holborn Gro. LS6: Leeds 6G 77
Holborn St. LS6: Leeds 6H 77
Holborn Ter. LS6: Leeds 6H 77
Holborn Towers LS6: Leeds 6H 77
Holborn Vw. LS6: Leeds 6G 77
Holborn Wlk. LS6: Leeds 6G 77
Holby Bus. Pk. HX6: Hal 6H 147
Holden Ing Way WF17: Bat 3C 136
Holden La. BD17: Bail 3D 52
(not continuous)
BD20: Sils 3G 15
BD22: Oxen 2A 84
Holden Rd. BD6: B'frd 4B 110
Holdforth Cl. LS12: Leeds 4E 97
Holdforth Gdns. LS12: Leeds 4E 97
Holdforth Grn. LS12: Leeds 4E 97
Holdforth Pl. LS12: Leeds 4E 97
HOLDSWORTH 1E 129
Holdsworth Bldgs. BD2: B'frd 5B 72
(off Elvey Cl.)
BD12: B'frd 3C 132
(off Huddersfield Rd.)
Holdsworth Pl. LS12: Leeds 4B 96
Holdsworth Rd. HX2: Hal 6E 107
Holdsworth Sq. BD2: B'frd 5B 72
Holdsworth St. BD1: B'frd 3F 91 (2E 7)
BD18: Ship 3C 70
Holdsworth Ter. HX1: Hal 4H 149
Holdsworth Yd. BD1: B'frd 4B 6
(off Thornton Rd.)
Hole BD22: Haw 3B 64
Holgate La. LS23: B Spa 3B 30
Holker St. BD8: B'frd 3B 90
BD21: Keigh 5A 34
Holland Mt. LS16: B'hpe 2F 43
Holland Rd. LS25: Kip 3A 124
Hollas La. HX6: Hal 1C 158
(not continuous)
Hollerton La. WF3: E Ard 1F 155
Hollies, The LS12: Leeds 4C 96
LS21: Pool 5F 25
Hollin Cl. La. BD2: B'frd 6E 71
(not continuous)
Hollin Ct. BD18: Ship 3C 70
LS16: Leeds 2D 76

Hollin Cres. LS16: Leeds 2D 76
Hollin Dr. LS16: Leeds 2E 77
Hollin Gdns. LS16: Leeds 2C 76
Hollin Ga. LS21: Otley 1B 22
Hollingbourne Rd. LS15: Leeds 1H 101
Holling Gro. HX6: Hal 4G 147
Hollin Greaves La. HX3: Hal 6H 129
Hollings, The LS26: Mick 4B 144
Hollings Rd. BD8: B'frd 2B 90
Hollings Sq. BD8: B'frd 3B 90
Hollings St. BD8: B'frd 3B 90
BD16: Bgly 2D 68
Hollings Ter. BD8: B'frd 3B 90
Hollingwood Av. BD7: B'frd 1H 109
Hollingwood Ct. BD7: B'frd 2G 109
Hollingwood Dr. BD7: B'frd 1G 109
Hollingwood Ga. LS29: I'ly 6B 10
Hollingwood La. BD7: B'frd 2F 109
Hollingwood Mt. BD7: B'frd 1H 109
Hollingwood Ri. LS29: I'ly 6B 10
Hollin Hall Dr. LS29: I'ly 6A 10
Hollin Hall Rd. BD18: Ship 3G 69
Hollin Head BD17: Bail 3F 53
Hollin Hill Av. LS8: Leeds 4G 79
Hollin Hill Dr. LS8: Leeds 4G 79
Hollin Hill Cotts. LS8: Leeds 4G 79
Hollinhurst WF10: Kip 1E 145
Hollin La. BD18: Ship 3D 70
HX2: Hal 2A 126
HX6: Hal 2A 158
LS16: Leeds 2D 76
Hollin M. LS16: Leeds 2D 76
Hollin Mt. LS16: Leeds 2C 76
HOLLIN PARK 4H 79
Hollin Pk. Av. LS8: Leeds 4H 79
Hollin Pk. Ct. LS28: Pud 3E 73
Hollin Pk. Cres. LS8: Leeds 4H 79
Hollin Pk. Mt. LS8: Leeds 3H 79
Hollin Pk. Pde. LS8: Leeds 4G 79
Hollin Pk. Pl. LS8: Leeds 4G 79
Hollin Pk. Rd. LS8: Leeds 4G 79
LS28: Pud 3E 73
Hollin Pk. Ter. LS8: Leeds 4G 79
Hollin Pk. Vw. LS8: Leeds 4G 79
Hollin Ri. BD18: Ship 3C 70
Hollin Rd. BD18: Ship 3C 70
LS16: Leeds 2D 76
Hollins HX2: Hal 4C 146
Hollins, The HX6: Hal 5H 147
Hollins Bank HX6: Hal 5H 147
Hollins Bank La. BD20: Stee 6D 14
Hollins Beck Cl. LS25: Kip 5G 123
Hollins Cl. BD20: Keigh 3F 33
Hollins Ga. HX2: Hal 4C 146
Hollins Gro. WF10: Kip 1F 145
Hollins Hey Rd. HX5: Hal 6H 159
Hollins Hill BD17: Bail 2G 53
LS20: Guis 2G 53
Hollins La. BD20: Keigh 2F 33
HX2: Hal 4B 146
(Cat La.)
HX2: Hal 2A 128
(Mixenden Cl.)
HX6: Hal 4G 147
Hollins Mill La. HX6: Hal 5G 147
Hollins Pk. LS25: Kip 4G 123
Hollin Ter. BD18: Ship 3C 70
HOLLINTHORPE 1A 122
Hollin Vw. LS16: Leeds 2D 76
Hollin Wood Cl. BD18: Ship 2G 69
Hollinwood Vw. BD16: Bgly 6H 35
Hollis Pl. LS3: Leeds 2F 97
Hollowfield Cft. BD12: B'frd 2H 133
Holly Av. LS16: Leeds 4F 57
Holly Bank HX5: Ell 6A 160
LS6: Leeds 3D 76
LS20: Guis 4B 40
LS25: Gar 5H 103
Holly Bank Ct. HX3: Hal 1F 151
Holly Bank Dr. HX3: Hal 1F 151
Hollybank Gdns. BD7: B'frd 2G 109
Hollybank Gro. BD7: B'frd 2G 109
Holly Bank Ho. HD6: Brigh 3H 161
(off Field La.)

Holly Bank Pk. HD6: Brigh 3G **161**
(off Hanson Rd.)
HD6: Brigh 3H **161**
(Field La.)
Holly Bank Rd. HD6: Brigh 3G **161**
Hollybank Rd. BD7: B'frd 2G **109**
Holly Bush Ct. LS23: B Spa 4C **30**
Hollybush Grn. LS22: Coll 3C **28**
Holly Cl. LS10: Leeds 3H **139**
Holly Ct. LS20: Guis 5B **40**
WF1: Wake 4G **157**
WF3: E Ard 3E **155**
Hollycroft Ct. LS16: Leeds 4A **58**
Hollycroft St. BD21: Keigh 1H **47**
Holly Dr. LS16: Leeds 4F **57**
Holly Gro. HX1: Hal 3E **149**
HX2: Hal 3E **127**
Holly Hall La. BD12: B'frd 3C **132**
Holly Mt. HX3: Hal 4A **150**
(off High Gro. La.)
Hollynsmill HX4: Hal 4H **159**
Hollyns Ter. HX4: Hal 4H **159**
Holly Pk. LS18: H'fth 6B **56**
Holly Pk. Dr. BD7: B'frd 1G **109**
Holly Pk. Gro. BD7: B'frd 1G **109**
Holly Pk. Mills LS28: Pud 3E **73**
Holly Rd. LS23: B Spa 3H **29**
Holly Royd HX3: Hal 5E **151**
Hollyshaw Cres. LS15: Leeds 3E **101**
Hollyshaw Gro. LS15: Leeds 3E **101**
Hollyshaw La. LS15: Leeds 2E **101**
Hollyshaw St. LS15: Leeds 3E **101**
Hollyshaw Ter. LS15: Leeds 3E **101**
Hollyshaw Wlk. LS15: Leeds 2E **101**
Holly St. BD6: B'frd 3F **109**
Holly Tree La. LS15: Leeds 5G **101**
Hollywell Gro. LS12: Leeds 3B **96**
Hollywell La. LS12: Leeds 4B **96**
Hollywood Bowl
Bradford 5F **91** (5E **7**)
Leeds 2D **96**
Holman Av. LS25: Gar 6F **103**
Holme Bank BD4: B'frd 1D **112**
Holmecarr Ct. BD16: Bgly 3C **50**
Holme Dr. HX2: Hal 3H **147**
Holme Farm Ct. LS12: Leeds 2F **115**
Holme Farm La. LS17: Bard, Coll . .1G **45**
LS23: Bard 1G **45**
Holmefield Vw. BD4: B'frd 1D **112**
Holme Gro. LS29: Burl W 4F **21**
Holme Ho. La. BD22: Keigh 1B **46**
(not continuous)
HX2: Hal 3E **127**
Holme Ings LS29: Add 2G **9**
Holme La. BD4: B'frd 2D **112**
Holme Mill La. BD22: Keigh 1F **47**
Holme Pk. LS29: Burl W 4F **21**
Holme Rd. HX2: Hal 3H **147**
Holmes Rd. HX6: Hal 5A **148**
Holmes St. BD1: B'frd 3D **90** (2A **6**)
LS11: Leeds 5A **98**
Holme's Ter. HX2: Hal 1C **148**
Holme St. BD5: B'frd 1D **110**
BD22: Oxen 1C **84**
HX3: Hal 2A **152**
HOLME TOP 1D **110**
Holme Top La. BD5: B'frd 1D **110**
Holme Top St. BD5: B'frd 1D **110**
Holme Vw. LS29: I'ly 5C **10**
HOLME VILLAGE 2D **112**
Holme Well Rd. LS10: Leeds 2C **140**
HOLME WOOD 2B **112**
Holme Wood BD22: Keigh 1G **47**
Holme Wood Rd. BD4: B'frd 2B **112**
BD22: Keigh 1F **47**
HOLMFIELD 2E **129**
Holmfield BD22: Oxen 2C **84**
Holmfield Cotts. LS26: Mick 4E **145**
Holmfield Ct. BD1: B'frd 4B **6**
Holmfield Dr. LS8: Leeds 6E **61**
Holmfield Gdns. HX2: Hal 2E **129**
Holmfield Ho. HX3: Hal 2E **129**
Holmfield Ind. Est. HX2: Hal 6E **107**
Holmfield Ind. Est. Rd. HX2: Hal . . .1E **129**

Holmfield St. BD1: B'frd 4D **90** (4B **6**)
Holmsley Crest LS26: Rothw 6C **120**
Holmsley Fld. Ct. LS26: Rothw 1E **143**
Holmsley Fld. La. LS26: Rothw 1D **142**
Holmsley Gth. LS26: Rothw 6D **120**
Holmsley Gro. LS26: Rothw 1C **142**
Holmsley La. LS26: Rothw 1C **142**
Holmsley Wlk. LS26: Rothw 1D **142**
Holmwood LS8: Leeds 5E **61**
Holmwood Av. LS6: Leeds 1E **77**
Holmwood Cl. LS6: Leeds 1F **77**
Holmwood Cres. LS6: Leeds 1F **77**
Holmwood Dr. LS6: Leeds 1E **77**
Holmwood Gro. LS6: Leeds 1F **77**
Holmwood Mt. LS6: Leeds 1F **77**
Holmwood Vw. LS6: Leeds 1F **77**
Holroyd Hill BD6: B'frd 4C **110**
Holroyd Mill La. BD16: Bgly 5A **36**
Holroyd St. LS7: Leeds 1B **98**
Holsworthy Rd. BD4: B'frd 3C **112**
Holt, The BD18: Ship 1C **70**
Holt Av. LS16: Leeds 2C **58**
Holt Gro. HX3: Hal 2A **152**
Holt Cl. LS16: Leeds 3C **58**
Holt Cres. LS16: Leeds 2H **57**
Holtdale App. LS16: Leeds 2G **57**
Holtdale Av. LS16: Leeds 2H **57**
Holtdale Cl. LS16: Leeds 2H **57**
Holtdale Cft. LS16: Leeds 2H **57**
Holtdale Dr. LS16: Leeds 2H **57**
Holtdale Fold LS16: Leeds 2H **57**
Holtdale Gdns. LS16: Leeds 2H **57**
Holtdale Gth. LS16: Leeds 2H **57**
Holtdale Grn. LS16: Leeds 2H **57**
Holtdale Gro. LS16: Leeds 2G **57**
Holtdale Lawn LS16: Leeds 2H **57**
Holtdale Pl. LS16: Leeds 2H **57**
Holtdale Rd. LS16: Leeds 2H **57**
Holtdale Vw. LS16: Leeds 2H **57**
Holtdale Way LS16: Leeds 2H **57**
Holt Dr. LS16: Leeds 2A **58**
Holt Farm Cl. LS16: Leeds 2H **57**
Holt Farm Ri. LS16: Leeds 2H **57**
Holt Gdns. BD10: B'frd 1G **71**
LS16: Leeds 2C **58**
Holt Ga. LS16: Leeds 2A **58**
Holt Grn. LS16: Leeds 2A **58**
Holt La. LS16: Leeds 2G **57**
Holt La. Ct. LS16: Leeds 3B **58**
HOLT PARK 2H **57**
Holt Pk. Av. LS16: Leeds 2A **58**
Holt Pk. Cl. LS16: Leeds 2A **58**
Holt Pk. Cres. LS16: Leeds 2A **58**
Holt Pk. Dr. LS16: Leeds 2A **58**
Holt Pk. Gdns. LS16: Leeds 2A **58**
Holt Pk. Ga. LS16: Leeds 2A **58**
Holt Pk. Grange LS16: Leeds 2A **58**
Holt Pk. Grn. LS16: Leeds 2A **58**
Holt Pk. Gro. LS16: Leeds 2H **57**
Holt Park Leisure Cen. 2H **57**
Holt Pk. Ri. LS16: Leeds 2A **58**
Holt Pk. Rd. LS16: Leeds 2A **58**
Holt Pk. Va. LS16: Leeds 2A **58**
Holt Pk. Vw. LS16: Leeds 2H **57**
Holt Pk. Way LS16: Leeds 2A **58**
Holt Ri. LS16: Leeds 2A **58**
Holt Rd. LS16: Leeds 2A **58**
Holts La. BD14: B'frd 6D **88**
Holt Ter. HX3: Hal 5H **149**
Holt Va. LS16: Leeds 2A **58**
Holt Wlk. LS16: Leeds 2A **58**
Holybrook Av. BD10: B'frd 3B **72**
HOLY CROFT 1H **47**
Holyoake Av. BD16: Bgly 6B **50**
Holy Rood La. LS25: Led 5H **125**
Holywell Ash La. BD8: B'frd 2D **90**
HOLYWELL GREEN 6F **159**
Holywell La. LS17: Leeds 2H **61**
Holywell Vw. LS17: Leeds 2H **61**
Home Farm Cl. BD6: B'frd 4F **109**

Homefield Av. LS27: Morl 5A **138**
Home Lea LS26: Rothw 6H **119**
Home Lea Dr. LS26: Rothw 1H **141**
Homepaddock Ho. LS22: Weth 3F **13**
Homestead Est. LS29: Men 6G **21**
Home Vw. Ter. BD8: B'frd 2B **90**
Honey Pot BD15: B'frd 6G **67**
Honey Pot La. BD17: Bail 4A **52**
Hoods, The HD6: Brigh 4H **161**
Hoopoe M. BD15: B'frd 4D **88**
Hopbine Av. BD5: B'frd 3E **111**
Hopbine Rd. BD5: B'frd 3E **111**
Hope Av. BD5: B'frd 3C **110**
BD18: Ship 1D **70**
Hopefield Chase LS26: Rothw 3F **141**
Hopefield Cl. LS26: Rothw 3F **141**
Hopefield Ct. LS26: Rothw 3F **141**
WF3: E Ard 2A **156**
Hopefield Cres. LS26: Rothw 3F **141**
Hopefield Dr. LS26: Rothw 3F **141**
Hopefield Gdns. LS26: Rothw 3F **141**
Hopefield Grn. LS26: Rothw 3F **141**
Hopefield Gro. LS26: Rothw 3F **141**
Hopefield M. LS26: Rothw 3F **141**
Hopefield Pl. LS26: Rothw 3F **141**
Hopefield Vw. LS26: Rothw 3F **141**
Hopefield Wlk. LS26: Rothw 3F **141**
Hopefield Way BD5: B'frd 4H **111**
LS26: Rothw 3F **141**
Hope Hall St. HX1: Hal 3G **149** (6C **164**)
Hope Hall Ter. HX1: Hal 6C **164**
Hope Hill Vw. BD16: Bgly 2C **68**
Hope La. BD17: Bail 3B **52**
Hope Pl. BD21: Keigh 2A **48**
Hope Rd. LS2: Leeds 3B **98** (3H **5**)
Hopes Farm Mt. LS10: Leeds 6D **118**
Hopes Farm Rd. LS10: Leeds 6D **118**
Hopes Farm Vw. LS10: Leeds 6D **118**
Hope St. HX1: Hal 2F **149** (3A **164**)
HX3: Hal 3D **130**
HX6: Hal 6H **147**
LS27: Morl 3A **138**
Hope Vw. BD18: Ship 2D **70**
Hopewell Pl. LS6: Leeds 1E **97**
Hopewell Ter. LS18: H'fth 2D **74**
LS25: Kip 4H **123**
Hopewell Vw. LS10: Leeds 2B **140**
Hopkinson Bldgs. HX3: Hal 4D **128**
(off Foundry St. Nth.)
Hopkinson Dr. BD4: B'frd 5A **112**
Hopkinson St. HX3: Hal 4D **128**
Hopkin St. BD4: B'frd 4C **112**
Hops La. HX3: Hal 5B **128**
Hopton Av. BD4: B'frd 4H **111**
Hopton Ct. LS12: Leeds 4B **96**
(off Hopton M.)
Hopton M. LS12: Leeds 4B **96**
Hopwood Bank LS18: H'fth 5E **57**
Hopwood Cl. LS18: H'fth 5E **57**
Hopwood La. HX1: Hal 3C **148** (5A **164**)
(not continuous)
Hopwood Rd. LS18: H'fth 5E **57**
Horace Waller VC Pde.
WF12: Dew 6A **154**
Horley Grn. La. HX3: Hal 6A **130**
Horley Grn. Rd. HX3: Hal 6A **130**
Hornbeam Cl. BD15: B'frd 5B **68**
Hornbeam Way LS14: Leeds 1E **81**
Hornby St. HX1: Hal 3D **148**
Hornby Ter. HX1: Hal 3D **148**
Horner's Bldgs. HX2: Hal 2E **129**
(off Shay La.)
Horners Fold BD20: Keigh 4H **35**
Horne St. HX1: Hal 2F **149**
Hornsea Dr. BD15: B'frd 5G **67**
Horse Cl. BD12: B'frd 3A **132**
Horsefair LS22: Weth 4F **13**
Horsefair Cen. LS22: Weth 4F **13**
Horseshoe Ct. BD15: B'frd 5F **67**
Horsfall Stadium 6B **110**
Horsfall St. HX1: Hal 4E **149**
LS27: Morl 1H **137**
HORSFORTH 1D **74**
Horsforth New Rd. LS13: Leeds 3A **74**

Horsforth Station (Rail) 4E 57	Howgate Hill HX3: Hal 4B 150	Hunslet La. LS10: Leeds 5A 98
Horsham Ct. BD22: Keigh 2E 47	Howgill Grn. BD6: B'frd 1A 132	(Crown Point Rd.)
Horsham Rd. BD4: B'frd 3C 112	Howley Pk. Cl. LS27: Morl 5H 137	LS10: Leeds 5A 98 (6F 5)
Horsley Fold HD6: Brigh 1E 163	Howley Pk. Rd. LS27: Morl 5H 137	(Hunslet Rd., not continuous)
Horsley St. BD6: B'frd 4C 110	Howley Pk. E. LS27: Morl 6H 137	Hunslet Rd. LS10: Leeds 5B 98
Horsman St. BD4: B'frd 4C 112	Howley Pk. Ter. LS27: Morl 5H 137	(Crown Point Rd., not continuous)
HORTON BANK 2F 109	Howley Pk. Trad. Est.	LS10: Leeds 4A 98 (6F 5)
HORTON BANK BOTTOM 3A 110	LS27: Morl 5H 137	(Waterloo St.)
Horton Bank Country Pk. 2F 109	Howley Pk. Vw. LS27: Morl 6C 138	Hunslet Trad. Est. LS10: Leeds . . .1D 118
Horton Cl. LS13: Leeds 5B 74	Howson Cl. LS20: Guis 4D 40	HUNSWORTH 5B 134
Horton Gth. LS11: Leeds 5B 74	Hoxton Mt. LS11: Leeds 2F 117	Hunsworth La. BD4: B'frd 3B 134
Horton Grange Rd. BD7: B'frd 5B 90	Hoxton St. BD8: B'frd 3A 90	BD19: Cleck 6B 134
Horton Hall Cl. BD5: B'frd 6D 90	Hoyle Ct. Av. BD17: Bail 4E 53	Hunter Hill Rd. HX2: Hal 2G 127
Horton Ind. Est. BD7: B'frd 2A 110	Hoyle Ct. Dr. BD17: Bail 4E 53	Hunterscombe Ct. BD16: Bgly 2F 51
Horton Pl. HX2: Hal 5D 106	Hoyle Ct. Rd. BD17: Bail 4E 53	Hunters Ct. BD9: B'frd 5E 69
Horton Ri. LS13: Leeds 5B 74	Hoyle Fold BD22: Keigh 2F 47	Hunters Grn. BD13: B'frd 2B 66
Horton St. HX1: Hal 3G 149 (5C 164)	Hoyle Ing Rd. BD13: B'frd 5B 88	Hunters Mdw. BD20: Sils 1E 15
Horton Ter. HX3: Hal 1D 150	Hoyle Syke BD22: Oxen 5B 64	Hunters Pk. Av. BD14: B'frd 6F 89
Hospital Cotts. LS25: Led 5H 125	HUBBERTON GREEN 6C 146	Hunters Wlk. LS22: Weth 1E 13
Hospital La. LS16: Leeds 5H 57	Hubberton Grn. Rd. HX6: Hal 6C 146	Huntingdon Av. HD2: Hud 6F 163
Hospital Rd. BD20: Keigh 4D 34	Hubert St. BD3: B'frd 5H 91	Huntingdon Rd. HD6: Brigh 2C 162
Hothfield St. BD20: Sils 2D 14	HX2: Hal 2B 148	Huntington Cres. LS16: Leeds 2C 76
Hough HX3: Hal 6B 130	Huddersfield Crematorium	Huntock Pl. HD6: Brigh 4H 151
Hough Cl. LS13: Leeds 3D 94	HD2: Hud 5A 162	Huntsman Ho. LS10: Leeds 5A 98
HOUGH END 3E 95	Huddersfield Rd. BD6: B'frd 1C 132	Huntsmans Cl. BD16: Bgly 2E 51
Hough End Av. LS13: Leeds 2F 95	BD12: B'frd, Brigh 1B 152	BD20: Keigh 5G 33
Hough End Cl. LS13: Leeds 2F 95	(not continuous)	Hunt Yd. BD7: B'frd 1A 110
Hough End Ct. LS13: Leeds 2F 95	HD6: Brigh 4B 162	Hurstville Av. BD4: B'frd 1D 134
Hough End Cres. LS13: Leeds 2E 95	HX3: Hal 4G 149	Husler Gro. LS7: Leeds 6B 78
Hough End Gdns. LS13: Leeds 2F 95	(not continuous)	Husler Pl. LS7: Leeds 6B 78
Hough End La. LS13: Leeds 2E 95	HX5: Ell 6D 160	Hustlergate BD1: B'frd 4E 91 (4D 6)
Hough Gro. LS13: Leeds 1E 95	WF17: Bat 6A 136	Hustler's Row LS6: Leeds 1D 76
Hough La. LS13: Leeds 1E 95	Hud Hill HX3: Hal 3D 130	Hustler St. BD3: B'frd 2G 91 (1H 7)
Houghley Av. LS12: Leeds 1H 95	Hudson, The BD12: B'frd 4C 132	Hutchinson La. HD6: Brigh 1B 162
Houghley Cl. LS13: Leeds 1G 95	Hudson Av. BD7: B'frd 1B 110	Hutchinson Pl. LS5: Leeds 6A 76
Houghley Cres. LS12: Leeds 1H 95	Hudson Cl. BD7: B'frd 2B 110	Hutson St. BD5: B'frd 1D 110
Houghley La. LS13: Leeds 1G 95	LS22: Weth 4E 13	Hutton Rd. BD5: B'frd 3C 110
Houghley Pl. LS12: Leeds 1H 95	Hudson Gdns. BD7: B'frd 1B 110	Hutton Ter. BD2: B'frd 4B 72
Houghley Rd. LS12: Leeds 1H 95	Hudson Gro. LS9: Leeds 2E 99	LS28: Pud 4A 94
Houghley Sq. LS12: Leeds 1H 95	Hudson M. LS23: B Spa 4C 30	Huxley Mt. BD2: B'frd 4A 72
HOUGH SIDE 4D 94	Hudson Pl. LS9: Leeds 2E 99	Hydale Cl. BD21: Keigh 2C 48
Hough Side Cl. LS28: Pud 4D 94	Hudson Rd. LS9: Leeds 1E 99	Hydale Ct. BD12: B'frd 1C 132
Hough Side La. LS28: Pud 4C 94	Hudson's Ter. LS19: Yead 6G 41	Hyde Gro. BD21: Keigh 5B 34
Hough Side Rd. LS28: Pud 4B 94	LS9: Leeds 2E 99	(off Kirby St.)
Hough Ter. LS13: Leeds 1E 95	LS28: Pud 2H 93	HYDE PARK 6E 77
Houghton Pl. BD1: B'frd 3D 90 (2B 6)	Hudson St. BD3: B'frd 4B 92	Hyde Pk. HX1: Hal 3E 149
Houghton St. HD6: Brigh 6B 152	LS9: Leeds 2E 99	Hyde Pk. Cl. LS6: Leeds 1F 97
Houghton Towers HX6: Hal 5H 147	LS28: Pud 1B 118	Hyde Pk. Cnr. LS6: Leeds 6F 77
Hough Top LS13: Leeds 4C 94	Huggan Row LS28: Pud 4B 94	Hyde Pk. Gdns. HX1: Hal 4E 149
Hough Tree Rd. LS13: Leeds 3E 95	(off Hammerton Gro.)	(off Haugh Shaw Rd.)
Hough Tree Ter. LS13: Leeds 3E 95	Hughenden Vw. LS27: Morl 1A 138	Hyde Pk. Pl. LS6: Leeds 6F 77
Hougomont BD13: B'frd 2G 107	Hughendon Dr. BD13: B'frd 5C 88	Hyde Pk. Rd. HX1: Hal 4E 149
Hoults La. HX4: Hal 3F 159	Hughendon Wlk. BD13: B'frd 5C 88	LS6: Leeds 1F 97
HOVE EDGE 4H 151	Hugill St. BD13: B'frd 5H 87	Hyde Pk. St. HX1: Hal 4E 149
Hovingham Av. LS8: Leeds 5E 79	Hulbert St. BD16: Bgly 5C 50	Hyde Pk. Ter. LS6: Leeds 6F 77
Hovingham Gro. LS8: Leeds 5E 79	Hullenedge Gdns. HX5: Ell 5H 159	Hyde Pl. LS2: Leeds 2G 97 (2A 4)
Hovingham Mt. LS8: Leeds 5E 79	Hullenedge La. HX4: Hal 5G 159	Hyde St. BD10: B'frd 6H 53
Hovingham Ter. LS8: Leeds 5E 79	Hullenedge Rd. HX5: Ell 5H 159	LS2: Leeds 2G 97 (2A 4)
Howard Av. LS15: Leeds 4B 100	Hullen Rd. HX5: Ell 5H 159	Hyde Ter. LS2: Leeds 2G 97 (1A 4)
Howard Ct. LS15: Leeds 4B 100	Hullett Cl. HX7: Heb B 6A 126	Hydro Cl. LS29: I'ly 6H 11
Howards Dean BD22: Haw 1D 64	Hullett Dr. HX7: Heb B 6A 126	Hyne Av. BD4: B'frd 4H 111
Howard St. BD5: B'frd 5D 90 (6B 6)	Hull St. LS27: Morl 3B 138	
HX1: Hal 1E 149	Hulme St. HX6: Hal 6H 147	
Howarth Av. BD2: B'frd 4G 71	(off Syke La.)	
Howarth Cres. BD2: B'frd 4G 71	HUNGATE 6H 143	**I**
Howbeck Av. BD20: Keigh 4E 35	Hungate La. LS26: Mick 6G 143	
Howbeck Dr. BD20: Keigh 5E 35	HUNGER HILL 6H 143	Ibbetson Cl. LS27: Morl 6A 116
Howcans La. HX3: Hal 2E 129	Hunger Hill HX1: Hal 3G 149 (6C 164)	Ibbetson Ct. LS27: Morl 6A 116
Howden Av. BD20: Keigh 3G 33	LS27: Morl 4A 138	Ibbetson Cft. LS27: Morl 6A 116
Howdenbrook HX3: B'frd 6G 109	LS29: I'ly 1D 10	Ibbetson Dr. LS27: Morl 6A 116
Howden Cl. BD4: B'frd 4D 112	Hunger Hill Rd. LS29: I'ly 1E 11	Ibbetson Oval LS27: Morl 6A 116
HOWDEN CLOUGH 5D 136	Hunger Hills Av. LS18: H'fth 6C 56	Ibbetson Ri. LS27: Morl 6A 116
Howden Clough Ind. Est.	Hunger Hills Dr. LS18: H'fth 6C 56	Ibbetson Rd. LS27: Morl 6A 116
WF17: Bat 4D 136	HUNSLET 1B 118	Ida's, The LS10: Leeds 3E 119
Howden Clough Rd. LS27: Morl 4E 137	Hunslet Bus. Pk. LS10: Leeds 6C 98	Ida St. BD5: B'frd 2C 110
Howden Gdns. LS6: Leeds 1E 97	HUNSLET CARR 4B 118	LS10: Leeds 3E 119
Howden Pl. LS6: Leeds 1E 97	Hunslet Distributor LS10: Leeds . . .1B 118	Iddesleigh St. BD4: B'frd 5B 92
Howden Rd. BD20: Sils 2E 15	Hunslet Grn. Retail Cen.	IDLE 1H 71
Howden Rough BD20: Keigh 1H 33	LS10: Leeds 2B 118	Idlecroft Rd. BD10: B'frd 1H 71
Howden Way LS27: Morl 4F 137	Hunslet Grn. Way LS10: Leeds 1B 118	IDLE MOOR 2F 71
Howes La. HX3: Hal 4B 130	Hunslet Hall Rd. LS11: Leeds 1H 117	Idle Rd. BD2: B'frd 4G 71
Howgate BD10: B'frd 1A 72	Hunslet Hawks RLFC	Idlethorp Way BD10: B'frd 2A 72
	(South Leeds Stadium) 5A 118	Ilbert Av. BD4: B'frd 4A 112
		Ilford St. LS27: Morl 3B 138

ILKLEY 5D 10
Ilkley Hall M. LS29: I'ly 6D 10
Ilkley Hall Pk. LS29: I'ly 6D 10
Ilkley Lawn Tennis & Squash Club
. . . . .4B 10
Ilkley Playhouse 5D 10
(off Castle Rd.)
Ilkley Pool & Lido 4D 10
Ilkley Rd. BD20: Keigh 3D 34
LS21: Otley 4C 22
LS29: Add 2E 9
LS29: Burl W 1D 20
Ilkley Station (Rail) 5D 10
Ilkley Toy Mus. 5D 10
(off Whitton Cft. Rd.)
ILLINGWORTH 1C 128
Illingworth Av. HX2: Hal 5C 106
Illingworth Bldgs. BD12: B'frd 3F 133
(off Illingworth Rd.)
Illingworth Cl. HX2: Hal 6C 106
LS19: Yead 2G 55
Illingworth Cres. HX2: Hal 6C 106
Illingworth Dr. HX2: Hal 6C 106
Illingworth Gdns. HX2: Hal 1C 128
Illingworth Gro. HX2: Hal 6C 106
Illingworth La. HX2: Hal 1C 128
Illingworth Rd. BD12: B'frd 3F 133
Illingworth Way HX2: Hal 6C 106
Imax Bus. Cen. BD19: Cleck 6B 134
(off Balme Rd.)
Imax Cinema 6C 6
Imperial Av. WF2: Wake 6D 156
Imperial Ter. LS12: Leeds 3B 96
Incline, The HX3: Hal 1A 150
Independent St. BD5: B'frd 2C 110
Industrial Av. WF17: Bat 6H 135
Industrial Mus. 2H 149 (4D 164)
Industrial Pl. HX1: Hal 5C 164
Industrial Rd. HX6: Hal 5H 147
Industrial St. BD16: Bgly 4B 50
BD19: Cleck 1F 153
BD22: Keigh 1G 47
HD6: Brigh 6B 152
LS9: Leeds 2D 98
Industrial Ter. HX1: Hal 4F 149
Infirmary St. BD1: B'frd 3D 90 (3B 6)
(not continuous)
LS1: Leeds 3H 97 (4D 4)
Ingester St. BD22: Haw 2B 64
(off West La.)
Ing Fld. BD12: B'frd 3G 133
Ingham Cl. HX2: Hal 5D 106
Ingham La. HX2: Hal 4C 106
Inghams Av. LS28: Pud 4F 93
Inghams Ct. HX3: Hal 6E 129
Inghams Ter. LS28: Pud 3F 93
Inghams Vw. LS28: Pud 3F 93
Ing Head Cotts. HX3: Hal 3E 131
Inghead Gdns. HX3: Hal 3D 130
Ing Head Ter. HX3: Hal 3D 130
(not continuous)
Ingle Av. LS27: Morl 1H 137
Ingleborough Cl. BD4: B'frd 2C 112
Ingleborough Dr.
LS27: Morl 4C 138
(not continuous)
Ingleby Pl. BD7: B'frd 5A 90
Ingleby Rd. BD7: B'frd 3A 90
BD8: B'frd 3A 90
Ingleby St. BD8: B'frd 4A 90
Ingleby Way LS10: Leeds 6C 118
Ingle Ct. LS27: Morl 2H 137
(Earlsmere Dr.)
LS27: Morl 1H 137
(Ingle Av.)
Ingle Cres. LS27: Morl 1A 138
Ingledew Cl. LS17: Leeds 3B 60
Ingledew Cres. LS8: Leeds 5F 61
Ingledew Dr. LS8: Leeds 6F 61
Ingle Gro. LS27: Morl 2H 137
Ingle Row LS7: Leeds 3B 78
Ingleton Cl. LS11: Leeds 2H 117
Ingleton Dr. LS15: Leeds 4A 100
Ingleton Gro. LS11: Leeds 2H 117

Ingleton Ho. BD4: B'frd 3C 112
(off Arlesford Rd.)
Ingleton Pl. LS11: Leeds 2H 117
Ingleton St. LS11: Leeds 2H 117
Inglewood App. LS14: Leeds 6D 80
Inglewood Dr. LS14: Leeds 6D 80
LS21: Otley 4D 22
Inglewood Est. LS21: Otley 4D 22
Inglewood Pl. LS14: Leeds 6D 80
Inglewood Ter. LS6: Leeds 5G 77
(off Delph La.)
Ingram Cl. LS11: Leeds 6F 97
Ingram Ct. LS11: Leeds 6F 97
Ingram Cres. LS11: Leeds 1F 117
Ingram Gdns. LS11: Leeds 6F 97
Ingram Pde. LS26: Rothw 2A 142
Ingram Rd. LS11: Leeds 1F 117
Ingram Row LS11: Leeds 5H 97
Ingram Sq. HX1: Hal 4E 149
Ingram St. BD21: Keigh 4H 47
HX1: Hal 4E 149
LS11: Leeds 5H 97
Ingram Vw. LS11: Leeds 6F 97
INGROW 3G 47
Ingrow Bri. BD21: Keigh 3H 47
Ingrow La. BD21: Keigh 3G 47
BD22: Keigh 3F 47
Ingrow West Station
Vintage Carriages Trust Mus. of
Rail Travel 3H 47
Ings, The HX3: Hal 3A 152
Ings Av. LS20: Guis 3B 40
Ings Cl. LS20: Guis 3A 40
Ings Cres. LS9: Leeds 4F 99
LS20: Guis 4A 40
Ings Cft. HX3: Hal 2E 131
Ings Dr. LS26: Mick 4E 145
Ings La. LS20: Guis 4A 40
LS21: Otley 3F 23
LS23: B Spa 3E 31
Ings Rd. BD20: Stee 4B 14
LS9: Leeds 4F 99
Ing St. BD3: B'frd 4B 92
Ings Vw. LS26: Mick 4E 145
Ings Way BD8: B'frd 3G 89
BD20: Sils 2E 15
Inkerman St. BD2: B'frd 5B 72
BD4: B'frd 1B 112
Inmoor Rd. BD7: B'frd 5B 70
Inner Ring Rd. LS1: Leeds 2G 97 (2B 4)
Innings, The BD10: B'frd 1G 71
Institute Rd. BD2: B'frd 4A 72
INTAKE 5C 74
Intake BD22: Keigh 1E 47
Intake, The LS25: Kip 4H 123
Intake Gro. BD2: B'frd 1A 92
Intake La. BD2: B'frd 1A 92
BD20: Stee 1A 32
BD22: Oxen 3A 84
LS10: Leeds 4A 140
LS13: Leeds 6B 74
LS14: T'ner 4F 63
LS19: Yead 4H 55
LS28: Leeds 6B 74
WF17: Bat 6B 136
Intake Mt. LS10: Leeds 3A 140
Intake Rd. BD2: B'frd 1A 92
LS28: Pud 3B 94
Intake Sq. LS10: Leeds 3A 140
Intake Ter. BD2: B'frd 2A 92
Intake Vw. LS10: Leeds 3A 140
LS13: Leeds 6C 74
Intercity Way LS13: Leeds 2B 94
Intermezzo Dr. LS10: Leeds 4F 119
Invargarry Cl. LS25: Gar 3H 103
Inverness Rd. LS25: Gar 4H 103
Invertrees Av. LS19: Yead 3G 55
Iona Pl. HX3: Hal 5G 129
(off Iona St.)
Iona St. HX3: Hal 5G 129
Iqbal Ct. BD3: B'frd 5B 92
Ireland Cres. LS16: Leeds 4H 57
Ireland St. BD16: Bgly 4A 50
Ireland Ter. BD16: Bgly 4A 50
IRELAND WOOD 6H 57

Ireton St. BD7: B'frd 5B 90
Irish La. BD22: Keigh 5A 46
Iron Row LS29: Burl W 2F 21
(Back La.)
LS29: Burl W 1F 21
(Gt. Pasture La.)
Ironwood App.
LS14: Leeds 6C 80
Ironwood Cres.
LS14: Leeds 6C 80
Ironwood Vw. LS14: Leeds 5C 80
Irvine St. HX1: Hal 4D 148
Irving Ter. BD14: B'frd 2E 109
Irwell St. BD8: B'frd 6G 91
Irwin App. LS15: Leeds 4B 100
Irwin St. LS28: Pud 1H 93
(not continuous)
Isaac St. BD8: B'frd 3B 90
Isabella Rd. LS25: Gar 3H 103
Islay Cl. LS26: Rothw 2B 142
Isle La. BD22: Oxen 4C 84
Isles St. BD8: B'frd 3H 89
ISLINGTON 1D 116
Ivanhoe Rd. BD7: B'frd 6B 90
Ivegate BD1: B'frd 4E 91 (4C 6)
LS19: Yead 6F 41
Ive Ho. La. HX2: Hal 1E 147
Iveson App. LS16: Leeds 5H 57
Iveson Cl. LS16: Leeds 5H 57
Iveson Ct. LS16: Leeds 5H 57
Iveson Cres. LS16: Leeds 5H 57
Iveson Dr. LS16: Leeds 5H 57
Iveson Gdns. LS16: Leeds 5H 57
Iveson Gth. LS16: Leeds 5A 58
Iveson Grn. LS16: Leeds 5H 57
Iveson Gro. LS16: Leeds 5H 57
Iveson Lawn LS16: Leeds 5A 58
Iveson Ri. LS16: Leeds 5A 58
Iveson Rd. LS16: Leeds 5H 57
Ives St. BD17: Ship 1B 70
(not continuous)
Ivey Way BD18: Ship 2A 70
Ivory St. LS10: Leeds 6A 98
Ivy Av. LS9: Leeds 3E 99
Ivy Bank BD12: B'frd 3C 132
Ivy Bank Ct. BD17: Bail 5D 52
(off Dewhirst Cl.)
Ivy Bank La. BD22: Haw 3C 64
Ivy Chase LS28: Pud 3D 94
Ivy Cotts. HX1: Hal 4E 149
(off Ivy St.)
Ivy Ct. LS7: Leeds 3B 78
LS29: I'ly 6D 10
Ivy Cres. HX3: Hal 2G 151
LS9: Leeds 3E 99
Ivy Gdns. LS13: Leeds 5F 75
Ivy Gth. LS7: Leeds 3B 78
Ivy Gro. BD18: Ship 2G 69
LS9: Leeds 4F 99
Ivy Ho. Rd. BD5: B'frd 3E 111
Ivy La. BD15: B'frd 2C 88
HX2: Hal 1B 128
LS9: Leeds 3E 99
Ivy Mt. HX3: Hal 1H 159
LS9: Leeds 3E 99
Ivy Pl. BD2: B'frd 5H 71
LS13: Leeds 5F 75
Ivy Rd. BD18: Ship 2G 69
BD21: Keigh 1C 48
LS9: Leeds 4E 99
Ivy St. BD21: Keigh 5H 33
HD6: Brigh 6H 151
HX1: Hal 4E 149
LS9: Leeds 3E 99
Ivy St. Sth. BD21: Keigh 4H 47
HX1: Hal 4E 149
Ivy Ter. BD6: B'frd 6B 110
BD21: Keigh 1D 48
HD6: Brigh 6H 151
(off Ivy St.)
HX1: Hal 4E 149
(off Ivy St.)
HX3: Hal 2G 151

Ivy Vw. LS9: Leeds 3E **99**
Ivy View Studios *3E 99*
(off Ivy Vw.)

J

Jacana Way BD6: B'frd 4E **109**
Jackdaw Cl. BD15: B'frd 4D **88**
Jackdaw La. LS23: B Spa 3A **30**
Jackie Smart Ct. LS7: Leeds 6C **78**
Jackie Smart Rd. BD5: B'frd ...1E **111**
Jack La. LS10: Leeds 1C **118**
(Oval, The)
LS10: Leeds 6A **98**
(Parkfield St.)
LS11: Leeds 6H **97**
(Nineveh Rd.)
LS11: Leeds 6A **98**
(Parkfield St.)
Jackman Dr. LS18: H'fth 1F **75**
Jackroyd HX3: Hal 5D **128**
Jackson Av. LS8: Leeds 2D **78**
Jackson Hill BD13: B'frd 6B **108**
(not continuous)
Jackson Rd. LS7: Leeds 6A **78**
Jackson St. BD3: B'frd ...5G **91** (6H **7**)
Jacky La. BD22: Haw 3C **64**
Jacobs Ct. LS5: Leeds 6B **76**
Jacobs Cft. BD14: B'frd 1D **108**
Jacobs La. BD22: Haw 1D **64**
Jacob St. BD5: B'frd 1D **110**
LS2: Leeds 2A **98** (2F **5**)
Jacobs Well BD1: B'frd ...5E **91** (5D **6**)
Jacques Fold BD20: Sils 2F **15**
Jacques Gro. BD20: Sils 2F **15**
Jail Yd. LS26: Rothw 2B **142**
Jakeman Ct. WF3: E Ard 1E **155**
Jakeman Ct. WF3: E Ard 1E **155**
Jakeman Dr. WF3: E Ard 1E **155**
Jakeman Fold WF3: E Ard 1E **155**
James Av. BD20: Stee 6A **14**
LS8: Leeds 1D **78**
James Baillie Pk. LS6: Leeds ...4F **77**
James Cl. LS25: Gar 4H **103**
James Ct. LS22: Coll *3B 28*
(off Station La.)
LS27: Morl *2C 138*
(off Harold Gdns.)
James Ga. BD1: B'frd 4E **91** (4C **6**)
James St. BD1: B'frd 4E **91** (3C **6**)
BD11: B'frd 1E **135**
BD13: B'frd 5H **87**
BD15: B'frd 2E **89**
BD22: Keigh 5B **46**
HD6: Brigh 5A **152**
HX5: Ell 5B **160**
LS19: Yead 3F **55**
James St. E. BD21: Keigh 1A **48**
James St. Mkt. BD1: B'frd 3C **6**
Jamie Cl. BD10: B'frd 3B **72**
Jane Grn. HX2: Hal 3B **106**
Jane Hills *BD17: Ship* *1A 70*
(off Riverside Est.)
Jane St. BD13: B'frd 2B **86**
BD18: Ship 1H **69**
BD22: Haw *2D 64*
(off Park St.)
Janesway LS25: Kip 3F **123**
Janet St. BD22: Haw 1E **65**
Japonica Way BD3: B'frd 2A **92**
Jaques Cl. LS6: Leeds 5B **76**
Jardine Rd. BD16: Bgly 4C **50**
Jardine St. BD16: Bgly 4C **50**
Jarratt St. BD8: B'frd 2B **90**
Jarratt St. E. BD8: B'frd 2B **90**
Jarrom Cl. BD4: B'frd 1B **112**
Jarvis Sq. WF3: Rothw 4E **141**
Jarvis Wlk. WF3: Rothw 4E **141**
Jasmine Gdns. HX1: Hal 3D **148**
Jasmin Ter. BD8: B'frd 3C **90**
Jasper St. BD10: B'frd 1H **71**
HX1: Hal 2D **148**
Javelin Cl. BD10: B'frd 3H **71**

JAW HILL 6G **155**
Jay Ho. La. HD6: Brigh 4C **152**
Jay St. BD22: Haw 2D **64**
(not continuous)
Jean Av. LS15: Leeds 4C **100**
Jemmy La. HX3: Hal 2C **164**
Jenkinson Cl. LS11: Leeds 6G **97**
Jenkinson Lawn LS11: Leeds ...6G **97**
Jenkinsons Pl. LS10: Leeds 5B **118**
Jennetts Cres. LS21: Otley 4D **22**
Jennings Cl. BD20: Sils 3F **15**
Jennings Pl. BD7: B'frd 1A **110**
Jennings St. BD7: B'frd 1A **110**
Jenny La. BD17: Bail 3D **52**
Jepson La. HX5: Ell 5B **160**
Jer Gro. BD7: B'frd 3G **109**
Jer La. BD7: B'frd 3G **109**
Jermyn St. BD1: B'frd 4F **91** (3F **7**)
Jerry Clay La. WF2: Wake 6B **156**
Jerry La. BD20: Sils 2D **16**
HX6: Hal 6G **147**
Jerry Spring Rd. HX2: Hal 3D **146**
Jersey Cl. WF12: Dew 6A **154**
Jerusalem Farm Camp Site
HX2: Hal 3D **126**
Jerusalem La. HX2: Hal 3C **126**
Jervaulx Cl. LS23: B Spa 4A **30**
Jervaulx Cres. BD8: B'frd ..3C **90** (1A **6**)
Jerwood Hill Cl. HX3: Hal 6H **129**
Jerwood Hill Rd. HX3: Hal 6H **129**
Jesmond Av. BD9: B'frd 1H **89**
Jesmond Gro. BD9: B'frd 1H **89**
Jessamine Av. LS11: Leeds 4F **117**
Jesse St. BD5: B'frd 6E **91**
BD8: B'frd 4F **89**
Jessop Row LS12: Leeds 4A **96**
Jester Pl. BD13: B'frd 3G **107**
Jewitt La. LS22: Coll 5B **28**
Jew La. BD22: Oxen 1C **84**
Jilley Royd La. HD2: Hud 6A **162**
(not continuous)
Jill Kilner Dr. LS29: Burl W 3D **20**
Jim Allen La. HX2: Hal 6C **126**
Jim Laker Pl. BD18: Ship 2H **69**
Jimmy Gees 1H **69**
Jinnah Ct. BD8: B'frd 3D **90** (1A **6**)
Jinny Moor La. LS26: Swil 5G **121**
Joba Av. BD3: B'frd 4H **91**
Joe Dean Recreation Cen. 4H **95**
Joffre Mt. *LS19: Yead* *1G 55*
(off Springwell Cl.)
John Charles Way LS12: Leeds ..1D **116**
John Escritt Rd. BD16: Bgly 5C **50**
John Gilmour Way LS29: Burl W ..3D **20**
John Hanson Ct. BD13: B'frd ...5C **86**
John Naylor La. HX2: Hal 4E **147**
John Nelson Cl. WF17: Bat 6B **136**
Johnny La. LS21: Otley 5E **23**
JOHN O'GAUNTS 6B **120**
John O'Gaunts Trad. Est.
LS26: Rothw 6A **120**
John O'Gaunts Wlk.
LS26: Rothw 1B **142**
John Ormsby VC Way
WF12: Dew 6A **154**
Johns Av. WF3: Wake 3G **157**
John Smeaton Sports Cen. 6G **81**
Johnson St. BD3: B'frd 4B **92**
BD16: Bgly 3B **50**
Johnsons St. LS29: Burl W 2F **21**
Johnson Ter. LS27: Morl 3B **138**
Johnston St. LS6: Leeds 6H **77**
John St. BD1: B'frd 4E **91** (3C **6**)
BD4: B'frd 4C **112**
BD13: B'frd 2B **86**
(Longlands La.)
BD13: B'frd 5H **87**
(Lwr. Kipping La.)
BD13: B'frd 3B **66**
(Old La.)
BD14: B'frd 1E **109**
BD17: Bail 6C **52**
BD18: Ship 1A **70**
BD22: Keigh 5D **46**

John St. HD6: Brigh 6A **152**
HX1: Hal 2G **149** (4B **164**)
HX4: Hal 4G **159**
HX5: Ell 5B **160**
LS6: Leeds 6E **77**
LS19: Yead 3F **55**
WF17: Bat 6A **136**
John St. W. HX6: Hal 5H **147**
John William St. BD19: Cleck ...6B **134**
HX5: Ell 5B **160**
Jonathan Gth. LS29: Add 1C **8**
Jonscroft BD13: B'frd 6H **107**
Jordan Rd. LS28: Pud 1C **94**
Jordan Way BD2: B'frd 2A **92**
Joseph Av. HX3: Hal 5C **130**
Joseph Crossley's Almshouses
HX1: Hal 3F **149**
Joseph St. BD1: B'frd 6G **91** (4G **7**)
(not continuous)
BD4: B'frd 4C **112**
LS10: Leeds 1C **118**
Joseph's Well LS3: Leeds 3B **4**
Joseph Wright Ct. *BD10: B'frd* ..*6G 53*
(off Greenfield La.)
Jowett Pk. Cres. BD10: B'frd ...5G **53**
Jowett St. BD1: B'frd 4C **90** (3A **6**)
Jowett Ter. LS27: Morl 5A **138**
Jowler HX2: Hal 3D **126**
Jubilee Av. WF1: Wake 5G **157**
Jubilee Cl. BD18: Ship 1C **70**
LS27: Morl *3B 138*
(off Marshall St.)
Jubilee Cres. BD11: B'frd 6C **114**
WF1: Wake 5G **157**
Jubilee Cft. BD11: B'frd 6B **114**
Jubilee Dr. BD21: Keigh 2G **47**
Jubilee Mt. HD6: Brigh 1H **161**
Jubilee Pl. LS27: Morl 3B **138**
Jubilee Rd. HX3: Hal 1H **159**
Jubilee St. BD8: B'frd 2D **90** (1B **6**)
HX3: Hal 3H **149**
LS27: Morl 3B **138**
Jubilee St. Nth. HX3: Hal 4E **129**
Jubilee Ter. *HX3: Hal* *3H 149*
(off Jubilee St.)
LS27: Morl 3B **138**
Jubilee Trees LS29: Burl W 4C **20**
Jubilee Way BD18: Ship 1D **70**
Julian Dr. BD13: B'frd 3E **109**
Jumb Beck Cl. LS29: Burl W 3F **21**
Jumble Dyke HD6: Brigh 3H **161**
Jumbles, The BD12: B'frd 4C **132**
Jumbles Ct. WF3: Rothw 6G **141**
Jumbles La. WF3: Rothw 6G **141**
Jumples HX2: Hal 3B **128**
Jumples Cl. HX2: Hal 3B **128**
Jumples Ct. HX2: Hal 3A **128**
Jumples Crag HX2: Hal 3B **128**
Junction 1 Retail Pk.
LS11: Leeds 3D **116**
Junction Rd. BD17: Ship 1C **70**
Junction Row *BD2: B'frd* *5H 71*
(off Bolton Rd.)
Junction St. LS10: Leeds 5A **98**
Junction Ter. *BD2: B'frd* *5H 71*
(off Bolton Rd.)
June St. BD21: Keigh 5A **34**
Juniper Av. LS26: Rothw 6G **121**
Juniper Cl. BD8: B'frd 3B **90**
Juniper Pl. LS9: Leeds 2F **99**

K

Karnac Rd. LS8: Leeds 5D **78**
Kart Skill 5C **98**
Katherine St. BD18: Ship 1H **69**
Kaycell St. BD4: B'frd 3H **111**
Kay Cl. LS27: Morl 6H **115**
Kay St. BD18: Ship 4C **70**
KEARBY TOWN END 1A **26**
Kearsley Ter. LS10: Leeds 3C **118**
Keasden Cl. BD10: B'frd 5G **53**
Keats Gro. WF3: Wake 3H **157**

Keats Ho. LS29: I'ly 5G 11
Keble Gth. LS25: Kip 3A 124
Kedleston Rd. LS8: Leeds 5D 60
Keeble Ho. BD2: B'frd 1B 92
(off St Clare's Av.)
Keelam Ga. HX7: Wads 1A 126
Keeldar Cl. BD7: B'frd 2B 110
KEELHAM .6C 86
Keelham Dr. LS19: Yead 3G 55
Keelham La. BD20: Keigh 3G 33
Keelham Pl. BD13: B'frd 6D 86
Keel Moorings LS13: Leeds 4B 74
Keeper La. BD4: B'frd 2H 113
Keeton St. LS9: Leeds 3D 98
KEIGHLEY .6A 34
Keighley & Worth Valley Railway
Exhibition Cen. 6C 64
Keighley Bus Mus. 3C 86
Keighley Cl. HX2: Hal 1B 128
Keighley Cougars RLFC (Cougar Pk.)
. . . . .4B 34
Keighley Crematorium
BD22: Keigh 4A 46
Keighley Dr. HX2: Hal 2C 128
Keighley Ind. Pk. BD21: Keigh 4A 34
Keighley Leisure Cen. 5B 34
Keighley Pl. LS28: Pud 1A 94
Keighley Playhouse 6H 33
Keighley Retail Pk. BD21: Keigh . . .4A 34
Keighley Rd. BD8: B'frd 5B 70
BD9: B'frd 5B 70
BD13: B'frd 2A 66
(Ellar Carr Rd.)
BD13: B'frd 6A 66
(Manywells Brow)
BD16: B'frd 2A 66
BD16: Bgly 3D 48
(Altar La.)
BD16: Bgly 1H 49
(Croft Rd.)
BD20: I'ly 4A 18
BD20: Sils 4D 14
BD20: Stee 6D 14
BD22: Keigh 5D 46
BD22: Oxen 6C 64
HX2: Hal 4B 106
(not continuous)
HX3: Hal 2C 128
LS29: I'ly 1B 18
Keighley Station (Rail) 6B 34
Keilder Grn. BD6: B'frd 3E 109
Kelbrook Ho. BD4: B'frd 3C 112
(off Muirhead Dr.)
Kelburn Gro. BD22: Keigh 4B 46
KELCLIFFE 3B 40
Kelcliffe Av. LS20: Guis 4C 40
Kelcliffe Gro. LS20: Guis 4C 40
Kelcliffe La. LS20: Guis 3B 40
Keldholme Cl. LS13: Leeds 4A 74
Keldholme Rd. LS13: Leeds 4A 74
Keldregate HD2: Hud 6E 163
Kell Beck LS21: Otley 1D 22
Kell Butts HX2: Hal 1F 127
Kellett Av. LS12: Leeds 1C 116
Kellett Bldgs. BD12: B'frd 2D 132
Kellett Cres. LS12: Leeds 1C 116
Kellett Dr. LS12: Leeds 1C 116
Kellett Gro. LS12: Leeds 1C 116
Kellett La. LS12: Leeds 6B 96
Kellett Mt. LS12: Leeds 1C 116
Kellett Pl. LS12: Leeds 1C 116
Kellett Rd. LS12: Leeds 6B 96
Kellett Ter. LS12: Leeds 1C 116
Kellett Wlk. LS12: Leeds 1C 116
Kell La. HX2: Hal 2E 127
HX3: Hal 4B 130
Kelloe St. BD19: Cleck 6B 134
Kell St. BD16: Bgly 4C 50
Kellymoor Wlk. BD10: B'frd 2F 71
Kelmore Gro. BD6: B'frd 1G 131
Kelmscott Av. LS15: Leeds 6F 81
Kelmscott Cres. LS15: Leeds 6F 81
Kelmscott Gdns. LS15: Leeds 6F 81
Kelmscott Gth. LS15: Leeds 5G 81

Kelmscott Grn. LS15: Leeds 6F 81
Kelmscott Gro. LS15: Leeds 6F 81
Kelmscott La. LS15: Leeds 6F 81
Kelsall Av. LS6: Leeds 1E 97
Kelsall Gro. LS6: Leeds 1E 97
Kelsall Ho. BD3: B'frd 2F 7
Kelsall Pl. LS6: Leeds 1E 97
Kelsall Rd. LS6: Leeds 1E 97
Kelsall Ter. LS6: Leeds 1E 97
Kelseys Ct. HX2: Hal 1C 148
(off Stretchgate La.)
Kelsey St. HX1: Hal 1D 148
Kelso Cl. LS3: Leeds 2F 97
Kelso Gdns.
LS2: Leeds 2F 97 (1A 4)
Kelso Hgts. LS3: Leeds 1F 97
Kelso Pl. LS2: Leeds 1F 97
Kelso Rd. LS2: Leeds 1F 97 (1A 4)
Kelso St. LS2: Leeds 2F 97 (1A 4)
Kelton Ho. BD5: B'frd 3G 111
(off Spring Wood Gdns.)
Kelvin Av. HX2: Hal 2B 148
Kelvin Cres. HX2: Hal 3B 148
Kelvin Ho. BD4: B'frd 2D 112
Kelvin Pl. BD4: B'frd 6G 91
Kelvin Rd. HX5: Ell 5A 160
Kelvin Way BD2: B'frd 1A 92
Kempton Rd. LS25: Kip 3G 123
Kemsing Wlk. LS15: Leeds 1H 101
Kendal Bank LS3: Leeds 2F 97 (2A 4)
Kendal Carr LS3: Leeds 2A 4
Kendal Cl. LS3: Leeds 2F 97 (2A 4)
Kendal Dr. LS15: Leeds 4A 100
Kendal Gro. LS3: Leeds 2G 97 (2A 4)
Kendal La. LS3: Leeds 2F 97 (2A 4)
Kendall Av. BD18: Ship 2G 69
Kendal Mellor Ct. BD21: Keigh 6H 33
Kendal Ri. LS3: Leeds 3A 4
Kendal Rd. LS3: Leeds 2G 97 (2A 4)
Kendal St. BD21: Keigh 1B 48
Kendal Wlk. LS3: Leeds 2A 4
Kendell St. LS1: Leeds 4A 98 (6F 5)
Kenilworth Av. LS27: Morl 1F 137
Kenilworth Dr. HX3: Hal 3A 152
Kenilworth Gdns. LS27: Morl 6F 115
Kenilworth Rd. LS12: Leeds 6C 96
Kenilworth St. BD4: B'frd 1H 111
Kenley Av. BD6: B'frd 3A 110
Kenley Mt. BD6: B'frd 3A 110
Kenley Pde. BD7: B'frd 3H 109
Kenmore Av. BD19: Cleck 6A 134
Kenmore Cl. BD19: Cleck 6A 134
Kenmore Cres. BD6: B'frd 3A 110
BD19: Cleck 1H 153
Kenmore Dr. BD6: B'frd 3A 110
Kenmore Gro. BD6: B'frd 3A 110
BD19: Cleck 1H 153
Kenmore Rd. BD6: B'frd 3A 110
BD19: Cleck 6A 134
WF2: Wake 5D 156
Kenmore Wlk. BD6: B'frd 3A 110
Kennedy Av. HD2: Hud 6A 162
Kennedy Cl. WF12: Dew 6A 154
Kennedy Ho. BD21: Keigh 3H 47
(off Hainworth La.)
Kennels La. LS14: Coll, S'cft 5H 45
Kennerleigh Av. LS15: Leeds 2E 101
Kennerleigh Cres. LS15: Leeds 2F 101
Kennerleigh Dr. LS15: Leeds 2E 101
Kennerleigh Gdns. LS15: Leeds 2F 101
Kennerleigh Glen LS15: Leeds 2E 101
Kennerleigh Gro. LS15: Leeds 2F 101
Kennerleigh Ri. LS15: Leeds 2F 101
Kennerleigh Wlk. BD4: B'frd 3D 112
LS15: Leeds 2E 101
Kenneth St. LS11: Leeds 6F 97
Kennet La. LS25: Gar 5G 103
Kennion St. BD5: B'frd 6D 90
Kensington Cl. HX5: Ell 5E 149
Kensington Ct. LS6: Leeds 6F 77
LS10: Leeds 5D 118
Kensington Gdns. HX5: Ell 5A 160
LS10: Leeds 6D 118
Kensington Rd. HX3: Hal 5E 149

Kensington St. BD8: B'frd 2A 90
BD21: Keigh 1H 47
Kensington Ter. LS6: Leeds 6F 77
LS25: Gar 4E 103
(off Main St.)
Kensington Way LS10: Leeds 6D 118
Kenstone Cres. BD10: B'frd 2G 71
Ken Syke Cotts. WF3: E Ard 2D 154
KENT 4A 94
Kent Av. BD20: Sils 2D 14
LS28: Pud 4C 94
Kent Cl. LS28: Pud 4C 94
Kent Cres. LS28: Pud 4C 94
Kent Dr. LS28: Pud 4C 94
Kentmere BD2: B'frd 3F 71
Kentmere App. LS14: Leeds 4A 80
Kentmere Av. BD12: Cleck 6E 133
LS14: Leeds 2B 80
LS25: Gar 5H 103
Kentmere Cl. LS14: Leeds 4C 80
Kentmere Cres. LS14: Leeds 3B 80
Kentmere Gdns. LS14: Leeds 3B 80
Kentmere Ga. LS14: Leeds 2B 80
Kentmere Grn. LS14: Leeds 3B 80
Kentmere Ri. LS14: Leeds 4C 80
Kent M. BD16: Bgly 5D 50
Kenton Way BD4: B'frd 1B 112
Kent Rd. BD16: Bgly 5D 50
LS28: Pud 4B 94
Kent St. BD1: B'frd 5E 91 (6D 6)
HX1: Hal 3F 149 (5A 164)
Kenwood M. LS18: H'fth 1F 75
Kenworthy Cl. LS16: Leeds 2A 58
Kenworthy Gdns. LS16: Leeds 2A 58
Kenworthy Gth. LS16: Leeds 2A 58
Kenworthy Ga. LS16: Leeds 2A 58
Kenworthy Ri. LS16: Leeds 2A 58
Kenworthy Va. LS16: Leeds 2A 58
Kenya Mt. BD21: Keigh 5F 33
Kenyon La. HX2: Hal 2B 148
Kepler Gro. LS8: Leeds 1C 98
Kepler Ho. BD4: B'frd 3A 112
(off Railway St.)
Kepler Mt. LS8: Leeds 1C 98
Kepler Ter. LS8: Leeds 1C 98
Keplestone M. LS17: Leeds 1C 60
Kepstorn Cl. LS5: Leeds 4A 76
Kepstorn Ri. LS5: Leeds 4A 76
Kepstorn Rd. LS16: Leeds 2B 76
Kerry Ct. LS18: H'fth 6D 56
(off Kerry Gth.)
Kerry Gth. LS18: H'fth 6D 56
Kerry Hill LS18: H'fth 1D 74
(not continuous)
Kerry St. LS18: H'fth 6D 56
Kerry Vw. LS18: H'fth 6E 57
Kershaw Ct. HX2: Hal 1D 146
Kershaw Dr. HX2: Hal 2D 146
Kershaw St. BD3: B'frd 4B 92
Kesteven Cl. BD4: B'frd 3D 112
Kesteven Ct. BD4: B'frd 3D 112
Kesteven Rd. BD4: B'frd 3C 112
Kestrel Cl. LS17: Leeds 3D 60
Kestrel Dr. BD2: B'frd 5G 71
Kestrel Gth. LS27: Morl 3D 138
Kestrel Gro. LS17: Leeds 3D 60
Kestrel Mt. BD2: B'frd 5G 71
Kestrel Vw. BD19: Cleck 6B 134
Keswick Cl. HX3: Hal 5A 150
Keswick Grange LS17: Bard 6E 27
Keswick La. LS17: Bard 1E 45
Keswick St. BD4: B'frd 6B 92
Keswick Vw. LS17: Bard 6G 27
Kettlewell Dr. BD5: B'frd 2B 110
Keverne Ho. BD5: B'frd 1D 110
(off Hutson St.)
Khalaq Ct. BD3: B'frd 3H 91
Khus Wlk. BD21: Keigh 3A 48
Kidacre St. LS10: Leeds 5A 98
LS11: Leeds 6A 98
Kilburn Ho. BD10: B'frd 3A 72
Kilburn Rd. LS12: Leeds 4C 96
Kildare Cres. BD15: B'frd 2C 88

Kildare Ter. LS12: Leeds 5E **97**
KILLINGBECK **2A 100**
Killingbeck Bri. LS14: Leeds 2A **100**
Killingbeck Dr. LS14: Leeds 2A **100**
Killingbeck Retail Pk.
  LS14: Leeds 1A **100**
Killinghall Av. BD2: B'frd 2H **91**
Killinghall Dr. BD2: B'frd 2H **91**
Killinghall Gro. BD2: B'frd 2H **91**
Killinghall Rd. BD2: B'frd 1H **91**
  BD3: B'frd 1H **91**
Kiln Bank BD20: Keigh 3C **34**
Kilner Ho. *BD2: B'frd* *1B 92*
                (off St Clares Av.)
Kilner Rd. BD6: B'frd 4A **110**
              (not continuous)
Kilners Cft. LS29: Add 1D **8**
Kiln Fold HD6: Brigh 6D **152**
Kilnsea Mt. BD4: B'frd 2C **112**
Kilnsey Fold BD20: Sils 1D **14**
Kilnsey M. BD17: Bail 4B **52**
Kilnsey Rd. BD3: B'frd 5H **91**
Kilroyd Av. BD19: Cleck 5B **134**
Kilroyd Dr. BD19: Cleck 5C **134**
Kimberley Pl. HX3: Hal 3E **129**
  LS9: Leeds 1F **99**
Kimberley Rd. LS9: Leeds 1F **99**
Kimberley St. BD3: B'frd 5A **92**
  HD6: Brigh 6B **152**
  HX3: Hal 3E **129**
  LS29: I'ly 4E **11**
Kimberley Vw. LS9: Leeds 2F **99**
Kinara Cl. BD21: Keigh 5C **34**
Kineholme Dr. LS21: Otley 5B **22**
King Alfred's Dr. LS6: Leeds 6G **59**
King Alfred's Grn. LS6: Leeds 6G **59**
King Alfred's Wlk. LS6: Leeds 6G **59**
King Alfred's Way LS6: Leeds 6G **59**
King Charles St.
  LS1: Leeds 3A **98** (4E **5**)
King Charles Wlk. *LS1: Leeds* *4E 5*
           (in Headrow Cen., The)
Kingcliff BD15: B'frd 3F **67**
King Cl. LS17: Leeds 3G **59**
KING CROSS **4C 148**
King Cross Rd. HX1: Hal 4D **148**
King Cross St. HX1: Hal 3F **149** (5A **164**)
King Dr. LS17: Leeds 3F **59**
King Edward Av. LS18: H'fth 1D **74**
  WF10: Kip 1F **145**
King Edward Cres. LS18: H'fth 6E **57**
King Edward Rd. BD13: B'frd 5H **87**
King Edward St.
  HX1: Hal 2G **149** (4C **164**)
  LS1: Leeds 3A **98** (4F **5**)
  LS29: Burl W 2F **21**
King Edward Ter. BD13: B'frd 5H **87**
King Edwins Ct. LS8: Leeds 4E **79**
Kingfield LS20: Guis 3D **40**
Kingfisher Cl. LS17: Leeds 3D **60**
Kingfisher Ct. *BD21: Keigh* *6A 34*
              (off East Pde.)
Kingfisher Gro. BD8: B'frd 4E **89**
Kingfisher M. LS27: Morl 4C **138**
Kingfisher Reach LS22: Coll 2B **28**
Kingfishers, The BD20: Sils 3E **15**
Kingfisher Way LS17: Leeds 3D **60**
King George Av. LS7: Leeds 2B **78**
  LS18: H'fth 6E **57**
  LS27: Morl 1B **138**
King George Cft. LS27: Morl 2B **138**
King George Gdns. LS7: Leeds 2B **78**
King George Gro. LS27: Morl 1B **138**
King George Rd. LS18: H'fth 6E **57**
King George St. WF1: Wake 6F **157**
King Ho. *LS29: I'ly* *5C 10*
             (off Kings Rd.)
Kings App. LS13: Leeds 1G **95**
Kings Av. LS6: Leeds 1E **97**
  LS29: I'ly 5C **10**
Kingsbury Pl. HX1: Hal 3D **148**
Kings Chase LS26: Rothw 1B **142**
Kings Cl. LS21: Otley 4G **23**
  LS29: I'ly 5A **10**

Kings Ct. BD16: Bgly 4B **50**
  HX1: Hal 3F **149** (5A **164**)
  LS17: Leeds 6A **60**
  WF17: Bat 6A **136**
Kings Cft. LS25: Gar 5D **102**
King's Cft. Gdns. LS17: Leeds 6B **60**
Kingsdale Av. BD2: B'frd 6G **71**
  BD11: B'frd 1A **136**
Kingsdale Ct. LS14: Leeds 3A **80**
             (not continuous)
Kingsdale Cres. BD2: B'frd 6G **71**
Kingsdale Dr. BD2: B'frd 6G **71**
Kingsdale Gdns. BD11: B'frd 1A **136**
Kingsdale Gro. BD2: B'frd 6F **71**
King's Dr. BD2: B'frd 3F **71**
  WF17: Bat 5A **136**
Kingsfield LS26: Rothw 2F **141**
King's Ga. BD1: B'frd 2E **91**
Kings Gro. BD16: Bgly 3C **50**
  BD21: Keigh 6G **51**
Kings Lea HX3: Hal 1F **159**
Kingsley Av. BD3: B'frd 6E **71**
  BD11: B'frd 3F **135**
  HX6: Hal 6F **147**
  LS16: Leeds 2B **58**
  WF1: Wake 4F **157**
Kingsley Cl. BD11: B'frd 3F **135**
  WF1: Wake 4F **157**
Kingsley Cres. BD11: B'frd 3F **135**
  BD17: Bail 5C **52**
Kingsley Dr. BD11: B'frd 3F **135**
  LS16: Leeds 2B **58**
Kingsley Gth. WF1: Wake 4F **157**
Kingsley Pl. HX1: Hal 3E **149**
Kingsley Rd. LS16: Leeds 2B **58**
Kingsmark Freeway BD12: B'frd . . .2F **133**
Kings Mead LS26: Rothw 1C **142**
Kingsmead LS14: Leeds 1C **80**
Kings Mdw. Cl. LS22: Weth 2D **12**
Kings Mdw. Dr. LS22: Weth 2D **12**
Kings Mdw. Gro. LS22: Weth 2D **12**
Kings Mdw. M. LS22: Weth 2D **12**
Kings Mdw. Vw. LS22: Weth 2D **12**
Kingsmill Cl. LS27: Morl 2H **137**
King's Mt. LS17: Leeds 1A **78**
Kings Pl. LS6: Leeds 5D **76**
Kings Rd. BD1: B'frd 1E **91**
  BD16: Bgly 1A **50**
  LS6: Leeds 1E **97**
  LS29: I'ly 5A **10**
Kingston Cl. BD15: B'frd 4G **67**
  HX1: Hal 3D **148**
Kingston Ct. HX1: Hal 3D **148**
Kingston Dr. HX1: Hal 3D **148**
Kingston Gdns. LS15: Leeds 1D **100**
Kingston Gro. BD10: B'frd 6H **53**
Kingston Ho. *BD10: B'frd* *3A 72*
           (off Rowantree Dr.)
Kingston Rd. BD10: B'frd 6H **53**
Kingston St. HX1: Hal 3D **148**
Kingston Ter. HX1: Hal 3D **148**
  LS2: Leeds 1H **97**
King St. BD2: B'frd 4A **72**
  BD11: B'frd 1A **136**
  BD20: Sils 2E **15**
  BD21: Keigh 1H **47**
  BD22: Haw 3C **64**
  HD6: Brigh 1B **162**
  HX1: Hal 2H **149** (3D **164**)
  HX5: Ell *5C 160*
             (off Brook St.)
  HX6: Hal 6E **147**
  LS1: Leeds 4H **97** (5C **4**)
  LS19: Yead 3E **55**
            (Alexandra Ter.)
  LS19: Yead 3E **55**
           (Micklefield La.)
  LS27: Morl 4A **138**
  LS28: Pud 2H **93**
Kings Vw. HX3: Hal 5C **150**
Kingsway BD2: B'frd 2F **71**
  BD11: B'frd 1A **136**
  BD16: Bgly 4C **50**

Kingsway BD20: Keigh 4E **35**
  LS15: Leeds 3E **101**
  LS25: Gar 5D **102**
  WF17: Bat 5A **136**
Kingsway Cl. LS17: Leeds 6B **60**
Kingsway Dr. LS29: I'ly 5C **10**
Kingsway Gth. LS25: Gar 5D **102**
Kingswear Cl. LS15: Leeds 2F **101**
Kingswear Cres. LS15: Leeds 2F **101**
Kingswear Gth. LS15: Leeds 2F **101**
Kingswear Glen LS15: Leeds 2F **101**
Kingswear Gro. LS15: Leeds 2F **101**
Kingswear Pde. LS15: Leeds 2F **101**
Kingswear Ri. LS15: Leeds 2F **101**
Kingswear Vw. LS15: Leeds 2F **101**
Kingswell Av. WF1: Wake 5G **157**
Kingswood Av. LS8: Leeds 4E **61**
Kingswood Cres. LS8: Leeds 4D **60**
Kingswood Dr. LS8: Leeds 4D **60**
Kingswood Gdns. LS8: Leeds 4D **60**
Kingswood Grn. HX3: Hal 6B **130**
Kingswood Gro. LS8: Leeds 4E **61**
Kingswood Pl. BD7: B'frd 1A **110**
Kingswood Rd. LS12: Leeds 5C **96**
Kingswood St. BD7: B'frd 1A **110**
Kingswood Ter. BD7: B'frd 1A **110**
Kinnaird Cl. HX5: Hal 3B **160**
Kinross Ho. *BD4: B'frd* *3C 112*
            (off Muirhead Dr.)
Kinsey M. *BD17: Bail* *4B 52*
            (off West La.)
Kipling Ct. BD10: B'frd 2B **72**
KIPPAX **3G 123**
KIPPAX COMMON **2F 123**
Kippax La. End LS25: Gar 6E **103**
Kippax Mt. LS9: Leeds 4D **98**
Kippax Pl. LS9: Leeds 4D **98**
Kippax Sports Cen. **5F 123**
Kipping La. BD13: B'frd 5H **87**
Kipping Pl. BD13: B'frd 5H **87**
Kirby Leas HX1: Hal 3G **149** (6B **164**)
Kirby St. BD21: Keigh 5B **34**
Kirk Beeston Cl. LS11: Leeds 3F **117**
Kirkbourne Gro. BD17: Bail 5E **53**
Kirkburn Pl. BD7: B'frd 5B **90**
Kirkby Av. LS25: Gar 6G **103**
Kirkby Gth. LS14: T'ner 1H **63**
Kirkby La. LS22: Kirkby 1A **26**
Kirkcroft BD13: B'frd 3B **86**
Kirkdale Av. LS12: Leeds 1B **116**
Kirkdale Cres. LS12: Leeds 2B **116**
Kirkdale Dr. LS12: Leeds 1B **116**
Kirkdale Gdns. LS12: Leeds 1B **116**
Kirkdale Gro. LS12: Leeds 1A **116**
Kirkdale Ho. *BD10: B'frd* *3A 72*
           (off Rowantree Dr.)
Kirkdale Mt. LS12: Leeds 2B **116**
Kirkdale Ter. LS12: Leeds 2B **116**
Kirkdale Vw. LS12: Leeds 2B **116**
Kirkdale Way BD4: B'frd 4D **112**
KIRK DEIGHTON **1D 12**
Kirk Dr. BD17: Bail 3D **52**
Kirkfield Dr. LS15: Leeds 4F **101**
Kirkfield Gdns. LS15: Leeds 4F **101**
Kirkfield La. LS14: T'ner 2H **63**
              (not continuous)
Kirkfields BD17: Bail 3E **53**
Kirkfields Ind. Cen. LS19: Yead 6E **41**
Kirkfield Vw. LS15: Leeds 4F **101**
Kirk Ga. BD11: B'frd 6D **112**
Kirkgate BD1: B'frd 4E **91** (4C **6**)
            (not continuous)
  BD18: Ship 1A **70**
  BD20: Sils 2E **15**
  LS1: Leeds 3A **98** (4F **5**)
  LS2: Leeds 4A **98** (5G **5**)
  LS21: Otley 3E **23**
              (not continuous)
  WF17: Bat 6H **135**
  WF17: Dew 6A **154**
Kirkgate Arc. LS21: Otley 4E **23**
Kirkgate Cen. BD1: B'frd 4E **91** (4C **6**)
Kirkgate Mall BD1: B'frd 4C **6**

Kirkgate Mkt. LS2: Leeds 3A 98 (4F 5)
Kirkham Av. WF2: Wake 6H 155
KIRKHAMGATE 6H 155
Kirkham Ho. BD5: B'frd 3F 111
(off Parkway)
Kirkham Rd. BD7: B'frd 6B 90
Kirkham St. LS13: Leeds 4B 74
Kirk Hills LS14: T'ner 2H 63
Kirklands LS14: T'ner 2H 63
Kirklands Av. BD13: B'frd 5A 88
BD17: Bail 4E 53
Kirklands Cl. BD17: Bail 5E 53
LS19: Yead 6E 41
LS29: Men 1G 39
Kirklands Gdns. BD17: Bail 4E 53
Kirklands La. BD17: Bail 4E 53
Kirklands Rd. BD17: Bail 4D 52
Kirkland Vs. LS28: Pud 5A 94
Kirk La. HX3: Hal 1E 151
LS19: Yead 6D 40
Kirklees Cl. LS28: Pud 5H 73
Kirklees Cft. LS28: Pud 5H 73
Kirklees Dr. LS28: Pud 5H 73
Kirklees Gth. LS28: Pud 5H 73
Kirklees Ri. LS28: Pud 5H 73
Kirklees Rd. BD15: B'frd 4D 88
Kirkley Av. BD12: B'frd 6C 132
KIRKSTALL 5A 76
Kirkstall Abbey (Remains) 4H 75
Kirkstall Av. LS5: Leeds 6H 75
Kirkstall Brewery LS5: Leeds 5H 75
(off Broad La.)
Kirkstall Gro. BD8: B'frd 4F 89
Kirkstall Hill LS4: Leeds 5B 76
LS5: Leeds 5B 76
Kirkstall Ind. Pk. LS4: Leeds 2D 96
Kirkstall La. LS5: Leeds 5A 76
LS6: Leeds 5A 76
Kirkstall Leisure Cen. 5A 76
Kirkstall Mt. LS5: Leeds 6H 75
Kirkstall Rd. LS3: Leeds 3F 97
LS4: Leeds 3F 97
Kirkstall Valley Nature Reserve . . .1B 96
Kirkstall Valley Retail Pk.
LS5: Leeds 6A 76
Kirkstone Dr. HX2: Hal 1H 147
Kirkwall Av. LS9: Leeds 4F 99
Kirkwall Dr. BD4: B'frd 2C 112
Kirkwood Av. LS16: Leeds 3F 57
Kirkwood Cl. LS16: Leeds 2F 57
Kirkwood Cres. LS16: Leeds 2G 57
Kirkwood Dr. LS16: Leeds 2F 57
Kirkwood Gdns. LS16: Leeds 2G 57
Kirkwood Gro. LS16: Leeds 3F 57
WF3: E Ard 1F 155
Kirkwood La. LS16: Leeds 2F 57
Kirkwood Ri. LS16: Leeds 2G 57
Kirkwood Vw. LS16: Leeds 2G 57
Kirkwood Way LS16: Leeds 2G 57
Kismet Gdns. BD3: B'frd 3A 92
Kitchener Av. LS9: Leeds 2F 99
Kitchener Gro. LS9: Leeds 1F 99
Kitchener Mt. LS9: Leeds 2F 99
Kitchener Pl. LS9: Leeds 2F 99
Kitchener St. BD12: B'frd 2G 133
LS9: Leeds 2F 99
LS26: Rothw 1E 143
Kite M. BD8: B'frd 4E 89
Kitson Cl. LS12: Leeds 5C 96
Kitson Gdns. LS12: Leeds 5C 96
Kitson La. HX6: Hal 2B 158
Kitson Rd. LS10: Leeds 6B 98
Kitson St. BD18: Ship 3C 70
LS9: Leeds 4D 98
WF3: E Ard 6D 138
Kitten Clough HX2: Hal 6C 128
Kitty Fold LS29: Add 1D 8
Kitwood Cl. BD4: B'frd 3D 112
Kliffen Pl. HX3: Hal 5H 149
Knavesmire LS26: Rothw 2F 141
Knightsbridge Ct. HD6: Brigh 6A 152
Knightsbridge Wlk. BD4: B'frd 6H 111
Knights Cl. LS15: Leeds 3E 101
Knights Cft. LS22: Weth 2F 13

Knightscroft Av. LS26: Rothw 1A 142
Knightscroft Dr. LS26: Rothw 1A 142
Knight's Fold BD7: B'frd 1A 110
Knightshill LS15: Leeds 3F 101
Knight St. HX1: Hal 3D 148
Knightsway LS15: Leeds 2E 101
LS25: Gar 6D 102
WF3: Rothw 5F 141
Knightsway Ct. BD3: B'frd 2D 92
Knoll, The LS28: Pud 1E 93
Knoll Gdns. BD17: Bail 6B 52
Knoll Pk. WF3: E Ard 2B 156
Knoll Pk. Dr. BD17: Bail 6B 52
Knoll Ter. BD17: Bail 6B 52
Knoll Vw. BD17: Bail 5B 52
Knoll Wood Pk. LS18: H'fth 1F 75
Knostrop La. LS9: Leeds 1F 119
KNOTFORD 2A 24
Knott La. LS19: Yead 1H 73
Knowle Av. LS4: Leeds 6D 76
Knowle Gro. LS4: Leeds 6D 76
Knowle La. BD21: Keigh 5D 132
Knowle Mt. LS4: Leeds 6D 76
KNOWLE PARK 2G 47
Knowle Pl. LS4: Leeds 6D 76
Knowle Rd. LS4: Leeds 6D 76
Knowles Av. BD4: B'frd 3B 112
Knowles La. BD4: B'frd 3A 112
BD19: Cleck 4F 135
Knowle Spring Rd. BD21: Keigh 3H 47
(Foster Rd.)
BD21: Keigh 2H 47
(Selborne Gro.)
Knowles Rd. HD6: Brigh 3A 162
Knowles St. BD4: B'frd 3A 112
BD13: B'frd 3B 86
Knowles Vw. BD4: B'frd 3B 112
Knowle Ter. LS4: Leeds 1C 96
Knowle Top Dr. HX3: Hal 1G 151
Knowle Top Rd. HX3: Hal 1G 151
Knowsley St. BD3: B'frd 4G 91 (4H 7)
KNOWSTHORPE 6C 98
Knowsthorpe Cres. LS9: Leeds 5D 98
Knowsthorpe Ga. LS9: Leeds 1F 119
Knowsthorpe La. LS9: Leeds, Swil . .6D 98
(not continuous)
Knowsthorpe Rd. LS9: Leeds 6G 99
Knowsthorpe Way LS9: Leeds 1F 119
Knox St. LS13: Leeds 4H 73
Knutsford Gro. BD4: B'frd 3C 112
Komla Cl. BD1: B'frd 3F 7
Kyffin Av. LS15: Leeds 4A 100
Kyffin Pl. BD4: B'frd 6C 92

L

LA Bowl 6H 97
Laburnum Cl. WF3: E Ard 2A 156
Laburnum Dr. BD17: Bail 3D 52
Laburnum Gro. BD19: Cleck 6E 135
BD22: Haw 1E 65
HX3: Hal 3A 152
Laburnum Pl. BD8: B'frd 2C 90
BD10: B'frd 1C 72
Laburnum Rd. BD18: Ship 4D 70
Laburnum St. BD8: B'frd 2C 90
LS28: Pud 2H 93
(New St.)
LS28: Pud 3G 93
(Oak St.)
Laburnum Ter. HX3: Hal 5A 132
(off Village St.)
Laceby Cl. BD10: B'frd 1A 72
Lacey Gro. LS22: Weth 5F 13
Lacey M. BD4: B'frd 3A 112
Lacy Way HX5: Ell 3C 160
Ladbroke Gro. BD4: B'frd 4C 112
Ladderbanks La. BD17: Bail 3D 52
(not continuous)
Ladstone Towers HX6: Hal 5H 147
Ladybeck Cl. LS2: Leeds 3B 98 (3G 5)
Lady Fld. BD13: B'frd 5H 87
(off West La.)

Lady in Trim 4C 100
Lady La. BD16: Bgly 1C 50
LS2: Leeds 3A 98 (4F 5)
Lady Pk. Av. BD16: Bgly 1C 50
Lady Pk. Ct. LS17: Leeds 3D 60
Lady Pit La. LS11: Leeds 1H 117
(not continuous)
Ladyroyd Dr. BD4: B'frd 1C 134
Ladysmith Rd. BD13: B'frd 5G 107
Ladywell Cl. BD5: B'frd 2E 111
Ladywell La. WF15: Liv 6H 153
LADY WOOD 2G 79
Ladywood Grange LS8: Leeds 3H 79
Ladywood Mead LS8: Leeds 3H 79
Ladywood Rd. LS8: Leeds 3F 79
Ladywood Ter. HX1: Hal 1E 149
LA Fitness 5E 5
Lairum Ri. LS23: B Spa 6B 30
LAISERDYKE 4B 92
Laisterdyke BD4: B'frd 5B 92
Laisteridge La. BD5: B'frd 5C 90
BD7: B'frd 5C 90 (6A 6)
Laith Cl. LS16: Leeds 4H 57
Laithe Cl. BD20: Sils 1E 15
Laithe Fld. HX4: Hal 6B 158
Laithe Gro. BD6: B'frd 4A 110
Laithe Rd. BD6: B'frd 4B 110
Laith Gdns. LS16: Leeds 4A 58
Laith Gth. LS16: Leeds 4H 57
Laith Grn. LS16: Leeds 4H 57
Laith Rd. LS16: Leeds 4H 57
Laith Wlk. LS16: Leeds 4H 57
Lakeland Ct. LS15: Leeds 5H 99
Lakeland Cres. LS17: Leeds 1G 59
Lakeland Dr. LS17: Leeds 1H 59
Lake Row BD4: B'frd 6H 91
Lakeside BD20: Keigh 3A 36
Lakeside Chase LS19: Yead 3G 55
Lakeside Cl. LS29: I'ly 4C 10
Lakeside Ct. LS10: Leeds 3B 118
Lakeside Gdns. LS19: Yead 3G 55
Lakeside Ind. Est. LS12: Leeds 4G 95
Lakeside Rd. LS12: Leeds 5G 95
Lakeside Ter. LS19: Yead 3G 55
Lakeside Vw. LS19: Yead 3G 55
Lakeside Wlk. LS19: Yead 3G 55
(off Lakeside Ter.)
Lake St. BD4: B'frd 6H 91
BD21: Keigh 4C 34
Lake Ter. LS10: Leeds 3B 118
Lake Vw. HX3: Hal 1F 149 (1A 164)
Lakeview Ct. LS8: Leeds 1G 79
Lamb Cote Rd. HD2: Hud 5D 162
Lambert Av. LS8: Leeds 3D 78
Lambert Cl. HX4: Hal 4H 159
Lambert Dr. LS8: Leeds 3D 78
Lambert Pl. BD2: B'frd 1H 91
(off Thirlmere Gdns.)
Lambert's Arc. LS1: Leeds 5F 5
Lambert St. HX4: Hal 4H 159
Lamberts Yd. LS26: Rothw 2A 142
Lambert Ter. LS18: H'fth 1G 75
(off Low La.)
LS18: H'fth 1C 74
(Park Side)
Lambourne Av. BD10: B'frd 4B 72
Lambrigg Cres. LS14: Leeds 5C 80
Lamb Springs La. BD17: Bail 1G 53
Lambton Gro. LS8: Leeds 5D 78
Lambton Pl. LS8: Leeds 5D 78
Lambton St. LS8: Leeds 5D 78
Lambton Ter. LS8: Leeds 5D 78
Lambton Vw. LS8: Leeds 5D 78
Lammas Ct. LS14: S'cft 6D 44
Lampards Cl. BD15: B'frd 1C 88
Lanark Dr. LS18: H'fth 3D 56
Lancaster Ct. BD21: Keigh 2H 47
(off Rutland St.)
Lancaster Pl. LS26: Rothw 3B 142
(off Springfield St.)
Lancastre Av. LS5: Leeds 6H 75
(not continuous)
Lancastre Gro. LS5: Leeds 6H 75
Lancefield Ho. WF1: Wake 4F 157

Lancet Ri.—Launton Way

Lancet Ri. WF3: Rothw 4E 141
Landemere Syke HX3: Hal 3C 130
Landford Ho. *BD5: B'frd 1D 110*
(off Park La.)
Landmark Ct. LS11: Leeds 2F 117
Landmark Ho. BD1: B'frd 4D 6
Landor St. BD21: Keigh 5B 34
Landscove Av. BD4: B'frd 3C 112
Landseer Av. LS13: Leeds 6G 75
WF3: E Ard 1E 155
Landseer Cl. LS13: Leeds 6F 75
Landseer Cres. LS13: Leeds 6G 75
Landseer Dr. LS13: Leeds 6F 75
Landseer Gdns. LS13: Leeds 6F 75
Landseer Grn. LS13: Leeds 6F 75
Landseer Gro. LS13: Leeds 6G 75
Landseer Mt. LS13: Leeds 6G 75
Landseer Ri. LS13: Leeds 6F 75
Landseer Rd. LS13: Leeds 6F 75
Landseer Ter. LS13: Leeds 6G 75
Landseer Vw. LS13: Leeds 6G 75
Landseer Wlk. *LS13: Leeds 6F 75*
(off Landseer Cl.)
Landseer Way LS13: Leeds 6F 75
Lands Head La. HX3: Hal 3B 130
Landsholme Ct. BD4: B'frd 3D 112
Lands La. BD10: B'frd 4A 72
LS1: Leeds 3A 98 (4E 5)
LS20: Guis 4C 40
Landsmoor Gro. BD16: Bgly 2D 50
Land St. LS28: Pud 6H 73
Lane, The LS9: Leeds 4C 98
LS17: Leeds 2F 59
Lane Ct. *HD6: Brigh 6B 152*
(off Old La.)
LANE END 1E 109
Lane End BD13: B'frd 5H 87
BD14: B'frd 2E 109
(off Station Rd.)
BD16: Bgly 6F 49
(off Spring Row)
BD17: Bail 4C 52
LS28: Pud 3B 94
(not continuous)
Lane End Ct. LS17: Leeds 2F 59
Lane End Cft. LS17: Leeds 2F 59
Lane End Fold LS28: Pud 3B 94
Lane End Mt. LS28: Pud 3B 94
Lane End Pl. LS11: Leeds 6H 97
LANE ENDS
Keighley 5B 46
Leeds 4B 56
Lane Ends HX2: Hal 2G 147
(Abbey La.)
HX2: Hal 6D 126
(Pin Hill La.)
HX3: Hal 5E 131
(Denholme Ga. Rd.)
HX3: Hal 1E 151
(Halifax Rd.)
HX3: Hal 5C 128
(Long La.)
HX6: Hal 5B 146
(Moor Bottom La.)
HX6: Hal 6A 148
(Spark Ho. La.)
Lane Ends Cl. BD8: B'frd 3H 89
Lane Ends Grn. HX3: Hal 1D 150
Lane Fox Ct. *LS19: Yead 1F 55*
(off Harper La.)
LANE HEAD 6H 151
Lane Head La. HX2: Hal 5A 106
Lane Ho. Gro. HX2: Hal 1E 147
Lanes, The LS28: Pud 3B 94
(not continuous)
Lane Side BD12: B'frd 3B 132
BD13: B'frd 2G 107
BD15: B'frd 5F 67
LS12: Leeds 1D 114
Laneside LS27: Morl 6B 116
Laneside Cl. LS27: Morl 6B 116
Laneside Fold LS27: Morl 6B 116
Laneside Gdns. LS27: Morl 6B 116
Laneside M. LS27: Morl 6B 116
Laneside Ter. LS27: Morl 6B 116
Lane Top BD13: B'frd 1B 86
Langbar App. LS14: Leeds 3F 81
Langbar Av. BD9: B'frd 6F 69
Langbar Cl. LS14: Leeds 3F 81
Langbar Gdns. LS14: Leeds 4F 81
Langbar Gth. LS14: Leeds 3F 81
Langbar Grange LS14: Leeds 4F 81
Langbar Grn. LS14: Leeds 3F 81
Langbar Gro. LS14: Leeds 4F 81
Langbar Pl. LS14: Leeds 3F 81
Langbar Rd. LS14: Leeds 4F 81
LS29: I'ly 3C 10
Langbar Sq. LS14: Leeds 4F 81
Langbar Towers *LS14: Leeds 4F 81*
(off Swarcliffe Av.)
Langbar Vw. LS14: Leeds 3F 81
Langdale Av. BD8: B'frd 3G 89
BD12: Cleck 6E 133
LS6: Leeds 4C 76
WF1: Wake 4H 157
Langdale Cl. LS22: Weth 3C 12
Langdale Ct. BD16: Bgly 3C 50
Langdale Cres. HX2: Hal 6C 128
Langdale Dr. BD13: B'frd 4H 107
Langdale Gdns. LS6: Leeds 5C 76
Langdale Rd. BD10: B'frd 5C 72
LS26: Rothw 1D 142
Langdales HX6: Hal 5G 147
Langdale St. HX5: Ell 5B 160
Langdale Ter. LS6: Leeds 5C 76
Langela Ter. HX3: Hal 1E 151
Langford Cl. LS29: Burl W 2E 21
Langford Ct. LS29: Burl W 2D 20
Langford La. LS29: Burl W 2E 21
Langford M. LS29: Burl W 2E 21
Langford Ride LS29: Burl W 2F 21
Langford Rd. LS29: Burl W 2E 21
Langlands Rd. BD16: Bgly 2C 68
Lang La. BD2: B'frd 4D 70
LANGLEY 1F 157
Langley Av. BD4: B'frd 4H 111
BD16: Bgly 3C 50
LS13: Leeds 5C 74
Langley Cl. LS13: Leeds 5C 74
Langley Cres. BD17: Bail 4E 53
LS13: Leeds 5D 74
Langley Gth. LS13: Leeds 5C 74
Langley Gro. BD16: Bgly 3C 50
Langley La. BD17: Bail 3E 53
Langley Mt. LS13: Leeds 5D 74
Langley Pl. LS13: Leeds 5C 74
Langley Rd. BD16: Bgly 3C 50
LS13: Leeds 5C 74
Langley Ter. LS13: Leeds 5C 74
Langport Cl. BD13: B'frd 4B 108
Langsett Cft. HD2: Hud 6E 163
Langthorne Ct. LS27: Morl 5C 138
Langton Av. BD4: B'frd 4H 111
Langton Cl. BD19: Cleck 5F 135
Langton Grn. LS12: Leeds 6C 96
Langton St. HX6: Hal 4H 147
Langtons Wharf LS2: Leeds 6G 5
Langwith Av. LS22: Coll 3A 28
Langwith Dr. LS22: Coll 3G 27
Langwith M. LS22: Coll 3A 28
Langwith Ter. LS22: Coll 3H 27
Langwith Valley Rd. LS22: Coll 3G 27
(not continuous)
Lanrick Ho. *BD4: B'frd 1C 112*
(off Broadstone Way)
Lansdale Ct. BD4: B'frd 3D 112
Lansdowne Cl. BD17: Bail 4F 53
Lansdowne Ho. *BD8: B'frd 2C 90*
(off Trenton Dr.)
Lansdowne Pl. BD5: B'frd 5D 90 (6B 6)
Lansdowne St. LS12: Leeds 5C 96
Lanshaw Cl. LS10: Leeds 1C 140
Lanshaw Cres. LS10: Leeds 2C 140
Lanshaw Pl. LS10: Leeds 1C 140
Lanshaw Rd. LS10: Leeds 1C 140
Lanshaw Ter. LS10: Leeds 1C 140
Lanshaw Vw. LS10: Leeds 1C 140
Lanshaw Wlk. LS10: Leeds 1C 140
Lapage St. BD3: B'frd 4A 92
Lapage Ter. BD3: B'frd 5A 92
Lapwing Cl. BD8: B'frd 4D 88
Larch Cl. BD22: Keigh 5D 46
WF17: Bat 5C 136
Larch Dr. BD6: B'frd 6C 110
Larchfield Home LS10: Leeds 1C 118
Larchfield Rd. LS10: Leeds 6C 98
Larch Gro. BD16: Bgly 2C 50
BD17: Bail 6G 51
Larch Hill BD6: B'frd 6D 110
Larch Hill Cres. BD6: B'frd 5D 110
Larch La. LS25: Gar 5H 103
Larchmont BD14: B'frd 1E 109
Larch St. BD21: Keigh 3H 47
Larch Wood LS14: S'cft 6E 45
Larchwood LS19: Yead 6G 55
LARKFIELD 3G 55
Larkfield BD9: B'frd 6H 69
BD20: Keigh 1C 34
Larkfield Av. LS19: Yead 3G 55
Larkfield Cres. LS19: Yead 3G 55
Larkfield Dr. LS19: Yead 3G 55
Larkfield Mt. LS19: Yead 3G 55
Larkfield Rd. LS19: Yead 3G 55
LS28: Pud 3A 94
Larkfield Ter. BD21: Keigh 1C 48
BD22: Keigh 5D 46
(off Keighley Rd.)
Lark Hill WF17: Bat 6C 136
Lark Hill Av. BD19: Cleck 3H 153
Lark Hill Cl. BD19: Cleck 3H 153
Larkhill Cl. LS8: Leeds 1C 78
Lark Hill Dr. BD19: Cleck 3H 153
Larkhill Grn. LS8: Leeds 6C 60
Larkhill Rd. LS8: Leeds 6C 60
Larkhill Vw. LS8: Leeds 1C 78
Larkhill Wlk. LS8: Leeds 6C 60
Larkhill Way LS8: Leeds 6C 60
Lark St. BD16: Bgly 4B 50
BD21: Keigh 6H 33
BD22: Haw 2D 64
BD22: Keigh 5D 46
Lark Va. BD16: Bgly 3E 51
Larne Ho. *BD5: B'frd 1D 110*
(off Roundhill St.)
Larwood Av. BD10: B'frd 5C 72
Lascelles Mt. *LS8: Leeds 6D 78*
(off Lascelles Rd. E.)
Lascelles Pl. LS8: Leeds 6D 78
Lascelles Rd. E. LS8: Leeds 6D 78
Lascelles Rd. W. LS8: Leeds 6D 78
Lascelles St. LS8: Leeds 6D 78
Lascelles Ter. LS8: Leeds 6D 78
Lascelles Vw. LS8: Leeds 6D 78
Lastingham Grn. BD6: B'frd 4G 109
Lastingham Rd. LS13: Leeds 4B 74
Latchmere Av. LS16: Leeds 1H 75
Latchmere Cl. LS16: Leeds 1A 76
Latchmere Crest LS16: Leeds 1H 75
Latchmere Cross LS16: Leeds 1H 75
Latchmere Dr. LS16: Leeds 1H 75
Latchmere Gdns. LS16: Leeds 6A 58
Latchmere Grn. LS16: Leeds 1H 75
Latchmere Rd. LS16: Leeds 1H 75
Latchmere Vw. LS16: Leeds 1H 75
(not continuous)
Latchmere Wlk. LS16: Leeds 6A 58
Latchmore Rd. LS12: Leeds 1E 117
Latchmore Rd. Ind. Pk.
LS12: Leeds 1D 116
Latham Ct. BD19: Cleck 5F 135
Latham La. BD19: Cleck 4E 135
Latham Lea BD19: Cleck 5E 135
Latimer Ho. *BD5: B'frd 1E 111*
(off Manchester Rd.)
Launceston Dr. BD4: B'frd 3C 112
Launton Way BD5: B'frd 1D 110

230 A-Z Leeds & Bradford

Laura St. HD6: Brigh 2A **162**
  HX3: Hal 6G **129** (1B **164**)
  LS12: Leeds 5F **97**
Laurel Bank BD12: Brigh 1C **152**
  BD16: Bgly 3E **51**
  HX2: Hal 6E **107**
    (Holdsworth Rd.)
  HX2: Hal 6E **127**
    (Stocks La.)
  LS15: Leeds 5F **81**
Laurel Bank Cl. HX2: Hal 1E **129**
Laurel Bank Ct. LS6: Leeds 5C **76**
Laurel Cl. HX3: Hal 6E **109**
  HX5: Ell 5A **160**
  LS17: Bard 6E **27**
Laurel Cres. BD20: Keigh 5H **33**
  HX2: Hal 4D **128**
Laurel Fold LS12: Leeds 4C **96**
Laurel Gro. BD16: Bgly 2A **50**
  BD20: Sils 2D **14**
  BD21: Keigh 5H **33**
  LS12: Leeds 4C **96**
Laurel Hill Av. LS18: Leeds 5F **101**
Laurel Hill Ct. LS15: Leeds 4F **101**
Laurel Hill Gdns. LS15: Leeds 4F **101**
Laurel Hill Gro. LS15: Leeds 4F **101**
Laurel Hill Vw. LS15: Leeds 5F **101**
Laurel Hill Way LS15: Leeds 5F **101**
Laurel Mt. HX1: Hal 4E **149**
  *HX6: Hal 4H **147**
    (off Bright St.)*
  LS7: Leeds 4B **78**
  LS28: Pud 3A **94**
Laurel Pk. BD15: B'frd 5G **67**
Laurel Pl. LS10: Leeds 4H **139**
  LS12: Leeds 4C **96**
Laurels, The BD16: Bgly 4D **50**
  LS8: Leeds 3D **78**
Laurel St. BD3: B'frd 5A **92**
  HX1: Hal 4E **149**
  LS12: Leeds 4C **96**
Laurel Ter. LS12: Leeds 4C **96**
  *LS15: Leeds 5F **81**
    (off Laurel Bank)*
  LS28: Pud 3A **94**
Laurence Ct. LS26: Rothw 6F **121**
Lavell M. BD2: B'frd 6A **72**
Lavender Ct. BD18: Ship 4D **70**
Lavender Hill BD10: B'frd 4A **72**
Lavender Wlk. LS9: Leeds 4D **98**
Laverack Fld. BD12: B'frd 4C **132**
Laverock Cres. HD6: Brigh 4H **151**
Laverock La. HD6: Brigh 4H **151**
Laverock Pl. *HD6: Brigh 4H **151**
    (off Huntock Pl.)*
Laverton Rd. BD4: B'frd 1H **111**
Lavinia Ter. BD14: B'frd 1F **109**
Lawcliffe Cres. BD22: Haw 1D **64**
Law Cl. LS22: Weth 2F **13**
Lawfield Av. LS26: Rothw 1G **141**
Lawkholme Cres.
  BD21: Keigh 6A **34**
Lawkholme La. BD21: Keigh 6A **34**
Law La. HX3: Hal 4B **150**
Lawler Cl. *HX3: Hal 4D **128**
    (off Rugby Ter.)*
Lawn Av. LS29: Burl W 2F **21**
Lawn Rd. LS29: Burl W 2F **21**
LAWNS 3C **156**
Lawns WF2: Wake 3C **156**
Lawns, The HX3: Hal 6F **149**
  *LS29: I'ly 5C **10**
    (off Church St.)*
Lawns Av. LS12: Leeds 2F **115**
Lawns Cl. LS12: Leeds 2F **115**
Lawns Ct. WF2: Wake 4C **156**
Lawns Cres. LS12: Leeds 2F **115**
Lawns Cft. LS12: Leeds 2F **115**
Lawns Dene LS12: Leeds 2F **115**
Lawns Dr. LS12: Leeds 2F **115**
Lawns Grn. LS12: Leeds 2F **115**
Lawns Hall Cl. LS16: Leeds 4B **58**

Lawns La. LS10: Leeds 2C **118**
  LS12: Leeds 1F **115**
  WF2: Wake 4C **156**
Lawns Mt. LS12: Leeds 2F **115**
Lawns Sq. LS12: Leeds 2F **115**
Lawns Ter. LS12: Leeds 2F **115**
  WF3: E Ard 2B **156**
LAWNSWOOD 5A **58**
Lawnswood Bus. Pk. LS16: Leeds . .6A **58**
Lawns Wood Crematorium
  LS16: Leeds 4B **58**
Lawnswood Gdns. LS16: Leeds 5B **58**
Lawnswood Rd. BD21: Keigh 2G **47**
Lawn Wlk. LS29: Burl W 2F **21**
Lawrence Av. LS8: Leeds 5G **79**
Lawrence Ct. LS28: Pud 5H **93**
Lawrence Cres. LS8: Leeds 5G **79**
Lawrence Dr. BD7: B'frd 3G **109**
Lawrence Gdns. LS8: Leeds 4G **79**
Lawrence Rd. HX3: Hal 6F **149**
  LS8: Leeds 5G **79**
Lawrence St. HX3: Hal 6E **129**
Lawrence Wlk. LS8: Leeds 5G **79**
Lawson Rd. HD6: Brigh 1B **162**
Lawson St. BD3: B'frd 3F **91** (1E **7**)
  LS12: Leeds 4B **96**
Lawson Wood Ct. LS6: Leeds 6F **59**
Lawson Wood Dr. LS6: Leeds 6F **59**
Law St. BD4: B'frd 3A **112**
  BD19: Cleck 6B **134**
Laxton Ho. *BD5: B'frd 1D **110**
    (off Launton Wlk.)*
LAYCOCK .6C **32**
Laycock La. BD22: Keigh 1B **46**
Laycock Pl. LS7: Leeds 6B **78**
Lay Gth. LS26: Rothw 2A **142**
Lay Gth. Cl. LS26: Rothw 3A **142**
Lay Gth. Ct. LS26: Rothw 3A **142**
Lay Gth. Fold LS26: Rothw 3A **142**
Lay Gth. Gdns. LS26: Rothw 3A **142**
Lay Gth. Grn. LS26: Rothw 3A **142**
Lay Gth. Mead LS26: Rothw 3A **142**
Lay Gth. Pl. LS26: Rothw 3A **142**
Lay Gth. Sq. LS26: Rothw 3A **142**
Laythorp Ter. BD20: Keigh 4H **35**
Layton Av. LS19: Yead 4H **55**
Layton Cl. LS19: Yead 5A **56**
Layton Cres. LS19: Yead 4H **55**
Layton Dr. LS19: Yead 4A **56**
Layton Ho. *BD5: B'frd 1D **110**
    (off Newall St.)*
Layton La. LS19: Yead 5A **56**
Layton Mt. LS19: Yead 4H **55**
Layton Pk. Av. LS19: Yead 5A **56**
Layton Pk. Cl. LS19: Yead 4H **55**
Layton Pk. Cft. LS19: Yead 5A **56**
Layton Pk. Dr. LS19: Yead 4H **55**
Layton Ri. LS18: H'fth 4B **56**
Layton Rd. LS18: H'fth 4A **56**
  LS19: H'fth, Yead 4A **56**
Lazenby Dr. LS22: Weth 3D **12**
Lazenby Fold LS22: Weth 3D **12**
Lea, The LS25: Gar 6F **103**
Lea Av. HX3: Hal 6G **149**
Leabank Av. LS25: Gar 6G **103**
Leach Cres. BD20: Keigh 3C **34**
Leach Ri. BD20: Keigh 3C **34**
Leach Rd. BD20: Keigh 3B **34**
Leach Way BD20: Keigh 3C **34**
Lea Cl. HD6: Brigh 5A **152**
Lea Ct. BD7: B'frd 3G **109**
Lea Cft. LS21: Otley 4E **23**
  LS23: B Spa 6B **30**
Leadenhall St. HX1: Hal 4D **148**
Leadwell La. LS26: Rothw 4F **141**
  WF3: Rothw 4F **141**
Lea Farm Cres. LS5: Leeds 3H **75**
Lea Farm Dr. LS5: Leeds 2H **75**
Lea Farm Gro. LS5: Leeds 3H **75**
Lea Farm Mt. LS5: Leeds 2G **75**
Lea Farm Pl. LS5: Leeds 3H **75**
Lea Farm Rd. LS5: Leeds 2G **75**

Lea Farm Row LS5: Leeds 3H **75**
Lea Farm Wlk. LS5: Leeds 2H **75**
Leafield Av. BD2: B'frd 5A **72**
Leafield Cl. LS17: Leeds 5H **59**
Leafield Cres. BD2: B'frd 5H **71**
Leafield Dr. BD2: B'frd 5A **72**
  LS17: Leeds 5H **59**
  LS28: Pud 6B **94**
Leafield Grange LS17: Leeds 5H **59**
Leafield Gro. BD2: B'frd 6A **72**
Leafield Ho. *BD5: B'frd 1D **110**
    (off Newall St.)*
Leafield La. LS21: Leat 1E **25**
Leafield Pl. LS19: Yead 6D **40**
Leafield Ter. BD2: B'frd 6A **72**
Leafield Towers LS17: Leeds 5H **59**
Leafield Vs. *LS19: Yead 6D **40**
    (off Leafield Pl.)*
Leafield Way BD2: B'frd 6A **72**
Leafland St. HX1: Hal 2E **149**
Leaf St. BD22: Haw 1E **65**
Leafsway BD6: B'frd 1H **131**
Leah Pl. LS12: Leeds 5F **97**
Leah Row LS12: Leeds 5F **97**
Lea Mill Pk. Cl. LS19: Yead 6E **41**
Lea Mill Pk. Dr. LS19: Yead 6E **41**
Leamington Dr. BD10: B'frd 1A **72**
Leamington Rd. LS29: I'ly 4E **11**
Leamington St. BD9: B'frd 1B **90**
Leamington Ter. LS29: I'ly 4E **11**
Leamside Wlk. BD4: B'frd 3C **112**
Lea Pk. Cl. LS10: Leeds 6D **118**
Lea Pk. Cft. LS10: Leeds 6E **119**
Lea Pk. Dr. LS10: Leeds 6D **118**
Lea Pk. Gdns. LS10: Leeds 6D **118**
Lea Pk. Gth. LS10: Leeds 6D **118**
Lea Pk. Gro. LS10: Leeds 6D **118**
Lea Pk. Va. LS10: Leeds 6E **119**
Leaside Dr. BD13: B'frd 4H **87**
Leasowe Av. LS10: Leeds 3C **118**
Leasowe Cl. LS10: Leeds 3C **118**
Leasowe Ct. *LS10: Leeds 3C **118**
    (off Woodhouse Hill Rd.)*
Leasowe Gdns. LS10: Leeds 3D **118**
Leasowe Gth. LS10: Leeds 3C **118**
Leasowe Rd. LS10: Leeds 3C **118**
Lea Ter. LS17: Leeds 6A **60**
Leather Bank LS29: Burl W 1E **21**
LEATHLEY .1C **24**
Leathley Av. LS29: Men 2H **39**
Leathley Cres. LS29: Men 2H **39**
Leathley Ho. *BD5: B'frd 1D **110**
    (off Hutson St.)*
Leathley La. LS21: Leat 1C **24**
  LS29: Men 1H **39**
Leathley Rd. LS10: Leeds 6A **98**
  LS29: Men 1H **39**
Leavens, The BD10: B'frd 1B **72**
LEAVENTHORPE 5E **89**
Leaventhorpe Av. BD8: B'frd 4F **89**
Leaventhorpe Cl. BD8: B'frd 4F **89**
Leaventhorpe Gro. BD13: B'frd 5E **89**
Leaventhorpe La. BD8: B'frd 5D **88**
  BD13: B'frd 5D **88**
Leaventhorpe Way BD8: B'frd 4F **89**
Lea Vw. LS18: H'fth 6D **56**
Leavington Cl. BD6: B'frd 1B **132**
Leconfield Cl. LS22: Weth 3C **12**
Leconfield Ho. BD10: B'frd 2A **72**
  *LS29: I'ly 5D **10**
    (off Cowparsley Rd.)*
Ledbury Av. LS10: Leeds 3D **140**
Ledbury Cl. LS10: Leeds 3D **140**
Ledbury Cft. LS10: Leeds 3D **140**
Ledbury Dr. LS10: Leeds 3D **140**
Ledbury Grn. LS10: Leeds 3D **140**
Ledbury Gro. LS10: Leeds 3C **140**
Ledbury Pl. BD4: B'frd 1H **111**
Ledgard Way LS12: Leeds 3C **96**
Ledger La. WF1: Wake 4F **157**
  WF3: Rothw 6G **141**
Ledger Pl. WF1: Wake 5F **157**

232 A-Z Leeds & Bradford

Lidgett Pl. LS8: Leeds 1D **78**
Lidgett Towers LS8: Leeds 6C **60**
Lidgett Wlk. LS8: Leeds 2D **78**
(not continuous)
Lifton Pl. LS2: Leeds 1G **97**
Light, The LS2: Leeds 3H **97** (3D **4**)
Light Bank La. BD20: Sils 5A **8**
LIGHTCLIFFE **2H 151**
Lightcliffe Rd. HD6: Brigh 4A **152**
Lightcliffe Royd La. HX4: Hal 5A **158**
Lightowler Cl. HX1: Hal 2E **149**
Lightowler Rd. HX1: Hal 2E **149**
Lightowler St. BD6: B'frd 4C **110**
Lightridge Rd. HD2: Hud 6H **161**
Lilac Cl. HD6: Brigh 6C **152**
LS29: Add 1E **9**
Lilac Gro. BD4: B'frd 5B **92**
BD18: Ship 4D **70**
BD19: Cleck 6E **135**
Lilacs, The LS20: Guis 4C **40**
Lilac St. HX3: Hal 6E **129**
Lilian St. BD4: B'frd 2A **112**
Lillands Av. HD6: Brigh 1H **161**
Lillands La. HD6: Brigh 1H **161**
Lillands Ter. HD6: Brigh 1H **161**
Lilly La. HX1: Hal 3H **149** (5D **164**)
(not continuous)
HX3: Hal 3H **149** (5D **164**)
Lilly St. HX6: Hal 6H **147**
Lilycroft BD8: B'frd 1B **90**
Lilycroft Pl. BD8: B'frd 1B **90**
Lilycroft Rd. BD9: B'frd 2A **90**
Lilycroft Wlk. BD9: B'frd 1A **90**
(not continuous)
Lily St. BD8: B'frd 1B **90**
Lilythorne Av. BD10: B'frd 1A **72**
Lime Cl. BD20: Keigh 4G **33**
LS29: Add 1B **8**
Lime Ct. BD16: Bgly 1A **50**
(off Aire St.)
Lime Gro. LS19: Yead 3E **55**
Limes Av. HX3: Hal 5G **149**
Lime St. BD7: B'frd 1A **110**
BD16: Bgly 4B **50**
BD21: Keigh 6H **33**
BD22: Haw 3C **64**
Lime Tree Av. HX5: Ell 5C **160**
LS17: Leeds 5C **60**
LS23: B Spa 3B **30**
Lime Tree Cl. LS26: Rothw 6F **121**
Lime Tree Cres. LS25: Kip 4A **124**
Lime Tree Gdns. LS23: B Spa 4C **30**
Limetree Gro. BD11: B'frd 6E **113**
Lime Tree Sq. BD18: Ship 6F **51**
Lime Va. Way BD6: B'frd 4G **109**
Limewood App. LS14: Leeds 2C **80**
Limewood Ct. LS14: Leeds 2C **80**
Limewood Rd. LS14: Leeds 3C **80**
Lincoln Cl. BD8: B'frd 2C **90**
Lincoln Ct. LS28: Pud 1H **93**
(off South Dr.)
Lincoln Grn. Ct. LS9: Leeds 2C **98**
Lincoln Grn. Rd.
LS9: Leeds 2C **98** (2H **5**)
Lincoln Rd. BD8: B'frd 3C **90**
LS9: Leeds 2C **98**
Lincoln St. BD15: B'frd 3E **89**
Lincoln Towers LS9: Leeds 2C **98**
(off Lincoln Rd.)
Lincoln Way HX3: Hal 6F **129**
Lincoln Way LS25: Kip 3A **124**
Lincs Wold WF15: Liv 5H **153**
Lindale Cl. LS10: Leeds 6B **118**
Lindale Gth. WF2: Wake 6A **156**
Lindale La. WF2: Wake 6A **156**
Linden Av. BD3: B'frd 3C **92**
LS11: Leeds 2H **117**

Linden Cl. HD6: Brigh 6C **152**
LS17: Bard 1F **45**
Linden Ct. LS16: Leeds 2D **76**
Linden Gdns. LS11: Leeds 2A **118**
Linden Gro. LS11: Leeds 2A **118**
Linden Mt. LS11: Leeds 2H **117**
Linden Pl. HX6: Hal 4A **148**
LS11: Leeds 2A **118**
Linden Ri. BD21: Keigh 2C **48**
Linden Rd. HX3: Hal 5G **149**
HX5: Ell 5A **160**
LS11: Leeds 2H **117**
Linden St. LS11: Leeds 2H **117**
Linden Ter. HX3: Hal 2E **151**
(off Barfield Rd.)
LS11: Leeds 2A **118**
Linden Way LS22: Weth 2D **12**
Lindholme Gdns. BD15: B'frd 3D **88**
Lindisfarne Rd. BD18: Ship 2H **69**
Lindley Dr. BD7: B'frd 3H **109**
Lindley Rd. BD5: B'frd 2D **110**
Lindon St. BD22: Haw 3C **64**
Lindrick Gro. HX2: Hal 6D **106**
Lindrick Wlk. HX2: Hal 6D **106**
Lindrick Way HX2: Hal 6D **106**
Lindsay Acre WF3: E Ard 1G **155**
Lindsay Rd. LS25: Gar 5F **103**
Lindsey Ct. LS9: Leeds 2C **98**
Lindsey Gdns. LS9: Leeds 2C **98**
Lindsey Mt. LS9: Leeds 2C **98**
(off Lindsey Rd.)
Lindsey Rd. LS9: Leeds 2C **98**
LINDWELL **3H 159**
Lindwell Av. HX4: Hal 4G **159**
Lindwell Gro. HX4: Hal 4G **159**
Lindwell Pl. HX4: Hal 4G **159**
(off Wellgate)
Linfoot Ct. LS21: Otley 4D **22**
Lingard St. BD1: B'frd 3F **91** (2E **7**)
LINGBOB **5G 67**
Ling Bob HX2: Hal 1B **148**
Ling Bob La. HX2: Hal 1B **148**
Lingbob Ct. BD15: B'frd 5G **67**
Ling Bob Cft. HX2: Hal 6B **128**
Ling Cft. LS23: B Spa 3H **29**
Lingcroft Grn. BD5: B'frd 3G **111**
(off Tristram Av.)
Lingdale Rd. BD6: B'frd 1A **132**
Lingfield App. LS17: Leeds 4H **59**
Lingfield Bank LS17: Leeds 4H **59**
Lingfield Cl. LS17: Leeds 4A **60**
Lingfield Cres. BD13: B'frd 3E **109**
LS17: Leeds 4H **59**
Lingfield Dr. BD22: Haw 6G **47**
LS17: Leeds 4A **60**
Lingfield Gdns. LS17: Leeds 4H **59**
Lingfield Gth. LS17: Leeds 4A **60**
Lingfield Ga. LS17: Leeds 4H **59**
Lingfield Gro. BD15: B'frd 4H **67**
LS17: Leeds 4H **59**
Lingfield Hill LS17: Leeds 3H **59**
Lingfield Ho. BD10: B'frd 3A **72**
(off Savile Av.)
Lingfield Mt. LS17: Leeds 4A **60**
Lingfield Rd. BD15: B'frd 4G **67**
LS17: Leeds 4H **59**
Lingfield Ter. BD13: B'frd 3E **109**
Lingfield Vw. LS17: Leeds 4H **59**
Lingfield Wlk. LS17: Leeds 4H **59**
Ling La. LS14: S'cft 6B **44**
LS17: S'cft 6B **44**
Lingmell Cres. BD4: B'frd 3D **112**
(off Simon Cl.)
Ling Pk. App. BD15: B'frd 5G **67**
Ling Pk. Av. BD15: B'frd 5G **67**
Ling Royd Av. HX2: Hal 1B **148**
Lingwell App. LS10: Leeds 3A **140**
Lingwell Av. LS10: Leeds 2A **140**
Lingwell Chase WF3: Wake 3G **157**
Lingwell Ct. LS10: Leeds 3A **140**
WF3: Wake 3E **157**

Lingwell Cres. LS10: Leeds 2A **140**
Lingwell Gdns. LS10: Leeds 3A **140**
LINGWELL GATE **2E 157**
Lingwell Ga. Cres. WF1: Wake 4F **157**
Lingwell Ga. Dr. WF1: Wake 4E **157**
Lingwell Ga. La. WF1: Wake 2D **156**
WF3: E Ard, Leeds 5D **140**
WF3: Wake 2D **156**
Lingwell Grn. LS10: Leeds 3A **140**
Lingwell Gro. LS10: Leeds 3A **140**
Lingwell M. LS10: Leeds 3A **140**
LINGWELL NOOK **1D 156**
Lingwell Nook Ct. WF3: Wake 3G **157**
Lingwell Nook La. WF3: Wake 1E **157**
(Lingwell Gate)
WF3: Wake 3F **157**
(Lofthouse Gate)
Lingwell Pk. Ct. LS10: Leeds 2A **140**
Lingwell Rd. LS10: Leeds 2A **140**
Lingwell Vw. LS10: Leeds 3A **140**
Lingwell Wlk. LS10: Leeds 3A **140**
Lingwood Av. BD8: B'frd 2H **89**
Lingwood Rd. BD8: B'frd 3H **89**
Lingwood Ter. BD8: B'frd 3H **89**
Link, The LS26: Swil 4H **121**
Links, The LS11: Leeds 6G **117**
Links Av. BD19: Cleck 6B **134**
Linkway BD16: Bgly 2C **68**
Linnburn M. LS29: I'ly 6D **10**
Linnet Cl. BD8: B'frd 3E **89**
Linnet St. BD21: Keigh 5A **34**
Linnhe Av. BD6: B'frd 1H **131**
LINTON **1B 28**
Linton Av. BD20: Sils 1E **15**
LS17: Leeds 3D **60**
LS22: Weth 3D **12**
Linton Cl. LS17: Leeds 3C **60**
Linton Comn. LS22: Coll 2H **27**
Linton Cres. LS17: Leeds 3D **60**
Linton Cft. LS16: Leeds 1H **75**
Linton Dr. LS17: Leeds 3C **60**
Linton Gro. HD6: Brigh 3G **161**
LS17: Leeds 3C **60**
Linton Hills Rd. LS22: Weth 4C **12**
Linton La. LS22: Coll, Weth 6C **12**
LS22: Weth 2A **12**
Linton Mdws. LS22: Weth 4C **12**
Linton Ri. LS17: Leeds 3C **60**
Linton Rd. LS17: Leeds 3C **60**
LS22: Coll 2A **28**
LS22: Weth 4C **12**
Linton St. BD4: B'frd 1F **111**
Linton Vw. LS17: Leeds 2C **60**
Lion Ct. LS29: Burl W 2F **21**
Lippersley La. BD20: Sils 5A **8**
(not continuous)
Lisbon Sq. LS1: Leeds 4A **4**
Lisbon St. LS1: Leeds 3G **97** (4B **4**)
Lisker Av. LS21: Otley 4F **23**
Lisker Ct. LS21: Otley 4F **23**
Lisker Dr. LS21: Otley 4F **23**
Lismore Cl. LS26: Rothw 2B **142**
Lismore Rd. BD20: Keigh 5H **33**
Lister Av. BD4: B'frd 2H **111**
Lister Cl. HX1: Hal 4B **164**
LS29: I'ly 5C **10**
(off Church St.)
Lister Gdns. BD8: B'frd 1D **90**
Lister Hill LS18: H'fth 5E **57**
LISTER HILLS **4C 90**
Listerhills Ind. Est.
BD1: B'frd 4D **90** (4A **6**)
Listerhills Rd. BD7: B'frd 5C **90**
Listerhills Science Pk. BD7: B'frd . . .4C **90**
Lister La. BD2: B'frd 1F **91**
HX1: Hal 2E **149** (4A **164**)
(not continuous)
Lister's Ct. HX1: Hal 2E **149**
Listers Rd. HX3: Hal 1A **150**
Lister St. BD4: B'frd 3A **112**
(Bela Av.)

Lister St. BD4: B'frd 4C **112**
    (Edward St.)
BD21: Keigh 1G **47**
HD6: Brigh 6A **152**
LS29: I'ly 5C **10**
Lister Vw. BD8: B'frd 2C **90**
Lister Ville BD15: B'frd 4G **67**
Lister Wlk. LS27: Morl 1H **137**
Lit. Baines St. HX1: Hal 2E **149**
Littlebeck Dr. BD16: Bgly 4E **51**
Lit. Bradley HX4: Hal 5G **159**
Lit. Church La. LS26: Mick 5C **144**
Little Cote BD10: B'frd 6G **53**
Lit. Cross St. BD5: B'frd 3E **111**
    LS1: Leeds 4E **5**
Littlefield Wlk. BD6: B'frd 5B **110**
Lit. Fountain St. LS27: Morl 4A **138**
Little Haley BD22: Oxen 6D **64**
Lit. Hew Royd BD10: B'frd 6F **53**
LITTLE HORTON 1C **110**
LITTLE HORTON GREEN 6D **90**
Lit. Horton Grn. BD5: B'frd 6D **90**
Lit. Horton La. BD5: B'frd . .6D **90** (6C **6**)
    (Bk. Trinity Ter., not continuous)
    BD5: B'frd 2C **110**
    (Canterbury Av.)
    BD5: B'frd 3B **110** (6B **6**)
    (Carr Bottom Rd.)
Lit. King St. LS1: Leeds 4H **97** (5D **4**)
Littlelands BD16: Bgly 2C **68**
Littlelands Ct. BD16: Bgly 2C **68**
Little La. BD9: B'frd 1H **89**
    BD20: Keigh 4A **36**
    HX3: Hal 2C **150**
    LS27: Morl 5C **116**
    LS29: I'ly 5D **10**
    WF3: Rothw 4A **142**
Lit. Lane Ct. LS27: Morl 5C **116**
LITTLE LONDON
    LS7 . . . . .1A **98** (1F **5**)
    LS19 . . . . .3E **55**
Little London HX3: Hal 3B **130**
LITTLE MOOR 4C **108**
Little Moor BD13: B'frd 4C **108**
LITTLEMOOR BOTTOM 6A **94**
Littlemoor Ct. LS28: Pud 5A **94**
Littlemoor Cres. LS28: Pud 6A **94**
Littlemoor Cres. Sth. LS28: Pud . . .6A **94**
Littlemoor Gdns. HX2: Hal 1C **128**
    LS28: Pud 6A **94**
Littlemoor La. LS14: T'ner 2H **63**
Lit. Moor Pl. LS12: Leeds 4B **96**
Littlemoor Rd. HX2: Hal 6C **106**
    LS28: Pud 5A **94**
Littlemoor Vw. LS28: Pud 5B **94**
Lit. Neville St. LS1: Leeds . . .4H **97** (6D **4**)
Little Pk. BD10: B'frd 6C **54**
LITTLE PRESTON 4B **122**
Little Preston Hall LS26: Swil 4B **122**
Lit. Queen St. LS1: Leeds 4G **97** (5B **4**)
Little St. BD22: Haw 2C **64**
Littleway LS17: Leeds 6A **60**
Littlewood Cl. BD6: B'frd 6C **110**
Littlewood Dr. BD19: Cleck 5B **134**
LITTLE WOODHOUSE 2G **97** (1A **4**)
Lit. Woodhouse HD6: Brigh 1A **162**
Lit. Woodhouse St.
    LS2: Leeds 2G **97** (2B **4**)
Littondale Cl. BD17: Bail 3E **53**
Litton Rd. BD22: Keigh 1G **47**
Litton Way LS14: Leeds 1D **80**
Liverpool Row HX2: Hal 3H **147**
    (off Stock La.)
Liversedge Row BD7: B'frd 2A **110**
    (off Perseverance La.)
Livingstone Cl. BD2: B'frd 3F **71**
Livingstone Rd. BD2: B'frd 5D **70**
    (Bolton Hall Rd.)
    BD2: B'frd 4F **71**
    (Cheltenham Rd.)
Livingstone St. HX3: Hal 6E **129**
Livingstone St. Nth. HX2: Hal 2E **129**

Livingston Ho. BD10: B'frd 3A **72**
Livinia Gro. LS7: Leeds 1A **98**
Lloyds Dr. BD12: B'frd 1E **133**
Locarno Av. BD9: B'frd 1G **89**
Lochore Ct. BD15: B'frd 2D **88**
Lochy Rd. BD6: B'frd 1H **131**
Locks, The BD16: Bgly 4C **50**
    (off Granville Ter.)
    BD16: Bgly 3B **50**
    (Wilson Rd.)
Lockside Rd. LS10: Leeds 2E **119**
Locksley Rd. HD6: Brigh 2D **162**
Lock St. HX3: Hal 3H **149**
Lock Vw. BD16: Bgly 3A **50**
    HX5: Ell 3C **160**
Lockwood Cl. LS11: Leeds 4A **118**
Lockwood Cl. LS11: Leeds 4A **118**
Lockwood Pk. LS11: Leeds 4A **118**
Lockwood St. BD6: B'frd 4C **110**
    BD12: B'frd 2E **133**
    BD18: Ship 1H **69**
Lockwood Way LS11: Leeds 4A **118**
Lode Pit La. BD16: Bgly 3F **51**
Lodge Av. HX5: Ell 4E **161**
Lodge Dr. HX5: Ell 4E **161**
Lodge Ga. Cl. BD13: B'frd 2C **86**
Lodge Hill BD17: Bail 4H **51**
    LS29: Add 1D **8**
    (off Main St.)
Lodge Hill Cl. LS12: Leeds 2G **115**
Lodge Hill Wlk. LS12: Leeds 2G **115**
Lodge La. LS11: Leeds 2H **117**
Lodge Pl. HX5: Ell 4E **161**
Lodge Rd. LS28: Pud 3H **93**
Lodge Row LS15: Leeds 1E **101**
    (off Tranquility Av.)
Lodge St. BD13: B'frd 3B **66**
    BD22: Haw 2B **64**
    LS2: Leeds 1H **97** (1C **4**)
    (not continuous)
Lodge Ter. LS11: Leeds 3H **117**
Lodore Av. BD2: B'frd 6G **71**
Lodore Pl. BD2: B'frd 6H **71**
Lodore Rd. BD2: B'frd 6G **71**
LOFTHOUSE 6G **141**
Lofthouse Farm Fold WF3: Wake . .2G **157**
LOFTHOUSE GATE 3F **157**
Lofthouse Pl. LS2: Leeds 1H **97**
Loft St. BD8: B'frd 3H **89**
Loiner Ct. LS9: Leeds 6G **99**
Lombard St. HX1: Hal 4D **148**
    LS15: Leeds 4B **100**
    LS19: Yead 3E **55**
Lomond Av. LS18: H'fth 3D **56**
Londesboro Gro. LS9: Leeds 4E **99**
Londesboro Ter. LS9: Leeds 4E **99**
London La. LS19: Yead 3E **55**
London Rd. HX6: Hal 6B **148**
London Sq. LS19: Yead 3E **55**
London St. LS19: Yead 3E **55**
Longacre La. BD22: Haw 1D **64**
Longacres BD22: Haw 1E **65**
Longbottom Av. BD20: Sils 2F **15**
Longbottom Ter. HX3: Hal 5H **149**
Longbow Av. LS26: Mick 4C **144**
Longbow Cl. HD2: Hud 6D **162**
Long C'way. BD13: B'frd 2F **85**
    BD22: B'frd 2F **85**
    HX2: Hal 2B **106**
    LS9: Leeds 6D **98**
    LS16: Leeds 5D **58**
Long Causeway, The HX2: Hal 3A **146**
Long Cl. BD12: B'frd 3B **132**
Long Cl. La. LS9: Leeds 4D **98**
Longcroft BD21: Keigh 1A **48**
Longcroft Link BD1: B'frd 4D **90** (3B **6**)
Longcroft Pl. BD1: B'frd 4D **90** (3B **6**)
Longcroft Rd. LS29: I'ly 6G **11**
Longdike Ct. LS25: Kip 4H **123**
Longdike La. LS25: Kip 5A **124**
Long Edge Low Rd. HX6: Hal 6B **146**

Long Edge Middle Rd. HX6: Hal 6A **146**
Long Edge Rd. HX6: Hal 6A **146**
    (not continuous)
Long Fallas Cres. HD6: Brigh 4B **162**
Longfield Av. HX3: Hal 6C **130**
    LS28: Pud 4B **94**
Longfield Ct. LS28: Pud 4B **94**
Longfield Dr. BD4: B'frd 2A **112**
    LS13: Leeds 4B **74**
    LS15: Leeds 3C **100**
Longfield Gth. LS13: Leeds 4B **74**
Longfield Gro. LS28: Pud 4B **94**
Longfield Mt. LS28: Pud 4B **94**
Longfield Rd. LS28: Pud 4B **94**
Longfield Ter. HX3: Hal 6C **130**
    (off Longfield Av.)
    LS28: Pud 4A **94**
Longfield Vw. LS28: Pud 6H **73**
    (off Croft St.)
Longford Ter. BD7: B'frd 6H **89**
Long Hall Pk. LS29: I'ly 4C **10**
Long Heys HX4: Hal 5G **159**
Longhouse Dr. BD13: B'frd 3B **86**
Longhouse La. BD13: B'frd 3B **86**
Long Ho. Rd. HX2: Hal 1A **128**
Longlands Dr. BD22: Haw 1D **64**
Longlands La. BD13: B'frd 2B **86**
Longlands St. BD1: B'frd 4D **90** (3B **6**)
    (Baptist Pl.)
    BD1: B'frd 4D **90** (3B **6**)
    (Providence St.)
Long La. BD9: B'frd 4F **69**
    BD13: B'frd 6H **107**
    BD15: B'frd 2H **87**
    BD16: Bgly 6E **49**
    HX3: Hal 2B **150**
    (Barrowclough La.)
    HX3: Hal 5C **128**
    (Lane Ends)
    HX6: Hal 6H **147**
    LS15: Bar E 2E **83**
    LS25: Bar E 2E **83**
LONG LEE .1C **48**
Long Lee La. BD21: Keigh 2B **48**
Long Lee Ter. BD21: Keigh 2C **48**
Longley's Yd. LS10: Leeds 3C **118**
Long Lover La. HX2: Hal 1C **148**
Long Mdw. Ct. LS25: Gar 6G **103**
Long Mdw. Ga. LS25: Gar 6F **103**
Long Mdws. BD2: B'frd 5E **71**
    LS16: B'hpe 3G **43**
    LS25: Gar 6F **103**
    LS29: Burl W 1E **21**
Long Preston Chase BD10: B'frd . . .2B **72**
Long Reach HX2: Hal 4G **127**
Long Riddings LS29: Add 1D **8**
Long Ridge HD6: Brigh 4A **162**
Long Row BD12: B'frd 2D **132**
    LS18: H'fth 6E **57**
    (not continuous)
Long Row Ct. BD5: B'frd 2E **111**
Longroyd BD10: B'frd 1F **71**
Longroyd Av. LS11: Leeds 2A **118**
Long Royd Cl. BD17: Bail 3D **52**
Longroyd Cres. LS11: Leeds 2A **118**
Longroyd Cres. Nth.
    LS11: Leeds 2A **118**
Long Royd Dr. BD17: Bail 3E **53**
Longroyde Cl. HD6: Brigh 3H **161**
Longroyde Gro. HD6: Brigh 3H **161**
Longroyde Rd. HD6: Brigh 2H **161**
Longroyd Gro. LS11: Leeds 2A **118**
Longroyd Pl. LS11: Leeds 2A **118**
Longroyd St. LS11: Leeds 2A **118**
Longroyd St. Nth.
    LS11: Leeds 2A **118**
Longroyd Ter. LS11: Leeds 2A **118**
Longroyd Vw. LS11: Leeds 2A **118**
Longside Hall BD7: B'frd 5C **90**
Longside La. BD7: B'frd 5C **90** (5A **6**)
Long St. BD4: B'frd 6H **91**
Long Thorpe La. WF3: Leeds 6D **140**

Long Wall HX4: Hal 4H 159
   HX5: Ell .4H 159
Longwood Av. BD16: Bgly 2H 49
Longwood Cl. HX3: Hal 6F 149
   LS17: Leeds 2F 61
   WF3: E Ard 1D 154
Longwood Ct. WF3: E Ard 1E 155
Longwood Cres. LS17: Leeds 2F 61
Longwood Fold WF3: E Ard 1E 155
Longwood Gth. WF3: E Ard 1E 155
Longwood Rd. WF3: E Ard 1D 154
Longwood Va. WF3: E Ard 1E 155
Longwood Way LS17: Leeds 2F 61
Lonsdale Mdws. LS23: B Spa 4B 30
Lonsdale Ri. WF3: E Ard 1E 155
Lonsdale Sq. LS10: Leeds 4B 118
Lonsdale St. BD3: B'frd 3H 91
Lord La. BD22: Haw 1B 64
Lord's Bldgs. LS27: Morl 5A 138
Lordsfield Pl. BD4: B'frd 4B 112
Lord's La. HD6: Brigh 2B 162
Lord St. BD21: Keigh 6A 34
   BD22: Haw 2D 64
   HX1: Hal 2G 149 (4B 164)
   HX6: Hal 4A 148
   LS12: Leeds 5F 97
Lord Ter. LS12: Leeds 5F 97
Loris St. BD4: B'frd 4B 112
Lorne St. BD4: B'frd 2H 111
   BD21: Keigh 5C 34
   BD22: Haw . . . . *.1F 65*
   (off Bingley Rd.)
Lotherton Way LS25: Gar 3F 103
Lot St. BD22: Haw 2D 64
Loughrigg St. BD5: B'frd 2E 111
Louisa St. BD10: B'frd 1H 71
Louis Av. BD5: B'frd 1C 110
Louis Ct. LS7: Leeds 6B 78
Louis Gro. LS7: Leeds 6C 78
Louis Ho. *LS27: Morl* *2B 138*
   (off Pullman Ct.)
Louis le Prince Ct. *LS8: Leeds* *6D 78*
   (off Bayswater Rd.)
Louis St. LS7: Leeds 6B 78
Lounge Picture House, The 4D 76
Love La. HX1: Hal 4F 149 (6A 164)
   LS26: Rothw 2A 142
Lovell Pk. Cl. LS7: Leeds . . .2B 98 (1G 5)
Lovell Pk. Ct. LS7: Leeds . . .2A 98 (1F 5)
Lovell Pk. Ga. LS7: Leeds . . .2A 98 (1F 5)
Lovell Pk. Grange LS7: Leeds 1G 5
Lovell Pk. Hgts. LS7: Leeds 1G 5
Lovell Pk. Hill LS7: Leeds . . .2A 98 (1F 5)
Lovell Pk. M. LS7: Leeds 2B 98 (1G 5)
Lovell Pk. Rd. LS2: Leeds . . .2A 98 (2F 5)
   LS7: Leeds 2A 98 (2F 5)
Lovell Pk. Towers LS7: Leeds 1F 5
Lovell Pk. Vw. LS7: Leeds . . .2B 98 (1G 5)
Low Ash Av. BD18: Ship 2D 70
Low Ash Cres. BD18: Ship 2D 70
Low Ash Dr. BD18: Ship 2D 70
Low Ash Gro. BD18: Ship 2D 70
Low Ash Rd. BD18: Ship 3E 71
LOW BAILDON 3D 52
LOW BANK 4B 46
Low Bank Dr. BD22: Keigh 4B 46
Low Bank La. BD22: Keigh 4B 46
LOW BANKS 3D 34
Low Banks BD20: Keigh 4D 34
Low Banks St. LS28: Pud 6H 73
Low Beck LS29: I'ly 4F 11
Low Bentley HX3: Hal 2G 131
Low Cl. BD16: Bgly 5D 50
   LS29: I'ly .3D 10
Low Cl. St. LS2: Leeds 6G 77
LOW COMMON 6E 145
Lowcroft LS22: Coll 3A 28
Low Cft. Ct. LS16: B'hpe 2G 43
Lowell Av. BD7: B'frd 6H 89
Lowell Gro. LS13: Leeds 3C 94
Lowell Pl. LS13: Leeds 3C 94

Lwr. Ainley HX2: Hal 1D 128
Lwr. Ashgrove BD5: B'frd 5D 90 (6B 6)
Lwr. Bankhouse LS28: Pud 1H 113
Lwr. Basinghall St.
   LS1: Leeds 3H 97 (4D 4)
Lwr. Bentley Royd HX6: Hal 5G 147
Lwr. Bracken Bank *BD22: Keigh* *3G 47*
   (off Diamond St.)
Lwr. Brea HX3: Hal 1C 150
Lwr. Brockholes HX2: Hal 6B 106
Lwr. Brockwell La. HX6: Hal 6F 147
Lwr. Brown Hurst HX2: Hal 4A 128
Lwr. Brunswick St.
   LS2: Leeds 2B 98 (2G 5)
Lwr. Clay Pits HX1: Hal 1D 148
Lwr. Clifton St. HX6: Hal 5A 148
Lwr. Clyde St. HX6: Hal 6H 147
Lwr. Constable Rd. LS29: I'ly 6F 11
Lwr. Copy BD15: B'frd 2D 88
Lwr. Crow Nest Dr. HX3: Hal 2B 152
LOWER EDGE BOTTOM 4D 160
Lwr. Edge Rd. HD6: Brigh 4D 160
   HX5: Brigh, Ell 4D 160
Lwr. Ellistones *HX4: Hal* *4E 159*
   (off Saddleworth Rd.)
Lwr. Exley HX3: Hal 2H 159
LOWER FAGLEY 6C 72
Lwr. Finkil St. HD6: Brigh 4G 151
Lwr. Fleet BD13: B'frd 4G 107
Lwr. Fold HD6: Brigh 5H 161
   HX1: Hal 4B 164
   HX4: Hal 5B 158
Lwr. Gaukrodger HX6: Hal 6F 147
Lwr. George St. BD6: B'frd 4B 110
Lwr. Gilbert Flds. HX4: Hal 5A 158
Lwr. Globe St. BD8: B'frd 3C 90
LOWER GRANGE 4D 88
Lwr. Grange HD2: Hud 5E 163
Lwr. Grange Cl. BD8: B'frd 4D 88
Lwr. Grattan Rd. BD1: B'frd . .4D 90 (4A 6)
Lower Grn. BD17: Bail 5B 52
Lwr. Green Av. BD19: Cleck 1F 153
Lwr. Hathershelf HX2: Hal 2B 146
Lwr. Hazelhurst BD13: B'frd 6A 108
Lwr. Heights Rd. BD13: B'frd 3G 87
Lwr. Hollins HX6: Hal 5H 147
Lwr. Holme BD17: Bail 6C 52
Lwr. Horley Grn. HX3: Hal 6A 130
Lwr. House Cl. BD10: B'frd 6F 53
Lower Ings HX2: Hal 4A 106
Lwr. Kipping La. BD13: B'frd 5H 87
Lwr. Kirkgate HX1: Hal 2H 149
Lower La. BD4: B'frd 1H 111
   (Fenby Av.)
   BD4: B'frd 1H 69
   (Hunsworth La.)
Lwr. Langwith LS22: Coll 3A 28
Lwr. Lark Hill BD19: Cleck 2H 153
LOWER MICKLETOWN 4F 145
Lwr. Mickletown LS26: Mick 4E 145
Lwr. Newlands BD6: Brigh 2B 162
Lwr. Ox Heys HX3: Hal 4H 131
Lwr. Park Grn. BD20: Sils 2C 14
Lwr. Pierce Cl. BD22: Haw 6F 47
Lwr. Quarry Rd. HD2: Hud 4F 163
   HD5: Hud 4F 163
Lwr. Range HX3: Hal 6G 129
Lwr. Range Ter. HX3: Hal 1C 164
Lwr. Rayleigh St. BD4: B'frd 1G 111
Lwr. Rushton Rd. BD3: B'frd 4C 92
Lwr. Saltonstall HX2: Hal 2D 126
Lower Sandhills LS14: T'ner 4G 63
Lwr. Scholes BD22: Keigh 1A 64
Lwr. School St. BD12: B'frd 1C 132
   BD18: Ship 1H 69
Lwr. Skircoat Grn. *HX3: Hal* *1G 159*
   (off Cow La.)
Lwr. Slack HX2: Hal 1F 127
Lwr. Tofts Rd. LS28: Pud 4A 94
LOWER TOWN 1D 84
Lowertown BD22: Oxen 1C 84
Lwr. Town St. LS13: Leeds 6F 75

Lwr. Wellgate HX4: Hal 4G 159
Lwr. Wellington Rd. LS29: I'ly 5E 11
Lwr. Westfield Rd. BD9: B'frd 2A 90
Lwr. Whiteshaw M. BD13: B'frd 1B 86
LOWER WOODLANDS 2H 133
LOWER WORTLEY 6C 96
Lwr. Wortley Rd. LS12: Leeds 6A 96
LOWER WYKE 1C 152
Lwr. Wyke Grn. BD12: Brigh 1B 152
Lwr. Wyke La. BD12: Brigh 1B 152
Loweswater Av. BD6: B'frd 1H 131
LOW FARM 3H 57
Low Farm LS26: Kip 5E 123
Lowfield Cl. BD12: B'frd 2E 133
Lowfield Cres. BD20: Sils 3F 15
Low Flds. Av. LS12: Leeds 1E 117
Lowfields Bus. Pk. HX5: Ell 3D 160
   (not continuous)
Lowfields Cl. HX5: Ell 3C 160
Low Flds. Rd. LS12: Leeds 1E 117
   (not continuous)
Low Flds. Way LS12: Leeds 1E 117
Lowfields Way HX5: Ell 3C 160
LOW FOLD
   LS12 . . . . .5G 95
   LS18 . . . . .1C 74
Low Fold BD2: B'frd 6F 71
   BD13: B'frd 3A 108
   BD17: Bail *3C 52*
   (off Moorgate)
   BD19: Cleck 1F 153
   BD20: Stee 6C 14
   LS9: Leeds 5C 98
   LS18: H'fth 2C 74
   LS19: Yead 3F 55
Low Gipton Cres. LS9: Leeds 6H 79
Low Grange Cres. LS10: Leeds 4C 118
Low Grange Vw. LS10: Leeds 5C 118
LOW GREEN 4G 55
Low Grn. BD7: B'frd 2A 110
   LS19: Yead 4G 55
Low Grn. Ter. BD7: B'frd 2B 110
Low Hall Cl. LS29: Men 1G 39
Low Hall Pl. LS11: Leeds 5G 97
Low Hall Rd. LS18: H'fth 1A 74
   LS19: H'fth 1A 74
   LS29: Men 1H 39
Low Hill BD17: Bail 1C 52
Low Ho. Dr. BD20: Sils 3E 15
Low Ho. Farm Ct. BD20: Sils 3E 15
Low Laithes HX6: Hal 6G 147
Low La. BD13: B'frd 2G 107
   BD14: B'frd 6B 88
   HD6: Brigh 3C 152
   HX2: Hal 1A 126
   LS18: H'fth 5E 57
   WF17: Bat 6A 136
Low Mill La. BD21: Keigh 6B 34
   LS29: Add .1F 9
Low Mills Rd. LS12: Leeds 1B 116
LOW MILL VILLAGE 2F 9
LOW MOOR 1C 132
LOW MOOR SIDE 3E 115
Low Moor Side LS12: Leeds 2F 115
Low Moorside Cl. LS12: Leeds 2G 115
Low Moorside Ct. LS12: Leeds 2G 115
Low Moor Side La. LS12: Leeds 3E 115
Low Moor St. BD12: B'frd 1D 132
Low Moor Ter. HX2: Hal 3B 148
   LS11: Leeds 3H 117
Lowood La. WF17: Bat 4A 136
Low Rd. LS10: Leeds 1C 118
Lowry Rd. WF3: E Ard 1D 154
Lowry Vw. BD21: Keigh 1A 48
Low Shops La. LS26: Rothw 1G 141
Low Spring Rd. BD21: Keigh 1C 48
LOW SPRINGS 6C 38
Low St. BD21: Keigh 6A 34
   (not continuous)
   WF3: E Ard 6E 139
Lowther Av. LS25: Gar 5E 103
Lowther Cres. LS26: Swil 3A 122

Lowther Dr.—Main St.

Lowther Dr. LS25: Gar .5E **103**
LS26: Swil .4H **121**
Lowther Gro. LS25: Gar .5E **103**
Lowther Rd. LS25: Gar .5E **103**
Lowther St. BD2: B'frd .1H **91**
LS8: Leeds .6D **78**
Lowther Ter. LS15: Swil .5A **102**
Lowtown LS28: Pud .3B **94**
LOW TOWN END .4B **138**
LOW UTLEY .3G **33**
Low Way LS23: B Spa .5B **30**
Low Well St. BD5: B'frd .2D **110**
Low Whitehouse Row
LS10: Leeds .6B **98**
Low Wood BD15: B'frd .5H **67**
Low Wood Ct. BD20: Keigh .2H **33**
Low Wood Head BD20: Keigh .2B **34**
Low Wood Ri. LS29: I'ly .6H **11**
Loxley Gro. LS22: Weth .1D **12**
Lucas Ct. LS6: Leeds .6A **78**
Lucas Pl. LS6: Leeds .5G **77**
Lucas St. LS6: Leeds .5G **77**
Lucy Av. LS15: Leeds .3A **100**
Lucy Hall Dr. BD17: Bail .5G **51**
Lucy St. HX3: Hal .1H **149**
LUDDENDEN .6E **127**
LUDDENDEN FOOT .2D **146**
Luddenden La. HX2: Hal .2D **146**
Luddendon Pl. *BD13: B'frd .3G* ***107***
(off Mill La.)
Ludgate Hill LS2: Leeds .3A **98** (4F **5**)
Ludlam St. BD5: B'frd .6E **91**
(not continuous)
Ludlow Av. LS25: Gar .4H **103**
Ludolf Dr. LS17: Leeds .3A **62**
Luke Rd. BD5: B'frd .1C **110**
Lulworth Av. LS15: Leeds .2F **101**
Lulworth Cl. LS15: Leeds .2F **101**
Lulworth Cres. LS15: Leeds .2F **101**
Lulworth Dr. LS15: Leeds .3F **101**
Lulworth Gth. LS15: Leeds .3F **101**
Lulworth Gro. BD4: B'frd .3B **112**
(not continuous)
Lulworth Vw. LS15: Leeds .2F **101**
Lulworth Wlk. LS15: Leeds .2F **101**
Lumb Bottom BD11: B'frd .6B **114**
Lumb Gill La. LS29: Add .3F **9**
Lumb La. BD8: B'frd .2C **90**
HX2: Hal .1F **127**
HX3: Hal .5F **129**
Lumbrook HX3: Hal .4E **131**
Lumbrook Cl. HX3: Hal .4E **131**
Lumby Cl. LS28: Pud .6B **94**
Lumby Gth. LS17: Bard .5D **26**
Lumby La. LS17: Bard .4C **26**
LS28: Pud .6B **94**
Lumby St. BD10: B'frd .1H **71**
Lumley Av. LS4: Leeds .6D **76**
Lumley Gro. LS4: Leeds .6D **76**
Lumley Mt. LS4: Leeds .6D **76**
Lumley Pl. LS4: Leeds .6D **76**
Lumley Rd. LS4: Leeds .6D **76**
Lumley St. LS4: Leeds .6D **76**
Lumley Ter. LS4: Leeds .6D **76**
Lumley Vw. LS4: Leeds .6D **76**
Lumley Wlk. LS4: Leeds .6D **76**
Lunan Pl. LS8: Leeds .5D **78**
Lunan Ter. LS8: Leeds .5D **78**
Lund La. BD22: Keigh .1B **46**
Lund St. BD8: B'frd .4G **89**
BD16: Bgly .4B **50**
BD21: Keigh .5A **34**
Lundy Ct. BD5: B'frd .2E **111**
Lune St. BD22: Haw .1F **65**
Lupton Av. LS9: Leeds .3E **99**
Lupton Flats LS6: Leeds .4D **76**
Lupton's Bldgs. LS12: Leeds .4B **96**
Lupton St. BD8: B'frd .2E **91**
LS10: Leeds .2C **118**
Lustre St. BD21: Keigh .6G **33**
Luther St. LS13: Leeds .4A **74**
Luther Way BD2: B'frd .6F **71**
Luton St. BD21: Keigh .6H **33**
HX1: Hal .2D **148**
Luttrell Cl. LS16: Leeds .5A **58**
Luttrell Cres. LS16: Leeds .5A **58**
Luttrell Gdns. LS16: Leeds .5A **58**
Luttrell Pl. LS16: Leeds .5A **58**
Luttrell Rd. LS16: Leeds .5A **58**
Lutyens, The *LS29: I'ly .5C* ***10***
(off Westville)
LS29: I'ly .5B **10**
(Warlbeck)
Luxor Av. LS8: Leeds .5D **78**
Luxor Rd. LS8: Leeds .5D **78**
Luxor St. LS8: Leeds .5D **78**
Luxor Vw. LS8: Leeds .5D **78**
Lydbrook Pk. HX3: Hal .1E **159**
Lyddon Ter. LS2: Leeds .1G **97** (1A **4**)
Lydford Ho. *BD5: B'frd .6E* ***91***
(off Grafton St.)
LYDGATE .2G **151**
Lydgate HX3: Hal .4C **130**
LS9: Leeds .2D **98**
Lydgate Pk. HX3: Hal .2G **151**
Lydgate Pl. LS28: Pud .2E **73**
Lydgate St. LS28: Pud .2E **73**
Lydia Hill *HD6: Brigh .2A* ***162***
(off East St.)
Lydia St. LS2: Leeds .4G **5**
Lyme Chase LS14: Leeds .1B **100**
Lymington Dr. BD4: B'frd .1C **112**
Lynch Av. BD7: B'frd .2H **109**
Lyncroft BD2: B'frd .5F **71**
Lyndale LS25: Kip .5G **123**
Lyndale Dr. BD18: Ship .2F **71**
WF2: Wake .6C **156**
(not continuous)
Lyndale Rd. BD16: Bgly .2E **51**
Lyndean Gdns. BD10: B'frd .2G **71**
Lynden Av. BD18: Ship .1E **71**
Lynden Ct. BD6: B'frd .6A **110**
Lyndhurst Av. HD6: Brigh .4A **162**
Lyndhurst Cl. LS15: Scho .2H **81**
Lyndhurst Cres. LS15: Scho .2H **81**
Lyndhurst Gro. BD15: B'frd .2E **89**
Lyndhurst Gro. Rd. HD6: Brigh .4A **162**
Lyndhurst Rd. HD6: Brigh .3A **162**
LS15: Scho .3H **81**
Lyndhurst Vw. LS15: Scho .3H **81**
Lyndon Av. LS25: Gar .4E **103**
Lyndon Ter. BD16: Bgly .4C **50**
Lyndsey Ct. BD22: Keigh .5B **46**
Lyndum Gro. LS25: Kip .3G **123**
Lynfield Dr. BD9: B'frd .6E **69**
WF15: Liv .4H **153**
Lynfield Mt. BD18: Ship .1E **71**
Lynmoor Ct. BD10: B'frd .2F **71**
Lynnfield Gdns. LS15: Scho .3H **81**
Lynsey Gdns. BD4: B'frd .6H **111**
Lynthorne Rd. BD9: B'frd .5C **70**
Lynton Av. BD9: B'frd .1H **89**
LS23: B Spa .3B **30**
WF3: Leeds .5C **140**
Lynton Dr. BD9: B'frd .1G **89**
BD18: Ship .2A **70**
BD20: Keigh .4D **34**
Lynton Gro. BD9: B'frd .1H **89**
HX2: Hal .4D **106**
Lynton Vs. BD9: B'frd .1H **89**
Lynwood Av. BD18: Ship .1E **71**
LS12: Leeds .6C **96**
LS26: Rothw .1F **143**
Lynwood Cl. BD11: B'frd .3F **135**
Lynwood Ct. BD22: Keigh .2E **47**
Lynwood Cres. HX1: Hal .4D **148**
LS12: Leeds .6C **96**
LS26: Rothw .1F **143**
Lynwood Gdns. LS28: Pud .4G **93**
Lynwood Gth. LS12: Leeds .6C **96**
Lynwood Gro. LS12: Leeds .1C **116**
Lynwood M. BD4: B'frd .3D **112**
Lynwood Mt. LS12: Leeds .6C **96**
Lynwood Ri. LS12: Leeds .6C **96**
Lynwood Vw. LS12: Leeds .6C **96**
Lyon Rd. BD20: Stee .5A **14**
Lyons St. BD13: B'frd .4B **108**
Lyon St. BD13: B'frd .4H **87**
Lytham Dr. BD13: B'frd .3D **108**
Lytham Gro. LS12: Leeds .1A **116**
Lytham Pl. LS12: Leeds .1A **116**
Lytham St. HX1: Hal .2D **148**
Lythe Ho. BD3: B'frd .2G **7**
Lytton Rd. BD8: B'frd .3H **89**
Lytton St. HX3: Hal .6G **129**
LS10: Leeds .2B **118**

M

M1 Ind. Est. LS10: Leeds .2B **118**
Mabel Royd BD7: B'frd .6H **89**
MABGATE .2B **98** (2G **5**)
Mabgate LS9: Leeds .3B **98** (3H **5**)
Mabgate Grn. LS9: Leeds .3B **98** (3H **5**)
Mabgate Mills Ind. & Commercial Cen.
LS9: Leeds .2C **98** (2H **5**)
Macaulay St. LS9: Leeds .2C **98** (3H **5**)
McBride Way LS22: Weth .4F **13**
McBurney Cl. HX3: Hal .5F **129**
Mackingstone Dr. BD22: Keigh .4B **46**
Mackingstone La. BD22: Keigh .3B **46**
Mackintosh St. HX1: Hal .3D **148**
McLaren Flds. LS13: Leeds .1F **95**
McMahon Dr. BD13: B'frd .3D **108**
McMillan Gdns. BD6: B'frd .6D **110**
Macturk Gro. BD8: B'frd .2A **90**
Maddocks St. BD18: Ship .1A **70**
Madewel Ho. HX5: Ell .6C **160**
Madison Av. BD4: B'frd .4C **112**
Madni Cl. HX1: Hal .2F **149**
Mafeking Av. LS11: Leeds .4G **117**
Mafeking Gro. LS11: Leeds .4G **117**
Mafeking Mt. LS11: Leeds .4G **117**
Mafeking Ter. BD18: Ship .4D **70**
Magdalene Cl. LS16: Leeds .4A **58**
Magdalin Dr. LS28: Pud .1C **94**
Magellan Ho. LS10: Leeds .5B **98** (6G **5**)
Magnolia Dr. BD15: B'frd .5B **68**
Magpie Cl. BD6: B'frd .4E **109**
Magpie La. LS27: Morl .4B **138**
Mahim Cres. BD17: Bail .5E **53**
Maidstone St. BD3: B'frd .4A **92**
Maidwell Way BD6: B'frd .1A **132**
Mail Cl. LS15: Leeds .6G **81**
Main Rd. BD13: B'frd .3B **86**
BD20: Keigh .5H **35**
BD20: Stee .5A **14**
Mainspring Rd. BD15: B'frd .4G **67**
Main St. BD12: B'frd .1E **133**
(Breaks Rd.)
BD12: B'frd .3C **132**
(Royd St.)
BD15: B'frd .4G **67**
BD16: Bgly .4B **50**
(Millgate)
BD16: Bgly .3D **68**
(Mnr. Farm Cl.)
BD17: B'frd .2A **54**
BD22: Haw .2C **64**
LS14: T'ner .3H **63**
LS15: Bar E .2D **82**
LS15: Scho .3H **81**
LS17: Bard .6E **27**
LS17: Leeds .2H **61**
LS20: Guis .5E **39**
LS21: Pool .4E **25**
LS22: Coll .3B **28**
(School La.)
LS22: Coll .1B **28**
(Stammergate La.)
LS24: Tad .4H **31**
LS25: Gar .4E **103**
LS26: Mick .4D **144**
LS29: Add .1C **8**
LS29: Burl W .1E **21**

236 A-Z Leeds & Bradford

Main St. LS29: Men 6F **21**
  WF3: E Ard 2B **156**
  WF3: Rothw 4H **141**
  WF10: Kip 3H **145**
Maister Pl. BD22: Keigh 4B **46**
Maitland Cl. BD15: B'frd 4D **88**
Maitland Pl. LS11: Leeds 1G **117**
Maize St. BD21: Keigh 3G **47**
Malden Rd. LS6: Leeds 6F **59**
Malham Av. BD9: B'frd 6E **69**
  HD6: Brigh 3G **161**
Malham Cl. LS14: Leeds 5C **80**
Malham Ct. BD20: Sils 3E **15**
         (off Ings Way)
Malham Rd. HD6: Brigh 4G **161**
Malin Rd. WF12: Dew 6A **154**
Mallard Cl. BD10: B'frd 4A **72**
  LS10: Leeds 6D **118**
Mallard Ct. BD8: B'frd 4E **89**
Mallard M. BD2: B'frd 4B **72**
Mallards, The BD20: Sils 2E **15**
Mallard Vw. BD22: Oxen 1C **84**
Mallard Way LS27: Morl 3D **138**
Mall La. LS20: Guis 2F **41**
Mallory Cl. BD7: B'frd 5H **89**
Malmesbury Cl. BD4: B'frd 4C **112**
  LS12: Leeds 5C **96**
Malmesbury Gro. LS12: Leeds 5C **96**
Malmesbury Pl. LS12: Leeds 5C **96**
Malmesbury Ter. LS12: Leeds 5C **96**
Malsis Cres. BD21: Keigh 1G **47**
Malsis Rd. BD21: Keigh 1G **47**
Maltby Ct. LS15: Leeds 4F **101**
Maltby Ho. BD5: B'frd 1D **110**
         (off Park La.)
Malthouse Cl. LS14: S'cft 5E **45**
Malting Cl. WF3: Rothw 4F **141**
Malting Ri. WF3: Rothw 4F **141**
Maltings, The BD20: Sils 1E **15**
  LS6: Leeds 1E **97**
      (off Alexandra Rd.)
  WF3: Rothw 4F **141**
Maltings Ct. LS11: Leeds 1A **118**
      (off Moorside Maltings)
Maltings Rd. HX2: Hal 5B **128**
  LS11: Leeds 2A **118**
Malt Kiln BD14: B'frd 1D **108**
       (off Gordon St.)
Malt Kiln La. BD13: B'frd 6F **87**
  LS25: Kip 4H **123**
Malton Ho. BD10: B'frd 3A **72**
      (off Rowantree Dr.)
Malton St. HX3: Hal 5G **129**
  HX6: Hal 4H **147**
Malt Shovel Yd. BD10: B'frd 1H **71**
        (off Town La.)
Malt St. BD22: Keigh 3G **47**
Malvern Brow BD9: B'frd 1F **89**
Malvern Cres. BD20: Keigh 2C **34**
Malvern Gro. BD9: B'frd 2F **89**
  LS11: Leeds 1G **117**
Malvern Ri. LS11: Leeds 1G **117**
Malvern Rd. BD9: B'frd 2F **89**
  LS11: Leeds 1G **117**
Malvern St. LS11: Leeds 1G **117**
Malvern Vw. LS11: Leeds 1G **117**
Manchester Rd.
  BD5: B'frd 3D **110** (6D **6**)
Manchester Sq. LS21: Otley 3E **23**
Mancot Ho. BD5: B'frd 1E **111**
     (off Manchester Rd.)
Mandale Gro. BD6: B'frd 5F **109**
Mandale Rd. BD6: B'frd 5F **109**
Mandarin Way LS10: Leeds 6D **118**
Mandela Cl. LS7: Leeds 4B **78**
Mandela Ho. LS7: Leeds 6B **78**
Mandeville Cres. BD6: B'frd 5H **109**
Manitoba Pl. LS7: Leeds 3C **78**
Manley Cl. LS25: Gar 6F **103**
Manley Dr. LS22: Weth 3B **12**
Manley Gro. LS29: I'ly 5F **11**
Manley Ri. LS29: I'ly 6F **11**

Manley Rd. LS29: I'ly 6F **11**
Manley St. HD6: Brigh 6A **152**
Manley St. Pl. HD6: Brigh 6A **152**
      (off Manley St.)
Mannheim Rd. BD9: B'frd 1B **90**
MANNINGHAM 1B **90**
Manningham La.
  BD8: B'frd 1C **90** (1B **6**)
Manningham La. Pk.
  BD1: B'frd 3D **90** (2B **6**)
Manningham Sports Cen. 2B **90**
Mann's Bldgs. WF17: Bat 5D **136**
Mann's Ct. BD1: B'frd 4D **6**
Mannville Gro. BD22: Keigh 1G **47**
Mannville Pl. BD22: Keigh 1G **47**
Mannville Rd. BD22: Keigh 2G **47**
Mannville St. BD22: Keigh 1G **47**
Mannville Ter. BD7: B'frd 5D **90** (5B **6**)
Mannville Wlk. BD22: Keigh 1G **47**
      (off Mannville St.)
Mannville Way BD22: Keigh 1G **47**
Manor, The LS8: Leeds 3G **79**
     (off Ladywood Rd.)
Manor Av. LS6: Leeds 5E **77**
Manor Barn Stables LS21: Otley . . .3E **23**
       (off Kirkgate)
Manor Cl. BD8: B'frd 3F **89**
  BD11: B'frd 6A **114**
  HX3: Hal 5F **149**
  LS16: B'hpe 2F **43**
  LS19: Yead 6F **41**
  LS26: Rothw 1A **142**
Manor Cott. M. LS14: S'cft 1E **63**
Manor Ct. BD16: Bgly 2C **68**
  BD19: Cleck 2F **153**
  LS11: Leeds 4E **117**
  LS17: Leeds 3B **62**
  LS21: Otley 3E **23**
      (off Bridge St.)
Manor Cres. LS21: Pool 4E **25**
  LS26: Rothw 1H **141**
Manor Cft. LS15: Leeds 4E **101**
Manor Dr. BD16: Bgly 1C **68**
  HX3: Hal 5F **149**
  LS6: Leeds 5E **77**
Manor Farm Cl. BD16: Bgly 3D **68**
  LS10: Leeds 1B **140**
  LS20: Guis 4C **40**
Manor Farm Ct. BD4: B'frd 6C **112**
Manor Farm Cres. LS27: Morl 5C **116**
Manor Farm Dr. LS10: Leeds 1A **140**
  LS27: Morl 5C **116**
  WF17: Bat 3A **154**
Manor Farm Gdns. LS10: Leeds . . .1A **140**
Manor Farm Grn. LS10: Leeds 1A **140**
Manor Farm Gro. LS10: Leeds 1A **140**
Manor Farm Ri. LS10: Leeds 1B **140**
Manor Farm Rd. LS10: Leeds 1B **140**
Manor Farm Wlk. LS10: Leeds 1B **140**
Manor Farm Way LS10: Leeds 2A **140**
Manorfield LS11: Leeds 2F **117**
Manor Fold BD16: Bgly 3D **68**
Manor Gdns. BD13: B'frd 4B **66**
  LS14: T'ner 1H **63**
  LS21: Pool 4E **25**
  WF12: Dew 6A **154**
Manor Gth. LS15: Leeds 4E **101**
  LS25: Led 5H **125**
Manor Gth. Rd. LS25: Kip 3H **123**
Manor Gro. BD20: Keigh 5E **35**
  LS7: Leeds 3B **78**
Manor Heath Pk. & Jungle Experience
  . . . . .5G **149**
Mnr. Heath Rd. HX3: Hal 5F **149**
Manor Ho. LS21: Otley 3E **23**
      (off Main St.)
Mnr. House Cft. LS16: Leeds 4D **58**
Manor Ho. La. LS17: Leeds 2D **60**
Manor Ho. Rd. BD15: B'frd 3G **67**
Manor Ho's. BD22: Keigh 5C **46**
      (off Colne La.)
Manor Ho. St. LS28: Pud 4A **94**

Manor La. BD18: Ship 2B **70**
      (not continuous)
  LS26: Rothw 2E **143**
     (off Aberford Rd.)
Manorley La. BD6: B'frd 1G **131**
Mnr. Mill La. LS11: Leeds 4E **117**
Manor Mills LS11: Leeds 4E **117**
Manor Pk. BD8: B'frd 3F **89**
  BD22: Keigh 5C **46**
  LS14: S'cft 6E **45**
  WF12: Dew 6B **154**
      (not continuous)
Manor Pk. Av. WF10: Kip 2G **145**
Manor Pk. Gdns. BD19: B'frd 4F **135**
Manor Ri. LS29: I'ly 5F **11**
Manor Rd. BD16: Bgly 2C **68**
  BD20: Keigh 3G **33**
  LS11: Leeds 5H **97**
  LS12: Leeds 6C **96**
  LS18: H'fth 1C **74**
  LS26: Rothw 1H **141**
  LS27: Morl 5C **116**
  WF17: Bat 4A **154**
Manor Row BD1: B'frd 4E **91** (2C **6**)
Manor Royd HX3: Hal 5G **149**
Manor Sq. LS19: Yead 6F **41**
  LS21: Otley 3E **23**
Manor St. BD2: B'frd 6H **71**
  BD19: Cleck 3F **153**
  LS7: Leeds 1B **98**
  LS21: Otley 3E **23**
Manor St. Ind. Est. LS7: Leeds 1C **98**
      (not continuous)
Manor Ter. BD2: B'frd 6H **71**
  LS6: Leeds 5E **77**
  LS19: Yead 6F **41**
  LS25: Kip 4H **123**
Manor Vw. BD20: Stee 6A **14**
      (off Moor La.)
  LS6: Leeds 5E **77**
  LS28: Pud 4A **94**
Manscombe Rd. BD15: B'frd 2E **89**
Manse Cres. LS29: Burl W 2E **21**
Mansel M. BD4: B'frd 4C **112**
Manse Rd. LS29: Burl W 2E **21**
Manse St. BD3: B'frd 4A **92**
Mansfield Av. BD16: Bgly 2E **51**
Mansfield Pl. LS6: Leeds 3D **76**
Mansfield Rd. BD8: B'frd 1C **90**
  LS29: Burl W 2D **20**
Mansion Ga. LS7: Leeds 3C **78**
Mansion Ga. Dr. LS7: Leeds 3C **78**
Mansion Ga. M. LS7: Leeds 3C **78**
Mansion Ga. Sq. LS7: Leeds 3C **78**
Mansion La. HX3: Hal 5G **149**
  LS8: Leeds 6F **61**
MANSTON 6F **81**
Manston App. LS15: Leeds 6E **81**
Manston Av. LS15: Leeds 6E **81**
Manston Cres. LS15: Leeds 6E **81**
Manston Dr. LS15: Leeds 6E **81**
Manston Gdns. LS15: Leeds 6F **81**
Manston Gro. LS15: Leeds 1E **101**
Manston La. LS15: Leeds 1F **101**
Manston Ri. LS15: Leeds 6E **81**
Manston Ter. LS15: Leeds 6E **81**
Manston Way LS15: Leeds 6E **81**
Mantra Ho. Bus. Cen.
  BD21: Keigh 1H **47**
      (off South St.)
Manywells Brow BD13: B'frd 5A **66**
      (not continuous)
Manywells Brow Ind. Est.
  BD13: B'frd 4B **66**
Manywells Cres. BD13: B'frd 4B **66**
Manywells La. BD13: B'frd 4H **65**
Maple Av. BD3: B'frd 3C **92**
  BD22: Keigh 5D **46**
Maple Ct. BD16: Bgly 5B **50**
      (off Ash Ter.)
  LS11: Leeds 3F **117**

Maple Cft. LS12: Leeds 6F **95**
  LS17: Leeds 4C **60**
Maple Dr. LS12: Leeds 6F **95**
  LS22: Weth 2E **13**
Maple Fold HX5: Ell 6A **160**
  LS12: Leeds 6F **95**
Maple Gdns. LS17: Bard 6G **27**
Maple Gro. BD17: Bail 6G **51**
  BD19: Cleck 6E **135**
  BD20: Keigh 4G **33**
  HD2: Hud 6A **162**
  LS12: Leeds 6G **95**
Maple Ri. LS26: Rothw 3A **142**
Maple St. HX1: Hal 4D **148**
Maple Ter. LS19: Yead 6D **40**
Maple Way LS14: Leeds 1E **81**
Marbridge Ct. BD6: B'frd 3B **110**
Marchant Way LS27: Leeds 4C **116**
Marchbank Rd. BD3: B'frd 3A **92**
March Cote La. BD16: Bgly 3B **68**
Marchmont Cres. LS25: Kip 5F **123**
Marchwood Gro. BD14: Thi 6F **89**
Marcia Cl. BD10: B'frd 3A **72**
Mardale Cres. LS14: Leeds 6C **80**
Margaret Av. LS17: Bard 1F **45**
Margaret Cl. LS27: Morl 2C **138**
Margaret St. BD21: Keigh 5G **33**
  HX1: Hal 2F **149**
  WF1: Wake 5E **157**
Margate LS26: Rothw 1E **143**
Margate Rd. BD4: B'frd 1G **111**
Margate St. HX6: Hal 6G **147**
Margerison Cres. LS29: I'ly 6G **11**
Margerison Rd. LS29: I'ly 6G **11**
Margram Bus. Cen. HX1: Hal 1F **149**
  (off Horne St.)
Marian Gro. LS11: Leeds 2H **117**
Marian Rd. LS6: Leeds 6H **77**
Marian Ter. LS6: Leeds 6H **77**
Maria St. LS29: Burl W 1E **21**
Marina Cres. LS27: Morl 4H **137**
Marina Gdns. HX6: Hal 5B **148**
  (off Park Rd.)
Marion Dr. BD18: Ship 2C **70**
Marion St. BD7: B'frd 4C **90**
  BD16: Bgly 4C **50**
  HD6: Brigh 5A **152**
Mark Cl. BD10: B'frd 1A **72**
Market Arc. HX1: Hal 4C **164**
Mkt. Balcony HX1: Hal 4C **164**
Market Bldgs. LS2: Leeds . . .3B **98** (4G **5**)
Market Bus. Cen., The
  HX1: Hal 2E **149**
Market Ct. BD13: B'frd 5A **88**
Market Hall LS27: Morl 3A **138**
  (off Hope St.)
Market Pl. BD18: Ship 1B **70**
  BD21: Keigh 6A **34**
  LS21: Otley 3E **23**
  LS22: Weth 4E **13**
  LS28: Pud 4A **94**
Market Sq. BD18: Ship 2B **70**
  LS27: Morl 3A **138**
  (off Queen St.)
Market St. BD1: B'frd 5E **91** (5C **6**)
  BD6: B'frd 4C **110**
  BD13: B'frd 5A **88**
  BD16: Bgly 4B **50**
  BD18: Ship 2B **70**
  (not continuous)
  BD20: Stee 6D **14**
  BD21: Keigh 1A **48**
  HD6: Brigh 1B **162**
  HX1: Hal 2G **149** (4C **164**)
  LS21: Otley 4E **23**
  WF17: Bat 6A **136**
Market St. Arc. LS1: Leeds . . .4A **98** (5F **5**)
Markfield Av. BD12: B'frd 2C **132**
Markfield Cl. BD12: B'frd 2C **132**
Markfield Cres. BD12: B'frd 2C **132**
Markfield Dr. BD12: B'frd 2C **132**

Markham Av. LS8: Leeds 5D **78**
  LS19: Yead 2G **55**
Markham Cres. LS19: Yead 2G **55**
Markham Cft. LS19: Yead 2G **55**
Markington M. LS10: Leeds 4A **140**
Markington Pl. LS10: Leeds 4A **140**
Mark La. LS2: Leeds 3A **98** (3E **5**)
Mark St. BD5: B'frd 2E **111**
Marland Rd. BD21: Keigh 5C **34**
Marlborough Av. HX3: Hal 5F **149**
Marlborough Cotts. *LS29: Men* 1H **39**
  (off Marlborough Ct.)
Marlborough Ct. LS14: S'cft 5F **45**
  LS29: Men 1H **39**
Marlborough Gdns. *LS2: Leeds* 1H **97**
  (off Bk. Blenheim Ter.)
Marlborough Grange LS1: Leeds 3A **4**
Marlborough Gro. *LS2: Leeds* 1H **97**
  (off Bk. Blenheim Ter.)
  LS29: I'ly 6F **11**
Marlborough Ho. *HX5: Ell* 4B **160**
  (off Southgate)
Marlborough Rd. BD8: B'frd 2C **90**
  BD10: B'frd 1A **72**
  BD18: Ship 2A **70**
  HD2: Hud 6B **162**
Marlborough Sq. LS29: I'ly 6F **11**
Marlborough St. BD21: Keigh 5B **34**
  LS1: Leeds 3G **97** (4A **4**)
Marlborough Towers
  LS1: Leeds 3G **97** (3A **4**)
Marlborough Vs. LS29: Men 1H **39**
Marldon Rd. HX3: Hal 6C **130**
MARLEY 1G **49**
Marley Activities & Coaching Cen.
  . . . . .5D **34**
Marley Cl. BD8: B'frd 3G **89**
Marley Ct. BD16: Bgly 6H **35**
Marley Gro. LS11: Leeds 2F **117**
Marley La. BD13: B'frd 2A **108**
Marley Pl. LS11: Leeds 2F **117**
Marley Rd. BD21: Keigh 5D **34**
Marley St. BD3: B'frd 4G **91** (3G **7**)
  BD21: Keigh 1H **47**
  LS11: Leeds 2F **117**
Marley Ter. LS11: Leeds 2F **117**
Marley Vw. BD16: Bgly 6H **35**
  LS11: Leeds 2F **117**
Marlo Rd. WF12: Dew 6A **154**
Marlowe Ct. BD18: Ship 1D **70**
Marlowe Cl. LS28: Pud 6B **94**
Marlowe Ct. *LS20: Guis* 4B **40**
  (off Renton Dr.)
  LS25: Gar 4F **103**
Marmion Av. BD8: B'frd 4E **89**
Marne Av. BD14: B'frd 2E **109**
Marne Cres. BD10: B'frd 2H **71**
Marquis Av. BD12: B'frd 2H **133**
Marriner Rd. BD21: Keigh 1A **48**
Marriner's Dr. BD9: B'frd 5B **70**
Marriner Wlk. BD21: Keigh 2A **48**
Marsden Av. LS11: Leeds 3G **117**
Marsden Ct. *LS28: Pud* 6H **73**
  (off Water La.)
Marsden Gro. LS11: Leeds 3G **117**
Marsden Memorial Homes
  LS28: Pud 1H **93**
  (off Parkside Rd.)
Marsden Mt. LS11: Leeds 3G **117**
Marsden Pl. LS11: Leeds 3G **117**
Marsden Vw. LS11: Leeds 3G **117**
Marsett Way LS14: Leeds 1D **80**
MARSH 5B **64**
Marsh LS28: Pud 4G **93**
Marsh, The BD4: B'frd 6D **112**
Marshall Av. LS15: Leeds 1F **101**
Marshall Cl. *LS27: Morl* 3A **138**
  (off Commercial St.)
Marshall Ct. LS11: Leeds 5G **97**
  LS19: Yead 6F **41**
Marshall Cres. LS27: Morl 5B **138**
Marshall Mills LS11: Leeds 5G **97**

Marshall St. BD20: Keigh 4H **33**
  LS11: Leeds 5H **97**
  LS15: Leeds 1E **101**
  LS19: Yead 6F **41**
  LS27: Morl 3A **138**
Marshall Ter. LS15: Leeds 1E **101**
Marsh Ct. LS28: Pud 4G **93**
Marsh Delves HX3: Hal 3B **150**
Marsh Delves La. HX3: Hal 3B **150**
Marshfield Pl. BD5: B'frd 2D **110**
MARSHFIELDS 3D **110**
Marshfield St. BD5: B'frd 2D **110**
Marsh Gro. BD5: B'frd 2C **110**
  (not continuous)
Marsh La. BD11: B'frd 2E **135**
  BD22: Oxen 6A **64**
  HX3: Hal 3A **150**
  LS9: Leeds 4B **98** (5H **5**)
  (not continuous)
Marsh Ri. LS28: Pud 4G **93**
Marsh St. BD5: B'frd 2D **110**
  LS6: Leeds 6G **77**
  LS26: Rothw 3A **142**
Marsh Ter. LS28: Pud 4G **93**
MARSH TOP 5C **64**
Marsh Va. LS6: Leeds 6G **77**
Marshway HX1: Hal 1E **149**
Marsland Ct. BD19: Cleck 5B **134**
Marsland Pl. BD3: B'frd 4B **92**
Marston Av. LS27: Morl 4A **138**
Marston Cl. BD13: B'frd 4B **108**
Marston Mt. *LS9: Leeds* 2C **98**
  (off Cherry Pl.)
Marston Way LS22: Weth 3C **12**
Marten Rd. BD5: B'frd 2C **110**
Martin Cl. LS27: Morl 3C **138**
Martin Ct. BD6: B'frd 4E **109**
  LS15: Leeds 3F **101**
Martindale Cl. BD2: B'frd 6B **72**
Martindale Dr. LS13: Leeds 2G **95**
Martindale Dr. LS10: Leeds 4A **140**
Martingale Fold LS15: Bar E 2D **82**
Martin Grn. La. HX4: Hal 4E **159**
  (not continuous)
Martin St. HD6: Brigh 6B **152**
  WF17: Bat 6A **136**
Martin Ter. LS4: Leeds 1C **96**
Martlett Dr. BD7: B'frd 3F **111**
Marton Ct. BD3: B'frd 4B **92**
Marton Hgts. HX6: Hal 5G **147**
Marwood Rd. LS13: Leeds 4G **95**
Maryfield Av. LS15: Leeds 1C **100**
Maryfield Cl. LS15: Leeds 1C **100**
Maryfield Ct. LS15: Leeds 1D **100**
Maryfield Cres. LS15: Leeds 1D **100**
Maryfield Gdns. LS15: Leeds 1C **100**
Maryfield Grn. LS15: Leeds 1C **100**
Maryfield M. LS15: Leeds 1C **100**
Maryfield Va. LS15: Leeds 1C **100**
Mary St. BD4: B'frd 6A **92**
  BD12: B'frd 3C **132**
  BD13: B'frd 5H **87**
  (George St.)
  BD13: B'frd 2B **86**
  (Minorca Mt.)
  BD18: Ship 1H **69**
  BD22: Oxen 1C **84**
  HD6: Brigh 5A **152**
  LS28: Pud 5A **74**
  WF3: E Ard 1C **156**
Mary St. Cvn. Site BD4: B'frd 6A **92**
Mary Sunley Ho. *LS8: Leeds* 6D **78**
  (off Banstead St. W.)
Maryville Av. HD6: Brigh 4G **151**
Masefield Av. BD9: B'frd 6E **69**
Masefield St. LS20: Guis 5D **40**
Masham Cl. LS6: Leeds 3D **76**
Masham Gro. LS12: Leeds 4D **96**
Masham Pl. BD9: B'frd 1H **89**
Masham St. LS12: Leeds 4D **96**
Masino Ter. *BD7: B'frd* 1A **110**
  (off Paternoster La.)

Masonic St. HX1: Hal 3C 148
Mason's Grn. HX2: Hal 2C 128
Mason Sq. HX2: Hal 4D 128
   (off Keighley Rd.)
Massey Flds. BD22: Haw 1D 64
Master La. HX2: Hal 5D 148
Matheson Ho. BD3: B'frd 2F 7
Matlock St. HX3: Hal 6E 129
Matrix Ct. LS11: Leeds 3H 117
Matthew Cl. BD20: Keigh 4C 34
Matthews Ct. HX3: Hal 5C 130
Matty La. LS26: Rothw 3F 141
Maud Av. LS11: Leeds 3H 117
Maude Av. BD17: Bail 5C 52
Maude Cres. HX6: Hal 6E 147
Maude St. HX3: Hal 3E 129
  HX4: Hal 4H 159
  LS2: Leeds 4B 98 (6G 5)
Maud Pl. LS11: Leeds 3H 117
Maudsley St. BD3: B'frd 4G 91 (4H 7)
Maud St. BD3: B'frd 5H 91
Maufe Way LS29: I'ly 6D 10
Maurice Av. HD6: Brigh 5H 151
Mavis Av. LS16: Leeds 1G 57
Mavis Gro. LS15: Leeds 2G 57
Mavis La. LS16: Leeds 1G 57
Mavis St. BD3: B'frd 4H 91 (3H 7)
Mawcroft Cl. LS19: Yead 2E 55
Mawcroft Grange Dr.
  LS19: Yead 2E 55
Mawcroft M. LS19: Yead 2F 55
Mawsdon Pl. HX4: Hal 4A 158
Mawson Ct. BD1: B'frd 4C 6
Mawson St. BD18: Ship 1H 69
Maw St. BD4: B'frd 6F 91
Maxwell Rd. BD6: B'frd 5H 109
  LS29: I'ly 6F 11
May Av. BD13: B'frd 5A 88
  LS27: Leeds, Morl 4C 116
Maybrook Ind. Pk.
  LS12: Leeds 3E 97
May Ct. LS27: Morl 4C 116
Mayfair BD5: B'frd 1D 110
Mayfair Way BD4: B'frd 6B 92
Mayfield HX3: Hal 6E 131
  (Northedge La.)
  HX3: Hal 5H 131
  (Norwood Grn. Hill)
Mayfield Av. BD12: B'frd 4C 132
  HD6: Brigh 1B 152
  HX1: Hal 3E 149
  LS29: I'ly 5F 11
Mayfield Cl. LS29: I'ly 5F 11
Mayfield Ct. LS18: H'fth 6E 57
Mayfield Dr. BD20: Keigh 5G 35
  HX1: Hal 3E 149
Mayfield Gdns. HX1: Hal 3E 149
  HX6: Hal 5B 148
  (off Park Rd.)
  LS29: I'ly 4F 11
Mayfield Gro. BD15: B'frd 3F 67
  BD17: Bail 4D 52
  HD6: Brigh 1B 152
  HX1: Hal 3E 149
Mayfield Mt. HX1: Hal 3E 149
Mayfield Pl. BD12: B'frd 4C 132
Mayfield Ri. BD12: B'frd 4D 132
Mayfield Rd. BD20: Keigh 5H 33
  LS15: Leeds 3D 100
  LS29: I'ly 5E 11
Mayfield St. HX1: Hal 4E 149
Mayfield Ter. BD12: B'frd 4D 132
  BD14: B'frd 2E 109
  HX1: Hal 2D 148
Mayfield Ter. Sth. HX1: Hal 4E 149
  (off Mayfield St.)
Mayfield Vw. BD12: B'frd 4D 132
Mayflower Ho. LS10: Leeds 3E 119
Maylea St. LS21: Otley 5B 22
Mayo Av. BD5: B'frd 3D 110
Mayo Cl. LS8: Leeds 3H 79
Mayo Cres. BD5: B'frd 4E 111

Mayo Dr. BD5: B'frd 4E 111
Mayo Gro. BD5: B'frd 4E 111
Mayo Rd. BD5: B'frd 4E 111
Maypole M. LS15: Bar E 1D 82
Mayroyde HX3: Hal 2F 151
Mayster Gro. HD6: Brigh 4G 161
Mayster Rd. HD6: Brigh 4H 161
May St. BD19: Cleck 6B 134
  BD21: Keigh 5A 34
  BD22: Haw 3D 64
May Ter. LS9: Leeds 5D 98
Maythorne Cres. BD14: B'frd 1F 109
Maythorne Dr. BD14: B'frd 1G 109
May Tree Cl. BD14: B'frd 6F 89
Mayville Av. BD20: Keigh 5F 35
  LS6: Leeds 6E 77
Mayville Pl. LS6: Leeds 6E 77
Mayville Rd. LS6: Leeds 6E 77
Mayville St. LS6: Leeds 6E 77
Mayville Ter. LS6: Leeds 6E 77
Mazebrook Av. BD19: Cleck 5C 134
Mazebrook Cres. BD19: Cleck 5C 134
Mead Cl. LS15: Leeds 5G 101
Meade, The LS25: Gar 4F 103
Mead Gro. LS15: Leeds 5G 101
Meadow, The LS14: S'cft 5F 45
Meadowbank Av. BD15: B'frd 2D 88
Meadowbrook Ct. LS27: Morl 4G 137
Meadow Cl. BD16: Bgly 6F 49
  HX3: Hal 1F 131
  LS17: Bard 5G 27
  LS23: B Spa 3A 30
  WF1: Wake 4H 157
  WF17: Bat 6C 136
Meadow Ct. BD13: B'frd 5H 87
  (off Chapel St.)
  BD15: B'frd 5C 68
  HD6: Brigh 1E 163
Meadow Cres. HX3: Hal 5C 128
Meadow Cft. BD11: B'frd 1H 135
  BD22: Keigh 1E 47
  HD2: Hud 6F 163
  HX4: Hal 6A 158
  LS11: Leeds 6H 97
  LS17: Bard 6E 27
  WF1: Wake 4G 157
Meadowcroft BD5: B'frd 4F 111
  LS29: Men 2G 39
Meadow Cft. Cl. BD10: B'frd 1F 71
Meadowcroft Cl. WF1: Wake 4H 157
Meadowcroft Ct. WF1: Wake 4H 157
Meadowcroft M. LS9: Leeds 4C 98
Meadowcroft Ri. BD4: B'frd 5A 112
Meadowcroft Rd. WF1: Wake 4H 157
Meadow Dr. HX3: Hal 5C 128
Meadow End LS16: B'hpe 3G 43
Meadow Fold BD15: B'hpe 5H 67
Meadow Gth. LS16: B'hpe 4H 43
  WF1: Wake 4G 157
Meadowgate Cft. WF3: Rothw 5F 141
Meadowgate Dr. WF3: Rothw 5F 141
Meadowgate Va. WF3: Rothw 6F 141
Meadowhurst Gdns. LS28: Pud 4H 93
Meadowlands BD19: Cleck 6E 133
Meadow La. BD20: Sils 4H 15
  HX3: Hal 5C 128
  LS11: Leeds 5A 98
Mdw. Park Cres. LS28: Pud 1F 93
Mdw. Park Dr. LS28: Pud 1F 93
Meadow Rd. BD10: B'frd 1C 72
  LS11: Leeds 5H 97
  LS25: Gar 4G 103
Meadows, The BD6: B'frd 4C 110
  LS16: Leeds 4C 58
  WF10: Kip 1F 145
Meadowside Rd. BD17: Bail 3E 53
Meadow Va. WF1: Wake 4G 157
Meadow Valley LS17: Leeds 2H 59
Meadow Vw. BD12: B'frd 6C 132
  BD22: Keigh 5D 46
  LS6: Leeds 6E 77
  LS15: Bar E 1E 83

Meadow Wlk. HX3: Hal 5C 128
  (off Meadow La.)
  LS7: Leeds 3C 78
Meadow Way LS17: Leeds 2G 59
  WF3: E Ard 2D 154
Mead Rd. LS15: Leeds 5G 101
Mead Vw. BD4: B'frd 2C 112
Mead Way LS15: Leeds 5G 101
Meadway BD6: B'frd 1G 131
Meagill Ri. LS21: Otley 1B 22
MEANWOOD 2F 77
Meanwood Cl. LS7: Leeds 5H 77
MEANWOOD GROVE 6E 59
Meanwood Gro. LS6: Leeds 6E 59
Meanwood Rd. LS6: Leeds 3F 77
  LS7: Leeds 5H 77
Meanwood Towers LS6: Leeds 1G 77
Meanwood Valley Cl. LS6: Leeds 3F 77
Meanwood Valley Dr. LS7: Leeds 3F 77
Meanwood Valley Grn. LS7: Leeds . . .3F 77
Meanwood Valley Gro. LS7: Leeds . . .3F 77
Meanwood Valley Mt. LS7: Leeds 3F 77
Meanwood Valley Urban Farm 4H 77
Meanwood Valley Wlk.
  LS7: Leeds 3F 77
Mearclough Rd. HX6: Hal 5B 148
Mecca Bingo
  Bradford 6C 6
  Cross Gates 1E 101
  Halifax 3B 164
  Hunslet 2B 118
  Leeds 5G 5
Medeway LS28: Pud 1G 93
Medhurst Av. LS25: Kip 3H 123
Medley La. HX3: Hal 3B 130
Medway BD13: B'frd 5B 108
Medway Av. LS25: Gar 6G 103
Meggison Gro. BD5: B'frd 1C 110
Megna Way BD5: B'frd 1E 111
Melba Rd. BD5: B'frd 2B 110
Melbourne Av. WF2: Wake 6D 156
Melbourne Gro. BD3: B'frd 3C 92
  LS13: Leeds 1E 95
Melbourne M. WF2: Wake 5C 156
Melbourne Mill Yd. LS27: Morl 3B 138
  (off Middleton Rd.)
Melbourne Pl. BD5: B'frd . . .6D 90 (6B 6)
Melbourne St. BD18: Ship 1A 70
  HX3: Hal 6E 129
  LS2: Leeds 2B 98 (2G 5)
  LS13: Leeds 1E 95
  LS27: Morl 3B 138
  LS28: Pud 1H 93
Melbourne Ter. BD5: B'frd . .6E 91 (6C 6)
Melcombe Wlk. BD4: B'frd 1C 112
Meldon Way BD6: B'frd 4E 109
Melford St. BD4: B'frd 3A 112
Melilot Cl. BD16: Bgly 5D 50
Mellor St. HD6: Brigh 1B 162
  HX1: Hal 4E 149
Mellor Ter. HX1: Hal 4E 149
Melrose BD22: Haw 3C 64
Melrose Ct. HX5: Ell 5A 160
Melrose Dr. LS29: Burl W 1E 21
Melrose Gro. LS18: H'fth 1G 75
Melrose Ho. BD4: B'frd 1C 112
  (off Ned La.)
Melrose Pl. LS18: H'fth 1F 75
  LS28: Pud 5H 93
Melrose St. BD7: B'frd 1A 110
  HX3: Hal 6E 129
  LS18: H'fth 1F 75
Melrose Vs. LS18: H'fth 1F 75
  (off Broadgate La.)
Melrose Wlk. LS18: H'fth 1F 75
Melton Av. LS10: Leeds 3D 140
Melton Cl. LS10: Leeds 3D 140
Melton Gth. LS10: Leeds 3D 140
Melton M. BD22: Haw 1D 64
Melton Ter. BD10: B'frd 5C 72
Melville Cl. LS6: Leeds 6H 77

Melville Gdns. LS6: Leeds 5H 77
Melville Gro. LS29: I'ly 5G 11
Melville Ho. *BD7: B'frd* 4C 90
   (off Preston St.)
Melville Pl. LS6: Leeds 5H 77
Melville Rd. LS6: Leeds 6H 77
Melville St. BD7: B'frd 4C 90
Memorial Dr. LS6: Leeds 2F 77
Mendip Cl. LS25: Gar 6F 103
Mendip Ho. Gdns. LS29: I'ly 2E 11
Mendip Way BD12: B'frd 1B 132
Menin Dr. BD17: Bail 2C 52
MENSTON 1F 39
Menston Dr. LS29: Men 2G 39
Menstone St. BD8: B'frd 3C 90 (2A 6)
Menston Hall LS29: Men 1H 39
Menston Old La. LS29: Burl W 5F 21
Menston Station (Rail) 6G 21
Merchants Ct. BD4: B'frd 6G 91
Merchants Quay
   LS9: Leeds 4B 98 (6H 5)
Mercia Way LS15: Leeds 6G 81
Mercury Row LS21: Otley 4E 23
Meriden Av. LS25: Gar 6F 103
Merlin Cl. LS27: Morl 4C 138
Merlin Ct. BD21: Keigh 2H 47
   WF17: Bat 6C 136
Merlin Gro. BD8: B'frd 4E 89
Merlinwood Dr. BD17: Bail 3D 52
Merlyn-Rees Av. LS27: Morl 3A 138
Merrion Cen. LS2: Leeds 2A 98 (2E 5)
Merrion Cres. HX3: Hal 4A 150
Merrion Pl. LS1: Leeds 3A 98 (3F 5)
   (not continuous)
Merrion St. HX3: Hal 4A 150
   LS1: Leeds 3A 98 (3F 5)
   LS2: Leeds 3A 98 (3E 5)
   (not continuous)
Merrion Way LS2: Leeds 2A 98 (2E 5)
Merrivale Rd. BD15: B'frd 3C 88
Merriville LS18: H'fth 2F 75
Merrydale Rd. BD4: B'frd 1G 133
Merton Av. LS28: Pud 1H 93
Merton Cl. LS25: Kip 3A 124
Merton Dr. LS28: Pud 1G 93
Merton Fold BD5: B'frd 1E 111
Merton Gdns. LS28: Pud 1G 93
Merton Rd. BD7: B'frd 6D 90 (6A 6)
Merville Av. BD17: Bail 2C 52
Metcalfe St. BD4: B'frd 1H 111
METHLEY 5C 144
Methley Dr. LS7: Leeds 3A 78
Methley Gro. LS7: Leeds 3A 78
METHLEY JUNCTION 6D 144
Methley La. LS7: Leeds 3B 78
   LS26: Rothw 3E 143
Methley Mt. LS7: Leeds 3B 78
Methley Pl. LS7: Leeds 3B 78
Methley Ter. LS7: Leeds 3B 78
Methley Vw. LS7: Leeds 3B 78
Methuen Oval BD12: B'frd 6C 132
Mexborough Av. LS7: Leeds 5B 78
Mexborough Ct. LS14: T'ner 2H 63
Mexborough Dr. LS7: Leeds 5B 78
Mexborough Gro. LS7: Leeds 5B 78
Mexborough Ho. *HX5: Ell* *4B 160*
   (off Gog Hill)
Mexborough Pl. LS7: Leeds 6B 78
Mexborough Rd. BD2: B'frd 4D 70
   LS7: Leeds 6B 78
Mexborough St. LS7: Leeds 5B 78
Meynell App. LS11: Leeds 6G 97
Meynell Av. LS26: Rothw 2A 142
Meynell Ct. LS15: Leeds 4F 101
Meynell Fold LS15: Leeds 5F 101
Meynell Hgts. LS11: Leeds 6G 97
Meynell Ho. BD10: B'frd 3A 72
Meynell La. LS15: Leeds 5F 101
Meynell Mt. LS26: Rothw 2B 142
Meynell Rd. LS15: Leeds 4F 101
Meynell Sq. LS11: Leeds 6G 97
Meynell Wlk. LS11: Leeds 6G 97

Meyrick Av. LS22: Weth 3G 13
Miall St. HX1: Hal 1E 149
Michael Av. WF3: Wake 4H 157
Mickledore Ridge BD7: B'frd 2G 109
MICKLEFIELD 4E 105
Micklefield Ct. LS19: Yead 3F 55
Micklefield La. LS19: Yead 3E 55
Micklefield Rd. LS19: Yead 3F 55
Micklefield Station (Rail) 5E 105
Micklemoss Dr. BD13: B'frd 3G 107
MICKLETHWAITE 6A 36
Micklethwaite Dr. BD13: B'frd 5A 108
Micklethwaite La. BD16: Bgly 1A 50
Micklethwaite Vw. LS22: Weth 5E 13
MICKLETOWN 4D 144
Mickletown Rd. LS26: Mick 4C 144
Mickley St. LS12: Leeds 4D 96
Middlebrook Cl. BD8: B'frd 4G 89
Middlebrook Cres. BD8: B'frd 5F 89
Middlebrook Dr. BD8: B'frd 4F 89
Middlebrook Hill BD8: B'frd 4F 89
Middlebrook Ri. BD8: B'frd 4F 89
Middlebrook Vw. BD8: B'frd 4G 89
Middlebrook Way BD8: B'frd 5F 89
Middlebrook Wlk. BD8: B'frd 4G 89
Middlecroft Cl. LS10: Leeds 5D 118
Middlecroft Rd. LS10: Leeds 5D 118
Middle Cross St. LS12: Leeds 4D 96
   (not continuous)
Middle Dean St. HX4: Hal 5G 159
Middle Ellistones *HX4: Hal* *4E 159*
   (off Saddleworth Rd.)
Middlefield Ct. BD20: Keigh 4F 35
Middle Fold LS9: Leeds 3B 98 (3H 5)
Middlegate WF17: Bat 6A 136
Middlegate Ct. BD4: B'frd 5H 111
Middleham Ct. BD4: B'frd 2D 112
Middleham Moor LS10: Leeds 4B 140
Middle La. BD14: B'frd 6E 89
   LS22: Coll 1C 28
Middlemoor LS14: Leeds 1D 80
Middle Rd. LS9: Leeds 3H 119
Middle St. BD1: B'frd 4E 91 (3D 6)
Middlethorne Cl. LS17: Leeds 2F 61
Middlethorne Ct. LS17: Leeds 2E 61
Middlethorne M. LS17: Leeds 2F 61
Middlethorne Ri. LS17: Leeds 2E 61
MIDDLETON
   Ilkley 2E 11
   Leeds 2H 139
   LS26: Rothw 2E 141
   LS29: I'ly 3D 10
Middleton Av. LS9: Leeds 2D 98
   LS26: Rothw 2E 141
   LS29: I'ly 3D 10
Middleton Cl. LS27: Morl 3B 138
Middleton Cres. LS11: Leeds 3H 117
Middleton District Cen.
   LS10: Leeds 2B 140
Middleton Gro. LS11: Leeds 4H 117
   LS27: Morl 3C 138
Middleton La. LS10: Leeds 4A 140
   LS26: Rothw 2E 141
   (not continuous)
   WF3: Leeds 4B 140
Middleton Leisure Cen. 3B 140
Middleton Pk. Av. LS10: Leeds 3H 139
Middleton Pk. Cir. LS10: Leeds 2H 139
Middleton Pk. Ct. LS10: Leeds 3H 139
Middleton Pk. Cres. LS10: Leeds 3A 140
Middleton Park Equestrian Cen. 5A 118
Middleton Pk. Grn. LS10: Leeds 3H 139
Middleton Pk. Gro. LS10: Leeds 2H 139
Middleton Pk. Mt. LS10: Leeds 3H 139
Middleton Pk. Rd. LS10: Leeds 2H 139
Middleton Pk. Ter. LS10: Leeds 3H 139
Middleton Railway 4A 118
Middleton Rd. LS10: Leeds 6C 118
   LS27: Morl 3B 138
   LS29: I'ly 5C 10
Middleton St. BD8: B'frd 2B 90
Middleton Ter. LS27: Morl 3C 138
Middleton Way LS10: Leeds 1D 140
Middle Wlk. LS8: Leeds 6G 61

Middle Way BD21: Keigh 6C 34
Middleway BD20: Sils 2F 15
Midge Hall Cl. LS29: Burl W 2E 21
Midgeham Gro. BD16: Bgly 6E 49
Midgeley Rd. BD17: Bail 6A 52
Midgley Gdns. LS6: Leeds 6G 77
Midgley Pl. LS6: Leeds 6H 77
Midgley Rd. HX7: Heb B 5A 126
   LS29: Burl W 2E 21
Midgley Row BD4: B'frd 4H 111
Midgley Ter. LS6: Leeds 6H 77
Midland Cl. LS10: Leeds 2D 118
Midland Gth. LS10: Leeds 2C 118
Midland Hill BD16: Bgly 4B 50
Midland Ho. *LS26: Rothw* *1F 143*
   (off Midland St.)
Midland Pas. LS6: Leeds 6F 77
Midland Pl. LS11: Leeds 5G 97
Midland Rd. BD8: B'frd 1D 90 (1C 6)
   BD9: B'frd 4C 70
   BD17: Bail 5D 52
   LS6: Leeds 6F 77
   LS10: Leeds 2C 118
Midland St. LS26: Rothw 1E 143
Midland Ter. BD2: B'frd 6D 70
   BD21: Keigh 5A 34
Mid Point BD3: Pud 3D 92
Mid Point Bus. Pk. BD3: Pud 3D 92
Midway Av. BD16: Bgly 2C 68
Milan Rd. LS8: Leeds 6D 78
Milan St. LS8: Leeds 6E 79
Mildred St. BD3: B'frd 2G 91 (1G 7)
Mile Cross Gdns. HX1: Hal 3C 148
Mile Cross Pl. HX1: Hal 3C 148
Mile Cross Rd. HX1: Hal 3C 148
Mile Cross Ter. HX1: Hal 3C 148
Miles Gth. LS17: Bard 5H 27
MILES HILL 3H 77
Miles Hill Av. LS7: Leeds 3H 77
Miles Hill Cres. BD4: B'frd 4A 112
   LS7: Leeds 3H 77
Miles Hill Dr. BD4: B'frd 4A 112
Miles Hill Gro. LS7: Leeds 3H 77
Miles Hill Mt. LS7: Leeds 2G 77
Miles Hill Pl. LS7: Leeds 2H 77
Miles Hill Rd. LS7: Leeds 2H 77
Miles Hill Sq. LS7: Leeds 3H 77
Miles Hill St. LS7: Leeds 3H 77
Miles Hill Ter. LS7: Leeds 3H 77
Miles Hill Vw. LS7: Leeds 3H 77
Milestone Ct. LS28: Pud 1B 94
Mile Thorn St. HX1: Hal 2D 148
Milford Gro. BD19: B'frd 4E 135
Milford Pl. BD9: B'frd 6A 70
   LS4: Leeds 2D 96
Millbank Ct. LS28: Pud 5B 94
Millbank Fold LS28: Pud 5B 94
Mill Banks BD20: Sils 2E 15
Millbank Vw. LS28: Pud 5B 94
Millbeck App. LS27: Morl 3C 138
Millbeck Cl. BD13: B'frd 5E 89
Millbeck Grn. LS22: Coll 3A 28
Mill Carr Hill Rd. BD4: B'frd 3H 133
   BD12: B'frd 2H 133
Mill Cotts. LS21: Pool 4F 25
Mill Ct. BD22: Oxen 1C 84
Millcroft LS21: Pool 4F 25
   WF3: Wake 3H 157
Millcroft Cl. WF3: Wake 3H 157
Millcroft Ri. WF3: Wake 3H 157
Mill Dam LS23: B Spa 6C 30
Millennium Sq.
   LS1: Leeds 2H 97 (2D 4)
Millennium Way LS11: Leeds 4H 117
Miller Cl. BD2: B'frd 6D 70
Millergate BD1: B'frd 4E 91 (4C 6)
Millers Cft. WF17: Bat 6D 136
Millers Dale LS27: Morl 1H 137
Millersdale Cl. BD4: B'frd 6G 111
Millfield End HX2: Hal 1C 146

Mill Fld. Rd. BD16: Bgly 2D 68
Millfields BD20: Sils 2D 14
Mill Fold LS27: Morl 6F 115
Mill Gth. LS27: Morl 6F 115
Millgarth Cl. LS22: Coll 3B 28
Millgarth St. LS2: Leeds ...3B 98 (4G 5)
Millgate BD16: Bgly 4B 50
   HX5: Ell 4B 160
MILL GREEN 4D 80
Mill Grn. LS11: Leeds 5F 97
Mill Grn. Cl. LS14: Leeds 4E 81
Mill Grn. Gdns. LS14: Leeds 4E 81
Mill Grn. Gth. LS14: Leeds 4E 81
Mill Grn. Pl. LS14: Leeds 4E 81
Mill Grn. Rd. LS14: Leeds 4E 81
Mill Grn. Vw. LS14: Leeds 4E 81
Mill Gro. HD6: Brigh 5H 151
Millhaven M. BD8: B'frd 2D 90
   (off Holywell Ash La.)
Mill Hey BD22: Haw 2D 64
Mill Hill BD22: Haw 2C 64
   HX2: Hal 1B 146
   LS1: Leeds 4A 98 (5E 5)
   LS26: Rothw 2A 142
   LS28: Pud 6A 94
Mill Hill Grn. LS26: Rothw 2A 142
Mill Hill La. HD6: Brigh 2F 163
   (Wakefield Rd.)
   HD6: Brigh 5G 151
   (Wood Bottom La.)
Mill Hill Sq. LS26: Rothw 2A 142
Mill Hill Top BD16: Bgly 1F 67
Mill Ho. Ri. BD5: B'frd 4H 111
Milligan Av. BD2: B'frd 4F 71
Milligan Ct. BD16: Bgly 6E 49
Mill La. BD4: B'frd 6E 91
   (Conway St.)
   BD4: B'frd 2B 114
   (Tong La.)
   BD5: B'frd 6E 91
   BD6: B'frd 1G 131
   BD11: B'frd 1E 135
   BD13: B'frd 3G 107
   BD16: Bgly 1E 51
   BD19: Cleck 4B 134
   BD20: Stee 6C 14
   BD22: Keigh 5B 46
   BD22: Oxen 6C 64
   HD5: Hud 6H 163
   HD6: Brigh 1B 162
   HX2: Hal 5E 127
   (Brook Ter.)
   HX2: Hal 6A 106
   (Hays La.)
   HX3: Hal 5F 129
   LS13: Leeds 6C 74
   LS17: Bard 1G 45
   LS20: Guis 6C 38
   LS21: Otley 3E 23
   LS21: Pool 4E 25
   LS22: Coll 3B 28
   LS22: Kirkby 1A 26
   LS23: B Spa 3C 30
   LS26: Mick 4C 144
   LS27: Morl 6F 115
   WF3: E Ard 1B 156
   WF17: Bat 5D 136
Millmoor Cl. BD9: B'frd 1F 89
Mill Pit La. LS26: Rothw 6H 119
   (not continuous)
Mill Pond Cl. LS6: Leeds 3E 77
Mill Pond Gro. LS6: Leeds 3E 77
Mill Pond La. LS6: Leeds 2E 77
Mill Pond Sq. LS6: Leeds 2E 77
Mill Row BD20: Stee 5A 14
Mill Royd St. HD6: Brigh 1B 162
MILL SHAW 4E 117
Millshaw LS11: Leeds 4D 116
Millshaw Mt. LS11: Leeds 5E 117
Millshaw Pk. Av. LS11: Leeds 5D 116
Millshaw Pk. Cl. LS11: Leeds 5D 116
Millshaw Pk. Dr. LS11: Leeds 4D 116

Millshaw Pk. La. LS11: Leeds 5D 116
Millshaw Pk. Trad. Est.
   LS11: Leeds 5E 117
Millshaw Pk. Way LS11: Leeds ...4D 116
Millshaw Rd. LS11: Leeds 6E 117
Millside Wlk. LS27: Morl 3C 138
Millside Way HX3: Hal 6H 149
Mill St. BD1: B'frd 3F 91 (2E 7)
   BD6: B'frd 4A 110
   BD13: B'frd 3B 66
   HX3: Hal 2E 159
   LS9: Leeds 4C 98 (5H 5)
   LS27: Morl 4A 138
Mill Vw. BD18: Ship 1A 70
   LS29: Burl W 1E 21
Millwright St. LS2: Leeds 2B 98 (2H 5)
Milne Ct. LS15: Leeds 5F 101
Milner Bank LS21: Otley 5B 22
Milner Cl. HX4: Hal 4G 159
Milner Fold LS28: Pud 6H 93
Milner Gdns. LS9: Leeds 5D 98
Milner Ga. HX2: Hal 3C 146
Milner Ing BD12: B'frd 3C 132
Milner La. HX4: Hal 4G 159
   LS14: S'cft, T'ner 5H 45
   WF3: Rothw 4E 141
   (not continuous)
Milner Pl. HX2: Hal 3D 146
Milner Rd. BD17: Bail 6B 52
Milner Royd La. HX6: Hal 6C 148
Milner's Rd. LS19: Yead 6D 40
Milner St. HX1: Hal 2F 149
Milnes St. LS12: Leeds 5E 97
Milne St. BD7: B'frd 4C 90
   (not continuous)
Milton Av. HX6: Hal 4H 147
Milton Dr. LS15: Scho 2H 81
Milton Pl. HX1: Hal 2F 149
   HX6: Hal 4H 147
   (off Milton St.)
Milton St. BD7: B'frd 4C 90
   BD13: B'frd 3C 86
   HX6: Hal 4H 147
Milton Ter. HX1: Hal 2F 149
   (not continuous)
   LS5: Leeds 5A 76
   LS19: Yead 6D 40
Minerva Ind. Est. LS26: Rothw ...6G 121
Minister Dr. BD4: B'frd 6B 92
Minnie St. BD21: Keigh 1H 47
   BD22: Haw 3C 64
Minor and Scurr's Yd. LS1: Leeds ..4E 5
Minorca Mt. BD13: B'frd 2B 86
Minstead Av. HX5: Brigh 4F 161
Minster Cl. HX4: Hal 4F 159
Minstrel Dr. BD3: B'frd 4A 108
Mint St. BD2: B'frd 1H 91
Miramar HD2: Hud 6D 162
Mirey La. HX6: Hal 5B 146
Mirfield Av. BD2: B'frd 4G 71
Mirycarr La. LS14: T'ner 5G 63
Miry La. HX7: Heb B 3A 146
   LS19: Yead 6H 41
   WF15: Liv 5H 153
Mission St. HD6: Brigh 2C 162
Mistal, The BD10: B'frd 1F 71
Mistral Cl. BD12: B'frd 5C 132
Mistral Gro. WF15: Liv 4H 153
Mistress La. LS12: Leeds 3C 96
Mitcham Dr. BD9: B'frd 1A 90
Mitchell Cl. BD10: B'frd 6A 54
Mitchell La. BD10: B'frd 6A 54
   BD20: Sils 2E 15
Mitchell Sq. BD5: B'frd 1E 111
   BD20: Sils 2E 15
   (off Elliot St.)
Mitchell St. BD21: Keigh 5B 34
   HD6: Brigh 6A 152
   HX6: Hal 5A 148
Mitchell Ter. BD16: Bgly 6B 50
Mitford Pl. LS12: Leeds 4D 96

Mitford Rd. LS12: Leeds 4D 96
Mitford Ter. LS12: Leeds 4D 96
Mitford Vw. LS12: Leeds 4D 96
Mitre Ct. BD4: B'frd 2B 112
Mitton St. BD5: B'frd 2C 110
   BD16: Bgly 3D 68
MIXENDEN 2A 128
Mixenden Cl. HX2: Hal 2A 128
Mixenden Ct. HX2: Hal 3B 128
   (off Mixenden Rd.)
Mixenden Grn. HX2: Hal 6A 106
Mixenden La. HX2: Hal 1B 128
Mixenden La. Ends HX2: Hal 3H 127
Mixenden Rd. HX2: Hal 1A 128
Mixenden Stones HX2: Hal 2A 128
Moat Cres. BD10: B'frd 1A 72
Moat End LS14: T'ner 2H 63
Moat Hill WF17: Bat 5B 136
Moat Hill Farm Dr. WF17: Bat 5C 136
Modder Av. LS12: Leeds 4B 96
Modder Pl. LS12: Leeds 4B 96
Model Av. LS12: Leeds 4D 96
Model Rd. LS12: Leeds 4D 96
Model Ter. LS12: Leeds 4D 96
Moderna Bus. Pk. HX7: Heb B 1A 146
Moderna Way HX7: Heb B 6A 126
Moffat Cl. BD6: B'frd 6H 109
Moffatt Cl. HX3: Hal 4C 128
Monarch Ga. BD13: B'frd 5C 86
Monckton Ho. BD5: B'frd 3F 111
   (off Parkway)
Mond Av. BD3: B'frd 2B 92
Monk Barn Cl. BD16: Bgly 3C 50
Monk Bri. Av. LS6: Leeds 3F 77
Monk Bri. Dr. LS6: Leeds 3E 77
Monk Bri. Gro. LS6: Leeds 3E 77
Monk Bri. Mt. LS6: Leeds 3E 77
Monk Bri. Pl. LS6: Leeds 3E 77
Monk Bri. Rd. LS6: Leeds 3E 77
Monk Bri. St. LS6: Leeds 3F 77
Monk Bri. Ter. LS6: Leeds 3E 77
Monk Ings WF17: Bat 6H 135
Monk Ings Av. WF17: Bat 6G 135
Monkmans Wharf BD20: Sils 2E 15
Monk St. BD7: B'frd 4C 90 (4A 6)
Monkswood LS5: Leeds 3H 75
Monkswood Av. LS14: Leeds 1B 80
Monkswood Bank LS14: Leeds 1B 80
Monkswood Cl. LS14: Leeds 1B 80
Monkswood Dr. LS14: Leeds 1B 80
Monkswood Ga. LS14: Leeds 1C 80
Monkswood Grn. LS14: Leeds 1B 80
Monkswood Hill LS14: Leeds 1B 80
Monkswood Ho. LS5: Leeds 5H 75
Monkswood Ri. LS14: Leeds 1B 80
Monkswood Wlk. LS14: Leeds 1C 80
Monkwood Rd. WF1: Wake 4F 157
Monson Av. LS28: Pud 3F 73
Montagu Av. LS8: Leeds 4F 79
Montagu Ct. LS8: Leeds 3F 79
Montagu Cres. LS8: Leeds 4G 79
Montagu Dr. LS8: Leeds 3F 79
Montague Ct. LS12: Leeds 4A 96
Montague Cres. LS25: Gar 3G 103
Montague Pl. LS25: Gar 4G 103
Montague St. BD5: B'frd 2C 110
   HX6: Hal 6G 147
Montagu Gdns. LS8: Leeds 4F 79
Montagu Gro. LS8: Leeds 4G 79
Montagu Pl. LS8: Leeds 4G 79
Montagu Ri. LS8: Leeds 4G 79
Montagu Rd. LS22: Weth 4G 13
Montagu Vw. LS8: Leeds 4F 79
Montcalm Cres. LS10: Leeds 3C 118
Monterey Dr. BD15: B'frd 6B 68
Montfort Cl. LS18: H'fth 4D 56
Montgomery Av. LS16: Leeds 2C 76
Montgomery Ho. BD8: B'frd 2C 90
   (off Trenton Dr.)
Mont Gro. BD5: B'frd 2C 110
   (off Montague St.)
Montpelier Ter. LS6: Leeds 5G 77

Montreal Av. LS7: Leeds 3B 78
Montreal Ter. LS13: Leeds 3C 94
Montrose Pl. BD13: B'frd 3G 107
Montrose St. BD2: B'frd 5D 70
Montserrat Rd. BD4: B'frd 4D 112
Moody St. BD4: B'frd 6F 91
Moon Cl. WF17: Bat 6B 136
MOOR ALLERTON 4A 60
Moor Allerton Av. LS17: Leeds ...5C 60
Moor Allerton Cen. LS17: Leeds ...5H 59
Moor Allerton Cres. LS17: Leeds ...5C 60
Moor Allerton Dr. LS17: Leeds ...5C 60
Moor Allerton Gdns.
   LS17: Leeds 5B 60
Moor Allerton Hall LS8: Leeds ...6D 60
Moor Allerton Way LS17: Leeds 5C 60
Moor Av. LS15: Leeds 4B 100
   LS23: B Spa 5B 30
Moor Bank BD4: B'frd 6E 113
Moorbank Ct. LS6: Leeds 4E 77
MOORBOTTOM 2H 153
Moor Bottom HX2: Hal 5G 127
Moorbottom BD19: Cleck 2H 153
Moor Bottom La. BD16: Bgly 4C 50
   BD21: Keigh 5H 47
   HX4: Hal 2E 159
               (not continuous)
   HX6: Hal 2A 158
        (Butterworth End La.)
   HX6: Hal 4A 146
                  (Mirey La.)
   HX7: Hal, Heb B 4A 146
Moor Bottom Rd. HX2: Hal 1D 128
Moor Cl. LS10: Leeds 3B 118
Moor Cl. Av. BD13: B'frd 5G 107
Moor Cl. Farm M. BD13: B'frd ...5G 107
Moor Cl. La. BD13: B'frd 5G 107
Moor Cl. Pde. BD13: B'frd 4G 107
Moor Cl. Rd. BD13: B'frd 5G 107
Moor Cres. LS11: Leeds 1A 118
Moor Cres. Chase LS11: Leeds ...1A 118
Moor Cft. LS16: Leeds 3D 58
Moorcroft BD3: B'frd 2B 92
   BD22: Keigh 4E 47
Moorcroft Dr. BD4: B'frd 4D 112
Moorcroft Rd. BD4: B'frd 4D 112
Moorcroft Ter. BD4: B'frd 4D 112
Moor Dr. BD22: Keigh 4C 46
   LS6: Leeds 3E 77
   LS21: Otley 3H 23
   LS28: Pud 6B 94
Moore Av. BD7: B'frd 2H 109
MOOR EDGE 5E 49
Moor Edge High Side BD16: Bgly ...5E 49
Moor Edge Low Side BD16: Bgly ...5E 49
Moorehouse Gro. LS9: Leeds 2C 98
MOOR END
   BD2 ....3G 71
   HX2 ....3H 127
   LS12 ....4A 96
MOOREND 6B 134
Moor End BD22: Haw 3D 64
   HX6: Hal 1B 158
   LS23: B Spa 3G 29
Moor End Av. HX2: Hal 6A 128
Moor End Gdns. HX2: Hal 6B 128
Moor End La. HX6: Hal 1B 158
               (not continuous)
Moor End Rd. HX2: Hal 2H 127
Moor End Vw. HX2: Hal 1C 148
Moore St. BD21: Keigh 1A 48
Moore Vw. BD7: B'frd 2H 109
Moor Farm Gdns. LS7: Leeds 2A 78
Moorfield LS27: Morl 6E 115
Moorfield Av. BD3: B'frd 2B 92
   BD19: Cleck 2E 153
   LS12: Leeds 3A 96
   LS29: Men 1F 39
Moorfield Bus. Pk. LS19: Yead ...1H 55
Moorfield Cl. LS19: Yead 1H 55
Moorfield Ct. LS19: Yead 1H 55

Moorfield Cres. LS12: Leeds 3A 96
   LS19: Yead 1G 55
   LS28: Pud 5H 93
Moorfield Cft. LS19: Yead 1H 55
Moorfield Dr. BD17: Bail 2C 52
   BD22: Keigh 4D 46
   LS19: Yead 1H 55
Moorfield Gdns. LS28: Pud 5G 93
Moorfield Gro. LS12: Leeds 3A 96
   LS28: Pud 5G 93
Moorfield Ind. Est. LS19: Yead ...6H 41
Moorfield Pl. BD10: B'frd 1H 71
               (not continuous)
Moorfield Rd. BD16: Bgly 2C 68
   LS12: Leeds 3A 96
   LS19: Yead 1H 55
   LS29: I'ly 5H 11
Moorfields LS13: Leeds 6E 75
   LS28: Pud 5B 60
Moorfield St. HX1: Hal 4E 149
   LS2: Leeds 6G 77
   LS12: Leeds 3A 96
Moorfield Ter. LS19: Yead 6G 41
Moorfield Way BD19: Cleck 2E 153
   LS29: I'ly 5H 11
Moor Flatts Av. LS10: Leeds 2A 140
Moor Flatts Rd. LS10: Leeds 2A 140
MOOR GARFORTH 3F 103
Moorgarth Av. BD3: B'frd 2B 92
MOOR GATE 3G 123
Moorgate BD17: Bail 3C 52
Moorgate Av. BD3: B'frd 2B 92
   LS25: Kip 2G 123
Moorgate Cl. LS25: Kip 3G 123
Moorgate Dr. LS25: Kip 3H 123
Moorgate Ri. LS25: Kip 3G 123
Moorgate Rd. LS25: Kip 2G 123
Moorgate St. HX1: Hal 4D 148
Moor Grange LS19: Yead 1H 55
Moor Grange Ct. LS16: Leeds 1H 75
Moor Grange Dr. LS16: Leeds 1A 76
Moor Grange Ri. LS16: Leeds 1A 76
Moor Grange Vw. LS16: Leeds 1A 76
Moorgreen Fold BD10: B'frd 2G 71
Moor Gro. HX3: Hal 6E 109
   LS28: Pud 6B 94
Moor Haven LS17: Leeds 4G 59
Moor Haven Ct. LS17: Leeds 4G 59
MOOR HEAD 5E 115
MOORHEAD 2G 69
Moorhead Cres. BD18: Ship 2G 69
Moorhead La. BD18: Ship 2G 69
Moorhead Ter. BD18: Ship 2G 69
Moor Hey La. HX5: Ell 6E 161
Moorhouse Av. BD2: B'frd 4G 71
   LS11: Leeds 4F 117
Moorhouse Bri. BD22: Oxen 6C 64
Moor Ho. Cl. BD22: Oxen 6C 64
Moor Ho. Ct. LS17: Leeds 3F 61
Moorhouse Ct. BD22: Oxen 6C 64
Moorhouse Dr. BD11: B'frd 6D 112
Moorhouse La. BD11: B'frd 6E 113
   BD22: Oxen 5B 64
Moorhouse Ter. HX3: Hal 6F 129
Moorings, The BD10: B'frd 1B 72
   LS10: Leeds 2F 119
   LS17: Leeds 2C 60
Moor Knoll Cl. WF3: E Ard 1B 156
Moor Knoll Dr. WF3: E Ard 1A 156
Moor Knoll La. WF3: E Ard 6A 140
Moorland Av. BD16: Bgly 2E 51
   BD17: Bail 3D 52
   LS6: Leeds 1F 97
   LS20: Guis 4C 40
   LS27: Morl 5D 114
Moorland Cl. HX2: Hal 4C 128
   LS17: Leeds 6B 60
   LS27: Morl 5E 115
Moorland Cres. BD17: Bail 3D 52
   LS17: Leeds 6A 60

Moorland Cres. LS20: Guis 3C 40
   LS27: Morl 5D 114
   LS28: Pud 3E 93
   LS29: Men 3A 40
                  (Bradford Rd.)
   LS29: Men 6G 21
                    (Chevin Av.)
Moorland Dr. BD11: B'frd 6F 113
   LS17: Leeds 6A 60
   LS20: Guis 3C 40
   LS28: Pud 2E 93
Moorland Gdns. LS17: Leeds 6B 60
Moorland Gth. LS17: Leeds 6A 60
Moorland Gro. LS17: Leeds 5A 60
   LS28: Pud 2E 93
Moorland Ings LS17: Leeds 6A 60
Moorland Leys LS17: Leeds 6A 60
Moorland Mills BD19: Cleck 6B 134
Moorland M. BD19: Cleck 3H 153
Moorland Pl. BD12: B'frd 2E 133
Moorland Ri. LS17: Leeds 6A 60
Moorland Rd. BD11: B'frd 1A 136
   LS6: Leeds 1F 97
   LS16: B'hpe 3D 42
   LS28: Pud 2E 93
Moorlands LS29: I'ly 1C 18
Moorlands, The LS17: Leeds 3C 60
   LS22: Weth 4F 13
   LS23: B Spa 3A 30
Moorlands Av. BD3: B'frd 2B 92
   BD11: B'frd 6E 113
   BD22: Keigh 3F 47
   HX2: Hal 4C 128
   LS19: Yead 1H 55
Moorlands Bus. Cen.
   BD19: Cleck 6B 134
               (off Balme La.)
Moorlands Ct. HX4: Hal 3F 159
   LS22: Weth 4F 13
Moorlands Cres. HX2: Hal 4C 128
Moorlands Dr. HX2: Hal 5C 128
   LS19: Yead 1H 55
Moorlands Pl. HX1: Hal 4F 149
Moorlands Rd. BD11: B'frd 6E 113
   HX4: Hal 3F 159
Moorlands Vw. HX1: Hal 4F 149
   LS22: Weth 4F 13
Moorland Ter. BD21: Keigh 1D 48
   LS25: Gar 5E 103
Moorland Vw. BD12: B'frd 2E 133
   BD15: B'frd 5H 67
   HX6: Hal 6F 147
   LS13: Leeds 5D 74
   LS17: Leeds 5A 60
Moorland Wlk. LS17: Leeds 5A 60
Moor La. BD17: B'frd 3G 135
   BD19: Cleck 5F 135
   BD20: Stee 6A 14
               (not continuous)
   HX2: Hal 3C 128
   LS17: Bard 5B 26
   LS20: Guis 2C 40
   LS21: Weston 1H 21
   LS23: Coll 5F 29
   LS29: Add 1A 8
   LS29: Burl W 4C 20
   LS29: Men 6D 20
Moorlea Dr. BD17: Bail 4D 52
Moorleigh Cl. LS25: Kip 3H 123
Moorleigh Dr. LS25: Kip 3H 123
Moor Lodge Cvn. Pk. LS17: Bard ...4C 44
Moor Pk. Av. LS6: Leeds 3D 76
Moor Pk. Cl. BD3: B'frd 3A 92
   LS29: Add 1B 8
Moor Pk. Cres. LS29: Add 1B 8
Moor Pk. Dr. BD3: B'frd 3B 92
   LS6: Leeds 3D 76
   LS29: Add 1B 8
Moor Pk. Gro. LS29: Add 1C 8
Moor Pk. Mt. LS6: Leeds 3D 76
Moor Pk. Rd. BD3: B'frd 3A 92
Moor Pk. Vs. LS6: Leeds 3E 77

Moor Pk. Way LS29: Add 1C 8
Moor Rd. LS6: Leeds 3D 76
  LS11: Leeds 1A 118
             (not continuous)
  LS16: B'hpe 2F 43
  LS23: B Spa 4A 30
  WF3: Wake 3H 157
Moor Road Station
  Middleton Railway 2B 118
Moor Royd HX3: Hal 5E 149
Moors Cen., The LS29: I'ly 5D 10
     (off Sth. Hawksworth St.)
MOOR SIDE
  Bradford 1H 91
  Low Moor 2C 132
MOORSIDE
  Bradford 2B 136
  Leeds 5E 75
Moor Side LS23: B Spa 3H 29
Moorside BD9: B'frd 1G 89
  BD17: Bail 2C 52
  BD19: Cleck 3G 153
           (not continuous)
Moorside App. BD11: B'frd 2B 136
Moorside Av. BD2: B'frd 1A 92
  BD11: B'frd 6E 113
        (Moorlands Rd.)
  BD11: B'frd 2B 136
        (Moorside Dr.)
  BD20: Stee 6A 14
Moorside Cl. BD2: B'frd 6A 72
  BD11: B'frd 2B 136
Moorside Ct. LS29: I'ly 6E 11
Moorside Cres. BD11: B'frd 2A 136
Moorside Cft. BD2: B'frd 1A 92
Moorside Dr. BD11: B'frd 2B 136
  LS13: Leeds 5E 75
Moorside Farm BD22: Oxen 6A 64
Moorside Gdns. BD2: B'frd 6A 72
  BD11: B'frd 2B 136
  HX3: Hal 3D 128
Moorside Grn. BD11: B'frd 1B 136
Moorside Ho. BD15: B'frd 5G 67
        (off Crooke La.)
Moor Side La. BD22: Haw, Oxen ..4A 64
Moorside La. BD3: B'frd 4B 92
  LS29: Add 5C 8
Moorside Maltings LS11: Leeds ..1A 118
Moorside M. BD2: B'frd 6A 72
Moorside Mt. BD11: B'frd 2A 136
Moorside Paddock BD19: Cleck ..3H 153
Moorside Pde. BD11: B'frd 2B 136
Moorside Pl. BD3: B'frd 4B 92
Moorside Ri. BD19: Cleck 2H 153
Moorside Rd. BD2: B'frd 5A 72
  BD3: B'frd 4B 92
        (off Moorside La.)
  BD11: B'frd 2A 136
  BD15: B'frd 5G 67
Moorside St. BD12: B'frd 1B 132
  LS13: Leeds 5E 75
Moorside Ter. BD2: B'frd 1B 92
  BD11: B'frd 2B 136
  LS13: Leeds 5E 75
Moorside Va. BD11: B'frd 1B 136
Moorside Vw. BD11: B'frd 2B 136
Moorside Wlk. BD11: B'frd 1B 136
Moor Smith Copse HX2: Hal 6C 106
Moor Stone Pl. HX3: Hal 2E 131
Moor St. BD13: B'frd 4A 108
  BD22: Keigh 4D 46
Moor Ter. BD2: B'frd 2A 92
      (off Glenmore Cl.)
Moorthorpe Av. BD3: B'frd 2B 92
MOOR TOP
  Bradford 1B 132
  Leeds 4B 96
Moor Top BD11: B'frd 1H 135
          (not continuous)
  LS12: Leeds 4E 115
  LS20: Guis 1B 40
  LS29: Guis, Otley 6B 22

Moor Top Gdns. HX2: Hal 5C 106
Moor Top Rd. BD12: B'frd 1B 132
  HX2: Hal 1H 147
MOORTOWN 4B 60
Moortown Cnr. LS17: Leeds 5B 60
Moor Valley Pk. LS20: Guis 6C 38
Moor Vw. BD4: B'frd 6E 113
  LS6: Leeds *6F 77*
      (off Hyde Pk. Rd.)
  LS11: Leeds 6G 97
  LS12: Leeds 4B 96
  LS19: Yead 6H 41
  LS26: Mick 4F 145
Moor Vw. Av. BD18: Ship 1A 70
Moor Vw. Ct. BD20: Keigh 6G 35
Moor Vw. Cres. BD16: Bgly 3A 68
Moorview Cft. LS29: Men 6F 21
Moorview Dr. BD16: Bgly 3A 68
  BD18: Ship 2F 71
Moorview Gro. BD21: Keigh 2B 48
Moorville Av. BD3: B'frd 2B 92
Moorville Cl. LS11: Leeds 1H 117
Moorville Ct. LS11: Leeds 1H 117
Moorville Dr. BD11: B'frd 6E 113
Moorville Gro. LS11: Leeds 1G 117
Moorville Rd. LS11: Leeds 1H 117
Moor Way BD22: Keigh 4C 46
Moorway LS20: Guis 4H 39
Moorwell Pl. BD2: B'frd 5A 72
Moravian Ho. HX3: Hal 2F 151
      (off Wakefield Rd.)
Moravian Pl. BD5: B'frd 1D 110
Moresby Rd. BD6: B'frd 1G 131
Moresdale La. LS14: Leeds 6B 80
Moreton Ho. BD3: B'frd 2G 7
MORLEY 2A 138
Morley Av. BD3: B'frd 2B 92
Morley Bottoms LS27: Morl 2A 138
MORLEY CARR 2D 132
Morley Carr Rd. BD12: B'frd 2D 132
Morley Hall La. HX2: Hal 3C 146
Morley Hall Ter. HX2: Hal 3C 146
MORLEY HOLE 2H 137
Morley Leisure Cen. 3A 138
Morley Mkt. *LS27: Morl* *3A 138*
      (off Queen St.)
Morley Station (Rail) 2C 138
Morley St. BD7: B'frd 5D 90 (6B 6)
Morley Vw. HX3: Hal 6A 150
Morningside BD8: B'frd 2B 90
  BD13: B'frd 1B 86
Morning St. BD21: Keigh 3H 47
Mornington Rd. BD16: Bgly 4C 50
  LS29: I'ly 5E 11
Mornington St. BD21: Keigh 5H 33
Mornington Vs. BD8: B'frd 2D 90
Morpeth Pl. LS9: Leeds 4C 98
Morpeth St. BD7: B'frd 4C 90
  BD13: B'frd 4A 108
Morrell Ct. BD4: B'frd 2B 112
Morrell Cres. WF2: Wake 6D 156
Morris Av. LS5: Leeds 4A 76
Morris Gro. LS5: Leeds 5A 76
Morris La. LS5: Leeds 4A 76
Morris Mt. LS5: Leeds 5A 76
Morris Pl. LS27: Morl 2H 137
Morris Vw. LS5: Leeds 5A 76
Morritt Av. LS15: Leeds 2D 100
Morritt Dr. LS15: Leeds 3B 100
Morritt Gro. LS15: Leeds 3B 100
Mortec Pk. LS15: Scho 2G 81
Mortimer Av. BD3: B'frd 2B 92
Mortimer Cl. LS25: Gar 5E 103
Mortimer Row BD3: B'frd 4B 92
Mortimer St. BD8: B'frd 3H 89
Morton Gro. BD20: Keigh 5H 35
Morton La. BD16: Bgly 5H 35
  BD20: Keigh 5H 35
Morton Rd. BD4: B'frd 6A 112
Mortons Cl. HX3: Hal 6A 150
Morton Ter. LS20: Guis 4B 40
Morwick Gro. LS15: Scho 3H 81

Morwick Ter. LS14: T'ner 1G 81
Moseley Pl. LS6: Leeds 6H 77
Moseley Wood App.
  LS16: Leeds 3F 57
Moseley Wood Av. LS16: Leeds ..1F 57
Moseley Wood Bank
  LS16: Leeds 2F 57
Moseley Wood Cl. LS16: Leeds ..3F 57
Moseley Wood Cres.
  LS16: Leeds 3F 57
Moseley Wood Cft. LS16: Leeds ..3E 57
Moseley Wood Dr. LS16: Leeds ..2F 57
Moseley Wood Gdns.
  LS16: Leeds 2F 57
Moseley Wood Grn. LS16: Leeds ..2F 57
Moseley Wood Gro. LS16: Leeds ..2F 57
Moseley Wood La. LS16: Leeds ..2G 57
Moseley Wood Ri. LS16: Leeds ..2F 57
Moseley Wood Vw. LS16: Leeds ..1G 57
Moseley Wood Wlk. LS16: Leeds ..3F 57
Moseley Wood Way LS16: Leeds ..1F 57
Moser Av. BD2: B'frd 4G 71
Moser Cres. BD2: B'frd 4G 71
Mosley Ho. *BD4: B'frd* *6B 92*
      (off Parsonage Rd.)
Moss Bri. Rd. LS13: Leeds 4B 74
Moss Carr Av. BD21: Keigh 2D 48
Moss Carr Gro. BD21: Keigh 2D 48
Moss Carr Rd. BD21: Keigh 2D 48
Moss Carr Ter. BD21: Keigh 1D 48
Mossdale Av. BD9: B'frd 6E 69
Moss Dr. HX2: Hal 1C 128
Moss Gdns. LS17: Leeds 2G 59
Moss La. HX2: Hal 1C 128
Mosslea LS27: Morl 6B 116
Moss Ri. LS17: Leeds 2G 59
Moss Row BD15: B'frd 3G 67
Moss Side BD9: B'frd 1G 89
Moss St. BD13: B'frd 4G 87
  BD22: Haw 1E 65
Moss Syke LS14: S'cft 5E 45
Mosstree Cl. BD13: B'frd 3G 107
Moss Valley LS17: Leeds 2G 59
Mossy Bank Cl. BD13: B'frd 3A 108
Mostyn Gro. BD6: B'frd 5A 110
Mostyn Mt. HX3: Hal 4E 129
Motley La. LS20: Guis 3C 40
Motley Row *LS20: Guis* *3C 40*
      (off Motley La.)
Mould Greave BD22: Oxen 5B 64
Moule Ri. LS25: Gar 2H 103
Moulson Cl. BD6: B'frd 4B 110
Moulson Ct. BD5: B'frd 2E 111
Moulson Ter. BD13: B'frd 3B 86
Mount, The BD17: Bail 5D 52
  LS15: Bar E 3D 82
  LS15: Leeds 2D 100
  LS17: Leeds 1H 59
  LS19: Yead 4H 55
  LS25: Kip 4G 123
  LS26: Rothw 6B 120
  LS27: Morl *6B 116*
      (off Elland Rd.)
  WF17: Bat 5A 136
MOUNTAIN 3G 107
Mountain Vw. BD18: Ship 3D 70
  HX2: Hal 1E 129
Mount Av. BD2: B'frd 4H 71
  HX2: Hal 2A 148
  WF2: Wake 6D 156
Mountbatten Av. WF1: Wake 4G 157
Mountbatten Ct. BD5: B'frd 3E 111
Mountbatten Cres. WF1: Wake ..5G 157
Mountbatten Gro. WF1: Wake ..5H 157
Mt. Cliffe Vw. LS27: Morl 6B 116
Mount Cres. BD19: Cleck 6B 134
  HX2: Hal 2A 148
Mount Dr. LS17: Leeds 1H 59
Mountfields HX3: Hal 1G 151
  LS2: Leeds 1A 4
Mount Gdns. BD19: Cleck 6B 134
  LS17: Leeds 1H 59

Mount Gro. BD2: B'frd 4H 71
Mount La. HD6: Brigh 4G 161
Mountleigh Cl. BD4: B'frd 1G 133
Mt. Pellon HX2: Hal 1D 148
Mt. Pellon Rd. HX2: Hal 1C 148
Mt. Pisgah LS21: Otley 4E 23
Mt. Pisgah Ter. LS21: Otley 4E 23
(off Well Hill)
Mount Pl. BD18: Ship 1A 70
MOUNT PLEASANT 4H 123
Mount Pleasant BD6: B'frd 6G 109
BD9: B'frd 1C 90
BD13: B'frd 3B 86
BD17: Bail 4C 52
BD20: Keigh 6G 35
HD6: Brigh 5G 161
HX2: Hal 6C 126
HX3: Hal 5C 150
HX6: Hal 6D 146
LS10: Leeds 2A 140
LS13: Leeds 5D 74
LS18: H'fth 1F 75
(off Broadgate La.)
LS20: Guis 3C 40
LS25: Kip 5H 123
LS29: Add 1D 8
LS29: I'ly 6E 11
Mt. Pleasant Av.
HX1: Hal 1F 149 (2A 164)
LS28: Leeds 4D 78
Mt. Pleasant Ct. LS28: Pud 3A 94
Mt. Pleasant Gdns. LS8: Leeds 4D 78
(off Sycamore Av.)
LS25: Kip 5H 123
Mount Pleasant Rd.
LS28: Pud 3A 94
Mt. Pleasant St. BD13: B'frd 4A 108
LS28: Pud 3B 94
Mt. Preston St. LS2: Leeds . . .2G 97 (1A 4)
Mount Ri. LS17: Leeds 1H 59
Mount Rd. BD2: B'frd 4A 72
BD6: B'frd 4A 110
Mount Royal LS18: H'fth 1D 74
Mt. Royd BD8: B'frd 1D 90
Mount St. BD2: B'frd 4H 71
BD3: B'frd 5G 91 (5H 7)
BD4: B'frd 5H 91
BD19: Cleck 6B 134
BD21: Keigh 6H 33
HX1: Hal 2G 149 (4B 164)
HX6: Hal 5H 147
Mt. Street W. HX2: Hal 1C 148
MOUNT TABOR 4G 127
Mt. Tabor Rd. HX2: Hal 2F 127
Mt. Tabor St. LS28: Pud 4G 93
Mount Ter. BD2: B'frd 4H 71
HX2: Hal 6C 126
(Jim Allen La.)
HX2: Hal 1C 148
(Sutcliffe St.)
Mt. Vernon Rd. LS19: Yead 3G 55
Mount Vw. BD13: B'frd 4H 107
BD16: Bgly 4D 50
BD22: Keigh 5B 46
HX2: Hal 4G 127
LS27: Morl 6B 116
Mt. View Dr. BD19: Cleck 1H 153
Mowat Ct. WF15: Liv 4H 153
Mowbray Chase
LS26: Rothw 6D 120
Mowbray Cl. BD13: B'frd 4A 66
Mowbray Ct. LS14: Leeds 6C 80
Mowbray Cres. LS14: Leeds 6C 80
Moxon Gro. WF1: Wake 6F 157
Moxon St. WF1: Wake 5G 157
Moxon Way WF1: Wake 5G 157
Moynihan Cl. LS8: Leeds 5F 79
Mozeley Dr. HX2: Hal 1D 128
Mucky La. HX5: Hal 6H 159
Muddy La. LS22: Coll 6B 12
Muff La. BD19: Cleck 6G 135
Muff St. BD4: B'frd 6H 91

Muff Ter. BD6: B'frd 4A 110
Muir Ct. LS6: Leeds 5D 76
(off St Michael's Gro.)
Muirhead Ct. BD4: B'frd 3C 112
Muirhead Dr. BD4: B'frd 3C 112
Muirhead Fold BD4: B'frd 3C 112
Muirlands, The HD2: Hud 6E 163
Mulberry Av. LS16: Leeds 3D 58
Mulberry Chase LS21: Pool 5F 25
Mulberry Gdns. LS26: Mick 5B 144
Mulberry Gth. LS16: Leeds 4E 59
LS23: B Spa 2C 30
Mulberry Ri. LS16: Leeds 3D 58
Mulberry St. BD21: Keigh 5B 34
LS28: Pud 4A 94
Mulberry Vw. LS16: Leeds 4D 58
Mulcture Hall Rd.
HX1: Hal 2H 149 (3D 164)
Mulgrave St. BD3: B'frd . . . 5H 91 (6H 7)
Mulhalls Mill HX6: Hal 5A 148
Mullins Ct. LS9: Leeds 4D 98
Mumford St. BD5: B'frd 2E 111
Munby St. BD8: B'frd 4G 89
Muncaster Rd. LS25: Gar 3H 103
Munster St. BD4: B'frd 2H 111
Munton Cl. BD6: B'frd 1G 131
Murdoch St. BD21: Keigh 5D 34
Murdstone Cl. BD5: B'frd 2E 111
Murgatroyd St. BD5: B'frd 3E 111
(not continuous)
BD18: Ship 1B 70
Murray St. BD5: B'frd 2C 110
Murton Cl. LS14: Leeds 5C 80
Murton Gro. BD20: Stee 6D 14
(off East Pde.)
Museum Ct. BD2: B'frd 1A 92
Museum St. LS9: Leeds 2D 98
Musgrave Bank LS13: Leeds 1G 95
Musgrave Bldgs. LS28: Pud 3B 94
Musgrave Dr. BD2: B'frd 1A 92
Musgrave Gro. BD2: B'frd 1A 92
Musgrave Mt. BD2: B'frd 1A 92
LS13: Leeds 1G 95
Musgrave Ri. LS13: Leeds 1G 95
Musgrave Rd. BD2: B'frd 1A 92
Musgrave St. WF17: Bat 6A 136
Musgrave Vw. LS13: Leeds 1G 95
Musgrave Ho. LS5: Leeds 5H 75
(off Broad La.)
Mushroom St. LS9: Leeds . . .2B 98 (1H 5)
Musselburgh St. BD7: B'frd 4C 90
Mutton Fold HX3: Hal 5C 130
(off Towngate)
Mutton La. BD15: B'frd 1H 87
Myers Av. BD2: B'frd 5G 71
Myers Cft. LS21: Otley 4E 23
Myers La. BD2: B'frd 5G 71
Myrtle Av. BD16: Bgly 5B 50
HX2: Hal 3C 128
Myrtle Bank HX3: Hal 5H 149
Myrtle Cl. BD16: Bgly 5B 50
Myrtle Dr. BD22: Haw 6F 47
HX2: Hal 3C 128
Myrtle Gdns. HX2: Hal 3C 128
Myrtle Gro. BD13: B'frd 6G 107
BD16: Bgly 5B 50
HX2: Hal 3C 128
Myrtle La. LS29: Burl W 6D 20
Myrtle Pl. BD16: Bgly 4B 50
BD18: Ship 1H 69
HX2: Hal 3C 128
Myrtle Rd. HX5: Ell 6B 160
Myrtle St. BD3: B'frd 5A 92
BD16: Bgly 4C 50
Myrtle Ter. BD22: Haw 6F 47
HX6: Hal 5H 147
Myrtle Vw. BD22: Keigh 4D 46
Myrtle Wlk. BD16: Bgly 4B 50
(off Ferncliffe Rd.)
MYTHOLMES 1C 64
Mytholmes BD22: Haw 1C 64

Mytholmes La. BD22: Haw 2C 64
(not continuous)
Mytholmes Ter. BD22: Haw 1C 64

N

NAB END 3E 109
Nab End BD12: B'frd 5D 132
Nab End Rd. HX4: Hal 4H 159
Nab La. BD18: Ship 2F 69
WF17: Bat 5C 136
(not continuous)
Naburn App. LS14: Leeds 6D 62
Naburn Chase LS14: Leeds 2E 81
Naburn Cl. LS14: Leeds 2D 80
Naburn Ct. LS14: Leeds 1D 80
Naburn Dr. LS14: Leeds 2D 80
Naburn Fold LS14: Leeds 2E 81
Naburn Gdns. LS14: Leeds 2D 80
Naburn Grn. LS14: Leeds 2D 80
Naburn Pl. LS14: Leeds 1D 80
Naburn Rd. LS14: Leeds 2D 80
Naburn Vw. LS14: Leeds 2E 81
Naburn Wlk. LS14: Leeds 2D 80
Nab Vw. BD20: Sils 1F 15
Nab Water La. BD22: Oxen 5B 84
NAB WOOD 2F 69
Nab Wood Bank BD18: Ship 2F 69
Nab Wood Cl. BD18: Ship 2G 69
Nab Wood Crematorium
BD18: Ship 1F 69
Nab Wood Cres. BD18: Ship 2F 69
Nab Wood Dr. BD18: Ship 3F 69
Nab Wood Gdns. BD18: Ship 2G 69
Nab Wood Gro. BD18: Ship 2F 69
Nab Wood Mt. BD18: Ship 2F 69
Nab Wood Pl. BD18: Ship 2F 69
Nab Wood Ri. BD18: Ship 2F 69
Nab Wood Rd. BD18: Ship 3F 69
Nab Wood School Sports Cen. . . . 2E 69
Nab Wood Ter. BD18: Ship 2F 69
Naden Cl. BD6: B'frd 3E 109
Nancroft Cres. LS12: Leeds 4C 96
Nancroft Mt. LS12: Leeds 4C 96
Nancroft Ter. LS12: Leeds 4C 96
Nanny Goat La. LS25: Gar 3D 102
Nansen Av. LS13: Leeds 1D 94
Nansen Gro. LS13: Leeds 1D 94
Nansen Mt. LS13: Leeds 1D 94
Nansen Pl. LS13: Leeds 1D 94
Nansen St. LS13: Leeds 1C 94
Nansen Ter. LS13: Leeds 1D 94
Nansen Vw. LS13: Leeds 1D 94
Napier Rd. BD3: B'frd 4B 92
HX5: Ell 5A 160
Napier St. BD3: B'frd 4B 92
BD13: B'frd 4B 108
BD21: Keigh 1B 48
Napier Ter. BD3: B'frd 4B 92
Naples St. BD8: B'frd 2B 90
Napoleon Bus. Pk. BD4: B'frd . . . 6H 91
Nares St. BD21: Keigh 6H 33
BD22: Haw 1E 65
Narrowboat Wharf LS13: Leeds . . 4B 74
Narrow La. BD16: Bgly 6F 49
Narrows, The BD16: Bgly 6F 49
Naseby Gdns. LS9: Leeds 3C 98
Naseby Gth. LS9: Leeds 3C 98
Naseby Grange LS9: Leeds 3C 98
(off Naseby Gdns.)
Naseby Ho. BD4: B'frd 4D 112
Naseby Pl. LS9: Leeds 3C 98
Naseby Ri. BD13: B'frd 4B 108
Naseby Ter. LS9: Leeds 3C 98
Naseby Vw. LS9: Leeds 3C 98
Naseby Wlk. LS9: Leeds 3C 98
Nashville Rd. BD22: Keigh 1G 47
Nashville St. BD22: Keigh 1G 47
Nashville Ter. BD22: Keigh 1G 47
(off Nashville Rd.)
Nassau Pl. LS7: Leeds 6C 78

Nateby Ri.—Newlands Ga.

Nateby Ri. WF3: Rothw 4H 141
Nathaniel Waterhouse Homes
HX1: Hal 5B 164
National Mus. of Photography, Film & Television, The 5E 91 (5C 6)
National Pk. LS10: Leeds 1C 118
National Rd. LS10: Leeds 6C 98
Natty Fields Cl. HX2: Hal 6C 106
Nature Way BD6: B'frd 1G 131
Navigation Cl. HX5: Ell 3C 160
Navigation Rd. HX3: Hal 3H 149
Navigation Wlk.
LS10: Leeds 4A 98 (6F 5)
Naylor Gth. LS6: Leeds 4F 77
Naylor La. HX2: Hal 1C 146
Naylor Pl. LS11: Leeds 1H 117
Naylor's Bldgs. *BD19: Cleck 1F 153*
(off Tabbs La.)
Naylor St. HX1: Hal 2D 148
Neal St. BD5: B'frd 5E 91 (6C 6)
Nearcliffe Rd. BD9: B'frd 1A 90
Near Crook BD10: B'frd 6F 53
Near Highfield BD22: Keigh 4C 46
Near Hob Cote BD22: Keigh 6A 46
Near Peat La. BD22: Oxen 4A 84
Near Royd HX3: Hal 4E 129
Neath Gdns. LS9: Leeds 6H 79
Necropolis Rd. BD7: B'frd 6H 89
Ned Hill Rd. HX2: Hal 3C 106
Ned La. BD4: B'frd 1C 112
Needless Inn La. LS26: Rothw 6E 121
Nelson Ct. LS26: Mick 4D 144
LS27: Morl 5H 137
LS29: I'ly 5D 10
(off Nelson Rd.)
Nelson Cft. LS25: Gar 5D 102
Nelson Pl. BD13: B'frd 4A 108
HX6: Hal 5B 148
LS27: Morl 2A 138
(off Sth. Nelson St.)
Nelson Rd. LS29: I'ly 5D 10
Nelson St. BD1: B'frd 5E 91 (6D 6)
BD13: B'frd 4A 108
BD15: B'frd 2E 89
BD22: Haw 1E 65
(Albion St.)
BD22: Haw 1E 65
(East Ter.)
HX6: Hal 5A 148
LS21: Otley 4E 23
WF17: Bat 6B 136
Nene St. BD5: B'frd 1C 110
Nepshaw La. LS27: Morl 2H 137
(Farm Hill Rd.)
LS27: Morl 3F 137
(Wakefield Rd.)
Nepshaw La. Nth. LS27: Morl 2G 137
Nepshaw La. Sth. LS27: Morl 2G 137
Neptune St. LS9: Leeds 4B 98 (6H 5)
NESFIELD 2G 9
Nesfield Cl. LS10: Leeds 1D 140
Nesfield Cres. LS10: Leeds 1D 140
Nesfield Gdns. LS10: Leeds 1C 140
Nesfield Gth. LS10: Leeds 1C 140
Nesfield Grn. LS10: Leeds 1C 140
Nesfield La. LS29: I'ly 1G 9
Nesfield Rd. LS10: Leeds 1C 140
LS29: I'ly 4B 10
Nesfield St. BD1: B'frd 3D 90 (1B 6)
Nesfield Vw. LS10: Leeds 1C 140
LS29: I'ly 5A 10
Nesfield Wlk. LS10: Leeds 1C 140
Nessfield Dr. BD22: Keigh 2F 47
Nessfield Gro. BD22: Keigh 2F 47
Nessfield Rd. BD22: Keigh 2F 47
Netherby St. BD3: B'frd 4H 91
Nethercliffe Cres. LS20: Guis 3B 40
Nethercliffe Rd. LS20: Guis 3B 40
Netherdale Ct. LS22: Weth 3G 13
Netherfield Cl. LS19: Yead 6F 41
Netherfield Ct. *LS20: Guis 4B 40*
(off Netherfield Rd.)
Netherfield Dr. LS20: Guis 3B 40
Netherfield Ri. LS20: Guis 4B 40
Netherfield Rd. LS20: Guis 3B 40
Netherfield Ter. LS19: Yead 6F 41
LS20: Guis 4B 40
(off Netherfield Rd.)
Netherhall Pk. *BD17: Bail 4D 52*
(off Netherhall Rd.)
Netherhall Rd. BD17: Bail 4D 52
Netherlands Av. BD6: B'frd 6C 110
BD12: B'frd 6C 110
Netherlands Sq. BD12: B'frd 6D 110
Nether Moor Vw. BD16: Bgly 4C 50
Nether St. LS28: Pud 6H 73
NETHERTOWN 6C 114
Netherwood BD13: B'frd 3B 86
NETHER YEADON 3F 55
Nettle Gro. HX3: Hal 6C 130
Nettleton Cl. BD4: B'frd 3A 114
Nettleton Ct. LS15: Leeds 3F 101
Neville App. LS9: Leeds 5G 99
Neville Av. BD4: B'frd 4H 111
LS9: Leeds 5G 99
Neville Cl. LS9: Leeds 5G 99
Neville Ct. BD18: Ship 1H 69
Neville Cres. LS9: Leeds 3H 99
Neville Gth. LS9: Leeds 5G 99
Neville Gro. LS9: Leeds 5G 99
LS26: Swil 3A 122
Neville Mt. LS9: Leeds 5G 99
Neville Pde. LS9: Leeds 5G 99
Neville Pl. LS9: Leeds 4H 99
Neville Rd. BD4: B'frd 1H 111
LS9: Leeds 3H 99
LS15: Leeds 3H 99
LS21: Otley 4F 23
Neville Row LS9: Leeds 5G 99
Neville Sq. LS9: Leeds 4H 99
Neville St. BD21: Keigh 5B 34
LS1: Leeds 5H 97 (6D 4)
LS11: Leeds 5H 97 (6D 4)
Neville Ter. LS9: Leeds 5G 99
Neville Vw. LS9: Leeds 5G 99
Neville Wlk. LS9: Leeds 4G 99
Nevill Gro. BD9: B'frd 6F 69
New Adel Av. LS16: Leeds 4A 58
New Adel Gdns. LS16: Leeds 4A 58
New Adel La. LS16: Leeds 5A 58
NEWALL 2D 22
Newall Av. LS21: Otley 2D 22
Newall Cl. LS21: Otley 2D 22
LS29: Men 6H 21
Newall Hall Pk. LS21: Otley 2E 23
Newall Mt. LS21: Otley 3D 22
Newall St. BD5: B'frd 1D 110
Newark Ho. *BD5: B'frd 1D 110*
(off Roundhill St.)
Newark Rd. BD16: Bgly 2B 50
Newark St. BD4: B'frd 6G 91
Newark Va. WF3: Rothw 4E 141
New Augustus St.
BD1: B'frd 5F 91 (6F 7)
New Bank HX3: Hal 1H 149 (1D 164)
New Bank Ri. BD4: B'frd 2B 112
New Bank St. LS27: Morl 2B 138
New Barton Rd. HX6: Hal 6C 146
NEW BLACKPOOL 1A 116
New Bond St. HX1: Hal 2F 149 (4A 164)
Newbridge Ind. Est. BD21: Keigh 6B 34
New Briggate LS1: Leeds 3A 98 (4F 5)
NEW BRIGHTON
Bingley 3E 69
Leeds 3A 138
New Brighton *BD12: B'frd 2G 133*
(off Dyehouse Rd.)
BD16: Bgly 3E 69
New Brook St. LS29: I'ly 5D 10
New Brunswick St.
HX1: Hal 2F 149 (4A 164)
Newburn Rd. BD7: B'frd 6B 90
Newbury Cl. BD17: Bail 3D 52
Newbury Rd. HD6: Brigh 4H 161
Newby Gth. LS17: Leeds 2F 61
Newby Ho. *BD2: B'frd 1H 91*
(off Otley Rd.)
Newby St. BD5: B'frd 1E 111
Newcastle Cl. BD11: B'frd 2H 135
Newcastle Ho. BD3: B'frd 3F 7
New Centaur Ho.
LS11: Leeds 4H 97 (6D 4)
New Cheapside BD1: B'frd 4E 91 (4D 6)
New Clayton Ter. BD13: B'frd 4B 66
New Cl. BD13: B'frd 6D 86
New Cl. Av. BD20: Sils 2E 15
New Cl. Rd. BD18: Ship 2E 69
New Clough Rd. HX6: Hal 1B 158
Newcombe St. HX5: Ell 6C 160
New Craven Ga. LS11: Leeds 6A 98
New Cres. LS18: H'fth 1D 74
New Cft. LS18: H'fth 1D 74
New Cross St. BD5: B'frd 3E 111
(not continuous)
BD12: B'frd 2H 133
New Delight HX2: Hal 6A 106
New England Rd. BD21: Keigh 2A 48
New Farmers Hill LS26: Rothw 6F 121
NEW FARNLEY 2F 115
Newfield Chase LS25: Gar 6H 103
Newfield Cres. LS25: Gar 1H 123
Newfield Dr. LS25: Gar 1H 123
LS29: Men 1G 39
Newfield La. LS25: Led 5H 125
New Fold BD6: B'frd 6G 109
Newforth Gro. BD5: B'frd 3C 110
New Grange Vw. HX2: Hal 5D 106
NEWHALL 4F 111
Newhall Bank LS10: Leeds 2B 140
Newhall Chase LS10: Leeds 1B 140
Newhall Cl. LS10: Leeds 1B 140
Newhall Cres. LS10: Leeds 1B 140
Newhall Cft. LS10: Leeds 6C 118
Newhall Dr. BD6: B'frd 5F 111
Newhall Gdns. LS10: Leeds 2B 140
Newhall Gth. LS10: Leeds 1B 140
Newhall Ga. LS10: Leeds 6B 118
Newhall Grn. LS10: Leeds 1C 140
Newhall Mt. BD6: B'frd 5F 111
LS10: Leeds 2B 140
Newhall Rd. BD4: B'frd 4H 111
LS10: Leeds 1B 140
Newhall Wlk. LS10: Leeds 1C 140
New Hey Rd. BD4: B'frd 1G 111
HD2: Hud 6E 161
HD6: Brigh, Hud 6F 161
Newhold LS25: Gar 3G 103
Newhold Ind. Est. LS25: Gar 3G 103
New Holme HX3: Hal 2E 151
New Holme Cotts. HX2: Hal 2F 127
New Holme Rd. BD22: Haw 3D 64
New Ho. La. BD13: B'frd 5D 108
Newill Cl. BD5: B'frd 3G 111
New Inn Ct. LS21: Otley 4E 23
New Inn St. LS12: Leeds 4A 96
New John St. BD1: B'frd 4D 90 (4C 6)
New Kirkgate BD18: Ship 1B 70
New Laithe HX2: Hal 2C 128
New Laithe Rd. BD6: B'frd 4A 110
Newlaithes Gdns. LS18: H'fth 2D 74
Newlaithes Gth. LS18: H'fth 3C 74
Newlaithes Rd. LS18: H'fth 3C 74
Newlands LS28: Pud 1H 93
Newlands, The HX6: Hal 6E 147
Newlands Av. BD3: B'frd 2B 92
HX3: Hal 3C 130
HX6: Hal 6E 147
LS19: Yead 5E 41
Newlands Cl. HD6: Brigh 2B 162
Newlands Cres. HX3: Hal 4C 130
LS27: Morl 3D 138
Newlands Dr. BD16: Bgly 1A 50
HX3: Hal 4C 130
LS27: Morl 2D 138
WF3: Wake 4H 157
Newlands Ga. HX2: Hal 2G 147

Newlands Gro. HX3: Hal 4C **130**
Newlands Pl. BD3: B'frd 2H **91** (1H **7**)
Newlands Ri. LS19: Yead 6E **41**
Newlands Rd. HX2: Hal 2G **147**
Newlands Vw. HX3: Hal 4C **130**
New La. BD3: B'frd 5B **92**
  BD4: B'frd 5B **92**
                (Laisterdyke)
  BD4: B'frd 3F **113**
                (Raikes La.)
  BD11: B'frd 5C **114**
  BD19: Cleck 3G **153**
  BD20: Kild 1A **14**
  HX2: Hal 4B **146**
  HX3: Hal 6E **149**
                (Birdcage La.)
  HX3: Hal 5H **149**
                (Whitegate)
  LS10: Leeds 2H **139**
  LS11: Leeds 5H **97**
  LS27: Morl 5D **114**
  WF3: E Ard 1H **155**
                (not continuous)
NEWLAY 3D **74**
Newlay Bridle Path LS18: H'fth . . .2D **74**
Newlay Cl. BD10: B'frd 2C **72**
Newlay Gro. LS18: H'fth 3D **74**
Newlay La. LS13: Leeds 5E **75**
  LS18: H'fth 2D **74**
Newlay La. Pl. LS13: Leeds 5E **75**
Newlay Mt. LS18: H'fth 3D **74**
Newlay Wood Av. LS18: H'fth 2E **75**
Newlay Wood Cl. LS18: H'fth 2E **75**
Newlay Wood Cres. LS18: H'fth . . .2E **75**
Newlay Wood Dr. LS18: H'fth 2E **75**
Newlay Wood Fold LS18: H'fth 2D **74**
Newlay Wood Gdns. LS18: H'fth . . .2E **75**
Newlay Wood Ri. LS18: H'fth 2E **75**
Newlay Wood Rd. LS18: H'fth 2D **74**
New Leeds LS13: Leeds 4D **74**
New Line BD10: B'frd 2B **72**
Newlyn Rd. BD20: Keigh 4E **35**
Newman St. BD4: B'frd 3H **111**
New Mkt. LS21: Otley 4E **23**
Newmarket App. LS9: Leeds 6F **99**
Newmarket Grn. LS9: Leeds 5F **99**
Newmarket La. LS9: Leeds 6F **99**
New Mkt. Pl. BD1: B'frd 4D **6**
                (off Hustlergate)
New Mkt. St. LS1: Leeds 4A **98** (5F **5**)
NEW MICKLEFIELD 6E **105**
New Marsh HX6: Hal 4H **147**
New Mill HX2: Hal 1E **127**
New Mill La. LS23: B Spa 6C **30**
New Occupation La. LS28: Pud 5G **93**
New Otley Rd. BD3: B'frd . . .3G **91** (2G **7**)
New Park Av. LS28: Pud 6A **74**
New Pk. Cl. LS28: Pud 6A **74**
New Pk. Cft. LS28: Pud 6A **74**
New Pk. Gro. LS28: Pud 6H **73**
New Pk. Pl. LS28: Pud 6A **74**
New Pk. Rd. BD13: B'frd 3H **107**
New Pk. St. LS27: Morl 4H **137**
New Pk. Va. LS28: Pud 6A **74**
New Pk. Vw. LS28: Pud 1A **94**
New Pk. Wlk. LS28: Pud 1H **93**
New Pk. Way LS28: Pud 6A **74**
New Pepper Rd. LS10: Leeds 2D **118**
New Popplewell La. BD19: Cleck . . .1F **153**
Newport Av. LS13: Leeds 1C **94**
Newport Cres. LS6: Leeds 6D **76**
Newport Gdns. LS6: Leeds 6D **76**
Newport Mt. LS6: Leeds 6D **76**
Newport Pl. BD8: B'frd 2C **90**
Newport Rd. BD8: B'frd 2C **90**
  LS6: Leeds 6D **76**
Newport Vw. LS6: Leeds 5D **76**
New Princess St. LS11: Leeds 6H **97**
New Pudsey Sq. LS28: Pud 2G **93**
New Pudsey Station (Rail) 2G **93**
New Rd. BD13: B'frd 3B **86**
  BD20: Sils 2D **14**

New Rd. HX1: Hal 3G **149** (5C **164**)
  HX2: Hal 6D **126**
  HX4: Hal 4E **159**
  LS19: Yead 6D **40**
  LS25: Led 4H **125**
  WF3: Rothw 4H **141**
New Rd. E. BD19: Cleck 1F **153**
NEW ROAD SIDE 3D **132**
New Rd. Side LS18: H'fth 1C **74**
  LS19: Yead 2F **55**
New Rd. Sq. HD6: Brigh 5G **161**
                (off New Hey Rd.)
New Row BD9: B'frd 1G **89**
  BD12: B'frd 5D **132**
  BD16: Bgly 1D **68**
  LS15: Leeds 5G **101**
  LS25: M'fld 4E **105**
  LS28: Pud 6D **72**
Newroyd Rd. BD5: B'frd 3E **111**
Newsam Ct. LS15: Leeds 4C **100**
Newsam Dr. LS15: Leeds 4A **100**
NEWSAM GREEN 3F **121**
Newsam Grn. Rd. LS26: Swil 3F **121**
NEW SCARBOROUGH
  LS13 . . . . .2F **95**
  LS19 . . . . .6D **40**
New Scarbro' Rd. LS13: Leeds 1F **95**
NEWSHOLME 3A **46**
Newsholme New Rd. BD22: Keigh . . .3A **46**
New Station St.
  LS1: Leeds 4H **97** (5D **4**)
Newstead Av. HX1: Hal 2C **148**
  WF1: Wake 4E **157**
Newstead Gdns. HX1: Hal 2C **148**
Newstead Gro. HX1: Hal 2C **148**
Newstead Heath HX1: Hal 2C **148**
Newstead Pl. HX1: Hal 2C **148**
Newstead Ri. BD20: Keigh 4F **35**
Newstead Rd. LS21: Otley 4E **23**
Newstead Ter. HX1: Hal 2C **148**
Newstead Wlk. BD5: B'frd 1D **110**
New St. BD4: B'frd 5H **111**
  BD10: B'frd 1H **71**
  BD12: B'frd 2H **133**
  BD13: B'frd 3B **86**
  BD16: Bgly 6A **36**
  BD22: Haw 3C **64**
  BD22: Keigh 5D **46**
  HD6: Brigh 6D **152**
                (Savile Rd.)
  HD6: Brigh 2B **152**
                (West St.)
  HX2: Hal 1C **148**
  HX3: Hal 5C **150**
  LS18: H'fth 1D **74**
  LS25: Kip 4H **123**
  LS28: Pud 2H **93**
                (Carlisle Rd.)
  LS28: Pud 2H **93**
                (Westfield)
New St. Cl. LS28: Pud 5A **94**
New St. Gdns. LS28: Pud 5A **94**
New St. Gro. LS28: Pud 5A **94**
New Sturton La. LS25: Gar 3H **103**
New Temple Ga. LS15: Leeds 5C **100**
NEW TOFTSHAW 5B **112**
New Toftshaw BD4: B'frd 5B **112**
Newton Cl. BD20: Sils 2D **14**
  LS26: Rothw 3F **141**
Newton Ct. LS8: Leeds 3G **79**
  LS26: Rothw 3F **141**
  WF1: Wake 5F **157**
Newton Dr. WF1: Wake 6G **157**
Newton Gth. LS7: Leeds 4C **78**
Newton Gro. LS7: Leeds 5C **78**
NEWTON HILL 6F **157**
Newton Hill Rd. LS7: Leeds 4B **78**
Newton La. WF1: Wake 5F **157**
Newton Lodge Cl. LS7: Leeds 4A **78**
Newton Lodge Dr. LS7: Leeds 4A **78**
Newton Pde. LS7: Leeds 4B **78**
Newton Pk. HD6: Brigh 3H **151**

Newton Pk. Ct. LS7: Leeds 4C **78**
Newton Pk. Dr. LS7: Leeds 4C **78**
Newton Pk. Vw. LS7: Leeds 5C **78**
Newton Pl. BD5: B'frd 1D **110**
Newton Rd. LS7: Leeds 5B **78**
Newton Sq. LS12: Leeds 2F **115**
Newton St. BD5: B'frd 1E **111**
                (Ripley St.)
  BD5: B'frd 2E **111**
                (St Stephen's Ter.)
  HX6: Hal 5H **147**
Newton Ter. HX6: Hal 6H **147**
Newton Vw. LS7: Leeds 4B **78**
Newton Vs. LS7: Leeds 3A **78**
Newton Wlk. LS7: Leeds 5C **78**
Newton Way BD17: Bail 3C **52**
NEW TOWN
  Ilkley 1D **8**
  Keighley 1G **47**
  Leeds 1C **98**
New Town Cl. BD21: Keigh 6H **33**
New Town Ct. BD21: Keigh 6H **33**
New Village M. LS27: Morl 5C **116**
                (off New Village Way)
New Village Way LS27: Leeds 4C **116**
New Wlk. LS8: Leeds 6F **61**
New Way LS20: Guis 4H **39**
New Windsor Dr. LS26: Rothw 1B **142**
New Works Rd. BD12: B'frd 2C **132**
NEW WORTLEY 4E **97**
New York Cotts. LS19: Yead 5H **55**
New York La. LS19: Yead 5H **55**
New York Rd. LS2: Leeds . . .3B **98** (3G **5**)
                (not continuous)
  LS9: Leeds 3B **98** (3G **5**)
New York St. LS2: Leeds 4B **98** (5F **5**)
Nialls Cl. BD10: B'frd 5H **53**
Nice Av. LS8: Leeds 5D **78**
Nice St. LS8: Leeds 5E **79**
Nice Vw. LS8: Leeds 5D **78**
Nicholas Cl. BD7: B'frd 4H **89**
Nichols Cl. LS22: Weth 4C **12**
Nicholson Cl. BD16: Bgly 1C **50**
Nicholson Ct. LS8: Leeds 3E **79**
Nichols Way LS22: Weth 4B **12**
Nichols Yd. HX6: Hal 5A **148**
Nickleby Rd. LS9: Leeds 3E **99**
Nicolsons Pl. BD20: Sils 2E **15**
Nidd App. LS22: Weth 1D **12**
Nidd Ct. BD20: Sils 2E **15**
Nidderdale Cl. LS25: Gar 6H **103**
Nidderdale Wlk. BD17: Bail 3E **53**
Nidd St. BD3: B'frd 5H **91**
Nightingale St. BD21: Keigh 5A **34**
                (off Linnet St.)
Nightingale Wlk. BD16: Bgly 3E **51**
Nijinsky Way LS10: Leeds 4F **119**
Nile Rd. LS29: I'ly 5D **10**
Nile St. BD22: Haw 1E **65**
  BD22: Keigh 1F **47**
  LS2: Leeds 2B **98** (2G **5**)
Nina Rd. BD7: B'frd 2H **109**
Ninelands La. LS25: Gar 6G **103**
Ninelands Spur LS25: Gar 5G **103**
Ninelands Vw. LS25: Gar 4G **103**
Ninevah La. WF10: Kip 2F **145**
Nineveh Gdns. LS11: Leeds 6G **97**
Nineveh Pde. LS11: Leeds 6G **97**
Nineveh Rd. LS11: Leeds 6G **97**
Ninth Av. WF15: Liv 4H **153**
Nippet La. LS9: Leeds 3C **98**
Nixon Av. LS9: Leeds 4F **99**
Noble St. BD7: B'frd 6B **90**
Nog La. BD9: B'frd 5A **70**
NOOK 6C **136**
Nook, The HX6: Hal 6H **147**
  LS17: Leeds 2B **60**
  WF3: E Ard 3E **155**
Nook Gdns. LS15: Scho 1H **81**
Nooking WF2: Wake 6H **155**
Nooking, The WF2: Wake 6H **155**

Nook Rd. LS15: Scho 1H **81**
Nooks, The LS27: Morl 6F **115**
Nook Vw. WF3: E Ard 3E **155**
NOON NICK 5E **69**
Nora Pl. LS13: Leeds 6C **74**
Nora Rd. LS13: Leeds 6C **74**
Nora Ter. LS13: Leeds 6C **74**
Norbreck Dr. BD22: Haw 1E **65**
Norbury Rd. BD10: B'frd 4C **72**
Norcliffe La. HX3: Hal 3C **150**
Norcroft Brow BD7: B'frd 5D **90** (5A **6**)
Norcroft Ind. Est.
    BD7: B'frd 4C **90** (4A **6**)
Norcroft St. BD7: B'frd 4C **90** (4A **6**)
Nordale Cl. LS29: I'ly 4E **11**
Norfield HD2: Hud 6A **162**
Norfolk Cl. LS7: Leeds 2B **78**
    LS26: Rothw 2F **143**
Norfolk Dr. LS26: Rothw 2F **143**
Norfolk Gdns. BD1: B'frd 5E **91** (5D **6**)
    LS7: Leeds 2B **78**
Norfolk Grn. LS7: Leeds 2B **78**
Norfolk Mt. LS7: Leeds 2B **78**
Norfolk Pl. HX1: Hal 3E **149**
    LS7: Leeds 2B **78**
Norfolk St. BD16: Bgly 4C **50**
Norfolk Ter. LS7: Leeds 2B **78**
Norfolk Vw. LS7: Leeds 2B **78**
Norfolk Wlk. LS7: Leeds 2B **78**
Norgarth CI. WF17: Bat 4A **154**
Norham Gro. BD12: B'frd 5D **132**
Norland Rd. HX4: Hal 4B **158**
    HX6: Hal 6H **147**
Norland St. BD7: B'frd 2H **109**
NORLAND TOWN 1B **158**
Norland Town Rd. HX6: Hal 1B **158**
Norland Vw. HX2: Hal 5E **149**
    (off Delph Hill Rd.)
    HX6: Hal 5B **148**
Norman Av. BD2: B'frd 4H **71**
    HX5: Ell 5C **160**
Norman Cres. BD2: B'frd 4H **71**
Norman Gro. BD2: B'frd 4H **71**
    HX5: Ell 5C **160**
    LS5: Leeds 5A **76**
Norman La. BD2: B'frd 4H **71**
Norman Mt. BD2: B'frd 4H **71**
    LS5: Leeds 5A **76**
Norman Pl. LS8: Leeds 5E **61**
Norman Row LS5: Leeds 5A **76**
Norman St. BD16: Bgly 4C **50**
    BD22: Haw 2D **64**
    HX1: Hal 4D **148**
    HX5: Ell 5C **160**
    LS5: Leeds 5A **76**
Norman Ter. BD2: B'frd 4H **71**
    HX5: Ell 5C **160**
    LS8: Leeds 5E **61**
Normanton Gro. LS11: Leeds 1G **117**
Normanton Pl. LS11: Leeds 1G **117**
Norman Towers LS16: Leeds 3A **76**
Norman Vw. LS5: Leeds 5A **76**
Norquest Ind. Pk. WF17: Bat 4C **136**
NORR 3H **67**
Norr Grn. Ter. BD15: B'frd 3H **67**
Nortech Cl. LS7: Leeds 1B **98**
Northallerton Rd. BD3: B'frd 2F **91**
Northampton St. BD3: B'frd 2F **91** (1F **7**)
North Av. BD8: B'frd 6D **70**
    LS21: Otley 3E **23**
Nth. Bank Rd. BD16: Bgly 4C **68**
North Beck Ho. BD21: Keigh 1H **47**
    (off Aireworth St.)
North Bolton HX2: Hal 6B **106**
North Bri. HX1: Hal 1G **149** (2C **164**)
North Bridge Leisure Cen.
    .....1G **149** (2C **164**)
North Bri. St. HX1: Hal 1G **149** (2C **164**)
Nth. Broadgate La. LS18: H'fth 6E **57**
Northbrook Pl. BD2: B'frd 2B **78**
Northbrook St. BD1: B'frd 3F **91** (2E **7**)
    LS7: Leeds 2B **78**

Nth. Byland HX2: Hal 6C **106**
North Cliffe HX6: Hal 6H **147**
Nth. Cliffe Av. BD13: B'frd 5B **88**
Nth. Cliffe CI. BD13: B'frd 4A **88**
Nth. Cliffe Dr. BD13: B'frd 5A **88**
Nth. Cliffe Gro. BD13: B'frd 4A **88**
Nth. Cliffe La. BD13: B'frd 4B **88**
Northcliffe Rd. BD18: Ship 3A **70**
North Cl. LS8: Leeds 3H **79**
Northcote Cres. LS11: Leeds 1H **117**
Northcote Dr. LS11: Leeds 1H **117**
Northcote Fold LS22: Coll 1B **28**
Northcote Grn. LS11: Leeds 1H **117**
Northcote Rd. BD2: B'frd 1H **91**
Northcote St. LS28: Pud 1H **93**
North Ct. LS2: Leeds 3A **98** (3F **5**)
Nth. Croft Gro. LS29: I'ly 5C **10**
Northcroft Ri. BD8: B'frd 2G **89**
North Cut HD6: Brigh 1H **161**
Northdale Av. BD5: B'frd 3C **110**
Northdale Cres. BD5: B'frd 3C **110**
Northdale Mt. BD5: B'frd 3C **110**
Northdale Rd. BD9: B'frd 4B **70**
Nth. Dean Av. BD22: Keigh 6E **33**
Nth. Dean Bus. Pk. HX4: Hal 2G **159**
Nth. Dean Rd. BD22: Keigh 6E **33**
    HX4: Hal 2E **159**
Nth. Dene Rd. BD20: Sils 1E **15**
North Dr. LS16: B'hpe 3H **43**
North Edge HX3: Hal 6E **131**
    (off Brighouse and Denholme Ga. Rd.)
Northedge La. HX3: Hal 6E **131**
Northedge Mdw. BD10: B'frd 3H **71**
Northedge Pk. HX3: Hal 6E **131**
Northern Ballet Theatre 2A **76**
    (in West Pk. Curriculum Cen.)
Northern CI. BD7: B'frd 3H **109**
Northern St. LS1: Leeds 4G **97** (5B **4**)
Nth. Farm Rd. LS8: Leeds 6F **79**
Northfield Av. LS22: Weth 3E **13**
    LS26: Rothw 3G **141**
Northfield CI. HX5: Ell 5B **160**
    (off Victoria Av.)
Northfield Cres. BD16: Bgly 2C **68**
Northfield Gdns. BD6: B'frd 4C **110**
Northfield Gro. BD6: B'frd 4C **110**
Northfield Ho. BD10: B'frd 2A **72**
Northfield M. LS22: Weth 3F **13**
Northfield Pl. BD8: B'frd 2C **90**
    LS22: Weth 3E **13**
    LS26: Rothw 3F **141**
Northfield Rd. BD6: B'frd 4B **110**
Northfield Ter. BD13: B'frd 4C **108**
North Fold BD10: B'frd 1H **71**
Northgate BD1: B'frd 4E **91** (3C **6**)
    BD17: Bail 3C **52**
    HX1: Hal 2G **149** (3C **164**)
    HX5: Ell 4B **160**
    LS26: Rothw 1E **143**
Northgate Ho. LS22: Weth 4E **13**
Northgate La. LS22: Coll, Weth 4A **12**
Northgate Ri. LS22: Coll 1B **28**
Northgates LS22: Weth 4E **13**
Nth. Grange M. LS6: Leeds 5F **77**
Nth. Grange Mt. LS6: Leeds 4E **77**
Nth. Grange Rd. LS6: Leeds 5E **77**
Nth. Grove App. LS22: Weth 2E **13**
Nth. Grove Av. LS22: Weth 2E **13**
Nth. Grove Cl. LS8: Leeds 3H **79**
Nth. Grove Ct. LS22: Weth 3E **13**
Nth. Grove Cres. LS22: Weth 2E **13**
Nth. Grove Dr. LS8: Leeds 3H **79**
    LS22: Weth 2E **13**
Nth. Grove Mt. LS22: Weth 3E **13**
Nth. Grove Ri. LS22: Weth 3H **79**
Nth. Grove Rd. LS22: Weth 2E **13**
Nth. Grove Way LS22: Weth 3E **13**
North Hall Av. BD10: B'frd 5G **53**
North Hill LS14: S'cft 5F **45**
Nth. Hill CI. LS8: Leeds 3G **79**
Nth. Hill Ct. LS6: Leeds 4F **77**

Nth. Hill Rd. LS6: Leeds 5F **77**
Nth. Holme St. BD1: B'frd 3E **91** (2D **6**)
North Ives BD22: Oxen 5C **64**
Nth. John St. BD13: B'frd 4A **108**
North La. LS6: Leeds 4D **76**
    LS8: Leeds 2G **79**
    LS26: Rothw 1E **143**
Nth. Lane Gdns. LS8: Leeds 3G **79**
North Lea HX6: Hal 5H **147**
    (off Tuel La.)
Northlea Av. BD10: B'frd 6G **53**
Nth. Lingwell Rd. LS10: Leeds 2A **140**
North Lodge BD13: B'frd 2C **86**
North Mead LS16: B'hpe 3H **43**
Northolme Av. LS16: Leeds 2B **76**
Northolme Cres. LS16: Leeds 2B **76**
NORTHOWRAM 4C **130**
Northowram Grn. HX3: Hal 4C **130**
North Pde. BD1: B'frd 4E **91** (3C **6**)
    BD15: B'frd 1C **88**
    HX1: Hal 2G **149** (3C **164**)
    LS16: Leeds 1A **76**
    LS21: Otley 3E **23**
    LS27: Morl 4B **138**
    (off Wide La.)
    LS29: Burl W 1E **21**
    LS29: I'ly 5E **11**
North Pk. Av. LS8: Leeds 1D **78**
North Pk. Gro. LS8: Leeds 1E **79**
North Pk. Pde. LS8: Leeds 6D **60**
North Pk. Rd. BD9: B'frd 6B **70**
    LS8: Leeds 1E **79**
    (not continuous)
North Pk. Ter. BD9: B'frd 1C **90**
Nth. Parkway LS14: Leeds 4A **80**
Nth. Queen St. BD21: Keigh 6A **34**
North Rd. BD6: B'frd 4B **110**
    LS15: Leeds 1E **99**
    LS18: H'fth 4D **56**
Northrop CI. BD8: B'frd 2H **89**
Northrops Yd. LS28: Pud 4A **94**
Nth. Royd HX3: Hal 6E **131**
Nth. Selby HX2: Hal 6B **106**
Northside Av. BD7: B'frd 5A **90**
Northside Bus. Pk. LS7: Leeds 1B **98**
Northside Family Shop. Cen.
    LS7: Leeds 2F **77**
Northside Rd. BD7: B'frd 5H **89**
Northside Ter. BD7: B'frd 5H **89**
North St. BD1: B'frd 4F **91** (3F **7**)
    BD10: B'frd 5H **53**
    BD12: B'frd 3G **133**
    BD20: Sils 1E **15**
    BD21: Keigh 6A **34**
    BD22: Haw 2B **64**
    HX4: Hal 6F **159**
    (Cross St.)
    HX4: Hal 4H **159**
    (Green La.)
    LS2: Leeds 2B **98** (2G **5**)
    LS7: Leeds 1B **98** (2G **5**)
    LS19: Yead 3F **55**
    LS21: Otley 3E **23**
    LS22: Weth 4E **13**
    LS28: Pud 3A **94**
    LS29: Add 1E **9**
North Ter. BD16: Bgly 5C **50**
    (off Leonard St.)
    LS15: Leeds 1E **101**
    (off Tranquility Av.)
    LS19: Yead 6F **41**
    WF17: Bat 6B **136**
Nth. Vale Ct. HD6: Brigh 2B **152**
North Vw. BD13: B'frd 3G **107**
    (Glazier Rd.)
    BD13: B'frd 4B **66**
    (Walker Ter.)
    BD15: B'frd 2C **88**
    (North Pde.)
    BD15: B'frd 4G **67**
    (Townfield)
    BD20: Stee 5A **14**

North Vw. HX3: Hal 1E **151**
HX4: Hal 6F **159**
LS8: Leeds 3H **79**
LS26: Rothw *3B 142*
(off Royds La.)
LS29: Burl W 2F **21**
LS29: Men 1G **39**
North Vw. Rd. BD3: B'frd 1F **91**
BD4: B'frd 6E **113**
North Vw. St. BD20: Keigh 4H **33**
LS28: Pud 1A **94**
North Vw. Ter. *BD20: Keigh* *5H 35*
(off Main Rd.)
BD22: Haw 1C **64**
LS28: Pud 1A **94**
North Wlk. BD16: Bgly 6E **49**
North Way LS8: Leeds 3H **79**
Northwell Ga. LS21: Otley 2C **22**
Northwest Bus. Pk. LS6: Leeds ...6H **77**
Nth. West Rd. LS6: Leeds 6H **77**
North Wing BD3: B'frd 3F **91** (2F **7**)
Northwood Cl. LS26: Rothw 6E **121**
LS28: Pud 6B **94**
Northwood Cres. BD10: B'frd 2A **72**
Northwood Falls LS26: Rothw 6E **121**
Northwood Gdns. LS15: Leeds 4G **101**
Northwood Mt. LS28: Pud 6B **94**
Northwood Pk. LS26: Rothw 6E **121**
Northwood Vw. LS28: Pud 6B **94**
Norton Cl. HX2: Hal 2H **147**
HX5: Ell 6B **160**
Norton Dr. HX2: Hal 2H **147**
Norton Rd. LS8: Leeds 5E **61**
Norton St. BD20: Sils 2D **14**
HX5: Ell 5B **160**
NORTON TOWER 2H **147**
Norton Twr. HX2: Hal 2H **147**
Norville Ter. *LS6: Leeds* *5E 77*
(off Headingley La.)
Norwich Av. LS10: Leeds 3B **118**
Norwood Av. BD11: B'frd 3F **135**
BD18: Ship 3B **70**
LS29: Burl W 2F **21**
Norwood Cl. LS29: Burl W 2F **21**
Norwood Cres. BD11: B'frd 3F **135**
LS28: Pud 1B **94**
Norwood Cft. LS28: Pud 1B **94**
Norwood Dr. BD11: B'frd 3F **135**
WF17: Bat 6B **136**
NORWOOD GREEN 5H **131**
Norwood Grn. Hill HX3: Hal 5H **131**
Norwood Gro. BD11: B'frd 3F **135**
LS6: Leeds 6E **77**
Norwood Pk. LS29: I'ly 5B **10**
Norwood Pl. BD18: Ship 3B **70**
LS6: Leeds 6E **77**
Norwood Rd. BD18: Ship 3B **70**
LS6: Leeds 6E **77**
Norwood St. BD5: Leeds 3D **110**
BD18: Ship 3B **70**
Norwood Ter. BD18: Ship 3B **70**
HX3: Hal 5A **132**
LS6: Leeds 6E **77**
LS29: Burl W 2F **21**
Norwood Vw. LS6: Leeds 6E **77**
Nostell Cl. BD8: B'frd 3D **90** (1A **6**)
Noster Gro. LS11: Leeds 2F **117**
Noster Hill LS11: Leeds 2F **117**
Noster Pl. LS11: Leeds 2F **117**
Noster Rd. LS11: Leeds 2F **117**
Noster St. LS11: Leeds 2F **117**
Noster Ter. LS11: Leeds 2F **117**
Noster Vw. LS11: Leeds 2F **117**
Nottingham Cl. WF3: Rothw 4E **141**
Nottingham St. BD3: B'frd 4C **92**
Nova La. WF17: Bat 5H **135**
Nowell App. LS9: Leeds 2F **99**
Nowell Av. LS9: Leeds 2F **99**
Nowell Cl. LS9: Leeds 2F **99**
Nowell Cres. LS9: Leeds 2F **99**

Nowell End Row LS9: Leeds 2F **99**
Nowell Gdns. LS9: Leeds 2F **99**
Nowell Gro. LS9: Leeds 2F **99**
Nowell La. LS9: Leeds 2F **99**
Nowell Mt. LS9: Leeds 2F **99**
Nowell Pde. LS9: Leeds 2F **99**
Nowell Pl. LS9: Leeds 2F **99**
Nowell St. LS9: Leeds 2F **99**
Nowell Ter. LS9: Leeds 2F **99**
Nowell Vw. LS9: Leeds 2F **99**
Nowell Wlk. LS9: Leeds 2F **99**
No. 7 Health Club *6H 33*
(off Devonshire St.)
Nunburnholme Wlk. BD10: B'frd ...1F **71**
Nunington Av. LS12: Leeds 3C **96**
Nunington St. LS12: Leeds 3C **96**
Nunington Ter. LS12: Leeds 3C **96**
Nunington Vw. LS12: Leeds 2C **96**
Nunlea Royd HX3: Hal 3A **152**
Nunnery La. HD6: Brigh 4F **161**
Nunroyd Av. LS17: Leeds 6B **60**
LS20: Guis 5D **40**
Nunroyd Gro. LS17: Leeds 6B **60**
Nunroyd Ho. *BD4: B'frd* *5B 92*
(off Sticker La.)
Nunroyd Lawn LS17: Leeds 6B **60**
Nunroyd Rd. LS17: Leeds 6B **60**
Nunroyd St. LS17: Leeds 6B **60**
Nunroyd Ter. LS17: Leeds 6B **60**
Nunthorpe Rd. LS13: Leeds 4B **74**
Nurser La. BD5: B'frd 1C **110**
Nurser Pl. BD5: B'frd 1C **110**
Nursery Av. HX3: Hal 4D **128**
Nursery Cl. BD17: Bail 5H **51**
BD20: Keigh 2G **33**
HX3: Hal 5D **128**
Nursery Gdns. BD16: Bgly 1B **68**
Nursery Gth. LS22: Weth 3F **13**
Nursery Gro. HX3: Hal 4D **128**
LS17: Leeds 3G **59**
Nursery La. HX3: Hal 4C **128**
LS17: Leeds 3G **59**
LS29: Add 1E **9**
Nursery Mt. LS10: Leeds 4C **118**
Nursery Mt. Rd. LS10: Leeds 3C **118**
Nursery Rd. BD7: B'frd 3H **109**
BD14: B'frd 1D **108**
LS20: Guis 2B **40**
Nursery Way LS23: B Spa 3H **29**
(Albion St.)
LS23: B Spa 3H **29**
(Holly Rd.)
Nussey Av. WF17: Bat 5A **136**
Nuthatch M. BD6: B'frd 4E **109**
Nuttall Rd. BD3: B'frd 4G **91** (3G **7**)
Nutter La. WF17: Bat 5G **135**
Nutting Gro. Ter. LS12: Leeds 6G **95**
Nutwood Wlk. BD6: B'frd 1G **131**

O

Oak Av. BD8: B'frd 1C **90**
BD16: Bgly 6B **50**
HX6: Hal 4H **147**
LS25: Gar 4F **103**
LS27: Morl 4B **138**
LS29: Burl W 3F **21**
Oak Bank BD16: Bgly 5C **50**
BD17: Bail 5C **52**
BD18: Ship 4D **70**
Oakbank Av. BD22: Keigh 2F **47**
Oakbank B'way. BD22: Keigh 3F **47**
Oakbank Ct. BD22: Keigh 3F **47**
Oakbank Cres. BD22: Keigh 3F **47**
Oakbank Dr. BD22: Keigh 2F **47**
Oakbank Gro. BD22: Keigh 3F **47**
Oakbank La. BD22: Keigh 3F **47**
Oakbank Mt. BD22: Keigh 3F **47**
Oakburn Rd. LS29: I'ly 6C **10**
Oak Cl. LS29: Burl W 3F **21**

Oak Cotts. LS23: B Spa 6B **30**
Oak Cres. LS15: Leeds 4B **100**
LS25: Gar 4F **103**
Oakdale BD16: Bgly 2C **50**
Oakdale Av. BD6: B'frd 4B **110**
BD18: Ship 3D **70**
Oakdale Cl. BD10: B'frd 6C **72**
HX3: Hal 5E **129**
WF3: Wake 3F **157**
Oakdale Cres. BD6: B'frd 4B **110**
Oakdale Dr. BD10: B'frd 6C **72**
BD18: Ship 3E **71**
Oakdale Gth. LS14: Leeds 6D **62**
Oakdale Gro. BD18: Ship 3E **71**
Oakdale Mdw. LS14: Leeds 6D **62**
Oakdale Pk. LS21: Pool 4F **25**
Oakdale Rd. BD18: Ship 3E **71**
Oakdale Ter. BD6: B'frd 4B **110**
Oakdene LS26: Rothw 6F **121**
Oakdene Cl. LS28: Pud 6B **94**
Oakdene Ct. LS17: Leeds 3E **61**
Oakdene Dr. LS17: Leeds 3E **61**
Oakdene Gdns. LS17: Leeds 3E **61**
Oakdene Mt. LS14: B'frd 2C **108**
Oakdene Va. LS17: Leeds 3E **61**
Oakdene Way LS17: Leeds 3E **61**
Oak Dr. LS16: Leeds 5B **58**
LS25: Gar 4F **103**
OAKENSHAW 2F **133**
Oakenshaw Cl. BD12: B'frd 5C **132**
Oakenshaw La. BD12: B'frd 5G **133**
BD19: B'frd 5G **133**
Oakfield LS6: Leeds 5E **77**
Oakfield Av. BD16: Bgly 5E **51**
LS26: Rothw 1A **142**
Oakfield Cl. HX5: Ell 5A **160**
LS25: Gar 5F **103**
LS29: Men 5G **21**
Oakfield Dr. BD17: Bail 5D **52**
Oakfield Gro. BD9: B'frd 1C **90**
Oakfield Rd. BD21: Keigh 3G **47**
Oakfield Ter. BD18: Ship 2D **70**
LS18: H'fth *1G 75*
(off Low La.)
Oakford Ter. LS18: H'fth 6G **57**
Oak Gro. BD20: Keigh 3D **34**
BD21: Keigh 4G **47**
LS25: Gar 4G **103**
LS27: Morl 4B **138**
Oakham M. LS9: Leeds 4F **99**
Oakhampton Ct. LS8: Leeds 1G **79**
Oakham Wlk. BD4: B'frd 1G **111**
Oakham Way LS9: Leeds 4F **99**
Oakhall Pk. BD13: B'frd 4H **87**
Oakham M. LS9: Leeds 4F **99**
Oakhampton Ct. LS8: Leeds 1G **79**
Oakham Wlk. BD4: B'frd 1G **111**
Oakham Way LS9: Leeds 4F **99**
Oakhall Pk. BD13: B'frd 4H **87**
Oakham M. LS9: Leeds 4F **99**
Oak Ho. LS5: Leeds 5H **75**
LS7: Leeds *2B 78*
(off Allerton Pk.)
LS15: Leeds 5A **100**
Oakhurst Av. LS11: Leeds 4G **117**
Oakhurst Ct. BD8: B'frd 1D **90**
Oakhurst Gro. LS11: Leeds 4F **117**
Oakhurst Mt. LS11: Leeds 4F **117**
Oakhurst Rd. LS11: Leeds 4F **117**
Oakhurst St. LS11: Leeds 4G **117**
Oaklands BD10: B'frd 1G **71**
BD18: Ship 2F **69**
HD6: Brigh 2H **161**
LS29: I'ly 6C **10**
WF3: Rothw 4E **141**
Oaklands Av. HX3: Hal 4C **130**
LS13: Leeds 4A **74**
LS16: Leeds 4D **58**
Oaklands Cl. LS16: Leeds 4D **58**
Oaklands Dr. LS16: Leeds 5D **58**
Oaklands Fold LS16: Leeds 4D **58**
Oaklands Gro. LS13: Leeds 4A **74**
LS16: Leeds 4D **58**
Oaklands Rd. LS13: Leeds 4A **74**
Oaklands Rd. Trad. Est.
LS13: Leeds 4A **74**
Oakland St. BD20: Sils 2D **14**

Oak La. BD9: B'frd 1B **90**
  HX1: Hal 2E **149**
Oaklea Gdns. LS16: Leeds 5D **58**
Oaklea Hall Cl. LS16: Leeds 5D **58**
Oaklea Rd. LS15: Scho 3H **81**
Oakleigh Av. BD14: B'frd 2D **108**
  (not continuous)
  HX3: Hal 6G **149**
Oakleigh Cl. BD14: B'frd 1D **108**
Oakleigh Gdns. BD14: B'frd 2D **108**
Oakleigh Gro. BD14: B'frd 2D **108**
  (not continuous)
Oakleigh M. BD22: Keigh 5C **46**
Oakleigh Rd. BD14: B'frd 2D **108**
Oakleigh Ter. BD14: B'frd 1D **108**
Oakleigh Vw. BD17: Bail 4B **52**
Oakley Gro. LS11: Leeds 2A **118**
Oakley Ho. BD5: B'frd 1D **110**
  (off Park La.)
Oakley St. WF3: E Ard 6C **140**
Oakley Ter. LS11: Leeds 3A **118**
Oakley Vw. LS11: Leeds 3A **118**
Oak Mt. BD8: B'frd 1D **90**
  HX3: Hal 1G **151**
Oak Pl. BD17: Bail 3F **53**
  HX1: Hal 2E **149**
  HX6: Hal 4H **147**
  LS25: Gar 4E **103**
Oak Ridge LS22: Weth 4C **12**
Oakridge Av. LS29: Men 1H **39**
Oakridge Ct. BD16: Bgly 3C **50**
Oak Ri. BD19: Cleck 5B **134**
Oak Rd. HD2: Hud 6G **163**
  LS7: Leeds 4B **78**
  LS12: Leeds 4E **97**
  LS15: Leeds 4B **100**
  LS25: Gar 4E **103**
  LS27: Morl 5H **137**
Oak Royd LS25: Gar 4F **103**
Oakroyd Av. BD6: B'frd 4C **110**
Oakroyd Cl. BD11: B'frd 2E **135**
  HD6: Brigh 4B **152**
Oak Royd Cotts. HX3: Hal 1F **159**
Oakroyd Dr. BD11: B'frd 3E **135**
  HD6: Brigh 4B **152**
Oakroyd Fold LS27: Morl 5C **116**
Oakroyd Mt. LS28: Pud 3A **94**
Oakroyd Rd. BD6: B'frd 4B **110**
Oakroyd Ter. BD8: B'frd 1D **90**
  BD17: Bail 5D **52**
  LS27: Morl 5C **116**
  LS28: Pud 3A **94**
Oakroyd Vs. BD8: B'frd 1D **90**
Oaks, The BD15: B'frd 3F **67**
  LS20: Guis 3C **40**
  LS27: Morl 6B **116**
Oaks Dr. BD15: B'frd 3E **89**
Oaksfield LS26: Mick 5D **144**
Oaks Fold BD5: B'frd 2E **111**
Oaks Grn. Mt. HD6: Brigh 4H **161**
Oakshaw Cl. BD4: B'frd 1G **111**
Oaks La. BD8: B'frd 4F **89**
  BD15: B'frd 3E **89**
  LS23: B Spa 3A **30**
Oak St. BD14: B'frd 1D **108**
  BD22: Haw 2D **64**
  BD22: Oxen 6C **64**
  HX5: Ell 5B **160**
  HX6: Hal 4H **147**
  LS27: Morl 6B **116**
  WF1: Wake 5G **157**
Oak Ter. HX1: Hal 2E **149**
  (off Acorn St.)
  HX6: Hal 4H **147**
  (off Oak Pl.)
  LS15: Leeds 6F **81**
  (off Church La.)
Oak Tree Bus. Pk.
  LS14: Leeds 2C **80**
Oak Tree Cl. LS9: Leeds 6G **79**

Oak Tree Ct. BD20: Sils 1D **14**
  LS9: Leeds 6G **79**
  (off Oak Tree Pl.)
Oak Tree Cres. LS9: Leeds 6G **79**
Oak Tree Dr. LS8: Leeds 6G **79**
Oak Tree Gro. LS9: Leeds 6G **79**
Oak Tree Mt. LS9: Leeds 6G **79**
Oak Tree Pl. LS9: Leeds 6G **79**
Oak Tree Wlk. LS9: Leeds 6G **79**
Oak Vw. BD20: Sils 1E **15**
Oak Vs. BD8: B'frd 1D **90**
Oakway BD11: B'frd 3F **135**
OAKWELL 4H **135**
Oakwell Av. LS8: Leeds 3E **79**
Oakwell Cl. BD7: B'frd 2B **110**
  BD11: B'frd 2C **136**
Oakwell Ct. LS13: Leeds 6D **74**
  LS28: Pud 6H **73**
  (off Water La.)
  WF17: Bat 4C **136**
  (not continuous)
Oakwell Cres. LS8: Leeds 3E **79**
Oakwell Dr. LS8: Leeds 3E **79**
Oakwell Gdns. LS8: Leeds 3E **79**
Oakwell Gro. LS13: Leeds 6E **75**
Oakwell Hall 4H **135**
Oakwell Hall Country Pk. 4G **135**
Oakwell Hall Farm Vis. Cen. 4H **135**
Oakwell Ind. Est. WF17: Bat 4H **135**
Oakwell Ind. Pk. WF17: Bat 4B **136**
Oakwell Mt. LS8: Leeds 3E **79**
Oakwell Oval LS8: Leeds 3E **79**
Oakwell Rd. BD11: B'frd 2C **136**
Oakwell Ter. LS28: Pud 6H **73**
Oakwell Way WF17: Bat 4C **136**
OAKWOOD 3G **79**
Oakwood Av. BD2: B'frd 5D **70**
  BD11: B'frd 3E **135**
  LS8: Leeds 3F **79**
Oakwood Boundary Rd.
  LS8: Leeds 3F **79**
Oakwood Cotts. BD16: Bgly 1C **50**
Oakwood Ct. BD8: B'frd 3C **90**
  LS8: Leeds 3G **79**
Oakwood Dr. BD16: Bgly 2B **50**
  LS8: Leeds 3G **79**
  LS26: Rothw 6H **119**
Oakwood Fitness Cen. 4G **79**
Oakwood Gdns. LS8: Leeds 3F **79**
  LS28: Pud 5A **94**
Oakwood Gth. LS8: Leeds 3G **79**
Oakwood Grange LS8: Leeds 3G **79**
Oakwood Grange La.
  LS8: Leeds 3G **79**
Oakwood Grn. LS8: Leeds 3G **79**
Oakwood Gro. BD8: B'frd 2A **90**
  LS8: Leeds 3F **79**
Oakwood La. LS8: Leeds 3F **79**
  LS9: Leeds 6H **79**
Oakwood Mt. LS8: Leeds 3F **79**
Oakwood Nook LS8: Leeds 3F **79**
Oakwood Pk. LS8: Leeds 4G **79**
Oakwood Pl. LS8: Leeds 3F **79**
Oakwood Ri. LS8: Leeds 3G **79**
Oak Wood Rd. LS22: Weth 2D **12**
Oakwood Ter. LS28: Pud 5A **94**
Oakwood Vw. LS8: Leeds 3G **79**
Oakwood Wlk. LS8: Leeds 3G **79**
OAKWORTH 5C **46**
Oakworth Hall BD22: Keigh 5C **46**
Oakworth Rd. BD21: Keigh 2F **47**
  BD22: Keigh 2F **47**
Oakworth Station
Keighley & Worth Valley Railway
  . . . . .6D **46**
Oakworth Ter. BD22: Keigh 5C **46**
  (off Dockroyd La.)
Oasby Cft. BD4: B'frd 4C **112**
Oast Ho. Cft. WF3: Rothw 4F **141**
Oastler Pl. BD12: B'frd 1D **132**
Oastler Rd. BD18: Ship 1H **69**
  LS28: Pud 3F **73**

Oastler Shop. Cen.
  BD1: B'frd 4E **91** (3C **6**)
Oatland Cl. LS7: Leeds 1A **98**
Oatland Ct. LS7: Leeds . . .1A **98** (1F **5**)
Oatland Dr. LS7: Leeds 1A **98**
Oatland Gdns. LS7: Leeds 1A **98**
Oatland Grn. LS7: Leeds 1A **98**
Oatland Hgts. LS7: Leeds 1G **5**
Oatland La. LS7: Leeds 1A **98**
Oatland Pl. LS7: Leeds 6A **78**
Oatland Rd. LS7: Leeds 1A **98**
Oatlands LS21: Otley 2E **23**
Oatland Towers LS7: Leeds . . .1A **98** (1F **5**)
Oats St. BD22: Keigh 3G **47**
Oban Cl. WF3: E Ard 6D **138**
Oban Pl. LS12: Leeds 3A **96**
Oban St. LS12: Leeds 3B **96**
Oban Ter. LS12: Leeds 3B **96**
  WF3: E Ard 6D **138**
Occupation La. BD22: Keigh 3D **46**
  HX2: Hal 1C **128**
  LS16: B'hpe 2D **42**
  LS28: Pud 5G **93**
Octagon Ter. HX2: Hal 5C **148**
Odda La. LS20: Guis 4E **39**
Oddfellows Ct. BD1: B'frd . . .4E **91** (4C **6**)
Oddfellows St. BD19: Cleck 1F **153**
  HD6: Brigh 6B **152**
Oddfellow St. LS27: Morl 3A **138**
Oddy Pl. BD6: B'frd 4B **110**
  LS6: Leeds 3D **76**
Oddy's Fold LS6: Leeds 1E **77**
Oddy St. BD4: B'frd 4C **112**
Odeon Cinema 3D **92**
ODSAL .5D **110**
Odsal Rd. BD6: B'frd 4C **110**
  (not continuous)
Odsal Stadium 5E **111**
ODSAL TOP 5E **111**
Office Row BD22: Haw 1C **64**
OGDEN .3B **106**
Ogden Cres. BD13: B'frd 1B **86**
Ogden Ho. BD4: B'frd 1D **112**
Ogden La. BD13: B'frd 1B **86**
  HD6: Brigh 3H **161**
  HX2: Hal 3B **106**
Ogden St. HX6: Hal 6G **147**
Ogden Vw. Cl. HX2: Hal 6B **106**
Ogden Water Vis. Cen. 3A **106**
Ogilby Ct. LS26: Rothw 6D **120**
Ogilby M. LS26: Rothw 6D **120**
O'Grady Sq. LS9: Leeds 4D **98**
Old Allen Rd. BD15: B'frd 6E **67**
Old Arc., The HX1: Hal 4C **164**
Old Bank HX3: Hal 2H **149**
  (not continuous)
Old Barn Cl. LS17: Leeds 2G **59**
Old Bell Ct. HX1: Hal 5B **164**
OLD BRAMHOPE 2C **42**
Old Brandon La. LS17: Leeds 3A **62**
Old Bri. Ri. LS29: I'ly 5F **11**
Old Canal Rd. BD1: B'frd . . .3E **91** (1D **6**)
Old Cawsey HX6: Hal 5A **148**
Old Cl. LS11: Leeds 5D **116**
Old Cock Yd. HX1: Hal . . .2G **149** (4C **164**)
Old Corn Mill, The BD4: B'frd 2B **112**
  HD6: Hud 3F **163**
Old Corn Mill La. BD7: B'frd 1A **110**
Old Dalton La. BD21: Keigh 6B **34**
Old Dan La. HX4: Hal 6G **159**
OLD DOLPHIN 3D **108**
Old Earth HX5: Ell 4D **160**
Old Farm App. LS16: Leeds 1H **75**
Old Farm Cl. LS16: Leeds 1A **76**
Old Farm Cres. BD4: B'frd 2H **111**
Old Farm Cross LS16: Leeds 1A **76**
Old Farm Dr. LS16: Leeds 1H **75**
Old Farm Gth. LS16: Leeds 1A **76**
Old Farm Pde. LS16: Leeds 1H **75**
Old Farm Wlk. LS16: Leeds 1H **75**
Oldfield Av. LS12: Leeds 5C **96**
Oldfield Cl. LS25: M'fld 4E **105**

Oldfield Ct. LS7: Leeds 3C 78
Oldfield Ga. BD22: Haw 2A 64
Oldfield La. BD22: Haw 1A 64
    LS12: Leeds 5C 96
    LS22: Coll, Weth 2D 28
Oldfield St. HX3: Hal 3E 129
    LS12: Leeds 5C 96
Old Fold LS28: Pud 6H 73
Old Forge M. LS16: B'hpe 2F 43
Old Fort BD13: B'frd 5C 86
Old Godley La. HX3: Hal 1A 150
Old Gt. North La. LS25: M'fld 3D 104
Old Guy Rd. BD13: B'frd 3G 107
Old Hall Cl. BD22: Haw 3C 64
Old Hall Rd. WF3: E Ard 1F 155
Oldham St. HD6: Brigh 2A 162
    (off Bridge End)
Old Haworth La. LS19: Yead 6F 41
Old Hollins Hill BD17: B'frd, Guis . . .1A 54
    LS20: Guis 1A 54
Old La. BD11: B'frd 6B 114
    (Lumb Bottom)
    BD11: B'frd 1E 135
    (Station La.)
    BD13: B'frd 3B 86
    HD2: Hud 6C 162
    HD6: Brigh 6B 152
    HX2: Hal 6D 126
    HX3: Hal 4E 129 (1A 164)
    LS11: Leeds 3F 117
    LS16: Yead 2C 42
    LS20: Guis 5D 38
    LS21: Otley, Yead 1A 42
    LS29: Add 3G 9
    LS29: I'ly 6F 11
Old Lane Ct. HD6: Brigh 6B 152
    (off Old La.)
Old Langley La. BD17: Bail 3D 52
Old Lee Bank HX3: Hal 6F 129
Old Lodge Hill LS29: I'ly 3B 10
Old Main St. BD16: Bgly 3B 50
Old Manse Cft. BD22: Oxen 1C 84
Old Mkt. HX1: Hal 2G 149 (4C 164)
Old Marsh HX6: Hal 4H 147
    (off Burnley Rd.)
    LS28: Pud 4G 93
OLD MICKLEFIELD 3D 104
Old Mill BD2: B'frd 5A 72
Old Mill Bus. Pk. LS10: Leeds 1D 118
Old Mill Cl. LS29: Burl W 1F 21
Old Mill Gro. HX1: Hal 3C 148
Old Mill La. LS10: Leeds 1C 118
    LS23: B Spa 6C 30
Old Oak Cl. LS16: Leeds 2A 76
Old Oak Dr. LS16: Leeds 2A 76
Old Oak Gth. LS16: Leeds 2H 75
Old Oak Lawn LS16: Leeds 2A 76
Old Orchard, The LS21: Pool 4E 25
    LS29: Men 1H 39
    (off Station Rd.)
Old Oxenhope La. BD22: Oxen 4B 64
Old Pk. Ct. BD3: B'frd 4G 91 (4G 7)
Old Park Rd. BD10: B'frd 1A 72
    LS8: Leeds 1E 79
    (not continuous)
Old Pool Bank LS21: Pool 1D 42
Old Popplewell La. BD19: Cleck 1E 153
Old Power Way HX5: Ell 3C 160
Old Riding La. HX2: Hal 4F 127
Old Rd. BD7: B'frd 3G 109
    BD13: B'frd 3B 86
    (New Rd.)
    BD13: B'frd 5B 88
    (Watkin Av.)
    LS27: Morl 5C 116
    LS28: Pud 2G 93
Oldroyd Cres. LS11: Leeds 3E 117
Old Run Rd. LS10: Leeds 3B 118
Old Run Vw. LS10: Leeds 5B 118
Old School, The LS29: Burl W 2E 21
    (off Albert Simmons Way)

Old School Gdns. HX3: Hal 6G 129
Old School Lofts LS12: Leeds 4A 96
Old School M. LS27: Morl 5C 116
Old Side Rd. BD20: Keigh 4A 36
Old Souls Way BD16: Bgly 1A 50
Old Station Rd. HX2: Hal 2D 146
Old Sta. Way LS29: Add 1D 8
Old Tannery BD16: Bgly 4B 50
    (off Industrial St.)
Old Vicarage Cl. BD16: Bgly 3D 68
Old Well Head
    HX1: Hal 4G 149 (6B 164)
Old Whack Ho. La. LS19: Yead 1D 54
Old Wood La. BD16: Bgly 4A 38
Olicana Pk. LS29: I'ly 4C 10
Olive Gro. BD8: B'frd 3G 89
Olive Pl. BD13: B'frd 4A 108
Oliver Cl. HX6: Hal 5H 147
Oliver Ct. BD11: B'frd 2H 135
Oliver Hill LS18: H'fth 2E 75
Oliver Mdws. HX5: Ell 4D 160
Oliver St. BD4: B'frd 6G 91
Olive Ter. BD16: Bgly 4C 50
Olivia's Ct. BD9: B'frd 1G 89
Ollerdale Av. BD15: B'frd 6C 68
    (not continuous)
Ollerdale Cl. BD15: B'frd 1C 88
Olrika Ct. LS7: Leeds 5B 78
Olympic Pk. BD12: B'frd 2E 133
Olympic Way BD12: B'frd 2E 133
One St. BD1: B'frd 4B 6
Onslow Cres. BD4: B'frd 3H 111
Ontario Pl. LS7: Leeds 3B 78
Opal St. BD22: Keigh 3G 47
Open University 5E 5
Orange St. BD3: B'frd 5A 92
    HX1: Hal 2G 149 (3A 164)
Orange Tree Gro. WF3: E Ard 2A 156
Orchard, The BD21: Keigh 6D 34
    LS23: B Spa 3B 30
    WF2: Wake 6D 156
Orchard Cl. HX2: Hal 3B 148
    WF2: Wake 6C 156
    WF3: E Ard 3B 156
Orchard Ct. LS16: Leeds 2D 76
    (off St Chads Rd.)
    LS20: Guis 4C 40
    (off Orchard La.)
Orchard Cft. LS15: Leeds 1D 100
    WF2: Wake 6C 156
Orchard Dr. LS22: Coll 6B 12
Orchard Ga. LS21: Otley 4E 23
    (off Market St.)
Orchard Gro. BD10: B'frd 2B 72
    LS29: Men 1G 39
Orchard Ho. LS23: B Spa 3B 30
    (off Albion St.)
Orchard La. LS20: Guis 4C 40
    LS29: Add 1E 9
Orchard Mt. LS15: Leeds 1E 101
Orchard Ri. HX6: Hal 6F 147
Orchard Rd. LS15: Leeds 1D 100
Orchards, The BD16: Bgly 2C 50
    BD19: Cleck 6G 135
    HD6: Brigh 3H 161
    LS15: Leeds 1D 100
    LS26: Mick 5C 144
Orchard Sq. LS15: Leeds 1D 100
Orchard St. LS21: Otley 4F 23
Orchard Vw. LS22: Weth 1E 13
Orchard Way HD6: Brigh 5A 152
    LS20: Guis 4C 40
    LS26: Rothw 1A 142
Orchid Cl. BD18: Ship 4D 70
Orchid Ct. WF3: Rothw 5F 141
Oriental St. LS12: Leeds 4C 96
Orion Cres. LS10: Leeds 6C 118
Orion Dr. LS10: Leeds 6C 118
Orion Gdns. LS10: Leeds 6D 118
Orion Pl. HX6: Hal 5H 147
    (off Greenups Ter.)
Orion Vw. LS10: Leeds 6D 118

Orion Wlk. LS10: Leeds 5D 118
Orleans St. BD6: B'frd 6H 109
Ormonde Ct. LS13: Leeds 2F 95
Ormonde Dr. BD15: B'frd 3C 88
Ormonde Pl. LS7: Leeds 6A 78
Ormond Rd. BD6: B'frd 4B 110
Ormondroyd Av. BD6: B'frd 5C 110
Ormond St. BD7: B'frd 1A 110
Orville Gdns. LS6: Leeds 5E 77
Osborne Gro. HX3: Hal 2F 151
Osborne St. BD5: B'frd 6D 90
    HX1: Hal 1D 148
Osborne Ct. LS13: Leeds 2F 95
Osbourne Dr. BD13: B'frd 4H 107
Osdal Rd. BD6: B'frd 5D 110
    (off Glenfield Mt.)
Osmond Ho. BD5: B'frd 6E 91
    (off Crosscombe Wlk.)
OSMONDTHORPE 3G 99
Osmondthorpe Cotts. LS9: Leeds . . .4G 99
Osmondthorpe La. LS9: Leeds 3G 99
Osmondthorpe Ter. LS9: Leeds 3F 99
Osprey Cl. LS17: Leeds 3D 60
    LS22: Coll 2B 28
Osprey Ct. BD8: B'frd 4E 89
Osprey Gro. LS17: Leeds 3D 60
Osprey Mdw. LS27: Morl 3D 138
Osterley Cres. BD10: B'frd 4C 72
Osterley Gro. BD10: B'frd 4C 72
Oswald Cl. LS20: Guis 4B 40
Oswald St. BD18: Ship 2D 70
Oswaldthorpe Av. BD3: B'frd 2B 92
OTLEY 4E 23
Otley La. LS19: Yead 6F 41
Otley Mt. BD20: Keigh 5A 36
Otley Mus. 3E 23
    (off Cross Grn.)
Otley Old Rd. LS16: Leeds 1A 42
    (Dean La.)
    LS16: Leeds 2G 57
    (Holt La.)
    LS18: Yead 1A 42
    LS19: H'fth, Leeds, Yead 1A 42
    LS21: Otley, Yead 1A 42
Otley Rd. BD2: B'frd 3G 91
    BD3: B'frd 4F 91 (1G 7)
    BD16: Bgly 5F 37
    BD18: Ship 3B 70
    BD20: Bgly, Keigh 4A 36
    LS6: Leeds 2C 76
    LS16: Leeds 1B 58
    LS20: Guis 4A 40
    LS29: Burl W 3G 21
    LS29: Men 6H 21
Otley St. BD21: Keigh 1H 47
    HX1: Hal 2D 148
Ottawa Pl. LS7: Leeds 3B 78
Otterburn Cl. BD5: B'frd 1D 110
Otterburn Gdns. LS16: Leeds 4B 58
Otterburn St. BD21: Keigh 5A 34
Otterwood Bank LS22: Weth 2F 13
Ouchthorpe Fold WF1: Wake 5G 157
Ouchthorpe La. WF1: Wake 6G 157
OULTON 2E 143
Oulton Dr. LS26: Rothw 4E 143
Oulton La. LS26: Rothw 2B 142
    (Rothwell)
    LS26: Rothw 6E 121
    (Woodlesford)
Oulton Ter. BD7: B'frd 6C 90
Ounsworth St. BD4: B'frd 1H 111
Ouse Dr. LS22: Weth 1D 12
OUSEL HOLE 3A 36
Ouse St. BD22: Haw 2D 64
Out Gang LS13: Leeds 6F 75
Out Gang La. LS13: Leeds 6G 75
Outlands Ri. BD10: B'frd 1B 72
Outside La. BD22: Oxen 6A 64
OUTWOOD .5F 157
Outwood Av. LS18: H'fth 2F 75
Outwood Chase LS18: H'fth 1F 75
Outwood La. LS18: H'fth 2E 75
Outwood Pk. Ct. WF1: Wake 5E 157

Outwood Station (Rail) 4E 157
Outwood Wlk. LS18: H'fth 2E 75
Ouzel Dr. BD6: B'frd 4E 109
OUZLEWELL GREEN 6H 141
Ouzlewell Grn. WF3: Rothw 5H 141
OVAL, THE 1B 100
Oval, The BD8: B'frd 3G 89
   BD16: Bgly 5D 50
   BD17: Bail 6B 52
   LS10: Leeds 1B 118
   LS14: Leeds 1B 100
   LS20: Guis 5A 40
   LS21: Otley 2D 22
   LS25: Gar 4G 103
   LS26: Rothw 2B 142
Ovendale Hall HX3: Hal 5E 129
(off Gro. Ct.)
OVENDEN .5D 128
Ovenden Av. HX3: Hal 6E 129
Ovenden Cl. HX3: Hal 6E 129
Ovenden Cres. HX3: Hal 5E 129
Ovenden Grn. HX3: Hal 5D 128
Ovenden Pk. 3D 128
Ovenden Rd. HX1: Hal 1F 149 (2B 164)
   HX3: Hal 4E 129
Ovenden Rd. Ter. HX3: Hal 5E 129
Ovenden Ter. HX3: Hal 5H 129
Ovenden Way HX3: Hal 5C 128
OVENDEN WOOD 5A 128
Ovenden Wood Rd. HX2: Hal 5A 128
Overdale Av. LS17: Leeds 2E 61
Overdale Cl. LS22: Weth 3D 12
Overdale Dr. BD10: B'frd 6F 53
Overdale Mt. HX6: Hal 4A 148
Overdale Ter. BD22: Haw 2C 64
   LS15: Leeds 3C 100
Overend St. BD6: B'frd 4A 110
Overgreen Royd HX2: Hal 3G 127
Overland Cres. BD10: B'frd 1B 72
Overland Trad. Est.
   LS27: Morl 2E 137
Over La. LS19: Yead 4G 55
Overmoor Fold BD10: B'frd 2G 71
Overton Dr. BD6: B'frd 3F 109
Overton Ho. BD5: B'frd 1D 110
(off Newstead Wlk.)
Ovington Dr. BD4: B'frd 4C 112
Owen Ct. BD16: Bgly 1C 50
Owlcotes Dr. LS28: Pud 3G 93
Owlcotes Gdns. LS28: Pud 3G 93
Owlcotes Gth. LS28: Pud 3F 93
Owlcotes La. LS28: Pud 3G 93
(Cemetery Rd.)
   LS28: Pud 2G 93
(Stanningley By-Pass, not continuous)
Owlcotes Rd. LS28: Pud 3F 93
Owlcotes Shop. Cen.
   LS28: Pud 2H 93
Owlcotes Ter. LS28: Pud 3G 93
Owler Ings Rd. HD6: Brigh 1A 162
Owler La. WF17: Bat 4A 136
Owler Pk. Rd. LS29: I'ly 2A 10
Owlers Cl. HD2: Hud 6F 163
OWLET 5D 70
Owlet Grange BD18: Ship 3C 70
Owlet Rd. BD18: Ship 2C 70
Owlett Mead WF3: E Ard 6C 140
Owlett Mead Cl. WF3: E Ard 6C 140
Owl La. WF12: Dew 6A 154
Owl Ridge LS27: Morl 4C 138
Owl St. BD21: Keigh 5B 34
(off Parson St.)
Oxenford Ct. LS16: Leeds 4A 58
OXENHOPE 1C 84
Oxenhope Station
   Keighley & Worth Valley Railway
   . . . . .6C 64
Oxford Av. LS20: Guis 3B 40
Oxford Cl. BD13: B'frd 5G 107
Oxford Cres. BD14: B'frd 1D 108
   HX3: Hal 5H 149
Oxford Dr. LS25: Kip 4F 123

Oxford La. HX3: Hal 5H 149
Oxford Pl. BD3: B'frd 3F 91 (1F 7)
   BD17: Bail 5C 52
   LS1: Leeds 3H 97 (3C 4)
   LS28: Pud 2A 94
Oxford Rd. BD2: B'frd 1G 91
   BD13: B'frd 5G 107
   BD19: Cleck 5F 135
   HX1: Hal 3G 149 (6B 164)
   LS7: Leeds 6A 78
   LS20: Guis 4B 40
   WF17: Bat 6A 136
Oxford Row LS1: Leeds 3H 97 (3C 4)
(not continuous)
Oxford St. BD14: B'frd 1D 108
   BD21: Keigh 1G 47
   HX6: Hal 5B 148
   LS20: Guis 4C 40
   LS27: Morl 5H 137
   WF3: E Ard 1C 156
Oxford Ter. BD17: Bail 5E 53
(off Union St.)
Oxford Vs. LS20: Guis 4C 40
Ox Heys Mdw. BD13: B'frd 5C 88
Oxley Gdns. BD12: B'frd 1A 132
Oxley St. BD8: B'frd 3C 90 (2A 6)
   LS9: Leeds 4D 98
Oxton Mt. LS9: Leeds 3D 98
Oxton Way LS9: Leeds 3D 98
Oyster Cl. LS27: Morl 4C 138

P

Pack Horse Yd. LS1: Leeds 4E 5
Packington St. BD13: B'frd 3G 87
Padan St. HX3: Hal 5H 149
Paddock BD9: B'frd 5C 70
   HX2: Hal 2B 130
Paddock, The BD13: B'frd 3B 66
   BD17: Bail 3F 53
   BD19: Cleck 1F 153
   BD20: Sils 2E 15
   LS6: Leeds 2F 77
   LS14: T'ner 2H 63
   LS17: Bard 5E 27
   LS26: Rothw 2A 142
Paddock Cl. BD11: B'frd 2A 136
   BD12: B'frd 6C 132
   LS25: Gar 5G 103
Paddock Cnr. LS15: Leeds 4E 101
(off Colton Rd.)
Paddock Dr. BD11: B'frd 2A 136
Paddock Grn. LS17: Bard 6E 27
Paddock Ho. La. LS22: Sick 1D 26
Paddock La. BD16: Bgly 1F 51
   HX2: Hal 1A 148
Paddock Rd. HX3: Hal 2A 130
Paddock Vw. LS17: Bard 6F 27
Padgate Ho. BD5: B'frd 1D 110
(off Park La.)
Padgum BD17: Bail 3C 52
Padma Cl. BD7: B'frd 4B 90
Padmans La. LS23: B Spa 3B 30
Padstow Av. LS10: Leeds 2G 139
Padstow Gdns. LS10: Leeds 2G 139
Padstow Pl. LS10: Leeds 3G 139
Padstow Row LS10: Leeds 3G 139
Page Hill HX2: Hal 4C 128
Paget St. BD21: Keigh 6G 33
Pagewood Ct. BD10: B'frd 6G 53
Paignton Ct. LS13: Leeds 2F 95
Paisley Gro. LS12: Leeds 3A 96
Paisley Pl. LS12: Leeds 3A 96
Paisley Rd. LS12: Leeds 3A 96
Paisley St. LS12: Leeds 3A 96
Paisley Ter. LS12: Leeds 3A 96
Paisley Vw. LS12: Leeds 3A 96
Pakington St. BD5: B'frd 1D 110
Paley Rd. BD4: B'frd 1G 111
Paley Ter. BD4: B'frd 1G 111
Palin Av. BD3: B'frd 2B 92

Palm Cl. BD6: B'frd 5B 110
Palmer Rd. BD3: B'frd 3H 91
Palmerston St. BD2: B'frd 1H 91
Palm St. HX3: Hal 5F 129
Pannal St. BD7: B'frd 2A 110
Pannel Hill WF10: Kip 6B 124
Panorama Dr. LS29: I'ly 1A 18
Paper Hall, The 3F 7
Papyrus Vs. LS24: Tad 5G 31
Parade, The BD4: B'frd 2C 112
   BD16: Bgly 2C 68
   LS6: Leeds 4D 76
(off North La.)
   LS9: Leeds 4C 98
   LS16: B'hpe 2G 43
   LS19: Yead 1D 54
(off Westfield Dr.)
   LS21: Otley 2C 22
Paradise HX2: Hal 1C 146
Paradise Fold BD7: B'frd 1G 109
PARADISE GREEN 1G 109
Paradise Gro. LS18: H'fth 1G 75
(off Hawksworth La.)
Paradise La. HX2: Hal 3H 147
Paradise Pl. LS18: H'fth 1G 75
Paradise Rd. BD9: B'frd 5H 69
Paradise St. BD1: B'frd 4D 90 (3A 6)
(not continuous)
   HX1: Hal 3F 149 (5A 164)
Paradise Vw. BD15: B'frd 3F 67
Parc Mont LS8: Leeds 1G 79
Paris Gates HX3: Hal 4H 149
(off Boys La.)
Parish Ghyll Dr. LS29: I'ly 6B 10
Parish Ghyll La. LS29: I'ly 6B 10
Parish Ghyll Rd. LS29: I'ly 6C 10
Parish Ghyll Wlk. LS29: I'ly 6C 10
PARK 3F 53
Park, The HX3: Hal 5C 150
Park & Ride
   King Lane 4H 59
Park Av. BD10: B'frd 5H 53
   BD11: B'frd 1A 136
   BD16: Bgly 5B 50
   BD18: Ship 1A 70
   BD21: Keigh 1H 47
   BD22: Keigh 5D 46
   HX5: Ell .5A 160
   LS8: Leeds 1G 79
   LS12: Leeds 3B 96
   LS15: Leeds 1F 101
   LS19: Yead 3G 55
(Batter La.)
   LS19: Yead 6E 41
(Swaine Hill Ter.)
   LS25: Kip 4A 124
   LS26: Swil 4A 122
   LS27: Morl 4H 137
   LS28: Pud 4A 94
   WF1: Wake 5E 157
   WF3: Wake 3G 157
Park Bottom BD12: B'frd 2C 132
Park Bldgs. LS21: Pool 4F 25
Park Cir. LS10: Leeds 2H 139
Park Cliffe Rd. BD2: B'frd 1G 91
Park Cl. BD10: B'frd 4A 72
   BD11: B'frd 1A 136
   BD13: B'frd 4H 107
   BD16: Bgly 3C 50
   BD21: Keigh 2A 48
   HX2: Hal 5H 127
   HX3: Hal 2G 151
   LS13: Leeds 6E 75
   LS29: Burl W 3E 21
Park Copse LS18: H'fth 6C 56
Park Cotts. LS8: Leeds 6F 61
Park Ct. BD9: B'frd 1C 90
   LS4: Leeds 1D 96
   LS13: Leeds 4F 75
   LS21: Pool 5F 25
Park Cres. BD3: B'frd 1G 91
   HX3: Hal 6E 129

Park Cres. HX6: Hal 5B **148**
(off Grove St.)
LS8: Leeds 5E **61**
LS12: Leeds 3B **96**
LS20: Guis 6A **40**
LS26: Rothw 1C **142**
LS27: Morl 1F **137**
LS29: Add 1E **9**
Parkcroft LS28: Pud 1H **93**
Park Cross St. LS1: Leeds 3H **97** (4C **4**)
Park Dale LS29: Men 1G **39**
Park Dr. BD9: B'frd 5A **70**
BD16: Bgly 2D **50**
HX1: Hal 3E **149**
HX2: Hal 4B **148**
LS18: H'fth 1B **74**
WF3: Wake 2G **157**
Park Dr. Rd. BD21: Keigh 2A **48**
Park Edge Cl. LS8: Leeds 2G **79**
Parker's La. BD20: Keigh 2G **33**
Parker St. WF3: E Ard 2A **156**
Park Farm Ind. Est. LS11: Leeds . .5H **117**
Park Fld. LS29: Men 1G **39**
Parkfield Av. HX5: Ell 5B **160**
LS11: Leeds 2G **117**
Parkfield Cl. LS25: Kip 3H **123**
LS28: Pud 4H **93**
Parkfield Ct. LS14: Leeds 6A **80**
Parkfield Dr. BD13: B'frd 4H **107**
HX6: Hal 6G **147**
LS23: B Spa 3A **30**
Parkfield Gro. LS11: Leeds 2G **117**
Parkfield La. HX6: Hal 6B **148**
Parkfield Mt. LS11: Leeds 2G **117**
LS28: Pud 4A **94**
Parkfield Pl. LS11: Leeds 2G **117**
Parkfield Rd. BD8: B'frd 1D **90**
BD18: Ship 1G **69**
LS11: Leeds 2G **117**
Parkfield Row LS11: Leeds 2G **117**
Park Flds. HX2: Hal 5H **127**
Parkfield St. LS11: Leeds 6A **98**
Parkfield Ter. LS28: Pud 4A **94**
(Church La.)
LS28: Pud 2A **94**
(Richardshaw Rd., not continuous)
Parkfield Vw. LS11: Leeds 2G **117**
Parkfield Way LS14: Leeds 6A **80**
Park Gdns. HX2: Hal 4B **148**
Park Ga. BD1: B'frd 4F **91** (3F **7**)
Park Ga. Cl. LS18: H'fth 1D **74**
Park Ga. Cres. LS20: Guis 5B **40**
Park Grn. BD20: Sils 1C **14**
HX3: Hal 6B **130**
Park Gro. BD9: B'frd 5C **70**
BD13: B'frd 4H **107**
BD18: Ship 1H **69**
BD21: Keigh 5A **34**
LS6: Leeds 3D **76**
LS10: Leeds 3A **140**
LS18: H'fth 1B **74**
LS19: Yead 6E **41**
LS26: Swil 5A **122**
LS27: Morl 1F **137**
Park Gro. Ct. BD9: B'frd 5C **70**
Park Halt
Middleton Railway 5B **118**
Parkhead Cl. BD6: B'frd 1A **132**
Park Hill HD2: Hud 5F **163**
Pk. Hill Cl. BD8: B'frd 2F **89**
Pk. Hill Dr. BD8: B'frd 2F **89**
Pk. Hill Gro. BD16: Bgly 3C **50**
Park Holme LS7: Leeds 5C **78**
Park Ho. Cl. BD12: B'frd 6E **111**
Park Ho. Cres. BD12: B'frd 6E **111**
Park Ho. Gro. BD12: B'frd 6E **111**
Park Ho. Rd. BD12: B'frd 1D **132**
Park Ho. Wlk. BD12: B'frd 6E **111**
Parkin La. BD10: B'frd 1D **72**
Parkinson App. LS25: Gar 3F **103**
Parkinson La. HX1: Hal 3C **148**
Parkinson Rd. BD13: B'frd 3C **86**

Parkinson St. BD5: B'frd 1D **110**
Parkland Av. LS27: Morl 4G **137**
Parkland Bus. Cen.
BD10: B'frd 2B **72**
Parkland Cres. LS6: Leeds 6G **59**
Parkland Dr. BD10: B'frd 2A **72**
LS6: Leeds 6G **59**
Parkland Gdns. LS6: Leeds 1G **77**
PARKLANDS 5C **80**
Parklands BD16: Bgly 2D **50**
LS16: B'hpe 2F **43**
LS29: I'ly 5F **11**
Parklands Cres. LS16: B'hpe 2G **43**
Parklands Ga. LS16: B'hpe 2G **43**
Parklands Wlk. LS16: B'hpe 3F **43**
Parkland Ter. LS6: Leeds 1G **77**
Parkland Vw. LS19: Yead 6F **41**
(off Town St.)
LS19: Yead 1F **55**
(Henshaw Av.)
Park La. BD5: B'frd 1D **110**
BD13: B'frd 4B **108**
BD14: B'frd 1D **108**
BD17: Bail 3F **53**
BD21: Keigh 1A **48**
HX3: Hal 1H **159**
LS1: Leeds 3G **97** (3B **4**)
LS3: Leeds 3F **97** (3A **4**)
LS8: Leeds 5F **61**
LS20: Guis 6A **40**
LS25: Kip 5A **124**
LS25: Led 4G **125**
(not continuous)
LS26: Mick 6A **144**
LS26: Rothw 2B **142**
WF10: Kip 3H **145**
Park La. Ct. LS17: Leeds 2G **61**
Park La. Ends HX2: Hal 5B **106**
Park La. Mt. LS17: Leeds 3F **61**
Park Lea HD2: Hud 5F **163**
LS10: Leeds 2A **140**
Parklee Ct. BD21: Keigh 1B **48**
Park Lodge BD15: B'frd 4G **67**
Park Mead BD10: B'frd 5H **53**
Parkmere Cl. BD4: B'frd 6H **111**
Park M. LS21: Pool 5F **25**
Park Mt. LS5: Leeds 5A **76**
LS12: Leeds 3A **96**
LS21: Pool 6D **24**
Park Mt. Av. BD17: Bail 4E **53**
Park Nook HX3: Hal 1B **160**
Park Pde. LS9: Leeds 5E **99**
LS27: Morl 4H **137**
Park Pl. BD10: B'frd 5H **53**
HX1: Hal 3E **149**
(off Warley St.)
LS1: Leeds 3H **97** (4C **4**)
LS8: Leeds 4H **79**
Park Pl. E. HX3: Hal 2G **151**
Park Pl. W. HX3: Hal 2G **151**
Park Ri. LS13: Leeds 5E **75**
Park Rd. BD5: B'frd 6E **91**
BD10: B'frd 5H **53**
(Ainsbury Rd.)
BD10: B'frd 4A **72**
(Victoria Rd.)
BD12: B'frd 6C **110**
BD16: Bgly 4B **50**
BD18: Ship 2C **70**
HX1: Hal 3F **149** (5A **164**)
HX5: Ell 3B **160**
HX6: Hal 4A **148**
LS12: Leeds 3A **96**
LS13: Leeds 6E **75**
LS15: Leeds 5F **101**
LS19: Yead 3F **55**
(Gladstone Rd.)
LS19: Yead 6E **41**
(Park Gro.)
LS20: Guis 6A **40**
LS23: B Spa 3A **30**
LS29: Men 1G **39**

Park Row HD6: Brigh 1B **162**
LS1: Leeds 3H **97** (4D **4**)
LS21: Otley 3F **23**
(off Cross Grn.)
LS28: Pud 2A **94**
LS29: Burl W 1F **21**
Park School M. BD16: Bgly 4B **50**
(off Lime St.)
PARKSIDE 3F **111**
Park Side BD14: B'frd 1D **108**
LS18: H'fth 1C **74**
Parkside BD16: Bgly 3C **50**
HX3: Hal 5F **149**
Parkside Av. BD13: B'frd 4H **107**
LS6: Leeds 2F **77**
Parkside Cl. LS6: Leeds 1F **77**
Parkside Ct. BD22: Haw 1E **65**
Parkside Cres. LS6: Leeds 1F **77**
Parkside Dr. BD9: B'frd 6A **70**
Parkside Gdns. LS6: Leeds 2F **77**
Parkside Grn. LS6: Leeds 2F **77**
Parkside Gro. BD9: B'frd 6A **70**
LS11: Leeds 4G **117**
Parkside Ind. Est. LS11: Leeds 4A **118**
Parkside La. LS11: Leeds 3A **118**
Parkside Lawns LS6: Leeds 2F **77**
Parkside Mt. LS11: Leeds 4G **117**
Parkside Pde. LS11: Leeds 4G **117**
Parkside Pl. LS6: Leeds 1F **77**
Parkside Rd. BD5: B'frd 3D **110**
LS6: Leeds 1F **77**
LS16: Leeds 6D **58**
LS28: Pud 1H **93**
Parkside Row LS11: Leeds 4G **117**
Parkside Ter. BD13: B'frd 3B **66**
Parkside Vw. LS6: Leeds 1F **77**
Parks La. LS29: I'ly 1C **10**
PARK SPRING 4F **95**
Park Spring Gdns. LS13: Leeds 2D **94**
Park Spring Ri. LS13: Leeds 3D **94**
Park Sq. BD6: B'frd 5H **109**
HX3: Hal 5C **130**
(off Hough)
LS21: Pool 5F **25**
LS28: Pud 4A **94**
WF3: Wake 3G **157**
Park Sq. E. LS1: Leeds 3H **97** (4C **4**)
Park Sq. Nth. LS1: Leeds 3H **97** (4C **4**)
Park Sq. Sth. LS1: Leeds 3H **97** (4C **4**)
Park Sq. W. LS1: Leeds 3H **97** (4C **4**)
Parkstone HD2: Hud 5F **163**
Parkstone Av. LS16: Leeds 6A **58**
Parkstone Dr. BD10: B'frd 4A **72**
Parkstone Grn. LS16: Leeds 6A **58**
Parkstone Gro. LS16: Leeds 6A **58**
Parkstone Mt. LS16: Leeds 6A **58**
Parkstone Pl. LS16: Leeds 6A **58**
Park Stone Ri. HX3: Hal 1D **130**
Park St. BD18: Ship 1A **70**
BD19: Cleck 3H **153**
BD22: Haw 2D **64**
HD6: Brigh 1B **162**
HX6: Hal 5C **148**
LS1: Leeds 3H **97** (3C **4**)
LS12: Leeds 3A **96**
LS15: Leeds 3D **100**
LS19: Yead 6E **41**
LS27: Morl 5C **116**
Park Ter. BD12: B'frd 1C **132**
(off Fold La.)
BD18: Ship 1A **70**
BD21: Keigh 1D **48**
(off Bank Top Way)
BD21: Keigh 6B **34**
(Dalton La.)
HX1: Hal 3E **149**
(not continuous)
HX3: Hal 6C **130**
(Leeds Rd.)
HX3: Hal 2F **151**
(Wakefield Rd.)

Park Ter. LS6: Leeds 3D **76**
   LS21: Otley *3F 23*
   (off Cross Grn.)
   LS21: Pool 6C 24
Park Top LS28: Pud 2A **94**
Pk. Top Cotts. BD16: Bgly 2D **50**
Pk. Top Row BD22: Haw 2C **64**
Park Vw. BD11: B'frd 2E **135**
   BD13: B'frd 3H 107
   BD19: Cleck 1H 153
   HX1: Hal 3E 149
   HX3: Hal 2G 151
   HX6: Hal *4H 147*
   (off Tuel La.)
   LS11: Leeds 2G 117
   LS13: Leeds 6E 75
   LS16: Leeds 3C 58
   LS25: Kip 4H 123
   LS26: Swil 4A 122
   LS28: Pud 4A **94**
   WF3: Wake 3G **157**
Park Vw. Av. BD22: Haw 1E **65**
   HX3: Hal 6C 130
   LS4: Leeds 6D 76
   LS19: Yead 3G 55
Parkview Ct. BD18: Ship 2A 70
   LS8: Leeds 5F 61
Park Vw. Cres. LS8: Leeds 6F 61
Park Vw. Gro. LS4: Leeds 6D 76
Park Vw. Rd. BD9: B'frd 6B 70
   LS4: Leeds 1D 96
Park Vw. Ter. BD9: B'frd 6B 70
   BD16: Bgly 5F 49
   LS15: Leeds *3C 100*
   (off Park St.)
   LS19: Yead 3F 55
Park Villa Ct. LS8: Leeds 6E 61
PARK VILLAS 5E **61**
Park Vs. *HX6: Hal* *5B 148*
   (off Grove St.)
   LS8: Leeds 6E 61
Parkville Pl. LS13: Leeds 6E 75
Parkville Rd. LS13: Leeds 6E 75
Park Way BD17: Bail 6H 51
   LS21: Pool 5F 25
   LS29: Men 1G 39
Parkway BD5: B'frd 3F **111**
   BD13: B'frd 4H 107
   BD20: Stee 6B 14
   (not continuous)
   BD21: Keigh 2A 48
   LS27: Morl 1E **137**
Parkway Cl. LS14: Leeds 5A 80
Parkway Ct. LS14: Leeds 6A 80
Parkway Grange LS14: Leeds 6A 80
Parkways LS26: Rothw 1D 142
Parkways Av. LS26: Rothw 2D 142
Parkways Cl. LS26: Rothw 1D 142
Parkways Ct. LS26: Rothw 1D 142
Parkways Dr. LS26: Rothw 1D 142
Parkways Gth. LS26: Rothw 2D 142
Parkways Gro. LS26: Rothw 1D 142
Parkway Towers LS14: Leeds 5A **80**
Parkway Va. LS14: Leeds 6A 80
   (not continuous)
Park W. LS26: Rothw 2A 142
PARKWOOD 1A **48**
Park Wood Av. LS11: Leeds 5F **117**
Parkwood Av. LS8: Leeds 2E **79**
Parkwood Cen. for Young People . . .1B **48**
Park Wood Cl. LS11: Leeds 6F **117**
Parkwood Ct. LS8: Leeds 1E **79**
Park Wood Crematorium
   HX5: Hal 2B **160**
Park Wood Cres. LS11: Leeds 6F **117**
Park Wood Dr. LS11: Leeds 5F **117**
Parkwood Gdns. LS8: Leeds 1A **48**
   LS28: Pud 3E **73**
Parkwood Ri. BD21: Keigh 1A **48**
Park Wood Rd. LS11: Leeds 6F **117**
Parkwood Rd. BD18: Ship 2H **69**
   LS28: Pud 3F **73**

Parkwood St. BD21: Keigh 1A 48
Park Wood Top BD21: Keigh 1B 48
Parkwood Vw. LS8: Leeds 2E **79**
Parkwood Way LS8: Leeds 2E **79**
Parliament Pl. LS12: Leeds 3D **96**
Parliament Rd. LS12: Leeds 4D **96**
Parlington Ct. LS15: Bar E 2E 83
Parlington La. LS25: Bar E 6F **83**
Parlington Mdw. LS15: Bar E 3E 83
Parma St. BD5: B'frd 6E **91**
Parnaby Av. LS10: Leeds 4D 118
Parnaby Rd. LS10: Leeds 4D 118
Parnaby St. LS10: Leeds 4D 118
Parnaby Ter. LS10: Leeds 4D **118**
Parratt Row BD3: B'frd 4B **92**
Parrott St. BD4: B'frd 4B **112**
Parry Cl. BD16: Bgly 6E **49**
Parry La. BD4: B'frd 6A **92**
Parsley M. LS26: Mick 4C **144**
Parsonage La. HD6: Brigh 6A **152**
   (not continuous)
Parsonage Rd. BD4: B'frd 6B **92**
   BD5: B'frd 2E 111
   LS26: Mick 4D 144
Parsonage St. HX3: Hal 6H **129**
Parsons Grn. LS22: Weth 4F 13
Parson's La. LS29: Add 1A **8**
   (not continuous)
Parsons Rd. BD9: B'frd 5A 70
Parson St. BD21: Keigh 5A 34
Partons Pl. WF3: Wake 3G **157**
Partridge Cl. LS27: Morl 3D **138**
Partridge Dr. BD6: B'frd 4E 109
Paslew Cl. BD20: Keigh 4F 35
Pasture Av. BD22: Keigh 6C **46**
   LS7: Leeds 2B 78
Pasture Cl. BD14: B'frd 1F **109**
Pasture Cres. LS7: Leeds 2B 78
Pasture Fold LS29: Burl W 1E 21
Pasture Gro. LS7: Leeds 2B 78
Pasture La. BD14: B'frd 1E **109**
   LS7: Leeds 2B 78
   LS22: Kirkby 2A 26
Pasture Mt. LS12: Leeds 3B **96**
Pasture Pde. LS7: Leeds 2B 78
Pasture Pl. LS7: Leeds 2B 78
Pasture Ri. BD14: B'frd 1F **109**
Pasture Rd. BD17: Bail 5D 52
   LS8: Leeds 5C 78
Pastureside Ter. E. BD14: B'frd 1F **109**
Pastureside Ter. W. BD14: B'frd 1E **109**
Pasture St. LS7: Leeds 2B 78
Pasture Ter. LS7: Leeds 2B 78
Pasture Vw. LS12: Leeds 3B **96**
Pasture Vw. Rd. LS26: Rothw 2A **142**
Pasture Wlk. BD14: B'frd 1E **109**
Patchett Sq. *BD13: B'frd* *4D 108*
   (off Highgate Rd.)
Patent St. BD9: B'frd 1B 90
Paternoster La. BD7: B'frd 1A **110**
Patricia Gdns. HX6: Hal 4G **147**
Patterdale App. LS22: Weth 4B 12
Patterdale Ho. *BD5: B'frd* *1D 110*
   (off Hutson St.)
Patterson Ct. WF2: Wake 6D **156**
Pattie St. BD20: Keigh 4H **33**
Paulena Ter. *LS27: Morl* *5B 138*
   (off Britannia Rd.)
Paul La. HD5: Hud 6H **163**
Pavement La. HX2: Hal 5C **106**
Pavilion Bus. Pk. LS12: Leeds 2C **116**
Pavilion Cl. LS28: Pud 1A **94**
Pavilion Ct. BD4: B'frd 5A **112**
Pavilion Gdns. LS26: Rothw 1E **143**
   LS28: Pud 1A **94**
Pavilion M. LS6: Leeds 6D **76**
Pavilion Way LS28: Pud 4H **93**
Paw La. BD13: B'frd 6B **108**
Pawson St. BD4: B'frd 5B **92**
   LS27: Morl 4H 137
   WF3: E Ard 1C **156**
   WF3: Rothw 5F **141**

Peabody St. HX3: Hal 6E **129**
Peace Mus., The 4D **6**
Peace St. BD4: B'frd 6A **92**
Peach Wlk. BD4: B'frd 1H **111**
Peacock Grn. LS27: Morl 4C **138**
Pearl St. BD22: Keigh 3G **47**
Pearson Av. LS6: Leeds 6E **77**
Pearson Fold BD12: B'frd 3F **133**
Pearson Gro. LS6: Leeds 6E **77**
Pearson La. BD9: B'frd 2F **89**
Pearson Rd. BD6: B'frd 5D **110**
Pearson Rd. W. BD6: B'frd 5D **110**
Pearson Row BD12: B'frd 4D **132**
Pearsons Bldgs. LS21: Otley 4F 23
Pearson St. BD3: B'frd 5A **92**
   BD19: Cleck 3H 153
   LS10: Leeds 6B 98
   LS28: Pud 2F 73
Pearson Ter. LS6: Leeds 6E **77**
Pear St. BD21: Keigh 4G **47**
   BD22: Oxen 1C **84**
   HX1: Hal 3D **148**
Pear Tree Acre LS23: B Spa 2C **30**
Pear Tree Ct. BD20: Sils 1E **15**
Pear Tree Gdns. LS15: Bar E 3E **83**
Peas Acre BD16: Bgly 5A **36**
Peasborough Vw. LS29: Burl W 3F **21**
Peasefold LS25: Kip 4H **123**
Peasehill Cl. LS19: Yead 3G **55**
Peasehill Pk. LS19: Yead 3G **55**
Peaselands BD18: Ship 2A **70**
Peckfield Cotts. LS25: Gar 1B **124**
Peckover Dr. LS28: Pud 2D **92**
Peckover St. BD1: B'frd 4F **91** (3F **7**)
Peel Cl. BD4: B'frd 5C **92**
Peel Ct. BD3: B'frd 1F **91**
Peel Ho. BD16: Bgly 5D **50**
Peel Mills Bus. Cen. LS27: Morl 3B **138**
Peel Pk. Dr. BD2: B'frd 1H **91**
Peel Pk. Ter. BD2: B'frd 1H **91**
Peel Pk. Vw. BD3: B'frd 2G **91**
Peel Pl. LS29: Burl W 1E **21**
Peel Row BD7: B'frd 1A **110**
Peel Sq. BD8: B'frd 3D **90** (2B **6**)
   LS5: Leeds 5A **76**
Peel St. BD13: B'frd 5H **87**
   (George St.)
   BD13: B'frd 4B **108**
   (Scarlet Hgts.)
   BD15: B'frd 5G **67**
   BD16: Bgly 4D **50**
   HX6: Hal 5H **147**
   LS27: Morl 3B **138**
Peep Grn. La. WF15: Liv 1H **163**
Pegholme Dr. LS21: Otley 5B **22**
Pelham Cl. BD2: B'frd 6H **71**
   LS10: Leeds 4B **140**
Pelham Pl. LS7: Leeds 2A **78**
Pelham Rd. BD2: B'frd 6H **71**
PELLON 1C **148**
Pellon La. HX1: Hal 1D **148** (2A **164**)
Pellon New Rd. HX2: Hal 1C **148**
Pellon Ter. BD10: B'frd 6H **53**
Pellon Wlk. BD10: B'frd 6H **53**
Pemberton Dr. BD7: B'frd 5D **90** (6A **6**)
Pembroke Cl. LS27: Morl 2H **137**
Pembroke Ct. *BD8: B'frd* *3H 89*
   (off St Leonards Rd.)
Pembroke Dr. LS27: Morl 2H **137**
   LS28: Pud 3A **94**
Pembroke Grange LS9: Leeds 1H **99**
Pembroke Ho. *BD4: B'frd* *3C 112*
   (off Launceston Dr.)
Pembroke Ri. LS25: Kip 3A **124**
Pembroke Rd. LS28: Pud 3A **94**
Pembroke St. BD5: B'frd 1E **111**
Pembroke Towers LS9: Leeds 6H **79**
Pembury Mt. LS15: Leeds 6H **81**
Penarth Rd. LS15: Leeds 1D **100**
Pendas Dr. LS15: Leeds 1F **101**
PENDAS FIELDS 6H **81**
Pendas Gro. LS15: Leeds 6F **81**

Pendas Wlk. LS15: Leeds 1F **101**
Pendas Way LS15: Leeds 1F **101**
Pendil Cl. LS15: Leeds 3E **101**
Pendle Ct. BD13: B'frd 6A **108**
Pendle Rd. BD16: Bgly 4D **50**
(not continuous)
Pendragon BD2: B'frd 6G **71**
Pendragon La. BD2: B'frd 6H **71**
Pendragon Ter. LS20: Guis 4B **40**
Penfield Gro. BD14: B'frd 1E **109**
Penfield Rd. BD11: B'frd 1B **136**
Pengarth BD16: Bgly 2D **50**
Penistone Hill Country Pk. 3A **64**
Penistone M. BD22: Haw 2C **64**
Penlands Cres. LS15: Leeds 4F **101**
Penlands Lawn LS15: Leeds 4F **101**
Penlands Wlk. LS15: Leeds 4F **101**
Pennard Ho. BD5: B'frd 1D **110**
(off Launton Way)
Penn Cl. BD2: B'frd 5H **71**
Pennine Cl. BD13: B'frd 6H **107**
Pennine Ind. Est. LS12: Leeds 4B **96**
Pennine Vw. WF17: Bat 4C **136**
Pennington Ct. LS6: Leeds 6G **77**
Pennington Gro. LS6: Leeds 5G **77**
Pennington La. LS26: Rothw 5D **142**
Pennington Pl. LS6: Leeds 6G **77**
Pennington St. LS6: Leeds 6G **77**
Pennington Ter. BD5: B'frd 1C **110**
LS6: Leeds 5G **77**
Pennithorne Av. BD17: Bail 3C **52**
Penn St. HX1: Hal 1E **149**
Pennwell Cft. LS14: Leeds 4F **81**
(off Whinmoor Way)
Pennwell Dean LS14: Leeds 4F **81**
Pennwell Fld. LS14: Leeds 4G **81**
Pennwell Gth. LS14: Leeds 4F **81**
Pennwell Ga. LS14: Leeds 4F **81**
Pennwell Grn. LS14: Leeds 4F **81**
Pennwell Lawn LS14: Leeds 4F **81**
Pennyfield Cl. LS6: Leeds 6F **59**
Pennygate BD16: Bgly 2F **51**
Penny Hill Cen., The
LS10: Leeds 1C **118**
Penny Hill Dr. BD14: B'frd 1F **109**
Penny La. Way LS10: Leeds 1B **118**
Pennythorne Ct. LS19: Yead 2E **55**
Pennythorne Dr. LS19: Yead 2E **55**
Penraevon 1 Light Ind. Est.
LS7: Leeds 6A **78**
Penraevon Av. LS7: Leeds 6A **78**
Penrith Gro. LS12: Leeds 5C **96**
Penrose Dr. BD7: B'frd 2H **109**
Penrose Pl. HX3: Hal 5C **130**
Pentland Av. BD14: B'frd 1E **109**
Pentland Cl. BD22: Keigh 1G **47**
Pentland Dr. LS25: Gar 6F **103**
Pentland Way LS27: Morl 4A **138**
Penuel Pl. HX3: Hal 6H **149**
Penzance Ct. BD8: B'frd 3B **90**
(off Fearnsides St.)
Pepper Gdns. LS13: Leeds 5G **75**
PEPPER HILL 1C **130**
Pepper Hills LS17: Leeds 3B **60**
Pepper La. LS10: Leeds 2D **118**
LS13: Leeds 5F **75**
Pepper Rd. LS10: Leeds 3D **118**
Percival St. BD3: B'frd 4G **91** (4H **7**)
LS2: Leeds 2H **97** (2D **4**)
Percy St. BD13: B'frd 3G **107**
BD16: Bgly 4C **50**
BD21: Keigh 3H **47**
LS12: Leeds 5D **96**
Peregrine Av. LS27: Morl 3D **138**
Peregrine Way BD6: B'frd 4E **109**
Perkin La. BD10: B'frd 6F **53**
(off Far Crook)
Per La. HX2: Hal 6B **106**
Perry Cl. BD22: Keigh 4G **47**
Perseverance La. BD7: B'frd 2A **110**
Perseverance Rd. BD13: B'frd 2E **107**
HX2: Hal 2E **107**

Perseverance St. BD12: B'frd 3C **132**
BD17: Bail 3D **52**
HX1: Hal 4E **149**
HX6: Hal 4H **147**
LS28: Pud 4G **93**
Perseverance Ter. LS26: Rothw 3A **142**
Perth Av. BD2: B'frd 6E **71**
Perth Dr. WF3: E Ard 1F **155**
Perth Ho. BD4: B'frd 6B **92**
(off Parsonage Rd.)
Perth Mt. LS18: H'fth 3D **56**
Peterborough Pl. BD2: B'frd 6H **71**
Peterborough Rd. BD2: B'frd 1H **91**
Peterborough Ter. BD2: B'frd 6H **71**
Peterhouse Dr. LS21: Otley 4G **23**
Peter La. HX2: Hal 2H **147**
LS27: Morl 2D **138**
Peter Laylock Ind. Est.
LS7: Leeds 6A **78**
Petersfield Av. LS10: Leeds 6C **118**
Petersgarth BD18: Ship 1G **69**
Petrel Cl. BD6: B'frd 4E **109**
Petrel Way LS27: Morl 4C **138**
Petrie Cres. LS13: Leeds 4H **73**
Petrie Gro. BD3: B'frd 4C **92**
Petrie Rd. BD3: B'frd 4C **92**
Petrie St. LS13: Leeds 4H **73**
Pevensey Gth. BD10: B'frd 3A **72**
(off Savile Av.)
Peverell Pl. BD4: B'frd 2C **112**
Peveril Mt. BD2: B'frd 6A **72**
Pheasant Dr. WF17: Bat 4C **136**
Pheasant St. BD21: Keigh 5B **34**
Philip Gth. WF1: Wake 4F **157**
Philippa Way LS12: Leeds 2C **116**
Philip's Gro. WF3: Wake 3G **157**
Phil May Ct. LS12: Leeds 5E **97**
(off Green La.)
Phoebe La. HX3: Hal 5H **149**
Phoebe La. Ind. Est. HX3: Hal 5H **149**
Phoenix Bldgs. BD7: B'frd 5C **90**
Phoenix Cl. LS14: Leeds 6C **80**
Phoenix St. HD6: Brigh 1B **162**
Phoenix Way BD4: Pud 5C **92**
Physiques Health Studio 3F **91**
Piccadilly BD1: B'frd 4E **91** (3C **6**)
Piccadilly Chambers BD1: B'frd . . .3C **6**
(off Up. Piccadilly)
Pickard Bank LS6: Leeds 4F **77**
Pickard Ct. LS15: Leeds 3E **101**
Pickard La. BD20: Sils 1E **15**
Pickering Av. LS25: Gar 3H **103**
Pickering Mt. LS12: Leeds 3D **96**
Pickerings, The BD13: B'frd 5A **108**
Pickering St. LS12: Leeds 3D **96**
PICKLES HILL 3H **109**
Pickles La. BD7: B'frd 3H **109**
Pickles St. BD21: Keigh 2H **47**
Pickpocket La. LS26: Rothw 6C **120**
Pickup Bus. Pk. LS28: Pud 1B **94**
Pickwood La. HX6: Hal 1C **158**
PICKWOOD SCAR 1C **158**
Picton Ho. BD8: B'frd 2C **90**
(off Green La.)
Picton St. BD8: B'frd 2D **90**
Piece Hall HX1: Hal 4D **164**
Piece Hall Yd. BD1: B'frd 4E **91** (4D **6**)
Piece Wood Rd. LS16: Leeds 4F **57**
Pigeon Cote Cl. LS14: Leeds 3C **80**
Pigeon Cote Rd. LS14: Leeds 3C **80**
Piggott St. HD6: Brigh 6A **152**
Pigman La. HX2: Hal 3G **147**
Pilden La. WF3: E Ard 3A **156**
Pilgrim Way LS28: Pud 1C **94**
Pilot St. LS9: Leeds 2C **98** (1H **5**)
Pinder Av. LS12: Leeds 1H **115**
PINDER GREEN 6C **144**
Pinder Gro. LS12: Leeds 1H **115**
Pinders Grn. Ct. LS26: Mick 6C **144**
Pinders Grn. Dr. LS26: Mick 6C **144**
Pinders Grn. Fold LS26: Mick 6C **144**
Pinders Grn. Wlk. LS26: Mick 6C **144**

Pinder St. LS12: Leeds 1H **115**
Pinder Vw. LS12: Leeds 1H **115**
Pinebury Dr. BD13: B'frd 4G **107**
Pine Cl. LS22: Weth 2E **13**
Pine Ct. LS2: Leeds 4B **98** (5G **5**)
Pine Cft. BD20: Keigh 4G **33**
Pinedale BD16: Bgly 2B **50**
Pines Gdns. LS29: I'ly 6B **10**
Pine St. BD1: B'frd 4F **91** (3F **7**)
BD22: Haw 3C **64**
HX1: Hal 3G **149** (5B **164**)
Pine Tree Av. LS23: B Spa 3C **30**
Pinewood Cl. LS29: I'ly 6C **10**
Pinfold BD14: B'frd 1E **109**
Pinfold Cl. LS26: Mick 4E **145**
Pinfold Ct. LS15: Leeds 3D **100**
Pinfold Grn. HX6: Hal 6E **147**
Pinfold Gro. LS15: Leeds 3C **100**
Pinfold Hill LS15: Leeds 3D **100**
Pinfold La. HX5: Ell 5F **161**
HX6: Hal 5D **146**
LS12: Leeds 4B **96**
LS15: Leeds 3C **100**
LS16: Leeds 1G **57**
LS25: Gar 4F **103**
LS26: Mick 4E **145**
Pinfold Mt. LS15: Leeds 4D **100**
Pinfold Rd. LS15: Leeds 3D **100**
Pinfold Sq. LS15: Leeds 3D **100**
Pin Hill La. HX2: Hal 6D **126**
Pink St. BD22: Haw 4C **64**
Pinnar Cft. HX3: Hal 5C **150**
Pinnar La. HX3: Hal 4B **150**
Pintail Av. BD6: B'frd 4E **109**
Pipe & Nook La. LS12: Leeds 4H **95**
Pipercroft BD6: B'frd 1G **131**
Piper La. LS21: Otley 4D **22**
Pipit Mdw. LS27: Morl 4C **138**
Pippins Grn. Av. WF2: Wake 6H **155**
Pirie Cl. BD2: B'frd 6F **71**
Pitchstone Ct. LS12: Leeds 4F **95**
Pitcliffe Way BD5: B'frd 1F **111**
Pitfall St. LS1: Leeds 4A **98** (6F **5**)
Pit Fld. Rd. WF3: Rothw 5H **141**
Pit Hill HX3: Hal 3H **149**
Pit La. BD6: B'frd 6H **109**
BD13: B'frd 3H **85**
(Drive, The)
BD13: B'frd 2G **107**
(Low La.)
BD19: Cleck 5F **135**
LS25: M'fld 1C **124**
(not continuous)
LS26: Mick 3D **144**
Pits La. BD19: Cleck 3E **153**
Pitt Row LS1: Leeds 4A **98** (6E **5**)
Pitts St. BD3: B'frd 1B **112**
Pitt St. BD21: Keigh 6B **34**
Pitt St. Bus. Cen. BD21: Keigh 6B **34**
Place's Rd. LS9: Leeds 4C **98**
Plaid Row LS9: Leeds 3C **98**
Plainfield HX6: Hal 4B **148**
Plains La. HX5: Hal 2B **160**
Plane Tree Av. LS17: Leeds 3D **60**
Plane Tree Cl. LS17: Leeds 3D **60**
Plane Tree Cft. LS17: Leeds 3D **60**
Plane Tree Gdns. LS17: Leeds 3D **60**
Plane Tree Gro. LS19: Yead 1H **55**
Plane Tree Nest HX2: Hal 3C **148**
Plane Tree Nest La. HX2: Hal 3C **148**
Plane Tree Ri. LS17: Leeds 3D **60**
Plane Tree Rd. HX6: Hal 4H **147**
Planes Trees HX2: Hal 1B **148**
Plane Trees Cl. BD19: Cleck 4B **134**
Planetrees Rd. BD3: B'frd 5A **92**
Planetrees St. BD15: B'frd 2C **88**
Plane Tree Vw. LS17: Leeds 3D **60**
Plantation Av. LS15: Leeds 4B **100**
LS17: Leeds 2E **61**
Plantation Fold BD22: Keigh 3F **47**
Plantation Gdns. LS17: Leeds 2E **61**
Plantation Pl. BD4: B'frd 1B **112**

Plantation Way. BD17: Bail 4D 52
Playfair Rd. LS10: Leeds 3B 118
Playground LS12: Leeds 2F 115
Playhouse, The 3F 149 (5A 164)
Playhouse Sq. LS2: Leeds . . .3B 98 (4H 5)
Pleasance, The LS26: Swil 4A 122
Pleasant Ct. LS6: Leeds 6G 77
(off Rampart Rd.)
Pleasant M. LS11: Leeds 6G 97
Pleasant Pl. BD15: B'frd 2C 88
LS11: Leeds 6G 97
Pleasant Row BD13: B'frd 5G 107
Pleasant St. BD7: B'frd 1A 110
HX6: Hal 5A 148
LS11: Leeds 6G 97
Pleasant Ter. LS11: Leeds 6G 97
Pleasant Vw. HX2: Hal 6C 126
WF3: Wake 2D 156
Pleasant Views BD13: B'frd 2C 86
Pleasant Vw. Ter. LS26: Rothw 3F 141
(off Copley La.)
Plevna St. LS10: Leeds 3E 119
Plevna Ter. BD16: Bgly 3B 50
Plimsoll St. BD4: B'frd 1G 111
Plockwood Cotts. LS25: Gar 1A 124
Ploughcroft La. HX3: Hal 5F 129
Ploughman's Cft. BD2: B'frd 5E 71
Plover St. BD5: B'frd 2C 110
BD21: Keigh 5A 34
Plover Way LS27: Morl 4C 138
Plowmans Wlk. LS19: Yead 1D 54
Plumpton Av. BD2: B'frd 3F 71
Plumpton Cl. BD2: B'frd 4G 71
Plumpton Dr. BD2: B'frd 3F 71
Plumpton End BD2: B'frd 3G 71
Plumpton Gdns. BD2: B'frd 3E 71
Plumpton Lea BD2: B'frd 3F 71
Plumpton Mead BD2: B'frd 3F 71
Plumpton St. BD8: B'frd 3A 90
Plumpton Wlk. BD2: B'frd 3F 71
Plum St. BD21: Keigh 4G 47
HX1: Hal 3D 148
Plymouth Gro. HX1: Hal 1E 149
(off Diamond St.)
Pochard Cl. BD6: B'frd 4E 109
Poets Pl. LS18: H'fth 5E 57
Pogson's Cotts. LS14: Leeds 4D 80
(off York Rd.)
Pohlman St. HX1: Hal 4D 148
Pole Position Indoor Karting 3B 90
Pole Rd. BD22: Keigh 5A 32
Pollard Av. BD16: Bgly 2D 50
BD19: Cleck 6F 135
Pollard Cl. BD19: Cleck 6F 135
Pollard La. BD2: B'frd 2H 91
LS13: Leeds 3D 74
Pollard St. BD4: B'frd 6F 91
BD16: Bgly 3D 68
WF3: Wake 3G 157
Pollard St. Nth.
HX3: Hal 1H 149 (2C 164)
Pollard Way BD19: Cleck 6F 135
Pollit Av. HX6: Hal 6E 147
Pomfret Pl. LS25: Gar 3H 103
Ponderosa Cl. LS8: Leeds 6D 78
Pond Farm Dr. HD6: Brigh 4G 151
Pondfields Cl. LS25: Kip 4H 123
Pondfields Crest LS25: Kip 3H 123
Pondfields Dr. LS25: Kip 3H 123
Pondfields Pl. LS25: Kip 3H 123
Pondfields Ri. LS25: Kip 3H 123
Pond St. BD21: Keigh 6A 34
Pond Ter. HD6: Brigh 4G 151
Pontefract Av. LS9: Leeds 4D 98
Pontefract La. LS9: Leeds, Swil 3D 98
(not continuous)
LS15: Swil 2C 120
Pontefract La. Cl. LS9: Leeds 4D 98
Pontefract Rd. LS10: Leeds 3E 119
LS26: Rothw 5H 119
Pontefract St. LS9: Leeds 4D 98
POOL 4E 25

Pool Bank Cl. LS21: Pool 4F 25
Pool Bank Ct. LS21: Pool 5F 25
Pool Bank New Rd.
LS16: Pool 1D 42
LS21: Pool 1D 42
Pool Ct. BD3: B'frd 4G 91 (3H 7)
Poole Cres. LS15: Leeds 2D 100
Poole Mt. LS15: Leeds 2D 100
Poole Rd. LS15: Leeds 1D 100
Poole Sq. LS15: Leeds 2D 100
Pool Rd. LS21: Otley 3G 23
Pope St. BD21: Keigh 5B 34
Poplar Av. BD7: B'frd 3H 109
BD18: Ship 4C 70
HX6: Hal 4A 148
LS15: Leeds 1F 101
LS22: Weth 2D 12
LS25: Gar 4E 103
Poplar Cl. LS13: Leeds 3H 95
LS29: Burl W 3F 21
Poplar Ct. BD7: B'frd 5B 90
LS13: Leeds 3G 95
Poplar Cres. BD18: Ship 3C 70
HX2: Hal 6D 106
WF3: Morl 6C 138
Poplar Cft. LS13: Leeds 3G 95
Poplar Dr. BD18: Ship 4C 70
BD20: Keigh 6G 35
LS18: H'fth 1B 74
Poplar Gdns. LS13: Leeds 3G 95
Poplar Gth. LS13: Leeds 3G 95
Poplar Ga. LS13: Leeds 3G 95
Poplar Grn. LS13: Leeds 3G 95
Poplar Gro. BD7: B'frd 3G 109
BD16: Bgly 6E 49
BD17: Bail 6G 51
BD18: Ship 4C 70
BD19: Cleck 3H 153
Poplar Mt. LS13: Leeds 3G 95
Poplar Pl. LS28: Pud 4F 93
Poplar Ri. LS13: Leeds 2G 95
Poplar Rd. BD7: B'frd 3A 110
BD18: Ship 3C 70
Poplars, The HX3: Hal 5A 132
LS6: Leeds 5E 77
LS16: B'hpe 3H 43
LS20: Guis 5H 39
WF3: Wake 1G 157
Poplars Pk. Rd. BD2: B'frd 5E 71
Poplar Sq. LS28: Pud 1H 93
Poplar St. HX3: Hal 1G 149 (1B 164)
WF3: Wake 3G 157
Poplar Ter. BD16: Bgly 5C 50
BD20: Keigh 6H 35
BD21: Keigh 6G 33
(off W. Leeds St.)
Poplar Vw. BD7: B'frd 3G 109
HX3: Hal 3A 152
LS13: Leeds 3G 95
Poplar Way LS13: Leeds 3G 95
Poplarwood Gdns. BD10: B'frd 4C 72
Popples HX2: Hal 6D 106
Popples Dr. HX2: Hal 6D 106
Poppleton Ct. WF3: E Ard 6E 139
Poppleton Cft. WF3: E Ard 1E 155
Poppleton Dr. WF3: E Ard 6E 139
Poppleton Ri. WF3: E Ard 1E 155
Poppleton Rd. WF3: E Ard 6E 139
Poppleton Way WF3: E Ard 6E 139
Popple Wells La. HX2: Hal 2F 147
Poppy Ct. BD6: B'frd 1H 131
Poppy Flds. LS22: Weth 3F 13
Porritt St. BD19: Cleck 6B 134
Portage Av. LS15: Leeds 4B 100
Portage Cres. LS15: Leeds 4A 100
Portland Cres. LS1: Leeds . . .2H 97 (2D 4)
Portland Ga. LS1: Leeds 2H 97 (2D 4)
(not continuous)
LS2: Leeds 2H 97 (2D 4)
Portland Ho. BD4: B'frd 5B 92
(off Fearnville Dr.)

Portland Ho. HX5: Ell 4B 160
(off Huddersfield Rd.)
Portland Pl. BD16: Bgly 5C 50
HX1: Hal 3G 149 (5C 164)
Portland Rd. HX3: Hal 1H 149 (1D 164)
LS12: Leeds 5C 96
Portland St. BD5: B'frd 5E 91 (6D 6)
BD22: Haw 2D 64
HX1: Hal 2G 149 (3C 4)
LS1: Leeds 3H 97 (3C 4)
LS28: Pud 3C 94
Portland Way LS1: Leeds . . .2H 97 (2D 4)
Portman St. LS28: Pud 3F 73
Portree Dr. BD6: B'frd 5G 109
Portslade Ho. BD8: B'frd 1A 6
(off Green La.)
Portsmouth Av. BD3: B'frd 2G 91
Portwood St. BD9: B'frd 1F 89
Post Hill Ct. LS12: Leeds 4F 95
Post Office Rd. BD2: B'frd 4A 72
Post Office Yd. LS29: Burl W 2G 21
Pothouse Rd. BD6: B'frd 5B 110
Pot La. BD20: Stee 6C 14
Potovens Ct. WF3: Wake 3G 157
Potovens La. WF1: Wake 4F 157
WF2: Wake 6D 156
WF3: Wake 4F 157
Potter Brow Rd. BD17: Bail 6C 38
Potter Cl. BD12: B'frd 2E 133
POTTERNEWTON 5B 78
Potternewton Av. LS7: Leeds 3H 77
Potternewton Ct. LS7: Leeds 3A 78
Potternewton Cres. LS7: Leeds 4H 77
Potternewton Gdns.
LS7: Leeds 3A 78
Potternewton Gro. LS7: Leeds 3H 77
Potternewton Hgts. LS7: Leeds 3A 78
Potternewton La. LS7: Leeds 3G 77
Potternewton Mt. LS7: Leeds 3H 77
Potternewton Vw. LS7: Leeds 3H 77
Potters Cft. WF3: Wake 3G 157
Potterton Cl. LS15: Bar E 1E 83
Potterton Ct. LS15: Bar E 1E 83
(off Potterton Cl.)
POTTERY FIELD 5B 98
Pottery La. LS26: Rothw 6F 121
Pottery Rd. LS10: Leeds 1B 118
Pottery St. WF10: C'frd 6H 145
Poulton Pl. LS11: Leeds 2A 118
Powell Av. BD5: B'frd 1C 110
Powell Rd. BD16: Bgly 4D 50
BD18: Ship 4D 70
Powell St. HX1: Hal 2G 149 (4B 164)
(not continuous)
Pratt La. BD18: Ship 3C 70
Premiere Pk. LS29: I'ly 6A 10
Premier Way HX5: Ell 3C 160
Prescott St. HX1: Hal 3G 149 (6B 164)
Prescott Ter. BD15: B'frd 2D 88
Preston Bldgs. BD19: Cleck 6F 133
(off Tabbs La.)
Preston La. HX2: Hal 6A 128
(not continuous)
LS26: Kip 6E 123
Preston Pde. LS11: Leeds 3G 117
Preston Pl. HX1: Hal 2E 149
Preston St. BD7: B'frd 4C 90
Preston Ter. BD16: Bgly 2B 50
(off Sleningford Rd.)
Preston Vw. LS26: Swil 4B 122
Prestwick Cl. LS21: Otley 5B 22
Pretoria Rd. BD3: B'frd 4B 92
Pretoria St. HX2: Hal 1B 148
PRIEST HILL 1D 12
Priest Hill Gdns. LS22: Weth 1D 12
PRIESTHORPE 5G 73
Priesthorpe Av. LS28: Pud 1F 93
Priesthorpe Ct. LS28: Pud 5H 73
Priesthorpe La. LS28: Pud 6F 73
Priesthorpe Rd. LS28: Pud 5E 73
(not continuous)
Priestley Av. BD6: B'frd 5C 110

Priestley Cen. for the Arts 4F 7
Priestley Cl. LS28: Pud 3B 94
Priestley Ct. LS28: Pud 3B 94
Priestley Dr. LS28: Pud 2B 94
Priestley Gdns. LS28: Pud 3B 94
PRIESTLEY GREEN 6G 131
Priestley Hill BD13: B'frd 1G 129
Priestley Pl. HX6: Hal 6G 147
Priestley Sq. WF17: Bat 5A 136
Priestley St. BD1: B'frd 3F 91 (2E 7)
    BD13: B'frd 5H 87
Priestley Ter. BD6: B'frd 4C 110
Priestley Vw. LS28: Pud 3B 94
Priestley Wlk. LS28: Pud 3B 94
Priestman Cl. BD8: B'frd 2C 90
Priestman St. BD8: B'frd 2C 90
PRIESTTHORPE 3C 50
Priestthorpe Cl. BD16: Bgly 3C 50
Priestthorpe La. BD16: Bgly 3C 50
Priestthorpe Rd. BD16: Bgly 4C 50
Primitive St. WF3: Rothw 4H 141
Primley Gdns. LS17: Leeds 3A 60
Primley Pk. Av. LS17: Leeds 3A 60
Primley Pk. Cl. LS17: Leeds 3B 60
Primley Pk. Ct. LS17: Leeds 2A 60
Primley Pk. Cres. LS17: Leeds 3A 60
Primley Pk. Dr. LS17: Leeds 3A 60
Primley Pk. Gth. LS17: Leeds 2B 60
Primley Pk. Grn. LS17: Leeds 2B 60
Primley Pk. Gro. LS17: Leeds 3A 60
Primley Pk. La. LS17: Leeds 3A 60
Primley Pk. Mt. LS17: Leeds 3B 60
Primley Pk. Ri. LS17: Leeds 3B 60
Primley Pk. Rd. LS17: Leeds 3A 60
Primley Pk. Vw. LS17: Leeds 2A 60
Primley Pk. Wlk. LS17: Leeds 2B 60
Primley Pk. Way LS17: Leeds 2A 60
Primrose Av. LS15: Leeds 3C 100
    LS26: Swil 4B 122
Primrose Bank BD16: Bgly 5D 50
Primrose Cl. LS15: Leeds 3C 100
Primrose Ct. LS17: Leeds 2B 60
    LS20: Guis 4C 40
        (off Orchard Way)
Primrose Cres. LS15: Leeds 2C 100
Primrose Dr. BD16: Bgly 5D 50
    LS15: Leeds 3C 100
Primrose Gdns. LS15: Leeds 2C 100
Primrose Gth. LS15: Leeds 3B 100
Primrose Gro. BD21: Keigh 6C 34
    LS15: Leeds 2C 100
Primrose Hill BD7: B'frd 6C 90
        (off Gt. Horton Rd.)
    BD16: Bgly 6E 51
    LS28: Pud 2A 94
Primrose Hill Cl. LS26: Swil 4B 122
Primrose Hill Dr. LS26: Swil 4B 122
Primrose Hill Gdns. LS26: Swil 4B 122
Primrose Hill Gth. LS26: Swil 5B 122
Primrose Hill Grn. LS26: Swil 5B 122
Primrose Hill Gro. LS26: Swil 4B 122
Primrose La. BD2: B'frd 5D 70
    BD16: Bgly 6D 50
    LS11: Leeds 2A 118
    LS15: Leeds 3B 100
        (not continuous)
    LS23: B Spa 4A 30
Primrose Rd. LS15: Leeds 3C 100
Primrose Row BD17: Bail 3F 53
Primrose St. BD8: B'frd 3C 90 (1A 6)
    BD21: Keigh 6C 34
Primrose Wlk. LS27: Morl 5C 116
Primrose Way HX3: Rothw 6F 109
Primrose Yd. LS26: Rothw 2E 143
Prince Albert Sq. BD13: B'frd 3D 108
Prince Edward Gro. LS12: Leeds 1A 116
Prince Edward Rd. LS12: Leeds 1A 116
Prince Henry Rd. LS21: Otley 1E 23
Princeroyd Way BD8: B'frd 4A 90
Princes Av. LS8: Leeds 2F 79
Prince's Ct. BD18: Ship 3B 70
    LS18: Leeds 6A 60

Prince's Cres. BD2: B'frd 6E 71
Prince's Ga. HX3: Hal 5F 149
Prince's Gro. LS6: Leeds 4D 76
Prince's Gym 1F 97
Princess Ct. LS15: Leeds 5F 101
    LS17: Leeds 4B 60
Princess Flds. LS15: Leeds 5F 101
Princes Sq. LS1: Leeds 4H 97 (6C 4)
Princess Rd. LS29: I'ly 6C 10
Princess St. HX1: Hal . . .2G 149 (3C 164)
    HX4: Hal 4H 159
    HX6: Hal 5A 148
    LS19: Yead 3E 55
    WF1: Wake 5F 157
Prince's St. BD6: B'frd 6G 109
        (Beck Hill)
    BD6: B'frd 5B 110
        (Pothouse Rd.)
Prince St. BD4: B'frd 4A 112
    BD20: Sils 2D 14
    BD22: Haw 2D 64
    WF10: Kip 6F 123
Prince's Way BD1: B'frd 5E 91 (5C 6)
Princeton Cl. HX2: Hal 6D 128
PRINCEVILLE 4B 90
Princeville Rd.
    BD7: B'frd 4A 90
Princeville St. BD7: B'frd 4B 90
Prior St. BD21: Keigh 5C 34
Priory Cl. BD16: Bgly 3C 50
    LS22: Weth 2F 13
Priory Ct. BD8: B'frd 3D 90 (1A 6)
    BD16: Bgly 3C 50
Priory Gro. BD16: Bgly 3C 50
Priory Ho. BD10: B'frd 2A 72
        (off Cavendish Rd.)
Priory Pl. HD2: Hud 6F 163
Priory Rd. HD6: Brigh 1C 162
Privet Dr. BD22: Keigh 5D 46
Privilege St. LS12: Leeds 4B 96
Proctor St. BD4: B'frd 3B 112
Prod La. BD17: Bail 5G 51
Progress Av. BD16: Bgly 6E 49
Prospect Av. BD18: Ship 2C 70
    HX2: Hal 5C 148
    LS13: Leeds 6E 75
    LS28: Pud 3H 93
Prospect Bldgs. WF3: E Ard 2A 156
        (off Bradford Rd.)
Prospect Cl. BD18: Ship 2C 70
    HX2: Hal 5C 148
Prospect Ct. HX2: Hal 1H 147
    LS14: T'ner 2H 63
Prospect Cres. BD22: Keigh 2E 47
    LS10: Leeds 2B 118
Prospect Dr. BD22: Keigh 2E 47
Prospect Gdns. LS15: Leeds 3D 100
Prospect Gro. BD18: Ship 2C 70
    LS28: Pud 3H 93
Prospect La. BD11: B'frd 2F 135
Prospect Mt. BD18: Ship 2C 70
    BD22: Keigh 2E 47
Prospect Pl. BD2: B'frd 1A 92
    BD9: B'frd 2H 89
    BD13: B'frd 4A 108
    HD6: Brigh 1A 162
    HX2: Hal 4D 128
        (Prospect Row)
    HX2: Hal 4G 127
        (Waindale Cres.)
    HX3: Hal 5A 132
        (off Village St.)
    LS13: Leeds 6E 75
    LS18: H'fth 1D 74
    LS26: Rothw 3B 142
    WF3: Rothw 5F 141
Prospect Rd. BD3: B'frd 3F 91 (1F 7)
        (not continuous)
    BD16: Bgly 2E 51
    LS29: Burl W 3E 21
Prospect Row HX2: Hal 4D 128
        (Prospect Pl.)

Prospect Row HX2: Hal 6A 106
        (Spring Row)
    LS29: Burl W 5C 20
Prospect Sq. LS28: Pud 1H 93
Prospect St. BD4: B'frd 6F 91
    BD6: B'frd 6H 109
    BD10: B'frd 4A 72
    BD13: B'frd 5A 88
    BD18: Ship 2C 70
    BD22: Haw 3C 64
    BD22: Keigh 1F 47
    HX3: Hal 1H 149 (1D 164)
    LS19: Yead 4G 55
    LS28: Pud 3G 93
        (Cemetery Rd.)
    LS28: Pud 6H 73
        (Town St.)
Prospect Ter. BD15: B'frd 2E 89
    BD20: Keigh 3D 34
    HX2: Hal 4E 147
    LS9: Leeds 4D 98
        (off Bk. Prospect Ter.)
    LS13: Leeds 6E 75
    LS13: Pud 4A 74
    LS18: H'fth 6E 57
    LS25: M'fld 5E 105
    LS26: Rothw 3B 142
    LS28: Pud 1H 93
Prospect Vw. BD13: B'frd 6G 107
    LS13: Leeds 6E 75
Prospect Vs. LS22: Weth 3E 13
Prospect Wlk. BD18: Ship 2C 70
Prospect Way HD6: Brigh 3B 152
Prosper St. LS10: Leeds 1C 118
Providence Av. BD17: Bail 3C 52
    LS6: Leeds 5G 77
Providence Bldgs. HX3: Hal 5C 150
        (off New St.)
Providence Ct. BD22: Keigh 5C 46
    LS27: Morl 2A 138
        (off Troy Rd.)
    LS27: Morl 2A 138
        (Bank St.)
    LS27: Morl 4B 138
        (Siskin Cl.)
Providence Cres. BD22: Keigh 5C 46
Providence La. BD22: Keigh 5C 46
Providence Pl. BD12: B'frd 3C 132
    HD6: Brigh 2C 162
    HX6: Hal 4E 147
    LS2: Leeds 2A 98 (1E 5)
    LS15: Swil 5A 102
    LS25: Gar 4E 103
    LS27: Morl 3G 137
    LS28: Pud 2A 94
    WF10: Kip 4H 145
Providence Rd. LS6: Leeds 5G 77
Providence Row BD2: B'frd 6H 71
    BD17: Bail 3C 52
    BD20: Keigh 3A 36
    HX2: Hal 4D 128
        (Club Ho's.)
    HX2: Hal 6A 106
        (Hebble Brook Bus. Pk.)
Providence St. BD1: B'frd 4D 90 (4B 6)
    BD19: Cleck 6E 133
    HX5: Ell 4B 160
    LS28: Pud 1H 93
        (not continuous)
Providence Ter. BD13: B'frd 5H 87
    LS2: Leeds 6G 77
Providence Vs. BD19: Cleck 6E 133
        (off Providence St.)
    LS23: B Spa 6B 30
Prune Pk. La. BD15: B'frd 6A 68
PUDSEY .3B 94
Pudsey Bus. Cen. LS28: Pud 4B 94
Pudsey Leisure Cen. 4A 94
Pudsey Rd. LS13: Leeds 3F 95
    LS13: Leeds, Pud 4D 94
Puffin Cl. BD6: B'frd 4E 109
Pule Grn. La. HX3: Hal 4F 129

PULE HILL 4F 129
Pullan Av. BD2: B'frd 5H 71
Pullan Dr. BD2: B'frd 5A 72
Pullan Gro. BD2: B'frd 5A 72
Pullan La. BD17: B'frd 2A 54
Pullan St. BD5: B'frd 6D 90
Pullman Ct. LS27: Morl 2B 138
Pulmans Pl. HX3: Hal 1G 159
(off Skircoat Grn.)
Pulmans Yd. HX3: Hal 1G 159
Pump La. HX3: Hal 1B 150
WF3: E Ard 4E 155
Pundles HX2: Hal 5C 106
Purbeck Ct. BD4: B'frd 3C 112
(off Dorchester Cres.)
Purbeck Gro. LS25: Gar 5F 103
Purcell Dr. BD20: Sils 1D 14
Purley Wlk. BD6: B'frd 5B 110
Pyebank BD15: B'frd 3F 67
PYE NEST 4D 148
Pye Nest Av. HX2: Hal 4B 148
Pye Nest Dr. HX2: Hal 5C 148
Pye Nest Gdns. HX2: Hal 4C 148
Pye Nest Gro. HX2: Hal 4C 148
Pye Nest Ri. HX2: Hal 5C 148
Pye Nest Rd. HX3: Hal 5B 148
HX6: Hal 5B 148
Pye Nook BD12: B'frd 6D 110
Pymont Ct. WF3: Rothw 6G 141
Pymont Dr. LS26: Rothw 6C 120
Pymont Gro. LS26: Rothw 6D 120
Pym St. LS10: Leeds 6B 98
Pyrah Fold BD12: B'frd 3C 132
Pyrah Rd. BD12: B'frd 6D 110
Pyrah St. BD12: B'frd 3D 132

Q

QBM Bus. Pk. WF17: Bat 5B 136
Quail Av. BD6: B'frd 4E 109
Quail St. BD21: Keigh 5B 34
Quaker Ho. LS2: Leeds 1G 97
Quaker La. BD5: B'frd 2B 110
Quakers La. LS19: Yead 2F 55
Quarrie Dene Ct.
LS7: Leeds 3A 78
Quarry, The LS17: Leeds 1G 59
LS22: Weth 3E 13
Quarry Bank Ct. LS5: Leeds 3H 75
Quarry Cotts. LS18: H'fth 6D 56
Quarry Dene Ct. HD6: Brigh 4G 151
(off Spout Ho. La.)
HX3: Hal 2A 150
Quarry Dene LS16: Leeds 1D 76
Quarry Dene Pk. LS16: Leeds 6C 58
Quarry Farm Rd. LS21: Pool 6C 24
Quarryfield Ter. WF3: E Ard 2B 156
Quarry Gap Row BD4: B'frd 5C 92
Quarry Gdns. LS17: Leeds 1G 59
QUARRY HILL 3B 98 (4H 5)
Quarry Hill HX6: Hal 6H 147
LS26: Rothw 2E 143
LS28: Pud 6H 73
(off Wesley St.)
Quarry Hill La. LS22: Weth 2D 12
(not continuous)
Quarry Ho. LS2: Leeds 3C 98 (4H 5)
Quarry La. LS27: Dew 2A 154
LS27: Morl 5B 138
WF12: Dew 3A 154
WF17: Bat 6B 136
Quarry Mt. LS6: Leeds 5G 77
LS19: Yead 6G 41
(off King St.)
Quarry Mt. Pl. LS6: Leeds 5G 77
Quarry Mt. St. LS6: Leeds 5G 77
Quarry Mt. Ter. LS6: Leeds 5G 77
Quarry Pl. BD2: B'frd 1H 91
LS6: Leeds 6G 77
Quarry Rd. HD6: Brigh 4A 162
HX3: Hal 5C 128

Quarry Rd. LS21: Pool 6C 24
LS26: Rothw 1F 143
Quarry St. BD9: B'frd 5A 70
BD21: Keigh 6B 34
LS6: Leeds 6G 77
Quarry Ter. LS18: H'fth 6D 56
Quaver La. BD15: B'frd 2D 88
Quayside BD18: Ship 1B 70
Quayside, The BD10: B'frd 1C 72
Quayside Ho. LS11: Leeds 6D 4
Quebec BD16: Bgly 3D 68
Quebec Ho. BD21: Keigh 1H 47
(off Aireworth St.)
Quebec St. BD1: B'frd 5E 91 (5C 6)
BD21: Keigh 1H 47
HX5: Ell 4C 160
LS1: Leeds 4H 97 (4D 4)
Queen Elizabeth St. WF1: Wake . . .5F 157
Queen's Arc. LS1: Leeds 4E 5
Queen's Av. BD2: B'frd 6F 71
QUEENSBURY 4A 108
Queensbury Av. WF1: Wake 4G 157
Queensbury Rd. HX3: Hal 3F 129
Queensbury Sq. BD13: B'frd 4A 108
Queensbury Swimming Pool 4A 108
Queens Cl. LS7: Leeds 1A 78
BD16: Bgly 5D 50
Queens Ct. LS1: Leeds 5F 5
BD16: Bgly 4B 50
BD18: Ship 1H 69
BD19: Cleck 5F 135
(off Queen St.)
LS17: Leeds 6A 60
LS28: Pud 3A 94
Queens Dr. LS29: I'ly 6B 10
HX3: Hal 5C 150
LS28: Pud 3H 93
WF3: Rothw 4H 141
Queen's Dr. La. LS29: I'ly 6B 10
Queen's Gdns. LS29: I'ly 6C 10
Queen's Ga. HX3: Hal 5F 129
Queensgate BD1: B'frd 4E 91 (4D 6)
Queen's Gro. BD21: Keigh 2H 47
LS27: Morl 4H 137
Queenshill App. LS17: Leeds 5A 60
Queenshill Av. LS17: Leeds 5A 60
Queenshill Cl. LS17: Leeds 5A 60
Queenshill Cft. LS17: Leeds 5A 60
Queenshill Cres. LS17: Leeds 4A 60
Queenshill Dr. LS17: Leeds 5H 59
Queenshill Gdns. LS17: Leeds 5H 59
Queenshill Gth. LS17: Leeds 5A 60
Queenshill Lawn LS17: Leeds 5A 60
(off Queenshill App.)
Queenshill Rd. LS17: Leeds 5A 60
Queenshill Vw. LS17: Leeds 5A 60
Queenshill Wlk. LS17: Leeds 5A 60
Queenshill Way LS17: Leeds 5A 60
Queens Mead HX3: Hal 4C 130
Queen's Pl. BD18: Ship 1H 69
LS21: Otley 4E 23
LS27: Morl 3B 138
Queen's Prom. LS27: Morl 2A 138
Queen Sq. LS2: Leeds 2A 98 (2E 5)
Queen Sq. Ct. LS2: Leeds 2H 97 (2D 4)
Queen's Ri. BD2: B'frd 6F 71
Queen's Rd. BD2: B'frd 1D 90
BD8: B'frd 1D 90
BD16: Bgly 1A 50
BD18: Ship 1H 69
BD21: Keigh 3G 47
HX1: Hal 2D 148
HX3: Hal 5H 131
LS6: Leeds 1E 97
LS23: B Spa 3A 30
LS27: Morl 4H 137
LS29: I'ly 6C 10
Queens Sports Club 4F 149
Queens Ter. LS20: Guis 4B 40
LS21: Otley 4E 23
Queensthorpe Av. LS13: Leeds 3F 95
Queensthorpe Cl. LS13: Leeds 3G 95

Queensthorpe Ri. LS13: Leeds 3F 95
Queen St. BD6: B'frd 6G 109
BD10: B'frd 2B 72
BD13: B'frd 3B 66
BD15: B'frd 5G 67
BD16: Bgly 4B 50
BD17: Bail 6C 52
BD19: Cleck 5F 135
BD20: Sils 2E 15
BD20: Stee 6C 14
BD22: Haw 3C 64
HX4: Hal 5G 159
HX6: Hal 6E 147
LS1: Leeds 4G 97 (4B 4)
LS10: Leeds 3E 119
LS19: Yead 3F 55
LS26: Kip 1E 145
LS27: Morl 2A 138
(not continuous)
WF1: Wake 5F 157
WF3: E Ard 1B 156
WF3: Rothw 4H 141
Queensview LS14: Leeds 4D 80
Queen's Wlk. LS6: Leeds 3A 76
Queensway BD16: Bgly 4D 50
BD21: Keigh 6A 34
(off Airedale Shop. Cen.)
HX1: Hal 1D 148
LS15: Leeds 3E 101
LS19: Yead 4D 40
LS20: Guis, Yead 4C 40
LS25: Gar 4D 102
LS26: Rothw 1A 142
LS27: Morl 3A 138
Queenswood Cl. LS6: Leeds 3A 76
Queenswood Ct. LS6: Leeds 2A 76
Queenswood Dr. LS6: Leeds 2A 76
Queenswood Gdns.
LS6: Leeds 5C 76
Queenswood Grn. LS6: Leeds 2A 76
Queenswood Hgts. LS6: Leeds . . .4C 76
Queenswood Mt. LS6: Leeds 4B 76
Queenswood Ri. LS6: Leeds 4B 76
Queenswood Rd. LS6: Leeds 4B 76
Queen Victoria Cres. HX3: Hal . . .4D 130
Queen Victoria St. LS1: Leeds 4F 5
Quincy Cl. BD2: B'frd 5A 72
Qureshi Vw. BD8: B'frd 2C 90

R

Raby Av. LS7: Leeds 6B 78
RABY PARK 3E 13
Raby Pk. LS22: Weth 4D 12
Raby St. LS7: Leeds 6B 78
Raby Ter. LS7: Leeds 6B 78
Race Moor La. BD22: Keigh 4B 46
Racemoor La. BD22: Keigh 4D 46
Radcliffe Av. BD2: B'frd 4G 71
Radcliffe Gdns. LS28: Pud 5A 94
Radcliffe Gro. LS28: Pud 5A 94
Radcliffe La. HX2: Hal 5C 126
LS28: Pud 4A 94
Radcliffe Ter. LS28: Pud 5A 94
Radfield Dr. BD6: B'frd 4E 111
Radfield Rd. BD6: B'frd 4E 111
Radnor St. BD3: B'frd 4A 92
LS12: Leeds 5E 97
Radwell Dr. BD5: B'frd 6E 91 (6C 6)
Raeburn Dr. BD6: B'frd 6A 110
Rae Ct. WF3: Wake 4H 157
Rae Rd. BD18: Ship 3B 70
Raglan Av. BD22: Keigh 1F 47
Raglan Ct. HX1: Hal 2E 149
(off Raglan St.)
Raglan Gdns. HX1: Hal 2E 149
(off Lister's Cl.)
Raglan Rd. LS2: Leeds 6G 77
(not continuous)
Raglan St. BD3: B'frd 4B 92
BD13: B'frd 4B 108

Raglan St. BD22: Keigh 1F 47
    HX1: Hal 2E 149
Raglan Ter. BD3: B'frd 4C 92
Raikes La. BD4: B'frd 3E 113
    (Holme La.)
    BD4: B'frd 5C 112
    (Toftshaw La.)
    WF17: Bat 5A 136
Rail Balk La. LS22: Weth 2D 12
    (not continuous)
Railes Cl. HX2: Hal 6D 126
Railes Cotts. HX2: Hal 6D 126
Railsfield Mt. LS13: Leeds 2E 95
Railsfield Ri. LS13: Leeds 2E 95
Railsfield Way LS13: Leeds 1F 95
Railway Cotts. LS25: M'fld 5E 105
Railway Rd. BD10: B'frd 1H 71
    LS15: Leeds 1E 101
    (not continuous)
    LS29: I'ly 5D 10
Railway St. BD4: B'frd 4A 112
    BD20: Keigh 4A 34
    HD6: Brigh 2B 162
    LS9: Leeds 4C 98 (5H 5)
Railway Ter. BD12: B'frd 2E 133
    HD6: Brigh *1C 162*
    (off Clifton Comn.)
    HX3: Hal 1E 159
    LS29: I'ly 5E 11
    WF1: Wake 4F 157
    WF3: E Ard 6A 140
Rainbow Leisure 2E 23
Rainbow M. BD6: B'frd 1H 131
Raincliffe Gro. LS9: Leeds 3E 99
Raincliffe Mt. LS9: Leeds 4E 99
Raincliffe Rd. LS9: Leeds 3E 99
Raincliffe St. LS9: Leeds 3E 99
Raincliffe Ter. LS9: Leeds 4E 99
Rainton Ho. *BD5: B'frd* *1D 110*
    (off Park La.)
Raistrick Way BD18: Ship 1D 70
Rake Bank HX2: Hal 3B 128
Rakehill Rd. LS15: Scho 2H 81
Raleigh St. HX1: Hal 4D 148
Rampart Rd. LS6: Leeds 6G 77
Ramsden Av. BD7: B'frd 6G 89
Ramsden Ct. BD21: Keigh 1A 110
Ramsden Pl. BD14: B'frd 6D 88
Ramsden St. HX3: Hal 5C 128
    LS25: Kip 5F 123
Ramsey St. BD5: B'frd 2D 110
Ramsey Ter. LS21: Otley 3E 23
Ramsgate WF3: Rothw 6F 141
Ramsgate Cres. WF3: Rothw 6F 141
Ramsgate St. HX1: Hal 2D 148
Ramsgill Cl. BD6: B'frd 5G 109
Ramshead App. LS14: Leeds 3C 80
Ramshead Cl. LS14: Leeds 2C 80
Ramshead Cres. LS14: Leeds 2B 80
Ramshead Dr. LS14: Leeds 2B 80
Ramshead Gdns. LS14: Leeds 2B 80
Ramshead Gro. LS14: Leeds 3C 80
Ramshead Hgts. LS14: Leeds 4C 80
    (Bailey's La.)
    LS14: Leeds 3C 80
    (Eastdean Rd.)
Ramshead Hill LS14: Leeds 3C 80
Ramshead Pl. LS14: Leeds 3C 80
Ramshead Vw. LS14: Leeds 3C 80
Randall Pl. BD9: B'frd 6A 70
Randall Well St. BD7: B'frd . . .5D 90 (5B 6)
Randolph St. BD3: B'frd 3C 92
    HX3: Hal 6G 129 (1B 164)
    LS13: Leeds 1C 94
Random Cl. BD22: Keigh 2F 47
Rand Pl. BD7: B'frd 6C 90
Rand St. BD7: B'frd 6C 90
Ranelagh Av. BD10: B'frd 4C 72
Range Bank HX3: Hal 6G 129 (1C 164)
Range Bank Top *HX3: Hal* *6G 129*
    (off Range La.)

Range Ct. HX3: Hal 1C 164
Range Gdns. HX3: Hal 6G 129
Range La. HX3: Hal 1G 149 (1C 164)
Ranger's Wlk. LS25: M'fld 1G 105
Range St. HX3: Hal 6G 129
Ransdale Dr. BD5: B'frd 2D 110
Ransdale Gro. BD5: B'frd 2D 110
Ransdale Rd. BD5: B'frd 2D 110
RASTRICK 3H 161
Rastrick Comn. HD6: Brigh 3A 162
Rastrick Community Sports Cen.
    . . . . .2H 161
Rathlin Rd. WF12: Dew 6A 154
Rathmell St. LS15: Leeds 4A 100
Rathmell St. BD5: B'frd 4D 110
Raven Bank HX2: Hal 3D 146
Raven Rd. LS6: Leeds 5E 77
Ravenscar Av. LS8: Leeds 3E 79
Ravenscar Mt. LS8: Leeds 3E 79
Ravenscar Ter. LS8: Leeds 3E 79
Ravenscar Vw. LS8: Leeds 3E 79
Ravenscar Wlk. LS8: Leeds 3E 79
RAVENSCLIFFE 5C 72
Ravenscliffe Av. BD10: B'frd 4B 72
Ravenscliffe Cl. HX3: Hal 1F 159
Ravenscliffe Rd. LS28: Pud 3D 72
Ravenscroft Rd. HX3: Hal 6F 149
Ravens Mt. LS28: Pud 4B 94
Ravenstone Dr. HX4: Hal 5G 159
Raven St. BD16: Bgly 4B 50
    BD21: Keigh 6H 33
    HX1: Hal 2D 148
Ravensworth Cl. LS15: Leeds 6H 81
Ravensworth Way LS15: Leeds 6H 81
Raven Ter. BD8: B'frd 4E 89
RAWDON 4H 55
Rawdon Crematorium LS19: Yead 6A 56
Rawdon Dr. LS19: Yead 4F 55
Rawdon Hall Dr. LS19: Yead 4F 55
Rawdon Rd. BD22: Haw 2C 64
    LS18: H'fth, Yead 5A 56
Rawdon St. BD22: Keigh 1G 47
Raw End Rd. HX2: Hal 6F 127
Rawfolds Av. WF17: Bat 5B 136
Raw Hill HD6: Brigh 3H 161
Raw La. HX2: Hal 2B 128
Raw La. Bottom HX6: Leeds 6D 146
Rawling St. BD21: Keigh 2H 47
Rawling Way LS6: Leeds 4G 77
RAW NOOK 1E 133
Rawnook BD12: B'frd 2F 133
Rawnsley Ho. *BD5: B'frd* *1D 110*
    (off Manchester Rd.)
Rawroyds HX4: Hal 6G 159
Rawson Av. BD3: B'frd 3B 92
    HX3: Hal 6F 149
Rawson Pl. BD1: B'frd 4E 91 (3C 6)
    HX6: Hal 6G 147
    LS11: Leeds 2A 118
Rawson Quarter Shop. Complex
    BD1: B'frd *3C 6*
    (off Rawson Pl.)
Rawson Rd. BD1: B'frd 4D 90 (3B 6)
Rawson Sq. BD1: B'frd 4E 91 (3C 6)
    (not continuous)
    BD10: B'frd 6H 53
Rawson St. BD12: B'frd 3D 132
    HX1: Hal 2G 149 (4B 164)
Rawson St. Nth. HX3: Hal 6F 129
Rawson Ter. LS11: Leeds 2A 118
Rawson Wood HX6: Hal 6E 147
Raygill Cl. LS17: Leeds 2F 61
Raylands Cl. LS10: Leeds 1D 140
Raylands Fold LS10: Leeds 1D 140
Raylands Gth. LS10: Leeds 1D 140
Raylands La. LS10: Leeds 1D 140
Raylands Pl. LS10: Leeds 1D 140
Raylands Rd. LS10: Leeds 1D 140
Raylands Way LS10: Leeds 2C 140
Rayleigh St. BD4: B'frd 1G 111
Raymond Dr. BD5: B'frd 3E 111

Raymond St. BD5: B'frd 3E 111
Raynbron Cres. BD5: B'frd 3F 111
Raynel App. LS16: Leeds 4A 58
Raynel Cl. LS16: Leeds 3H 57
Raynel Dr. LS16: Leeds 4A 58
Raynel Gdns. LS16: Leeds 3A 58
Raynel Gth. LS16: Leeds 4A 58
Raynel Grn. LS16: Leeds 4A 58
Raynel Mt. LS16: Leeds 3A 58
Raynel Way LS16: Leeds 3H 57
Rayner Av. BD8: B'frd 2H 89
Rayner Dr. HD6: Brigh 5A 152
Rayner Mt. BD15: B'frd 3C 88
Rayner Rd. HD6: Brigh 5A 152
Raynham Cres. BD21: Keigh 5E 33
Raynor Ter. LS28: Pud 3B 94
Raynville App. LS13: Leeds 1G 95
Raynville Av. LS13: Leeds 6G 75
Raynville Cl. LS13: Leeds 6G 75
Raynville Ct. LS13: Leeds 1G 95
Raynville Cres. LS12: Leeds 1H 95
Raynville Dene LS12: Leeds 6H 75
Raynville Dr. LS13: Leeds 6G 75
Raynville Grange *LS13: Leeds* *1G 95*
    (off Raynville Rd.)
Raynville Grn. LS13: Leeds 1G 95
Raynville Gro. LS13: Leeds 6G 75
Raynville Mt. LS13: Leeds 6G 75
Raynville Pl. LS13: Leeds 1G 95
Raynville Ri. LS13: Leeds 1G 95
Raynville Rd. LS12: Leeds 6G 75
    LS13: Leeds 6F 75
Raynville St. LS13: Leeds 6G 75
Raynville Ter. LS13: Leeds 6G 75
Raynville Wlk. LS13: Leeds 1G 95
Raywood Cl. LS19: Yead 5E 41
Rebecca St. BD1: B'frd 3D 90 (2A 6)
Recreation Av. LS11: Leeds 1G 117
Recreation Cres. LS11: Leeds 1F 117
Recreation Gro. LS11: Leeds 1F 117
Recreation La. HX5: Ell 5A 160
Recreation Mt. LS11: Leeds 1F 117
Recreation Pl. LS11: Leeds 1F 117
Recreation Rd. HX6: Hal 5A 148
    LS11: Leeds 3F 117
Recreation Row LS11: Leeds 1F 117
Recreation St. LS11: Leeds 1F 117
Recreation Ter. LS11: Leeds 1F 117
Recreation Vw. LS11: Leeds 1F 117
Rectory Cl. LS25: Gar 4F 103
Rectory Dr. WF17: Bat 6C 136
Rectory Row BD21: Keigh 6H 33
Rectory St. LS9: Leeds 2C 98
Redbeck Cotts. LS18: Yead 1A 74
Red Beck Rd. HX3: Hal 6B 130
Red Beck Va. BD18: Ship 4A 70
Red Brick La. HX6: Hal 6C 146
Red Brink La. HX6: Hal 6B 146
Redburn Av. BD18: Ship 4A 70
Redburn Dr. BD18: Ship 4A 70
Redburn Rd. BD18: Ship 4B 70
Redcar La. BD20: Stee 3B 32
Redcar Rd. BD10: B'frd 3C 72
Redcar St. HX1: Hal 2D 148
Redcliffe Av. BD21: Keigh 6G 33
Redcliffe Gro. BD21: Keigh 6G 33
Redcliffe St. BD21: Keigh 6G 33
Redcote La. LS12: Leeds 3B 96
    (not continuous)
Redesdale Gdns. LS16: Leeds 4A 58
Red Hall App. LS14: Leeds 6C 62
Red Hall Av. LS17: Leeds 6B 62
Red Hall Chase LS14: Leeds 6C 62
Redhall Cl. LS11: Leeds 4E 117
Red Hall Ct. LS14: Leeds 6C 62
Redhall Cres. LS11: Leeds 4E 117
Red Hall Cft. LS14: Leeds 6C 62
Red Hall Dr. LS14: Leeds 6C 62
Red Hall Gdns. LS17: Leeds 6B 62
Red Hall Gth. LS14: Leeds 6C 62
Redhall Ga. LS11: Leeds 4E 117
Red Hall Grn. LS14: Leeds 6C 62

Red Hall La. LS14: Leeds 6B **62**
  LS17: Leeds 6B **62**
Red Hall Va. LS14: Leeds 1C **80**
Red Hall Vw. LS14: Leeds 6C **62**
Red Hall Wlk. LS14: Leeds 6C **62**
Red Hall Way LS14: Leeds 6C **62**
Redhill Av. WF3: E Ard 4E **155**
Redhill Cl. BD4: B'frd 5E **113**
  WF3: E Ard 4E **155**
Redhill Cres. WF3: E Ard 4E **155**
Redhill Dr. WF3: E Ard 4E **155**
Red Ho. Gdns. LS29: Men 2G **39**
Redhouse La. LS7: Leeds 2C **78**
Red House Mus. 6F **135**
Red La. LS28: Pud 6G **73**
Red Lodge Cl. LS8: Leeds 5H **79**
Redman Cl. BD22: Haw 2B **64**
Redman Gth. BD22: Haw 2B **64**
Redmire Cl. LS14: Leeds 5C **80**
Redmire Dr. LS14: Leeds 5C **80**
Redmire St. BD3: B'frd 4C **92**
Redmire Vw. LS14: Leeds 5C **80**
Redpoll Way BD6: B'frd 4E **109**
Redshank Cl. BD6: B'frd 4E **109**
Redshaw Rd. LS12: Leeds 5D **96**
Red Va. BD19: Cleck 5F **135**
Redvers Cl. LS16: Leeds 6A **58**
Redwald Dr. LS20: Guis 4B **40**
Redwing Dr. BD6: B'frd 4E **109**
Redwood Av. WF3: E Ard 1G **155**
Redwood Cl. BD21: Keigh 2C **48**
  LS19: Yead 6E **41**
  LS26: Rothw 1G **143**
Redwood Dr. HD2: Hud 6D **162**
Redwood Gro. LS19: Yead 6D **40**
Redwood Way LS19: Yead 6D **40**
Reedling Dr. LS27: Morl 4C **138**
Reed Rd. LS12: Leeds 5D **96**
Reedsdale Av. LS27: Morl 6E **115**
Reedsdale Dr. LS27: Morl 6E **115**
Reedsdale Gdns. LS27: Morl 6E **115**
Rees Way BD3: B'frd 3F **91** (1F **7**)
Reeth Rd. HD6: Brigh 3G **161**
Reevy Av. BD6: B'frd 6H **109**
Reevy Cres. BD6: B'frd 6G **109**
Reevy Dr. BD6: B'frd 5A **110**
Reevylands Dr. BD6: B'frd 5A **110**
Reevy Pk. Ct. BD6: B'frd 5G **109**
Reevy Rd. BD6: B'frd 5H **109**
Reevy Rd. W. BD6: B'frd 5F **109**
Reevy St. BD6: B'frd 4A **110**
Reevy Yd. BD6: B'frd 5B **110**
           (off Green End Rd.)
Reform St. BD19: Cleck 6F **135**
Regal Pde. LS15: Leeds 1D **100**
Regency Ct. BD8: B'frd 3B **90**
  LS6: Leeds 5E **77**
  LS29: I'ly 6C **10**
Regency Gdns. WF3: E Ard 1G **155**
Regency Pk. Gro.
  LS28: Pud 6A **94**
Regency Pk. Rd. LS28: Pud 6A **94**
Regency Vw. BD3: B'frd 1G **91**
Regent Av. LS18: H'fth 2E **75**
Regent Cl. HD6: Brigh 5G **161**
  LS18: H'fth 2E **75**
Regent Ct. LS1: Leeds 5F **5**
  LS18: H'fth 2E **75**
Regent Cres. LS18: H'fth 2D **74**
Regent Ho. HX5: Ell 4B **160**
Regent Pde. HX6: Hal 5A **148**
              (off Wharf St.)
Regent Pk. Av. LS6: Leeds 5F **77**
Regent Pk. Cross Av. LS6: Leeds . . .5F **77**
          (off Regent Pk. Av.)
Regent Pk. Ter. LS6: Leeds 5F **77**
Regent Pl. BD10: B'frd 6G **53**
  HX6: Hal 4H **147**
Regent Rd. LS18: H'fth 2D **74**
  LS29: I'ly 5C **10**
Regent St. BD10: B'frd 2B **72**
            (Haigh Hall Rd.)

Regent St. BD10: B'frd 6G **53**
             (Northlea Av.)
  BD13: B'frd 4B **108**
  BD22: Haw 2D **64**
  HX1: Hal 3G **149** (5A **164**)
  LS2: Leeds 3B **98** (3H **5**)
  LS7: Leeds 2B **78** (3H **5**)
Regent Ter. LS6: Leeds 1F **97**
  LS7: Leeds 2B **78**
Regina Dr. LS7: Leeds 3B **78**
Regina Ho. LS13: Leeds 3F **95**
Reginald Mt. LS7: Leeds 5B **78**
Reginald Pl. LS7: Leeds 5B **78**
Reginald Row LS7: Leeds 5B **78**
Reginald St. BD5: B'frd 2D **110**
  LS7: Leeds 5B **78**
Reginald Ter. LS7: Leeds 5B **78**
Reginald Vw. LS7: Leeds 5B **78**
Reighton Cft. BD10: B'frd 3C **72**
Rein, The LS14: Leeds 3B **80**
Rein Gdns. WF3: E Ard 1C **154**
Rein M. WF3: E Ard 1C **154**
Rein Rd. LS18: H'fth 3D **74**
           (not continuous)
  LS27: Morl 6B **138**
  WF3: Morl 6C **138**
Reins Av. BD17: Bail 6B **52**
Reins Rd. HD6: Brigh 3G **161**
Rein St. LS27: Morl 6C **138**
Reinwood Av. LS8: Leeds 4H **79**
Rembrandt Av. WF3: E Ard 1F **155**
Renaissance Ct. LS27: Morl 5C **116**
Renaissance Dr. LS27: Morl 5C **116**
Renee Cl. BD4: B'frd 5A **112**
Renshaw St. BD10: B'frd 6H **53**
Renton Av. LS20: Guis 4B **40**
Renton Dr. LS20: Guis 5B **40**
Renton Lea LS20: Guis 5B **40**
Reservoir Pl. BD13: B'frd 3G **107**
Reservoir Rd. HX2: Hal 1C **148**
Reservoir Vw. BD13: B'frd 5G **87**
Restmore Av. LS20: Guis 3B **40**
Retford Pl. BD7: B'frd 6C **90**
Reva Cl. BD16: Bgly 3D **50**
Reva Syke Rd. BD14: B'frd 2D **108**
Revie Rd. LS11: Leeds 2F **117**
Revie Rd. Ind. Est. LS11: Leeds 2F **117**
Rex Cinema 4B **160**
Reyden M. LS12: Leeds 5C **96**
Reydon Wlk. BD6: B'frd 4H **109**
Reyhill Gro. BD5: B'frd 6E **91** (6D **6**)
Reyner Ho. BD5: B'frd 6E **91**
          (off Manchester Rd.)
Reyner Ho. M. BD5: B'frd 6E **91**
Reynolds Av. BD7: B'frd 6G **89**
Rhine St. BD4: B'frd 6G **91**
Rhodes Gdns. WF3: Wake 3G **157**
Rhodesia Av. BD15: B'frd 3E **89**
  HX3: Hal 6G **149**
Rhodes La. LS23: B Spa 5H **29**
Rhodes Pl. BD17: Ship 1B **70**
Rhodes St. BD18: Ship 1A **70**
  HX1: Hal 2F **149** (4A **164**)
Rhodes Ter. BD2: B'frd 5H **71**
  LS12: Leeds 5E **97**
Rhodesway BD8: B'frd 4F **89**
Rhodesway Pool 3F **89**
Rhondda Pl. HX1: Hal 3C **148**
Rhum Cl. BD6: B'frd 1H **131**
Rhyddings Gdns. LS29: I'ly 5F **11**
Rhylstone Mt. BD7: B'frd 4H **89**
Ribble Ct. BD20: Sils 2E **15**
           (off Howden Rd.)
Ribblesdale Av. LS25: Gar 5H **103**
Ribble St. BD21: Keigh 5C **34**
Ribbleton Gro. BD3: B'frd 3G **91** (2H **7**)
Riccall Nook BD10: B'frd 2A **72**
Richard Dunn Sports Cen. 4D **110**
Richard Gossop Ct. LS29: Burl W . . .2E **21**
Richard Pl. HD6: Brigh 5A **152**
           (off Richard St.)
Richardshaw Dr. LS28: Pud 2A **94**

Richardshaw La. LS28: Pud 2A **94**
Richardshaw Rd. LS28: Pud 2A **94**
Richardson Av. BD6: B'frd 5C **110**
Richardson Cres. LS9: Leeds 4F **99**
Richardson Rd. LS9: Leeds 4F **99**
Richardson St. BD12: B'frd 3G **133**
Richmond Av. BD3: B'frd 4G **91** (4G **7**)
  HD6: Brigh 5A **152**
Richmond Av. HX6: Hal 6F **147**
  LS6: Leeds 5E **77**
Richmond Cl. HX1: Hal . . .1G **149** (2B **164**)
  LS13: Leeds 1C **94**
  LS26: Rothw 1B **142**
  LS27: Morl 4A **138**
Richmond Ct. LS9: Leeds 4D **98**
  LS26: Rothw 1B **142**
  LS29: I'ly 6E **11**
         (off Richmond Pl.)
Richmond Cft. LS9: Leeds 4D **98**
Richmondfield Av. LS15: Bar E 3E **83**
Richmondfield Cl. LS15: Bar E 3E **83**
Richmondfield Cres. LS15: Bar E 3E **83**
Richmondfield Cross
  LS15: Bar E 3E **83**
Richmondfield Dr. LS15: Bar E 2E **83**
Richmondfield Gth. LS15: Bar E 2E **83**
Richmondfield Gro. LS15: Bar E 3E **83**
Richmondfield La. LS15: Bar E 3E **83**
Richmondfield Mt. LS15: Bar E 3E **83**
Richmondfield Wlk. LS15: Bar E 3E **83**
Richmondfield Way LS15: Bar E 3E **83**
Richmond Gdns. HX6: Hal 6F **147**
  LS28: Pud 4C **94**
Richmond Gro. BD19: Cleck 5F **135**
RICHMOND HILL 4D **98**
Richmond Hill App. LS9: Leeds 4C **98**
Richmond Hill Cl. LS9: Leeds 4C **98**
Richmond Hill Sports & Recreation Cen.
  . . . . .3D **98**
Richmond Ho. *LS8: Leeds* 5F **61**
          (off Street La.)
Richmond M. BD18: Ship 1H **69**
Richmond Mt. LS6: Leeds 5E **77**
Richmond Pl. BD18: Ship 1H **69**
  LS29: I'ly 6E **11**
Richmond Rd. BD7: B'frd . . .4C **90** (4A **6**)
  BD18: Ship 1H **69**
  HX1: Hal 1F **149** (2A **164**)
  LS6: Leeds 5E **77**
  LS28: Pud 1G **93**
Richmond St. BD21: Keigh 5H **33**
  HX1: Hal 1F **149** (2A **164**)
  LS9: Leeds 4C **98** (6H **5**)
Richmond Ter. HX2: Hal 6E **127**
           (off High St.)
  LS20: Guis 4B **40**
  LS21: Otley 4D **22**
  LS28: Pud 4C **94**
Richmond Way LS25: Gar 6F **103**
Rickard St. LS12: Leeds 5F **97**
Ridding Ga. LS21: Otley 2C **22**
Riddings Rd. LS29: I'ly 6D **10**
RIDDLESDEN 3E **35**
Riddlesden St. BD20: Keigh 4D **34**
Riddlesden Vw. BD21: Keigh 6D **34**
Rider Rd. LS6: Leeds 5H **77**
Rider St. LS9: Leeds 3C **98**
Ridge, The LS22: Coll 6C **12**
Ridge Cl. LS20: Guis 5A **40**
Ridge Gro. LS7: Leeds 4G **77**
Ridge Hill HD6: Brigh 2G **161**
Ridge Lea HD6: Brigh 2H **161**
Ridge Mt. LS6: Leeds 5G **77**
Ridgemount Rd. BD20: Keigh 3C **34**
Ridge Rd. LS7: Leeds 5H **77**
  LS25: Kip, Leds 5B **124**
Ridge Ter. LS6: Leeds 4E **77**
Ridge Vw. LS13: Leeds 3E **95**
Ridge Vw. HX5: Ell 5E **161**
Ridge Vw. Gdns. BD10: B'frd 2A **72**
Ridge Vw. Rd. HD6: Brigh 2H **161**
Ridge Way LS8: Leeds 3D **78**

Ridgeway BD13: B'frd 5B 108
  BD15: B'frd 3C 88
  BD18: Ship 3E 71
  LS20: Guis 5H 39
Ridge Way Cl. LS8: Leeds 3D 78
Ridgeway Dr. WF17: Bat 6C 136
Ridgeway Gdns. HD6: Brigh 4G 151
Ridgeway Mt. BD22: Keigh 2F 47
Ridgeway Ter. LS6: Leeds 5G 77
  (off Delph La.)
Ridgewood Cl. BD17: Bail 4E 53
Riding Head La. HX2: Hal 6E 127
Riding Hill HX3: B'frd 1G 131
Riding La. HX2: Hal 4A 128
Ridings, The BD20: Keigh 2H 33
Ridings Bus. Pk. HX1: Hal 3D 148
Ridings Cl. WF3: Wake 3F 157
Ridings Ct. WF3: Wake 3F 157
Ridings Cft. BD5: B'frd 4H 111
Ridings Gdns. WF3: Wake 3F 157
Ridings La. WF3: Wake 3F 157
Ridings M. WF3: Wake 3F 157
Ridings Sports Cen., The 4D 128
Ridings Way BD6: B'frd 4G 109
  WF3: Wake 3F 157
Ridleys Fold LS29: Add 1D 8
Rievaulx Av. BD8: B'frd ...3C 90 (1A 6)
Rievaulx Cl. LS23: B Spa 4A 30
Riffa Bus. Pk. LS21: Leat 1H 25
Rigton App. LS9: Leeds 3C 98
Rigton Bank LS17: Bard 1F 45
Rigton Cl. LS9: Leeds 3D 98
Rigton Dr. LS9: Leeds 3C 98
Rigton Grn. LS9: Leeds 3C 98
  LS17: Bard 1G 45
RIGTON HILL 5G 27
Rigton Lawn LS9: Leeds 3C 98
Rigton M. LS9: Leeds 3C 98
Rigton St. BD5: B'frd 2D 110
Riley La. HX2: Hal 5D 106
Rillbank La. LS3: Leeds 2F 97
Rillbank St. LS3: Leeds 2F 97
  (off Rillbank La.)
Rillington Mead BD10: B'frd 3B 72
Rills Mead LS21: Otley 4E 23
Rilston St. BD7: B'frd 5B 90
Rimswell Holt BD10: B'frd 3C 72
Ringby La. HX3: Hal 3F 129
Ring Hay Rd. BD4: B'frd 4E 113
Ring Rd. Adel LS16: Leeds 5D 58
Ring Rd. Beeston LS12: Leeds 1C 116
Ring Rd. Beeston Pk.
  LS10: Leeds 5G 117
  LS11: Leeds 5G 117
Ring Rd. Bramley LS13: Leeds 3F 95
Ring Rd. Cross Gates LS15: Leeds ..6E 81
Ring Rd. Farnley LS12: Leeds 3F 95
Ring Rd. Farsley
  LS13: Leeds, Pud 1F 93
  LS28: Pud 1F 93
Ring Rd. Halton LS15: Leeds 2E 101
Ring Rd. Horsforth LS16: Leeds ...1G 75
  LS18: H'fth 1G 75
Ring Rd. Lwr. Wortley
  LS12: Leeds 5H 95
Ring Rd. Meanwood LS6: Leeds ...5E 59
  LS16: Leeds 5E 59
  LS17: Leeds 5E 59
Ring Rd. Middleton LS10: Leeds ..2B 140
Ring Rd. Moortown LS6: Leeds 5G 59
  LS17: Leeds 5G 59
Ring Rd. Seacroft LS14: Leeds 1B 80
Ring Rd. Shadwell LS17: Leeds ...4G 61
Ring Rd. Weetwood LS16: Leeds ..6B 58
Ring Rd. W. Pk. LS16: Leeds 6H 57
Ringway LS25: Gar 5D 102
Ringwood Av. LS14: Leeds 1B 80
Ringwood Ct. WF1: Wake 4H 157
Ringwood Cres. LS14: Leeds 6C 62
Ringwood Dr. LS14: Leeds 1C 80
Ringwood Edge HX5: Ell 5H 159
Ringwood Gdns. LS14: Leeds 1C 80

Ringwood Mt. LS14: Leeds 1C 80
Ringwood Rd. BD5: B'frd 2B 110
Ripley La. LS20: Guis 2C 40
Ripley Rd. BD4: B'frd 2F 111
  (Bowling Pk. Dr.)
  BD4: B'frd 1F 111
  (Ripley La.)
Ripley St. BD4: B'frd 1F 111
  BD5: B'frd 1E 111
  (not continuous)
  BD15: B'frd 1C 88
  BD20: Keigh 4D 34
  HX3: Hal 2A 152
Ripon Ho. HX5: Ell 4B 160
Ripon St. HX1: Hal 3C 148
Ripon Ter. HX3: Hal 6F 129
Rise, The HX3: Hal 5C 130
  LS5: Leeds 4A 76
  LS25: Kip 4G 123
Risedale Av. WF17: Bat 5D 136
Risedale Cl. WF17: Bat 5D 136
Rishworthian Ct. HX3: Hal 2E 159
Rishworth St. BD22: Keigh 1F 47
Rivadale Vw. LS29: I'ly 4D 10
River Bank Way HX5: Ell 2D 160
Riverdale LS22: Weth 5F 13
Riverdale Ct. LS21: Otley 3E 23
Riverdale Gdns. LS21: Otley 3E 23
  LS23: B Spa 4D 30
Riverdale Rd. LS21: Otley 3E 23
River Mt. BD20: Keigh 4C 34
Riverside BD21: Keigh 6C 34
Riverside Av. LS21: Otley 1F 23
Riverside Bus. Pk.
  LS29: I'ly 4E 11
Riverside Cl. LS21: Otley 2F 23
Riverside Ct. BD17: Ship 6A 52
  LS1: Leeds 4A 98 (6F 5)
Riverside Cres. LS21: Otley 1F 23
Riverside Dr. BD19: Cleck 6B 134
  LS21: Otley 1F 23
Riverside Est. BD17: Ship 1A 70
Riverside Landings BD16: Bgly 4B 50
  (off Ferrand La.)
Riverside Pk. LS21: Otley 2F 23
Riverside Wlk. LS29: I'ly 4B 10
Riverside Way LS1: Leeds ...4G 97 (6B 4)
River St. BD21: Keigh 4C 34
  BD22: Haw 2D 64
  HD6: Brigh 2C 162
River Vw. LS18: H'fth 6D 56
  LS23: B Spa 4D 30
  LS29: I'ly 4G 11
  WF10: C'frd 6H 145
River Wlk. BD16: Bgly 4B 50
  HX6: Hal 6H 147
Riverwood Dr. HX3: Hal 1F 159
Riviera Gdns. LS7: Leeds 3A 78
Rivock Av. BD20: Keigh 2F 33
  BD20: Stee 5D 14
Rivock Gro. BD20: Keigh 2F 33
Roach Grange Av. LS25: Kip 2G 123
Road End HX4: Hal 4G 159
Roans Brae BD10: B'frd 3C 72
Robb Av. LS11: Leeds 4G 117
Robb St. LS11: Leeds 4G 117
Robert Ho. LS27: Morl 2B 138
  (off Pullman Ct.)
Roberts Av. LS9: Leeds 1F 99
Roberts Bldgs. HX2: Hal 2B 148
  (off Gibbet St.)
Roberts Pl. BD1: B'frd 3D 90 (2B 6)
  LS9: Leeds 2F 99

Roberts St. BD22: Keigh 1C 46
  LS26: Rothw 1E 143
Robert St. BD3: B'frd 5G 91 (5G 7)
  BD22: Haw 1F 65
  HX3: Hal 5E 129
Robert St. Nth. HX3: Hal 5G 129
Robina Cl. LS23: B Spa 4A 30
Robin Chase LS28: Pud 4B 94
Robin Cl. BD2: B'frd 5A 72
Robin Dr. BD2: B'frd 5A 72
  BD20: Stee 5B 14
Robin Hill WF17: Bat 6C 136
ROBIN HOOD 4F 141
Robin Hood Way HD6: Brigh 1E 163
Robin La. LS28: Pud 4A 94
Robins, The LS29: Burl W 3E 21
Robin's Gro. LS26: Rothw 2B 142
Robinson Ct. BD7: B'frd 5H 89
Robinson La. LS25: Kip 4H 123
Robinson St. WF10: Kip 3H 145
Robin St. BD5: B'frd 1C 110
Robin Wlk. BD18: Ship 3D 70
Robinwood Ct. LS8: Leeds 6E 61
Rochdale Rd. HX2: Hal 4B 148
  HX4: Hal 4B 158
  HX6: Hal 6G 147
  (Stubbing La.)
  HX6: Hal 4B 148
  (Willow Dell Dr.)
Rocheford Cl. LS10: Leeds 2D 118
Rocheford Ct. LS10: Leeds 2D 118
Rocheford Gdns. LS10: Leeds 2D 118
Rocheford Gro. LS10: Leeds 2D 118
Rocheford Wlk. LS10: Leeds 2D 118
Rochester Gdns. LS13: Leeds 6B 74
Rochester Pl. HX5: Ell 5B 160
  (off Saville Rd.)
Rochester Rd. WF17: Bat 4A 136
Rochester St. BD3: B'frd 4A 92
  BD18: Ship 3C 70
Rochester Ter. LS6: Leeds 5D 76
Rochester Wynd LS17: Leeds 3E 61
Rockcliffe Av. BD17: Bail 6C 52
Rock Cliffe Mt. HX2: Hal 2D 146
Rock Ct. LS27: Morl 2B 138
Rockery Cft. LS18: H'fth 5E 57
Rockery Rd. LS18: H'fth 5E 57
Rockfield LS19: Yead 6G 41
  (off Rockfield Ter.)
Rockfield Ter. LS19: Yead 6G 41
Rockhill Cl. WF17: Bat 6B 136
Rockhill La. BD4: B'frd 6G 111
  (not continuous)
Rockingham Cl. LS15: Leeds 6H 81
Rockingham Rd. LS15: Leeds 6H 81
Rockingham Way LS15: Leeds 6H 81
Rockland Cres. BD7: B'frd 6G 89
Rocklands Av. BD17: Bail 3C 52
Rocklands Pl. BD17: Bail 3C 52
Rock La. BD13: B'frd 3G 87
  LS13: Leeds 5D 74
Rock Lea BD13: B'frd 4B 108
Rockley Grange Gdns.
  LS25: Gar 6D 102
Rockley Hall Yd. LS1: Leeds 4F 5
Rocks La. HX2: Hal 5B 106
Rocks Rd. HX3: Hal 6E 149
Rock St. HD6: Brigh 6A 152
Rocks Vw. HX2: Hal 5E 149
Rock Ter. BD8: B'frd 2D 90
  BD13: B'frd 5H 87
  BD22: Keigh 2B 46
  HX3: Hal 1F 151
  LS15: Leeds 3B 100
  LS27: Morl 3D 138
  WF12: Dew 3B 154
Rock Vw. HX4: Hal 6G 159
Rockville Ter. HX1: Hal 4E 149
  LS19: Yead 1G 55
  (off South Vw. Ter.)
Rockwell La. BD10: B'frd 3A 72
Rockwood Cl. HD2: Hud 5E 163

Rockwood Cres. LS28: Pud 1E **93**
Rockwood Gro. LS28: Pud 6F **73**
Rockwood Hill Ct. LS28: Pud 1E **93**
Rockwood Rd. LS28: Pud 1E **93**
Roderick St. LS12: Leeds 4B **96**
Rodin Av. BD8: B'frd 4F **89**
RODLEY **4A 74**
Rodley La. LS13: Leeds 5C **74**
(Airedale Quay)
LS13: Leeds 3G **73**
(Brookfield Av.)
LS28: Leeds, Pud 3G **73**
Rods Vw. LS27: Morl 4B **138**
Roebuck St. WF17: Bat 6B **136**
Roeburn Way BD6: B'frd 4G **109**
Roedhelm Rd. BD20: Keigh 4F **35**
Roe Ho. BD17: Bail *6B 52*
(off Fairview Ct.)
Roger Ct. BD2: B'frd 1H **91**
Roger Fold LS25: Kip 4H **123**
Rogerson Sq. HD6: Brigh 6A **152**
Rogers Pl. LS28: Pud 3B **94**
Roils Head Rd. HX2: Hal 2H **147**
Rokeby Gdns. BD10: B'frd 3C **72**
LS6: Leeds 4C **76**
Roker La. LS28: Pud 6B **94**
ROKER LANE BOTTOM 1C **114**
Roman Av. LS8: Leeds 5E **61**
Romanby Shaw BD10: B'frd 3B **72**
Roman Ct. LS8: Leeds 5F **61**
Roman Cres. LS8: Leeds 5F **61**
Roman Dr. LS8: Leeds 5F **61**
Roman Gdns. LS8: Leeds 5E **61**
Roman Gro. LS8: Leeds 5E **61**
Roman Mt. LS8: Leeds 5F **61**
Roman Pl. LS8: Leeds 5F **61**
Roman Ter. LS8: Leeds 5E **61**
Roman Vw. LS8: Leeds 5F **61**
Rombalds Av. LS12: Leeds 3C **96**
Rombalds Ct. LS29: Men 1F **39**
Rombalds Cres. BD20: Sils 3F **15**
LS12: Leeds 2C **96**
Rombalds Cft. LS19: Yead 6F **41**
Rombalds Dr. BD16: Bgly 4D **50**
Rombalds Gro. LS12: Leeds 3C **96**
Rombalds La. LS29: I'ly 6G **11**
Rombalds Pl. LS12: Leeds 2C **96**
Rombalds St. LS12: Leeds 2C **96**
Rombalds Ter. LS12: Leeds 3C **96**
Rombalds Vw. LS29: I'ly 4F **11**
LS12: Leeds 2C **96**
LS21: Otley 1B **22**
Romford Av. LS27: Morl 4A **138**
Romford Ct. BD6: B'frd 1H **131**
Romney Mt. LS28: Pud 6C **94**
Romsey Gdns. BD4: B'frd 2B **112**
Romsey M. BD4: B'frd 2B **112**
Rona Cft. LS26: Rothw 2C **142**
Ronald Dr. BD7: B'frd 5A **90**
Ron Lawton Cres. LS29: Burl W ...3D **20**
Rookery HX3: Hal 6H **149**
Rookery, The LS29: Add 1D **8**
Rookery La. HX3: Hal 6H **149**
Rookery Pl. HD6: Brigh 6B **152**
Rookes Av. BD6: B'frd 5C **110**
Rookes La. HX3: Hal 6A **132**
Rookes La. Top HX3: Hal 5A **132**
Rookes Vw. HX3: Hal 5A **132**
Rook La. BD4: B'frd 3H **111**
Rooks Av. BD19: Cleck 6A **134**
Rooks Cl. BD12: Cleck 6D **132**
Rook's Nest Rd. WF1: Wake 5G **157**
WF3: Wake 5G **157**
Rook St. BD16: Bgly 4B **50**
Rookwith Pde. BD10: B'frd 3B **72**
Rookwood Av. LS9: Leeds 3G **99**
LS25: Kip 5G **123**
Rookwood Cres. LS9: Leeds 3G **99**
Rookwood Cft. LS9: Leeds 4G **99**
Rookwood Gdns. LS9: Leeds 3G **99**
Rookwood Hill LS9: Leeds 3G **99**
Rookwood Mt. LS9: Leeds 3G **99**

Rookwood Pde. LS9: Leeds 3H **99**
Rookwood Pl. LS9: Leeds 3G **99**
Rookwood Rd. LS9: Leeds 3G **99**
Rookwood Sq. LS9: Leeds 3H **99**
Rookwood St. LS9: Leeds 4G **99**
Rookwood Ter. LS9: Leeds 3G **99**
Rookwood Va. LS9: Leeds 4G **99**
Rookwood Vw. LS9: Leeds 3G **99**
Rookwood Wlk. LS9: Leeds 3G **99**
Rooley Av. BD6: B'frd 5D **110**
Rooley Banks HX6: Hal 6E **147**
Rooley Cl. BD5: B'frd 4E **111**
Rooley Ct. HX6: Hal 6D **146**
Rooley Cres. BD6: B'frd 4E **111**
Rooley Hgts. HX6: Hal 6D **146**
ROOLEY HILL 6D **146**
Rooley La. BD4: B'frd 4F **111**
BD5: B'frd 4D **110**
HX6: Hal 6D **146**
ROOMS 5H **115**
Rooms Fold LS27: Morl 1A **138**
Rooms La. LS27: Morl 5H **115**
Roper Av. LS8: Leeds 1D **78**
Roper Gdns. HX2: Hal 3B **128**
Roper Grn. HX2: Hal 3B **128**
Roper Gro. LS8: Leeds 1D **78**
Roper Ho. HX2: Hal 3B **128**
Roper La. BD13: B'frd 2F **107**
HX2: Hal 5D **106**
Roper St. BD21: Keigh 6H **33**
Rope Wlk. HX2: Hal 1F **127**
Roscoe St. LS7: Leeds 1B **98**
Roscoe Ter. LS12: Leeds 4B **96**
Roseate Grn. LS27: Morl 4C **138**
Rose Av. LS18: H'fth 2D **74**
Rose Bank *BD8: B'frd* *2C 90*
(off E. Squire La.)
BD12: B'frd 3D **132**
HX2: Hal 4D **148**
LS29: Burl W 3E **21**
Rosebank Cres. LS3: Leeds 1F **97**
Rosebank Gdns. LS3: Leeds 2F **97**
Rosebank Ho. LS3: Leeds 1F **97**
Rose Bank Pl. BD8: B'frd 4G **89**
Rosebank Rd. LS3: Leeds 2F **97**
Rosebank Row LS3: Leeds 2F **97**
Roseberry St. BD22: Keigh 5D **46**
Rosebery Av. BD18: Ship 2C **70**
HX3: Hal 5H **149**
Rosebery Mt. BD18: Ship 2D **70**
Rosebery Rd. BD8: B'frd 1C **90**
Rosebery St. HX5: Ell 5B **160**
LS28: Pud 3G **93**
Rosebery Ter. HX1: Hal 1E **149**
LS28: Pud 1B **94**
Rosebud Wlk. LS8: Leeds 1C **98**
Rosechapel Cl. BD6: B'frd 1H **131**
Rosecliffe Mt. LS13: Leeds 6D **74**
Rosecliffe Ter. LS13: Leeds 1E **95**
Rose Ct. LS25: Gar 4G **103**
Rose Cft. LS17: Bard 5E **27**
Rosedale LS26: Rothw 1B **142**
Rosedale Av. BD15: B'frd 1B **88**
Rosedale Bank LS10: Leeds 4B **118**
Rosedale Cl. BD17: Bail 5A **52**
Rosedale Ct. BD4: B'frd 6C **112**
Rosedale Gdns. LS10: Leeds 4B **118**
(not continuous)
Rosedale Grn. LS10: Leeds 4B **118**
Rosedale Ho. BD10: B'frd 3B **72**
HX6: Hal *6H 147*
(off Sowerby St.)
Rosedale Ri. LS23: B Spa 4A **30**
Rosedale Wlk. LS10: Leeds 4B **118**
Rose Gro. HX2: Hal 4E **127**
HX6: Hal 4G **147**
LS26: Rothw 1H **141**
Rose Gro. La. HX2: Hal 4F **147**
HX6: Hal 4F **147**
Rose Heath HX2: Hal 6B **106**
Rose Hill *HX6: Hal* *5A 148*
(off Beech Rd.)

Rose Hill Cres. BD12: B'frd 3C **132**
Rosehip Ri. BD14: B'frd 2D **108**
Roselee Cl. HX3: Hal 6A **150**
Rose Lynn Ter. *BD6: B'frd* *6H 109*
(off Halifax Rd.)
Rosemary Av. *LS12: Leeds* *4D 96*
(off Armley Gro. Pl.)
Rosemary Cl. HD6: Brigh 2A **162**
Rosemary Gdns. BD15: B'frd 2C **88**
Rosemary Gro. HX3: Hal 6A **150**
(not continuous)
Rosemary Hill HX3: Hal 1A **160**
Rosemary La. HD6: Brigh 3A **162**
HX3: Hal 6A **150**
Rosemary Pl. *HD6: Brigh* *3A 162*
(off Rosemary La.)
Rosemary Ter. HX3: Hal 6A **150**
Rose Mdws. BD22: Keigh 2E **47**
Rosemont Av. LS13: Leeds 1E **95**
LS28: Pud 3B **94**
Rosemont Dr. LS28: Pud 3B **94**
Rosemont Gro. LS13: Leeds 1D **94**
Rosemont La. BD17: Bail 5E **53**
Rosemont Pl. LS13: Leeds 1E **95**
Rosemont Rd. LS13: Leeds 1E **95**
Rosemont St. LS13: Leeds 1E **95**
LS28: Pud 3B **94**
Rosemont Ter. LS13: Leeds 1E **95**
LS28: Pud 3B **94**
Rosemont Vw. LS13: Leeds 1D **94**
Rosemont Vs. LS28: Pud 3B **94**
Rosemont Wlk. LS13: Leeds 1E **95**
ROSEMOUNT 5C **160**
Rose Mt. BD2: B'frd 6G **71**
BD4: B'frd 5E **113**
HX2: Hal 5E **149**
Rosemount *LS7: Leeds* *3A 78*
(off Henconner La.)
Rosemount Av. HX5: Ell 5C **160**
Rosemount Cl. *BD21: Keigh* *6H 33*
(off Well St.)
Rose Mt. Pl. LS12: Leeds 5D **96**
Rosemount Ter. HX5: Ell 5C **160**
Rosemount Wlk. *BD21: Keigh* *6H 33*
(off Well St.)
Roseneath Pl. LS12: Leeds 5D **96**
Roseneath St. LS12: Leeds 5D **96**
Roseneath Ter. LS12: Leeds 5D **96**
Rose Pl. HX2: Hal 4E **147**
Rose St. BD8: B'frd 2B **90**
BD21: Keigh 6D **34**
BD22: Haw 3C **64**
HX1: Hal 3D **148**
LS18: H'fth 1D **74**
Rose Ter. *HX1: Hal* *2E 149*
(off West St.)
HX2: Hal 5E **149**
LS18: H'fth 1C **74**
LS29: Add 1D **8**
Rosetta Dr. BD8: B'frd 4H **89**
Roseville Rd. LS8: Leeds 1C **98** (1H **5**)
Roseville St. LS8: Leeds 1C **98**
Roseville Ter. *LS15: Leeds* *6F 81*
(off Church La.)
Roseville Way LS8: Leeds 1C **98**
Rosewood Av. BD20: Keigh 4D **34**
LS25: Kip 2F **123**
Rosewood Ct. LS26: Rothw 6B **120**
Rosewood Gro. BD4: B'frd 6B **92**
Rosgill Dr. LS14: Leeds 4B **80**
Rosgill Grn. LS14: Leeds 4C **80**
Rosgill Wlk. LS14: Leeds 4B **80**
Rosley Mt. BD6: B'frd 1H **131**
Roslyn Pl. BD7: B'frd 5B **90**
Rossall Rd. LS8: Leeds 5D **78**
Rossefield App. LS13: Leeds 2F **95**
Rossefield Av. LS13: Leeds 1F **95**
Rossefield Chase LS13: Leeds 1F **95**
Rossefield Cl. LS13: Leeds 1F **95**
Rossefield Dr. LS13: Leeds 1F **95**
Rossefield Gdns. LS13: Leeds 1F **95**
Rossefield Gth. LS13: Leeds 1F **95**

Rossefield Grn. LS13: Leeds 1F **95**
(off Rossefield Dr.)
Rossefield Gro. LS13: Leeds 1F **95**
Rossefield Lawn LS13: Leeds 1F **95**
Rossefield Pde. LS13: Leeds 1F **95**
(off Rossefield Gro.)
Rosse Fld. Pk. BD9: B'frd 5B **70**
Rossefield Pl. LS13: Leeds 1F **95**
Rossefield Rd. BD9: B'frd 5A **70**
Rossefield Ter. LS13: Leeds 1F **95**
Rossefield Vw. LS13: Leeds 1F **95**
Rossefield Wlk. LS13: Leeds 1F **95**
Rossefield Way LS13: Leeds 1F **95**
Rossendale Pl. BD18: Ship 2A **70**
Rosse St. BD8: B'frd 4A **90**
BD18: Ship 1B **70**
Rossett Bus. Pk. LS13: Leeds 5D **74**
Rossett Ho. BD3: B'frd 2F **7**
Ross Gro. LS13: Leeds 5C **74**
Rossington Gro. LS8: Leeds 5C **78**
Rossington Pl. LS8: Leeds 5C **78**
Rossington Rd. LS8: Leeds 4E **79**
Rossington St. LS2: Leeds . . .3H **97** (3D **4**)
Rosslyn Gro. BD22: Haw 3C **64**
Rossmore Dr. BD15: B'frd 2E **89**
Ross Ter. LS13: Leeds 5C **74**
Rothbury Gdns. LS16: Leeds 4B **58**
Rothery Ct. HX1: Hal 1E **149**
(off Crossley Gdns.)
Rothesay Ter. BD7: B'frd 5C **90**
ROTHWELL 2A **142**
Rothwell Dr. HX1: Hal 4F **149**
ROTHWELL HAIGH 1H **141**
Rothwell La. LS26: Rothw 1C **142**
Rothwell Mt. HX1: Hal 4F **149**
Rothwell Rd. HX1: Hal 4F **149** (6A **164**)
Rothwell Sports Cen. 3E **143**
Rough Hall La. HX2: Hal 2F **127**
Roundell Av. BD4: B'frd 5H **111**
Roundfield Pl. BD13: B'frd 4H **87**
(off West La.)
ROUNDHAY 6E **61**
Roundhay Av. LS8: Leeds 4D **78**
Roundhay Cres. LS8: Leeds 4D **78**
Roundhay Gdns. LS8: Leeds 4D **78**
Roundhay Gro. LS8: Leeds 4D **78**
Roundhay Mt. LS8: Leeds 5D **78**
Roundhay Pk. Cvn. & Camping Site
LS8: Leeds 1H **79**
Roundhay Pk. La. LS17: Leeds 2F **61**
Roundhay Pl. LS8: Leeds 4D **78**
Roundhay Rd. LS7: Leeds 1B **98**
LS8: Leeds 5E **79**
Roundhay Vw. LS8: Leeds 4D **78**
Roundhead Fold BD10: B'frd 1C **72**
Round Hill BD13: B'frd 5G **107**
(off Rope La.)
HX2: Hal 1D **128**
Roundhill Av. BD16: Bgly 1D **68**
Round Hill Cl. BD13: B'frd 3D **108**
HX2: Hal 1D **128**
Round Hill Pl. BD13: B'frd 3D **108**
Roundhill Mt. BD16: Bgly 2D **68**
Round Hill Pl. BD13: B'frd 3D **108**
Roundhill Pl. BD1: B'frd 4D **90** (4B **6**)
Roundhill St. BD5: B'frd 1D **110**
Roundhouse Bus. Pk.
LS12: Leeds 4F **97** (6A **4**)
Round St. BD5: B'frd 2E **111**
(not continuous)
Round Thorn Pl. BD8: B'frd 3A **90**
Roundway, The LS27: Morl 3G **137**
Roundwood BD18: Ship 2G **69**
Roundwood Av. BD10: B'frd 4C **72**
BD17: Bail 4F **53**
Roundwood Glen
BD10: B'frd 2C **72**
Roundwood Rd. BD17: Bail 4E **53**
Roundwood Vw. BD10: B'frd 3C **72**
Rouse Fold BD4: B'frd 6F **91** (6F **7**)
Row, The LS19: Yead 3E **55**
Rowan Av. BD3: B'frd 4C **92**
Rowanberry Cl. BD2: B'frd 5H **71**

Rowan Cl. LS21: Pool 5G **25**
WF17: Bat 5C **136**
Rowan Ct. BD2: B'frd 2A **92**
LS19: Yead 2F **55**
LS26: Rothw 1G **143**
Rowan Dr. HD6: Brigh 6C **152**
Rowan Pl. LS25: Gar 5H **103**
Rowans, The BD17: Bail 4H **51**
LS13: Leeds 6B **74**
LS16: B'hpe 3H **43**
LS22: Weth 3G **13**
Rowan St. BD20: Keigh 3G **33**
Rowantree Av. BD17: Bail 3B **52**
Rowantree Dr. BD10: B'frd 3H **71**
Row Bottom Ter. HX6: Hal 5D **146**
Rowland Pl. LS11: Leeds 2H **117**
Rowland Rd. LS11: Leeds 2H **117**
Rowland Ter. LS11: Leeds 2H **117**
Row La. HX6: Hal 6D **146**
Rowlestone Ri. BD10: B'frd 3C **72**
Rowley Dr. LS29: I'ly 6H **11**
Rowsley St. BD21: Keigh 6A **34**
Rowton Thorpe BD10: B'frd 3C **72**
Roxburgh Gro. BD15: B'frd 3D **88**
Roxby Cl. LS9: Leeds 2C **98**
Roxby St. BD5: B'frd 2D **110**
Roxholme Av. LS7: Leeds 4C **78**
Roxholme Gro. LS7: Leeds 4C **78**
Roxholme Ho. BD4: B'frd 3A **112**
(off Prince St.)
Roxholme Pl. LS7: Leeds 4C **78**
Roxholme Rd. LS7: Leeds 4C **78**
Roxholme Ter. LS7: Leeds 4C **78**
Royal Arc. BD21: Keigh 6A **34**
Royal Armouries Mus., The
. . . . .5B **98** (6H **5**)
Royal Cl. BD7: B'frd 2H **109**
LS10: Leeds 3B **118**
Royal Ct. LS10: Leeds 3B **118**
Royal Dr. LS10: Leeds 3B **118**
Royal Gdns. LS10: Leeds 3B **118**
Royal Gro. LS10: Leeds 3B **118**
Royal Ind. Pk. HX1: Hal . . .2F **149** (4A **164**)
Royal Lofts, The HX6: Hal 6H **147**
(off Sowerby St.)
Royal London Ind. Est., The
LS11: Leeds 4F **117**
Royal Pk. Av. LS6: Leeds 6F **77**
Royal Pk. Gro. LS6: Leeds 6F **77**
Royal Pk. Mt. LS6: Leeds 6F **77**
Royal Pk. Rd. LS6: Leeds 1E **97**
Royal Pk. Ter. LS6: Leeds 6F **77**
Royal Pk. Vw. LS6: Leeds 6F **77**
Royal Pl. LS10: Leeds 3B **118**
Royal Ter. LS23: B Spa 3B **30**
Royd HX6: Hal 6E **147**
Royd Cres. HX1: Hal 1C **148**
Royden Gro. BD9: B'frd 1A **90**
Royd Farm HX2: Hal 6C **106**
(off Causeway Foot)
Royd Ho. Gro. BD21: Keigh 2C **48**
Royd Ho. Rd. BD21: Keigh 2C **48**
Royd Ho. Wlk. BD21: Keigh 2C **48**
Royd Ho. Way BD21: Keigh 2C **48**
Royd Ings Av. BD21: Keigh 4A **34**
Roydlands St. HX3: Hal 1F **151**
Roydlands Ter. HX3: Hal 2F **151**
Royd La. BD20: Keigh 4H **33**
HX2: Hal 6C **106**
HX3: Hal 3E **129**
Royd Mill Bus. Pk. HD6: Brigh 2C **162**
Royd Moor Rd. BD4: B'frd 4D **112**
Royd Mt. HX3: Hal 5G **129**
Royd Pl. HX3: Hal 5G **129**
Royds, The HX3: Hal 6F **149**
Royds Av. BD11: B'frd 2F **135**
HD6: Brigh 1B **152**
Roydscliffe Dr. BD9: B'frd 5H **69**
Roydscliffe Rd. BD9: B'frd 6H **69**

Royds Cl. LS12: Leeds 1C **116**
Royds Ct. LS26: Rothw 2B **142**
(off Marsh St.)
Royds Cres. HD6: Brigh 2B **152**
Roydsdale Way BD4: B'frd 1G **133**
Royds Farm Rd. LS12: Leeds 3C **116**
ROYDS GREEN 5C **142**
Royds Gro. WF1: Wake 4G **157**
Royds Hall Av. BD6: B'frd 5C **110**
Royds Hall La. BD6: B'frd 1A **132**
(Alderholt Dr.)
BD6: B'frd 2A **132**
(Lingdale Rd.)
BD12: B'frd 4A **132**
Royds Hall Rd. LS12: Leeds 1C **116**
Royds La. LS12: Leeds 1C **116**
LS26: Rothw 3B **142**
Royds Pk. LS12: Leeds 1C **116**
Royds Pk. Cres. BD12: B'frd 3D **132**
Roydstone Rd. BD3: B'frd 3B **92**
Roydstone Ter. BD3: B'frd 3B **92**
Royd St. BD12: B'frd 3C **132**
BD13: B'frd 5G **87**
BD15: B'frd 5G **67**
BD20: Keigh 3H **33**
(not continuous)
Royds Wood BD18: Ship 4A **70**
Royd Vw. LS28: Pud 5G **93**
Royd Way BD21: Keigh 4A **34**
Royd Well BD11: B'frd 2F **135**
Royd Wood BD22: Oxen 5D **64**
Roydwood Ter. BD13: B'frd 3B **66**
Roy Rd. BD6: B'frd 4F **109**
Royston Cl. WF3: E Ard 3B **156**
Royston Hill WF3: E Ard 3B **156**
Ruby St. BD22: Keigh 3G **47**
LS9: Leeds 2C **98** (1H **5**)
Rudding Av. BD15: B'frd 2C **88**
Rudding Cres. BD15: B'frd 2C **88**
Rudd St. BD7: B'frd 1A **110**
Rudgate LS23: W'ton 1G **31**
LS24: Tad 5H **31**
Ruffield Side BD12: B'frd 2C **132**
Rufford Av. LS19: Yead 1F **55**
Rufford Bank LS19: Yead 1G **55**
Rufford Cl. LS19: Yead 1G **55**
Rufford Cres. LS19: Yead 1G **55**
Rufford Dr. LS19: Yead 1G **55**
RUFFORD PARK 1F **55**
Rufford Pl. HX3: Hal 5F **149**
Rufford Ridge LS19: Yead 1G **55**
Rufford Ri. LS19: Yead 1G **55**
Rufford Rd. HX3: Hal 5F **149**
HX5: Ell 5B **160**
Rufford St. BD3: B'frd 4A **92**
Rufford Vs. HX3: Hal 5F **149**
Rufforth Ho. BD10: B'frd 3A **72**
(off Rowantree Dr.)
Rufus St. BD5: B'frd 2B **110**
BD21: Keigh 5A **34**
Rugby Av. HX3: Hal 4D **128**
Rugby Dr. HX3: Hal 4D **128**
Rugby Gdns. HX3: Hal 4D **128**
Rugby League Hall of Fame 3E **143**
Rugby Mt. HX3: Hal 4D **128**
Rugby Pl. BD7: B'frd 5B **90**
Rugby Ter. HX3: Hal 4D **128**
Rugby Training Cen. 6A **76**
Rumple Cft. LS21: Otley 1C **22**
Runnymede Ct. BD10: B'frd 2H **71**
(off Cobden St.)
Runswick Av. LS11: Leeds 6F **97**
Runswick Gro. BD5: B'frd 4D **110**
Runswick Pl. LS11: Leeds 6F **97**
Runswick St. BD5: B'frd 4D **110**
LS11: Leeds 6F **97**
Runswick Ter. BD5: B'frd 4D **110**
LS11: Leeds 6G **97**
Rupert Rd. LS29: I'ly 4C **10**
Rupert St. BD21: Keigh 5A **34**
BD22: Haw 1F **65**

Rush Cft. BD10: B'frd 6F 53
Rushcroft Ter. BD17: Bail 4C 52
Rushdene Ct. BD12: B'frd 6C 132
Rushmoor Rd. BD4: B'frd 3B 112
Rusholme Dr. LS28: Pud 6G 73
Rushton Av. BD3: B'frd 3C 92
Rushton Hill HX2: Hal 6A 128
Rushton Hill Cl. HX2: Hal 6A 128
Rushton Rd. BD3: B'frd 3B 92
Rushton St. HX1: Hal 1D 148
LS28: Pud 3F 73
Rushton Ter. BD3: B'frd 4C 92
Rushworth St. HX3: Hal 6E 129
Ruskin Av. BD9: B'frd 6F 69
WF1: Wake 6E 157
Ruskin Cres. LS20: Guis 5D 40
Ruskin St. LS28: Pud 2G 93
Ruskin Ter. HX3: Hal 6E 129
Russel Ho. *BD10: B'frd* *3A 72*
(off Yewdall Way)
Russell Av. BD13: B'frd 5A 108
Russell Ct. LS17: Bard 2F 45
Russell Gro. BD11: B'frd 2F 135
LS8: Leeds 5D 78
Russell Hall La. BD13: B'frd 4A 108
Russell Rd. BD13: B'frd 5H 107
Russell St. BD5: B'frd 6D 90 (6B 6)
BD13: B'frd 4A 108
BD18: Ship 4C 70
BD21: Keigh 6H 33
HX1: Hal 2G 149 (4C 164)
LS1: Leeds 3H 97 (4D 4)
Russell Way HD6: Brigh 5B 152
Russetts, The HX3: Hal 1A 150
Rustic Av. HX3: Hal 5C 150
Rustless Cl. BD19: Cleck 3G 153
Ruswarp Cres. BD10: B'frd 3B 72
Ruth Ho. *BD3: B'frd* *3G 7*
(off Otley Rd.)
Ruth St. BD22: Haw 1E 65
Ruthven Av. LS8: Leeds 6E 79
Rutland Cl. LS25: Kip 3H 123
LS26: Rothw 1F 143
Rutland Ct. *LS28: Pud* *3A 94*
(off Richardshaw La.)
Rutland Dr. LS25: Kip 3H 123
Rutland Ho. *BD16: Bgly* *4C 50*
(off Lyndon Ter.)
Rutland Mt. LS3: Leeds 3F 97 (3A 4)
Rutland St. BD4: B'frd 1G 111
BD21: Keigh 2H 47
LS3: Leeds 3G 97 (3A 4)
Rutland Ter. LS3: Leeds 3F 97 (3A 4)
Ryan Gro. BD22: Keigh 5D 32
Ryan Pl. LS8: Leeds 5E 79
Ryan St. BD5: B'frd 2D 110
Ryburn Bldgs. *HX6: Hal* *6H 147*
(off Town Hall St.)
Ryburn Ct. *HX1: Hal* *2D 148*
(off Hanson La.)
Ryburn Ho. *HX1: Hal* *2D 148*
(off Clay St.)
Ryburn St. HX6: Hal 6H 147
Ryburn Ter. HX1: Hal 2D 148
Ryburn Vw. HX2: Hal 4C 148
Rycroft Av. BD16: Bgly 3C 68
LS13: Leeds 2C 94
Rycroft Cl. LS13: Leeds 2D 94
Rycroft Ct. LS13: Leeds 2D 94
Rycroft Dr. LS13: Leeds 2D 94
Rycroft Grn. LS13: Leeds 2D 94
Rycroft Pl. LS13: Leeds 2D 94
Rycroft Sq. LS13: Leeds 2D 94
Rycroft St. BD18: Ship 4D 70
Rycroft Towers LS13: Leeds 2C 94
Rydal Av. BD9: B'frd 5C 70
BD17: Bail 6G 51
LS25: Gar 5F 103
Rydal Cres. LS27: Morl 2D 138
Rydal Dr. LS27: Morl 2D 138
Rydale Ho. HX6: Hal 6H 147
Rydall Pl. LS11: Leeds 6F 97

Rydall St. LS11: Leeds 6F 97
Rydall Ter. LS11: Leeds 6F 97
Rydal St. BD21: Keigh 1G 47
Ryder Gdns. LS8: Leeds 2E 79
Rydings, The *HD6: Brigh* *6A 152*
(off Halifax Rd.)
Rydings Av. HD6: Brigh 6A 152
Rydings Cl. HD6: Brigh 6H 151
Rydings Dr. HD6: Brigh 6H 151
Rydings Wlk. HD6: Brigh 6H 151
Rye Cft. HX2: Hal 1D 128
Ryecroft BD16: Bgly 6D 48
Ryecroft Cl. WF1: Wake 4G 157
Ryecroft Cres. HX2: Hal 6B 128
Ryecroft La. HD6: Brigh 3C 162
HX2: Hal 1B 148
Ryecroft Rd. BD16: B'frd 5B 48
Ryecroft Ter. HX2: Hal 6B 128
Ryedale Av. LS12: Leeds 1B 116
Ryedale Ct. LS14: Leeds 4B 80
Ryedale Holt LS12: Leeds 6C 96
Ryedale Pk. LS29: I'ly 6F 11
Ryedale Way BD15: B'frd 1C 88
WF3: E Ard 2E 155
Ryefield Av. BD14: B'frd 6D 88
Rye Gth. LS22: Weth 1D 12
Ryelands Gro. BD9: B'frd 5F 69
Rye La. HX2: Hal 6A 127
Rye Pl. LS14: Leeds 2B 100
Rye St. BD21: Keigh 3H 47
Rylands Av. BD16: Bgly 4D 50
Rylands Mdw. BD22: Haw 1E 65
Rylstone Gdns. BD3: B'frd 2G 91
Rylstone Rd. BD17: Bail 5H 51
Rylstone St. BD21: Keigh 5B 34
Rylston Gdns. HX3: Hal 6F 149
Rylston Gdns. HX3: Hal 6F 149
Ryshworth Av. BD16: Bgly 6H 35
Ryshworth Bri. BD16: Bgly 1H 49
Ryshworth Cres. BD16: Bgly 6H 35
Ryton Dale BD10: B'frd 3C 72

S

Sable Crest BD2: B'frd 5F 71
Sackville App. LS7: Leeds 6A 78
Sackville Rd. BD20: Sils 1E 15
Sackville St. BD1: B'frd 4E 91 (4C 6)
LS7: Leeds 5A 78
Saddlers Cft. LS29: I'ly 5C 10
Saddleworth Rd. HX4: Hal 6A 158
HX5: Ell 4A 160
Sadler Cl. LS16: Leeds 3C 58
Sadler Copse LS16: Leeds 3C 58
Sadler St. BD12: B'frd 3C 132
Sadlers Wlk. LS22: Weth 3F 13
Sadler Way LS16: Leeds 3C 58
Saffron Dr. BD15: B'frd 2D 88
Sage St. BD5: B'frd 1C 110
Sahara Ct. BD8: B'frd 1D 90
St Abbs Cl. BD6: B'frd 6C 110
St Abbs Dr. BD6: B'frd 6C 110
St Abbs Fold BD6: B'frd 6C 110
St Abbs Ga. BD6: B'frd 6C 110
St Abbs Wlk. BD6: B'frd 6C 110
St Abbs Way BD6: B'frd 6C 110
St Aidans Rd. BD17: Bail 5D 52
LS26: Kip 5E 123
St Aidans Sq. *BD16: Bgly* *1A 50*
(off Micklethwaite La.)
St Alban App. LS9: Leeds 2G 99
St Alban Cl. LS9: Leeds 2G 99
St Alban Cres. LS9: Leeds 2G 99
St Alban Gro. LS9: Leeds 2G 99
St Alban Mt. LS9: Leeds 2G 99
St Alban Rd. LS9: Leeds 2G 99
St Albans Av. HX3: Hal 6G 149
(not continuous)
St Albans Cft. HX3: Hal 5H 149
St Alban's Pl. LS2: Leeds 2A 98 (2F 5)
St Albans Rd. HX3: Hal 6G 149

St Alban Vw. LS9: Leeds 2G 99
St Andrews Av. LS27: Morl 4G 137
St Andrews Cl. HX2: Hal 2E 129
LS13: Leeds 4A 74
LS19: Yead 5G 41
LS27: Morl 4G 137
St Andrews Ct. *LS3: Leeds* *3F 97*
(off Cavendish St.)
LS19: Yead *5G 41*
(off St Andrew's Rd.)
HD6: Brigh *5A 152*
(off Mary St.)
St Andrews Cres. BD12: B'frd 3G 133
St Andrew's Cft. LS17: Leeds 3H 59
St Andrews Dr. LS17: Leeds 3A 60
HD6: Brigh 5A 152
St Andrews Gro. LS27: Morl 4H 137
St Andrews Pl. BD7: B'frd 5C 90
LS3: Leeds 3F 97
St Andrew's Rd. LS19: Yead 5G 41
St Andrew's Sq. *BD16: Bgly* *1A 50*
(off Micklethwaite La.)
St Andrew's St. LS3: Leeds 3F 97
St Andrews Ter. LS27: Morl 5H 137
St Andrew's Vs. BD7: B'frd 4C 90
St Andrew's Wlk. LS17: Leeds 3A 60
St Anne's Dr. LS4: Leeds 5C 76
St Anne's Rd. HX3: Hal 1G 159
LS6: Leeds 4C 76
St Anne's Roman Catholic Cathedral
. . . . .3H 97 (3D 4)
St Anne's St. LS2: Leeds 3H 97 (3D 4)
St Annes Ter. BD17: Bail 5D 52
St Ann's Cl. LS4: Leeds 6C 76
St Ann's Gdns. LS4: Leeds 6C 76
St Ann's Grn. LS4: Leeds 5C 76
St Ann's La. LS4: Leeds 5C 76
St Ann's Mt. LS4: Leeds 6D 76
St Ann's Pl. *HX1: Hal* *1E 149*
(off Pellon La.)
St Ann's Ri. LS4: Leeds 6B 76
St Anns Sq. LS4: Leeds 6C 76
LS9: Leeds 3C 98
(off Shannon St.)
St Ann's Way LS4: Leeds 6C 76
St Anthony's Dr. LS11: Leeds 3F 117
St Anthonys Gdns. *BD18: Ship* *3D 70*
(off Snowden Rd.)
St Anthony's Rd. LS11: Leeds 3E 117
St Anthony's Ter. LS11: Leeds 4E 117
St Armands Ct. LS25: Gar 4F 103
St Augustines Ct. *LS8: Leeds* *6D 78*
(off Harehills Pl.)
St Augustine's Ter.
BD3: B'frd 2G 91 (1G 7)
HX1: Hal 2E 149
St Barnabas Rd. LS11: Leeds 5H 97
St Bartholomews Cl.
LS12: Leeds 4C 96
St Benedicts Chase LS13: Leeds 4F 75
St Benedicts Dr. LS13: Leeds 4G 75
St Benedicts Gdns. LS13: Leeds 4G 75
St Bevan's Rd. HX3: Hal 6G 149
St Blaise Ct. BD5: B'frd 6E 91 (6D 6)
St Blaise Sq. BD1: B'frd 4E 91 (3D 6)
St Blaise Way BD1: B'frd 4E 91 (3D 6)
St Catherines Cres. LS13: Leeds 5F 75
St Catherine's Dr. LS13: Leeds 5F 75
St Catherines Grn. LS13: Leeds 5F 75
St Catherine's Hill LS13: Leeds 5F 75
St Catherines Wlk. LS8: Leeds 3E 79
St Chad's Av. HD6: Brigh 4G 151
LS6: Leeds 3C 76
St Chad's Dr. LS6: Leeds 3C 76
St Chad's Gro. LS6: Leeds 3C 76
St Chads Pde. LS16: Leeds 3D 76
St Chad's Ri. LS6: Leeds 3C 76
St Chads Rd. BD8: B'frd 2B 90
LS16: Leeds 3D 76
St Chad's Vw. LS6: Leeds 4C 76

St Christopher's Av.—St Matthias St.

St Christopher's Av.
LS26: Rothw 2B 142
St Christophers Dr. LS29: Add 1D 8
St Clair Rd. LS21: Otley 3F 23
(not continuous)
St Clair St. LS21: Otley 3F 23
St Clair Ter. LS21: Otley 3F 23
(off St Clair Rd.)
St Clare's Av. BD2: B'frd 1B 92
St Clements Av. LS26: Rothw 3A 142
St Clements Cl. LS26: Rothw 3H 141
St Clements Ri. LS26: Rothw 2H 141
St Cyprian's Gdns. LS9: Leeds 1F 99
St Davids Cl. WF3: Rothw 5F 141
St Davids Ct. HX3: Hal 6F 129
St Davids Gth. WF3: Rothw 5F 141
St Davids Rd. LS21: Otley 1C 22
WF3: Rothw 5F 141
St Edmunds Ct. LS8: Leeds 5E 61
St Edward's Ter. LS23: B Spa 6B 30
(off High St.)
St Elmo BD13: B'frd 6G 107
St Elmo Gro. LS9: Leeds 3E 99
St Eloi Av. BD17: Bail 3C 52
St Enoch's Rd. BD6: B'frd 4B 110
St Francis Gdns. HD2: Hud 6A 162
St Francis Pl. LS11: Leeds 5H 97
St George's Av. LS26: Rothw 6G 119
St George's Concert Hall 5E 7
St Georges Cres. LS26: Rothw 6G 119
HX3: Hal 6F 129
St George's Pl. BD4: B'frd 1H 111
BD5: B'frd 6E 91
St Georges Rd. HX3: Hal 6E 129
LS1: Leeds 2H 97 (2C 4)
LS10: Leeds 2B 140
St George's Sq. HX3: Hal 6F 129
St George's St. BD3: B'frd 5H 91 (5H 7)
St George's Ter. HX3: Hal 6F 129
St Giles Cl. HD6: Brigh 4G 151
St Giles Ct. HX3: Hal 2G 151
St Giles Gth. LS16: B'hpe 2G 43
St Giles Rd. HD6: Brigh 3G 151
HX3: Hal 2G 151
St Helena BD13: B'frd 2C 86
St Helena Rd. BD6: B'frd 4B 110
St Helenas Cvn. Pk.
LS18: H'fth 4E 43
St Helens Av. LS16: Leeds 4D 58
St Helens Cl. LS16: Leeds 4D 58
(not continuous)
St Helens Cft. LS16: Leeds 4C 58
St Helen's Dr. LS25: M'fld 3D 104
St Helens Gdns. LS16: Leeds 4C 58
St Helens Gro. LS16: Leeds 4C 58
St Helens La. LS16: Leeds 4B 58
St Helens M. LS24: Tad 5H 31
St Helen's St. LS10: Leeds 6B 98
St Helens Way LS29: I'ly 5F 11
LS16: Leeds 4D 58
St Helier Gro. BD17: Bail 3D 52
St Hilda's Av. LS9: Leeds 5D 98
St Hilda's Cres. LS9: Leeds 5D 98
St Hilda's Gro. LS9: Leeds 5D 98
St Hilda's Mt. LS9: Leeds 5D 98
St Hilda's Pl. LS9: Leeds 5D 98
St Hilda's Rd. LS9: Leeds 5D 98
St Hilda's Ter. BD3: B'frd 3C 92
St Ians Cft. LS29: Add 2D 8
St Ives Est. BD16: Bgly 5G 49
St Ives Gdns. HX3: Hal 6G 149
St Ives Gro. BD16: Bgly 5G 49
LS12: Leeds 3A 96
St Ives Mt. LS12: Leeds 3A 96
St Ives Pl. BD16: Bgly 5G 49
St Ives Rd. BD16: Bgly 4H 49
(Cross Gates La.)
BD16: Bgly 5G 49
(St Ives Pl.)
HX3: Hal 6G 149
St James App. LS14: Leeds 5C 80
St James Av. LS18: H'fth 6E 57
St James Bus. Pk.
BD1: B'frd 5G 91 (5G 7)
St James Cl. LS12: Leeds 3H 95
St James Ct. HD6: Brigh 6B 152
HX1: Hal 3B 164
St James Cres. LS28: Pud 4F 93
St James Dr. LS18: H'fth 6F 57
St James M. LS12: Leeds 3H 95
LS15: Leeds 6F 81
St James Pl. BD17: Bail 3F 53
(off Otley Rd.)
St James Rd. BD17: Bail 3F 53
HX1: Hal 2G 149 (3B 164)
LS29: I'ly 6C 10
St James's Ct. LS9: Leeds 1C 98
St James's Mkt.
BD4: B'frd 5G 91 (6G 7)
St James Sq. HX3: Hal 5C 130
St James's Sq. BD5: B'frd 6E 91
St James's St. LS22: Weth 4E 13
St James St. HX1: Hal 2G 149 (3B 164)
St James Ter. LS18: H'fth 6F 57
St James Wlk. LS18: H'fth 6F 57
St Johns LS29: I'ly 6C 10
St Johns Av. LS6: Leeds 1F 97
LS14: T'ner 2H 63
LS28: Pud 1H 93
LS29: Add 1D 8
St John's Cen. LS2: Leeds 3A 98 (3E 5)
St John's Cl. LS6: Leeds 1F 97
St John's Ct. BD17: Bail 5E 53
BD20: Keigh 3G 33
(off St John's Rd.)
LS7: Leeds 5B 78
LS14: T'ner 2H 63
LS19: Yead 1E 55
St Johns Cres. BD8: B'frd 3G 89
St John's Cross HX2: Hal 5E 107
St John's Dr. LS19: Yead 1E 55
St John's Gro. LS6: Leeds 1F 97
St John's La. HX1: Hal 3G 149 (6B 164)
St Johns M. BD13: B'frd 3B 66
(off Station Rd.)
St John's Pk. LS29: Men 6F 21
St John's Pl. BD11: B'frd 1E 135
LS5: Leeds 5B 76
St John's Rd. BD20: Keigh 3G 33
LS3: Leeds 2F 97 (2A 4)
LS19: Yead 1E 55
LS23: B Spa 4B 30
LS29: I'ly 5G 11
St John's St. BD20: Sils 2E 15
LS26: Rothw 2E 143
St John's Ter. LS3: Leeds 1F 97
St John St. HD6: Brigh 2A 162
St John's Vw. LS23: B Spa 4A 30
St Johns Way LS19: Yead 1E 55
BD22: Keigh 1F 47
St John's Yd. LS26: Rothw 2E 143
St Josephs Ct. LS19: Yead 5F 55
LS25: Gar 4E 103
St Jude's Pl. BD1: B'frd 3D 90 (1B 6)
St Jude's St. BD8: B'frd 3D 90 (1A 6)
HX1: Hal 4F 149
St Laurence's Cl. BD2: B'frd 4D 70
St Lawrence Cl. LS28: Pud 4H 93
St Lawrence St. LS7: Leeds 3B 78
St Lawrence Ter. LS28: Pud 4A 94
St Leonards Cl. LS29: Add 2D 8
St Leonards Ct. BD8: B'frd 2H 89
St Leonard's Gro. BD8: B'frd 2H 89
St Leonard's Rd. BD8: B'frd 2H 89
St Lukes Cl. BD19: Cleck 2H 153
LS23: B Spa 6B 30
BD5: B'frd 6D 90
St Luke's Cres. LS11: Leeds 1G 117
St Luke's Grn. LS11: Leeds 1G 117
St Luke's Rd. LS11: Leeds 1G 117
St Luke's St. LS11: Leeds 1G 117
St Luke's Ter. BD19: Cleck 2H 153
BD20: Keigh 5H 35
St Luke's Vw. LS11: Leeds 1G 117
St Margaret's Av. BD4: B'frd 3B 112
LS8: Leeds 3E 79
LS18: H'fth 6D 56
LS26: Mick 4D 144
St Margaret's Cl. LS18: H'fth 5D 56
St Margaret's Dr. LS8: Leeds 3E 79
LS18: H'fth 5D 56
St Margaret's Gro. LS8: Leeds 3E 79
St Margaret's Pl. BD7: B'frd 6B 90
St Margaret's Rd. BD7: B'frd 5B 90
LS18: H'fth 5D 56
LS26: Mick 4D 144
St Margaret's Ter. BD7: B'frd 6B 90
LS29: I'ly 6D 10
St Margaret's Vw. LS8: Leeds 3E 79
St Mark's Av. BD12: B'frd 2C 132
LS2: Leeds 1G 97
St Mark's Flats LS2: Leeds 6G 77
(off Low Cl. St.)
St Mark's Pl. BD12: B'frd 2C 132
St Mark's Rd. LS2: Leeds 1H 97
LS6: Leeds 6G 77
(not continuous)
St Mark's St. LS2: Leeds 1G 97
St Mark's Ter. BD12: B'frd 2C 132
St Martins Av. LS7: Leeds 4A 78
LS21: Otley 1D 22
BD7: B'frd 4C 90
St Martins Ct. WF3: Rothw 5F 141
St Martin's Cres. LS7: Leeds 4B 78
St Martin's Dr. LS7: Leeds 3B 78
St Martins Fold WF3: Rothw 5F 141
St Martin's Gdns. LS7: Leeds 4A 78
St Martin's Gro. LS7: Leeds 4B 78
St Martin's Rd. LS7: Leeds 4B 78
St Martin's Ter. LS7: Leeds 4B 78
St Martin's Vw. HD6: Brigh 6A 152
LS7: Leeds 4B 78
St Mary Magdalenes Cl.
BD8: B'frd 3D 90 (1A 6)
St Mary's Av. BD12: B'frd 5C 132
LS26: Swil 4A 122
St Marys Cl. BD12: B'frd 5B 132
LS7: Leeds 4B 78
LS12: Leeds 5D 96
LS25: Gar 5F 103
WF3: E Ard 2C 154
LS29: I'ly 5E 11
St Mary's Ct. HX2: Hal 2B 128
LS7: Leeds 4B 78
WF10: Kip 3H 145
St Mary's Cres. BD12: B'frd 6B 132
St Mary's Dr. BD12: B'frd 5C 132
St Mary's Gdns. BD12: B'frd 5C 132
St Mary's Gth. LS17: Bard 6D 26
St Mary's Ga. HX5: Ell 4B 160
St Mary's Hgts. HX2: Hal 2B 128
St Mary's Mt. BD12: B'frd 5B 132
St Mary's Pk. App. LS12: Leeds 3H 95
St Mary's Pk. Ct. LS12: Leeds 3H 95
St Mary's Pk. Cres. LS12: Leeds 3H 95
St Mary's Pk. Grn. LS12: Leeds 3H 95
St Mary's Rd. BD4: B'frd 6B 92
BD9: B'frd 1C 90
BD20: Keigh 3D 34
LS7: Leeds 4B 78
St Mary's Sq. BD12: B'frd 5C 132
LS27: Morl 3A 138
St Mary's St. LS9: Leeds 3B 98 (3H 5)
LS23: B Spa 3B 30
St Mary St. HX1: Hal 3F 149 (5A 164)
St Mary's Wlk. LS25: M'fld 4D 104
St Matthews Cl. BD15: B'frd 5F 67
St Matthew's Dr. HX3: Hal 4C 130
St Matthews Gro. BD15: B'frd 5G 67
St Matthews Rd. BD5: B'frd 4D 110
St Matthew's St. LS11: Leeds 6G 97
St Matthews Wlk. LS7: Leeds 1A 78
St Matthias Ct. LS4: Leeds 1D 96
St Matthias Gro. LS4: Leeds 1D 96
St Matthias St. LS4: Leeds 2D 96
(not continuous)

St Matthias Ter.—Sandringham Cl.

St Matthias Ter. LS4: Leeds 1D **96**
St Michael Ct. LS13: Leeds 6E **75**
St Michaels Cl. BD16: Bgly 3D **68**
St Michael's Ct. LS6: Leeds 4D **76**
St Michael's Cres. LS6: Leeds 5D **76**
St Michael's Gro. LS6: Leeds 5D **76**
St Michael's La. LS4: Leeds 6C **76**
LS6: Leeds 5D **76**
St Michael's Rd. BD8: B'frd 3C **90**
LS6: Leeds 5D **76**
St Michael's Ter. LS6: Leeds 5D **76**
St Michael's Vs. *LS6: Leeds 5D* ***76***
(off St Michael's Cres.)
St Michaels Way LS29: Burl W 3F **21**
LS29: Add 1D **8**
St Nicholas Rd. LS29: I'ly 4C **10**
St Oswald's Gth. LS20: Guis 4D **40**
St Oswald's Ter. LS20: Guis 4C **40**
St Paul's Av. BD6: B'frd 5B **110**
BD11: B'frd 2F **135**
St Paul's Bldgs *HX5: Ell 5B* ***160***
(off Langdale St.)
St Paul's Cl. *BD8: B'frd 2C* ***90***
(off Church St.)
St Paul's Gro. BD6: B'frd 5B **110**
LS29: I'ly 5F **11**
St Paul's Pl. LS1: Leeds 3H **97** (4C **4**)
St Pauls Ri. LS29: Add 2D **8**
St Paul's Rd. BD6: B'frd 5B **110**
BD8: B'frd 1C **90**
(not continuous)
BD11: B'frd 2F **135**
BD18: Ship 2A **70**
BD21: Keigh 1B **48**
HX1: Hal 4D **148**
St Paul's St. LS1: Leeds 3G **97** (4B **4**)
LS27: Morl 4B **138**
St Peter's Av. HX6: Hal 6E **147**
LS26: Rothw 2B **142**
St Peter's Bldgs.
LS9: Leeds 4B **98** (5H **5**)
St Peters Cl. LS21: Otley 3F **23**
WF17: Bat 6H **135**
St Peters Ct. LS11: Leeds 1A **118**
LS13: Leeds 6F **75**
LS29: Add 2D **8**
St Peter's Cres. LS27: Morl 1A **138**
St Peter's Gdns. LS13: Leeds 6E **75**
St Peter's Gth. LS14: T'ner 1H **63**
St Peter's Mt. LS13: Leeds 1F **95**
St Peter's Pl. LS9: Leeds 3B **98** (4H **5**)
St Peters Sq. LS2: Leeds 3B **98** (4H **5**)
HX6: Hal 6E **147**
St Peter's St. LS2: Leeds 3B **98** (4G **5**)
St Peter's Way LS29: Men 1F **39**
St Philip's Av. LS10: Leeds 2H **139**
St Philip's Cl. LS10: Leeds 2H **139**
LS29: Burl W 3F **21**
St Philip's Dr. LS29: Burl W 3F **21**
St Philip's Way LS29: Burl W 2F **21**
St Phillips Ct. *BD8: B'frd 2A* ***90***
(off Thorn St.)
St Richard's Rd. LS21: Otley 1C **22**
St Stephen's Ct. BD20: Stee 5C **14**
HX3: Hal 1E **159**
LS9: Leeds 3D **98**
St Stephen's Rd. BD5: B'frd 2D **110**
BD20: Stee 6C **14**
LS9: Leeds 3D **98**
LS28: Pud 2E **73**
St Stephen's St. HX3: Hal 1E **159**
St Stephen's Ter. BD5: B'frd 2E **111**
HX3: Hal 1F **159**
Saint St. BD7: B'frd 1A **110**
St Thomas Gdns. HD2: Hud 5F **163**
St Thomas Row LS2: Leeds . . .2B **98** (2G **5**)
St Thomas's Rd. BD1: B'frd . . .4D **90** (3B **6**)
St Vincent Rd. LS28: Pud 5A **94**
St Wilfrid's Av. LS8: Leeds 5E **79**
(not continuous)
St Wilfrid's Cir. LS8: Leeds 6F **79**
St Wilfrid's Cl. BD7: B'frd 6H **89**
St Wilfrid's Cres. BD7: B'frd 6H **89**
LS8: Leeds 5F **79**
St Wilfrid's Dr. LS8: Leeds 5E **79**
St Wilfrid's Gth. LS8: Leeds 6F **79**
St Wilfrid's Gro. LS8: Leeds 5E **79**
St Wilfrid's Rd. BD7: B'frd 6H **89**
St Wilfrid's St. LS28: Pud 2F **73**
St Wilfrids Ter. *LS21: Pool 4E* ***25***
(off Main St.)
St Winifred's Cl. HX2: Hal 2B **128**
Salcombe Pl. BD4: B'frd 3C **112**
Salem Pl. LS10: Leeds 5A **98** (6F **5**)
LS25: Gar 4E **103**
Salem St. BD1: B'frd 3E **91** (2C **6**)
BD13: B'frd 4H **107**
Salisbury Av. BD17: Bail 4C **52**
LS12: Leeds 3C **96**
Salisbury Ct. LS18: H'fth 6F **57**
Salisbury Gro. LS12: Leeds 3C **96**
Salisbury M. LS18: H'fth 6F **57**
WF3: E Ard 6D **138**
Salisbury Pl. HX3: Hal 6F **129**
LS28: Pud 3E **73**
Salisbury Rd. BD9: B'frd 4C **70**
BD12: B'frd 1C **132**
BD19: Cleck 1F **153**
BD22: Keigh 1G **47**
LS12: Leeds 3C **96**
Salisbury St. HX6: Hal 6G **147**
LS19: Yead 3F **55**
LS28: Pud 3E **73**
Salisbury Ter. HX3: Hal 6F **129**
LS12: Leeds 3C **96**
Salisbury Vw. LS12: Leeds 3C **96**
LS18: H'fth 6F **57**
Salmon Cres. LS18: H'fth 6E **57**
Sal Nook Cl. BD12: B'frd 6D **110**
Sal Royd Rd. BD12: B'frd 2E **133**
SALTAIRE **1H 69**
Saltaire BD22: Haw 1F **65**
Saltaire Rd. BD16: Bgly 2F **51**
BD18: Ship 1H **69**
Saltaire Station (Rail) **6H 51**
Saltburn Pl. BD9: B'frd 1H **89**
Saltburn St. HX1: Hal 2D **148**
SALTERHEBBLE **6H 149**
Salterhebble Hill HX3: Hal 1H **159**
Salterhebble Ter. *HX3: Hal 6H* ***149***
(off Huddersfield Rd.)
Salterlee HX3: Hal 5A **130**
Salters Gdn. *LS28: Pud 4A* ***94***
(off Crawshaw Rd.)
Salt Horn Cl. BD12: B'frd 2F **133**
Saltonstall La. HX2: Hal 2D **126**
Salts Mill BD18: Ship 6A **52**
Salts Mill Rd. BD18: Ship 1A **70**
Salt St. BD8: B'frd 2C **90**
HX1: Hal 1E **149**
Samuel St. BD21: Keigh 6H **33**
Sandacre Cl. BD10: B'frd 6C **72**
Sandale Wlk. BD6: B'frd 6H **109**
Sandall Cl. LS25: Kip 3H **123**
Sandal Magna HX3: B'frd 6G **109**
Sandals Rd. BD17: Bail 4C **52**
Sandal Ter. HX6: Hal 6A **148**
Sandal Way WF17: Bat 6B **136**
Sandbeck Ct. LS22: Weth 2F **13**
Sandbeck Ind. Est. LS22: Weth 2F **13**
Sandbeck La. LS22: Weth 2F **13**
(not continuous)
Sandbeck Pk. LS22: Weth 2F **13**
Sandbeck Way LS22: Weth 2F **13**
Sandbed Ct. LS15: Leeds 6F **81**
Sandbed La. LS15: Leeds 6F **81**
Sandbed Lawns LS15: Leeds 6F **81**
Sand Beds BD13: B'frd 4A **108**
Sandbeds Cres. HX2: Hal 6C **128**
Sandbeds Rd. HX2: Hal 1B **148**
Sandbeds Ter. HX2: Hal 6C **128**
Sanderling Ct. BD8: B'frd 4E **89**
Sanderling Gth. LS10: Leeds 2B **140**
Sanderling Way LS10: Leeds 2B **140**
Sanderson Av. BD6: B'frd 4C **110**
Sanderson La. LS26: Rothw 5C **142**
Sandfield Av. LS6: Leeds 3E **77**
Sandfield Gth. LS6: Leeds 3E **77**
Sandfield Rd. BD10: B'frd 3H **71**
Sandfield Vw. *LS6: Leeds 3E* ***77***
(off Sandfield Av.)
SANDFORD **5G 75**
Sandford Pl. LS5: Leeds 5A **76**
Sandford Rd. BD3: B'frd 4A **92**
(not continuous)
LS5: Leeds 6B **76**
Sandforth Av. HX3: Hal 5G **129**
Sandgate Dr. LS25: Kip 2H **123**
Sandgate La. LS25: Kip 4A **124**
(not continuous)
Sandgate Ri. LS25: Kip 3A **124**
Sandgate Ter. LS25: Kip 4A **124**
Sandgate Wlk. BD4: B'frd 3D **112**
Sandhall Av. HX2: Hal 2B **148**
Sandhall Cres. *HX2: Hal 1B* ***148***
(off Sandhall Grn.)
Sandhall Dr. HX2: Hal 2B **148**
Sandhall Grn. HX2: Hal 2B **148**
(not continuous)
Sandhall La. HX2: Hal 2B **148**
Sandhill Ct. LS17: Leeds 4B **60**
Sandhill Cres. LS17: Leeds 3C **60**
Sandhill Dr. LS17: Leeds 3B **60**
Sandhill Fold BD10: B'frd 2G **71**
Sandhill Gro. LS17: Leeds 2C **60**
Sand Hill La. LS17: Leeds 4B **60**
Sandhill Lawns LS17: Leeds 4B **60**
Sandhill Mt. BD10: B'frd 3H **71**
LS17: Leeds 2C **60**
Sandhill Oval LS17: Leeds 2C **60**
SANDHILLS **4G 63**
Sandhill Vs. LS14: T'ner 4G **63**
Sandholme Cres. HX3: Hal 2F **151**
Sandholme Dr. BD10: B'frd 3H **71**
LS29: Burl W 3F **21**
Sandholme Fold HX3: Hal 2F **151**
Sandhurst Av. LS8: Leeds 6E **79**
Sandhurst Gro. LS8: Leeds 6E **79**
Sandhurst Mt. LS8: Leeds 5E **79**
Sandhurst Pl. LS8: Leeds 6E **79**
Sandhurst Rd. LS8: Leeds 6E **79**
Sandhurst St. LS28: Pud 2E **73**
Sandhurst Ter. LS8: Leeds 6E **79**
Sandiford Cl. LS15: Leeds 6F **81**
Sandiford Ter. LS15: Leeds 6F **81**
Sandleas Way LS15: Leeds 1H **101**
Sandlewood Cl. LS11: Leeds 6G **97**
Sandlewood Ct. LS6: Leeds 6F **59**
Sandlewood Cres. LS6: Leeds 6F **59**
Sandlewood Grn. LS11: Leeds 6H **97**
Sandmead Cl. BD4: B'frd 2C **112**
LS27: Morl 1A **138**
Sandmead Cft. LS27: Morl 1A **138**
Sandmead Way LS27: Morl 1A **138**
Sandmoor Av. LS17: Leeds 1B **60**
Sandmoor Chase LS17: Leeds 2B **60**
Sandmoor Cl. BD13: B'frd 5A **88**
LS17: Leeds 2B **60**
Sandmoor Ct. LS17: Leeds 2B **60**
Sandmoor Dr. LS17: Leeds 1B **60**
Sandmoor Gdns. HX3: Hal 2D **130**
Sandmoor Gth. BD10: B'frd 6H **53**
Sandmoor Grn. LS17: Leeds 1A **60**
Sandmoor La. LS17: Leeds 1B **60**
Sandmoor M. LS17: Leeds 2B **60**
Sandon Gro. LS10: Leeds 3C **118**
Sandon Mt. LS10: Leeds 3C **118**
Sandon Pl. LS10: Leeds 3C **118**
Sandown Av. HX2: Hal 3C **128**
Sandown Rd. HX2: Hal 3C **128**
Sandpiper App. LS27: Morl 4C **138**
Sandpiper M. BD8: B'frd 4E **89**
Sandringham App. LS17: Leeds 4C **60**
Sandringham Av. LS28: Pud 5A **94**
Sandringham Cl. BD14: B'frd 6F **89**
LS27: Morl 2C **138**

A-Z Leeds & Bradford 265

Sandringham Ct. BD14: B'frd 6F 89
  HD2: Hud 6D 162
Sandringham Cres. LS17: Leeds 4B 60
Sandringham Dr. LS17: Leeds 4B 60
Sandringham Fold LS27: Morl 2C 138
Sandringham Grn. LS17: Leeds 3C 60
Sandringham Gdns. LS17: Leeds 4B 60
Sandringham Mt. LS17: Leeds 4C 60
Sandringham Rd. BD14: B'frd 6F 89
  LS22: Weth 3E 13
Sandringham Way LS17: Leeds 4B 60
Sandsend Cl. BD9: B'frd 6F 69
Sandside Cl. BD5: B'frd 3F 111
Sandstone Dr. LS12: Leeds 4E 95
Sand St. BD21: Keigh 6A 34
  BD22: Haw 3C 64
Sandway LS15: Leeds 1D 100
Sandway Gdns. LS15: Leeds 1D 100
Sandway Gro. LS15: Leeds 1D 100
Sandyacres LS26: Rothw 1B 142
Sandyacres Cres. LS26: Rothw 1B 142
Sandyacres Dr. LS26: Rothw 1B 142
Sandy Bank Av. LS26: Rothw 1B 142
Sandy Banks BD16: Bgly 1F 67
Sandy Beck BD15: B'frd 6C 68
Sandyfoot HX4: Hal 6A 158
Sandy Fore HX2: Hal 3F 127
Sandy Ga. BD20: Keigh 5G 33
Sandygate Ter. BD4: B'frd 6B 92
Sandy Gro. LS26: Rothw 1B 142
SANDY LANE 5C 68
Sandy Lobby LS21: Pool 5E 25
Sandymoor BD15: B'frd 5C 68
Sandy Wlk. LS16: B'hpe 3H 43
Sandy Way LS19: Yead 6F 41
Sandywood Ct. LS18: H'fth 2E 75
Sandywood St. BD21: Keigh 5A 34
Sangster Way BD5: B'frd 4G 111
Santa Monica Cres.
  BD10: B'frd 2G 71
Santa Monica Gro. BD10: B'frd 2G 71
Santa Monica Rd. BD10: B'frd 2G 71
Santon Ho. BD5: B'frd 1E 111
  (off Manchester Rd.)
Sapgate La. BD13: B'frd 5A 88
Sapling Gro. Cotts. HX2: Hal 5D 148
Saplin St. BD8: B'frd 2B 90
Sarah St. WF3: E Ard 1B 156
Sardinia St. LS10: Leeds 6B 98
Savannah Way LS26: Leeds 5F 119
Savile Av. BD10: B'frd 3A 72
  LS7: Leeds 6B 78
Savile Cl. HD6: Brigh 6D 152
Savile Cres. HX1: Hal 3F 149 (6A 164)
Savile Dr. HX1: Hal 4F 149 (6A 164)
  LS7: Leeds 5B 78
Savile Glen HX1: Hal 3F 149 (6A 164)
Savile Grn. HX1: Hal 3G 149 (6B 164)
Savile La. HD6: Brigh 6D 152
Savile Lea HX1: Hal 3F 149 (6A 164)
Savile M. HX1: Hal 4F 149 (6A 164)
Savile Mt. HX1: Hal 4F 149 (6A 164)
  LS7: Leeds 6B 78
Savile Pde. HX1: Hal 4F 149
SAVILE PARK 4E 149
Savile Pk. HX1: Hal 4E 149
  HX3: Hal 5F 149
Savile Pk. Gdns. HX1: Hal 4F 149
Savile Pk. Mills HX1: Hal 4E 149
  (off Moorfield St.)
Savile Pk. Rd. BD19: Cleck 4B 134
  HX1: Hal 4F 149 (6A 164)
Savile Pk. St. HX1: Hal 4E 149
Savile Pk. Ter. HX1: Hal 4E 149
  (off Moorfield St.)
Savile Pl. LS7: Leeds 6B 78
Savile Rd. HX1: Hal 3F 149 (6A 164)
  HX5: Ell 5B 160
  LS7: Leeds 6B 78
  LS26: Mick 4D 144
Savile Row HX1: Hal 3F 149 (6A 164)
Savile Royd HX1: Hal 4F 149 (6A 164)

Savile St. BD19: Cleck 6B 134
Savile Ter. HX1: Hal 4E 149
  (off Savile Pk. Rd.)
Savile Way HX5: Ell 3C 160
Saville Cl. WF3: Rothw 6G 141
Saville Ct. LS21: Otley 4D 22
Saville Grn. LS9: Leeds 3D 98
Saville Pk. HX1: Hal 4D 148
Saville's Sq. LS27: Morl 3A 138
  (off Queen St.)
Savins Mill Way LS5: Leeds 5A 76
Sawley St. BD21: Keigh 1H 47
Saw Mill La. LS29: Add 1E 9
Saw Mill Rd. BD20: Keigh 4F 35
Saw Mill Yd. LS11: Leeds 5H 97
SAWOOD 2F 85
Sawood La. BD22: Oxen 2F 85
Sawrey Pl. BD5: B'frd 5D 90 (6B 6)
Sawyers Gth. LS29: Add 1F 9
Saxilby Rd. BD20: Keigh 4F 35
Saxon Cl. BD12: B'frd 4B 132
  LS17: Leeds 4H 59
Saxon Ga. LS17: Leeds 5H 59
Saxon Grn. LS17: Leeds 5G 59
Saxon Gro. LS17: Leeds 4G 59
Saxon Mt. LS17: Leeds 4H 59
Saxon Rd. LS17: Leeds 5G 59
Saxon St. BD8: B'frd 3C 90
  HX1: Hal 2D 148
Saxstead Ri. LS12: Leeds 5C 96
Saxton Av. BD6: B'frd 4G 109
Saxton Ct. LS25: Gar 3F 103
Saxton Gdns. LS9: Leeds 4C 98
  (off Drive, The)
Saxton Ho. LS19: Yead 1F 55
Saxton La. LS9: Leeds 4C 98 (5H 5)
Sayers Cl. LS5: Leeds 5B 76
Sayle Av. BD4: B'frd 4H 111
Sayner La. LS10: Leeds 5B 98
Sayner Rd. LS10: Leeds 5B 98
Scala Ct. LS10: Leeds 6B 98
Scalebor Pk. Cl. LS29: Burl W 3E 21
Scalebor Sq. LS29: Burl W 3D 20
Scales La. BD4: B'frd 6A 112
Scaley St. BD3: B'frd 4B 92
Scandinavia Ter. BD19: Cleck 6B 134
Scarborough Gro. BD18: Ship 2A 70
Scarborough Junc. LS13: Leeds 2E 95
Scarborough La. WF3: E Ard 6D 138
Scarborough Rd. BD18: Ship 2A 70
  LS21: Otley 4D 22
Scarborough St. WF3: E Ard 6D 138
Scarborough Ter. HX5: Ell 5B 160
SCAR BOTTOM 5D 148
Scar Bottom La. HX4: Hal 4D 158
SCARCROFT 5E 45
Scarcroft Ct. LS14: S'cft 5F 45
SCARCROFT HILL 6G 45
Scarcroft Ho. BD5: B'frd 4F 111
  (off Parkway)
Scarcroft Vw. LS17: S'cft 1B 62
Scargill Bldgs. LS27: Morl 3D 138
Scargill Cl. LS9: Leeds 2D 98
Scargill Grange LS9: Leeds 3D 98
Scargill Ho. BD3: B'frd 2G 7
Scar Head Rd. HX6: Hal 6H 147
SCARLET HEIGHTS 4B 108
Scarlet Hgts. BD13: B'frd 4B 108
Scarr Bottom Rd HX2: Hal 5D 148
Scarsdale La. LS17: Bard 5G 27
Scarsdale Ridge LS17: Bard 5G 27
Scarth Av. LS9: Leeds 1E 99
Scarwood Cl. BD16: Bgly 3C 50
Scatchard La. LS27: Morl 4H 137
Scatcherd Pk. Av. LS27: Morl 2A 138
Scatcherd's Bldgs. LS27: Morl 1B 138
Schofield St. LS27: Morl 3A 138
  (off Queensway)
Scholars Wlk. BD2: B'frd 6H 71
SCHOLEBROOK 2G 113
Scholebrook Ct. BD4: B'frd 4C 112
  (off Broadfield Cl.)
Scholebrook La. BD4: B'frd 2G 113

SCHOLEMOOR 6H 89
Scholemoor Av. BD7: B'frd 6G 89
Scholemoor Crematorium
  BD7: B'frd 5G 89
Scholemoor La. BD7: B'frd 6G 89
Scholemoor Rd. BD7: B'frd 6H 89
SCHOLES
  Cleckheaton 1F 153
  Keighley 6A 46
  Leeds 2H 81
Scholes La. BD19: Cleck 1F 153
  HX4: Hal 2E 159
  LS15: Scho 1G 81
Scholes St. BD5: B'frd 3D 110
Scholey Av. HD6: Brigh 3A 162
SCHOLEY HILL 6A 144
Scholey Rd. HD6: Brigh 3A 162
School Cl. HX2: Hal 6D 106
  LS12: Leeds 2F 115
School Cote Brow HX3: Hal 1F 129
School Cote Ter. HX3: Hal 1F 129
School Cres. HX2: Hal 6D 106
School Cft. LS26: Rothw 1A 142
School Fold BD12: B'frd 1B 132
Schoolgate LS15: Bar E 2E 83
SCHOOL GREEN 5C 88
School Grn. BD13: B'frd 5C 88
  HD6: Brigh 3A 162
  LS16: B'hpe 3G 43
School Grn. Av. BD13: B'frd 5B 88
School Ho. HX3: Hal 4C 130
School Ho. Fold BD20: Keigh 3D 34
School La. BD5: B'frd 3C 110
  BD6: B'frd 4B 110
  BD21: Keigh 6B 34
  HX2: Hal 1D 128
  HX3: Hal 6C 150
  (not continuous)
  LS6: Leeds 3E 77
  LS7: Leeds 3A 78
  LS15: Leeds 5G 101
  (Colton Rd. E.)
  LS15: Leeds 3C 100
  (Pinfold Gro.)
  LS17: Bard 6E 27
  LS22: Coll 3B 28
  LS29: Add 1C 8
School M. LS12: Leeds 4C 96
School Pl. BD12: B'frd 3C 132
School Ridge BD13: B'frd 3G 87
School Rd. BD22: Keigh 6F 33
  LS22: Weth 3F 13
School Sq. BD3: B'frd 4B 92
School St. BD1: B'frd 4E 91 (3D 6)
  (not continuous)
  BD4: B'frd 2A 112
  (Cutler Hgts. La.)
  BD4: B'frd 5H 111
  (Shetcliffe Rd.)
  BD6: B'frd 6G 109
  BD12: B'frd 1C 132
  (Bowler Cl.)
  BD12: B'frd 3G 133
  (Bradford Rd.)
  BD13: B'frd 3B 66
  (Ashdene Ct.)
  BD13: B'frd 3C 86
  (Parkinson Rd.)
  BD14: B'frd 1D 108
  BD15: B'frd 4G 67
  BD16: Bgly 2D 68
  BD19: Cleck 3H 153
  BD20: Keigh 3G 33
  BD20: Stee 6C 14
  HX1: Hal 3H 149 (5D 164)
  HX4: Hal 3F 159
  LS27: Morl 5C 116
  (Old Rd.)
  LS27: Morl 3B 138
  (South Pde.)
  LS28: Pud 6H 73
  (Back La.)

School St. LS28: Pud 5H **93**
  (Greenside, not continuous)
  WF3: E Ard 4D **154**
  WF17: Bat 6B **136**
School Ter. BD19: Cleck 1F **153**
  LS25: Gar 3G **103**
School Vw. LS6: Leeds 6E **77**
School Wlk. BD22: Keigh 6F **33**
School Yd. Vw. HX3: Hal 6G **129**
Sconce La. BD16: Bgly 5A **38**
  BD17: Bgly 5A **38**
Score Hill HX3: Hal 3C **130**
Scoresby St. BD1: B'frd 4F **91** (4F **7**)
Scotchman Cl. LS27: Morl 5H **137**
Scotchman La. LS27: Morl 6G **137**
Scotchman Rd. BD9: B'frd 1H **89**
Scotch Pk. Trad. Est. LS12: Leeds . .3D **96**
SCOTLAND 2D **56**
Scotland HX2: Hal 5C **126**
Scotland Cl. LS18: H'fth 4D **56**
Scotland La. HX2: Hal 5B **126**
  LS18: H'fth 5C **42**
Scotland Mill La. LS6: Leeds 5F **59**
  LS17: Leeds 5F **59**
Scotland St. WF17: Bat 5G **135**
Scotland Way LS18: H'fth 3C **56**
Scotland Wood Rd. LS17: Leeds 5F **59**
Scott Bldgs. LS6: Leeds 3D **76**
  (off Oddy Pl.)
Scott Cl. LS26: Swil 4A **122**
SCOTT GREEN 6D **114**
Scott Grn. LS27: Morl 5D **114**
Scott Grn. Cres. LS27: Morl 5D **114**
Scott Grn. Dr. LS27: Morl 5D **114**
Scott Grn. Gro. LS27: Morl 5E **115**
Scott Grn. Mt. LS27: Morl 5D **114**
Scott Grn. Vw. LS27: Morl 5E **115**
SCOTT HALL 4A **78**
Scott Hall Av. LS7: Leeds 4A **78**
Scott Hall Cres. LS7: Leeds 3H **77**
Scott Hall Dr. LS7: Leeds 5A **78**
Scott Hall Grn. LS7: Leeds 4A **78**
Scott Hall Gro. LS7: Leeds 4A **78**
Scott Hall Pl. LS7: Leeds 4A **78**
Scott Hall Rd. LS7: Leeds 2H **77**
  LS17: Leeds 2H **77**
Scott Hall Row LS7: Leeds 5B **78**
Scott Hall Sports Cen. 3A **78**
Scott Hall Sq. LS7: Leeds 4A **78**
Scott Hall St. LS7: Leeds 5A **78**
Scott Hall Ter. LS7: Leeds 5A **78**
Scott Hall Wlk. LS7: Leeds 5A **78**
Scott Hall Way LS7: Leeds 3A **78**
Scott La. BD19: Cleck 6F **135**
  BD20: Keigh 3C **34**
  LS22: Weth 4E **13**
  LS27: Morl 5F **137**
Scott La. W. BD20: Keigh 3B **34**
Scott M. LS22: Weth 4E **13**
Scotts Almshouse's LS10: Leeds . .4C **118**
Scotts Hill Cl. LS14: T'ner 2H **63**
Scott St. BD21: Keigh 6H **33**
  LS28: Pud 5B **94**
Scott Wood La. LS7: Leeds 4H **77**
  (not continuous)
Scotty Bank HD6: Brigh 1A **162**
  (off Bridge End)
Scotty Cft. La. HD6: Brigh 2A **162**
  (off Bramston St.)
Scout Bottom La. HX7: Heb B 1A **146**
Scout Rd. HX7: Heb B 1A **146**
Scratcherd Gro. LS27: Morl 3H **137**
Scriftain La. LS22: Weth 1E **13**
Sculptor Pl. HD6: Brigh 6A **152**
  (off Waterloo Rd.)
SDH Ind. Pk. HX6: Hal 6H **147**
SEACROFT 4C **80**
Seacroft Av. LS14: Leeds 4D **80**
Seacroft Cres. LS14: Leeds 4D **80**
Seacroft Family Activity Cen. 6C **80**
Seacroft Ga. LS14: Leeds 4D **80**
  (not continuous)

Seacroft Ho. BD10: B'frd 3A **72**
  (off Rowantree Dr.)
Seacroft Ind. Est. LS14: Leeds 1D **80**
  (Coal Rd., not continuous)
  LS14: Leeds 2C **80**
  (Limewood Rd.)
Seaforth Av. LS9: Leeds 6E **79**
Seaforth Gro. LS9: Leeds 6E **79**
Seaforth Mt. LS9: Leeds 6E **79**
Seaforth Pl. LS9: Leeds 6E **79**
Seaforth Rd. LS9: Leeds 6E **79**
Seaforth Ter. LS9: Leeds 6E **79**
Seaton St. BD3: B'frd 4H **91** (4H **7**)
Second Av. BD3: B'frd 2A **92**
  BD21: Keigh 1H **47**
  HX3: Hal 5F **149**
  LS12: Leeds 4E **97**
  LS17: Bard 6G **27**
  LS19: Yead 2G **55**
  LS22: Weth 4F **13**
  LS26: Rothw 6B **120**
  WF1: Wake 6F **157**
  WF15: Liv 5H **153**
Second St. BD12: B'frd 1E **133**
Sedan St. HX1: Hal 5B **164**
Sedbergh Dr. LS29: I'ly 6E **11**
Sedburgh Rd. LS29: I'ly 6D **10**
Sedburgh Chambers LS29: I'ly 6D **10**
  (off Chantry Dr.)
Sedburgh Cl. LS15: Leeds 4H **99**
Sedburgh Rd. HX1: Hal 4H **149**
  HX3: Hal 4H **149**
Sedgegarth LS14: T'ner 1H **63**
Sedge Gro. BD22: Haw 1C **64**
Sedgewick St. WF17: Bat 6A **136**
Sedgfield Ter. BD1: B'frd . . .4D **90** (3A **6**)
Sedgwick Cl. BD8: B'frd . . .3D **90** (2A **6**)
Seed Hill Ter. BD20: Stee 1H **7**
  HX2: Hal 1A **128**
Seed Row BD4: B'frd 5H **111**
Seed St. BD12: B'frd 1D **132**
See Mill La. HX3: Hal 5F **129**
Sefton Av. HD6: Brigh 4H **151**
  LS11: Leeds 2G **117**
Sefton Cres. HD6: Brigh 4H **151**
Sefton Dr. HD6: Brigh 4H **151**
  LS29: I'ly 6D **10**
Sefton Gro. BD2: B'frd 6H **71**
Sefton Pl. BD2: B'frd 6H **71**
  BD21: Keigh 5A **34**
Sefton St. BD21: Keigh 5A **34**
  HX1: Hal 1E **149**
  LS11: Leeds 2H **117**
Sefton Ter. HX1: Hal 1E **149**
  LS11: Leeds 2G **117**
Selborne Gro. BD9: B'frd 6B **70**
  BD21: Keigh 2G **47**
Selborne Mt. BD9: B'frd 1C **90**
Selborne Ter. BD9: B'frd 1B **90**
  BD18: Ship 3B **70**
Selborne Vs. BD9: B'frd 1B **90**
  (off Selborne Gro.)
Selbourne Vs. BD14: B'frd 2E **109**
Selby HX2: Hal 1B **128**
Selby Av. LS9: Leeds 3A **100**
Selby Rd. LS9: Leeds 3A **100**
  LS15: Leeds 4C **100**
  LS25: Gar, Led, Leds, M'fld
  . . . . .6D **102**
  LS25: Led, Leds, M'fld 1C **124**
Seldon St. BD5: B'frd 2B **110**
Selene Cl. BD19: Cleck 5G **135**
SELLARS FOLD 1A **110**
Sellerdale Av. BD12: B'frd 6D **132**
Sellerdale Dr. BD12: B'frd 5D **132**
Sellerdale Ri. BD12: B'frd 5D **132**
Sellerdale Way BD12: B'frd 6D **132**
Sellers Fold BD7: B'frd 1A **110**
Selside Ho. BD10: B'frd 1A **72**
  (off Garsdale Av.)
Seminary St. LS2: Leeds 2G **97** (1B **4**)
Semon Av. BD2: B'frd 4F **71**

Senior Way BD5: B'frd 5E **91** (6C **6**)
  (not continuous)
Serin Wlk. BD6: B'frd 4F **109**
Servia Dr. LS7: Leeds 6A **78**
Servia Gdns. LS7: Leeds 6A **78**
Servia Hill LS6: Leeds 6H **77**
  LS7: Leeds 6H **77**
Servia Rd. LS7: Leeds 6H **77**
Service Rd. LS9: Leeds 3G **119**
Seven Acres BD13: B'frd 3B **86**
Sevenoaks Mead BD15: B'frd 2D **88**
Seventh Av. LS26: Rothw 6C **120**
  WF15: Liv 4H **153**
Severn Dr. LS25: Gar 6H **103**
Severn Rd. BD2: B'frd 6G **71**
  LS10: Leeds 2D **118**
Severn Way LS10: Leeds 1D **118**
Sewage Works Rd. LS9: Leeds 2G **119**
Sewell Rd. BD3: B'frd 5H **91**
Seymour St. BD3: B'frd 5G **91** (5H **7**)
Shackleton Ter. BD16: Bgly 6E **49**
SHADWELL 3B **62**
Shadwell La. LS17: Leeds 5B **60**
Shadwell Pk. Av. LS17: Leeds 2G **61**
Shadwell Pk. Cl. LS17: Leeds 2G **61**
Shadwell Pk. Ct. LS17: Leeds 3G **61**
Shadwell Pk. Dr. LS17: Leeds 3G **61**
Shadwell Pk. Gdns. LS17: Leeds 2G **61**
Shadwell Pk. Gro. LS17: Leeds 3G **61**
Shadwell Wlk. LS17: Leeds 4C **60**
Shaftesbury Av. BD9: B'frd 1F **89**
  BD18: Ship 2C **70**
  HD6: Brigh 4B **162**
  LS8: Leeds 6E **61**
Shaftesbury Ct. BD8: B'frd 2F **89**
  BD9: B'frd 2F **89**
Shaftesbury Pde. LS9: Leeds 2G **99**
Shaftesbury Rd. LS8: Leeds 5E **61**
Shafton La. LS11: Leeds 6F **97**
Shafton Pl. LS11: Leeds 6F **97**
Shafton St. LS11: Leeds 6F **97**
Shafton Vw. LS11: Leeds 6F **97**
Shakespeare App. LS9: Leeds 2D **98**
Shakespeare Av. LS9: Leeds 2D **98**
Shakespeare Cl.
  BD3: B'frd 3G **91** (2H **7**)
  LS9: Leeds 2D **98**
  LS20: Guis 5D **40**
Shakespeare Ct. LS9: Leeds 2D **98**
  (off Shakespeare App.)
Shakespeare Gdns. LS9: Leeds 2D **98**
Shakespeare Grange LS9: Leeds 2D **98**
Shakespeare Lawn LS9: Leeds 2D **98**
Shakespeare Rd. LS20: Guis 5C **40**
Shakespeare St.
  HX1: Hal 3G **149** (4C **164**)
  LS9: Leeds 1D **98**
Shakespeare Towers LS9: Leeds 2D **98**
Shakespeare Va. LS9: Leeds 2D **98**
Shakespeare Wlk. LS9: Leeds 2D **98**
Shalimar St. HX1: Hal 2D **148**
Shambles, The LS22: Weth 4E **13**
Shann Av. BD21: Keigh 5F **33**
Shann Cres. BD21: Keigh 5F **33**
Shann La. BD20: Keigh 5F **33**
Shannon Cl. HD6: Brigh 4G **161**
  LS29: I'ly 6B **10**
Shannon Rd. HD6: Brigh 4G **161**
  LS9: Leeds 3C **98**
Shannon St. LS9: Leeds 3C **98**
Shapers Health & Fitness Cen. 1E **151**
Shapla Cl. BD22: Keigh 1G **47**
Sharp Av. BD6: B'frd 5C **110**
Sharpe St. BD5: B'frd 5E **91** (6C **6**)
Sharp Ho. Rd. LS10: Leeds 3C **140**
Sharp La. LS10: Leeds 2C **140**
  (Dolphin Rd.)
  LS10: Leeds 2B **140**
  (Ring Rd. Middleton)
  WF3: Rothw 3E **141**
Sharp M. LS6: Leeds 4F **77**

Sharp Row LS28: Pud 5A **94**
Sharp St. BD6: B'frd 4C **110**
SHAW 1B **84**
Shaw Barn Cft. LS22: Weth 4C **12**
Shaw Barn La. LS22: Weth 4C **12**
Shaw Booth La. HX2: Hal 3F **127**
Shaw Cl. HX4: Hal 6G **159**
  LS20: Guis 5D **40**
  LS25: Gar 6G **103**
SHAW CROSS 6A **154**
Shaw Hill HX1: Hal 4G **149**
  (not continuous)
Shaw Hill La. HX3: Hal 4H **149**
SHAW LANE 5E **41**
Shaw La. BD13: B'frd 1B **130**
  BD21: Keigh 5B **48**
  BD22: Oxen 1B **84**
  HX3: Hal 4H **149**
  HX5: Ell 3E **161**
  HX6: Hal 2A **158**
  LS6: Leeds 4D **76**
  LS20: Guis 4D **40**
Shaw La. Gdns. LS20: Guis 4D **40**
Shaw Leys LS19: Yead 5E **41**
Shaw Lodge HX1: Hal 4H **149**
Shaw Mt. HX2: Hal 1E **147**
Shaw Royd LS14: Leeds 5E **41**
Shaw Royd Ct. LS19: Yead 5E **41**
  (off Shaw Royd)
Shaws La. LS15: Bar E 3C **82**
Shaw St. BD12: B'frd 1B **132**
  BD19: Cleck 2H **153**
  HX4: Hal 6G **159**
Shaw Vs. LS20: Guis 4D **40**
  (off Queensway)
Shay, The 4G **149** (6C **164**)
SHAY BROW 6B **68**
Shay Cl. BD9: B'frd 5H **69**
Shay Ct. LS6: Leeds 6H **77**
Shay Cres. BD9: B'frd 5G **69**
Shay Dr. BD9: B'frd 5G **69**
Shayfield La. WF3: Rothw 5G **141**
Shay Fold BD9: B'frd 5G **69**
Shay Gap Rd. BD22: Keigh 1C **46**
Shaygate BD15: B'frd 5A **68**
Shay Grange BD9: B'frd 4G **69**
Shay Gro. BD9: B'frd 5H **69**
Shay La. BD4: B'frd 2D **112**
  BD7: B'frd 4G **69**
  BD15: B'frd 4H **67**
  HX3: Hal 4E **129**
Shay St. LS6: Leeds 6H **77**
Shay Syke HX1: Hal 3H **149** (6D **164**)
Sheaf St. LS10: Leeds 5B **98**
SHEARBRIDGE 5B **90** (4A **6**)
Shearbridge Grn. BD7: B'frd 5C **90**
Shearbridge Pl. BD7: B'frd 5C **90**
Shearbridge Rd. BD7: B'frd 5C **90**
Shearbridge Ter. BD7: B'frd 5C **90**
Shear's Yd. LS2: Leeds 4B **98** (5G **5**)
Shed St. BD21: Keigh 6A **34**
Sheep Hill La. BD13: B'frd 3D **129**
SHEEPSCAR 6B **78**
Sheepscar Ct. LS7: Leeds 1B **98**
Sheepscar Gro. LS7: Leeds . .2B **98** (1G **5**)
Sheepscar Row LS7: Leeds 1B **98**
Sheepscar St. Nth. LS7: Leeds . . .6A **78**
Sheepscar St. Sth.
  LS7: Leeds 1B **98** (1H **5**)
Sheepscar Way LS7: Leeds 6B **78**
Sheila Henry Dr. BD13: B'frd 4E **109**
Shelby Grange BD10: B'frd 3A **72**
Sheldon Ridge BD4: B'frd 6H **111**
Sheldrake Av. BD8: B'frd 4E **89**
Shelf Hall La. HX3: Hal 2D **130**
Shelf Moor HX3: Hal 6E **109**
Shelf Moor Rd. HX3: Hal 6E **109**
Shelldrake Dr. LS10: Leeds 2B **140**
Shelley Cl. LS26: Rothw 4E **143**
Shelley Cres. LS26: Rothw 4E **143**
Shelley Gro. BD8: B'frd 3G **89**
Shell La. LS28: Pud 3F **73**

Shelton Ct. BD13: B'frd 2C **86**
Shepcote Cl. LS16: Leeds 4H **57**
Shepcote Cres. LS16: Leeds 4H **57**
Shepherds Cft. BD22: Haw 2D **64**
Shepherds Fold HX3: Hal 4B **130**
Shepherd's Gro. LS7: Leeds 5C **78**
Shepherd's La. LS7: Leeds 5C **78**
  LS8: Leeds 5C **78**
Shepherd's Pl. LS8: Leeds 5C **78**
Shepherds Thorn La. HD2: Hud . .4B **162**
  HD6: Brigh 4B **162**
Shepherd St. BD7: B'frd 1A **110**
Shepton Apartments BD5: B'frd . . .6E **91**
  (off Park Rd.)
Sherborne Dr. BD22: Keigh 2E **47**
Sherborne Rd. BD7: B'frd . . .5D **90** (6A **6**)
  BD10: B'frd 6H **53**
Sherbourne Dr. LS6: Leeds 6E **59**
Sherbrooke Av. LS15: Leeds 4B **100**
Sherburn App. LS14: Leeds 3E **81**
Sherburn Cl. BD11: B'frd 1F **135**
  LS14: Leeds 3E **81**
  (off Sherburn Pl.)
Sherburn Ct. LS14: Leeds 3E **81**
  (off York Rd.)
Sherburn Gro. BD11: B'frd 1F **135**
Sherburn Pl. LS14: Leeds 3E **81**
Sherburn Rd. HD6: Brigh 3F **161**
  LS14: Leeds 3E **81**
Sherburn Rd. Nth. LS14: Leeds . . .1D **80**
Sherburn Row LS14: Leeds 3E **81**
  (off York Rd.)
Sherburn Sq. LS14: Leeds 3E **81**
  (off Sherburn Pl.)
Sherburn Wlk. LS14: Leeds 3E **81**
  (off York Rd.)
Sheridan Cl. LS28: Pud 5B **94**
Sheridan Ct. LS28: Pud 5B **94**
Sheridan Ho. LS27: Morl 1E **137**
Sheridan St. BD4: B'frd 1G **111**
  WF1: Wake 4G **157**
Sheridan Way LS28: Pud 5B **94**
Sherwell Gro. BD15: B'frd 2E **89**
Sherwell Ri. BD15: B'frd 2E **89**
Sherwood Av. HD2: Hud 6F **163**
Sherwood Cl. BD16: Bgly 2E **51**
Sherwood Gdns. WF3: Rothw 5F **141**
Sherwood Grn. WF3: Rothw 4E **141**
Sherwood Gro. BD18: Ship 1G **69**
Sherwood Ind. Est. WF3: Rothw . .4F **141**
Sherwood Pl. BD2: B'frd 1H **91**
Sherwood Rd. HD6: Brigh 1C **162**
Sherwood Works HD6: Brigh 2D **162**
Shetcliffe La. BD4: B'frd 5H **111**
Shetcliffe Rd. BD4: B'frd 5H **111**
Shetland Cl. BD2: B'frd 5F **71**
Shibden Fold HX3: Hal 6A **130**
Shibden Gth. HX3: Hal 2C **150**
Shibden Grange Dr. HX3: Hal 6B **130**
Shibden Hall 1B **150**
Shibden Hall Cft. HX3: Hal 1C **150**
Shibden Hall Rd. HX3: Hal 1A **150**
SHIBDEN HEAD 1G **129**
Shibden Head Cl. BD13: B'frd 6G **107**
Shibden Head La. BD13: B'frd 6G **107**
Shibden Mill Fold HX3: Hal 4A **130**
Shibden Vw. BD13: B'frd 6H **107**
Shiela Henry Dr. BD6: B'frd 4E **109**
Shield Cl. LS15: Leeds 6G **81**
Shield Hall La. HX6: Hal 5C **146**
SHIPLEY 2B **70**
Shipley Airedale Rd.
  BD1: B'frd 5F **91** (5F **7**)
  BD3: B'frd 3F **91** (2E **7**)
Shipley Flds. Rd. BD18: Ship 4B **70**
  (not continuous)
Shipley Lanes 2B **70**
Shipley Station (Rail) 2B **70**
Shipley Swimming Pool 2A **70**
Ship St. HD6: Brigh 1B **162**
Shipton M. LS27: Morl 4B **138**

Ship Yd. LS1: Leeds 4E **5**
Shire Cl. BD6: B'frd 6H **109**
  LS27: Morl 5B **138**
Shire Ct. LS27: Morl 6B **138**
Shiredene LS6: Leeds 4E **77**
Shire Gro. LS27: Morl 6A **138**
Shire Oak Rd. LS6: Leeds 4E **77**
Shire Oak St. LS6: Leeds 4D **76**
Shire Rd. LS27: Morl 5B **138**
Shires Bus. Pk. BD7: B'frd 6A **90**
Shirley Av. BD12: B'frd 6B **132**
  WF17: Bat 5H **135**
Shirley Cl. LS21: Otley 4F **23**
Shirley Cres. BD12: B'frd 6B **132**
Shirley Dr. LS13: Leeds 5E **75**
Shirley Gro. BD19: Cleck 6F **135**
  HX3: Hal 2A **152**
Shirley Mnr. Gdns. BD12: B'frd . . .6B **132**
Shirley Pl. BD12: B'frd 6C **132**
Shirley Rd. BD4: B'frd 4B **112**
  BD7: B'frd 5B **90**
  BD19: Cleck 6F **135**
Shirley St. BD13: B'frd 2C **86**
  BD18: Ship 1H **69**
  BD22: Haw 2B **64**
Shoebridge Av. BD20: Stee 5A **14**
Sholebroke Av. LS7: Leeds 5B **78**
Sholebroke Ct. LS7: Leeds 5B **78**
Sholebroke Mt. LS7: Leeds 5A **78**
Sholebroke Pl. LS7: Leeds 5B **78**
Sholebroke St. LS7: Leeds 5A **78**
Sholebroke Ter. LS7: Leeds 4B **78**
Sholebroke Vw. LS7: Leeds 5B **78**
Shone Ct. LS27: Morl 5B **138**
Shop La. WF3: Wake 1F **157**
Shoreham Rd. LS12: Leeds 4C **96**
Short Cl. BD12: B'frd 2B **132**
Short La. LS7: Leeds 2A **78**
Short Row BD12: B'frd 1D **132**
Short Way LS28: Pud 2E **93**
Shortway BD13: B'frd 5C **88**
Showcase Cinemas 3D **136**
Shrike Cl. BD6: B'frd 4E **109**
Shroggs, The BD20: Stee 6C **14**
Shroggs Rd. HX3: Hal . . .5D **128** (1A **164**)
Shroggs St. HX1: Hal 1E **149**
Shroggs Vue Ter. HX1: Hal 1E **149**
Shuttleworth La. BD8: B'frd 3G **89**
Shuttle Fold BD22: Haw 1D **64**
Shuttocks Cl. LS25: Kip 2G **123**
Shuttocks Fold LS25: Kip 2H **123**
Shutts, The LS26: Rothw 2G **141**
Shutts La. HX3: Hal 5G **131**
Sickleholme Cl. HD2: Hud 6E **163**
Sicklinghall Rd. LS22: Weth 4A **12**
SIDDAL .6A **150**
Siddal Gro. HX3: Hal 5H **149**
Siddal La. HX3: Hal 5A **150**
Siddall St. LS11: Leeds 5H **97**
Siddal New Rd. HX3: Hal 4H **149**
Siddal Pl. HX3: Hal 6A **150**
Siddal St. HX3: Hal 6A **150**
Siddal Top La. HX3: Hal 5A **150**
Siddal Vw. HX3: Hal 5A **150**
Side Copse LS21: Otley 3F **23**
Sidings, The BD18: Ship 1C **70**
  LS20: Guis 4B **40**
Sidings Cl. BD2: B'frd 6D **70**
Sidney St. LS1: Leeds 3A **98** (4F **5**)
Siegen Cl. LS27: Morl 3A **138**
Siegen Mnr. LS27: Morl 3A **138**
  (off Wesley St.)
Silk Mill App. LS16: Leeds 5G **57**
Silk Mill Av. LS16: Leeds 4F **57**
Silk Mill Bank LS16: Leeds 5F **57**
Silk Mill Cl. LS16: Leeds 4F **57**
Silk Mill Dr. BD20: Keigh 4A **36**
  LS16: Leeds 5F **57**
Silk Mill Gdns. LS16: Leeds 5F **57**
Silk Mill Grn. LS16: Leeds 5G **57**
Silk Mill M. LS16: Leeds 5H **57**
Silk Mill Rd. LS16: Leeds 5F **57**

Silk Mill Way LS16: Leeds 5G 57
Silkstone Cl. LS25: Gar 2H 103
Silkstone Ct. LS15: Leeds 2E 101
Silkstone Rd. BD3: B'frd 4H 91
Silkstone Way LS15: Leeds 2E 101
Silk St. BD9: B'frd 1A 90
Silsbridge St. BD1: B'frd 4A 6
SILSDEN 2E 15
Silsden Ho. Gdns. BD20: Sils 1C 14
Silsden Rd. BD20: Keigh 1C 34
  LS29: Add .2A 8
Silson La. BD17: Bail 3E 53
Silver Birch Av. BD12: B'frd 5D 132
Silver Birch Cl. BD12: B'frd 5D 132
Silver Birch Dr. BD12: B'frd 5D 132
Silver Birch Gro. BD12: B'frd 5D 132
Silver Ct. LS13: Leeds 2B 94
Silverdale Av. BD20: Keigh 4C 34
  LS17: Leeds 2F 61
  LS20: Guis 5C 40
Silverdale Cl. LS20: Guis 6C 40
Silverdale Cres. LS20: Guis 5C 40
Silverdale Dr. LS20: Guis 6C 40
Silverdale Grange
  LS20: Guis 6C 40
Silverdale Gro. LS20: Guis 6B 40
Silverdale Mt. LS20: Guis 6C 40
Silverdale Rd. BD5: B'frd 3E 111
  LS20: Guis 6B 40
Silverdale Ter. HX4: Hal 5E 159
Silverhill Av. BD3: B'frd 2B 92
Silverhill Dr. BD3: B'frd 2B 92
Silverhill Rd. BD3: B'frd 2A 92
Silver Ho. LS2: Leeds 1E 5
Silver La. LS19: Yead 6F 41
Silver Mill Hill LS21: Otley 5F 23
Silver Royd Av. LS12: Leeds 5H 95
Silver Royd Cl. LS12: Leeds 5H 95
Silver Royd Dr. LS12: Leeds 5H 95
Silver Royd Gth. LS12: Leeds 5H 95
Silver Royd Gro. LS12: Leeds 5H 95
SILVER ROYD HILL 5H 95
Silver Royd Hill LS12: Leeds 5H 95
Silver Royd Pl. LS12: Leeds 5H 95
Silver Royd Rd. LS12: Leeds 5H 95
Silver Royd St. LS12: Leeds 5H 95
Silver Royd Ter. LS12: Leeds 5H 95
Silver Royd Way LS12: Leeds 5H 95
Silver St. BD8: B'frd 2B 90
  HX1: Hal 2G 149 (4B 164)
  LS11: Leeds 5G 97
  WF1: Wake 6F 157
Silvertrees LS16: B'hpe 2F 43
Silverwood HX2: Hal 6A 128
  (not continuous)
Silverwood Av. HX2: Hal 6A 128
  (not continuous)
Silwood Dr. BD2: B'frd 6A 72
Simes St. BD1: B'frd 4D 90 (3B 6)
Simm Carr HX3: Hal 3H 129
Simm Carr La. HX3: Hal 3H 129
Simmonds La. HX1: Hal 4H 149
Simmons Ct. LS9: Leeds 5D 98
Simmons Way LS8: Leeds 5F 79
Simms Dene BD15: B'frd 5C 68
Simon Cl. BD4: B'frd 3D 112
Simon Fold BD12: B'frd 5C 132
Simon Marks Ct. LS12: Leeds 6C 96
  (off Lynwood Gth.)
SIMPSON GREEN 6A 54
Simpson Gro. BD10: B'frd 6A 54
  LS12: Leeds 4D 96
Simpsons Fold E.
  LS10: Leeds 4A 98 (6F 5)
Simpsons Fold W. LS10: Leeds 6F 5
Simpson St. BD21: Keigh 6G 33
  HX3: Hal 5F 129
  WF3: E Ard 1C 156
Sinclair Rd. BD2: B'frd 4F 71
Sinden M. BD10: B'frd 5H 53
Singleton St. BD1: B'frd 3E 91 (1D 6)
Sion Hill HX3: Hal 6A 150

Sir Francis Crossley's Almshouses
  HX1: Hal .2F 149
  (off Margaret St.)
Sir George Martin Dr.
  LS16: Leeds 3D 58
Sir Isaac Holden Pl. BD7: B'frd 4B 90
Sir Karl Cohen Sq. LS12: Leeds 4B 96
Sir Wilfred Pl. BD10: B'frd 1H 71
Siskin Ct. LS27: Morl 4B 138
Siskin Dr. BD6: B'frd 4E 109
Sissons Av. LS10: Leeds 3H 139
Sissons Cres. LS10: Leeds 3H 139
Sissons Dr. LS10: Leeds 3H 139
Sissons Grn. LS10: Leeds 3H 139
Sissons Gro. LS10: Leeds 3H 139
Sissons La. LS10: Leeds 3H 139
Sissons Mt. LS10: Leeds 4G 139
Sissons Pl. LS10: Leeds 2H 139
Sissons Rd. LS10: Leeds 3G 139
Sissons Row LS10: Leeds 3H 139
Sissons St. LS10: Leeds 3H 139
Sissons Ter. LS10: Leeds 3G 139
Sissons Vw. LS10: Leeds 4G 139
Sixth Av. BD3: B'frd 2A 92
  LS26: Rothw 6C 120
  WF15: Liv .4H 153
Sizers Ct. LS19: Yead 2E 55
Skelda Ri. LS29: I'ly 6D 10
Skellow Dr. BD4: B'frd 4E 113
Skelton Av. LS9: Leeds 3F 99
Skelton Cres. LS9: Leeds 3F 99
Skelton Grange Cotts.
  LS9: Leeds 2G 119
Skelton Grange Rd. LS10: Leeds 3F 119
Skelton Mt. LS9: Leeds 3F 99
Skelton Pl. LS9: Leeds 3F 99
  (off Skelton Av.)
Skelton Rd. LS9: Leeds 3F 99
Skeltons La. LS14: Leeds, T'ner 6D 62
Skelton St. LS9: Leeds 3F 99
Skelton Ter. LS9: Leeds 3F 99
Skelton Wlk. BD10: B'frd 2B 72
Skelwith App. LS14: Leeds 1C 100
Skelwith Wlk. LS14: Leeds 1C 100
Skinner La. BD8: B'frd 1C 90
  LS7: Leeds 2B 98 (1G 5)
Skinner St. LS1: Leeds 4A 4
Skippon Ter. LS14: T'ner 2H 63
Skipton Ri. LS25: Gar 4H 103
Skipton Rd. BD20: Keigh 2F 33
  BD20: Sils 2B 14
  BD20: Stee 6B 14
  BD21: Keigh 5A 34
  LS29: Add .1C 8
  LS29: I'ly 4G 9
SKIRCOAT GREEN 1F 159
Skircoat Grn. HX3: Hal 1G 159
Skircoat Grn. Rd. HX3: Hal 6G 149
Skircoat Lodge HX3: Hal 6F 149
Skircoat Moor Cl. HX3: Hal 5E 149
Skircoat Moor Rd. HX1: Hal 4D 148
Skircoat Rd. HX1: Hal 3G 149 (6C 164)
Skirrow St. BD16: Bgly 3D 68
Skye Vw. LS26: Rothw 2B 142
Skylark Av. BD6: B'frd 4E 109
Slack Bottom Rd. BD6: B'frd 5A 110
Slack End BD6: B'frd 6H 109
Slack La. BD22: Keigh 4A 46
  HX2: Hal 3B 126
SLACK SIDE 4H 109
Sladdin Row BD13: B'frd 5G 107
Slade Cl. LS23: B Spa 4B 30
Slade Ho. BD2: B'frd 1B 92
  (off St Clares Av.)
Slade La. BD20: Keigh 3C 34
  HD6: Brigh 5G 161
Sladen Bri. BD22: Haw 2A 64
Sladen St. BD21: Keigh 6G 33
Slade Wlk. WF17: Bat 6B 136
SLAID HILL .2F 61
Slaid Hill Ct. LS17: Leeds 2F 61
Slate Quarry La. BD16: Bgly 3D 50

Slaters Rd. LS28: Pud 2A 94
Slates La. LS29: I'ly 2C 10
Slaymaker La. BD22: Keigh 4B 46
Slead Av. HD6: Brigh 5H 151
Slead Cl. HD6: Brigh 5H 151
Slead Ct. HD6: Brigh 5H 151
Slead Gro. HD6: Brigh 5H 151
Slead Royd HD6: Brigh 5H 151
SLEAD SYKE 5G 151
Slead Syke Sports Cen. 4H 151
Slead Vw. HD6: Brigh 5H 151
Sledmere Cft. LS14: Leeds 3E 81
Sledmere Gth. LS14: Leeds 3E 81
Sledmere Grn. LS14: Leeds 3E 81
  (off Sledmere Pl.)
Sledmere La. LS14: Leeds 3E 81
  (not continuous)
Sledmere Pl. LS14: Leeds 3E 81
Sledmere Sq. LS14: Leeds 3E 81
  (off Sledmere Pl.)
Sleningford Gro. BD18: Ship 1G 69
Sleningford Ri. BD16: Bgly 2B 50
Sleningford Rd. BD16: Bgly 2A 50
  BD18: Ship 1G 69
Sleningford Ter. BD16: Bgly 2B 50
  (off Sleningford Rd.)
Slicer's Yd. BD16: Bgly 4B 50
  (off Busfield St.)
Slingsby Cl. BD10: B'frd 1B 72
Slippy La. HX2: Hal 2A 128
  (not continuous)
Smalewell Cl. LS28: Pud 5H 93
Smalewell Dr. LS28: Pud 5G 93
Smalewell Gdns. LS28: Pud 5G 93
Smalewell Grn. LS28: Pud 5H 93
Smalewell Rd. LS28: Pud 5G 93
  (New Occupation La.)
  LS28: Pud .5F 93
  (Tyersal La.)
Small Page BD13: B'frd 4A 108
  (off Albert Rd.)
Small Page Fold BD13: B'frd 4A 108
Smallwood Gdns. WF12: Dew 6B 154
Smallwood Rd. WF12: Dew 6A 154
  (not continuous)
Smeaton App. LS15: Leeds 6G 81
Smeaton Gro. LS26: Swil 4A 122
Smiddles La. BD5: B'frd 3D 110
Smith Art Gallery 6A 152
Smith Av. BD6: B'frd 4C 110
Smith Cres. HD6: Brigh 3G 161
Smitherd's St. BD21: Keigh 1H 47
Smithfield Av. HX3: Hal 1E 151
Smith Ho. Av. HD6: Brigh 4A 152
Smith Ho. Cl. HD6: Brigh 4A 152
Smith Ho. Cres. HD6: Brigh 4A 152
  (not continuous)
Smith Ho. Dr. HD6: Brigh 3A 152
Smith Ho. Gro. HD6: Brigh 4A 152
Smith Ho. La. HD6: Brigh 4A 152
Smithies La. WF17: Bat 6A 136
Smith Rd. BD7: B'frd 2A 110
Smiths Cotts. LS16: Leeds 3D 76
  (off Weetwood La.)
Smithson St. LS26: Rothw 3B 142
Smith's Ter. HX3: Hal 4E 129
Smith St. BD4: B'frd 5H 111
  BD7: B'frd 4D 90 (4A 6)
  BD16: Bgly 3D 68
  BD21: Keigh 5G 33
Smithville BD20: Keigh 4D 34
Smithy Carr La. HD6: Brigh 5A 152
Smithy Ct. BD19: Cleck 6F 133
  LS22: Coll .2B 28
Smithy Fold BD13: B'frd 3E 109
  HX5: Ell 5E 161
Smithy Greaves LS29: Add 2G 9
Smithy Hill BD6: B'frd 4C 110
  BD13: B'frd 4C 86
  BD22: Keigh 3F 47
  (off Keighley Rd.)

Smithy La. BD15: B'frd 3G 67
  LS16: Leeds 1G 57
  LS17: Bard 3E 45
  LS29: Burl W 3E 21
  WF3: E Ard 1F 155
Smithy Mills La. LS16: Leeds 5D 58
Smithy St. HX1: Hal 2H 149 (3D 164)
Smools La. LS27: Morl 6B 116
Snaith Wood Dr. LS19: Yead 6G 55
Snaith Wood M. LS19: Yead 6G 55
Snake Hill BD12: B'frd 2G 133
Snake La. LS9: Leeds 5E 99
Snape Dr. BD7: B'frd 3F 109
Snape St. BD21: Keigh 3A 48
Snelsins La. BD19: Cleck 6A 134
Snelsins Rd. BD19: Cleck 6A 134
Snowden App. LS13: Leeds 6G 75
Snowden Cl. LS13: Leeds 1F 95
Snowden Cres. LS13: Leeds 1F 95
Snowden Fold LS13: Leeds 1F 95
Snowden Gdns. LS13: Leeds 1G 95
Snowden Grn. LS13: Leeds 1F 95
                (off Aston Rd.)
Snowden Gro. LS13: Leeds 1F 95
Snowden Lawn LS13: Leeds 1F 95
Snowden Rd. BD18: Ship 3D 70
             (not continuous)
Snowden Royd LS13: Leeds 6F 75
Snowden St. BD1: B'frd 3E 91 (2C 6)
Snowdens Wlk. BD14: B'frd 1F 109
Snowden Va. LS13: Leeds 1F 95
Snowden Wlk. LS13: Leeds 1F 95
Snowden Way LS13: Leeds 6F 75
Snowdrop M. BD15: B'frd 3D 88
SNOW HILL 6E 157
Soaper Ho. La. HX3: Hal 5E 131
Soaper La. BD6: B'frd 5F 109
  HX3: Hal 6E 109
Sod Ho. Grn. HX3: Hal 4E 129
Soho Mills BD1: B'frd 4B 6
Soho St. BD1: B'frd 4D 90 (4B 6)
  HX1: Hal 2D 148
SOIL HILL 2C 106
Solomon Hill HX2: Hal 6D 126
Somerdale Cl. LS13: Leeds 2F 95
Somerdale Gdns. LS13: Leeds 2F 95
Somerdale Gro. LS13: Leeds 2F 95
Somerdale Wlk. LS13: Leeds 2F 95
Somerset Av. BD17: Bail 3B 52
  HD6: Brigh 4B 162
Somerset Rd. LS28: Pud 3A 94
Somers Pl. LS12: Leeds 4C 4
Somers St. LS1: Leeds 3H 97 (4B 4)
Somerton Dr. BD4: B'frd 3B 112
Somerville Av. BD6: B'frd 6B 110
  LS14: Leeds 1B 100
Somerville Dr. LS14: Leeds 1B 100
Somerville Grn. LS14: Leeds 1B 100
Somerville Gro. LS14: Leeds 6B 80
Somerville Mt. LS14: Leeds 1B 100
Somerville Pk. BD6: B'frd 6B 110
Somerville Ter. LS21: Otley 3F 23
Somerville Vw. LS14: Leeds 1B 100
Sommerville M. LS28: Pud 2G 93
Sonning Rd. BD15: B'frd 3D 88
Soothill La. WF17: Bat, Dew 4A 154
Sorrel Way BD17: Bail 3F 53
Sorrin Cl. BD10: B'frd 1G 71
Soureby Cross Way BD4: B'frd 6D 112
            (off Green, The)
  BD4: B'frd 6D 112
           (Hunsworth La.)
Sth. Accommodation Rd.
  LS9: Leeds 6C 98
  LS10: Leeds 6B 98
Southampton St.
  BD3: B'frd 2F 91 (1F 7)
South Bank BD3: B'frd 4B 108
  LS17: Bard 5E 27
South Bolton HX2: Hal 6B 106
Southbrook Ter. BD7: B'frd . . .5D 90 (5B 6)
South Carr HX2: Hal 6D 126

South Cliffe BD13: B'frd 5A 88
  HX2: Hal 2E 129
Southcliffe HX3: Hal 4A 150
           (off Bank Top)
Southcliffe Dr. BD17: Bail 6B 52
Southcliffe Way BD17: Bail 6C 52
South Cl. LS20: Guis 5H 39
Sth. Clough Head
  HX2: Hal 2G 147
Southcote Pl. BD10: B'frd 1H 71
Southcote St. LS28: Pud 1H 93
           (off Northcote St.)
Sth. Croft Av. BD11: B'frd 1E 135
Sth. Croft Dr. BD11: B'frd 6E 113
Sth. Croft Ga. BD11: B'frd 1E 135
Southdown Cl. BD9: B'frd 1G 89
Southdown Ct. BD9: B'frd 1G 89
         (off Southdown Cl.)
Southdown Rd. BD17: Bail 6B 52
South Dr. LS20: Guis 5H 39
  LS28: Pud 6H 73
South Edge BD18: Ship 2G 69
  BD20: Keigh 5G 33
  HX3: Hal 2F 151
Southedge Ter. HX3: Hal 2F 151
South End Av. LS13: Leeds 2G 95
South End Ct. LS13: Leeds 1G 95
South End Gro. LS13: Leeds 2G 95
South End Mt. LS13: Leeds 2G 95
South End Ter. LS13: Leeds 2G 95
Sth. Farm Cres. LS9: Leeds 1G 99
Sth. Farm Rd. LS9: Leeds 1G 99
Southfield LS16: B'hpe 3H 43
Southfield Av. BD6: B'frd 5C 110
  BD20: Keigh 3D 34
  LS17: Leeds 5C 60
Southfield Dr. BD20: Keigh 3E 35
  LS17: Leeds 5C 60
Southfield La. BD5: B'frd 2B 110
  BD7: B'frd 1A 110
  LS29: Add 1C 8
Southfield Mt. BD20: Keigh 3D 34
  LS10: Leeds 4C 118
         (off South Vw. Rd.)
  LS12: Leeds 4C 96
Southfield Rd. BD5: B'frd 2C 110
  BD16: Bgly 6C 50
  LS29: Add 1D 8
  LS29: Burl W 2E 21
Southfield Sq. BD8: B'frd 2C 90
Southfield St. LS12: Leeds 4C 96
Southfield Ter. BD11: B'frd 1E 135
  HX3: Hal 6E 131
  LS12: Leeds 4C 96
         (off Southfield St.)
  LS29: Add 1D 8
Southfield Way BD20: Keigh 3E 35
Southgate BD1: B'frd 4E 91 (4C 6)
         (not continuous)
  HX1: Hal 2G 149 (4C 164)
  HX5: Ell 4B 160
  LS20: Guis 6H 39
  LS26: Rothw 1E 143
South Gro. BD18: Ship 2F 69
  HD6: Brigh 4G 151
South Hawksworth St. LS29: I'ly . . .5D 10
South Hill LS10: Leeds 6D 118
Sth. Hill Cl. LS10: Leeds 6D 118
Sth. Hill Cft. LS10: Leeds 6D 118
Sth. Hill Dr. BD16: Bgly 5E 51
Sth. Hill Gdns. LS10: Leeds 6D 118
Sth. Hill Gro. LS10: Leeds 6D 118
Sth. Hill Ri. LS10: Leeds 6D 118
Sth. Hill Way LS10: Leeds 6D 118
Sth. Holme La. HD6: Brigh 5G 151
Southlands BD17: Bail 6B 52
  HX2: Hal 4D 106
  LS18: H'fth 6D 56
Southlands Av. BD13: B'frd 5E 89
  BD16: Bgly 6C 50
  BD20: Keigh 4E 35

Southlands Av. LS17: Leeds 1A 78
  LS19: Yead 5H 55
Southlands Cl. LS17: Leeds 6A 60
Southlands Cres. LS17: Leeds 1A 78
Southlands Dr. BD20: Keigh 4E 35
  LS17: Leeds 1A 78
Southlands Gro. BD13: B'frd 5D 88
  BD16: Bgly 6B 50
  BD20: Keigh 4E 35
Southlands Gro. W. BD20: Keigh . . .3E 35
Southlands Mt. BD20: Keigh 4E 35
Southlands Rd. BD20: Keigh 3E 35
South La. HX3: Hal 6D 108
South La. Gdns. HX5: Ell 6B 160
South Lea WF3: E Ard 6F 139
Southlea BD12: B'frd 2G 133
Southlea Av. BD22: Keigh 5E 47
South Lee LS18: H'fth 6D 56
Sth. Leeds Bus. Cen.
  LS11: Leeds 6A 98
South Leeds Sports Cen. 6H 97
South Leeds Stadium 5A 118
South Leeds Tennis Cen. 5A 118
Southleigh Av. LS11: Leeds 5G 117
Southleigh Cres. LS11: Leeds 5G 117
Southleigh Cft. LS11: Leeds 5H 117
Southleigh Dr. LS11: Leeds 5G 117
Southleigh Gdns. LS11: Leeds 5G 117
Southleigh Gth. LS11: Leeds 5H 117
Southleigh Grange LS11: Leeds 5H 117
Southleigh Gro. LS11: Leeds 5G 117
Southleigh Rd. LS11: Leeds 5G 117
Southleigh Vw. LS11: Leeds 5G 117
South Mead LS16: B'hpe 3H 43
Southmere Av. BD7: B'frd 2A 110
Southmere Cres. BD7: B'frd 2A 110
Southmere Dr. BD7: B'frd 2H 109
              (Bartle Pl.)
  BD7: B'frd 2A 110
           (Southmere Rd.)
Southmere Gro. BD7: B'frd 2A 110
Southmere Oval BD7: B'frd 3H 109
Southmere Rd. BD7: B'frd 2A 110
Southmere Ter. BD7: B'frd 2A 110
South Mt. LS17: Bard 5D 26
Sth. Nelson St. LS27: Morl 2A 138
Southolme Cl. LS5: Leeds 3H 75
SOUTHOWRAM 5C 150
Southowram Bank HX3: Hal 2H 149
South Pde. BD8: B'frd 2D 90
  BD19: Cleck 1H 153
  HX1: Hal 3H 149 (6D 164)
  HX5: Ell 6B 160
  LS1: Leeds 3H 97 (4D 4)
  LS6: Leeds 4D 76
  LS21: Otley 4F 23
            (off Albion St.)
  LS27: Morl 3B 138
  LS28: Pud 5H 93
  LS29: I'ly 5C 10
Sth. Parade Cl. LS28: Pud 5A 94
Sth. Pk. Ter. LS28: Pud 1B 114
South Pk. Way WF2: Wake 5D 156
Sth. Parkway LS14: Leeds 6A 80
          (not continuous)
Sth. Parkway App. LS14: Leeds 6A 80
South Pl. LS27: Morl 3B 138
            (off South St.)
Sth. Queen St. LS27: Morl 4B 138
South Ridge LS25: Kip 4G 123
South Rd. BD9: B'frd 5C 70
  BD13: B'frd 4B 66
South Row LS18: H'fth 6E 57
Sth. Royd Av. HX3: Hal 5G 149
Southroyd Pde. LS28: Pud 6A 94
            (off Fartown)
Southroyd Pk. LS28: Pud 6A 94
          (not continuous)
Southroyd Ri. LS28: Pud 6A 94
Southroyd Vs. LS28: Pud 6A 94
South Selby HX2: Hal 1B 128
South Sq. BD13: B'frd 5H 87

Sth. Square Cen. BD13: B'frd 5H **87**
(off South Sq.)
South St. BD5: B'frd 2C **110**
BD12: B'frd 3G **133**
BD13: B'frd 3B **86**
(Main Rd.)
BD13: B'frd 4H **87**
(West La.)
BD20: Keigh 5H **35**
BD21: Keigh 2H **47**
HD6: Brigh 6A **152**
HX1: Hal 3F **149** (5A **164**)
HX4: Hal 6F **159**
LS19: Yead 3F **55**
LS27: Morl 3B **138**
South Ter. HX3: Hal 4C **130**
South Vw. BD6: B'frd 1G **131**
BD9: B'frd 5C **70**
BD10: B'frd 2B **72**
BD13: B'frd 3G **107**
BD15: B'frd 4G **67**
BD19: Cleck 2F **153**
BD20: Keigh 4F **35**
BD22: Haw 2C **64**
HX2: Hal 2E **129**
(off Blackmires)
HX2: Hal 4F **147**
(Warley Wood Av.)
HX3: Hal 5C **150**
(Towngate)
HX3: Hal 5A **150**
(Whitegate Top)
LS15: Leeds 1E **101**
(off Selby Rd.)
LS18: H'fth 2E **75**
LS19: Yead 6D **40**
LS20: Guis 4C **40**
LS22: Coll 3H **27**
LS22: Weth 1E **13**
LS23: B Spa 6B **30**
LS26: Rothw 1A **142**
LS27: Morl 6B **116**
LS28: Pud 4B **94**
(Kent Rd.)
LS28: Pud 2G **93**
(New Pudsey Sq.)
LS29: Men 2G **39**
WF3: E Ard 4D **154**
WF17: Bat 6B **136**
Southview Bus. Pk. LS20: Guis 6C **40**
South Vw. Cl. BD4: B'frd 6C **112**
LS19: Yead 6D **40**
South Vw. Cotts. LS17: Leeds 4B **62**
South Vw. Ct. HX3: Hal 3F **151**
South Vw. Cres. LS19: Yead 6D **40**
South Vw. Dr. BD4: B'frd 6D **112**
South Vw. Rd. BD4: B'frd 6D **112**
LS19: Yead 6F **41**
South Vw. Ter. BD16: Bgly 2E **51**
BD17: Bail 4C **52**
BD20: Sils 2D **14**
HX1: Hal 1D **148**
(off Queen's La.)
LS19: Yead 1G **55**
LS21: Otley 4F **23**
(off Bermondsey St.)
Southwaite Cl. LS14: Leeds 5B **80**
Southwaite Gth. LS14: Leeds 5B **80**
Southwaite La. LS14: Leeds 5B **80**
Southwaite Lawn LS14: Leeds 5B **80**
Southwaite Pl. LS14: Leeds 5B **80**
South Wlk. BD16: Bgly 6E **49**
South Way BD4: B'frd 6C **112**
BD18: Ship 2F **69**
Southway BD16: Bgly 2D **50**
LS18: H'fth 4C **56**
LS20: Guis 5G **39**
LS29: I'ly 6F **11**
Southwood Cl. LS14: Leeds 5E **81**
Southwood Cres. LS14: Leeds 5E **81**
Southwood Ga. LS14: Leeds 5E **81**
Southwood Rd. LS14: Leeds 5E **81**

Sovereign Bus. Pk. LS10: Leeds 5B **98**
Sovereign Cl. WF17: Bat 6B **136**
Sovereign Ct. LS17: Leeds 1C **60**
Sovereign Pk. BD17: Bail 3E **53**
Sovereign Quay LS1: Leeds 6E **5**
Sovereign St. HX1: Hal 2F **149** (4A **164**)
LS1: Leeds 4A **98** (6D **4**)
Sowden Bldgs. BD2: B'frd 1H **91**
Sowden Grange BD13: B'frd 5H **87**
(James St.)
BD13: B'frd 5H **87**
(Lane End)
Sowden La. BD12: B'frd 4A **132**
HX3: Hal 4H **131**
(not continuous)
Sowden Rd. BD9: B'frd 6F **69**
Sowden St. BD7: B'frd 2B **110**
Sowden's Yd. LS6: Leeds 2H **75**
(off Moor Rd.)
SOWERBY 6E **147**
SOWERBY BRIDGE 5A **148**
Sowerby Bridge Pool 5H **147**
Sowerby Bridge Station (Rail) 6A **148**
Sowerby Cft. HX6: Hal 1A **158**
Sowerby Cft. La. HX6: Hal 6H **147**
Sowerby Grn. HX6: Hal 6D **146**
Sowerby La. HX2: Hal 2B **146**
Sowerby New Rd. HX6: Hal 6E **147**
Sowerby St. HX6: Hal 6H **147**
Sowerby Town HX6: Hal 6D **146**
Sowood St. LS4: Leeds 1C **96**
Spa Bldgs. LS29: I'ly 5D **10**
(off Parish Ghyll Rd.)
Spa Ind. Est. LS7: Leeds 5A **78**
Spa La. BD16: Bgly 2C **50**
LS23: B Spa 4C **30**
Spalding Towers LS9: Leeds 2C **98**
(off Lindsey Gdns.)
Spa M. LS23: B Spa 4C **30**
Spandola Ct. BD21: Keigh 5F **33**
Spanfield La. HX2: Hal 3F **127**
Sparable La. BD16: Bgly 4E **51**
Spark Ho. La. HX6: Hal 6A **148**
Spartal La. WF10: Leds 5C **124**
Spartan Rd. BD12: B'frd 2D **132**
Spear Fir LS17: Bard 3C **44**
Spearhead Way BD21: Keigh 5A **34**
Speedwell Mt. LS6: Leeds 6H **77**
Speedwell St. LS6: Leeds 6H **77**
Speeton Av. BD7: B'frd 3G **109**
Speeton Gro. BD7: B'frd 3F **109**
Speights Pl. BD4: B'frd 3A **112**
(off Dawson La.)
Spen App. LS16: Leeds 2H **75**
Spen Bank LS16: Leeds 2H **75**
Spence La. LS12: Leeds 5F **97**
Spenceley St. LS2: Leeds 6G **77**
(not continuous)
Spencer Av. BD7: B'frd 6A **90**
BD20: Sils 1E **15**
LS27: Morl 5A **138**
Spencer Mt. LS8: Leeds 6C **78**
Spencer Pl. LS7: Leeds 6C **78**
Spencer Rd. BD7: B'frd 6H **89**
(not continuous)
Spencer St. BD21: Keigh 6G **33**
(not continuous)
Spen Cl. BD4: B'frd 6H **111**
Spen Cres. LS16: Leeds 2H **75**
Spen Dr. BD16: Leeds 1A **76**
Spen Gdns. LS16: Leeds 1B **76**
Spen Grn. LS16: Leeds 2H **75**
Spen Hill LS16: Leeds 2A **76**
Spen La. BD19: Cleck 6E **135**
LS5: Leeds 3A **76**
LS6: Leeds 3A **76**
LS16: Leeds 6A **58**
(not continuous)
Spen Lawn LS16: Leeds 2H **75**
Spen M. LS16: Leeds 2A **76**
Spennithorne Av. LS16: Leeds 5A **58**
Spennithorne Dr. LS16: Leeds 6A **58**

Spen Rd. LS16: Leeds 1A **76**
Spenser Ri. LS20: Guis 5D **40**
Spenser Rd. LS20: Guis 5D **40**
Spens Ho. LS2: Leeds 1D **4**
Spenslea Gro. LS27: Morl 5A **138**
Spen Vw. La. BD4: B'frd 6H **111**
Spen Wlk. LS16: Leeds 2H **75**
Spen Way LS16: Leeds 3A **76**
Spibey Cres. LS26: Rothw 6H **119**
Spibey La. LS26: Rothw 6H **119**
Spicer St. BD5: B'frd 2C **110**
Spiers Gth. BD6: B'frd 4D **110**
Spiggs HX3: Hal 4B **130**
Spindle Point HX3: Hal 2E **129**
Spindles, The LS10: Leeds 5B **118**
Spindle St. HX2: Hal 2E **129**
Spink Pl. BD8: B'frd 3D **90** (2A **6**)
Spinks Gdns. LS14: Leeds 5D **80**
Spink St. BD8: B'frd 3D **90** (2A **6**)
Spinkwell Cl. BD3: B'frd 2F **91** (1E **7**)
Spink Well La. WF3: E Ard 6F **139**
Spinners Chase LS28: Pud 4A **94**
Spinners Way BD19: Cleck 1F **153**
BD22: Haw 3C **64**
Spinney, The BD20: Keigh 5H **35**
HD6: Brigh 4A **152**
LS9: Leeds 4C **98**
LS17: Leeds 5C **60**
LS19: Yead 5E **55**
LS22: Weth 3D **12**
Spinneyfield Ct. LS9: Leeds 4C **98**
Spinney Ri. BD4: B'frd 4D **112**
Spinning Mill, The BD22: Haw 1C **64**
Spinning Mill Ct. BD18: Ship 6G **51**
(Hirst La.)
BD18: Ship 1G **69**
(Sherwood Gro.)
Spion Kop LS14: T'ner 2H **63**
Spire Hgts. BD16: Bgly 4F **51**
Spofforth Hill LS22: Weth 3C **12**
Spofforth Wlk. LS25: Gar 4H **103**
Spout Hill HD6: Brigh 5G **161**
Spout Ho. La. HD6: Brigh 3G **151**
Spring Av. BD21: Keigh 1C **48**
LS27: Morl 6E **115**
SPRING BANK 3A **48**
Spring Bank BD13: B'frd 4A **66**
HX6: Hal 4G **147**
LS5: Leeds 5A **76**
Springbank HX2: Hal 1E **147**
LS19: Yead 4E **55**
LS25: Gar 6C **102**
Springbank Av. LS27: Morl 6E **115**
LS28: Pud 6A **74**
Springbank Cl. LS28: Pud 6H **73**
Spring Bank Cres. LS6: Leeds 5E **77**
Springbank Cres. LS25: Gar 5C **102**
LS27: Morl 5E **115**
Springbank Dr. LS28: Pud 6A **74**
Springbank Gro. LS28: Pud 6A **74**
Spring Bank Ind. Est. HX6: Hal 6H **147**
Springbank M. WF3: Wake 2D **156**
Spring Bank Pl. BD8: B'frd 2D **90**
Spring Bank Ri. BD21: Keigh 3A **48**
Springbank Ri. LS28: Pud 6A **74**
Springbank Rd. LS27: Morl 5E **115**
LS28: Pud 6H **73**
Spring Bank Ter. LS20: Guis 4C **40**
Springcliffe BD8: B'frd 2B **90**
Springcliffe St. BD8: B'frd 2B **90**
Spring Cl. BD16: Bgly 5D **50**
BD21: Keigh 1C **48**
LS25: Gar 5H **103**
(Firtree Av.)
LS25: Gar 3G **103**
(Newhold)
Spring Cl. Av. LS9: Leeds 5D **98**
Spring Cl. Gdns. LS9: Leeds 5D **98**
Spring Cl. St. LS9: Leeds 5C **98**
Spring Cl. Wlk. LS9: Leeds 5D **98**
Springdale Cres. BD10: B'frd 1A **72**
Spring Dr. BD21: Keigh 1C **48**

Spring Edge—Stainbeck Rd.

Spring Edge HX1: Hal .5E 149
Spring Edge Nth. HX1: Hal .4E 149
Spring Edge W. HX1: Hal .4D 148
Spring Farm La. BD16: Bgly .6E 49
Spring Farm M. BD15: B'frd .4G 67
SPRINGFIELD .3H 71
Springfield BD13: B'frd .4H 107
HX2: Hal .6C 126
HX3: Hal .1E 151
HX6: Hal .6G 147
LS23: B Spa .6B 30
(Church Vw. M.)
LS23: B Spa .3A 30
(Oaks La.)
Springfield Av. BD7: B'frd .6H 89
LS27: Morl .1H 137
LS29: I'ly .5E 11
Springfield Cl. LS18: H'fth .6G 57
Springfield Commercial Cen.
LS28: Pud .5A 74
Springfield Ct. BD20: Keigh .5G 33
LS19: Yead .5E 41
Springfield Cres. LS27: Morl .1A 138
Springfield Dr. WF15: Liv .4H 153
Springfield Gdns. BD20: Keigh .5G 33
LS18: H'fth .6F 57
LS28: Pud .5B 94
Springfield Grn. LS10: Leeds .3C 118
Springfield Gro. BD16: Bgly .3B 50
HD6: Brigh .4A 152
Springfield La. BD4: B'frd .3A 114
LS27: Morl .1A 138
Springfield Mt. LS2: Leeds . . .2G 97 (1A 4)
LS12: Leeds .3A 96
LS18: H'fth .6F 57
LS29: Add .1D 8
Springfield Pl. BD1: B'frd 3D 90 (1B 6)
BD10: B'frd .2H 71
LS10: Leeds .3C 118
(Leasowe Rd.)
LS10: Leeds .3E 119
(Pontefract Rd.)
LS20: Guis .4C 40
LS21: Otley .4D 22
LS25: Gar .5C 102
Springfield Ri. LS18: H'fth .6F 57
LS26: Rothw .3B 142
Springfield Rd. BD17: Bail .3B 52
BD20: Keigh .5G 33
HX5: Ell .4D 160
LS20: Guis .5C 40
LS27: Morl .1H 137
Springfield St. BD8: B'frd .3C 90
BD13: B'frd .5A 88
LS26: Rothw .3B 142
Spring Fld. Ter. HX3: Hal .1E 151
Springfield Ter. BD8: B'frd .3C 90
BD13: B'frd .4C 66
BD19: Cleck .6F 133
HX2: Hal .6C 126
LS17: Leeds .3E 61
LS20: Guis .5C 40
LS28: Pud .2H 93
Springfield Vw. *LS25: Kip* .*4H 123*
(off Hanover Pl.)
Springfield Vs. LS27: Morl .5D 114
Springfield Wlk. LS18: H'fth .6F 57
Spring Gdn. Cotts. *BD20: Sils* .*2D 14*
(off South Vw. Ter.)
SPRING GARDENS .1B 136
Spring Gdns. BD1: B'frd 3E 91 (1B 6)
BD11: B'frd .1B 136
BD20: Sils .*2D 14*
(off Elliott St.)
HX2: Hal .4C 128
HX3: Hal .5H 131
HX6: Hal .4H 147
LS27: Morl .6C 116
LS29: Burl W .2F 21
Spring Gdns. La. BD20: Keigh .3G 33
Spring Gdns. Mt. BD20: Keigh .4H 33
Spring Gdns. Rd. BD9: B'frd .6A 70
Spring Gdn. St. BD13: B'frd .4A 108
Spring Gro. BD10: B'frd .2H 71
HX1: Hal .2C 148
LS6: Leeds .1E 97
Spring Gro. Av. LS6: Leeds .1E 97
Spring Gro. Vw. LS6: Leeds .1E 97
Spring Gro. Wlk. LS6: Leeds .1E 97
Spring Hall Cl. HX3: Hal .2D 130
Spring Hall Ct. HX1: Hal .1C 148
Spring Hall Dr. HX2: Hal .3C 148
Spring Hall Gdns. HX2: Hal .2C 148
Spring Hall Gro. HX2: Hal .2C 148
Spring Hall La. HX1: Hal .3C 148
Spring Hall Pl. HX1: Hal .2C 148
Spring Head BD22: Keigh .1B 64
HX2: Hal .6C 128
HX3: Hal .2E 131
Springhead Mills BD22: Haw .1C 64
Spring Head Rd. BD13: B'frd .5A 88
BD22: Haw .1B 64
Springhead Rd. LS26: Rothw .1C 142
Spring Head Ter. BD13: B'frd .4G 87
Spring Hill BD15: B'frd .4G 67
BD17: Bail .4H 51
BD18: Ship .2E 71
LS16: Leeds .3E 59
Springhill Cl. WF1: Wake .4E 157
Spring Hill Cotts. *LS6: Leeds* .*3E 77*
(off Monk Bri. Ter.)
Spring Hill Pl. BD15: B'frd .4G 67
Springhills WF1: Wake .4E 157
Spring Hill Ter. *LS6: Leeds* .*3E 77*
(off Monk Bri. Rd.)
Spring Holes La. BD13: B'frd .4G 87
Springhurst Rd. BD18: Ship .2A 70
Spring La. BD16: Bgly .1F 51
HX4: Hal .4E 159
LS22: Weth .4H 13
Springlodge Pl. BD8: B'frd .2D 90
Springmead Dr. LS25: Gar .5F 103
Spring Mill St. BD5: B'frd .6E 91
Spring Mt. BD21: Keigh .2C 48
Spring Pk. Rd. BD15: B'frd .3G 67
Spring Pl. BD7: B'frd 6C 90 (6A 6)
BD21: Keigh .2C 48
Spring Ri. BD21: Keigh .1C 48
Spring Rd. LS6: Leeds .5E 77
Spring Rock HX4: Hal .6G 159
Spring Row BD13: B'frd .4A 108
BD16: Bgly .6F 49
BD21: Keigh .1H 47
(not continuous)
BD22: Haw .1F 65
BD22: Oxen .2E 85
HX2: Hal .6A 106
Spring Royd HX2: Hal .1C 146
Springroyd Ter. BD8: B'frd .3H 89
Springs La. LS29: I'ly .5E 11
Springs Rd. LS19: B'frd .1C 54
Springs Ter. LS29: I'ly .5E 11
Spring St. BD10: B'frd .2H 71
BD15: B'frd .6C 68
BD21: Keigh .5A 34
BD22: Haw .*1F 65*
(off Bingley Rd.)
HD6: Brigh .1A 162
Springswood Av. BD18: Ship .2A 70
Springswood Pl. BD18: Ship .2A 70
Springswood Rd. BD18: Ship .2A 70
Spring Ter. BD21: Keigh .1C 48
HX3: Hal 1H 149 (2D 164)
HX6: Hal .1A 158
Spring Valley LS28: Pud .2A 94
Spring Valley Av. LS13: Leeds .2E 95
Spring Valley Cl. LS13: Leeds .2E 95
Spring Valley Ct. LS13: Leeds .2E 95
Spring Valley Cres.
LS13: Leeds .2E 95
Spring Valley Cft. LS13: Leeds .2E 95
Spring Valley Dr. LS13: Leeds .2E 95
Spring Valley Vw. LS13: Leeds .2E 95
Spring Valley Wlk. LS13: Leeds .2E 95
Spring Vw. *BD13: B'frd* .*3G 87*
(off Up. Heights Rd.)
HX2: Hal .3D 146
LS27: Morl .5F 115
Spring Vw. Rd. HX2: Hal .3D 146
Springville Ter. BD10: B'frd .2H 71
Spring Way BD21: Keigh .1C 48
Springwell Av. LS26: Swil .4A 122
Springwell Cl. LS19: Yead .1G 55
Springwell Ct. LS12: Leeds .5F 97
WF3: E Ard .6E 139
Springwell Dr. BD5: B'frd .1E 111
Springwell Rd. LS12: Leeds .5F 97
LS26: Swil .4A 122
Spring Wells BD22: Keigh .3C 46
Springwell St. LS12: Leeds .5F 97
Springwell Ter. BD6: B'frd .4A 110
LS19: Yead .1G 55
Springwell Vw. LS11: Leeds .5G 97
WF17: Bat .*6B 136*
(off South Vw.)
Spring Wood Av. HX3: Hal .1F 159
Springwood Av. BD5: B'frd .2F 111
Springwood Ct. *LS8: Leeds* .*3F 79*
(off Bk. Wetherby Rd.)
Spring Wood Dr. HX3: Hal .1F 159
Spring Wood Gdns. BD5: B'frd .3F 111
HX3: Hal .2F 159
Springwood Gdns. LS8: Leeds .3F 79
Springwood Gro. LS8: Leeds .3G 79
Springwood Pl. *BD2: B'frd* .*1E 91*
(off Bolton Rd.)
Springwood Rd. LS8: Leeds .3F 79
LS19: Yead .4E 55
Springwood Ter. *BD2: B'frd* .*1E 91*
(off King's Rd.)
Spruce St. BD21: Keigh .5B 34
Spruice Hgts. HD6: Brigh .3A 152
Spur Dr. LS15: Leeds .6G 81
Square HX2: Hal .1F 127
HX3: Hal .4C 130
Square, The BD8: B'frd .4E 89
HX3: Hal .4A 150
LS23: B Spa .4C 30
LS25: Kip .4G 123
Square Chapel Cen. for the Arts
. . . . .2H 149 (4D 164)
Square Rd. HX1: Hal 2H 149 (4D 164)
Square St. BD4: B'frd .6G 91
Squire Grn. BD8: B'frd .2H 89
Squire La. BD8: B'frd .2H 89
BD9: B'frd .2H 89
Squirrel La. BD13: B'frd .6F 87
Squirrel Way LS17: Leeds .3D 60
Stable Ct. *LS28: Pud* .*3F 73*
(off Bk. Thornhill St.)
Stable Fold BD12: B'frd .5D 132
Stable La. HX3: Hal .6F 129
Stable M. BD16: Bgly .2A 68
Stables, The *LS21: Otley* .*3E 23*
(off Wesley St.)
Stables La. LS23: B Spa .4C 30
Stackgarth HD6: Brigh .3A 162
Stadium Rd. BD6: B'frd .5E 111
Stadium Way LS11: Leeds .2E 117
Stafford Av. HX3: Hal .5G 149
Stafford Grn. HX3: Hal .6G 149
Stafford Pde. HX3: Hal .6G 149
Stafford Pl. HX3: Hal .5G 149
Stafford Rd. HX3: Hal .6G 149
Stafford Sq. HX3: Hal .6H 149
Stafford St. BD4: B'frd .1H 111
LS10: Leeds .1C 118
LS27: Morl .5H 137
WF10: C'frd .6H 145
Stainbeck Av. LS7: Leeds .3F 77
Stainbeck Cnr. *LS7: Leeds* .*2A 78*
(off Harrogate Rd.)
Stainbeck Gdns. BD6: B'frd .5F 109
LS7: Leeds .3H 77
Stainbeck La. LS7: Leeds .2G 77
Stainbeck Rd. LS7: Leeds .3F 77

Stainbeck Wlk.—Staygate Grn.

Stainbeck Wlk. LS7: Leeds 3H **77**
Stainburn Av. LS17: Leeds 6C **60**
Stainburn Cres. LS17: Leeds 6B **60**
Stainburn Dr. LS17: Leeds 6B **60**
Stainburn Gdns. LS17: Leeds 6C **60**
Stainburn Mt. LS17: Leeds 1C **78**
Stainburn Pde. LS17: Leeds 6B **60**
Stainburn Rd. LS17: Leeds 1B **78**
Stainburn Ter. LS17: Leeds 1B **78**
Stainburn Vw. LS17: Leeds 6C **60**
Staincliffe Ct. BD20: Sils 2D **14**
Stainland Rd. HX4: Hal 2H **159**
(Exley)
HX4: Hal 6A **158**
(Rishworth Rd.)
HX4: Hal 6F **159**
(Stainland)
Stainmore Cl. LS14: Leeds 6C **80**
Stainmore Pl. LS14: Leeds 6C **80**
Stainton Cl. BD6: B'frd 5G **109**
Stainton La. WF3: Rothw 3H **141**
Staircase La. LS16: B'hpe 5F **25**
LS21: Pool 5F **25**
Stairfoot Cl. LS16: Leeds 2D **58**
Stair Foot La. LS16: Leeds 2D **58**
LS17: Leeds 2D **58**
Stairfoot Vw. LS16: Leeds 2D **58**
Stairfoot Wlk. LS16: Leeds 2D **58**
Staithe Av. LS10: Leeds 2B **140**
Staithe Cl. LS10: Leeds 2B **140**
Staithe Gdns. LS10: Leeds 2B **140**
Staithes, The *BD17: Bail* *4C* ***52***
(off Baildon Rd.)
Staithgate La. BD6: B'frd 4F **111**
Stake La. HX7: Heb B 2A **146**
Stallabrass St. BD8: B'frd 3C **90** (2A **6**)
Stamford St. BD4: B'frd 6H **91**
Stammergate La. LS22: Coll 2B **28**
Stamp Hill Cl. LS29: Add 1B **8**
Stanacre Pl. BD3: B'frd 3F **91** (1F **7**)
Stanage La. HX3: Hal 6E **109**
Stanbeck Ct. LS7: Leeds 1A **78**
Standale Av. LS28: Pud 3H **93**
Standale Cres. LS28: Pud 3H **93**
Standale Ho. *BD4: B'frd* *3A* ***112***
(off Prince St.)
Standale Ri. LS28: Pud 3H **93**
Standard Vs. LS12: Leeds 1B **116**
Stanhall Av. LS28: Pud 2H **93**
Stanhope Av. LS18: H'fth 5E **57**
Stanhope Cl. LS18: H'fth 5E **57**
Stanhope Cotts. *LS21: Pool* *4E* ***25***
(off Old Orchard, The)
Stanhope Dr. LS18: H'fth 1D **74**
Stanhope Gdns. WF3: E Ard 6C **140**
Stanhope Rd. WF3: E Ard 6C **140**
STANKS **4F 81**
Stanks App. LS14: Leeds 5F **81**
Stanks Av. LS14: Leeds 5F **81**
Stanks Cl. LS14: Leeds 5G **81**
Stanks Cross LS14: Leeds 5G **81**
Stanks Dr. LS14: Leeds 3E **81**
Stanks Gdns. LS14: Leeds 4F **81**
Stanks Gth. LS14: Leeds 5G **81**
Stanks Grn. LS14: Leeds 5G **81**
Stanks Gro. LS14: Leeds 5F **81**
Stanks La. Nth. LS14: Leeds 3E **81**
Stanks La. Sth. LS14: Leeds 5F **81**
Stanks Pde. LS14: Leeds 5F **81**
Stanks Ri. LS14: Leeds 5G **81**
Stanks Rd. LS14: Leeds 5F **81**
Stanks Way LS14: Leeds 5F **81**
Stanley Av. LS9: Leeds 1D **98**
Stanley Ct. *HX1: Hal* *2D* ***148***
(off Queen's Rd.)
Stanley Dr. LS8: Leeds 5F **61**
Stanley Gro. LS20: Guis 5C **40**
Stanley La. WF1: Wake 5H **157**
Stanley Pl. LS9: Leeds 1E **99**
Stanley Rd. BD2: B'frd 5D **70**
BD22: Keigh 3G **47**
HX1: Hal 3D **148**
Stanley Rd. LS7: Leeds 6B **78**
LS9: Leeds 1D **98**
Stanley St. BD10: B'frd 2B **72**
(Fieldgate Rd.)
BD10: B'frd 1H **71**
(Moorfield Pl.)
BD16: Bgly 4C **50**
BD18: Ship 4C **70**
BD21: Keigh 5H **33**
BD22: Haw 1E **65**
HD6: Brigh 6B **152**
HX6: Hal 5A **148**
Stanley St. Nth. *HX2: Hal* *2E* ***129***
(off Shay La.)
Stanley St. W. *HX6: Hal* *6H* ***147***
(off Salisbury St.)
Stanley Ter. LS9: Leeds 1E **99**
(not continuous)
LS12: Leeds 4C **96**
Stanley Vw. LS12: Leeds 4C **96**
Stanmore Av. LS4: Leeds 6C **76**
Stanmore Cres. LS4: Leeds 6C **76**
Stanmore Gro. LS4: Leeds 6C **76**
Stanmore Hill LS4: Leeds 6D **76**
Stanmore Mt. LS4: Leeds 6C **76**
Stanmore Pl. BD7: B'frd 6A **90**
LS4: Leeds 6C **76**
Stanmore Rd. LS4: Leeds 6C **76**
Stanmore St. LS4: Leeds 6C **76**
Stanmore Ter. LS4: Leeds 6C **76**
Stanmore Vw. LS4: Leeds 6C **76**
Stannary Pl. HX1: Hal 1F **149** (2A **164**)
Stannery End La. HX7: Heb B 2A **146**
STANNINGLEY **1B 94**
Stanningley Av. HX2: Hal 2H **127**
Stanningley By-Pass LS13: Leeds 3A **94**
LS28: Pud 2G **93**
Stanningley Dr. HX2: Hal 2H **127**
Stanningley Fld. Cl. LS13: Leeds 2C **94**
Stanningley Grn. HX2: Hal 1A **128**
Stanningley Ind. Est. LS28: Pud 2H **93**
Stanningley Rd. HX2: Hal 2H **127**
LS12: Leeds 2G **95**
LS13: Leeds 2G **95**
LS28: Pud 1B **94**
Stansfield Cl. HX1: Hal 2E **149**
Stansfield Ct. HX6: Hal 6H **147**
Stansfield Pl. BD10: B'frd 6H **53**
Stanwick Ho. BD2: B'frd 5D **70**
Staples La. BD21: Haw 2G **65**
Stapleton Ho. BD2: B'frd 5D **70**
Stapper Grn. BD15: B'frd 3F **67**
Star Health & Fitness Club ***3E 99***
(off Glenthorpe Cres.)
Starkie St. BD21: Keigh 1H **47**
Starling M. *BD15: B'frd* *4D* ***88***
(off Bell Dean Rd.)
Star St. BD5: B'frd 2C **110**
Star Ter. HD6: Brigh 4G **161**
Starting Post BD10: B'frd 2F **71**
Station App. HX1: Hal 3H **149** (5D **164**)
LS29: Burl W 3E **21**
Station Av. LS13: Leeds 1D **94**
Station Bri. *BD21: Keigh* *6B* ***34***
(off Bradford Rd.)
Station Cl. LS25: Gar 4F **103**
Station Cotts. LS14: T'ner 1H **63**
LS24: Tad 5G **31**
Station Ct. BD1: B'frd 4F **91** (4E **7**)
LS15: Leeds 2E **101**
LS25: Gar 4F **103**
Station Cres. LS12: Leeds 4B **96**
Station Flds. LS25: Gar 4F **103**
Station Gdns. LS22: Weth 4D **12**
Station Ho. *LS25: M'fld* *5E* ***105***
(off Old Great Nth. Rd.)
Station Ind. Pk. HX2: Hal 2D **146**
Station La. BD11: B'frd 1E **135**
HX4: Hal 3H **159**
LS14: T'ner 1H **63**
LS22: Coll 3B **28**
LS26: Rothw 6F **121**
Station La. WF3: E Ard 6B **140**
(Bidder Dr.)
WF3: E Ard 6E **139**
(Thorpe La.)
WF3: Leeds 5E **139**
Station Mt. LS13: Leeds 1D **94**
Station Pde. LS5: Leeds 5B **76**
Station Pl. LS13: Leeds 1E **95**
Station Plaza *LS29: I'ly* *5D* ***10***
(off Station Rd.)
Station Rd. BD2: B'frd 1E **91**
BD11: B'frd 2A **136**
BD12: B'frd 5A **132**
(Hill End Cl.)
BD12: B'frd 2E **133**
(Olympic Way)
BD13: B'frd 3B **108**
(Bridle Stile La.)
BD13: B'frd 3B **86**
(Main Rd.)
BD13: B'frd 3A **66**
(Turf La.)
BD14: B'frd 1E **109**
BD15: B'frd 6D **66**
BD17: B'frd 1H **53**
BD17: Bail 4C **52**
BD18: Ship 1B **70**
BD20: Stee 6D **14**
BD22: Haw 2C **64**
BD22: Keigh 5D **46**
BD22: Oxen 6C **64**
HD2: Hud 6G **163**
HD6: Brigh 1C **162**
HX2: Hal 2D **146**
HX3: B'frd, Hal 5A **132**
HX3: Hal 2E **129**
(Burton St.)
HX3: Hal 2E **151**
(Hill End Cl.)
HX6: Hal 6H **147**
LS12: Leeds 4B **96**
LS15: Leeds 1E **101**
LS15: Scho 2H **81**
LS18: H'fth 5E **57**
LS20: Guis 4B **40**
LS21: Arth 6H **25**
LS21: Otley 4E **23**
LS25: Gar 4F **103**
LS25: Kip 5F **123**
LS26: Mick 4B **144**
LS27: Morl 2A **138**
LS29: Burl W 3E **21**
LS29: I'ly 5D **10**
LS29: Men 1H **39**
WF10: Kip 3H **145**
Station Rd. Ind. Est. LS25: Kip 6F **123**
Station St. LS28: Pud 5H **93**
Station Ter. LS13: Leeds 1E **95**
Station Vw. BD20: Stee 6D **14**
BD22: Oxen 6C **64**
LS15: Leeds 2E **101**
Station Wlk. LS27: Morl 2B **138**
Station Way LS12: Leeds 4B **96**
Station Works Ind. Pk.
BD21: Keigh 6C **34**
Staups La. HX3: Hal 5B **130**
Staveley Ct. BD16: Bgly 3C **50**
BD18: Ship 1F **69**
BD22: Keigh 3G **47**
Staveley Dr. BD18: Ship 2F **69**
Staveley Gro. BD22: Keigh 4G **47**
Staveley M. BD16: Bgly 3C **50**
Staveley Rd. BD7: B'frd 5B **90**
BD16: Bgly 3C **50**
BD18: Ship 1F **69**
BD22: Keigh 4G **47**
Staveley Way BD22: Keigh 3G **47**
Staverton Gro. BD13: B'frd 4A **88**
Staverton St. HX2: Hal 2C **148**
Staybrite Av. BD16: Bgly 2C **68**
STAYGATE **4E 111**
Staygate Grn. BD6: B'frd 4E **111**

A-Z Leeds & Bradford 273

Staynton Cres. HD2: Hud 6F 163
   (not continuous)
STEAD 2A 20
Stead Hill Way BD10: B'frd 6F 53
Steadings Way BD22: Keigh 2E 47
Stead La. BD16: Bgly 1F 51
  LS14: T'ner 2H 63
  LS29: Burl W 3B 20
Steadman St. BD3: B'frd 5H 91
Steadman Ter. BD3: B'frd 5H 91
Stead Rd. BD4: B'frd 5C 112
Stead St. BD18: Ship 1B 70
  HX1: Hal 2F 149 (4A 164)
   (not continuous)
Steads Yd. LS18: H'fth 5E 57
Steander LS9: Leeds 4B 98 (6H 5)
Steel Ter. LS26: Rothw 2B 142
   (off Blackburn Ct.)
Steep Bank Side HX3: Hal 3A 150
Steeplands HD2: Hud 5F 163
STEEP LANE 5B 146
Steep La. HD2: Hud 5F 163
  HX6: Hal 5A 146
Steeple Cl. LS27: Morl 6B 138
Steerforth Cl. BD5: B'frd 2E 111
   (off Mumford St.)
STEETON .6C 14
Steeton & Silsden Station (Rail) . .5D 14
Steeton Gro. BD20: Stee 5C 14
Steeton Hall Gdns. BD20: Stee 5C 14
Stell Hill BD22: Keigh 2D 46
Stephen Cl. HX3: Hal 6C 130
Stephen Cres. BD2: B'frd 6E 71
Stephen Rd. BD6: B'frd 3H 109
Stephen Row HX3: Hal 5C 130
   (off Windmill La.)
Stephenson Dr. LS12: Leeds 2F 115
Stephenson Ho. LS27: Morl 2B 138
   (off Pullman Ct.)
Stephenson Rd. BD15: B'frd 1H 87
Stephenson St. BD7: B'frd 2B 110
Stephensons Way LS29: I'ly 5D 10
Stephenson Way LS12: Leeds 2F 115
  WF2: Wake 4D 156
Stepping Stones BD20: Keigh 5A 36
Steps, The HX6: Hal 4A 148
Steps La. HX6: Hal 4A 148
Ster Century Cinema 3H 97
Sterling St. WF3: Morl 5E 139
Sterling Way WF3: Morl 5D 138
Stewart Cl. BD2: B'frd 4A 72
  LS15: Leeds 4E 101
Stewart St. BD22: Haw 1E 65
Sticker La. BD4: B'frd 2A 112
Stile Hill Way LS15: Leeds 4H 101
Stillington Ho. BD2: B'frd 5D 70
Stirling Cres. BD4: B'frd 2C 112
  LS18: H'fth 3C 56
Stirling Rd. LS29: Burl W 2D 20
Stirling St. BD20: Sils 1E 15
  HX1: Hal 3F 149 (5A 164)
Stirling Way LS25: Gar 4H 103
Stirrup Gro. BD2: B'frd 5F 71
Stirton St. BD5: B'frd 2D 110
STOCKBRIDGE 4D 34
Stockeld Rd. LS29: I'ly 5C 10
Stockeld Way LS29: I'ly 4C 10
Stockheld La. LS15: Scho 6H 63
Stockhill Fold BD10: B'frd 1B 72
   (not continuous)
Stockhill Rd. BD10: B'frd 2B 72
Stockinger La. LS29: Add 1D 8
   (not continuous)
Stock La. HX2: Hal 3H 147
Stocks App. LS14: Leeds 5D 80
Stocksfield Vw. BD13: B'frd 4D 108
Stocks Hill LS11: Leeds 6G 97
  LS12: Leeds 3C 96
  LS26: Mick 4D 144
   (off Hicks La.)
  LS29: Men 1F 39
Stocks Hill Cl. BD20: Keigh 4H 35

Stocks Hill Gth. LS29: Men 1F 39
   (off Stocks Hill)
Stocks La. BD13: B'frd 3D 108
  HX2: Hal 6E 127
  HX6: Hal 6E 147
Stocks Ri. LS14: Leeds 5D 80
Stocks Rd. LS14: Leeds 5E 81
Stocks St. LS7: Leeds 6A 78
Stotd Fold HX2: Hal 5A 106
Stogden Hill BD13: B'frd 4D 108
Stone Acre Ct. BD5: B'frd 3E 111
Stonebridge BD10: B'frd 1H 71
   (off Idlecroft Rd.)
Stonebridge App. LS12: Leeds 5G 95
Stonebridge Av. LS12: Leeds 5H 95
Stonebridge Gro. LS12: Leeds 5G 95
Stonebridge La. LS12: Leeds 6G 95
Stone Brig Grn. LS26: Rothw 3H 141
Stone Brig La. LS26: Rothw 3H 141
STONE CHAIR 3D 130
Stonechat Ri. LS27: Morl 3C 138
Stone Cliffe HX3: Hal 5E 149
   (off Wakefield Ga.)
Stonecliffe Bank LS12: Leeds 5G 95
Stonecliffe Cl. LS12: Leeds 5G 95
Stonecliffe Cres. LS12: Leeds 5G 95
Stonecliffe Dr. LS12: Leeds 5G 95
Stonecliffe Gdns. LS12: Leeds 5G 95
Stonecliffe Gth. LS12: Leeds 5G 95
Stonecliffe Grn. LS12: Leeds 5G 95
Stonecliffe Gro. LS12: Leeds 5G 95
Stonecliffe Lawn LS12: Leeds 5G 95
Stonecliffe Mt. LS12: Leeds 5G 95
Stonecliffe Pl. LS12: Leeds 6G 95
   (off Stonecliffe Way)
Stonecliffe Ter. LS12: Leeds 5G 95
Stonecliffe Vw. LS12: Leeds 5G 95
Stonecliffe Wlk. LS12: Leeds 6G 95
Stonecliffe Way LS12: Leeds 5G 95
Stone Ct. BD20: Keigh 5H 35
Stonecroft BD2: B'frd 5A 72
Stonedale Cl. LS21: Pool 5G 25
Stonedene LS6: Leeds 1F 77
Stonedene Pk. LS22: Weth 3F 13
Stonefield LS14: S'cft 5F 45
Stonefield Cl. BD2: B'frd 4H 71
Stonefield Pl. WF17: Bat 6B 136
Stonefield St. BD19: Cleck 3G 153
Stonefield Ter. LS27: Morl 5C 116
Stone Fold BD17: Bail 5A 52
Stonegate BD16: Bgly 2C 50
  LS7: Leeds 6A 78
   (not continuous)
Stonegate App. LS7: Leeds 3F 77
Stonegate Chase LS7: Leeds 3F 77
Stonegate Cl. LS17: Leeds 4B 60
Stonegate Cres. LS7: Leeds 2G 77
Stonegate Dr. LS7: Leeds 2G 77
Stonegate Edge LS7: Leeds 2G 77
Stonegate Farm Cl. LS7: Leeds 2F 77
Stonegate Gdns. LS7: Leeds 2F 77
Stonegate Grn. LS7: Leeds 3F 77
Stonegate Gro. LS7: Leeds 2G 77
Stonegate La. LS7: Leeds 2F 77
Stonegate M. LS7: Leeds 3F 77
Stonegate Pl. LS7: Leeds 3F 77
Stonegate Rd. BD10: B'frd 3H 71
  LS6: Leeds 2F 77
Stonegate Vw. LS7: Leeds 2F 77
Stonegate Wlk. LS7: Leeds 3G 77
Stone Gro. BD20: Stee 6C 14
   (not continuous)
Stone Hall M. BD2: B'frd 5A 72
Stone Hall Rd. BD2: B'frd 5H 71
Stonehaven Ct. BD21: Keigh 2C 48
Stone Hill BD16: Bgly 3D 50
Stone Ho. Dr. BD13: B'frd 5G 107
Stone Ho. Fold BD22: Keigh 5B 46
Stonehurst LS14: Leeds 5F 81
Stone La. BD22: Oxen 1A 84

Stonelea BD4: B'frd 5E 113
Stonelea Ct. LS6: Leeds 4D 76
  LS7: Leeds 2G 77
Stonelea Dr. HD6: Brigh 4H 161
Stoneside BD13: B'frd 4B 108
Stoneleigh Av. LS17: Leeds 3D 60
Stoneleigh Cl. LS17: Leeds 3D 60
Stoneleigh Ct. BD19: Cleck 6E 133
  LS17: Leeds 3D 60
Stoneleigh Gth. LS17: Leeds 4D 60
Stoneleigh La. LS17: Leeds 4D 60
Stoneleigh Way LS17: Leeds 4D 60
Stone Mill App. LS6: Leeds 2E 77
Stone Mill Ct. LS6: Leeds 2E 77
Stone Mill Way LS6: Leeds 2E 77
Stone Pits La. LS27: Morl 1F 137
Stone Stay Fold LS29: Add 1C 8
Stone St. BD1: B'frd 4E 91 (3D 6)
  BD13: B'frd 3G 107
   (off South Vw.)
  BD15: B'frd 6C 68
  BD17: Bail 5E 53
  BD22: Haw 3C 64
   (off Sun St.)
Stone Ter. BD16: Bgly 5F 49
Stone Vs. LS6: Leeds 3D 76
Stoney Battery
  HX3: Hal 1G 149 (1C 164)
Stoney Brow HX3: Hal 5A 150
Stoneycroft LS18: H'fth 1D 74
  LS19: Yead 3G 55
   (off Batter La.)
Stoneycroft La. BD20: Keigh 3H 33
Stoney Hill HD6: Brigh 1A 162
Stoneyhurst Sq. BD4: B'frd 2C 112
Stoneyhurst Way BD4: B'frd 2C 112
Stoney La. HX2: Hal 4D 148
  HX3: Hal 4E 129
   (Ovenden Rd.)
  HX3: Hal 4E 151
   (Walter Clough La.)
  HX3: Hal 3A 152
   (West Av.)
  HX7: Heb B 5A 126
  LS17: S'cft 2C 62
  LS18: H'fth 1D 74
  LS29: Burl W 5C 20
  WF2: Wake 4B 156
  WF3: E Ard 4A 156
Stoney Ridge Av. BD9: B'frd 5D 68
Stoney Ridge Rd. BD16: Bgly 5D 68
Stoney Ri. LS18: H'fth 1D 74
Stoney Rock Ct. LS9: Leeds 2D 98
Stoney Rock Gro. LS9: Leeds 2D 98
Stoney Rock La. LS9: Leeds 2D 98
STONEY ROYD 4H 149
Stoney Royd LS29: Burl W 1E 21
   (off Main St.)
Stoney Royd Ter. HX3: Hal 5H 149
Stoneys Fold BD15: B'frd 3F 67
Stoney Springs Ho. HX2: Hal 1B 146
Stoney Springs Ind. Units
  HX2: Hal 1B 146
Stoney St. BD20: Keigh 3H 33
Stoneythorpe LS18: H'fth 1D 74
Stony Cft. La. HX4: Hal 6A 158
Stony La. BD2: B'frd 4A 72
  BD15: B'frd 1B 88
  BD22: Keigh 1A 46
  HX4: Hal 3E 159
Stony Royd LS28: Pud 6G 73
Stoodley Ter. HX2: Hal 3C 148
Storey Pl. LS14: Leeds 2A 100
Storiths LS29: Add 2D 8
Stormer Hill HX6: Hal 1B 158
Stormer Hill La. HX6: Hal 1B 158
Storr Hill BD12: B'frd 3C 132
Storr Hill Ter. BD12: B'frd 3C 132
Storth Lea HX5: Ell 6D 160
Storth Vw. HX5: Ell 6D 160
Story Stones BD16: Bgly 2F 51
Stott Gap BD13: B'frd 4H 87

Stott Hill BD1: B'frd 4F **91** (3E **7**)
Stott Rd. LS6: Leeds 6E **77**
Stott St. LS12: Leeds 4D **96**
Stott Ter. BD2: B'frd 5B **72**
STOURTON 4F **119**
Stourton St. LS29: I'ly 4B **10**
Stowe Gro. LS9: Leeds 3G **99**
Stowell Mill St. BD5: B'frd 1D **110**
Stradbroke Way LS12: Leeds 5C **96**
Stradmore Rd. BD13: B'frd 3C **86**
Strafford Way BD10: B'frd 1C **72**
Straight Acres La.
    BD10: B'frd 4B **72**
Straight La. HX2: Hal 2B **128**
    LS29: Add 4A **8**
Straits BD17: Bail 3C **52**
Strand BD16: Bgly 3D **68**
Strangford Ct. BD10: B'frd 1B **72**
Stratford Av. LS11: Leeds 2G **117**
Stratford Ct. LS7: Leeds 3A **78**
Stratford Rd. BD7: B'frd 6B **90**
Stratford St. LS11: Leeds 3H **117**
Stratford Ter. LS11: Leeds 2H **117**
Strathallan Dr. BD17: Bail 4D **52**
Strathmore Av. LS9: Leeds 1E **99**
Strathmore Cl. BD2: B'frd 6H **71**
Strathmore Dr. BD17: Bail 3B **52**
    LS9: Leeds 6E **79**
Strathmore Rd. LS29: I'ly 5G **11**
Strathmore St. LS9: Leeds 1F **99**
Strathmore Ter. LS9: Leeds 6E **79**
Strathmore Vw. LS9: Leeds 1E **99**
Stratton Cl. HD6: Brigh 2B **162**
Stratton Pk. HD6: Brigh 2B **162**
Stratton Rd. HD6: Brigh 2B **162**
Stratton Vw. BD4: B'frd 1C **112**
Stratton Wlk. BD15: B'frd 3C **88**
Strawberry Av. LS25: Gar 5E **103**
Strawberry Flds. BD21: Keigh 5A **34**
Strawberry La. LS12: Leeds 4C **96**
    (not continuous)
Strawberry Rd. LS12: Leeds 4C **96**
Strawberry St. BD20: Sils 2D **14**
    BD21: Keigh 5A **34**
Straw Vw. BD10: B'frd 1F **71**
Stray, The BD10: B'frd 3G **71**
Stream Cl. BD20: Keigh 4F **35**
Stream Head BD13: B'frd 2F **87**
Stream Head Rd. BD13: B'frd 1F **87**
Streamside LS6: Leeds 3E **77**
Street, The LS29: Add 2C **8**
    (Hart Rhydding La.)
    LS29: Add 1B **8**
    (Stamp Hill Cl.)
Street 1 LS23: W'ton 3E **31**
Street 2 LS23: W'ton 3F **31**
Street 3 LS23: W'ton 2F **31**
Street 5 LS23: W'ton 1F **31**
Street 6 LS23: W'ton 1F **31**
Street 7 LS23: W'ton 1F **31**
Street 8 LS23: W'ton 1G **31**
Street La. BD20: Keigh 2F **35**
    LS8: Leeds 5E **61**
    LS17: Leeds 5A **60**
    LS27: Morl 2E **137**
Strensall Grn. BD6: B'frd 5G **109**
Stretchgate La. HX2: Hal 1C **148**
Stretton Av. LS6: Leeds 6E **59**
Strickland Av. LS17: Leeds 3B **62**
Strickland Cl. LS17: Leeds 3B **62**
Strickland Cres. LS17: Leeds 3B **62**
Stringer Cl. BD4: B'frd 5A **112**
Strone, The BD10: B'frd 6D **54**
STRONG CLOSE 6C **34**
Strong Cl. Gro. BD21: Keigh 6C **34**
Strong Cl. Rd. BD21: Keigh 6C **34**
Strong Cl. Way BD21: Keigh 6C **34**
    (off Strong Cl. Rd.)
Stuart Ct. BD5: B'frd 1E **111**
    (off Swarland Gro.)
Stuart Pl. HD2: Hud 6F **163**
Stubbing La. HX4: Hal 6C **158**

Stubbings Farm (Cvn. Site)
    LS21: Otley 5A **24**
Stubbings Rd. BD17: Bail 5H **51**
Stubbing Way BD18: Ship 3C **70**
    (not continuous)
Stubbs La. WF3: E Ard 2C **156**
Stubham Ri. LS29: I'ly 4C **10**
Stubs Beck La. BD19: Cleck 5B **134**
Stub Thorn La. HX3: Hal 3B **150**
Studdards Fold BD7: B'frd 1A **110**
Studdley Cres. BD16: Bgly 4D **50**
Studfold Vw. LS14: Leeds 6C **80**
Studio Rd. LS3: Leeds 6B **4**
Studleigh Ter. HD6: Brigh 4G **151**
    (off Brooklyn Ter.)
Studley Av. BD6: B'frd 6B **110**
Studley Cl. BD20: Keigh 4H **35**
Studley Rd. BD3: B'frd 1F **91**
Studley Ter. LS28: Pud 3A **94**
STUMP CROSS 6B **130**
Stumps, The BD18: Ship 6E **53**
Sturges Gro. BD2: B'frd 1H **91**
Sturton Av. LS25: Gar 3G **103**
Sturton Grange La. LS25: Gar 4H **103**
Sturton Gro. HX2: Hal 6C **106**
Sturton La. HX2: Hal 6C **106**
    LS25: Gar 3G **103**
Stutely Gro. HD2: Hud 6E **163**
Styebank La. LS26: Rothw 1B **142**
Styes La. HX2: Hal 5D **146**
    HX6: Hal 5D **146**
Sty La. BD16: Bgly 1A **50**
Styveton Way BD20: Stee 5B **14**
Suffield Cl. LS27: Morl 5D **114**
Suffield Cres. LS27: Morl 5D **114**
Suffield Dr. LS27: Morl 5D **114**
Suffield Rd. LS27: Morl 5D **114**
Suffolk Cl. LS19: Yead 6F **41**
Suffolk Pl. BD2: B'frd 5F **71**
SUGAR HILL 6C **136**
Sugar Hill LS29: Add 1D **8**
Sugar Hill St. LS26: Rothw 4E **143**
Sugar Well App. LS7: Leeds 4G **77**
Sugar Well Cl. LS7: Leeds 5H **77**
Sugar Well Mt. LS7: Leeds 4G **77**
Sugar Well Rd. LS7: Leeds 4G **77**
Sugden Bank HX6: Hal 3A **162**
    (off Sunny Bank St.)
Sugden Cl. HD6: Brigh 3A **162**
Sugden End BD22: Haw 2F **65**
Sugden Ho. Farm BD21: Haw 2H **65**
Sugden Pl. BD6: B'frd 6G **109**
    (off Beck Hill)
Sugden's Almshouses
    BD22: Keigh 4D **46**
Sugden St. BD1: B'frd 4C **90** (3A **6**)
    BD12: B'frd 3F **133**
Sulby Gro. BD10: B'frd 2C **72**
Summerbank Cl. BD11: B'frd 6B **114**
Summerbridge Cres. BD10: B'frd . . .4B **72**
    BD19: Cleck 5G **135**
Summerbridge Dr. BD10: B'frd 4B **72**
Summerdale BD19: Cleck 5F **135**
Summerfield Av. HD6: Brigh 3B **152**
    LS13: Leeds 6C **74**
Summerfield Cl. BD17: Bail 4A **52**
Summerfield Cl. HX2: Hal 2E **129**
Summerfield Dr. BD17: Bail 4B **52**
    LS13: Leeds 6C **74**
Summerfield Gdns. LS13: Leeds 6C **74**
Summerfield Grn. BD17: Bail 4B **52**
    LS13: Leeds 6C **74**
Summerfield Gro. BD17: Bail 4A **52**
Summerfield Pk. BD17: Bail 4B **52**
Summerfield Pl. LS13: Leeds 6C **74**
    LS28: Pud 6C **74**
    (off Richardshaw La.)
Summerfield Rd. BD10: B'frd 3A **72**
    LS13: Leeds 6C **74**
Summerfield Wlk. LS13: Leeds 6C **74**
Summergate Pl. HX1: Hal 3D **148**
Summergate St. HX1: Hal 3D **148**

Summer Hall Ing BD12: B'frd 3B **132**
Summerhill Av. BD20: Stee 5D **14**
Summerhill Dr. BD20: Stee 5D **14**
Summerhill Gdns. LS8: Leeds 5F **61**
Summerhill Gro. LS25: Gar 5D **102**
Summerhill Pl. BD20: Stee 5D **14**
Summerhill Pl. LS8: Leeds 5F **61**
Summer Hill Rd. LS26: Mick 4D **144**
Summerhill Rd. LS25: Gar 4D **102**
Summer Hill St. BD7: B'frd 6A **90**
Summerlands Gro. BD5: B'frd 3G **111**
Summerland Ter. HX6: Hal 5B **148**
Summer Lea BD10: B'frd 1G **71**
Summerley Ct. BD10: B'frd 2H **71**
Summerscale St. HX1: Hal 1E **149**
Summerseat LS19: Yead 4H **55**
Summerseat Pl. BD7: B'frd 6C **90**
Summerset Pl. BD2: B'frd 1H **91**
    (off Green Pl.)
Summersgill Sq. LS18: H'fth 1D **74**
Summer St. HX1: Hal 4D **148**
Summerville Rd. BD7: B'frd 5C **90**
    LS28: Pud 2G **93**
Summit St. BD21: Keigh 5H **33**
Sunbeam Av. LS11: Leeds 2H **117**
Sunbeam Gro. LS11: Leeds 2H **117**
Sunbeam Pl. LS11: Leeds 2H **117**
Sunbeam Ter. LS11: Leeds 2H **117**
    WF3: E Ard 6E **139**
Sunbridge Rd. BD1: B'frd . . .4D **90** (2A **6**)
Sun Bldgs. HX2: Hal 2F **127**
Sunderland Cl. HD6: Brigh 6A **152**
    (off Thornhill Bri. La.)
Sunderland Rd. BD9: B'frd 1B **90**
Sunderland St. BD21: Keigh 1H **47**
    BD22: Haw 1F **65**
    HX1: Hal 2F **149** (4A **164**)
Sundown Av. BD7: B'frd 1G **109**
Sun Fld. LS28: Pud 2H **93**
Sunfield Cl. LS28: Pud 1H **93**
Sunfield Dr. LS28: Pud 1H **93**
Sunfield Gdns. LS28: Pud 1H **93**
Sunfield Pl. LS28: Pud 2H **93**
Sun Fold HX1: Hal 3H **149** (6D **164**)
Sunhill Dr. BD17: Bail 5G **51**
Sunhurst Cl. BD22: Keigh 5C **46**
Sunhurst Dr. BD22: Keigh 5C **46**
Sun La. BD22: Haw 2A **64**
    LS29: Burl W 1D **20**
    (not continuous)
Sunningdale BD8: B'frd 3F **89**
    LS25: M'fld 3D **104**
Sunningdale Av. LS17: Leeds 3G **59**
Sunningdale Cl. LS17: Leeds 3G **59**
Sunningdale Cres. BD13: B'frd 4C **66**
Sunningdale Dr. LS17: Leeds 3G **59**
Sunningdale Grn. LS17: Leeds 3G **59**
Sunningdale Wlk. LS17: Leeds 3G **59**
Sunningdale Way LS17: Leeds 3G **59**
SUNNYBANK 4F **159**
Sunny Bank BD12: B'frd 3E **133**
    BD13: B'frd 4B **108**
    BD18: Ship 2B **70**
    HX3: Hal 5H **131**
    LS28: Pud 4D **78**
    LS27: Morl 5C **116**
    (off Sunny Gro.)
Sunnybank LS25: M'fld 5F **105**
Sunnybank Av. BD3: Pud 2D **92**
    BD5: B'frd 4D **110**
    LS18: H'fth 2D **74**
Sunnybank Cl. BD19: Cleck 2F **153**
Sunnybank Cl. LS19: Yead 6H **41**
Sunnybank Cres. HX4: Hal 4F **159**
    LS19: Yead 6H **41**
Sunny Bank Dr. HX6: Hal 5A **148**
Sunnybank Dr. HX4: Hal 4F **159**
Sunnybank Grange HD6: Brigh 1A **162**
Sunny Bank Gro. LS8: Leeds 4D **78**
Sunnybank Gro. BD3: Pud 2D **92**
Sunny Bank Ho. LS28: Pud 6H **73**
Sunny Bank La. HX3: Hal 4D **150**

Sunnybank La.—Syke La.

Sunnybank La. BD3: Pud .2D **92**
HX4: Hal .4F **159**
Sunny Bank Mills LS28: Pud .6H **73**
Sunny Bank Rd. BD5: B'frd .4D **110**
HD6: Brigh .1A **162**
HX2: Hal .2H **127**
Sunnybank Rd. HX4: Hal .4E **159**
LS18: H'fth .2D **74**
Sunny Bank St. HX6: Hal .5A **148**
Sunnybank St. LS18: H'fth .2D **74**
Sunny Bank Ter. HX3: Hal .6G **129**
Sunnybank Ter. HD6: Brigh .6A **152**
LS18: H'fth .2D **74**
Sunny Bank Vw. LS8: Leeds .4D **78**
Sunny Brae Cres. BD16: Bgly .5D **50**
Sunny Brow La. BD9: B'frd .1F **89**
Sunny Cliffe HX3: Hal .2G **151**
Sunnycliffe BD20: Keigh .5H **35**
Sunny Dale BD13: B'frd .1B **86**
Sunnydale Av. HD6: Brigh .3A **162**
Sunnydale Cres. LS21: Otley .5B **22**
Sunnydale Gro. BD21: Keigh .1D **48**
Sunnydale Pk. BD20: Keigh .4A **36**
Sunnydale Ridge LS21: Otley .5B **22**
Sunnydene LS14: Leeds .2B **100**
Sunnyfield WF3: E Ard .2A **156**
Sunny Gro. LS27: Morl .5C **116**
Sunny Gym .**4E 13**
Sunnyhill Av. BD21: Keigh .2F **47**
Sunnyhill Gro. BD21: Keigh .2F **47**
Sunny Lee Est. LS21: Otley .3E **23**
Sunny Mt. BD16: Bgly .6F **49**
BD20: Keigh .6G **35**
BD21: Keigh .5H **33**
BD22: Keigh .5E **33**
HX3: Hal .2E **151**
Sunnymount Ter. *WF17: Bat .6B **136***
(off Moon Cl.)
Sunnyridge Av. LS28: Pud .3F **93**
Sunny Side HX3: Hal .2G **151**
Sunnyside HD6: Brigh .3D **162**
*WF3: E Ard .1D **154***
(off Dewsbury Rd.)
Sunnyside Av. WF3: E Ard .1D **154**
Sunnyside La. BD3: B'frd .2F **91**
Sunnyside Rd. LS13: Leeds .2D **94**
Sunny Side St.
HX3: Hal .6G **129** (1C **164**)
Sunnyview WF3: E Ard .2A **156**
Sunnyview Av. LS11: Leeds .2F **117**
Sunnyview Gdns. LS11: Leeds .2F **117**
Sunny Vw. Ter. BD13: B'frd .5G **107**
Sunnyview Ter. LS11: Leeds .2F **117**
Sunrise Ct. LS27: Morl .6E **115**
Sunset Av. LS6: Leeds .1E **77**
Sunset Cres. HX3: Hal .4A **150**
Sunset Dr. LS6: Leeds .2E **77**
LS29: I'ly .4F **11**
Sunset Hilltop LS6: Leeds .1E **77**
Sunset Mt. LS6: Leeds .2E **77**
Sunset Ri. LS6: Leeds .1E **77**
Sunset Rd. LS6: Leeds .1E **77**
Sunset Ter. LS29: I'ly .4G **11**
Sunset Vw. LS6: Leeds .1E **77**
Sunshine Ct. BD6: B'frd .6H **109**
Sunshine Mills LS12: Leeds .4A **96**
Sun St. BD1: B'frd .3F **91** (2F **7**)
BD20: Stee .6A **14**
BD21: Keigh .1A **48**
BD22: Haw .3C **64**
LS19: Yead .6G **41**
LS28: Pud .2A **94**
Sun Way HX3: Hal .4B **150**
Sun Wood Av. HX3: Hal .3D **130**
Sun Wood Ter. HX3: Hal .3D **130**
Suresnes Rd. BD21: Keigh .6H **33**
Surgery St. BD22: Haw .3D **64**
Surrey Gro. BD5: B'frd .1E **111**
LS28: Pud .3A **94**
Surrey Rd. LS28: Pud .3A **94**
Surrey St. BD21: Keigh .5C **34**
HX1: Hal .3C **148**
Sussex App. LS10: Leeds .2D **118**
Sussex Av. LS10: Leeds .2D **118**
LS18: H'fth .4E **57**
Sussex Gdns. LS10: Leeds .2D **118**
Sussex Grn. LS10: Leeds .2D **118**
Sussex Pl. LS10: Leeds .2D **118**
Sussex St. BD21: Keigh .5C **34**
LS9: Leeds .4C **98**
(not continuous)
Sutcliffe Ct. *HX3: Hal .4A **150***
(off Bank Top)
Sutcliffe Fold BD13: B'frd .4C **108**
Sutcliffe Pl. BD6: B'frd .5D **110**
Sutcliffe Rd. HX3: Hal .2E **151**
Sutcliffe St. HX2: Hal .1C **148**
Sutcliffe Ter. *HX3: Hal .6G **129***
(off Amblers Ter.)
Sutcliffe Wood La. HD6: Hal .2E **151**
HX3: Brigh, Hal .2E **151**
Sutherland Av. LS8: Leeds .6E **61**
Sutherland Cres. LS8: Leeds .5E **61**
Sutherland Mt. LS9: Leeds .1E **99**
Sutherland Rd. HX3: Hal .1G **151**
LS9: Leeds .1E **99**
Sutherland St. LS12: Leeds .5E **97**
Sutherland Ter. LS9: Leeds .1E **99**
Sutton App. LS14: Leeds .2A **100**
Sutton Av. BD2: B'frd .4F **71**
Sutton Ct. BD16: Bgly .5B **50**
Sutton Cres. BD4: B'frd .1C **112**
LS14: Leeds .2A **100**
Sutton Dr. BD13: B'frd .4B **66**
Sutton Gro. BD4: B'frd .6C **92**
LS27: Morl .4A **138**
Sutton Ho. BD4: B'frd .6C **92**
Sutton Rd. BD4: B'frd .6C **92**
Sutton St. LS12: Leeds .5F **97**
Swaine Hill Cres. LS19: Yead .6E **41**
Swaine Hill St. LS19: Yead .6E **41**
Swaine Hill Ter. LS19: Yead .6E **41**
SWAIN GREEN .**6B 92**
SWAIN HOUSE .**4F 71**
Swain Ho. Cres. BD2: B'frd .4G **71**
Swain Ho. Rd. BD2: B'frd .4G **71**
Swain Mt. BD2: B'frd .4G **71**
SWAIN ROYD LANE BOTTOM .**6A 68**
Swale Ct. *BD20: Sils .3E **15***
(off Ings Way)
Swale Cres. LS25: Gar .5H **103**
Swaledale Ho. *HX6: Hal .6H **147***
(off Sowerby St.)
Swale Ri. LS22: Weth .1D **12**
Swales Moor Rd. HX3: Hal .2F **129**
Swallow Av. LS12: Leeds .5A **96**
Swallow Cl. LS17: Leeds .3D **60**
LS21: Pool .5F **25**
Swallow Cres. LS12: Leeds .5H **95**
Swallow Dr. LS17: Leeds .3D **60**
LS21: Pool .5F **25**
Swallow Fold BD8: B'frd .4E **89**
SWALLOW HILL .**4H 95**
Swallow Hill WF17: Bat .6C **136**
Swallow Mt. LS12: Leeds .5A **96**
Swallow St. BD21: Keigh .5B **34**
Swallow Va. LS27: Morl .3D **138**
Swan Av. BD16: Bgly .4E **51**
Swan Bank La. HX3: Hal .4H **149**
Swan Hill BD9: B'frd .5C **70**
Swan St. BD5: B'frd .6E **91** (6C **6**)
LS1: Leeds .4E **5**
SWARCLIFFE .**5E 81**
Swarcliffe App. LS14: Leeds .5E **81**
Swarcliffe Av. LS14: Leeds .5E **81**
Swarcliffe Bank LS14: Leeds .4E **81**
Swarcliffe Dr. LS14: Leeds .4E **81**
Swarcliffe Dr. E. LS14: Leeds .5F **81**
Swarcliffe Grn. LS14: Leeds .5F **81**
Swarcliffe Pde. LS14: Leeds .5E **81**
Swarcliffe Rd. LS14: Leeds .4E **81**
Swardale Grn. LS14: Leeds .5E **81**
Swardale Rd. LS14: Leeds .5E **81**
Swarland Gro. BD5: B'frd .1E **111**
SWARTHA .**1G 15**
Swartha La. BD20: Sils .1G **15**
Sweet St. LS11: Leeds .5H **97**
Sweet St. W. LS11: Leeds .5G **97**
(not continuous)
Swift Dr. BD6: B'frd .4E **109**
SWILLINGTON .**4A 122**
Swillington La. LS15: Swil .6A **102**
LS26: Swil .4H **121**
Swincar Av. LS19: Yead .6E **41**
SWINCLIFFE .**3E 135**
Swincliffe Cl. BD19: B'frd .3E **135**
Swincliffe Cres. BD19: B'frd .4E **135**
Swinegate LS1: Leeds .4A **98** (6E **5**)
Swine La. BD20: Keigh .5F **35**
Swine Mkt. HX1: Hal .4B **164**
SWINNOW .**1C 94**
Swinnow Av. LS13: Leeds .2C **94**
Swinnow Cl. LS13: Leeds .2C **94**
Swinnow Cres. LS28: Pud .1C **94**
Swinnow Dr. LS13: Leeds .2C **94**
Swinnow Gdns. LS13: Leeds .2C **94**
Swinnow Gth. LS13: Leeds .3C **94**
Swinnow Grn. LS28: Pud .2B **94**
Swinnow Gro. LS13: Leeds .2C **94**
Swinnow La. LS13: Leeds .1C **94**
SWINNOW MOOR .**3D 94**
Swinnow Rd. LS13: Leeds .3B **94**
LS28: Leeds, Pud .3B **94**
Swinnow Vw. LS13: Leeds .2C **94**
Swinnow Wlk. LS13: Leeds .2C **94**
Swinton Pl. BD7: B'frd .6B **90**
Swinton Ter. HX1: Hal .4D **148**
Swires Rd. BD2: B'frd .2A **92**
HX1: Hal .3F **149** (6A **164**)
Swires Ter. HX1: Hal .3F **149** (6A **164**)
Swithen's Ct. LS26: Rothw .3B **142**
Swithen's Dr. LS26: Rothw .3A **142**
Swithen's Gro. LS26: Rothw .3A **142**
Swithen's La. LS26: Rothw .3B **142**
Swithen's St. LS26: Rothw .3B **142**
Sycamore Av. BD7: B'frd .4H **89**
BD16: Bgly .5B **50**
LS8: Leeds .4D **78**
LS15: Leeds .3C **100**
LS25: Kip .3F **123**
WF2: Wake .6D **156**
Sycamore Chase LS28: Pud .4B **94**
Sycamore Cl. BD3: B'frd .3G **91** (1G **7**)
LS6: Leeds .5G **77**
LS7: Leeds .2F **77**
LS16: B'hpe .4H **43**
Sycamore Ct. BD3: B'frd .3G **91** (1G **7**)
LS8: Leeds .3G **79**
Sycamore Cft. LS11: Leeds .2H **117**
Sycamore Dr. BD19: Cleck .2H **153**
HX3: Hal .3A **152**
HX5: Ell .5H **159**
LS29: Add .1E **9**
Sycamore Fold LS11: Leeds .2H **117**
LS21: Pool .5F **25**
Sycamore Gro. BD20: Stee .6A **14**
Sycamore Row LS13: Leeds .5C **74**
Sycamores, The LS16: B'hpe .4H **43**
LS20: Guis .3C **40**
Sycamore Vw. BD22: Keigh .1F **47**
HD6: Brigh .6H **151**
Sycamore Wlk. LS28: Pud .1H **93**
Sycamore Way WF17: Bat .6B **136**
Sydenham Pl. BD3: B'frd .1G **91**
Sydenham Rd. LS11: Leeds .5F **97**
Sydenham St. LS11: Leeds .5F **97**
Sydney St. BD16: Bgly .4C **50**
LS26: Rothw .1F **143**
LS28: Pud .1H **93**
Syke Av. WF3: E Ard .2D **154**
Syke Cl. WF3: E Ard .2C **154**
Syke Gdns. WF3: E Ard .2D **154**
Syke Grn. LS14: S'cft .5E **45**
Syke Ho. La. HX4: Hal .5D **158**
Syke La. BD13: B'frd .6A **108**
HX2: Hal .3C **106**

Syke La.—Terrace, The

Syke La. HX3: Hal .6G **131**
HX6: Hal .6H **147**
LS14: S'cft .6C **44**
Syke Rd. BD9: B'frd .6A **70**
LS22: Weth .4G **13**
WF3: E Ard .2D **154**
Sykes Bottom BD22: Keigh .5D **46**
Sykes Head BD22: Keigh .4D **46**
Syke Side BD20: Keigh .3H **33**
Sykes La. BD12: B'frd .3G **133**
BD20: Sils .3D **14**
BD22: Keigh .4D **46**
WF17: Bat .5A **154**
Sykes Yd. *HX1: Hal .4D* ***148***
(off King Cross Rd.)
Syke Ter. WF3: E Ard .2C **154**
Sylhet Cl. BD1: B'frd .3D **90** (2B **6**)
Sylvan Av. BD13: B'frd .5H **107**
Sylvan Vw. LS18: H'fth .6E **57**
Syringa Av. BD15: B'frd .5C **68**

T

Tabbs Ct. BD19: Cleck .6F **133**
Tabbs La. BD19: Cleck .6E **133**
Tagore Ct. BD3: B'frd .5B **92**
Talbot Av. LS4: Leeds .6C **76**
LS8: Leeds .5C **60**
LS17: Leeds .5C **60**
Talbot Ct. LS8: Leeds .6D **60**
Talbot Cres. LS8: Leeds .5D **60**
Talbot Fold LS8: Leeds .6D **60**
Talbot Gdns. LS8: Leeds .5D **60**
Talbot Gro. LS8: Leeds .5D **60**
Talbot Ho. HX5: Ell .5B **160**
Talbot Mt. LS4: Leeds .6C **76**
Talbot Ri. LS17: Leeds .5D **60**
Talbot Rd. LS8: Leeds .5D **60**
Talbot St. BD7: B'frd .4B **90**
BD21: Keigh .6G ***33***
(off Bk. Sladen St.)
Talbot Ter. LS4: Leeds .6C **76**
LS26: Rothw .3A **142**
Talbot Vw. LS4: Leeds .6C **76**
Talbot Yd. LS26: Mick .4E **145**
Tall Trees LS17: Leeds .4A **60**
Tamar St. BD5: B'frd .1C **110**
Tamworth St. BD4: B'frd .5C **92**
Tandy Trad. Est., The
LS12: Leeds .2D **96**
Tanfield Dr. LS29: Burl W .1E **21**
Tanglewood LS11: Leeds .6G **117**
Tanglewood Ct. BD6: B'frd .4A **110**
Tan Ho. Ct. BD4: B'frd .6H **111**
Tanhouse Hill HX3: Hal .2E **151**
LS18: H'fth .1G **75**
Tan Ho. La. BD15: B'frd .3E **67**
HX3: Hal .3C **130**
Tanhouse Pk. HX3: Hal .2E **151**
Tan Ho. Yd. LS27: Leeds .4C **116**
Tan La. BD4: B'frd .1H **133**
Tannerbrook Cl. BD14: B'frd .1F **109**
Tanner Hill Rd. BD7: B'frd .2G **109**
Tanner St. WF15: Liv .4H **153**
Tannery Bus. Cen., The
HX3: Hal .4C **130**
Tannery Ct. BD10: B'frd .1B **72**
LS28: Pud .3A **94**
Tannery Sq. LS6: Leeds .2E **77**
Tannery Yd. LS28: Pud .4B **94**
Tannett Grn. BD5: B'frd .3F **111**
Tansy End BD22: Oxen .2E **85**
Tanton Cres. BD14: B'frd .1F **109**
Tanton Wlk. BD14: B'frd .1F **109**
Tarn Ct. BD20: Keigh .5F **33**
LS29: I'ly .6E ***11***
(off Moorside Ct.)
WF1: Wake .6F **157**
Tarnhill M. BD5: B'frd .1E **111**
Tarn La. BD22: Keigh .5A **32**
LS17: Leeds, S'cft .6A **44**
Tarn M. *LS29: I'ly .6E* ***11***
(off Moorside Ct.)
Tarnside Dr. LS14: Leeds .6B **80**
Tarn Vw. Rd. LS19: Yead .6H **41**
Tatefield Gro. LS25: Kip .5G **123**
Tatefield Pl. LS25: Kip .4G **123**
Tatham's Ct. *HX1: Hal .4D* ***148***
(off High Shaw Rd. W.)
Tatham Way LS8: Leeds .3G **79**
Taunton Ho. *BD5: B'frd .6E* ***91***
(off Crosscombe Wlk.)
Taunton St. BD18: Ship .1A **70**
Taverngate LS20: Guis .5E **39**
Tavistock Cl. LS12: Leeds .5D **96**
Tavistock M. LS12: Leeds .5D **96**
Tavistock Pk. LS12: Leeds .5D **96**
Tavistock Way LS12: Leeds .5D **96**
Tawny Beck LS12: Leeds .3E **95**
Tawny Cl. BD4: B'frd .4C **112**
LS27: Morl .3D **138**
Tay Ct. BD2: B'frd .4B **72**
Taylor Av. BD20: Sils .2D **14**
Taylor Gro. LS26: Mick .4E **145**
Taylor La. HX2: Hal .2D **106**
LS15: Scho .3B **82**
Taylor Rd. BD6: B'frd .5D **110**
(not continuous)
Taylors Cl. LS14: Leeds .5D **80**
Tealbeck App. LS21: Otley .4F **23**
Tealbeck Ho. LS21: Otley .4F **23**
Tealby Cl. LS16: Leeds .5G **57**
Teal Ct. BD20: Stee .5B **14**
Teal Dr. LS27: Morl .3D **138**
Teale Ct. LS7: Leeds .4C **78**
Teale Dr. LS7: Leeds .4C **78**
Teal La. HX3: Hal .3B **130**
(not continuous)
Teal M. LS10: Leeds .2B **140**
Teasdale St. BD4: B'frd .2H **111**
(not continuous)
Teasel Cl. BD12: B'frd .2G **133**
Techno Cen. LS18: H'fth .5E **57**
Tees St. BD5: B'frd .2C **110**
Telephone Pl. LS7: Leeds .2B **98** (1H **5**)
Telford Cl. BD20: Sils .3F **15**
LS10: Leeds .3C **118**
Telford Ct. BD7: B'frd .5B **90**
Telford Gdns. LS10: Leeds .3C **118**
Telford Pl. LS10: Leeds .3C **118**
Telford St. LS10: Leeds .3C **118**
Telford Ter. LS10: Leeds .3C **118**
Telford Wlk. LS10: Leeds .3C **118**
Telford Way WF2: Wake .4C **156**
Telscombe Dr. BD4: B'frd .3B **112**
Temperance Ct. LS18: H'fth .1D **74**
Temperance Fld. BD12: B'frd .4C **132**
BD19: Cleck .1F **153**
Temperance St. LS28: Pud .2A **94**
Tempest Grn. *BD6: B'frd .4C* ***110***
(off Chapel St.)
Tempest Pl. LS11: Leeds .2G **117**
Tempest Rd. LS11: Leeds .2G **117**
Templar Gdns. LS22: Weth .2F **13**
Templar La. LS2: Leeds .3B **98** (3G **5**)
LS15: Leeds .5F **81**
Templar Pl. LS2: Leeds .3B **98** (4G **5**)
Templars Cl. HX4: Hal .4E **159**
Templar St. LS2: Leeds .3A **98** (3F **5**)
Templars Way BD8: B'frd .3G **89**
LS25: Gar .5F **103**
Temple Av. LS15: Leeds .5C **100**
LS26: Rothw .6B **120**
Temple Cl. LS15: Leeds .5C **100**
Temple Ct. LS15: Leeds .4B **100**
LS26: Rothw .6B **120**
Temple Cres. LS11: Leeds .2G **117**
Temple Ga. LS15: Leeds .4D **100**
Templegate Av. LS15: Leeds .5C **100**
Templegate Cl. LS15: Leeds .4D **100**
Templegate Cres. LS15: Leeds .5D **100**
Temple Ga. Dr. LS15: Leeds .4C **100**
Templegate Grn. LS15: Leeds .4D **100**
Templegate Ri. LS15: Leeds .5C **100**
Templegate Rd. LS15: Leeds .5C **100**
Templegate Vw. LS15: Leeds .5C **100**
Templegate Wlk. LS15: Leeds .4D **100**
Templegate Way LS15: Leeds .5D **100**
Temple Grn. LS26: Rothw .6C **120**
Temple Gro. LS15: Leeds .4C **100**
Temple La. LS15: Leeds .4D **100**
Temple Lawn LS26: Rothw .6C **120**
Temple Lea LS15: Leeds .4C **100**
Temple Newsam Country Pk. .1C **120**
Temple Newsam Home Farm
(Rare Breeds) .6D **100**
Temple Newsam House .6D **100**
Templenewsam Rd. LS15: Leeds .4B **100**
Templenewsam Vw. LS15: Leeds .5B **100**
Temple Pk. Cl. LS15: Leeds .4C **100**
Temple Pk. Gdns. LS15: Leeds .4C **100**
Temple Pk. Grn. LS15: Leeds .4C **100**
Temple Rhydding BD17: Bail .5C **52**
Temple Rhydding Dr. BD17: Bail .5C **52**
Temple Ri. LS15: Leeds .5C **100**
Temple Row *BD21: Keigh .6A* ***34***
(off Temple St.)
LS15: Leeds .5G **101**
Temple Row Cl. LS15: Leeds .5G **101**
Templer Ter. LS27: Morl .5B **138**
Templestowe Cres. LS15: Leeds .2E **101**
Templestowe Dr. LS15: Leeds .3E **101**
Templestowe Gdns. LS15: Leeds .3D **100**
Templestowe Hill LS15: Leeds .2D **100**
Temple St. BD9: B'frd .1B **90**
BD21: Keigh .6H **33**
Temple Vw. WF3: Rothw .6G **141**
Temple Vw. Gro. LS9: Leeds .4E **99**
(not continuous)
Temple Vw. Pl. LS9: Leeds .4D **98**
Temple Vw. Rd. LS9: Leeds .3D **98**
Temple Vw. Ter. LS9: Leeds .4D **98**
Temple Vue *LS6: Leeds .3D* ***76***
(off Mansfield Pl.)
Temple Wlk. LS15: Leeds .3D **100**
Tenbury Fold BD4: B'frd .2C **112**
Tenby Ter. *HX1: Hal .1D* ***148***
(off Osborne St.)
Tennis Av. BD4: B'frd .4C **112**
Tennis Way BD17: Bail .6A **52**
Tennyson Av. HX6: Hal .6F **147**
WF3: Wake .3H **157**
Tennyson Cl. LS28: Pud .5B **94**
Tennyson Ho. *LS29: I'ly .4G* ***11***
(off Blackthorn Rd.)
Tennyson Pl. BD3: B'frd .3G **91**
HX3: Hal .1E **151**
Tennyson Rd. BD6: B'frd .5B **110**
Tennyson St. BD21: Keigh .2H **47**
HX3: Hal .6E **129**
LS20: Guis .5D **40**
LS27: Morl .3B **138**
LS28: Pud .5B **94**
(Tennyson Cl.)
LS28: Pud .1H **93**
(Victoria Rd.)
Tennyson Ter. LS27: Morl .3B **138**
Tentercroft BD17: Bail .3C **52**
Tenterden Way LS15: Leeds .6H **81**
Tenterfield Ri. HX3: Hal .6C **130**
Tenterfields BD10: B'frd .1B **72**
HX2: Hal .4E **147**
Tenterfields Bus. Pk. HX2: Hal .4E **147**
Tenterfield Ter. HX3: Hal .6C **130**
Tenter Hill BD14: B'frd .1D **108**
Tenth Av. WF15: Liv .4H **153**
Ten Yards La. BD13: B'frd .2D **86**
Terminus Pde. *LS15: Leeds .1E* ***101***
(off Farm Rd.)
Ternhill Gro. BD5: B'frd .6E **91**
Tern Pk. LS22: Coll .2B **28**
Tern St. BD5: B'frd .2B **110**
Terrace, The BD3: B'frd .1F **91**
LS23: B Spa .4C **30**
LS28: Pud .1A **114**

Terrace Gdns. HX3: Hal 6F 129
Terracotta Dr. BD15: B'frd 2C 88
Terrington Crest BD14: B'frd 1F 109
Terry Rd. BD12: B'frd 2E 133
Tetley Dr. BD11: B'frd 3E 135
Tetley La. HX3: Hal 5C 130
Tetley Pl. BD2: B'frd 6F 71
Tetley St. BD1: B'frd 4D 90 (4B 6)
Teville Ct. BD4: B'frd 1G 111
Tewit Cl. HX2: Hal 6D 106
Tewit Gdns. HX2: Hal 6D 106
(Tewit Cl.)
HX2: Hal 6D 106
(Tewit Grn.)
Tewit Grn. HX2: Hal 6D 106
Tewit Hall Gdns. HX2: Hal 1D 128
Tewit Hall Rd. BD3: B'frd 3A 92
Tewit La. HX2: Hal 6D 106
Tewitt Cl. BD20: Stee 5B 14
Tewitt La. BD13: B'frd 1D 86
BD16: Bgly 1D 50
Texas St. LS27: Morl 5B 138
Thackeray Medical Mus. 1D 98
Thackeray Rd. BD10: B'frd 5B 72
Thacker Ga. Rd. HX6: Hal 4A 146
HX7: Hal 4A 146
THACKLEY 6G 53
Thackley Av. BD10: B'frd 5G 53
Thackley Ct. BD18: Ship 1C 70
THACKLEY END 6G 53
Thackley Old Rd. BD18: Ship 1C 70
Thackley Rd. BD10: B'frd 5G 53
Thackley Vw. BD10: B'frd 5G 53
Thackray St. HX2: Hal 2B 148
LS27: Morl 4A 138
Thames Dr. LS25: Gar 5G 103
Thanet Gth. BD20: Sils 3E 15
Thane Way LS15: Leeds 6G 81
Thatchers Way BD19: B'frd 6E 135
Theaker La. LS12: Leeds 3B 96
Theakston Mead
BD14: B'frd 1E 109
Thealby Cl. LS9: Leeds 3C 98 (3H 5)
Thealby Lawn LS9: Leeds 2C 98
Thealby Pl. LS9: Leeds 3C 98 (3H 5)
Thearne Grn. BD14: B'frd 1F 109
Theatre in the Mill, The 5C 90
Theatre Wlk. LS1: Leeds 4E 5
(in Headrow Cen., The)
Theodore St. LS11: Leeds 4G 117
Third Av. BD3: B'frd 2A 92
BD21: Keigh 1H 47
HX3: Hal 5F 149
LS12: Leeds 5D 96
LS22: Weth 4F 13
LS26: Rothw 6B 120
WF1: Wake 6G 157
WF15: Liv 5H 153
Third St. BD12: B'frd 1E 133
Thirkhill Ct. BD5: B'frd 1E 111
Thirkleby Royd BD14: B'frd 1E 109
Thirlmere Av. BD12: Cleck 6E 133
HX5: Ell 4D 160
Thirlmere Cl. LS11: Leeds 5E 117
Thirlmere Dr. LS22: Weth 3B 12
WF3: E Ard 1G 155
Thirlmere Gdns. BD2: B'frd 1H 91
LS11: Leeds 5E 117
Thirlmere Gro. BD17: Bail 6G 51
(not continuous)
Thirsk Dr. LS25: Kip 3G 123
Thirsk Grange BD14: B'frd 1F 109
Thirsk Gro. LS10: Leeds 4B 140
Thirsk Row LS1: Leeds 4H 97 (5C 4)
Thirteenth Av. WF15: Liv 4H 153
Thistle Way LS27: Morl 2F 137
Thistlewood Rd. WF1: Wake 4H 157
Thomas Cl. BD6: B'frd 4C 110
Thomas Duggan Ho. BD18: Ship . . .2B 70
(off Well Cft.)
Thomas Fold BD2: B'frd 1H 91
(off Idle Rd.)

Thomas Pl. BD18: Ship 2C 70
Thomas St. BD22: Haw 3D 64
HD6: Brigh 2A 162
HX1: Hal 2G 149 (4C 164)
HX4: Hal 6F 159
HX5: Ell 5C 160
LS6: Leeds 6G 77
Thomas St. Sth. HX1: Hal 3D 148
Thomas St. W. HX1: Hal 4E 149
Thompson Av. BD2: B'frd 4F 71
Thompson Cl. HX3: Hal 2E 151
Thompson Dr. WF2: Wake 6D 156
Thompson Grn. BD17: Bail 5A 52
Thompson La. BD17: Bail 6A 52
Thompson St. BD18: Ship 1A 70
Thoresby Gro. BD7: B'frd 2A 110
Thoresby Pl. LS1: Leeds 3H 97 (3C 4)
Thornaby Dr. BD14: B'frd 1E 109
Thornacre Cres. BD18: Ship 3E 71
Thornacre Rd. BD18: Ship 2E 71
Thorn Av. BD2: B'frd 5E 69
Thornbank Av. BD22: Keigh 3F 47
Thornber Bank BD20: Sils 1E 15
(off Thornber Gro.)
Thornber Gro. BD20: Sils 1E 15
Thornberry Dr. WF15: Liv 4H 153
Thornbridge M. BD2: B'frd 5H 71
THORNBURY 4C 92
Thornbury Av. BD3: B'frd 3B 92
LS16: Leeds 2C 76
Thornbury Cres. BD3: B'frd 3B 92
Thornbury Dr. BD3: B'frd 3B 92
Thornbury Gro. BD3: B'frd 3B 92
Thornbury Pk. BD3: B'frd 4B 92
Thornbury St. BD3: B'frd 4B 92
Thorncliffe Rd. BD8: B'frd 2D 90
BD22: Keigh 1F 47
Thorn Cl. BD18: Ship 3E 71
LS8: Leeds 6F 79
Thorn Cres. LS8: Leeds 6F 79
Thorncroft Rd. BD6: B'frd 4H 109
Thorn Cross LS8: Leeds 5G 79
Thorndale Rd. BD2: B'frd 5E 71
Thorndene Way BD4: B'frd 6E 113
Thorn Dr. BD9: B'frd 5F 69
BD13: B'frd 6G 107
LS8: Leeds 6F 79
Thorne Cl. LS28: Pud 3F 93
Thornefield Cres. WF3: E Ard 1D 154
Thorne Gro. LS26: Rothw 1B 142
THORNER 2H 63
Thorner La. LS14: S'cft 5F 45
LS14: T'ner 5G 63
Thornes Farm App. LS9: Leeds 6H 99
Thornes Farm Way LS9: Leeds 6H 99
Thornes Pk. BD18: Ship 4D 70
HD6: Brigh 2A 162
Thorneycroft Rd. BD20: Keigh 4F 35
Thorney La. HX2: Hal 6C 126
Thornfield BD16: Bgly 3A 50
BD22: Haw 2D 64
Thornfield Av. BD6: B'frd 5D 110
LS28: Pud 6G 73
Thornfield Cl. LS15: Leeds 1D 100
Thornfield Dr. LS15: Leeds 1D 100
Thornfield Hall BD13: B'frd 5A 88
(off Thornton Rd.)
Thornfield M. BD16: Bgly 6A 36
LS15: Leeds 1D 100
Thornfield Mt. WF17: Bat 6C 136
Thornfield Pl. BD2: B'frd 6A 72
Thornfield Ri. HX4: Hal 4F 159
Thornfield Rd. LS16: Leeds 1B 76
Thornfield Sq. BD2: B'frd 6A 72
Thornfield St. HX4: Hal 4F 159
Thornfield Ter. BD15: B'frd 5F 67
Thornfield Way LS15: Leeds 1D 100
Thorn Gth. BD19: Cleck 3H 153
BD20: Keigh 4G 33
Thorngate BD13: B'frd 1D 86
Thorn Gro. BD9: B'frd 5F 69
LS8: Leeds 6F 79

Thornhill Av. BD18: Ship 4D 70
BD22: Keigh 4E 47
Thornhill Bri. La. HD6: Brigh 6A 152
Thornhill Cl. LS28: Pud 2F 73
Thornhill Ct. LS12: Leeds 5C 96
Thornhill Cft. LS12: Leeds 5B 96
Thornhill Dr. BD18: B'frd 4D 70
LS28: Pud 1D 72
Thornhill Gro. BD18: Ship 4D 70
BD20: Stee 5B 14
LS28: Pud 2F 73
Thornhill Ho. BD3: B'frd 3C 92
(off Thornhill Pl.)
Thornhill Pl. BD3: B'frd 3C 92
HD6: Brigh 2A 162
LS12: Leeds 5B 96
Thornhill Rd. BD20: Stee 4B 14
HD6: Brigh 3H 161
LS12: Leeds 5B 96
THORNHILLS 5C 152
Thornhills Beck La. HD6: Brigh 5B 152
Thornhills La. HD6: Brigh 5C 152
Thornhill St. LS12: Leeds 5B 96
LS28: Pud 2F 73
Thornhill Ter. BD3: B'frd 3B 92
THORNHURST 6G 27
Thorn La. BD9: B'frd 5F 69
(not continuous)
LS8: Leeds 2D 78
Thornlea Cl. LS19: Yead 2D 54
Thorn Lee HX2: Hal 6E 127
Thornleigh Gdns. LS9: Leeds 5D 98
Thornleigh Gro. LS9: Leeds 5D 98
Thornleigh Mt. LS9: Leeds 5D 98
Thornleigh St. LS9: Leeds 5D 98
Thornleigh Vw. LS9: Leeds 5D 98
Thornmead Rd. BD17: Bail 5D 52
Thorn Mt. LS8: Leeds 5G 79
Thorn Royd Dr. BD4: B'frd 3D 112
Thornsgill Av. BD4: B'frd 2A 112
Thorn St. BD8: B'frd 2H 89
BD22: Haw 1E 65
WF17: Bat 6A 136
Thorn Ter. HX2: Hal 6E 127
LS8: Leeds 5F 79
THORNTON 5H 87
Thornton Av. LS12: Leeds 4A 96
Thornton Cl. WF17: Bat 4B 136
Thornton Ct. BD8: B'frd 3H 89
(off Lane Ends Cl.)
Thornton Gdns. LS12: Leeds 4A 96
Thornton Gro. LS12: Leeds 4A 96
Thornton La. BD5: B'frd 2C 110
Thornton Moor Rd. BD13: Oxen 3G 85
BD22: B'frd, Oxen 3G 85
(not continuous)
Thornton Old Rd. BD8: B'frd 4F 89
Thornton Recreation Cen. 5D 88
Thornton Rd. BD1: B'frd 3A 90 (5C 6)
BD7: B'frd 3A 90
BD8: B'frd 3A 90
BD13: B'frd 6C 86
(Halifax Rd.)
BD13: B'frd 3H 107
(Harp La.)
HD6: Brigh 1A 162
Thornton's Arc. LS1: Leeds . . .3A 98 (4E 5)
Thorntons Dale LS18: H'fth 3D 74
Thornton Sq. BD5: B'frd 3D 110
(off Delamere St.)
HD6: Brigh 1A 162
(off Commercial St.)
Thornton St. BD1: B'frd 4C 90 (3A 6)
BD19: Cleck 3G 153
HX1: Hal 4D 148
LS29: Burl W 1E 21
Thornton Ter. HX1: Hal 4D 148
Thornton Vw. BD14: B'frd 2E 109
Thornton Vw. Rd. BD14: B'frd 2E 109
Thorn Tree Cotts. HX2: Hal 4C 148
(off Warley Rd.)
HX3: Brigh 5F 151

Thorntree St. HX1: Hal 4D **148**
Thorn Vw. HX2: Hal 6E **127**
  HX3: Hal 5G **129**
  HX5: Ell 5C **160**
  LS8: Leeds 6G **79**
Thornville LS27: Morl 6B **116**
Thornville Av. LS6: Leeds 1E **97**
Thornville Ct. BD8: B'frd 1C **90**
  LS6: Leeds 1E 97
  (off Thornville Rd.)
Thornville Cres. LS6: Leeds 6E **77**
Thornville Gro. LS6: Leeds 1E **97**
Thornville Mt. LS6: Leeds 1E **97**
Thornville Pl. LS6: Leeds 1E **97**
Thornville Rd. LS6: Leeds 1E **97**
Thornville Row LS6: Leeds 1E **97**
Thornville St. LS6: Leeds 1E **97**
Thornville Ter. LS6: Leeds 1E **97**
Thornville Vw. LS6: Leeds 1E **97**
Thorn Wlk. LS8: Leeds 6G **79**
Thorny Bank HX6: Hal 1B **158**
Thorold Ho. *BD10: B'frd* 2A **72**
  (off Fairhaven Grn.)
THORP ARCH 2C **30**
Thorp Arch Grange LS23: W'ton . .1D **30**
Thorp Arch Pk. LS23: B Spa 2C **30**
Thorp Arch Trad. Est. LS23: W'ton . .1F **31**
THORPE 2A **72**
Thorpe Av. BD13: B'frd 5C **88**
Thorpe Cl. LS20: Guis 5H **39**
Thorpe Ct. LS10: Leeds 4A **140**
Thorpe Cres. LS10: Leeds 4A **140**
Thorpe Dr. LS20: Guis 4A **40**
THORPE EDGE 2A **72**
Thorpe Gdns. LS10: Leeds 3A **140**
Thorpe Gth. LS10: Leeds 4H **139**
Thorpe Gro. BD13: B'frd 5D **88**
  LS10: Leeds 3A **140**
Thorpe La. LS10: Leeds 6F **139**
  LS20: Guis 5G **39**
  WF3: E Ard, Leeds 6E **139**
Thorpe Lwr. La. WF3: Leeds 5D **140**
Thorpe Mt. LS10: Leeds 4H **139**
THORPE ON THE HILL 5B **140**
Thorpe Pk. LS15: Leeds 4H **101**
Thorpe Pl. HX6: Hal 6C **146**
Thorpe Rd. BD13: B'frd 5C **88**
  LS10: Leeds 3A **140**
  LS28: Pud 3H **93**
  WF3: E Ard 2A **156**
Thorpe Sq. LS10: Leeds 3B **140**
Thorpe St. BD21: Keigh 5A **34**
  HX3: Hal 5F **129**
  LS10: Leeds 3A **140**
  LS15: Leeds 3C **100**
Thorpe Ter. HX2: Hal 1D **146**
  (Carr Vw.)
  HX2: Hal 6D **126**
  (Solomon Hill)
Thorpe Vw. LS10: Leeds 4A **140**
Thorp Gth. BD10: B'frd 2H **71**
Thorverton Dr. BD4: B'frd 5C **112**
Thorverton Gro. BD4: B'frd 5C **112**
Threadneedle St. *HX1: Hal* 4D **148**
  (off Dundas St.)
Threap Cft. HX2: Hal 1D **128**
Threelands Grange BD11: B'frd 1E **135**
Three Nooked M. *BD10: B'frd* 2H **71**
  (off Brecon Cl.)
Threshfield BD17: Bail 4C **52**
Threshfield Cres. BD11: B'frd 1F **135**
Thrice Fold BD10: B'frd 1F **71**
Thrift Way BD16: Bgly 5B **50**
Throstle Av. LS10: Leeds 4H **139**
Throstle Bank *HX2: Hal* 4D **148**
  (off Gainest)
Throstle Dr. LS10: Leeds 4G **139**
Throstle Hill LS10: Leeds 4H **139**
Throstle La. LS10: Leeds 4H **139**
Throstle Mt. HX2: Hal 4F **147**
  LS10: Leeds 4H **139**
Throstle Nest Cl. LS21: Otley 1B **22**

Throstle Nest Rd. BD20: Sils 1D **14**
Throstle Nest Vw. LS18: H'fth 2E **75**
Throstle Pde. LS10: Leeds 4H **139**
Throstle Pl. LS10: Leeds 4H **139**
Throstle Rd. LS10: Leeds 4A **140**
Throstle Rd. Nth. LS10: Leeds 2C **140**
Throstle Row LS10: Leeds 4H **139**
Throstle Sq. LS10: Leeds 4B **140**
Throstle St. LS10: Leeds 4H **139**
Throstle Ter. LS10: Leeds 4A **140**
Throstle Vw. LS10: Leeds 4B **140**
Throstle Wlk. LS10: Leeds 4H **139**
Throxenby Way BD14: B'frd 1E **109**
Thrum Hall Cl. HX1: Hal 2D **148**
Thrum Hall Dr. HX1: Hal 2D **148**
Thrum Hall Ind. Pk. HX2: Hal 1C **148**
Thrum Hall La. HX1: Hal 2D **148**
Thrush St. BD21: Keigh 5A **34**
Thryberg St. BD3: B'frd 4G **91** (5H **7**)
Thurlestone Ct. BD20: Keigh 5F **35**
Thurley Dr. BD4: B'frd 3H **111**
Thurley Rd. BD4: B'frd 3H **111**
Thurnscoe Rd. BD1: B'frd . . .3D **90** (1B **6**)
  (not continuous)
Thursby St. BD3: B'frd 4H **91** (4H **7**)
Thurston Gdns. BD15: B'frd 3D **88**
THWAITE GATE 2D **118**
Thwaite Ga. LS10: Leeds 2D **118**
Thwaite La. LS10: Leeds 2E **119**
Thwaite Mills Watermill Mus. 2F **119**
THWAITES 6D **34**
Thwaites Av. LS29: I'ly 5E **11**
Thwaites Bank BD21: Keigh 6D **34**
Thwaites Bri. BD21: Keigh 6C **34**
THWAITES BROW 1D **48**
Thwaites Brow Rd. BD21: Keigh 2D **48**
Thwaites La. BD21: Keigh 6C **34**
Tibgarth LS22: Coll 6B **12**
Tichborne Rd. BD5: B'frd 2E **111**
Tichborne Rd. W. BD5: B'frd 2E **111**
Tickhill St. BD3: B'frd 5H **91** (5H **7**)
Tilbury Av. LS11: Leeds 1F **117**
Tilbury Gro. LS11: Leeds 1F **117**
Tilbury Mt. LS11: Leeds 1F **117**
Tilbury Pde. LS11: Leeds 1F **117**
Tilbury Rd. LS11: Leeds 1F **117**
Tilbury Row LS11: Leeds 1F **117**
Tilbury Ter. LS11: Leeds 1F **117**
Tilbury Vw. LS11: Leeds 1F **117**
Tile La. LS16: Leeds 4D **58**
  (not continuous)
Tile St. BD8: B'frd 2B **90**
Tile Ter. HD6: Brigh 2A **162**
Tiley Sq. BD5: B'frd 1E **111**
Till Carr La. HX3: Hal 2A **152**
Tillotson Av. HX6: Hal 6G **147**
Tillotson's Bldgs. HX2: Hal 2D **146**
Tillotson St. BD20: Sils 1D **14**
Timber St. BD21: Keigh 5C **34**
  HX5: Ell 5B **160**
Timble Beck LS9: Leeds 5B **98** (6H **5**)
Timble Dr. BD16: Bgly 3D **50**
Tim La. BD22: Keigh 5B **46**
Timmey La. HX6: Hal 4G **147**
TINGLEY .6E **139**
Tingley Av. WF3: E Ard 6E **139**
Tingley Comn. LS27: Morl 5B **138**
Tingley Cres. WF3: Morl 6C **138**
Tinkler Stile BD10: B'frd 1F **71**
TINSHILL 3F **57**
Tinshill Av. LS16: Leeds 4G **57**
Tinshill Cl. LS16: Leeds 4G **57**
Tinshill Cres. LS16: Leeds 3G **57**
Tinshill Dr. LS16: Leeds 3G **57**
Tinshill Gth. LS16: Leeds 3G **57**
Tinshill Gro. LS16: Leeds 3G **57**
Tinshill La. LS16: Leeds 4F **57**
TINSHILL MOOR 2G **57**
Tinshill Mt. LS16: Leeds 3G **57**
Tinshill Rd. LS16: Leeds 4F **57**
Tinshill Vw. LS16: Leeds 3G **57**
Tinshill Wlk. LS16: Leeds 2G **57**

Tintern Av. BD8: B'frd 4F **89**
Tisma Dr. BD4: B'frd 5A **112**
Titan Cen. BD12: B'frd 5C **132**
Tithe Barn Fold LS15: Bar E 2D **82**
Tithe Barn La. LS17: Bard 3D **44**
Tithe Barn Vw. HD6: Brigh 3C **162**
Tithe Ho. Way HD2: Hud 5E **163**
Titus St. BD18: Ship 1H **69**
Tiverton Ho. BD5: B'frd 6C **6**
Tiverton Wlk. BD4: B'frd 3C **112**
Tivoli Pl. BD5: B'frd 2C **110**
  LS29: I'ly 6E **11**
Toby La. BD7: B'frd 6A **90**
Todd Ter. BD7: B'frd 1B **110**
Todley Hall Rd. BD22: Keigh 1A **46**
Todwell La. BD5: B'frd 2C **110**
Tofts Av. BD12: B'frd 5C **132**
Tofts Gro. HD6: Brigh 4H **161**
Tofts Gro. Fold HD6: Brigh 4H **161**
Tofts Gro. Gdns. HD6: Brigh 4H **161**
Tofts Gro. Pl. *HD6: Brigh* 4H **161**
  (off Tofts Gro.)
TOFTSHAW 5B **112**
Toftshaw Fold BD4: B'frd 5B **112**
Toftshaw La. BD4: B'frd 5C **112**
Toftshaw New Rd. BD4: B'frd 5B **112**
Tofts Ho. Cl. LS28: Pud 4A **94**
Tofts Rd. LS28: Pud 4H **93**
Toft St. LS12: Leeds 5D **96**
Toller Dr. BD9: B'frd 6G **69**
Toller Gro. BD9: B'frd 6H **69**
Toller La. BD8: B'frd 1H **89**
  BD9: B'frd 6G **69**
Toller Pk. BD9: B'frd 6H **69**
Tollgate Ct. BD8: B'frd 2A **90**
Tolworth Fold BD15: B'frd 3D **88**
Tomling Cote La. BD20: Sils 3G **15**
Tomlinson Bldgs. BD10: B'frd 6G **53**
Tonbridge Cl. BD6: B'frd 5H **109**
TONG 3H **113**
Tong App. LS12: Leeds 5F **95**
Tong Dr. LS12: Leeds 4F **95**
Tong Ga. LS12: Leeds 4F **95**
Tong Grn. LS12: Leeds 4F **95**
Tong Hall Bus. Pk. BD4: B'frd 3H **113**
Tong La. BD4: B'frd 5G **113**
TONG PARK 3F **53**
Tong Pk. BD17: Bail 3F **53**
Tong Rd. LS12: Leeds 1D **114**
Tong Sports College 5E **113**
TONG STREET 4C **112**
Tong St. BD4: B'frd 3A **112**
Tongue La. LS6: Leeds 1F **77**
Tong Wlk. LS12: Leeds 4F **95**
Tong Way LS12: Leeds 4F **95**
Tonson St. BD21: Keigh 5A **34**
Tony Miller App. BD17: Ship 1C **70**
TOOTHILL 4A **162**
Toothill Av. HD6: Brigh 4A **162**
Toothill Bank HD6: Brigh 3A **162**
Toothill La. HD6: Brigh 5A **162**
Toothill La. Sth. HD6: Hud 6H **161**
TOPCLIFFE 5C **138**
Topcliffe Av. LS27: Morl 3D **138**
Topcliffe Ct. LS27: Morl 3D **138**
Topcliffe Fold LS27: Morl 5C **138**
Topcliffe Grn. LS27: Morl 3D **138**
Topcliffe Gro. LS27: Morl 5C **138**
Topcliffe La. LS27: Morl 5C **138**
  WF3: Morl 4D **138**
Topcliffe Mead LS27: Morl 3D **138**
Topcliffe M. LS27: Morl 3D **138**
Top Fold LS12: Leeds 5B **96**
Top Moor Side LS11: Leeds 6G **97**
Tops Health Club 5F **157**
  (off Cobham Pde.)
Tor Av. BD12: B'frd 6C **132**
Torcote Cres. HD2: Hud 6C **162**
Tordoff Av. BD7: B'frd 6G **89**
Tordoff Grn. BD6: B'frd 5B **110**
Tordoff Pl. LS5: Leeds 5A **76**
Tordoff Rd. BD12: B'frd 1E **133**

Tordoff Ter. LS5: Leeds 5A 76
Tornwood Cl. BD22: Keigh 5C 46
Toronto Pl. LS7: Leeds 3B 78
Toronto St. LS1: Leeds 3H 97 (4D 4)
  LS6: Leeds 1E 97
    (off Queen's Rd.)
Torre Cl. LS9: Leeds 3E 99
Torre Cres. BD6: B'frd 4F 109
  LS9: Leeds 3F 99
Torre Dr. LS9: Leeds 2E 99
Torre Gdns. LS9: Leeds 3D 98
Torre Grn. LS9: Leeds 3D 98
Torre Gro. BD6: B'frd 4F 109
  LS9: Leeds 2E 99
Torre Hill LS9: Leeds 3F 99
Torre La. LS9: Leeds 3F 99
Torre Mt. LS9: Leeds 2E 99
Torre Pl. LS9: Leeds 3F 99
Torre Rd. BD6: B'frd 4F 109
  LS9: Leeds 3D 98
Torre Sq. LS9: Leeds 2F 99
Torre Vw. LS9: Leeds 2F 99
Torre Wlk. LS9: Leeds 2F 99
Torridon Cres. BD6: B'frd 1G 131
TOULSTON 5G 31
Tourist Info. Cen.
  Bradford 5E 91 (5D 6)
  Halifax 2H 149 (4D 164)
  Haworth 2B 64
  Ilkley 5D 10
  Leeds Station 4H 97 (5D 4)
  Morley 3A 138
  Otley 3E 23
  Wetherby 4E 13
Towcester Av. LS10: Leeds 4B 140
Tower Ct. LS12: Leeds 3D 96
Tower Dr., The LS21: Pool 5G 25
Tower Gdns. HX2: Hal 5D 148
Tower Gro. LS12: Leeds 3A 96
Tower Hill HX6: Hal 5H 147
Tower Ho. St. LS2: Leeds ...2A 98 (2F 5)
Tower La. LS12: Leeds 3H 95
    (not continuous)
Tower Pl. LS12: Leeds 3H 95
Tower Rd. BD18: Ship 1G 69
Towers Sq. LS6: Leeds 1G 77
Tower St. BD2: B'frd 1H 91
Towers Way LS6: Leeds 1G 77
Tower Vw. HX2: Hal 4C 148
    (off Plane Tree Nest La.)
Tower Works LS11: Leeds 4H 97 (6C 4)
Town Cl. LS18: H'fth 6D 56
Townclose Vw. LS25: Kip 5F 123
TOWN END
  BD14 ....1C 108
  LS12 ....6B 96
  LS13 ....1G 95
  LS27 ....3B 138
  WF3 ....6G 141
Town End BD7: B'frd 1A 110
  LS25: Gar 3E 103
    (off Middleton Rd.)
  LS27: Morl 3B 138
    (Harthill Ri.)
Town End Cl. LS13: Leeds 2G 95
Townend Pl. LS28: Pud 3B 94
Town End Rd. BD14: B'frd 6D 88
Townend Rd. LS12: Leeds 6B 96
Town End Yd. LS13: Leeds 1F 95
Townfield BD15: B'frd 4G 67
Town Flds. Rd. HX5: Ell 5A 160
Town Ga. BD10: B'frd 1H 71
  BD12: B'frd 5C 132
  BD19: Cleck 1F 153
  HX2: Hal 6B 126
  HX6: Hal 6D 146
  LS20: Guis 4C 40
  LS28: Pud 2F 73
Towngate BD17: Bail 3D 52
    (off Northgate)
  BD18: Ship 2D 70

Towngate BD21: Keigh 6A 34
  HD6: Brigh 6D 152
  HX3: Hal 1E 151
    (Kirk La.)
  HX3: Hal 5C 150
    (Law La.)
  HX3: Hal 5C 130
    (Tetley La.)
Towngate Av. HD6: Brigh 6D 152
Town Ga. Cl. LS20: Guis 4C 40
Towngate Ho. HX5: Ell 5B 160
Town Hall Bldgs. HX5: Ell 5B 160
    (off Southgate)
Town Hall Ct. HX6: Hal 5H 147
Town Hall Sq. LS19: Yead 6F 41
Town Hall St. BD21: Keigh 6A 34
  HX5: Ell 5B 160
  HX6: Hal 6H 147
Town Hall St. E.
  HX1: Hal 2G 149 (3C 164)
TOWN HEAD 1F 15
Townhead Fold LS29: Add 1C 8
Town Hill St. BD16: Bgly 3D 68
Town La. BD10: B'frd 6H 53
Townley Av. HX3: Hal 5C 150
Town St. BD11: B'frd 1E 135
  LS7: Leeds 2B 78
  LS10: Leeds 2H 139
  LS11: Leeds 3E 117
  LS12: Leeds 3A 96
  LS13: Leeds 6E 75
    (Bell La.)
  LS13: Leeds 4A 74
    (St Andrew's Cl.)
  LS18: H'fth 1D 74
  LS19: Yead 4H 55
    (Billing Vw.)
  LS19: Yead 6F 41
    (Haworth La.)
  LS20: Guis 4C 40
  LS27: Morl 6E 115
  LS28: Pud 6H 73
    (Prospect St.)
  LS28: Pud 2A 94
    (Richardshaw La.)
  LS28: Pud 3F 73
    (Town Wells Dr.)
  WF3: Rothw 4H 141
Town St. M. LS7: Leeds 2B 78
Town St. Wlk. LS7: Leeds 2B 78
Town Wells Dr. LS28: Pud 3F 73
Trackside BD7: B'frd 2F 133
Trafalgar Gdns. LS27: Morl 4A 138
Trafalgar Rd. LS29: I'ly 5D 10
Trafalgar Sq. HX1: Hal 4E 149
Trafalgar St. BD1: B'frd 3E 91 (2C 6)
  HX1: Hal 4E 149
  LS2: Leeds 3B 98 (3G 5)
Trafford Av. LS9: Leeds 1F 99
Trafford Gro. LS9: Leeds 6E 79
Trafford Ter. LS9: Leeds 1F 99
Train FX 2F 31
Tramways BD12: B'frd 2F 133
  LS20: Guis 4H 39
Tranbeck Rd. LS20: Guis 4H 39
Tranfield Av. LS20: Guis 4A 40
Tranfield Cl. LS20: Guis 4A 40
Tranfield Ct. LS20: Guis 4A 40
Tranfield Gdns. LS20: Guis 4A 40
Tranmere Ct. LS20: Guis 4A 40
Tranmere Dr. LS20: Guis 4A 40
TRANMERE PARK 4A 40
Tranquility LS15: Leeds 1E 101
Tranquility Av. LS15: Leeds 1E 101
Tranquility Ct. LS15: Leeds 1E 101
    (off Tranquility Av.)
Tranquility Wlk. LS15: Leeds 1E 101
Transformations Fitness Cen. 4E 97
Tranter Gdns. BD4: B'frd 6C 92
Tranter Pl. LS15: Leeds 3A 100
Tray Royd HX2: Hal 5C 126
Tredgold Av. LS16: B'hpe 3G 43

Tredgold Cl. LS16: B'hpe 3G 43
Tredgold Cres. LS16: B'hpe 3G 43
Tredgold Gth. LS16: B'hpe 3G 43
Treefield Ind. Est. LS27: Morl 1F 137
Tree La. HX2: Hal 2F 127
Trees St. BD8: B'frd 2C 90
Tree Tops Ct. LS8: Leeds 2G 79
Tree Top Vw. BD13: B'frd 3G 107
Trelawn Av. LS6: Leeds 4D 76
Trelawn Cres. LS6: Leeds 4D 76
Trelawn Pl. LS6: Leeds 4D 76
Trelawn St. LS6: Leeds 4D 76
Trelawn Ter. LS6: Leeds 4D 76
Tremont Gdns. LS10: Leeds 3C 118
Trenam Pk. Dr. BD10: B'frd 5G 53
Trenance Dr. BD18: Ship 2H 69
Trenance Gdns. HX4: Hal 4E 159
Trenholme Av. BD6: B'frd 1B 132
Trenic Cres. LS6: Leeds 6D 76
Trenic Dr. LS6: Leeds 6D 76
Trent Av. LS25: Gar 6H 103
Trentham Av. LS11: Leeds 2H 117
Trentham Gro. LS11: Leeds 2H 117
Trentham Pl. LS11: Leeds 2H 117
Trentham Row LS11: Leeds 2H 117
Trentham St. LS11: Leeds 3H 117
Trentham Ter. LS11: Leeds 2H 117
Trenton Dr. BD8: B'frd 2C 90
Trent Rd. LS9: Leeds 3D 98
Trent St. LS11: Leeds 6H 97
Trescoe Av. LS13: Leeds 2G 95
Trevelyan Sq. LS1: Leeds 4A 98 (5E 5)
Trevelyan St. HD6: Brigh 4A 152
Trevor Foster Way BD5: B'frd 3F 111
Trevor Ter. WF2: Wake 3C 156
Triangle Bus. Pk. WF17: Bat 4C 136
Trimmingham La. HX2: Hal 3B 148
Trimmingham Rd. HX2: Hal 3B 148
Trimmingham Vs. HX2: Hal 3C 148
Trim 'n' Shape 4B 6
Trinity Bus. Cen. HX1: Hal 6C 164
Trinity Cl. HX2: Hal 1E 129
Trinity Ct. LS8: Leeds 2C 78
Trinity Fold HX1: Hal 5B 164
Trinity One LS9: Leeds 4B 98 (6C 6)
Trinity Pl. BD16: Bgly 5C 50
  HX1: Hal 3G 149 (5B 164)
Trinity Ri. LS21: Otley 4F 23
Trinity Rd. BD5: B'frd 6D 90
  HX1: Hal 3G 149 (5B 164)
Trinity Row HX1: Hal 3G 149 (5B 164)
    (not continuous)
Trinity St. BD21: Keigh 5A 34
    (off East Av.)
  HX1: Hal 3G 149 (5B 164)
  LS1: Leeds 3A 98 (4E 5)
Trinity St. Arc. LS1: Leeds ...4A 98 (5E 5)
Trinity Ter. WF17: Bat 6H 135
Trinity Vw. BD12: B'frd 6E 111
  HX3: Hal 3H 149
Trinity Wlk. BD12: B'frd 6E 111
Trip Gth. LS22: Coll 1B 24
Trip La. LS22: Coll 1H 27
Tristram Av. BD5: B'frd 3G 111
Tristram Cen., The LS12: Leeds ...1E 117
Triumph Cl. LS11: Leeds 5G 97
Trooper La. HX3: Hal 4H 149
Trooper Ter. HX3: Hal 4H 149
Tropical World 6F 61
Trough La. BD13: B'frd 6H 65
  BD22: B'frd 2F 85
Troughton Pl. LS28: Pud 6B 94
Troughton St. LS28: Pud 6B 94
Trough Well La. WF2: Wake 5C 156
Troutbeck Av. BD17: Bail 6G 51
    (not continuous)
TROY 5E 57
TROYDALE 5D 94
Troydale Gdns. LS28: Pud 6D 94
Troydale Gro. LS28: Pud 6D 94
Troydale La. LS28: Pud 5C 94
TROY HILL 2B 138

Troy Hill LS18: H'fth 5E **57**
  LS27: Morl 2A **138**
Troy Ri. LS27: Morl 2B **138**
Troy Rd. LS18: H'fth 5E **57**
  LS27: Morl 3A **138**
Trueman Ct. BD12: B'frd 1E **133**
TRUNCLIFFE 4D **110**
Truncliffe BD5: B'frd 4D **110**
Truncliffe Ho. BD5: B'frd 4D **110**
  (off Truncliffe)
Truro St. LS12: Leeds 3C **96**
Tudor Barn Ct. BD18: Ship 2D **70**
Tudor Cl. LS28: Pud 1G **93**
Tudor Ct. BD5: B'frd 6E **91**
  (off Swarland Gro.)
Tudor Cft. HD2: Hud 6F **163**
Tudor Gdns. LS11: Leeds 3E **117**
Tudor Lawns LS8: Leeds 2G **79**
  WF2: Wake 4C **156**
Tudor St. BD5: B'frd 1D **110**
Tuel La. HX6: Hal 4H **147**
Tufton St. BD20: Sils 2D **14**
Tulip Retail Pk. LS10: Leeds 2B **118**
Tulip St. BD22: Haw 4C **64**
  LS10: Leeds 2B **118**
Tumbling Hill St.
  BD7: B'frd 5D **90** (5A **6**)
Tunnel St. BD13: B'frd 3B **86**
Tunnicliffe Pl. BD20: Sils 2D **14**
Tunstall Grn. BD4: B'frd 2C **112**
Tunstall Rd. LS11: Leeds 2A **118**
Tunwell La. BD2: B'frd 5A **72**
Tunwell St. BD2: B'frd 5A **72**
Turbary Av. LS28: Pud 1A **94**
Turbury La. HX4: Hal 3C **158**
Turf Ct. BD13: B'frd 4A **66**
Turf La. BD13: B'frd 3A **66**
Turkey Hill LS28: Pud 5B **94**
  (not continuous)
Turks Head Yd. LS1: Leeds 4E **5**
Turlow St. LS9: Leeds 4B **98** (6H **5**)
Turnberry Av. LS17: Leeds 3H **59**
Turnberry Cl. LS17: Leeds 3H **59**
  WF3: E Ard 1D **154**
Turnberry Ct. BD20: Keigh 2G **33**
Turnberry Dr. LS17: Leeds 3H **59**
  WF3: E Ard 1D **154**
Turnberry Fold LS17: Leeds 3H **59**
Turnberry Gdns. WF3: E Ard 1D **154**
Turnberry Gro. LS17: Leeds 3H **59**
Turnberry Pk. Rd. LS27: Morl 3F **137**
Turnberry Pl. LS17: Leeds 3H **59**
Turnberry Ri. LS17: Leeds 3H **59**
Turnberry Vw. LS17: Leeds 3H **59**
Turnbull Ct. LS8: Leeds 4H **79**
Turner Av. BD7: B'frd 6H **89**
Turner Av. Nth. HX2: Hal 2B **128**
Turner Av. Sth. HX2: Hal 2C **128**
Turner Cl. WF3: E Ard 1E **155**
Turner Cres. LS21: Otley 2F **23**
Turner Dr. WF3: E Ard 1E **155**
Turner Farm HX2: Hal 6C **106**
  (off Causeway Foot)
Turner Ho. LS5: Leeds 5H **75**
Turner La. HX3: Hal 6H **129** (1D **164**)
  (not continuous)
  LS29: Add 1A **8**
  (Addingham Wharfedale Rd.)
  LS29: Add 3A **8**
  (Cocking La.)
Turner Pl. BD7: B'frd 6B **90**
  HX2: Hal 3C **128**
Turners Ct. HX3: Hal 5F **129**
Turner St. LS28: Pud 6H **73**
Turner's Yd. LS13: Leeds 1F **95**
  LS28: Pud 6H **73**
Turner Vw. HX2: Hal 3C **128**
  (off Bank Edge Rd.)
Turney St. HX3: Hal 5E **129**
  (not continuous)
Turn Lea HX2: Hal 6D **126**
Turnpike St. HX5: Ell 4C **160**

Turnshaw Rd. BD22: Keigh 5A **46**
Turnsteads Av. BD19: Cleck 1H **153**
Turnsteads Dr. BD19: Cleck 6A **134**
Turnstone Ct. LS10: Leeds 2B **140**
Turnways, The LS6: Leeds 5C **76**
Turton Grn. LS27: Morl 6F **115**
Turton Va. LS27: Morl 1F **137**
Tweed Cl. WF17: Bat 6C **136**
Tweedy St. BD15: B'frd 4G **67**
Twelfth Av. WF15: Liv 4H **153**
Twickenham Ct. BD8: B'frd 1D **90**
Twine La. HX7: Heb B 6A **126**
Twinge La. HX3: Hal 3B **150**
Tyas Gro. LS9: Leeds 4F **99**
TYERSAL 5C **92**
Tyersal Av. BD4: Pud 4D **92**
Tyersal Cl. BD4: Pud 5D **92**
Tyersal Ct. BD4: Pud 5C **92**
Tyersal Cres. BD4: Pud 5D **92**
Tyersal Dr. BD4: Pud 5D **92**
Tyersal Gth. BD4: Pud 5D **92**
TYERSAL GATE 1C **112**
Tyersal Grn. BD4: Pud 5D **92**
Tyersal Gro. BD4: Pud 5D **92**
Tyersal La. BD4: B'frd, Pud 1C **112**
  LS28: B'frd, Pud 5F **93**
Tyersal Pk. BD4: Pud 5D **92**
Tyersal Rd. BD4: Pud 5C **92**
Tyersal Ter. BD4: Pud 5C **92**
Tyersal Vw. BD4: Pud 5C **92**
Tyersal Wlk. BD4: Pud 5D **92**
Tyler Ct. BD10: B'frd 1A **72**
Tyndale La. LS7: Leeds 3G **77**
Tyne St. BD3: B'frd 3F **91** (2F **7**)
  BD21: Keigh 6B **34**
  BD22: Haw 2D **64**
Tynwald Cl. LS17: Leeds 5G **59**
Tynwald Dr. LS17: Leeds 4G **59**
Tynwald Gdns. LS17: Leeds 5G **59**
Tynwald Grn. LS17: Leeds 4G **59**
Tynwald Hill LS17: Leeds 5G **59**
Tynwald Mt. LS17: Leeds 4G **59**
Tynwald Rd. LS17: Leeds 5G **59**
Tynwald Wlk. LS17: Leeds 4G **59**
Tyrls, The BD1: B'frd 5E **91** (5C **6**)
Tyrrel St. BD1: B'frd 4E **91** (4D **6**)
  (not continuous)
Tyson St. BD1: B'frd 3D **90** (2B **6**)
  HX1: Hal 3C **148**

U

UK Workout 5B **136**
Ullswater Cl. HX5: Ell 4D **160**
Ullswater Cres. LS15: Leeds 4A **100**
  LS26: Rothw 1E **143**
Ullswater Dr. BD6: B'frd 1H **131**
Ullswater Ri. LS22: Weth 3C **12**
UNDERCLIFFE 1G **91**
Undercliffe BD3: B'frd 2G **91**
Undercliffe Old Rd. BD2: B'frd 2H **91**
Undercliffe Ri. LS29: I'ly 1G **19**
Undercliffe Rd. BD2: B'frd 6H **71**
Undercliffe St. BD3: B'frd 2H **91**
Undercliffe Ter. HX2: Hal 5D **148**
  (off Scar Bottom Rd.)
Underwood Dr. LS19: Yead 5F **55**
Underwood Ho. BD3: B'frd 2F **7**
Union Cl. LS21: Otley 4D **22**
Union Cross Yd.
  HX1: Hal 2G **149** (3C **164**)
Union Ho. BD13: B'frd 3E **109**
Union Ho. Cl. BD13: B'frd 3E **109**
Union Ho. La. BD13: B'frd 3E **109**
Union La. HX2: Hal 5B **106**
Union Pl. LS11: Leeds 5H **97**
Union Rd. BD7: B'frd 6B **90**
  BD12: B'frd 6C **110**
Union St. BD13: B'frd 4A **108**
  BD16: Bgly 6A **36**

Union St. BD17: Bail 5E **53**
  HX1: Hal 2G **149** (4C **164**)
  HX4: Hal 4H **159**
  HX6: Hal 4A **148**
  LS2: Leeds 3B **98** (4F **5**)
  LS21: Otley 4D **22**
  LS27: Morl 5C **116**
  WF17: Bat 6A **136**
Union Ter. LS7: Leeds 3A **78**
Union Yd. BD10: B'frd 1H **71**
Unity Cl. LS6: Leeds 5H **77**
Unity Ct. HD6: Brigh 3H **161**
Unity St. BD20: Keigh 3D **34**
  WF3: Rothw 4H **141**
Unity St. Nth. BD16: Bgly 5B **50**
Unity St. Sth. BD16: Bgly 5B **50**
Unity Ter. HX1: Hal 3C **148**
University of Bradford
  Dennis Bellamy Hall 6C **90**
  Laisteridge Lane Campus 6C **90**
  Revis Barber Hall 6C **90**
  School of Health Studies 6D **90**
  School of Management 5B **70**
  Shearbridge Grn. 5C **90** (5A **6**)
  Trinity Hall 6C **90**
University of Bradford Sports Cen.
  . . . . .5C **90** (6A **6**)
University of Leeds 1G **97** (1B **4**)
University Rd. LS2: Leeds 1G **97**
Unwin Pl. BD9: B'frd 1G **89**
Upcroft Ct. BD13: B'frd 3G **107**
Upland Cres. LS8: Leeds 4E **79**
Upland Gdns. LS8: Leeds 5E **79**
Upland Gro. LS8: Leeds 4E **79**
Upland Rd. LS8: Leeds 5E **79**
Uplands BD20: Keigh 4G **33**
Uplands Av. BD13: B'frd 3D **108**
Uplands Cl. BD13: B'frd 3D **108**
Uplands Cres. BD13: B'frd 3D **108**
Uplands Gro. BD13: B'frd 3D **108**
Up. Accommodation Rd.
  LS9: Leeds 3C **98**
Up. Ada St. BD18: Ship 1H **69**
Up. Addison St. BD4: B'frd . . .6F **91** (6F **7**)
Up. Allerton La. BD15: B'frd 3A **88**
UPPER ARMLEY 2H **95**
Upper Armley Tennis Club 2A **96**
Up. Ashley La. BD17: Ship 1B **70**
Up. Basinghall St.
  LS1: Leeds 3H **97** (3D **4**)
Up. Batley La. WF17: Bat 6B **136**
Up. Batley Low La. WF17: Bat 5D **136**
Up. Bell Cft. HX3: Hal 5C **150**
Up. Bell Hall HX1: Hal 4E **149**
Up. Bentley Royd HX6: Hal 6G **147**
  (not continuous)
Up. Bolton Brow HX6: Hal 4B **148**
Up. Bonegate HD6: Brigh 6B **152**
UPPER BROCKHOLES 5B **106**
Up. Calton St. BD21: Keigh 2H **47**
Up. Carr La. LS28: Pud 3E **73**
Up. Castle St. BD5: B'frd 1E **111**
Up. Chelsea St. BD21: Keigh 2H **47**
UPPER COMMON 3D **132**
Up. Ellistones HX4: Hal 4E **159**
  (off Martin Grn. La.)
Up. Ellistones Ct. HX4: Hal 4E **159**
UPPER EXLEY 2A **160**
UPPER FAGLEY 1B **92**
Up. Ferndown Grn. BD15: B'frd . . .2C **88**
Up. Field Ho. La. HX6: Hal 6D **146**
Upper Forge HX1: Hal 2G **149** (4B **164**)
Up. Fountain St. HX6: Hal 5H **147**
Up. Fyfe La. BD17: Bail 4E **53**
Up. Gaukroger HX6: Hal 6F **147**
Up. George St. BD6: B'frd 4B **110**
Up. Grange Av. BD15: B'frd 3D **88**
UPPER GREEN
  Bradford 1G **109**
  Wakefield 2D **154**
Upper Grn. BD7: B'frd 2H **109**
  BD17: Bail 5B **52**

Up. Green Av. BD19: Cleck 1F **153**
   WF3: E Ard 2D **154**
Up. Green Cl. WF3: E Ard 2E **155**
Up. Green Dr. WF3: E Ard 2E **155**
Up. Green La. HD6: Brigh 4G **151**
Up. Grn. Royd HX2: Hal 3G **127**
Up. Green Way WF3: E Ard 2D **154**
Upper Haley BD22: Oxen 6D **64**
Up. Hall Fold HX4: Hal 6A **158**
Up. Hall Vw. HX3: Hal 4C **130**
Up. Haugh Shaw HX1: Hal 4E **149**
Up. Headley BD13: B'frd 6H **87**
Up. Heights Rd. BD13: B'frd 3G **87**
Up. High Lees HX2: Hal 5C **126**
Up. Hird St. BD21: Keigh 2G **47**
Up. House Cotts. BD13: B'frd 3C **108**
Up. House St. BD4: B'frd 6H **91**
Up. Hoyle Ing BD13: B'frd 4B **88**
Up. Jackroyd HX3: Hal 6D **128**
Up. Kell HX2: Hal 1F **127**
Up. Kingston HX1: Hal 3C **148**
Up. Kirkgate HX1: Hal 2H **149** (4D **164**)
Upper La. HX3: Hal 3B **130**
Up. Langwith LS22: Coll 3G **27**
Up. Lombard St. LS19: Yead 3E **55**
UPPER MARSH 4A **64**
Upper Marsh HX3: Hal 4B **150**
Up. Marsh La. BD22: Oxen 4A **64**
Up. Martin Grn. HX4: Hal 4E **159**
Up. Mary St. BD18: Ship 1H **69**
Upper Mdws. BD13: B'frd 5A **108**
Up. Mill Cotts. BD17: B'frd 2H **53**
Up. Millergate BD1: B'frd 4C **6**
Up. Mill Row BD20: Keigh 3A **36**
Uppermoor LS28: Pud 4G **93**
Uppermoor Cl. LS28: Pud 5H **93**
UPPER MOOR SIDE 3D **114**
Up. Mosscar St. BD3: B'frd . .4G **91** (4H **7**)
Up. Nidd St. BD3: B'frd 5H **91**
Up. Parish Ghyll La.
   LS29: I'ly 6B **10**
Up. Park Ga. BD1: B'frd 4F **91** (3F **7**)
Up. Piccadilly BD1: B'frd 4E **91** (3C **6**)
Up. Pierce Cl. BD22: Haw 6F **47**
Upper Pikeley BD15: B'frd 3H **87**
Up. Quarry Rd. HD2: Hud 5G **163**
Up. Range HX3: Hal 6G **129**
   (off Woodlands Gro.)
Up. Reap Hurst HX2: Hal 3G **127**
Up. Rushton Rd. BD3: B'frd 2B **92**
Up. School St. BD20: Stee 6C **14**
Up. Seymour St.
   BD3: B'frd 5H **91** (5H **7**)
Up. Slack HX2: Hal 1F **127**
Upper St. WF3: E Ard 6F **139**
   (off Bradford Rd.)
Up. Sutherland Rd. HX3: Hal 1G **151**
Up. Tewit HX2: Hal 6D **106**
UPPER TOWN 1C **84**
Upper Town BD22: Oxen 1C **84**
Up. Town St. LS13: Leeds 6E **75**
Up. Washer La. HX2: Hal 4D **148**
Up. Well Royd HX2: Hal 2A **148**
Up. Westlock Av. LS9: Leeds 2E **99**
Up. W. Scausby HX2: Hal 5D **106**
Up. White Lees HX7: Heb B 6A **126**
Up. Willow Hill HX2: Hal 3B **148**
Up. Woodlands Rd. BD8: B'frd 2A **90**
Up. Woodview Pl. LS11: Leeds 3H **117**
   (off Woodview St.)
UPPER WORTLEY 5B **96**
Up. Wortley Dr. LS12: Leeds 4B **96**
Up. Wortley Rd. LS12: Leeds 4B **96**
UPPER WYKE 4D **132**
Upton's Yd. LS1: Leeds 4E **5**
Upton Wlk. BD15: B'frd 3D **88**
Upwood Holiday Pk. BD22: Oxen . . .6E **65**
Upwood La. BD20: Keigh 3H **35**
Ures Cres. BD8: B'frd 3D **90** (1A **6**)
Ure Gro. LS22: Weth 1D **12**
Usher St. BD4: B'frd 6G **91**
Uttley St. HX3: Hal 5F **129**

V

Vale, The LS6: Leeds 4F **77**
   LS22: Coll 3A **28**
Vale Av. LS8: Leeds 5E **61**
Vale Gro. BD13: B'frd 4B **108**
   BD20: Sils 2D **14**
Vale Mill La. BD22: Haw 6D **46**
Valentine Ct. BD13: B'frd 4A **88**
Valentine M. WF3: Wake 1G **157**
Vale St. BD21: Keigh 4C **34**
   HD6: Brigh 6A **152**
Vale Ter. BD22: Keigh 6D **46**
Vale Vw. BD20: Sils 2D **14**
Valley, The LS17: Leeds 1G **59**
Valley Av. HX3: Hal 1A **152**
Valley Cl. LS17: Leeds 1G **59**
Valley Ct. BD1: B'frd 2E **91**
   LS17: Leeds 1B **78**
   (off Allerton Grange Gdns.)
Valley Dr. LS15: Leeds 2C **100**
   LS26: Kip 5E **123**
   LS29: I'ly 5F **11**
Valley Farm Rd. LS10: Leeds 4E **119**
Valley Farm Way LS10: Leeds 4E **119**
Valley Fold BD13: B'frd 5A **108**
Valley Gdns. LS7: Leeds 1A **78**
Valley Grn. LS28: Pud 5B **94**
Valley Gro. HX2: Hal 6D **106**
   LS28: Pud 5B **94**
Valley Hgts. BD17: B'frd 2B **86**
Valley Mills BD11: B'frd 5D **114**
Valley Mills Ind. Est. BD10: B'frd . . .1C **72**
Valley Mt. LS13: Leeds 3C **94**
   LS25: Kip 3F **123**
Valley Parade 2D **90**
Valley Pde. BD8: B'frd 2D **90**
Valley Pl. BD1: B'frd 2E **91**
Valley Ridge LS25: Kip 2F **123**
   (not continuous)
Valley Ri. LS13: Leeds 4E **75**
   BD18: Ship 2B **70**
   BD21: Keigh 6D **34**
   LS13: Leeds 4E **75**
   LS25: Kip 2F **123**
   LS27: Morl 2B **138**
   LS28: Pud 5A **94**
   LS29: I'ly 4F **11**
Valley Rd. Retail Pk.
   BD1: B'frd 3E **91** (1D **6**)
Valley Sq. LS28: Pud 5B **94**
Valley Vw. LS16: Leeds 4D **60**
Valley Vw. BD16: Bgly 6E **49**
   BD17: Bail 6B **52**
   HX2: Hal 6D **106**
   HX3: Hal 5H **131**
   LS21: Arth 5H **25**
   LS21: Pool 6D **24**
Valley Vw. Cl. BD22: Keigh 4E **47**
Valley Vw. Gdns. BD22: Haw 1E **65**
Valley Vw. Gro. BD2: B'frd 6G **71**
Valley Way HX2: Hal 6D **106**
Vancouver Pl. LS7: Leeds 3C **78**
Vantage Point LS27: Morl 6H **137**
Varley St. LS28: Pud 2H **93**
   (not continuous)
Varleys Yd. LS28: Pud 4B **94**
Vaughan St. BD1: B'frd 4D **90** (3A **6**)
   HX1: Hal 4D **148**
Vegal Cres. HX3: Hal 5D **128**
Ventnor Dr. BD19: Cleck 5F **135**
Ventnor St. BD3: B'frd 4G **91** (4H **7**)
Ventnor Ter. HX3: Hal 5F **149**
Vento Cl. BD6: B'frd 5B **110**
Verdun Rd. BD6: B'frd 5A **110**
Vere Sq. BD5: B'frd 1E **111**
Veritys Pl. LS28: Pud 3B **94**
Verity Spur LS9: Leeds 3A **100**
Verity St. BD4: B'frd 6D **112**
Verity Vw. LS9: Leeds 2A **100**

Vermont St. LS13: Leeds 1C **94**
Vernon Ct. BD20: Keigh 5H **33**
Vernon Pl. BD2: B'frd 1H **91**
   BD13: B'frd 6G **107**
   LS28: Pud 2A **94**
Vernon Rd. LS1: Leeds 2H **97** (1C **4**)
Vernon St. BD22: Haw 1F **65**
   LS2: Leeds 2H **97** (2D **4**)
Vesper Cl. LS5: Leeds 3H **75**
Vesper Ct. LS5: Leeds 3G **75**
Vesper Ct. Dr. LS5: Leeds 3G **75**
Vesper Gdns. LS5: Leeds 4H **75**
Vesper Ga. Cres. LS5: Leeds 4H **75**
Vesper Ga. Dr. LS5: Leeds 3G **75**
Vesper Ga. Mt. LS5: Leeds 4H **75**
Vesper Gro. LS5: Leeds 5A **76**
Vesper La. LS5: Leeds 4H **75**
Vesper Mt. LS5: Leeds 5A **76**
Vesper Pl. LS5: Leeds 5A **76**
Vesper Ri. LS5: Leeds 3G **75**
Vesper Rd. LS5: Leeds 3F **75**
Vesper Ter. LS5: Leeds 5A **76**
Vesper Wlk. LS5: Leeds 4G **75**
Vesper Way LS5: Leeds 3G **75**
Vestry St. BD4: B'frd 2H **111**
Viaduct Rd. LS4: Leeds 2D **96**
Viaduct St. LS28: Pud 2H **93**
Viaduct Theatre 1B **164**
   (in Dean Clough)
Vicarage Av. LS5: Leeds 5B **76**
Vicarage Cl. BD12: B'frd 5C **132**
   WF1: Wake 4F **157**
Vicarage Dr. LS28: Pud 4H **93**
Vicarage Gdns. BD11: B'frd 2E **135**
   HD6: Brigh 3H **161**
   LS21: Otley 4E **23**
Vicarage Pl. LS5: Leeds 5B **76**
Vicarage Rd. BD18: Ship 1E **71**
   LS6: Leeds 1F **97**
Vicarage St. LS5: Leeds 5B **76**
Vicarage Ter. LS5: Leeds 5B **76**
Vicarage Vw. LS5: Leeds 5B **76**
Vicar La. BD1: B'frd 4F **91** (4E **7**)
   (not continuous)
   LS1: Leeds 3A **98** (4F **5**)
Vicar Pk. Dr. HX2: Hal 1H **147**
Vicar Pk. Rd. HX2: Hal 2H **147**
Vicars Rd. LS8: Leeds 5D **78**
Vicars Ter. LS8: Leeds 5D **78**
   WF10: Kip 3H **145**
Vickerman St. HX1: Hal 3D **148**
Vickers Av. LS5: Leeds 6H **75**
Vickersdale LS28: Pud 1A **94**
Vickersdale Ct. LS28: Pud 1A **94**
Vickersdale Gro. LS28: Pud 1A **94**
   (off Haydn's Ter.)
Vickers Pl. LS28: Pud 1A **94**
Vickers St. LS27: Morl 5H **137**
Vickers Yd. LS28: Pud 2H **93**
Victor Dr. LS20: Guis 5C **40**
Victoria Av. BD2: B'frd 5B **72**
   BD18: Ship 1H **69**
   BD21: Keigh 6A **34**
   BD22: Haw 1C **64**
   HD6: Brigh 6C **152**
   HX1: Hal 3D **148**
   HX5: Ell 5A **160**
   HX6: Hal 5A **148**
   LS9: Leeds 3E **99**
   LS18: H'fth 2C **74**
   LS19: Yead 1H **55**
   LS26: Rothw 3A **142**
   LS27: Morl 2A **138**
   LS29: I'ly 5B **10**
   LS29: Men 6F **21**
   WF1: Wake 6H **157**
Victoria Chase HD6: Brigh 1B **152**
Victoria Cl. LS18: H'fth 2C **74**
   LS19: Yead 6H **41**
   LS29: I'ly 5C **10**
   WF10: Kip 3H **145**

Victoria Ct. *BD18: Ship* 1H **69**
 (off Victoria Av.)
 BD21: Keigh 6H **33**
 LS15: Leeds 5F **81**
 LS27: Morl *2A* **138**
 (off Victoria M.)
 WF17: Bat 6B **136**
Victoria Ct. M. LS6: Leeds 6E **77**
Victoria Cres. HX5: Ell 5B **160**
 LS18: H'fth 2C **74**
 LS28: Pud 4G **93**
Victoria Dr. BD2: B'frd 5B **72**
 HX3: Hal 4D **130**
 LS18: H'fth 2C **74**
 LS27: Morl 1B **138**
 LS29: I'ly 5B **10**
Victoria Gdns. LS18: H'fth 2D **74**
 LS28: Pud 4G **93**
 LS29: I'ly 5B **10**
Victoria Grange Dr. LS27: Morl . . .2A **138**
Victoria Grange Way LS27: Morl . . .2A **138**
Victoria Gro. LS9: Leeds 3F **99**
 LS18: H'fth 3C **74**
 LS28: Pud 4G **93**
 LS29: I'ly 5B **10**
Victoria Hall
 Eastwood 5B **34**
 Saltaire *1H* **69**
 (off Victoria Rd.)
Victoria Ind. Est. BD2: B'frd 5A **72**
Victoria Ind. Pk. LS14: Leeds 2D **80**
Victoria M. *BD21: Keigh* *6H* **33**
 (off Drewry Rd.)
 HX5: Ell *5B* **160**
 (off John St.)
 LS18: H'fth 2C **74**
 LS27: Morl 2A **138**
Victoria Mt. LS18: H'fth 1C **74**
Victorian Arc. *LS29: I'ly* *5D* **10**
 (off Church St.)
Victorian Museum of Reed Organs &
 Harmonicas 1H **69**
 (in Victoria Hall)
Victoria Pk. BD18: Ship 2H **69**
 HX1: Hal 2E **149**
Victoria Pk. Av. LS13: Leeds 6G **75**
Victoria Pk. Gro. LS5: Leeds 6H **75**
 LS13: Leeds 6G **75**
Victoria Pk. St. BD21: Keigh 5B **34**
Victoria Pk. Vw. BD21: Keigh 5B **34**
Victoria Pl. BD10: B'frd 4A **72**
 HD6: Brigh 2B **162**
 HX2: Hal 4E **147**
 HX3: Hal 4D **130**
 LS11: Leeds 5H **97**
 LS19: Yead 6E **41**
 LS23: B Spa 6B **30**
 LS26: Mick 4C **144**
Victoria Quarter LS1: Leeds . . .3A **98** (4F **5**)
Victoria Ri. LS28: Pud 4G **93**
Victoria Rd. BD6: B'frd 5A **110**
 BD10: B'frd 4A **72**
 BD18: Ship 1H **69**
 BD21: Keigh 1H **47**
 BD22: Haw 2D **64**
 BD22: Keigh 5D **46**
 HD6: Brigh 2B **152**
 HX1: Hal 2E **149**
 HX3: Hal 2F **151**
 HX5: Ell 6H **159**
 HX6: Hal 6H **147**
 LS5: Leeds 5A **76**
 LS6: Leeds 6E **77**
 LS11: Leeds 5H **97**
 LS14: Leeds 2D **80**
 LS20: Guis 5B **40**
 LS26: Rothw 1H **141**
 LS27: Morl 2A **138**
 LS28: Pud 1H **93**
 (Northcote St.)
 LS28: Pud 4G **93**
 (Uppermoor)

Victoria Rd. LS29: Burl W 2E **21**
 LS29: I'ly 5B **10**
Victoria Sq. LS1: Leeds 3H **97** (3C **4**)
Victoria St. BD1: B'frd 3D **90** (1B **6**)
 BD2: B'frd 1A **92**
 BD10: B'frd 5H **53**
 BD13: B'frd 4B **108**
 (Brighouse Rd.)
 BD13: B'frd 3C **66**
 (Brunswick St.)
 BD14: B'frd 1D **108**
 BD15: B'frd 5G **67**
 (Albert St.)
 BD15: B'frd 6C **68**
 (Cottingley Rd.)
 BD16: Bgly 6A **36**
 (Ferncliffe Rd.)
 BD16: Bgly 6A **36**
 (New St.)
 BD17: Bail 6C **52**
 BD17: Ship 1B **70**
 BD19: Cleck 6B **134**
 BD22: Keigh *5D* **46**
 (off Victoria Rd.)
 HD6: Brigh 2B **152**
 (Railway St.)
 HD6: Brigh 6C **152**
 (Victoria Av.)
 HX1: Hal 2G **149** (3B **164**)
 HX4: Hal 4H **159**
 HX6: Hal 6H **147**
 LS3: Leeds 2F **97** (2A **4**)
 LS7: Leeds 2B **78**
 LS22: Weth 4E **13**
 LS27: Morl 6C **116**
 (Back Grn.)
 LS27: Morl 2H **137**
 (Kingsmill Cl.)
 LS28: Pud 3E **73**
 WF1: Wake 5F **157**
 WF10: Kip 3H **145**
 WF17: Bat 6B **136**
Victoria Ter. BD18: Ship 6H **51**
 BD21: Keigh *6B* **34**
 (off Dalton La.)
 HX1: Hal *3E* **149**
 (off Park Dr.)
 HX2: Hal 4E **147**
 (Rose Pl.)
 HX2: Hal 5E **149**
 (Rose Ter.)
 HX3: Hal 2F **97** (2A **4**)
 LS3: Leeds 2F **97** (2A **4**)
 LS5: Leeds 5A **76**
 LS6: Leeds 3D **76**
 LS19: Yead 6G **41**
 LS20: Guis *4C* **40**
 (off Lands La.)
 LS28: Pud 1B **94**
 LS29: Add *1D* **8**
 (off Main St.)
Victoria Theatre, The 5B **164**
Victoria Vs. LS28: Pud 2A **94**
Victoria Wlk. *LS1: Leeds* *4E* **5**
 (in Headrow Cen., The)
 LS18: H'fth 2C **74**
Victoria Way WF1: Wake 6F **157**
Victoria Works HX2: Hal 6E **107**
Victor Rd. BD9: B'frd 1B **90**
Victor St. BD3: B'frd 4C **92**
 BD9: B'frd 1B **90**
Victor Ter. BD9: B'frd 1B **90**
 HX1: Hal 1E **149**
Victory Rd. LS29: I'ly 5D **10**
View, The LS8: Leeds 1D **78**
 LS17: Leeds 1F **59**
View Cft. Rd. BD17: Ship 1C **70**
Viewlands Cres. LS29: Men 6B **22**
Viewlands Mt. LS29: Men 6B **22**
Viewlands Ri. LS29: Men 1B **40**
View Rd. BD20: Keigh 5G **33**
View Row BD15: B'frd 3E **89**

Vignola Ter. BD14: B'frd 6E **89**
Village, The LS23: B Spa 2C **30**
Village Av. LS4: Leeds 1D **96**
Village Gdns. LS15: Leeds 5F **101**
 (not continuous)
Village Hotel & Leisure Club 1C **76**
Village M. BD15: B'frd 4G **67**
Village Pl. LS4: Leeds 1D **96**
Village St. HX3: Hal 4H **131**
Village St., The LS4: Leeds 1D **96**
Village Ter. LS4: Leeds 6D **76**
Villa Gro. BD16: Bgly 3C **50**
Villa Mt. BD12: B'frd 6C **132**
Villa Rd. BD16: Bgly 3C **50**
Villa St. HX6: Hal 5A **148**
Villier Ct. BD15: B'frd 2D **88**
Vincent Av. BD20: Stee 6A **14**
Vincent St. BD1: B'frd 4D **90** (4B **6**)
 HX1: Hal 3D **148**
Vine Cl. HD6: Brigh 1D **162**
Vine Ct. HD6: Brigh 1D **162**
 LS20: Guis 5C **40**
Vine Gth. HD6: Brigh 6D **152**
Vine Gro. HD6: Brigh 1D **162**
Vine Ind. Est. HD6: Brigh 6H **151**
Vine Pl. BD2: B'frd 6H **71**
Vinery Av. LS9: Leeds 3E **99**
Vinery Gro. LS9: Leeds 3E **99**
Vinery Mt. LS9: Leeds 4E **99**
Vinery Pl. LS9: Leeds 4E **99**
Vinery Rd. LS4: Leeds 1D **96**
Vinery St. LS9: Leeds 3E **99**
Vinery Ter. LS9: Leeds 4E **99**
Vinery Vw. LS9: Leeds 4E **99**
Vine St. BD7: B'frd 6B **90**
 BD19: Cleck 6B **134**
Vine Ter. BD13: B'frd 5H **87**
 HX1: Hal 3F **149** (6A **164**)
Vine Ter. E. BD8: B'frd 3G **89**
Vine Ter. W. BD8: B'frd 3G **89**
Vint Ri. BD10: B'frd 2G **71**
Violet St. BD22: Haw 4C **64**
 HX1: Hal 2E **149**
Violet St. Nth. HX1: Hal 1E **149**
Violet Ter. HX6: Hal 5A **148**
Virginia Cl. WF3: Wake 3E **157**
Virginia Dr. WF3: Wake 3E **157**
Virginia Gdns. WF3: Wake 3E **157**
Virginia St. BD14: B'frd 2E **109**
Virginia Ter. *BD14: B'frd* *2E* **109**
 (off Virginia St.)
 LS14: T'ner 2H **63**
Vivian Pl. BD7: B'frd 2A **110**
Vivien Rd. BD8: B'frd 3E **89**
Vogue Ladies Slimming & Fitness Club
 . . . . .6H **145**
Vollan's Ct. LS14: Leeds 4C **80**
Vue Cinema 2D **96**
Vulcan St. BD4: B'frd 4B **112**
 HD6: Brigh 2C **162**

W

Waddington St. BD21: Keigh 1A **48**
Wade Ho. Av. HX3: Hal 1E **131**
Wade Ho. Rd. HX3: Hal 2E **131**
Wade La. LS2: Leeds 3A **98** (3E **5**)
Wade St. BD1: B'frd 5E **91** (4C **6**)
 HX1: Hal 2G **149** (3C **164**)
 LS28: Pud 6H **73**
Wadlands Cl. LS28: Pud 6H **73**
Wadlands Dr. LS28: Pud 6G **73**
Wadlands Gro. LS28: Pud 5G **73**
Wadlands Ri. LS28: Pud 6G **73**
Wadsworth Ct. HX1: Hal 1E **149**
Wadsworth St. HX1: Hal 1D **148**
 (not continuous)
Wadworth BD22: Oxen 2C **84**
Wagon La. BD16: Bgly 6C **50**
Wagtail Cl. BD6: B'frd 4E **109**

Waides Bldgs. LS26: Mick 4E 145
Waincliffe Cres. LS11: Leeds 4F 117
Waincliffe Dr. LS11: Leeds 5F 117
Waincliffe Gth. LS11: Leeds 4F 117
Waincliffe Ho. *BD4: B'frd* *5B 92*
(off Fearnville Dr.)
Waincliffe Mt. LS11: Leeds 4F 117
Waincliffe Pl. LS11: Leeds 4F 117
Waincliffe Sq. LS11: Leeds 4F 117
Waincliffe Ter. LS11: Leeds 5F 117
Waindale Cl. HX2: Hal 4G 127
Waindale Cres. HX2: Hal 4G 127
Wainfleet Ho. *BD3: B'frd* *3C 92*
(off Rushton Rd.)
Wainhouse Rd. HX1: Hal 4D 148
Wainhouse Ter. *HX2: Hal* *4D 148*
(off Burnley Rd.)
Wainman Sq. BD12: B'frd 4C 132
Wainman St. BD12: B'frd 4C 132
BD17: Bail 3D 52
BD17: Ship 1B 70
HX1: Hal 2D 148
WAINSTALLS 1F 127
Wainstalls La. HX2: Hal 2E 127
Wainstalls Lodge La.
HX2: Hal 2E 127
Wainstalls Rd. HX2: Hal 1F 127
Waites Ter. LS21: Otley 4F 23
Wakefield 41 Ind. Pk.
WF2: Wake 3D 156
(Lingwell Ga. La.)
WF2: Wake 4D 156
(Telford Way)
Wakefield Av. LS14: Leeds 2B 100
Wakefield Ga. HX3: Hal 5D 148
Wakefield Rd. BD4: B'frd 5F 91 (6F 7)
(not continuous)
BD11: B'frd 1B 136
(not continuous)
HD6: Brigh, Hud 1B 162
(not continuous)
HD6: Wake, Brigh 2F 151
HX3: Hal 2F 151
HX6: Hal 5B 148
LS10: Leeds 3D 118
LS25: Gar 5C 102
LS26: Kip, Swil 5G 121
LS26: Rothw 2F 141
(Castlefields)
LS26: Rothw 6D 142
(Sanderson La.)
LS27: Morl 2E 137
WF14: Brigh, Hud 2F 163
Walden Dr. BD9: B'frd 6E 69
Waldron Ho. *BD5: B'frd* *6E 91*
(off Elizabeth St.)
Walesby Ct. LS16: Leeds 5G 57
Walford Av. LS9: Leeds 3E 99
Walford Gro. LS9: Leeds 3E 99
Walford Mt. LS9: Leeds 3E 99
Walford Rd. LS9: Leeds 3E 99
Walford Ter. LS9: Leeds 3E 99
Walk, The BD21: Keigh 1A 48
LS28: Pud 1G 93
Walker Av. BD7: B'frd 6G 89
(not continuous)
Walker Dr. BD8: B'frd 3A 90
Walkergate LS21: Otley 4E 23
Walker Ho. LS5: Leeds 5H 75
Walker La. HX6: Hal 5B 148
Walker Pl. BD18: Ship 1D 70
(not continuous)
LS27: Morl 6B 116
Walker Rd. BD12: B'frd 3F 133
LS18: H'fth 6D 56
LS29: Men 1F 39
Walker's Grn. LS12: Leeds 1C 116
Walker's La. LS12: Leeds 1C 116
(not continuous)
Walkers Mt. LS6: Leeds 4F 77
Walker's Pl. BD20: Sils 3E 15
Walkers Row LS19: Yead 6E 41

Walker St. BD4: B'frd 5H 111
BD19: Cleck 1F 153
Walker Ter. BD4: B'frd 1H 111
BD13: B'frd 4B 66
Walker Wood BD17: Bail 5H 51
Wallace Gdns. WF3: Wake 3F 157
Wallace St. HX1: Hal 3D 148
Wallbank Dr. BD18: Ship 3C 70
Wallingford Mt. BD15: B'frd 4D 88
Wallis St. BD8: B'frd 4H 89
(not continuous)
HX6: Hal 5H 147
Wall Rd. BD21: Keigh 4C 34
Wall St. BD22: Keigh 1F 47
Walmer Gro. LS28: Pud 6B 94
Walmer Vs. BD8: B'frd 2D 90
Walmsley Rd. LS6: Leeds 6E 77
Walnut Bus. Pk. HX1: Hal 2E 149
Walnut Cl. LS14: Leeds 1E 81
Walnut St. BD3: B'frd 5A 92
BD21: Keigh 3H 47
HX1: Hal 2E 149
Walshaw St. BD7: B'frd 1A 110
Walsh La. BD16: Bgly 1B 50
HX3: Hal 6F 129
LS12: Leeds 3E 115
Walsh's Sq. *HX1: Hal* *4E 149*
(off Mellor Ter.)
Walsh St. HX1: Hal 2D 148
Walter Clough La. HX3: Hal 4D 150
Walter Cres. LS9: Leeds 4D 98
Walter St. BD2: B'frd 5D 70
BD10: B'frd 1H 71
LS4: Leeds 2D 96
Walton Dr. BD11: B'frd 1B 136
Walton Gth. BD11: B'frd 2B 136
Walton La. BD19: Brigh, Cleck 4E 153
Walton Rd. LS22: Weth 4F 13
LS23: B Spa, W'ton 2D 30
Walton's Bldgs. HX2: Hal 3D 128
Walton St. BD4: B'frd 6F 91
HX6: Hal 5H 147
LS10: Leeds 1C 118
LS11: Leeds 5H 97
Walt Royd HX2: Hal 4B 128
Waltroyd Dr. BD19: Cleck 2H 153
Wand La. HX3: Hal 1E 151
Wansford Dr. BD4: B'frd 3C 112
Wanstead Cres. BD15: B'frd 3D 88
WAPPING 3F 91 (2E 7)
Wapping Rd. BD3: B'frd . . .3F 91 (1E 7)
Warburton Pl. BD6: B'frd 4C 110
Ward Ct. HD6: Brigh 4H 161
Ward End BD13: B'frd 3H 87
Ward La. LS10: Leeds 4B 118
Wardle Cres. BD21: Keigh 5F 33
Wardman St. BD21: Keigh 5F 33
Ward's End HX1: Hal 3G 149 (5C 164)
Ward St. BD7: B'frd 2A 110
BD21: Keigh 1H 47
Wareham Cnr. BD4: B'frd 3C 112
Warehouse, The *LS5: Leeds* *5H 75*
(off Broad La.)
Warhurst Rd. HX5: Ell 3C 160
WARING GREEN 6A 152
Warings Bldgs. WF3: E Ard 2D 154
Warlbeck LS29: I'ly 5B 10
Warley Av. BD3: B'frd 3B 92
Warley Dene HX2: Hal 3H 147
Warley Dr. BD3: B'frd 4B 92
Warley Edge HX2: Hal 2A 148
Warley Edge La. HX2: Hal 2H 147
Warley Gro. BD3: B'frd 3B 92
HX2: Hal 2B 148
Warley Rd. HX2: Hal 2B 148
Warley St. HX1: Hal 3E 149
WARLEY TOWN 3H 147
Warley Town La. HX2: Hal 2G 147
Warley Vw. HX2: Hal 2B 148
LS13: Leeds 5D 74
Warley Wood HX2: Hal 4F 147
Warley Wood Av. HX2: Hal 4F 147

Warley Wood La. HX2: Hal 4E 147
Warm La. LS19: Yead 2E 55
Warmleigh Pk. BD13: B'frd 4F 107
Warneford Sq. *HX1: Hal* *4D 148*
(off King Cross Rd.)
Warnford Gro. BD4: B'frd 2B 112
Warrel's Av. LS13: Leeds 6E 75
Warrel's Ct. LS13: Leeds 1E 95
Warrel's Gro. LS13: Leeds 1E 95
Warrel's Mt. LS13: Leeds 1E 95
Warrel's Pl. LS13: Leeds 6E 75
Warrel's Rd. LS13: Leeds 6E 75
Warrel's Row LS13: Leeds 1E 95
Warrel's Ter. LS13: Leeds 1E 95
Warren Av. BD16: Bgly 2D 50
Warren Dr. BD16: Bgly 3D 50
Warren Ho. Cotts. LS25: M'fld 1D 124
Warren Ho. La. LS19: Yead 4H 41
Warren La. BD16: Bgly 2D 50
LS21: Arth 5H 25
Warren Pk. HD6: Brigh 4G 151
Warren Pk. Cl. HD6: Brigh 4G 151
Warrenside HD2: Hud 6E 163
Warrens La. BD11: B'frd 2A 136
WF17: Bat, B'frd 4H 135
Warren Ter. BD16: Bgly 4E 51
Warrenton Pl. BD7: B'frd 6A 90
Warton Av. BD4: B'frd 4H 111
Warwick Cl. BD4: B'frd 1H 111
HX3: Hal *5F 149*
(off Free School La.)
Warwick Ct. LS18: H'fth 2E 75
Warwick Dr. BD4: B'frd 1H 111
Warwick Rd. BD4: B'frd 1H 111
Waryn Ho. *BD10: B'frd* *2A 72*
(off Fairhaven Grn.)
Washburn Ct. *BD20: Sils* *2E 15*
(off Wharfe Cl.)
LS22: Weth 1D 12
Washer La. HX2: Hal 5C 148
Washer La. Ind. Est. HX2: Hal 5D 148
Washington Pl. LS13: Leeds 3C 94
Washington St. BD8: B'frd 2H 89
HX3: Hal 6E 129
LS3: Leeds 3E 97
LS13: Leeds 3C 94
Washington Ter. LS13: Leeds 3C 94
Wastwater Dr. BD6: B'frd 1H 131
Watercock St. BD4: B'frd 6G 91
Waterfront M. BD10: B'frd 1C 72
Water Gdns. LS26: Rothw 6H 119
Watergate HX3: Hal 2E 151
LS26: Mick 6A 144
Water Hill HX6: Hal 4G 147
Water Hill La. HX2: Hal 4G 147
HX6: Hal 4G 147
Water Ho. Ct. LS18: H'fth 2D 74
Waterhouse Ct. *LS10: Leeds* *1B 118*
(off Oval, The)
Waterhouse Dr. WF3: E Ard 2H 155
Waterhouse St. BD21: Keigh 6G 33
HX1: Hal 2G 149 (4B 164)
Watering La. LS27: Morl 4D 138
WF3: Morl 4D 138
Watering Mdw. LS27: Morl 3D 138
Water La. BD1: B'frd 4C 90 (4A 6)
(not continuous)
BD21: Keigh 1H 47
HX1: Hal 3H 149 (6D 164)
HX3: Hal 3H 149 (6D 164)
LS11: Leeds 4A 98 (6F 5)
(Hunslet Rd.)
LS11: Leeds 5G 97 (6C 4)
(Triumph Cl.)
LS12: Leeds 4F 95
LS18: H'fth 6B 56
LS28: Pud 6H 73
Waterloo Cres. BD10: B'frd 1D 72
LS13: Leeds 6F 75
Waterloo Fold BD12: B'frd 5D 132
Waterloo Gro. LS28: Pud 4F 93

Waterloo La. LS13: Leeds 6F 75
Waterloo Mt. LS28: Pud 3F 93
Waterloo Rd. BD16: Bgly 4B 50
  HD6: Brigh 6A 152
  LS10: Leeds 1C 118
  LS28: Pud 3F 93
Waterloo St. LS7: Leeds 4A 98 (6F 5)
Waterloo Ter. HX6: Hal 3A 148
Waterloo Way LS13: Leeds 6F 75
Water Mill Ct. BD22: Keigh 1B 46
Waterside BD16: Bgly 2H 49
  BD20: Sils 3F 15
  BD22: Oxen 1C 84
  HX3: Hal 3H 149
Waterside LS13: Leeds 4B 74
Waterside Ind. Pk. LS10: Leeds 2F 119
Waterside Rd. BD8: B'frd 3A 90
  LS10: Leeds 3F 119
Watersole La. LS22: Weth 5G 13
Water Stalls Rd. HX7: Heb B 6A 146
  (not continuous)
Water St. HD6: Brigh 6B 152
  HX6: Hal 6H 147
Waterwood Cl. WF3: E Ard 2F 155
Watery La. BD20: Sils 1F 15
Watford Av. HX3: Hal 4H 131
Watkin Av. BD13: B'frd 5B 88
Watkinson Av. HX2: Hal 2D 128
Watkinson Bungs. *HX2: Hal* *3C 128*
  (off Cumberland Cl.)
Watkinson Dr. HX2: Hal 3D 128
Watkinson Rd. HX2: Hal 3D 128
Watmough St. BD7: B'frd 2A 110
Watson Cl. BD22: Oxen 1C 84
Watson Mill La. HX6: Hal 6H 147
Watson Rd. LS14: Leeds 2B 100
Watsons's La. LS24: Tad 6G 31
Watson St. LS27: Morl 4H 137
Wattlesyke LS22: Coll 2D 28
  LS23: Coll 2D 28
Watts St. BD14: B'frd 1D 108
Watt St. BD4: B'frd 6B 92
Watty Hall Av. BD6: B'frd 3A 110
Watty Hall La. BD6: B'frd 3B 110
Watty Hall Rd. BD6: B'frd 3A 110
Wauds Gates *BD17: Bail* *6C 52*
  (off Baildon Rd.)
Waveney Rd. LS12: Leeds 5C 96
Waverley Av. BD7: B'frd 6B 90
  BD20: Keigh 5F 35
Waverley Cres. HX3: Hal 2E 151
Waverley Pl. BD7: B'frd 6B 90
Waverley Rd. BD7: B'frd 6B 90
  HX5: Ell 6B 160
Waverley Ter. BD7: B'frd 6B 90
  HX3: Hal 2E 151
Waverton Grn. BD6: B'frd 6H 109
Wavertree Pk. Gdns.
  BD12: B'frd 3C 132
Wayland App. LS16: Leeds 3D 58
Wayland Cl. LS16: Leeds 3D 58
Wayland Ct. LS16: Leeds 3D 58
Wayland Cft. LS16: Leeds 3D 58
Wayland Dr. LS16: Leeds 3D 58
Wayside Av. LS14: S'cft 4F 45
Wayside Cl. BD20: Keigh 3G 33
Wayside Cres. BD2: B'frd 4H 71
  LS14: S'cft 3F 45
WAYSIDE GARDENS 4F 45
Wayside Mt. LS14: S'cft 3F 45
Weardale Cl. BD4: B'frd 4A 112
Weatherhead Pl. BD20: Sils 2F 15
Weatherhouse Ter. HX2: Hal 6B 128
Weaver Ct. *BD10: B'frd* *1H 71*
  (off Moorfield Pl.)
Weaver Gdns. LS27: Morl 4D 138
Weaver Grn. BD20: Pud 4A 94
Weavers Cotts. *BD22: Oxen* *1C 84*
  (off Waterside)
Weavers Ct. LS12: Leeds 4B 96
  LS28: Pud 6B 94

Weavers Cft. BD10: B'frd 5G 53
  HX2: Hal 3A 148
  LS28: Pud 5B 94
Weavers Grange LS20: Guis 3C 40
Weavers Hill BD22: Haw 3C 64
Weavers La. BD13: B'frd 3B 66
Weavers Row LS28: Pud 5B 94
Weaver St. LS4: Leeds 2D 96
Weavers Wlk. BD20: Sils 1E 15
Weaverthorpe Retail Pk.
  BD4: B'frd 4C 112
Weaverthorpe Rd. BD4: B'frd 4C 112
Weaving Shed, The *HX6: Hal* *5A 148*
  (off Old Cawsey)
Webb Dr. BD2: B'frd 1G 91
Webb's Ter. HX3: Hal 1H 149
Weber Ct. *BD3: B'frd* *4A 92*
  (off Amberley St.)
Webster Pl. BD3: B'frd 4H 91 (3H 7)
Webster Row LS12: Leeds 5B 96
Webster St. BD3: B'frd 4H 91
Webton Ct. LS7: Leeds 2B 78
Wedgemoor Cl. BD12: B'frd 3C 132
Wedgewood Cl. LS8: Leeds 6E 61
Wedgewood Dr. LS8: Leeds 1E 79
Wedgewood Gro. LS8: Leeds 1E 79
Weetlands Cl. LS25: Kip 3H 123
WEETWOOD 2B 76
Weetwood Av. LS16: Leeds 2D 76
Weetwood Ct. LS16: Leeds 1C 76
Weetwood Cres. LS16: Leeds 1D 76
Weetwood Grange Gro.
  LS16: Leeds 1B 76
Weetwood Ho. Ct.
  LS16: Leeds 1B 76
Weetwood La. LS16: Leeds 6C 58
Weetwood Mnr. LS16: Leeds 1C 76
Weetwood Mill La. LS16: Leeds 1D 76
Weetwood Pk. Dr. LS16: Leeds 1B 76
Weetwood Rd. BD8: B'frd 3A 90
  LS16: Leeds 1B 76
Weetwood Ter. LS16: Leeds 1D 76
Weetwood Wlk. LS16: Leeds 1C 76
Welbeck Dr. BD7: B'frd 1G 109
Welbeck Ri. BD7: B'frd 1G 109
Welbeck Rd. LS9: Leeds 4E 99
  WF17: Bat 5B 136
Welburn Av. HX3: Hal 2F 151
  LS16: Leeds 2B 76
Welburn Dr. LS16: Leeds 2B 76
Welburn Gro. LS16: Leeds 2B 76
Welburn Mt. BD6: B'frd 5G 109
Welbury Dr. BD8: B'frd 1C 90
Weldon Ct. BD4: B'frd 1C 112
Welfare Av. LS15: Bar E 2E 83
Welham Wlk. BD3: B'frd 3G 91 (1G 7)
Welland Dr. LS25: Gar 5G 103
Wellands Grn. BD19: Cleck 2H 153
Wellands La. BD19: Cleck 1F 153
Wellands Ter. BD3: B'frd 4A 92
Well Bank Rd. BD4: B'frd 2B 112
Well Cl. LS19: Yead 4G 55
  LS26: Kip 5E 123
  LS29: Add 1C 8
Well Cl. Ri. HD6: Brigh 6A 152
Well Cl. Ri. LS7: Leeds 1A 98
Well Cl. St. HD6: Brigh 6B 152
Well Cft. BD18: Ship 2B 70
Wellcroft LS21: Otley 4F 23
Wellcroft Gro. WF3: E Ard 2F 155
Weller Cl. *BD5: B'frd* *5B 92*
  (off Boynton St.)
Wellesley Ho. *BD4: B'frd* *5B 92*
  (off Wellington St.)
Wellesley St. BD1: B'frd 4F 91 (3F 7)
Wellfield Gdns. BD13: B'frd 2H 107
Wellfield La. LS29: Burl W 1E 21
Wellfield Pl. *LS6: Leeds* *4D 76*
  (off Chapel St.)
Wellfield Ter. LS27: Morl 6E 115
Well Fold BD10: B'frd 1H 71
Well Gth. LS15: Leeds 1E 101

Wellgarth BD6: B'frd 6H 109
  HX1: Hal 4G 149 (6A 164)
Well Gth. Bank LS13: Leeds 5D 74
Well Gth. Mt. LS15: Leeds 1E 101
Well Gth. Vw. LS13: Leeds 5E 75
Wellgate HX4: Hal 3G 159
Well Grn. Ct. BD4: B'frd 6C 112
Well Grn. La. HD6: Brigh 4H 151
Well Gro. HD6: Brigh 4H 151
Wellhead Cl. LS16: B'hpe 2G 43
Well Head Dr. HX1: Hal . .3G 149 (6B 164)
Well Head Ho. *HX1: Hal* *6C 164*
  (off Well Head Dr.)
Well Head La.
  HX1: Hal 4G 149 (6B 164)
  HX6: Hal 6C 146
Well Head Ri. HX1: Hal 4G 149
WELL HEADS 4E 87
Well Heads BD13: B'frd 5D 86
Well Hill LS19: Yead 6F 41
  LS21: Otley 4D 22
Well Hill Ct. *LS19: Yead* *1F 55*
  (off Well Hill)
Wellholme HD6: Brigh 6B 152
Well Holme Mead LS12: Leeds 2G 115
Well Ho. Av. LS8: Leeds 4E 79
Well Ho. Ct. LS8: Leeds 4E 79
Well Ho. Cres. LS8: Leeds 4E 79
Well Ho. Dr. LS8: Leeds 4E 79
Well Ho. Gdns. LS8: Leeds 4E 79
Well Ho. Rd. LS8: Leeds 4E 79
Wellington Arc. *HD6: Brigh* *1B 162*
  (off Briggate)
Wellington Bri. St.
  LS1: Leeds 4F 97 (5A 4)
  LS3: Leeds 3F 97 (4A 4)
Wellington Bus. Cen. HX5: Ell 4C 160
Wellington Ct. BD11: B'frd 1E 135
  HX2: Hal 1C 148
Wellington Cres. BD18: Ship 2A 70
Wellington Gdns. LS13: Leeds 6F 75
Wellington Gth. LS13: Leeds 5F 75
Wellington Gro. BD2: B'frd 1H 91
  LS13: Leeds 5F 75
  LS28: Pud 4G 93
WELLINGTON HILL 1B 80
Wellington Hill LS17: Leeds 5C 62
Wellington Mt. LS13: Leeds 5F 75
Wellington Pl. BD2: B'frd 6A 72
  HX1: Hal 3G 149 (5D 164)
  LS1: Leeds 4G 97 (5A 4)
Wellington Rd. BD2: B'frd 6H 71
  BD15: B'frd 5F 67
  BD21: Keigh 1A 48
  LS1: Leeds 5E 97
  (Copley Hill)
  LS1: Leeds 4F 97 (5A 4)
  (Gotts Rd.)
  LS12: Leeds 5E 97
  LS29: I'ly 5D 10
Wellington Rd. Ind. Est.
  LS12: Leeds 4F 97
Wellington St. BD1: B'frd 4F 91 (3E 7)
  BD2: B'frd 6H 71
  BD4: B'frd 5B 92
  BD10: B'frd 2H 71
  BD11: B'frd *1E 135*
  (off Bradford Rd.)
  BD13: B'frd 4B 108
  BD15: B'frd 2E 89
  (Nelson St.)
  BD15: B'frd 5G 67
  (Peel St.)
  BD16: Bgly 4B 50
  LS3: Leeds 3F 97 (4A 4)
  (not continuous)
  LS27: Morl 3A 138
Wellington St. Sth.
  HX1: Hal 3H 149 (5D 164)
Wellington St. W.
  HX1: Hal 3F 149 (6A 164)
Wellington Ter. LS13: Leeds 5F 75

Well La. BD19: Cleck 6F 133
  HD6: Brigh 3H 161
    (Castlefields Dr.)
  HD6: Brigh 1E 163
    (Westgate)
  HX1: Hal 2H 149 (3D 164)
  LS7: Leeds 2B 78
  LS19: Yead 4G 55
    (Low Grn.)
  LS19: Yead 1F 55
    (Parkland Vw.)
  LS20: Guis 4C 40
  LS25: Kip 4G 123
Well Royd Av. HX2: Hal 2A 148
Well Royd Cl. HX2: Hal 2B 148
  (not continuous)
Wells, The HX2: Hal 2A 148
    (Roils Head Rd.)
  HX2: Hal 4C 148
    (Willowfield Ter.)
Wells Ct. HX3: Hal 6F 129
  LS19: Yead 1F 55
    (off Well La.)
  LS29: I'ly 6D 10
    (off Wells Prom.)
Wells Cft. LS6: Leeds 2E 77
Wells Gro. LS20: Guis 4C 40
Wells Ho. HX6: Hal 5A 148
    (off Church Vw.)
Wells M. LS29: I'ly 6D 10
    (off Wells Prom.)
Wells Prom. LS29: I'ly 5D 10
Wells Rd. LS20: Guis 4C 40
  LS29: I'ly 1C 18
Wells Ter. BD22: Keigh 6C 32
  HX3: Hal 5A 132
    (off Village St.)
Wellstone Av. LS13: Leeds 2D 94
Wellstone Dr. LS13: Leeds 2D 94
Wellstone Gdns. LS13: Leeds 3D 94
Wellstone Gth. LS13: Leeds 3D 94
Wellstone Grn. LS13: Leeds 2D 94
Wellstone Ri. LS13: Leeds 3D 94
Wellstone Rd. LS13: Leeds 3D 94
Wellstone Way LS13: Leeds 3D 94
Well St. BD1: B'frd 4F 91 (4E 7)
  BD13: B'frd 3B 86
  BD15: B'frd 4G 67
  BD21: Keigh 6H 33
  HX4: Hal 6F 159
  LS20: Guis 4C 40
    (off Well Ter.)
  LS28: Pud 6H 73
Wells Wlk. LS29: I'ly 6D 10
Well Ter. LS20: Guis 4C 40
Well Vw. LS20: Guis 4C 40
Welton Gro. LS6: Leeds 6E 77
Welton Mt. LS6: Leeds 6E 77
Welton Pl. LS6: Leeds 6E 77
Welton Rd. LS6: Leeds 6E 77
Welwyn Av. BD18: Ship 2F 71
Welwyn Dr. BD17: Bail 5C 52
  BD18: Ship 2F 71
Welwyn Rd. WF12: Dew 6A 154
Wembley Av. BD13: B'frd 5B 88
Wenborough La. BD4: B'frd 2D 112
Wendel Av. LS15: Bar E 2D 82
Wendover Ct. LS16: Leeds 4D 58
Wendron Way BD10: B'frd 2H 71
Wenlock St. BD3: B'frd 5G 91 (5G 7)
Wenning St. BD22: Keigh 5C 34
Wensley Av. BD18: Ship 2A 70
  LS7: Leeds 2A 78
Wensley Bank BD13: B'frd 5G 87
Wensley Bank Ter. BD13: B'frd 5G 87
Wensley Bank W. BD13: B'frd 5G 87
Wensley Cres. LS7: Leeds 2A 78
Wensleydale Av. LS12: Leeds 1H 95
Wensleydale Cl. LS12: Leeds 1H 95
Wensleydale Ct. LS7: Leeds 2A 78
    (off Stainbeck La.)

Wensleydale Cres. LS12: Leeds 1H 95
Wensleydale Dr. LS12: Leeds 1H 95
Wensleydale M. LS12: Leeds 1H 95
Wensleydale Pde.
  WF17: Bat 6A 136
Wensleydale Ri. BD17: Bail 3E 53
  LS12: Leeds 1H 95
Wensley Dr. LS7: Leeds 1H 77
Wensley Gdns. LS7: Leeds 1H 77
Wensley Grn. LS7: Leeds 2H 77
Wensley Gro. HD6: Brigh 3G 161
  LS7: Leeds 2A 78
Wensley Ho. BD10: B'frd 3B 72
Wensley Lawn LS10: Leeds 3A 140
Wensley Rd. LS7: Leeds 1H 77
Wensley Vw. LS7: Leeds 2A 78
Wentworth Av. LS17: Leeds 3H 59
Wentworth Cl. LS29: Men 1G 39
Wentworth Ct. HD6: Brigh 4H 161
Wentworth Cres. LS17: Leeds 3A 60
Wentworth Dr. HX2: Hal 6D 106
Wentworth Farm Res. Pk.
  LS12: Leeds 3F 115
Wentworth Ga. LS22: Weth 3B 12
Wentworth Gro. HX2: Hal 6D 106
Wentworth Ter. LS19: Yead 4H 55
    (off Town St.)
Wentworth Way
  LS17: Leeds 3A 60
Wepener Mt. LS9: Leeds 2F 99
Wepener Pl. LS9: Leeds 2F 99
Wesleyan St. BD4: B'frd 2A 112
Wesley App. LS11: Leeds 3F 117
Wesley Av. BD12: B'frd 6E 111
  LS12: Leeds 4C 96
Wesley Av. Sth. BD12: B'frd 1E 133
Wesley Cl. LS11: Leeds 2F 117
Wesley Ct. HX1: Hal 2G 149 (3C 164)
  LS6: Leeds 6G 77
    (off Woodhouse St.)
  LS11: Leeds 3F 117
Wesley Cft. LS11: Leeds 2F 117
Wesley Dr. BD12: B'frd 6E 111
Wesley Gth. LS11: Leeds 2F 117
Wesley Grn. LS11: Leeds 3F 117
Wesley Gro. BD10: B'frd 6A 54
Wesley Ho. LS11: Leeds 3F 117
WESLEY PLACE 1D 132
Wesley Pl. BD12: B'frd 1E 133
    (off Main St.)
  BD20: Sils 2E 15
  BD21: Keigh 4G 47
  HX6: Hal 6D 146
  LS9: Leeds 4C 98
  LS12: Leeds 4C 96
  LS29: Add 1D 8
Wesley Rd. LS12: Leeds 4C 96
  LS28: Pud 2G 93
Wesley Row LS28: Pud 3A 94
Wesley Sq. LS28: Pud 4A 94
Wesley St. LS11: Leeds 2F 117
  LS21: Otley 3E 23
  LS27: Morl 3A 138
  LS28: Pud 1H 93
    (Sunfield Pl.)
  LS28: Pud 6H 73
    (Town St.)
Wesley Ter. LS9: Leeds 4C 98
    (off Wesley Pl.)
  LS13: Leeds 4B 74
    (Wesley St.)
  LS13: Leeds 6F 75
    (Westover St.)
  LS25: Gar 4F 103
  LS28: Pud 4A 94
Wesley Vw. LS13: Leeds 4B 74
  LS28: Pud 4A 94
West 26 Ind. Est.
  BD19: Cleck 5A 134

Westacres HD6: Brigh 3B 162
WEST ARDSLEY 1E 155
West Av. BD15: B'frd 6B 68
  BD17: Bail 4C 52
  HX3: Hal 5F 149
    (Queen's Ga.)
  HX3: Hal 2A 152
    (Stoney La.)
  LS8: Leeds 1G 79
  LS23: B Spa 3A 30
West Bank BD9: B'frd 5H 69
  BD20: Sils 1D 14
  BD22: Keigh 5F 33
    (off W. Bank Ri.)
  HX2: Hal 3B 128
    (not continuous)
West Bank Cl. BD22: Keigh 5F 33
W. Bank Gro. BD20: Keigh 3C 34
W. Bank Ri. BD22: Keigh 5F 33
W. Bank Rd. BD20: Keigh 3B 34
West Bolton HX2: Hal 6B 106
Westborough Dr. HX2: Hal 2B 148
W. Bottom HX6: Hal 1A 158
Westbourne Av. LS11: Leeds 2H 117
  LS25: Gar 5D 102
    (not continuous)
Westbourne Cl. LS21: Otley 5C 22
  LS25: Gar 5D 102
Westbourne Cres. HX3: Hal 6H 149
  LS25: Gar 5D 102
Westbourne Dr. LS20: Guis 4A 40
  LS25: Gar 5D 102
  LS29: Men 6F 21
Westbourne Gdns. LS25: Gar 5D 102
Westbourne Gro. HX3: Hal 6H 149
  LS21: Otley 5C 22
  LS25: Gar 5D 102
Westbourne Mt. LS11: Leeds 2H 117
Westbourne Pl. LS11: Leeds 2H 117
  LS28: Pud 2H 93
Westbourne Rd. BD8: B'frd 1B 90
Westbourne St. LS11: Leeds 2H 117
Westbourne Ter. BD13: B'frd 4A 108
    (off Albert Rd.)
  HX3: Hal 6H 149
  LS25: Gar 5D 102
West Breary 2H 43
WEST BOWLING 2E 111
WEST BREARY 2H 43
Westbrook Cl. LS18: H'fth 5D 56
Westbrook Ct. HX1: Hal 2A 164
Westbrook La. LS18: H'fth 5D 56
Westburn Av. BD22: Keigh 1F 47
Westburn Cres. BD22: Keigh 2F 47
Westburn Gro. BD22: Keigh 2F 47
Westburn Pl. BD19: Cleck 2H 153
Westburn Way BD22: Keigh 2F 47
Westbury Cl. BD4: B'frd 6B 92
Westbury Ct. HX1: Hal 3C 148
Westbury Gro. LS10: Leeds 3D 118
Westbury Mt. LS10: Leeds 4D 118
Westbury Pl. HX1: Hal 3C 148
Westbury Pl. Nth. LS10: Leeds 3D 118
Westbury Pl. Sth. LS10: Leeds 4D 118
Westbury Rd. BD6: B'frd 4F 109
Westbury St. BD4: B'frd 6B 92
  HX5: Ell 4C 160
  LS10: Leeds 4D 118
Westbury Ter. HX1: Hal 3C 148
  LS10: Leeds 4D 118
W. Busk La. LS21: Otley 5A 22
W. Byland HX2: Hal 6C 106
WEST CARLTON 2F 41
West Chevin Rd. LS21: Otley 6B 22
  LS29: Men 6B 22
Westcliffe Av. BD17: Bail 3B 52
Westcliffe Dr. HX2: Ship 2B 148
Westcliffe M. BD18: Ship 2B 70
    (off Westcliffe Rd.)
Westcliffe Rd. BD18: Ship 2A 70
Westcombe Av. LS8: Leeds 5E 61
Westcombe Ct. BD12: B'frd 3C 132
W. Cote Dr. BD10: B'frd 6F 53

Westcott Ho. BD8: B'frd 1A **6**
West Ct. LS8: Leeds 1G **79**
  LS13: Leeds 2E **95**
West Cft. BD12: B'frd 5C **132**
  LS29: Add 1D **8**
Westcroft Av. HX3: Hal 3D **130**
Westcroft Rd. BD7: B'frd 1A **110**
West Dale LS23: B Spa 2A **30**
Westdale Dr. LS28: Pud 3H **93**
Westdale Gdns. LS28: Pud 3H **93**
Westdale Gro. LS28: Pud 3H **93**
Westdale M. LS28: Pud 3H **93**
  (off Westdale Gro.)
Westdale Ri. LS28: Pud 3H **93**
Westdale Rd. LS28: Pud 3H **93**
West Dene BD20: Sils 1E **15**
  LS17: Leeds 1D **60**
West Dr. BD22: Oxen 6C **64**
WEST END
  Bradford 5H **107**
  Cleckheaton 1H **153**
  Leeds 6B **56**
West End BD13: B'frd 5H **107**
  BD19: Cleck 1H **153**
  HX1: Hal 3C **148**
  LS12: Leeds 2F **115**
  LS23: B Spa 2A **30**
  LS27: Morl 6E **115**
West End App. LS27: Morl 4F **137**
West End Cl. LS18: H'fth 6B **56**
West End Dr. BD19: Cleck 3H **153**
  LS18: H'fth 6B **56**
West End Gro. LS18: H'fth 6B **56**
West End La. LS18: H'fth 6B **56**
Westend La. BD1: B'frd 3B **6**
West End Ri. LS18: H'fth 6B **56**
West End Rd. HX1: Hal 3C **148**
  LS28: Pud 3F **73**
West End St. BD1: B'frd 4D **90** (4B **6**)
West End Ter. BD2: B'frd 4H **71**
  BD18: Ship 1A **70**
  LS20: Guis 4A **40**
Westercroft HX3: Hal 4D **130**
Westercroft La. HX3: Hal 4C **130**
Westercroft Vw. HX3: Hal 4D **130**
Westerley Cres. BD20: Sils 2C **14**
Westerly Cft. LS12: Leeds 3C **96**
Westerly Ri. LS12: Leeds 3C **96**
  (off Stocks Hill)
Western Av. BD20: Keigh 2A **34**
  WF17: Bat 6C **136**
Western Gro. LS12: Leeds 6B **96**
Western Mt. LS12: Leeds 6B **96**
Western Pl. BD13: B'frd 4D **108**
Western Rd. LS12: Leeds 6B **96**
Western St. LS12: Leeds 6B **96**
Western Way BD6: B'frd 6A **110**
WESTERTON 2F **155**
Westerton Cl. WF3: E Ard 1H **155**
Westerton Ct. BD12: B'frd 2H **133**
Westerton Rd. WF3: E Ard 2D **154**
Westerton Wlk. WF3: E Ard 1H **155**
W. Farm Av. LS10: Leeds 2H **139**
WESTFIELD 1D **54**
West Fld. HX6: Hal 1A **158**
Westfield BD13: B'frd 5C **88**
  HX3: Hal 6B **150**
  LS7: Leeds 2A **78**
  LS28: Pud 2H **93**
Westfield Av. HX3: Hal 2F **151**
  LS12: Leeds 3H **95**
  LS19: Yead 1D **54**
  LS25: Kip 4G **123**
  WF10: Kip 2G **145**
Westfield Bungs. WF10: Kip 2G **145**
Westfield Cl. LS19: Yead 1D **54**
  LS26: Rothw 3G **141**
Westfield Cotts. LS25: Kip 4H **123**
  (off High St.)

Westfield Ct. LS3: Leeds 2F **97**
  (off Westfield Rd.)
  LS26: Rothw 3G **141**
Westfield Cres. BD2: B'frd 2H **91**
  BD18: Ship 3E **71**
  BD20: Keigh 3D **34**
  LS3: Leeds 1F **97**
  (Bk. Rosebank Cres.)
  LS3: Leeds 2F **97**
  (Westfield Rd.)
  WF2: Wake 6H **155**
Westfield Dr. BD20: Keigh 4D **34**
  HX3: Hal 2F **151**
  LS19: Yead 1C **54**
Westfield Gdns. HX3: Hal 2F **151**
  LS25: Kip 3F **123**
Westfield Gro. BD10: B'frd 1G **71**
  BD18: Ship 3E **71**
  LS19: Yead 1D **54**
  WF10: Kip 2G **145**
Westfield Ho. BD10: B'frd 2H **71**
  (off Buckfast Ct.)
Westfield Ind. Est. LS19: Yead 1E **55**
Westfield La. BD10: B'frd 1F **71**
  BD12: B'frd 5C **132**
  BD18: Ship 3E **71**
  BD19: Cleck 5C **132**
  LS14: T'ner 3G **63**
  LS25: Kip 3F **123**
Westfield M. BD13: B'frd 5C **88**
Westfield Mt. LS19: Yead 1D **54**
Westfield Oval LS19: Yead 1C **54**
Westfield Pl. BD19: Cleck 6E **133**
  HX1: Hal 3E **149**
  LS27: Morl 3A **138**
  WF2: Wake 6H **155**
Westfield Rd. BD9: B'frd 1A **90**
  BD3: B'frd 1D **108**
  BD20: Keigh 4D **34**
  LS3: Leeds 2F **97**
  LS26: Rothw 4G **141**
  LS27: Morl 3A **138**
  WF3: Rothw 4G **141**
Westfield St. HX1: Hal 3F **149** (5A **164**)
Westfield Ter. BD2: B'frd 2H **91**
  BD14: B'frd 1D **108**
  BD17: Bail 3C **52**
  HX1: Hal 1E **149**
  LS3: Leeds 2F **97**
  LS7: Leeds 2A **78**
  WF10: Kip 2G **145**
Westfield Yd. LS12: Leeds 6B **96**
West Fold BD17: Bail 3C **52**
WEST GARFORTH 6D **102**
Westgarth LS22: Coll 6B **12**
W. Garth M. BD17: Bail 5B **52**
WESTGATE 1G **157**
West Ga. BD21: Keigh 6H **33**
  LS22: Weth 4E **13**
Westgate BD1: B'frd 3D **90** (2A **6**)
  BD2: B'frd 5A **72**
  BD17: Bail 3C **52**
  BD18: Ship 1B **70**
  HD6: Brigh 1E **163**
  HX1: Hal 2G **149** (4C **164**)
  HX5: Ell 4B **160**
  LS1: Leeds 3G **97** (4A **4**)
  (not continuous)
  LS20: Guis 5G **39**
  LS21: Otley 4D **22**
Westgate Cl. WF3: Wake 1G **157**
Westgate Ct. WF3: Rothw 1G **157**
Westgate Gdns. BD21: Keigh 1H **47**
  (off Aireworth St.)
Westgate Gro. WF3: Wake 1G **157**
WESTGATE HILL 5E **113**
Westgate Hill St. BD4: B'frd 5D **112**
Westgate La. WF3: Wake 1F **157**
Westgate Mall BD1: B'frd 4C **6**
Westgate Mkt.
  HX1: Hal 2G **149** (4C **164**)
Westgate Pl. BD4: B'frd 5E **113**

Westgate Ter. BD4: B'frd 5E **113**
W. Grange Cl. LS10: Leeds 4B **118**
W. Grange Dr. LS10: Leeds 4B **118**
W. Grange Fold LS10: Leeds 4B **118**
W. Grange Gdns. LS10: Leeds 4B **118**
W. Grange Gth. LS10: Leeds 4B **118**
W. Grange Grn. LS10: Leeds 4B **118**
W. Grange Rd. LS10: Leeds 5B **118**
W. Grange Wlk. LS10: Leeds 4B **118**
West Gro. BD17: Bail 3C **52**
West Gro. St. BD1: B'frd 4D **90** (3A **6**)
  LS28: Pud 2H **93**
W. Grove Ter. HX1: Hal . . .2F **149** (4A **164**)
West Hall LS19: Yead 1G **55**
W. Hall La. LS29: I'ly 1F **9**
W. Hill Av. LS7: Leeds 2A **78**
Westhill Av. BD13: B'frd 4C **66**
W. Hill St. HX1: Hal 2E **149**
W. Hill Ter. LS7: Leeds 2A **78**
Westholme Rd. HX1: Hal 2D **148**
Westholme St. BD1: B'frd 5D **90** (4B **6**)
West Ho. HX5: Ell 4B **160**
  (off Gog Hill)
Westland Ct. LS11: Leeds 5H **117**
Westland Rd. LS11: Leeds 4H **117**
Westlands Dr. BD15: B'frd 2D **88**
Westlands Gro. BD15: B'frd 2E **89**
Westland Sq. LS11: Leeds 5H **117**
West La. BD13: B'frd 4H **87**
  BD17: Bail 4H **51**
  (not continuous)
  BD19: Cleck 6F **135**
  BD21: Keigh 5F **33**
  BD22: Haw 2B **64**
  HX3: Hal 6B **150**
  LS23: B Spa 2A **30**
Westlea Av. BD20: Keigh 4D **34**
W. Lea Cl. LS17: Leeds 6H **59**
W. Lea Cres. LS19: Yead 1D **54**
  WF3: E Ard 2D **154**
W. Lea Dr. LS17: Leeds 6H **59**
  WF3: E Ard 2D **154**
W. Lea Gdns. LS17: Leeds 6H **59**
W. Lea Gth. LS17: Leeds 6H **59**
W. Lea Gro. LS19: Yead 1D **54**
W. Leeds St. BD21: Keigh 6G **33**
Westleigh BD16: Bgly 3C **50**
Westleigh Cl. BD17: Bail 5A **52**
Westleigh Dr. BD17: Bail 5A **52**
Westleigh Rd. BD17: Bail 4A **52**
Westleigh Way BD17: Bail 5A **52**
Westlock Av. LS9: Leeds 2E **99**
West Lodge LS29: Burl W 3E **21**
W. Lodge Gdns. LS7: Leeds 3A **78**
Westmead LS28: Pud 2E **93**
Westminster Av. BD14: B'frd 1C **108**
Westminster Cl. LS13: Leeds 5B **74**
Westminster Cres. BD14: B'frd 1C **108**
  LS15: Leeds 4A **100**
Westminster Cft. LS13: Leeds 5B **74**
Westminster Dr. BD14: B'frd 1C **108**
  LS13: Leeds 5B **74**
Westminster Gdns. BD14: B'frd 1C **108**
Westminster Pl. BD3: B'frd . . .2F **91** (1F **7**)
Westminster Rd. BD3: B'frd 2F **91**
  HX3: Hal 3F **151**
Westminster Ter. BD3: B'frd . .2F **91** (1F **7**)
Westmoor Av. BD17: Bail 3B **52**
Westmoor Cl. BD17: Bail 3B **52**
Westmoor Pl. LS13: Leeds 6D **74**
Westmoor Ri. LS13: Leeds 6D **74**
Westmoor Rd. LS13: Leeds 6D **74**
Westmoor St. LS13: Leeds 6D **74**
Westmoreland Mt. LS13: Leeds 5F **75**
WEST MORTON 3G **35**
W. Mount Pl. HX1: Hal 1E **149**
  (off W. Mount St.)
W. Mount St. HX1: Hal 1E **149**
  LS11: Leeds 2G **117**
Westmuir Ho. BD5: B'frd 1D **110**
  (off Launton Way)
WESTON 1H **21**

Weston Av. BD13: B'frd 4H 107
Weston Cres. LS21: Otley 2C 22
Weston Dr. LS21: Otley 1B 22
Weston Hall 1H 21
Weston La. LS21: Otley 2B 22
Weston Pk. Vw. LS21: Otley 1B 22
Weston Ridge LS21: Otley 1C 22
Weston Rd. LS29: I'ly 5D 10
Weston St. BD22: Keigh 2F 47
Weston Va. Rd. BD13: B'frd 5H 107
Westover Av. LS13: Leeds 6E 75
Westover Cl. LS13: Leeds 6F 75
Westover Gdns. LS28: Pud 4G 93
Westover Grn. LS13: Leeds 6E 75
Westover Gro. LS13: Leeds 6E 75
Westover Mt. LS13: Leeds 6E 75
Westover Rd. LS13: Leeds 6E 75
Westover St. LS13: Leeds 6E 75
Westover Ter. LS13: Leeds 6E 75
Westover Vw. LS13: Leeds 6E 75
West Pde. HX1: Hal 3F 149 (5A 164)
HX6: Hal 5B 148
LS16: Leeds 1A 76
LS20: Guis 4C 40
LS26: Rothw 2B 142
LS29: I'ly 5E 11
West Pde. Flats HX1: Hal 5A 164
(off West Pde.)

WEST PARK
Leeds 1A 76
Wetherby 2A 30
West Pk. LS20: Guis 3A 40
LS28: Pud 4H 93
West Pk. Av. LS8: Leeds 4F 61
West Pk. Chase LS8: Leeds 4E 61
West Pk. Cl. LS8: Leeds 4E 61
West Pk. Ct. LS8: Leeds 4F 61
West Pk. Cres. LS8: Leeds 5F 61
West Pk. Dr. LS16: Leeds 1A 76
W. Park Dr. E. LS8: Leeds 4E 61
W. Park Dr. W. LS8: Leeds 4D 60
West Pk. Gdns. LS8: Leeds 5F 61
West Pk. Gro. LS8: Leeds 4E 61
West Pk. Ind. Est.
BD7: B'frd 1H 109
West Pk. Pl. LS8: Leeds 5F 61
West Pk. Rd. BD8: B'frd 3H 89
LS8: Leeds 5F 61
West Pk. St. HD6: Brigh 1B 162
West Pk. Ter. BD8: B'frd 3H 89
W. Pasture Cl. LS18: H'fth 6B 56
West Point LS1: Leeds 4H 97 (5C 4)
West Riding Folk Mus. 1B 150
West Rd. LS9: Leeds 2G 119
West Rd. Nth. LS9: Leeds 2G 119
WEST ROYD 1E 71
West Royd BD15: B'frd 4G 67
HX3: Hal 1E 151
Westroyd LS28: Pud 5G 93
W. Royd Av. BD2: B'frd 5H 71
BD18: Ship 1D 70
HX1: Hal 3E 149
Westroyd Av. BD19: Cleck 4B 134
LS28: Pud 5G 93
W. Royd Cl. BD18: Ship 1E 71
HX1: Hal 4E 149
W. Royd Cres. BD18: Ship 1E 71
Westroyd Cres. LS28: Pud 6G 93
W. Royd Dr. BD18: Ship 1E 71
Westroyd Gdns. LS28: Pud 5G 93
W. Royd Gro. BD18: Ship 1E 71
WESTROYD HILL 5H 93
W. Royd Mt. BD18: Ship 1E 71
W. Royd Rd. BD18: Ship 1E 71
W. Royd Ter. BD18: Ship 1E 71
W. Royd Vs. HX1: Hal 4E 149
(off W. Royd Cl.)
W. Royd Wlk. BD18: Ship 1E 71
W. Scausby Pk. HX2: Hal 6C 106
WEST SCHOLES 2H 107
West Shaw BD22: Oxen 6B 64
W. Shaw La. BD22: Oxen 6A 64

Westside Ct. BD8: B'frd 3A 90
(off Bk. Girlington Rd.)
W. Side Retail Pk. LS20: Guis 6D 40
Westside Vw. BD11: B'frd 1A 136
(off West St.)
West Vw. St. BD1: B'frd 5F 91 (5F 7)
BD2: B'frd 6H 71
BD11: B'frd 2A 136
BD17: Bail 3C 52
BD19: Cleck 6F 135
HD6: Brigh 6A 152
(New St.)
HD6: Brigh 6A 152
(South St.)
HX1: Hal 2E 149
HX3: Hal 3D 130
HX4: Hal 6F 159
HX6: Hal 6H 147
LS3: Leeds 3F 97 (4A 4)
LS20: Guis 4C 40
LS27: Morl 4B 138
LS28: Pud 3A 94
LS29: I'ly 5D 10
W. Terrace St. LS28: Pud 2H 93
WEST VALE 4H 159
West Va. LS12: Leeds 6E 97
Westvale St. LS13: Leeds 2G 95
West Vw. BD4: B'frd 1G 111
(off New Hey Rd.)
BD11: B'frd 3F 135
BD16: Bgly 2E 51
BD17: Bail 3C 52
(off Newton Way)
BD19: Cleck 6F 133
BD20: Sils 1E 15
HX1: Hal 3D 148
(off Hopwood La.)
HX3: Hal 5F 129
HX4: Hal 6E 159
HX6: Hal 5A 148
LS11: Leeds 1G 117
LS19: Yead 6D 40
LS21: Arth 5H 25
LS21: Otley 4F 23
LS25: Kip 3H 123
LS25: M'fld 5F 105
LS26: Rothw 2E 143
LS28: Pud 1H 93
(off West La.)
LS29: I'ly 6D 10
WF2: Wake 6H 155
West Vw. Av. BD18: Ship 2E 71
HX2: Hal 2C 148
LS29: Burl W 2E 21
Westview Cl. BD18: Ship 2E 71
West Vw. Ct. LS19: Yead 6D 40
Westview Ct. BD20: Keigh 5G 33
West Vw. Cres. HX2: Hal 2C 148
West Vw. Dr. HX2: Hal 2B 148
Westview Gro. BD20: Keigh 5G 33
West Vw. Rd. HX3: Hal 5F 129
LS29: Burl W 2E 21
West Vw. St. BD22: Haw 1F 65
West Vw. Ter. HX2: Hal 1D 106
(Bradshaw La.)
HX2: Hal 1C 148
(Stretchgate La.)
Westview Way BD20: Keigh 5H 33
W. Villa Rd. LS20: Guis 4C 40
West Ville BD13: B'frd 5H 87
Westville LS29: I'ly 5C 10
Westville Av. LS29: I'ly 5C 10
Westville Cl. LS29: I'ly 5C 10
Westville Rd. LS29: I'ly 5C 10
Westville Way BD13: B'frd 5H 87
Westward Ho. HX3: Hal 3E 129
West Way BD18: Ship 2F 69
LS1: Leeds 3G 97 (4A 4)
Westway BD9: B'frd 1E 89
BD16: Bgly 2D 50
BD20: Keigh 5F 33

Westway LS20: Guis 5H 39
LS25: Gar 5D 102
LS28: Pud 6G 73
Westways WF2: Wake 6D 156
Westways Cl. WF2: Wake 6D 156
Westways Dr. LS8: Leeds 2G 79
West Winds LS29: Men 6E 21
Westwinn Gth. LS14: Leeds 1E 81
Westwinn Vw. LS14: Leeds 6E 63
Westwood BD9: B'frd 5H 69
Westwood Av. BD2: B'frd 4H 71
Westwood Cl. LS27: Morl 1B 138
Westwood Cotts. LS23: B Spa 6C 30
W. Wood Cl. LS10: Leeds 2G 139
Westwood Cres. BD16: Bgly 1C 68
Westwood Dr. LS29: I'ly 1B 18
Westwood Gro. BD2: B'frd 4H 71
Westwood Ho. BD13: B'frd 4A 108
Westwood Ri. LS27: Morl 1B 138
LS29: I'ly 1B 18
W. Wood Rd. LS10: Leeds 3F 139
LS27: Leeds 3F 139
Westwood Side LS27: Morl 6A 116
Westwood St. HD5: Hud 5G 163
Westwood Way LS23: B Spa 4B 30
Westy Bank Cft. BD20: Stee 3C 32
W. Yorkshire Ind. Est. BD4: B'frd . . .5B 112
West Yorkshire Playhouse, The
. . . . .3B 98 (4H 5)
W. Yorkshire Retail Pk.
WF17: Bat 3C 136
WETHERBY 4E 13
Wetherby Bus. Pk. LS22: Weth 3F 13
Wetherby Grange LS22: Weth 1G 29
Wetherby Gro. LS4: Leeds 1C 96
Wetherby Leisure Cen. 5E 13
Wetherby Pl. LS4: Leeds 1D 96
Wetherby Race Course 3H 13
Wetherby Rd. LS8: Leeds 3F 79
LS14: Bard, Leeds, S'cft 2A 80
LS14: S'cft 6B 62
LS17: Bard 1E 63
LS17: Leeds 6B 62
LS22: Coll, Weth 2D 28
LS22: Weth 1E 13
LS24: Tad 5F 31
Wetherby Ter. LS4: Leeds 1C 96
Wetton Ct. BD3: B'frd 4B 92
Wetville BD22: Oxen 6C 64
Weybridge Ho. BD8: B'frd 2C 90
(off Trenton Dr.)
Weyhill Dr. BD15: B'frd 3D 88
Weymouth Av. BD15: B'frd 3C 88
Weymouth St. HX1: Hal . . .2G 149 (3B 164)
Whack Ho. LS19: Yead 1D 54
(off Westfield Av.)
Whack Ho. Cl. LS19: Yead 1E 55
Whack Ho. La. LS19: Yead 1E 55
Whalley La. BD13: B'frd 1B 86
Wharfe Bank LS22: Coll 3G 27
Wharfebank Bus. Cen.
LS21: Otley 4C 22
Wharfe Cl. LS16: Leeds 3D 58
Wharfe Ct. BD20: Sils 2E 15
LS29: Burl W 2F 21
Wharfe Cres. LS21: Pool 4F 25
Wharfedale Av. LS7: Leeds 5H 77
Wharfedale Ct. LS14: Leeds 4B 80
LS21: Otley 3E 23
LS21: Pool 4F 25
(off Main St.)
Wharfedale Cres. LS25: Gar 6F 103
Wharfedale Dr. LS29: I'ly 5E 11
Wharfedale Gdns. BD17: Bail 3E 53
Wharfedale Gro. LS7: Leeds 5H 77
Wharfedale Ho. HX6: Hal 6H 147
(off Quarry Hill)
Wharfedale Lawns LS22: Weth 4E 13
Wharfedale M. LS21: Otley 3F 23
Wharfedale Mt. HX3: Hal 2D 130
LS7: Leeds 5H 77

Wharfedale Pl. LS7: Leeds 5H 77
Wharfedale Ri. BD9: B'frd 1E 89
  WF3: E Ard 2D 154
Wharfedale Rd. BD4: B'frd 6G 111
Wharfedale St. LS7: Leeds 5H 77
Wharfedale Ter. LS22: Coll 2B 28
Wharfedale Vw. LS7: Leeds 5H 77
  LS29: Add 1C 8
  LS29: Men 1G 39
Wharfe Grange LS22: Weth 4D 12
Wharfe Gro. LS22: Weth 4D 12
Wharfe Pk. LS29: Add 1E 9
Wharfe Rein LS22: Coll 3G 27
Wharfeside LS23: B Spa 4D 30
Wharfeside La. LS29: I'ly 4E 11
Wharfe St. LS21: Otley 3F 23
  LS22: Weth 4D 12
Wharfe Vw. LS21: Pool 4E 25
  LS22: Weth 4D 12
Wharfe Vw. Rd. LS29: I'ly 5D 10
Wharf St. BD3: B'frd 3F 91 (2E 7)
  BD17: Ship 1B 70
  HD6: Brigh 1B 162
  HX6: Hal 5A 148
  LS2: Leeds 4B 98 (5G 5)
Wharncliffe Cres. BD2: B'frd 5B 72
Wharncliffe Dr. BD2: B'frd 5B 72
Wharncliffe Gro. BD2: B'frd 5B 72
  BD18: Ship 3B 70
Wharncliffe Rd. BD18: Ship 4B 70
Whartons, The LS21: Otley 1E 23
Wharton Sq. BD13: B'frd 4D 108
           (off Highgate Rd.)
Wheater Rd. BD7: B'frd 6A 90
Wheatfield Ct. LS28: Pud 5H 93
Wheat Head Cres. BD22: Keigh 2E 47
Wheat Head Dr. BD22: Keigh 2F 47
Wheathead La. BD22: Keigh 2E 47
Wheatlands LS28: Pud 6G 73
  LS29: I'ly 5E 11
Wheatlands Av. BD9: B'frd 1G 89
Wheatlands Cres. BD9: B'frd 1G 89
Wheatlands Dr. BD9: B'frd 1G 89
Wheatlands Gro. BD9: B'frd 1G 89
Wheatlands Sq. BD9: B'frd 1G 89
WHEATLEY 5C 128
Wheatley Av. LS29: I'ly 6G 11
Wheatley Cl. HX3: Hal 6E 129
Wheatley Ct. HX2: Hal 3B 128
Wheatley Gdns. LS29: I'ly 6G 11
Wheatley Gro. LS29: I'ly 6G 11
Wheatley La. HX3: Hal 6E 129
  LS29: I'ly 6G 11
Wheatley Ri. LS29: I'ly 6G 11
Wheatley Rd. HX3: Hal 5C 128
           (Denfield La.)
  HX3: Hal 6D 128
           (Shroggs Rd.)
  LS29: I'ly 6E 11
Wheaton Av. LS15: Leeds 3C 100
Wheaton Ct. LS15: Leeds 3C 100
           (off Wheaton Av.)
Wheat St. BD22: Keigh 3G 47
Wheelwright Av. LS12: Leeds 6A 96
Wheelwright Cl. LS12: Leeds 6A 96
          (not continuous)
Whernside Mt. BD7: B'frd 3G 109
Whernside Way HX2: Hal 4G 127
Wherwell Rd. HD6: Brigh 2B 162
Whetley Cl. BD8: B'frd 3C 90
Whetley Gro. BD8: B'frd 2A 90
Whetley Hill BD8: B'frd 2B 90
Whetley La. BD8: B'frd 3A 90
Whetley St. BD8: B'frd 3C 90
           (off Denby St.)
Whetley Ter. BD8: B'frd 3C 90
Whewell St. WF17: Bat 6A 136
Whiddon Cft. LS29: Men 6F 21
Whimbrel Cl. BD8: B'frd 4E 89
Whimbrel M. LS27: Morl 4C 138
Whinberry Pl. WF17: Bat 4B 136
Whinbrook Ct. LS17: Leeds 6A 60
Whinbrook Cres. LS17: Leeds 6A 60

Whinbrook Gdns. LS17: Leeds 6A 60
Whinbrook Gro. LS17: Leeds 6A 60
Whincover Bank LS12: Leeds 6H 95
Whincover Cl. LS12: Leeds 6H 95
Whincover Cross LS12: Leeds 6H 95
Whincover Dr. LS12: Leeds 6G 95
Whincover Gdns. LS12: Leeds 6H 95
Whincover Grange LS12: Leeds 6H 95
Whincover Gro. LS12: Leeds 6H 95
Whincover Hill LS12: Leeds 6H 95
Whincover Mt. LS12: Leeds 6H 95
Whincover Rd. LS12: Leeds 6G 95
Whincover Vw. LS12: Leeds 6H 95
Whincup Gdns. LS10: Leeds 3C 118
      (off Woodhouse Hill Rd.)
Whiney Hill BD13: B'frd 4B 108
           (off Sand Beds)
Whinfield LS16: Leeds 3B 58
Whinfield Av. BD22: Keigh 6E 33
Whinfield Cl. BD22: Keigh 5F 33
Whinfield Dr. BD22: Keigh 5E 33
Whingate LS12: Leeds 3A 96
Whingate Av. LS12: Leeds 4A 96
Whingate Bus. Pk. LS12: Leeds 4B 96
Whingate Cl. LS12: Leeds 4A 96
Whingate Ct. LS12: Leeds 4B 96
Whingate Grn. LS12: Leeds 4A 96
Whingate Gro. LS12: Leeds 4A 96
Whingate Rd. LS12: Leeds 4A 96
Whin Knoll Av. BD21: Keigh 5F 33
WHINMOOR 1D 80
Whinmoor Ct. LS14: Leeds 6C 62
Whinmoor Cres. LS14: Leeds 6C 62
Whinmoor Gdns. LS14: Leeds 6B 62
Whinmoor La. LS17: Leeds 4A 62
Whinmoor Way LS14: Leeds 4F 81
         (Brayton Grange)
  LS14: Leeds 5E 81
           (Naburn Cl.)
  LS14: Leeds 4F 81
         (Pennwell Grn.)
Whinney Brow BD10: B'frd 1F 71
Whinney Fld. HX3: Hal 5G 149
Whinney Hill BD4: B'frd 6C 92
Whinney Hill Pk. HD6: Brigh 4A 152
Whinney Royd La. HX3: Hal 2C 130
Whinn Wood Grange LS14: Leeds . . .1D 80
Whins La. LS23: B Spa 2D 30
Whin St. BD21: Keigh 6G 33
Whiskers La. HX3: Hal 4A 130
Whisperwood Cl. WF1: Wake 4H 157
Whisperwood Rd. WF1: Wake 4H 157
Whitaker Av. BD2: B'frd 6A 72
Whitaker Cl. BD2: B'frd 6A 72
Whitaker St. LS28: Pud 2H 93
Whitaker Wlk. BD22: Oxen 1C 84
Whitburn Way BD15: B'frd 3D 88
Whitby Rd. BD8: B'frd 2A 90
Whitby Ter. BD8: B'frd 2A 90
Whitcliffe Mount Sports Cen. 1H 153
Whitcliffe Rd. BD19: Cleck 1H 153
White Abbey Rd.
  BD8: B'frd 3C 90 (1A 6)
Whitebeam La. LS10: Leeds 5B 118
Whitebeam Wlk. BD2: B'frd 4H 71
White Birch Ter. HX3: Hal 5C 128
Whitebridge Av. LS9: Leeds 3A 100
Whitebridge Cres. LS9: Leeds 2A 100
Whitebridge Spur LS9: Leeds 2A 100
Whitebridge Vw. LS9: Leeds 2A 100
White Castle Ct. BD13: B'frd 3F 107
Whitechapel Cl. LS8: Leeds 3F 79
Whitechapel Gro. BD19: Cleck 6G 133
Whitechapel Rd. BD19: Cleck 6F 133
Whitechapel Way LS8: Leeds 3F 79
Whitecliffe Cres. LS26: Swil 3A 122
Whitecliffe Dr. LS26: Swil 3A 122
Whitecliffe La. LS26: Swil 3A 122
Whitecliffe Ri. LS26: Swil 3A 122
WHITECOTE 5E 75
Whitecote Gdns. LS13: Leeds 5D 74
Whitecote Hill LS13: Leeds 5D 74

Whitecote Ho. LS13: Leeds 4D 74
Whitecote La. LS13: Leeds 5D 74
Whitecote Ri. LS13: Leeds 5D 74
WHITE CROSS 3A 40
White Cross HD2: Hud 6E 163
Whitefield Pl. BD8: B'frd 3A 90
White Ga. HX2: Hal 6B 106
Whitegate HX3: Hal 5H 149
  LS17: Bard 5E 27
Whitegate Dr. HX3: Hal 5H 149
Whitegate Rd. HX3: Hal 4H 149
Whitegate Ter. HX3: Hal 5H 149
Whitegate Top HX3: Hal 5A 150
White Gro. LS8: Leeds 1E 79
Whitehall Av. BD12: B'frd 6C 132
Whitehall Cft. LS26: Rothw 2B 142
Whitehall Gro. BD11: B'frd 2F 135
           (Royds Av.)
  BD11: B'frd 1H 135
         (Whitehall Rd.)
Whitehall Ind. Est. LS12: Leeds 1H 115
White Hall La. HX2: Hal 1G 127
Whitehall Pk. LS12: Leeds 1H 115
Whitehall Quay LS1: Leeds . . .4H 97 (5C 4)
Whitehall Rd. BD11: B'frd 1A 136
  BD12: B'frd, Brigh, Cleck 6D 132
  HX3: Hal 6H 131
  LS1: Leeds 5F 97 (6A 4)
  LS12: Leeds 4D 114 (6A 4)
Whitehall Rd. E. BD11: B'frd 3E 135
Whitehall Rd. W. BD11: B'frd 5C 134
  BD19: Cleck 5C 134
Whitehall St. HX3: Hal 2F 151
Whitehall Vs. HX3: Hal 1G 151
Whitehaven Cl. BD6: B'frd 6H 109
Whitehead Gro. BD2: B'frd 2A 92
Whitehead Pl. BD2: B'frd 1A 92
Whitehead's Ter. HX1: Hal 2D 148
Whitehead St. BD3: B'frd 5H 91
Whitehill Cotts. HX2: Hal 2C 128
Whitehill Cres. HX2: Hal 1C 128
Whitehill Dr. HX2: Hal 1C 128
Whitehill Grn. HX2: Hal 1D 128
Whitehill Rd. HX2: Hal 1C 128
White Holme Dr. LS21: Pool 5G 25
White Horse Cl. WF17: Bat 5D 136
Whitehouse Av. LS26: Kip 5D 122
Whitehouse Cres. LS26: Kip 5E 123
Whitehouse Dr. LS26: Kip 5D 122
Whitehouse La. LS19: Yead 5A 42
  LS26: Swil, Kip 2C 122
Whitehouse St. LS10: Leeds 6B 98
White Laithe App. LS14: Leeds 1D 80
White Laithe Av. LS14: Leeds 1D 80
White Laithe Cl. LS14: Leeds 1D 80
White Laithe Ct. LS14: Leeds 1D 80
White Laithe Cft. LS14: Leeds 1D 80
White Laithe Gdns. LS14: Leeds 1D 80
White Laithe Gth. LS14: Leeds 6D 62
White Laithe Grn. LS14: Leeds 1E 81
Whitelaithe Gro. LS14: Leeds 1E 81
White Laithe Rd. LS14: Leeds 1D 80
White Laithe Wlk. LS14: Leeds 1E 81
White Lands LS19: Yead 3E 55
Whitelands LS28: Pud 3B 94
Whitelands Cres. BD17: Bail 4D 52
Whitelands Rd. BD17: Bail 4D 52
White La. BD6: B'frd 4D 110
  BD22: Keigh 5A 46
White La. Top BD6: B'frd 4D 110
           (off White La.)
White Lee Cft. HX7: Heb B 6A 126
Whiteley Av. HX6: Hal 6F 147
Whiteley Cft. LS21: Otley 4E 23
Whiteley Cft. Cl. LS21: Otley 4E 23
Whiteley Cft. Gth. LS21: Otley 4D 22
Whiteley Cft. Ri. LS21: Otley 4E 23
Whiteley Cft. Rd. LS21: Otley 4D 22
Whitelock St. LS7: Leeds 2B 98 (1G 5)
White Moor La. BD22: Oxen 4C 84
Whitemoor Way BD13: B'frd 5C 86
White Rose Av. LS25: Gar 4F 103

White Rose Mead LS25: Gar 4G 103
White Rose Shop. Cen., The
  LS11: Leeds 6E 117
White Rose Way LS25: Gar 4G 103
Whites Cl. BD9: B'frd 6F 69
White's Ter. BD8: B'frd 2B 90
Whitestone Cres. LS19: Yead ...6F 41
Whitestone Dr. BD20: Keigh 4H 35
White St. LS26: Rothw 1F 143
White's Vw. BD8: B'frd 3B 90
Whiteways BD2: B'frd 6E 71
White Wells Spa Cottage 1D 18
White Windows Cotts. HX6: Hal ..6G 147
Whitfield Av. LS10: Leeds 1C 118
Whitfield Gdns. LS10: Leeds 1C 118
Whitfield Pl. LS10: Leeds 1C 118
Whitfield Sq. LS10: Leeds 1C 118
Whitfield St. LS8: Leeds 6D 78
Whitfield Way LS10: Leeds 1C 118
Whitham Cl. LS23: B Spa 3B 30
Whitham Rd. BD18: Ship 1G 69
WHITKIRK 2E 101
Whitkirk Cl. LS15: Leeds 3G 101
Whitkirk La. LS15: Leeds 3F 101
WHITKIRK LANE END 3F 101
Whitlam St. BD18: Ship 1H 69
Whitley Dr. HX2: Hal 1D 128
Whitley Gdns. LS8: Leeds 6C 78
  (off Bayswater Rd.)
WHITLEY HEAD 1C 32
Whitley La. HX3: Hal 4C 150
Whitley Pl. WF10: Kip 3H 145
Whitley Rd. BD21: Keigh 2G 47
Whitley St. BD3: B'frd 4G 91 (4G 7)
  BD16: Bgly 4B 50
  HX1: Hal 3F 149 (5A 164)
Whittle Cres. BD14: B'frd 6D 88
Whitton Cft. Rd. LS29: I'ly 5D 10
Whitty La. HX6: Hal 3H 147
Whitwell Av. HX5: Ell 4D 160
Whitwell Dr. HX5: Ell 4D 160
Whitwell Grn. La. HX5: Ell 5D 160
Whitwell Gro. HX5: Ell 4D 160
Whitwell St. BD4: B'frd 6G 91
Whitwood La. HD6: Brigh 2C 152
  (not continuous)
Whyment Cl. LS27: Leeds 4C 116
Whytecote End BD12: B'frd 3C 132
WIBSEY 4B 110
Wibsey Bank BD6: B'frd 4D 110
Wibsey Pk. Av. BD6: B'frd 5H 109
Wicken Cl. BD10: B'frd 3A 72
Wicken La. BD13: B'frd 4H 87
Wicket, The LS28: Pud 2F 73
Wickets, The BD2: B'frd 1A 92
  LS6: Leeds 5D 109
  LS15: Leeds 4G 101
Wickets Cl. BD6: B'frd 5D 110
Wickham Av. BD6: B'frd 5C 110
  LS23: B Spa 4A 30
Wickham Cl. LS23: B Spa 3A 30
Wickham St. BD19: Cleck 1F 153
  LS11: Leeds 2G 117
Wide La. BD22: Keigh 4A 46
  LS27: Morl 4B 138
Wigan St. BD1: B'frd 4D 90 (4A 6)
  (not continuous)
Wigeon App. LS27: Morl 3C 138
Wighill La. LS23: W'ton 1G 31
Wightman St. BD3: B'frd 2G 91
Wignall St. BD20: Keigh 3H 33
Wigton Chase LS17: Leeds 2E 61
Wigton Cl. LS17: Leeds 1C 60
Wigton Grn. LS17: Leeds 1D 60
Wigton Gro. LS17: Leeds 1C 60
Wigton La. LS17: Leeds 1C 60
Wigton Pk. Cl. LS17: Leeds 1D 60
WIKE 4A 44
Wike La. LS17: Bard 3B 44
Wike Ridge Av. LS17: Leeds 2E 61
Wike Ridge Cl. LS17: Leeds 1F 61
Wike Ridge Ct. LS17: Leeds 1F 61

Wike Ridge Fold LS17: Leeds 1E 61
Wike Ridge Gdns. LS17: Leeds ...2F 61
Wike Ridge Gro. LS17: Leeds 2F 61
Wike Ridge La. LS17: Leeds 2F 61
Wike Ridge M. LS17: Leeds 2F 61
Wike Ridge Mt. LS17: Leeds 2F 61
Wike Ridge Vw. LS17: Leeds 2E 61
Wilday Cl. BD16: Bgly 1A 50
Wilderness Rd. HX5: Ell 5E 161
Wild Gro. LS28: Pud 4E 93
Wilfred St. BD14: B'frd 1F 109
  LS15: Leeds 3D 100
Wilfred Ter. LS12: Leeds 1A 116
Wilkinson Fold BD12: B'frd 4C 132
Wilkinson Ter. BD7: B'frd 5H 89
Wilkinson Way LS21: Otley 2C 22
Wilkin St. BD21: Keigh 6H 33
Willerton Cl. WF12: Dew 6B 154
Williamson St. HX1: Hal 1E 149
William Dr. BD20: Stee 6B 14
William Fison Ride LS29: Burl W ..3D 20
William Foster Way LS29: Burl W ..3D 20
William Henry St. BD18: Ship 6H 51
  HD6: Brigh 6A 152
William Hey Ct. LS9: Leeds 1F 99
William Ri. LS15: Leeds 3A 100
Williams Dr. BD20: Stee 6B 14
Williams Rd. BD20: Stee 6B 14
William St. BD4: B'frd 4B 112
  BD5: B'frd 5E 91 (6C 6)
  BD6: B'frd 6H 109
  BD13: B'frd 2B 86
  HD6: Brigh 2A 162
  HX4: Hal 5H 159
  LS6: Leeds 6E 77
  LS27: Morl 5C 116
  LS28: Pud 1B 94
    (Milestone Ct.)
  LS28: Pud 2H 93
    (Sun Fld.)
William Vw. LS15: Leeds 3A 100
Willians Av. LS26: Rothw 6A 120
Willis St. LS9: Leeds 4C 98
Willoughby Ter. LS11: Leeds 6F 97
Willow App. LS4: Leeds 2E 97
Willow Av. BD2: B'frd 3G 71
  LS4: Leeds 2E 97
  LS23: B Spa 5B 30
Willow Bank HX1: Hal 4E 149
  HX2: Hal 3D 146
Willow Cl. BD6: B'frd 6C 110
  HX2: Hal 3B 148
  LS4: Leeds 2E 97
  LS20: Guis 4C 40
  LS29: Burl W 2E 21
Willow Ct. LS21: Pool 5F 25
Willow Cres. BD2: B'frd 3G 71
  HX6: Hal 4A 148
  LS15: Leeds 4B 100
  LS23: B Spa 5B 30
Willow Cft. LS29: Men 1G 39
Willowcroft BD19: Cleck 2H 153
Willow Dene Av. HX2: Hal 4B 148
Willow Dr. BD6: B'frd 6C 110
  HX2: Hal 3B 148
Willow Gdns. BD2: B'frd 3G 71
  HX2: Hal 4C 148
  LS20: Guis 4C 40
Willow Gth. LS4: Leeds 2E 97

Willow Gth. Av. LS14: Leeds 1D 80
Willow Gth. Cl. LS14: Leeds 1D 80
Willow Glade LS23: B Spa 6B 30
Willow Grn. WF1: Wake 6F 157
Willow Gro. BD2: B'frd 3G 71
  BD21: Keigh 4G 47
  LS23: B Spa 6B 30
  LS25: Kip 2F 123
Willow Hall Rd. HX5: Ell 4B 148
Willow Hall Fold HX6: Hal 4B 148
    (off Bairstow La.)
Willow Hall La. HX6: Hal 4B 148
Willow Ho. LS7: Leeds 2B 78
Willow Ho's. HX6: Hal 4B 148
    (off Rochdale Rd.)
Willow Ind. Complex HX6: Hal ...6G 147
Willow La. LS20: Bail, Guis 1F 53
  LS23: B Spa 5B 30
Willow Mt. HX3: Hal 1F 131
    (off Witchfield Hill)
  HX6: Hal 4A 148
    (off Overdale Mt.)
Willow Pk. WF1: Wake 6F 157
Willow Pk. Dr. HX3: Hal 1F 131
Willow Ri. HX2: Hal 3B 148
Willow Rd. LS4: Leeds 2E 97
  LS28: Pud 1G 93
Willows, The BD16: Bgly 6F 49
  BD17: Bail 5G 51
  HX2: Hal 6C 106
  LS17: Leeds 5A 60
Willow Sq. LS26: Rothw 2E 143
Willow St. BD8: B'frd 3H 89
  BD19: Cleck 6B 134
  HX1: Hal 3E 149
  HX6: Hal 5B 148
Willow Ter. HX6: Hal 4A 148
  LS1: Leeds 2G 97 (1B 4)
Willow Tree Cl. BD21: Keigh 3G 47
Willow Tree Gdns. BD16: Bgly ...2E 51
  LS29: Burl W 1F 21
Willow Va. LS22: Weth 2D 12
Willow Vw. HX6: Hal 4B 148
    (off Bairstow Mt.)
Willow Vs. BD2: B'frd 3G 71
Willow Well Cl. LS15: Leeds 3B 100
Wills Gill LS20: Guis 4D 40
Will St. BD4: B'frd 1B 112
Wilman Hill BD6: B'frd 4B 110
    (not continuous)
Wilmer Dr. BD9: B'frd 5A 70
  BD18: Ship 4A 70
Wilmer Rd. BD9: B'frd 6A 70
Wilmington Gro. LS7: Leeds 6A 78
Wilmington St. LS7: Leeds 1B 98
Wilmot Rd. LS29: I'ly 5E 11
Wilmur Mt. HX2: Hal 3E 147
WILSDEN 4G 67
Wilsden Hill Rd. BD15: B'frd 4F 67
Wilsden Old Rd. BD16: Bgly 6F 49
Wilsden Rd. BD15: B'frd 5A 68
  BD16: Bgly 6F 49
Wilson Av. BD20: Stee 5B 14
Wilson Ct. WF1: Wake 5G 157
Wilson Dr. WF1: Wake 5F 157
Wilson Fold BD12: B'frd 2D 132
Wilson Rd. BD12: B'frd 3D 132
  BD16: Bgly 3B 50
  HX1: Hal 4D 148
Wilson's Row LS26: Mick 4F 145
Wilson St. BD8: B'frd 2C 90
  LS28: Pud 2H 93
Wilton Av. HD2: Hud 5E 163
Wilton Gro. LS6: Leeds 3E 77
Wilton Rd. LS29: I'ly 6C 10
Wilton St. BD5: B'frd 5D 90 (6B 6)
  HD6: Brigh 6H 151
Wimborne Dr. BD15: B'frd 2E 89
Wimburn Cl. LS25: Kip 5F 33
Winbrooke Ter. BD6: B'frd 4A 110
Winburg Rd. BD7: B'frd 6A 90
Winburn Ter. HX2: Hal 3H 147

Winchester Gdns. BD4: B'frd 6B **92**
Winchester Ho. *HX6: Hal* *5A 148*
            (off Church Vw.)
Winchester St. LS12: Leeds 4D **96**
Winden Cl. WF3: Wake 4G **157**
Winden Gro. WF3: Wake 4F **157**
Windermere Av. LS29: Men 5G **21**
Windermere Dr. LS17: Leeds 1F **59**
   LS25: Gar 5F **103**
Windermere Ri. HD6: Brigh 3B **152**
Windermere Rd. BD7: B'frd 2G **109**
   BD17: Bail 6H **51**
             (not continuous)
Windermere Ter. BD7: B'frd 2G **109**
Winders Dale LS27: Morl 1H **137**
Windgate BD20: Sils 3F **15**
WINDHILL .2C **70**
Windhill Old Rd.
   BD10: B'frd 6F **53**
Winding Rd. HX1: Hal 2G **149** (3C **164**)
Winding Way LS17: Leeds 2H **59**
Windle Royd La. HX2: Hal 2A **148**
Windmill App. LS10: Leeds 5C **118**
Windmill Chase LS26: Rothw 3A **142**
Windmill Cl. LS10: Leeds 6C **118**
Windmill Cotts. *LS15: Leeds* 4F *101*
             (off Colton La.)
Windmill Ct. LS14: Leeds 3D **80**
Windmill Cres. HX3: Hal 5C **130**
Windmill Dr. HX3: Hal 5C **130**
Windmill Fld. Rd. LS26: Rothw . . .3A **142**
Windmill Fold *LS19: Yead* 6G *41*
            (off Windmill La.)
Windmill Gdns. LS15: Leeds 4F *101*
WINDMILL HILL 5G **93**
Windmill Hill BD6: B'frd 4A **110**
   HX3: Hal 6C **130**
   LS28: Pud 5G **93**
Windmill La. BD6: B'frd 4C **110**
   HX3: Hal 5C **130**
   LS19: Yead 1G **55**
   LS26: Rothw 3A **142**
   LS27: Morl 1F **137**
   LS29: Men 1B **40**
   WF17: Bat 6C **136**
Windmill Pl. *LS19: Yead* 1G *55*
            (off Windmill La.)
Windmill Rd. LS10: Leeds 5C **118**
   LS23: B'ham 6C **30**
Windsor Av. BD20: Sils 2D **14**
   LS15: Leeds 3D **100**
Windsor Cl. LS25: Kip 3G **123**
   WF12: Dew 6B **154**
Windsor Ct. *BD5: B'frd* 6E *91*
         (off Swarland Gro.)
   BD18: Ship 2B *70*
            (off Manor La.)
   LS13: Leeds 1F **95**
   LS17: Leeds 5C **60**
   LS27: Morl 3A **138**
   WF12: Dew 6A **154**
Windsor Cres. BD22: Keigh 5B **46**
   HX2: Hal 6C **128**
   LS26: Rothw 1A **142**
Windsor Gdns. WF12: Dew 6B **154**
Windsor Grn. LS25: Gar 4H **103**
Windsor Gro. BD13: B'frd 5H **87**
   BD22: Keigh 5B **46**
Windsor Mt. LS15: Leeds 3D **100**
Windsor Oval WF3: E Ard 4D **154**
Windsor Pl. HD2: Hud 6E **163**
Windsor Rd. BD18: Ship 2B **70**
   BD22: Keigh 5B **46**
   WF12: Dew 6A **154**
   WF17: Bat 6C **136**
Windsor St. BD4: B'frd 6G **91**
   HX1: Hal 3G **149** (6B **164**)
Windsor Ter. HX6: Hal 6H **147**
   LS27: Morl 6F **115**
Windsor Vw. WF12: Dew 6B **154**
Windsor Vs. HX3: Hal 5H **131**

Windsor Wlk. HX3: Hal 3A **152**
   WF17: Bat 5D **136**
Windy Bank La. BD13: B'frd 1F **129**
   WF15: Liv 4H **153**
Windy Gro. BD15: B'frd 5H **67**
Wine Tavern La. HX6: Hal 6B **146**
Wine Tavern Rd. HX6: Hal 6B **146**
             (not continuous)
Winfield Dr. BD4: B'frd 1C **134**
Winfield Gro. *LS2: Leeds* 1H *97*
         (off Blenheim Av.)
Winfield Pl. LS2: Leeds 1H **97**
Winfield Ter. *LS2: Leeds* 1H *97*
         (off Winfield Pl.)
Wingate Av. BD22: Keigh 1F **47**
Wingate Way BD22: Keigh 1F **47**
Wingfield Ct. BD16: Bgly 3C **50**
Wingfield Mt. BD3: B'frd 3H **91**
Wingfield St. BD3: B'frd 3H **91**
Winnard Row BD5: B'frd 3F **111**
Winnipeg Pl. LS7: Leeds 3B **78**
Winnow La. LS23: B Spa 4G **29**
Winrose App. LS10: Leeds 6C **118**
Winrose Av. LS10: Leeds 5B **118**
Winrose Cl. BD12: B'frd 3C **132**
Winrose Cres. LS10: Leeds 5B **118**
Winrose Dr. LS10: Leeds 5B **118**
Winrose Gth. LS10: Leeds 5C **118**
Winrose Gro. LS10: Leeds 5C **118**
Winrose Hill LS10: Leeds 4C **118**
Winscar Av. BD6: B'frd 4E **109**
Winslow Rd. BD10: B'frd 5C **72**
Winstanley Ter. *LS6: Leeds* 6E *77*
         (off Victoria Rd.)
Winston Gdns. LS6: Leeds 4C **76**
Winston Mt. LS6: Leeds 4C **76**
Winstons Health Club 4A **4**
             (off West St.)
Winston Ter. BD7: B'frd 6A **90**
Winterbourne Av. LS27: Morl 1B **138**
Winterburn Hill HX2: Hal 3G **147**
Winterburn La. HX2: Hal 2G **147**
Winterburn St. BD21: Keigh 5A **34**
Winter Ct. BD15: B'frd 6C **68**
Winter Hill HX3: Hal 6C **150**
Winterneb HX2: Hal 4E **147**
Winter St. HX1: Hal 4D **148**
Winterton Dr. BD12: B'frd 2C **132**
Winthorpe Av. WF3: Leeds 5B **140**
Winthorpe Cres. WF3: Leeds 5B **140**
Winthorpe St. LS6: Leeds 3F **77**
Winthorpe Vw. WF3: Leeds 5C **140**
Winton Grn. BD6: B'frd 1B **132**
Winton Ho. *BD5: B'frd* 1D *110*
          (off Hutson St.)
Winton Mill HX6: Hal 1A **148**
Wintoun St. LS7: Leeds 2B **98** (1G **5**)
Wira Ho. LS16: Leeds 6H **57**
WIRING FIELD 4C **96**
         (Elland Riorges Link)
Wistons La. HX5: Ell 3C **160**
   HX5: Ell 3C **160**
          (Old Power Way)
WITCHFIELD 1F **131**
Witchfield Ct. *HX3: Hal* 1F *131*
         (off Shelf Moor Rd.)
Witchfield Grange HX3: Hal 1E **131**
Witchfield Hill HX3: Hal 1F **131**
Witham Way LS25: Gar 5G **103**
Withens Hill Cft. HX2: Hal 6B **106**
Withens New Rd. HX2: Hal 3A **106**
             (not continuous)
Withens Rd. HX2: Hal 1F **127**
   WF17: Bat 5A **136**
Withinfield Ct. HX3: Hal 5C **150**
Within Flds. HX3: Hal 5C **150**
Withins Cl. BD5: B'frd 3B **110**
Woburn Ho. *BD5: B'frd* 1D *110*
            (off Park La.)
Woburn Ter. BD14: B'frd 1D **108**
Wold Cl. BD13: B'frd 3H **87**
Wolley Av. LS12: Leeds 2F **115**

Wolley Ct. LS12: Leeds 2F **115**
Wolley Dr. LS12: Leeds 2F **115**
Wolley Gdns. LS12: Leeds 2F **115**
Wolseley Rd. LS4: Leeds 2D **96**
             (not continuous)
Wolseley St. BD14: B'frd 6E **89**
Wolston Cl. BD4: B'frd 3C **112**
Womersley Pl. LS28: Pud 5H **93**
           (Carlisle Rd.)
   LS28: Pud 2F **93**
         (Woodhall Pk. Gdns.)
Womersley St. HX1: Hal 2D **148**
Woodacre Cres. LS17: Bard 2E **45**
Woodacre Grn. LS17: Bard 1E **45**
Woodacre La. LS17: Bard 1E **45**
Woodale Av. BD9: B'frd 6F **69**
Woodbine Gro. BD10: B'frd 2H **71**
Woodbine St. BD3: B'frd 4G **91** (3G **7**)
   HX1: Hal 4E **149**
Woodbine Ter. BD10: B'frd 2H **71**
   HX1: Hal 4E *149*
         (off Woodbine St.)
   LS6: Leeds 3E **77**
   LS13: Leeds 6E **75**
   LS18: H'fth 2E *75*
            (off Wood La.)
WOODBOTTOM 1H **73**
Wood Bottom LS19: Yead 1H **73**
Wood Bottom La. HD6: Brigh 4F **151**
Woodbourne LS8: Leeds 2G **79**
Woodbourne Av. LS17: Leeds 6A **60**
Woodbridge Av. LS25: Gar 2A **104**
Woodbridge Cl. LS6: Leeds 4B **76**
Woodbridge Cres. LS6: Leeds 3A **76**
Woodbridge Fold LS6: Leeds 4A **76**
Woodbridge Gdns. LS6: Leeds 4A **76**
Woodbridge Gth. LS6: Leeds 4B **76**
Woodbridge Grn. LS6: Leeds 4B **76**
Woodbridge Lawn LS6: Leeds 4A **76**
Woodbridge Pl. LS6: Leeds 4A **76**
Woodbridge Rd. LS6: Leeds 4A **76**
Woodbridge Va. LS6: Leeds 4A **76**
Woodbrook Av. HX2: Hal 2A **128**
Woodbrook Cl. HX2: Hal 2A **128**
Woodbrook Pl. HX2: Hal 2A **128**
Woodbrook Rd. HX2: Hal 2A **128**
Wood Cl. BD17: Bail 5B **52**
   LS7: Leeds 2A **78**
   LS26: Rothw 1H **141**
Woodcot Av. BD17: Bail 5D **52**
Wood Cote Fold BD22: Keigh 1B **46**
Wood Cres. LS26: Rothw 1H **141**
Wood Cft. HD6: Brigh 3H **161**
   HX6: Hal 6E **147**
Woodcross LS27: Morl 1A **138**
Woodcross End LS27: Morl 6A **116**
Woodcross Fold LS27: Morl 1A **138**
Woodcross Gdns. LS27: Morl 1A **138**
Woodcross Gth. LS27: Morl 6A **116**
Wood Dr. LS26: Rothw 1G **141**
WOODEND
   Castleford 2F **145**
   Shipley .2D **70**
Woodend WF10: Kip 1F **145**
Wood End Cl. HX3: Hal 6F **149**
Woodend Ct. BD5: B'frd 3F **111**
Wood End Cres. BD18: Ship 1D **70**
Woodend Cres. WF10: Kip 2F **145**
Wood End La. HX4: Hal 5B **158**
Woodeson Ct. LS13: Leeds 4B **74**
Woodeson Lea LS13: Leeds 4B **74**
Woodfield Av. HX4: Hal 4F **159**
Woodfield Cl. BD10: B'frd 1A **72**
Woodfield Dr. HX4: Hal 5F **159**
Woodfield Rd. BD13: B'frd 2C **66**
Woodfield Ter. *LS28: Pud* 5B *94*
         (off Sheridan Way)
Woodford Av. HX4: Hal 5H **149**
Woodford Cl. BD15: B'frd 3C **88**
Woodgarth Gdns. BD4: B'frd 2D **112**
Wood Gro. LS12: Leeds 4F **95**
WOODHALL 1E **93**

Woodhall Av. BD3: B'frd 3C **92**
LS5: Leeds 3G **75**
Woodhall Cl. LS28: Pud 1E **93**
Woodhall Ct. LS15: Leeds 5F **101**
LS28: Pud 4E **73**
Woodhall Cres. HX3: Hal 6E **149**
Woodhall Ct. LS28: Pud 1E **93**
Woodhall Dr. LS5: Leeds 3G **75**
Woodhall Gro. LS26: Mick 4D **144**
(not continuous)
WOODHALL HILLS 6E **73**
Woodhall Hills LS28: Pud 6D **72**
Woodhall La. LS28: Pud 6E **73**
WOODHALL PARK 1F **93**
Woodhall Pk. Av. LS28: Pud 1E **93**
Woodhall Pk. Cres. E. LS28: Pud . .2F **93**
Woodhall Pk. Cres. W. LS28: Pud . .2E **93**
Woodhall Pk. Dr. LS28: Pud 2E **93**
Woodhall Pk. Gdns. LS28: Pud 2F **93**
Woodhall Pk. Gro. LS28: Pud 2E **93**
Woodhall Pk. Mt. LS28: Pud 1E **93**
Woodhall Pl. BD3: B'frd 2C **92**
Woodhall Retail Cen., The
BD3: B'frd 2C **92**
Woodhall Rd. BD3: B'frd 3C **92**
BD3: Pud 2C **92**
LS28: Pud 5E **73**
Woodhall Ter. BD3: B'frd 2C **92**
Woodhall Vw. BD3: B'frd 2D **92**
Woodhead LS29: Burl W, I'ly, Men . .2H **19**
Woodhead La. HD6: Brigh 2E **163**
LS27: Morl 6E **115**
Woodhead Rd. BD7: B'frd 6B **90**
WF17: Bat 4D **136**
Woodhead St. HX2: Hal 1C **148**
Wood Hill LS26: Rothw 1H **141**
Wood Hill Ct. LS16: Leeds 3F **57**
Wood Hill Cres. LS16: Leeds 4E **57**
Wood Hill Gdns. LS16: Leeds 3F **57**
Wood Hill Gth. LS16: Leeds 3F **57**
Wood Hill Gro. LS16: Leeds 4E **57**
Wood Hill Ri. LS16: Leeds 3F **57**
Woodhill Ri. BD10: B'frd 1C **72**
Wood Hill Rd. LS16: Leeds 4F **57**
Woodhill Vw. LS22: Weth 3E **13**
WOODHOUSE
Brighouse 3C **162**
Keighley 2A **48**
Leeds 1H **97**
Woodhouse BD16: Bgly 5C **50**
Woodhouse Av. BD21: Keigh 2A **48**
WOODHOUSE CARR 6H **77**
WOODHOUSE CLIFF 5G **77**
Woodhouse Cliff LS6: Leeds 5G **77**
Woodhouse Cl. BD21: Keigh 2A **48**
WF3: E Ard 3H **155**
Woodhouse Dr. BD21: Keigh 2A **48**
Woodhouse Flats LS2: Leeds 6G **77**
(off St Mark's St.)
Woodhouse Gdns. HD6: Brigh 3C **162**
Woodhouse Gro. BD15: B'frd 5C **68**
BD21: Keigh 2A **48**
WOODHOUSE HILL 3B **118**
Woodhouse Hill Av. LS10: Leeds . . .3C **118**
Woodhouse Hill Gro.
LS10: Leeds 3C **118**
Woodhouse Hill Pl. LS10: Leeds . .3C **118**
Woodhouse Hill Rd. LS10: Leeds . . .3C **118**
(not continuous)
Woodhouse La. HD6: Brigh 4B **162**
HX3: Hal 6E **149**
LS1: Leeds 1G **97** (1D **4**)
LS2: Leeds 6G **77** (1C **4**)
WF2: E Ard 6G **155**
WF3: E Ard 6G **155**
Woodhouse Rd. BD21: Keigh 2A **48**
Woodhouse Sq.
LS3: Leeds 3G **97** (3B **4**)
Woodhouse St. LS6: Leeds 6G **77**
Woodhouse Ter. BD6: B'frd 5E **111**
Woodhouse Wlk. BD21: Keigh 2A **48**
Woodhouse Way BD21: Keigh 2A **48**

WOODKIRK 2D **154**
Woodkirk Av. WF3: E Ard 1C **154**
Woodkirk Gdns. WF12: Dew 3B **154**
Woodkirk Gro. BD12: B'frd 6C **132**
WF3: E Ard 1D **154**
Woodland Av. LS26: Swil 4A **122**
Woodland Cl. BD9: B'frd 5E **69**
LS15: Leeds 3E **101**
Woodland Ct. LS8: Leeds 4E **79**
Woodland Cres. BD9: B'frd 5D **68**
LS26: Rothw 1H **141**
LS26: Swil 4A **122**
Woodland Cft. LS18: H'fth 5E **57**
Woodland Dr. HD6: Brigh 6H **151**
HX2: Hal 4B **148**
LS7: Leeds 2B **78**
LS26: Swil 4H **121**
Woodland Gro. BD9: B'frd 4E **69**
LS7: Leeds 5C **78**
LS26: Swil 4A **122**
Woodland Hill LS15: Leeds 3D **100**
Woodland Ho. BD10: B'frd 2A **72**
(off Garsdale Av.)
Woodland La. LS7: Leeds 2B **78**
Woodland Mt. LS7: Leeds 5C **78**
Woodland Pk. LS26: Rothw 3E **143**
Woodland Pk. Rd.
LS6: Leeds 4E **77**
Woodland Ri. LS15: Leeds 3E **101**
Woodland Rd. LS15: Leeds 3D **100**
Woodlands BD12: B'frd 2G **133**
BD17: Bail 3E **53**
BD22: Keigh 5C **46**
LS17: Leeds 5C **60**
LS29: I'ly 5F **11**
WF3: E Ard 2A **156**
Woodlands, The LS21: Pool 5G **25**
LS26: Rothw 2E **143**
(off Farrer La.)
Woodlands Av. BD13: B'frd 4D **108**
BD19: Cleck 6E **135**
HX3: Hal 6G **129**
LS28: Pud 2G **93**
Woodlands Cl. BD10: Pud 6D **54**
HD2: Hud 5G **163**
LS14: S'cft 5E **45**
LS29: I'ly 5B **10**
WF3: E Ard 2A **156**
Woodlands Ct. BD8: B'frd 2A **6**
BD16: Bgly 2A **50**
LS16: Leeds 6B **58**
LS25: Kip 5H **123**
(off Woodlands Cft.)
LS28: Pud 6H **93**
Woodlands Cres. BD19: Cleck 6E **135**
Woodlands Cft. LS25: Kip 5H **123**
Woodlands Dr. BD10: Pud 6D **54**
BD19: Cleck 6E **135**
LS19: Yead 5E **55**
LS25: Gar 5H **103**
LS27: Morl 1H **137**
WF3: E Ard 2H **155**
Woodlands Fold BD11: B'frd 2F **135**
Woodlands Gdns. LS14: S'cft 1E **63**
Woodlands Gro. BD13: B'frd 4C **108**
BD16: Bgly 2D **68**
BD17: Bail 5H **51**
HX3: Hal 6G **129**
LS25: Kip 5A **124**
LS28: Pud 2G **93**
LS29: I'ly 5B **10**
Woodlands Leisure Cen. 6F **137**
Woodlands Mt. HX3: Hal 5G **129**
(not continuous)
Woodlands Pk. BD19: B'frd 4H **133**
LS14: S'cft 3A **45**
Woodlands Pk. Gro. LS28: Pud 6H **93**
Woodlands Pk. Rd. BD28: Pud 6H **93**
Woodland Sq. HD6: Brigh 2C **162**
LS12: Leeds 3H **95**
Woodlands Ri. BD22: Haw 4C **64**
LS29: I'ly 5A **10**

Woodlands Rd. BD8: B'frd 3A **90**
BD13: B'frd 4C **108**
BD16: Bgly 3E **51**
BD19: Cleck 6E **135**
HX3: Hal 6G **129**
HX5: Hal 3B **160**
WF17: Bat 6C **136**
Woodlands St. BD8: B'frd 3C **90**
Woodlands Ter. BD8: B'frd 2A **90**
BD12: B'frd 2H **133**
LS28: Pud 2G **93**
Woodlands Vw. BD19: Cleck 6E **135**
HX3: Hal 6G **129**
(off Range St.)
LS14: S'cft 6E **45**
LS25: Kip 5A **124**
Woodland Ter. HX3: Hal 6G **129**
LS7: Leeds 2G **77**
Woodland Vw. LS7: Leeds 2B **78**
LS28: Pud 2E **73**
WF3: E Ard 4D **154**
Wood Land Vs. LS14: Leeds 5F **81**
Wood La. BD2: B'frd 5E **71**
(not continuous)
BD16: Bgly 6B **36**
HD6: Hal 1F **161**
HX2: Hal 1B **126**
(Catherine Ho. La.)
HX2: Hal 6B **128**
(Doctor Hill)
HX3: Hal 6D **130**
(Bird Holme La.)
HX3: Hal 6D **150**
(Dark La.)
HX6: Hal 6E **147**
LS6: Leeds 4D **76**
LS7: Leeds 2A **78**
(not continuous)
LS12: Leeds 3F **95**
(Ring Rd. Farnley)
LS12: Leeds 3F **115**
(Wentworth Farm Res. Pk.)
LS13: Leeds 5E **75**
(Bellmount Pl.)
LS13: Leeds 3F **95**
(Ring Rd. Farnley)
LS15: Leeds 4G **81**
LS17: Bard 2F **45**
LS18: H'fth 2E **75**
LS23: B Spa 1C **30**
LS26: Kip 1E **145**
LS26: Rothw 6F **119**
LS28: Pud 2F **73**
Wood La. Ct. LS6: Leeds 4E **77**
Woodlark Cl. BD6: B'frd 4F **109**
Woodlea LS23: B Spa 3B **30**
Woodlea App. LS6: Leeds 6F **59**
LS19: Yead 1D **54**
Woodlea Av. LS6: Leeds 6F **59**
Woodlea Chase
LS6: Leeds 1F **77**
Woodlea Cl. LS19: Yead 2D **54**
Woodlea Ct. LS6: Leeds 1F **77**
LS17: Leeds 3F **61**
Woodlea Cft. LS6: Leeds 6F **59**
LS19: Yead 2D **54**
Woodlea Dr. LS6: Leeds 6F **59**
LS19: Yead 2D **54**
Woodlea Fold LS6: Leeds 6F **59**
Woodlea Gdns. LS6: Leeds 6F **59**
Woodlea Gth. LS6: Leeds 6F **59**
Woodlea Ga. LS6: Leeds 1F **77**
Woodlea Grn. LS6: Leeds 6F **59**
Woodlea Gro. LS6: Leeds 1F **77**
LS11: Leeds 2F **117**
(off Woodlea St.)
LS19: Yead 1D **54**
Woodlea Holt LS6: Leeds 6F **59**
Woodlea La. LS6: Leeds 6F **59**
Woodlea Lawn LS6: Leeds 6F **59**
Woodlea Mt. LS11: Leeds 2F **117**
LS19: Yead 1D **54**
Woodlea Pk. LS6: Leeds 1F **77**

Woodlea Pl. LS6: Leeds 6F **59**
LS11: Leeds 2G **117**
Woodlea Rd. LS19: Yead 1D **54**
Woodlea Sq. LS6: Leeds 1F **77**
Woodlea St. LS11: Leeds 2F **117**
Woodlea Vw. LS6: Leeds 1F **77**
LS19: Yead 2D **54**
Woodleigh Av. BD5: B'frd 4E **111**
LS25: Gar 4E **103**
(off Lyndon Av.)
Woodleigh Hall Vw. LS19: Yead . . .6A **56**
WOODLESFORD 6E **121**
Woodlesford HX2: Hal 6A **128**
Woodlesford Cres. HX2: Hal 5H **127**
Woodlesford Station (Rail) 6F **121**
Woodliffe Ct. LS7: Leeds 2A **78**
Woodliffe Cres. LS7: Leeds 2A **78**
Woodliffe Dr. LS7: Leeds 2A **78**
Woodman Av. HD2: Hud 6F **163**
HX5: Ell 6B **160**
Woodman Ct. BD6: B'frd 1G **131**
Woodman St. LS15: Leeds 3C **100**
Woodman Works HX5: Ell 6B **160**
Woodman Yd. LS16: Leeds 3D **76**
(off Otley Rd.)
Wood Mt. HX2: Hal 5D **148**
LS26: Rothw 1G **141**
Woodnook Cl. LS16: Leeds 5F **57**
Woodnook Dr. LS16: Leeds 5F **57**
Woodnook Gth. LS16: Leeds 5F **57**
Woodnook Rd. LS16: Leeds 4F **57**
Wood Nook La. HX6: Hal 4A **148**
Woodnook Rd. LS16: Leeds 4F **57**
Wood Nook Ter. LS28: Pud 2G **93**
Woodpecker Cl. BD15: B'frd 4D **88**
Woodpecker Rd. LS29: Burl W 1E **21**
Wood Pl. BD8: B'frd 3C **90** (1A **6**)
BD9: B'frd 5C **70**
Wood Rd. BD5: B'frd 1E **111**
BD9: B'frd 5C **70**
WOOD ROW 4B **144**
Wood Row LS26: Mick 4B **144**
Woodrow Cres. LS26: Mick 4A **144**
Woodrow Dr. BD12: B'frd 1E **133**
Woodroyd HX2: Hal 4F **147**
Woodroyd Av. BD5: B'frd 3F **111**
Woodroyd Cres. HX6: Hal 4G **147**
Woodroyd Dr. HX3: Hal 5D **128**
Woodroyd Gdns. HX2: Hal 4F **147**
LS29: I'ly 6H **11**
Woodroyd Rd. BD5: B'frd 2E **111**
(not continuous)
Woodroyd Ter. BD5: B'frd 3F **111**
WOODSIDE
Bradford 6A **110**
Halifax 1G **149** (1B **164**)
Wood Side HX4: Hal 6B **158**
Woodside BD18: Ship 1D **70**
BD20: Keigh 4G **33**
LS26: Mick 4A **144**
WF2: Wake 6C **156**
Woodside Av. BD16: Bgly 2B **68**
BD18: Ship 1G **69**
LS4: Leeds 1C **96**
LS7: Leeds 2F **77**
WF2: Wake 6C **156**
Woodside Cl. LS27: Morl 1A **138**
Woodside Ct. BD13: B'frd 3B **86**
LS16: Leeds 6H **57**
LS18: H'fth 1G **75**
LS29: I'ly 3C **10**
Woodside Cres. BD16: Bgly 2B **68**
HX3: Hal 6F **129** (1A **164**)
Woodside Dr. BD16: Bgly 2B **68**
LS27: Morl 6A **116**
WF2: Wake 6C **156**
Woodside Gdns. LS27: Morl 6A **116**
Woodside Gro. HX3: Hal 6G **129**
HX4: Hal 5G **159**
WF10: Kip 1F **145**
Woodside Hill Cl. LS18: H'fth 1G **75**
Woodside La. HD2: Hud 6B **162**
LS27: Morl 6A **116**

Woodside Lawn LS12: Leeds 4F **95**
Woodside M. LS7: Leeds 2F **77**
Woodside Mt. HX3: Hal . . .1F **149** (1A **164**)
Woodside Pk. Av. LS18: H'fth 1F **75**
Woodside Pk. Dr. LS18: H'fth 1F **75**
Woodside Pl. HX3: Hal . . .6F **129** (1A **164**)
LS4: Leeds 1C **96**
Woodside Rd. BD12: B'frd 4C **132**
BD20: Sils 2C **14**
HX3: Hal 1F **149** (1A **164**)
LS23: B Spa 4H **29**
Woodside St. WF10: Kip 1F **145**
Woodside Ter. HX3: Hal 6G **129**
HX4: Hal 5H **159**
LS4: Leeds 1C **96**
Woodside Vw. BD16: Bgly 2B **68**
HX3: Hal 6F **129** (1A **164**)
HX4: Hal 5H **159**
(off Woodside Ter.)
LS4: Leeds 6C **76**
WF3: Wake 1F **157**
Woodsley Grn. LS6: Leeds 1F **97**
Woodsley Rd. BD10: B'frd 3G **71**
LS2: Leeds 2E **97**
LS3: Leeds 2E **97**
LS6: Leeds 2E **97**
Woodsley Ter. LS2: Leeds . . .2G **97** (1A **4**)
Woods M. LS29: I'ly 5E **11**
Woods Row LS28: Pud 2A **94**
Woodstock Cl. LS16: Leeds 4D **58**
Woodstock Wlk. BD5: B'frd 6E **91**
(off Park Rd.)
Wood St. BD8: B'frd 3C **90** (1A **6**)
BD12: B'frd 1D **132**
BD15: B'frd 2E **89**
BD16: Bgly 1A **50**
BD17: Bail 6C **52**
BD20: Stee 6C **14**
BD22: Haw 3C **64**
HD6: Brigh 1B **162**
HX5: Ell 5C **160**
LS18: H'fth 5E **57**
LS27: Morl 6A **116**
WF3: E Ard 1B **156**
Woodthorne Cft. LS17: Leeds 3E **61**
Woodthorpe BD13: B'frd 3B **86**
Wood Top BD18: Ship 1D **70**
Woodtop HD6: Brigh 4G **151**
Woodvale Cl. BD4: B'frd 6C **92**
Woodvale Cres. BD16: Bgly 2C **50**
Woodvale Gro. BD7: B'frd 6G **89**
Woodvale Office Pk. HD6: Brigh . . .5B **152**
Woodvale Rd. HD6: Brigh 6B **152**
Woodvale Ter. LS18: H'fth 2F **75**
Woodvale Way BD7: B'frd 6G **89**
Wood Vw. BD8: B'frd 6D **70**
BD12: B'frd 3G **133**
BD17: Bail 6A **52**
HX3: Hal 5E **149**
LS27: Morl 5D **116**
LS29: I'ly 4F **11**
Woodview BD11: B'frd 6H **113**
BD13: B'frd 6A **66**
BD22: Keigh 3E **47**
Woodview Av. BD17: Bail 3F **53**
Woodview Cl. LS18: H'fth 5E **57**
Woodview Ct. LS16: Leeds 5F **81**
Wood Vw. Dr. BD2: B'frd 1A **92**
Woodview Gro. LS11: Leeds 3H **117**
Woodview M. LS14: Leeds 4F **81**
Woodview Mt. LS11: Leeds 3H **117**
Woodview Pl. LS11: Leeds 3H **117**
Woodview Rd. BD22: Keigh 3F **47**
LS11: Leeds 3H **117**
Woodview St. LS11: Leeds 3H **117**
Wood Vw. Ter. LS27: Morl 5D **116**
WF12: Dew 3B **154**
Woodview Ter. BD8: B'frd 6D **70**
BD21: Keigh 3H **47**
(off Haincliffe Pl.)
LS11: Leeds 3H **117**

Woodville Av. LS18: H'fth 6F **57**
Woodville Ct. LS8: Leeds 6F **61**
Woodville Cres. LS18: H'fth 6G **57**
Woodville Gro. BD22: Haw 1F **65**
LS10: Leeds 4C **118**
LS18: H'fth 6F **57**
Woodville Mt. LS10: Leeds 4C **118**
Woodville Pl. BD9: B'frd 5H **69**
HD2: Hud 5E **163**
LS18: H'fth 6G **57**
Woodville Rd. BD20: Keigh 5H **33**
Woodville Sq. LS10: Leeds 4C **118**
Woodville St. BD18: Ship 1D **70**
HX3: Hal 6E **129**
LS18: H'fth 6G **57**
Woodville Ter. BD5: B'frd 6D **90**
BD18: Ship 1D **70**
BD22: Haw 1F **65**
(off Vernon St.)
LS18: H'fth 6F **57**
Wood Vine St. LS28: Pud 2G **93**
Woodway BD16: Bgly 2B **68**
LS18: H'fth 2E **75**
Woodway Dr. LS18: H'fth 2E **75**
Woodworth Gro. BD21: Keigh 4H **47**
Woolcomb Ct. BD9: B'frd 1B **90**
Wooler Av. LS11: Leeds 3G **117**
Wooler Dr. LS11: Leeds 3G **117**
Wooler Gro. LS11: Leeds 3G **117**
Wooler Pl. LS11: Leeds 3F **117**
Wooler Rd. LS11: Leeds 3F **117**
Wooler St. LS11: Leeds 3F **117**
Wool Exchange, The BD1: B'frd 4D **6**
(off Market St.)
Woolford Way WF3: Wake 3H **157**
Wool Ga. BD16: Bgly 2D **68**
Wooller Rd. BD12: B'frd 2D **132**
Woollin Av. WF3: E Ard 4E **155**
Woollin Cres. WF3: E Ard 3E **155**
Woolpack HX1: Hal 2G **149** (3C **164**)
(not continuous)
Woolrow La. HD6: Brigh 3C **152**
Woolshops HX1: Hal 2G **149** (4C **164**)
Wootton St. BD5: B'frd 1E **111**
Worcester Av. LS10: Leeds 3D **140**
Worcester Cl. WF3: E Ard 6A **140**
Worcester Dr. LS10: Leeds 3D **140**
Worcester Pl. BD4: B'frd 1G **111**
Worden Gro. BD7: B'frd 1G **109**
Wordsworth Ct. LS26: Rothw 4E **143**
Wordsworth Dr. LS26: Rothw 4E **143**
Wordsworth Ho. LS29: I'ly 4G **11**
(off Blackthorn Rd.)
Wordsworth Way BD16: Bgly 2C **50**
Workhouse La. HX2: Hal 2G **147**
(Newlands Rd.)
HX2: Hal 5B **126**
(Scotland La.)
HX4: Hal 5H **159**
(not continuous)
Workouts Health & Fitness Cen. 1G **47**
(off Oakworth Rd.)
World Class Sports 3E **23**
World's End LS19: Yead 6G **41**
Wormald Lea BD4: B'frd 2C **112**
(off Stirling Cres.)
Wormald Row LS2: Leeds 3A **98** (3E **5**)
Worrall St. LS27: Morl 4H **137**
Worsnop Bldgs. BD12: B'frd 3C **132**
Worsnop St. BD12: B'frd 1D **132**
Worstead Rd. BD22: Haw 6F **47**
Worth Av. BD21: Keigh 4C **34**
Worth Bri. Rd. BD21: Keigh 6C **34**
Worthing Head Cl. BD12: B'frd 4D **132**
Worthing Head Rd. BD12: B'frd 4D **132**
Worthing St. BD12: B'frd 4D **132**
Worthington Ct. BD8: B'frd 2A **6**
Worthington St. BD8: B'frd . . .3C **90** (2A **6**)
Worth Vw. BD22: Keigh 5D **46**
Worth Vw. BD22: Keigh 4E **47**
WORTH VILLAGE 5C **34**
Worthville Cl. BD21: Keigh 2A **48**

Worth Way BD21: Keigh 1A 48
WORTLEY .5C 96
Wortley Hgts. LS12: Leeds 5D 96
Wortley La. LS11: Leeds 5F 97
　　LS12: Leeds 5F 97
Wortley Moor La. Trad. Est.
　　LS12: Leeds 5B 96
Wortley Moor Pde. LS12: Leeds 4A 96
Wortley Moor Rd. LS12: Leeds 4A 96
Wortley Pk. LS12: Leeds 5D 96
Wortley Rd. LS12: Leeds 4A 96
Wortley St. BD16: Bgly 4D 50
Wortley Towers LS12: Leeds 5E 97
Wrangthorn Av. LS6: Leeds 6F 77
Wrangthorn Pl. LS6: Leeds 6F 77
Wrangthorn Ter. LS6: Leeds 6F 77
Wren Av. BD7: B'frd 6G 89
Wrenbeck Av. LS21: Otley 1E 23
Wrenbeck Cl. LS21: Otley 1E 23
Wrenbeck Dr. LS21: Otley 1E 23
Wrenbury Av. LS16: Leeds 2F 57
Wrenbury Cres. LS16: Leeds 2F 57
Wrenbury Gro. LS16: Leeds 2G 57
Wren Dr. LS27: Morl 4D 138
Wren Hill WF17: Bat 6C 136
Wren St. BD21: Keigh 5A 34
　　BD22: Haw 2D 64
Wrenthorpe Rd. WF2: Wake 6D 156
Wrexham Rd. LS29: Burl W 2D 20
Wright Av. BD22: Keigh 4D 46
Wright St. BD22: Keigh 5D 46
Wrigley HX2: Hal 1C 128
Wrigley Av. BD4: B'frd 4H 111
Wrigley Hill HX2: Hal 2C 128
Wroe Cres. BD12: B'frd 4C 132
Wroe Pl. BD12: B'frd 4C 132
Wroe Ter. BD12: B'frd 4C 132
WROSE 3D 70
Wrose Av. BD2: B'frd 4G 71
　　BD18: Ship 3D 70
Wrose Brow Rd. BD18: Ship 1D 70
Wrosecliffe Gro. BD10: B'frd 1F 71
Wrose Dr. BD18: Ship 3D 70
Wrose Gro. BD2: B'frd 3F 71
　　BD18: Ship 3D 70
Wrose Hill Pl. BD2: B'frd 4D 70
Wrose Mt. BD18: Ship 3E 71
Wrose Rd. BD2: B'frd 3F 71
　　BD18: Ship 3D 70
Wrose Vw. BD17: Bail 3C 52
　　BD18: Ship 3D 70
Wycliffe Cl. LS13: Leeds 4H 73
Wycliffe Dr. LS17: Leeds 5B 60
Wycliffe Gdns. BD18: Ship 1A 70
Wycliffe Rd. BD18: Ship 1A 70
　　LS13: Leeds 4H 73
Wycoller Rd. BD12: B'frd 3C 132
Wycombe Grn. BD4: B'frd 2C 112
WYKE 4C 132
Wykebeck Av. LS9: Leeds 4H 99
Wykebeck Cres. LS9: Leeds 3H 99
Wykebeck Gdns. LS9: Leeds 3H 99
Wykebeck Gro. LS9: Leeds 3H 99
Wykebeck Mt. LS9: Leeds 4H 99
Wykebeck Pl. LS9: Leeds 3A 100
Wykebeck Rd. LS9: Leeds 3H 99
Wykebeck Sq. LS9: Leeds 3H 99
Wykebeck St. LS9: Leeds 3H 99
Wykebeck Ter. LS9: Leeds 3H 99
Wykebeck Valley Rd. LS9: Leeds 1H 99
Wykebeck Vw. LS9: Leeds 3H 99
Wyke Bottoms BD12: B'frd 3F 133
WYKE COMMON 5D 132

Wyke Cres. BD12: B'frd 5D 132
Wyke La. BD12: B'frd 5C 132
Wykelea Cl. BD12: B'frd 4D 132
Wyke Old La. HD6: Brigh 2B 152
Wyncliffe Ct. LS17: Leeds 5A 60
Wyncliffe Gdns. LS17: Leeds 5B 60
Wyncroft Ct. LS15: Bar E 3E 83
Wyncroft Gro. LS16: B'hpe 3H 43
Wyncroft Ri. BD18: Ship 4D 70
Wyndham Av. BD2: B'frd 6F 71
Wyndy Ridge BD13: B'frd 4G 87
Wynford Av. LS16: Leeds 6B 58
Wynford Gro. LS16: Leeds 6B 58
Wynford Mt. LS16: Leeds 6A 58
Wynford Ri. LS16: Leeds 6A 58
Wynford Ter. LS16: Leeds 6A 58
Wynford Way BD12: B'frd 5E 111
Wynmore Av. LS16: B'hpe 3G 43
Wynmore Cres. LS16: B'hpe 3H 43
Wynmore Dr. LS16: B'hpe 3H 43
Wynne St. BD1: B'frd 3D 90 (2A 6)
Wynyard Dr. LS27: Morl 3H 137
Wyre Cl. BD6: B'frd 4G 109
Wyther Av. LS5: Leeds 6H 75
Wyther Dr. LS5: Leeds 6A 76
Wyther Grn. LS5: Leeds 6A 76
Wyther La. LS5: Leeds 6H 75
Wyther La. Ind. Est. LS5: Leeds 6A 76
Wyther Pk. Av. LS12: Leeds 2H 95
Wyther Pk. Cl. LS12: Leeds 2H 95
Wyther Pk. Cres. LS12: Leeds 2H 95
Wyther Pk. Gro. LS12: Leeds 1H 95
Wyther Pk. Hill LS12: Leeds 1H 95
Wyther Pk. Mt. LS12: Leeds 2H 95
　　　　(not continuous)
Wyther Pk. Pl. LS12: Leeds 1H 95
Wyther Pk. Rd. LS12: Leeds 2G 95
　　　　(not continuous)
Wyther Pk. Sq. LS12: Leeds 1G 95
Wyther Pk. St. LS12: Leeds 2H 95
Wyther Pk. Ter. LS12: Leeds 2H 95
Wyther Pk. Vw. LS12: Leeds 1H 95
Wyvern Cl. BD7: B'frd 6H 89
Wyvern Pl. HX2: Hal 1C 148
Wyvern Ter. HX2: Hal 1C 148
Wyvil Cres. LS29: I'ly 5G 11
Wyvil Rd. LS29: I'ly 4G 11

Y

Yarborough Cft. HX3: Hal 3C 130
Yardley Way BD12: B'frd 1E 133
Yard No. 4 WF17: Bat 6B 136
Yarn St. LS10: Leeds 6C 98
Yarra Ct. LS27: Morl 6F 115
Yarwood Gro. BD7: B'frd 2G 109
Yateholm Dr. BD6: B'frd 4E 109
Yate La. BD22: Oxen 1C 84
Yates Flat BD18: Ship 3D 70
YEADON 6F 41
Yeadon Airport Ind. Est.
　　LS19: Yead 4B 42
Yeadon Dr. HX3: Hal 5C 150
Yeadon Moor Rd. LS19: Yead 1A 56
　　　　(Bayton La.)
　　LS19: Yead 6C 42
　　　　(Whitehouse La.)
Yeadon Row LS18: H'fth 2E 75
　　　　(off South Vw.)
Yeadon Stoops LS19: Yead 1H 55
　　　　(off Bayton La.)
Ye Farre Cl. HD6: Brigh 5A 152
Yeoman Ct. BD6: B'frd 3E 109

Yewbank Cl. LS29: I'ly 5C 10
Yewbank Ter. LS29: I'ly 5C 10
Yewdall Rd. LS13: Leeds 4H 73
Yewdall Way BD10: B'frd 3A 72
Yew La. LS25: Gar 5H 103
Yew Pk. HD6: Brigh 4G 151
YEWS GREEN 2A 108
Yew Tree Av. BD8: B'frd 2F 89
Yew Tree Cl. BD18: Ship 3D 70
Yew Tree Cotts. HX2: Hal 6C 126
Yew Tree Cres. BD8: B'frd 2G 89
Yew Tree Cft. HX2: Hal 6C 126
Yew Tree Dr. LS26: Rothw 1G 143
Yew Tree Gro. BD8: B'frd 2G 89
Yew Tree La. BD15: B'frd 3H 87
　　LS15: Leeds 4G 101
Yew Trees HX3: Hal 5C 150
Yew Trees Av. HX3: Hal 4C 130
York Cres. BD16: Bgly 5C 50
York Ga. LS21: Otley 6C 22
York Gate Garden 2D 58
York Ho. BD10: B'frd 2A 72
　　　　(off Fairhaven Grn.)
　　BD10: B'frd 2A 72
　　　　(Billing Vw.)
　　HX5: Ell 4B 160
　　　　(off Gog Hill)
　　HX6: Hal 5A 148
　　　　(off Beech Rd.)
　　LS28: Pud 1H 93
　　　　(off South Dr.)
York Pl. LS1: Leeds 3H 97 (4C 4)
　　LS22: Weth 3E 13
York Rd. LS9: Leeds 3C 98
　　　　(not continuous)
　　LS14: Leeds 2A 100
　　LS15: T'ner 3D 80
　　LS22: Weth 3F 13
　　LS29: Burl W 2F 21
York Rd. Ind. Est. LS22: Weth 3F 13
Yorkshire Academy of Cricket, The
　　. . . . . .1C 110
Yorkshire County Cricket (Headingley)
　　. . . . . .5D 76
Yorkshire Dr. BD5: B'frd 4G 111
Yorkshire Way BD7: B'frd 2B 110
York St. BD8: B'frd 4G 89
　　BD13: B'frd 4H 107
　　BD16: Bgly 5C 50
　　HD6: Brigh 2A 162
　　　　(off Thomas St.)
　　HD6: Brigh 2A 162
　　　　(Capel St.)
　　HX1: Hal 3F 149 (5A 164)
　　LS2: Leeds 4B 98 (5G 5)
　　LS9: Leeds 4B 98 (5G 5)
York Ter. HX3: Hal 6F 129
　　LS29: Burl W 2F 21
York Towers LS9: Leeds 3E 99
York Towers Pde. LS9: Leeds 3E 99
　　　　(off Lupton Av.)
Young St. BD8: B'frd 3H 89
Young St. Ind. Est. BD8: B'frd 3H 89

Z

Zealand St. BD4: B'frd 1B 112
Zermatt Gro. LS7: Leeds 3A 78
Zermatt Mt. LS7: Leeds 3A 78
Zermatt St. LS7: Leeds 3B 78
Zermatt Ter. LS7: Leeds 3B 78
Zetland Pl. LS8: Leeds 6D 78
Zoar St. LS27: Morl 3A 138

HOSPITALS and HOSPICES
covered by this atlas.

N.B. Where Hospitals and Hospices are not named on the map, the reference
given is for the road in which they are situated.

AIREDALE GENERAL HOSPITAL 5B **14**
Skipton Road
Steeton
KEIGHLEY
BD20 6TD
Tel: 01535 652511

BINGLEY HOSPITAL 4D **50**
Fernbank Drive
BINGLEY
BD16 4HD
Tel: 01274 563438

BRADFORD ROYAL INFIRMARY 2G **89**
Duckworth La.
BRADFORD
BD9 6RJ
Tel: 01274 542200

CALDERDALE ROYAL HOSPITAL, THE 6H **149**
Huddersfield Road
HALIFAX
HX3 0PW
Tel: 01422 357171

CHAPEL ALLERTON HOSPITAL 4B **78**
Chapeltown Road
LEEDS
LS7 4SA
Tel: 0113 2623404

COOKRIDGE HOSPITAL 5G **57**
Hospital Lane
LEEDS
LS16 6QB
Tel: 0113 2673411

CORONATION HOSPITAL (ILKLEY) 6E **11**
Springs Lane
ILKLEY
LS29 8TG
Tel: 01943 609666

ELLAND BUPA HOSPITAL 4C **160**
Elland Lane
ELLAND
HX5 9EB
Tel: 01422 324000

LEEDS BUPA HOSPITAL........................1E **79**
Jackson Avenue
LEEDS
LS8 1NT
Tel: 0113 2693939

LEEDS CHEST CLINIC 3F **5**
74 New Briggate
LEEDS
LS1 6PH
Tel: 0113 2951100

LEEDS DENTAL INSTITUTE 2G **97** (2B **4**)
Clarendon Way
LEEDS
LS2 9LU
Tel: 0113 2440111

LEEDS GENERAL INFIRMARY 2H **97** (2C **4**)
Great George Street
LEEDS
LS1 3EX
Tel: 0113 2432799

LEEDS NUFFIELD HOSPITAL 3G **97** (3B **4**)
2 Leighton Street
LEEDS
LS1 3EB
Tel: 0113 3882000

LEEDS ROAD HOSPITAL 4H **91**
Leeds Road
BRADFORD
BD3 9LH
Tel: 01274 494194

LYNFIELD MOUNT HOSPITAL 1F **89**
Heights Lane
BRADFORD
BD9 6DP
Tel: 01274 494194

MALHAM HOUSE DAY HOSPITAL 2G **97** (2A **4**)
25 Hyde Terrace
LEEDS
LS2 9LN
Tel: 0113 2926716

MANORLANDS (SUE RYDER) HOSPICE 6C **64**
Keighley Road
Oxenhope
KEIGHLEY
BD22 9HJ
Tel: 01535 642308

MARIE CURIE CENTRE (BRADFORD) 4H **91**
Maudsley Street
BRADFORD
BD3 9LH
Tel: 01274 337000

MARTIN HOUSE HOSPICE 4C **30**
Grove Road, Boston Spa
WETHERBY
LS23 6TX
Tel: 01937 845045

METHLEY PARK BUPA HOSPITAL 4A **144**
Methley Lane, Methley
LEEDS
LS26 9HG
Tel: 01977 518518

OVERGATE HOSPICE 5H **159**
30 Hullen Edge Road
ELLAND
HX5 0QY
Tel: 01422 379151

ST CATHERINES HOSPITAL 1C **90**
St Mary's Road
BRADFORD
BD8 7QG
Tel: 01274 227599

Hospitals & Hospices

ST GEMMA'S HOSPICE 5B **60**
329 Harrogate Road
LEEDS
LS17 6QD
Tel: 0113 2185500

ST JAMES'S UNIVERSITY HOSPITAL 1D **98**
Beckett Street
LEEDS
LS9 7TF
Tel: 0113 2433144

ST LUKE'S HOSPITAL (BRADFORD) 1D **110**
Little Horton La.
BRADFORD
BD5 0NA
Tel: 01274 734744

ST MARY'S HOSPITAL 3H **95**
Greenhill Road
LEEDS
LS12 3QE
Tel: 0113 2790121

SEACROFT HOSPITAL 2C **100**
York Road
LEEDS
LS14 6UH
Tel: 0113 2648164

SHIPLEY HOSPITAL 2A **70**
90 Kirkgate
SHIPLEY
BD18 3LT
Tel: 01274 773390

STONEY RIDGE HOSPITAL 4E **69**
Stoney Ridge Road
BINGLEY
BD16 1UL
Tel: 01274 322924

WHARFEDALE GENERAL HOSPITAL 1D **22**
Newall Carr Road
OTLEY
LS21 2LY
Tel: 01943 465522

WHEATFIELDS SUE RYDER HOSPICE 4E **77**
Wood Lane, Headingley
LEEDS
LS6 2AE
Tel: 0113 2787249

YORKSHIRE CLINIC, THE 2E **69**
Bradford Road
BINGLEY
BD16 1TW
Tel: 01274 560311